Sports Law and Regulation

ASPEN CASEBOOK SERIES

Sports Law and Regulation

Cases, Materials, and Problems

Third Edition

Matthew J. Mitten

Professor of Law and Director
National Sports Law Institute and
L.L.M. in Sports Law Program for Foreign Lawyers
Marquette University Law School

Timothy Davis

John W. & Ruth H. Turnage Professor of Law
Wake Forest University School of Law

Rodney K. Smith

Distinguished Professor of Law
Director, Center for Sports Law and Policy
Thomas Jefferson School of Law

N. Jeremi Duru

Professor of Law
Washington College of Law
American University

Wolters Kluwer
Law & Business

Published by Wolters Kluwer Law & Business in New York.

Wolters Kluwer Law & Business serves customers worldwide with CCH, Aspen Publishers, and Kluwer Law International products. (www.wolterskluwerlb.com)

To contact Customer Service, e-mail customer.service@wolterskluwer.com, call 1-800-234-1660, fax 1-800-901-9075, or mail correspondence to:

Wolters Kluwer Law & Business
Attn: Order Department
PO Box 990
Frederick, MD 21705

Printed in the United States of America.

1 2 3 4 5 6 7 8 9 0

ISBN 978-1-4548-1072-8

Library of Congress Cataloging-in-Publication Data

Mitten, Matthew J., 1959-
   Sports law and regulation : cases, materials, and problems / Matthew J. Mitten, professor of law and director, National Sports Law Institute and L.L.M. in sports law for foreign lawyers, Marquette University Law School; Timothy Davis, John W. & Ruth H. Turnage professor of law, Wake Forest University School of Law; Rodney K. Smith, distinguished professor of law, director Center for Sports Law and Policy, Thomas Jefferson School of Law; N. Jeremi Duru, professor of law, American University Washington College of Law. — Third edition.
      pages cm
   Includes index.
   ISBN 978-1-4548-1072-8
   1. Sports—Law and legislation—United States—Cases.   I. Davis, Timothy. II. Smith, Rodney K. III. Duru, N. Jeremi. IV. Title.

   KF3989.S6775 2013
   344.73′099—dc23

                                                              2013003812

About Wolters Kluwer Law & Business

Wolters Kluwer Law & Business is a leading global provider of intelligent information and digital solutions for legal and business professionals in key specialty areas, and respected educational resources for professors and law students. Wolters Kluwer Law & Business connects legal and business professionals as well as those in the education market with timely, specialized authoritative content and information-enabled solutions to support success through productivity, accuracy and mobility.

Serving customers worldwide, Wolters Kluwer Law & Business products include those under the Aspen Publishers, CCH, Kluwer Law International, Loislaw, Best Case, ftwilliam.com and MediRegs family of products.

CCH products have been a trusted resource since 1913, and are highly regarded resources for legal, securities, antitrust and trade regulation, government contracting, banking, pension, payroll, employment and labor, and healthcare reimbursement and compliance professionals.

Aspen Publishers products provide essential information to attorneys, business professionals and law students. Written by preeminent authorities, the product line offers analytical and practical information in a range of specialty practice areas from securities law and intellectual property to mergers and acquisitions and pension/benefits. Aspen's trusted legal education resources provide professors and students with high-quality, up-to-date and effective resources for successful instruction and study in all areas of the law.

Kluwer Law International products provide the global business community with reliable international legal information in English. Legal practitioners, corporate counsel and business executives around the world rely on Kluwer Law journals, looseleafs, books, and electronic products for comprehensive information in many areas of international legal practice.

Loislaw is a comprehensive online legal research product providing legal content to law firm practitioners of various specializations. Loislaw provides attorneys with the ability to quickly and efficiently find the necessary legal information they need, when and where they need it, by facilitating access to primary law as well as state-specific law, records, forms and treatises.

Best Case Solutions is the leading bankruptcy software product to the bankruptcy industry. It provides software and workflow tools to flawlessly streamline petition preparation and the electronic filing process, while timely incorporating ever-changing court requirements.

ftwilliam.com offers employee benefits professionals the highest quality plan documents (retirement, welfare and non-qualified) and government forms (5500/PBGC, 1099 and IRS) software at highly competitive prices.

MediRegs products provide integrated health care compliance content and software solutions for professionals in healthcare, higher education and life sciences, including professionals in accounting, law and consulting.

Wolters Kluwer Law & Business, a division of Wolters Kluwer, is headquartered in New York. Wolters Kluwer is a market-leading global information services company focused on professionals.

Third Edition

> In memory of Robert C. Berry,
> our friend, colleague, and coauthor.

Second Edition

> To my wife, Brenda,
> who inspires me with her love and creativity.
>
> —Matthew J. Mitten

> To my wife, Ida,
> and my daughter, Adia,
> for their love and support
> and to my students, who inspire me.
>
> —Timothy Davis

> To my parents,
> who always emphasized the student
> in student-athlete; to Gus Klekas, a coach who always
> believed in me; and to my wife, Danielle, and my children,
> Will, Hyrum, Mary, Heber, Lacey, Rod, Georgi, and Charlie,
> all of whom have been very supportive.
>
> —Rodney K. Smith

> To Professor Carole Berry,
> as we two emeriti continue to share ideas in our
> latest writing endeavors, taking it one book at a time.
>
> —Robert C. Berry

First Edition

> To my parents,
> Robert and Carol Mitten,
> for providing me with an excellent education; to
> Professors Ron Raitt and Bruce Burton for mentoring me
> as a law student, lawyer, and law professor; to my lifelong
> friends Mark Shiple, Tony Siravo, Doug Gerrick, Dan Streb,
> Joe Leonard, Greg Kelly, and Bob Leahy for encouraging
> my love of sports; and to Brenda Kurowski for her love and support.
>
> —Matthew J. Mitten

To my mother and father
for emphasizing the importance of education;
to my wife, Ida, and my daughter, Adia, for their love
and support; and to my friends Michael Poston, Keith Smith,
Vincent James, and Carolyn Mayes for their encouragement
and support through the years.

—Timothy Davis

To my parents,
who always emphasized the student
in student-athlete; to Gus Klekas, a coach who always
believed in me; and to my wife, Danielle, and my children,
Will, Hyrum, Mary, Heber, Lacey, Rod, Georgi, and Charlie,
all of whom have been very supportive.

—Rodney K. Smith

To Carole, another Professor Berry, my life companion and
collaborator. We continue to learn from each other.

—Robert C. Berry

Summary of Contents

Contents

Preface

Third Edition

To provide users of our book with the most current and comprehensive sports law text available, we have revised and updated the third edition of our book to include a discussion of the most significant legal developments affecting high school, college, Olympic, and professional sports that have occurred since our second edition was published in April 2009. Our third edition provides new landmark judicial decisions (e.g., *American Needle v. NFL*) as well as significant NCAA infractions cases and Olympic sports arbitration awards. It also provides revised text, updated notes, and some new questions and problems to facilitate understanding, analysis, and discussion of legal issues arising out of the dynamic evolution and development of the amateur and professional sports industries. To provide a more streamlined and unified presentation of the complex issues raised by the application of antitrust, labor, and intellectual property law to sports, the principal materials concerning legal regulation of the professional sports industries have been reorganized and consolidated into two chapters, Chapter 6 ("Professional Sports League Governance and Legal Regulation") and Chapter 7 ("Labor Relations in Professional Sports"), and parts of Chapter 12 ("Intellectual Property Issues in Sports") have been reorganized. We miss the friendship, insights, and wisdom of Bob Berry, who passed away in November 2011. Although Bob is irreplaceable, we are happy to welcome Jeremi Duru to our team. We trust that you will find our third edition to be an excellent text for the study of sports law, which will satisfy the objectives of your course. Please feel free to contact any of us with your comments and suggestions for improving our book: Matt (matt.mitten@marquette.edu), Tim (davistx@wfu.edu), Rod (rsmith@tjls.edu), or Jeremi (duru@wcl.american.edu).

Matthew J. Mitten
Timothy Davis
Rodney K. Smith
N. Jeremi Duru

March 2013

Second Edition

Since the first edition of this book was published in 2005, the amateur and professional sports industries have continued to evolve, and new legal issues have arisen. The second edition of the book has been revised and updated to include a discussion of the most significant legal developments affecting interscholastic athletics, intercollegiate athletics, Olympic and international sports, and professional sports. Throughout the second edition there is revised text, new principal cases, updated notes, and new problems to facilitate analysis and discussion of the key legal topics and issues covered in each chapter. Because sports is becoming more international and global in scope, materials have been added in several chapters to provide a comparative law perspective and to discuss the key differences between the European and North American models of professional sports as well as how European Union law regulates professional sports labor markets.

Several chapters in the second edition have been reorganized to provide a more unified and streamlined discussion of the topics covered therein. In particular, Chapters 3 ("Regulating Intercollegiate Athletics") and 4 ("Regulating Olympic and International Athletics") have been reorganized and revised significantly to provide better coverage of these topics. The principal materials concerning legal regulation of the professional sports industries have been reorganized into three chapters: Chapter 6 ("Regulating Professional Athletics"), Chapter 7 ("Labor Law and Relations"), and Chapter 8 ("League Governance, Rival Leagues, and Developing Global Issues").

We hope you enjoy our second edition and that it provides a useful tool for understanding, and stimulating discussion of, legal regulation of amateur and professional sports within the United States and internationally. As always, your comments and suggestions for improving our book are welcome. Please feel free to contact any of us: Matt (matt.mitten@marquette.edu), Tim (davistx@ wfu.edu), Rod (rodney.smith@svu.edu), or Bob (lawprofs@tampabay.rr.com).

Matthew J. Mitten
Timothy Davis
Rodney K. Smith
Robert C. Berry

February 2009

First Edition

This book facilitates study and analysis of the significant legal, historical, economic, and sociological issues affecting the development of both the amateur and professional sports industries in the twenty-first century. It provides sports law professors and students with a comprehensive, multipurpose text of cases, materials, and problems that gives a balanced perspective on how some of America's largest and most popular industries are regulated by our legal system. The book takes an in-depth look at the legal regulation of interscholastic athletics, intercollegiate athletics, Olympic and international sports, and professional sports.

In our experience, law students most effectively learn about legal regulation of the sports industries by understanding the underlying historical, economic, and sociological factors influencing the developing nature of the various legal relationships that exist therein (e.g., athlete and team, university and NCAA, professional team and league, etc.). To accomplish this objective, this book initially covers the respective internal regulatory mechanisms for the different levels of athletic competition (e.g., high school, college, Olympic, and professional sports); then it considers the primary bodies of public law that shape and constrain them. Individual chapters of this book focus on racial and gender equity issues in sports and facilitate multidisciplinary consideration of these important, contemporary topics. The book considers economic policy and consumer welfare issues as part of its coverage of how courts have applied antitrust law to the sports industries. This interdisciplinary examination of sports and law also is intended to appeal to upper-division undergraduate and graduate students.

This book provides a vehicle for applying general principles typically covered in first-year courses, such as contracts, torts, constitutional law, criminal law, and civil procedure, to sports-related legal issues and problems. For example, it includes coverage of the following issues: the nature of a university's contractual obligations to its student-athletes, tort liability of an athletic event participant to another participant, a state high school athletic association's status as a state actor and high school students' federal constitutional rights, criminal liability for on-field violence, and the implications of American courts' lack of personal jurisdiction over international sports governing bodies.

A sports law course also provides a means of initially exposing students to specialized areas of law such as antitrust, labor, intellectual property, and workers compensation laws as well as relatively new legislation such as the Americans with Disabilities Act. Our book considers how each of these areas of law (and others) regulates the sports industries. It also provides introductory materials and hypothetical problems to facilitate students' understanding of these legal principles and their application to the sports industries and society in general.

This book incorporates the strengths of existing casebooks while also providing broader coverage of contemporary sports law issues. It includes the leading historical and recent sports law cases and provides detailed explanatory material, notes, and questions to facilitate students' understanding of complex legal doctrines. It also raises some of the deeper philosophical, sociological, psychological, and economic policy issues that arise in the sports context. This approach both mirrors the practice of law in the twenty-first century generally and heightens students' understanding of sports-related legal issues. In addition, this book includes some negotiation exercises and problems designed to develop students' client counseling and transactional skills. These unique features combine both theoretical and practical components to provide sports law students with a well-rounded learning experience.

The breadth and depth of this book provide the flexibility necessary to achieve a wide range of teaching and learning objectives. It is suitable for use as a primary text in either a two- or three-credit-hour general sports law course covering individually selected amateur and sports law topics as well as issues common to both industries. It also can be used in separate two-hour or three-hour courses focusing primarily on either amateur or professional sports law issues.

Alternatively, it can be used for two separate one-semester courses designated Sports Law I and Sports Law II. In addition, this book provides a suitable text for use in sports management programs and other academic disciplines studying sports law.

A sports law course provides several important educational benefits in addition to providing students with an understanding of the legal framework governing the amateur and professional sports industries. Perhaps the most important one is that the study of sports law provides students with a package of readily transferable knowledge and skills applicable to a wide variety of legal and non-legal careers. It is one of the relatively few law school courses not limited to consideration of a single, discrete area of substantive law. This book enables thoughtful study of how several different bodies of law combine to regulate the amateur and professional sports industries. It also facilitates students' ability to synthesize several different discrete bodies of law, to recognize how they combine to govern sports, and to understand how laws that conflict are harmonized. In doing so, the book also encourages student examination of the role of sport in our culture and how law responds to serious cultural and moral questions.

In whatever form this book is used, we trust that students and faculty alike will enjoy their engagement with the material as much as we have. We have found that sports law deals with issues that merit deep study and reflection. We hope that this book encourages such study.

Matthew J. Mitten
Timothy Davis
Rodney K. Smith
Robert C. Berry

March 2005

Acknowledgments

Third Edition

We thank our editors at Wolters Kluwer and Aspen Publishers, particularly Peter Skagestad, for their assistance and suggestions regarding the third edition of this book, as well as Newgen–Austin and Rebecca Logan for their work in connection with its production. As always, we very much appreciate the comments from professors who have used the previous editions of our book in their sports law courses and their useful suggestions regarding how to improve our third edition. Matthew Mitten expresses his gratitude to Aaron Hernandez for his research assistance and comments regarding this edition of our book. He also thanks Jessica Berman for her review of portions of Chapter 7 and provision of updated information. Timothy Davis thanks Wake Forest University School of Law for its generous research support and Wake Forest law students Thailer Buari and Nathan Harrill for their research assistance. Rodney Smith thanks his research assistants, Lindsay Demery and Brian McMillen, for their able research assistance and Dean Rudy Hasl for his continuing support. Jeremi Duru is grateful to Dan La Luz, Angad Patheja, Amanda Naldjieff, and Michelle Winters for their research assistance.

Second Edition

We thank the people at Wolters Kluwer and Aspen Publishers, particularly Taylor Kearns, for their assistance and suggestions regarding the content of the second edition of this book, as well as Newgen North America and Andy Sieverman for their editorial assistance. We are grateful for the helpful comments and suggestions regarding how to improve our second edition from professors who have used the first edition of the book in their sports law courses. Matthew Mitten expresses his gratitude to Kaitlyn Wild for her research assistance and comments regarding the second edition of our book. He also regrets his inadvertent failure to acknowledge Jeffrey Benz's insightful review and comments on Chapter 4 as well as Kristin Muenzin's research assistance in connection with our book's first edition. Timothy Davis acknowledges the research assistance and comments provided by David Ginzer and David Rea. He also expresses gratitude for the research support provided by Wake Forest University School of Law. Rodney Smith expresses his gratitude to his assistant, Pat Griffin, who readily offers a helping hand, and to his coauthors for understanding the difficulties that attend having a college president as a teammate.

First Edition

We thank many people for their support and assistance in preparing this book. We begin by thanking the many people at Aspen Publishers for their helpful guidance and editorial support. We also thank students in our sports law classes who generously commented on the manuscript of this book. In addition, we acknowledge the insightful commentary offered by the professors who provided reviews of our manuscript.

Robert Berry expresses his gratitude and deep appreciation to long-time colleagues who have worked with him on various writings dealing with sports and legal regulation—in particular, William B. Gould IV, Stanford University, and Glenn M. Wong, University of Massachusetts–Amherst. He also is indebted to colleagues and students over the years at his home school, Boston College, and at various other law schools where he has visited—most notably, Capital University and the Ohio State University.

Timothy Davis acknowledges the conscientious research assistance provided by the following dedicated students at Wake Forest University: Nancy Ladson, Jeffrey Lepchenske, Antonio Lewis, Stephen Marshall, and Kenneth Menzel. He is also grateful for the excellent secretarial and computer assistance provided by Beverly Marshall and Beth Malone. Finally, he expresses gratitude for the research support provided by Wake Forest University School of Law.

Matthew J. Mitten thanks Jefferson Read, Robert Koch, Mark Dodds, William Appleton, Melissa Vittone, and Susan Jones for their helpful research assistance and Professor Eric Goldman for his thoughtful review of Chapter 12. He also appreciates the secretarial and computer assistance provided by Carrie Kratochvil and Peter Hackl as well as proofreading of portions of our manuscript by Jenna Merten.

Rodney Smith gratefully acknowledges the able research assistance provided by his former students Christie Woodruff, Jay Fowler, Thor Larsen, Robert Walker, and Leanne Austin. He also appreciates the excellent secretarial support offered by Karol Usmani. Finally, he acknowledges the support of Dean Don Polden, Provost Ralph Faudree, President Shirley Raines, and funding from the Herff Chair of Excellence at Cecil C. Humphreys School of Law at the University of Memphis.

We also thank the following authors, publishers, and copyright holders for permitting us to include excerpts from these works:

American Law Institute, Restatement, Second, Torts. Copyright © 1977 by The American Law Institute. Reproduced with permission. All rights reserved.

Athlete Graduation Rates Continue to Climb, NCAA News, Sept. 1, 2003. Copyright © National Collegiate Athletic Association. 2013. All rights reserved.

Bean, Lori L., Note, *Ambush Marketing: Sport Sponsorship Confusion and the Lanham Act*, 75 Boston University Law Review 1099 (1995). Copyright © 1995 by Lori B. Geisinger. Reprinted with permission.

Brake, Deborah L., & Verna L. Williams, *The Heart of the Game: Putting Race and Educational Equity at the Center of Title IX*, 7 Va. Sports & Ent. L.J. 199 (2008).

Collective Bargaining Agreement, National Basketball Association and National Basketball Players Association. Copyright © 1999 by National Basketball Association and National Basketball Players Association. Reprinted with Permission.

Collective Bargaining Agreement between The NFL Management Council and the NFL Players Association, 2002-2008, as amended Jan. 28, 2002. Copyright © 2002 by The NFL Management Council and the NFL Players Association. Reprinted with permission.

Could Doping Be Effectively Legalized, Regulated?, Bus. Pundit, May 20, 2010.

Davis, Timothy, *The Myth of the Superspade: The Persistence of Racism in College Athletics*, 22 Fordham Urban Law Journal 615 (1995). Copyright © 1995 Fordham Urban Law Journal. Reprinted with permission.

Davis, Timothy, *What Is Sports Law?*, 11 Marq. Sports L.J. 211 (2001). Copyright © 2001 Marquette Sports Law Journal. Reprinted with permission.

Dolley, Jeff, *The Four R's: Use of Indian Mascots in Educational Facilities*, 32 J.L. & Educ. 21, 26-27 (2003).

Former Head Men's Basketball Coach University of Minnesota, Twin Cities Public Infractions Appeals Committee Report, April 6, 2001. Copyright © National Collegiate Athletic Association. 2013. All rights reserved.

Gould, William B. IV, The Cambridge Lectures, Queens College, University of Cambridge, England, 1995. Copyright © 1995 by University of Cambridge. Reprinted with permission.

Hair Absent Showing of Actual Disruption Violates High School Student's Constitutional Rights, 84 Harv. L. Rev. 1702 (1971).

Harry, Chris, *NFL Owners in a League of Their Own*, Orlando Sentinel, March 17, 2002, at C1.

Idelman, Scott C., *Religious Freedom and the Interscholastic Athlete*, 12 Marq. Sports L. Rev. 295 (2001).

Marburger, Daniel R., & Nancy Hogshead-Makar, *Is Title IX Really to Blame for the Decline in Intercollegiate Men's Nonrevenue Sports?*, 14 Marq. Sports L. Rev. 65 (2003).

Meggyesy, David, *Let Players Decide Who Coaches Will Be*, Sports Bus. J., Oct. 21-27, 2002. Reprinted with permission from SportsBusiness Journal and David Meggyesy.

Mitten, Matthew J., *Emerging Issues in Sports Medicine: A Synthesis, Summary, and Analysis*, 76 St. John's Law Review 5 (2002). Copyright © 2002 by St. John's Law Review. Reprinted with permission.

Mitten, Matthew J., *Enhanced Risk of Harm to One's Self as a Justification for Exclusion from Athletics*, 8 Marq. Sports L. Rev. 189 (1998).

Mitten, Matthew J., & Timothy Davis, *Athlete Eligibility Requirements and Legal Protection of Sports Participation Opportunities*, 8 Va. Sports & Ent. L.J. 71 (2009).

National Basketball Players Association Regulations Governing Player Agents. Copyright © 2004 by National Basketball Players Association Regulations Governing Player Agents.

National Collegiate Athletic Association, 2012-13 NCAA Division I Manual (2012). Copyright © National Collegiate Athletic Association. 2013. All rights reserved.

National Collegiate Athletic Association, National Letter of Intent. Copyright © National Collegiate Athletic Association. 2013. All rights reserved.

Sports Law and Regulation

CHAPTER
1

An Introduction to the Study of Sports Law

A. WHAT IS SPORTS LAW?[1]

Should sports law be recognized as an independent substantive area of the law like torts, contracts, or employment law? Scholars have debated this question.

1. The Traditional View: "Sports Law" Does Not Exist

The traditional view is that sports law represents nothing more than an amalgamation of various substantive areas of the law that are relevant in the sports context. According to this perspective, the term *sports law* is a misnomer given that sport represents a form of activity and entertainment that is governed by the legal system in its entirety. Adherents to the traditional perspective argue that "sports law simply entails the application of basic legal precepts to a specific industry" that are drawn from other substantive areas of the law. Michael J. Cozzillio and Mark S. Levinstein, Sports Law 7 (1997). Consequently, no separately identifiable body of law exists that can be characterized as sports law.

2. The Moderate Position: "Sports Law" May Develop into a Field of Law

Other commentators have begun increasingly to question the traditional view that no corpus of law exists that can be characterized as an independent field of law called sports law. Some have staked out what represents a middle ground. Professor Kenneth Shropshire acknowledges that developments, such as state and federal legislation impacting sports (for example, state statutes regulating sports agents, and federal statutes such as Title IX), suggest a "growing sports-only corpus" of law. Kenneth L. Shropshire, *Introduction: Sports Law?*, Am. Bus. L.J. 181, 182 (1998).

---

1. This section is adapted from Timothy Davis, *What Is Sports Law?*, 11 Marq. Sports L. Rev. 211 (2001).

Professor Burlette Carter argues that sports law is in the midst of an exciting, yet challenging, transformative process. According to Professor Carter, this process parallels the increased focus by law schools on sports and the growing significance of sports regulation to participants, organizations, and communities. She believes that these developments will better shape the contours of this emerging field of study. This in turn, will eventually transform sports law from "a course without a corpus" to a widely recognized independent substantive area of law. Burlette Carter, *Introduction: What Makes a "Field" a Field?*, 1 Va. J. Sports & L. 234, 245 (1999).

3.   *"Sports Law": A Separate Field of Law*

Others argue that sports law currently exists as a field of law. Adherents to this view emphasize the growing body of case and statutory law specific to the sports industry as evidence of the existence of a separately identifiable body of law. Pointing to the increasing body of judicial and legislative law specific to sports, Professor Simone Gardiner argues:

> [I]t is true to say that [sports law] is largely an amalgam of interrelated legal disciplines involving such areas as contract, taxation, employment, competition and criminal law but dedicated legislation and case law has developed and will continue to do so. As an area of academic study and extensive practitioner involvement, the time is right to accept that a new legal area has been born—sports law.

Simon Gardiner et al., Sports Law 74 (1998).

Commentators also propose that references to sports law as merely an amalgamation of various other substantive areas of the law ignore an important present-day reality—very few substantive areas of the law fit into separate categories that are divorced from and independent of other substantive areas of the law. Doctrinal overlap exists not only within sports law, but within other areas of law as well. According to Professor Carter, "the field of sports law has moved beyond the traditional antitrust and labor law boundaries into sports representation and legal ethics, sports and corporate structure, sports and disability, sports and race, sports and gender, sports and taxation, international issues in sports law and numerous other permutations." Carter, *supra*, at 239-240.

Proponents of the sports law designation and those sympathetic to the view also argue that reticence to recognize sports law as a specific body of law may reflect attitudes regarding the intellectual seriousness of sports. In this regard, they emphasize the tendency to marginalize the study of sports rather than treat it as any other form of business. The intellectual marginalization of sport has been attributed, in part, to the belief that social relations extant in sports were not deemed proper subjects for reconstruction into legal relationships. Thus, private and public law were considered "inappropriate [mechanisms for] controlling the social norms of sport." Gardiner, *supra* at 45. The competing and increasingly predominant view, however, casts sports as a significant economic activity suitable, like other big businesses, to regulation, whether it be internal or external.

In the end, whether sports law is recognized as an independent field of law may turn on the perceptions of those who practice, teach, and engage in scholarship related to sports law. Professor Carter asks that we consider the following:

But what makes a field a field? The answer is that a field becomes a field not because it is inherently so but because in our public legal dealings we shape it as such, defining the concepts and legal norms that will prevail uniquely in that context. It becomes a field because enough people with power on all sides are so affected by it to require some special treatment of it in the law.

Carter, *supra* at 244-245.

Regardless of the position that is adopted regarding the "what is sports law" debate, most would agree that matters arising in the sports law context implicate diverse substantive areas of law. Moreover, sports-related cases are sculpting a body of law particularly applicable in the sports context and influencing the development of general legal principles. According to Professor Daniel Lazaroff:

> On both the federal and state levels, sports related cases have not only had a profound impact on the narrow questions raised by the facts of particular disputes, but have also significantly influenced more general jurisprudential trends. . . . The growing body of sports-based legal authority has shaped the face of general legal doctrine in several important areas. In federal law, antitrust and labor doctrine have been significantly shaped by cases originating in the sports industries. In addition, constitutional principles involving drug testing and search and seizure have been influenced by sports law cases. On the state level, important tort doctrine has been and will continue to be affected by disputes arising in the context of sports. Undoubtedly, other areas of the law will be similarly influenced by sports litigation.

Huge influence

Daniel E. Lazaroff, *The Influence of Sports Law on American Jurisprudence*, 1 Va. Sports & Ent. L.J. 1, 2 (2001).

As sport evolves at the national and global levels, its impact on the development of a special and influential body of law is evident. A recent article examining the development of international, comparative, and national sports law concludes that sport is an important contributor to the global economy and culture, which has resulted in the development of a body of sports law that is globally significant. Matthew J. Mitten and Hayden Opie, "*Sports Law": Implications for the Development of International, Comparative, and National Law and Dispute Resolution*, 85 Tul. L. Rev. 269 (2010).

NOTE AND QUESTION

Scholars have identified several factors that provide indicia that an area of law has matured to the point of common acceptance. Among them are (1) the unique application by courts of law from other disciplines to a specific context; (2) factual peculiarities within a specific context that produce problems that require specialized analysis; (3) "within the proposed discipline, [the] elements of its subject matter must connect, interact, or interrelate"; (4) the proposed discipline significantly affects "the nation's (or the world's) business, economy, culture, or society"; (5) the development of interventionist legislation to regulate specific relationships; (6) development and publication of legal casebooks, law journals, and other publications that specifically focus on the proposed discipline; and (7) acceptance of the proposed field as a separate substantive area by law schools and legal associations, such as bar associations. Timothy Davis, *What Is Sports Law?*, 11 Marq. Sports L.J. 211 (2001). As you continue your studies this semester, consider which of the foregoing factors support designating sports law as a separate corpus of law.

For further discussion of whether sports law is a separately identifiable substantive area of the law, see Michael J. Cozzillio, Mark S. Levenstein, Michael R. Dimino, Sr., and Gabriel Feldman, Sports Law: Cases and Materials (2d ed. 2007); Simone Gardiner et al., Sports Law (4th ed. 2011); John C. Weistart and Cym H. Lowell, The Law of Sports xviii (1979); W. Burlette Carter, *Introduction: What Makes a "Field" a Field?*, 1 Va. J. Sports & L. 235 (1999); Kenneth L. Shropshire, *Introduction: Sports Law?*, 35 Am. Bus. L.J. 181, 182 (1998). See also Peter W. Hohenhaus, An Introductory Perspective on Computer Law: Is It, Should It Be, and How Do We Best Develop It As, Separate Discipline, 1991 WL 330761; Gail Crummie Washington, *Entertainment Law: Is There Such an Animal and Could There Be One in Alabama?*, 53 Ala. Law. 400 (Nov. 1992).

B.   IS THE STUDY OF SPORTS LAW MARGINALIZED?

Notwithstanding its widespread influence, only recently has sport become recognized as a "legitimate subject of intellectual inquiry." What accounts for the historical and continued marginalization of sport? Given our preoccupation with sports, it is remarkable, as Professors Gorn and Oriard note, "that athletics have remained so far beyond the boundary of intellectual discourse, [despite the fact that the] study of sport can take us to the very heart of critical issues in the study of culture and society." Elliott J. Gorn and Michael Oriard, *Taking Sports Seriously*, Chron. Higher Educ., Mar. 24, 1995, at A52.

Other academics strongly agree. Professor Drew Hyland notes:

> There is a long tradition that calls on the academy, as one of its central tasks, to reflect on and analyze social phenomenon that play an important role in a given culture. Thus, there are many varied considerations of the role of politics, religion, music, and the arts by the various disciplines in the academy, certainly including philosophy. Arguably, however, that social phenomenon in American life which has the biggest impact on our culture, yet which receives the least serious attention from our intellectual standard-bearers, is sport and athletics. There seems to be a longstanding prejudice of professorial philosophy.

Drew A. Hyland, Philosophy of Sport xiii (1990).

Announcing the establishment of the first multidisciplinary scholarly journal devoted exclusively to the study of intercollegiate sports, Professor Scott Krechmar stated that "college sport, given its centrality and influence in American culture and higher education, has been given less attention than it is due." R. Scott Krechmar, *Research, Sport, and Higher Education: An Introduction to the Journal of Intercollegiate Sport*, 1 J. Intercollegiate Sport 1, 1 (2008). He opines:

> Perhaps this broader neglect of sport and "things physical" is related to the lingering effects of mind-body dualism, or to distinctions between high versus low or popular culture, or to long-standing academic traditions that separate intellectual procedures like writing from motor acts [like] hitting a tennis ball, or even more fundamentally to epistemological commitments that favor theory or "knowing

that" over practice or "knowing how." In all likelihood, several of these factors working together account for the academy's relative neglect of sport as a theme for scholarly inquiry.

NOTE AND QUESTIONS

Why has sports been marginalized as an area of serious academic study?

Despite the continuing discussion in American studies of "the body" (of how human beings conceive of themselves physically), athletes' bodies remain curiously off-limits. . . . Is "the body" as conceived in cultural studies a rhetorical construction, while the bodies of athletes are too palpably real? Are we, as intellectuals, just uncomfortable with physicality, because our own bailiwick is the life of the mind? Could it be that professors are creatures of words while the language of athletics is fundamentally non-verbal? Or are we simply playing out the long-standing faculty antagonism to the distorted priorities of universities with multimillion-dollar athletics programs?

Elliott J. Gorn and Michael Oriard, *Taking Sport Seriously*, Chron. Higher Educ. (Mar. 24, 1995), A52. Academics' treatment of sport as a marginal social and cultural phenomenon transcends national boundaries. Hans Ulrich Gumbrecht, In Praise of Athletic Beauty 21 (2006). Gumbrecht offers several explanations for the global academic devaluation of sport, including intellectuals' preference to attach a higher status to those things that are metaphysical in contrast to those things deemed "material (or merely corporeal)." *Id.* at 30.

Do the reasons suggested by scholars adequately explain the reticence to examine sports as a matter of serious scholarly inquiry? Is the trivialization of sports by academics a consequence of stereotypes concerning the intellectual abilities of athletes, and particularly African American athletes, who dominate certain highly visible and popular sports? Does the treatment of sport stem from the perception that sport is more a matter of entertainment than business and therefore not worthy of serious academic interest? Will a failure to seriously study sport "distort our view of culture" as suggested by Professors Gorn and Oriard?

C.   THE SIGNIFICANCE OF SPORT AND SPORTS LAW

1.   *The Role of Sport in Society*

There is a reciprocal relationship between sports and societal values. Sport incorporates society's existing values and reinforces these values on the playing field, in its rules, and through its established institutions. Sport also exports its principles and the lessons learned from participating in athletics and its governance to society in general.

Matthew J. Mitten, *Foreword* to *Symposium: Sports Law as a Reflection of Society's Law and Values*, 38 S. Tex. L. Rev. 999 (1997). The following discussion initially analyzes the significance of sport in relation to its role in shaping and reflecting societal values. The discussion then provides specific illustrations of how sport intersects with other important aspects of American society.

As a predicate to this discussion, we attempt to define sports. Although definitions vary, we adopt one offered by a leading sociologist. "Sports are institutionalized competitive activities that involve rigorous physical exertion or the use of relatively complex physical skills by participants motivated by personal enjoyment and external rewards." Jay Coakley, Sport in Society: Issues and Controversies 6 (10th ed. 2008). See also D. Stanley Eitzen and George H. Sage, Sociology of North American Sport 15 (8th ed. 2008) (defining sport as "any competitive physical activity that is guided by established rules").

These definitions inevitably lead to additional questions, including why some activities are considered sports and others are not. Is an activity a sport merely because it possesses the unique features suggested in the preceding definition, such as formalized structures (i.e., informal and formal rules enforced by regulatory bodies), off-field cooperation necessary to produce on-field competition, and uncertain outcomes? Is whether an activity is considered a sport more a function of other variables, including cultural and historical tradition, the amount of television coverage an activity garners, and political processes (e.g., the ability of particular countries to export their values and traditions to other nations, as the English did with soccer)? See Stefan Szymanski and Andrew Zimbalist, National Pastime 48-83 (2006).

The designation of an activity as a sport is not merely a matter of intellectual curiosity since the resolution of disputes may hinge on such a designation. In *Biediger v. Quinnipiac University*, 667 F.3d 910 (2d Cir. 2012), the court found that cheerleading was not a sport for Title IX purposes. In reaching that conclusion, the court looked at the characteristics of athletic competition and concluded that cheerleading as then constituted at Quinnipiac University was an activity and not a sport. See also *Fontes v. Irvine Unified Sch. Dist.*, 30 Cal. Rptr. 521 (Cal. App. 1994) (noting characteristics of a sport). Looking ahead to our discussion of gender equity in Chapter 10, the significance of designating cheerleading and dance as sports is controversial, particularly given the Title IX implications of such a characterization.

See Supplement

a.   Positive Values Associated with Sport

Some sociologists argue that sport "is infused with themes consistent with the American Dream." Howard L. Nixon II and James H. Frey, A Sociology of Sport 41 (1996). These themes include "competition, individualism, [and] achievement." Eitzen and Sage, *supra*, at 10. Sport has also been viewed as holding the potential to instill within its participants values of teamwork, perseverance, sacrifice, and hard work. What has been called the "American Sports Creed" stands for the proposition that "sport builds character, teaches discipline, develops competitiveness, prepares participants to compete in life, enhances physical and mental fitness, and contributes to a belief in (Christian) religion and a patriotic belief in America." Nixon and Frey, *supra*, at 41.

Similarly, academics argue that sport is premised on doctrines of equality of opportunity, sportsmanship, and fair play. This premise comports with a liberal jurisprudential approach that "conceives meritocracy as a system in which benefits and burdens are distributed in accord with one's deeds—presumably the products of rational choice—rather than characteristics over which one has no apparent control." Timothy Davis, *The Myth of the Superspade: The Persistence of Racism in College Athletics*, 22 Fordham Urb. L.J. 615, 639-640 (1995).

The judiciary has been influenced by positive values associated with sports. A California appellate court's resolution of an issue—the availability of assumption of the risk as a defense to a negligence claim—was influenced by the court's vision of the values associated with sport:

> For many, sports are part of the school learning experience, among other things teaching students how to deal properly with both success and failure, and instilling in them an understanding of the importance of teamwork, good sportsmanship, discipline, and respect for coaches, teammates and opposing players. Another important part of the experience is that students and their parents learn about accepting responsibility for the consequences of one's choices and actions. By choosing to participate in a sport that poses the obvious possibility of injury, the student athlete must learn to accept an adverse result of the risks inherent in the sport.
> In other words, application of the doctrine of primary assumption of the risk in the extracurricular school sports setting is consistent with, rather than inimical to, the goals and responsibilities of elementary and secondary schools.

Lilley v. Elk Grove Unified Sch. Dist., 68 Cal. App. 4th 939, 946, 80 Cal. Rptr. 2d 638, 643 (1998).

Judicial opinions also often express notions of meritocracy that are central to the traditional vision of sport. "It must also be made clear that the mandate of equality of opportunity does not dictate a disregard of differences in talents and abilities among individuals. There is no right to a position on an athletic team. There is a right to compete for it on equal terms." *Hoover v. Meiklejohn*, 430 F. Supp. 164, 171 (D. Colo. 1977).

Scholars attribute significant benefits arising from sports participation:

> Significant educational and physical benefits have been identified as arising from athletic participation at competitive and recreational levels. For example, some academics maintain that participation in competitive athletics is analogous to participation on the part of many students in a basic biology class, teaching the student memorization and basic analytical skills. . . . The same concept can be applied to a complex football playbook—the athlete learns to analyze how to respond to a unique set of complex situations by memorizing and applying an elaborate set of fundamental rules or plays that are designed to respond to certain situations as they arise.

Rodney K. Smith, *When Ignorance Is Not Bliss: In Search of Racial and Gender Equity in Intercollegiate Athletics*, 61 Mo. L. Rev. 329, 335-336, 339 (1996). For a more recent elaboration of the benefits derived from participation in sports, see Matthew J. Mitten et al., *Targeted Reform of Commercialized Intercollegiate Athletics*, 47 San Diego L. Rev. 779, 797-798 (2010).

Some proponents of increased athletic participation by women assert that sport assists in the development of qualities and skills such as self-esteem, strategic thinking, team building, leadership, and the willingness to take risks. Mindy Bingham and Sandy Stryker, Things Will Be Different for My Daughter 271-276 (1995). In the landmark gender equity case, *Cohen v. Brown University*, 991 F.2d 888 (1st Cir. 1993), the court commented on short- and long-term benefits associated with participating in college sports.

> For college students, athletics offers an opportunity to [develop] leadership skills, learn teamwork, build self-confidence, and perfect self-discipline. In addition, for many student-athletes, physical skills are a passport to college admissions and

scholarships, allowing them to attend otherwise inaccessible schools. These opportunities, and the lessons learned on the playing fields, are invaluable in attaining career and life successes in and out of professional sports.

Id.

Sport has also been identified as a unifying mechanism that provides a sense of community among increasingly diverse constituents of larger bodies. This important function of sport is adroitly described by Professor Rodney Smith in the following excerpt:

In our diverse culture, characterized by a wide variety of ethnic, religious, socio-economic and other groups, there may well be no other force quite like sport, in terms of bringing people of diverse backgrounds together in pursuit of a common purpose. People from all walks of life are able to sense some unity of purpose as they gather to participate in or watch competitive athletics. With growing divisiveness on the basis of ethnic, religious and cultural differences, the capacity of sport to unify may be of increasing significance, particularly if teams are not divided on the basis of race, religion or culture. Deep friendships that transcend such difference are often forged in the crucible of athletic competition. The need for such a sense of connection or community is significant, although the capacity of sport to contribute to connectedness may be discounted by those who refuse to embrace sport as anything more than mere fun and games.

Rodney K. Smith, *When Ignorance Is Not Bliss: In Search of Racial and Gender Equity in Intercollegiate Athletics*, 61 Mo. L. Rev. 329, 341 (1996).

b. Negative Values Associated with Sport

In contrast to the vision of sport just discussed, others focus on aspects of sport that mirror negative societal qualities. Such values include "selfishness, envy, conceit, [and] hostility," and a heightened level of competitiveness that may produce a winning-at-all-costs mentality. D. Stanley Eitzen, *Ethical Dilemmas in American Sport*, 62 Vital Speeches of the Day 182, 185 (1996). Notes Professor Eitzen, the winning-at-all-costs philosophy "leads to dehumanization of athletes and to their alienation from themselves and from their competitors." *Id.* Illustrations abound of the negative consequences of the winning-at-all-costs mentality that is pervasive in sport and often leads to questionable strategies aimed at attempting to gain a competitive advantage. A desire to secure a starting position on the University of Northern Colorado's football team resulted in Mitch Cozad's conviction and sentence of seven years in prison for the 2007 stabbing of his teammate Rafael Mendoza. In 1999, Ben Christensen, a pitcher for Wichita State University, threw a fastball at Anthony Molina, a player for the University of Evansville. *Molina v. Christensen*, 2001 Kan. App. LEXIS 1265, at *3 (Kan. Ct. App. 2001). Molina sustained serious injury to his eye and cheek after being struck by a pitch. The pitch was thrown during Christensen's warm-up while Molina was near or in the on-deck circle. In attempting to justify his actions, Christensen claimed that his coach instructed him to throw the pitch at Molina as a warning to dissuade Molina from standing too close to home plate when he came to bat in an effort to time Christensen's pitches. *Id.*

In 2002, the NCAA imposed penalties on the University of Alabama (Tuscaloosa) for infractions of NCAA rules involving, among other things, prohibited recruiting inducements, such as providing cash to a prospect if he agreed to play for the university, and offering money to a high school coach who would seek to secure a recruit's commitment to play for the university. The NCAA Infractions Committee stated:

> The ingrained culture of non-compliance evident among certain of the university's athletics representatives was particularly troubling to the committee. While rogue athletics representatives are new neither to infractions cases generally nor to the infractions history of this university, their level of involvement and spending, is an increasingly visible and major problem in intercollegiate athletics. . . . Even if sincere, their claimed motivation for cheating—helping a university to recruit blue-chip athletes—betrays a lack of integrity and a "win-at-all-costs" attitude that undermines and cheapens athletics competition and corrupts the ethics and maturation process of the young people they claim to be "helping."

NCAA Committee on Infractions, University of Alabama, Tuscaloosa, Public Infraction Report 2 (Feb. 2, 2002).

In 2012, in an unprecedented action, the NCAA and Penn State University entered into a binding consent decree imposed by the NCAA on and agreed to by the university. In introducing what may be the most significant sanctions ever imposed by the NCAA, the decree declared:

> The NCAA concludes that [the evidence in this case] presents an unprecedented failure of institutional integrity leading to a culture in which a football program was held in higher esteem than the values of the institution, the values of the NCAA, the values of higher education, and most disturbingly the values of human decency. The sexual abuse of children on a university campus by a former [football coach]—and even the active concealment of that abuse—while despicable, ordinarily would not be actionable by the NCAA. Yet, in this instance, it was fear of or deference to the omnipotent football program that enabled a sexual predator to attract and abuse his victims. Indeed, the reverence for Penn State football permeated every level of the University community. That imbalance of power and its result are antithetical to the model of intercollegiate athletics embedded in higher education. Indeed, the culture exhibited at Penn State is an extraordinary affront to the values all members of the Association have pledged to uphold and calls for extraordinary action.
>
> As a result, the NCAA has determined that the University's sanctions be designed to not only penalize the University for contravention of the NCAA Constitution and Bylaws, but also to change the culture that allowed this activity to occur and realign it in a sustainable fashion with the expected norms and values of intercollegiate athletics.

Consent Decree Imposed by the National Collegiate Athletic Association and Agreed to by the Penn State University 4 (July 23, 2012).

Youth sports provide an excellent context within which to view the negative consequences of placing undue emphasis on winning. In one incident, six high school students severely beat the leading scorer of an opposing team in an apparent attempt to prevent him from playing against their team in a tournament game. In 2003, police had to quell a melee that occurred at the end of a high school football game after the winning team blocked an extra point attempt that would have tied the game. A parent filed a complaint accusing former Detroit Tigers baseball player Pete Incaviglia of yelling obscenities and threatening the parent's son. See Dianna K. Fiore, *Parental Rage and Violence in Youth Sports: How*

Can We Prevent "Soccer Moms" and "Hockey Dads" from Interfering in Youth Sports and Causing Games to End in Fistfights Rather than Handshakes?, 10 Vill. Sports & Ent. L.J. 103 (2003). A 2005 study published in the *Journal of Research in Character Education* documented ethical problems in youth sports that included athletes cheating, arguing with officials, and intentionally attempting to injure opponents, and coaches encouraging athletes to cheat.

One of the more notorious instances of parental violence in youth sports occurred in 2001, when Thomas Junta was convicted of involuntary manslaughter and sentenced to six to ten years in prison. Junta beat another father, Michael Costin, to death following a hockey practice in which their sons participated. Although Junta's conduct may be an aberration, parents engage in improper behavior at youth games and practices that often manifests as physical and verbal assaults on officials, other parents, and children. The desire to be number one in our competitive society is one of the social and psychological factors that contribute to such behaviors. One commentator notes, "Whether it's a reflection of our confrontational, win-at-all-costs society or the desperate desire some parents have to see their kids earn a college scholarship or get their names in the papers, this is a problem that is not only very real but also very threatening to the purity of youth and high school sports." Patricia Babcock McGraw, *Games Kids Play Can Make Parents Behave in a Bad Way*, Chi. Daily Herald, Feb. 1, 2002, at 1. See Kevin P. Polansky, Note, *Parental Violence at Youth Sporting Events: Should Landowners Be Liable?*, 39 Suffolk U.L. Rev. 561 (2006) (advocating landowner liability as a means of attempting to curb parental violence in sports).

The role of money in sports also cannot be ignored. Money becomes the bait that not only lures individuals and entities into sports, but also becomes an impediment to sports' regulation. Parents push children to excel in sports as a means of increasing a child's chances of obtaining a college athletic scholarship or a lucrative contract with a professional sports team. See Fiore, *supra*. As discussed later in this chapter, the quest for financial rewards nurtures the win-at-all-cost mentality evident in big-time intercollegiate athletics. Communications, athletic apparel, and merchandising companies invest billions of dollars into amateur and professional sports. The real and perceived financial interests of the various participants in the sports industry influence their openness to regulation, particularly if regulation may lead to changes that will upset the financial status quo.

Thus sport produces a fundamental dichotomy: the inherent conflict between values associated with competition, individualism, and the unrelenting pursuit of self-interest and those associated with teamwork, fair play, moral responsibility, and interdependence. As such, sport reproduces the tension between values that favor unrestricted personal autonomy and those that favor external regulation as a means of inserting community norms into the sports realm.

This tension leads to a concern about how sport should be regulated. When sport conflicts with other values, should sport or the other values prevail? What is different about sport as an object of regulation? Too much regulation reduces our freedom. Too little arguably does the same by giving sport leeway that would not be granted in other aspects of society.

Finally, sport reflects the group struggles of the larger society. Does sport encourage diversity? Does sport provide a forum within which barriers based on gender, race, or disability impede equity? But is sport a forum within which discrimination and power undermine the ideas of meritocracy commonly associated with sport? These issues are addressed in Chapters 9, 10, and 11.

2.   *Sport and Its Various Intersections*

Any serious effort to study sport must begin from the premise that sport interfaces with other important cultural institutions. Commenting on the relevance of studying the intersection of sport and other social institutions, one sociologist notes that "there exist numerous *institutional interconnections* among the basic institutions of a society, and changes in one sphere reverberate into others because of their systemic connections." Wilbert M. Leonard II, A Sociological Perspective of Sport IX (5th ed. 1998). Professor Burlette Carter's observations concerning the importance of recognizing the interdisciplinary nature of sports law are equally applicable to sport generally. "[I]n the real world, there is no contracts case that does not bump into some other legal field—at the very least evidence, civil procedure and legal ethics, but possibly too corporations, antitrust, labor law, securities law and others." W. Burlette Carter, *Introduction: What Makes a "Field" a Field?*, 1 Va. J. Sports & L. 235, 243 (1999). Just as with sports law, sport cannot be critically assessed apart from its cultural, economic, political, and philosophical dimensions to which we now turn.

a.   Sport, Culture, and Metaphors

Sport's influence intrudes into various aspects of our culture. We make decisions regarding clothing and other products that we purchase based on the attire that is worn and the products that are used and endorsed by sports heroes. NBA superstar Michael Jordan has added millions of dollars to Nike's bottom line for his signature "Air Jordan" shoes and clothing. Despite his marital infidelities, Tiger Woods earned approximately $55 million in 2011 for endorsing several popular consumer products and services. These and numerous other athletes' endorsements seek to persuade consumers that their affiliations with various products and services warrant their purchase of them.

i.   *Metaphors*

Expressions used in sport filter into popular culture. Terms and figures of speech that had their genesis in sport, such as cheap shot, pinch-hit, go to bat, and ballpark figure, are commonly used in nonsport contexts. Habitual criminal statutes adopted by California and other states are commonly referred to as "three strikes and you're out" laws. Professor Elizabeth Thornburg argues that expressions in sport have had a profound impact on the American litigation system. She argues that sport-, war-, and love-related metaphors and the values that underlie them influence the development of rules that foster competition rather than cooperation in our litigation system.

> Some sports metaphors . . . have to do with roles. They portray trial lawyers as game players, boxers, team members, or forensic athletes. Judges, not surprisingly, are referees or umpires.
>   Other metaphors compare lawsuits to particular sports or games: blind man's bluff, hide and seek, chess, a game of chance, a game of wits and strategy, a cat and mouse game, a poker game, a football game, a boxing match, tennis, fishing, a tug of war, dice, [and] a race. Metaphors using sports as a reference for litigation

activities are also common. For example, litigants sometimes play with one hand tied behind their backs, skate close to the edge, strike a blow, lay their cards on the table, go close to the line, bluff, coach witnesses, ask for an extra inning, or get an elbow in the eye.

Sports metaphors also illustrate litigation strategy. As in war, the goal is to win. The players must know the rules of the game. Lawyers employ stratagems and devices; they need gamesmanship and game plans. As in chess, successful litigators make moves and need defensive gambits; as in cards, they need a poker face; as in wrestling they "go to the mat." Litigators can be hard hitting, play rough, or play tough but fair. It is currently extremely popular, despite frequent criticism, to play hardball. . . .

The complex use of game metaphors also reinforces competitive values and behaviors. The sin here is not playing too hard, but failing to take the game seriously. Many judges state that litigation is not a game because the game image fails to recognize the seriousness of the competition or suggest that the outcome might be somewhat random. Nevertheless, metaphors describing game activities are frequently used to describe what goes on in litigation, and are used approvingly to describe the strategic and competitive aspects of lawsuits.

Elizabeth G. Thornburg, *Metaphors Matter: How Images of Battle, Sports, and Sex Shape the Adversary System,* 10 Wis. Women's L.J. 225, 239, 242 (1995).

Professor Thornburg concludes that sport and game metaphors can be but are rarely used to emphasize values such as teamwork. Consequently, sport metaphors stress "winning at all costs rather than fair play and rules." She argues that ultimately these and other metaphors impede efforts to modify procedural and ethical rules so that they reflect values of cooperation and community.

ii.   Shaping Gender Identity

Some sociologists argue that sport as a social institution has historically contributed to shaping gender identity. Specifically, sport has traditionally amounted to an external dynamic that socialized boys and helped them to sculpt their developing gender identities. Some feminist scholars go further and argue that sport has significantly contributed to the construction of a male identity that is often harmful to women. For example, Professor Michael Messner argues:

> Sport is a social institution, that, in its dominant forms, was created by and for men. . . . [T]he gendered values of the institution of sport [make] it extremely unlikely that [young men will] construct anything but the kinds of personalities and relationships that [are] consistent with the dominant values and power relations of the larger gender order. . . . The fact that winning was premised on physical power, strength, discipline, and willingness to take, ignore, or deaden pain inclined men to experience their bodies as machines, instruments of power and domination— and to see other peoples' bodies as objects of their power and domination.

Michael A. Messner, Power at Play 54 (1992).

iii. Sport and Religion: The Ultimate Metaphor or Something More?

Considerable controversy revolves around the relationship, if any, between sport and religion. Some argue that sport and religion constitute unique cultural practices because the nature of religion and the nature of sport are essentially different. According to this view, "religious beliefs, meaning, rituals, and events are grounded in the sacred and supernatural realm, while sport beliefs, meanings, rituals, and events are grounded in the profane realm." Coakley, *supra*, at 461.

Other scholars argue that sport is a "new form of religion." This view is based on the notion that sport involves expressions of beliefs and meanings that take on greater relevance in people's lives than those associated with traditional religions. According to one scholar, "Sport constitutes the primary lived world of the vast majority of Americans. The holy trinity—baseball, basketball, and football . . . are not simply interludes but the basic substratum of our intellectual and emotional lives. Play provides the fundamental metaphors and the paradigmatic experiences for understanding the other elements of life." Michael Novak, *The Natural Religion*, in Sport Inside Out 353, 363 (David L. Vanderwerken and Spencer K. Wertz eds., 1985).

An intermediate perspective suggests a connection between sport and religion, but stops short of identifying sport as a "new form of religion." Proponents of this view propose that sport and religion share common characteristics, including the presence of gods in both sport and religion (e.g., saints, priests, and superstars); places of worship and communal gathering; a desire to achieve "perfection in body, mind, and spirit"; structured organizations with hierarchical systems of authority; and organized events that celebrate and reflect core values. Coakley, *supra*, at 459-460. Notwithstanding such parallels, these academics argue that sport fails to fulfill key functions of traditional religion, such as exploring the purpose of human existence on earth and life after death. Eitzen and Sage, *supra*, at 171.

Several questions emerge from efforts exploring the relationship between sport and religion. For example, does it demean religion to attempt to equate sport with religion? Does the willingness of some to equate sport with religion itself say something about sport's role in society? If so, what?

Sport and religion have on occasion intersected in a pragmatic context. For example, former NBA basketball player Chris Jackson changed his name to Mahmoud Abdul-Rauf after he converted to Islam. During the 1995-1996 NBA season, Abdul-Rauf decided that his religious beliefs precluded him from demonstrating respect for the American flag or the national anthem. Abdul-Rauf's stance conflicted with NBA rules that require players to stand respectfully during the playing of the national anthem before each game. After unsuccessful efforts to reach a compromise, NBA commissioner David Stern suspended Abdul-Rauf for his failure to comply with league rules. Abdul-Rauf promised, after a one-game suspension, that he would stand for the playing of the national anthem but with his eyes closed and his face cupped in his hands while he prayed to Allah. In response to his promise, the NBA ended the suspension, and Abdul-Rauf completed the season.

Tim Tebow's outward expressions of his religious faith on the field, as a collegiate and professional football player, have been praised and criticized. For example, Khaled Hamideh, chairman of the board of the Colorado Muslim Society, reacted positively to Tebow's religious acts, stating, "I know I'm a Muslim and he's a Christian, but I admire somebody who thanks God for everything that he gave him." See Billy Hallowell, *Muslims and Jews Defend Tim Tebow's Dedication to His Faith*, Blaze, Dec. 12, 2011, http://www.theblaze.com/stories/muslims-jews-defend-tim-tebows-dedication-to-his-faith/. Others are less positive. Jake Plummer, quarterback for the Phoenix Cardinals, for example, noted that he wishes that Tebow would not use football as a means of proselytizing.

See Michael David Smith, *Jake Plummer Wishes Tim Tebow Would Cut Down on the Religion Talk*, NBC Sports, Nov. 21, 2011, http://profootballtalk.nbcsports .com/2011/11/21/jake-plummer-wishes-tim-tebow-would-cut-down-on-the-religion-talk/. What is very clear is that religion and sport become intermixed, and when they do, the reaction is often mixed.

b.   Sport and Economics

The pervasiveness of sport has also had profound effect on our national economy. According to Plunkett Research, an estimated $435 billion was spent on sports in the United States during 2012, placing it in the top ten largest industries in the United States. Sporting equipment retail sales account for approximately $41.5 billion. In 2011, U.S. sporting goods manufacturers earned $77.3 billion in wholesale revenues. In 2001, sports teams, leagues, and other sports properties generated an estimated $31.76 billion in revenue. During 2011-2012, the major four professional sports leagues in the United States, the National Football League (NFL), National Basketball Association (NBA), Major League Baseball (MLB), and National Hockey League (NHL), had combined annual revenues of over $20 billion. The average annual revenue per worker across all sports teams in 2007 was estimated at over $325,000. In 1988, three companies secured "naming rights" to arenas and stadiums for a total of $25 million. By 2004, 66 companies entered into naming rights deals worth an estimated $3.6 billion. Richard Sandomir, *At (Your Name Here) Arena*, N.Y. Times, May 30, 2004, Sec. 3, at 1. In 2007, the *Sports Business Journal* reported that over the past decade more than $6.14 billion had been committed to new facility naming rights deals in five sports alone: the NFL, the NBA, the NHL, MLB, and MLS (Major League Soccer). Andy Carter and David Broughton, *Name Your Price: $6.14 Billion*, Sports Bus. J., Apr. 28, 2008, at 52A. Over the same time period, $27 billion was spent on the construction of sports facilities for major league, minor league, and college teams. *Id.* at 71A.

The foregoing numbers present an impressive picture of the extent of the economic influence of sport in the United States. Yet they tell only part of the story. On the other side of the ledger lies, by way of example, the "athletic arms race" in college sports that results in most university athletic departments operating at a loss, the payment of exorbitant salaries to many coaches in men's basketball and football, and pressure to win that produces for many a win-at-all-cost attitude. Between 1995 and 2000, average athletic budgets at Division I schools increased 25 percent. Mary Jo Sylwester and Tom Witosky, *Athletic Spending Grows as Academic Funds Dry Up*, USA Today, Feb. 18, 2004, at 1A. Similarly, between 2004 and 2006, revenues at Division I's Football Bowl Subdivision (FBS) increased by 16 percent, but expenses increased by 23 percent.[2] Between

---

2. Daniel L. Fulks, 2004-06 NCAA Revenues and Expenses of Division I Intercollegiate Athletics Programs Report 7 (2008). This report also found that only 19 of 119 Football Bowl Subdivision institutions generated revenues in excess of expenses. *Id.* Other findings included the following: "The median FBS football program generated approximately $10.6 million in revenues (up from $8.3 million in 2004). The median for football program expenses was approximately $8.5 million (versus $7.5 million in 2004). The median FBS's men's basketball program generated approximately $4.0 million in revenue in 2006, and had $2.7 in expenses. The revenue and expense numbers were up from $3.2 million and $2.5 million, respectively, in 2004." *Id.*

2010 and 2011, median revenues generated at FBS institutions increased by 9.7 percent, and median total expenses increased by 8.8 percent.[3] With respect to the "athletic arms race," as early as 2001, the Knight Foundation Commission on Intercollegiate Athletics was emphasizing the move toward excess:

> Too much in major college sports is geared to accommodating excess. Too many athletic directors and conference commissioners serve principally as money managers, ever alert to maximizing revenues. And too many have looked to their stadiums and arenas to generate more money. In the last seven years, capital expenditures at Division I-A institutions (e.g., construction or remodeling of athletics facilities, capital equipment, etc.) increased 250 percent. From east to west, north to south, the test becomes who can build the biggest stadiums, the most luxurious skyboxes. Every one of the 12 schools in one major conference has built a new football stadium or refurbished its old one in recent years. All seem to have assumed they could not afford to do otherwise. The building boom in college sports facilities now under way across the nation will cost well over $4 billion, with the resulting debt stretching far into the future.

Knight Foundation Commission on Intercollegiate Athletics, A Call to Action: Reconnecting College Sports and Higher Education 17 (June 2001).

In its report, *Restoring the Balance: Dollars, Values, and the Future of College Sports* (2010), the Knight Commission noted that the top ten athletic budgets had grown significantly since 2005: from $69 million in 2005 to $98 million in 2009. In that same report, the Knight Commission projects that the top ten athletic budgets will be at the $165 million figure, representing an increase of nearly 140 percent in little over a decade. These figures may prove to be conservative, given the addition of a BCS-sponsored national championship in FBS football, which will clearly be quite lucrative and will surely contribute to an increased "arm's war" among the most powerful programs and those that desire to join this elite group.

This growth in athletic budgets at the most powerful programs has occurred during a downturn in the economy and a time of general cost-containment in higher education. These economic factors have created an imbalance between commercially successful intercollegiate athletic programs (e.g., men's basketball and football) and programs that do not generate significant revenues. At page 7 of its *Restoring the Balance* report, the Knight Commission warns:

> The current downturn should be a wake-up call for all programs. It has significantly refocused academic priorities and even forced some institutions to ratchet back spending on sports—primarily by paring teams in lower-profile sports, thus curtailing opportunities for student-athletes. However, even with this new reality, top programs are expected to have athletics budgets exceeding $250 million by 2020, based on data from the past five years. Even for the largest and best-positioned universities, a $250 million athletics budget serving an average of 600 students is untenable.

The debate concerning public financing of sports stadiums illustrates that often factors other than dollars and cents are at play. Despite uncertainty as to

---

3. Daniel L. Fulks, 2004-2011 NCAA Division I Intercollegiate Athletics Programs Report 12 (2012). This report found that 23 FBS institutions generated revenues in excess of expenses. *Id.* at 13.

the extent to which public financing of sport stadiums in most communities results in significant economic benefits, communities nevertheless have been willing to invest public funds in building stadiums as a means of attracting or retaining a professional sports franchise. What prompts community leaders to act so as to defy economic logic? Supporters of public financing argue that the impact of a professional sports franchise lies not only in direct benefits (e.g., tax revenue, stadium lease payments by teams) but also in the indirect benefits. They argue that the indirect benefits that communities derive from having a sports franchise include the sense of identity and stature that accompanies having a sports franchise.

Some view the NBA's Washington Wizards' basketball arena, the Verizon Center, as a model of the benefits that can be reaped from stadium construction. The Verizon Center, which was constructed in an economically depressed section of Washington, D.C., has been viewed as providing the cornerstone of the redevelopment of the city's downtown core. As of 2007, close to $5 billion in economic development was reportedly completed in the area within close proximity to the stadium. Tim Lemke, *Change on the Verizon After Arena Revived D.C., City Set to Return the Favor*, Wash. Times, Oct. 29, 2007, at A01.

In discussing the economics of sports franchises, Professor Kenneth Shropshire strikes a discordant note:

> Direct and indirect economic benefits such as increased tourism, arena or stadium income, sports franchise expenditures in the city, taxes, and employment are often mythically thought to be guaranteed by the acquisition of a professional sports franchise. Such is the proverbial carrot at the end of the stick that cities chase. In reality, the only reward a city that successfully attracts a sports franchise may receive is the public perception that their metropolis has been thrust into that class of cities nebulously described as "big-league."

Kenneth L. Shropshire, The Sports Franchise: Cities in Pursuit of Sports Franchises, Events, Stadiums, and Arenas 8 (1995). Shropshire concludes that despite most recent empirical studies that fail to find a significant positive correlation between professional sports teams and economic development, decisions regarding whether to pursue a franchise turn largely on subjective considerations. *Id.* For comprehensive economic analyses of professional sports franchises and events, see Robert A. Baade, Robert Baumann, and Victor A. Matheson, *Selling the Game: Estimating the Economic Impact of Professional Sports through Taxable Sales*, 74 S. Econ. J. 794 (2008); Dennis Coates, *Stadiums and Arenas: Economic Development or Economic Redistribution?*, 25 Contemp. Econ. Pol'y, 565 (2007); Andrew Zimbalist, The Economics of Sport 287 (2001); Roger G. Noll and Andrew Zimbalist, Sports, Jobs, and Taxes: The Economic Impact of Sports Teams and Stadiums (1997). For a recent analysis of operating a major league franchise in challenging times, see Paul M. Anderson and W.S. Millier, *Sonic Bust: Trying to Retain Major League Franchises in Challenging Economic Times*, 21 J. Legal Aspects of Sport 117 (2011).

c. Sport and Politics

Organized competitive sports long have been connected with politics, government, and the nation-state. **Politics** refers to power and how it is gained and used in social life, and **government** refers to formal organizations and agencies that have the authority to make rules regulating people's behavior. Politics is involved in all social relationships and organizations, including those related to sports.

Coakley, *supra*, at 386.

Sociologists Stanley Eitzen and George Sage address the characteristics inherent in sport that make politics endemic to it. They first note that sport participants hold allegiances to particular ideologies that manifest in slogans, insignias, and music. In addition, as sports became organized, teams, regulatory bodies, and other organizations emerged. Political conflict arises when the interests of these groups are in conflict. Finally, Eitzen and Sage argue that a systemic entwinement between sport and politics arises because sport as a social institution typically reinforces societal values, including those of a political nature. Consequently, sport "serves as a preserver and a legitimator of the existing order." Eitzen and Sage, *supra*, at 194. Helpful discussions of the interconnectedness of sport and politics include John M. Hoberman, Sport and Political Ideology 20 (1984); Wilbert M. Leonard II, A Sociological Perspective of Sport (1998); and Martin B. Vinokur, More Than a Game: Sports and Politics (1988).

The intersection of sport and politics to which these scholars refer is multidimensional. It plays out at local, national, and international levels. Title IX and efforts by sports leagues to stymie athletes' use of performance-enhancing drugs illustrate how issues in sports can become highly politicized. The politics surrounding construction of sports facilities, public support for recreational activities, and laws such as "no-pass, no-play" legislation provide illustrations of the relationship between sport and politics at the local level. The politics of sport also involves diverse players, including governmental authorities, multinational corporations, other institutional entities, and individuals. Governmental involvement in sport may cover a broad range of activities, including enacting laws regulating sport-related activities, expending public funds to promote physical fitness among citizens, using sport to heighten national prestige, and using sport to forge a sense of national identity among a diverse populace. Governments have also used sport to promote particular values or ideologies and to take political positions on controversial issues. See Coakley, *supra*, at 391.

In this regard, important and dramatic illustrations of the politics of sport have occurred in the international arena in the context of the Olympic Games. Reflecting on the politics of the Olympics, Professor Alfred Senn states:

> Although many sports fans consider "politics" an unwelcome intruder in the Olympic Games, politics are in fact an integral part of the Games. The glamour and attractiveness of the Olympic Games and the fact people care give Olympic performances great political significance and weight. Lord Killanin, the head of the IOC in the 1970s, confirmed this, writing, "[n]inety-five percent of my problems as president of the IOC involved national and international politics." In practice, the political dimensions of the Games are diverse and complicated, ranging from the certification of national teams, through the interplay and intrigues of the various international sports organizations, to the infighting of the IOC. Governments have tried to exploit the Games for their own ends, and at times the IOC has itself put pressure on governments. It is no surprise, then, that the Games have served as a focus for national rivalries and ideological rivalries between states.

Alfred E. Senn, Power, Politics, and the Olympic Games X (1999).

Specific illustrations of the Olympic politics to which Professor Senn refers include Nazi Germany's efforts to use the 1936 Olympic Games to promote its political ideology of Aryan supremacy, the United States and Canada's boycott of the 1980 Games to protest Soviet actions in Afghanistan, and the retaliatory boycott of the 1984 Games by the USSR and its allies in protest of commercialization. At the 1968 Olympics, when a proposed boycott did not materialize, some African American athletes developed a list of demands that focused on racial discrimination in athletics. Two African Americans, John Carlos and Tommie Smith, who finished first and third in the 200-meter dash, raised black-gloved fists and socks and bowed their heads as they stood on the medal stand while "The Star-Spangled Banner" played. Alfred D. Mathewson, *Grooming Crossovers*, 4 J. Gender Race & Just. 225, 236 (2001).

Sport has also been a vehicle for protest at the international level, both within and outside of the Olympic Games. The organized boycott of sports competitions involving teams from South Africa that began in the 1960s contributed to the end of apartheid by focusing international attention on racial oppression in that country. A recent illustration of the complexity of the politics of sports involves accusations that sporting goods manufacturers exploit workers in poorer countries whose labor produces the merchandise sold by these companies.

Another dimension of the endemic political nature of sport is its use by politicians. Apart from trumpeting their own personal past involvement in sport, politicians use the sporting venue for political purposes. It is very common for politicians to promote ties between themselves and athletes or sports teams. U.S. Senator Herbert Kohl owns the Milwaukee Bucks NBA team. Presidents of the United States extend "White House" invitations to championship professional and amateur teams in the more popular sports. Such high-profile events attract considerable favorable media for presidents. Politicians also actively seek the support of athletes who, because of their popularity, are effective in getting the vote for candidates whom they support. See Eitzen and Sage, *supra*, at 199-200.

Several former athletes currently hold political office, including New Jersey Congressman Jon Runyan, a former NFL and University of Michigan football player; Detroit Mayor Dave Bing, a seven-time NBA all-star player whose number was retired by the Detroit Pistons; and Sacramento Mayor Kevin Johnson, who played in the NBA for 12 years. Examples of former athletes who have recently held political office are President George W. Bush, who captained Yale's varsity baseball team; California Governor Arnold Schwarzenegger, winner of six consecutive Mr. Olympia bodybuilding championships between 1970 and 1975 and a seventh in 1980; Florida Governor Charles Crist, Jr., who played college football; U.S. Senator Jim Bunning, a Hall of Fame Major League Baseball pitcher; U.S. Representative Heath Shuler, former NFL quarterback; and U.S. Representative Jim Ryun, Olympic silver medalist in the 1,500-meter run. Other notable politicians who competed as athletes include former President Gerald Ford (collegiate football), former President Ronald Reagan (collegiate football), former President Richard Nixon (collegiate football), former Maryland Governor Robert Ehrlich (captain of the Princeton football team), former U.S. Senator Ben Nighthorse Campbell (captain of the 1964 U.S. Olympic judo team), former U.S. Representative Steve Largent (NFL wide receiver), former U.S. Representative Tom Osborne (University of Nebraska head football coach), former U.S. Representative J.C. Watts (college football), former U.S. Representative Jack Kemp (professional football), former U.S. Senator Bill Bradley (professional basketball), and former Minnesota Governor Jesse Ventura (professional wrestler).

Sports teams and associations are also politically active. *Forbes* reported the following lobbying expenses from 2007-2011: the NFL spent $6.528 million; MLB spent $3.6 million, the NBA spent $907,000, the NCAA spent $840,000, and the BCS spent $960,000. See Darren Heitner, *Why Obama and Romney Should Pay Careful Attention to Professional Sports*, Forbes, Aug. 6, 2012, http://www.forbes .com/sites/darrenheitner/2012/08/06/why-obama-and-romney-should-pay-careful-attention-to-professional-sports/. Lobbying also occurs at the state level. It is clear that associations and individual clubs or institutions are expending significant sums to increase their political influence. Finally, some commentators propose that sport has become transformed at the international level. According to this view, the increased significance of nongovernmental groups and organizations, such as multinational corporations that operate independently of national governments, redefines the politics of sports as transnational rather than international. Nike entered into a $200 million deal with Brazil's soccer team that allowed the company to use the team to promote its Nike products through 2005. Some argue that one consequence of such emerging relationships is the redefinition of the politics of sports. For example, messages promoting the interests of corporate entities may become more prevalent than themes that focus on patriotism or nationalism. See Coakley, *supra*, at 397-399; Senn, *supra*, at xii.

NOTES AND QUESTIONS

1. *The Value of Sports Participation.* This chapter introduced you to the idea that sport reflects and reinforces cultural themes, both empowering and harmful, that pervade our society. See, e.g., Eitzen and Sage, *supra*, at 13 (stating that sport provides a useful institution for examining the complexities of larger society because it represents a microcosm of the society in which it is embedded); Harry Edwards, *Playoffs and Payoffs: The African-American Athlete as an Institutional Resource*, in The State of Black America 85, 85 (Billy J. Tidwell ed., 1994) (discussing how sport reflects and recapitulates America's evolving social realities). In justifying the need to expand sports-related opportunities, one commentator opined that "values we learn from participation in sports [include] teamwork, standards, leadership, discipline, work ethics, self-sacrifice, pride in accomplishment [and] strength of character." Rodney K. Smith, *When Ignorance Is Not Bliss: In Search of Racial and Gender Equity in Intercollegiate Athletics*, 61 Mo. L. Rev. 329, 340 (1996) (quoting Norma Cantu). Do you agree?

2. *Sport and the Construction of Gender Identity.* Does sport contribute to the construction of male identity in ways that are potentially harmful to women? What variables shape male and female identity? Is sport a critical variable? Will increased opportunities for women to participate in organized sport alter the way in which sport influences the shaping of male and female identity? How women view themselves?

   For thoughtful discussions of these issues, see Lois Bryson, *Sport and Maintenance of Masculine Hegemony, in* Women, Sport, and Culture 47, 60 (Susan Birrell and Cheryl L. Cole eds., 1994) (arguing that sport supports male hegemony, in part, because of the public's exposure to position-sanctioned use of aggression and violence by men); Mary Jo Kane and Lisa J. Disch, *Sexual Violence and the Reproduction of Male Power in the Locker Room:*

The "Lisa Olson Incident," Soc. Sport J., Dec. 1993, at 331, 334 (citations omitted) ("[s]port is an institution that creates and reproduces male power and domination in this culture"). See also Jeff Benedict, Public Heroes, Private Felons: Athletes and Crimes Against Women 215 (1997); Ellen E. Dabbs, *Intentional Fouls: Athletes and Violence Against Women,* 31 Colum. J.L. & Soc. Probs. 167 (1998) (urging professional leagues to support penalizing players who commit acts of violence against women); Michael M. O'Hear, *Blue-Collar Crimes/White-Collar Criminals: Sentencing Elite Athletes Who Commit Violent Crimes,* 12 Marq. Sports L. Rev. 427 (2001) (addressing whether courts should consider the macho subculture when sentencing athletes who have been convicted of criminally proscribed acts of violence against women). See also Suzanne Janusz, *The NFL's Strict Enforcement of its Personal Conduct Policy for Crimes Against Women: A Useful Tool for Combating Violence or an Attempt to Punish Morality?,* 22 Seton Hall J. Sports & Ent. L. 93 (2012) (analyzing the use of the NFL's personal conduct policy for crimes against women); Bethany P. Withers, *The Integrity of the Game: Professional Athletes and Domestic Violence,* 1 Harv. J. Sports & Ent. 145 (2010) (exploring ethical issues raised by violence against women in professional athletics); and Dionne L. Koller, *Not Just One of the Boys: A Post-Feminist Critique of Title IX's Vision for Gender Equity in Sports,* 43 Conn. L. Rev. 401 (2010) (critiquing the vision and role of Title IX from a "post-feminist" viewpoint).

3. *Sport and Religion.* One sociologist describes the relationship between sport and religion as follows:

> The purpose of religion is to transcend the circumstances and conditions of material life in the pursuit of spiritual goals and eternal life, while the purpose of sport is to focus on material issues, such as victories and the regards they bring in this life. Religion is fundamentally rooted in faith, while sport is fundamentally rooted in concrete factual rules and relationships. Religion involves cooperation among believers, while sport involves competition. Religion emphasizes a spirit of service and love of others, while sports emphasizes a spirit of personal achievement and defeat of others.

Coakley, *supra,* at 461. Does the foregoing accurately cast the relationship between sport and religion?

4. *Sport and Religious Organizations.* Evangelism is a central activity of organizations such as the Fellowship of Christian Athletes (FCA) and Athletes in Action (AIA). AIA was founded with the mission to give "100 people annually the opportunity to hear the gospel" and to build a "global movement of 15,000 spiritually mature athletic influencers." Athletes in Action, *About Athletes in Action,* http://athletesinaction.org/about/ (accessed Aug. 24, 2012). The FCA identifies its mission as follows: "To present to athletes and coaches and all whom they influence the challenge and adventure of receiving Jesus Christ as Savior and Lord, serving Him in their relationships and in the fellowship of the church." Fellowship of Christian Athletes, *Mission and Vision,* http://www.fca.org/AboutFCA/ (accessed Aug. 24, 2012).

The evangelistic activities of AIA, FCA, and similar organizations have prompted some to coin the phrase "Sportianity" to identify this movement. Eitzen and Sage, *supra,* at 176 (noting that the effectiveness of athletes as evangelists is in part because of the prestige, visibility, and access that allows them to reach people, particularly the young, who a preacher or priest might not be able to reach). What are the consequences of organizations using athletes to evangelize? Should such organizations focus on matters other than religion that arise in sports? See Coakley, *supra*, at 482 (critically assessing the evangelistic activities of such groups).

3.   The Study of Sports Law

In the next several chapters, you will be introduced to issues related to the regulation of sports primarily in four areas of athletic competition: the interscholastic (high school), intercollegiate, Olympic, and professional levels. During your studies, note the similarities and differences in the levels of competition:

> At the professional and Olympic sport levels, athletic participation produces economic benefits including money earned from player contracts, prize earnings, and endorsement contracts as well as the psychological and social rewards for achieving athletic excellence. At the collegiate level, many thousands of the participating student-athletes receive an athletic scholarship that is worth thousands of dollars. Indirect economic benefits include the prospective monetary gain that will be realized by college athletes who are talented enough to use college as a training ground for a career in professional sports. Although relatively few of the more than 7 million high school student-athletes or 400,000 National Collegiate Athletic Association student-athletes have the exceptional talent necessary to play a professional or Olympic sport, recent empirical research proves that they derive important intangible benefits from organized sports competition, including educational and character development with lifelong individual and social effects.

Matthew J. Mitten and Timothy Davis, *Athlete Eligibility Requirements and Legal Protection of Sports Participation Opportunities*, 8 Va. Sports & Ent. L.J. 71, 73-74 (2009).

   Throughout your studies, consider how these and other similarities and differences in the levels of athletic competition impact their legal regulation. For example, at all levels of sports competition, monolithic sports leagues and governing bodies (e.g., the National Football League, the International Olympic Committee, the National Collegiate Athletic Association, and state interscholastic athletic associations) establish eligibility requirements and conditions that must be satisfied for an individual to participate in athletics. Most of these governing bodies possess "broad, exclusive authority to regulate a single sport or group of sports on either an international, national, or state-wide basis," which provides the corresponding power to exclude or limit athletic participation opportunities. In some instances, unilaterally established eligibility rules either completely preclude an individual from athletic participation, or condition his or her right to participate upon compliance with several requirements." *Id.* You will also have the opportunity, however, to consider whether differences between the levels of competition help to explain the greater process and substantive protections afforded athlete participation rights at the professional and Olympic levels of competition in contrast with the paucity of such protections afforded athletes at the high school and collegiate levels.

   Because of the increasing globalization of sports and the historical European domination of the governance of Olympic and international sports competition, it is important to have a basic understanding of the differences between the U.S. and European models of sport. In the United States there is an autonomous governing body for each sport (e.g., soccer) at each level of competition (e.g., youth, high school, college, Olympic, and professional). Sport generally is separately and privately funded at each level of competition, with no government subsidization (with the exception of state-funded public high school and university athletic programs) or direct government regulation.

Traditionally, European sport has been based on a sociocultural model, with the objective of promoting athletic participation opportunities for all through club sports. In Europe there is a hierarchical or pyramid system of governance for both "amateur" and "professional" competition in a sport, with a worldwide regulatory authority at its apex. For example, within each country there are regional federations that govern soccer in their respective local areas; these regional federations are members of a national federation, which in turn is part of the Union of European Football Associations (UEFA), a confederation of 53 national federations recognized by soccer's international governing body, the Federation Internationale de Football Association (FIFA). Pursuant to a vertical solidarity system, the grassroots amateur clubs traditionally have received some financial support from the country's national federation and top-tier professional clubs, as well as some government subsidies. In contrast to U.S. professional sports leagues, European sports leagues are "open" and have a promotion and relegation system. Each year the best two to four teams in a league are promoted to the next higher league and the corresponding worst teams are relegated to the next lower league. See generally Richard Parish and Samuli Miettinen, The Sporting Exception in European Union 17-22 (2008); *European and North American Models of Sports Organization,* in Research Handbook on International Sports Law 88-111 (James A.R. Nafziger and Stephen F. Ross, eds.) (Edward Elgar Publishing 2011).

We begin our study of sports law by examining legal regulation of interscholastic sports (Chapter 2) and intercollegiate sports (Chapter 3), two levels of athletic competition that are prevalent in the United States but not in Europe or the rest of the world.

STOP

CHAPTER 2

Regulating Interscholastic (High School) Athletics

A. INTERSCHOLASTIC ATHLETICS: THE RISE OF REGULATION AT THE STATE AND NATIONAL LEVELS

1. *Historical Overview*

By 1821 the Latin School for girls of Salem, Massachusetts, encouraged athletic activity in the form of simple gymnastics for educational and recreational reasons. Mabel Lee, A History of Physical Education and Sports in the U.S.A. 34 (1983). Soon thereafter, Catherine Beecher started using calisthenics in her school in Hartford, Connecticut. *Id.* The first recognition of physical education as "a real part of a school program came shortly after the Round Hill School was established in 1823. From its inception, Round Hill School provided a rich program of physical activities, which included archery, baseball, boxing, camping, dancing, football, hiking, running, skating, swimming, and wrestling." *Id.* at 34-35. Initially, these athletic activities were informally organized, but in 1827 physical education was formalized as part of the curriculum, with the entire school being divided into classes, which met for an hour three times each week for instruction in gymnastics. *Id.* at 35.

Other schools began to implement physical education in some form, and by 1851 the state superintendent of schools for Minnesota called for an acre or more of land to be "set aside for the physical development of [students]." *Id.* During the coming decades, secondary schools were established throughout the United States and were increasingly involved in providing athletic activity of some form for their students.

A Detroit high school football team existed in 1888, and by 1892 a Detroit high school baseball team traveled to Ann Arbor for an interscholastic game. *Id.* at 196. By the latter part of the nineteenth century, "[f]ollowing the pattern set by college men, high school boys formed their own student-directed athletic associations." *Id.* at 196. As was the case with their collegiate counterparts, however, these student-run athletic associations and activities were plagued by economic challenges, and a "win-at-all-costs philosophy often resulted in the recruiting of ineligible players." Richard A. Swanson and Betty Spears, History of Sport and Physical Education in the United States 199 (4th ed. 1995). Thus, in 1902, "[t]he 15th Educational Conference of Academics and High Schools . . . recommended strict faculty control of sports and the establishment of state associations to oversee competition. By 1923 all but three had associations." *Id.*

Actually, the first state athletic associations for secondary schools predated the action of the 15th Educational Conference. In late 1895 and early 1896, a series of meetings was held in Wisconsin, "involving people interested in promoting (but not necessarily regulating) athletic competition between Wisconsin high schools." See *About WIAA*, http://www.wiaawi.org/aboutwiaa.aspx (last visited February 6, 2013). After the formal organization of the Wisconsin Interscholastic Athletic Association, state athletic associations began to proliferate throughout the United States, and the predecessor to the National Federation of State High School Associations was formed in 1923.

In 1903 the Public School Athletic League (PSAL) was formed in New York to supervise interscholastic sports. By 1910 this league was being praised as "the world's greatest athletic organization." Swanson and Spears, *supra*, at 199. The successful rise of interscholastic athletics, however, was not confined to New York. A survey of Nebraska high schools in 1909 "revealed that 95 percent of them had interscholastic sports; 91 percent of those said that discipline was improved, 92 percent that scholastic standards became higher, and 97 percent that school spirit was better." *Id.* The early favorable response to the benefits of interscholastic athletics in Nebraska and elsewhere has continued.

In November 2010, the National Women's Law Center filed administrative complaints with the U.S. Department of Education's Office of Civil Rights against the Chicago Public Schools (CPS) and 11 other school districts nationwide, including Houston and New York City, alleging that the schools within those districts are failing to provide equal opportunities for girls to participate in athletics and therefore are not in compliance with Title IX. Each complaint alleges that the schools are failing to provide a proportionate amount of athletic opportunities for high school girls based on their overall enrollment. In July 2012, the U.S. Department of Education announced that its Office for Civil Rights reached agreements with 4 of the 12 school districts, including districts in Raleigh, Phoenix, Columbus, and Houston. Complaints involving the other 8 school districts, including Chicago and New York City, remain open. In June 2012, the NWLC reported that in most states at least 25 percent and as many as 75 percent of schools report large participation gaps between the girls enrolled and girls who play.

Title IX has been slow in coming to interscholastic athletics, but these efforts by the National Women's Law Center may be the harbinger of things to come. Given the economic challenges facing most school districts, this movement could have a significant impact on the nature of interscholastic athletics in the near future

Participation in interscholastic athletics has grown on almost a yearly basis. Indeed, for the past 22 years, the number of high school students participating in interscholastic athletics has increased annually, setting an all-time high for participation in the 2010-2011 school year of 7,667,955. Participation numbers for both girls and boys increased in 2010-2011: participation by girls eclipsed the previous all-time high set the previous year, with 3,173,549 participants, and participation by boys finally surpassed the previous all-time high with 4,494,406 participants. Participation by girls has consistently increased since the passage of Title IX in 1972, which was adopted to help ensure equality of opportunity for girls desiring to participate in interscholastic and intercollegiate athletics.

Participation by girls, however, continues to lag behind boys and is not increasing at a rate commensurate with participation by boys. An interesting development in participation by girls has been an increasing trend toward participation in traditionally male sports. For example, in 2009-2010, 1,009 schools had women's wrestling, with 6,134 girls participating. In 2010-2011, 1,215 schools had wrestling for girls, with 7,351 girls participating. Weightlifting for girls increased significantly as well. Participation in competitive cheer declined during the same time period, after having experienced significant increases in prior years.

With these increases in participation and the competitiveness of our culture, it is not surprising that interscholastic athletics has spawned significant regulation. State associations have had to develop increasingly sophisticated and elaborate regulations to govern interscholastic athletics. State and federal legislation has impacted interscholastic athletics and will continue to do so. Courts have had to play a role in overseeing the operation of interscholastic athletics. Like intercollegiate athletics, interscholastic athletics has developed much of the appearance of a regulated industry.

2.   *Interscholastic Athletics Regulatory Structure, Governance, and Administrative Processes*

Every state has its own independent association, generally made up of public and private high schools, that has responsibility for promulgating and enforcing regulations related to the governance of interscholastic athletics. The National Federation of High Schools (NFHS) is made up of the 50 individual state high school athletic and activities associations, together with the District of Columbia and affiliate associations in the U.S. territories, Canada, and other countries.

Although local schools are given broad autonomy in determining what general policies should apply in their participation in interscholastic athletics, state associations play a significant role by providing a set of rules for the governance of interscholastic athletics within the state. The vision and mission of a typical state association, the California Interscholastic Federation (CIF), is available at http://cifstate.org/index.php/vision-a-mission.

Interscholastic athletics is largely regulated under the rules formulated at the state level by state athletic associations and voted on by institutions that are members of that state athletic association. Such rules, based on their general terms or individual application, may give rise to litigation. These rules implicate matters of association-wide concern such as transfer from one institution to another, participation in club sports, eligibility of homeschooled students, and age of participants.

Another source of litigation or controversy in the interscholastic athletics area finds its basis in rules developed at the local school district level or by individual schools or coaches. Institutional rules of this sort include those that require good conduct by student-athletes or regulate their grooming and appearance.

Cases raising legal issues relating to both associational and institutional rules and regulations are examined in this chapter. An aggrieved party will generally be required to first attempt to resolve the dispute through available internal administrative processes (i.e., the party will be expected to exhaust administrative remedies before turning to the courts) at either the institutional or associational level. A student-athlete (and his/her parents or guardian) must raise any issues regarding the application or enforcement of an institutional rule with a coach or school administrators. For example, if a school rule is the basis of the underlying dispute (e.g., a grade point or academic requirement that is more stringent than the minimum required by the high school athletic association), then the issue must be raised at the institutional level. On the other hand, if an associational rule is in dispute, then the student-athlete generally must petition association officials for administrative relief. If a student-athlete is unable to obtain the desired relief at the institutional or associational level, litigation may result that raises a host of federal or state law issues, including federal constitutional law claims if the school or association is a state actor. *Public Schools*

There are also occasions when legislative relief may be available through the political process. Some state legislatures are demonstrating a willingness to enact laws pertaining to some aspects of interscholastic athletics. For example, many states recently have passed statutory provisions authorizing the participation of homeschooled students in athletics and other extracurricular activities provided by high schools. This trend is important because it demonstrates a willingness of at least some state legislatures to recognize that a student-athlete's opportunity to participate in high school sports merits legal protection and may also evidence an increased willingness on the part of legislatures to directly regulate at least some aspects of interscholastic sports within the state. On the other hand, courts continue to be deferential to state athletic associations as well as to local school districts and individual high schools regarding the unilateral terms and conditions they may establish as prerequisites for participation in interscholastic athletics, which is generally viewed as a privilege rather than a legal right subject to judicial protection. See, e.g., *Delbuono v. Massachusetts Interscholastic Athletic Association*, 2006 WL 1345563 (Mass. 2006) (rejecting a student-athlete's request for judicial relief that would enable him to participate in a high school hockey game and reaffirming that there is no federal constitutional right to participate in athletics).

Lawyers that handle matters involving interscholastic athletics must be familiar with the internal administrative processes at both the state association and local school levels, each of which has its own culture and manner of dealing with particular issues. Lawyers are often involved in the early stages of a dispute as advisors to administrators (or as administrators) or as counsel representing a student-athlete or other party to the dispute. To provide effective counsel and advice, a lawyer must recognize potential legal issues and provide decision makers and their clients with relevant information that will aid them in making wise decisions. An attorney must be sensitive to the context of the dispute and the personalities of individual association or school decision makers because courts generally defer to their decisions and provide minimal judicial scrutiny.

B. JUDICIAL REGULATION OF INTERSCHOLASTIC ATHLETICS

The following cases and problems illustrate how legal issues arising in the context of interscholastic sports are judicially analyzed. Courts initially consider jurisdictional issues before examining the merits of the case, which requires consideration of relevant state athletic association and school district rules and internal administrative decisions as well as applicable legal precedent. As a general rule, courts will provide relief to an aggrieved party only if the subject rule, application, or enforcement is found to be arbitrary and capricious or violates an applicable federal or state statute or constitutional law provision. For example, in *Brown v. Oklahoma Secondary School Activities Assn.*, 125 P.3d 1219, 1220 (Okla. 2005), the court stated, "We may not interject ourselves in the Association's internal affairs if the rules are reasonable, lawful, in keeping with public policy, and are interpreted fairly and reasonably and enforced uniformly and not arbitrarily." See also *Jones v. Washington Interscholastic Athletic Assn.*, 2009 U.S. App. LEXIS 13240 (9th Cir. June 3, 2009) (affirming the lower court's holding that a state association's denial of a waiver which would have enabled a student to participate in interscholastic athletics on the grounds that the agency had not acted in an arbitrary and capricious manner where the agency acted honestly and on due consideration); *Suburban Scholastic Council v. Section 2 of the New York State Public High School Athletic Assn., Inc.*, 803 N.Y.S.2d 270, 271 (N.Y. App. Div. 2005) ("courts should not interfere with the internal affairs, proceedings, rules and orders of a high school athletic association unless there is evidence of acts which are arbitrary, capricious or an abuse of discretion").

As it relates to athletics, it is important to ask why courts are typically so deferential in such matters. Is it because the issues arise in an educational context, a context in which courts are historically deferential? Is it because courts are reluctant to get involved in overseeing sports or lack confidence in their competence to do so? Or is it for some other reason?

Professor Burlette Carter articulates three theories that provide the bases on which courts have historically deferred to the National Collegiate Athletic Association (NCAA) in matters involving challenges to NCAA regulations:

> First, historically, the courts have deferred to the leaders of educational institutions on matters of educational policy on the view that they are experts at making such judgments. Second, courts have long recognized a right of private associations to set their own rules of conduct for members. . . . Finally, . . . the cases demonstrate a judicial deference unique to the NCAA to its member schools as the recognized regulators of amateur athletic policy.

W. Burlette Carter, *Student-Athlete Welfare in a Restructured NCAA*, 2 Va. J. Sports & L. 1, 69-70 (2000).

In the cases that follow, consider whether any or all of these theories underlie the considerable deference courts afford to interscholastic sports governing bodies and high schools. It is important to recognize the reasons for such judicial deference, to analyze whether they are valid and justifiable, and to consider the effects of such deference on the decision making of sports governing body administrators, school officials, and coaches.

If the case cannot be decided on any other grounds, courts will examine federal and state constitutional issues. It is important to recognize that, in some instances, a state constitution may provide a stronger right or require that a higher standard be met to justify infringing such a right than the corresponding federal constitutional provision. For example, if a student-athlete asserts that she has a right to participate in interscholastic athletics, this assertion generally is rejected on federal constitutional grounds, but it may be recognized in some jurisdictions on state constitutional grounds. Therefore, lawyers should be aware of the potential dispositive role of state constitutional law in the interscholastic athletics context.

This section initially considers the important issue of "state action," specifically whether a state high school athletic association is a state actor for federal constitutional law purposes and the legally permissible scope of its regulatory authority over its member schools. Next, it considers several rules and regulations established by a state athletic association, local school district, or individual high school that delineate student-athletes' eligibility to participate in interscholastic sports. It then examines some cases that impact multiple dimensions of student-athletes' lives and raise significant federal constitutional law issues, such as mandatory drug testing and claims alleging infringement of their free speech, association, and religious rights.

1.   State Action

As a prerequisite to bringing a claim alleging infringement of a federal constitutional right, it must be established that its deprivation occurred as the result of state action. If an educational institution or state interscholastic sports association is not a state actor, it is not required to respect the constitutional rights secured by the Constitution of the United States, and a court will not address the merits of the substantive federal constitutional law issues. *Brentwood I* and *II* effectively illustrate this dynamic between state action and substantive constitutional claims.

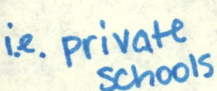 *i.e. private schools*

The question of whether a state athletic association is a state actor was a troublesome issue for many years, with varying jurisdictions reaching differing results on that issue. In the following 2001 case, *Brentwood I,* the Supreme Court resolved this issue, although it did so in a fact-specific manner that may not be determinative as to all high school athletic associations, given that the history, structure, and activities of high school athletic associations differ from state to state. As you read *Brentwood I,* think of the outcome-determinative facts in the case and how changing facts might give rise to a different decision on the state action issue. Note that the Court is closely divided, 5-4, in this case and that different facts might result in a judicial ruling regarding whether another state intercollegiate athletic association is a state actor.

BRENTWOOD ACADEMY v. TENNESSEE
SECONDARY SCHOOL ATHLETIC ASSN. (BRENTWOOD I)

531 U.S. 288 (2001)

Justice SOUTER delivered the opinion of the Court.

The issue is whether a statewide association incorporated to regulate interscholastic athletic competition among public and private secondary schools may be regarded as engaging in state action when it enforces a rule against a member school. The association in question here includes most public schools located within the State, acts through their representatives, draws its officers from them, is largely funded by their dues and income received in their stead, and has historically been seen to regulate in lieu of the State Board of Education's exercise of its own authority. We hold that the association's regulatory activity may and should be treated as state action owing to the pervasive entwinement of state school officials in the structure of the association, there being no offsetting reason to see the association's acts in any other way.

I

. . . [The District Court relied on language in the *Tarkanian* case, excerpted in Chapter 3, implying that state athletic associations might be state actors, even though the NCAA was not, in holding that the Tennessee Secondary School Athletic Association was a state actor.] The United States Court of Appeals for the Sixth Circuit reversed. . . . It said the District Court was mistaken in seeing a symbiotic relationship between the State and the Association, it emphasized that the Association was neither engaging in a traditional and exclusive public function nor responding to state compulsion, and it gave short shrift to the language from *Tarkanian* on which the District Court relied. . . .

We granted certiorari to resolve the conflict and now reverse.

A

. . . If the Fourteenth Amendment is not to be displaced . . . its ambit cannot be a simple line between States and people operating outside formally governmental organizations, and the deed of an ostensibly private organization or individual is to be treated sometimes as if a State had caused it to be performed. Thus, we say that state action may be found if, though only if, there is such a "close nexus between the State and the challenged action" that seemingly private behavior "may be fairly treated as that of the State itself." *Jackson, supra*, at 351, 95 S.Ct. 449.

To be sure, it is not the strict holding in *Tarkanian* that points to our view of this case, for we found no state action on the part of the NCAA. We could see, on the one hand, that the university had some part in setting the NCAA's rules, and the Supreme Court of Nevada had gone so far as to hold that the NCAA had been delegated the university's traditionally exclusive public authority over personnel. *Id.*, at 190, 109 S.Ct. 454. But on the other side, the NCAA's policies were shaped not by the University of Nevada alone, but by several hundred member institutions, most of them having no connection with Nevada, and exhibiting no color of Nevada law. *Id.*, at 193, 109 S.Ct. 454. Since it was difficult to see the NCAA, not as a collective membership, but as surrogate for the one State, we held the organization's connection with Nevada too insubstantial to ground a state action claim. *Id.*, at 193, 196, 109 S.Ct. 454.

But dictum in *Tarkanian* pointed to a contrary result on facts like ours, with an organization whose member public schools are all within a single State. "The situation would, of course, be different if the [Association's] membership consisted entirely of institutions located within the same State, many of them public institutions created by the same sovereign." *Id.*, at 193, n. 13, 109 S.Ct. 454. . . .

B

Just as we foresaw in *Tarkanian*, the "necessarily fact-bound inquiry," *Lugar*, 457 U.S., at 939, 102 S.Ct. 2744, leads to the conclusion of state action here. The nominally private character of the Association is overborne by the pervasive entwinement of public institutions and public officials in its composition and workings, and there is no substantial reason to claim unfairness in applying constitutional standards to it.

The Association is not an organization of natural persons acting on their own, but of schools, and of public schools to the extent of 84% of the total. Under the Association's bylaws, each member school is represented by its principal or a faculty member, who has a vote in selecting members of the governing legislative council and board of control from eligible principals, assistant principals and superintendents.

[T]o the extent of 84% of its membership, the Association is an organization of public schools represented by their officials acting in their official capacity to provide an integral element of secondary public schooling. There would be no recognizable Association, legal or tangible, without the public school officials, who do not merely control but overwhelmingly perform all but the purely ministerial acts by which the Association exists and functions in practical terms. Only the 16% minority of private school memberships prevents this entwinement of the Association and the public school system from being total and their identities totally indistinguishable.

To complement the entwinement of public school officials with the Association from the bottom up, the State of Tennessee has provided for entwinement from top down. State Board members are assigned ex officio to serve as members of the board of control and legislative council, and the Association's ministerial employees are treated as state employees to the extent of being eligible for membership in the state retirement system.

It is, of course, true that the time is long past when the close relationship between the surrogate association and its public members and public officials acting as such was attested frankly. As mentioned, the terms of the State Board's Rule expressly designating the Association as regulator of interscholastic athletics in public schools was deleted in 1996, the year after a Federal District Court held that the Association was a state actor because its rules were "caused, directed and controlled by the Tennessee Board of Education," *Graham v. TSSAA*, No. 1:95-CV-044, 1995 WL 115890, (E.D. Tenn., Feb. 20, 1995).

But the removal of the designation language from Rule 0520-1-2-.08 affected nothing but words. Today the State Board's member-designees continue to sit on the Association's committees as nonvoting members, and the State continues to welcome Association employees in its retirement scheme. The close relationship is confirmed by the Association's enforcement of the same preamendment rules and regulations reviewed and approved by the State Board (including the recruiting Rule challenged by Brentwood), and by the State Board's continued willingness to allow students to satisfy its physical education requirement by taking part in interscholastic athletics sponsored by the Association. The most one can say on the evidence is that the State Board once freely acknowledged the Association's official character but now does it by winks and nods. . . .

The entwinement down from the State Board is therefore unmistakable, just as the entwinement up from the member public schools is overwhelming. Entwinement will support a conclusion that an ostensibly private organization ought to be charged with a public character and judged by constitutional standards; entwinement to the degree shown here requires it.

Save for the Sixth Circuit, every Court of Appeals to consider a statewide athletic association like the one here has found it a state actor. . . . A reversal of the judgment here portends nothing more than the harmony of an outlying Circuit with precedent otherwise uniform.

Nor do we think there is anything to be said for the Association's contention that there is no need to treat it as a state actor since any public school applying the Association's rules is itself subject to suit under § 1983 or Title IX of the Education Amendments of 1972, 86 Stat. 373, 20 U.S.C. §§ 1681-1688. Brief for Respondents 30. . . . Its position boils down to saying that the Association should not be dressed in state clothes because other, concededly public actors are; that Brentwood should be kept out of court because a different plaintiff raising a different claim in a different case may find the courthouse open. Pleas for special treatment are hard to sell, although saying that does not, of course, imply anything about the merits of Brentwood's complaint; the issue here is merely whether Brentwood properly names the Association as a § 1983 defendant, not whether it should win on its claim.

The judgment of the Court of Appeals for the Sixth Circuit is reversed, and the case is remanded for further proceedings consistent with this opinion.

It is so ordered.

Justice THOMAS, with whom THE CHIEF JUSTICE, Justice SCALIA, and Justice KENNEDY join, dissenting.

faulty reasoning

We have never found state action based upon mere "entwinement." Until today, we have found a private organization's acts to constitute state action only when the organization performed a public function; was created, coerced, or encouraged by the government; or acted in a symbiotic relationship with the government. The majority's holding—that the Tennessee Secondary School Athletic Association's (TSSAA) enforcement of its recruiting rule is state action—not only extends state-action doctrine beyond its permissible limits but also encroaches upon the realm of individual freedom that the doctrine was meant to protect. I respectfully dissent.

Regardless of these various tests for state action, common sense dictates that the TSSAA's actions cannot fairly be attributed to the State, and thus cannot constitute state action. The TSSAA was formed in 1925 as a private corporation to organize interscholastic athletics and to sponsor tournaments among its member schools. Any private or public secondary school may join the TSSAA by signing a contract agreeing to comply with its rules and decisions. Although public schools currently compose 84% of the TSSAA's membership, the TSSAA does not require that public schools constitute a set percentage of its membership, and, indeed, no public school need join the TSSAA. The TSSAA's rules are enforced not by a state agency but by its own board of control, which comprises high school principals, assistant principals, and superintendents, none of whom must work at a public school. . . .

The State of Tennessee did not create the TSSAA. The State does not fund the TSSAA and does not pay its employees. In fact, only 4% of the TSSAA's revenue comes from the dues paid by member schools; the bulk of its operating budget is derived from gate receipts at tournaments it sponsors. The State does not permit the TSSAA to use state-owned facilities for a discounted fee, and it does not exempt the TSSAA from state taxation. No Tennessee law authorizes the State to coordinate interscholastic athletics or empowers another entity to organize interscholastic athletics on behalf of the State. The only state pronouncement acknowledging the TSSAA's existence is a rule providing that the State Board of Education permits public schools to maintain membership in the TSSAA if they so choose.

Moreover, the State of Tennessee has never had any involvement in the particular action taken by the TSSAA in this case: the enforcement of the TSSAA's recruiting rule prohibiting members from using "undue influence" on students or their parents or guardians "to secure or to retain a student for athletic purposes." App. 115. There is no indication that the State has ever had any interest in how schools choose to regulate recruiting. In fact, the TSSAA's authority to enforce its recruiting rule arises solely from the voluntary membership contract that each member school signs, agreeing to conduct its athletics in accordance with the rules and decisions of the TSSAA.

B

Even approaching the issue in terms of any of the Court's specific state-action tests, the conclusion is the same: The TSSAA's enforcement of its recruiting rule against Brentwood Academy is not state action.

The TSSAA has not performed a function that has been "traditionally exclusively reserved to the State." *Jackson v. Metropolitan Edison Co.*, 419 U.S. 34-5 352, 95 S.Ct. 449, 42 L.Ed.2d 477 (1974). The organization of interscholastic sports is neither a traditional nor an exclusive public function of the States. . . . Certainly, in Tennessee, the State did not even show an interest in interscholastic athletics until 47 years after the TSSAA had been in existence and had been orchestrating athletic contests throughout the State. Even then, the State Board of Education merely acquiesced in the TSSAA's actions and did not assume the role of regulating interscholastic athletics. . . .

It is also obvious that the TSSAA is not an entity created and controlled by the government for the purpose of fulfilling a government objective. . . . No one claims that the State of Tennessee played any role in the creation of the TSSAA as a private corporation in 1925. The TSSAA was designed to fulfill an objective—the organization of interscholastic athletic tournaments—that the government had not contemplated, much less pursued. And although the board of control currently is composed of public school officials, and although public schools currently account for the majority of the TSSAA's membership, this is not required by the TSSAA's constitution.

In addition, the State of Tennessee has not "exercised coercive power or . . . provided such significant encouragement [to the TSSAA], either overt or covert," *Blum*, 457 U.S., at 1004, 102 S.Ct. 2777, that the TSSAA's regulatory activities must in law be deemed to be those of the State. The State has not promulgated any regulations of interscholastic sports, and nothing in the record suggests that the State has encouraged or coerced the TSSAA in enforcing its recruiting rule. . . . Finally, there is no "symbiotic relationship" between the State and the TSSAA. *Moose Lodge, supra*, at 175, 92 S.Ct. 1965; cf. *Burton v. Wilmington Parking Authority*, 365 U.S. 715, 81 S.Ct. 856, 6 L.Ed.2d 45 (1961). Contrary to the majority's assertion, *see ante*, at 932-933, the TSSAA's "fiscal relationship with the State is not different from that of many contractors performing services for the government." *Rendell-Baker, supra*, at 843, 102 S.Ct. 2764. The TSSAA provides a service—the organization of athletic tournaments—in exchange for membership dues and gate fees, just as a vendor could contract with public schools to sell refreshments at school events. Certainly the public school could sell its own refreshments, yet the existence of that option does not transform the service performed by the contractor into a state action. Also, there is no suggestion in this case that, as was the case in Burton, the State profits from the TSSAA's decision to enforce its recruiting rule.

Because I do not believe that the TSSAA's action of enforcing its recruiting rule is fairly attributable to the State of Tennessee, I would affirm.

NOTES AND QUESTIONS

1. *Analysis of* Brentwood I. In *NCAA v. Tarkanian*, 488 U.S. 179 (1988), the Supreme Court, in a 5-4 decision, previously held that the National

Collegiate Athletic Association was not a state actor. In *Brentwood I*, another 5-4 decision rendered 12 years later, the Court holds that the Tennessee Secondary School Athletic Association (TSSAA) is a state actor. How does Justice Souter, writing for the majority, distinguish the TSSAA from the NCAA in holding that the former is a state actor but the latter is not? What is the legal standard the majority adopts to determine whether a state high school athletic association is a state actor? What factors are relevant in determining whether this standard is satisfied? If a state athletic association asked you, as its legal counsel, to minimize the likelihood that it would be held to be a state actor after *Brentwood I*, what would you suggest that it do and not do? The majority makes many references to the record. Why is the making of a record so critical in a case like *Brentwood I*?

The four dissenters strongly disagree with the majority's view. Why do they argue that the TSSAA is not a state actor? Do you agree with the dissenters or the majority?

2. *Lower Courts' Application of* Brentwood I. In *Communities for Equity v. Michigan High School Athletic Assn.*, 377 F.3d 504 (6th Cir. 2004), the Sixth Circuit relied on *Brentwood I* and held that the Michigan High School Athletic Association is a state actor: "MHSAA's stated purpose, '[t]o create, establish and provide for, supervise and conduct interscholastic athletic programs throughout the state,' is virtually identical to that of its Tennessee counterpart. Like TSSAA, MHSAA's membership is composed primarily of public schools. And, similar to TSSAA, public school teachers, administrators, and officials dominate MHSAA's leadership. Another common feature is that the bulk of MHSAA's revenue comes from ticket sales for state championship tournaments. Finally, MHSAA employees who had state teaching certificates were, until January of 1988, considered state employees and were therefore eligible to participate in the state's retirement system. Employees who started working for MHSAA before January of 1988 continue to be members of the state employees' retirement system. We therefore conclude that MHSAA is so entwined with the public schools and the state of Michigan, and that there is 'such a close nexus between the State and the challenged action,' that MHSAA should be considered a state actor." *Id.* at 511-512. But see *Bukowski v. Wisconsin Interscholastic Athletic Assn.*, 726 N.W.2d 326 (Wis. App. 2004) (in contrast to *Brentwood I*, plaintiff "failed to produce any evidence, by affidavit or otherwise, that the WIAA is a state actor"); *Mayo v. West Virginia Secondary Schools Activities Comm'n*, 672 S.E.2d 224, 229 (W. Va. 2008) (West Virginia state high school governing body is not a "state agency;" court's analysis suggests it is not a state actor).

3. *Governing Bodies That Are State Actors Not Necessarily Immune from Antitrust and Tort Liability.* In *Brentwood Academy v. Tennessee Secondary School Athletic Assn.*, 442 F.3d 410 (6th Cir. 2006), the Sixth Circuit reversed the district court's ruling that a state high school athletic association deemed to be a state actor has antitrust immunity. The Sixth Circuit held that a Tennessee statute delegating general authority to the State Board of Education regarding the operation of public high schools does not evidence the legislature's intent to authorize an anticompetitive regulatory program to be conducted by the Tennessee state high school athletic association. Moreover, the court found no record evidence that the State of Tennessee actively supervised the athletic association's regulation of high school athletics. See also *Brentwood Academy v. Tennessee Secondary Schools Athletic Assn.*, 2008 WL 2811307 (M.D. Tenn) (association's anti-recruiting rule and its enforcement against a

member school is a noncommercial restraint that does not have any anti-competitive economic effects). See also *Wissel v. Ohio High School Athletic Assn.*, 605 N.E.2d 458 (Ohio App. 1992) (no sovereign immunity from tort liability merely because governing body for high school athletics is a "state actor").

In *Brentwood II*, which made its way back to the Supreme Court in 2007, the Court considered the merits of the plaintiff high school's federal constitutional law challenges to the TSSAA's anti-recruiting rule on free speech and due process grounds.

TENNESSEE SECONDARY SCHOOL ATHLETIC ASSOCIATION v. BRENTWOOD ACADEMY (BRENTWOOD II)

551 U.S. 291 (2007)

Justice STEVENS delivered the opinion of the Court with respect to Parts I, II-B, III, and IV, concluding:

The principal issue before us is whether the enforcement of a rule prohibiting high school coaches from recruiting middle school athletes violates the First Amendment. We also must decide whether the sanction imposed on respondent for violating that rule was preceded by a fair hearing.

I

Although this case has had a long history, the relevant facts may be stated briefly. The Tennessee Secondary School Athletic Association (TSSAA) is a not-for-profit membership corporation organized to regulate interscholastic sports among its members, which include some 290 public and 55 private high schools in Tennessee. Brentwood Academy is one of those private schools.

Since the early 1950's, TSSAA has prohibited high schools from using "undue influence" in recruiting middle school students for their athletic programs. In April 1997, Brentwood's football coach sent a letter to a group of eighth-grade boys inviting them to attend spring practice sessions. The letter explained that football equipment would be distributed and that "getting involved as soon as possible would definitely be to your advantage." It was signed "Your Coach." While the boys who received the letter had signed a contract signaling their intent to attend Brentwood, none had enrolled within the meaning of TSSAA rules [which defined "enrolled" as having "attended 3 days of school"]. All of the boys attended at least some of the spring practice sessions. As the case comes to us, it is settled that the coach's pre-enrollment solicitation violated the TSSAA's antirecruiting rule and that he had ample notice that his conduct was prohibited.

TSSAA accordingly sanctioned Brentwood. After proceeding through two layers of internal TSSAA review, Brentwood brought this action against TSSAA and its executive director in federal court under Rev.Stat. § 1979, 42 U.S.C. § 1983. As relevant here, Brentwood made two claims: first, that enforcement of the rule was state action in violation of the First and Fourteenth Amendments; and second, that TSSAA's flawed adjudication of its appeal had deprived the school of due process of law. . . .

[handwritten: π arg 2]

II

The First Amendment protects Brentwood's right to publish truthful information about the school and its athletic programs. It likewise protects the school's right to try to persuade prospective students and their parents that its excellence in sports is a reason for enrolling. But Brentwood's speech rights are not absolute. It chose to join TSSAA, an athletic league [association] and a state actor invested with a three-fold obligation to prevent the exploitation of children, to ensure that high school athletics remain secondary to academics, and to promote fair competition among its members. TSSAA submits that these interests adequately support the enforcement against its member schools of a rule prohibiting coaches from trying to recruit impressionable middle school athletes. Brentwood disagrees, and maintains that TSSAA's asserted interests are too flimsy and its rule too broad to support what the school views as a serious curtailment of its constitutional rights. Two aspects of the case taken together persuade us that TSSAA should prevail.

[handwritten: TSSAA (state actor)]

A

The anti-recruiting rule strikes nowhere near the heart of the First Amendment. TSSAA has not banned the dissemination of truthful information relating to sports, nor has it claimed that it could.

[Relying on *Ohralik v. Ohio State Bar Assn.*, 436 U.S. 447 (1978), in which the Court held the First Amendment did not prevent a state bar association from disciplining a lawyer for in-person solicitation of clients, and other examples, the Court opined that] the dangers of undue influence and overreaching that exist when a lawyer chases an ambulance are also present when a high school coach contacts an eighth grader. . . . After all, it is a heady thing for an eighth-grade student to be contacted directly by a coach—here, "Your Coach"—and invited to join a high school sports team. In too many cases, the invitation will come accompanied with a suggestion, subtle or otherwise, that failure to accept will hurt the student's chances to play high school sports and diminish the odds that she could continue on to college or (dream of dreams) professional sports. Such a potent entreaty, playing as it does on youthful hopes and fears, could well exert the kind of undue pressure that "disserve[s] the individual and societal interest . . . in facilitation 'informed and reliable decisionmaking.'" Given that TSSAA member schools remain free to send brochures, post billboards, and otherwise advertise their athletic programs, TSSAA's limited regulation of recruiting conduct poses no significant First Amendment concerns.

[handwritten: this would be undue influence]

[handwritten: they can still send things → not a 1st Amend violation]

B

Brentwood made a voluntary decision to join TSSAA and to abide by its anti-recruiting rule. Just as the government's interest in running an effective workplace can in some circumstances outweigh employee speech rights, so too can an athletic league's interest in enforcing its rules sometimes warrant curtailing the speech of its voluntary participants. . . . This is not to say that TSSAA has unbounded authority to condition membership on the relinquishment of any and all constitutional rights. As we recently emphasized in the employment context, "[s]o long as employees are speaking as citizens about matters of public concern, they must face only those speech restrictions that are necessary for their employers to operate efficiently and effectively." Assuming, without deciding, that the coach in this case was "speaking as [a] citize[n] about matters of public concern," TSSAA can similarly impose only those conditions on such speech that are necessary to managing an efficient and effective state-sponsored high school athletic league.

That necessity is obviously present here. We need no empirical data to credit TSSAA's common-sense conclusion that hard-sell tactics directed at middle school students could lead to exploitation, distort competition between high school teams, and foster an environment in which athletics are prized more highly than academics. . . . [T]he First Amendment does not excuse Brentwood from abiding by the same anti-recruiting rule that governs the conduct of its sister schools. To hold otherwise would undermine the principle, succinctly articulated by the dissenting judge at the Court of Appeals, that "[h]igh school football is a game. Games have rules."

III

The decision to sanction Brentwood for engaging in prohibited recruiting was preceded by an investigation, several meetings, exchanges of correspondence, an adverse written determination from TSSAA's executive director, a hearing before the director and an advisory panel composed o three members of TSSAA's Board of Directors. During the investigation, Brentwood was notified of all the charges against it. At each of the two hearings, Brentwood was represented by counsel and given the opportunity to adduce evidence. No evidence offered by Brentwood was excluded.

Even accepting the questionable holding [of the Sixth Circuit] that TSSAA's closed-door deliberations were unconstitutional, we can safely conclude that any due process violation was harmless beyond a reasonable doubt. . . . Brentwood's claim of prejudice rests on the unsupported premise that it would have adopted a different and more effective strategy at the board hearing had it been given an opportunity to cross-examine the investigators and review their notes. Despite having had nearly a decade since the hearing to undertake that cross-examination and review, Brentwood has identified nothing the investigators shared with the board that Brentwood did not already know.

Justice KENNEDY, with whom THE CHIEF JUSTICE, Justice SCALIA, and Justice ALITO join, concurring in part and concurring in the judgment.

Although I have little difficulty concluding that the regulation at issue does not contravene the First Amendment, I do not agree with the principal opinion's reliance on *Ohralik*. . . . In my view it is both unnecessary and ill advised to rely upon *Ohralik* in the instant matter. By doing so, the principal opinion, at a minimum, is open to the implication that the speech at issue is subject to state regulation whether or not the school has entered a voluntary contract with a state-sponsored association in order to promote a code of conduct affecting solicitation. To allow free-standing state regulation of speech by coaches and other representatives of nonmember schools would be a dramatic expansion of *Ohralik* to a whole new field of endeavor. Yet by relying on *Ohralik* the principal opinion undermines the argument that, in the absence of Brentwood

Academy's consensual membership in the [TSSAA], the speech by the head coach would be entitled to First Amendment protection.

Justice THOMAS, concurring in the judgment.

Until today, *Pickering* governed limitations on the speech rights of government employees and contractors. The Court uproots *Pickering* from its context and applies it to speech by a private school that is a member of a private athletic association. The need to stretch *Pickering* to fit this case was occasioned by the Court when it held that TSSAA, a private organization, was a state actor. Because *Brentwood I* departed so dramatically from our earlier state-action cases, it is unsurprising that no First Amendment framework readily applies to this case. Rather than going through the bizarre exercise of extending obviously inapplicable First Amendment doctrine to these circumstances, I would simply overrule *Brentwood I.*

meaning the 1st Amendment issue?

NOTES AND QUESTIONS

1. *Analysis of First Amendment Issues.* Although a majority of the Court does not agree with his reasoning in Part II-A of his opinion, Justice Stevens asserts that recruiting eighth graders is like ambulance chasing. Does recruiting young student-athletes necessarily result in exploitation? Should impressionable young people be shielded from recruiting efforts of this sort by state high school athletic associations? Can parents effectively insulate their minor children from exploitive recruiting efforts? Is the age and impressionability of the student-athletes critical to the decision (i.e., if the letter came from a college coach, might it be protected speech)?

Some scholars argue that widening the scope of state action, as the Court did in *Brentwood I,* may have the unintended effect of limiting the underlying free speech right. In other words, when the Court recognizes more parties as state actors, it increases the number of instances in which constitutional rights claims may need to be adjudicated. This, in turn, puts pressure on the courts to limit those rights, if the government is to function. Is this case likely to have an impact in areas other than the recruitment of student-athletes?

In *Rottman v. PIAA*, 349 F. Supp. 2d 922 (W.D. Pa. 2004), the Pennsylvania Interscholastic Athletic Association's "anti-recruiting rule" was upheld against a claim that it was an impermissible content-based ban on protected speech. In finding the rule to be constitutional, the court applied an intermediate scrutiny test and found that the rule served the substantial governmental interests of prioritizing academics over athletics and protecting young student-athletes from exploitation.

In *Isler v. New Mexico Activities Assn.*, 2010 WL 8522978 (D.N.M. Feb. 19, 2010), a case involving termination of a high school basketball coach for his alleged violation of a New Mexico state governing body rule prohibiting "undue influence" in connection with school transfers by student-athletes, the court distinguished *Brentwood II* and held that this rule was unconstitutionally vague. The rule prohibited communications between school personnel and students or parents that "might be construed as inducement for them to attend a particular school." The court concluded that it "provides no guidance whatsoever as to the meaning of the phrase 'might be

similar case

construed as an inducement' and thus no guidance as to what conduct is actually prohibited. . . . While the NMAA does point out that the term 'undue influence' is defined in the appendices of the NMAA Handbook as '[i]nappropriate, unethical, and prohibited acts by which [a] coach, sponsor or agent of the school persuades or attempt to persuade a potential athlete to transfer into his/her school,' this definition does little to clarify the ambiguity embodied in Bylaw 6.1.3(K). No examples of what would be considered 'inappropriate' or 'unethical' are provided and nothing in this definition would put Mr. Isler on notice that the conduct at issue here would be prohibited by the NMAA; clearly his supervisor, Mr. Stacy, was not put on notice either. Moreover, apart from this vague definition, the NMAA has failed to provide any written guidance whatsoever." *Id.* at *8-9.

2. *Analysis of Procedural Due Process Issues.* What argument was raised regarding due process? Why did Brentwood Academy assert that its hearing before the TSSAA was deficient? On what ground did the Court reject this argument?

3. *Future of* Brentwood I. Justice Thomas concurs in the judgment because of his view the TSSAA is not a state actor, making it unnecessary for him to address the underlying constitutional issues. In short, he argues for the overruling of *Brentwood I.* Is he trying to send a signal that with changes in the Court's membership subsequent to *Brentwood I*'s 5-4 decision, in the future interscholastic athletic associations might not be held to be state actors on facts similar to those in *Brentwood I*?

4. *Other Constitutional Issues.* In *Christian Heritage Academy v. Oklahoma Secondary School Activities Assn.*, 483 F.3d 1025 (10th Cir. 2007), the Tenth Circuit held that the Oklahoma Secondary School Activity Association's (OSSAA) membership requirements for nonpublic schools violated the Equal Protection Clause of the Fourteenth Amendment. The court held that despite the fact that OSSAA had offered a number of legitimate purposes supporting a rule that distinguished between nonpublic and public schools, its rule requiring majority approval for nonpublic schools to be admitted to membership was not rationally related to any of those legitimate purposes. The court found that the only remaining reason for the decision to deny membership to Christian Heritage Academy (the plaintiff) was a growing animus against nonpublic schools because they were often more competitive, in an athletic sense, than their public counterparts. The court concluded that this justification was insufficient for equal protection purposes. A third judge concurred in the judgment, but disagreed with the majority's reasoning, because he concluded that Christian Heritage Academy was discriminated against because other similarly situated schools, both public and nonpublic, had been granted membership. The judges were also concerned that there were no voting standards or guidelines tied to the proffered rational bases, which made for a "complete disconnect" between the legitimate purposes behind the rule and its application.

2. *Athlete Eligibility Issues*

The remainder of this chapter deals with substantive issues that have been raised by student-athletes and their parents challenging the nature and scope of associational (state athletic association) and institutional (high school) governance of interscholastic athletics. The principal cases consider eligibility issues

[handwritten margin note: there was flawed adjudication ↓ they were given an opportunity]

arising out of the application and enforcement of transfer, "outside competition," good conduct, maximum age, personal appearance and grooming, and homeschool rules. Other cases address mandatory random drug testing and alleged infringement of student-athletes' federal constitutional rights to freedom of expression and religion. The cases could be divided into two separate categories—namely, claims against state athletic associations and those against a high school. However, cases sometimes involve legal claims against both institutional and associational actions. While reading the following cases, think about the different types of associational and institutional rules and actions typically challenged by student-athletes and their parents. In doing so, consider whether courts provide (or should provide) more or less deference to a state athletic association or individual educational institutions.

To think about...

The principal cases are organized by reference to the specific rule or its application in an individual case so that multiple legal claims are considered in the same judicial opinion. Often there is a blend of federal constitutional issues and state law issues that arise in a given case. In reading these cases it is important to distinguish among these claims and to identify their differing legal standards and elements. State athletic associations, whether deemed to be "state actors" or not, and both public and private high schools must comply with their own procedural rules for resolving eligibility disputes and applicable state laws. Public high schools and state athletic associations judicially characterized as state actors must respect student-athletes' federal constitutional due process, equal protection, and other rights.

Federal due process claims raise the threshold issue of whether a constitutionally protected property or liberty interest is being deprived. As you are reading these cases, consider whether participation in interscholastic athletics (with or without the prospect of earning a future college athletic scholarship) is sufficiently important to be constitutionally protected and how courts have resolved this issue. Procedural due process typically requires consideration of whether fair notice and an opportunity to be heard have been provided by a state athletic association or high school before a student-athlete is denied eligibility to participate in interscholastic athletics. On occasion, substantive due process claims alleging that an eligibility rule, its application to a student-athlete's particular circumstances, or disciplinary action resulting in a loss of athletic eligibility is arbitrary or capricious or violates a protected property or liberty interest (e.g., privacy rights) regardless of the level of procedural process provided have been raised in cases such as *Brands, infra*. Some student-athletes have argued, with little success, that substantive due process protects an independent right to participate in athletics or similar activities that are arguably of great value in her life. As the cases unfold in these various contexts, think about whether participation in athletics should trigger either procedural or substantive due process protection. Federal equal protection requires that similarly situated parties be treated alike, with the level of judicial scrutiny varying based on whether or not there is any discrimination based on innate characteristics such as race, ethnicity, national origin, or gender.

Procedural

substantive not a very successful claim

Regarding the extent to which an opportunity to participate in interscholastic athletics is worthy of legal protection and to what extent, consider the following:

In our increasingly technology-driven, isolated society, participation in interscholastic athletics provides a means of establishing social networks with one's peers and developing a community-based identity with corresponding positive academic effects. Finding a link between high school students' sense of identity, patterns of extracurricular involvement, and indicators of successful and risky adolescent development, a 1999 study found that female and male students who participate in high school team sports through the 12th grade have a school-based identity that correlates to positive academic performance (e.g., an increased 12th-grade GPA and an increased probability of being enrolled in college full-time at age 21). This highly positive finding is consistent with prior research evidencing that sports participation, relative to participation in other extracurricular activities such as student government and academic clubs, is "linked to lower likelihood of school dropout and higher rates of college attendance."

Matthew J. Mitten and Timothy Davis, *Athlete Eligibility Requirements and Legal Protection of Sports Participation Opportunities*, 8 Va. Sports and Ent. L.J. 137 (2008).

a.   Transfer Rules

Student-athletes often challenge transfer rules and regulations, which typically are adopted and enforced by state interscholastic athletic associations, that limit their eligibility to participate in interscholastic athletics. A transfer rule limits the ability of student-athletes to participate immediately in interscholastic competition after the athlete moves from one school to another. A common type of transfer rule renders a student-athlete who transfers from one high school to another within the same school district without a corresponding change in his or her parents' residence ineligible to engage in interscholastic competition for a period of time.

Carlberg provides an illustration of how courts have resolved a variety of federal and state law legal challenges to transfer rules. While reading this case, consider the purposes for which transfer rules are promulgated. Reasons typically cited in support of transfer rules include: deterring recruitment of student-athletes (i.e., protecting student-athletes from the pressure and harassment of zealous coaches and fans that might ensue from unregulated recruiting) and affording academics a higher priority than athletics. *Parker v. Ariz. Interscholastic Assn.*, 59 P.3d 806, 813 (Ariz. Ct. App. 2002) ("The purpose of the AIA transfer rule is to deter athletically motivated transfers and recruitment of students and promote 'the educational philosophy that participation in athletics is a privilege which should not take a dominate role over academics'"). Ironically, is the protection of an institution's athletic-related interests the reason schools support transfer rules?

PROBLEM 2-1

On June 25, 2009, the California Interscholastic Federation (CIF) issued *Understanding the Transfer Eligibility Procedure: A Parent Guideline Handbook*. In an effort to limit transfers between schools for athletic purposes, the CIF generally limits eligibility for students transferring from one school to another and outlines a waiver procedure permitting the waiver of ineligibility when the transfer was not for athletic purposes. As you review the language of the waiver provision below, think about how the following situations should be handled: (1) An all-state student-athlete, who has been living with his single mother, moves to live with his sister in another community because his mother feels that she has to work full time and lacks the discipline in her home necessary for her son's welfare. (2) Would it make a difference in question 1 if the parent was sick and legally named her daughter as legal guardian of her son? (3) A student-athlete's parents, who live on a military base that has a weak music program, want their daughter, who is an accomplished violinist and has also competed in softball at the varsity level during the past 12 months at the school on the military base, to transfer to live with her grandparents, who are in a school district with a nationally acclaimed music program and symphony. (4) Would it make a difference in question 3 if the base was in a dangerous area and the parents wanted their child to move to a safer area? As a lawyer working in this area, how would you counsel your clients in each of the cases noted in these four questions? What problems do you foresee? What kind of record or proof would you want to develop? How important is a letter from the school that the student is transferring from? Should such cases be decided on a case-by-case basis under a broad waiver provision, or should associations strongly enforce rules that limit transfers?

HARDSHIP WAIVERS

The CIF recognizes that, in certain circumstances, students may transfer from one school to another due to a compelling need or situation beyond a student's control. In such cases the Section may waive the transfer limitation imposed on a student when the case meets the definition of a hardship. (See "A" below.)

Consideration of any hardship request . . . requires documented proof of the hardship circumstance, and all facts to be considered must be submitted at the time of the application. Consideration will be give to those situations in which there is no evidence of athletic motivation, undue influence, pending disciplinary action or falsification of information.

A. A hardship is defined as an unforeseeable, unavoidable and uncorrectable act, condition or event that causes the imposition of a severe and non-athletic burden upon the student and his/her family. [A regional section of the CIF] may only waive the transfer limitation the transfer limitation if the conditions of hardship are met, and there is sufficient documentation to support the hardship claim. Sections may not waive the applicable rule if the conditions of hardship are not met.

B. Consideration of any hardship request to a Section requires documentation. Such documents may include, but not be limited to copies of current transcripts, financial documents, medical statements and /or supportive statements from the previous school attended.

In the following case, the Indiana Supreme Court considered whether the state athletic association's transfer rule itself, and as applied to the plaintiff, was legally enforceable.

Trial court held that this is a violation of the Const.

INDIANA HIGH SCHOOL ATHLETIC ASSOCIATION v. CARLBERG

694 N.E.2d 222 (Ind. 1997)

SULLIVAN, Justice.

[EDS. After attending Brebeuf Preparatory School as a freshman (where he swam on the varsity swim team), Jason Carlberg, who lives with his parents near Indianapolis, transferred to Carmel High School for academic reasons. The Indiana High School Athletic Association (IHSAA) is a voluntary association of public and private high schools that adopts and enforces rules regarding eligibility and similar matters related to interscholastic athletic competition. *R* Applying Rule 19 (the "Transfer Rule"), the IHSAA determined that Carlberg transferred for nonathletic reasons without a change of permanent residence by his parents or guardians. Therefore, he had only limited athletic eligibility for 365 days following enrollment (i.e., he was immediately eligible to participate in all interscholastic sports except as a member of a varsity athletic team).

π
violates Equal Protection Clause

After exhausting available administrative remedies, including a hearing before the IHSAA Executive Committee, which denied his appeal, Carlberg alleged, *inter alia*, that application of the Transfer Rule violated his constitutional rights under the due process and equal protection clauses of the Fourteenth Amendment of the U.S. Constitution, and was arbitrary and capricious in violation of Indiana common law. Agreeing with his contentions, the trial court enjoined the IHSAA from enforcing the Transfer Rule and ordered that Carlberg be allowed to participate on the Carmel High School varsity swimming team, which ruling was affirmed by an intermediate appellate court.

In its appeal to the Indiana Supreme Court, the IHSAA argued that the Transfer Rule is subject to the rule of limited judicial interference in the affairs of private voluntary membership associations, and that the trial court wrongly interfered with its internal affairs.

The Indiana Supreme Court held that "decisions of the IHSAA with respect to student-athletes constitute 'state action.'" It observed that the IHSAA's "very existence is entirely dependent upon the absolute cooperation and support of the public school systems of the State of Indiana" that "is derived from the lawful delegation from public schools to the IHSAA of authority conferred upon public schools by the legislature." The court also noted that "(i) the salaries of *State Action* most the principals and coaches involved in interscholastic athletics are derived from tax funds; (ii) most of the athletic contests are held in, or on, athletic facilities which have been constructed and maintained with tax funds; and (iii) IHSAA rules are adopted by tax-supported schools and their enforcement may have a substantial impact upon the rights of students enrolled in these tax-supported institutions."

Regarding his due process claim, the court ruled that Carlberg has no constitutional right to participate in interscholastic athletics and was not entitled to procedural due process before the IHSAA's adverse eligibility determination. Moreover, Carlberg was granted a hearing before the IHSAA Executive *Procedure was fine* Committee and did not contend this procedure was inadequate or denied him a fair opportunity to be heard.

Regarding his equal protection claim, the court held that "[a]bsent a burden upon the exercise of a constitutionally protected right (none is at stake here) or creation of a suspect class (none is alleged here), the general standard of review of state action challenged under the equal protection clause is the rational basis test." It found that the Transfer Rule's objectives of preserving the integrity of interscholastic athletics and preventing recruiting and school transfers for athletic reasons are legitimate and concluded that the Transfer Rule is rationally related to achieving these goals.]

. . . We find resolution of challenges to IHSAA rules and enforcement actions well within the ambit of Indiana common law. Our state constitution specifically recognizes that "knowledge and learning" are "essential to the preservation of a free government" and so mandates a statewide system of free public education. Ind. Const. art. VIII, § 1. We believe athletics are an integral part of this constitutionally-mandated process of education. . . .

The substantial educational benefits derived from interscholastic athletics, together with the rationale that underlies the determination that IHSAA decisions constitute "state action," help explain why Indiana courts have been so willing to adjudicate disputes between the IHSAA and parties aggrieved by the association's decisions. We reaffirm our common law jurisdiction in this regard today and turn to an examination of the common law principles applicable in IHSAA cases. . . .

The rule in Indiana is that courts exercise limited interference with the internal affairs and rules of a voluntary membership association: A voluntary association may, without direction or interference by the courts, for its government, adopt a constitution, by-laws, rules and regulations which will control as to all questions of discipline, or internal policy and management, and its right to interpret and administer the same is as sacred as the right to make them. . . .

. . . Although we will continue to review for arbitrariness and capriciousness IHSAA decisions affecting students, we see little justification for such review when it comes to the IHSAA's member schools. As to its member schools, the IHSAA is a voluntary membership association. Those members have the internal procedures of their own association available to them to adjudicate disputes and, if necessary, change rules or leadership; there is no need for courts to micro-manage these matters. We hold in [*IHSAA v. Reyes*, 694 N.E.2d 249 (Ind. 1997)] and reiterate here, that judicial review of IHSAA decisions with respect to its member schools will be limited to those circumstances under which courts review the decisions of voluntary membership associations-fraud, other illegality, or abuse of civil or property rights having their origin elsewhere.

When it comes to student challenges, however, we reach a different result. Perhaps Judge Cummings said it best when he observed that "for a student athlete in public school, membership in IHSAA is not voluntary, and actions of the IHSAA arguably should be held to a stricter standard of judicial review." *Freeman*, 51 F.3d at 1363. Therein lies what is for us a crucial distinction between this case and *Reyes*: as a student, Carlberg has not voluntarily subjected himself to the rules of the IHSAA; he has no voice in its rules or leadership. We note as well the relatively short span of time a student spends in high school compared to the amount of time often required for institutional policies to change. These factors all point to the propriety of judicial scrutiny of IHSAA decisions with respect to student challenges.

But what should be the standard of review? This Court has never applied *de novo* review to IHSAA decisions and emphatically rejects it here. Rather than *de novo* review, . . . the appellate courts of this state have applied an "arbitrary and capricious" standard in reviewing the decisions of the IHSAA. (Citations omitted.)

While the doctrinal basis for judicial review of IHSAA decisions for arbitrariness and capriciousness is not clear from the cases, we believe that it is similar to that which justifies the conclusion that IHSAA decisions constitute "state action." The facts that make IHSAA decisions "state action" for purposes of federal and state constitutional analysis also suggest an analogy with government agency decisions: if IHSAA decisions are "state action," then they are like government agency decisions. We conclude that the "arbitrary and capricious" standard of review probably grows out of this similarity. That is, just as courts review IHSAA decisions in approximately the same way as those of government agencies for purposes of constitutional law, courts review IHSAA decisions in approximately the same way as those of government agencies for purposes of common law. . . .

In summary, as a matter of state common law, the courts of Indiana have jurisdiction to review challenges to IHSAA rules and enforcement decisions applicable to a particular student, assuming those challenges are brought by non-IHSAA members with standing. Such rules and decisions will not be reviewed *de novo* but in a manner analogous to judicial review of government agency action, recognizing, however, that the IHSAA is not a government agency and the common law will have to accommodate that difference.

The provisions of the IHSAA Transfer Rule at issue in this case apply to a student who changes schools without a corresponding change of residence by the student's parents. Such a student may participate as a member of a junior varsity or freshman team at his or her new school unless the transfer was either primarily for athletic reasons or as a result of undue influence. However, such a student may not participate in interscholastic athletics as a member of a *varsity* athletic team during the first 365 days after enrollment unless (i) the student meets one of the special criteria set forth in Rule 19-6.1 or (ii) is declared eligible under the IHSAA "Hardship Rule."

Carlberg agrees that he changed schools without a corresponding change of residence by his parents and that none of the special criteria of Rule 19-6.1 nor the Hardship Rule apply. For its part, the IHSAA acknowledges that the transfer was neither for primarily athletic reasons nor as a result of undue influence. Carlberg argues that the IHSAA acted arbitrarily and capriciously when it enforced the Transfer Rule against him where it was undisputed that his transfer was neither primarily for athletic reasons nor as a result of undue influence.

[W]e review the challenged IHSAA decision for arbitrariness or capriciousness. "Arbitrary and capricious" is a narrow standard of review and the reviewing court may not substitute its judgment for the judgment of the IHSAA. The rule or decision will be found to be arbitrary and capricious "only where it is willful and unreasonable, without consideration and in disregard of the facts or circumstances in the case, or without some basis which would lead a reasonable and honest person to the same conclusion." *Dep't of Natural Resources v. Indiana Coal Council, Inc.*, 542 N.E.2d 1000, 1007 (Ind. 1989) (citation omitted).

We do not find the IHSAA decision that Carlberg was ineligible for varsity athletics for 365 days following his transfer to be "willful and unreasonable, without consideration and in disregard of the facts or circumstances in the case, or without some basis which would lead a reasonable and honest person to the same conclusion." First, . . . there is no contention that the IHSAA failed to publicize its interpretation of the rule or failed to apply consistently its interpretation of the rule.

Second, by establishing objective standards for eligibility "governing residence and transfer," including the provision allowing for only limited eligibility upon a transfer not accompanied by a parental change of residence, Rule 19(c) acts as a deterrent to athletically motivated transfers. . . .

Third, the operation of the rule does not sweep too broadly in its proscription. While it is true that some students who change schools neither primarily for athletic reasons nor as a result of undue influence are denied varsity eligibility for one year, conducting a factual inquiry into the motivation for every transfer would impose a considerable burden on both the IHSAA and its member schools. IHSAA Commissioner Gardner testified that to the effect that the IHSAA could not afford to investigate individually each transfer: "Regular detailed investigations by the IHSAA are cost prohibitive, could not be staffed by the current IHSAA personnel, and would have limited success in identifying those athletic transfers thinly disguised as nonathletic transfers." The IHSAA has balanced these competing interests by (i) creating the thirteen special criteria for immediate eligibility under Rule 19-6.1, (ii) granting immediate eligibility under the Hardship Rule, and (iii) permitting students immediate eligibility at the junior varsity and freshman level.

While we do not find the IHSAA's application of the Transfer Rule to Carlberg to be either arbitrary or capricious, we believe fairness to Carlberg's position requires that we give additional consideration to his common law claim. That is, Carlberg's claim might fairly be categorized as a challenge to the validity of the Transfer Rule itself, asking whether the IHSAA has the authority to enforce a rule denying varsity athletic eligibility to a student who transfers schools whether the transfer is neither primarily for athletic reasons nor as a result of undue influence. To put the distinction in administrative law terms, Carlberg may be seen to argue that the IHSAA has abused its rulemaking authority rather than its adjudicatory authority.

Judicial review of whether a governmental agency has abused its rulemaking authority is highly deferential. But government agency rulemaking is not exempt from judicial review. Among the factors analyzed are whether the challenged agency rule (i) falls within the scope of the agency's enabling legislation, (ii) is arbitrary or unreasonable, (iii) is consistent and harmonious with the legislative pronouncement under which it operates, and (iv) does not expand or vary the legislature's enactment.

We have already found that this rule is not arbitrary or unreasonable. [T]he IHSAA does not derive its authority directly from the legislature but instead from a delegation of authority from member schools. As such, the analysis with respect to the three factors that concern authorizing legislation is conducted best by examining the challenged rule's consistency with the IHSAA's purpose in general and the purpose of the Transfer Rule in particular.

The IHSAA exists "to encourage, regulate, and give direction to wholesome amateur interschool athletic competition between schools who are members." IHSAA Articles of Incorporation, art. II; IHSAA By-Laws, art. II. To further this purpose, the IHSAA Articles and By-Laws mandate that it "determine qualifications of individual contestants . . . and provide written communications to establish standards for eligibility." *Id.* We find authority to take such action, and to delegate that authority to the IHSAA, to be within the powers granted Indiana public school corporations by the legislature. We further find Rule 19-6.2 to fall within the scope of, to be consistent and harmonious with, and not to expand or vary this authority. . . .

[W]e vacate the opinion of the Court of Appeals and reverse the decision of the trial court.

DICKSON, Justice, concurring and dissenting.

I agree with the majority that the Indiana State High School Athletics Association ("IHSAA") is subject to common law oversight in Indiana's courts and that IHSAA action is equivalent to "state action" subjecting it to judicial enforcement for violations of the federal or state constitutions. . . . I am convinced that the trial court was correct in finding the IHSAA's attempts to apply its Transfer Rule . . . to be arbitrary and capricious and thus improper. . . .

Jason Carlberg attended Brebeuf Preparatory School, a private school, his ninth-grade year and also participated in their swimming program. However, Jason did not thrive academically in the environment at Brebeuf. Because Jason's parents, James and Donna Carlberg, believed that he would do better in a more structured environment, they transferred Jason to the public school in their area for the tenth grade. The parents' choice of schools proved to be well-founded, as Jason's grades improved significantly. . . .

The choices faced by the Carlbergs are choices all parents face: what school and type of education is best for their children. For some, one facet of that education is athletics. As noted by the majority, "athletics are an integral part of this constitutionally-mandated process of education." Physical fitness lowers mortality rates, promotes cardiovascular and muscular fitness, generates a general feeling of well-being, and reduces the symptoms of depression and anxiety. U.S. Dep't of Health and Human Servs., Physical Activity and Health: a Report of the Surgeon General 85-136 (1996). The "potentially positive outcomes of organized sport competition" have been documented. Wilbert Marcellus Leonard II, A Sociolgical Perspective of Sport 124 (1993). Among these outcomes are enhanced decision-making skills, self-image, character, morality, independence, and opportunities for youth to experience a sense of achievement. *Id.* Witnesses for both sides also testified that athletics provided several benefits, including "learning how to be part of a team, the process of goal setting and working hard, individually and within a team, to achieve goals, and how to deal with successes and overcome the failures provided in sports."

In addition, for the student who is not academically inclined, participation in sports requires a certain amount of academic progress and provides motivation for the athlete to meet those standards in order to compete. . . .

The IHSAA's action against Jason is blatantly contrary to the expressed purpose of the IHSAA Transfer Rule. The IHSAA rules provide that, "Standards governing residence and transfer are a necessary prerequisite to participation in interschool activities because: . . . (5) *they keep the focus of students* and educators *on the fact that they attend school to receive an education first* and participate in athletics second." The trial court found that the Carlbergs have always put Jason's education first and the IHSAA officials "indicated they had no reason to believe Jason Carlberg's transfer was athletically motivated." Thus, the arbitrariness of the IHSAA's application of its rule becomes apparent in the present case: A rule purporting to limit athletically-motivated transfers and promote education as the primary value of school in fact punishes a student whom the IHSAA found did *not* transfer for an athletic reason and where the uncontradicted evidence points only to academic reasons for the transfer. Common sense instructs that application of the Transfer Rule to limit Jason's opportunities for participation would be blatantly arbitrary and capricious. The trial court was correct in making such a finding.

NOTES AND QUESTIONS

[handwritten: same manner as the judicial review of a gov't agency action (not de novo)]

1. *Analysis of* Carlberg. What standard of judicial review did *Carlberg* adopt with regard to a student's challenge to state governing body rules and decisions, and why did the court adopt that standard? By comparison, what standard of review applies in the case of an institutional member's challenge to such rules or decisions? Do you agree with the court's distinction and its far more deferential standard of review as to educational institutions?

    Jason Carlberg did not change schools primarily for reasons related to participation in interscholastic athletics. What reasons warrant strict enforcement of the transfer rule against him? Do they justify rendering him ineligible to participate in varsity athletics for one year? The association argues that the transaction costs of investigating individual cases warrant enforcement of a general rule that may prohibit student-athletes from participating even though the transfer is not primarily made for athletic reasons. Do you agree with this reasoning? What is the countervailing student-athlete interest, and is it being given sufficient weight by the majority? Do you prefer the dissent's view? *[handwritten: No!]*

2. *Judicial Deference.* Courts generally are very deferential to state athletic association eligibility determinations for transfer students. See, e.g., *Morgan v. Oklahoma Secondary Sch. Activities Assn.*, 207 P.3d 362 (Okla. 2009) (holding that student's eligibility for waiver of transfer rule should have been reserved for the Association). In *Art Gaines Baseball Camp, Inc. v. Houston*, 500 S.W.2d 735, 740-41 (Mo. App. 1973), the Missouri court of appeals provided the following reasons why judicial intervention should be minimal:

[handwritten: I agree w/ the view, but not the reasoning. Too hard to look @ case by case basis though!]

> Along with entrusting the education of our children to teachers and administrators, we also entrust the control and supervision of the extracurricular activities incident to that education. Implicit in the responsibility for these activities is the power to make reasonable rules and regulations. . . . As members of this association, [schools] may, by majority vote, enact rules to govern their interaction. It is obvious that chaos would result without such rules. It is also obvious that the members are in the most advantageous position to appreciate the regulations under which they must act to achieve desired goals.

In *Indiana High School Athletic Assn. v. Watson*, 938 N.E.2d 672 (Ind. 2010), the Indiana Supreme Court explained, "[A]n IHSAA determination is arbitrary and capricious 'only where it is willful and unreasonable, without consideration and in disregard of the facts or circumstances in the case, or without some basis which would lead a reasonable and honest person to the same conclusion.'" *Id.* at 680. Concluding that the evidence failed to establish that the defendant had acted arbitrarily and capriciously, the court stated, "While the IHSAA may not enforce its rules with arbitrary inconsistency, it must possess a level of discretion in sanctioning schools and athletes based on the language in the rules, the evidence available, and the overall justice of the situation." *Id.* at 682. Commenting on the trial court's ruling, the court stated that rather than inquiring into whether there was substantial evidence to support the athletic association's ruling, the trial court had substituted its own judgment for that of IHSAA.

What arguments may be raised in favor of judicial deference to decisions made by high school athletic associations and personnel? Is a court competent to resolve these disputes fairly and effectively? Should courts defer because these cases involve education and athletics? On the other hand, given the importance of athletic participation opportunities to student-athlete, is such deference warranted?

3.   *Federal Constitutional Claims.* In *In re: United States ex rel. MSHSAA*, 682 F.2d 147 (8th Cir. 1982), the Eighth Circuit held that a Missouri State High School Activities Association rule barring a student's participation in interscholastic athletics for a period of one year after the student transfers from one high school to another did not violate the student's federal constitutional rights to travel or association. Rejecting the right to travel argument, the court stated:

> Plaintiffs argue that the transfer rule burdens their exercise of the fundamental right to travel interstate. . . . When a student alters his or her place of residence from one state to another without an accompanying change by his or her parents . . . the rule prohibits the student from participating in interscholastic athletics for one year. Classifications which penalize the exercise of the right to travel are subject to strict scrutiny. But most cases which implicate the rule's sanction do not involve interstate travel and, those which do, implicate the sanction because they involve school transfers and not because they involve interstate travel. The rule's minimal impact on interstate travel does not require strict scrutiny.

Id. at 151-152.

The court also dispensed with the student's right of association argument:

> Plaintiffs also argue the rule burdens the right to freely associate by penalizing students' choice to change schools and thus to alter the body of people with which they associate. Students have no indefeasible right to associate through choice of school. Mandatory assignment to public schools based on place of residence or other factors is clearly permissible. The transfer rule does not prevent association through private schooling nor discriminate against any such association. Thus no right is burdened and the rule is not thereby subject to strict scrutiny.

Id. at 152.

See also *Menard v. La. High School Athletic Assn.*, 30 So. 3d 790, 795 (La. App. 2009) (dismissing plaintiff's due process and equal protection claims because "classification made by the transfer rule and the bona fide change of residence rule is not arbitrary or inherently suspect, and does not encroach upon a fundamental constitutional right"); *Dziewa v. PIAA*, 2009 WL 113419 (E.D. Pa.) (rejecting claim that the transfer rule violated privacy rights by requiring reason for student's transfer to another school—namely, parents' separation).

Once again, it is worth asking whether these federal constitutional doctrines have been applied in a more deferential manner in the athletics context than they would be applied in other educational or related contexts.

4.   *State Constitutional Issues.* In *Indiana High School Athletic Assn., Inc. v. Avant*, 650 N.E.2d 1164 (Ind. App. 1995), the court determined that the Indiana state constitution's equal protection clause provides a higher level of protection to a student-athlete challenging a transfer rule than is afforded under the federal equal protection clause. The court noted that the IHSAA had

to show that "1. The classification must be based upon distinctive, inherent characteristics which rationally distinguish the unequally treated class [transfer students], and the disparate treatment accorded by the [rule] must be reasonably related to such distinguishing characteristics; and 2. The classification must be open to any and all persons who share the inherent characteristics which distinguish and justify the classification, with any special treatment accorded to any particular classification extended equally to all such persons." *Id.* at 1170. Under federal constitutional law, equal protection challenges, unless based on the deprivation of a fundamental right or racial or gender-based discrimination, generally are decided based on a less stringent and very deferential standard (i.e., if there is any rational basis for supporting the decision made by the association, then the court will not find a deprivation of equal protection). Many lawyers representing student-athletes fail to heed the lesson that ought to be learned from reading cases like *Avant*: State constitutional provisions may be interpreted as providing the student-athlete with more (but not less) protection than that offered under the federal constitution, in terms of equal protection and other protected rights (e.g., freedom of association, educational opportunity, free exercise of religion, free speech, privacy). To effectively represent their clients, advocates for student-athletes must examine the particular state constitution to determine if it is applicable (sometimes coverage includes persons in addition to public entities and state actors) and arguably provides greater protection for their clients (what is sometimes referred to as a ratchet—state constitutions may provide greater but not lesser protection than the federal constitution).

5. *Restitution Rules.* Pending final resolution of all judicial appeals, a high school may be reluctant, notwithstanding a successful legal challenge at the trial court level, to allow a student-athlete to participate who was deemed ineligible by a state athletic association. If an appellate court ultimately upholds the association's finding of ineligibility, a high school risks sanctions imposed pursuant to an association's restitution rules, which may permit the imposition of retrospective sanctions for permitting an ineligible athlete to participate. The legal validity of such rules is discussed in Chapter 3.

6. *Mootness Doctrine.* It is common in transfer cases for mootness issues to arise. For example, in *Walsh v. Louisiana High School Athletic Assn.*, 613 F.2d 152 (5th Cir. 1980), the student-athlete's one-year period of ineligibility had expired by the time the case was heard on appeal. The court rejected the association's argument that the case was moot after applying the "capable of repetition, yet evading review" exception, which provides that (1) the challenged action was too short in duration to be fully litigated (i.e., the time to litigate exceeded the year of ineligibility under the transfer rule); and (2) there was a reasonable expectation that the same rule would be applied to the same party (in *Walsh*, the plaintiff had siblings who might be adversely affected by the rule) or another similarly aggrieved party. Mootness issues reflect a very practical problem in such cases—most parties will not spend the time and energy necessary to try a case when there is little left to win because their athletic ineligibility is limited in duration and often ends before a case is heard. Does this seem to argue for requiring a more expedited hearing process for students? Does it undercut the transaction cost arguments raised by the association?

7. *Penalizing Coaches for Recruiting Students.* Concerns regarding efforts by coaches to recruit students from one high school to another are being addressed by state governing bodies. For example, beginning with the 2012-2013 year, the Alabama High School Athletic Association will impose stiffer penalties on coaches for recruiting violations. Under the new Alabama rule, coaches found guilty of recruiting will be placed on probation, and his or her team will be prohibited from participating in the state play-offs for a year. Coaches involved in recruiting in violation of the association's rules may also be banned from coaching for a year. See Dennis Lin and Doug Segrest, *New Rules Try to Sideline Recruiting Among High Schools*, AL.com, April 30, 2012, http://highschoolsports.al.com/news/article/5618907589460379959/new-rules-try-to-sideline-recruiting-among-high-schools/. Interestingly, a high school football coach in Florida complained about a coach from the University of Alabama encouraging one of the high school football coach's players to transfer to another high school to help ensure his intercollegiate eligibility at Alabama. See Graham Watson, *High School Coach Takes Issues with Alabama's Recruiting Tactics*, Yahoo! Sports, Aug. 9, 2012, http://sports.yahoo.com/blogs/ncaaf-dr-saturday/high-school-coach-takes-issues-alabama-recruiting-tactics-213239312–ncaaf.html.

b. "Outside Competition" Rules

In the following case, the court of appeals considered whether the state athletic association rule limiting eligibility for students who are engaged in outside competition was enforceable.

LETENDRE v. MISSOURI STATE HIGH SCHOOL ACTIVITIES ASSN.

86 S.W.3d 63 (Mo. App. 2002)

Claire Letendre seeks to enjoin the Missouri State High School Activities Association (MSHSAA) from enforcing by-law 235, which prohibits students from competing on both a school and a non-school team in the same sport during the school team's season. . . .

The MSHSAA is a voluntary association of 750 secondary public, private and parochial schools in Missouri. It is charged with developing uniform and equitable standards of eligibility for students and schools to participate in interscholastic activities. The rules ostensibly work to avoid interference with the educational program of the school by outside activities; to prevent exploitation of high school youth and the programs of member schools by special interest groups; and to provide a means of evaluating and controlling local, state, and national contests affecting secondary schools. The association is governed by a Constitution and by-laws adopted by its members. Claire's high school, St. Joseph's Academy, is a member of the MSHSAA.

At the time of trial, Claire was a 15-year-old sophomore earning good grades. She did not participate in any school-sponsored sports, clubs, student government, or organized activities, other than a prayer group, because she "loves to swim." Claire has been a member of the private Parkway Swim Club since the age of three, swimming in competitive meets since the age of five. She practices and competes with the private swim club team all year long, participating in regional and national meets that require out-of-state travel. Her swim club's practice schedule is Monday through Friday from 4:30 to 7:30 p.m. and on Saturdays from 6:15 to 9:30 a.m., swimming from 5,000 to 9,000 yards daily. Claire testified that her coach at the Parkway Swim Club enters her in every single event offered during her swim club seasons. Claire claimed her short-term goal is to qualify for the Senior Nationals and, ultimately, the Olympics.

On January 31, 2001, Claire attended a meeting for students interested in joining the school swim team. They discussed health forms, practice times, the season schedule and MSHSAA eligibility rules. On February 12, 2001, Claire attended another school swim team meeting held immediately prior to the first practice. Claire testified that after this meeting she knew she would become ineligible for school swimming if she chose to swim with the club team.

By-law 235(1)(a) provides that "during the sport season a student . . . shall neither practice nor compete as a member of a non-school team nor as an individual participant in organized non-school competition in that same sport."

. . . Unlike other St. Joseph Academy students who also swam for Parkway Swim Club, Claire chose to practice with her swim club team rather than her school team. . . .

The power of a court to review the quasi-judicial actions of a voluntary association is limited to determining: (1) whether there are inconsistencies between the association's charter and by-laws and any action taken in respect to them; (2) whether the member has been treated unfairly, i.e., denied notice, hearing, or an opportunity to defend; (3) whether the association undertakings were prompted by malice, fraud or collusion; and (4) whether the charter or by-laws contravene public policy or law.

Courts have no power to usurp the function of the tribunals of [voluntary] associations, [like the MSHSAA] and can interfere only when those tribunals proceed without evidence or in bad faith or violate a valid part of the constitution and rules in dealing with a member, or attempt to enforce against him, to his injury, invalid provisions thereof. It is only upon the clearest showing that the rules have been violated by a decision of the association's tribunal that courts should intercede.

Claire agrees that the Association has acted consistently with its rules, given her due process and did not act out of malice. But instead argues that by-law 235 is against public policy because it is arbitrary, capricious and violates her Constitutional rights to equal protection and free association as guaranteed by the Fourteenth Amendment of the United States Constitution.

The specific inequity she claims is that by-law 235 is internally inconsistent in that it does not affect those who wish to participate in non-athletic activities both in and outside of school; it does not affect those who participate in one sport in school and another sport outside of school; and it does not apply to athletes who participate in national or Olympic development competitions during a sport season. She maintains that the prohibition of simultaneous same-sport competition is irrational and unrelated to any legitimate goal of the association and asks us to declare by-law 235 unconstitutional as applied to her.

The Fourteenth Amendment guarantees that no person shall be denied equal protection of the law. It assures all individuals fair treatment if fundamental rights are at stake. It also eliminates distinctions based on impermissible criteria such as race, age, religion, or gender. Where there is no suspect classification or Impingement on a fundamental right explicitly or implicitly protected by the U.S. Constitution, Equal Protection claims are reviewed by this Court under the "rational relationship" standard. . . .

Claire's claim is not based upon a suspect classification, such as race, religion, national origin, or gender. Nor is it based upon a claim that her fundamental rights were violated, because she recognizes there is no fundamental right to play high school athletics. Accordingly, our inquiry is confined to whether there is a "rational relationship" between by-law 235 and any legitimate interest of the MSHSAA. . . .

We have reviewed the history of the MSHSAA non-school competition standard. Since 1959 the rule has been reconsidered and modified fifteen times. The express purpose of these reconsiderations and modifications is to create standards that purport to serve the largest number of students. At trial the Executive Director of the MSHSAA identified several reasons for the adoption of by-law 235, including: (1) preventing or reducing interference with a school's academic program; (2) preventing interference with athletic programs by organized non-school athletics; (3) promoting and protecting competitive equity; (4) avoiding conflicts in coaching philosophy and scheduling; and (5) encouraging students not to overemphasize athletic competition.

The director of the MSHSAA testified that the association's 76 years of experience allowed them to conclude that the potential for harm is not as great in activities such as music, speech, debate and academics as in extracurricular sports. The Association has made, however, an exception for Olympic competitors because it is required by federal law. 36 U.S.C. 220501 et seq. The Amateur Sports Act of 1978 allows Olympic competitors to participate in interscholastic competitions, but gives organizations such as MSHSAA exclusive jurisdiction over such competitions. 36 U.S.C. 220526(a). The Amateur Sports Act also requires that national sports organizations minimize conflicts in scheduling of all practices and competitions through coordination with organizations such as the MSHSAA. 36 U.S.C. 220524(2). The National Federation of State High School Associations, including the MSHSAA, pledged to enact limited exceptions to their non-school participation restrictions to accommodate the national objectives reflected in The Amateur Sports Act. All state associations have an exception similar to this.

The issue for us, then, is not whether we agree with the Association, but whether the challenged rule bears a rational relationship to a reasonable goal of the MSHSAA. A rule of a quasi-judicial voluntary association "will not be set aside if any state of facts reasonably may be conceived to justify it." (Citation omitted.)

If the classification has some "reasonable basis" it does not offend the Constitution simply because "in practice it results in some inequality." (Citation omitted.) We conclude that there are reasonable grounds for by-law 235 because a reasonable person could believe that a legitimate goal of the Association is furthered by the rule.

In *Schoenlaub*, the Missouri Supreme Court adopted the following test for reasonableness:

the court must determine if the board's action is so willful and unreasoning, without consideration of the facts and circumstances, and in such disregard of them as to be arbitrary and capricious. Where there is room for two opinions on the matter, such action is not "arbitrary and capricious," even though it may be believed that an erroneous conclusion has been reached.

507 S.W.2d at 359.

Since its inception 75 years ago, the MSHSAA has received a mandate to value the best interests of all student athletes. In 1975, the Association identified outside competition during the school year as one of the "principal areas of problems facing high schools and state associations." A reasonable person could conclude that it is not in the best interest of the majority of high school students to compete in the same sport at the same time on two different teams, with different coaches, different rules, different practice schedules, and different competition schedules. The Executive Director of MSHSAA explained that one purpose of the Association is to have standards that will be in the best interest of the larger number of high school students. Here there is substantial evidence to conclude that by-law 235 is rationally related to the legitimate goal of protecting that interest. Claire's Equal Protection argument must fail.

Claire's second argument is that by preventing her from simultaneously competing on her school and swim club teams the MSHSAA has violated her right to free association. The First Amendment assures the freedom of expression, including the implied right of association. The Supreme Court first recognized this right in *NAACP v. Alabama*, 357 U.S. 449, 460-61, 78 S.Ct. 1163, 2 L.Ed.2d 1488 (1958), declaring that freedom to engage in association for the advancement of beliefs and ideas is an inseparable aspect of liberty.

The Court has made clear that the right of association encompasses only two distinct cases: (1) those involving "intimate" human relationships fundamental to personal liberty and (2) those involving activities expressly protected by the First Amendment such as speech, assembly, petitioning for redress of grievances and the exercise of religion. (citation omitted.) By-law 235 does not impinge upon intimate human relationships nor core First Amendment freedoms. There is, consequently, no First Amendment right for a high school student to associate simultaneously with both a school and a non-school swim team. . . .

While we might personally believe that a better rule could be drafted, one that would allow a student athlete who is getting good grades, such as Claire, to compete simultaneously on both her school and non-school swim teams, the law does not permit us to interject our personal beliefs in the name of the Constitution. Claire's constitutional challenges must fail because by-law 235 is rationally related to the MSHSAA's purpose of drafting rules that protect the welfare of the greatest number of high school athletes possible. The judgment of the trial court is, therefore, affirmed.

NOTE AND QUESTIONS

Letendre provides an example of judicial reluctance to second-guess an athletic governing body's judgment in formulating eligibility rules for high school students. Courts have uniformly rejected legal challenges to "outside competition" rules, even if the rule only applies to certain sports and prohibits participation in the same sport outside the time period for interscholastic competition in that sport. See, e.g., *Burrows v. Ohio High School Athletic Assn.*, 891 F.2d 122 (6th Cir. 1989); *Zuments v. Colo. High School Activities Assn.*, 737 P.2d 1113 (Colo. Ct. App. 1987); *Eastern New York Youth Soccer Assn. v. New York State Public High School*

Athletic Assn., 108 A.D.2d 39, 488 N.Y.S.2d 293 (N.Y. App. Div. 1985); *University Interscholastic League v. North Dallas Chamber of Commerce Soccer Assn.*, 693 S.W.2d 513 (Tex. App. 1985); *Caso v. New York State Public High School Athletic Assn.*, 78 A.D.2d 41, 434 S.W.2d 60 (N.Y. App. Div. 1980). To comply with the Amateur Sports Act of 1978's objective of furthering the development of Olympic sports, "outside competition" rules generally provide waivers to enable high school students to try out and qualify for spots on American Olympic teams.

By generally upholding "outside competition" rules, the prevailing judicial view is that "all students are free to compete, or otherwise participate in any or all non-school events. Rather than impinging upon their right of free association, the rule merely delineates under what terms and conditions they may participate in interscholastic athletics." *Zuments*, 737 P.2d at 1115. As one court explained:

> Petitioners urge that the outside competition rule, either as originally written or as amended, unconstitutionally interferes with parental rights to control the upbringing of children, including the right to determine whether the children can physically and academically contend with participation in school and nonschool athletic competition. While parents have a right to bring up their children as they see fit, the right is not free from legislative restrictions. . . . The instant rule does not interfere with parental privacy rights. The choice of whether to participate in school or nonschool teams remains with the parents and their children.
>
>   The other aspect of the issue, however, has to do with the obligation of public school officials to protect the well-being of their students. (Citation omitted.) Respondent's concern that students not overtax themselves is a legitimate interest and the outside competition rule is rationally related to that concern.

Eastern New York Youth Soccer Assn., 488 N.Y.S.2d at 294-295.

Do you agree that high school athletic governing bodies should have broad authority to effectively prohibit students' participation in competitive club sports as a condition of participating in interscholastic athletics?

c. Age Rules

PROBLEM 2-2

You represent a young woman, who is 12 years old, and her family. The young woman has been promoted, because of high academic performance, to the twelfth grade. As such, this will be her last opportunity to participate in varsity athletics at the interscholastic level. She is 5′5″ tall and weighs 123 pounds and wants to participate in varsity lacrosse. The coach refused to permit her to try out for the varsity team, suggesting that she would be at risk if she were to play at the varsity level because of her age. He suggested that she try out for the freshman or middle school team. However, she wants to play at the varsity level. What advice would you give her and her family?

What if your client were 19 and just returned to finish her senior year after being overseas with her family (her father was serving in a diplomatic capacity in a foreign country) for two years? The coach wants her to play, but the rule limits participation by a 19-year-old. What advice would you give?

Most interscholastic associations impose rules that prohibit the right of student-athletes to engage in interscholastic competition once they reach the age of 19. One commentator summarizes the reasons underlying this rule as follows:

This rule serves a variety of purposes, including reducing the competitive advantage of teams with older athletes, protecting younger students from injury, discouraging students from delaying their education to enhance athletic performance, and preventing coaches from red-shirting athletes. The age nineteen rule also aims to prevent older students from preempting participation by younger students, maintain uniformity of standards regarding participant's age, and retain a level playing field.

Brooke A. Fredrickson, *The Age Nineteen Rule and Students with Disabilities: Discrimination Against Disabled Students with Athletic Ability*, 25 T. Jefferson L. Rev. 635, 640 (2003).

The following case explores the constitutionality of rules prohibiting 19-year-old students from participating in interscholastic athletics. As you read *Tiffany*, consider the reasons that underlie the imposition of age limits on athletic participation and which of them are furthered by categorically excluding 19-year-old students.

TIFFANY v. ARIZONA INTERSCHOLASTIC ASSN., INC.

726 P.2d 231 (Ariz. Ct. App. 1986)

MEYERSON, Judge.

Does a high school student have a constitutional right to participate in interscholastic athletic competition during his senior year in high school? This is the primary question raised in this appeal. As explained more fully herein, we hold that defendant-appellant Arizona Interscholastic Association, Inc. (AIA) did not violate the due process clause of the fourteenth amendment when it refused to grant plaintiff-appellee John Tiffany a hardship waiver from its nineteen-year-old eligibility rule. We concur with the trial court, however, that AIA acted unlawfully by failing to follow its own bylaws in considering the request for the waiver.

I. FACTS

Tiffany began his senior year at St. Mary's High School in Phoenix during the 1983-84 school term. He had been held back in kindergarten and first grade because of a learning disability. Thus, he turned nineteen years of age on August 5, 1983, the month before his senior year would begin. Tiffany had participated in athletics throughout grade school and during high school. He wanted to participate in athletic competition during his senior year.

AIA is a voluntary association composed of all public and most private high schools in Arizona. AIA formulates and promulgates rules and regulations pertaining to, among other things, interscholastic athletic competition among its members. Under AIA's bylaws, if a student turns nineteen before September 1 of the school year, he is not eligible to participate in interscholastic athletics. AIA bylaws provide, however, that:

The Executive Board in individual cases may, at its discretion and upon such terms and conditions as it may impose, waive or modify any eligibility rule when in its opinion there are circumstances beyond the control of the student or parent whereby enforcement of the rule would work an undue hardship on the student. . . .

The parties have stipulated that the decision to hold Tiffany back in the early grades was made by his teachers and school administrators with his parents' approval. AIA does not contest that these circumstances were beyond the control of Tiffany and his parents.

At a hearing before the Executive Board of AIA, Tiffany presented evidence that he very much enjoyed his participation in interscholastic athletics, the friendship of those with whom he would compete, and the benefits from the discipline and regulation involved in playing varsity athletics. Tiffany indicated to the Executive Board that his motivation in studying came from the fact that in order to be eligible for interscholastic athletics a certain grade point average must be maintained. The Executive Board denied the request for the waiver. It is agreed by the parties that AIA has a policy of not making any exceptions to the nineteen-year-old eligibility rule.

Tiffany subsequently filed a complaint requesting that AIA be enjoined from disqualifying him from interscholastic athletic competition. He requested that AIA's actions be declared unconstitutional as a denial of due process. The trial court granted a preliminary injunction allowing Tiffany to play during the 1983-84 school year. Final judgment was entered in 1985. Because Tiffany requested attorney's fees, the trial court determined that the controversy was not moot.

The trial court held that AIA's Executive Board acted "unreasonably, capriciously and arbitrarily" when it failed to exercise its discretion in considering Tiffany's request for a waiver. The trial court also ruled that Tiffany possessed a "sufficient liberty or property interest or personal stake in participating in high school athletics" such that AIA's actions violated his constitutional rights. Tiffany was awarded attorney's fees in the amount of $2,500 pursuant to 42 U.S.C. § 1988. AIA has filed this appeal from that judgment. In order to determine whether the trial court could properly award attorney's fees to Tiffany pursuant to 42 U.S.C. § 1988, we must first decide whether the trial court correctly found that AIA violated Tiffany's constitutional rights.

II.   CONSTITUTIONAL CLAIMS

. . . In order to decide whether Tiffany's exclusion from interscholastic athletics during his senior year in high school violated due process (and therefore 42 U.S.C. § 1983), it first must be determined whether Tiffany had any property or liberty interest in participating in high school sports during the 1983-84 school year. The beginning point in analyzing this constitutional issue is the decision of the United States Supreme Court in *Goss v. Lopez*, 419 U.S. 565, 95 S.Ct. 729, 42 L.Ed.2d 725 (1975). In *Goss*, the Supreme Court held that a school could not suspend a student for ten days without insuring due process safeguards. The Court reasoned that a "State is constrained to recognize a student's legitimate entitlement to a public education as a property interest which is protected by the Due Process Clause and which may not be taken away for misconduct without adherence to the minimum procedures required by that Clause." *Id.* at 574, 95 S.Ct. at 736.

[E]ducation is perhaps the most important function of state and local governments, and the total exclusion from the educational process for more than a trivial period, and certainly if the suspension is for ten days, is a serious event in the life of the suspended child. Neither the property interest in educational benefits temporarily denied nor the liberty interest in reputation, which is also implicated, is so insubstantial that suspensions may constitutionally be imposed by any procedure the school chooses, no matter how arbitrary.

Id. at 576, 95 S.Ct. at 737 (citation omitted). We now proceed to apply the ruling of *Goss* to the case before us. . . .

Most courts which have considered this issue have declined to hold that participation in a single year of high school athletic competition rises to the level of a constitutionally protectable property interest. . . . For example, in *Albach v. Odle*, 531 F.2d 983 (10th Cir. 1976), the plaintiff challenged a rule automatically barring from interscholastic high school athletic competition for one year any student who transferred from his home district to a boarding school or from a boarding school to his home district. The court found that the ruling in *Goss v. Lopez* was limited to the "educational process." In language which has been cited repeatedly by other courts, the court declared:

The educational process is a broad and comprehensive concept with a variable and indefinite meaning. It is not limited to classroom attendance but includes innumerable separate components, such as participation in athletic activity and participation in school clubs and social groups, which combine to provide an atmosphere of intellectual and moral advancement. We do not read *Goss* to establish a property interest subject to constitutional protection in each of these separate components.

Id. at 985. In *Karmanos v. Baker*, 617 F. Supp. 809 (E.D.Mich. 1985), the court concluded that the plaintiff had not demonstrated that he had a property interest in participating in intercollegiate hockey. The court noted that the plaintiff had not alleged any acts which deprived him of educational or vocational opportunities other than the opportunity to play hockey.

Finally, in *Kulovitz v. Illinois High School Ass'n*, 462 F. Supp. 875 (N.D. Ill. 1978), the court rejected the plaintiff's constitutional claim arising out of his exclusion from participation in high school athletics during a single school year. The court held that "participation in interscholastic athletics is not a constitutionally protected civil right." *Id.* at 877. . . .

Under certain limited circumstances, however, courts have found that participation in interscholastic sports rises to the level of a constitutionally protected property interest. For example, in *Boyd v. Board of Directors*, 612 F. Supp. 86 (E.D. Ark. 1985), the court held that a student could not be suspended from the high school football team without procedural due process of law protections. The court found that the plaintiff-student was an outstanding athlete and that the 1983 season was his last opportunity to participate in football at the high school level. The testimony indicated that participation in high school sports was "vital and indispensable to a college scholarship and, in essence, a college education." *Id.* at 93. The court found that the plaintiff's continued status on the team was "very important" to his "development educationally and economically in the future." *Id.* Accordingly, the court found that his participation in interscholastic athletics must be deemed a property interest protected by the due process clause of the fourteenth amendment. . . .

In *Florida High School Activities Ass'n, Inc. v. Bryant*, 313 So.2d 57 (Fla. Dist. Ct. App. 1975), the court affirmed the trial court which ordered the defendant to allow the plaintiff to participate in athletics during the 1974-75 school year. Although the court did not express its ruling in due process terms, it accepted the trial court's finding that basketball was an important and vital part of the plaintiff's life "'providing an impetus to his general scholastic and social development and rehabilitation from his prior problems as a juvenile delinquent.'" *Id.* at 57.

As the above cases demonstrate, in the realm of constitutional law, there are very few absolutes. We are persuaded that under certain circumstances a high school student can properly establish an entitlement to due process protection in connection with a suspension or exclusion from high school athletics. We believe that an appropriate extension of the holding in *Goss v. Lopez* was expressed by the court in *Pegram v. Nelson*, 469 F. Supp. 1134 (M.D.N.C. 1979). In that case, a high school student was suspended from school for ten days and was also excluded from after-school activities for a period of four months. The court acknowledged that the "opportunity to participate in extracurricular activities is not, by and in itself, a property interest." *Id.* at 1139. The court recognized, however, that:

> *Total exclusion* from participation in that part of the educational process designated as extracurricular activities for a *lengthy period of time* could, depending upon the particular circumstances, be a sufficient deprivation to implicate due process.

Id. at 1140.

It is not necessary in this case to define the precise parameters of the circumstances under which due process must be afforded to a student excluded from high school athletics. This is so because Tiffany has not asserted any cognizable interest beyond his claim to mere participation in one year of interscholastic sports. Tiffany argues that he very much enjoys his participation in athletics, the friendship of those that he competes with and the benefit he derives from the discipline and regulation involved in playing varsity sports. Such interests, albeit important to him, simply do not rise to the level of constitutional magnitude necessary to invoke the protection of the due process clause. We likewise conclude that the scholastic benefit derived from the incentive to maintain a certain grade point average to remain eligible for athletic competition is also an interest which is outside the scope of constitutional protection. Unlike the "deprivation of a previously granted scholarship [which] would invoke the protections of procedural due process," *Colorado Seminary v. National Collegiate Athletic Ass'n*, 417 F. Supp. 885, 895 (D. Colo. 1976), *aff'd*, 570 F.2d 320 (10th Cir. 1978), the educational stimulus Tiffany claims to derive from athletic participation is, in constitutional terms, a "mere subjective 'expectation,'" *Perry v. Sindermann*, 408 U.S. 593, 603, 92 S.Ct. 2694, 2700, 33 L.Ed.2d 570, 580 (1972) and not protected by procedural due process. In short, Tiffany has failed to demonstrate the type of serious damage to his "later opportunities for higher education and employment," *Goss v. Lopez*, 419 U.S. at 575, 95 S.Ct. at 736, which would raise his interest in interscholastic athletics to a level warranting the safeguards of the due process clause.

III.   FAILURE TO EXERCISE DISCRETION

Although we reject Tiffany's constitutional claim, we sustain the trial court's ruling that the Executive Board of AIA acted unlawfully when it failed to exercise its discretion at the eligibility hearing. As noted above, despite the fact that AIA's bylaws specifically provide that its Executive Board will exercise discretion in considering hardship waivers to its eligibility rules, it is undisputed that the Executive Board has adopted a policy of not making any exceptions to the nineteen-year-old eligibility requirement.

It is hornbook law that an administrative board must follow its own rules and regulations. . . . An administrative agency's failure to follow its own rules and regulations does not create a constitutional due process right on behalf of a party who suffers some wrong at the hands of the administrative body. . . . Rather, the obligation of such a body to follow its own rules and regulations is founded in principles of administrative law. . . .

In Arizona, the procedure by which one can compel an administrative board to exercise its discretion is through the filing of a mandamus, *Eastman v. Southworth*, 87 Ariz. 394, 351 P.2d 992 (1960), now a special action. Rule 1, Rules of Procedure for Special Actions; *see* A.R.S. § 12-2021. Although Tiffany's complaint was not denominated a special action, the record of the trial court proceedings reflects that the mandamus issue was implicitly tried by the parties. We hold that the trial court was correct in concluding that the Executive Board of AIA acted "unreasonably, capriciously and arbitrarily" when it failed to exercise its discretion in considering Tiffany's request for a waiver.

Affirmed in part, reversed in part.

NOTES AND QUESTIONS

1. *Analysis of* Tiffany. What reasons were offered by John Tiffany as to why the defendant should waive its 19-year-old eligibility rule so he could participate for an additional year? On what basis did the court reject Tiffany's arguments? How was defendant's exercise of discretion limited? Is the approach adopted by the court similar to that which is taken in other cases in which student-athletes assert challenges to rules limiting their ability to engage in interscholastic participation?

2. *Rationale for Age Limits.* What is the rationale for imposing an age limitation on the ability of players to participate in interscholastic sport? Will older, more experienced athletes necessarily have a competitive advantage over younger players? Will older players expose younger and less physically developed players to a greater risk of physical harm? What other reasons may underlie age limitations on athletic participation?

In *Baisden v. West Virginia Secondary Schools Activities Commission*, 568 S.E.2d 32 (W. Va. 2002), the defendant's interscholastic regulations rendered students who reach the age of 19 prior to a certain date ineligible to participate in interscholastic competition. The plaintiff sought a permanent injunction prohibiting the defendant from enforcing its age rule against him based on Virginia's Human Rights Act, which requires reasonable accommodations for persons with disabilities. The lower court ruled that the age rule was unenforceable against the plaintiff. Its decision was based on evidence that the plaintiff's learning disability with respect to math and reading required him to repeat two years of education. According to the lower court, enforcing the ban would constitute discrimination against the plaintiff on the basis of his learning disability.

In addressing this question, the West Virginia Supreme Court first noted that the issue of the plaintiff's eligibility to participate in interscholastic sports is moot because he had graduated from high school. However, because of the importance of the substantive issue and the probability that it will affect the rights of students under similar circumstances, the court elected to address it. In reversing the lower court, the appellate court observed that age limitations "are typically strictly enforced, based upon safety issues raised by permitting older, larger, more experienced players to compete against younger students." *Id.* at 37. The court held:

Big kid!

While we decide . . . that individualized assessments are required in cases of this nature and that reasonable accommodations may be made through waiver of the nineteen age rule under certain circumstances, we do not believe that the facts of this case justify waiver as an accommodation. Mr. Baisden turned nineteen on July 27, 2001. He is six feet four inches tall and weighs 280 pounds. He runs the forty-yard-dash in 5.3 seconds. His participation in high school football would permit him to compete in this contact sport against students approximately five years younger. The safety of younger, smaller, more inexperienced students would be unreasonably compromised. In our view, this would fundamentally alter the structure of the interscholastic athletic program, a result which is not required by reasonable accommodation standards in anti-discrimination law.

Id. at 44.

Separate from education cirriculum

3. *Fifth-Year Student Rule.* In *Mancuson v. Massachusetts Interscholastic Athletic Assn.*, 900 N.E.2d 518 (Mass. 2009), the court upheld the MIAA's "fifth-year student rule," in a case involving a student who had repeated the ninth grade. The court rejected the student's argument that her due process rights were deprived because she had a property right in participation in athletics as an outgrowth of her right to education. The court found that there was no such right because athletics were "by their very nature" separate from the curriculum and were not, therefore, an outgrowth of the student's right to education. Do you agree?

4. *Federal and State Disability Discrimination Claims.* State governing body rules prohibiting 19-year-olds from participating in high school sports are increasingly the subject of challenges by learning and physically impaired student-athletes who allege that such age rules violate federal legislation such as the Americans with Disabilities Act and similar state laws. *Cruz v. Pennsylvania Interscholastic Athletic Association, Inc.*, 157 F. Supp. 2d 485 (E.D. Pa. 2001), in Chapter 11, examines this issue.

d. Academic Eligibility Requirements

PROBLEM 2-3

You represent a school district with three high schools and have been asked by the board to respond to the following question: May the school district legally adopt a minimum grade point average in a set of core courses for students participating in interscholastic sports that is higher than the 2.0 requirement set forth in the state athletic association rules? Would doing so be good policy? One member of the board supports raising the grade point average to 2.2, believing that a higher grade point average will cause students who desire to participate to take their core academic subjects seriously so that they can maximize their opportunities to pursue higher education. Another member disagrees, believing that a higher grade point requirement would cause more students to drop out or to lose interest in school. May a district adopt a more lenient requirement than that required at the state level? In responding to the board, think about the impact such requirements have had in other contexts.

———————

Eligibility rules commonly referred to as "no-pass, no-play" rules were initially promulgated in the early 1980s as state legislatures and athletic associations sought to strike an appropriate balance between academics and athletics. No-pass, no-play rules condition participation in extracurricular activities, including sports, on students achieving a certain academic performance. The first no-pass, no-play statute, which was enacted in Texas, provided that

> [a] student, other than a mentally retarded student, enrolled in a school district in this state shall be suspended from participation in any extracurricular activity sponsored or sanctioned by the school district during the grade reporting period after a grade reporting period in which the student received a grade lower than the equivalent of 70 on a scale of 100 in any academic class.

Spring Branch I.S.D. v. Stamos, 695 S.W.2d 556, 560 (Tex. 1985).

No-pass, no-play rules have been controversial, and questions have been raised regarding whether they achieve their ultimate objective—better academic performance. One commentator describes the debate as follows:

> Proponents of the rules argue that they advance education by giving the student who fails to meet minimum academic standards an incentive to do better, and more free time to devote to studies. However, opponents of the rules question this logic. They contend that the rules may in fact lead more students to either drop out of school altogether, or to pursue academic course work which does not present any substantial challenge.

David J. Shannon, *No Pass, No Play: Equal Protection Analysis Under the Federal and State Constitutions*, 63 Ind. L.J. 161, 161-162 (1987/1988).

Students deemed ineligible to participate in interscholastic sports have challenged the legality of no-pass, no-play rules on equal protection and due process grounds. Starting from the premise that participation in extracurricular activities is neither a fundamental right nor an infringement on the rights of a suspect class, courts have applied a rational basis test in addressing equal protection challenges. The application of such a standard invariably leads them to conclude that no-pass, no-play rules are rationally related to their intended goals. Similarly, courts have rejected due process challenges to no-pass, no-play rules because a student's interest in participating in extracurricular activities is not a protected property or liberty interest.

Bailey v. Truby, 321 S.E.2d 302 (W. Va. 1984) illustrates the prevailing judicial approach in these cases. A West Virginia State Board of Education policy required students to maintain a 2.0 or "C" grade point average and not receive a failing grade in any subject in order to participate in extracurricular activities.

The plaintiff, a basketball student-athlete, maintained a 2.0 grade point average but was declared academically ineligible to play basketball after he failed an English class. He asserted a denial of due process and violation of his federal and state equal protection guarantees. Agreeing with the majority of courts that have not recognized any fundamental right of students to participate in extracurricular activities and that there is no constitutionally protected property or liberty interest in interscholastic athletics, the court rejected the plaintiff's due process and equal protection challenges. On the question of whether the no-pass, no-play rule bore a rational relationship to a legitimate governmental purpose, the court defined the government's interests as follows:

> Unquestionably, the encouragement of academic excellence is a legitimate concern of the . . . Board of Education. The regulation of nonacademic extracurricular activity is a common method of achieving this fundamental goal. Part of this regulatory activity traditionally includes academic achievement standards as a prerequisite to participation in nonacademic extracurricular activities, particularly in the area of interscholastic sports. As one commentator has noted:
>
> > Since amateur athletics are ordinarily conducted as a part of the educational activities of high schools and colleges, it is also common for there to be rules which limit eligibility of those who maintain a required grade average. Such a rule will ordinarily be a proper exercise of institutional authority, because it is normally both authorized and reasonable. It will be authorized because the fostering of scholastic, not athletic, achievement is the primary objective of the academic institution, and denying participation in extracurricular activities to those who are unable to render satisfactory performance is directly related to that objective. (Quoting W. Lowell, The Law of Sports §1.21 (1979))

321 S.E.2d at 316. Accord *Bartmess v. Board of Trustees of Sch. Dist. No. 1*, 726 P.2d 801, 805 (Mont. 1986) (denying student-athlete's challenge of academic eligibility rule, court reasons that rule provides incentive for students wishing to participate in extracurricular activities and "promotes adequate study time for those students who have not maintained a 2.0 grade average"); *Spring Branch I.S.D. v. Stamos*, 695 S.W.2d 556, 560 (Tex. 1985) (rejecting due process argument because participation in extracurricular interscholastic does not rise to level of constitutionally protected property or liberty interest and concluding that grade eligibility rule was rationally related to legitimate state interest because it promoted improved academic performance by students); *Thompson v. Fayette County Public Schs.*, 786 S.W.2d 879, 882 (Ky. App. 1990) (eligibility rule requiring minimum 2.0 to participate in interscholastic sports upheld because plaintiff possessed neither a property nor a liberty interest in participating on high school wrestling team). But see *Fontes v. Irvine Unified Sch. Dist.*, 30 Cal. Rptr. 2d 521 (Cal. App. 4th Dist. 1994) (eligibility rule imposing higher academic requirements on cheerleaders than student-athletes violates equal protection rights under California constitution). For commentary regarding no-pass, no-play rules, see Thomas H. Sawyer, *The New Academic Requirements for Amateur Sports: No Pass, No Play*, 16 Loy. L.A. Ent. L.J. 105 (1995); Barbara Ferguson, *The Legal and Political Challenges to Academic Eligibility Requirements*, 2 Marq. Sports L.J. 103, 142 (1991); Anne Y. Koester, *No Pass, No Play Rules: An Incentive or an Infringement?*, 19 U. Tol. L. Rev. 87 (1987).

e. Exclusion of Homeschooled Students from Athletic Participation

In two recent cases, courts have addressed the issue of the eligibility of home-schooled students to participate in extracurricular sporting activities. In *Jones v. West Virginia State Board of Education*, 622 S.E.2d 289 (W. Va. 2005), plaintiffs sought to have their 11-year-old child, whom they homeschooled, try out for the Mannington Middle School wrestling team. The West Virginia Secondary School Activities Commission (WVSSAC) denied their request on the ground that only full-time students were permitted to participate in interscholastic athletics. Plaintiffs filed a complaint, seeking declaratory, equitable, and injunctive relief. The trial court found in favor of plaintiffs and entered the injunction.

On appeal, the West Virginia Supreme Court addressed three issues: (1) Did the WVSSAC breach a statutory duty by not allowing homeschoolers to participate in interscholastic athletics? (2) Did the WVSSAC violate the West Virginia equal protection rights of homeschool children by prohibiting them from participating in interscholastic athletics? (3) Did the WVSSAC breach its duty to promulgate reasonable rules and regulations by implementing a total ban on allowing homeschooled children to participate in interscholastic athletics?

The court held in favor of the WVSSAC on all three issues. With respect to the alleged breach of a statutory duty, the court held the plain language of the relevant statute imposed an obligation on the school superintendent to provide assistance and resources to the person providing the homeschool instruction (here, the student's mother). The statute did not, however, require that resources, including interscholastic athletics, be provided to the homeschooled student himself.

The court also held that the WVSSAC did not violate plaintiffs' equal protection rights. In reaching this conclusion, the court first found that participation in interscholastic athletics is neither a fundamental nor a constitutional right under the West Virginia constitution. Consequently, any classification affecting participation in interscholastic athletics will be upheld as long as it is rationally related to a legitimate state interest. Among the several grounds offered by defendant as providing a rational basis for excluding homeschooled children, the court focused on two as offering sufficient justification: "(a) promoting academics over athletics, and (2) protecting the economic interests of the county school systems." *Id.* at 295. With respect to the former, the court examined the grade requirements for participating in extracurricular activities. It found that homeschooled children are graded on different standards than public school children and converting such grades would impose a burden on the school district. Moreover, the different grading standards would impede the ability of school officials to maintain the academic standards required for participation in interscholastic sports. The court noted that a parent could withdraw an under-performing student from the public school system and homeschool him or her in order to retain the student athlete's eligibility.

As it relates to protecting the economic interests of the county school system, the court emphasized that money is apportioned to schools based on attendance in class. According to the court, requiring counties to spend limited funds to support athletic participation of homeschooled students (from whom no funds are allocated) would create a financial burden. Finally, the court held that the WVSSAC did not breach its duty to promulgate reasonable rules and regulations. Even though homeschooled students are totally banned from inter-scholastic athletics participation, the court held it is not arbitrary and capricious because it is rationally related to the two legitimate state purposes discussed above.

In *Reid v. Kenowa Hills Public Schools*, 680 N.W.2d (Mich. Ct. App. 2004), the court similarly resolved a homeschooled student's challenge to a rule of the MHSAA providing that only students enrolled in school for at least 20 hours may participate in extracurricular sports. The court held that nonenrolled, homeschooled children have no fundamental right to participate in athletic activities, which is a privilege rather than a right.

Thirty states now have laws permitting homeschooled students to participate in interscholastic sports. These rules have been dubbed "Tim Tebow" laws, after Tim Tebow, who had been homeschooled, gained notoriety on the football field at the collegiate and professional levels. See *Tim Tebow's Impact Reaches to South Carolina with Home School Law*, Sporting News, Aug. 21, 2012, http://aol.sport ingnews.com/nfl/story/2012-08-21/tim-tebow-new-york-jets-quarterback-law-home-schooled-students-south-carolina. Not surprisingly, success on the part of homeschooled students has been primarily legislative in nature and not through litigation. Given the growth of the homeschool movement in the United States, and its power in a lobbying or legislative sense, it is likely that legislative success at the state level will continue. Should homeschool students be permitted to participate in athletic competition sponsored by a state athletic association as a matter of public policy or law? If you were a lawyer for a homeschool associa-tion what would you argue and what counterarguments should you anticipate? Paul J. Batista and Lance C. Hatfield, *Learn at Home, Play at School: A State-by-State Examination of Legislation, Litigation and Athletic Association Rules Governing Public School Athletic Participation by Homeschool Students*, 15 J. Legal Aspects Sports 213 (2005) (presenting a survey of the different legal, judicial, and athletic asso-ciation responses to the issue of homeschool students' participation in public school sports).

f.   Good Conduct Rules

Individual high schools generally have broad authority to discipline and impose sanctions (such as the loss of their athletic eligibility) on student-athletes who engage in conduct that is considered inappropriate. Good conduct rules vary and prohibit a range of in-school and outside-of-school activities, including the consumption and use of drugs, tobacco, and alcohol; violations of the law; and conduct that violates community norms of appropriate behavior. Larry D. Bartlett, *The Courts' View of Good Conduct Rules for High School Student Athletes*, 82 Educ. L. Rep. 1087 (1993). Student-athletes who are punished for violating good conduct rules have asserted various legal challenges, including the lack of a sufficient nexus between the rule and a legitimate objective of their schools, and that such rules violate constitutionally protected interests. However, as the following case reveals, such challenges have met with only limited success. Courts afford considerable, albeit not complete, deference to schools and interscholas-tic sports governing bodies to use good conduct rules to regulate student-athlete behavior. One particularly interesting legal issue is the nature and scope of their authority to promulgate rules governing student-athletes' off-campus behavior and their legitimate interests in regulating such conduct.

*Procedura
(@ party)
— no I wasn't*

PROBLEM 2-4

Craig, a 17-year-old senior at Valley High School, is an outstanding wrestler. Although a "C" student, Craig planned to attend college and major in nursing and physical therapy. Because Craig's parents could not fund his college education, Craig hoped to obtain a wrestling scholarship. Craig is the defending state champion in his weight class and has not lost a match this season. He was expected to successfully defend his title at the state championship finals in March, where college coaches assess talent when offering wrestling scholarships.

At the beginning of the school year, parents and students were provided with a parent/student handbook that included the "eligibility policy" and "good conduct rules" for participation in extracurricular activities. The handbook provided in part as follows:

To retain eligibility for participation in Valley High School extracurricular activities, students must conduct themselves as good citizens both in and out of school 24 hours a day and 365 days a year. Students who represent the school in an activity are expected to serve as role models to other students and to the members of the community. Students who wish to have the *privilege* of participating in extracurricular activities must conduct themselves in accordance with board policy, administrative rules and the rules as set forth by the coaches/sponsors of the individual activities. In essence, the student must refrain from activities that are illegal, immoral, unhealthy or highly inappropriate. *Notice?*

Specific violations of the Good Conduct Rule include:

1. Possession, use or purchase of alcoholic beverages, including beer or wine (use includes having the odor of alcohol on one's breath); and
2. Being in attendance at a function or party where alcohol or other illegal drugs are being consumed by minors.

want a lot of discretion b/c not a right but still have to provide fair notice

Violators were subject to punishment ranging from a two-week period of ineligibility to participate in one sport to permanent ineligibility to participate in any sports. Students were required to admit a violation within 48 hours of the time at which the violation occurred, otherwise their punishment would be *wow* doubled.

The handbook stated that Valley could take disciplinary action against a student only after completion of a "thorough investigation of the alleged violation."

On a Saturday in mid-February, a number of Valley students attended a party where alcohol was served to minors. According to the school rumor mill, David Craig was one of the students who attended the party. On the following Wednesday during girls' volleyball practice, the coaches informed the girls that they knew about the party and they wanted any team members who had attended to come forward and admit their conduct. There was no response. The coaches then said that everyone on the team would run laps until those who attended the party admitted to it. After about ten minutes, three members of the team approached the coaches and admitted to having attended the party. Although the "admission" by the three girls occurred after the expiration of the 48-hour period, they were suspended from the volleyball team for only two weeks. None of these girls had their punishment doubled; they were all treated as if their good conduct code violations had been admitted within the required 48-hour period. During Thursday's wrestling practice, the coaches tried a similar

Foran police report no protected due process

5 days later

approach with the boys. None of them admitted to having attended the party. Thereafter, an assistant coach individually met with each wrestler, including Craig. Craig was asked several times if he had attended the party; each time he responded no. The next day, Valley's principal called Craig into his office and informed him that he had evidence that Craig had attended the party, which constituted a violation of the good conduct code, and that his failure to admit being there would result in a doubling of his punishment to a one-month suspension from wrestling.

The principal had no evidence that Craig had attended the party; Craig's suspension was based on information that the principal had received from a police officer who had stopped Craig the night of the party and given him an alcohol sobriety test that tested positive. Craig and the three female volleyball players were the only Valley students to be punished for having attended the party. Craig's punishment will prevent him from participating in the state wrestling championship.

Craig's parents appealed his punishment to the superintendent, who upheld the punishment after a 15-minute meeting. The school board did the same after a one-hour hearing. Craig's parents have filed a lawsuit seeking a court order that will allow him to continue wrestling.

Consider Craig's potential legal claims and their likely success.

In the following case, a federal district court in Iowa considered whether a student could be punished by the state athletic association for conduct occurring off campus in non-school hours, which provides a legal framework for analyzing the above problem.

BRANDS v. SHELDON COMMUNITY SCHOOL

671 F. Supp. 627 (N.D. Iowa 1987)

O'BRIEN, Chief Judge.

This matter comes to the Court on plaintiff's motions for temporary restraining order or preliminary injunction. . . .

FINDINGS OF FACT

The plaintiff is a student at Sheldon Community High School. As a member of his school's wrestling team, he has amassed a nearly perfect record in four years of competition, and is a defending state champion. His performance and the equally outstanding performance of his twin brother have attracted the attention of the state media and college coaches . . . , and each brother hopes to attend college on a wrestling scholarship.

The events leading to this decision began on January 25, 1987. The plaintiff has been understandably reluctant to give his account of what took place at his home that day, but the Sheldon Community School Board ultimately concluded that the plaintiff "as well as three other male youths engaged in multiple acts of sexual intercourse with a sixteen-year-old female student of the Sheldon Community School District. . . . " The Court makes no judgment as to whether a preponderance of the evidence, clear and convincing evidence, or evidence beyond a reasonable doubt supports this finding.

As rumors about this incident spread throughout Sheldon Community High School, Principal David Kapfer began an investigation and interviewed the plaintiff and other parties rumored to have been involved. On February 4, the plaintiff and his mother were sent letters from Kapfer declaring the plaintiff ineligible for the remainder of the wrestling season. . . . These letters stated that he "committed a breach of discipline by engaging in conduct which interfered with the maintenance of school discipline and by engaging in behavior which was antagonistic to the rights of (name redacted) to attain her education." The letters further stated that he violated Section III of the Discipline Policy because his conduct on January 25 was "detrimental to the best interests of the Sheldon Community School District." In a section of the letter to the plaintiff, Kapfer stated that the plaintiff's conduct "was a breach of discipline in that you: (1) engaged in bullying behavior; (2) committed an assault on (same name) in that you took acts against her resulting in physical contact which was insulting and offensive and which caused her emotional injury; (3) willfully injured (same name) by doing an unjustified act causing her serious emotional and mental injury; and (4) participated in multiple acts of sexual intercourse involving (same name) which took place on January 25, 1987. . . . The Court makes no judgment as to whether a preponderance of the evidence, clear and convincing evidence, or evidence beyond a reasonable doubt supports these charges.

The period of ineligibility declared by the principal included the dates of the sectional, district and state wrestling tournaments. Thus, any reinstatement which would preserve the plaintiff's chance to again become a state champion would have to occur before 8:30 a.m. on February 14, when weigh-ins would take place for the sectional tournament.

Following an appeal to Superintendent Jerry Peterson on February 5 . . . , Peterson sent letters to the plaintiff and his mother affirming the principal's decision which were nearly identical to the February 4 letters. These letters were dated February 9. . . . On February 10, the plaintiff and his mother requested a closed hearing before the School Board . . . which began Thursday morning, February 12, and ended late that night. The Board deliberated for several hours on February 12 and 13 before reaching a decision which affirmed the administration's decision. Extensive findings of fact were made by the Board. . . . The complaint and motions presently before this Court were filed within three hours of the Board's decision.

It became clear at this Court's February 13 hearing that the Court could not fairly consider all of the evidence admitted in time to fully resolve this matter prior to weigh-ins. This dilemma significantly increased the risk of irreparable harm, and for this reason, the Court entered a temporary restraining order which permitted the plaintiff to compete and advance in the sectional tournament. The TRO expired at the beginning of the February 16 hearing.

CONCLUSIONS OF LAW

Whether a temporary restraining order or preliminary injunction should issue involves consideration of (1) the threat of irreparable harm to the movant; (2) the state of the balance between this harm and the injury that granting the injunction will inflict upon other parties litigant; (3) the probability that movant will succeed on the merits; and (4) the public interest. *Dataphase Systems, Inc. v. C L Systems, Inc.*, 640 F.2d 109, 113 (8th Cir. 1981) (en banc). For the reasons stated below, the Court finds that the probability that the plaintiff will succeed on the merits is not great enough to satisfy that element of the *Dataphase* test, even if the plaintiff's allegations of irreparable harm, a favorable balance of interests and the public interest were accepted as true. Such relief is therefore improper.

The plaintiff asserts that he has been deprived of five constitutional rights—his Fourteenth Amendment rights to equal protection, substantive due process and procedural due process, his Eighth Amendment right to be free from cruel and unusual punishment, and his Sixth Amendment right to counsel. The equal protection claim must be rejected because the plaintiff has not alleged that he was treated differently because of his race, ethnicity, gender, or any other suspect classification, and his interests in wrestling or receiving a college scholarship are not among the small set of rights fundamental enough to warrant separate protection under the equal protection clause. *San Antonio Ind. School District v. Rodriguez*, 411 U.S. 1, 29-39, 93 S.Ct. 1278, 1294-1300, 36 L.Ed.2d 16 (1973). Likewise, the Eighth Amendment claim must be rejected because school discipline does not implicate Eighth Amendment concerns, as the Supreme Court held in *Ingraham v. Wright*, 430 U.S. 651, 668, 97 S.Ct. 1401, 1410, 51 L.Ed.2d 711 (1977). Because the Constitution limits the scope of Sixth Amendment rights to "all criminal prosecutions," U.S. Const. Amend. VI, that argument must be rejected. If any rights were violated, they can only be substantive or procedural due process rights.

PROCEDURAL DUE PROCESS

The majority of the plaintiff's complaints—including those concerning the vagueness of the school's standard of conduct, the School Board's reliance upon hearsay, the timing of his hearing, and the sufficiency of the evidence—are most relevant to his right to procedural due process. To consider those complaints, however, the Court must first find that the plaintiff is being deprived of liberty or property by the defendant. If not, no procedural protections were "due" to the plaintiff under the Constitution. *Board of Regents v. Roth*, 408 U.S. 564, 92 S.Ct. 2701, 33 L.Ed.2d 548 (1972).

The Supreme Court has consistently held that the existence of a protected liberty or property interest does not depend upon the seriousness of the loss the plaintiff would suffer as a result of the government's action. "[T]o determine whether due process requirements apply in the first place, we must look not to the 'weight' but to the *nature* of the interest at stake." *Smith v. Organization of Foster Families*, 431 U.S. 816, 841, 97 S.Ct. 2094, 2107, 53 L.Ed.2d 14 (1977)....

A clear majority of courts addressing this question in the context of interscholastic or intercollegiate athletics has found that athletes have no legitimate entitlement to participate. (Citations omitted.) In *In re U.S. Ex. Rel. Missouri State High School Activities Association*, 682 F.2d 147 (8th Cir. 1982), the Eighth Circuit stated that "a student's interest in participating in a single year of interscholastic athletics amounts to a mere expectation rather than a constitutionally protected claim of entitlement." *Id.* at 153 n. 8....

In *Boyd v. Bd. of Directors of McGehee School District*, 612 F. Supp. 86 (E.D. Ark. 1985), a court recognized a property interest where the plaintiff's interest "was something more than a desire to participate in a single season of interscholastic athletics without the belief and desire to realizing any tangential benefits accruing to him in the future." *Id.* at 93. That court found that the plaintiff's "continued status as a member of the McGehee High School football team during his last year was very important to [his] development educationally and economically in the future." *Id.* Yet the fact that this plaintiff's performance in the tournament may help him receive a college scholarship does not change the nature of the interest at stake; it merely raises its value while leaving the degree of entitlement unchanged.

Once awarded, a college scholarship may give rise to a property interest in its continuation. *Hall v. University of Minnesota*, 530 F. Supp. 104 (D. Minn. 1982). "But there is not automatic entitlement to a college education." *Fluitt v. University of Nebraska*, 489 F. Supp. 1194, 1203 (D. Neb. 1980). When scholarships are awarded at the discretion of a college coach, and such discretion has not yet been exercised, no property interest in the receipt of a scholarship can exist, and the plaintiff cannot invoke his expectation that he would earn a scholarship at the state tournament in order to claim a property interest in wrestling there.

If any property interest of the plaintiff is involved in this case, it is a property right created by the defendant's own Disciplinary Policy and Administrative Rules. When a government must follow mandatory laws or regulations which limit its discretion to make a decision in any way or for any reason, those laws or regulations can create a property right which is deprived if those regulations are not followed. However, the plaintiff was not deprived of this right because (1) the basis for the defendant's action was a permissible basis for this sanction under Sections III and V(E) of the Disciplinary Policy, (2) the procedures in part IV of the Administrative Rules were followed, and (3) the sanction chosen was authorized in § 9.14(5) of Board Policy 503.6.

Even if this Court were to recognize a protected interest in participation, the Court is satisfied that the plaintiff received all process due to him. The plaintiff and his mother were notified of the charges against him and were told of opportunities for appeal. . . . The plaintiff was given an opportunity to explain his side of the story to the principal prior to the suspension. . . . He was given a five- to six-hour evidentiary hearing within ten days of the initial suspension, which was also early enough to permit the Board to reverse the administration's decision before the plaintiff would be precluded from participating in the state tournament. Evidence was presented on the administration's behalf by an independent attorney. The plaintiff was represented by legal counsel, who called several witnesses and rigorously cross-examined the administration's witnesses. All witnesses were sworn prior to their testimony.

The plaintiff objects that the description of the incident presented to the Board was based upon hearsay, and that the administration did not present testimony from anyone who was present when it took place. This claim is supported in the hearing record. However, the Due Process Clause does not require courtroom standards of evidence to be used in administrative hearings.

As long as a decision rests upon "some evidence," due process may have been satisfied. *Superintendent v. Hill*, 472 U.S. 445, 105 S.Ct. 2768, 2770, 86 L.Ed.2d 356 (1985). . . . Hearsay which has a "rational probative force" can constitute substantial evidence, which is a higher standard than "some evidence." . . .

In this case there appears to be little or no evidence in the hearing record directly contradicting the Board's hearsay-based finding that the plaintiff "as well as three other male youths engaged in multiple acts of sexual intercourse with a sixteen year old female student of the Sheldon Community School District on or about January 25, 1987. . . ." The factual disagreement primarily concerned the effect of that incident upon the school and the female. Reliable and credible evidence was presented by Instructor Patti Thayer about the disruptive effect upon the school, and expert testimony was presented concerning the potential effect of such acts upon the female involved and upon student attitudes concerning sexuality, women and rape. While the Board was required to speculate about whether the female involved would react in the same way as the hypothetical female in the expert's answer . . . , that is not enough to prevent the testimony from constituting "some evidence." Further, it does not require experts to clearly demonstrate that such acts would, as it has in Sheldon, disrupt a good portion of the town and not just the school. . . .

For all of these reasons, the Court finds that the plaintiff's procedural due process rights were respected.

SUBSTANTIVE DUE PROCESS

The plaintiff can show that his right to substantive due process was denied if the Board's decision was arbitrary or capricious, *Littlefield v. City of Afton*, 785 F.2d 596, 607 (8th Cir. 1986); or if it violated one of the substantive due process rights such as the right to privacy, which cannot be deprived no matter how much procedural protection is used. *Griswold v. Connecticut*, 381 U.S. 479, 85 S.Ct. 1678, 14 L.Ed.2d 510 (1965).

The Court is persuaded that the Board's decision was not arbitrary or capricious. The Board's objectives were legitimate. The Iowa Supreme Court has described the set of permissible school board objectives in this area in broad, sweeping terms. *Bunger v. Iowa High School Athletic Association*, 197 N.W.2d 555, 564-65 (Iowa 1972). "To some extent at least, school authorities may base disciplinary measures on immoral acts or acts definitely contrary to current mores." *Id.* at 565. The *Bunger* court also held that:

> The present case involves the advantages and enjoyment of an extracurricular activity provided by the school, a consideration which we believe extends the authority of a school board somewhat as to participation in that activity. The influence of the students involved is an additional consideration. Standout students, whether in athletics, forensics, dramatics, or other interscholastic activities, play a somewhat different role from the rank and file. Leadership brings additional responsibility. These student leaders are looked up to and emulated. They represent the school and depict its character. We cannot fault a school board for expecting somewhat more of them as to eligibility for their particular extracurricular activities.

Id. at 564.

The means chosen to achieve their objectives were not arbitrary or capricious. As the Nebraska Supreme Court found in a similar case involving alcohol use by athletes who were then suspended from a team:

> The rule involved in this case, even though the penalty of expulsion for the season might be deemed severe by some persons, clearly serves a legitimate rational interest and directly affects the discipline of student athletes. It cannot be said that the prescribed penalty was an arbitrary and unreasonable means to attain the legitimate end of deterrence of the use of alcoholic liquor by student athletes.

Braesch v. DePasquale, 200 Neb. 726, 265 N.W.2d 842, 846 (1978).

The plaintiff argues that he should not have been given a penalty more severe than penalties allegedly given in the past to other students for conduct the plaintiff considers to be more serious than his own. The record adequately demonstrates that the school's treatment of those students involved to the same degree in this incident could hardly have been more consistent; even the female involved was suspended from extracurricular activities. To go further and evaluate the Board's "consistency" across different times and different factual settings would require the Court to substitute its judgment concerning the relative seriousness of different acts for that of the School Board; the "arbitrary or capricious" standard of review is too narrow to authorize this kind of analysis.

During the February 16 hearing, the plaintiff sought to introduce a statement one member of the School Board made after the Board's hearing but before the end of deliberations which purported to show a predisposition to affirm the suspension. However probative this statement may be, the Court cannot consider it. When a board has made formal findings, a court may not look beyond those findings to question the integrity of decision-makers or the decision-making process without a "strong showing of bad faith or improper behavior." *Overton Park*, 401 U.S. at 420, 91 S.Ct. at 825; *United States v. Morgan*, 313 U.S. 409, 422, 61 S.Ct. 999, 1004, 85 L.Ed. 1429 (1941). No such showing has been made here. In his testimony before the School Board, the plaintiff would not admit or deny that the incident took place because he believed it was a private matter. . . .[5] A limited right to privacy is protected by the Due Process Clause. *Griswold v. Connecticut*, 381 U.S. 479, 85 S.Ct. 1678, 14 L.Ed.2d 510 (1965). However, that right does not keep the state and its instrumentalities from regulating private sexual conduct. *Bowers v. Hardwick*, 478 U.S. 186, 106 S.Ct. 2841, 92 L.Ed.2d 140 (1986); Note, *Fornication, Cohabitation and the Constitution*, 77 Mich. L. Rev. 252 (1978).[6] The Board's findings indicate that it was not merely trying to impose its moral standard upon the plaintiff; the Board found that his acts injured another student and disrupted the school. These are legitimate school board concerns. Moreover, the school has not regulated the plaintiff as a student; by revoking his eligibility without suspending or expelling him, it has regulated him as a representative of the school, and has chosen a sanction which limits his ability to represent the school without limiting his basic rights as a student. For these reasons, the Court finds that whatever right the plaintiff has to sexual privacy after *Bowers* was not violated in this case, and the last possible ground for finding a likelihood that his substantive due process rights were violated is rejected.

CONCLUSION

The Court finds that the likelihood the plaintiff can prove that his constitutional rights were violated is not great enough to warrant a temporary restraining order or preliminary injunction — nothing more and nothing less. The Court neither approves nor disapproves of the defendant's action, for that particular question

---

5. It should be noted that the plaintiff admits that a fellow wrestler was present when the incident took place, and this individual has admitted that he "was involved in an incident with (female's name redacted) on Sunday night Jan. 25, 1987. . . ."

6. *Bowers* may not have undermined all earlier decisions recognizing privacy rights of consenting adults engaged in private sexual conduct. *See, e.g., State v. Pilcher*, 242 N.W.2d 348 (Iowa 1976); *Erb v. Iowa State Board of Public Instruction*, 216 N.W.2d 339 (Iowa 1974). But in light of the public school system's responsibility to "inculcate the habits and manners of civility" in students, *Bethel School District v. Fraser*, 478 U.S. 675, 106 S.Ct. 3159, 3162, 92 L.Ed.2d 549 (1986), the Court is hesitant to grant high school students the same degree of protection afforded adults.

has never been before it. However, it is the fervent hope of this judge that if or when this legal dispute is over, the parties and their respective supporters in the community have not burned so many bridges that a mutually beneficial reconciliation cannot be reached.

IT IS HEREBY ORDERED that the plaintiff's motions for a temporary restraining order or preliminary injunction are denied.

Cannot wrestle!

NOTES AND QUESTIONS

1. *Procedural Due Process Rights.* As the *Brands* court observes, most courts have held that student-athletes do not possess a constitutionally protected property interest in interscholastic sports participation that requires procedural due process before being limited or denied by public school officials. See, e.g., *Mayo v. West Virginia Secondary Schools Activities Comm'n*, 672 S.E.2d 224, 229 (W. Va. 2008) ("Because there is no property or liberty interest that attaches to extracurricular activities, 'procedural due process protections' do not apply").

   Although courts generally rule that no property interest in athletic participation exists, *Brands* holds that a school's student disciplinary rules and procedures may create a property right for student-athletes. Similarly, in *Butler v. Oak Creek-Franklin Sch. Dist.*, 172 F. Supp. 2d 1102 (E.D. Wis. 2001), a high school football player received a 12-month athletic suspension for allegedly violating municipal ordinances prohibiting possession of intoxicants by a minor and fireworks. He appealed his suspension alleging, *inter alia,* that it violated his due process rights. He had previously been suspended for violating good-conduct rules prohibiting smoking, drinking alcohol, and using marijuana. The court held that several documents, including the rules of the Wisconsin Interscholastic Athletic Association and the high school student/parent handbook, combined to grant student-athletes a property right in continued participation in interscholastic athletics, which is sufficient to trigger procedural due process protections. *Id.* at 1110. Having found the requisite property interest, the court identified the necessary due process as including a pre-deprivation hearing, notice of charges, an impartial decision, and a decision that rests on evidence presented at a hearing. See also Larry D. Bartlett, *The Courts' View of Good Conduct Rules for High School Student Athletes,* 82 Educ. L. Rep. 1087, 1098 (1993) ("A property interest exists because students may participate under those policies and rules until they are acted upon by school officials to deprive the students of those expectations"). Why did *Brands* reject the student-athlete's denial of procedural due process claim?

2. *Substantive Due Process Rights.* Courts generally refuse to recognize an independent right to participate in interscholastic athletics for purposes of substantive due process. In *A.C. v. Board of Education for the Cambridge Community Unit District #227,* 2005 WL3560658 (C.D. Ill. 2005), the court refused to reinstate a high school student-athlete's eligibility after the student discharged a look-alike weapon in the school parking lot after class hours and reaffirmed that playing high school sports is not a liberty or property interest giving rise to a substantive due process claim if it is denied. In rendering its decision, the court noted that participation in athletics is not an "integral" part of education. Do you agree? If it is not an integral part of education, why do school districts spend so many resources and so much

[handwritten: although it may be integral, it is not necessary.]

time fostering competitive athletic programs? If interscholastic athletics were considered to be an integral part of a student's education, what would the implications be for students seeking to participate? What rights would they be afforded?

However, the *Brands* court states that a student-athlete's substantive due process rights are violated if removal from an athletic team is arbitrary or capricious (suggesting there is a liberty interest in not being treated in this fashion) or violates an independent right such as the right to privacy. Does a school district have a legitimate interest in regulating student-athlete behavior outside school? Does this include consensual sexual activity among students? Does it make a difference whether the involved students are minors? See *Lawrence v. Texas*, 539 U.S. 558, 572 (2003) (constitutionally protected right to liberty "gives substantial protection to adult persons in deciding how to conduct their private life in matters pertaining to sex").

[handwritten: I think so]

[handwritten: this wasn't criminal though (no one was harmed)]

Courts generally have rejected claims that discipline imposed on student-athletes by public schools for violating rules prohibiting drinking alcoholic beverages off campus, *L.P.M. v. Sch. Bd. of Seminole County*, 753 So. 2d 130 (Fla. Dist. Ct. App. 2000); *Farver v. Bd. of Educ. of Carroll County*, 40 F. Supp. 2d 323 (D. Md. 1999) or drug use, *Jordan v. O'Fallon Township High Sch. Dist. No. 203*, 706 N.E.2d 137 (Ill. App. Ct. 1999), violates their constitutionally protected property or liberty interests.

3. *Other Constitutional Challenges.* In *Brands*, the court summarily rejected three of the student-athlete's five constitutional challenges to his high school's good conduct rules—alleged Eighth Amendment prohibition against cruel and unusual punishment, Sixth Amendment right to counsel, and Fourteenth Amendment right to equal protection claims. Courts have rejected claims that good conduct rules violate other constitutional rights. See, e.g., *Bush v. Dassel-Cokato Bd. of Educ.*, 745 F. Supp. 562 (D. Minn. 1990) (rejecting argument that suspension for violation of rule prohibiting student-athlete's presence at parties where alcohol is being served violated her right to associate socially with her friends under the First Amendment); *Farver v. Bd. of Educ. of Carroll County*, 40 F. Supp. 2d 323 (D. Md. 1999) (same).

[handwritten: stupid]

4. *Vagueness Defense.* In *Brands*, the student-athlete was punished by being declared ineligible to participate in the state wrestling tournament because his conduct was "detrimental to the best interests of the school district." Courts tend to be unreceptive to claims that good conduct rules are unconstitutionally vague and do not provide sufficient notice for due process purposes. In *Bush v. Dassel-Cokato Bd. of Educ.*, 745 F. Supp. 562 (D. Minn. 1990), a member of an interscholastic swim team was prohibited from participating in a swim meet because of a violation of a good conduct rule that imposed sanctions for "attending parties where alcohol and/or illegal drugs as defined by state law are *present.*" *Id.* at 572 (italics included). Taking a commonsense approach, the court rejected his arguments that the term *present* rendered this portion of the rule unconstitutionally vague. "[P]ersons of common intelligence would not need to guess at the meaning of the language in order to determine that it applied to the situation involved in this case." *Id.* at 572-573.

As noted by one commentator,

The issue of vagueness of school rules is part of the bigger issue of whether the student had notice of proscribed conduct. Was the rule stated and publicized in such a way that students would reasonably know that their conduct could result in suspension of eligibility from school activities? . . .

One common approach taken by schools to give notice is to provide all students copies of handbooks containing school discipline rules, including the good conduct rule. Another is to read various portions of the school rules orally to students.

Larry D. Bartlett, *The Courts' View of Good Conduct Rules for High School Student Athletes*, 82 Educ. L. Rep. 1087, 1096 (1993) (footnotes omitted).

When will the language of a good conduct rule be impermissibly vague? What harm ensues from vagueness that should be constitutionally protected against?

5. *Problem and Questions.* As the attorney for a state interscholastic athletic association or an educational institution, how would you answer the following questions: What kind of rules should be promulgated at the association-wide level regarding good conduct? What kind of rules should be promulgated at the institutional level? Can and should student-athletes be treated differently than other students generally or other students involved in extracurricular activities for good conduct purposes?

g.   Personal Appearance and Grooming Cases

PROBLEM 2-5

The Salem Board of Education recently adopted a written "Hair and Dress" policy for Salem Public Schools. The policy prohibits male students whose hair and dress do not conform to certain guidelines from taking part in the public performances of extracurricular activities such as sports. For example, a boy's hair cannot extend below the top of his collar. In addition, the top of a boy's pants cannot fall more than an inch below his waistline. Boys are also prohibited from wearing bandanas of any type whether on their head or any other part of their body or attire.

Marcus Williams, a 16-year-old, is a star member of Salem High School's football team. Marcus is very proud of his braids, which fall several inches below the top of his shirt collar, and which have taken him several months to grow. He also wears popular fashions such as baggy pants that hang several inches below his waistline. In addition, Marcus will often style his hair into a ponytail, holding it in place with the type of blue bandana worn by members of a gang in the part of the city where he resides.

After the implementation of the Hair and Dress Code, Salem High's head football coach informed Marcus that he would have to cut his hair, discontinue wearing the bandana, and make certain that his pants do not fall more than an inch below his waistline, because he is in violation of the written policy. Marcus objected, arguing that none of these things have negatively affected his performance in the classroom or on the athletic field. Shortly after an assembly at which the Hair and Dress policy was announced, Marcus played in an interscholastic football game. Following the game the football coach informed Marcus that he would not be able to play in another football game until he conformed to the Hair and Dress policy. He would be permitted, however, to practice with the team.

If Marcus challenges the dress policy, what is the likelihood he will prevail in light of the following legal precedent and commentary?

_____

Most cases involving the validity of personal appearance and grooming rules arose during the turbulent period of time from 1965 to 1975 in the United States In a case not involving college sports, *Tinker v. Des Moines Independent Community Sch. Dist.*, 393 U.S. 503 (1969), a public school dress code prohibited students from wearing black armbands. Finding that the prohibition violated the students' First Amendment rights, the Supreme Court concluded:

> The problem posed by the present case does not relate to regulation of the length of skirts or the type of clothing, to hair style, or deportment. . . . It does not concern aggressive, disruptive action or even group demonstrations. Our problem involves direct, primary First Amendment rights akin to "pure speech." . . .
>
> The school officials banned and sought to punish petitioners for a silent, passive expression of opinion, unaccompanied by any disorder or disturbance on the part of petitioners. There is here no evidence whatever of petitioners' interference, actual or nascent, with the schools' work or of collision with the rights of other students to be secure and to be let alone. Accordingly, this case does not concern speech or action that intrudes upon the work of the schools or the rights of other students.

Id. at 514.

In an article appearing in the *Harvard Law Review* in 1971, the author summarized legal challenges to grooming rules that commonly arose during that time period:

> Along with the recent trend toward longer hair has come a striking willingness on the part of high school students and their parents to challenge, often at the price of temporary suspension, the efforts of school authorities to enforce rules which demand that long hair be cut and facial hair be removed. Perhaps encouraged by the Supreme Court's ruling in *Tinker v. Des Moines Independent Community School District*, long-haired and bearded students have argued, in a spate of federal court cases over the past three years, that the enforcement of such regulations deprives them of their constitutionally protected right to fashion their own appearances and thereby to express their individual personalities.
>
> Students have lost in a slim majority of the cases, as courts have taken widely divergent positions on the hair issue. Several courts . . . have failed to find any constitutional merit in the students' claims, and thus have upheld hair regulations simply on the basis of a showing of some "reasonable connection" between the rule and the maintenance of an effective educational system.

Hair Absent Showing of Actual Disruption Violates High School Student's Constitutional Rights, 84 Harv. L. Rev. 1702 at 1702-1703 (1971).

The subject continues to arise today and presents a number of interesting issues. The following case involves a "clean shaving" policy and illustrates the current judicial approach of deferring to the judgment of coaches and educators in such matters. With the rise of gang members among high school students, it is not surprising that courts are inclined to find that potential disruption of the school's educational functions may warrant deference to the decisions of school districts and coaches to develop and enforce grooming and appearance standards.

In reading this case, think of how you would counsel a student-athlete whose chosen grooming standards are contrary to a coach's (or school's) standards. Also consider what advice you would give to a school district faced with a claim by a student-athlete that his legal rights are being infringed by the school's grooming standards.

DAVENPORT v. RANDOLPH COUNTY BOARD OF EDUCATION

730 F.2d 1395 (11th Cir. 1984)

KRAVITCH, Circuit Judge.

The plaintiffs, Jonathan Davenport and Micky Lazar O'Neal, are high school students who brought suit to challenge the "clean shaven" policy of defendant Ronald Watters, coach of the football and basketball teams at Randolph County High School (RCHS). Defendant Watters suspended Davenport from the RCHS basketball team in December 1981 for refusing to shave and barred both plaintiffs from participating on the football team for the 1982 season because of their refusal to abide by his grooming policy.

Defendant Watters' grooming policy prohibited team members from having beards, wearing mustaches extending beyond the corners of their mouths, or growing sideburns below the ear lobes. The plaintiffs' fathers approved of their sons' decisions not to abide by the coach's policy because they had suffered skin problems when shaving as youths and thus did not want their sons to shave. Defendant Randolph County School Board first considered the issue in March 1982 and recommended that coaches not require a minor to shave if the parents objected. At a later meeting, however, the Board reversed its position and endorsed Coach Watters' "clean shaven" policy. Plaintiffs proceeded to institute this suit pursuant to 42 U.S.C. § 1983 and the fourteenth amendment, requesting declaratory judgment and issuance of an injunction to prevent the defendants from refusing to allow the plaintiffs to participate in athletics at RCHS.

 The plaintiffs contend that the "clean shaven" policy is unconstitutional because it is arbitrary and unreasonable to require fourteen and fifteen year-old adolescents to shave in order to participate in high school athletics. This court has previously ruled that in the high school environment there is "a per se rule that [grooming regulations] are constitutionally valid." *Karr v. Schmidt*, 460 F.2d 609, 617 (5th Cir. 1972) (en banc); *see also, Stevenson v. Board of Education of Wheeler County, Georgia*, 426 F.2d 1154 (5th Cir.), *cert. denied*, 400 U.S. 957, 91 S.Ct. 355, 27 L.Ed.2d 265 (1970) ("clean shaven" policy not irrational). The rule announced in *Karr* is founded on the premise that "grooming regulations are a reasonable means of furthering the school board's undeniable interest in teaching hygiene, instilling discipline, asserting authority, and compelling uniformity." *Domico v. Rapides Parish School Board*, 675 F.2d 100, 102 (5th Cir. 1982) (discussing holding in *Karr*).

This case falls squarely within the holdings of *Karr* and *Stevenson*. The district court found that the policy was "adopted to accomplish the legitimate objective of presenting the school in the light deemed most favorable to the school by the students and coaches at the school." The court further found, and the plaintiffs do not disagree, that there was no evidence that the policy was racially motivated.

The plaintiffs attempt to distinguish the above cases primarily on the ground that their objections to the grooming code are based on a concern that shaving will cause them skin problems. The plaintiffs' fathers testified that they had suffered such problems as youths, and the district court recognized that blacks are prone to such medical problems. No evidence, however, was presented to the court or the school board that the plaintiffs themselves would be likely to suffer from such problems, and defendant Watters testified that he would not enforce the policy if it would have injurious results. Without such medical evidence, we find it unnecessary to decide whether enforcement of the "clean shaven" policy in such a context would amount to a constitutional violation outside the holding of *Karr's* per se rule. *Cf. Karr*, 460 F.2d at 617 n. 26 (per se rule does not apply if grooming policy has arbitrary effect or is discriminatorily enforced).

Finally, the plaintiffs argue that the "clean shaven" policy deprives them of property without due process of law because their inability to participate in high school athletics diminishes their chances of receiving athletic scholarships to college. This court has held that "[t]he privilege of participating in interscholastic activities must be deemed to fall . . . outside the protection of due process." *Mitchell v. Louisiana High School Athletic Association*, 430 F.2d 1155, 1158 (5th Cir. 1970); *see also Walsh v. Louisiana High School Athletic Association*, 616 F.2d 152, 159 (5th Cir. 1980). . . . We fail to perceive any principled distinction for due process purposes between the effect of the eligibility rides in *Mitchell* and *Walsh* in barring athletic participation and the plaintiffs' refusal to abide by the grooming regulations resulting in their ineligibility to compete in high school sports.

Having found that the disputed policy is within the school board's power to regulate grooming and that the plaintiffs have not proven unique circumstances that would render the policy arbitrary or unreasonable, the district court's denial of relief is AFFIRMED.

NOTES AND QUESTIONS

1. *Constitutionality of Grooming Regulations.* The *Davenport* court holds that grooming regulations do not deprive plaintiffs of any constitutionally recognized rights:

> The plaintiffs make two additional arguments in an attempt to distinguish the cases. First, they argue that the relevant focus here is whether there is a rational link between athletic performance and requiring a student to shave. The argument, however, ignores the district court's finding that the policy was aimed not at athletic performance but at presenting the school in a favorable light. Second, they contend that because RCHS is the only school in the county with a "clean shaven" policy, they have been denied equal protection relative to other county student-athletes. The argument fails to realize, however, that *Karr* and *Stevenson* stand for the proposition that grooming regulations at the high school level do not deprive the plaintiffs of any constitutionally recognized rights in the first place. It would be anomalous, therefore, to hold that the plaintiffs have no constitutional right to not shave, but if other schools do not adopt such a policy the plaintiffs' refusal to shave is transformed into a constitutionally protected activity.

730 F.2d at 1397, n.3. The court leaves open, however, the possibility of proving a denial of equal protection if plaintiffs can prove that the rule

was racially motivated or treated protected classes differently. Grooming and related regulations can also raise religious liberty issues. See *Menora v. Illinois High School Athletic Association, infra.* It should be noted, however, that *Menora* raises potential health and safety justifications that may not be present in most grooming cases.

Which of the school's interests, if any, do you think are sufficient to justify a grooming regulation applied to students generally or to student-athletes? In *Davenport,* might the result have been different if the plaintiffs had produced medical evidence showing that shaving would create individual skin problems?

2. *Other Cases.* Consistent with *Davenport,* other courts also defer to schools regarding appropriate grooming rules. See, e.g., *Zeller v. Donegal Sch. Dist. Bd. of Educ.,* 517 F.2d 600 (3d Cir. 1975) (high school student's claim that hair-length regulations of athletic code violated his constitutional rights was not one for which relief could be granted); *Board of Trustees of Bastrop Indep. Sch. Dist. v. Toungate,* 958 S.W.2d 365 (Tex. 1997) (upholding four-month "in-school suspension" of male elementary school student for violation of hair-length provision of school grooming code, which student claimed was discrimination based on sex). However, some courts are more likely to find infringement of a constitutionally protected right or interest and less likely to defer to a school's proffered justifications for its grooming rules. See, e.g., *Holsapple v. Woods,* 500 F.2d 49 (7th Cir. 1974) (a student's right to wear one's hair at any length or in any desired manner is an ingredient of personal freedom protected by the United States Constitution); *Gorman v. St. Raphael's Academy,* 2002 WL 31455570 (R.I. Super. Ct.) (academy's regulation of the hair of male students is arbitrary and capricious because it bears no rational relation to the legitimate mission statement of the school; nor does it in any way inhibit or enhance the learning process or order and discipline of the school); *Dostert v. Berthold Public Sch. Dist.,* 391 F. Supp. 876 (D. N.D. 1975) (invalidating school rule that prohibited participation in extracurricular activities, including sports, unless male students' hair conformed to a certain length).

3. *Requisite Justification.* Some cases hold that for the grooming regulation to be constitutionally valid, the justification must be compelling or necessary, whereas others require only that the justification have a reasonable or rational basis. Regulations required to meet the compelling standard generally fail. *Long v. Zopp,* 476 F.2d 180 (4th Cir. 1973) (holding that awards could not be used to enforce compliance with a "hair code," for the enforcement of which there was no compelling necessity); *Dunham v. Pulsifer,* 312 F. Supp. 411 (D. Vt. 1970) (finding the asserted justifications of preventing dissension, improving performance, aiding team discipline, and promoting conformity/uniformity were not compelling or necessary and not served by the grooming code, which was therefore invalid). However, cases applying the lower standard of a reasonable or rational basis are much more likely to be upheld. *Humphries v. Lincoln Parish Sch. Bd.,* 467 So. 2d 870 (2d Cir. 1985) (grooming policy that was a part of a "total discipline program" promoted athletic and academic excellence, both constitutionally permissible objectives and reasonably intended to accomplish their goals).

3. First and Fourth Amendment Constitutional Rights Issues

Cases in the prior sections often raised federal and state constitutional questions regarding student-athletes' eligibility to participate in interscholastic athletics; in particular and commonly, procedural due process (adequate notice and a fair hearing are required when a liberty or property interest is implicated), substantive due process (infringement of a privacy or personal autonomy right), and denial of equal protection of the law issues. Constitutional claims also arise out of alleged violations of student-athletes' First Amendment freedom of speech and religion rights, as well as Fourth Amendment protections against unreasonable searches and seizures, which may require more than very deferential rational basis judicial scrutiny.

a. Drug Testing

Like society at large, drug use pervades all levels of athletic competition, including among high school athletes. The National Federation of State High Schools does not require that high schools develop a drug-testing program for athletes. Nevertheless, some high school districts throughout the country recently have implemented random drug-testing programs that require students to consent to testing as a condition of being eligible to participate in interscholastic athletics. These policies vary by individual school district, with testing done for illegal recreational drugs such as marijuana and performance-enhancing drugs such as anabolic steroids, the use of which is a growing problem among high school athletes. See E. Tim Walker, Comment, *Missing the Target; How Performance Enhancing Drugs Go Unnoticed and Endanger the Lives of Athletes*, 10 Vill. Sports & Ent. L.J. 181 (2003).

Prior to 1995, lower federal courts were split on whether drug testing of high school athletes by public schools violates the Fourth or Fourteenth Amendments, as unreasonable searches or violations of due process, respectively. See, e.g., *Schaill v. Tippecanoe County Sch. Corp.*, 864 F.2d 1309 (7th Cir. 1988); *Brooks v. East Chambers Consol. Independent Sch. Dist.*, 730 F. Supp. 759 (S.D. Tex. 1989); *Moule by & Through Moule v. Paradise Valley Unified Sch. Dist.*, 863 F. Supp. 1098 (D. Ariz. 1994). See also Diane Heckman, *The Evolution of Drug Testing of Interscholastic Athletes*, 9 Vill. Sports & Ent. L.J. 209 (2002) (presenting an overview of the testing of interscholastic athletes pre- and post-*Vernonia* and the impact of the *Earls* case).

In the following case, the United States Supreme Court considered whether suspicionless random drug testing of high school athletes for recreational drugs is constitutional.

VERNONIA SCHOOL DISTRICT 47J v. ACTON
515 U.S. 646 (1995)

Justice SCALIA delivered the opinion of the Court.

[EDS. The Student Athlete Drug Policy adopted by School District 47J in the town of Vernonia, Oregon, authorizes random urinalysis drug testing of students who participate in the district's school athletics programs. Drugs had not been a major problem in Vernonia schools. In the mid- to late 1980s, however, teachers and administrators observed a sharp increase in drug use. Students began to speak out about their attraction to the drug culture, and to boast that there was nothing the school could do about it. Along with more drugs came more disciplinary problems.

Not only were student athletes included among the drug users, athletes were also the leaders of the drug culture. This caused the district's administrators particular concern, since drug use increases the risk of sports-related injury. Expert testimony at the trial confirmed the deleterious effects of drugs on motivation, memory, judgment, reaction, coordination, and performance. The high school football and wrestling coach witnessed a severe sternum injury suffered by a wrestler, and various omissions of safety procedures and misexecutions by football players, all attributable in his belief to the effects of drug use.

Initially, the district responded to the drug problem by offering special classes, speakers, and presentations designed to deter drug use. However, the drug problem persisted. Ultimately, the district adopted the Student Athlete Drug Policy (Policy) at a meeting, to which parents in attendance gave their unanimous approval.

The school board approved the Policy for implementation in the fall of 1989. Its expressed purpose was to prevent student-athletes from using drugs, to protect their health and safety, and to provide drug users with assistance programs.

The Policy applied to all students participating in interscholastic athletics. Students wishing to play sports must sign a form consenting to the testing and must obtain the written consent of their parents. Athletes are tested at the beginning of the season for their sport. In addition, once each week of the season the names of the athletes are placed in a "pool" from which a student, with the supervision of two adults, blindly draws the names of 10 percent of the athletes for random testing. Those selected are notified and tested that same day, if possible. Students to be tested enter an empty locker room accompanied by an adult monitor of the same sex and provide a urine sample. After the sample is produced, it is given to the monitor, who checks it for temperature and tampering and then transfers it to a vial.

The samples are sent to an independent laboratory, which routinely tests them for amphetamines, cocaine, and marijuana. Other drugs, such as LSD, may be screened at the request of the district, but the identity of a particular student does not determine which drugs will be tested. The laboratory's procedures are 99.94 percent accurate. The district follows strict procedures regarding the chain of custody and access to test results. The laboratory does not know the identity of the students whose samples it tests. It is authorized to mail written test reports only to the superintendent and to provide test results to district personnel by telephone only after the requesting official recites a code confirming his authority. Only the superintendent, principals, vice principals, and athletic directors have access to test results, and the results are not kept for more than one year.

If a sample tests positive, a second test is administered as soon as possible to confirm the result. If the second test is negative, no further action is taken. If the second test is positive, the athlete's parents are notified, and the school principal convenes a meeting with the student and the parents, at which the student is given the option of (1) participating for six weeks in an assistance program that includes weekly urinalysis or (2) suffering suspension from athletics for the remainder of the current season and the next athletic season. The student is then retested prior to the start of the next athletic season for which he or she is eligible. The Policy states that a second offense results in automatic imposition of option (2); a third offense results in suspension for the remainder of the current season and the next two athletic seasons.

In the fall of 1991, respondent James Acton, then a seventh grader, signed up to play football at one of the district's grade schools. He was denied participation, however, because he and his parents refused to sign the testing consent forms. The Actons filed suit, seeking declaratory and injunctive relief from enforcement of the Policy on the grounds that it violated the Fourth and Fourteenth Amendments to the United States Constitution and Article I, §9, of the Oregon Constitution. The District Court entered an order denying the claims on the merits and dismissing the action, but the Ninth Circuit reversed, holding that the Policy violated both the Fourth and Fourteenth Amendments and Article I, §9, of the Oregon Constitution. 23 F.3d 1514 (1994).]

II

. . . In *Skinner v. Railway Labor Executives' Assn.*, 489 U.S. 602, 617, 109 S.Ct. 1402, 1413, 103 L.Ed.2d 639 (1989), we held that state-compelled collection and testing of urine, such as that required by the Policy, constitutes a "search" subject to the demands of the Fourth Amendment. See also *Treasury Employees v. Von Raab*, 489 U.S. 656, 665, 109 S.Ct. 1384, 1390, 103 L.Ed.2d 685 (1989).

As the text of the Fourth Amendment indicates, the ultimate measure of the constitutionality of a governmental search is "reasonableness." At least in a case such as this, where there was no clear practice, either approving or disapproving the type of search at issue, at the time the constitutional provision was enacted, whether a particular search meets the reasonableness standard "'is judged by balancing its intrusion on the individual's Fourth Amendment interests against its promotion of legitimate governmental interests.'" (Citation omitted.) Where a search is undertaken by law enforcement officials to discover evidence of criminal wrongdoing, this Court has said that reasonableness generally requires the obtaining of a judicial warrant, *Skinner, supra*, at 619, 109 S.Ct., at 1414. Warrants cannot be issued, of course, without the showing of probable cause required by the Warrant Clause. But a warrant is not required to establish the reasonableness of *all* government searches; and when a warrant is not required (and the Warrant Clause therefore not applicable), probable cause is not invariably required either. A search unsupported by probable cause can be constitutional, we have said, "when special needs, beyond the normal need for law enforcement, make the warrant and probable-cause requirement impracticable." (Citation omitted.)

We have found such "special needs" to exist in the public school context. There, the warrant requirement "would unduly interfere with the maintenance of the swift and informal disciplinary procedures [that are] needed," and "strict adherence to the requirement that searches be based upon probable cause" would undercut "the substantial need of teachers and administrators for freedom to maintain order in the schools." *T.L.O.*, 469 U.S., at 340, 341, 105 S.Ct., at 742. The school search we approved in *T.L.O.*, while not based on probable cause, *was* based on individualized *suspicion* of wrongdoing. As we explicitly acknowledged, however, "'the Fourth Amendment imposes no irreducible requirement of such suspicion,'" (citation omitted). We have upheld suspicion-less searches and seizures to conduct drug testing of railroad personnel involved in train accidents, see *Skinner, supra;* to conduct random drug testing of federal customs officers who carry arms or are involved in drug interdiction, see *Von Raab, supra;* and to maintain automobile checkpoints looking for illegal immigrants and contraband, *Martinez-Fuerte, supra,* and drunk drivers, *Michigan Dept. of State Police v. Sitz,* 496 U.S. 444, 110 S.Ct. 2481, 110 L.Ed.2d 412 (1990).

III

The first factor to be considered is the nature of the privacy interest upon which the search here at issue intrudes. . . . Central, in our view, to the present case is the fact that the subjects of the Policy are (1) children, who (2) have been committed to the temporary custody of the State as schoolmaster.

Traditionally at common law, and still today, unemancipated minors lack some of the most fundamental rights of self-determination—including even the right of liberty in its narrow sense, *i.e.,* the right to come and go at will. They are subject, even as to their physical freedom, to the control of their parents or guardians. See 59 Am. Jur. 2d, Parent and Child § 10 (1987). When parents place minor children in private schools for their education, the teachers and administrators of those schools stand *in loco parentis* over the children entrusted to them. In fact, the tutor or schoolmaster is the very prototype of that status. . . .

Fourth Amendment rights, no less than First and Fourteenth Amendment rights, are different in public schools than elsewhere; the "reasonableness" inquiry cannot disregard the schools' custodial and tutelary responsibility for children. For their own good and that of their classmates, public school children are routinely required to submit to various physical examinations, and to be vaccinated against various diseases. . . . Particularly with regard to medical examinations and procedures, therefore, "students within the school environment have a lesser expectation of privacy than members of the population generally." [Citation omitted.]

Legitimate privacy expectations are even less with regard to student athletes. School sports are not for the bashful. They require "suiting up" before each practice or event, and showering and changing afterwards. Public school locker rooms, the usual sites for these activities, are not notable for the privacy they afford. The locker rooms in Vernonia are typical: No individual dressing rooms are provided; shower heads are lined up along a wall, unseparated by any sort of partition or curtain; not even all the toilet stalls have doors. As the United States Court of Appeals for the Seventh Circuit has noted, there is "an element of 'communal undress' inherent in athletic participation," *Schaill by Kross v. Tippecanoe County School Corp.,* 864 F.2d 1309, 1318 (1988).

There is an additional respect in which school athletes have a reduced expectation of privacy. By choosing to "go out for the team," they voluntarily subject themselves to a degree of regulation even higher than that imposed on students generally. In Vernonia's public schools, they must submit to a preseason physical exam (James testified that his included the giving of a urine sample, App. 17), they must acquire adequate insurance coverage or sign an insurance waiver, maintain a minimum grade point average, and comply with any "rules of conduct, dress, training hours and related matters as may be established for each sport by the head coach and athletic director with the principal's approval." Record, Exh. 2, p. 30, ¶ 8. Somewhat like adults who choose to participate in a "closely regulated industry," students who voluntarily participate in school athletics have reason to expect intrusions upon normal rights and privileges, including privacy. (Citation omitted.)

IV

Having considered the scope of the legitimate expectation of privacy at issue here, we turn next to the character of the intrusion that is complained of. . . . Under the District's Policy, male students produce samples at a urinal along a wall. They remain fully clothed and are only observed from behind, if at all. Female students produce samples in an enclosed stall, with a female monitor standing outside listening only for sounds of tampering. These conditions are nearly identical to those typically encountered in public restrooms, which men, women, and especially schoolchildren use daily. Under such conditions, the privacy interests compromised by the process of obtaining the urine sample are in our view negligible.

The other privacy-invasive aspect of urinalysis is, of course, the information it discloses concerning the state of the subject's body, and the materials he has ingested. In this regard it is significant that the tests at issue here look only for drugs, and not for whether the student is, for example, epileptic, pregnant, or diabetic. Moreover, the drugs for which the samples are screened are standard, and do not vary according to the identity of the student. And finally, the results of the tests are disclosed only to a limited class of school personnel who have a need to know; and they are not turned over to law enforcement authorities or used for any internal disciplinary function.

V

Finally, we turn to consider the nature and immediacy of the governmental concern at issue here, and the efficacy of this means for meeting it. In both *Skinner* and *Von Raab*, we characterized the government interest motivating the search as "compelling." [Citations omitted.] Relying on these cases, the District Court held that because the District's program also called for drug testing in the absence of individualized suspicion, the District "must demonstrate a 'compelling need' for the program." 796 F. Supp., at 1363. The Court of Appeals appears to have agreed with this view. See 23 F.3d, at 1526. It is a mistake, however, to think that the phrase "compelling state interest," in the Fourth Amendment context, describes a fixed, minimum quantum of governmental concern, so that one can dispose of a case by answering in isolation the question: Is there a compelling state interest here? Rather, the phrase describes an interest that appears *important enough* to justify the particular search at hand, in light of other factors that show the search to be relatively intrusive upon a genuine expectation of privacy. Whether that relatively high degree of government concern is necessary in this case or not, we think it is met.

That the nature of the concern is important—indeed, perhaps compelling—can hardly be doubted. Deterring drug use by our Nation's schoolchildren is at least as important as enhancing efficient enforcement of the Nation's laws against the importation of drugs, which was the governmental concern in *Von Raab, supra,* 489 U.S., at 668, 109 S.Ct., at 1392, or deterring drug use by engineers and trainmen, which was the governmental concern in *Skinner, supra,* at 628, 109 S.Ct., at 1419. School years are the time when the physical, psychological, and addictive effects of drugs are most severe. . . . And of course the effects of a drug-infested school are visited not just upon the users, but upon the entire student body and faculty, as the educational process is disrupted. In the present case, moreover, the necessity for the State to act is magnified by the fact that this evil is being visited not just upon individuals at large, but upon children for whom it has undertaken a special responsibility of care and direction. Finally, it must not be lost sight of that this program is directed more narrowly to drug use by school athletes, where the risk of immediate physical harm to the drug user or those with whom he is playing his sport is particularly high. Apart from psychological effects, which include impairment of judgment, slow reaction time, and a lessening of the perception of pain, the particular drugs screened by the District's Policy have been demonstrated to pose substantial physical risks to athletes. Amphetamines produce an "artificially induced heart rate increase, [p]eripheral vasoconstriction, [b]lood pressure increase, and [m]asking of the normal fatigue response," making them a "very dangerous drug when used during exercise of any type." Hawkins, *Drugs and Other Ingesta: Effects on Athletic Performance,* in H. Appenzeller, Managing Sports and Risk Management Strategies 90, 90-91 (1993). Marijuana causes "[i]rregular blood pressure responses during changes in body position," "[r]eduction in the oxygen-carrying capacity of the blood," and "[i]nhibition of the normal sweating responses resulting in increased body temperature." *Id.,* at 94. Cocaine produces "[v]asoconstriction[,] [e]levated blood pressure," and "[p]ossible coronary artery spasms and myocardial infarction." *Ibid.*

dangerous effects

    As for the immediacy of the District's concerns: We are not inclined to question—indeed, we could not possibly find clearly erroneous—the District Court's conclusion that "a large segment of the student body, particularly those involved in interscholastic athletics, was in a state of rebellion," that "[d]isciplinary actions had reached 'epidemic proportions,'" and that "the rebellion was being fueled by alcohol and drug abuse as well as by the student's misperceptions about the drug culture." . . .

VI

Taking into account all the factors we have considered above—the decreased expectation of privacy, the relative unobtrusiveness of the search, and the severity of the need met by the search—we conclude Vernonia's Policy is reasonable and hence constitutional.

    We caution against the assumption that suspicionless drug testing will readily pass constitutional muster in other contexts. The most significant element in this case is the first we discussed: that the Policy was undertaken in furtherance of the government's responsibilities, under a public school system, as guardian and tutor of children entrusted to its care. . . .

    We may note that the primary guardians of Vernonia's schoolchildren appear to agree. The record shows no objection to this districtwide program by any parents other than the couple before us here—even though, as we have described, a public meeting was held to obtain parents' views. We find insufficient basis to contradict the judgment of Vernonia's parents, its school board, and the District Court, as to what was reasonably in the interest of these children under the circumstances.

The Ninth Circuit held that Vernonia's Policy not only violated the Fourth Amendment, but also, by reason of that violation, contravened Article I, § 9, of the Oregon Constitution. Our conclusion that the former holding was in error means that the latter holding rested on a flawed premise. We therefore vacate the judgment, and remand the case to the Court of Appeals for further proceedings consistent with this opinion.

reversed and remanded

Justice O'CONNOR, with whom Justice STEVENS and Justice SOUTER join, dissenting.

The population of our Nation's public schools, grades 7 through 12, numbers around 18 million. *See U.S. Dept. of Education, National Center for Education Statistics, Digest of Education Statistics* 58 (1994) (Table 43). By the reasoning of today's decision, the millions of these students who participate in interscholastic sports, an overwhelming majority of whom have given school officials no reason whatsoever to suspect they use drugs at school, are open to an intrusive bodily search. . . .

As an initial matter, I have serious doubts whether the Court is right that the District reasonably found that the lesser intrusion of a suspicion-based testing program outweighed its genuine concerns for the adversarial nature of such a program, and for its abuses. For one thing, there are significant safeguards against abuses. The fear that a suspicion-based regime will lead to the testing of "troublesome but not drug-likely" students, for example, ignores that the required level of suspicion in the school context is objectively *reasonable* suspicion. . . . Moreover, any distress arising from what turns out to be a false accusation can be minimized by keeping the entire process confidential. . . .

The record here indicates that the Vernonia schools are no exception. The great irony of this case is that most (though not all) of the evidence the District introduced to justify its suspicionless drug testing program consisted of first- or second-hand stories of particular, identifiable students acting in ways that plainly gave rise to reasonable suspicion of in-school drug use—and thus that would have justified a drug-related search under our *T.L.O.* decision. . . .

In light of all this evidence of drug use by particular students, there is a substantial basis for concluding that a vigorous regime of suspicion-based testing would have gone a long way toward solving Vernonia's school drug problem while preserving the Fourth Amendment rights of James Acton and others like him. And were there any doubt about such a conclusion, it is removed by indications in the record that suspicion-based testing could have been supplemented by an equally vigorous campaign to have Vernonia's parents encourage their children to submit to the District's *voluntary* drug testing program. In these circumstances, the Fourth Amendment dictates that a mass, suspicionless search regime is categorically unreasonable. . . .

I find unpersuasive the Court's reliance on the widespread practice of physical examinations and vaccinations, which are both blanket searches of a sort. . . .

It might also be noted that physical exams (and of course vaccinations) are not searches for conditions that reflect wrongdoing on the part of the student, and so are *wholly* nonaccusatory and have no consequences that can be regarded as punitive. . . .

. . . I find unreasonable the school's choice of student athletes as the class to subject to suspicionless testing—a choice that appears to have been driven more by a belief in what would pass constitutional muster (indicating that the original program was targeted at students involved in any extracurricular activity) than by a belief in what was required to meet the District's principal disciplinary concern. . . . [I]t seems quite obvious that the true driving force behind the District's adoption of its drug testing program was the need to combat the rise in drug-related disorder and disruption in its classrooms and around campus. I mean no criticism of the strength of that interest. On the contrary, where the record demonstrates the existence of such a problem, that interest seems self-evidently compelling. . . . And the record in this case surely demonstrates there was a drug-related discipline problem in Vernonia of "'epidemic proportions.'" 796 F. Supp., at 1357. The evidence of a drug-related sports injury problem at Vernonia, by contrast, was considerably weaker. . . .

Having reviewed the record here, I cannot avoid the conclusion that the District's suspicionless policy of testing all student athletes sweeps too broadly, and too imprecisely, to be reasonable under the Fourth Amendment.

not reasonable!

NOTES AND QUESTIONS

1. What is the legal standard for determining whether drug testing of interscholastic athletes by a public high school violates the Fourth Amendment? Why does the *Acton* majority uphold suspicionless testing of high school athletes for recreational drug use? Would suspicion-based drug testing accomplish high school administrators' legitimate objectives equally well without intruding on students' privacy rights? The Court upheld the drug-testing program premised in part on the belief that athletes serve as role models and deterring athletes' use of drugs through testing will help to resolve the greater societal problem. Do you agree?

2. *Performance-Enhancing Drugs.* In *Board of Education of Indep. Sch. Dist. No. 92 of Pottawatomie County v. Earls,* 536 U.S. 822 (2002), the Supreme Court upheld the constitutionality of mandatory suspicionless drug testing of all students participating in high school extracurricular activities such as the Academic Team, Future Farmers of America, band, choir, pom-pom, cheerleading, and athletics. The only consequence of a positive test for illegal drugs was to limit the student's privilege of participating in extracurricular activities; it did not result in the imposition of any other discipline or have any academic consequences.

like Carterville

Writing for a narrow majority of five justices, Justice Thomas concluded that "the safety interest furthered by drug testing is undoubtedly substantial for all children, athletes and nonathletes alike." 536 U.S. at 837. The majority held that "testing students who participate in extracurricular activities is a reasonably effective means of addressing the School District's legitimate concerns in preventing, deterring, and detecting drug use." *Id.* The four dissenting justices asserted that "[i]nterscholastic athletics similarly require close safety and health regulation; a school's choir, band, and academic team do not." 536 U.S. at 846.

Given that protection of high school students' health and safety is a legitimate reason for drug testing, would testing for performance-enhancing drugs such as anabolic steroids (or instead of recreational drugs) be constitutional? See Thomas Proctor, Comment, *Constitutionality of Testing High School Male Athletes for Steroids Under* Vernonia School District v. Acton *and* Board of Education v. Earls, 2005 BYU L. Rev. 1335 (2005) (analyzing random, suspicionless testing of male high school athletes for steroid use under the *Acton* and *Earls* cases).

I think so — still a health risk to students

The legality of testing college athletes for usage of performance-enhancing and recreational drugs is considered in Chapter 3.

3. *State Constitutional Protections.* Although *Earls* gives broad approval under the Fourth Amendment of the United States Constitution to mandatory drug testing of all students wishing to participate in extracurricular activities, such policies may still face challenges under state constitutional provisions. In *York v. Wahkiakum*, 178 P.3d 995 (Wash. 2008), the Washington Supreme Court considered the constitutionality of a school district's blanket suspicionless random drug testing program for student-athletes. Although the court acknowledged that the district's drug testing policy did not violate the Fourth Amendment of the U.S. Constitution, it concluded that the Washington state constitution provided a higher level of protection. It held that the district's drug testing policy violated a provision of the state constitution that provides, "No person shall be disturbed in his private affairs, or his home invaded, without authority of law." *Id.* at 306. See also *Theodore v. Delaware Valley Sch. Dist.*, 836 A.2d 76 (Pa. 2003) (invalidating suspicionless drug-testing of all middle and high school students desiring to participate in extracurricular activities because it violates Pennsylvania's constitution).

can violate the State Const. even if no the U.S. Const.

But see *Hageman v. Goshen County School Dist. No. 1*, 256 P.3d 487 (Wyo. 2011), in which the Supreme Court of Wyoming was not persuaded by *York* and held that a public school system's policy requiring all students who participate in extracurricular activities to submit to random drug and alcohol testing does not violate Wyoming constitution, which the court declared to be more like the federal constitution than the Washington state constitution). The Wyoming Supreme Court examined both equal protection and due process issues under their state constitution, which makes it clear that advocates supporting the rights of student-athletes in such cases should invoke state constitutions rather than relying solely on the federal Constitution.

4. *State Governing Body Drug Testing Programs.* In 2005 the California Interscholastic Federation, which regulates high school athletics in the state, adopted a policy to curb steroid use that requires a student and his or her parents to agree in writing that the athlete will not use steroids without a physician's prescription. It also requires that coaches complete a certification program having a significant component regarding steroids and performance-enhancing dietary supplements, and prohibits school personnel from selling, distributing, or advocating the use of muscle-building dietary supplements.

In 2006 New Jersey became the first state to institute random steroid testing of high school student-athletes whose schools qualify for state championship games. Student-athletes who test positive will be banned from participating in state championship games, although their teams remain eligible to participate without them. During the 2006-2007 academic year, New Jersey's random drug testing program tested 500 student-athletes who qualified for state championship competition, with only one student-athlete testing positive for performance-enhancing drugs.

During the 2007-2008 school year, Texas implemented a mandatory random steroid testing program for high school athletes in all sports, with a 30-day suspension from athletic competition for first-time offenders. After spending $6 million since February 2008 to randomly test more than 50,000 high school athletes, which resulted in fewer than 30 confirmed positive tests, Texas reduced funding for the state's high school drug testing program to $1.5 million for the 2012 and 2013 school years, with testing to focus on football, baseball, and track.

In February 2009 Florida's high school drug testing program was scrapped for financial reasons. Florida's pilot program cost found the state over $100,000 and found only one steroid user among 600 students tested at 53 high schools. The Florida High School Athletic Association maintains a formal policy prohibiting the use of performance-enhancing drugs, but now there is no testing program in place to detect violations.

At its June 2012 meeting, the Illinois High School Association's Board of Directors approved continuation of the association's steroid testing program. Any student who participates in an IHSA-sponsored or sanctioned athletic event is subject to testing to determine usage of steroids. The board of directors also approved a recommendation requiring that each coach for a sport sponsored or sanctioned by the IHSA at or above the ninth grade level shall be required to complete an educational program on the prevention of abuse of performance-enhancing substances. Coaches shall also be required to complete an examination developed by the IHSA showing a minimum understanding of methods to prevent the abuse of performance-enhancing substances by students.

b.   Freedom of Speech and Association

In the following case, the Eighth Circuit considers whether a student's free speech rights were violated when her continued participation on the sophomore basketball team was conditioned on her issuing an apology for a letter she wrote regarding her coach.

WILDMAN v. MARSHALLTOWN SCHOOL DISTRICT

249 F.3d. 768 (8th Cir. 2001)

BRIGHT, Circuit Judge.

Rebecca Wildman appeals from the district court's summary judgment dismissal of her action. Wildman filed this action under 42 U.S.C. § 1983 and § 1988 as a high school student against the school principal, school athletic director, varsity girls' basketball coach, as well as the school district, alleging that they violated her rights under the Free Speech Clause of the First Amendment when they conditioned her continued participation on the sophomore basketball team on her apologizing to her teammates for writing a letter which criticized the varsity coach. We affirm.

I.   BACKGROUND

We take the facts in the light most favorable to Wildman. In January 1998, Wildman was a sophomore student at Marshalltown High School in Marshalltown, Iowa, and a member of the school's basketball team. Wildman hoped to play on the varsity team and she testified that Coach Rowles, the high school girls' varsity basketball coach, promised in conversations with her before the season that he would promote her to the varsity team. When the promotion never materialized, Wildman testified that she "became frustrated and decided to write a letter to [her] teammates" and that her "purpose was to find out what they thought of the situation and Coach Rowles." She composed a letter on her home computer and distributed it to her teammates in the school's locker room on Saturday, January 24, 1998. The letter stated:

> To all of my teammates:
>   Everyone has done a great job this year and now is the time that we need to make ourselves stronger and pull together. It was a tough loss last night but we will get it back. We have had some bumps in the road to success but every team does and the time is here for us to smoothen it out. Everyone on this team is important whether they think so or not. After watching last nights [*sic*] Varsity game and seeing their sophomores play up I think and I think [*sic*] that some of you are think [*sic*] the same thing. I think that we have to fight for our position. Am I the only one who thinks that some of us should be playing Varsity or even JV? We as a team have to do something about this. I want to say something to Coach Rowles. I will not say anything to him without the whole teams [*sic*] support. He needs us next year and the year after and what if we aren't there for him? It is time to give him back some of the bullshit that he has given us. We are a really great team and by the time we are seniors and we ALL have worked hard we are going to have an AWESOME season. We deserve better then [*sic*] what we have gotten. We now need to stand up for what we believe in!!!

She included below her statement a poem about geese in flight titled "We Makes Me Stronger."

The following week, Wildman's sophomore team coach received a telephone call from Charlotte Baltes, a parent of one of Wildman's teammates, who expressed concern about the letter her daughter brought home from the locker room. Coach Rowles received a copy of the letter from another player's parent, Diana Swanson, who worked as the attendance secretary at the high school. Both coaches, who stated in their depositions that they were alarmed by the letter's tone and language, met with athletic director Funk and principal Stephens to discuss how to handle the matter. On January 29, 1998, the coaches met with Wildman alone to discuss the letter with her. They told her the letter was disrespectful and demanded that she apologize to her teammates. Wildman claims that they did not ask her to explain what she hoped to accomplish with her letter. She contends that she did not advocate a strike or boycott but that the school did not give her a chance to explain herself before setting the condition for her continued participation in the basketball program. The coaches gave her twenty-four hours to apologize, and, if she did not, she would not be allowed to return to the team. Wildman refused to apologize and did not practice with the team or play in the season's remaining six games. She also complains that she was not invited to attend the postseason awards banquet and that

Coach Rowles declined to give her a participation award because "she did not finish the season." Following the school year, Wildman and her family moved to another school district where she enrolled in high school.

On September 2, 1999, Wildman brought this suit for damages. On November 2, 1999, the defendants filed a motion for summary judgment. On April 6, 2000, the district court granted defendants' motion for summary judgment, holding that Wildman's letter materially interfered or substantially disrupted a school activity. . . . Wildman appeals the summary judgment dismissal of her action.

II.   DISCUSSION

. . . For reversal, Wildman argues that the First Amendment prevents the school from disciplining her for distributing a letter which was a personal communication to other students containing her personal expression. Both parties agree that, as the Supreme Court acknowledged in *Tinker v. Des Moines Indep. Cnty. Sch. Dist.*, 393 U.S. 503, 506, 89 S.Ct. 733, 21 L.Ed.2d 731 (1969), students do not "shed their constitutional rights to freedom of speech or expression at the schoolhouse gate." *Tinker* involved an attempt by high school students to wear black armbands on school property to symbolize their protest against the Vietnam War. The Supreme Court struck down school authorities' efforts to discipline this expression of opinion (suspending the students from school until they would come back without their armbands) and stated that "undifferentiated fear or apprehension of disturbance is not enough to overcome the right to freedom of expression." *Tinker*, 393 U.S. at 508, 89 S.Ct. 733.

However, this right to express opinions on school premises is not absolute. It is well within the parameters of school officials' authority to prohibit the public expression of vulgar and offensive comments and to teach civility and sensitivity in the expression of opinions. . . .

Marshalltown had in place a handbook for student conduct in 1997-1998, as well as a Marshalltown Bobcat Basketball Handbook, drafted by Coach Rowles and distributed to Wildman and her teammates at the start of the season. Both handbooks indicated that disrespect and insubordination will result in disciplinary action at the coach's discretion. Appellees argue that they acted properly and lawfully in their reaction to Wildman's letter. They point to their interest in affording Wildman's teammates an educational environment conducive to learning team unity and sportsmanship and free from disruptions and distractions that could hurt or stray the cohesiveness of the team.

Wildman admits that her speech contained one profane word but contends that because there was no specific evidence of a material disruption of a school activity, her speech is protected. We disagree with the claim of protection.

The parties perhaps could have achieved with minimal creativity and flexibility a solution more amicable or less humiliating to the student. However, the school sanction only required an apology. The school did not interfere with Wildman's regular education. A difference exists between being in the classroom, which was not affected here, and playing on an athletic team when the requirement is that the player only apologize to her teammates and her coach for circulating an insubordinate letter. We agree with the district court's conclusions that the letter did suggest, at the least, that the team unite in defiance of the coach (where Wildman wrote that the coach "needs us next year and the year after and what if we aren't there for him?" and "[i]t is time to give him back some of the bullshit that he has given us" and "[w]e now need to stand up for what we believe in" and "I think that we have to fight for our position") and that the actions taken by the coaches in response were reasonable. Moreover, coaches deserve a modicum of respect from athletes, particularly in an academic setting.

This suit does not present a case like *Seamons v. Snow*, 206 F.3d 1021 (10th Cir. 2000), cited by Wildman for the proposition that dismissal of a high school player from an athletic team for refusing to apologize for the exercise of free speech rights amounts to an unconstitutional action. In that case, the Tenth Circuit Court of Appeals reversed the district court's summary judgment dismissal and remanded because of disputed issues of fact. The student athlete in *Seamons* asserted that the football coach asked the player to apologize to the football team for reporting to the police and to school authorities a hazing incident in which the player was assaulted in the high school locker room by a group of his teammates, forcibly restrained, and bound to a towel rack with adhesive athletic tape. *Id.* at 1027. The coach presented a different version, claiming that the player's ultimate failure to be involved with the football team was unrelated to his speech or refusal to speak. *Id.* The court determined that "[t]here [were] ample facts in the record to indicate that Brian's suspension and dismissal from the football team were directly related to his failure to apologize for reporting the assault." *Seamons*, 206 F.3d at 1028. Implicitly the court acknowledged that Brian's report of the assault was protected free expression.

In contrast, Wildman's letter, containing the word "bullshit" in relation to other language in it and motivated by her disappointment at not playing on the varsity team, constitutes insubordinate speech toward her coaches. Here, in an athletic context void of the egregious conduct which spurred the football player's speech about the hazing incident in *Seamons* and where Wildman's speech called for an apology, no basis exists for a claim of a violation of free speech.

III. CONCLUSION

Accordingly, we affirm the summary judgment of dismissal of Wildman's claim of alleged violation of her rights under the Free Speech Clause of the First Amendment.

NOTES AND QUESTIONS

1. *Student's Free Speech Rights.* Why did the court reject the student-athlete's free speech claim? If the student-athlete had not included the word "bullshit" in her letter, would the court have rendered a different decision? What kinds of comments by a student-athlete about her coach are constitutionally protected? Do student-athletes effectively shed much of their constitutional right of free speech at the gymnasium door? If a group of student-athletes decided to wear a black headband as a way of protesting poor coaching, would this be protected speech? For discussions of free speech challenges to interscholastic rules and regulations, see David W. Dulabon, *First [Amendment] & Goal: High School Recruiting and State Actor Theory*, 2 Vand. J. Ent. L. & Prac. 219 (2000).

The *Wildman* court states that "[t]he parties could have achieved with minimal creativity and flexibility a solution more amicable or less humiliating to the student." What would you have recommended?

In *Pinard v. Clatskanine School District 6J*, 446 F.3d 964 (9th Cir. 2006), a group of student-athletes alleged that the school's decision to remove them from the basketball team was in retaliation against their speaking out in opposition to the coach and expressing their desire that he be removed because of his abusive and intimidating behavior. The court found that the players' written, signed petition requesting that the school remove the coach was protected speech, but that the players' decision to refuse to board the bus to an away game was not protected, since it "[disrupted or interfered] with the [scheduled] activity." The court remanded the retaliation claim on the ground that there was an insufficient factual record presented on appeal, but in doing so, the court added, "[I]f the plaintiffs can show that their protected speech was a 'substantial or motivating factor' in the defendant's decision to suspend them from the team permanently, and the defendants fail to show that they 'would have taken the same action even in the absence' of that speech, then the defendants violated plaintiffs' First Amendment rights."

On remand, the district court held that there was sufficient evidence to survive summary judgment. With regard to the timing issue, there was evidence that the players may have been suspended in part for retaliatory purposes and the boycott was not enough to cut off the possible link between the petition and suspension. The court noted that there was no serious dispute with regard to the defendants having opposed the speech of the players and there was sufficient evidence to support the theory that a school official withheld information that could have averted the boycott. The court also noted that there was not an identifiable school policy requiring permanent suspension in such a case. *Pinard v. Clatskanie School District*, 2008 WL 410097 (D. Or.).

In *Doe v. Silsbee Independent School District*, 402 Fed. Appx. 852 (5th Cir. 2010), *cert. denied*, 131 S. Ct. 2875 (2011), a cheerleader cheered with her teammates throughout the game but refused to cheer, preferring to stand still with her arms crossed, when a young man who had pleaded guilty of sexual assault against her was shooting a free throw. After refusing to cheer for the young man, she was expelled from the cheerleading squad. She then filed suit claiming that her dismissal from the cheer squad for refusing to cheer under these circumstances constituted a violation of her First Amendment right of free speech. The district court dismissed her suit on the ground that a cheerleader agrees to represent the school, and therefore waives her right of free speech in that capacity. The court also upheld her dismissal from the cheer squad and ordered her to reimburse the school $45,000 for costs associated with the litigation. The Fifth Circuit affirmed and the Supreme Court refused to grant certiorari. What would you have done as superintendent? Would you have permitted the young man to play? Would you require the young woman to cheer for the young man?

2. *Parent's Free Speech Rights.* In *Parker v. The Waldron, Arkansas, School District*, 2006 WL 663401 (W.D. Ark. 2006), the district court held that a parent who published a letter in a local newspaper concerning the poor treatment of students on the school's sport teams had sufficiently alleged that he was being retaliated against by the school system for exercising his First Amendment

right of free speech. The court also held that evidence establishing that the school had penalized children following parental criticism of the coaching staff implied that the school remained indifferent or tacitly authorized such retaliation. See also *Besler v. Board of Educ. of West-Windsor-Plainsboro Reg'l Sch. Dist.*, 993 A.2d 805 (N.J. 2010) (parent's free speech rights violated when he was denied the opportunity to complete his statement alleging that a high school coach verbally abused students including his daughter). On the other hand, schools have the right to restrict persons, including parents, from entering onto campuses when their speech or conduct poses a threat to the safety of others. In *Cunningham v. Lenape Regional High Dist. Bd. of Educ.*, 2007 WL 1821010 (D. N.J.), the father of a high school wrestler brought suit against his son's school district after he was banished from the school's premises and instructed not to communicate with any coach or member of the wrestling team on the ground that the district's action violated his right of assembly under the First Amendment. The school district asserted that its decision was made to ensure public safety because the parent in question had engaged in behavior on six occasions that gave rise to complaints that he was aggressive and belittling and made people feel unsafe. Agreeing with the school district, the court ruled that schools have the right to impose restrictions to protect public safety and observed that a school district does not have to wait until such harm actually occurs but does need to have evidence of inappropriate and hostile behavior that could result in public harm.

c.   Freedom of Religion

Free exercise and establishment of religion issues may arise in the context of interscholastic sports under either federal or state constitutions. The Free Exercise Clause protects the rights of students, coaches, and other individuals to act on their religious beliefs. Establishment Clause issues focus on limiting the power of a state actor such as a public school to engage in or permit activities that could be considered state endorsement or approval of particular religious activities, such as prayers before athletic events.

i.   *Free Exercise Issues*

In his article, *Religious Freedom and the Interscholastic Athlete*, 12 Marq. Sports L. Rev. 295 (2001), Professor Scott Idleman observes:

> [A]thletic participation and religious observance appear to be two of Americans' most cherished endeavors. When these endeavors collide, and when the collision is due partly to a governmental regulation or policy, the Free Exercise Clause may very well dictate how this conflict between competition and conscience is resolved. The First Amendment's principal message in this regard is that regulations must be religiously neutral and generally applicable, and that religious requests for accommodation must be treated with at least the same solicitude that administrators display towards nonreligious requests (although more favorable treatment is in many instances permissible as well). The government may also have to bend its regulations where the athlete's predicament implicates not only free exercise, but also a conjunctive constitutional claim such as free speech or the right of parents

to direct their children's education. To the extent that governments abide by these norms, the First Amendment otherwise permits them generally to regulate in any rational manner, and pursue any legitimate objectives, which they deem appropriate.

Id. at 344-345.

Professor Idleman also notes the role of other federal and state laws, including state constitutional provisions:

[O]ther federal and especially state laws . . . might also be implicated . . . , depending on the jurisdiction, the legal status of the educational institution, the nature of the athletic regulation, and the particular circumstances of the alleged religious infringement. In some states, for example, strict scrutiny may apply to government regulations even if they are neutral and generally applicable. In others, the rights of students or student-athletes may be specifically protected. While in others, or in certain interscholastic venues, the regulations themselves may provide for certain forms of religious accommodation.

Id. at 345.

Some early cases evidence the propensity of courts to defer to institutions and interscholastic associations even when they act in a manner that clearly limits the free exercise of religion rights of a student-athlete or coach. In *Walsh v. Louisiana High School Athletic Assn.*, 616 F.2d 152 (5th Cir. 1980), the court upheld a transfer rule against a claim that it burdened a student's free exercise of religion rights. The parents sought to have their children educated in Lutheran schools, as a matter of faith, and argued that the transfer rule prohibiting their children from participating for a period of time in interscholastic athletics infringed their free exercise rights. Similarly, in *Menora v. Illinois High School Assn.*, 683 F.2d 1030 (7th Cir. 1982), the court upheld a rule that forbade student-athletes from wearing hats or other headwear (with the sole exception of a headband no wider than two inches) while playing basketball against a claim that this rule infringed on the religious freedom of Orthodox Jews who sought to wear yarmulkes during play. The court accepted the association's assertion that the rule preserved the safety of players by insuring that a player would not trip over a yarmulke that had fallen from a player's head.

The likelihood that a court will provide such a significant degree of deference, even when the challenged conduct implicates First Amendment free exercise of religion rights, is even greater today. In *Employment Division v. Smith*, 494 U.S. 872 (1990), the Supreme Court held that neutral laws of general applicability—laws that do not intentionally discriminate against religion or religious exercise—do not violate the Free Exercise Clause. It should be noted, however, that statutory or regulatory accommodations of religious exercise are permissible. Athletic associations may create rules or grant waivers that accommodate the free exercise of religion. For example, some athletic associations have promulgated rules that enable their religious school members to refrain from participating in interscholastic competitions on their Sabbath. Thus, it is now clear that the Louisiana High School Athletic Association, in the *Walsh* case noted above, could have permitted the student-athlete's transfer on religious grounds without any loss of eligibility to participate in sports. Indeed, that is one of the lessons of *Employment Division v. Smith*, which leaves such matters largely to the democratic or regulatory process at the state and federal levels. Many states (approximately half of them) responded to *Employment Division v. Smith* by passing religious freedom restoration acts. These state constitutional provisions provide stronger support for free exercise rights, but have not been invoked with any regularity in the interscholastic athletics context. Lawyers, however, need to remember that the best legal recourse for their clients is at the state constitutional level, not under the U.S. Constitution. Thus, they may be able to successfully argue that a religious accommodation or exemption is required under a state constitutional right of free exercise provision, which may be interpreted to provide broader rights than the U.S. Constitution's Free Exercise Clause.

NOTES AND QUESTIONS

1. *Individual's Free Exercise Rights.* The First Amendment offers little protection to parents, student-athletes, or coaches unless they can establish they are actually being discriminated against on religious grounds (a difficult burden of proof to satisfy), or they can persuade an educational institution or governing body to provide them with an accommodation to avoid infringing their free exercise of religion rights. Do you agree with the judicial precedent making it very difficult to assert successfully infringement of a religious liberty right in this context, and should courts be so deferential with regard to the right of conscience? Should student-athletes effectively be forced to waive their constitutional rights in exchange for the privilege of participating in interscholastic athletics?

    Courts occasionally have found that the free exercise of religion rights of student-athletes have been violated. In *Hadley v. Rush Henrietta Central School District*, 409 F. Supp. 2d 164 (W.D.N.Y. 2006), the court granted an injunction allowing a high school lacrosse player to participate in this sport despite his refusal to get a required tetanus vaccination for religious reasons. The court acknowledged that participation in interscholastic athletics is not a constitutionally protected right but concluded that the school district's failure to extend a vaccination waiver granted to students generally, but not to students desiring to participate in athletics, likely constituted illegal discrimination on the basis of religion.

    In *Trefelner v. Burrelle School District*, 655 F. Supp. 2d 581 (2009), the court held that a public school district must permit a private school student to participate in the public high school's jazz and marching bands. In keeping with state law, the school district's policy permitted homeschool, charter school, and cyberschool students to participate in extracurricular activities. The law did not expressly require the district to permit private school students to participate, but the student argued successfully that he had been denied his equal protection and free exercise of religion rights as a result of the district's refusal to permit him to participate despite the fact that his parents had elected to enroll him in a private religious school. The court found no reason that would warrant differentiating between religiously motivated homeschool programs and a religious private school for such purposes and held that the student's right to participate was protected by his right of free exercise of religion.

2. *School's Free Exercise Rights.* In *Cornerstone Christian Schools v. University Interscholastic League*, 563 F.3d 127 (5th Cir. 2009), the Fifth Circuit ruled that a state high school athletic association's refusal to admit a Christian school did not constitute an infringement of federal free exercise rights

because the challenged provision relied on by the association to make its decision was religiously neutral, generally applicable, and did not by its terms distinguish between private and parochial schools. See also *Evans v. Kentucky High Sch. Athletic Assn.*, 2010 WL 1643758 (W.D. Ky.), *affirmed*, 2011 WL 6415055 (6th Cir.) (applying a rational basis test to bylaw that applies to all nonpublic schools equally, court rejects claim that it discriminates against Roman Catholic schools by rendering students who receive more than 25 percent of their tuition from merit-based financial aid ineligible to participate in KHSAA-sponsored interscholastic athletics).

On the other hand, in *Nakashima v. Board of Education*, 185 P.3d 429 (2008), the Oregon Supreme Court ruled that the state school board violated a state law prohibiting discrimination based on religion when it approved the Oregon School Activities Association's refusal to accommodate an Adventist school's request that it adjust a basketball tournament schedule to enable students to avoid having to choose between participating in athletics on their Sabbath or refusing to play. It also awarded attorney fees to the ACLU chapter that represented the Adventist school.

ii.   Establishment Clause Issues

PROBLEM 2-6

A coach at a public high school has been bringing players together regularly for a prayer prior to practices and games. Does the coach have a free exercise right to offer a prayer for his or her team? Does such a prayer constitute an establishment of religion violation? If the coach learned that the prayer was constitutionally questionable and came to you with the following possible recommendations (in descending order of attractiveness to him), which ones, if any, do you believe may be constitutionally acceptable: (1) the coach selects a team chaplain; (2) the team elects a person to pray prior to practices and competition; (3) the coach invites a member of the team, on a noncompulsory basis, to join a representative of the Fellowship of Christian Athletes or some other religious group for a prayer prior to practice or competition; (4) the members of the team take turns offering a prayer or inspirational thought prior to practice or competition; (5) the coach asks the team members to join in a moment of silent reflection or prayer prior to practice and competition. Are there other possible ways in which religious interests of public school coaches and students are constitutionally permissible? If you were an attorney representing a public school district that wanted to recognize prayer in some form in the athletics context, what would you advise the district to do?

The First Amendment provides that "Congress shall make no law respecting an establishment of religion." This provision prohibits state actors from engaging in activities that have the effect of establishing a religion. One issue that regularly arises is the question of whether prayers may be offered prior to, or as a part of, interscholastic athletic events sponsored by public schools. In *Santa Fe Independent School District v. Doe*, 530 U.S. 290 (2000), the Court held that the school's policy permitting student-led prayer at football games was unconstitutional. Writing for the majority, Justice Stevens, held that pre-game prayers delivered "on school property, at school-sponsored events, over the school's public address system, by a speaker representing the student body, under the supervision of school faculty, and pursuant to a school policy that explicitly and implicitly encourages public prayer" are public speech and there-fore prohibited. Justice Stevens and the majority applied an objective test and found that students in the district "will unquestionably perceive the inevitable pregame prayer as stamped with her school's seal of approval." Chief Justice Rehnquist, joined by Justices Scalia and Thomas, believed the Court was acting prematurely because the policy had not been put in to practice. The dissenters were not convinced that speech (a prayer) under the policy would necessarily violate the Establishment Clause, because the speaker would be a private indi-vidual (not a public official) and the prayer, therefore, would be private rather than school-sponsored speech. Given changes in the membership of the Court, it is not clear that *Santa Fe Independent School District v. Doe* will be followed in subsequent cases.

NOTES AND QUESTIONS

1. *What Is Permissible?* The majority in the *Santa Fe* case indicated that religious activities may still occur in the interscholastic athletics context if a public school or state high schools athletics association determined to be a state actor is not viewed as sponsoring or endorsing the religious activity. What activities might be appropriate? If the captain of a public high school team led his team in prayer without the participation or knowledge of the coach, would that be permissible? If the coach learned that the captain did so and planned to do so in the future, would he need to prevent the captain from leading the team in a prayer in the future (i.e., would the coach's acquies-cence be sufficient reason to find undue state involvement)? What if an ath-lete was injured and his teammates spontaneously knelt in prayer around him? If a school's mascot is the crusaders or the saints, should the school be prohibited from using that name on establishment grounds?

2. *Relationship to Freedom of Speech and Free Exercise of Religion.* Cases involving prayer by public high school student-athletes and coaches often raise both free speech and free exercise issues in addition to establishment of religion issues, as was the case in *Santa Fe Independent School District*. In *Borden v. School District of the Township of East Brunswick*, 523 F.3d 153 (3d Cir. 2008), the Third Circuit ruled that a public school's refusal to permit a coach to silently bow his head during premeal grace and kneel with his team dur-ing a student-initiated locker room prayer did not constitute a violation of the coach's right of free speech and that the coach's doing so violated the Establishment Clause. Is this an appropriate balancing and accommodation of these three important provisions of the First Amendment?

3. *Preliminary Issues.* In the course of his opinion in the *Santa Fe* case, Justice Stevens argues that the policy adopted in the Santa Fe Independent School District silences the speech of students who are in a minority, because they will seldom be able to offer the prayer or may oppose prayer generally. Do you agree? The Court did not consider evidence on this issue, because the policy was being challenged and had not been put in practice. The Court simply held, as a theoretical matter, that the challenged prayers might

silence the speech of students who are in the minority. The majority and dissenters in *Santa Fe* disagreed regarding the extent to which actual evidence of a prayer being given should be required before invalidating a statute on facial grounds. Who is right?

4. *Voluntariness.* Since students did not have to participate and attendance at games was voluntary and after school hours, the school district argued that attendance at a football game was voluntary and, therefore, did not constitute a violation of the Establishment Clause of the First Amendment. Do you agree?

CHAPTER
3

Regulating Intercollegiate Athletics

A.   INTRODUCTION

This chapter initially provides a general overview and history of the governance of intercollegiate athletics, particularly within the National Collegiate Athletic Association (NCAA). Consideration of the nature of the legal relationship between a university and its student-athletes and First Amendment rights issues arising in connection with intercollegiate athletics follows. Next, the NCAA's legal status as a private regulatory body, its internal rules enforcement process, and external legal limits on its regulatory authority, such as the law of private associations and federal antitrust law, are examined.

B.   A BRIEF HISTORY: NCAA GOVERNANCE OF INTERCOLLEGIATE ATHLETICS

The NCAA's basic purpose "is to maintain intercollegiate athletics as an integral part of the educational program and the athlete as an integral part of the student body and, by so doing, retain a clear line of demarcation between intercollegiate athletics and professional sports." *National Collegiate Athletic Assn. Constitution*, art. 1.3.1, in 2011-2012 NCAA Division I Manual (2011). The NCAA includes over 1,000 colleges and universities organized into three divisions based on the nature of their intercollegiate athletic programs. Division I offers full athletic scholarships to many of its athletes and is the highest level of competition in most sports; Division II also offers athletic scholarships and competes at an intermediate competitive level; and Division III does not offer athletic scholarships and is the lowest and most student-centered competitive level. Differences among the divisions are described on the NCAA website at http://www.ncaa.org/wps/wcm/connect/public/ncaa/about+the+ncaa+old/who+we+are/differences+among+the+divisions/division+i/about+division+i. The discussion in this chapter focuses on Division I (D-I) intercollegiate athletics, but much of it is equally applicable to legal regulation of Divisions II and III.

There are other national associations engaged in the regulation of intercollegiate athletics. The National Association of Intercollegiate Athletics (NAIA) includes more than 360 colleges and universities and conducts numerous national championships. It is also developing programs designed to enhance the experience of student-athletes, including their Champions of Character program that encourages schools to take actions designed to develop character traits among student-athletes. The National Christian College Athletic Association (NCCAA) was incorporated to provide an association for Christ-centered collegiate institutions that are committed to athletic competition as an integral component of education, evangelism, and encouragement. The United States Collegiate Athletic Association (USCAA), another smaller national organization, was organized for the purpose of holding national championships in a number of sports for very small schools. The National Junior College Athletic Association (NJCAA) is made up of more than 500 junior and community colleges throughout 24 regions in the United States that sponsor men's and women's intercollegiate athletic teams, which compete for national championships in three divisions, based on levels of competitiveness. California also has a community college athletic association that governs athletics within California. These collegiate athletic associations have rules and standards by which its member schools are governed and through which student-athletes' participation is regulated, but the focus of this chapter is on the NCAA. Although the rules and governance structures differ among the various national associations that govern intercollegiate athletics, much of what you will learn by examining how the NCAA is legally regulated is relevant to all of these governing bodies.

Students, with some faculty oversight, initially were the major force in running intercollegiate athletics. With the deaths of 18 intercollegiate football players in 1905, President Theodore Roosevelt invited university officials to participate in a White House Conference to review football rules. These efforts to reform football rules led to the formation of a Rules Committee and the formation of the Intercollegiate Athletic Association, which in 1910 was renamed the National Collegiate Athletic Association. *NCAA*

Interest in intercollegiate sports and attendant increases in commercialization led the highly respected Carnegie Foundation for the Advancement of Education to issue, in 1929, a significant report regarding intercollegiate athletics, which concluded:

> [A] change of values is needed in a field that is sodden with the commercial and the material and the vested interests that these forces have created. Commercialism in college athletics must be diminished and college sport must rise to a point where it is esteemed primarily and sincerely for the opportunities it affords to mature youth.

Howard J. Savage et al., *The Growth of College Athletics*, in American College Athletics 13 (Carnegie Foundation for the Advancement of Teaching 1929).

After the Depression and World War II, with a dramatic increase in access to higher education on the part of all segments of society, largely through government support for returning military personnel to cover the costs of attending college, public interest in intercollegiate athletics expanded significantly. Commercial pressures intensified with the advent of television, the presence of radio in the vast majority of homes in the United States, and the broadcasting of major sporting events. These factors, coupled with a series of gambling scandals

and recruiting excesses, caused the NCAA to promulgate additional rules, resulting in an expansion of its governance authority. In 1948, the NCAA enacted
the so-called "Sanity Code," which was designed to "alleviate the proliferation
of exploitive practices in the recruitment of student-athletes." To enforce the
rules in the "Sanity Code," the NCAA created the Constitutional Compliance
Committee. Neither the Sanity Code with its rules nor the Constitutional
Compliance Committee with its enforcement responsibility was particularly
successful because their only sanction was expulsion, which was so severe that
enforcement of the rules was ineffectual.

Two other developments in the 1950s contributed to the transformation of
the NCAA into a major regulatory body: (1) Walter Byers became executive
director of the NCAA and personally contributed to strengthening the NCAA
and its enforcement division, and (2) the NCAA negotiated its first contract to
televise intercollegiate football, valued in excess of $1 million, opening the door
to increasingly lucrative future television contracts.

In the coming decades, the NCAA gained broader enforcement power but
found itself caught between two critiques. On the one hand, it was criticized for
responding inadequately to the increased commercialization of intercollegiate
athletics, with all its attendant excesses. On the other hand, it was criticized for
unfairly exercising its regulatory authority.

In difficult economic times for higher education in the 1980s, presidents
increasingly found themselves caught between the pressures applied by influential members of boards of trustees and graduates, who often demanded winning athletic programs, and faculty, who feared the rising commercialization
of athletics and its impact on academic values and their institution's budget. In
the mid-1980s, the presidents became increasingly involved in the governance
of intercollegiate athletics through the NCAA, taking some of the power away
from athletics directors and faculty representatives who had previously largely
controlled governance of intercollegiate athletics.

In 1984, in *NCAA v. Board of Regents of the University of Oklahoma*, 468 U.S. 85
(1984), the United States Supreme Court held that the NCAA television plan
for Division I football violated federal antitrust law. This decision ultimately gave
birth to the Bowl Championship Series. *Bowl Games*

In 1989, the Knight Commission, with support in the form of a $2 million
grant from the Knight-Ridder newspaper chain, recommended a series of significant reforms that included more presidential involvement and control and
has also become a major force in offering reform recommendations on a periodic basis. With guidance from groups like the Knight Commission, NCAA college and university presidents began to become increasingly concerned with
cost containment and ensuring that academic values continue to be central to
the governance of intercollegiate athletics. The pressure to produce income
largely through the revenue-producing sports of football and men's basketball (at some institutions other sports produce revenue as well), however, has
made it difficult to ensure academic values. Nevertheless, the presidents and
others have been successful in implementing some reforms that are helping to
increase graduation rates of student-athletes participating in the major revenue-
producing sports.

With the challenge of budgetary issues associated with achieving gender
equity in intercollegiate athletics and proliferating expenses in athletics during difficult economic times, presidents' efforts to gain further control of the
NCAA's governance process intensified and resulted in restrictions within the

NCAA, giving presidents primary control of legislative and administrative processes within the NCAA and conferences. These efforts, in turn, have led to the consolidation of the most profitable university athletics programs into large, major conferences. Conference realignments for monetary and nonmonetary reasons have become increasingly commonplace and are a becoming a significant factor in the second decade of the twenty-first century. See, e.g., Benjamin I. Leibovitz, *Avoiding the Sack: How Nebraska's Departure from the Big 12 Changed College Football and What Athletic Conferences Must Do to Prevent Defection in the Future*, 22 Marq. Sports L. Rev. 675 (2012).

With the move to consolidate and expand major conferences and the commercial growth of the Bowl Championship Series (BCS) in D-I football, serious questions have been raised regarding the role of the BCS and the overcommercialization of big-time college football. Strong support on the part of many university presidents within the NCAA, the Knight Commission, and others for a play-off resulted in a decision during the summer of 2012 to create a four-team national championship play-off for football beginning in 2014. The Knight Commission and others continue to question the commercialization of big-time football and raise concerns regarding how funds from such a play-off will be disbursed. The NCAA has retained control over the broadcasting of "March Madness," the national championship tournament in D-I basketball, which generates hundreds of millions of dollars on an annual basis and is the major source of funding for the NCAA. There is some support for the NCAA regaining control over the BCS to help ensure that funds are used to further student welfare and related concerns.

The last two decades of the twentieth century were active ones for the NCAA. With the meteoric rise in television and related revenues, the commercialization of intercollegiate athletics continued to grow at a pace that placed significant strain on institutions and the NCAA. These commercial pressures, together with rapidly increasing costs and a budgetary crisis related to a downturn in the economy that has affected both public and private institutions, continue to place substantial strain on big-time intercollegiate athletics. These challenges make it more difficult to maintain a viable enforcement process and a level playing field, while ensuring that student-athletes continue to have an opportunity to obtain an education. It is clear, however, these pressures, coupled with the rise of presidential involvement in the governance of intercollegiate athletics, have led to major efforts to implement academic reform in intercollegiate athletics.

In June 2010, the Knight Commission on Intercollegiate Athletics issued a report calling for reform in intercollegiate athletics and recommending:

- Greater transparency in intercollegiate athletics spending, including "comparisons of the growth rate in athletics spending and in education-related spending per institution."
- Creation of an "Academic-Athletics Balance Fund" that draws from Division I Men's Basketball Championship and Bowl Championship Series revenue and is distributed based on teams' academic success.
- Determining teams' eligibility for NCAA championships at the start of each academic year based on a projection of at least a 50 percent graduation rate (according to the NCAA's Graduation Success Rate metric).
- A reduction of eight to ten football scholarships at the Football Bowl Subdivision level.

Gary Brown, *NCAA Backs Knight Commission's Reform Principles*, NCAA News, June 17, 2010. Brown adds, "The Commission's three focus areas—greater transparency in athletics spending, making academics a priority and ensuring student-athletes are students first and foremost—are the cornerstones of a reform movement started by the late NCAA President Myles Brand almost seven years ago." *Id.*

Concerns regarding concussions and other sports-related injuries are giving rise to heightened scrutiny of intercollegiate athletics to ensure that student welfare is in fact being prioritized. Numerous bills have been introduced in the United States Senate and House of Representatives, but none have been enacted. Litigation has been initiated by former college athletes, including Adrian Arrington of Eastern Illinois University, who have filed a class-action lawsuit alleging that the NCAA's failure to protect players from concussions caused them to experience brain injuries. It is not clear whether plaintiffs will prevail against the NCAA; if successful, such a suit could be very costly and is illustrative of mounting concern in this area. See *Arrington v. NCAA* (N.D. Ill., filed Sept. 12, 2011).

On April 27, 2010, the NCAA named another university president, Mark Emmert, a member of the Presidential Task Force on the Future of Intercollegiate Athletics and a member of the Fiscal Responsibility Subcommittee, to succeed President Myles Brand as NCAA president. Because Emmert was the former president of the University of Washington and Louisiana State University (members of BCS conferences with highly commercialized athletic programs), there were initial doubts that he would do much to limit or restructure the commercialized nature of intercollegiate athletics at the D-I level. However, in a speech given on June 22, 2010, to a group of D-II presidents, President Emmert emphasized that his priorities would be to protect "student-athlete well-being and the collegiate model" and stated that intercollegiate athletics should remain "part of the whole academic experience."

Since taking office, Emmert has evidenced an understanding that the NCAA needs to be more transparent. He has responded with a willingness to promote reform within the NCAA in furtherance of academic values and student welfare. For example, he has suggested increasing financial aid for student-athletes and has expressed concerns regarding student-athletes' graduation rates and injuries. In addition, he acted with the Executive Committee of the NCAA to impose very significant sanctions on Penn State University for the alleged failure of its football coach and president, together with other university officials, to exercise institutional control and deal ethically with sex abuse of minors by a former assistant football coach. The NCAA's Committee on Infractions and the Infractions Appeals Committee have also significantly increased sanctions for violations of NCAA rules by Division I universities during President Emmert's tenure.

In October 2012, under President Emmert's leadership, the Division I Board of Directors approved a new rules enforcement process or structure that will enable the NCAA's investigative and adjudication processes to move more quickly, with more severe penalties imposed for serious violations. The new structure provides a four-tier violation hierarchy that ranges from severe rules violations to incidental infractions. The intent of this significant reform is "to develop a culture of compliance" by increasing the responsibility and accountability of coaches and other personnel consistent with the NCAA's commitment to the student-athlete. For a detailed look at this new structure and its purposes, see Gary Brown, *Board Adopts Tougher, More Efficient Enforcement Program*, NCAA .org, Oct. 30, 2012, https://www.ncaa.org/wps/wcm/connect/public/ncaa/ resources/latest+news/2012/october/board+adopts+tougher+more+efficient+ enforcement+program.

In a recent state legislative development in September 2012, the governor of California signed SB 1525, known as the Student Athlete Bill of Rights, into law. Under that legislation, California becomes the first state to mandate financial protections for student-athletes who suffer career-ending injuries in some of the state's top college sports programs. SB 1525 protects athletes at the four universities in California that receive more than $10 million annually in sports media revenue—the University of Southern California, UCLA, Berkeley, and Stanford. Those universities are required to provide academic scholarships to students who lose their athletic scholarships if injured while playing their sport as well as to pay insurance deductibles and health care premiums and cover future medical costs for on-the-field injuries suffered by some student-athletes. Given that only four schools are covered by this legislation, it is unclear whether it will have much impact in California or elsewhere. It does, however, illustrate a willingness of state governments to act to protect student-athletes if the NCAA and others fail to do so.

If the NCAA, entities like the Knight Commission, and even governmental bodies, as was the case in California, continue to act forcefully and push for reforms and strong action to protect student welfare in the face of a highly commercialized culture driven by an apparent "win at all costs" mentality, the second decade of the twenty-first century may be a decade of significant change that advances the interests of student-athletes and academic values.

NOTES AND QUESTIONS

1. *Importance of Historical Context.* Why is it important for a lawyer working in intercollegiate athletics to have a sense of the historical development of regulation in that area? In their thoughtful book, *College Sports and Educational Values: The Game of Life* (Princeton University Press, 2002), James L. Shulman and William G. Bowen assert that "[d]evising ways of regulating recruitment of athletes . . . depends on detailed knowledge of differences in the circumstances and needs of individual schools within [a given league or conference], the predilections of various presidents and boards of trustees, the requirements associated with managing specific sports, and the implications of broader NCAA developments." *Id.* at 288. Are they correct? Calls for regulatory reform within intercollegiate athletics regularly appear in the media. If those calls are not grounded in a sense of the historical development of the regulatory rubric governing intercollegiate athletics, are they likely to be successful? How can history be of assistance in litigation about athletics? See W. Burlette Carter, *Student-Athlete Welfare in a Restructured NCAA*, 2 Va. J. of Sports & L. 1, 9 (2000) (providing a detailed discussion of the history of the NCAA and the multiple concerns that led to its creation).

Shulman and Bowen also raise the following question:

> In embracing intercollegiate athletics, colleges and universities gambled on their ability to "control the beast"—to harness the energies and many good qualities of sports to their own purposes, rather than to be subverted by

them. The open question is whether the gamble was a good one: whether colleges and universities can rise to the challenge of re-balancing objectives and strengthening what we regard as the purer values of athletic competition.

Shulman at 277. In retrospect, do you think that the gamble of "embracing intercollegiate athletics" was a good one? If you were representing a university that was considering dropping its major athletics program, what kinds of issues do you think would have to be addressed? If you were asked for your recommendation, what factors would you want to consider in helping your client, the institution, make the "right" decision?

yes, I think so
• revenue
• education
• enrollment
• facilities

2. *Role of Presidents.* Do you think that presidents of major universities were wise in seeking to gain control of the governing processes in the NCAA? Or would it be better to leave the governance of intercollegiate athletics to athletics departments and their administrators? Given many existing demands on their time, are presidents capable of effectively maintaining control of big-time intercollegiate athletics? *not alone*

— presidents too — STUDENT Athletes, not just athletes

3. *Commercialization and Academic Values.* Many have argued that intercollegiate athletics has become too commercialized and that such commercialization will continue to compromise educational values. Can highly commercialized athletics programs be consistent with academic values? If so, what kinds of regulations can best assure adherence to academic values? Is President Emmert being realistic when he asserts that the NCAA must reclaim academic values and focus on the welfare of student-athletes?

— yes, look @ the students who get academic All-American

sure, more focus on academics.
(i.e. study tables)

C.   DEFINING THE STUDENT-ATHLETE AND UNIVERSITY RELATIONSHIP

1.   Contractual and Related Aspects

The express contractual relationship between a student-athlete and his or her institution arises out of several documents, including the Statement of Financial Assistance, the National Letter of Intent, and university publications such as bulletins and catalogues. These documents largely define the nature of the obligations that student-athletes owe to their colleges or universities and the obligations these educational institutions owe to their student-athletes.

Student-athletes who obtain athletic scholarships sign form documents commonly referred to as a Statement of Financial Assistance. Pursuant to a Statement of Financial Assistance, a college agrees to extend financial aid to student-athletes to the extent of tuition, fees, room, board, and books. The purpose of the financial aid award is to assist and enable a student-athlete to pursue a program of study and to participate in the educational process of the institution. In exchange for the university's commitment, a student-athlete promises to attend a particular college and to participate in athletics. A student-athlete's right to continue to receive financial assistance is contingent on the athlete remaining academically eligible to participate in the institution's athletic program and participating in his or her sport. Student-athletes also promise to comply with the rules and regulations of their teams, institutions, athletic conferences (e.g., ACC and SEC), and the athletic association (e.g., NCAA). As discussed below, a student-athlete's right to continue to receive financial assistance also is contingent on the institution annually renewing its financial commitment to an athlete in instances in which the financial commitment is for less than four years.

The other key document that defines the student-athlete and university relationship is the National Letter of Intent (NLI). By signing an NLI, a prospective student-athlete agrees for a period of one year to attend the institution named in the Letter of Intent (hereinafter referred to as "named institution"). Thereafter, other institutions must cease all recruiting contacts with the student-athlete. Conversely, the named institution may freely contact the student-athlete. The NLI is not effective unless the student-athlete has received a promise in writing from the named institution to provide financial aid for an entire academic year. If the student-athlete complies with NCAA financial aid eligibility requirements and is admitted to the named institution, the athlete is entitled to a scholarship for a minimum of one full academic year from the named institution. A student-athlete who fails to attend the named institution will be penalized by having to serve one academic year in residence and losing one year of athletic eligibility to compete in all sports at the new institution in which he or she enrolls.

Notwithstanding the documents that create the terms of their express contract, litigation has ensued over the scope of the respective obligations that arise out of the parties' relationship. Much of this litigation has revolved around efforts by student-athletes to broaden the scope of the obligations their institutions owe to them. Student-athletes argue that gaps in the contractual relationship, occasioned by the failure of the express contract documents to clearly and specifically state colleges' obligations to them, support the implication of terms into the agreement. It also has been asserted that the Letter of Intent component of this contractual relationship constitutes an adhesion contract.

The text of the NLI may be found at http://www.ncaa.org/wps/wcm/con nect/nli/nli/nli+provisions/index.html. The following excerpts are from some key provisions of the NLI.

THE NATIONAL LETTER OF INTENT

* * *

1. **Initial Enrollment in Four-Year Institution.** This NLI applies only to prospective student-athletes who will be entering four-year institutions for the first time as full-time students. It is also permissible for 4-2-4 transfer student-athletes who are graduating from a two-year to sign the NLI. No prospective student-athlete enrolling at midyear shall sign an NLI, with the exception of midyear two-year college transfer student athletes in football, who must graduate at midyear for this NLI to be valid.

2. **Financial Aid Requirement.** At the time I sign this NLI, I must receive a written offer of athletics financial aid applicable for the entire . . . academic year from the institution named in this document. The offer must list the terms, conditions and amount of the athletics award. . . . In order for this NLI to be valid, my parent/legal guardian and I must sign the NLI and I must also sign the offer of athletics aid . . . prior to submission to the institution named in this document, and any other stated conditions must also be met. If the conditions stated on the financial aid offer are not met, this NLI shall be declared null and void. . . .

4. Basic Penalty. I understand that if I do not attend the institution named in this document for one full academic year, and I enroll in another institution participating in the NLI program, I may not compete in intercollegiate athletics until I have completed one full academic year in residence at the latter institution. Further, I understand I shall be charged with the loss of one season of intercollegiate athletics competition in *all sports*. This is in addition to any seasons of competition expended at any institution. . . .

7. Letter Becomes Null and Void. This NLI shall be declared null and void if any of the following occur:

   a. Admissions Requirement. This NLI shall be declared null and void if the institution named in this document notifies me in writing that I have been denied admission or, by the opening day of classes in the fall . . . , has failed to provide me with written notice of admission, provided I have submitted a complete admission application. . . .

   b. Eligibility Requirements. This NLI shall be declared null and void if, by the opening day of classes in the fall . . . , I have not met (1) the NCAA initial eligibility requirements; (2) the NCAA, conference or institution's requirements for financial aid to student-athletes; or (3) the two-year college transfer requirements, provided I have submitted all necessary documents for eligibility determinations. . . .

   c. One-Year Absence. This NLI shall be declared null and void if I have not attended any institution (two-year or four-year) for at least one academic year, provided my request for athletics financial aid for a subsequent fall term is denied by the signing institution. I may still apply this provision if I initially enrolled in an NLI member institution but have been absent for at least one academic year. . . .

   d. Service in the U.S. Armed Forces. Church Mission. This NLI shall be declared null and void after serving active duty with the armed forces of the United States or on an official church mission for at least twelve (12) months.

   e. Discontinued Sport. This NLI shall be null and void if the institution named in the document discontinues my sport.

   f. Recruiting Rules Violation. If eligibility reinstatement by the NCAA student-athlete reinstatement staff is necessary due to NCAA and/or conference recruiting rules violations, the institution must notify me that I have an option to have the NLI declared null and void due to the rules violation. It is my decision to have the NLI remain valid or to have the NLI declared null and void, permitting me to be recruited and not subject to NLI penalties.

8. Recruiting Ban After Signing. I understand all participating conferences and institutions are obligated to respect my signing and shall cease to recruit me after my signing this NLI. I shall notify any recruiter who contacts me that I have signed an NLI. Once I enroll in the institution named in this document, the NLI Recruiting Ban is no longer in effect, and I shall be governed by applicable NCAA bylaws.

9. 14-Day Signing Deadline. If my parent/legal guardian and I fail to sign this NLI and accompanying offer of athletics financial aid . . . within 14 days after the date of issuance, it will be invalid. In that event, another NLI may be issued within the appropriate signing period. **Signing Deadline (November Only):** The NLI must be signed between the dates of November 9-16. . . .

Additionally, the institution must file the NLI with its conference office within 21 days of the date of final signature, otherwise the NLI is invalid.

10. Statute of Limitations. This NLI is in full force and effect for a period of four years, commencing with the date I sign this NLI. I am subject to the NLI penalty if I do not fulfill the agreement; however, once four years has elapsed, the NLI is no longer binding. . . .

11. Coaching Changes. I understand I have signed this NLI with the institution and not for a particular sport or coach. If the coach leaves the institution or the sports program (e.g., not retained, resigns), I remain bound by the provisions of this NLI. I understand it is not uncommon for a coach to leave his or her coaching position.

even if coach leaves

can't they give a release though?

NOTES AND QUESTIONS

1. *National Letter of Intent Program.* The National Letter of Intent Program, which began in 1964 with seven conferences and eight independent institutions as its members, now includes "more than 620 Division I and II participating institutions." National Letter of Intent, *About the National Letter of Intent (NLI),* http://www.ncaa.org/wps/wcm/connect/nli/nli/about+the+nli/index.html (accessed June 2, 2012). For a detailed discussion of the contractual relationship between student-athletes and their institutions and of the National Letter of Intent see Michael Cozzillio, *The Athletic Scholarship and the College National Letter of Intent: A Contract by Any Other Name,* 35 Wayne L. Rev. 1275 (1989). See also Stacey Meyer, *Unequal Bargaining Power: Making the National Letter of Intent More Equitable,* 15 Marq. Sports L. Rev. 227 (2004) (proposing changes to the National Letter of Intent Program in order to equalize the balance of power in the recruiting process).

to make it not an adhesion contract

2. *Conduct of Coaches.* The propriety of conduct (e.g., revocation of scholarship offers and over-signing) engaged in by coaches during the recruiting process has been subject to increased scrutiny. For helpful discussions of the legal and ethical dimensions of such conduct, see Alfred C. Yen, *Early Scholarship Offers and the NCAA,* 52 Boston Col. L. Rev. 585 (2011) (addressing revocation of scholarship offers); Jonathan D. Bateman, *When the Numbers Don't Add Up: Oversigning in College Football,* 22 Marq. Sports L. Rev. 7 (2011) (discussing over-signing); Jamie U. Nomura, *Refereeing the Recruiting Game: Applying Contract Law to Make the Inter-Collegiate Recruiting Process Fair,* 32 U. Haw. L. Rev. 275 (2009).

PROBLEM 3-1

MY PROBLEM!

Consider the following questions regarding the NLI: *National Letter of Intent*

a. What conditions must be met before the National Letter of Intent effectively commits a student-athlete to a particular institution?

b. A college coach provides a prospective student-athlete with extra benefits totaling $110.00 in violation of NCAA regulations. Will the coach's conduct invalidate the NLI? What factors must be considered?

c. A student-athlete is recruited to participate in a college's intercollegiate wrestling program. After the athlete signs an NLI but before he arrives on campus, the wrestling program is discontinued. Does the discontinuance of the program affect the enforceability of the NLI?

d.   You are a student-athlete whose decision to sign an NLI with a college is influenced by your desire to play for a certain coach. After you sign an NLI and before you arrive on campus, the coach leaves to work at another college. Can you follow the coach to the new institution? What are the consequences of your doing so?

Despite legal theories such as the implied duty of good faith, which provide a basis for implication, as the following cases illustrate, the judiciary has been reluctant to impose obligations on institutions different from or in addition to those expressly delineated in the contract documents.

TAYLOR v. WAKE FOREST UNIVERSITY
191 S.E.2d 379 (N.C. App. 1972)

CAMPBELL, Judge.

[EDS. Gregg Taylor, a student-athlete at Wake Forest University, and his father alleged that the university wrongfully terminated the athlete's football scholarship after he refused to participate in football because of his poor academic performance. Taylor's grade point average for the first semester of his freshman year was 1.0 on a 4.0 scale. As a result of this poor academic showing, Taylor refused, and in fact was ineligible, to play football during the spring term of his freshman year. Taylor's second semester grade point average improved to 1.9, which restored his academic eligibility to participate (at that time, Wake Forest required a 1.35 grade point average after freshman year). He refused, however, to play football during his sophomore year. Following a hearing before the university's Faculty Athletic Committee, Wake Forest terminated Taylor's scholarship after his sophomore year because of his failure to participate in the football program. Taylor, who ultimately received a degree from Wake Forest, sought to recover expenses that he incurred in completing his junior and senior years at the university.]

wants $

Plaintiffs contend that there was a genuine issue as to a material fact and that a jury should determine whether Gregg Taylor acted reasonably and in good faith in refusing to participate in the football program at Wake Forest when such participation interfered with reasonable academic progress.

The plaintiffs' position depends upon a construction of the contractual agreement between plaintiffs and Wake Forest. As stated in the affidavit of George J. Taylor, the position of the plaintiffs is that it was orally agreed between plaintiffs and the representative of Wake Forest that: "[I]n the event of any conflict between educational achievement and athletic involvement, participation in athletic activities could be limited or eliminated to the extent necessary to assure reasonable academic progress." And plaintiffs were to be the judge as to what "reasonable academic progress" constituted.

We do not agree with the position taken by plaintiffs. The scholarship application filed by Gregg Taylor provided: "I agree to maintain eligibility for intercollegiate athletics under both Conference and Institutional rules. Training rules for intercollegiate athletics are considered rules of the Institution, and I agree to abide by them."

Both Gregg Taylor and his father knew that the application was for "Football Grant-In-Aid or A Scholarship," and that the scholarship was "awarded for academic and athletic achievement." It would be a strained construction of the contract that would enable the plaintiffs to determine the "reasonable academic progress" of Gregg Taylor. Gregg Taylor, in consideration of the scholarship award, agreed to maintain his athletic eligibility and this meant both physically and scholastically. As long as his grade average equaled or exceeded the requirements of Wake Forest, he was maintaining his scholastic eligibility for athletics. Participation in and attendance at practice were required to maintain his physical eligibility. When he refused to do so in the absence of any injury or excuse other than to devote more time to studies, he was not complying with his contractual obligations.

The record disclosed that Wake Forest fully complied with its agreement and that Gregg Taylor failed to do so. There was no "genuine issue as to any material fact" and summary judgment was proper.

In determining the terms of the athletic scholarship between a university and its student-athletes, it is important to consider current NCAA rules governing this contractual relationship.

NCAA BYLAW, ARTICLE 15

FINANCIAL AID

15.3   TERMS AND CONDITIONS OF AWARDING INSTITUTIONAL FINANCIAL AID

15.3.3   Period of Institutional Financial Aid Award

15.3.3.1   Period of Award. If a student's athletics ability is considered in any degree in awarding financial aid, such aid shall neither be awarded for a period less than one academic year nor for a period that would exceed the student-athletes five-year period of eligibility. . . . (*Revised: 4/27/06, effective 8/1/2012*).

15.3.4   Reduction and Cancellation During Period of Award

15.3.4.1   Increase Permitted. Institutional financial aid may be increased for any reason at any time.

15.3.4.2   Reduction or Cancellation Permitted. Institutional financial aid based in any degree on athletics ability may be reduced or canceled during the period of the award if the recipient: (*Revised: 1/11/94, 1/10/95*)

(a) Renders himself or herself ineligible for intercollegiate competition;

(b) Fraudulently misrepresents any information on an application, letter of intent or financial aid agreement (see Bylaw 15.3.4.2.3);

(c) Engages in serious misconduct warranting substantial disciplinary penalty (see Bylaw 15.3.4.2.4); or

(d) Voluntarily (on his or her own initiative) withdraws from a sport at any time for personal reasons; however, the recipient's financial aid may not be awarded to another student-athlete in the academic term in which the aid was reduced or canceled. A student-athlete's request for written permission to contact another four-year collegiate institution regarding a possible transfer does not constitute a voluntary withdrawal. (*Revised: 1/10/92, 1/11/94, 1/10/95, 1/9/96, 12/13/05, 9/11/07*)....

15.3.4.3   Reduction or Cancellation Not Permitted. Institutional financial aid based in any degree on athletics ability may not be reduced or canceled during the period of its award: (*Adopted: 1/16/93; Revised: 1/11/94, 12/11/07*)

(a) On the basis of a student-athlete's athletics ability, performance or contribution to a team's success;

(b) Because of an injury, illness, or physical or mental medical condition (except as permitted pursuant to Bylaw 15.3.4.2); or (*Revised: 1/14/08*)

(c) For any other athletics reason. . . .

15.3.5   Renewals and Nonrenewals

15.3.5.1   Institutional Obligation. The renewal of institutional financial aid based in any degree on athletics ability shall be made on or before July 1 prior to the academic year in which it is to be effective. The institution shall promptly notify in writing each student-athlete who received an award the previous academic year and who has eligibility remaining in the sport in which financial aid was awarded the previous academic year (under Bylaw 14.2) whether the grant has been renewed or not renewed for the ensuing academic year. Notification of financial aid renewals and nonrenewals must come from the institution's regular financial aid authority and not from the institution's athletics department. (*Revised: 1/10/95*)

15.3.5.2   Reconsideration of Nonrenewal. It is permissible for an institution that had notified a student-athlete that he or she will not be provided institutional financial aid for the next academic year subsequently to award financial aid to that student-athlete.

The 2011-2012 NCAA Division I Manual can be accessed at http://www.ncaa publications.com/productdownloads/D112.pdf.

NOTES AND QUESTIONS

1year

1. *Duration of Scholarship.* What is the duration of a student-athlete's contract with his or her college or university? Pursuant to legislation the NCAA adopted in 1973, its rules restricted institutions to awarding to student-athletes one-year renewable athletic scholarships. Effective August 2012, however, NCAA-amended legislation permits institutions to award multi-year scholarships of up to five years. 2012-2013 NCAA Division I Manual §15.02.7. See Ray Yasser, *The Case for Reviving the Four-Year Deal*, 86 Tul. L. Rev. 987 (2012) (arguing in favor of awarding multiyear scholarships to student-athletes); Louis Hakim, Note, *The Student-Athlete vs. the Athlete Student: Has the Time Arrived for an Extended-Term Scholarship Contract?*, 2 Va. J. Sports & L. 145 (2000) (arguing the same).

2. *Limiting Discretion in Renewing Scholarships.* What limitations, if any, are imposed on the discretion afforded institutions to refuse to renew a student-

athlete's scholarship? Are these limitations sufficient? Does the discretion afforded institutions encourage particular forms of conduct by coaches?

3. *Incorporation by Reference.* It is important to note that NCAA and university athletic conference rules are incorporated as terms of a student-athlete's financial aid agreement with a university. For example, a student-athlete must comply with the NCAA's drug testing program and its amateurism rules (which, among other things, prohibit the receipt of any "extra benefits" from university employees or representatives of its athletics interests (NCAA Bylaw 16.02.3), or any "preferential treatment" because of one's athletics reputation or skill (NCAA Bylaw 12.1.2.1.6)). Student-athletes who violate NCAA (or conference) rules risk losing their eligibility to participate in intercollegiate athletes and athletic scholarships.

ROSS v. CREIGHTON UNIVERSITY
957 F.2d 410 (7th Cir. 1992)

RIPPLE, Circuit Judge.

Kevin Ross filed suit against Creighton University (Creighton or the University) for negligence and breach of contract arising from Creighton's alleged failure to educate him. The district court dismissed Mr. Ross' complaint for failure to state a claim. For the following reasons we affirm in part and reverse in part the judgment of the district court.

I. BACKGROUND

A. FACTS

In the spring of 1978, Mr. Ross was a promising senior basketball player at Wyandotte High School in Kansas City, Kansas. Sometime during his senior year in high school, he accepted an athletic scholarship to attend Creighton and to play on its varsity basketball team.

Creighton is an academically superior university. Mr. Ross comes from an academically disadvantaged background. At the time of his enrollment at Creighton, Mr. Ross was at an academic level far below that of the average Creighton student. For example, he scored in the bottom fifth percentile of college-bound seniors taking the American College Test, while the average freshman admitted to Creighton with him scored in the upper twenty-seven percent. According to the complaint, Creighton realized Mr. Ross' academic limitations when it admitted him, and, to induce him to attend and play basketball, Creighton assured Mr. Ross that he would receive sufficient tutoring so that he "would receive a meaningful education while at CREIGHTON." . . .

Mr. Ross attended Creighton from 1978 until 1982. During that time he maintained a D average and acquired 96 of the 128 credits needed to graduate. However, many of these credits were in courses such as Marksmanship and Theory of Basketball, and did not count towards a university degree. Mr. Ross alleges that he took these courses on the advice of Creighton's Athletic Department, and that the department also employed a secretary to read his assignments and prepare and type his papers. Mr. Ross also asserts that Creighton failed to provide him with sufficient and competent tutoring that it had promised.

When he left Creighton, Mr. Ross had the overall language skills of a fourth grader and the reading skills of a seventh grader. Consequently, Mr. Ross enrolled, at Creighton's expense, for a year of remedial education at the Westside Preparatory School in Chicago. At Westside, Mr. Ross attended classes with grade school children. He later entered Roosevelt University in Chicago, but was forced to withdraw because of a lack of funds. In July 1987, Mr. Ross suffered what he terms a "major depressive episode," during which he barricaded himself in a Chicago motel room and threw furniture out the window. . . . To Mr. Ross, this furniture "symbolized" Creighton employees who had wronged him. . . .

B. DISTRICT COURT PROCEEDINGS

Creighton moved to dismiss the complaint under Federal Rule of Civil Procedure 12(b)(6), and the district court granted this motion. . . .

II. ANALYSIS

B. THE NEGLIGENCE CLAIMS

Mr. Ross advances three separate theories of how Creighton was negligent towards him: educational malpractice for not educating him, a new tort of "negligent admission" to an educational institution, and negligent infliction of emotional distress. We believe that, on the facts of this case, Illinois law would deny Mr. Ross recovery on all three theories.

1. Educational Malpractice

Illinois courts have never ruled on whether a tort cause of action exists against an institution for educational malpractice. However, the overwhelming majority of states that have considered this type of claim have rejected it. (citation omitted.) Only Montana allows these claims to go forward, and its decision was based on state statutes that place a duty of care on educators, a circumstance not present here. *B.M. v. State*, 200 Mont. 58, 649 P.2d 425, 427-28 (Mont. 1982).

Courts have identified several policy concerns that counsel against allowing claims for educational malpractice. First, there is the lack of a satisfactory standard of care by which to evaluate an educator. . . . Theories of education are not uniform, and "different but acceptable scientific methods of academic training [make] it unfeasible to formulate a standard by which to judge the conduct of those delivering the services." *Swidryk v. St. Michael's Medical Center*, 201 N.J. Super. 601, 493 A.2d 641, 643 (N.J. Super. Ct. Law Div. 1985) (citing *Peter W. v. San Francisco Unified School Dist.*, 60 Cal. App. 3d 814, 131 Cal. Rptr. 854, 859 (Ct. App. 1976)). Second, inherent uncertainties exist in this type of case about the cause and nature of damages. . . . "Factors such as the student's attitude, motivation, temperament, past experience and home environment may all play an essential and immeasurable role in learning." *Donohue v. Copiague Union Free School Dist.*, 47 N.Y.2d 440, 418 N.Y.S.2d 375, 391 N.E.2d 1352, 1355 (N.Y. 1979) (Wachtler, J., concurring). Consequently, it may be a "practical impossibility [to] prov[e] that the alleged malpractice of the teacher proximately caused the learning deficiency of the plaintiff student." *Id.* A third reason for denying this cause of action is the potential it presents for a flood of litigation against schools. . . . As the district court noted, "education is a service rendered on an immensely greater scale than other professional services." *Ross v. Creighton Univ.*,

740 F. Supp. 1319, 1329 (N.D. Ill. 1990). The sheer number of claims that could arise if this cause of action were allowed might overburden schools. *Id.* This consideration also suggests that a common-law tort remedy may not be the best way to deal with the problem of inadequate education. *Id.* A final reason courts have cited for denying this cause of action is that it threatens to embroil the courts into overseeing the day-to-day operations of schools. . . . This oversight might be particularly troubling in the university setting where it necessarily implicates considerations of academic freedom and autonomy. . . .

We believe that the Illinois Supreme Court would find the experience of other jurisdictions persuasive and, consequently, that these policy considerations are compelling. Consequently, the Illinois Supreme Court would refuse to recognize the tort of educational malpractice. We therefore affirm the district court's dismissal of Mr. Ross' claim based on that theory.

2. *"Negligent Admission"*

In his complaint, Mr. Ross alleges that Creighton owed him a duty "to recruit and enroll only those students reasonably qualified and able to academically perform at CREIGHTON." . . . He then contends that Creighton breached this duty by admitting him, not informing him of how unprepared he was for studies there, and then not providing tutoring services or otherwise enabling him to receive a meaningful education. As a result, Mr. Ross underwent undue stress, which brought about, among other things, the incident at the motel.

We believe that Illinois would reject this claim for "negligent admission" for many of the same policy reasons that counsel against recognizing a claim for educational malpractice. First, this cause of action would present difficult, if not insuperable, problems to a court attempting to define a workable duty of care. . . . Mr. Ross suggests that the University has a duty to admit only students who are "reasonably qualified" and able to perform academically. However, determining who is a "reasonably qualified student" necessarily requires subjective assessments of such things as the nature and quality of the defendant institution and the intelligence and educability of the plaintiff. Such decisions are not open to ready determination in the judicial process. Second, such a cause of action might unduly interfere with a university's admissions decisions, to the detriment of students and society as a whole. *Ross*, 740 F. Supp. at 1330. As the district court noted, if universities and colleges faced tort liability for admitting an unprepared student, schools would be encouraged to admit only those students who were certain to succeed in the institution. The opportunities of marginal students to receive an education therefore would likely be lessened. *Id.* Also, the academic practice of promoting diversity by admitting students from disadvantaged backgrounds might also be jeopardized. . . .

3. *Negligent Infliction of Emotional Distress*

Finally, Mr. Ross argues that his allegations that Creighton wrongfully admitted him, and then caused him emotional harm, present a claim under the traditional tort theory of negligent infliction of emotional distress. In *Corgan v. Muehling*, 158 Ill. Dec. 489, 493, 574 N.E.2d 602, 606 (Ill. 1991), the Illinois Supreme Court made clear that the "essential question" when evaluating whether a complaint states a claim for negligent infliction of emotional distress "is whether the plaintiff properly alleged negligence on the part of the defendant." We have already held that policy reasons would compel Illinois not to recognize Mr. Ross' claims for educational malpractice and negligent admission.

We believe that these same concerns would cause it to refuse to recognize in this situation a claim for negligent infliction of emotional distress.

C.   THE CONTRACT CLAIMS

In counts two and three of his complaint, Mr. Ross alleges that Creighton breached an oral or a written contract that it had with him. When read as a totality, these allegations fairly allege that Creighton agreed, in exchange for Mr. Ross' promise to play on its basketball team, to allow him an opportunity to participate, in a meaningful way, in the academic program of the University despite his deficient academic background. The complaint further alleges, when read as a totality, that Creighton breached this contract and denied Mr. Ross any real opportunity to participate in and benefit from the University's academic program when it failed to perform five commitments made to Ross: (1) "to provide adequate and competent tutoring services," (2) "to require [Mr. Ross] to attend tutoring sessions," (3) to afford Mr. Ross "a reasonable opportunity to take full advantage of tutoring services," (4) to allow Mr. Ross to red-shirt, and (5) to provide funds to allow Mr. Ross to complete his college education. . . .

[π failed to perform 5 commitments]

It is held generally in the United States that the "basic legal relation between a student and a private university or college is contractual in nature. The catalogues, bulletins, circulars, and regulations of the institution made available to the matriculant become a part of the contract." *Zumbrun v. University of Southern California*, 25 Cal. App. 3d 1, 101 Cal. Rptr. 499, 504 (Ct. App. 1972) (collecting cases from numerous states). Indeed, there seems to be "no dissent" from this proposition. *Wickstrom v. North Idaho College*, 111 Idaho 450, 452, 725 P.2d 155, 157 (Idaho 1986) (quoting *Peretti v. Montana*, 464 F. Supp. 784, 786 (D. Mont. 1979), *rev'd on other grounds*, 661 F.2d 756 (9th Cir. 1981)). As the district court correctly noted, Illinois recognizes that the relationship between a student and an educational institution is, in some of its aspects, contractual. *See Steinberg v. Chicago Medical School*, 69 Ill. 2d 320, 13 Ill. Dec. 699, 371 N.E.2d 634 (Ill. 1977) (agreement that medical school application would be evaluated according to the criteria described by the medical school in its literature). . . . It is quite clear, however, that Illinois would not recognize all aspects of a university-student relationship as subject to remedy through a contract action. *DeMarco* makes the point quite clearly. "A contract between a private institution and a student confers duties upon both parties which cannot be arbitrarily disregarded and may be judicially enforced." *DeMarco*, 352 N.E.2d at 361-62. However, "a decision of the school authorities relating to the academic qualification of the students will not be reviewed. . . . Courts are not qualified to pass an opinion as to the attainments of a student . . . and . . . courts will not review a decision of the school authorities relating to academic qualifications of the students." *Id.*

There is no question, we believe, that Illinois would adhere to the great weight of authority and bar any attempt to repackage an educational malpractice claim as a contract claim. As several courts have noted, the policy concerns that preclude a cause of action for educational malpractice apply with equal force to bar a breach of contract claim attacking the general quality of an education. . . .

To state a claim for breach of contract, the plaintiff must do more than simply allege that the education was not good enough. Instead, he must point to an identifiable contractual promise that the defendant failed to honor. Thus, as was suggested in *Paladino*, if the defendant took tuition money and then provided no education, or alternately, promised a set number of hours of instruction and then failed to deliver, a breach of contract action may be available. *Paladino*, 454

[when it is available]

N.Y.S.2d at 873; *see also Zumbrun*, 25 Cal. App. 3d 1, 101 Cal. Rptr. 499 (breach of contract action allowed against university when professor declined to give lectures and final exam, and all students received a grade of "B"). Similarly, a breach of contract action might exist if a student enrolled in a course explicitly promising instruction that would qualify him as a journeyman, but in which the fundamentals necessary to attain that skill were not even presented. *See Wickstrom*, 725 P.2d at 156-58. In these cases, the essence of the plaintiff's complaint would not be that the institution failed to perform adequately a promised educational service, but rather that it failed to perform that service at all. Ruling on this issue would not require an inquiry into the nuances of educational processes and theories, but rather an objective assessment of whether the institution made a good faith effort to perform on its promise.

We read Mr. Ross' complaint to allege more than a failure of the University to provide him with an education of a certain quality. Rather, he alleges that the University knew that he was not qualified academically to participate in its curriculum. Nevertheless, it made a specific promise that he would be able to participate in a meaningful way in that program because it would provide certain specific services to him. Finally, he alleges that the University breached its promise by reneging on its commitment to provide those services and, consequently, effectively cutting him off from any participation in and benefit from the University's academic program. To adjudicate such a claim, the court would not be required to determine whether Creighton had breached its contract with Mr. Ross by providing deficient academic services. Rather, its inquiry would be limited to whether the University had provided any real access to its academic curriculum at all.

Accordingly, we must disagree respectfully with our colleague in the district court as to whether the contract counts of the complaint can be dismissed at the pleadings stage. In our view, the allegations of the complaint are sufficient to warrant further proceedings. We emphasize, however, the narrow ground of our disagreement. We agree—indeed we emphasize—that courts should not "take on the job of supervising the relationship between colleges and student-athletes or creating in effect a new relationship between them." *Ross*, 740 F. Supp. at 1332. We also recognize a formal university-student contract is rarely employed and, consequently, "the general nature and terms of the agreement are usually implied, with specific terms to be found in the university bulletin and other publications; custom and usages can also become specific terms by implication." *Wickstrom*, 725 P.2d at 157 (quoting *Peretti*, 464 F. Supp. at 786). Nevertheless, we believe that the district court can adjudicate Mr. Ross' specific and narrow claim that he was barred from *any* participation in and benefit from the University's academic program without second-guessing the professional judgment of the University faculty on academic matters. . . .

Accordingly, the judgment of the district court is affirmed in part and reversed and remanded in part for proceedings consistent with this opinion.

AFFIRMED in part, REVERSED in part and REMANDED.

[EDS. Ross eventually settled his lawsuit for $30,000.]

PROBLEM 3-2

Rogers, a high school student-athlete, and his parents were considering athletic scholarship offers from several major universities for Rogers to play intercollegiate basketball when they arrived at Big-Time University for an official recruiting visit. Big-Time's head men's basketball coach, Blum, gave Rogers and his parents a tour of Big-Time campus during their visit. As Blum drove them by Big-Time's law school, Rogers stated, "I want to be a lawyer." In response, Blum stated, "I can get you into Big-Time's law school; I can also make certain that your law school tuition is paid for." Blum's statements sold Rogers on attending Big-Time. At the beginning of his senior year, Rogers applied to Big-Time's law school as well as others. Rogers requested that Blum deliver on his promise to get him into Big-Time's highly competitive law school. Blum informed Rogers that there was nothing he could do. Does Rogers have any cause of action against Blum?

NOTES AND QUESTIONS

1. *Analysis of* Ross. In rejecting Ross's educational malpractice claim, the district and appellate courts relied on the reasoning adopted in cases in which courts have uniformly rejected such suits by nonathlete students against colleges and universities. See, e.g., *Vurimindi v. Fuqua Sch. of Bus.*, 435 Fed. Appx. 129, 133 (3d Cir. 2011) (refusing to recognize contract claims based on general complaints regarding the quality of the education a student received). But see Hazel G. Beh, *Student Versus University: The University's Implied Obligations of Good Faith and Fair Dealing*, 59 Md. L. Rev. 183, 184 (2000) (arguing all students, under limited circumstances, should be able to sue their institutions for educational malpractice).

   In *Ross*, was the court's reliance on such cases justified? Is the student-athlete's relationship with his or her university distinguishable from the nonathlete student's relationship with his or her university? Commentators disagree as to whether student-athletes should be able to sue their institutions for educational malpractice based on the unique character of their relationships with colleges and universities. Harold B. Hilborn, *Student Athletes and Judicial Inconsistency: Establishing a Duty to Educate as a Means of Fostering Meaningful Reform of Intercollegiate Athletics*, 89 Nw. U. L. Rev. 741 (1995); Timothy Davis, *Examining Educational Malpractice Jurisprudence: Should a Cause of Action Be Created for Student-Athletes?*, 69 Denv. U. L. Rev. 57 (1992); Derek Q. Johnson, Note, *Educating Misguided Student Athletes: An Application of Contract Theory*, 85 Colum. L. Rev. 96 (1985).

   Some authors argue that an imbalance exists in the student-athlete/university relationship that results in an unfair advantage to the institutions. Do you agree? See Rodney K. Smith and Neil Millhiser, *The BCS and Big-Time Intercollegiate Football Receive an "F": Reforming A Failed System*, 2 Wake Forest J.L. & Pol'y 45 (2012); Amy C. McCormick and Robert A. McCormick, *Race and Interest Convergence in NCAA Sports*, 2 Wake Forest J.L. & Pol'y 17 (2012); Michael J. Riella, Notes, *Leveling the Playing Field: Applying the Doctrine of Unconscionability and Condition Precedent to Effectuate Student-Athlete Intent Under the National Letter of Intent*, 43 Wm. & Mary L. Rev. 2181 (2002); Rodney K. Smith and Robert D. Walker, *From Inequity to Opportunity: Keeping the Promises Made to Big-Time Intercollegiate Student Athletes*, 1 Nev. L.J. 160 (2001). See *Gulf South Conference v. Boyd*, 369 So. 2d 553 (Ala. 1979) ("The individual athlete has no voice or participation in the formulation or interpretation of these rules and regulations governing his scholarship; even though these materially control his conduct on and off the field. Thus in some circumstances the college athlete may be placed in an *unequal bargaining position*"). For a comprehensive economic analysis of the student-athlete/university relationship, see Ahmed E. Taha, *Are College Athletes Economically Exploited?*, 2 Wake Forest J.L. & Pol'y 69 (2012).

2. *Student-Athlete Stipends.* The issue of whether student-athletes should be paid stipends often arises in discussions of whether equity resides in the relationship. In 2012, the Division I Board of Directors reaffirmed its support for a controversial measure that would permit schools to pay student-athletes a $2,000 miscellaneous expense allowance. Following objection from many institutions, rather than approve the measure outright, the Board instructed the NCAA's Student-Athlete Well-Being working group to develop a recommendation for the board's approval after taking into account concerns relating to Title IX, student-athlete financial need, and the potential for institutions to stockpile. Is allowing such a payment sound public policy? What problems might flow from instituting such a policy? For differing perspectives on whether student-athletes should receive cash payments for their services, see Mary Grace Miller, *The NCAA and the Student Athlete: Reform Is on the Horizon*, 46 U. Rich. L. Rev. 1141 (2012) (advocating the implementation of a pay scheme for student-athletes emulous of the Olympic model); Taylor Branch, *The Shame of College Sports*, Atlantic Magazine, Oct. 2011, http://www.theatlantic.com/magazine/archive/2011/10/the-shame-of-college-sports/8643/2/?single_page=true (arguing that despite prevailing concerns regarding the preservation of amateurism, student-athletes are being taken advantage of and the commercialization of intercollegiate athletics requires compensation for these athletes); Seth Davis, *Should College Athletes Be Paid? Why, They Already Are*, Sports Illustrated, Sept. 21 2011, http://sportsillustrated.cnn.com/2011/writers/seth_davis/09/21/Branch.rebuttal/index.html (opines that payment for tuition, room, board, books, and so forth is payment enough for student-athletes, and they need not be compensated more than they are); Kristi Dosh, *The Problems with Paying College Athletes*, Forbes, June 9, 2011, http://www.forbes.com/sites/sportsmoney/2011/06/09/the-problems-with-paying-college-athletes/ (identifies concerns related to paying student-athletes, including which athletes will be paid, how will they be paid, how much will they be paid, and Title IX implications of paying college athletes).

3. *Disclosure Laws.* Student-athletes and their parents are often unaware of the terms and conditions of athletes' contracts with their schools. For example, many athletes and their parents incorrectly assume that scholarships are guaranteed for a four-year period as long as the athlete remains academically and athletically eligible. On September 30, 2010, Governor Schwarzenegger signed into law the California Student-Athletes' Right to Know Act that requires university coaches who recruit athletes in California to disclose institutional and NCAA policies regarding payment of student-athlete medical expenses, scholarship renewals, and transfers to other institutions. The goal of this act is to provide increased disclosure to student-athletes to help them make wise choices. West's Ann. Cal. Educ. Code §67365 (West, Westlaw through Ch. 22 of 2012 Reg. Sess.). Connecticut has adopted similar legislation. Conn. Gen. Stat. Ann. §10a-55k (West, Westlaw through Public Acts approved on or before May 14, 2012); Kathleen Megan, *Legislators Hear Testimony on Need to Spell Out Details on Athletic Scholarships, Medical Expenses*, Hartford Courant, Feb. 9, 2011, http://articles.courant

.com/2011-02-09/news/hc-college-sport-scholarships-0209-20110208_1_ athletic-scholarship-athletic-recruiters-national-college-players-association. Other states are considering whether to adopt similar legislation. *Laws Force Disclosure of Scholarships' Fine Print*, CBSSports.com, June 25, 2011, http:// www.cbssports.com/collegefootball/story/15267318/laws-force-disclosure-of-scholarships-fine-print.

Is the adoption of disclosure laws by individual states wise public policy? Is a national law with uniform requirements needed?

[handwritten: I think so — for injury.]

4. *Express Promises to Provide Academic Support*. Although the court rejected Ross's breach-of-contract claim to the extent it merely restated a tort claim for educational malpractice, what is the narrow exception to the general rule of no institutional liability for a student-athlete's substandard or failing academic performance that the court recognized? Related to this exception, what factual issue was to be determined on remand? See Timothy Davis, *Absence of Good Faith: Defining a University's Educational Obligation to Student-Athletes*, 28 Hous. L. Rev. 743, 783 (1991) (questioning judicial reliance on the academic abstention doctrine in the university/student-athlete context).

5. *Implied Contract Terms*. Another leading case, *Jackson v. Drake University*, 778 F. Supp. 1490 (S.D. Iowa 1991), reveals the reluctance of courts to imply terms into the agreement as a means of expanding the obligations that a university owes to student-athletes. In *Jackson*, a basketball player alleged that the coaching staff of the men's basketball team engaged in improper conduct, such as failing to provide adequate tutoring and counseling and requiring him to turn in plagiarized work, which undermined the athlete's ability to play basketball and to succeed academically. According to Jackson, the coaching staff's conduct amounted to a breach of contract because "the express contract between him and Drake implicitly granted him the right to an educational opportunity and the right to play basketball for a Division I school." *Id.* at 1493. The court held that "the financial aid agreements do not implicitly contain a right to play basketball." *Id.* The court also refused to impose an implied obligation on Drake to provide Jackson with an educational opportunity. Do athletes have a reasonable expectation that, as long as they follow team rules and remain academically eligible, they will be allowed to participate on the intercollegiate athletic team for which they were recruited? Does judicial reticence to imply terms into the contractual relationship as a means of policing the relationship perpetuate an imbalance in the student-athlete/university relationship? What conceptualization of contract law is reflected by judicial refusal to imply terms into the student-athlete/university relationship?

[handwritten: A lot of MVC schools]

[handwritten: coaches encouraged]

[handwritten: this would be a slippery slope!]

6. *Discontinuation of Sports*. Student-athletes also have been unsuccessful in their attempts to imply into their agreement limitations on an institution's discretion to discontinue a particular sport. In *Soderbloom v. Yale University*, 1992 Conn. Super. LEXIS 256, student-athletes alleged that termination of the wrestling program amounted to a breach of contract "to provide a varsity wrestling program as part of the four-year undergraduate educational program." *Id.* at *8. The court rejected the plaintiffs' contention that such a contract arose by implication from the contract documents, including university publications and written and oral communications of the wrestling coach. Accord *Cooper v. Peterson*, 626 N.Y.S.2d 432 (N.Y. Sup. 1995) (rejecting contract as basis for enjoining university from discontinuing wrestling program). See also *Equity in Athletics, Inc. v. Dep't of Educ.*, 675 F. Supp. 2d 660

[handwritten: What about NLI?]

(W.D. VA. 2009) (discontinuance of seven men's sports and three women's sports in an effort to bring its athletic program into compliance with Title IX did not impinge on the substantive and procedural due process rights of the student-athletes). The question presented in these cases implicates the broader topic of whether student-athletes possess a property interest in participating in intercollegiate athletics, which is discussed *infra*.

7. *Oral Promises*. In *Fortay v. University of Miami*, 1994 U.S. Dist. LEXIS 1865, a student-athlete maintained that his contract with the University of Miami (UM) impliedly obligated the university to provide the guidance necessary to allow him to develop his football talents. He asserted that oral promises by then outgoing head coach Jimmy Johnson, his successor coach, and other UM officials supported a breach of contract claim. These promises allegedly included representations that UM would provide guidance that would enable Fortay to develop his football skills, that UM would not recruit other quarterbacks, and that Fortay would be UM's starting quarterback by his third year. Adhering to precedent from other jurisdictions, a federal district court ruled that the Letter of Intent and other contract documents did not give rise to the alleged implied obligations. Accord *Lesser v. Neosho County Community Coll.*, 741 F. Supp. 854, 865 (D. Kan. 1990) (refusing to imply promise that plaintiff would have position on baseball team). The district court ruled, however, that Fortay alleged facts sufficient to support a breach of an oral contract claim. The district court also refused to dismiss Fortay's negligent hiring and supervision claims stemming from the conduct of a Miami athletic official that pertained to Fortay and other athletes' involvement in a Pell Grant scandal.

The limits of a student-athlete's ability to rely on oral representations were more recently addressed in *Giuliani v. Duke University*, 2010 WL 1292321 (M.D.N.C.) (March 30, 2010). The late Duke golf coach, Rod Myers, recruited plaintiff to play golf at the university. Plaintiff asserted that his decision to enroll at Duke was strongly influenced by Myers's promises of "life-time access" to Duke's training facilities and the opportunity that would be afforded plaintiff to compete with his teammates to earn spots in NCAA tournaments. In the spring of 2007, Coach Myers unexpectedly passed away, and Orin Daniel Vincent took over as head coach. On February 11, 2008, Vincent announced that he was immediately and indefinitely suspending plaintiff's eligibility to participate in Duke's athletic program. Plaintiff filed claims against Duke and Vincent asserting breach of contract, breach of the covenant of good faith and fair dealing, promissory estoppel, and tortious interference with contract. In dismissing all of plaintiff's claims, the federal district court judge held that neither Myers's oral statements nor the provisions of the university's policy manuals were enforceable as binding contracts. With respect to Myers's alleged statements giving rise to a contract, the court concluded the evidence failed to establish the mutual assent necessary to create a binding contract. It also concluded that the plaintiff failed to identify a contract that specifically incorporated Duke's policy manuals by reference.

What impediments may confront a student-athlete who seeks to recover for breach of an oral promise? In *Searles v. Trustees of St. Joseph's College*, 695 A.2d 1206 (Me. 1997), a student-athlete allegedly suffered permanent injuries while playing basketball for his college. Searles sought to recover, among other things, reimbursement for medical expenses. He alleged that

St. Joseph's orally agreed to pay his medical bills if he continued to play on the school's basketball team. In granting defendant summary judgment on this contract claim, the court concluded that a mere promise to pay for medical expenses would not suffice. "In order to be legally operative and to create a power of acceptance, it is necessary that the offer shall contain all the terms of the contract to be made. It is not enough for one party to promise to do something." *Id.* at 1211. See *Reed v. University of North Dakota*, 589 N.W.2d 880, 883 (N.D. 1999) (rejecting scholarship student-athlete's claim of breach of oral contract to pay medical expenses because of plaintiff's failure to identify breach of a specific provision that conditioned his agreement to play hockey on provision of health care by the university; moreover, the Letter of Intent contains no specific provision that imposes such an obligation); *Hartman v. Univ. of Tennessee*, 1998 Tenn. App. LEXIS 620 (recognizing validity of applying parol evidence rule in context of contractual relationship between student-athletes and universities); *Cooper v. Peterson*, 626 N.Y.S.2d 432 (1995) (relying in part on statute of frauds as a basis for dismissing student-athlete's breach of contract claim).

8. *Promissory Estoppel.* In *Hall v. NCAA*, 985 F. Supp. 782 (N.D. Ill. 1997), the court did not reject the viability of promissory estoppel in the student-athlete/university context. It rejected plaintiff's claim, however, based on his failure to offer evidence sufficient to establish the elements of promissory estoppel, which the court stated consists of (1) an unambiguous promise; (2) reliance on that promise by the promisee; (3) of a type that was expected and foreseeable to the promisor; and (4) promisee actually relied to his or her detriment on the promise. *Id.* at 796.

   Similarly in *Williams v. University of Cincinnati*, 752 N.E. 2d 367 (Ohio Misc. 2001), an Ohio court did not reject promissory estoppel as a viable theory but dismissed the promissory estoppel claim of a former basketball player at the University of Cincinnati after evidence indicated that he was ruled ineligible "because of his own failures, not because of any . . . unfulfilled promises." *Id.* at 377. See Jamie U. Nomura, *Refereeing the Recruiting Game: Applying Contract Law to Make the Inter-Collegiate Recruiting Process Fair*, 32 U. Haw. L. Rev. 275 (2009) (arguing in favor of promissory estoppel as a basis for enforcing oral promises made by coaches to prospective student-athletes).

9. *Alleged Characterizations of the University/Student-Athlete Relationship.*
   a. *Fiduciary Relationship.* Is the student-athlete relationship with his or her institution imbued with the characteristics of a fiduciary relationship? Illustrations of fiduciary relationships that arise as a matter of law include those between a husband and wife and a minister and parishioner. An example of such a relationship that is the product of express agreement is the principal/agent relationship. The key characteristics of a fiduciary relationship are trust, confidence, and dominance by one party over the other. Thus, a "fiduciary relation arises where 'one person reposes trust or confidence or reliance in another' and where 'there is established an inequality of footing between the parties.' In these situations, courts feel justified in holding the more powerful party to a higher standard of care." Alvin L. Goldman, *The University and the Liberty of Its Students—a Fiduciary Theory*, 54 Ky. L.J. 643, 667 (1966). Are such features present in the student-athlete/university relationship? See Richard Salgado, *A Fiduciary Duty to Teach Those Who Don't Want to Learn: The Potentially*

Dangerous Oxymoron of "College Sports," 17 Seton Hall J. Sports & Ent. L. 135 (2007) (arguing that under certain limited circumstances a fiduciary relationship exists between student-athletes and their institutions); Timothy Davis, *Student-Athlete Prospective Economic Interests: Contractual Dimensions,* 19 T. Marshall L. Rev. 585, 618-623 (1994) (considering whether characteristics attendant to the student-athlete/university relationship warrant extending fiduciary concepts into the relationship).

Hendricks v. Clemson University, 578 S.E.2d 711 (S.C. 2003), arose out of an academic advisor's erroneous advice regarding course selection that contributed to a student-athlete's ineligibility to play baseball. Hendricks sued Clemson University alleging, *inter alia,* breach of fiduciary duty; the South Carolina Tort Claims Act shielded Clemson, a public university, from negligence liability. Noting that historically the imposition of fiduciary duties have been reserved for legal or business settings in which one entrusts money to another, the South Carolina Supreme Court refused to recognize the relationship between a student and a university academic advisor as fiduciary in nature. See also *Knelman v. Middlebury Coll.,* 2012 WL 4481470 (D. Vt. 2012) (concluding it is highly unlikely that the Vermont Supreme Court would recognize a fiduciary relationship between a student-athlete and university); *Brown v. Compton Unified Sch. Dist.,* 80 Cal. Rptr. 2d 171 (Cal. App. 1998) (rejecting negligence and breach of contract claims asserted by high school student who alleged inaccurate advice of high guidance counselor prevented him from satisfying NCAA eligibility requirements and led to the revocation of his athletic scholarship).

b. *Respondeat Superior.* Courts have also addressed the question of whether student-athletes' relationships with their institution can give rise to, on the basis of respondeat superior, institutional liability for acts committed by student-athletes. In *Hanson v. Kynast,* 494 N.E.2d 1091 (Ohio 1986), the court answered this question in the negative. Hanson, a lacrosse player for Ohio State University, sustained serious injuries after he was thrown to the ground by Kynast, a player on Ashland University's lacrosse team. In a lawsuit against Kynast and Ashland, Hanson turned to respondeat superior as a basis for holding Ashland responsible for Kynast's conduct. In rejecting this theory, the court articulated the rule that a master and servant or a principal and agent relationship exists only where one party exercises control of the other whose actions are directed toward attaining an objective sought by the master or principal. It found that a student is a buyer of educational services that he or she retains for his or her own benefit and is therefore not an agent of the institution. On the question of control the court concluded:

> [A] student who attends a university of his choice, receives no scholarship or compensation, voluntarily becomes a member of the university lacrosse team that engages in intercollegiate contests with other universities for which games no attendance fee is charged, who purchases his own equipment and who receives instructions from a coach while preparing for and playing such games, but is not otherwise controlled by the coach, and who participates in the games as a part of his total educational experience while attending school, is not an agent of the university at the time he is playing the game of lacrosse.

Id. at 1096. Does this rationale apply to student-athletes who have an athletic scholarship?

c.   *Special Relationship.* In addition to tort claims asserting educational malpractice, student-athletes have argued that their "special relationship" with colleges justifies the imposition of a legal duty to protect them from foreseeable, unreasonable risks of physical harm on the playing field, an issue discussed more fully in Chapter 11.

In *McFadyen v. Duke University*, 786 F. Supp. 2d 887 (M.D.N.C. 2011), three lacrosse players were accused of the sexual assault and rape of a woman who attended a party hosted by the three players. Throughout its investigation, Duke University released some of the players' financial records and unredacted reports of the players' transaction activities on their university-issued cards to the Durham Police. On several occasions, the university also advised the players that it would not be necessary to seek counsel. The players asserted that the relationship they had with the university was one of special trust and confidence, which Duke had not maintained. *Id.* at 986. The court held that there is no fiduciary duty between a student and university administrators. *Id.* The court further held that the Family Education Rights and Privacy Act (FERPA) does not establish a fiduciary relationship between a student and a university. *Id.* at 987. The players further asserted that the university was negligent by failing to properly advise them to seek counsel and failing to provide a supervisor to oversee the investigations. *Id.* at 995. The court held that even though a special relationship existed between the university and the lacrosse players as student-athletes, the duty of cared owed to the players is limited to the context of athletics and does not extend to all facets of student life. *Id.* at 997. The court then determined that there is generally no duty of care between a university advisor and a student for academic advice or guidance. *Id.* Accordingly, the court held that, where an advisor voluntarily undertakes to provide a student with advice, such advice gives rise to an actionable tort claim of negligence only if it leads to a student-athlete's physical injury. *Id.* at 998. Otherwise, "administrators and other advisors should be free to communicate and advise students without creating potential tort liability, even if that advice turns out to be misguided or inadequate." *Id.*

STOP !

2.   NCAA Academic Reform Legislation

a.   Academic Reform — Generally

How likely is it that a Kevin Ross–type scenario would occur today? NCAA rules seek, in part, to reduce the likelihood that a student-athlete will leave college after three or four years with the learning deficiencies of a Kevin Ross. These rules include "initial eligibility standards" and "satisfactory progress rules." With respect to the latter, NCAA rules require that, as a condition to eligibility for participation, student-athletes take a curriculum that allows them to make progress toward obtaining a degree. In 2002 the NCAA heightened these requirements. The changes in "satisfactory progress rules" were a part of Division I academic reforms enacted by the NCAA between 2002 and 2004. Another component of the NCAA's reform efforts were the significant revisions made to its initial eligibility rules; NCAA-revised eligibility rules deemphasize standardized test scores (i.e., the SAT and ACT), place greater emphasis on high school grades, and increase the number of core course requirements. (The history of and changes to initial eligibility requirements are detailed in Chapter 9.) The NCAA adopted another component of its academic reform legislation with its 2004 approval of the Academic Progress Rate (APR), which is an "incentive/disincentive program" and is discussed *infra*.

Some academics and college administrators lauded the revisions as likely to achieve their goal of improving graduation rates. Others, however, warned that the revised rules may have a negative impact on academic achievement. Some are concerned that more athletes will be steered toward "jock majors"—fields of study that allow student-athletes to "maneuver through the maze of academic requirements and remain eligible to compete." Welch Suggs, *Jock Majors*, Chron. Higher Educ., Jan. 17, 2003, at A33. As expressed by one commentator, "[T]he march toward tougher standards and, the NCAA hopes, higher graduation rates begs a crucial question, however: What do numbers matter if players are being sent into academic programs that won't give them a meaningful education or marketable skills?" *Id.* at A34. The clustering of players in particular majors is not a new phenomenon. Whether the revised standards will contribute to this practice is uncertain at this time. For a recent examination of majors by football players see David Biderman, *Why Football Players Don't Speak Spanish*, Wall St. J., Sept. 16, 2010, http://online.wsj.com/article/SB10001424052748703743504575493773613076844.html.

In 2011, the NCAA Board of Directors again considered enhanced academic performance measures. In addition to changes to the APR, discussed *infra*, the board also approved changes to the eligibility requirements for entering students and transfer students. For example, with respect to entering student-athletes, new initial eligibility standards increase the minimum core course grade point average from 2.0 to 2.3 for first-year student-athletes to be eligible for immediate access to competition. Students with a 2.0 grade point average would be eligible for athletically related financial aid during their first year of enrollment. These student-athletes would also be eligible to practice during their first term of enrollment. For a summary of these and additional changes to academic standards, see Michelle Brutlag Hosick, *DI Board Could Change Academic Standards, Financial Aid Opportunities*, NCAA.org, Oct. 25, 2011, http://www.ncaa.org/wps/wcm/connect/public/NCAA/Resources/Latest+News/2011/October/DI+Board+could+change+academic+standards,+financial+aid+opportunities.

b.   Academic Reform—Academic Progress Rate

In May 2004, the NCAA adopted legislation that instituted a metric known as the Academic Progress Rate (APR). It was designed to give a real-time "snapshot" into the academic progress of individual teams at member institutions. In commenting on this reform, then NCAA president, the late Myles Brand, stated, "For the first time, the NCAA will have the ability to hold institutions and teams accountable for the academic progress of their student athletes." Welch Suggs, *NCAA Weighs New Penalties for Academic Laggards*, Chron. Higher Educ., April 23, 2004, A42 (discussing NCAA's incentives/disincentives program).

To calculate an institution's APR, the NCAA examines each scholarship student-athlete on an intercollegiate team at a member institution and determines whether the player has remained academically eligible to participate in intercollegiate athletics and whether the student has chosen to remain enrolled at the school. Teams are awarded one point for meeting each of these standards during a given semester, resulting in each athlete earning the school a possible maximum of two points per semester and four points per year if the institution uses a two-semester calendar; alternatively, schools that use a quarter system can be awarded a maximum of eight total points per athlete. After determining each athlete's individual score, each team gets a final APR score; 1,000 is the maximum APR a team can earn. The NCAA initially established 925 as the minimum score an institution should achieve to avoid being immediately (or contemporaneously) penalized. The failure of a team to reach a 925 benchmark exposes a college to the assessment of penalties including scholarship and recruiting restrictions and a team's loss of eligibility for postseason competition. For a discussion of how the Academic Progress Rate is calculated, see NCAA, *Division I: Academic Progress Rate (APR)*, NCAA.org, July 9, 2012, http://www.ncaa.org/wps/wcm/connect/public/NCAA/Academics/Division+I/Academic+Progress+Rate. Also see Michelle B. Hosick, *Academic Success Stories Transcend Improved APRs*, NCAA News, June 9, 2010; Michelle B. Hosick, *Division I Beginning Major APR Assessment*, NCAA News, June 9, 2010.

Overall APR numbers released over the past several years indicate positive trends. NCAA officials attribute improved student-athlete academic performance, as measured by the APR, to several policy adjustments, including (1) more stringent progress-toward-degree requirements, (2) a rule allowing student-athletes who fit a certain academic profile to transfer, (3) increased core course requirements for incoming student-athletes, and (4) a requirement that transfer student-athletes earn an eligibility point in order to receive financial aid at the school to which they are transferring.

Apart from student-athletes' improved academic performance, the success of the APR program can be measured by the way in which it and other academic measures are becoming part of the fabric of Division I institutions. For example, the NCAA created a head coach APR portfolio, a database that was first made public in 2010 and provided details of the APRs earned by teams associated with a head coach. Some institutions are also incorporating APR clauses into coaching contracts, which give monetary incentives and disincentives for coaches who achieve or fail to achieve APR benchmarks.

Figures released in 2012 are illustrative of the positive trends and remaining challenges. The overall four-year rate rose to 973, which represented a 3-point increase over 2011 figures. APRs in three high-profile sports—baseball, football, and men's basketball—also showed improved four-year rates. *Most Division I Teams Deliver Top Grades: Latest Data Show Continued Impact of Academic Reform*, NCAA, June 20, 2012, http://www.ncaa.org/wps/wcm/connect/public/NCAA/Resources/Latest+News/2012/June/Most+Division+I+teams+deliver+top+grades. Nevertheless, APRs posted for football and men's basketball and for low-resource institutions reveal some of the remaining challenges. Football and men's basketball together have shown improvement since APRs were first released but continue to post comparatively lower multiyear Division I APRs. Low-resource institutions, many of which are also historically black colleges and universities (HBCU), have posted low APRs, especially with regard to their men's basketball teams. For detailed analysis of 2012 by sport see NCAA, *National and*

Sport-Group APR Average, Trends and Penalties, June 20, 2012, http://www.ncaa
.org/wps/wcm/connect/public/ncaa/pdfs/2012/apr+2012+trends.

In 2011, the NCAA Board of Directors enacted enhanced academic performance measures. One change, which takes effect in 2012-2013, increases the
APR benchmark to 930 (which corresponds to a 50 percent graduation rate),
and modifies the penalty structure in several ways including requiring teams to
achieve at least a 930 four-year APR to be eligible for postseason competition.
The potential impact of the changes to the APR penalty structure were realized
in dramatic fashion when the NCAA declared that because of a low four-year
APR, the University of Connecticut men's basketball team, which in 2011 was
the NCAA national champion, would be ineligible to participate in postseason
play during the 2012-2013 season. Connecticut appealed the NCAA's penalty
arguing that its men's basketball team's APR for 2010-2011 and the first semester of 2011 were perfect. Its appeal was rejected.

Student-athlete progress-toward-degree requirements from the 2011-2012
NCAA Division I Manual (2011) are as follows.

NCAA BYLAW, ARTICLE 14

Eligibility: Academic and General Requirements

14.4   Progress-Toward-Degree Requirements
14.4.1   Progress-Toward-Degree Requirements.
To be eligible to represent an institution in intercollegiate athletics competition, a student-athlete shall maintain progress toward a baccalaureate
or equivalent degree at that institution as determined by the regulations
of that institution subject to controlling legislation of the conference(s)
or similar association of which the institution is a member and applicable
NCAA legislation. (*Revised 4/15/09*)
14.4.2   Eligibility for Financial Aid and Practice.
Eligibility for institutional financial aid and practice during each academic year after a student-athlete's initial year in residence or after the
student-athlete has utilized one season of eligibility in a sport shall be based
upon the rules of the institution and the conference(s), if any, of which the
institution is a member.
14.4.3   Eligibility for Competition
14.4.3.1   Fulfillment of Credit-Hour Requirements. Eligibility for
competition shall be determined by the student-athlete's academic
record in existence at the beginning of the fall term or at the beginning
of any other regular term of that academic year, based upon satisfactory
completion of at least: (*Revised: 1/10/92, 10/31/02, effective 8/1/03*). . . .
(a) Twenty-four semester or 36 quarter hours of academic credit prior to
     start of the student-athlete's second year of collegiate enrollment (i.e.,
     third semester, fourth quarter); (*Revised: 10/31/02, effective 8/1/03*)
(b) Eighteen semester or 27 quarter hours of academic credit since the
     beginning of the previous fall term or since the beginning of the cer-
     tifying institution's preceding regular two semesters or three quar-
     ters (hours earned during the summer may not be used to fulfill this
     requirement); and (*Revised: 10/31/02, effective 8/1/03*. . . .)

(c) Six semester or six quarter hours of academic credit during the preceding regular academic term (e.g., fall semester, winter quarter) in which the student-athlete has been enrolled full-time at any collegiate institution. (*Revised: 10/31/02, effective 8/1/03*). . . .

14.4.3.1.7 Designation of Degree Program. A student-athlete shall designate a program of studies leading toward a specific baccalaureate degree at the certifying institution prior to participating in competition that occurs during or immediately before the third year of enrollment (fifth semester or seventh quarter) and thereafter shall make progress toward that specific degree. . . . (*Revised 2/27/08*)

14.4.3.2 Fulfillment of Percentage of Degree Requirements. A student-athlete who is entering his or her third year of collegiate enrollment shall have completed successfully at least 40 percent of the course requirements in the student's specific degree program. A student-athlete who is entering his or her fourth year of collegiate enrollment shall have completed successfully at least 60 percent of the course requirements in the student's specific degree program. A student-athlete who is entering his or her fifth year of collegiate enrollment shall have completed successfully at least 80 percent of the course requirements in the student's specific degree program. The course requirements must be in the student's specific degree program (as opposed to the student's major). (*Adopted: 1/10/92, effective 8/1/92; Revised: 1/9/96, 10/31/02, effective 8/1/03.*)

PROBLEM 3-3 *Read Facts carefully then read cases*

Skip Baxter, the starting center for his high school basketball team and consensus All-American, was recruited by more than 100 colleges and universities. Over the course of his senior year, Baxter received numerous letters from University of Denton (UD) personnel touting UD's (1) elite basketball program and its penchant for developing National Basketball Association (NBA) quality players, (2) academic requirements for scholarship athletes, (3) health and training facilities, and (4) academic and vocational resources. Baxter visited UD to meet the staff and view the school. Shortly thereafter, he made a verbal commitment *nothing in writing* to attend UD, which the UD basketball staff acknowledged by letter and e-mail.

Prior to making the verbal commitment, Baxter received visits at his home in North Carolina. On one occasion, Baxter was visited by the head coach, assistant coach, and athletic trainer. During the group visit, head coach David Lyons told Baxter that if he made a verbal commitment to attend UD, Lyons would *verbal* discontinue efforts to recruit another center in Baxter's class. Lyons, who had a reputation for developing college basketball players, particularly centers who left college to play in the NBA, also told Baxter that he and his coaching staff would do everything possible to develop Baxter's basketball skills. Lyons stated: *verbal* "You will start as center during your freshman year. We will build the team around you. We will also provide you with the resources to enable you to remain academically eligible and earn a degree in four or five years." Lyons also told Baxter, "Under no circumstances will I accept a head coaching position at any *verbal* other institution during the four years that you play for UD. If a player makes a commitment to me, I make one to the player. I love it here and plan to remain for years to come."

Baxter and his mother signed a National Letter of Intent that formalized his decision to attend UD in exchange for an athletic scholarship. Two weeks later, Coach Lyons signed an agreement with a highly regarded NBA team. Shortly thereafter, UD appointed a new basketball coach, Richard Douglas, who contacted Baxter and assured him that the commitments, goals, and play system used by the Lyons regime would not be changed. Around the same time, however, Baxter learned via the Internet and other media that another highly regarded center, John Williams, had signed a Letter of Intent with UD. Lyons had recruited Williams.

During fall practice, Baxter competed with Williams for the starting center position. In contrast to Williams, virtually no attention was directed toward developing Baxter's basketball skills during fall practice (or thereafter). Nevertheless, Baxter outperformed Williams during fall practice and the first two games of the season (the only games in which Baxter played; he started in neither game). Notwithstanding Baxter's performance, Douglas decided that Williams would be his center because he possessed a better attitude than Baxter. When questioned by the local media about what some viewed as an irrational decision, Coach Douglas stated that he and Baxter had a few personality clashes and that Williams possessed a better attitude. When pressed by one reporter at a press conference, Douglas said, "I didn't recruit Baxter, I don't like his entitlement attitude, and I don't have to play him. I'm the coach of this team, not Baxter. He'll be lucky if I offer him a scholarship next year."

To make matters worse, Baxter did not perform well academically. Coach Douglas and his basketball staff limited the time Baxter could meet with academic tutors to two hours per week. This is substantially less time than is afforded other players on the team.

Baxter and his mother are extremely unhappy with developments at UD and have come to you for advice as to what options, including litigation, are available to Baxter. What would you advise? In responding, identify any additional facts that would assist you in your analysis of Baxter's options.

3.   Constitutionally Protected Property or Liberty Interests

Under the United States Constitution, before a person is deprived of life, liberty, or property by "state action," procedural due process—adequate notice and a fair hearing—must be given. Substantive due process also provides a party with a means of determining whether a constitutionally protected substantive right such as one's privacy rights have in fact been infringed. In such cases, (1) the plaintiff must establish the requisite "state action"; (2) the party must be a person; and (3) an interest in life, liberty, or property must be threatened or infringed. Then, the court must determine whether these property interests were violated without either procedural or substantive due process. The state action requirement (which is satisfied by a public university's conduct) is addressed at length *infra* in section E of this chapter. In the case of student-athletes, coaches, or other personnel, the requirement that the party be a person is easily met. The major issue remaining generally is whether a property or liberty interest has been implicated.

The question of whether a student-athlete possesses a property or liberty interest most often arises in the context of an NCAA rule or regulation that renders the student-athlete ineligible to compete in intercollegiate competition.

In attempting to maintain their eligibility, student-athletes challenge NCAA eligibility determinations or institutional actions that terminate athletes' ability to continue to engage in intercollegiate competition. In asserting these challenges, student-athletes assert that the Fourteenth Amendment protects against deprivation of property without due process. The materials that follow examine whether student-athletes possess a property interest in athletic participation. In reviewing the cases, consider the rationales on which athletes rely in asserting the existence of a property interest. Also, consider the factors that influence judicial determinations in this regard. Is there a model of intercollegiate athletics on which courts primarily rely in determining whether to recognize a property interest in athletic participation?

PROBLEM 3-4

You serve as legal counsel to a legislative committee. One of the members of your committee has indicated that she wants you to draft legislation that would recognize a property interest in participation in intercollegiate athletics. The legislator is irate because her daughter was not permitted to try out for the football team at her public university. Her daughter believes that she could earn an athletic scholarship if she had the opportunity to demonstrate her ability as a kicker, and that she could increase her future job opportunities by playing college football. When the legislator and her daughter asked the coach why she was not permitted to try out, the coach simply said he thought it was best. When he was pressed for further reasons, he simply said he did not want to offer any. When the legislator discussed the matter with her lawyer, he said it was unlikely that a court would review why her daughter was not being permitted to participate because she does not have a property interest that would trigger federal due process protection. Considering the following case, was the lawyer's advice correct? What advice would you give to the legislator regarding the pros and cons of such a law? Would it be appropriate to advise the legislator to use her position as leverage to get the university administration, which is in the midst of budgetary hearings, to talk with the coach?

HYSAW v. WASHBURN UNIVERSITY OF TOPEKA

690 F. Supp. 940 (D. Kan. 1987)

SAFFELS, Judge.

This civil rights and breach of contract case arises out of a dispute early in Washburn University's 1986 football season. Several black football players complained that they were being treated in a racially-discriminatory manner by the coaching staff and administration. The dispute culminated in those players boycotting team practices and the administration removing those players from the team. The players now claim defendants infringed upon their free speech, liberty and property rights in violation of 42 U.S.C. § 1983, violated 42 U.S.C. § 1981, and breached their contracts with Washburn University. Defendants ask for summary judgment on all of plaintiffs' claims.

The court has reviewed the uncontroverted facts submitted by defendants, plaintiffs' responses to them, and supporting documents and deposition testimony, and has determined that for purposes of this motion, the uncontroverted facts are as follows:

1. Plaintiffs are all black Americans recruited to play football for Washburn University.
2. Defendant John L. Green is the president of defendant Washburn University.
3. Defendant Jerry Robertson is the Athletic Director at defendant Washburn University.
4. Defendant Larry Elliott is the head football coach at defendant Washburn University.
5. Each of the plaintiffs were awarded football scholarships for the 1986-87 school year. Plaintiffs Neil Chapman ("Chapman"), Vernon Hysaw ("Hysaw"), and Eugene Battle ("Battle") were told they would receive scholarships to cover tuition, fees, books, room and board. Plaintiff Randy Craven received a scholarship to cover tuition, fees and books; a federally-funded Pell Grant was to cover the cost of his room and board. Plaintiff Tony McDonald also was to receive a scholarship sufficient to cover tuition, fees and books, with a Pell Grant to pay for his room and board.
6. Before receiving their scholarships, each of the plaintiffs executed an agreement indicating that they accepted the financial aid awards. The written agreements did not promise that the plaintiffs would be allowed to play football for Washburn.
7. Early in the 1986 football season, several black football players on the Washburn team began expressing discontent with their scholarships. They complained that promises of full scholarships had not been carried out; many also felt that white players on the team were being favored by the coaching staff and that lesser white players had been awarded better scholarships than some of the black players.
8. On August 26, 1986, several of the black players, along with the president of the Washburn Black Student Alliance (B.S.A.), met with defendants Green and Robertson about their concerns. The following day, the players met with defendant Elliott and with financial aid officials.
9. After those meetings, the B.S.A. president composed a letter to defendant Green outlining the concerns of the black players.
10. The players again met with the B.S.A. president after football practice on August 27, 1986. At that meeting, they decided that they were not satisfied with the administration's response to their complaints. To protest the administration's response, the players agreed to boycott team practice.
11. The players prepared a letter containing a list of those players who would be boycotting; the letter indicated that the boycott was due to their dissatisfaction with the administration's response to their complaints.
12. On August 28, 1986, the players did not attend team practice.
13. On August 29, 1986, defendant Robertson responded to the players' boycott; he outlined the administration's position on their complaints. He also indicated that "missing practice without an excuse from the coaching staff is a violation of disciplinary rules affecting all players and will be treated in the same manner as any player's unexcused absence."
14. The players voted on August 29, 1986, to continue their boycott of practice and positional meetings.

15. Several additional meetings were held between the players and the administration. Some players were subsequently allowed to rejoin the team by meeting certain conditions set out by the administration.

16. On September 1, 1986, defendant Robertson met with the plaintiffs. Robertson told them that they would be allowed to retain their scholarships if they met the following conditions: 1) issue an apology through the news media to Washburn and its administration, 2) apologize to the football team at a team meeting, 3) participate in five early morning practices, 4) agree to be kept out of the first game that season, and 5) "exhibit total commitment and support to the Washburn University football program."

17. Plaintiffs refused to comply with the administration's requests.

18. Defendants then refused to allow plaintiffs to return to the team.

19. Defendants claim that the reasons plaintiffs were not allowed to return to the team were that they had missed practice and positional meetings and had failed to show leadership. Plaintiffs claim they were not allowed to return because they boycotted in protest of the alleged racial mistreatment of black football players at Washburn.

20. All plaintiffs received the financial aid allocations promised them for the 1986-87 school year. . . .

I. VIOLATIONS OF 42 U.S.C. § 1981

Defendants argue summary judgment is in order on plaintiffs' section 1981 claims because plaintiffs had no contractual interest in playing football for Washburn University. The facts do establish that defendants complied with their obligations under the written contracts. Therefore, there can be no violation of section 1981 with regard to any claims plaintiffs have that they were denied scholarship monies awarded under the 1986-87 agreements or prevented from playing football as allegedly promised by their contracts. However, a review of the Pre-trial Order in this case indicates that plaintiffs' section 1981 claims go far beyond the issue of whether defendants breached the 1986-87 written scholarship agreements. They claim that throughout their playing careers at Washburn, white players with equal or less ability were given greater opportunities to make more beneficial scholarship contracts and were allowed greater opportunities to participate in the Washburn football program. If proven, these actions might constitute violations of 42 U.S.C. § 1981. While the court does not express any opinion concerning the merits of this claim, it is unable to grant summary judgment at the present time because defendants have not addressed plaintiffs' claim in full. . . .

II. VIOLATIONS OF 42 U.S.C. § 1983

Plaintiffs claim defendants infringed on their property, liberty, and free speech rights in violation of 42 U.S.C. § 1983. The court will grant partial summary judgment in favor of defendants.

A. PROPERTY RIGHTS

Plaintiffs first argue that defendants violated their property rights without affording them due process. They argue they held a property interest in contractual rights to play football for Washburn, and argue that by breaching their scholarship contracts the defendants have deprived them of a property right without due process.

Our analysis begins with *Board of Regents v. Roth*, 408 U.S. 564, 33 L.Ed.2d 548, 92 S.Ct. 2701 (1972). In *Roth*, the United States Supreme Court set out the standard for determining whether an alleged deprivation of a property right violated due process. We must determine whether plaintiffs possessed a property right protected under the Constitution. Property rights "are created and their dimensions are defined by existing rules or understandings that stem from an independent source such as state law." *Roth*, 408 U.S. at 577. Only after a protectable property interest has been established do we then determine whether due process was afforded.

Plaintiffs claim defendants deprived them of their contractual rights under the scholarship agreements to play football for Washburn University. However, plaintiffs have only established a property right in the scholarship funds. No deprivation of those funds took place. Plaintiffs had no other protectable property interest. "To have a property interest in a benefit, a person clearly must have more than an abstract need or desire for it. He must have more than a unilateral expectation of it. He must, instead, have a legitimate claim of entitlement to it." *Roth*, 408 U.S. at 577. Plaintiffs concede that the only source for their alleged property interest is their scholarship agreements. The court has determined that the only interests created by those agreements are interests in receiving scholarship funds. Any other terms plaintiffs attempt to read into those agreements are, without supporting evidence, no more than "unilateral expectations." The court will therefore grant defendants' summary judgment motion on this claim.

B.   LIBERTY INTERESTS

Plaintiffs Battle and Chapman next argue that defendants infringed upon their liberty interests in pursuing a college football career. This claim arises out of those plaintiffs' efforts to be recruited by the nearby Emporia State University football team after they were dismissed from the Washburn team. The additional uncontroverted facts for purposes of this portion of the motion are as follows. . . .

4. After they were dismissed from the Washburn team, plaintiffs Battle and Chapman sought recruitment by the Emporia State University football team.
5. The head coach at Emporia spoke with defendant Elliott about the two plaintiffs.
6. Defendant Elliott commented to the Emporia coach about the plaintiffs' failure to attend practice and positional meetings. He allegedly told the coach the plaintiffs were lazy and were troublemakers.
7. Based on this information, the Emporia coach did not recruit Battle and Chapman.

Again, the court must start its analysis with *Board of Regents v. Roth*. A due process claim is made out only if the liberty interest allegedly violated is protectable under the Constitution. Again we look to an independent source of law to determine whether plaintiffs held a legitimate interest in the right to pursue a college football career. Only if this right is a protected liberty right under state law have plaintiffs made out a Section 1983 violation.

[handwritten: π — why would the π argue this?]

The plaintiffs concede that no right to pursue a college football career exists under well-established Tenth Circuit law. *See, e.g., Colorado Seminary (Univ. of Denver) v. NCAA*, 570 F.2d 320, 321 (10th Cir. 1978) (interest of student athlete in participating in intercollegiate sports did not rise to level of constitutionally protected right invoking due process); *see also Justice v. NCAA*, 577 F. Supp. 356, 366 (D. Ariz. 1983) (participation in intercollegiate athletics is not a constitutionally protected interest). Furthermore, the court rejects plaintiffs' contention that the rule of *Paul v. Davis*, 424 U.S. 693, 47 L.Ed.2d 405, 96 S. Ct. 1155 (1976), commands a denial of summary judgment here. The Court in *Paul* held that damage to an individual's reputation by a state official is not enough to establish a due process violation. Something more must be shown; a tangible interest must be established. *Paul*, 424 U.S. at 709-10.

[handwritten: ✳]

The court finds no tangible interest here. *Roth* held that defamatory comments made by a government employer which cast a cloud over an employee's future employment prospects could constitute a deprivation of liberty. Plaintiffs now ask this court to extend the holding in *Roth* to the present situation; in effect, they are asking the court to equate government employment with a football scholarship. The court is unwilling to take such a giant leap. While no constitutional right to a government job exists, the Supreme Court has noted that qualification for a government job is a "privileg[e] of first-class citizenship." *Anti-Fascist Committee v. McGrath*, 341 U.S. 123, 183, 95 L.Ed. 817, 71 S. Ct. 624 (1950) (J. Douglas, concurring). Plaintiffs have offered no reason why a right to pursue a collegiate athletic career should be afforded the same status, and the court likewise sees no reason to do so.

[handwritten: π]

If plaintiffs have made out any claim here, it is one for defamation under Kansas law. The rule in *Paul* dictates that every violation of state tort law does not rise to a violation of section 1983 when committed by a state official. Even claims of defamation are not enough, standing alone, to invoke the protections of section 1983. Plaintiffs have shown nothing in addition to their defamation charges which would justify invoking section 1983, and defendants' motion on this issue will be granted. . . .

[handwritten: for Δ school]

C. FREE SPEECH INTERESTS

Plaintiffs next claim that defendants violated their first amendment right to free speech by removing them from the team after they protested racial mistreatment. Defendants first argue summary judgment is appropriate because the players were removed from the team simply for missing practices and a positional meeting. They allege the discharge had nothing to do with the players' protest, and they point to the team policy that unexcused absences from team practices or positional meetings may result in disciplinary action, including dismissal from the team.

[handwritten: Δ]

However, plaintiffs point out that in defendant Elliott's deposition, he admitted that if a player were to miss practice in protest of racial mistreatment, the absence would be excused. If this were the case, then plaintiffs' absences may have been excused, and defendants' reasons for dismissing the players would be inadequate. If the facts were to establish that the plaintiffs were disciplined for protesting racial mistreatment, defendants may have infringed upon plaintiffs' first amendment rights. Summary judgment would therefore be inappropriate. . . .

[handwritten: π]

[handwritten: need more facts... TBD]

III. BREACH OF CONTRACT

Plaintiffs finally claim that defendants breached their scholarship contracts. Defendants argue that summary judgment is in order, because the only promise made in those contracts was to pay plaintiffs their scholarship money, and this was done. No other promises were made.

The law in Kansas is well-established that when a written contract exists and its language is clear and unambiguous, the language controls. . . . Plaintiffs argue they were promised that they would be allowed to play football during the 1986-87 season. Yet the written scholarship contracts they signed make no indication of such promises. In fact, the only promises in those written contracts were that the players would receive money. Plaintiffs provide no other evidence, other than "understandings" and "expectations," that they were promised a position on the 1986 team.

We then turn to the written language of the scholarship agreement to ascertain whether defendants breached those terms. The court finds that defendants met all obligations under the contracts. They promised to pay Chapman, Hysaw and Battle "full" scholarships for the 1986-87 school year, and Craven and McDonald were to receive "partial" scholarships. Plaintiffs concede that they received all disbursements on time. Defendants therefore met all their obligations under the contracts.

The court rejects the assertion that defendants' threats on September 1, 1986, constituted a breach of their scholarship agreements. They argue that any disbursements made after September 3, 1986, when suit was filed, only constitute mitigation of damages. However, the evidence does not indicate that the administration announced on September 1, 1986, "We hereby revoke your scholarships." Plaintiff has only shown the court that on September 1, defendants threatened to pull the scholarships. The evidence also indicates that the administration chose not to follow through with that threat, and instead paid all amounts promised. Whether the administration chose to comply with the agreement because of the suit the players had filed or for any other reason, their motivation is not controlling. The facts plainly indicate that all terms of the scholarship contracts were met, and plaintiffs concede this point. No breach of contract occurred, and summary judgment will be granted. . . .

IT IS BY THE COURT THEREFORE ORDERED that defendants' motion for summary judgment is granted in part and denied in part. Summary judgment is granted in favor of the defendants on plaintiffs' claims of property and liberty deprivation under 42 U.S.C. 1983 and on plaintiffs' claims of breach of contract. Summary judgment is denied on plaintiffs' claims under 42 U.S.C. § 1981 and for first amendment violations under 42 U.S.C. § 1983.

NOTES AND QUESTIONS

1. *Theoretical Perspectives.* According to one commentator, student-athletes have most often advanced four theories in arguing that they possess a constitutionally protected property interest in sports eligibility. He summarizes these theories as follows:

> The economic rationale views intercollegiate athletics as a training ground for professional sports and argues that the property right is derived from the

collegians' economic interests in uninterrupted preparation for lucrative careers as professional athletes. . . .

The educational rationale views participation in college athletics as an integral facet of the student athlete's educational experience. As a substantial element of the educational process, athletic eligibility should not be permitted to be sacrificed in the absence of due process. This reasoning is premised upon the longstanding recognition that the opportunity to pursue an education is a sufficiently important interest that it cannot be impaired without due process. . . .

The scholarship per se rationale claims that the loss of an athletic scholarship per se is a denial of a property interest in athletic eligibility. The athletes who suffer such losses are likely to incur financial hardships which may cut off the opportunity to continue attending college and to earn a degree. The deprivation of the scholarships then, is also a deprivation of benefits to which the athletes were entitled according to the terms of their awards; the continued receipt of those benefits is a property interest which cannot be denied without due process. . . .

The contractual rationale maintains that a property right to athletic eligibility is created by the contractual provisions of the athletic scholarship. The scholarships are contracts which have conferred upon the athletes certain benefits, including the right to participate in intercollegiate athletics, which cannot be denied without due process.

like youth handbook

Brian L. Porto, Note, *Balancing Due Process and Academic Integrity in Intercollegiate Athletics: The Scholarship Athlete's Limited Property Interest in Eligibility*, 62 Ind. L.J. 1151, 1158-1159 (1987).

2. *The Economic Rationale.* The foregoing author concludes that most courts have rejected the economic rationale. "Because so few former college athletes ever sign a professional contract, college athletes' economic interests in professional sports opportunities are speculative and not of constitutional dimensions." *Id.* at 1158. Illustrative of the judicial reticence to adopt the economic rationale as laying the groundwork for a property interest is *Colorado Seminary v. NCAA*, 417 F. Supp. 885 (D. Colo. 1976), *affirmed*, 580 F.2d 320 (10th Cir. 1978), wherein the court rejected plaintiffs' argument that a constitutionally protected property interest in athletic participation stems from the vital role college athletics plays in providing a training ground for a career in professional sports.

Pro too speculative

[W]hile plaintiffs' characterization of the distinctive importance of collegiate athletics as a forum may be a sadly accurate reflection of the true significance of today's amateur athletic competition, the interest in future professional careers must . . . be considered speculative and not of constitutional dimensions. . . . Nor do the interests in postseason competition or appearances on television seem to be of a constitutionally greater magnitude. The Court is therefore constrained by precedent in this circuit to conclude that the plaintiff student-athletes have no constitutionally protected property or liberty interest in participation in intercollegiate athletics, postseason competition, or appearances on television.

Id. at 24-25. See also *NCAA v. Yeo*, 171 S.W.3d 863, 869 (Tex. 2005) (rejecting student-athlete's claim that she possessed a property or liberty interest under the Texas constitution because of her unique "reputation as a world-class athlete in home country of Singapore, which was separate and apart from her intercollegiate swimming career"); *Hall v. NCAA*, 985 F. Supp. 782, 799 (N.D. Ill. 1997) ("There is no protected economic interest in an athletic scholarship because, while a college degree enhances one's ability to earn a livelihood, the lack of a scholarship does not prohibit a person from pursuing a college degree").

Although a clear majority of courts follow the precedent set forth in *Colorado Seminary*, a few cases from the 1970s and 1980s did not consider the student-athlete's future economic interests as too speculative. See, e.g., *Hall v. Univ. of Minnesota*, 530 F. Supp. 104 (D. Minn. 1982); *Buckton v. NCAA*, 366 F. Supp. 1152 (D. Mass. 1973); *Behagen v. Int'l Conference of Faculty Representatives*, 346 F. Supp. 602 (D. Minn. 1972). As suggested previously, however, courts no longer follow the precedent established in these cases.

3. *The Contract Rationale.* Scholars overwhelmingly support the notion that contract rationale justifies creating a property interest in athletic participation on behalf of student-athletes. See, e.g., Timothy Davis, *Student-Athlete Perspective Economic Interests: Contractual Dimensions*, 19 T. Marshall L. Rev. 585 (1994); John P. Sahl, *College Athletes and Due Process*, 21 Ariz. St. L.J. 621 (1989); John H. Mairo, Comment, *The College Athletic Scholarship: A Contract That Creates a Property Interest in Eligibility*, 3 Seton Hall J. Sport L. 149 (1993); Brian L. Porto, Note, *Balancing Due Process and Academic Integrity in Intercollegiate Athletics: The Scholarship Athlete's Limited Property Interest in Eligibility*, 62 Ind. L.J. 1150 (1987). Arguing in support of the contractual rationale, a commentator states:

> Even if a court did not agree that an athletic scholarship is an explicit contract which confers a property interest upon an awardee, that court could agree that where an athlete is recruited by a university and both parties anticipate the athlete's participation in athletics, an implied contract has been formed, creating a property interest in continued eligibility. . . .
>
> Implied contracts exist where the schools and the student athletes anticipate the latter's participation in the athletic program. . . . In college athletics, intense recruiting battles among schools for the services of highly skilled athletes are commonplace. These battles indicate that the combatant universities anticipate that the scholarship athletes who enroll at each institution will represent that institution in athletics competition. The scholarship agreement is the sort of "mutually explicit understanding," . . . which supports a claim of entitlement to participate in intercollegiate athletics.

Id. at 1168-1169.

Despite scholarly support, courts have largely rejected the contract rationale as providing an adequate basis for establishing a property interest in intercollegiate athletics participation. *Lesser v. Neosho County Community Coll.*, 741 F. Supp. 854, 865 (D. Kan. 1990) (relying on *Hysaw*, determining that the contract language promised plaintiff financial aid but not a position on the baseball team). What are the shortcomings of the foregoing rationales that have resulted in judicial unwillingness to be favorably disposed toward finding a property interest based on them?

4. *Discipline for Rules Violations.* Student-athletes have asserted claims alleging deprivation of a constitutionally protected property interest when a public university's sanctions imposed for rules violations resulted in the loss of athletes' athletic scholarships. In *Conard v. University of Washington*, 834 P.2d 17 (Wash. 1992), the University of Washington (UW) refused to renew the

scholarships of two student-athletes who were involved in a series of incidents that UW claimed violated football team rules. These incidents included the athletes' alleged theft of a food credit card, assaulting and threatening other students, vandalism, and an attempt to extort money from a student. The athletes alleged they were entitled to their athletic scholarships for four to five years. They based this understanding on what they characterized as the common understanding as to the duration of scholarships as set forth in the financial aid documents. The university asserted that scholarships were typically renewed for four to five years absent a finding of serious misconduct, which was not defined in writing but was "evaluated generally in light of UW's student conduct code and specifically by the team rules promulgated by [the head football coach]." *Id.* at 19.

Plaintiffs sued UW alleging, *inter alia,* breach of contract. The trial court granted summary judgment in favor of UW. The appellate court upheld the trial court's dismissal of plaintiff's breach of contract action, but sua sponte held that plaintiffs had a constitutionally protected entitlement to renewal of their scholarships. See *Conard v. University of Washington*, 62 Wash. App. 664, 671, 814 P.2d 1242 (1991). The Washington Supreme Court granted review "solely to determine if the University's termination of petitioners' athletic scholarships violated their due process rights and, if so, what remedy is appropriate." In framing the issue, the court stated: "Unless a legitimate claim of entitlement to the renewal of plaintiffs' scholarships was created by the terms of the contract, by a mutually explicit understanding, or by substantive procedural restrictions on the part of the decisionmaker, plaintiffs have no constitutional due process protections." *Id.* at 22.

With respect to the student-athletes' scholarship, the court concluded that its duration was for only one year and none of its terms established any entitlement to renewal. As to plaintiffs' assertion of a mutual understanding of renewal, the court stated, "[T]he fact that scholarships are, in fact, normally renewed does not create a 'common law' of renewal, absent other consistent and supportive UW policies or rules." *Id.* at 22. The court found plaintiffs not only failed to present evidence of such supportive rules or policies, but plaintiffs had failed to establish they had met the terms for renewal given their misconduct. Finally, the court acknowledged that procedural guarantees that limit a decision maker's discretion may create a protected property interest. It concluded, however, that the

> discretion of the decision-makers in this case is not sufficiently limited to create a protected property interest. Therefore, even though the DIA manual speaks to due process, such a procedural guaranty cannot create a protected property interest in a vacuum. There must be some substantive standard and explicitly mandatory language to give the hearing substance.

Id. at 26. Accord *Marsh v. Delaware State Univ.*, 2006 WL 141680 (D. Del.) (rejecting procedural and substantive due process claims of student-athlete who was expelled and lost athletic scholarship and intercollegiate athletic eligibility after violation of university's drug and weapons policies). But see *Richard v. Perkins*, 373 F. Supp. 2d 1211, 1219 (D. Kan. 2005) (adopting the general rule that participation in intercollegiate athletics is not a fundamental right, but suggesting that an athletic association may not enact and enforce rules that are arbitrary and capricious).

Is the issue regarding the existence of a property interest in athletic participation related to the question of the nature of the relationship between student-athletes and their institutions? See Porto, *supra* at 1152 (suggesting issue is part of a larger debate regarding the student-athlete and university relationship). For example, what parallels, if any, exist in the claims raised by the plaintiffs in *Hysaw* and contract claims asserted by plaintiffs in *Ross v. Creighton University* and *Jackson v. Drake University*? Did the courts in *Hysaw* and *Conard* take a literal approach in analyzing the student-athlete/university contract, or one based on reasonable expectations of the parties thereto?

5. *Subsequent Cases.* Courts continue to adhere to the position adopted by the courts in *Hysaw* and *Conard*. An apt illustration is *Hart v. NCAA*, 550 S.E.2d 79 (W. Va. 2001). Plaintiff, a fifth-year senior at Appalachian State University, participated on the school's intercollegiate wrestling team. Plaintiff sought to compete in a lower weight class than that in which he had previously competed. An NCAA regulation prevented wrestlers from competing in a weight class that differed from the class in which they had competed prior to a certain date. The NCAA rejected plaintiff's request for a waiver of the regulation and his request that he be afforded a fifth year of eligibility. Plaintiff eventually filed suit asserting a denial of an opportunity to fulfill his scholarship contract and to compete in intercollegiate competition. The lower court granted a preliminary injunction that ordered that plaintiff be allowed to compete in intercollegiate wrestling during the 2000-2001 academic year. The West Virginia Supreme Court reversed. In vacating the injunction, the court ruled that student-athletes do not possess a constitutionally protected property interest in participating in intercollegiate athletics.

[A] student's ability to participate in athletic contests is not a right recognized by the law of this State. "[P]articipation in interscholastic athletics . . . does not rise to the level of a constitutionally protected 'property' or 'liberty' interest. . . ." As Hart has no enforceable right to compete in collegiate wrestling contests, he has no existing right meriting protection by way of a preliminary injunction against the NCAA or the [Southern Conference].

Id. at 86. Accord *Equity in Athletics, Inc. v. Dep't of Educ.*, 675 F. Supp. 2d 660, 681 (W.D. Va. 2009) (adopting the majority rule that college athletes possess no property interest in athletic participation).

PROBLEM 3-5

You are general counsel at a Division I university. Your faculty athletics representative (FAR), who also serves as chairman of your institution's faculty athletics committee (FAC), which is given authority to hear scholarship termination cases, has asked you for advice regarding the creation of guidelines or standards for that process. At present, the FAC has broad discretion to hear such cases, and there are no institutional rules or guidelines. In responding to the FAR's request, consider the benefits and difficulties associated with discretion and with written guidelines. You should also consider whether the FAC should maintain written records of their deliberations and decisions as well as the nature of any such records.

4. *Student-Athletes as Employees: Eligibility for Workers' Compensation Benefits*

Generally, a person injured while performing services for compensation is considered an employee if two elements are present: (1) an express or implied contract to hire and (2) employee status. A contract to hire binds an employer to pay compensation to an employee who performs services, sets forth the place to perform such services and work to be performed, and sets the compensation for the performance of the work. Assuming the existence of a contract to hire, the inquiry shifts to whether the contract gives rise to an employer-employee relationship.

Courts often adopt one of the following standards to determine an employment relationship: (1) the right to control the details of the work test or (2) the relative nature of the work test. The right to control test examines whether the employer possessed the right to control the manner, means, and details of the worker's performance. Factors that demonstrate the requisite right of control include the terms of the employment agreement, the actual exercise of control, the method of payment, the furnishing of equipment, and the right to terminate the worker. An alternative standard used by an increasing number of courts is the relative nature of the work test. Pursuant to this test, "employees are those who as a matter of economic reality are dependent upon the business to which they render service." Leo L. Lam, Comment, *Designer Duty: Extending Liability to Manufacturing for Violation of Labor Standards in Garment Industry Sweatshops*, 141 U. Pa. L. Rev. 623, 651 (1992). This test is likely to be satisfied when a worker performs tasks integral to the employer's regular business and does not provide an independent business or professional service vis-à-vis the employer. The principal consideration under the nature of the work test is the relationship between the services provided and the regular business of the alleged employer.

Although historically courts were divided over the question of whether scholarship student-athletes are covered by workers' compensation statutes, the modern trend is not to afford employee status to student-athletes. While reading the following case, *Waldrep v. Texas Employers Insurance Association*, consider which test the court applied in rejecting the student-athlete's claim to workers' compensation benefits. Also consider the broader economic, legal, and policy implications of defining student-athletes as employees, and the extent to which the *Waldrep* court was influenced by such concerns.

WALDREP v. TEXAS EMPLOYERS INSURANCE ASSN.

21 S.W.3d 692 (Tex. Ct. App. 2000)

YEAKEL, Judge.

Appellant Alvis Kent Waldrep, Jr. was awarded workers' compensation benefits by the Texas Workers' Compensation Commission (the "Commission") for an injury he sustained while playing football for Texas Christian University ("TCU"). Appellee Texas Employers Insurance Association ("TEIA"), in receivership, Texas Property and Casualty Insurance Guaranty Association appealed the award to the district court. Following a trial *de novo*, a jury found that Waldrep had failed to prove that he was an employee of TCU at the time of his injury. The district court rendered judgment that Waldrep take nothing against TEIA.

Waldrep appeals the judgment, claiming that (1) he was an employee as a matter of law. . . . We will affirm the district court's judgment.

BACKGROUND

Waldrep graduated from high school in Alvin, Texas in 1972. During his junior and senior years, TCU was among many schools interested in recruiting Waldrep, a young man known for his athletic ability as well as his good academic record. Tommy Runnels, a TCU assistant football coach, visited Waldrep frequently at his home and school, attempting to interest Waldrep in TCU's football and academic programs. During one home visit, Waldrep's mother asked Runnels what would happen if Waldrep were injured during his football career at TCU. Runnels assured Waldrep and his family that TCU would "take care of them" and emphasized that Waldrep would keep his scholarship even if he were injured and could not play football.

Waldrep was very impressed with the facilities at TCU and believed that his abilities would fit in well with TCU's football program. He was also aware that recruitment and his future involvement in athletics at TCU were governed by the rules of the Southwest Athletic Conference ("Southwest Conference")[3] and the National Collegiate Athletic Association ("NCAA"). To affirm his intent to attend school at TCU and participate in TCU's football program, Waldrep signed two documents. First, Waldrep signed a pre-enrollment form ("Letter of Intent") . . . , which demonstrated his formal desire to play football for TCU and penalized him if he decided to enter a different school within the Southwest Conference. . . . Waldrep later signed a financial aid agreement ("Financial Aid Agreement") . . . , ensuring that Waldrep's room, board, and tuition would be paid while attending TCU and that Waldrep would receive ten dollars per month for incidentals. This cash payment was generally referred to as "laundry money." Both documents were contingent on Waldrep's meeting TCU's admission and scholastic requirements for athletic awards.

In August 1972, Waldrep enrolled at TCU. In October 1974, while playing football for TCU against the University of Alabama, Waldrep was critically injured. He sustained a severe injury to his spinal cord and was paralyzed below the neck. Today, Waldrep has no sensation below his upper chest. In 1991, Waldrep filed a workers' compensation claim for his injury.

DISCUSSION

STATUS AS AN EMPLOYEE FOR WORKERS' COMPENSATION PURPOSES

The question presented to this Court is whether there is some evidence (more than a mere scintilla) supporting the jury's failure to find that Waldrep was an employee of TCU at the time of his injury. Stated another way, could any reasonable and fair-minded person conclude that Waldrep was not employed by TCU when injured? We answer this question affirmatively.

---

3. At the time, TCU was a member of the Southwest Conference. That athletic conference no longer exists.

We are confronted with a situation novel to Texas jurisprudence: whether, for workers' compensation law purposes, a recipient of a scholarship or financial aid from a university becomes that university's employee by agreeing in return to participate in a university-sponsored program. Cases decided under the various workers' compensation statutes in effect from time to time have almost uniformly determined the existence of an employer-employee relationship by an analysis of whether the claimant of workers' compensation benefits was an *employee* as distinguished from an *independent contractor*. . . . These authorities do not conveniently overlay the facts presented here, as there is no allegation that Waldrep was an independent contractor. Yet they are instructive in one significant aspect: one may receive a benefit from another in return for services and not become an employee.

The jury charge defined "employee" as "a person in the service of another under a contract of hire, express or implied, oral or written, whereby the employer has the right to direct the means or details of the work and not merely the result to be accomplished. . . ." (Footnote omitted.) Thus, in failing to find that Waldrep was TCU's employee, the jury may have believed that there was no contract of hire between Waldrep and TCU or, if there was, it did not give TCU the right to direct the means or details of Waldrep's "work." We will examine both possibilities. . . .

EXISTENCE OF CONTRACT OF HIRE

For the purpose of workers' compensation law, the employer-employee relationship may be created *only* by a contract. . . . Waldrep strongly urges that the Letter of Intent and Financial Aid Agreement are express contracts of hire that set forth the terms of Waldrep's "employment." However, we do not find these documents to be so clear. At best, they only partially set forth the relationship between Waldrep and TCU. By their terms, they generally bound Waldrep to TCU to the exclusion of other Southwest Conference schools, if he intended to participate in athletics, and extended him financial aid so long as he complied with the admission and scholastic requirements of TCU and the rules and regulations of both TCU and the Southwest Conference. These requirements, rules, and regulations are not specifically described in either of the agreements. Nor does the record in this case set them forth in any detail. The Letter of Intent and Financial Aid Agreement are also silent with regard to whether any rules or regulations of the NCAA would apply to Waldrep or affect his relationship with TCU. Yet it is undisputed that before Waldrep signed the Letter of Intent and Financial Aid Agreement, both he and TCU understood that his recruitment and future football career at TCU would be governed by and subject to the rules of the NCAA.

TEIA, on the other hand, posits that Waldrep clearly and simply did not have a contract of hire. . . .

Mindful of the district court's definition of employee, the jury was left to determine if there was a "contract of hire" between Waldrep and TCU. We observe that "the most basic policy of contract law . . . is the protection of the justified expectations of the parties." *DeSantis v. Wackenhut Corp.*, 793 S.W.2d 670, 677 (Tex. 1990). Was it the expectation of Waldrep and TCU that Waldrep would become TCU's employee? To form a contract, the parties must mutually assent to its terms. Whether there is such assent is determined "based on objective standards of what the parties said and did and not on their alleged subjective states of mind." *American Nat'l Ins. Co. v. Paul*, 927 S.W.2d 239, 244

(Tex. App.—Austin 1996, writ denied) (quoting *Adams v. Petrade Int'l, Inc.*, 754 S.W.2d 696, 717 (Tex. App.—Houston [1st Dist.] 1988, writ denied)). Because the Letter of Intent and Financial Aid Agreement do not evidence the entire agreement between Waldrep and TCU, we consider them against "the background of circumstances surrounding [their] execution." *Brown*, 395 S.W.2d at 702 (citing *Allison v. Campbell*, 117 Tex. 277, 298 S.W. 523 (Tex. Comm. App. 1927, opinion adopted)). We may also look to the parties' conduct after execution of the documents, and such conduct "may be a strong factor in determining just what the real agreement contemplated." *Maryland Cas. Co. v. Brown*, 131 Tex. 404, 115 S.W.2d 394, 396 (Tex. 1938).

On the facts of this record, any contract of hire must have been a contract whereby TCU hired Waldrep to attend the university, remain in good standing academically, and play football. However, if Waldrep played football for pay, he would have been a professional, not an amateur. The evidence reflects that the actions of both Waldrep and TCU were consistent with a joint intention that Waldrep be considered an amateur and not a professional. It is undisputed that before Waldrep signed the Letter of Intent and Financial Aid Agreement, both he and TCU understood that his recruitment and future football career at TCU would be governed by and subject to the rules of the NCAA. The record indicates that the NCAA's policies and rules in effect at that time exhibited a concerted effort to ensure that each school governed by these rules made certain that student-athletes were not employees. Indeed, the rules declared that the fundamental policy of the NCAA was "to maintain intercollegiate athletics as an integral part of the educational program and the athlete as an integral part of the student body, and, by so doing, retain a clear line of demarcation between college athletics and professional sports." (citation omitted). Following its policy, the evidence reflects that the NCAA rules made the principle of amateurism foremost and established several requirements to ensure that the student-athlete would not be considered a professional. . . . For example, the NCAA had strict rules against student-athletes taking pay for participation in sports, and student-athletes were ineligible to participate if they were receiving or had received a salary from a professional sports organization.

Additionally, the record reflects that Waldrep and TCU did not treat the financial aid Waldrep received as "pay" or "income." First, as previously noted, the NCAA rules provided that student-athletes would be ineligible if they used their skill for pay in any form; however, that same rule goes on to state that "a student-athlete may accept scholarships or educational grants-in-aid from his institution" as these benefits do not conflict with the NCAA rules. (Citation omitted.) As the NCAA rules were based upon a principle of amateurism and strictly prohibited payment for play, these two provisions together indicate that the NCAA and its participating institutions did not consider the acceptance of financial aid from the institution to be "taking pay." Moreover, the rules provided that any financial aid that exceeded tuition and fees, room and board, required course-related supplies and books, and incidental expenses of fifteen dollars per month would be considered "pay" for participation in intercollegiate athletics. . . . TCU gave Waldrep financial aid for these items but nothing more, indicating that TCU did not intend to pay Waldrep for his participation. Of equal significance, TCU never placed Waldrep on its payroll, never paid him a salary, and never told him that he would be paid a salary. There is no evidence that Waldrep expected a salary. No social security or income tax was withheld from Waldrep's grant-in-aid. *See Continental Ins. Co. v. Wolford*, 526 S.W.2d 539,

540 (Tex. 1975) (withholding taxes is *indicia* of employee status). Waldrep never filed a tax return reporting his financial aid.

The evidence further reflects that Waldrep and TCU intended that Waldrep participate at TCU as a *student,* not as an *employee.* During the recruitment process, TCU never told Waldrep that he would be an employee, and Waldrep never told TCU that he considered himself to be employed. Moreover, a basic purpose of the NCAA, which governed Waldrep's intercollegiate football career, was to make the student-athlete an integral part of the student body. *See NCAA Manual* at 5. According to the NCAA rules, "an amateur student-athlete is one who engages in athletics for the education, physical, mental and social benefits he derives therefrom, and to whom athletics is an avocation." *NCAA Manual* at 6. Of importance is the evidence that Waldrep was aware when he signed the Letter of Intent and Financial Aid Agreement that he would still receive financial aid even if hurt or unable to play football, as long as he complied with the rules of the Southwest Conference. Thus, TCU could not "fire" Waldrep as it could an employee. . . . In addition, when Waldrep signed the agreements, he still had to meet the scholastic requirements for athletic awards and qualify for admission to TCU in order to enroll and participate in the football program. Waldrep testified that he knew when he signed the agreements that in order to play football at TCU he would have to maintain certain academic requirements as a student. Thus, his academic responsibilities dictated whether he could continue to play football.

Financial-aid awards are given to many college and university students based on their abilities in various areas, including music, academics, art, and athletics. Sometimes these students are required to participate in certain programs or activities in return for this aid. But, as the Supreme Court of Indiana observed, "scholarship recipients are considered to be students seeking advanced educational opportunities and are not considered to be professional athletes, musicians or artists employed by the university for their skill in their respective areas." *Rensing v. Indiana State Univ. Bd. of Trustees,* 444 N.E.2d 1170, 1174 (Ind. 1983).

Although the record in this case contains facts from which the jury could have found that Waldrep and TCU were parties to a contract of hire, there is also probative evidence to the contrary. Viewing the evidence in the light most favorable to the jury's verdict, we hold that the record before us reflects more than a mere scintilla of evidence that Waldrep was not in the service of TCU under a contract of hire.

RIGHT TO DIRECT THE MEANS OR DETAILS OF WALDREP'S WORK

If, however, we assume the jury found that a contract existed between Waldrep and TCU, we must determine whether there is some evidence concerning TCU's right to direct the means or details of Waldrep's "work." The definition of "employee" submitted to the jury correctly states the recognized test to determine whether an employer-employee relationship exists: the *right* of the employer to direct or control the means or details of the employee's work. *See Mayo,* 688 S.W.2d at 243 (ultimate test in deciding employment question is right of alleged employer to control specifics of worker's performance) (citing *Hartsfield,* 390 S.W.2d at 471). To determine whether there is a right of control, "we first must look to the terms of the employment contract." *Allstate Ins. Co. v. Scott,* 511 S.W.2d 412, 414 (Tex. Civ. App.—El Paso 1974, writ ref'd n.r.e.). Where there is no express contract or where the terms of the contract are indefinite, the *exercise* of control "may be the best evidence available to show the actual terms of the contract." *Newspapers, Inc. v. Love,* 380 S.W.2d 582, 590 (Tex. 1964); *see Scott,* 511 S.W.2d at 414. However, "'the *right* to control' remains the supreme test and the 'exercise of control' necessarily presupposes a right to control which must be related to some agreement expressed or implied." *Love,* 380 S.W.2d at 590 (emphasis added); *see Scott,* 511 S.W.2d at 414 ("the exercise of control, while evidentiary only and not the true test, is the best evidence available in determining the right of control").

The record reflects that TCU *exercised* direction and control over all of the athletes in its football program, including non-scholarship players, while they were participating in the *football program.* Waldrep admitted that his high school coaches exercised the same type of control over his participation in sports as the coaches at TCU. Waldrep further testified that he did everything that the coaches told him to do because he wanted to, because he loved the game, and because he wanted to be the best, not because he had to. The evidence is clear that TCU did not have the right to direct or control all of Waldrep's activities during his tenure at the school. The NCAA rules protected Waldrep's financial-aid award even if his physical condition prevented him from playing football for any reason. *See NCAA Manual* at 8. Moreover, TCU could not simply cancel Waldrep's grant-in-aid based on his "athletic ability or his contribution to [the] team's success," or even, in certain circumstances, if he quit. *Id.*

The fact that the athletic department at TCU established practice and meeting times to be observed by those playing football does not establish that TCU had the *right* to direct and control all aspects of the players' activities while enrolled in the university. Waldrep's acceptance of financial aid from TCU did not subject him to any extraordinary degree of control over his academic activities.

Waldrep clearly presented evidence that TCU *exercised* direction or control over some of his activities while a student at the university. Perhaps the jury might have found this sufficient to prove that TCU had the *right* to direct the means or details of Waldrep's activities, but the jury declined to do so. Viewing the evidence in the light most favorable to the jury's verdict, we hold that the record before us reflects more than a mere scintilla of evidence disputing TCU's right of control.

The district court properly left the jury to determine the issue of employment. The circumstances presented in the record before us do not establish an employer-employee relationship as a matter of law. We hold that there is some evidence to support the jury's verdict declining to find that Waldrep was an employee of TCU at the time of his injury.

CONCLUSION

In conclusion, we note that we are aware college athletics has changed dramatically over the years since Waldrep's injury. Our decision today is based on facts and circumstances as they existed almost twenty-six years ago. We express no opinion as to whether our decision would be the same in an analogous situation arising today; therefore, our opinion should not be read too broadly. Having disposed of all of the issues before us, we affirm the district court's judgment.

Affirmed.

right to control test

(1) terms of K
(2) exercise of control

NOTES AND QUESTIONS

1. *Employment Status.* What test was adopted in *Waldrep* to determine if the plaintiff was an employee for workers' compensation benefits? What are the elements of the standard adopted? The court affirmed the jury's finding that Waldrep was not a university employee when he suffered a permanently disabling injury during a game. Although Waldrep received an athletic scholarship for participating in university-sponsored athletics, the court found that it was not the expectation of the parties that he thereby became a paid university employee. According to the court, what was the parties' expectation regarding the nature of Waldrep's relationship with TCU? On what sources did the court rely in arriving at its characterization of the parties' expectations regarding their relationship?

2. *Requisite Degree of Control for Employment Status.* The *Waldrep* court concludes that even though the university "*exercised* direction and control over all of the athletes in its football program" (emphasis in original), TCU did not have the "right to direct or control all of Waldrep's activities during his tenure at the school."

   Moreover, Waldrep's participation in football "did not subject him to any extraordinary degree of control over his academic activities." What is the relevance of the right of control? Is the court's analysis of the degree of control exercised by athletic departments over student-athletes naïve? Which factor seems most influential in the court's assessment that the requisite right to control for workers' compensation purposes is absent?

   exercise of control

   The *Waldrep* court relied on TCU's inability to terminate its contract with Waldrep during the one-year term. Is this an accurate assessment of the realities of the student-athlete/university relationship? Is the unilateral right of a university not to renew the relationship akin to the right of an employer to terminate an employee in other settings?

   In *University of Colorado v. Derdeyn*, 863 P.2d 929 (Colo. 1993), the university argued that its drug-testing program did not violate the federal or Colorado constitutions, in part, because of student-athletes' lessened expectation of privacy. In support of its defense, the university emphasized the extent of control that universities exercise over student-athletes. Consider the following comments of the Colorado Supreme Court:

   > CU argues that student athletes' expectations of privacy with regard to urinalysis are diminished because they submit to extensive regulation of their on- and off-campus behavior, including maintenance of required levels of academic performance, monitoring of course selection, training rules, mandatory practice sessions, diet restrictions, attendance at study halls, curfews, and prohibitions on alcohol and drug use. . . .
   >
   > CU's athletic director testified in relevant part that the NCAA sets limits on financial aid awards, playing seasons, squad size, and years of eligibility; that the NCAA requires that CU maintain records of each athlete's academic performance; that the "athletes that eat at training tables are football and men's basketball and the other athletes eat in the dorms or at their off-campus residences"; that some coaches within their discretion impose curfews; that athletes are required to show up for practice; that athletes are "advised . . . on what they should take for classes"; that "we have a required study hall in the morning and in the evening"; and that it is "fair to say that the athletes are fairly well regulated." A student athlete testified in relevant part that "Yes,"

"if you are an NCAA athlete, you have to keep a certain grade average," and "Yes," "if your grades drop below that average, then you are not eligible for competition."

Although it is obviously not amenable to precise calculation, it is at least doubtful that the testimony relied upon by CU fully supports CU's assertion that its student athletes are "extensively regulated in their on and off-campus behavior," especially with regard to all of the particulars that CU asserts.

Id. at 940-941.

3. *Statutory Exclusion.* Might the Texas legislature have intervened if a different result had been reached in *Waldrep*? Some early cases held that an injured intercollegiate athlete could recover workers' compensation benefits if he held a university job unrelated to athletics. See, e.g., *Van Horn v. Indus. Accident Comm'n*, 33 Cal. Rptr. 169 (Cal. Ct. App. 1963); *Univ. of Denver v. Nemeth*, 257 P.2d 423 (Colo. 1953). After *Van Horn*, the California legislature amended its workers' compensation statute to expressly exclude student-athletes from its coverage. See Cal. Lab. Code §3352(k) (Deering Supp. 2011). See also Haw. Rev. Stat. Ann. §386-1 (Michie Supp. 2011) (worker or employee "shall not include a person engaged in amateur sports even if an employer contributes to support of such sports"); N.Y. Workers' Comp. §2(4) (McKinney 2012) ("'employee' shall not include persons who are members of a supervised amateur athletic activity operated on a non-profit basis"). Oregon and Vermont by virtue of Or. Rev. Stat. §656.027(13) (2008) and 21 Vt. Stat. Ann. §601(14(b)) (LexisNexis 2009), respectively, also exclude student-athletes from coverage pursuant to their workers' compensation laws. In contrast, Nebraska has established an administrative system for providing medical and disability benefits to injured university athletes. See, e.g., Neb. Rev. Stat. §85-106.05 (2011).

4. *Judicial Interpretations.* Most states do not expressly include or exclude scholarship athletes from coverage under their respective workers' compensation statutes or provide a system of compensation for injured university athletes. Thus, courts must determine whether or not scholarship athletes are covered "employees."

Despite some early contrary authority, as illustrated by *Van Horn* and *Nemeth*, courts now generally hold that athletes who suffer injuries while participating in intercollegiate athletics are not entitled to workers' compensation benefits. See *Rensing v. Indiana State Univ. Bd. of Trustees*, 444 N.E.2d 1170 (Ind. 1983); *Coleman v. Western Mich. Univ.*, 336 N.W.2d 224 (Mich. Ct. App. 1983); *State Compensation Ins. Fund v. Industrial Comm'n*, 314 P.2d 288 (Colo. 1957). Courts have refused to find that a student's receipt of an athletic scholarship establishes an employment relationship with a university, a prerequisite for workers' compensation coverage. These courts usually reach this conclusion for policy reasons, mainly based on a reluctance to characterize college athletes as professionals who are paid to play sports.

For example, in *Rensing v. Indiana State Univ. Bd. of Trustees*, 444 N.E.2d 1170 (Ind. 1983), the Indiana Supreme Court held that a football player could not recover workers' compensation benefits for an injury suffered during spring football practice that left him a quadriplegic. The court found no employer/employee relationship because the university and injured student did not intend to create a contract of employment. The four-year financial aid package received by plaintiff was not considered "pay" by either the parties or the Internal Revenue Service. *Id.* Rather, plaintiff was "still first and foremost a student," and the scholarship benefits were awarded, based on previously demonstrated athletic ability, to enable him to receive a college education. *Id.* at 1174. Accord *Coleman v. Western Mich. Univ.*, 336 N.W.2d 224 (Mich. Ct. App. 1983) (applying "economic reality" to find that although the plaintiff's athletic scholarship constituted "wages," and the university had a limited right to control the plaintiff's activities and discipline him, conducting a football program was not an integral part of the university's business, which was to provide an academic education). *Id.* at 226-227.

[handwritten: same reasoning here]

In *Shephard v. Loyola Marymount Univ.*, 102 Cal. App. 4th 837 (Cal. App. 2 Dist. 2002), the court held that a student-athlete was not an employee for the purpose of bringing a lawsuit pursuant to the California Fair Employment and Housing Act (FEHA). In reaching this decision, the court analogized the FEHA to California's workers' compensation law that excludes student-athletes. The court also based its decision on NCAA amateurism provisions that impliedly provide that student-athletes are not employees of their institutions as well as on relevant federal and state income tax provisions that specifically exclude athletic scholarships from gross income. See also *Kavanagh v. Trustees of Boston Univ.*, 795 N.E.2d 1170 (Mass. 2003) (provision of scholarship or other financial aid to student-athletes does not create an employment relationship for purposes of respondeat superior); *Korellas v. Ohio State Univ.*, 121 Ohio Mis. 2d 16, 779 N.E.2d 1112 (2002) (scholarship student-athlete on university's football team is not an employee of the institution and therefore not entitled to governmental immunity in a civil action).

5. *Scholarly Views.* Several legal commentators have criticized courts' refusals to include injured scholarship athletes within the coverage of workers' compensation statutes. See Larson, *supra* note 253, §22.21(c); Frank P. Tiscione, *College Athletics and Workers' Compensation: Why the Courts Get It Wrong in Denying Student-Athletes Workers' Compensation Benefits When They Get Injured*, 14 Sports Law. J. 137 (2007); Sean Alan Roberts, Comment, *College Athletes, Universities, and Workers' Compensation: Placing the Relationship in the Proper Context by Recognizing Scholarship Athletes as Employees*, 37 S. Tex. L. Rev. 1315 (1996); Mark R. Whitmore, Note, *Denying Scholarship Athletes Worker's Compensation: Do Courts Punt Away a Statutory Right?*, 76 Iowa L. Rev. 763 (1991).

Scholars have also debated whether student-athletes should be considered employees of their schools. See Robert A. McCormick and Amy Christian McCormick, *Myth of the Student-Athlete: The College Athlete as Employee*, 81 Wash. L. Rev. 71 (2006); Nathan McCoy and Kerry Knox, Comment, *Flexing Union Muscle — Is It the Right Game Plan for Revenue Generating Student-Athletes in Their Contest for Benefits Reform with the NCAA?*, 69 Tenn. L. Rev. 1051 (2002); Peter C. Goplerud, *Pay for Play for College Athletes: Now, More Than Ever*, 38 S. Tex. L. Rev. 1081 (1997).

6. *Competing Models.* Professor Timothy Davis posits that two models of intercollegiate athletics emerge from judicial decisions and scholarly discourse. Under the amateur/education model, the student-athlete is viewed as an amateur, and college athletics is considered an integral part of the educational purpose of universities. The competing model, the commercial/education model, assumes that college sport is a commercial enterprise subject to the same economic considerations as any other industry. Despite the considerable impact of economic factors on college sports, education remains

[handwritten: Model 1]
[handwritten: Model 2]

a component of the conceptualization of college sports. In the following excerpt, Professor Davis comments on the influence of judicial conceptualizations of college sports pursuant to one of these models on the resolution of cases involving student-athlete entitlement to workers' compensation.

> [L]egal doctrine and philosophical visions of college athletics combine to shape the judicial response to a student-athlete's status as an employee for worker's compensation purposes. Courts declining to define student-athletes as employees adopt the views of intercollegiate athletics embodied in the amateur/education model of college sports. The judiciary in these cases perceives college sports as serving an academic function where intercollegiate athletics are simply an avocation of the student.
>
> Juxtaposed with these decisions are cases in which the judiciary recognizes the impact of commercialism on college sports and on the student-athlete's relationship with his university. Here, the duality of the student-athlete's role, as a student on the one hand and an employee on the other, provides the framework from which the relevant issues are analyzed. Employment status stems from the quid pro quo that earmarks the contractual obligations between a student-athlete and his institution. Nevertheless, these cases recognize that the student-athlete is still a student, hence creating an educational component to college sports.
>
> The student-athlete worker's compensation decisions also illustrate the significant extent to which a court's reliance on a particular conceptual model influences the ultimate disposition of the case. Recognizing these judicial tendencies, parties to disputes arising within intercollegiate athletics construct their policy and legal arguments upon these two competing conceptual schemes.

Timothy Davis, *Intercollegiate Athletics: Competing Models and Conflicting Realities*, 25 Rutgers L.J. 269 (1994).

7. *Institutional Payment of Medical Expenses.* If an injury prevents a student-athlete from participating in intercollegiate athletics, NCAA bylaws permit a university to continue his or her scholarship so that the athlete can complete his or her education. Courts have held that a public university's gratuitous payment of medical expenses for athletes injured in intercollegiate sports, made from a fund generated by athletic department revenue, is a proper expenditure furthering a legitimate public purpose. See *State ex rel. Bd. of Governors of W. Va. Univ. v. Sims*, 59 S.E.2d 705, 710-711 (W. Va. 1950). However, absent a valid contract, a university has no obligation to pay for an injured athlete's medical expenses. See *Searles v. Trs. of St. Joseph's Coll.*, 695 A.2d 1206, 1211-1212 (Me. 1997); *Reed v. Univ. of N.D.*, 543 N.W.2d 106, 110 (Minn. Ct. App. 1996); *Reed v. Univ. of N.D.*, 589 N.W.2d 880, 884 (N.D. 1999); *Cardamone v. Univ. of Pittsburgh*, 384 A.2d 1228, 1232-1233 (Pa. Super. Ct. 1978). Moreover, an athlete's past service to a university as an intercollegiate athlete is not valid consideration for the university's agreement to pay for medical expenses arising out of an athletic injury. See *Cardamone*, 384 A.2d at 1232-1233. On the other hand, NCAA schools are required to certify that student-athletes have health insurance. The NCAA permits schools to require student-athletes to have their own insurance or to be covered by their parents' policy, but many universities provide medical care or health insurance for their student-athletes.

If a TCU athletic official had orally promised Waldrep that the university would provide him with all necessary medical treatment for future sustained injuries as an inducement to play a sport, would this promise be

[handwritten: Promissory estoppel?]

enforceable? See *Eberhart v. Morris Brown Coll.*, 352 S.E.2d 832, 834 (Ga. Ct. App. 1987) (limiting recovery to only those medical expenses incurred in connection with an athletic injury).

8. *NCAA Insurance Programs.* Since August 1, 1992, the NCAA has provided cata-strophic athletic injury insurance covering the more than 400,000 student-athletes who suffer serious injuries while participating in intercollegiate athletics at member institutions. This plan, which provides for a maximum lifetime benefit of $20 million, compensates for educational benefits and lost earnings, as well as lifetime rehabilitation, medical costs, and dental expenses. Catastrophic injuries that fall within a covered loss are defined as:

[handwritten: Waldrep would have recovered under this]

> i. The inability of the Insured Person, as the result of a Covered Accident, to engage in substantially the same activities as the Insured Person had engaged in immediately prior to the Covered Accident; and
>
> ii. The irrevocable loss suffered by the Insured Person, as a result of the Covered Accident, of: a) speech; or b) hearing of both ears; or c) sight in both eyes; or d) use of both arms; or e) use of both legs; or f) use of one arm and one leg; or g) severely diminished mental capacity due to brain stem or other neurological injury such that the Insured Person is unable to perform normal daily functions.

NCAA Catastrophic Injury Insurance Program Benefit Summary for 8/1/11 through 7/31/12, at p. 7, http://www.ncaa.org/wps/wcm/connect/public/ncaa/pdfs/2011/catastrophic+injury+insurance+program+benefit+summary.

The NCAA also has established a program that enables qualified "excep-tional" student-athletes to obtain a preapproved loan to purchase disabil-ity insurance. This policy is designed to protect talented student-athletes against the loss of expected future earnings should they suffer a disabling injury or illness while in college. When the NCAA initiated the program in 1990, exceptional student-athletes in football and men's basketball could obtain coverage. Thereafter, the program was expanded periodically such that it now includes exceptional student-athletes in baseball, men's ice hockey, and women's basketball. *Exceptional Student-Athlete Disability Insurance Program*, NCAA, Aug. 30, 2011, http://www.ncaa.org/wps/wcm/connect/public/ncaa/ncaa+insurance+programs/student+athlete+insurance+pro grams/exceptional+student+athlete+disability+insurance+program.

9. *California "Student Athlete Bill of Rights."* In September 2012, California enacted a law (effective with the 2013-2014 academic year) that requires any California four-year university whose athletic program receives $10 million or more in media revenues (currently Stanford University; the University of California, Berkeley; the University of California, Los Angeles; and the University of Southern California) to provide an academic scholarship for up to five academic years, or until he or she graduates, to a student-athlete who suffers a career-ending injury causing the loss of an athletic scholarship.

D. FIRST AMENDMENT RIGHTS ISSUES

As is the case in the interscholastic area (see Chapter 2), student-athletes, coaches, and others may raise issues regarding alleged violations of their rights under the First Amendment of the United States Constitution by state actors (e.g., public universities). Lawsuits seeking to protect alleged infringement of such rights arise in a number of contexts. For example, coaches and student-athletes have alleged that their free speech rights have been violated. In *Crue v. Aiken*, 370 F.3d 668 (7th Cir. 2004), a group of university students alleged that university rules preventing them from contacting prospective student-athletes violated their right of free speech. The students sought to inform athletes of the University of Illinois's controversial use of a Native American mascot in connection with its intercollegiate athletics teams.

It is clear, as well, that the courts consider maturation issues (the maturity of the student-athletes involved) in determining whether rights have been infringed. High school or younger students are often treated differently than more mature college students. Secondary schools often act in an *in loco parentis* (in the place of the parent) capacity. High schools are, therefore, often afforded greater power to regulate the speech and expression of their students than is afforded to colleges and universities. As you read the following cases, reflect on how First Amendment and other constitutional standards may be different at the intercollegiate and interscholastic or high school levels.

As the following materials demonstrate, alleged violations of First Amendment rights have been raised with respect to athletic department officials' and student-athletes' interaction with the media as well as alleged violations of an athlete's freedom of religion by a public university. The materials in this section are only intended to be illustrative of the kinds of issues that arise and are not intended to be exhaustive in their treatment of the First Amendment area.

1. The First Amendment and the Media

Athletic administrators, coaches, and student-athletes often have conflicts with broadcast and print media. With the public attention and commercialization of sport, it is not surprising that the media has extended its coverage into matters that might have been deemed, in other contexts, to be private in nature. For example, criminal accusations or other comments in the media that deal with the private lives of student-athletes and coaches may be given broad coverage in the media, particularly in the case of high-profile coaches, student-athletes, and administrators. High-profile administrators, coaches, and student-athletes receive less protection against incursions by the media into their private lives than most individuals do, under defamation law and the right of privacy, because they have been held to be public figures.

If a high-profile administrator, coach, or student-athlete decides to pursue recovery for defamatory falsehoods against the media, he or she must prove that the media acted with "actual malice," "knowing falsity," or "reckless disregard for the truth" in publishing a falsehood (truth is a defense in such cases) as required under applicable First Amendment case law. Such proof is not easy to muster, and it is clearly difficult for a high-profile athletic figure to recover if he or she is deemed to be a public figure.

The landmark Supreme Court case *Curtis Publishing Co. v. Butts*, 388 U.S. 130 (1967), arose from the accusations in a newspaper accusing Butts, the athletic director at the University of Georgia, of attempting to "fix" a 1962 football game between the Universities of Georgia and Alabama. In a libel action filed in federal court, Butts sought $5 million compensatory and $5 million punitive damages. The jury returned a verdict for $60,000 in general damages and for

$3 million in punitive damages. The trial court reduced the total to $460,000 by remittitur.

In a strongly divided set of opinions, the Court held that the *New York Times* actual malice (knowing falsity or reckless disregard for the truth) standard applied in the case of someone in the position of Athletic Director Butts. In his plurality opinion, Justice Harlan suggested that Athletic Director Butts could meet the burden of proof regarding reckless disregard for the truth by proving that the defendant engaged in "highly unreasonable conduct constituting an extreme departure from the standards of investigation and reporting ordinarily adhered to by responsible publishers." *Id.* at 153-155. This standard came to be referred to as the "professional standard rule," but it was generally rejected in *Harte-Hanks Communications, Inc. v. Connaughton*, 491 U.S. 657 (1989). In *Harte-Hanks*, Justice Stevens opined:

> In *Butts* the evidence showed that the *Saturday Evening Post* had published an accurate account of an unreliable informant's false description of the Georgia athletic director's purported agreement to "fix" a college football game. Although there was reason to question the informant's veracity, just as there was reason to doubt Thompson's story, the editors did not interview a witness who had the same access to the facts as the informant and did not look at films that revealed what actually happened at the game in question. This evidence of an intent to avoid the truth was not only sufficient to convince the plurality that there had been an extreme departure from professional publishing standards, but it was also sufficient to satisfy the more demanding *New York Times* standard applied by Chief Justice Warren.

491 U.S. 657 at 692-693.

Even though the public-figure status makes it very difficult for someone in the position of Butts to prevail in a defamation action, the *Butts* and *Harte-Hanks* cases provide a means by which a party might prevail—by proving reckless disregard with full knowledge of the harm that is likely to result from the publication. Butts ultimately prevailed on just such a ground.

The following case shows that student-athletes also have been characterized as public figures in a privacy action against two newspapers for an article published about the team.

BILNEY v. THE EVENING STAR NEWSPAPER CO.

43 Md. App. 560, 406 A.2d 652 (1979)

Appellants are six young men who, in 1977, were undergraduate students at the University of Maryland (College Park Campus) and members of the University's varsity basketball team. Feeling aggrieved by articles appearing in the November 1, 1977, editions of the *Washington Star* and the student publication, the *Diamondback*, they sued the publishers of those newspapers and a number of individuals who allegedly participated in the writing and editing of the articles for invasions of privacy and intentional infliction of mental distress. The Circuit Court for Prince George's County entered summary judgment in favor of all defendants save one, which it dismissed on motion raising preliminary objection; and this appeal followed.

. . . College basketball, particularly at the University of Maryland, is a "big time" sport. It generates a great deal of interest and excitement, not only among the students but among sports enthusiasts in most of the Baltimore-Washington megalopolis and, indeed, because of the team's frequent national ranking, among sports-minded people throughout the country. It also generates a lot of money legally for the University and the Atlantic Coast Conference, of which the University is a member, and illicitly for those who wager on college sporting events. Newspapers in the area follow the team's prospects and achievements with great interest and regularity.

The interest in the team, of course, spills over to the individual players. Their recruitment by the University and their individual performances as team members are given wide publicity, much of which is initiated or controlled by the University and its officials. Appellants, in their brief, concede that, by virtue of their status as members of the basketball team, they were "public figures" that, as team members they were the subject and object of widespread public interest.

Pursuant to certain regulations adopted by the National Collegiate Athletic Association and the University of Maryland, students at the University who have completed 45 credits must maintain a grade-point average of 1.95 or above (essentially equivalent to a C) and must earn at least 24 "quality points" per semester. Failure to meet these standards will cause a student to be placed on academic probation; and, of central importance in this case, if a student is on academic probation in two consecutive semesters, he is subject to dismissal from the University. If dismissed, of course, he becomes ineligible to play on the school basketball team.

Each of these appellants was the recipient and beneficiary of an athletic scholarship, awarded by the University, that defrayed all or a major part of his college expenses. Academic success of a University athlete is encouraged and given wide publicity. The University publicly posts a list of all of its athletes earning a grade point average of 3.0 or better, and it gives special publicity to those who achieve more notable success.

Thus it is that the academic prowess of these appellants, and their colleagues, was of significant public interest and concern not only in terms of the University's policy of encouraging scholastic success, but also from the perspective of their continuing eligibility to play varsity basketball.

On the morning of November 1, 1977, the *Washington Post* published an article quoting the University's basketball coach, "Lefty" Driesell, as admitting that four of the team's eight returning players were on academic probation for failing to meet grade requirements in the previous semester, and that two others had recently been taken off such probation. Although not directly identifying the four players, the article proceeded to permit their easy identification by a process of elimination. It named the eight veterans, stated that two appellants Boston and Davis had recently been taken off probation, and noted that two others, not involved in this case but who were named, were on the Atlantic Coast Conference honor roll. That, of course, left the four remaining appellants Bilney, Bryant, Gibson, and Hunter as those who were currently on probation. No action has been filed with respect to this article.

Later that morning, the *Star* printed two articles concerning appellants Bilney, Bryant, Gibson, and Hunter. Prominently displayed on page one were photographs of the four players, under which appeared their names and the statement: "The University of Maryland's basketball program is in danger of collapse because of poor schoolwork. The Star has learned that four of eight returning players Larry Gibson, Jo Jo Hunter, Billy Bryant and John Bilney are on academic probation and in danger of flunking." The full story appeared on the first page of the sports section. Under the by-line of appellee Dick Heller, identified as a *Star* "Staff Writer," the article recited that the *Star* had learned "from university records" that the four named players were "on academic probation and in danger of flunking" at the end of the fall semester. It went on to quote comments from Coach Driesell, Chancellor Gluckstern, Athletic Director Kehoe, other University officials and faculty members, and former University basketball stars, all dealing either with appellants' particular dilemma or the general problem of satisfying minimum academic requirements. At the end of the article, it was noted that appellees Kram, Burke, and Blum "also contributed to this report." The second article in the *Star* was a column also under Heller's by-line that dealt primarily with Coach Driesell.

The third newspaper to comment on this matter was the *Diamondback*. On that same day, November 1, in an article written by appellees Burke and Kram, it was again reported that Bilney, Bryant, Gibson, and Hunter were on probation and "in danger of being academically dismissed." More specifically, this article stated that "According to records, Bilney finished last semester with a 1.5 grade point average, Bryant with a 1.24, Gibson with a 1.88 and Hunter with a 1.1." It said also that appellant Boston had been "academically dismissed" the previous spring, but had been reinstated, and that appellant Davis, while having a 2.2 grade point average, had been temporarily placed on probation for a quality point deficiency which was subsequently corrected.

Appellants named as defendants in their action the publishers of the *Star* and the *Diamondback* (appellees Evening Star Newspaper Company and Maryland Media, Inc.); and various individuals including the editor and sports editor of the *Star* (appellees Bellows and Beitchman); Richard Heller (the *Star* staff reporter); Eric Blum, a "stringer" for the *Star*; and the two authors of the *Diamondback* article who also were credited with contributing to the *Star* story (appellees Burke and Kram). The gravamen of their complaint, both in terms of the invasion of privacy and intentional infliction of mental distress counts, was that appellees willfully, wrongfully, and maliciously invaded appellants' confidential University records and published private and privileged facts about their private lives. Both torts rested upon the unlawful obtention (sic) of confidential school records and the unlawful publication of such records.

Maryland Media, Inc. sought and obtained preliminary dismissal under Maryland Rule 323 on the basis of eleemosynary immunity. For reasons shortly to be explained, it is not necessary for this Court to consider the propriety of that decision, although appellants have raised it as an issue in their appeal. After extensive discovery and the filing of voluminous affidavits, deposition transcripts, and other assorted documents, all other parties moved for summary judgment. Following a recorded oral argument, the court, as noted, denied the motion filed by appellants and granted those filed by appellees. . . .

(3) Right to Publicize Scholastic Standing

We . . . [now] consider the propriety of its publication in the context of the tort of invasion of privacy.[3] Conceding that they were public figures and that the

---

3. Appellants' argument as to the propriety of publishing this information is couched solely in terms of whether the publication was an invasion of their privacy. They do not discuss whether such publication also amounted to an intentional infliction of emotional distress, and neither shall we.

information printed was true, appellants maintain that their scholastic status was a purely private matter unaffected by any public interest or concern.

That invasion of privacy would be recognized as a separate tort in Maryland and redress provided for its commission was first suggested by the Court of Appeals in *Carr v. Watkins*, 227 Md. 578, 177 A.2d 841 (1962). Although, at that time, more than 70 years had elapsed since the American nativity of the tort in the famous article by Warren and Brandeis (*The Right to Privacy*, 4 Harv. L. Rev. 193 (1890)) and the tort had already been recognized throughout most of the United States, there had yet to be reached any real consensus among courts and commentators as to its precise nature. The *Carr* Court observed only that it emanated from the right "to be let alone" and had a certain kinship with the tort of defamation. 227 Md. at 586, 177 A.2d 841.

In the years following *Carr*, however, a good bit of "fleshing out" and molding occurred, notably with the drafting and adoption of new sections 652A-652I of the Restatement of Torts (2d), and the tort was given a more precise and standard description. When it next dealt with the matter, in *Household Fin. Corp. v. Bridge*, 252 Md. 531, 250 A.2d 878 (1969), the Court of Appeals recognized these later developments and, in general, blessed by adoption their product.

. . . Restatement (2d), § 652A describes four ways in which one may tortiously invade the privacy of another. At issue here is the third of these methods § 652A(2Xc) "unreasonable publicity given to the other's private life, as stated in § 652D." Section 652D provides: "One who gives publicity to a matter concerning the private life of another is subject to liability to the other for invasion of his privacy, if the matter publicized is of a kind that:

(a) Would be highly offensive to a reasonable person, and
(b) Is not of legitimate concern to the public."

Comment e to § 652D deals with "voluntary public figures." Not all of it is relevant here, but this much, we think, is: "One who voluntarily places himself in the public eye, by engaging in public activities, or by assuming a prominent role in institutions or activities having general economic, cultural, social or similar public interest, or by submitting himself or his work for public judgment, cannot complain when he is given publicity that he has sought, even though it may be unfavorable to him. . . . In such a case, however, the legitimate interest of the public in the individual may extend beyond those matters which are themselves made public, and to some reasonable extent may include information as to matters that would otherwise be private."

The concept described in the emphasized portion of comment e is touched on in greater detail in comment h. That says, in relevant part:

> Permissible publicity to information concerning either voluntary or involuntary public figures is not limited to the particular events that arouse the interest of the public. That interest, once aroused by the event, may legitimately extend, to some reasonable degree, to further information concerning the individual and to facts about him, which are not public and which, in the case of one who had not become a public figure, would be regarded as an invasion of his purely private life. . . .
>
> The extent of the authority to make public private facts is not, however, unlimited. . . . In determining what is a matter of legitimate public interest, account

must be taken of the customs and conventions of the community; and in the last analysis what is proper becomes a matter of the community mores. The line is to be drawn when the publicity ceases to be the giving of information to which the public is entitled, and becomes a morbid and sensational prying into private lives for its own sake, with which a reasonable member of the public, with decent standards, would say that he had no concern. The limitations, in other words, are those of common decency, having due regard to the freedom of the press and its reasonable leeway to choose what it will tell the public, but also due regard to the feelings of the individual and the harm that will be done to him by the exposure. Some reasonable proportion is also to be maintained between the event or activity that makes the individual a public figure and the private facts to which publicity is given.

Our Court of Appeals summarized these principles most cogently in *Beane v. McMullen*, 265 Md. 585, 600, 291 A.2d 37, 45 (1972) when it stated that "reasonableness under the facts presented is the determining factor." *See also Hollander*, *supra*, 277 Md. at 60, 351 A.2d 42, 1.

Appellants achieved the status of public figures solely by virtue of their membership on the University basketball team. Their possible exclusion from the team whether for academic or any other reason was therefore a matter of legitimate public interest. Had they quit the team or withdrawn from the University, the public would be entitled to ask and to speculate as to the reasons for such action. That the threat of exclusion was academically based does not lessen the legitimacy of the public interest. Appellants were not in the same posture as other students, whose scholastic standing, in its entirety, was purely of private concern; when their standing reached the point of affecting their eligibility to play basketball for the University, the privacy of that status became somewhat attenuated. Publication of that eligibility-threatening status was not unreasonable and did not trample upon community mores. Having sought and basked in the limelight, by virtue of their membership on the team, appellants will not be heard to complain when the light focuses on their potentially imminent withdrawal from the team. We thus concur with the circuit court that, upon the undisputed evidence in this case, the publications in question did not constitute a tortious invasion of privacy.

NOTES AND QUESTIONS

1. *Coaches as Public Figures.* Should coaches be treated as public figures for defamation and privacy purposes? If you were representing a basketball coach at a major Division I-A institution who was concerned about falsehoods printed in a local paper, what advice would you give him or her? Would your advice differ if the falsehoods were related to a matter regarding the coach's private life (e.g., an alleged extramarital affair)? Would your advice differ if the coach of a non-revenue-producing and non-high-profile sport asked you to represent him or her in a defamation action related to an article dealing with his or her sexual orientation?
2. *Student-Athletes as Public Figures.* Should student-athletes be treated as public figures for defamation and privacy purposes? Was the *Bilney* case correctly decided? What if the student-athletes were complaining about falsehoods in an article claiming that the team members were engaged in alleged drug

use? These kinds of cases present challenging counseling problems, because you must explain why the law is unlikely to protect alleged victims against the harms done by such falsehoods. See Rodney K. Smith and Patrick Shea, *Religion and the Press: Keeping First Amendment Values in Balance*, 2002 Utah L. Rev. 177, an article discussing the challenges that attend advising a public figure in the defamation and privacy contexts.

3. *Athletics Administrators as Public Figures.* Should presidents and other athletics administrators at a university be considered public figures? Where should the line be drawn in determining which individuals at a university are public figures? Should student-athletes in major sports be held to be public figures while a law school dean would not be?

2. Religious Liberty Issues

As noted previously, religious liberty issues often arise in the interscholastic athletics context. Religious liberty issues are discussed in greater length in Chapter 2, dealing with interscholastic athletics. Similar issues arise at the intercollegiate level. For an excellent article examining these issues at the interscholastic and intercollegiate levels, see Scott C. Idleman, *Religious Freedom and the Interscholastic Athlete*, 12 Marq. Sports L. Rev. 295 (2001).

Some of the areas in which it can be anticipated that religious liberties will be implicated in the intercollegiate athletic context include the following: (1) recognition of religious activity on the part of student-athlete, coaches, and athletic personnel (see, e.g., Gil Fried and Lisa Bradley, *Applying the First Amendment to Prayer in a Public University Locker Room: An Athlete's and Coach's Perspective*, 4 Marq. Sports L.J. 301 (1994)); (2) accommodating the religious interests of competitors (e.g., coaches and conferences have been known to be sensitive to the religious interests of student-athletes and have rescheduled events and have relieved student-athletes of practice and other obligations so that they could exercise their religious conscience); and (3) accommodating religious institutions (e.g., Brigham Young University refuses to participate in athletic events on Sunday, the Sabbath for members of the Church of Jesus Christ of Latter-day Saints, and that refusal has resulted in their being placed in brackets in the NCAA Men's Basketball Tournament that will permit them to avoid having to violate their Sabbath and play on a Sunday).

Courts have been increasingly reluctant to recognize rights of religious conscience by requiring institutions or associations to accommodate the religious conscience of administrators, coaches, and student-athletes. Nevertheless, although the NCAA, conferences, and coaches have been willing to permit such accommodations, this is not always the case. The courts have indicated, however, a willingness to intervene to avoid discrimination against certain religious groups. For example, it is likely that a court would hold that a Christian coach who, on religious grounds, permitted his student-athletes to avoid practice on Christmas but refused to allow similar exemptions or accommodations to Jewish student-athletes on Rosh Hashanah would be found to be acting in a discriminatory fashion. Of course, it should be noted that proving religious discrimination is very difficult—few individuals admit to having acted in a religiously discriminatory fashion, and it is difficult to prove such discrimination based on nonsubjective factors.

NOTES AND QUESTIONS

1. *Religious Exemptions.* Even though it is not subject to the constraints of the federal constitution because it is not a state actor (see *NCAA v. Tarkanian, infra*), the NCAA has exempted brief religious observances by student-athletes, including pausing to pray or express religious gratitude in the end zone after scoring a touchdown, from its general rule that prohibits players from celebrating or drawing attention to themselves on the football field. Do you agree with this exemption? Does it prefer religion over other significant interests of student-athletes? It also should be noted that federal statutes and state constitutional provisions might provide athletes with greater protection, in the form of exemptions and otherwise, than is currently required of the NCAA.

2. *Relevence of Student Maturity.* Student-athletes at the intercollegiate level are generally older and more mature than high school or interscholastic student-athletes. For example, prayers in a high school locker room, particularly if they are led or sponsored by the coach, are arguably more offensive to impressionable high school athletes than they might be to intercollegiate student-athletes. Does this distinction in levels of maturity provide a legitimate basis for permitting more religion or religious exercise on the part of intercollegiate student-athletes?

3. *State Constitutional Law.* As noted in Chapter 2, which discusses high school athletics, state constitutional issues may arise in the First Amendment and other areas. For example, although federal constitutional law does not require that the religious conscience of student-athletes be recognized, state constitutional law may do so. In evaluating First Amendment and other constitutional law issues, therefore, it is imperative that sources of state constitutional law be consulted to determine whether the state has provided more (it may not provide less) protection than that available under federal constitutional law.

4. *Privacy Law.* In *National Collegiate Athletic Assn. v. Associated Press*, 18 So. 3d 1201 (Fla. Dist. Ct. App. 2009), the Associated Press sought to obtain records regarding the Committee on Infractions decision imposing penalties against Florida State University and vacating wins by the football program that would adversely impact Coach Bobby Bowden's quest to be the winningest coach in Division I history. The NCAA refused to provide the Associated Press with the transcript of the hearings before the Committee on Infractions, which the NCAA deemed to be confidential and shielded by privacy. The Associated Press filed suit. The appellate court affirmed the lower court decision holding that the transcript and response were public records under state law, that the state law was constitutional, and that the records were not exempt from disclosure under federal statutory law. The court emphasized that the state constitution gave the public broad rights to inspect governmental records. The NCAA provided those materials which they deemed to be confidential to counsel for Florida State University, and the court found that the law firm qualified as an agent of the state and that the transcripts and related documents were being viewed by counsel as a part of its fulfillment of a public function. The court also held that the materials were not shielded by federal privacy law, because FERPA protects only educational records, which have been defined as records containing information that relates directly to a student.

This case demonstrates how the NCAA's involvement with state actors can on occasion subject it to federal law and provides an excellent bridge to the *Tarkanian* case that follows. For an interesting article discussing the role of the state in governing Sunday play and end zone celebrations, see Kevin J Worthen, *The NCAA and Religion: Insights About Non-State Governance from Sunday Play and End Zone Celebrations,* 2010 Utah L. Rev. 123 (2010).

PROBLEM 3-6

You are general counsel at a major university, and a Muslim student-athlete has asked to meet with you to discuss a dispute he has with his coach. The coach insists that student-athletes maintain a rigorous diet, which includes eating certain meals each day. The Muslim student desires to follow his religious conscience and fast on certain days and avoid eating some of the meals prescribed by the coach. He also eats a more vegetarian diet than the high-protein fare established by the coach. Before the meeting, you call the coach, and he says that although he respects the student-athlete for his religious conviction, it is imperative that he eat with the team for health purposes and to maintain team morale. He is fearful that yielding to this student-athlete's religious beliefs would simply open a Pandora's box, permitting student-athletes to contrive all kinds of reasons for getting out of his strict dietary regimen. The coach also indicated that the diet was devised in conjunction with his athletic trainer and is believed to maximize performance on the part of student-athletes.

What do you say to the student-athlete? Is it likely that he has a cognizable legal action, on First Amendment grounds, against the coach and university? Will you indicate a willingness to try to persuade the coach to accommodate the religious conscience of the student-athlete? If so, what would you say? Would your analysis change depending on whether the sport in which the student-athlete participates is football or golf?

3.   *Free Speech and Retaliation Issues*

In *Ridpath v. Board of Governors Marshall University,* 447 F.3d 292 (4th Cir. 2006), a compliance officer at Marshall University became aware of a number of violations of NCAA rules, including the school's practice of providing student-athletes with jobs at "above-market" wages. After bringing this information to the attention of university officials, the compliance officer alleged he was prevented from assisting in the investigation, blamed for the violations, and subjected to "corrective action" and transferred to another position on campus that significantly diminished his ability to obtain future employment in his chosen occupation of athletic compliance. The court denied the university's immunity defense and found that the compliance officer had a liberty interest in his reputation or choice of occupation for due process purposes. The court held, in this regard, that the transfer was in fact a demotion and was only labeled as a transfer as a way of avoiding potential liability for demoting the compliance officer.

The court next examined the First Amendment issue and confirmed that a public employer "contravenes a public employee's First Amendment rights when it discharges or refuses to rehire the employee or when it makes decisions relating to the promotion, transfer, recall and hiring in the exercise of that employee's free speech rights." *Id.* at 316. The court held that the plaintiff had sufficiently alleged that he was speaking as a private citizen and not as a public employee, and that his interest in exercising his First Amendment rights was not outweighed by the university's interest in his speech because the school was unable to show how the plaintiff's remarks had interfered with its legitimate operations. The plaintiff also produced testimony that supported his claim that "but for" his speaking out against the school's conduct in its compliance process, he would not have been terminated from his position as compliance officer. Given that the evidence suggested that university administrators attempted to use their positions to intimidate the plaintiff so that he would remain silent regarding the investigation, the court found that he had properly alleged claims for retaliation and chilling of his free speech rights.

On the other hand, in *Richardson v. Sugg*, 448 F.3d 1046 (8th Cir. 2006) (discussed in Chapter 10), the court held that the firing of an African American head basketball coach was not an abridgment of his First Amendment rights or racially motivated. As to the First Amendment claim, the court held that the detrimental impact of Richardson's comments regarding the university outweighed any free speech right he may have asserted. The *Richardson* and *Ridpath* cases illustrate the nature of proof that must be proffered to prevail on free speech and retaliation grounds and how public universities must respond to such allegations.

E.   NCAA REGULATORY AUTHORITY AND LEGAL LIMITS THEREON

1.   Federal Constitutional Law

The U.S. Constitution imposes constraints on the regulatory authority of the NCAA's member public institutions, whose conduct constitutes state action. However, the following Supreme Court case holds that the NCAA is a private association and demonstrates judicial reluctance to impose federal constitutional limits on its regulation of intercollegiate athletics.

NCAA v. TARKANIAN
488 U.S. 179 (1988)

Justice STEVENS delivered the opinion of the Court.

When he became head basketball coach at University of Nevada, Las Vegas (UNLV) in 1973, Jerry Tarkanian inherited a team with a mediocre 14-14 record. Four years later the team won 29 out of 32 games and placed third in the championship tournament sponsored by the National Collegiate Athletic Association (NCAA), to which UNLV belongs.

Yet in September 1977 UNLV informed Tarkanian that it was going to suspend him. No dissatisfaction with Tarkanian, once described as "the 'winningest' active basketball coach," motivated his suspension. Rather, the impetus was a report by the NCAA detailing 38 violations of NCAA rules by UNLV personnel, including 10 involving Tarkanian. The NCAA had placed the University's basketball team on probation for two years and ordered UNLV to show cause why the NCAA should not impose further penalties unless UNLV severed all ties during the probation between its intercollegiate athletic program and Tarkanian.

Facing demotion and a drastic cut in pay, Tarkanian brought suit in Nevada state court, alleging that he had been deprived of his Fourteenth Amendment due process rights in violation of 42 U.S.C. § 1983. Ultimately Tarkanian obtained injunctive relief and an award of attorney's fees against both UNLV and the NCAA. . . . NCAA's liability may be upheld only if its participation in the events that led to Tarkanian's suspension constituted "state action" prohibited by the Fourteenth Amendment and were performed "under color of state law within the meaning of § 1983. . . ."

I

THE NCAA INVESTIGATION OF UNLV

On November 28, 1972, the Committee on Infractions notified UNLV's president that it was initiating a preliminary inquiry into alleged violations of NCAA requirements by UNLV. As a result of that preliminary inquiry, some three years later the Committee decided that an "Official Inquiry" was warranted and so advised the UNLV president on February 25, 1976. That advice included a series of detailed allegations concerning the recruitment of student athletes during the period between 1971 and 1975. Many of the allegations implicated Tarkanian. It requested UNLV to investigate and provide detailed information concerning each alleged incident.

With the assistance of the Attorney General of Nevada and private counsel, UNLV conducted a thorough investigation of the charges. On October 27, 1976, it filed a comprehensive response containing voluminous exhibits and sworn affidavits. The response denied all of the allegations and specifically concluded that Tarkanian was completely innocent of wrongdoing. Thereafter, the Committee conducted four days of hearings at which counsel for UNLV and Tarkanian presented their views of the facts and challenged the credibility of the NCAA investigators and their informants. Ultimately the Committee decided that many of the charges could not be supported, but it did find 38 violations of NCAA rules, including 10 committed by Tarkanian. Most serious was the finding that Tarkanian had violated the University's obligation to provide full cooperation with the NCAA investigation. . . .

The Committee proposed a series of sanctions against UNLV. The Committee also requested UNLV to show cause why additional penalties should not be imposed against UNLV if it failed to discipline Tarkanian by removing him completely from the University's intercollegiate athletic program during the probation period. UNLV appealed most of the Committee's findings and proposed sanctions to the NCAA Council. After hearing arguments from attorneys representing UNLV and Tarkanian, the Council on August 25, 1977 unanimously approved the Committee's investigation and hearing process and adopted all its recommendations.

UNLV'S DISCIPLINE OF TARKANIAN

Promptly after receiving the NCAA report, the president of UNLV directed the University's vice president to schedule a hearing to determine whether the

Committee's recommended sanctions should be applied. Tarkanian and UNLV were represented at that hearing, the NCAA was not. Although the vice president expressed doubt concerning the sufficiency of the evidence supporting the Committee's findings, he concluded that "given the terms of our adherence to the NCAA we cannot substitute—biased as we must be—our own judgment on the credibility of witnesses for that of the infractions committee and the Council." . . . [H]e advised the president that he had three options:

1. Reject the sanction requiring us to disassociate Coach Tarkanian from the athletic program and take the risk of still heavier sanctions, e.g., possible extra years of probation.
2. Recognize the University's delegation to the NCAA of the power to act as ultimate arbiter of these matters, thus reassigning Mr. Tarkanian from his present position—though tenured and without adequate notice—even while believing that the NCAA was wrong.
3. Pull out of the NCAA completely on the grounds that you will not execute what you hold to be their unjust judgments. . . .

[T]he president accepted the second option and notified Tarkanian that he was to be completely severed of any and all relations, formal or informal, with the University's Intercollegiate athletic program during the period of the University's NCAA probation.

so not fired?

TARKANIAN'S LAWSUIT AGAINST UNLV

The day before his suspension was to become effective, Tarkanian filed an action in Nevada state court for declaratory and injunctive relief against UNLV and a number of its officers. He alleged that these defendants had, in violation of 42 U.S.C. § 1983, deprived him of property and liberty without the due process of law guaranteed by the Fourteenth Amendment to the United States Constitution. Based on a stipulation of facts and the testimony offered by Tarkanian, the trial court enjoined UNLV from suspending Tarkanian on the ground that he had been denied procedural and substantive due process of law. UNLV appealed.

π

The NCAA, which had not been joined as a party, filed an amicus curiae brief arguing that there was no actual controversy between Tarkanian and UNLV; thus, the suit should be dismissed. Alternatively, the NCAA contended that the trial court had exceeded its jurisdiction by effectively invalidating the enforcement proceedings of the NCAA, even though the Association was not a party to the suit. Should a controversy exist, the NCAA argued, it was a necessary party to litigate the scope of any relief. Finally, it contested the trial court's conclusion that Tarkanian had been denied due process. The Nevada Supreme Court concluded that there was an actual controversy but agreed that the NCAA was a necessary party and therefore reversed and remanded to permit joinder of the NCAA. *University of Nevada v. Tarkanian*, 95 Nev. 389, 594 P.2d 1159 (1979).

NCAA

THE LAWSUIT AGAINST NCAA

Tarkanian consequently filed a second amended complaint adding the NCAA. . . . [T]he trial judge conducted a two-week bench trial and resolved the issues in Tarkanian's favor. The court concluded that NCAA's conduct constituted state action for jurisdictional and constitutional purposes, and that its decision was arbitrary and capricious. It reaffirmed its earlier injunction barring

UNLV from disciplining Tarkanian or otherwise enforcing the Confidential Report. Additionally, it enjoined the NCAA from conducting "any further proceedings against the University," from enforcing its show-cause order, and from taking any other action against the University that had been recommended in the Confidential Report. . . .

. . . The Nevada Supreme Court agreed that Tarkanian had been deprived of both property and liberty protected by the Constitution and that he was not afforded due process before suspension. It thus affirmed the trial court's injunction insofar as it pertained to Tarkanian, but narrowed its scope "only to prohibit enforcement of the penalties imposed upon Tarkanian in Confidential Report No. 123(47) and UNLV's adoption of those penalties. . . ."

As a predicate for its disposition, the State Supreme Court held that the NCAA had engaged in state action. Several strands of arguments supported this holding. First, the court assumed that it was reviewing "UNLV's and the NCAA'[s] imposition of penalties against Tarkanian," . . . [and not] the NCAA's proposed sanctions against UNLV if it failed to discipline Tarkanian appropriately. Second, it regarded the NCAA's regulatory activities as state action because "many NCAA member institutions were either public or government supported. . . ." Third, it stated that the right to discipline a public employee "is traditionally the exclusive prerogative of the state" and that UNLV could not escape its responsibility for such disciplinary action by delegating that duty to a private entity. . . . Summing up its holding that the NCAA's activities constituted state action, the Nevada Supreme Court stated:

> The first prong [of *Lugar v. Edmondson Oil Co.*, 457 U.S. 922 (1982)] is met because no third party could impose disciplinary sanctions upon a state university employee unless the third party received the right or privilege from the university. Thus, the deprivation which Tarkanian alleges is caused by the exercise of a right or privilege created by the state. Also, in the instant case, both UNLV and the NCAA must be considered state actors. By delegating authority to the NCAA over athletic personnel decisions and by imposing the NCAA sanctions against Tarkanian, UNLV acted jointly with the NCAA.

II

Embedded in our Fourteenth Amendment jurisprudence is a dichotomy between state action, which is subject to scrutiny under the Amendment's Due Process Clause, and private conduct, against which the Amendment affords no shield, no matter how unfair that conduct may be. . . .

In this case, Tarkanian argues that the NCAA was a state actor because it misused power that it possessed by virtue of state law. He claims specifically that UNLV delegated its own functions to the NCAA, clothing the Association with authority both to adopt rules governing UNLV's athletic programs and to enforce those rules on behalf of UNLV. Similarly, the Nevada Supreme Court held that UNLV had delegated its authority over personnel decisions to the NCAA. Therefore, the court reasoned, the two entities acted jointly to deprive Tarkanian of liberty and property interests, making the NCAA as well as UNLV a state actor.

These contentions fundamentally misconstrue the facts of this case. In the typical case raising a state action issue, a private party has taken the decisive conduct as state action. This may occur if the State creates the legal framework governing the conduct . . . if it delegates its authority to the private actor, . . . or sometimes if it knowingly accepts the benefits derived from unconstitutional behavior. . . . [I]n the usual case we ask whether the State provided a mantle of authority that enhanced the power of the harm-causing individual actor.

This case uniquely mirrors the traditional state action case. Here the final act challenged by Tarkanian—his suspension—was committed by UNLV. When *public* it decides to impose a serious disciplinary sanction upon one of its tenured employees, it must comply with the terms of the Due Process Clause of the Fourteenth Amendment to the Federal Constitution. . . .

The mirror image presented in this case requires us to step through an analytical looking glass to resolve it. Clearly UNLV's conduct was influenced by the rules and recommendations of the NCAA, the private party. But it was UNLV, the state entity, that actually suspended Tarkanian. Thus the question is not whether UNLV participated to a critical extent in the NCAA's activities, but whether UNLV's actions in compliance with the NCAA rules and recommendations turned the NCAA's conduct into state action. *Issue (1)*

We examine first the relationship between UNLV and the NCAA regarding the NCAA's rule-making. UNLV is among the NCAA's members and participated in promulgating the Association's rules; it must be assumed, therefore, that Nevada had some impact on the NCAA's policy determinations. Yet the NCAA's several hundred other public and private member institutions each similarly affected those policies. Those institutions, the vast majority of which were located in states other than Nevada, did not act under color of Nevada law. It necessarily follows that the source of the legislation adopted by the NCAA is not Nevada but the collective membership, speaking through an organization *not NV law* that is independent of any particular State. . . .

State action nonetheless might lie if UNLV, by embracing the NCAA's rules, transformed them into state rules and the NCAA into a state actor. . . . UNLV engaged in state action when it adopted the NCAA's rules to govern its own behavior, but that would be true even if UNLV had taken no part in the promulgation of those rules. UNLV retained the authority to withdraw from the NCAA and establish its own standards. The University alternatively could have stayed in the Association and worked through the Association's legislative process to amend rules or standards it deemed harsh, unfair, or unwieldy. Neither UNLV's decision to adopt the NCAA's standards nor its minor role in their formulation is a sufficient reason for concluding that the NCAA was acting under color of Nevada law when it promulgated standards governing athlete recruitment, eligibility, and academic performance.

Tarkanian further asserts that the NCAA's investigation, enforcement proceedings, and consequent recommendations constituted state action because *π* they resulted from a delegation of power by UNLV. UNLV, as an NCAA member, subscribed to the statement in the Association's bylaws that NCAA "enforcement procedures are an essential part of the intercollegiate athletic program of each member institution. . . ." [A s]tate may delegate authority to a private party and thereby make that party a state actor. . . . But UNLV delegated no power to the NCAA to take specific action against any University employee. The commitment by UNLV to adhere to NCAA enforcement procedures was enforceable only by sanctions that the NCAA might impose on UNLV itself.

Indeed, the notion that UNLV's promise to cooperate in the NCAA enforcement proceedings was tantamount to a partnership agreement or the transfer of certain University powers to the NCAA is belied by the history of this case. It is quite obvious that UNLV used its best efforts to retain its winning coach—a goal diametrically opposed to the NCAA's interest in ascertaining the truth of its investigators' reports. During the several years that the NCAA investigated the alleged violations, the NCAA and UNLV acted much more like adversaries than like partners engaged in a dispassionate search for the truth. The NCAA cannot be regarded as an agent of UNLV for purposes of that proceeding. It is more correctly characterized as an agent of its remaining members which, as competitors of UNLV, had an interest in the effective and evenhanded enforcement of NCAA's recruitment standards. . . .

The NCAA enjoyed no governmental powers to facilitate its investigation. It had no power to subpoena witnesses, to impose contempt sanctions, or to assert sovereign authority over any individual. Its greatest authority was to threaten sanctions against UNLV, with the ultimate sanction being expulsion of the University from membership. Contrary to the premise of the Nevada Supreme Court's opinion, the NCAA did not—indeed, could not—directly discipline Tarkanian or any other state university employee. The express terms of the Confidential Report did not demand the suspension unconditionally; rather, it requested "the university . . . to show cause" why the NCAA should not impose additional penalties if UNLV declines to suspend Tarkanian. . . . Even the university's vice president acknowledged that the Report gave the university options other than suspension: UNLV could have retained Tarkanian and risked additional sanctions, perhaps even expulsion from the NCAA, or it could have withdrawn voluntarily from the Association.

Finally, Tarkanian argues that the power of the NCAA is so great that the UNLV had no practical alternative to compliance with its demands. We are not at all sure this is true . . . , but even if we assume that a private monopolist can impose its will on a state agency by a threatened refusal to deal with it, it does not follow that such a private party is therefore acting under color of state law. . . .

It would be ironic indeed to conclude that the NCAA's imposition of sanctions against UNLV—sanctions that UNLV and its counsel, including the Attorney General of Nevada, steadfastly opposed during protracted adversary proceedings—is fairly attributable to the State of Nevada. It would be more appropriate to conclude that UNLV has conducted its athletic program under color of the policies adopted by the NCAA, rather than that those policies were developed and enforced under color of Nevada law.

The judgment of the Nevada Supreme Court is reversed and the case is remanded to that court for further proceedings not inconsistent with this opinion.

It is so ordered.

Justice WHITE, with whom Justice BRENNAN, Justice MARSHALL, and Justice O'CONNOR join, dissenting.

. . . I agree with the majority that this case is different on its facts from many of our prior state action cases. As the majority notes, in our "typical case raising a state action issue, a private party has taken the decisive step that caused the harm to the plaintiff." . . . In this case, however, the final act that caused the harm to Tarkanian was committed, not by a private party, but by a party conceded to be a state actor.

But the situation presented by this case is not unknown to us and certainly is not unique. In both *Adickes v. S.H. Kress & Co.*, 398 U.S. 144 (1970), and *Dennis v. Sparks*, 449 U.S. 24 (1980), we faced the question of whether private parties could be held to be state actors in cases in which the final or decisive act was carried out by a state official. In both cases we held that the private parties could be found to be state actors, if they were "jointly engaged with state officials in the challenged action. . . ."

On the facts of the present case, the NCAA acted jointly with UNLV in suspending Tarkanian. First, Tarkanian was suspended for violations of NCAA rules, which UNLV embraced in its agreement with the NCAA. . . .

Second, the NCAA and UNLV also agreed that the NCAA would conduct the hearings concerning violations of its rules. Although UNLV conducted its own investigation into the recruiting violations alleged by the NCAA, the NCAA procedures provide that it is the NCAA Committee on Infractions that "determine[s] facts related to alleged violations," subject to an appeal to the NCAA Council. . . .

Third, the NCAA and UNLV agreed that the findings of fact made by the NCAA at the hearings it conducted would be binding on UNLV. By becoming a member of the NCAA, UNLV did more than merely "promise to cooperate in the NCAA enforcement proceedings." . . . [T]he NCAA's findings were final and not subject to further review by any other body . . . , and it was for that reason that UNLV suspended Tarkanian, despite concluding that many of those findings were wrong. . . .

In short, it was the NCAA's findings that Tarkanian had violated NCAA rules, made at NCAA-conducted hearings, all of which were agreed to by UNLV in its membership agreement with the NCAA, that resulted in Tarkanian's suspension by UNLV. [T]he majority relies on the fact that the NCAA did not have any power to take action directly against Tarkanian as indicating that the NCAA was not a state actor. . . . But the same was true in [our decision in *Dennis*]: the private parties did not have any power to issue an injunction against the plaintiff. Only the trial judge, using his authority granted under state law, could impose the injunction.

Next, the majority points out that UNLV was free to withdraw from the NCAA at any time. . . . But of course the trial judge in *Dennis* could have withdrawn from his agreement at any time as well. That he had that option is simply irrelevant to finding that he had entered into agreement. What mattered was not that he could have withdrawn, but rather that he did not do so.

Finally, the majority relies extensively on the fact that the NCAA and UNLV were adversaries throughout the proceedings before the NCAA. . . . But this opportunity for opposition, provided for by the terms of the membership agreement between UNLV and the NCAA, does not undercut the agreement itself. Surely our decision in *Dennis* would not have been different had the private parties permitted the trial judge to seek to persuade them that he should not grant the injunction before finally holding the judge to his agreement with them to do so. The key there, as with any conspiracy, is that ultimately the parties agreed to take the action.

The majority states in conclusion that "[I]t would be ironic indeed to conclude that the NCAA's imposition of sanctions against UNLV—sanctions that UNLV and its counsel, including the Attorney General of Nevada, steadfastly opposed during protracted adversary proceedings—is fairly attributable to the State of Nevada." . . . Had UNLV refused to suspend Tarkanian, and the NCAA responded by imposing sanctions against UNLV, it would be hard indeed to find any state action that harmed Tarkanian. But that is not this case. Here, UNLV did suspend Tarkanian, and it did so because it embraced the NCAA

I agree... good reasoning

rules governing conduct of its athletic program and adopted the results of the hearings conducted by the NCAA concerning Tarkanian, as it had agreed that it would. Under these facts, I would find that the NCAA acted jointly with UNLV and therefore is a state actor.

I respectfully dissent.

NOTES AND QUESTIONS

1. *Lower Court Precedent.* Prior to *Tarkanian,* a number of lower courts had held that the NCAA was a state actor for constitutional purposes. See George W. Schubert et al., Sports Law at 64-66 (1986). Despite acknowledging that most courts had held that the NCAA was a state actor, those authors opined, "[I]t is certainly conceivable that a court may find that government action is not present on public function or any other grounds, particularly given the courts' propensity to defer to the decisions of amateur athletic and other institutions in a sports context." *Id.* at 68. Why are courts inclined to defer to sports governing bodies, including those with a substantial number of public school members? Is there something special about athletics that warrants judicial deference?

2. *Comparing* Brentwood *and* Tarkanian. Considering both recent changes in the composition of the Supreme Court and the Court's 2001 *Brentwood Academy* decision holding that the Tennessee State High School Athletic Association is a state actor (see Chapter 2), is *Tarkanian* likely to be overruled in the near future? What would be the implications if the NCAA were held to be a state actor? These issues continue to be discussed in the law review literature. See, e.g., Vikram David Amar, *The NCAA As Regulator, Litigant, and State Actor,* 52 B.C. L. Rev. 415 (2011) (arguing that the NCAA should be deemed to be a state actor).

3. *Impact of Restructuring.* Professor Burlette Carter has pointed out that even though the NCAA is not a state actor, some states have adopted the NCAA's rules and regulations or embraced them either legislatively or through the common law. Thus, this is the unusual situation of a private group making rules that the government has embraced. W. Burlette Carter, *Student-Athlete Welfare in a Restructured NCAA,* 2 Va. J. of Sports & L. 1, 84 (2000). She also argues that the restructuring of NCAA governance may have a profound impact on whether courts continue to adhere to the view that the NCAA is not a state actor. "The courts must now assess *Tarkanian* through new eyes, aware of the new post-Restructuring facts that could establish both delegation and conspiracy. In Division I those facts include the delegation of legislative authority to the Board and the new legislative process that limits individual institutional input." *Id.* at 93. Do you agree that this "delegation of authority" will or should affect *Tarkanian*'s holding that the NCAA is not a state actor?

4. *Subsequent NCAA Revisions to Enforcement Process.* After *Tarkanian,* the NCAA created a special commission to evaluate the due process provided institutional members and their personnel in the enforcement process. As discussed *infra,* many changes were made, including the addition of the Infractions Appeals Committee. Does the NCAA currently provide an adequate level of due process to coaches and others indirectly regulated by its rules? As

you read the Consent Decree in the Penn State University case discussed later in this chapter, ask yourself whether Penn State and its personnel were afforded sufficient due process by the NCAA.

5. *Dormant Commerce Clause Limit on State Regulatory Authority.* In response to *Tarkanian,* the Nevada legislature enacted a statute requiring "any national collegiate athletic association to provide a Nevada institution, employee, student-athlete, or booster who is accused of a rules infraction with certain procedural due process protections during an enforcement proceeding in which sanctions may be imposed." *NCAA v. Miller,* 10 F.3d 633, 637 (9th Cir. 1993). The federal district court upheld the statute, but the Ninth Circuit reversed:

> The Statute would force the NCAA to regulate the integrity of its product in every state according to Nevada's procedural rules. Thus, if a university in state X ("U of X") engaged in illicit practices while recruiting a high school quarterback from state Y, the NCAA would have to conduct its enforcement proceeding according to Nevada law in order to maintain uniformity in its rules. Nevada procedures do not allow the Committee on Infractions to consider some types of evidence, like hearsay and unsworn affidavits, that it can consider under the NCAA Bylaws. As a result, if its case against the U of X were based on unsworn affidavits from unavailable witnesses, the NCAA might not have enough admissible evidence to prove that there was a violation of the recruiting rules. The NCAA could be forced to allow the U of X to use an illegally recruited quarterback from state Y because it could not prove a rules violation under the strictures of Nevada law. In this way, the Statute could control the regulation of the integrity of a product in interstate commerce that occurs wholly outside Nevada's borders. That sort of extraterritorial effect is forbidden by the Commerce Clause.
>
> The Statute's extraterritorial reach also violates the Commerce Clause because of its potential interaction or conflict with similar statutes in other jurisdictions. "Generally speaking, the Commerce Clause protects against inconsistent legislation arising from the projection of one state regulatory regime into the jurisdiction of another State." [Citation omitted.]
>
> Nevada is not the only state that has enacted or could enact legislation that establishes procedural rules for NCAA enforcement proceedings. Florida, Illinois, and Nebraska have also adopted due process statutes and similar legislation has been introduced in five other states. Those statutes could easily subject the NCAA to conflicting requirements. For example, suppose that state X required proof of an infraction beyond a reasonable doubt, while state Y only required clear and convincing evidence, and state Z required infractions to be proven by a preponderance of the evidence. Given that the NCAA must have uniform enforcement procedures in order to accomplish its fundamental goals, its operation would be disrupted because it could not possibly comply with all three statutes. Nor would it do to say that it need only comply with the most stringent burden of persuasion (beyond a reasonable doubt), for a state with a less stringent standard might well consider its standard a maximum as well as a minimum. The serious risk of inconsistent obligations wrought by the extra-territorial effect of the Statute demonstrates why it constitutes a per se violation of the Commerce Clause.

Id. at 639-640. What state regulation of the NCAA is permissible? Are state constitutional provisions applicable to the NCAA? See *Brennan v. Board of Trustees for University of Louisiana System, infra.*

6. In *Cohane v. NCAA*, 2005 WL 2373472 (W.D.N.Y. 2005), the district court held that an NCAA investigation of a men's basketball coach did not constitute state action despite cooperation in the investigation on the part of his employer, a public university. On appeal, however, the Second Circuit concluded that the district court erred in concluding that the coach could not prove a set of facts showing that the NCAA was a state actor by willfully participating in joint activity with a public university. The complaint alleged that the university forced the coach's resignation immediately upon learning of the charges in an attempt to placate the NCAA, actively participated in the case against the coach, and intimidated witnesses into giving false statements to NCAA investigators. These allegations, combined with others, if proved, could show joint activity between the university and the NCAA to deprive the coach of his liberty. The court further stated that the coach may be able to show that without the state's assistance, pursuant to the university's actions and the exercise of its authority over student witnesses, the NCAA could not have issued the defamatory report and imposed sanctions. *Cohane v. NCAA*, 215 Fed. Appx. 13, 2007 WL 247710 (2d Cir. 2007), *cert. denied*, 128 S. Ct. 641 (2007). How does this decision potentially impact the holding in the *Tarkanian* case? Does *Cohane* provide a way for plaintiffs to have the NCAA judicially characterized as a state actor because of its relationship to state institutions? If so, how do you think the Supreme Court would respond?

2. NCAA Rules Enforcement Process

In 1954, to ensure fairness and a level playing field in intercollegiate athletics, the NCAA formed the Committee on Infractions (COI) to interpret NCAA rules and impose penalties on member institutions for rules violations. Concerns were frequently raised regarding the manner in which the COI enforced the rules against member institutions. In *NCAA v. Tarkanian, supra*, the Supreme Court held that the NCAA did not have to afford constitutionally mandated procedural due process in its investigative processes or to those appearing before the COI. Nevertheless, member institutions continued to be concerned about the need for greater due process in the infractions procedure. A Special Committee to Review the National Collegiate Athletic Association Enforcement and Infractions Process (Review Committee) was formed to evaluate the enforcement process of the NCAA to ensure timeliness, fairness, and consistency. The Review Committee issued a report in 1991 that included a series of recommended reforms designed to bring greater fairness to the NCAA's enforcement and infractions processes. The Infractions Appeals Committee (IAC), which was formed in 1993, was based on one of these recommendations. The investigative and hearings processes are described on the NCAA website. See *Hearings*, NCAA.org, March 29, 2012, http://www.ncaa.org/wps/wcm/connect/public/ncaa/enforcement/process/hearings.

Working collectively, the COI, IAC, Management Council, conferences, and member institutions and personnel play the critical role in fulfilling the mission of the NCAA enforcement program, which is summarized in Bylaw 19.01.1, in the NCAA Manual:

It shall be the mission of the NCAA enforcement program to eliminate violations of NCAA rules and impose appropriate penalties should violations occur. The program is committed to fairness of procedures and the timely and equitable resolution of infractions cases. The achievement of those objectives is essential to the conduct of a viable and effective enforcement program. Further, an important consideration in imposing penalties is to provide fairness to uninvolved student-athletes, coaches, administrators, competitors and other institutions.

Bylaw 19.01.2, in turn, provides that all representatives of member institutions shall cooperate fully with the NCAA enforcement staff, COI, IAC, and Management Council to further the objectives of the NCAA and its enforcement program. Indeed, for the system to work well, institutions and institutional personnel must be proactive in uncovering and disclosing possible violations of the rules and regulations of the NCAA.

On October 30, 2012, the board of directors for Division I adopted major reforms to the rules infractions structure and process. All of these changes are designed to strengthen a culture among head coaches, the compliance community, institutional leadership, and conferences to assume a shared responsibility for upholding the values of intercollegiate athletics. The new structure provides a four-tier violation hierarchy that ranges from severe breaches of conduct to incidental infractions. The structure replaces the current two-tier approach (major and secondary violations) with an approach that designates four levels of violations. Level I (severe breach of conduct) is used to designate "[v]iolations that seriously undermine or threaten the integrity of the NCAA collegiate model as set forth in the Constitution and bylaws, including any violation that provides or is intended to provide a substantial or extensive recruiting, competitive or other advantage, or a substantial or extensive impermissible benefit." Level II (significant breach of conduct), consists of "[v]iolations that provide or are intended to provide more than a minimal but less than a substantial or extensive recruiting, competitive or other advantage . . . or . . . conduct that may compromise the integrity of the NCAA collegiate model as set forth in the Constitution and bylaws." Level III (breach of conduct) consists of "[v]iolations that are isolated or limited in nature; provide no more than a minimal recruiting, competitive or other advantage; and do not include more than a minimal impermissible benefit. Multiple Level IV violations may collectively be considered a breach of conduct." Level IV (incidental issues) consists of "[m]inor infractions that are inadvertent and isolated, technical in nature and result in a negligible, if any, competitive advantage. Level IV infractions generally will not affect a student-athlete's eligibility for intercollegiate athletics. (This level may be revised or even eliminated pending outcomes from the Rules Working Group's efforts to streamline the Division I Manual.)" For a more detailed discussion of these reform efforts, see Gary Brown, *Board Adopts Tougher, More Efficient Enforcement Program*, NCAA.org, Oct. 30, 2012, https://www.ncaa.org/wps/wcm/connect/public/ncaa/resources/latest+news/2012/october/board+adopts+tougher+more+efficient+enforcement+program.

As you read the following infractions cases, think about what level of violation—I through IV—would in all likelihood be assessed by the COI or IAC in a given case. In making this assessment, remember that the NCAA has now created a "presumption of responsibility on the part of coaches." Also remember that "[a]ll of these changes are designed to develop a culture among head coaches, the compliance community, institutional leadership and conferences to assume a shared responsibility for upholding the values of intercollegiate athletics." In addition, consider the appropriate penalties in each case. Under the new structure, "Penalty guidelines include imposed suspensions that can range from 10 percent of the season to an entire season [for coaches]." The new structure also is intended to offer "harsh consequences (postseason bans, scholarship reductions, recruiting limits, head coach suspensions, show-cause orders and financial penalties), but seeks to align those penalties more predictably with the severity of the violations, placing emphasis on aggravating and mitigating circumstances in each case." *Id.*

To expedite handling of cases, the 2012 reform more than doubles the number of voting members on the Committee on Infractions in an effort to provide many more smaller panels to reduce the backlog of cases. It will be interesting to see how cases are resolved under the new structure.

A growing body of private law is developing in the NCAA regulatory area, with reported trial-like decisions rendered by the COI and appellate decisions made by the IAC. This developing area of the law has increased the role of lawyers in the regulatory process, at all levels. Many university athletic departments now hire personnel who are legally trained to deal with the complex issues of the type raised in the following cases and to assist in the rules compliance process. Most of the members of the COI and IAC, together with their staff members, possess legal training. In turn, virtually all institutions appearing before the COI and IAC choose to be represented by legal counsel. Indeed, many institutions are represented by their own internal university legal counsel and by outside law firms.

The NCAA's enforcement process continues to be the subject of scholarly critical attention. See, e.g., Jerry R. Parkinson, *Scoundrels: An Inside Look at the NCAA Infractions and Enforcement Processes*, 12 Wyo. L. Rev. 215 (2012); Josephine (Jo) R. Potuto and Jerry R. Parkinson, *If It Ain't Broke, Don't Fix It: An Examination of the NCAA Division I Infractions Committee's Composition and Decision-Making Process*, 89 Neb. L. Rev. 437 (2011); Maureen A. Weston, *NCAA Sanctions: Assigning Blame Where It Belongs*, 52 B.C. L. Rev. 551 (2011); Megan Fuller, *Where's the Penalty Flag? The Unauthorized Practice of Law, the NCAA, and Athletic Compliance Directors*, 54 N.Y.L. Sch. L. Rev. 495 (2010); Glenn Wong et al., *The NCAA's Infractions Appeals Committee: Recent Case History, Analysis and the Beginning of a New Chapter*, 9 Va. Sports & Ent. L.J. 47 (2009); Gene A. Marsh, *A Call for Dissent and Further Independence in the NCAA Infractions Process*, 26 Cardozo Arts & Ent. L.J. 695 (2009).

The following excerpts from reported decisions of the IAC are illustrative of procedural and substantive issues that often arise in the NCAA rules enforcement process. The principal cases, together with those discussed in the footnotes, demonstrate how detailed the decision-making process is at the institutional (in terms of both athletics and nonathletics staff), conference, and NCAA levels. Given the nature of these cases, it is clear that institutions need to develop educational, monitoring, and compliance programs that enable athletic department personnel, coaches, student-athletes, and others to deal with the detailed rules and regulations that govern intercollegiate athletics. IAC major infractions case decisions can be accessed at https://web1.ncaa.org/LSDBi/exec/miSearch.

a.   Institutions and the Infractions Process

In the enforcement process, historically, the COI and the IAC have imposed penalties on NCAA member institutions and indirectly on institutional personnel (e.g., athletics administrators, coaches, boosters) and student-athletes. A major institutional issue that arises in the infractions process is whether the conduct and activities of the institution demonstrate a lack of institutional control. As to institutional control, or the lack thereof, the Constitution of the NCAA provides, in pertinent part, as follows (see 2012-13 NCAA Division I Manual (2012)).

NCAA CONSTITUTION—SELECTED PROVISIONS

2.1   THE PRINCIPLE OF INSTITUTIONAL CONTROL AND RESPONSIBILITY

2.1.1   Responsibility for Control. It is the responsibility of each member institution to control its intercollegiate athletics program in compliance with the rules and regulations of the Association. The institution's president or chancellor is responsible for the administration of all aspects of the athletics program, including approval of the budget and audit of all expenditures. . . .

2.1.2   Scope of Responsibility. The institution's responsibility for the conduct of its intercollegiate athletics program includes responsibility for the actions of its staff members and for the actions of any other individual or organization engaged in activities promoting the athletics interests of the institution.

6.01   GENERAL PRINCIPLE

6.01.1   Institutional Control. The control and responsibility for the conduct of intercollegiate athletics shall be exercised by the institution itself and by the conference(s), if any, of which it is a member. Administrative control or faculty control, or a combination of the two, shall constitute institutional control.

6.1   INSTITUTIONAL GOVERNANCE

6.1.1   President or Chancellor. A member institution's chief executive officer has ultimate responsibility and final authority for the conduct of the intercollegiate athletics program and the actions of any board in control of that program.

6.1.2   Athletics Board. A board in control of athletics or an athletics advisory board, which has responsibility for advising or establishing athletics policies and making policy decisions, is not required. However, if such a board exists, it must conform to the following provisions.

6.1.3   Faculty Athletics Representative. A member institution shall designate an individual to serve as faculty athletics representative. An individual so designated after January 12, 1989, shall be a member of the institution's faculty or an administrator who holds faculty rank and shall not hold an administrative or coaching position in the athletics department. Duties of the faculty athletics representative shall be determined by the member institution.

6.1.4   Student-Athlete Advisory Committee. Each institution shall establish a student-athlete advisory committee for its student-athletes. The composition and duties of the committee shall be determined by the institution.

6.2   BUDGETARY CONTROL

6.2.1   Normal Budgeting Procedures. The institution's annual budget for its intercollegiate athletics programs shall be controlled by the institution and subject to its normal budgeting procedures. . . .

6.2.3   Financial Audit. All expenditures for or in behalf of a member institution's intercollegiate athletics programs, including those by any outside organization, agency or group of individuals (two or more) shall be subject to an annual financial audit (in addition to any regular financial audit policies and procedures of the institution). . . .

6.4   RESPONSIBILITIES FOR ACTIONS OF OUTSIDE ENTITIES

6.4.1   Independent Agencies or Organizations. An institution's "responsibility" for the conduct of its intercollegiate athletics program shall include responsibility for the acts of an independent agency, corporate entity (e.g., apparel or equipment manufacturer) or other organization when a member of the institution's executive or athletics administration, or an athletics department staff member, has knowledge that such agency, corporate entity or other organization is promoting the institution's intercollegiate athletics program.

6.4.2   Representatives of Athletics Interests. An institution's "responsibility" for the conduct of its intercollegiate athletics program shall include responsibility for the acts of individuals, a corporate entity (e.g., apparel or equipment manufacturer) or other organization when a member of the institution's executive or athletics administration or an athletics department staff member has knowledge or should have knowledge that such an individual, corporate entity or other organization:

(a) Has participated in or is a member of an agency or organization as described in Constitution 6.4.1;

(b) Has made financial contributions to the athletics department or to an athletics booster organization of that institution;

(c) Has been requested by the athletics department staff to assist in the recruitment of prospective student-athletes or is assisting in the recruitment of prospective student-athletes;

(d) Has assisted or is assisting in providing benefits to enrolled student-athletes; or

(e) Is otherwise involved in promoting the institution's athletics program.

6.4.2.1   Agreement to Provide Benefit or Privilege. Any agreement between an institution (or any organization that promotes, assists or augments in any way the athletics interests of the member institution, including those identified per Constitution 6.4.1) and an individual who, for any consideration, is or may be entitled under the terms of the agreement to any benefit or privilege relating to the institution's athletics program, shall contain a specific clause providing that any such benefit or privilege may be withheld if the individual has engaged in conduct that is determined to be a violation of NCAA legislation. The clause shall provide for the withholding of the benefit or privilege from a party to the agreement and any other person who may be entitled to a benefit or privilege under the terms of the agreement.

6.4.2.2   Retention of Identity as "Representative." Any individual participating in the activities set forth in Constitution 6.4.2 shall be considered a "representative of the institution's athletics interests," and once so identified as a representative, it is presumed the person retains that identity.

The following cases involving three major universities with highly successful football programs examine ways in which institutions have violated the NCAA Constitution and Bylaws, particularly lack of institutional control, ethical conduct, and compliance with amateurism requirements. As you read the following case involving the University of Alabama, get a feel for the manner in which the IAC evaluates a case and the underlying issues, including the sanctions or penalties imposed by the COI. Also, reflect on how the handling of the case might differ after adoption of the new rules enforcement structure and in light of subsequent cases involving the University of Southern California and the Ohio State University.

UNIVERSITY OF ALABAMA, TUSCALOOSA
PUBLIC INFRACTIONS APPEALS COMMITTEE REPORT
September 17, 2002

III-A.   RECRUITING INDUCEMENTS; IMPERMISSIBLE RECRUITING CONTACTS — family

In academic years 1995-96 and 1996-97, while recruiting prospect 1, athletics representative B provided $20,000 cash, lodging and entertainment to prospect 1 and his parents to induce the young man to sign a National Letter of Intent with the university. Further, athletics representative B told prospect 1's family that athletics representative A was the source of the cash. Finally, athletics representatives A, B, and C made impermissible recruiting contacts with the young man and his family. . . .

III-B.   RECRUITING INDUCEMENTS THROUGH HIGH-SCHOOL COACH . . .

Between May 1999 and February 2000, the university recruited a prospective student-athlete (henceforth, "prospect 2") from a Memphis high school. Athletics representative A offered a substantial amount of money to the high school's head football coach (henceforth, "head high-school coach 1") to secure the prospect's commitment to attend the university. Head high-school coach 1 (who told coaches from at least five other NCAA member institutions who were interested in recruiting prospect 2 that they would have to provide him money or money and vehicles before he would allow prospect 2 to consider their school) accepted athletics representative A's offer. In fulfillment of the agreement, athletics representative A provided several large cash payments to head high-school coach 1 prior to the February 2000 National Letter of Intent signing day. . . . [EDS. In addition to the violations just described, the COI found other major violations including (1) a booster providing $1,600 and $55,000 loans to an assistant football coach, (2) recruiting violations during prospects' official and unofficial visits to the institution, (3) a booster allowing a student-athlete to use an automobile, (4) a booster making four $100 payments to a student-athlete, (5) improper booster contact with prospective student-athletes, and (6) excessive entertainment (including a party at which female strippers performed) of prospects during a recruiting visit. The COI also found that the university had committed several secondary violations relating to improper recruiting; provision of extra benefits; and allowing an NCAA nonqualifier to compete, practice, and receive athletically related financial aid.]

V. Corrective Actions Taken and Penalties (Proposed or Self-Imposed) by the University

In determining the appropriate penalties to impose, the committee considered the institution's self-imposed corrective actions and penalties. [Eds. Those self-imposed penalties included dissociation of the athletics representatives, reductions in scholarships, reductions in paid campus visits by prospects, limited recruiting in the Memphis area, reduction in the number of coaches permitted to recruit off-campus, and a series of other corrective actions designed to limit the broad autonomy of the football program and the athletic department. The COI imposed more stringent sanctions, including a postseason ban, further reductions in scholarships, public reprimand, and probation. Those increased penalties were the basis for this appeal. In its discussion regarding penalties, the IAC also examined the issue of whether the "death penalty" (suspension of the football program) should be imposed.] . . .

IX. Infractions Appeals Committee's Resolution of the Issues Raised on Appeal

A showing that there was some information that might have supported a contrary result will not be sufficient to warrant setting aside a finding nor will a showing that such information might have outweighed the information on which the committee based a finding. The Infractions Appeals Committee . . . will set aside a finding only on a showing that information that might have supported a contrary result clearly outweighed the information on which the Committee on Infractions based the finding. The Committee on Infractions determines the credibility of the evidence. (University of Mississippi Public Infractions Appeals Committee Report, at page 10, May 1, 1995).

A penalty imposed by the Committee on Infractions may be set aside on appeal if the penalty is "excessive or inappropriate based on all the evidence and circumstances."

[Eds. The IAC first found that the violations were not barred by the NCAA's four-year statute of limitations, Bylaw 32.5.2 (now 32.6.3). It also rejected the university's arguments regarding alleged procedural errors.]

The institution also appealed several of the penalties in this case, particularly focusing on the two-year ban on postseason competition (III-B-3) and the five-year probation (III-B-2). The institution contended on appeal that the conduct of its athletics representatives should not result in an institutional penalty without a showing of fault by the institution.

We have addressed violations by athletics representatives in a number of prior cases. The issue in the University of Nevada, Las Vegas, case was whether it was appropriate to impose a ban on postseason competition against an institution whose athletics representatives had made cash payments to a prospective student-athlete and an enrolled student-athlete. We held that such a penalty was appropriate as a deterrent to future violations by bringing the "violations to the attention of the institution's boosters as well as the institution." (UNLV Public Infractions Appeals Committee Report, page 11, February 16, 2001). In that case, we discussed the application of Bylaw 19.6.2. 1-(f). We found it unnecessary to decide there whether one of the three conditions of the bylaw must be satisfied as a condition to imposing a postseason ban because the case was subject to the repeat violator Bylaw 19.6.2.3.

In this case, we have a similar situation because the institution is subject to the repeat violator bylaw. The Committee on Infractions has discretion to ban post-season competition under this bylaw if such a penalty is not excessive or inappropriate. We have already concluded that such a ban is not inappropriate in a case involving violations by athletics representatives.

A ban on postseason competition is one of the most serious penalties that can be imposed on an institution. It deprives the institution and its student-athletes of the opportunity to achieve the highest level of success in . . . their sport. It also prevents the fans and other supporters of the program from enjoying the full success of a season of competition. Because the violations in this case were numerous and particularly egregious, we conclude that the imposition of such a penalty is appropriate under the facts of the case.

The institution contended that, although it is responsible for the conduct of its athletics representatives, it was not, and was not found to be, at fault with respect to their actions. Without institutional fault, the institution argued that it is inappropriate to impose penalties on it for violations committed by its athletics representatives. This argument is based on the fact that the Committee on Infractions did not make a finding of lack of institutional control or failure to monitor. As discussed above, we upheld the institutional sanction of a post-season ban in the UNLV case based on athletics representative violations for a repeat violator where there were no findings of lack of institutional control or failure to monitor. Moreover, the Committee on Infractions noted in this case that the athletics representatives were "not the typical representatives" due to their "favored access and insider status" (Committee on Infractions report page 3). The Committee found this status:

> not only gives credence to their claims of authority within a program but also, and however unintended, serves to reward them for the illicit activities in which they engage. Moreover, special access and insider status likely ease the way for illicit conduct by rogue representatives both by identifying prospects for them and by fostering (or contributing to) the belief of prospects and their parents that the representative's conduct is sanctioned by the university and in its best interest as well as that of the prospect. (Committee on Infractions report page 3)

The Committee concluded that this favored access and insider status created "greater university responsibility for any misconduct in which they engage." (Committee on Infractions report page 3). We agree.

The remaining question is whether the penalty is excessive. The two-year post-season ban imposed here is one of the longest imposed by the Committee on Infractions. However, in its report, the Committee on Infractions indicated that it seriously considered imposing the repeat violator penalty set forth in Bylaw 19.6.2.3.2-(a) and prohibiting outside competition in football (the "death penalty"). Its articulated bases for considering this penalty were the institution's status as a "two-time repeat violator" (1995 and 1999), the very serious nature of the recruiting violations and its view that the institution "bears some responsibility for the special status . . . within the athletics department" enjoyed by two of the athletics representatives. (Committee on Infractions report page 29). Although finding this a "very close question," the Committee on Infractions declined to impose the death penalty due to "the particular circumstances of this case and of the university's infractions history." (Committee on Infractions report page 29).

Although the Committee did not elaborate in the report on what it meant by the "particular circumstances" of the institution's infractions history, it appears that the Committee considered cooperation of the institution in reporting the 1999 violation as a mitigating factor. This is consistent with the view the Committee took in its 1999 report on this matter. In that report, the Committee recognized that the institution had made great strides after the 1995 violation by creating "an environment of compliance" and stated: "Rather than impose institutional penalties, the Committee commends the university for its effective institutional control and proactive compliance (Public Infractions Report for the University of Alabama, Tuscaloosa, page 3, February 9, 1999). The Infractions Appeals Committee agrees with this assessment of the 1999 report. However, even if the nature of the 1999 case mitigates the institution's status as a two-time repeat violator, the institution remains a repeat violator as a result of the 1995 report.

In further explaining why it did not impose the death penalty, the Committee on Infractions contrasted this case with the prior case (Southern Methodist University, February 25, 1987) in which this penalty was imposed. In that case, the Committee noted that there was "a demonstrated blatant disregard for NCAA rules that permeated throughout the entire university and its governance structure." (Committee on Infractions report page 29). The Committee found the circumstances of this case in sharp contrast. Here "university officials cooperated fully with the enforcement staff, often at great personal criticism, in a diligent effort to develop complete information regarding the violations." (Committee on Infractions report page 29). The Committee concluded "[h]ad this candor and cooperation been lacking, the death penalty (as well as substantial penalties in addition to those imposed in this case) would have been imposed." (Committee on Infractions report pages 29-30). . . .

Finally, the institution argued that the two-year postseason ban and five-year probation are excessive compared to the penalties imposed in other cases involving repeat violators. . . . In this case, the Committee on Infractions carefully considered the nature, number and seriousness of the violations, the conduct and motives of those involved in the violations, the corrective actions taken by the institution, the institution's exemplary cooperation and its repeat violator status.

The Committee on Infractions compared this case with the only case in which the death penalty was imposed and appropriately distinguished this case from that one. In the hearing on appeal, it adequately demonstrated the consistency of the result in this case with other recent cases.

There is one other circumstance present in this case which deserves comment. In 1996, the NCAA enforcement staff received a letter alleging that one of the athletics representatives who was involved in the 1995-96 violations reviewed in this case had committed recruiting violations involving a prospective student-athlete. The enforcement staff noted in its records that the information should be given to the institution. This was not done. All the parties regretted this lapse by the enforcement staff.

The institution argued on appeal that it was disadvantaged by the enforcement staff's failure to notify it of the allegation and that this lapse should be a mitigating factor in imposing penalties. . . . The Committee on Infractions did consider an enforcement lapse when deciding the University of Minnesota, Twin Cities, infractions case (July 2, 2002). At the hearing in this case, the appeals coordinator for the Committee on Infractions agreed that an enforcement lapse should be a mitigating factor. The report in this case does not, however, indicate how or the extent to which the factor was so considered by the Committee. We do not find it necessary to decide in this particular case whether a lapse in the enforcement process is a mitigating factor. We note, however, that should this issue arise in a future case, the Committee on Infractions' report should include an explanation of the effect of such an enforcement lapse.

For all of the foregoing reasons, we conclude that the two-year postseason ban and five-year period of probation imposed in this case are not excessive or inappropriate, and affirm. . . .

same sanctions!

X.   CONCLUSION

The findings and penalties in this case are affirmed.

NOTE AND QUESTIONS

Strict Liability Offense: Appropriate Sanctions. Many assumed that the University of Alabama was going to receive the "death penalty," based on the fact that the infractions were clearly major rules violations. Given that Alabama was not found guilty of lack of institutional control or failure to monitor, it has been suggested that the university was held to a strict liability standard. As you read the following later cases, you will note that the COI and IAC appear to be holding commercially powerful institutions like Alabama, USC, and Ohio State to higher standards for monitoring and program oversight. Additionally, the NCAA's newly adopted four-tier enforcement structure is based on a presumption of responsibility, which sounds very much like strict liability. If this is the case, do you believe that such heightened responsibility is warranted?

Postseason bans have been and remain a major significant penalty imposed in cases involving Division I universities with prominent and commercially successful athletic programs. Such bans remain controversial, but clearly will play a significant role in the newly adopted enforcement and penalty structure. In *The University of California, Berkeley Public Infractions Appeals Committee Report* (11/18/2002), the IAC noted:

> The committee has consistently recognized that in most cases a ban on post-season competition will affect innocent student-athletes. As we have pointed out before, this is inherent in the nature of the penalty (citations omitted). The NCAA's legislation provides that a ban on postseason competition is a presumptive penalty for a major violation. (Bylaw 19.6.2.1) In considering this issue, the Infractions Appeals Committee noted that a penalty that would allow a postseason competition to take place, but deny the university the financial rewards of that contest, might be a more appropriate sanction under Bylaw 1.9.6.2.1. Such a penalty would minimize the adverse impact on student-athletes, who individually have done nothing wrong, and instead would penalize the institution, which has failed in its responsibilities. Neither the Committee on Infractions nor this committee has authority from the NCAA to fashion such a penalty. Accordingly, we suggest that legislative authorities of the NCAA consider possible postseason competition penalties that would permit the Committee on Infractions to fashion penalties more appropriate to the violation in particular cases.

good reasoning

Consideration

Is it appropriate for the IAC propose legislation and should its proposed legislation be adopted by the NCAA? What are the arguments in favor of and opposed to such a legislative proposal? Why does the NCAA impose bans on postseason competition, particularly on very competitive and commercially successful football programs such as those at Alabama (and USC and Penn State)? The cases that follow, involving USC and Penn State, respectively, further evidence the inclination of the NCAA to impose such penalties.

In the following case, which involves serious violations of the NCAA's amateurism rules and related issues, the University of Southern California, a repeat offender, appeals a series of penalties imposed by the COI on the ground that they are inconsistent with past precedent and are unfair.

THE UNIVERSITY OF SOUTHERN CALIFORNIA PUBLIC INFRACTIONS APPEALS COMMITTEE REPORT

May 26, 2011

[EDS. Summary of facts and disposition of initial issues: Beginning in October 2004 and continuing until November 2005, the former football student-athlete, his stepfather, and his mother agreed to form a partnership with two individuals to form a sports agency. Shortly after the agreement was reached the former football student-athlete and his family began asking for financial and other assistance from the partners. During the course of this relationship, the agency partners gave the former football student-athlete and his family impermissible benefits including several thousand dollars, an automobile, housing, a washer and dryer, air travel, hotel lodging, and transportation, among others. Because of the receipt of these benefits, the former football student-athlete competed while ineligible.

On January 8, 2006, one of the agency partners called the assistant football coach asking for assistance in convincing the former student-athlete to adhere to the agency agreement or reimburse the partners for money and benefits they provided. The assistant football coach failed to alert the university compliance staff of this information and later provided false and misleading information to the enforcement staff regarding his knowledge of the violations. Based on these actions, the Committee on Infractions (COI) found that the assistant football coach violated NCAA ethical conduct rules and violated NCAA legislation by failing to report knowledge of possible violations.

The former football student-athlete and his family also received benefits from another sports marketing agency during his time at the university. On a number of occasions from November 2005 to January 2006, an individual who triggered NCAA agent rules provided impermissible benefits to the former football student-athlete, as well as his friends and family. These benefits included air travel, transportation, lodging, and repairs to the automobile that was purchased by the previous agency partners.

Although the former football student-athlete participated in an interview with enforcement staff, he refused to cooperate fully with the investigation. He failed to provide the requested information that, if it existed, could have substantiated his claim that he was not involved in NCAA rules violations.

The case also includes multiple impermissible inducements and extra benefits for a former men's basketball student-athlete, his brother, his girlfriend, and his girlfriend's mother. From August 2006 through May 2008, a representative affiliated with a professional sports agency and his associate provided cash, lodging, transportation, meals, air travel, professional personal trainers, a cell phone, wireless service, a television, watches, shoes, and clothing, among other benefits.

basketball

The former head men's basketball coach, assistant men's basketball coach, institutional compliance staff, faculty athletics representative, and athletics director all knew this representative had previously committed two separate NCAA violations. One of these violations involved the former men's basketball student-athlete, and in the other violation the representative was found to have provided benefits to a student-athlete. These university officials also knew that the representative was acting as the point person in the recruitment of the former men's basketball student-athlete, yet failed to take steps to monitor the recruitment.

The COI also found the football program violated coaching staff limit rules. In August 2008, the former head football coach hired a consultant for the entire 2008 regular playing season. The consultant attended practice sessions, analyzed video footage of contests, and discussed with the former head football coach his observations and analyses of the university's special teams. These activities led the university to exceed the maximum number of countable coaches.

football

Further, from November 2006 to March 2009, a former women's tennis student-athlete used an athletics department long-distance access code to make 123 unauthorized international telephone calls to family members. The total value of the calls is more than $7,000.

tennis

The COI acknowledged the difficulty of the investigation. Investigations of amateurism cases are often laborious given the significant effort by those involved to avoid leaving a paper trail or other evidence. It also noted that a number of key individuals, including the former football and basketball student-athletes, refused to cooperate fully with the investigation.

In determining the penalties, the committee considered the university's self-imposed penalties, corrective actions, and cooperation. The committee seriously contemplated imposing a television ban penalty in this case. However, after careful consideration, it ultimately decided that the penalties imposed adequately responded to the nature of violations and the level of institutional responsibility.

The penalties include four-year probation; a two-year football postseason ban; a one-year basketball postseason ban; vacation of regular and postseason wins for all three involved sports; scholarship reductions for football and basketball; and recruiting restrictions for men's basketball. They also include a $5,000 financial penalty; forfeiture of revenue from the 2008 NCAA Division I Men's Basketball Championship Tournament; and limitations for access granted to boosters and non-university personnel to team charters, sidelines, practices, locker rooms, and camps for men's basketball and football. The university must also disassociate itself from three boosters, including the former football and men's basketball student-athletes involved in the case. As part of the disassociation, the university will not be able to accept financial contributions or other assistance for the athletics department from these individuals or provide them with any benefit or privileges. In addition, the assistant football coach received a one-year show-cause penalty, which prohibits him from engaging in any recruiting activity with prospective student-athletes.

self-imposed penalties (?)

Issues on appeal include the following: (1) the penalties imposed on the University of Southern California (USC) should be reduced because they "are not supported by the facts and are excessive," and (2) the COI's findings of certain violations should be set aside as contrary to the evidence.

The IAC also rejected the university's assertion that the COI had "erred in concluding that sports marketer A, sports marketer B, and agency were representatives of USC's athletic interests" on the ground that the IAC was persuaded that there was sufficient evidence for the COI's conclusions regarding these issues.

The IAC rejected the university's argument that the COI's finding of lack of institutional control "should be set aside because some of the facts found by the [COI] did not constitute a violation of NCAA rules, and the [COI] failed to consider a number of mitigating factors." One of the institution's principal arguments regarding this point was that the COI had imposed a heightened duty to monitor elite student-athletes and that "NCAA bylaws do not establish a 'heightened duty' standard, nor do they differentiate between 'elite' athletes and other student-athletes." The IAC did find that the COI's statements inappropriately established a new or different standard not permitted by the applicable bylaws.

Despite these and related arguments, the IAC found no basis on which to reverse the COI's finding of lack of institutional control. More particularly, the IAC determined that there was evidence sufficient to permit the COI to hold that the institution had devoted inadequate resources to its compliance program, especially when the institution learned that problems with the compliance program were developing.]

The institution argues that the penalties imposed by the COI were excessive. More specifically, the institution argues that (a) the COI "has imposed significantly lesser sanctions in major infractions cases based on similar violations"; (b) "abused its discretion in imposing a two-year post-season ban and drastic scholarship reductions in football for the violations in this case"; and (c) "the scholarship reductions are excessive, particularly when considering the unintended actual impact."

The committee states in the Alabama State case as follows:

An abuse of discretion in the imposition of a penalty occurs if the penalty: (1) was not based on a correct legal standard or was based on a misapprehension of the underlying substantive legal principles; (2) was based on a clearly erroneous factual finding; (3) failed to consider and weigh material factors; (4) was based on a clear error of judgment, such that the imposition was arbitrary, capricious, or irrational; or (5) was based in significant part on one or more irrelevant or improper factors. . . .

Guided by that standard, we find no error or abuse of discretion in the imposition of either the two-year postseason ban or the grants-in-aid reduction. We note in particular the [COI's] recognition that this was the institution's sixth major infraction case involving football, and that the institution had last been before the [COI] in June 2001, fewer than four years before the violations which occurred in this case. Thus, the institution was a "repeat violator" under Bylaw 19.5.2.3 and therefore at risk for enhanced penalties set forth in Bylaw 19.5.2.3.2. As the [COI] stated in its response to the institution's appeal:

Although the COI ultimately chose not to impose any of the enhanced penalties, it noted that "stiff sanctions are warranted in light of the serious violations found by the committee and the fact that the institution is a 'repeat violator.'" Those stiff penalties are particularly warranted because the school failed to take to heart the lessons it should have learned in 2001.

Thus, we believe that the penalties imposed make clear to other institutions the message which the [COI] intended to convey:

> Similar strong penalties will be meted out to institutions that do [not] take the problems of sports agents and their runners seriously. It is not enough for institutions simply to educate student athletes about the dangers of unscrupulous agents. Schools must have appropriate staff and procedures in place to combat this significant problem. An institution that does not foster a climate of compliance on its campus should expect serious consequences.

In reaching this decision, this committee [IAC] closely considered both the institution and the [COI's] substantial arguments regarding the application to this case of prior decisions of both the [COI] and this committee [citations omitted]. Indeed, we have recognized since the University of Mississippi (May 1, 1995) case that a "factor of particular significance in considering an appeal of penalties is the review and analysis of the penalty or penalties imposed when compared with the penalty or penalties imposed in other cases with similar characteristics." [citation omitted] Given this latitude afforded the [COI], there is no basis on which to conclude that the [COI] departed from prior decisions, much less to any impermissible extent.[2]

The institution placed particular reliance on the [COI's] decision in the 1996 Florida State case, arguing that the case "illustrates how the [COI] historically has penalized universities for amateurism violations." [citation omitted] While the institution's observation regarding that case may be correct, we also must make clear the principle of guidance from prior decisions is not an unyielding directive. It is instead a matter of considered judgment to be applied along with all other factors which this committee has recognized should guide the [COI] and this committee. And, one very important factor in the application of that principle, and in determining the extent to which a prior decision should guide a present decision, is change in the matters to which the decision of the [COI] and this committee are directed. The [COI] should not be strictly bound to a decision made fifteen years earlier, when the circumstances of intercollegiate athletics were qualitatively different than those which presently obtain. This, of course, does not mean that prior decisions provide no restraint on or guidance to the [COI] and this committee, or that insignificant changes in the environment in which NCAA member institutions operate can justify ignoring those prior decisions. It means only that the guidance provided by prior decisions is, and always has been, a matter of judgment. In this case, we cannot say that the [COI] improperly exercised that judgment.

---

2. We note in particular the [COI's] extensive discussion of the Alabama, Michigan, and Florida State cases [citation omitted]. While we do not necessarily agree with all of the [COI's] points made there, the discussion makes clear that none of the facts of, or penalties imposed in, those cases demonstrate an abuse of discretion in this case.

NOTES AND QUESTIONS

1. *Repeat Major Offenders and the "Death Penalty."* Like the University of Alabama in the preceding case, the University of Southern California was a repeat offender, with six prior major infractions. Should USC's football program have been suspended, as was the case with Southern Methodist University a number of years ago? Both Alabama and USC quickly regained their national status and power by being highly ranked in football shortly after receiving what were considered to be stringent penalties. What sanctions are most effective in cases involving highly successful and competitive programs like those at Alabama and USC to maintain academic values and student welfare in the world of highly commercialized and competitive intercollegiate athletics? Under the new enforcement structure, what penalties are likely to be used in such cases?

2. *IAC Precedent and the Rule of Law.* In the *USC* case the IAC makes it clear that past precedent is not binding but is merely a "matter of judgment." Which cases should institutions rely on and to what extent? The IAC seems to imply that cases decided in the mid-1990s reflect a different era and therefore carry less precedential weight. What support does the IAC offer for this significant assertion, and is this wise policy? What has changed in big-time intercollegiate athletics in the past 15 years that warrants minimizing the role of cases from that era? If you represent a university, how much weight should you give to precedent from that time period?

3. *High-Profile Student-Athletes.* While the IAC indicates that it is not adopting a new standard or institutional duty for higher profile student-athletes, hasn't it done just that? Aren't institutions with higher profile student-athletes being held to a different standard, a standard that requires closer scrutiny of their activities and relationships? If so, then what steps should USC and other institutions with higher profile student-athletes take? On July 8, 2011, after the decision in the *USC* case and in the midst of serious problems in its own football program, officials at the Ohio State University altered its oversight of its student-athletes, many of whom are higher profile. See Encarnacion Pyle and Bill Rabinowitz, *Ohio State Alters Oversight of Athletes*, Columbus Dispatch, July 8, 2011. In that article Pyle and Rabinowitz, for example, quote Gene Smith the athletic director at OSU as stating, "We want to go further than where we've been." That article then goes on to set forth a series of steps that OSU is taking to oversee the purchases and relationships of its student-athletes, including receiving in-depth information regarding automobile purchases and usage, checking of game passes to ascertain whether there might be any improper relationships that might jeopardize a student-athlete's amateur status, and even examining the bank accounts of student-athletes. Is this fair to student-athletes?

4. *The Ohio State University Case.* On December 20, 2011, in *The Ohio State Public Infractions Report*, the Ohio State University was cited for failure to monitor along with preferential treatment and extra benefit violations in its football program, according to findings by the COI. Eight football student-athletes received more than $14,000 in cash payments or preferential treatment from the owner of a Columbus, Ohio, tattoo parlor. In addition to free or discounted tattoos and cash for memorabilia received by these student-athletes, one football student-athlete received a loan and discount on a car.

The COI also found that former head coach Jim Tressel concealed these NCAA violations after he was notified of the situation. In its report, the COI expressed "great concern" over the "fact that the former head coach became aware of these violations and decided not to report the violations to institutional officials, the Big Ten Conference or the NCAA." The COI found that Tressel engaged in unethical conduct for not reporting these NCAA rule violations; as a sanction, he received a five-year show-cause order that limits his athletically related duties and applies to any NCAA member school which may consider employing him. Sanctions on coaches are discussed at greater length after the *Haskins* case, *infra*. The penalties imposed on Ohio State, some of which were self-imposed by the university and adopted by the committee, included a one-year postseason ban for the 2012 football season, scholarship reductions, disassociation of both an involved booster and a former student-athlete, forfeiture of almost $340,000, and forfeiture of all of the team's wins during the 2010 season.

5. *The University of North Carolina Case.* On March 12, 2012, the COI determined that the University of North Carolina, Chapel Hill was responsible for multiple violations, including academic fraud, impermissible agent benefits, ineligible participation, and a failure to monitor its football program. Over the course of three seasons, six football student-athletes competed while ineligible as a result of these violations. Multiple student-athletes received over $30,000 in impermissible benefits. While employed by the university, a former assistant football coach failed to disclose income or compensation he received from a sports agent for the access he provided to student-athletes and failed to disclose the income to the university. The former assistant coach and a former tutor, who had engaged in academic fraud by doing work for the student-athletes, both were found to have committed unethical conduct. They also failed to cooperate with the investigation. Penalties imposed on the university included a one-year postseason ban, reduction of 15 football scholarships, vacation of records, and three years' probation.

6. *Latest Cases and the New Enforcement Structure.* Are these newly decided cases involving USC, Ohio State, and North Carolina consistent with the new enforcement structure and penalties? Can it be argued that they effectively foreshadow the new four-tier structure and heightened obligations of major programs in the interests of academic values and student welfare?

7. Guillory v. NCAA. In late October 2010, Rodney Guillory and O.J. Mayo, the basketball player involved in the USC case, filed a $25 million defamation, false light invasions of privacy, and negligent misrepresentation lawsuit against the NCAA. The NCAA Infractions Report accused Gillory of giving Mayo automobile transportation, skills instruction, dinner at no cost, free clothing, and other inducements. Guillory contends that the report fails to take into consideration the fact that the ride was in Guillory's car, the meals were home-cooked, the skills instruction was not prearranged or paid for by anyone, and the clothing was left over from a variety of basketball camps. The NCAA moved to strike Guillory's complaint, because (1) the report is a protected matter of public interest, and (2) Guillory is unlikely to prevail at trial. (Code Civ. Proc. §425.16.) The trial court granted the NCAA's motion, which was affirmed. *Guillory v. National Collegiate Athletic Assn.*, B234302, 2012 WL 2831806 (Cal. Ct. App. June 4, 2012). In its decision, the COI did

not address these facts. Should the COI and IAC have addressed these seemingly mitigating factors? In their respective decisions, should the COI and IAC make it clear that all relevant facts, including ones that have a potential to mitigate, were considered?

On November 17, 2011, NCAA President Emmert wrote a letter to Penn State President Rodney Erickson in which he stated, in pertinent part:

As we have discussed, on November 5, 2011, the NCAA first learned about allegations of sexual abuse of young boys occurring in the athletic facilities of Pennsylvania State University, perpetrated by a former assistant head football coach. Further, at the same time the NCAA learned that these alleged acts occurred over two decades and that individuals with present or former coaching responsibilities may have been aware of this behavior. The recount of these tragic events in the Grand Jury Report is deeply troubling, and if true, individuals who were in a position to monitor and act upon learning of potential abuses appear to have been acting starkly contrary to the values of higher education, as well as the NCAA. I am writing to notify you that the NCAA will examine Penn State's exercise of institutional control over its intercollegiate athletics program, as well as the actions, and inactions, of relevant responsible personnel.

President Emmert then stated the NCAA constitutional and bylaw provisions requiring institutional control, monitoring, and ethical conduct and added:

[T]o prepare for potential inquiry, the university should provide relevant information and data in response to the following questions:

1. How has Penn State and/or its employees complied with the Articles of the [NCAA] Constitution and bylaws [implicated in this case?]
2. How has Penn State exercised institutional control over the issues identified in and related to the Grand Jury Report? Were there procedures in place that were or were not followed? What are the institution's expectations and policies to address conduct that has been alleged in this matter upon discovery by any party?
3. Have each of the alleged persons to have been involved or have notice of the issues identified in and related [to this matter] behaved consistent with principles and requirements governing ethical conduct and honesty? If so, how? If not, how?
4. What policies and procedures does Penn State have in place to monitor, prevent and detect the issues identified in [this case] or to take disciplinary or corrective action if such behaviors are found?

Penn State responded quickly, hiring the law firm of Judge Louis Freeh, former FBI director, to investigate the matter. In compiling that report, Freeh's law firm and those working with them interviewed 430 university and other individuals and reviewed over 3.5 million e-mails and documents. The Freeh report concluded, "Our most saddening finding is the total disregard [by Penn State officials] for the safety and welfare of [the abuse] victims."

Rather than engaging in further investigation or hearings, President Emmert and the Executive Committee of the NCAA, in turn, responded quickly by proposing a Binding Consent Decree. In a press release regarding the Decree, the NCAA noted:

> By perpetuating a "football first" culture that ultimately enabled serial child sexual abuse to occur, The Pennsylvania State University leadership failed to value and uphold institutional integrity, resulting in a breach of the NCAA constitution and rules. The NCAA Division I Board of Directors and NCAA Executive Committee directed Association President Mark Emmert to examine the circumstances and determine appropriate action in consultation with these presidential bodies.
>
> "As we evaluated the situation, the victims affected by Jerry Sandusky and the efforts by many to conceal his crimes informed our actions," said Emmert. "At our core, we are educators. Penn State leadership lost sight of that."
>
> According to the NCAA conclusions and sanctions, the Freeh Report "presents an unprecedented failure of institutional integrity leading to a culture in which a football program was held in higher esteem than the values of the institution, the values of the NCAA, the values of higher education, and most disturbingly the values of human decency."

Penn State Failures Draw Unprecedented NCAA Sanctions, NCAA.org, July 2012, http://www.ncaa.org/wps/wcm/connect/public/NCAA/Resources/Latest+News/2012/July/21207231.

The sanctions imposed in the Penn State Consent Decree include the following, according to a summary published by the NCAA:

> **$60 million fine**. The NCAA imposes a $60 million fine, equivalent to the approximate average of one year's gross revenues from the Penn State football program, to be paid over a five-year period beginning in 2012 into an endowment for programs preventing child sexual abuse and/or assisting the victims of child sexual abuse. The minimum annual payment will be $12 million until the $60 million is paid. The proceeds of this fine may not be used to fund programs at the University. No current sponsored athletic team may be reduced or eliminated in order to fund this fine.
>
> **Four-year postseason ban**. The NCAA imposes a four-year postseason ban on participation in postseason play in the sport of football, beginning with the 2012-2013 academic year and expiring at the conclusion of the 2015-2016 academic year. Therefore, the University's football team shall end its 2012 season and each season through 2015 with the playing if its last regularly scheduled, in-season contest and shall not be eligible to participate in any postseason competition, including a conference championship, any bowl game, or any postseason playoff competition.
>
> **Four-year reduction of grants-in-aid**. For a period of four years commencing with the 2013-2014 academic year and expiring at the conclusion of the 2016-2017 academic year, the NCAA imposes a limit of 15 initial grants-in-aid (from a maximum of 25 allowed) and for a period of four years commencing with the 2014-2015 academic year and expiring at the conclusion of the 2017-2018 academic year a limit of 65 total grants-in-aid (from a maximum of 85 allowed) for football during each of those specified years. In the event the total number of grants-in-aid drops below 65, the University may award grants-in-aid to non-scholarship student-athletes who have been members of the football program as allowed under Bylaw 15.5.6.3.6.
>
> **Five years of probation**. The NCAA imposes this period of probation, which will include the appointment of an on-campus, independent Integrity Monitor and periodic reporting as detailed in the Corrective Component of this Consent Decree. Failure to comply with the Consent Decree during this probationary period may result in additional, more severe sanctions.

Vacation of wins since 1998. The NCAA vacates all wins of the Penn State football team from 1998 to 2011. The career record of Coach "Joe" Paterno will reflect the vacated records.

Waiver of transfer rules and grant-in-aid retention. Any entering or returning football student-athlete will be allowed to immediately transfer and will be eligible to immediately compete at the transfer institution, provided he is otherwise eligible. Any football student-athlete who wants to remain at the University may retain his athletic grant-in-aid, as long as he meets and maintains applicable academic requirements, regardless of whether he competes on the football team.

Individual penalties to be determined. The NCAA reserves the right to initiate a formal investigatory and disciplinary process and impose sanctions on individuals after the conclusion of any criminal proceedings related to any individual involved.

Corrective

Adoption of all recommendations presented in Chapter 10 of the Freeh Report. The NCAA requires the university to adopt all recommendations for reform delineated in Chapter 10 of the Freeh Report. The university shall take all reasonable steps to implement the recommendations in spirit and substance by December 31, 2013.

Implementation of Athletics Integrity Agreement. The Freeh Report includes a number of recommendations related to the University's athletics department. Specifically, in Chapter 10, Section 5.0, the report addresses the integration of the athletics department into the greater university community. Within 10 days of this consent decree, the university will be required to enter into an "Athletics Integrity Agreement" (AIA) with the NCAA and the Big Ten Conference, which obligates the University to adopt all of the recommendations in Section 5.0 of the Free Report as described in the above paragraph and, at a minimum, the following additional actions:

- **Compliance Officer for Athletics.** Establish and select an individual for a position of a compliance officer or equivalent who is, at a minimum, responsible for the ethical and compliance obligations of the athletics department.
- **Compliance Council.** Create a Compliance Council (or Council Subcommittee) composed of faculty, senior university administrators and the compliance officer for athletics, which shall be responsible for review and oversight of matters related to ethical, legal and compliance obligations of the athletics department.
- **Disclosure Program.** Create a reporting mechanism, including a hotline, for named or anonymous individuals to disclose, report or request counsel on any identified issues or questions regarding compliance with (i) the AIA; (ii) the athletics department's policies, conduct, practices or procedures or (iii) the NCAA Constitution, bylaws or the principles regarding institutional control, responsibility, ethical conduct and integrity reflected in the Constitution and bylaws.
- **Internal Accountability and Certifications.** Appoint a named coach, manager or administrator for each of the university's NCAA-sanctioned intercollegiate athletics teams who shall be assigned to monitor and oversee activities within his or her team and shall annually certify to the Compliance Council that his or her team is compliant with all relevant ethical, legal, compliance and university standards and obligations.
- **External Compliance Review/Certification Process.** The athletics director shall annually certify to the Compliance Council, the board of trustees and the NCAA that the athletics department is in compliance with all ethical, compliance, legal and university obligations. If the department fails to earn a certification, the board of trustees (or subcommittee thereof) or an appropriate university administrator shall take appropriate action against the athletics department, including the possibility of reduction in athletics funding.

- **Athletics Code of Conduct.** Create or update any code of conduct for the athletics department to codify the values of honesty, integrity and civility.
- **Training and Education.** In addition to Chapter 10, Section 5.5 of the Free Report, require all student-athletes and university employees associated with the athletics department, including faculty and staff to complete a yearly training course that addresses issues of ethics, integrity, civility, standards of conduct and reporting of violations. Each person who is required to complete training shall certify, in writing, that he or she has received such training. All training shall be overseen by the Compliance Council. The board of trustees also should receive training and education on these issues, including its relationship, role and responsibilities regarding the athletics program.

If the NCAA determines, in its sole discretion, that the university materially breached any provision of the AIA, such action shall be considered grounds for extending the term of the AIA or imposing additional sanctions, up to and including a temporary ban on participation in certain intercollegiate athletic competition and additional fines. The NCAA shall be permitted to accept as true and take into consideration all factual findings of the Freeh Report in imposing additional sanctions related to breach of the AIA and may initiate further NCA investigative and administrative proceedings. The NCAA will provide the university notice of the allegation of a material breach and an opportunity to respond, but the final determination rests with the NCAA.

Appointment of an independent Athletics Integrity Monitor for a five-year period. The NCAA requires that the university appoint an independent Athletics Integrity Monitor for a five-year period, at the university's expense. The monitor will prepare a quarterly report to the university's board of trustees, the Big Ten Conference, and the NCAA regarding the university's execution and maintenance of the provisions of the AIA. The monitor will make recommendations to the university to take any steps he or she reasonably believes are necessary to comply with the terms of the AIA and to enhance compliance with NCAA rules and regulations. The Monitor will operate under the following conditions:

- He or she will be selected by the NCAA, in consultation with the university and the Big Ten Conference.
- He or she will have access to any university facilities, personnel and non-privileged documents and records as are reasonably necessary to assist in the execution of his or her duties. The university shall preserve all such records as directed by the monitor.
- He or she will have the authority to employ legal counsel, consultants, investigators, experts and other personnel reasonably necessary to assist in the proper discharge of his or her duties. His or her expenses will be paid by the university, and the university shall indemnify and hold harmless the monitor and his or her professional advisors from any claim by any third party except for conduct: a) outside the scope of the monitor's duties; b) undertaken in bad faith; or c) constituting gross negligence or willful misconduct.

Sanctions, NCAA.org, July 2012, http://www.ncaa.org/wps/wcm/connect/public/NCAA/Resources/Latest+News/2012/July/21207232.

In the press release noted above, the NCAA added:

"There has been much speculation on whether or not the NCAA has the authority to impose any type of penalty related to Penn State," said Ed Ray, Executive Committee chair and Oregon State president. "This egregious behavior not only goes against our rules and constitution, but also against our values."

Because Penn State accepted the Freeh Report factual findings, which the university itself commissioned, the NCAA determined traditional investigative proceedings would be redundant and unnecessary.

"We cannot look to NCAA history to determine how to handle circumstances so disturbing, shocking and disappointing," said Emmert. "As the individuals charged with governing college sports, we have a responsibility to act. These events should serve as a call to every single school and athletics department to take an honest look at its campus environment and eradicate the 'sports are king' mindset that can so dramatically cloud the judgment of educators."

Penn State fully cooperated with the NCAA on this examination of the issues and took decisive action in removing individuals in leadership who were culpable.

"The actions already taken by the new Penn State Board of Trustees chair Karen Peetz and Penn State President Rodney Erickson have demonstrated a strong desire and determination to take the steps necessary for Penn State to right these severe wrongs," said Emmert.

See *Penn State Failures Draw Unprecedented NCAA Sanctions, supra.*

NOTES AND QUESTIONS

1. *NCAA Authority to Sanction Penn State.* It has been argued that the NCAA did not have any authority to intervene in a case involving sexual abuse of young men by a former coach. Proponents of this position argue that it should have been left to the legal system, which found the coach guilty of multiple counts. Should the NCAA have intervened? Opponents of the action also argue that the NCAA acted improvidently when it did not follow its own hearing and investigative processes, choosing rather to simply rely on the Freeh report, which had been commissioned by Penn State. Was it wise for the NCAA to act promptly? Why do you think it did so? Early in 2013, Governor Tom Corbett of Pennsylvania announced that he intended to sue the NCAA on antitrust grounds for their sanctioning of Penn State University. See Christian Red, *Pennsylvania Governor Tom Corbett Will Sue NCAA over "Unprecedented and Aggressive" Sanctions for Penn State,* N.Y. Daily News, Jan. 2, 2013, http://www.nydailynews.com/sports/i-team/pa-gov-suit-claims-ncaa-crippled-penn-state-article-1.1231786. For an argument that it is inappropriate for Governor Corbett to sue the NCAA, see Rodney K. Smith, *Picking Politics and Football over Education,* USA Today, Jan. 3, 2013, http://www.usatoday.com/story/opinion/2013/01/03/penn-state-ncaa-sanctions-sandusky-tom-corbett/1805189/. Do you agree?

2. *Sanctions.* The sanctions in this case were "unprecedented." Do you think the sanctions were excessive? It has been reported that the NCAA leadership seriously considered the suspension of the football program (the "death penalty"), but they refrained from doing so, in part because they believed that they had tailored the penalties in a manner that was designed to penalize Penn State and help the university avoid such actions in the future. The willingness to not suspend the football program also was an inducement to Penn State to enter into the Consent Decree. Should the NCAA have invoked the "death penalty"? What would the implications of the "death penalty" have been on the Penn State program? Could they have maintained their membership in the Big Ten Conference?

3. *Changing Role of the NCAA.* The USC, Ohio State, and Penn State cases evidence that the NCAA is imposing stronger sanctions for rules violations occurring at "BCS" institutions with commercially successful and well-known football programs. President Emmert has also taken a much more active role than his predecessors, as evidenced by his actions in the Penn State case. All of this may be contributing to a major change in the approach of the NCAA, in an effort to maintain academic integrity and student welfare. These decisions, together with the NCAA's new four-tier rules enforcement structure, clearly evidence an effort on the part of the NCAA and its leadership to re-enshrine academic values and student-welfare concerns in the governance and operation of big-time intercollegiate athletics. Can the NCAA succeed in this effort which appears to cut against the prevailing win-at-all-costs culture that may drive competition at this level? The Penn State, USC, and Ohio State cases involved very successful, even revered, coaches who were penalized by removal from their coaching positions (Jim Tressel and Joe Paterno) or who left to coach in the NFL (Pete Carroll). In the Penn State case, other university personnel, including the athletics director; vice president, whose duties included overseeing the athletic department; and president were removed from their positions by the university. The following section takes a closer look at the sanctioning of coaches and other university personnel for NCAA rules violations.

4. *The Costs of Monitoring Compliance with NCAA Rules.* In *Boise State University* (9/13/2011) the COI found numerous major violations involving more than 75 prospects and student-athletes in five sports over the course of five years, including football, men's and women's cross country and track and field, and men's and women's tennis. One of the lessons learned from the Boise State case is that failure to monitor one sport, even a minor sport, may adversely impact other sports, including revenue producing sports. What is now required in terms of monitoring? In an October 2012 compliance report filed with the NCAA, Ohio State reported that it is devoting significantly more financial and personnel resources to ensure compliance with NCAA rules; for example, it increased the size of its compliance department to 12 full-time employees, including one that focuses exclusively on its football program and another whose primary responsibility is to counsel and oversee elite student-athletes likely to play professional sports after their intercollegiate career. In announcing its new enforcement structure announced on October 30, 2012, the NCAA noted, "Penalties in the previous structure relied on whether the head coach knew of the violations or whether there was 'a presumption of knowledge.' But under the new structure, rather than focus on knowledge or the presumption of it, the bylaw will be amended to presume only responsibility. Accordingly, if a violation occurs, the head coach is presumed responsible, and if he or she can't overcome that presumption, charges will be forthcoming." Gary Brown, *Board Adopts Tougher, More Efficient Enforcement Program,* NCAA.org, Oct. 30, 2012, https://www.ncaa.org/wps/wcm/connect/public/ncaa/resources/latest+news/2012/october/board+adopts+tougher+more+efficient+enforcement+program.

The USC and Ohio State cases were decided prior to the October 30, 2012, NCAA announcement, but it may be argued that the high level of monitoring expected in those cases essentially held them to a presumption of responsibility, the basis for the new enforcement structure. Is it feasible for less commercially successful athletic programs to provide such monitoring, given their economic constraints (the vast majority of NCAA university athletic programs do not generate net revenues)?

b. Coaches and Other Internal Institutional Personnel and the Infractions Process

As illustrated by *NCAA v. Tarkanian, supra,* the NCAA has indirect authority to sanction coaches and other university employees for violations of its rules. Some of the rules commonly involved in cases dealing with coaches and other institutional personnel include the following:

NCAA REGULATIONS—SECTIONS 10 AND 11

10 ETHICAL CONDUCT

10.01 GENERAL PRINCIPLES

10.01.1 Honesty and Sportsmanship. Individuals employed by (or associated with) a member institution to administer, conduct or coach intercollegiate athletics and all participating student-athletes shall act with honesty and sportsmanship at all times so that intercollegiate athletics as a whole, their institutions and they, as individuals, shall represent the honor and dignity of fair play and the generally recognized high standards associated with wholesome competitive sports.

10.1 ETHICAL CONDUCT

Unethical conduct by a prospective or enrolled student-athlete or current or former institutional staff member (e.g., coach, professor, tutor, teaching assistant, student manager, student trainer) may include but is not limited to, the following. . . .

(a) Refusal to furnish information relevant to an investigation or a possible violation of an NCAA regulation when requested to do so by the NCAA or the individual's institution;

(b) Knowing involvement in arranging for fraudulent academic credit or false transcripts for a prospective or enrolled student-athlete;

(c) Knowing involvement in offering or providing a prospective or an enrolled student-athlete an improper inducement or extra benefit or improper financial aid;

(d) Knowingly furnishing or knowingly influencing others to furnish the NCAA or the individual's institution false or misleading information concerning the individual's involvement in or knowledge of matters relevant to a possible violation of an NCAA regulation;

(e) Receipt of benefits by an institutional staff member for facilitating or arranging a meeting between a student-athlete and an agent, financial advisor or a representative of an agent of advisor (e.g., "runner");

(f) Knowing involvement in providing a banned substance or impermissible supplement to student-athletes . . .

(g) Failure to provide complete and accurate information to the NCAA . . . or an institution's admissions office regarding an individual's academic record . . . ;

(h) Fraudulence or misconduct in connection with entrance or placement examinations;

(i) Engaging in any athletics competition under an assumed name or with intent to deceive; or

(j) Failure to provide complete and accurate information to the NCAA. . . .

11.1   CONDUCT OF ATHLETICS PERSONNEL

11.1.1   Honesty and Sportsmanship. Individuals employed by or associated with a member institution to administer, conduct or coach intercollegiate athletics shall act with honesty and sportsmanship at all times so that intercollegiate athletics as a whole, their institutions and they, as individuals, represent the honor and dignity of fair play and the generally recognized high standards associated with wholesome competitive sports. . . .

11.1.2   Responsibility for Violations. Institutional staff members found in violation of NCAA regulations shall be subject to disciplinary or corrective action as set forth in the provisions of the NCAA enforcement procedures, whether such violations occurred at the certifying institution or during the individual's previous employment at another member institution.

11.1.2.1   Responsibility of Head Coach. It shall be the responsibility of the head coach to promote an atmosphere for compliance within the program supervised by the coach and to monitor the activities regarding compliance of all assistant coaches and other administrators involved with the program who report directly or indirectly to the coach.

See 2012-13 NCAA Division I Manual (2012).

In the following case and accompanying notes, unethical conduct and related violations by coaches and other personnel are considered. This IAC decision involves Clem Haskins, the former head basketball coach at the University of Minnesota, who was sanctioned with a seven-year order to show cause for a series of major violations, which effectively terminated his college coaching career. Other members of the athletic department were removed from their positions as part of a series of corrective actions taken by the University of Minnesota in the case.

FORMER HEAD MEN'S BASKETBALL COACH
UNIVERSITY OF MINNESOTA, TWIN CITIES
PUBLIC INFRACTIONS APPEALS COMMITTEE REPORT

April 6, 2001

II.   BACKGROUND . . .

On October 24, 2000, the Committee on Infractions issued Infractions Report No. 176 in which the committee found violations of NCAA legislation in Minnesota's men's basketball program. On the basis of those findings, the Committee on Infractions determined that this was a major infractions case and imposed penalties accordingly. . . .

This case primarily involved the men's basketball program at Minnesota and involved violations of NCAA bylaws governing academic fraud, extra benefits, academic eligibility, unethical conduct and lack of institutional control. The case centered around three individuals, one of whom was the former head coach, whose actions resulted in the violations found by the Committee on Infractions. There were also secondary violations in several sports programs at the university.

[EDS. The COI found major infractions consisting of (1) academic fraud—from 1994 to 1998 a secretary prepared coursework consisting of typing, composing papers, completing homework assignments, and preparing take-home exams for at least 18 men's basketball student-athletes; (2) provision of extra benefits—from 1994-1995 through the 1998-1999 academic years, the men's basketball coaching staff provided substantially discounted rates at a local hotel for parents and friends of men's basketball student-athletes; the head coach and other basketball coaches provided cash payments to men's basketball student-athletes; (3) improper recruiting inducements—the head coach invited a prospective student-athlete to his home for dinner; and (4) supplement pay provisions—the head coach made monthly car lease payments for the academic counselor without the knowledge of university administrators. The COI found that the head coach violated the principle of ethical conduct by "(1) committing the violations alleged against him in this report; (2) providing false and misleading information during interviews with the university and enforcement staff; and (3) directing the four men's basketball student-athletes named in the Pioneer Press to give false and misleading information to the university regarding their involvement in the academic fraud." It also found that the head coach committed a secondary violation.] . . .

IV. PENALTIES IMPOSED BY THE COMMITTEE ON INFRACTIONS

The Committee on Infractions imposed additional penalties because of the seriousness of the violations and "because they involved the active complicity of the head coach and because they involved a men's basketball program for which the university previously had been cited for a failure of institutional control." The penalties in which the former head coach were cited are:

Regarding the 1994, 1995 and 1997 NCAA Division I Men's Basketball Tournaments, and the 1996 and 1998 National Invitational Tournaments (NIT), the university will vacate its team record as well as the individual records of any student-athlete who engaged in academic fraud as set forth in this report. Further, the university's records regarding men's basketball as well as the record of the former head coach will be reconfigured to reflect the vacated records and so recorded in all publications in which men's basketball records for the 1993-94 through the 1998-99 seasons are reported. . . .

The former head coach and the former academic advisor will be informed in writing by the NCAA that, due to their involvement in certain violations of NCAA legislation found in this case, if they seek employment or affiliation in an athletically-related position at an NCAA member institution during a seven-year period, they and any involved institution shall be requested to appear before the Committee on Infractions to consider whether the member institution(s) should be subject to the show-cause procedures from Bylaw 19.6.2.2-(1), which could limit athletically-related duties of the head coach and academic advisor at any such institution for a designated period. . . .

VII.   Infractions Appeals Committee's
Resolution of the Issues Raised on Appeal

... [The issues on appeal] may be divided into two major categories: A. Whether the Committee on Infraction's findings of violations should be set aside; and B. Whether the penalties imposed by the committee are excessive or inappropriate and should be set aside.

A.   Whether the Committee on Infraction's findings of violations should be set aside

Bylaw 32.10.2, provides that:

> A finding of violation by the Committee on Infractions may be set aside on appeal only if the Infractions Appeals Committee determines that:
>
> 1.   The finding is clearly contrary to the evidence presented to the committee;
> 2.   The facts found do not constitute a violation; or
> 3.   A procedural error affected the reliability of the information that was used to support the finding.

There are really four general issues raised by the former head coach on appeal in his effort to support his position that findings of violations by the Committee on Infractions should be set aside:

1.   Whether alleged procedural errors in the investigation and the decision by the Committee on Infractions adversely affected the former head coach's rights;
2.   Whether the evidence was sufficient to sustain the findings on issues of academic integrity by the Committee on Infractions;
3.   Whether the evidence was sufficient to sustain the findings on issues of unethical conduct by the Committee on Infractions; and
4.   Whether the evidence was sufficient to sustain the findings on other issues by the Committee on Infractions.

1.   Procedural Matters

a.   Access to pertinent documents during the investigation.

The former head coach alleges that the NCAA failed to comply with its own bylaws by failing to produce certain documents—chiefly, transcripts and audio tapes of witness interviews—in a timely fashion prior to the Committee on Infractions hearing. Bylaw 32.5.4 provides, in pertinent part, that, "within 30 days following the filing of an official inquiry in an infractions case, the enforcement staff shall make available to the member institution and to the involved individuals reasonable access to all pertinent evidentiary materials, including tape recordings of interviews and documents, upon which the inquiry is based."

... For us to find a violation of Bylaw 32.5.4, we must conclude that former head coach was denied "reasonable access" to these materials. A respondent in former head coach's position has the burden of showing that he was denied reasonable access. ...

b.   Contact between the NCAA and federal law enforcement authorities.

The former head coach devotes a considerable portion of his rebuttal to an allegation that a member of the enforcement staff spoke to an attorney in the

U.S. Department of Justice and several FBI agents on February 28, 2000, in reference to possible federal law enforcement interest in the allegations of impropriety in the University of Minnesota basketball program. The former head coach contends that he "just recently discovered" an internal NCAA memorandum of this conversation and that he was prejudiced in that he "should have been allowed to delay" the Committee on Infractions hearing, which was held on August 11, 2000 "pending the completion of the federal investigation."

. . . In order for new evidence to be considered on appeal, it must not only be "evidence that could not reasonably be ascertained" prior to the hearing by the Committee on Infractions; it must also be "directly related to the findings in the case." The former head coach has not shown how this conversation is related, directly or indirectly, to any of the findings of the case. . . .

c. *Participation in the hearing by the former head coach's attorney alone.*

On July 31, 2000, prior to the Committee on Infractions hearing, the former head coach's attorney notified the Committee on Infractions that the former head coach would not attend the hearings, but that his attorneys would. On August 1, 2000 the chair of the Committee on Infractions replied that the attorneys would not be allowed to attend the hearing unless they accompanied the former head coach. The former head coach now argues that this was error.

We disagree. Bylaw 32.7.4.1 states that institutional officials who have been requested to appear at a Committee on Infractions hearing "are expected to appear in person and may be accompanied by personal legal counsel." There is no provision for appearance by attorneys alone. . . .

2. *Academic Integrity*

The most serious charges against the former head coach are those that he knew of the secretary's fraudulent assistance to student-athletes. The findings of the Committee on Infractions bear repeating here:

> The numerous violations found by the committee are among the most serious academic fraud violations to come before it in the past 20 years. The violations were significant, widespread and intentional. More than that, their nature—academic fraud—undermined the bedrock foundation of a university and the operation of its intercollegiate athletics program. By purposeful acts of commission, and, through the absence of effective oversight, serious acts of omission, these violations damaged the academic integrity of the institution.

The Committee also found that the former head coach "knew of the secretary's preparation of course work on behalf of the student-athletes identified by the academic counselor. [He] also knew that her work constituted academic fraud." In support of its findings, the Committee on Infractions discussed at length the facts and circumstances that led it to conclude that the former head coach "knew and was complicit in" the fraudulent activities. These facts included the former head coach's payment of $3000 to the secretary (a payment he consistently denied making until he turned over a $3000 check used for the payment, at which point he "corrected" his earlier denials); the secretary's constant and open contact with student-athletes (including her attendance at study halls) of which the former head coach could not have been ignorant; her own admissions that she told the former head coach that she was assisting the student-athletes; his caution to her that the papers she was writing "can't be too good"; his apology to her after a student-athlete had admitted to the associate director of athletics that she was giving him academic assistance; another student-athlete's statement that he told the former head coach that the secretary was working with him on course work; evidence that the secretary's assistance to student-athletes was common knowledge in the basketball program; and, evidence that the former head coach tightly controlled the academic counselor and indeed "all aspects of the men's basketball program." In addition, the Committee found that the secretary was generally credible, in that much of her information was independently corroborated by other evidence, and that the former head coach's credibility was undermined by his untruthful denials of payments to the secretary. . . .

The former head coach's chief argument on appeal is that the Committee on Infractions erroneously based its findings on what the former head coach should have known rather than on what he actually knew. This error, he argues, violates Bylaw 10.1 provides that unethical conduct consists among other things of "[k]nowing involvement" in academic fraud. He essentially argues that since there was no direct evidence of his "knowing" involvement in fraud, he should have been exonerated.

We disagree and uphold the Committee on Infractions' findings and conclusions. In doing so, we make the following observations:

a.   The Committee on Infractions' standard.

It is clear from the Committee on Infractions' decision that it applied the subjective standard of the former head coach's actual knowledge and not the objective standard of what a head coach in the former head coach's position should have known. As noted above, the Committee concluded that the former head coach "knew of the secretary's preparation of course work" and "also knew that her work constituted academic fraud." It stated its "very firm conclusion" that the former head coach "knew about and supported" the illicit activities. At no point in its decision does the Committee on Infractions refer to what the former head coach "should have known."

b.   The difference between an objective and a subjective standard proven.

At the heart of the former head coach's argument that the Committee on Infractions applied an objective "should have known" standard is his confusion between an objective standard and a subjective standard proven by indirect or substantial evidence. The applicable standard of knowledge that is an element of wrong-doing, and the means of proving that standard, are entirely separate matters.

"Knowingly" is a subjective standard, which requires that the individual actually have knowledge of the matters at issue. "Should have known" is an objective standard; that is, it considers what a person in the individual's position should have known based on all the facts and circumstances, whether the actual respondent knew it or not. . . .

Like any other element of an offense, the standard of knowledge—objective or subjective—must be proven. Proof can be by direct evidence, or by indirect (sometimes called "circumstantial") evidence. Direct evidence is that evidence that, in and of itself, demonstrates the requisite element. Indirect or circumstantial evidence is that evidence that properly justifies an inference that the element exists. . . .

c. The evidence in this case.

In this case, there was both direct and circumstantial evidence. The direct evidence consisted of the secretary's statements that she discussed with the former head coach her academic assistance, including fraudulent assistance such as the writing of papers for students, and that he warned her that her papers couldn't be "too good," and a student-athlete's statement that he likewise discussed with the former head coach the improper nature of the secretary's academic assistance. This evidence, if credible (and the Committee on Infractions found that it was), directly establishes the former head coach's knowledge of the academic fraud. The circumstantial evidence included the former head coach's payment, without satisfactory explanation, of $3000 to the secretary; the testimony that the coach tightly controlled the men's basketball program and that it was common knowledge in that program that the secretary was writing papers for students; the extensive and unconcealed contact between the secretary and the student-athletes, including her presence in study halls; and, the extended period (1994 to 1998) that this conduct covered. In appraising this evidence, both direct and circumstantial, the Committee on Infractions properly took into account its conclusion that the secretary was much more credible than the former head coach.

We agree with the Committee on Infractions that this evidence satisfactorily established, both directly and by permissible inference from the circumstances, the former head coach's knowing involvement in academic fraud.

d. An objective standard of knowledge of academic fraud.

Although it is not necessary for us to decide whether Bylaw 10.1 permits a finding of unethical conduct based on what a head coach should have known, we address that question in light of the former head coach's argument that the bylaw does not allow it, and also because we think the question is an important one.

First, it is not at all clear that Bylaw 10.1 requires actual knowledge of academic fraud and thus precludes a finding of unethical conduct against an individual who should have known of fraud. The bylaw states that unethical conduct "may include, but is not limited to" actual knowledge of the academic fraud. This at least leaves open the possibility that an objective standard may be applied.

We believe that the objective, "should have known" standard may well be appropriate to assess the responsibility of a person, such as the head coach of an athletics program, who is expected to know what those in the program are doing. To conclude otherwise would be to encourage coaches or others in similarly responsible positions to close their eyes and ears to what is happening in areas for which they are accountable. It would be irresponsible for this committee, the NCAA, or any member institution to tolerate, let alone encourage, such intentional ignorance.

A head coach's responsibility goes beyond merely acting upon academic fraud that comes to his attention. A coach should take reasonable steps to see that it does not happen in the first place. This is not to say that he is absolutely liable for every instance of academic fraud that might occur; it is to say, however, that his accountability should be measured by more than what he actually knew. It should be measured by what a reasonably vigilant observant, and diligent person in his position should have known. If he does nothing to discourage academic fraud, nothing to observe those circumstances in which it might be occurring, and nothing to see that those in the program are carrying out their responsibilities honestly, he should not be shielded from accountability merely because his inaction insulates him from knowledge of what is happening. To do so, would be to encourage the evasion of responsibility on the part of those of whom the NCAA, and the public expect responsibility.

It is no answer to say, as the former head coach does in this case, that the secretary who took part in illicit activities reported to an academic counselor who was not in the former head coach's direct line of command as a basket-ball coach. The responsibility of a head coach is not based on a chain of command — it arises from the fact that he is one of those who are responsible for the integrity of the program and, specifically, for the welfare of student-athletes in the program.

We see no difference here. This is not a case in which a secretary provided isolated or well-concealed assistance that a vigilant and responsible coach could not reasonably have been expected to uncover. The evidence was uncontro-verted that her assistance was extensive, visible and notorious. We agree with the Committee on Infractions that the evidence taken as a whole establishes that the former head coach in fact knew of it. But even if we were somehow persuaded that he lacked actual knowledge, we have no doubt that he should have known of it, and we would find in Bylaw 10.1 sufficient warrant to conclude that a head coach's unethical conduct consists not only of the academic fraud he knows of, but also that of which he clearly should have known.

should have known

3. Unethical Conduct

In challenging the findings of unethical conduct made by the Committee on Infractions, the former head coach asserts that the Committee erred in finding:

1. That the former head coach provided false and misleading information regarding the $3,000 payment to the secretary; and
2. That the former head coach gave instructions to student-athletes to provide false, and misleading information to University officials.

As to the first point, the former head coach argues that "the committee did not find that the $3,000 payment an indicator that the former head coach knew the secretary was involved in academic fraud." Given that we have upheld the Committee's findings regarding academic fraud, including the fact that the for-mer head coach was aware that the payment was being made for fraudulent purposes, there is no remaining support for the former head coach's argument that he did not provide false and misleading information regarding the secre-tary payment.

With regard to the second point, the former head coach offers support for his assertion that, "the overwhelming evidence was that the former head coach told the players to be truthful during their meetings with investigators, and is con-trary to the findings of the Committee on Infractions." Once again, the former head coach is simply disagreeing with the weight of the factual basis supporting the Committee on Infractions' finding that the former head coach told the students to give false or misleading statements. The Committee itself concluded that "the evidence is not fully consistent," but it found that the clear weight of the evidence showed that the former head coach attempted to influence young men to provide false and misleading information and, in doing so, violated NCAA standards of ethical conduct. . . .

The Committee on Infractions' finding in this regard is not clearly contrary to the evidence presented to the Committee.

4.   *Other Issues*

The former head coach challenges virtually every finding of the Committee on Infractions. He asserts that the following findings were clearly contrary to the evidence:

1. That he arranged hotel rooms for student-athletes and their families at a substantially discounted rate;
2. That he provided various recruiting inducements to prospective student-athletes and improper benefits to student-athletes; and
3. That he made payments on a car lease for the academic counselor in violation of NCAA rules.

Once again, we uphold the Committee on Infractions' findings in each of these areas on the grounds that they are not clearly contrary to the evidence presented in the case.

The Committee on Infractions found that the former head coach had provided extra benefits to student-athletes and their families from 1994-1999, by helping to arrange for parents and friends of men's basketball student-athletes to stay at the Ramada Plaza Hotel at a discounted rate. The evidence certainly supports the Committee's finding in this regard, given that parents and friends of five student-athletes stayed at the Ramada Plaza Hotel at a rate of $30 per night, which is substantially less than the $79 per night minimum daily rate.

Similarly, the former head coach's assertion that the Committee's findings that he had provided cash to student-athletes was clearly contrary to the evidence is unfounded. In his own brief, the former head coach "admitted that he gave [the student-athlete] a $200 loan, based on the fact that the [student-athlete's] wallet had been stolen just prior to his return home for Christmas." Bylaw 16.02.3 provides that, "An extra benefit is any special arrangement by an institutional employee or representative of the institution's athletics interests to provide a student-athlete . . . a benefit not expressly authorized by NCAA legislation." Certainly, a cash payment to a student-athlete would violate this provision. Even if this were a loan, and there is no evidence to indicate that it was a loan that was ever memorialized or paid back, it would constitute an extra benefit, because it is not "expressly authorized by NCAA legislation." [T]here was [also] sufficient evidence in the record to support the committee's findings relative to the former head coach's payments to another student-athlete. This is another instance of the evidence being conflicted, but the committee's finding was not clearly contrary to existing evidence. Finally, the record was sufficient to support the committee's finding that the former head coach provided improper recruiting inducements to a prospective student-athlete by having the prospect over to his home for dinner. The former head coach asserts that the prospect was a family friend. In support of his position, the former head coach argues that the prospect was a friend of [the former head coach's] family since he was in the 5th grade, when he first attended a basketball camp offered by the former head coach. Given that the former head coach came to know the prospect through the basketball program and was involved in recruiting him, the committee was warranted in finding that the prospect was not a family friend for the purposes of the dinner.

The former head coach also contends that the evidence was insufficient to support the Committee on Infractions' finding that the former head coach's making of car lease payments to an academic counselor, who was an employee of the academic counseling center rather than the athletics department, was a violation of NCAA rules. Once again, the former head coach is asserting that he did not know that making the lease payments was a violation of NCAA rules. The Committee did find that the former head coach knew that he was not permitted to supplement the salary of a university employee in this manner, particularly in an instance in which the University had deemed it inappropriate for the counselor to be provided a car.

B. WHETHER THE PENALTIES IMPOSED BY THE COMMITTEE ARE EXCESSIVE OR INAPPROPRIATE AND SHOULD BE SET ASIDE

The Committee on Infractions noted Minnesota's "prompt and decisive" corrective actions and self-imposed penalties. It nonetheless imposed penalties on Minnesota and upon the former head coach and certain other individuals. Only the penalty imposed on the coach is before us. That penalty is a seven-year period (until October 24, 2007) during which the former head coach is subject to the show-cause procedures of Bylaw ¶6.2.2-(1). He asks us to set this aside under Bylaw 32.10.2, which authorizes us to reduce or vacate a penalty that is excessive or inappropriate based on all the evidence and circumstances.

The former head coach's argument is based on a number of factors, including his age, his belief that the penalty "essentially prohibits [him] from ever being able to coach at an NCAA institution again" (Br. 44), the fact that previous cases have imposed shorter periods under Bylaw 19.6.2.2-(1), the fact that the Committee on Infractions imposed lesser penalties in this case on others who were involved and his assertion (which we have rejected) that the evidence failed to establish his "knowing" violation of NCAA rules.

We have considered all these factors carefully, and we have also considered, independent of the former head coach's arguments, whether the penalty was either "excessive" or "inappropriate" based on all the evidence and circumstances.

We affirm the penalty. We recognize, as the Committee on Infractions did, that the penalty is a serious one, but it is commensurate with the conduct that gave rise to it. We adopt the characterization of the Committee on Infractions: "[T]his case involved numerous and repeated violations that occurred over many years and whose nature, academic fraud, strikes at the heart of institutional integrity. Furthermore, the academic fraud clearly violated the principles relating to the educational welfare of student-athletes and the maintenance of sound academic standards as set forth in NCAA Constitution 2.2.1 and 2.5."

The most severe penalties are appropriate when the academic mission of the university has been compromised. The former head coach was not the only one who bears responsibility for the damage; as the Committee on Infractions' report demonstrates, others in the program, and Minnesota itself, also failed in their responsibilities. The former head coach's appeal is the only one before us. We have no doubt that his conduct, fully established by the evidence in this case, justifies the penalty imposed.

Penalties Affirmed.

VIII. CONCLUSION

As discussed in the preceding section, we affirm each of the findings made by the Committee on Infractions. We also affirm the penalty imposed against the former head coach.

NOTES AND QUESTIONS

1. *Scapegoating or Appropriate Corrective Action?* The University of Minnesota's president responded to the NCAA's investigation by seeking the resignations of athletics administrators and coaches as part of the institution's corrective efforts made prior to the hearing before the COI. Was he seeking scapegoats in an effort to placate the NCAA, or to show institutional control over the university's athletics department, or perhaps both? As legal counsel, would you recommend such strong action as a part of your institution's voluntary corrective efforts? In such cases, highly successful coaches are often removed, as was the case at Penn State, Ohio State, and the University of Minnesota. How far should the NCAA go in the direction of penalizing other personnel associated with the university? For example, would it be appropriate for the NCAA to seek removal of the university's president or replacement of its board of trustees?

2. *Practical Lawyering Issues.* As legal counsel for Coach Haskins, what would you have advised him to do once the NCAA and University of Minnesota began its investigation? Would you have advised him to refuse to appear before the COI? What was his best defense?

3. *Notoriety and Power of Coaches.* It is clear that Clem Haskins was a very powerful and successful coach at the University of Minnesota. In the Penn State and other cases, the NCAA has expressed concern regarding the power of nationally prominent coaches and its potential adverse effects on the broader university community. Do you know the names of coaches in major athletic programs in your region of the country? Do you know the names of the presidents at the same institutions? Given this apparent disparity in notoriety, popularity, and perhaps even de facto power, is it surprising that presidents and athletic directors are often hesitant to deal directly with or investigate prominent coaches when they may have engaged in inappropriate activity in running their highly visible programs? What causes coaches to violate NCAA rules: a-win-at-all-costs philosophy, economic incentives created by the overcommercialization of intercollegiate athletics, lack of knowledge or concern about NCAA rules, or other factors? As legal counsel, is there anything that you might suggest doing to help the president and athletic director in their efforts to restrain a prominent coach inclined to violate NCAA rules?

4. *Objective Knowledge Standard for Head Coaches.* In its Haskins opinion, the IAC engages in a lengthy discussion regarding the distinction between a head coach's subjective and objective knowledge for the purpose of assessing culpability in a case like this. Why do you think the IAC did so? Was it appropriate to do so? What did you learn from this discussion that might be helpful in representing a coach or institution in the future? The new enforcement structure, adopted in October 2012, continues to emphasize strong penalties for coaches, like Coach Haskin, who personally violate NCAA rules.

Under the new structure, rather than focusing on knowledge or the presumption of it, the bylaws will be amended to presume only responsibility: if a violation occurs, the head coach is presumed responsible, and if he or she is unable to overcome that presumption, charges will be forthcoming. The new enforcement structure has also "enhance[d] head coach responsibility/accountability and potential consequences for head coaches who fail to direct their staffs and student-athletes to uphold NCAA bylaws. Penalties include imposed suspensions that can range from 10 percent of the season to an entire season." Head coaches are also expected to provide practice and training materials to instruct their assistant coaches. If they do so, such instruction may mitigate the head coach's presumed responsibility in the case of a "rogue" assistant coach. If such training does not occur, the head coach will be held accountable for the acts of a "rogue" assistant coach, even if the head coach was unaware of the assistant coach's violation of the rules. In short, coaches are being held to an even higher level of responsibility under the new structure.

5. *Significant Sanctions Imposed on Coaches.* Institutions are now self-imposing penalties on coaches that include termination and permanent dissociation from the program and the university. See, e.g., University of South Alabama (5/12/2009) (NCAA added to the penalty imposed on the coach by the institution, limiting his coaching duties at the university, by requiring his appearance before the NCAA Committee on Infractions on an order to show cause prior to him being permitted to seek athletically related employment at another NCAA institution). In May 2011 Ohio State University forced head football coach Jim Tressel to "retire" for failing to disclose that two players received impermissible extra benefits (e.g., cash for selling sports memorabilia and discounted tattoos) and permitted them to play in games during the 2010 season. On February 22, 2011, the NCAA Division I Committee on Infractions penalized the University of Connecticut and head basketball coach Jim Calhoun for violations in its men's basketball program. The case included more than $6,000 in improper recruiting inducements, impermissible phone calls and text messages to prospective student-athletes, failure to monitor and promote an atmosphere for compliance by the head coach, failure to monitor by the university, and unethical conduct by the former operations director, among other violations. Penalties include suspension of the head coach for three conference games during the 2011-2012 season, scholarship reductions for three academic years, recruiting restrictions, permanent disassociation of a booster and three years' probation. As stated in the COI's report, this case involved facts related to "extraordinary steps" taken by the university to recruit a high-profile or top prospective student-athlete to its men's basketball program. The COI's emphasis on the high-profile nature of the student-athlete made it clear that a very high standard will be applied to oversight or monitoring of such recruiting efforts. The University of Oklahoma committed major violations in its men's basketball program, according to findings by the NCAA Division I Committee on Infractions (11/11/2011). The violations in this case included unethical conduct by a former assistant men's basketball coach, extra benefits, preferential treatment, and ineligible participation. Penalties in this case include recruiting restrictions, a scholarship reduction, vacation of records, a $15,000 fine, and three years of probation for the university. A former assistant men's basketball coach also

received a two-year show-cause order, which restricts his recruiting activity at any NCAA member institution during that time. A March 2012 case involving the University of North Carolina brought to light serious violations by a former assistant football coach, who was compensated by a sports agent for the access he provided to student-athletes and failed to disclose the income to the university. The former assistant coach and a former tutor both committed unethical conduct and failed to cooperate with the investigation. The NCAA noted that "[the North Carolina] case should serve as a cautionary tale to all institutions to vigilantly monitor the activities of those student-athletes who possess the potential to be top professional prospects." Penalties for the case include a one-year postseason ban, reduction of 15 football scholarships, vacation of records, and three years' probation. The former assistant coach received a three-year show-cause penalty restricting any recruiting activity.

6. *Penalties Imposed on Other Personnel.* The imposition of stiff penalties on athletically related personnel has extended to others such as tutors, learning specialists, and academic advisors who violate major NCAA rules. See, e.g., Florida State University (3/6/2009), for a case involving academic fraud with regard to online courses and typing portions of papers for students, in which a learning specialist was placed under a four-year order to show cause before he could be rehired at a member institution, a tutor was placed under a three-year order to show cause, and an academic advisor was placed under a five-year order to show cause, with an additional year being added because he failed to cooperate with the NCAA's investigation. (This case is also significant because the Committee on Infractions also required the vacation of victories in football games, which adversely affected Bobby Bowden's quest for the most Division I wins; this penalty serves as a strong reminder to coaches of the importance of compliance and oversight.) See also University of District of Columbia (10/29/2008), in which the NCAA prohibited the former athletic director from performing duties beyond the normal duties of a coach, and the faculty athletics representative was prohibited from holding any athletically related position at any NCAA member institution for a five-year period. In the Penn State case, a number of administrators, including the president, a vice president, and the athletic director, were pressured to resign as part of the corrective action being taken by the university. The NCAA also criticized the board of trustees. In *Bucknell University Infractions Appeals Report* (3/7/2000), the IAC discussed the role of the president in failing to act promptly with regard to his personal knowledge that infractions had occurred in that case. The committee did not sanction the president directly but implied that such a sanction remains a possibility and may be more likely under the new enforcement structure which has increased accountability for coaches and other university officials. Should a president be given an order to show cause in a case in which he or she failed to act, given the expectation that a university's president or chancellor is responsible for overseeing the program? What kind of message would such an order send and what would be its effect (i.e., similar to a show cause order, would it preclude employment as a university president for a designated period of time)? See generally Rodney K. Smith, *Increasing Presidential Accountability in Big-Time Intercollegiate Athletics*, 10 Vill. Sports & Ent. L.J. 297 (2003).

PROBLEM 3-7

Midwestern State University was highly interested in seeing Joe Fastball, a junior college baseball star, don a Midwestern State baseball uniform and compete for the team in the upcoming season. In an effort to recruit Fastball, Midwestern State's assistant baseball coach promised the junior college star that his wife would be able to travel with the baseball team to each away game. Furthermore, the assistant coach assured Fastball that he would help Fastball's wife secure full-time employment.

Fastball accepted the assistant coach's "offer" and enrolled in Midwestern State. Fastball was happy to see that the assistant coach was true to his word in that he immediately arranged for Fastball's wife to work part-time before switching to a full-time job in the mailroom of the apartment complex where the assistant baseball coach both lives and works part-time as a manager. In an additional gesture of gratitude toward Fastball, the assistant coach loaned his automobile to Fastball and his wife on several occasions so the two of them could run local errands.

Joe was not the only member of the Fastball family who, in the eyes of the assistant coach, had an aptitude for the game of baseball. On several occasions, the assistant coach called on Joe's father, Scout Fastball, to watch a prospective student-athlete compete in a high school baseball game and share his opinion of the prospective student-athlete's performance with the assistant coach. As the relationship between Scout and the assistant coach continued to grow, the assistant coach gave more and more recruitment-related responsibilities to Scout. On one occasion, Scout was asked to hand-deliver a National Letter of Intent to a prospective student-athlete. On another occasion, Scout introduced a different prospective student-athlete and his family to the Midwestern State's head baseball coach.

Although Scout was in regular contact with the assistant baseball coach, he was never compensated by Midwestern State for his efforts. According to the NCAA, Scout was not actually a certified recruiter; he was merely a representative of Midwestern State's athletic interests.

Fastball was not the only student-athlete for whom the assistant baseball coach performed favors. While in Oklahoma for winter break, the assistant coach offered to provide Sam Slugger, a Midwestern State baseball player, with transportation from Oklahoma to Midwestern State's campus (a distance of 1,350 miles) so Slugger could enroll in the institution for the spring semester. Slugger accepted this offer. Upon returning to Midwestern State's campus, the assistant baseball coach allowed Slugger to borrow his automobile for personal errands on approximately two occasions.

When baseball season arrived, Midwestern State certified both Fastball and Slugger as initial enrollees with four years of eligibility. Both were allowed to practice, travel with the team, compete, and receive financial aid. Fastball and Slugger, however, had both previously attended and competed for other institutions: Fastball for a junior college and Slugger for both a junior college and a four-year institution. The assistant baseball coach knew that both individuals had competed as student-athletes for other institutions and thus could not be eligible under NCAA rules governing transfers from two- and four-year institutions.

During the following summer, three Midwestern State student-athletes, one of whom was Fastball, were awarded academic credit for classes in which they did not perform any work, take any exams, or even attend. In fact, none of the three student-athletes was aware that he was enrolled in the class in question. When two of the student-athletes, after finding they had received a grade of "A," approached the assistant coach, he told them not to be concerned about the situation. After being informed that the credits may have been fraudulent, the assistant coach took no action to report or investigate the matter.

Although the academic credits were indeed fraudulent, Fastball was certified as eligible to compete for Midwestern State the following season.

How many NCAA violations can you spot in this particular fact pattern?

Assume the NCAA sanctions Midwestern State University for rules violations. How blameworthy is Joe Fastball? If he is culpable, what action should be taken by Midwestern State against Fastball?

PROBLEM 3-8

You are vice president and legal counsel for a large public Division I-A institution. The president of the university has given you responsibility for acting as her liaison with the athletics program regarding possible infractions of NCAA rules. Your men's football and basketball teams have regularly been ranked in the top 25 in the nation. Your coaches are well known in the local community and nationally, are quite popular, and are well liked by legislators throughout the state. Indeed, they are better known and more popular than the president in whose administration you serve. Not surprisingly, therefore, the coaches have been given wide budgetary latitude (they are able to raise and allocate funds within their respective programs, for example). They have raised and allocated funds for the hiring of additional academic advisors and tutors to work with their student-athletes in an effort to increase their graduation rates and avoid possible disincentives that might be applied to their programs if they fail to increase graduation rates among their players.

It is December, and your football and basketball teams have each enjoyed substantial success. Your football team is scheduled to play in a BCS Bowl and your basketball team is 10-1 and ranked fifth in the country. Needless to say, the community is thrilled by the successes of your most visible programs. However, your institution's faculty athletics representative (FAR) has asked to meet with you and the athletic director as soon as possible to relate some concerns that have been raised by some faculty and staff members on campus. When notified of the meeting, the athletic director has also indicated that he has heard some rumors that he thinks he should share with you, although with the upcoming bowl game he is very busy and would like to put off the meeting until after the first of the year.

When you suggest the possibility of putting off the meeting until after the first of the year to your FAR, she responds by indicating that the problems she wants you to consider are significant and may implicate the eligibility of players on the men's basketball and football teams. This certainly was not what you wanted to hear, but it makes it clear that you need to hold the meeting as soon as possible. You communicate this to the athletic director, who reluctantly agrees.

At the meeting, the FAR states that staff members associated with the university's academic support program have indicated that they have strong reason to believe that the academic advisors and tutors working directly with the basketball and football teams may have helped student-athletes research and write papers during the recently concluded finals period. Additionally, the FAR noted that she was contacted immediately after finals by a professor who is concerned about possible cheating by a number of student-athletes in his class. The professor teaches a large psychology class, and he gave a multiple-choice exam that could be taken at the testing center on campus at any time. After discovering that a number of students in the class, almost all of whom were prominent student-athletes, did so well on the exam that they raised their grades in the class from the D range to the B range, the faculty member examined the grade sheets and discovered that the student-athletes missed only five to seven questions on a 100-question exam. Of even greater concern to the professor was the fact that the student-athletes overwhelmingly missed the same questions. The student-athletes suspected of cheating include an All-American linebacker on the football team and the star center on the basketball team, as well as three other starters on the football team and one other starter on the basketball team.

cheating

The athletic director, who joins you in being stunned by the professor's allegations of possible cheating among student-athletes, then shares his concerns. He has learned that a major donor at the university, who owns three major car dealerships, may have loaned cars to a couple of student-athletes. The athletic director confesses that he received a call from a reporter with the local newspaper who said he saw the quarterback on the football team driving a new Ford Explorer, which caused him to spend a day observing student-athletes arriving and departing from the athletics facilities on campus. When he did so, the reporter noted that at least four other student-athletes arrived in new cars that could be traced, based on their plates, to the dealerships owned by the major donor. Upon inquiring of the student-athletes and the donor, the athletic director was told by the student-athletes that they were permitted to use the cars because their older cars were in the shop. The donor, in turn, confirmed the student-athlete's statements and added, when asked whether this was common practice, "Sure, we commonly do this for our best customers." The athletic director was hesitant to inquire further at the time, but he was unsettled about the donor's response.

You are obviously quite concerned about these statements. After the meeting, you call the president on her cell phone and relate what has happened. She instructs you to call the coaches and see what they have to say about the matter and set up meetings for you to discuss your concerns with the student-athletes suspected of cheating. She then wants you to get back to her so that she can determine whether a full investigation is in order. When told about the cars, she muses, "I wondered about that. Last week, I went to a banquet at the athletic department and noticed that a number of the athletes were driving what appeared to be new, high-priced automobiles." She said that she will personally contact the donor, because she is involved in delicate discussions with him regarding a multimillions-dollar gift from his family to the university that could be used to build an addition on the business building that would be named after the donor.

When you call the coaches regarding possible cheating, each of them responds by requesting the identity of the faculty member and the names of the student-athletes. When you are reluctant to give the names at this stage, each coach responds indicating his belief it was Professor Norse in the psychology department, who has long been an opponent of athletics at the university.

They add that they are not surprised that the athletes missed the same questions because they generally study together. Both coaches are reluctant to help set up meetings with the student-athletes until school starts after the first of the year, arguing that it would be very disruptive to their practice and playing schedules and that the students were going home for the holidays on the few days that they have off during December. When told of allegations that the basketball and football academic advisors and tutors may have helped write papers, the coaches scoff, again noting that there is bad blood between the university's academic support staff and the basketball and football advisors and tutors, because the university personnel think the athletic academic advisors get preferential treatment and perks, including necessary traveling with the teams to provide academic and tutoring support on the road. They agree to talk with the advisors and the student-athletes and get back with you to set up a meeting after the first of the year.

schedules are not a legit. excuse!

After these conversations with the coaches, which you found to be disheartening and unhelpful, you call the president to ask whether she can help get the coaches to set up meetings with the student-athletes, the academic advisors and tutors, and the donor as soon as possible. She responds that she will do her best and get back to you. You do not hear from her for a week despite two follow-up e-mails you sent to her during the week. When you finally reach her, she apologizes for not getting back to you sooner and indicates that, after speaking with the coaches, she thinks it would be best to wait to set up the meetings until after the first of the year, when the student-athletes are back on campus on a full-time basis and athletics personnel are not busy preparing for the football bowl game and two prestigious holiday tournaments that the basketball team is participating in during December.

Pres. wants to wait

In analyzing the preceding factual scenario, consider the following questions:

a. Who is your client? Do you see any potential conflicts of interest (consider which individuals may have violated NCAA rules), and if so, what steps should you take to comply with your ethical duties as an attorney?

My client = the institution and the President — meet immediately or self report

b. Are you satisfied with the responses you received from the president and the coaches? Should you do anything to try to expedite the interviews? If so, what might you do? Are there possible implications for you personally if you fail to take appropriate action until after the first of the year? What role, if any, do the public relations aspects of this scenario play in determining how you should proceed?

certain consequences, yes + threaten turning them in - the media would be tough, but better than finding out school covered it up later

Ethical Conduct, impermissible benefit, academic integrity

c. If any of the allegations are true, what possible NCAA rules may have been violated? Should you be concerned about possible failure to monitor the athletic department or lack of institutional control in this case? Whom do you want to interview? What facts are you trying to discover?

d. If you find that the allegations are true, what action would you recommend that the university take to fulfill its self-reporting obligation? What other voluntary self-corrective actions would you advise? What if the university president refuses to follow your advice?

Notify the NCAA and begin my own investigation. Interview AD, Students, Coaches, Car person, Psych prof., tutors looking for impermissible benefits

e. What would you advise with regard to the new rules enforcement structure, which might well apply in this case? If that new structure in fact heightens responsibility, accountability, and liability, how will that affect the advice you are giving to the individuals involved? To the respective administrators and coaches?

Probably a level II. Advice that expidites the process and informs of the serious consequences.

f.   Going forward, what is your advice to prevent similar problems from arising in the future (i.e., what reporting, follow-up, or other investigative procedures designed to deal with possible infractions should be implicated)?

[handwritten: Hiring compliance for just football and men's basketball. Tutor advisor]

3.   Federal and State Civil Rights Laws

Virtually all public and private universities receive some federal funds, and therefore must comply with federal civil right statutes such as Title IX and the Rehabilitation Act of 1972. As the following case illustrates, this does not necessarily mean that the NCAA is subject to these federal laws.

NCAA v. SMITH
525 U.S. 459 (1999)

GINSBURG, Justice.

   This case concerns the amenability of the National Collegiate Athletic Association (NCAA or Association) to a private action under Title IX of the Education Amendments of 1972. . . . Title IX proscribes sex discrimination in "any education program or activity receiving Federal financial assistance." 20 U.S.C. § 1681(a).

   . . . Renee M. Smith, sued the NCAA under Title IX alleging that the Association discriminated against her on the basis of her sex by denying her permission to play intercollegiate volleyball at federally assisted institutions. . . . The Third Circuit held that the NCAA's receipt of dues from federally funded member institutions would suffice to bring the Association within the scope of Title IX. We reject that determination as inconsistent with the governing statute, regulation, and Court decisions. Dues payments from recipients of federal funds, we hold, do not suffice to render the dues recipient subject to Title IX. We do not address alternative grounds, urged by respondent and the United States as *amicus curiae*, in support of Title IX's application to the NCAA in this litigation, and leave resolution of those grounds to the courts below on remand.

[handwritten right margin: Lower court held that the NCAA could be subject to a Title IX claim]

I

Rules adopted by the NCAA govern the intercollegiate athletics programs of its member colleges and universities; "[b]y joining the NCAA, each member agrees to abide by and enforce [the Association's] rules." *National Collegiate Athletic Assn.v. Tarkanian*, 488 U.S. 179, 183, 109 S.Ct. 454, 102 L.Ed.2d 469 (1988); see 1993-1994 NCAA Manual, NCAA Const., Arts. 1.2(h), 1.3.2, p. 1. Among these rules is the Postbaccalaureate Bylaw, which allows a postgraduate student-athlete to participate in intercollegiate athletics only at the institution that awarded her undergraduate degree. . . .[1]

   Respondent Smith enrolled as an undergraduate at St. Bonaventure University, an NCAA member, in 1991. Smith joined the St. Bonaventure inter-collegiate

---

1. The Postbaccalaureate Bylaw is an exception to the general NCAA rule restricting participation in intercollegiate athletics to students enrolled in a full-time program of studies leading to a baccalaureate degree.

volleyball team in the fall of 1991 and remained on the team throughout the 1991-1992 and 1992-1993 athletic seasons. She elected not to play the following year.

Smith graduated from St. Bonaventure in 2 1/2 years. During the 1994-1995 athletic year, she was enrolled in a postgraduate program at Hofstra University; for the 1995-1996 athletic year, she enrolled in a different postgraduate program at the University of Pittsburgh. Smith sought to play intercollegiate volleyball during these athletic years, but the NCAA denied her eligibility on the basis of its postbaccalaureate restrictions. At Smith's request, Hofstra and the University of Pittsburgh petitioned the NCAA to waive the restrictions. Each time, the NCAA refused to grant a waiver.

In August 1996, Smith filed this lawsuit *pro se*, alleging, among other things, that the NCAA's refusal to waive the Postbaccalaureate Bylaw excluded her from participating in intercollegiate athletics at Hofstra and the University of Pittsburgh on the basis of her sex, in violation of Title IX. . . . The complaint did not attack the Bylaw on its face, but instead alleged that the NCAA discriminates on the basis of sex by granting more waivers from eligibility restrictions to male than female postgraduate student-athletes. . . .

The NCAA moved to dismiss Smith's Title IX claim on the ground that the complaint failed to allege that the NCAA is a recipient of federal financial assistance. In opposition, Smith argued that the NCAA governs the federally funded intercollegiate athletics programs of its members, that these programs are educational, and that the NCAA benefited economically from its members' receipt of federal funds. . . .

II

. . . Under the Civil Rights Restoration Act of 1987 (CRRA), 102 Stat. 28, 20 U.S.C. § 1687, a "program or activity" includes "all of the operations of . . . a college, university, or other postsecondary institution, or a public system of higher education . . . any part of which is extended Federal financial assistance." § 1687(2)(A). The CRRA also provides institution-wide coverage for entities "principally engaged in the business of providing education" services, § 1687(3) (A)(ii), and for entities created by two or more covered entities, § 1687(4). Thus, if any part of the NCAA received federal assistance, all NCAA operations would be subject to Title IX.

We have twice before considered when an entity qualifies as a recipient of federal financial assistance. In *Grove City College v. Bell*, 465 U.S. 555, 563-570, 104 S.Ct. 1211, 79 L.Ed.2d 516 (1984), we held that a college receives federal financial assistance when it enrolls students who receive federal funds earmarked for educational expenses. Finding "no hint" that Title IX distinguishes "between direct institutional assistance and aid received by a school through its students," we concluded that Title IX "encompass[es] *all* forms of federal aid to education, direct or indirect." *Id.* at 564. [Internal quotation marks omitted.]

In [*U.S. Department of Transportation v. Paralyzed Veterans of America*, 477 U.S. 597, 106 S. Ct. 2705, 91 L. Ed. 2d 494 (1986)], we considered the scope of § 504 of the Rehabilitation Act of 1973, 29 U.S.C. § 794, which prohibits discrimination on the basis of disability in substantially the same terms that Title IX uses to prohibit sex discrimination. In that case, a group representing disabled veterans contended that the Department of Transportation had authority to enforce

§ 504 against commercial air carriers by virtue of the Government's extensive program of financial assistance to airports. We held that airlines are not recipients of federal funds received by airport operators for airport construction projects, even when the funds are used for projects especially beneficial to the airlines. Application of § 504 to all who benefited economically from federal assistance, we observed, would yield almost "limitless coverage." 477 U.S., at 608, 106 S.Ct. 2705. We concluded that "[t]he statute covers those who receive the aid, but does not extend as far as those who benefit from it." *Id.*, at 607, 106 S.Ct. 2705. . . . Entities that receive federal assistance, whether directly or through an intermediary, are recipients within the meaning of Title IX; entities that only benefit economically from federal assistance are not.

The Third Circuit's conclusion that the NCAA would be subject to the requirements of Title IX if it received dues from its federally funded members is inconsistent with this precedent. Unlike the earmarked student aid in *Grove City*, there is no allegation that NCAA members paid their dues with federal funds earmarked for that purpose. At most, the Association's receipt of dues demonstrates that it indirectly benefits from the federal assistance afforded its members. This showing, without more, is insufficient to trigger Title IX coverage. . . .

III

Smith, joined by the United States as *amicus curiae*, presses two alternative theories for bringing the NCAA under the prescriptions of Title IX. First, she asserts that the NCAA directly and indirectly receives federal financial assistance through the National Youth Sports Program NCAA administers. Second, Smith argues that when a recipient cedes controlling authority over a federally funded program to another entity, the controlling entity is covered by Title IX regardless whether it is itself a recipient.

. . . We do not decide in the first instance issues not decided below. . . .

For the reasons stated, we conclude that the Court of Appeals erroneously held that dues payments from recipients of federal funds suffice to subject the NCAA to suit under Title IX. Accordingly, we vacate the judgment of the Third Circuit and remand the case for further proceedings consistent with this opinion.

It is so ordered.

NOTE AND QUESTIONS

Like *Tarkanian*, *Smith* holds that certain laws applicable to its member institutions do not apply to the NCAA. Is this good policy? Note that educational institutions acting collectively through the NCAA may legally accomplish what cannot be done individually. In *Cureton v. NCAA*, 198 F.3d 107 (3d Cir. 1999), the Third Circuit considered the two issues not decided by *Smith*. The *Cureton* plaintiffs alleged that the NCAA's Proposition 16 minimum standardized test score requirement for freshman student-athlete eligibility has a racially discriminatory impact in violation of Title VI of the Civil Rights Act of 1964, 42 U.S.C. §§2000d et seq., which applies to any program or activity receiving federal financial assistance. The court rejected plaintiffs' contention that the NCAA is subject to Title VI based on federal funds received by the National Youth Sports program or the degree of its control over its member institutions. It found no evidence that the National Youth Sports program's practices affected the NCAA's broader practices, including adoption and enforcement of Proposition 16. Relying on *Tarkanian*, the court held that the NCAA does not in fact "control" its members:

> Similarly, the ultimate decision as to which freshmen an institution will permit to participate in varsity intercollegiate athletics and which applicants will be awarded athletic scholarships belongs to the member schools. The fact that the institutions make these decisions cognizant of NCAA sanctions does not mean that the NCAA controls them, because they have the option, albeit unpalatable, of risking sanctions or voluntarily withdrawing from the NCAA.

Id. at 117.

However, in some instances, courts have held that federal antidiscrimination laws such as Title VI, the Americans with Disabilities Act of 1990, and the Rehabilitation Act of 1972 apply to the NCAA. See Chapters 9 and 11.

The NCAA's drug testing program, applicable to all student-athletes, was initiated in 1986. It was created so that no one participant could gain an artificially induced advantage, so that no one participant might be pressured to use chemical substances in order to remain competitive, and to safeguard the health and safety of student-athletes. See NCAA Drug-Testing Program 2011-12 at http://150.174.33.55/~jjunot/special/2011_NCAA_DTProgrambook.pdf. As a condition to participating in intercollegiate athletics, student-athletes are required to provide written consent to random drug testing for substances prohibited by the NCAA during NCAA championship competition and out-of-season testing programs. The NCAA's list of banned substances includes performance-enhancing drugs such as anabolic steroids, stimulants (e.g., cocaine and amphetamines), and certain illegal recreational drugs such as marijuana and heroin.

In effect, a student-athlete's compliance with the NCAA's drug testing program, which has been alleged to violate his or her civil rights protected by state law, is a condition of eligibility to compete in intercollegiate athletics. As illustrated by the following case, courts also provide significant deference to the NCAA in its efforts to prevent student-athletes from using banned substances and its imposition of disciplinary sanctions for doing so.

BRENNAN v. BOARD OF TRUSTEES FOR UNIVERSITY OF LOUISIANA SYSTEMS
691 So. 2d 324 (La. App. 1997)

LOTTINGER, Chief Judge.

Plaintiff, John Patout Brennan (Brennan), a student-athlete at the University of Southwestern Louisiana (USL), tested positive for [use of the banned anabolic steroid testosterone in the second of three random drug tests administered by the NCAA]. Brennan requested and received two administrative appeals in which he contended that the positive test results were "false" due to a combination of factors, including heavy drinking and sexual activity the night before the test, and his use of nutritional supplements. Following the unsuccessful appeals, USL complied with the NCAA regulations and suspended Brennan from intercollegiate athletic competition for one year. Brennan brought this action against USL's governing body, the Board of Trustees for University of Louisiana Systems (Board of Trustees), seeking to enjoin enforcement by USL of the suspension.

In his petition, Brennan alleged that, by requiring him to submit to the NCAA's drug testing program, USL violated his right of privacy and deprived him of a liberty and property interest without due process in contravention of Article I, Sections 2 and 5 of the Louisiana Constitution. The NCAA moved to intervene on the grounds that the drug testing policies and procedures that Brennan placed at issue were developed, administered, conducted and enforced by the NCAA. The intervention was granted. . . .

VALIDITY OF THE DRUG TEST

. . . After reviewing the record in this case in its entirety, we conclude that the trial judge committed manifest error in finding that the drug test results were flawed. . . .[2]

Upon close review, we find that the record does not contain a reasonable factual basis for the trial judge's conclusion that the test results were flawed. According to the experts, sex and alcohol alone could not have caused the drastic increase in Brennan's T/E ratio. Brennan admitted to taking nutritional supplements which likely contained testosterone. Experts testified that Brennan's elevated T/E ratio was consistent with having consumed nutritional supplements which likely contained testosterone. The pattern established by Brennan's three drug tests indicated that he had been exposed to testosterone. Considering the evidence contained in the record, we conclude that the trial judge was clearly wrong in finding that the test results were flawed. . . .

A.   BRENNAN'S CONSTITUTIONAL CLAIMS

Brennan claims that his constitutional rights to privacy and due process were violated. The Louisiana Constitution's protection of privacy provisions contained in Article 1, § 5 does not extend so far as to protect private citizens against the actions of private parties. *Carr v. City of New Orleans*, 622 So.2d 819, 822 n. 3 (La. App. 4th Cir.), *writ denied*, 629 So.2d 404 (La. 1993). Nor do the due process provisions of Article 1, § 2 provide a cause of action against private actors. *Delta Bank & Trust Company v. Lassiter*, 383 So.2d 330, 334 (La. 1980). Thus, in order to prevail on the merits of either constitutional claim, Brennan must first show that USL was a state actor when it enforced the NCAA's rules and recommendations. . . .

In the present case, Brennan asserts that USL, not the NCAA, violated his constitutional rights to privacy and due process. Without question, USL is a

2. Brennan tested positive for the anabolic steroid testosterone. Testosterone that is introduced into the body from external sources (exogenous testosterone) appears in the urine. To identify the presence of exogenous testosterone, the urine is tested to measure the ratio of testosterone to another hormone called epitestosterone (the T/E ratio). The NCAA has adopted a 6 to 1 ratio as a standard for a positive test result for the presence of exogenous testosterone.

state actor even when acting in compliance with NCAA rules and recommenda-tions. While we conclude that there is state action in this case, the preliminary injunction could only be issued on the constitutional claims if Brennan made a prima facie showing that he had a privacy interest which was invaded or that he had a property or liberty interest which was entitled to due process protection.

2. Brennan's Privacy Interest

In determining whether USL violated Brennan's right of privacy, we are guided by the California Supreme Court's recent decision in *Hill v. National Collegiate Athletic Association*, 7 Cal. 4th 1, 26 Cal. Rptr. 2d 834, 865 P.2d 633 (Cal. 1994). Therein several student-athletes filed suit against the NCAA challenging its drug testing program as an invasion of the right of privacy. While the court recognized that the drug testing program impacts privacy interests, it reasoned that there was no constitutional violation when the student-athletes' lower expectations of privacy were balanced against the NCAA's countervailing interests.

After discussing aspects of communal undress, the necessity of physical exam-inations, as well as the fact that student-athletes share personal information with their coaches and trainers on a routine basis, the court concluded that student-athletes have a diminished expectation of privacy. The court further noted that:

> Drug testing has become a highly visible, pervasive, and well accepted part of ath-letic competition, particularly on intercollegiate and professional levels. It is a rea-sonably expected part of the life of an athlete, especially one engaged in advanced levels of competition, where the stakes and corresponding temptations are high.
>
> The student athlete's reasonable expectation of privacy is further diminished by two elements of the NCAA's drug testing program—advance notice and the opportunity to consent to testing.

Id. at 860, 865 P.2d at 658-59. Balanced against the diminished privacy inter-ests of the student-athletes, the *Hill* court found that the drug testing program was reasonably calculated to further the NCAA's interests of safeguarding the integrity of intercollegiate athletic competition and in protecting the health and safety of student-athletes.

Although Brennan filed suit against USL, the state actor, rather than the NCAA, we conclude, as did the court in *Hill*, that there was no violation of a privacy interest. Brennan, like the student-athletes in *Hill*, has a diminished expectation of privacy. Additionally, we note that USL shares the NCAA's inter-ests in ensuring fair competition in intercollegiate sports as well as in protecting the health and safety of student-athletes. While a urine test may be an invasion of privacy, in this case, it is reasonable considering the diminished expectation of privacy in the context of intercollegiate sports and there being a significant interest by USL and the NCAA that outweighs the relatively small compromise of privacy under the circumstances.

Because Brennan could not make a prima facie showing that he had a privacy interest which was unjustly violated, he could not prevail on the merits of the right of privacy claim.

3. Brennan's Property or Liberty Interest

To prevail on the due process claim, Brennan must show the existence of some property or liberty interest which has been adversely affected by state action. *Delta Bank & Trust Company v. Lassiter*, 383 So.2d at 334. However, it is clear that participation in intercollegiate athletics is not a property right, but is a privilege not protected by Constitutional due process safeguards. *See Marino v. Waters*, 220 So.2d 802, 806 (La. App. 1st Cir. 1969); *La. State Bd. of Educ. v. NCAA*, 273 So.2d 912, 916 (La. App. 3rd Cir. 1973). Because a student-athlete has no liberty or property interest in participating in intercollegiate athletics, Brennan could not make a prima facie showing that he would prevail on the merits of his due process claim.

In sum, Brennan could not make a prima facie showing that he would prevail on the merits of either constitutional claim; therefore, these claims could not be the basis for the issuance of the preliminary injunction. . . .

For the foregoing reasons, the judgment of the trial court issuing the preliminary injunction is reversed.

NOTES AND QUESTIONS

The *Brennan* court rejected the plaintiff's indirect challenge to the NCAA's drug testing program. Do you agree with the court's conclusion that the NCAA's justifications for drug testing outweigh the student-athlete's privacy interests? Does the NCAA have a valid justification for testing adult student-athletes for usage of recreational drugs that are not performance enhancing?

NCAA rules impose an affirmative duty on an institution to notify and educate its student-athletes regarding the NCAA's banned substances list and drug protocol. Regarding plaintiff's contention that USL negligently failed to provide this information, the *Brennan* court held:

> While Brennan claimed not to have received adequate information or warnings, the overwhelming evidence supports a conclusion to the contrary. According to the documentary evidence, Brennan was aware of and given the opportunity to review the NCAA drug testing program, he was provided a summary of NCAA rules, given an opportunity to ask questions about the rules and to review the NCAA manual. Brennan was told to inquire of the USL athletic department before taking anything at all, prescription or non-prescription. Thus, the only possible basis for a tort claim was USL's failure to specifically warn against taking nutritional supplements. However, in light of the warnings which were given by USL and the information which was received by Brennan, we cannot say that the relevant jurisprudence supports a finding that USL was negligent in failing to specifically warn against consuming nutritional supplements.

691 So. 2d at 331.

The sanction generally imposed on a student-athlete who tests positive for a banned substance is ineligibility to participate in any intercollegiate sports for one calendar year and loss of one season of eligibility. (Athletes ineligible to participate in Olympic or international sports competition for violating the World Anti-Doping Code also are ineligible to participate in NCAA intercollegiate sports during the period of their suspension.) The student-athlete, in conjunction with his or her institution, has the right to appeal the finding of a positive drug test to the NCAA's Committee on Competitive Safeguards and Medical Aspects of Sports. Effective August 1, 2005, the NCAA's drug-testing protocol was modified to make it more consistent with the World Anti-Doping Code (discussed in Chapter 4) by now allowing consideration of a reduced penalty based on the student-athlete's relative degree of fault for a doping violation. After a hearing, the committee may reduce the length of the student-athlete's suspension to one-half season of competition in the particular sport or determine that no suspension is appropriate based on extenuating circumstances.

A 2012 Associated Press investigation analyzing weight gains for more than 61,000 players suggests that the NCAA's drug testing program does not effectively prevent the use of anabolic steroids by intercollegiate football players despite annual positive tests results of less than 1 percent. See Matt Apuzzo, Adam Goldman, and Jack Gillum, *Steroids Loom in Major-College Football,* Yahoo! News, Dec. 31, 2012, http://news.yahoo.com/steroids-loom-major-college-football-182028506–spt.html.

4.   Contract and Private Associations Law

Courts generally are quite deferential to the NCAA regarding its interpretation and enforcement of its own rules and regulations, particularly its student-athlete eligibility rules. As you read the following case, consider whether such judicial deference is warranted and results in a fair and principled resolution of the matter at issue.

BLOOM v. NCAA

93 P.3d 621 (Colo. App. 2004)

DAILEY, J.

I.   BACKGROUND

Bloom, a high school football and track star, was recruited to play football at CU. Before enrolling there, however, he competed in Olympic and professional World Cup skiing events, becoming the World Cup champion in freestyle moguls. During the Olympics, Bloom appeared on MTV, and thereafter was offered various paid entertainment opportunities, including a chance to host a show on Nickelodeon. Bloom also agreed to endorse commercially certain ski equipment, and he contracted to model clothing for Tommy Hilfiger.

Bloom became concerned that his endorsements and entertainment activities might interfere with his eligibility to compete in intercollegiate football. On Bloom's behalf, CU first requested waivers of NCAA rules restricting student-athlete endorsement and media activities and, then, a favorable interpretation of the NCAA rule restricting media activities.

The NCAA denied CU's requests, and Bloom discontinued his endorsement, modeling, and media activities to play football for CU during the 2002 fall season. However, Bloom instituted this action against the NCAA for declaratory and injunctive relief, asserting that his endorsement, modeling, and media activities were necessary to support his professional skiing career, something which the NCAA rules permitted.

In his complaint, Bloom alleged: (1) as a third-party beneficiary of the contract between the NCAA and its members, he was entitled to enforce NCAA bylaws permitting him to engage in and receive remuneration from a professional sport different from his amateur sport; (2) as applied to the facts of this case, the NCAA's restrictions on endorsements and media appearances were arbitrary and capricious; and (3) those restrictions constituted improper and unconscionable restraints of trade.

For these reasons, Bloom requested that the NCAA restrictions be declared inapplicable, and that the NCAA and CU be enjoined from applying them, to activities originating prior to his enrollment at CU or wholly unrelated to his prowess as a football player. . . .

IV. STANDING

[handwritten: NCAA argued that π lacked standing]

We reject the NCAA's assertion that Bloom lacked standing to pursue claims for breach of contract or arbitrary and capricious action on the part of the NCAA. *[handwritten: ①]*

[handwritten: Standing]

A party has standing to seek relief when he or she has suffered actual injury to a legally protected interest. . . .

A person not a party to an express contract may bring an action on the contract if the parties to the agreement intended to benefit the nonparty, provided that the benefit claimed is a direct and not merely incidental benefit of the contract. While the intent to benefit the nonparty need not be expressly recited in the contract, the intent must be apparent from the terms of the agreement, the surrounding circumstances, or both. . . .

Here, the trial court found, and we agree, that the NCAA's constitution, bylaws, and regulations evidence a clear intent to benefit student-athletes. And because each student-athlete's eligibility to compete is determined by the NCAA, we conclude that Bloom had standing in a preliminary injunction hearing to contest the meaning or applicability of NCAA eligibility restrictions. *See Hall v. NCAA*, 985 F. Supp. 782, 796-97 (N.D. Ill. 1997) (given importance of NCAA's function to benefit student-athletes, and NCAA's role in determining eligibility of student-athletes, court assumed student-athlete was likely to succeed in proving third-party beneficiary standing vis-a-vis the contract between the NCAA and its members); *see also NCAA v. Brinkworth*, 680 So.2d 1081, 1083 (Fla. Dist. Ct. App. 1996).

With respect to a claim of arbitrary and capricious action, the Kentucky Supreme Court observed that "relief from our judicial system should be available if voluntary athletic associations act arbitrarily and capriciously toward student-athletes." *NCAA v. Lasege*, 53 S.W.3d 77, 83 (Ky. 2001). . . . *[handwritten: ②]*

Courts are reluctant to intervene, except on the most limited grounds, in the internal affairs of voluntary associations. . . . Even then, it would appear that a plaintiff must ordinarily allege an invasion of some type of civil or property right to have standing. *See Van Valkenburg v. Liberty Lodge No. 300, supra*, 619 N.W.2d at 609; *see also Levant v. Whitley*, 755 A.2d 1036, 1043-44 n. 11 (D.C. 2000) (surveying circumstances in which courts intervene in disputes involving voluntary membership associations).

Here, Bloom is not a member of the NCAA, and he does not have a constitutional right to engage in amateur intercollegiate athletics at CU. *See, e.g., Graham v. NCAA*, 804 F.2d 953, 955 (6th Cir. 1986); *Colo. Seminary (Univ. of Denver) v. NCAA*, 570 F.2d 320, 321 (10th Cir. 1978); *Hart v. NCAA*, 209 W.Va. 543, 550 S.E.2d 79, 86 (2001). Nor does he assert any property interest in playing football for CU.

However, to the extent Bloom's claim of arbitrary and capricious action asserts a violation of the duty of good faith and fair dealing that is implied in the contractual relationship between the NCAA and its members, his position as a third-party beneficiary of that contractual relationship affords him standing to pursue this claim. *See O'Reilly v. Physicians Mut. Ins. Co.*, 992 P.2d 644, 646 (Colo. App. 1999) (implied duty of good faith and fair dealing requires "parties to the agreement to perform their contractual obligations in good faith and in a reasonable manner"); *see also Hall v. NCAA, supra*, 985 F. Supp. at 784 (implied duty of good faith and fair dealing "requires that a party vested with contractual discretion exercise that discretion reasonably, not arbitrarily or capriciously"); *Dayan v. McDonald's Corp.*, 125 Ill. App. 3d 972, 991, 81 Ill. Dec. 156, 466 N.E.2d 958, 972 (1984) (implied duty to deal fairly and in good faith requires party vested with discretion to act reasonably and not "arbitrarily, capriciously, or in a manner inconsistent with the reasonable expectations of the parties").

In sum, we conclude that Bloom has third-party beneficiary standing to pursue what in essence are two claims for violation of his contractual rights.

V.   PROBABILITY OF SUCCESS

Bloom contends that the trial court erred in assessing the probability of success on his contract claims. We disagree.

Initially, we note that, as a third-party beneficiary, Bloom has rights no greater than those of the parties to the contract itself, here, the NCAA and its member institutions. . . .

A.   INTERPRETATION OF NCAA BYLAWS

In interpreting a contract, we seek to give effect to the intent and the reasonable expectations of the parties. . . . To determine the intent and expectations of the parties, we view the contract in its entirety, not in isolated portions, . . . and we give words and phrases their plain meaning according to common usage.

If its meaning is clear and unambiguous, the contract is enforced as written. . . . If, however, the contract is susceptible of more than one reasonable interpretation, it is ambiguous, and its meaning must be determined as an issue of fact. . . . In resolving an ambiguity, a court will follow the construction placed upon it by the parties themselves before the controversy arose. . . .

The interpretation of a contract and the determination whether it is ambiguous are questions of law subject to de novo review by this court. . . .

Bloom relies on NCAA Bylaw 12.1.2, which states that "[a] professional athlete in one sport may represent a member institution in a different sport." He asserts that, because a professional is one who "gets paid" for a sport, a student-athlete is entitled to earn whatever income is customary for his or her professional sport, which, in the case of professional skiers, primarily comes from endorsements and paid media opportunities.

We recognize that, like many others involved in individual professional sports such as golf, tennis, and boxing, professional skiers obtain much of their income from sponsors. We note, however, that none of the NCAA's bylaws mentions, much less explicitly establishes, a right to receive "customary income" for a sport.

To the contrary, the NCAA bylaws prohibit every student-athlete from receiving money for advertisements and endorsements. In this regard, NCAA Bylaw 12.5.2.1 states:

Subsequent to becoming a student-athlete, an individual shall not be eligible for participation in intercollegiate athletics if the individual: (a) Accepts any remuneration for or permits the use of his or her name or picture to advertise, recommend or promote directly the sale or use of a commercial product or service of any kind, or (b) Receives remuneration for endorsing a commercial product or service through the individual's use of such product or service.

amateurism

Additionally, while NCAA Bylaw 12.5.1.3 permits a student-athlete to continue to receive remuneration for activity initiated prior to enrollment in which his or her name or picture is used, this remuneration is only allowed, if, as pertinent here, "the individual became involved in such activities for reasons independent of athletics ability; . . . no reference is made in these activities to the individual's name or involvement in intercollegiate athletics; [and] . . . the individual does not endorse the commercial product."

Further, NCAA Bylaw 12.4.1.1 prohibits a student-athlete from receiving "any remuneration for value or utility that the student-athlete may have for the employer because of the publicity, reputation, fame or personal following that he or she has obtained because of athletics ability."

Unlike other NCAA bylaws, the endorsements and media appearance bylaws do not contain any sport-specific qualifiers. *See, e.g.*, NCAA Bylaw 12.3.1 (ineligibility of student-athlete to compete in intercollegiate sport based on agreement with agent to market athlete's athletic ability or reputation "in that sport").

not sport-specific

In our view, when read together, the NCAA bylaws express a clear and unambiguous intent to prohibit student-athletes from engaging in endorsements and paid media appearances, without regard to: (1) when the opportunity for such activities originated; (2) whether the opportunity arose or exists for reasons unrelated to participation in an amateur sport; and (3) whether income derived from the opportunity is customary for any particular professional sport.

clear language

The clear import of the bylaws is that, although student-athletes have the right to be professional athletes, they do not have the right to simultaneously engage in endorsement or paid media activity and maintain their eligibility to participate in amateur competition. And we may not disregard the clear meaning of the bylaws simply because they may disproportionately affect those who participate in individual professional sports.

meaning of the rule

Further, the record contains ample evidence supporting the trial court' conclusion that this interpretation is consistent with both the NCAA's and its member institutions' construction of the bylaws. An NCAA official testified that both the endorsement and media appearance provisions have been consistently applied and interpreted in a nonsport-specific manner. Indeed, another NCAA official related that association members had resisted efforts to change the endorsement rule to be sport-specific. Although the evidence is conflicting, the record supports the trial court's conclusion that, from the beginning, CU understood that the endorsement and media activity rules were nonsport-specific in scope.

Thus, even if the bylaws were viewed as ambiguous, the record supports the trial court's conclusion that the bylaws would ultimately be interpreted in accordance with the NCAA's and its member institutions' construction of those bylaws.

B.   APPLICATION OF BYLAWS TO BLOOM

The United States Supreme Court has recognized the NCAA as "the guardian of an important American tradition," namely, amateurism in intercollegiate athletics. *See NCAA v. Bd. of Regents*, 468 U.S. 85, 101, 104 S.Ct. 2948, 2960, 82 L.Ed.2d 70 (1984).

Under that tradition, "college sports provided an important opportunity for teaching people about character, motivation, endurance, loyalty, and the attainment of one's personal best—all qualities of great value in citizens. In this sense, competitive athletics were viewed as an extracurricular activity, justified by the university as part of its ideal objective of educating the whole person." James J. Duderstadt, Intercollegiate Athletics and the American University 70 (Univ. Mich. Press 2003).

The NCAA's "Principle of Amateurism" states:

> Student-athletes shall be amateurs in an intercollegiate sport, and their participation should be motivated primarily by education and by the physical, mental and social benefits to be derived. Student participation in intercollegiate athletics is an avocation, and student-athletes should be protected from exploitation by professional and commercial enterprises.

NCAA Const. art. 2.9.

The NCAA's purpose, in this regard, is not only "to maintain intercollegiate athletics as an integral part of the educational program," but also to "retain a clear line of demarcation between intercollegiate athletics and professional sports." NCAA Const. art. 1, § 1.3.1.

Here, the trial court found that application of the endorsement and media appearance rules in Bloom's case was rationally related to the legitimate purpose of retaining the "clear line of demarcation between intercollegiate athletics and professional sports."

The trial court noted that salaries and bonuses are an acceptable means for attaining income from professional sports, but endorsement income is not acceptable if a student-athlete wishes to preserve amateur eligibility. According to NCAA officials: (1) endorsements invoke concerns about "the commercial exploitation of student-athletes and the promotion of commercial products"; and (2) it is not possible to distinguish the precise capacity in which endorsements are made. A CU official related that generally, the endorsement rule prevents students from becoming billboards for commercialism, and in Bloom's case, there would "be no way to tell whether he is receiving pay commensurate with his . . . football ability or skiing ability."

In this respect, the trial court observed:

> In an honest world where there is no attempt to avoid an ideal, there wouldn't be an impact on amateurism if Mr. Bloom was allowed to be compensated as is customary for professional skiers; however, it's naive to think that we live in such a world. There are those who would be less than honest and seek profit for profit's sake. . . .
>
> If Mr. Bloom was allowed to receive the [endorsement] income that is customary for professional skiers, it is not difficult for me to imagine that some in other professional sports would decide that in addition to direct monetary compensation . . . endorsements or promotion of goods would become customary.

Similar concerns underlie the NCAA's prohibition on paid entertainment activity. Paid entertainment activity may impinge upon the amateur ideal if the opportunity were obtained or advanced because of the student's athletic ability or prestige, even though that activity may further the education of student-athletes such as Bloom, a communications major. As the trial court noted, there are "various shades of gray within which such events could fall." And, as should be evident, the NCAA does not prohibit *unpaid* internships, externships, or other educational opportunities in the entertainment field.

In this case, Bloom presented evidence that some of his acting opportunities arose not as a result of his athletic ability but because of his good looks and on-camera presence. However, the record contains evidence that Bloom's agent and the Tommy Hilfiger company marketed Bloom as a talented multi-sport athlete, and a representative from a talent agency intimated that Bloom's reputation as an athlete would be advantageous in obtaining auditions for various entertainment opportunities. Further, the NCAA indicated, when asked to interpret its rules, that it was unable, due to insufficient information, to determine which of Bloom's requested media activities were, in fact, unrelated to his athletic ability or prestige.

Under these circumstances, we perceive no abuse of the trial court's discretion in failing to fault the NCAA for refusing to waive its rules, as requested by CU, to permit Bloom "to pursue any television and film opportunities while he is a student-athlete at CU." *See Cole v. NCAA*, 120 F. Supp. 2d 1060, 1071-72 (N.D. Ga. 2000) (NCAA decisions regarding "challenges of student-athletes are entitled to considerable deference," and courts are reluctant to replace the NCAA as the "decision-maker on private waiver applications"); *see also NCAA v. Lasege, supra,* 53 S.W.3d at 83 (voluntary athletic associations "should be allowed to 'paddle their own canoe' without unwarranted interference from the courts").

Bloom also asserts that the NCAA is arbitrary in its application of the endorsement and media bylaws. He notes that, while the NCAA would bar him from accepting commercial endorsements, it will allow colleges to commercially endorse athletic equipment by having students wear the equipment, with identifying logos and insignias, while engaged in intercollegiate competition. But the trial court determined, and we agree, that this application of the bylaws has a rational basis in economic necessity: financial benefits inure not to any single student-athlete but to member schools and thus to all student-athletes, including those who participate in programs that generate no revenue.

Bloom further argues that the NCAA is arbitrary in the way it applies its bylaws among individual students. Bloom presented evidence that, in one instance, a student-athlete was permitted to make an unpaid, minor appearance in a single film. But the NCAA could rationally conclude that this situation was different: Bloom did not seek permission to make an unpaid appearance in one specific instance; he wanted to take advantage of any number of television and film opportunities, and he wanted to be paid. Bloom also presented evidence that a second student-athlete was permitted to appear on television while he participated in his professional sport. But Bloom did not show that the NCAA would prohibit him from appearing on television while participating in his professional sport.

In a "supplemental authority" filed with this court, . . . Bloom presented us with new evidence relating to the NCAA's treatment of the second student-athlete. Because this evidence was never presented to the trial court, however, we may not now consider it. . . .

Bloom has thus failed to demonstrate any inconsistency in application which would lead us to conclude that the NCAA was arbitrarily applying its rules.

Finally, we are not convinced that the NCAA treated Bloom unfairly in the manner in which it denied the requests to waive or interpret its rules.

Although Bloom is correct that he was not permitted to personally petition the NCAA, he effectively submitted three petitions to the NCAA with the full assistance and support of CU. The trial court's finding that Bloom had "an ability to fully present his . . . position through the membership institution" is amply supported by the record.

Further, the court found, with record support, that the NCAA requested additional information on CU's petition (evidencing that the NCAA was not acting arbitrarily or capriciously), and that there was no evidence that the NCAA gave CU's petition any less consideration than its other "hundreds of administrative and waiver requests."

The record thus supports the trial court's findings that the NCAA's administrative review process is reasonable in general and that it was reasonably applied in this case. As such, these findings, as well as those with respect to the NCAA's application of its bylaws, are not manifestly arbitrary, unreasonable, or unfair. . . .

For these reasons, we agree with the trial court that Bloom failed to demonstrate a reasonable probability of success on the merits.

VI. OTHER ISSUES

. . . In light of this conclusion, we need not address whether, as the trial court found, Bloom also failed to show that a preliminary injunction would not disserve the public interest and was justified by the balance of equities in the case. Consequently, we do not address the parties' remaining arguments, including the validity of the NCAA's restitution rule, NCAA Bylaw 19.8, or the effect, if any, of the federal Commerce Clause on the trial court's ability to fashion a remedy for Bloom in this case.

Accordingly, the trial court's order is affirmed.

NOTES AND QUESTIONS

1. *Judicial Deference to Private Associations.* As is true of other private associations, courts afford considerable deference to the NCAA in enforcing its rules and regulations. *NCAA v. Brinkworth*, 680 So. 2d 1081, 1085 (Fla. Ct. App. 1996) (in upholding NCAA procedures for considering student-athlete's request for waiver of rule that requires completion of four years of intercollegiate competition within five years, the court concludes that because the "procedures were adequate and fair, there was no basis on which to intervene in the internal affairs of the NCAA"); *Hispanic College Fund, Inc. v. NCAA*, 826 N.E.2d 652, 657 (Ind. App. 2005) (upholding NCAA decision to add twelfth Division 1-A regular season game because no allegation that "NCAA's actions were fraudulent, otherwise illegal, or that they abused civil or property rights having their origin elsewhere").

Notwithstanding the policy of judicial abstention from interference, courts will intervene into the affairs of private associations when the association has acted in violation of its own rules, regulations, and policies. *Gulf South Conference v. Boyd*, 369 So. 2d 553, 557 (Ala. 1979) (holding that "the general non-interference doctrine concerning voluntary associations does not apply in cases involving disputes between college athletes themselves and college athletic associations . . . because "the athlete is not even a member of the athletic association" and "has no voice or bargaining power concerning [its] rules and regulations"; finding student eligible to play football because athletic conference incorrectly declared him ineligible in violation of its own rules); *California State Univ., Hayward v. NCAA,* 121 Cal. Rptr. 85, 88-89 (Cal. App. 1975) ("It is true that courts will not interfere with the disciplining or expelling of members of such associations where the action is taken in good faith and in accordance with its adopted laws and rules. But if the decision of the tribunal is contrary to its laws and rules, it is not authorized by the bylaws of the association, a court may review the ruling of the board and direct the reinstatement of the member.").

What was the significance of third-party beneficiary contract law in *Bloom?* Why did the *Bloom* court hold that the NCAA's application of its endorsement and media bylaws was not arbitrary or capricious? For law review commentary regarding *Bloom,* see, e.g., Michael A. Corgan, *Permitting Student-Athletes to Accept Endorsement Deals: A Solution to the Financial Corruption of College Athletics Created by Unethical Sports Agents and the NCAA's Revenue-Generating Scheme,* 19 Vill. Sports & Ent. L.J. 371 (2012); Bill Cross, *The NCAA As Publicity Enemy Number One,* 58 U. Kan. L. Rev. 1221 (2010); Joel Eckert, *Student-Athlete Contract Rights in the Aftermath of Bloom v. NCAA,* 59 Vand. L. Rev. 905 (2006). In contrast to *Bloom,* in *Knelman v. Middlebury Coll.,* 2012 WL 4481470 (D. Vt. 2012), the court refused to grant third-party beneficiary status to a student-athlete. It concluded that the student-athlete failed to demonstrate that Middlebury College and the NCAA intended to confer on the athlete the benefit of provisions in the NCAA manual articulating the responsibility of institutions to ensure that coaches exhibit fairness and honesty in their relationships with student-athletes.

In *Oliver v. National Collegiate Athletic Assn.,* 920 N.E.2d 203 (Ohio Ct. Common Pleas, 2009), a college baseball player sued the NCAA, alleging breach of contract and tortious interference with contractual relations and seeking declaratory and injunctive relief to prevent it from rendering him ineligible for violating its rules. After a bench trial, an Ohio Court of Common Pleas held that (1) the NCAA bylaw prohibiting an attorney representing a student-athlete from being present during contract negotiations between the athlete and a professional sports organization violated the NCAA's contractual obligation of good faith and fair dealing to its member universities' student-athletes; (2) the NCAA bylaw allowing the NCAA to impose penalties on student-athletes and institutions after an injunction allowing an athlete to play was overturned on appeal (i.e., "restitution rule") violated its contractual obligation of good faith and fair dealing; and (3) an injunction was necessary to prevent the plaintiff from suffering irreparable harm. The court's decision subsequently was vacated pursuant to a settlement between the parties. For scholarly discussion of the *Oliver* case, see Brandon D. Morgan, Oliver v. NCAA: *NCAA's No Agent Rule Called Out, But Remains Safe,* 17 Sports Law. J. 303 (2010); T. Matthew Lockhart, Oliver v. NCAA: *Throwing a Contractual Curveball at the NCAA's "Veil of Amateurism,"* 35 U. Dayton L. Rev. 175 (2010); James Halt, *Andy Oliver Strikes Out the NCAA's "No-Agent" Rule for College Baseball,* 19 J. Legal Aspects Sport 185 (2009). What kinds of problems does the *Oliver* decision portend for the NCAA?

2. In *NCAA v. Lasege,* 53 S.W.3d 77 (Ky. 2001), the Supreme Court of Kentucky ruled in favor of the NCAA, which had prohibited a University of Louisville

basketball player from participating in intercollegiate sports. Prior to his matriculation at Louisville, Lasege played basketball in Russia under a professional contract and engaged in other conduct that the NCAA found violated its amateurism rules. Consequently, the NCAA deemed him ineligible to participate in intercollegiate competition. Louisville declared Lasege ineligible but subsequently requested that the NCAA reinstate his eligibility. The NCAA rejected the request, concluding that Lasege had compromised his amateur status by accepting "preferential treatment, benefits, or services" for his participation in the Russian basketball league. *Id.* at 2.

After Louisville exhausted its appeals within the NCAA regulatory process, Lasege filed an action against the NCAA in which he sought a temporary injunction to reverse the NCAA's decision and reinstate his eligibility. The trial court granted Lasege's request. It found that a substantial question existed as to whether the NCAA acted arbitrarily and capriciously. The trial court stated that the NCAA ignored overwhelming mitigating circumstances (e.g., economic and cultural disadvantage, ignorance of NCAA rules, and coercion associated with execution of the profession contract) and engaged in disparate treatment with respect to Lasege. Accordingly, it issued the injunction, and Lasege played during the 2000-2001 basketball season.

The Kentucky Supreme Court reversed the trial court's decision in favor of the plaintiff and the court of appeals' affirmance thereof. It characterized the trial court's order as clearly erroneous. Moreover, it identified the NCAA as the party in the best position to determine a player's eligibility.

> We have held that a ruling is arbitrary and capricious only where it is "clearly erroneous, and by 'clearly erroneous' we mean unsupported by substantial evidence." Here, the NCAA's ruling has strong evidentiary support—Lasege unquestionably signed contracts to play professional basketball and unquestionably accepted benefits. Contrary to the trial court's allegations of disparate treatment, the NCAA submits that no individual has ever had his or her eligibility reinstated after committing a combination of rules violations akin to those compiled by Lasege. The NCAA's eligibility determinations are entitled to a presumption of correctness—particularly when they stem from conceded violations of NCAA regulations. Although we recognize that Lasege's mitigation evidence is relevant to review of the NCAA's determination, we believe the trial court simply disagreed with the NCAA as to the weight which should be assigned to this evidence. Accordingly, we believe the trial court abused its discretion when it found that Lasege had a high probability of success on the merits of his claim.

Id. at 85.

3. *Judicial Deference and the Federal Government.* Not surprisingly, courts are more reluctant to defer to the NCAA in litigation involving the federal government. In *United States Department of Education v. NCAA*, 481 F.3d 936 (7th Cir. 2007), the Seventh Circuit held that the NCAA was not entitled to a protective order limiting a subpoena from the Department of Education (DOE) seeking information that the NCAA considered confidential. The court acknowledged that the NCAA "was stung by a recent incident in which it received information from a head football coach at the University of Tennessee, Phillip Fulmer, concerning possible violations of NCAA rules by another university. It gave the information to a grand jury pursuant to a subpoena. The information became public, precipitating a defamation suit

against Fulmer and the NCAA seeking $60 million in damages." *Id.* at 939. However, it deemed the NCAA's burden of compliance, based on its assertion of confidentiality, speculative and outweighed by the DOE's investigatory needs. The NCAA is dependent on self-reporting if it is to be successful in its enforcement efforts and believes that such self-reporting is strengthened by strong confidentiality rules. Although the court acknowledged that "those incentives [to self-report] are diminished not only by the threat of a defamation suit but also by the fact that, the fewer whistleblowers there are, the less likely violators of the NCAA's rules are to be caught and so the less incentive they have to turn themselves in," it nevertheless found that the government's interest in obtaining the information for purposes of litigation outweighed any confidentiality concerns on the part of the NCAA. *Id.* Do you agree? Is this a case of the court protecting its own terrain — refusing to be as deferential to the NCAA as in other instances that do not involve its inherent judicial authority?

4. *Proposed Heightened Judicial Review.* Consider the following view:

> To ensure that student-athletes are not denied the lifetime educational benefits of athletic participation opportunities without adequate justification, courts should apply a higher level of judicial scrutiny than the traditional common law rational basis or arbitrary and capricious standards. We do not advocate *de novo* or strict judicial review, but the significant educational and potential economic benefits of athletic participation (e.g., a scholarship or professional sports career) warrant more than courts merely asking the very deferential and frequently outcome determinative question of whether an eligibility rule or its application is merely rational or arbitrary and capricious. We propose a uniform heightened level of judicial scrutiny that allows a student-athlete to prove, by clear and convincing evidence, that his or her exclusion from athletic participation does not substantially further an important and legitimate interest of an interscholastic or intercollegiate sports governing body or educational institution.

> This standard would better balance the parties' respective interests in an athletic eligibility dispute, but it poses the risk of unwarranted judicial micromanagement of high school and college athletics and potentially more litigation. On the other hand, because a student-athlete has a significant burden of persuasion to satisfy, an adverse eligibility determination will be judicially vacated in relatively few cases.

Matthew J. Mitten and Timothy Davis, *Athlete Eligibility Requirements and Legal Protection of Sports Participation Opportunities*, 8 Va. Sports & Ent. L.J. 71 (2008). Do you agree?

5. *Legality of Restitution Rule.* The *Lasege* court also validated NCAA Bylaw 19.8, which permits the organization to seek restitution from its member institutions as a result of rules violations such as those that Louisville committed when it allowed Lasege to play.

> By becoming a member of the NCAA, a voluntary athletic association, U of L agreed to abide by its rules and regulations. NCAA Bylaw 19.8 is one of those regulations, and it specifically provides that the NCAA can attempt to restore competitive equity by redistributing wins and losses and imposing sanctions upon a member institution which allows an ineligible player to participate under a subsequently-vacated court order, even if that order requires the institution to allow the player to participate.

Id. at 87.

Quoting from an Indiana Supreme Court decision involving the Indiana High School Athletic Association (IHSAA), the court explained:

> Undeniably, the Restitution Rule imposes hardship on a school that, in compliance with an order of a court which is later vacated, fields an ineligible player. On the other hand, use of an ineligible player imposes a hardship on other teams that must compete against the teams fielding ineligible players. While schools will contend that is unfair when they have to forfeit victories earned with an ineligible player on the field because they complied with a court order, competing schools will reply that it is unfair when they have to compete against a team with an ineligible student athlete because a local trial judge prohibited the school or the IHSAA from following the eligibility rules. The Restitution Rule represents the agreement of IHSAA members on how to balance those two competing interests. The Restitution Rule may not be the best method to deal with such situations. However, it is the method which the member schools have adopted. And in any event, its enforcement by the IHSAA does not impinge upon the judiciary's function. [Citation omitted.]

Id. at 87-88.

Do you agree with the court? See also Richard G. Johnson, *Submarining Due Process: How the NCAA Uses Its Restitution Rule to Deprive College Athletes of Their Right of Access to the Courts . . . Until* Oliver v. NCAA, 11 Fla. Coastal L. Rev. 459 (2010).

[handwritten margin note: Collection of federal and state laws, which regulates the conduct and organization of business corporations, generally to promote fair competition for the benefit of consumers.]

F. ANTITRUST LAW

In addition to contract and private association law, antitrust law provides an important limit on the NCAA's regulatory authority.

1. Introduction

Despite the more than 100-year history of the NCAA's national governance of college sports through the collective action of its members, federal antitrust law has only recently had a significant role in regulating the NCAA. There was virtually no antitrust litigation challenging the NCAA's rules, enforcement activities, or other conduct prior to the early 1970s, when the financial rewards for fielding winning big-time football and basketball programs escalated as public demand for intercollegiate sports viewing and television revenues skyrocketed. Since then, there have been several antitrust suits against the NCAA and its member universities asserting that their conduct unreasonably restrains trade to some party's economic detriment.

[handwritten margin note: typical argument]

Ideally, intercollegiate athletics is intended to be an extracurricular activity for talented students who attend college for the primary purpose of earning a degree. This view is exemplified by former Ohio State University football coach Woody Hayes, who stated, "The coach will squeeze every bit of football from each player that he can, but in return the coach must give that man every legitimate measure of help he needs to get 'the rest' of his education. . . .

I like that!

[W]e feel that the man who plays college football and does not graduate has been cheated." Woody Hayes, You Win with People! 12 (Typographic Printing Co. 2d ed. 1975). For most sports and most students, this student-athlete model of intercollegiate athletics still applies. See generally Timothy Davis, *Intercollegiate Athletics: Competing Models and Conflicting Realities*, 25 Rutgers L.J. 269 (1994).

Today's economic realities, however, have reshaped the idealistic student-athlete model of intercollegiate athletics for sports such as NCAA Division I men's basketball and Football Bowl Subdivision (FBS) football (formerly Division I-A) because the tremendous popularity of these sports creates a substantial revenue-generating capacity that has been exploited by television for the benefit of schools that sponsor these sports. This trend toward commercialism in big-time football and men's basketball has continued until today, and intercollegiate athletics is now a multibillion-dollar industry. In recent years, the NCAA has sought to capitalize on the popularity of its members' athletic programs and enable university athletic departments to increase their revenues. For example, the NCAA has increased the maximum allowable number of football games during a season, stimulated conference expansion by permitting championship games to be played by conferences with 12 or more members, and certified new postseason football bowl games. Beginning in 2011 the NCAA increased to 68 the total number of teams participating in its popular "March Madness" postseason basketball tournament that culminates in the Final Four championship round. In 2014 a four-team football national championship play-off system will be implemented, which is expected to generate millions more in revenues than its predecessor, the Division 1-A football Bowl Championship Series.

Membership in the NCAA is unquestionably an economic necessity if a school desires to participate in "big-time" intercollegiate athletics. Nonmembers cannot compete in NCAA championship events, do not have the prestige and visibility to consistently attract a large number of quality athletes to their programs, and do not generate the substantial economic revenues from gate receipts and television contracts that NCAA schools do. Perhaps because there is no viable existing alternative, some universities whose individual economic interests have been harmed by NCAA regulations and rules enforcement actions have brought antitrust litigation against the NCAA.

NCAA really only option

Many NCAA rules and regulations are specifically directed toward and indirectly govern players, coaches, boosters, and alumni, even though these parties are not members of the NCAA and lack effective representation in the NCAA's rule-making and enforcement process. See Peter C. Carstensen and Paul Olszowski, *Antitrust Law, Student-Athletes, and the NCAA: Limiting the Scope and Conduct of Private Economic Regulation*, 1995 Wis. L. Rev. 545, 549-552. Thus, in governing the association's affairs, the NCAA effectively possesses and exercises significant regulatory power over persons without a voice or vote, often to their economic detriment. Antitrust suits against the NCAA have been brought by coaches, student-athletes, competing athletics governing bodies, television broadcasters, and others whose economic interests have been allegedly adversely affected by the NCAA's pervasive regulation of intercollegiate athletics. Thus far, there have been few reported antitrust cases relating to intercollegiate athletics filed by consumers. See *McCormack v. NCAA*, 845 F.2d 1338 (5th Cir. 1988) (where court held that Southern Methodist University (SMU) alumni did not have standing to challenge NCAA sanctions imposed on their alma mater for rules violations). The federal government has not instituted any antitrust litigation against the NCAA, but there have been several congressional hearings regarding the Division 1-A football Bowl Championship Series and the Department of Justice's Antitrust Division has filed amicus briefs in some college sports antitrust litigation.

2.   Nature and Scope of Antitrust Limits

The NCAA has no blanket exemption from the federal antitrust laws merely because it is a nonprofit organization whose members are predominantly colleges and universities with educational objectives. In *Hennessey v. NCAA*, 564 F.2d 1136 (5th Cir. 1977), the Fifth Circuit observed that "[w]hile the participating athletics [*sic*] may be amateurs, intercollegiate athletics in its management is clearly business, and big business at that." *Id.* at 1150. The court concluded, "[w]hile organized as a non-profit organization, the NCAA and its member institutions are, when presenting amateur athletics to a ticket-paying, television-buying public, engaged in a business venture of far greater magnitude than the vast majority of 'profit-making' enterprises." *Id.* at 1149, n.14.

Federal antitrust litigation against the NCAA generally has been brought under §1 of the Sherman Act (15 U.S.C. §1), which provides that "[e]very contract, combination . . . or conspiracy in restraint of trade or commerce" is illegal. The NCAA also is subject to §2 of the Sherman Act (15 U.S.C. §2), which prohibits monopolization or attempts to monopolize trade or commerce, although litigation asserting §2 claims against the NCAA historically has been unsuccessful. See, e.g., *Association of Intercollegiate Athletics for Women v. NCAA*, 735 F.2d 577 (D.C. Cir. 1984) (rejecting allegation that NCAA unlawfully used its monopoly regulatory power over men's intercollegiate sports to facilitate its entry into the regulation of women's intercollegiate sports and to force the Association of Intercollegiate Athletics for Women, a competing national governing body, out of existence). Both statutory provisions apply only to restraints affecting interstate trade or commerce.

For a court to have Sherman Act jurisdiction, the challenged activity must have (1) an interstate nexus or effect, and (2) constitute or affect trade or commerce. *Summit Health, Ltd. v. Pinhas*, 111 S. Ct. 1841 (1991). Courts have consistently held that the NCAA's general business activities and regulation of intercollegiate athletics have a national scope, thereby evidencing their interstate character. *NCAA v. Miller*, 10 F.3d 633 (9th Cir. 1993); *Hennessey v. NCAA*, 564 F.2d 1136 (5th Cir. 1977); *Justice v. NCAA*, 577 F. Supp. 356 (D. Ariz. 1983). For example, the NCAA conducts national championships in various men's and women's sports and sells the national television and radio broadcasting rights to these events, promulgates rules that apply to its member schools located throughout the country, and engages in a nationwide system of policing and rules enforcement activities. Today, it is undisputed that the NCAA's business activities and regulatory conduct are interstate in nature and that this jurisdictional requirement is easily satisfied.

The collective adoption and enforcement of NCAA rules by its member universities as well as other agreements concerning the production, marketing, and regulation of intercollegiate athletics is considered concerted action for purposes of §1 of the Sherman Act. As a result, virtually all NCAA rules and agreements among NCAA members are potentially subject to antitrust challenge. However, §1's broad statutory language has been judicially interpreted to prohibit only unreasonable restraints of trade in economic terms.

The purpose of the antitrust laws is to preserve a competitive marketplace and protect consumer welfare. Competition is hurt when conduct harms the market's ability to achieve lower prices, better products, and more efficient methods of production, all of which benefit consumers. *Sullivan v. NFL*, 34 F.3d 1091, 1097 (1st Cir. 1994), *cert. denied*, 513 U.S. 1190 (1995) ("injury to competition" is "measured by a reduction in output and an increase in prices in the relevant market"). In the context of intercollegiate athletics, one of the key issues courts must address in evaluating the antitrust validity of a challenged NCAA rule is whether it has a predominantly anticompetitive commercial effect that harms college sports fans (i.e., it is an unreasonable restraint of trade) or whether it is a valid regulation that benefits fans more than unbridled market competition among universities producing intercollegiate athletics (i.e., it is a reasonable restraint of trade).

The following landmark Supreme Court case addresses how the federal antitrust laws limit the NCAA's regulatory authority and establishes the legal framework for determining whether an NCAA rule or decision unreasonably restrains trade.

a. Output Market

This case addresses how antitrust law limits the NCAA's regulatory authority in the output market in which goods or services are produced for public consumption; in particular, televised college football games.

**NCAA v. BOARD OF REGENTS
OF THE UNIVERSITY OF OKLAHOMA**

468 U.S. 85 (1984)

Justice STEVENS delivered the opinion of the Court.

The University of Oklahoma and the University of Georgia contend that the National Collegiate Athletic Association has unreasonably restrained trade [in violation of §1 of the Sherman Act] in the televising of college football games. . . .

. . . With the exception of football, the NCAA has not undertaken any regulation of the televising of athletic events. . . .

[EDS. In separate agreements, the NCAA granted the American Broadcasting Company (ABC) and the Columbia Broadcasting System (CBS) the right to each telecast 14 regular season football games in accordance with certain "ground rules." Each network agreed to pay a specified "minimum aggregate compensation to the participating NCAA member institutions" during the four-year period in an amount that totaled $131,750,000.

The ground rules provided that the carrying networks make alternate selections of those games they wished to televise, and thereby obtain the exclusive right to submit a bid at an essentially fixed price to the institutions involved. The plan also contained "appearance requirements" and "appearance limitations" which pertained to each of the two-year periods that the plan was in effect. The basic requirement imposed on each of the two networks was that it must schedule appearances for at least 82 different member institutions during each two-year period. Under the appearance limitations no member institution was eligible to appear on television more than a total of six times and more than four times nationally, with the appearances to be divided equally between the two carrying networks. The number of exposures specified in the contracts also set an absolute maximum on the number of games that could be broadcast.

Thus, although the current plan was more elaborate than any of its predecessors, it retained the essential features of each of them. It limited the total amount of televised intercollegiate football and the number of games that any one team could televise. No NCAA member university was permitted to make any sale of television rights except in accordance with the basic plan.

Some years ago, five major conferences together with major football-playing independent institutions organized the College Football Association (CFA). The original purpose of the CFA was to promote the interests of major football-playing schools within the NCAA structure. The Universities of Oklahoma and Georgia, respondents in this Court, were members of the CFA.

Beginning in 1979, CFA members began to advocate that colleges with major football programs should have a greater voice in the formulation of football television policy than they had in the NCAA. They developed an independent television plan and entered into a 1981 contract with the National Broadcasting Co. (NBC) that would have permitted a greater number of its members games to be televised, and would have increased the overall football television revenues realized by CFA members. In response the NCAA publicly announced that it would take disciplinary action against any CFA member that complied with the CFA-NBC contract, which would apply to other sports as well as football. Although respondents obtained a preliminary injunction against the NCAA's threatened disciplinary action, most CFA members were reluctant to enter into the proposed contract with NBC and the agreement was never consummated.]

II

There can be no doubt that the challenged practices of the NCAA constitute a "restraint of trade" in the sense that they limit members' freedom to negotiate and enter into their own television contracts. In that sense, however, every contract is a restraint of trade, and as we have repeatedly recognized, the Sherman Act was intended to prohibit only unreasonable restraints of trade.

It is also undeniable that these practices share characteristics of restraints we have previously held unreasonable. The NCAA is an association of schools which compete against each other to attract television revenues, not to mention fans and athletes. As the District Court found, the policies of the NCAA with respect to television rights are ultimately controlled by the vote of member institutions. By participating in an association which prevents member institutions from competing against each other on the basis of price or kind of television rights that can be offered to broadcasters, the NCAA member institutions have created a horizontal restraint—an agreement among competitors on the way in which they will compete with one another. A restraint of this type has often been held to be unreasonable as a matter of law. Because it places a ceiling on the number of games member institutions may televise, the horizontal agreement places an artificial limit on the quantity of televised football that is available to broadcasters and consumers. By restraining the quantity of television rights available for sale, the challenged practices create a limitation on output;

our cases have held that such limitations are unreasonable restraints of trade. Moreover, the District Court found that the minimum aggregate price in fact operates to preclude any price negotiation between broadcasters and institutions, thereby constituting horizontal price fixing, perhaps the paradigm of an unreasonable restraint of trade.

Horizontal price fixing and output limitation are ordinarily condemned as a matter of law under an "illegal per se" approach because the probability that these practices are anticompetitive is so high; a per se rule is applied when "the practice facially appears to be one that would always or almost always tend to restrict competition and decrease output." *Broadcast Music, Inc. v. Columbia Broadcasting System, Inc.*, 441 U.S. 1, 19-20, 99 S.Ct. 1551, 1562, 60 L.Ed.2d 1 (1979). In such circumstances a restraint is presumed unreasonable without inquiry into the particular market context in which it is found. Nevertheless, we have decided that it would be inappropriate to apply a per se rule to this case. This decision is not based on a lack of judicial experience with this type of arrangement, on the fact that the NCAA is organized as a nonprofit entity, or on our respect for the NCAA's historic role in the preservation and encouragement of intercollegiate amateur athletics. Rather, what is critical is that this case involves an industry in which horizontal restraints on competition are essential if the product is to be available at all.

As Judge Bork has noted: "[S]ome activities can only be carried out jointly. Perhaps the leading example is league sports. When a league of professional lacrosse teams is formed, it would be pointless to declare their cooperation illegal on the ground that there are no other professional lacrosse teams." R. Bork, The Antitrust Paradox 278 (1978). What the NCAA and its member institutions market in this case is competition itself—contests between competing institutions. Of course, this would be completely ineffective if there were no rules on which the competitors agreed to create and define the competition to be marketed. A myriad of rules affecting such matters as the size of the field, the number of players on a team, and the extent to which physical violence is to be encouraged or proscribed, all must be agreed upon, and all restrain the manner in which institutions compete. Moreover, the NCAA seeks to market a particular brand of football—college football. The identification of this "product" with an academic tradition differentiates college football from and makes it more popular than professional sports to which it might otherwise be comparable, such as, for example, minor league baseball. In order to preserve the character and quality of the "product," athletes must not be paid, must be required to attend class, and the like. And the integrity of the "product" cannot be preserved except by mutual agreement; if an institution adopted such restrictions unilaterally, its effectiveness as a competitor on the playing field might soon be destroyed. Thus, the NCAA plays a vital role in enabling college football to preserve its character, and as a result enables a product to be marketed which might otherwise be unavailable. In performing this role, its actions widen consumer choice—not only the choices available to sports fans but also those available to athletes—and hence can be viewed as procompetitive.

Respondents concede that the great majority of the NCAA's regulations enhance competition among member institutions. Thus, despite the fact that this case involves restraints on the ability of member institutions to compete in terms of price and output, a fair evaluation of their competitive character requires consideration of the NCAA's justifications for the restraints.

Our analysis of this case under the Rule of Reason, of course, does not change the ultimate focus of our inquiry. Both per se rules and the Rule of Reason are employed "to form a judgment about the competitive significance of the restraint." . . .

III

Because it restrains price and output, the NCAA's television plan has a significant potential for anticompetitive effects.[28] The findings of the District Court indicate that this potential has been realized. The District Court found that if member institutions were free to sell television rights, many more games would be shown on television, and that the NCAA's output restriction has the effect of raising the price the networks pay for television rights. Moreover, the court found that by fixing a price for television rights to all games, the NCAA creates a price structure that is unresponsive to viewer demand and unrelated to the prices that would prevail in a competitive market. And, of course, since as a practical matter all member institutions need NCAA approval, members have no real choice but to adhere to the NCAA's television controls.

The anticompetitive consequences of this arrangement are apparent. Individual competitors lose their freedom to compete. Price is higher and output lower than they would otherwise be, and both are unresponsive to consumer preference. This latter point is perhaps the most significant, since "Congress designed the Sherman Act as a 'consumer welfare prescription.'" *Reiter v. Sonotone Corp.*, 442 U.S. 330, 343, 99 S.Ct. 2326, 2333, 60 L.Ed.2d 931 (1979). A restraint that has the effect of reducing the importance of consumer preference in setting price and output is not consistent with this fundamental goal of antitrust law. Restrictions on price and output are the paradigmatic examples of restraints of trade that the Sherman Act was intended to prohibit. At the same time, the television plan eliminates competitors from the market, since only those broadcasters able to bid on television rights covering the entire NCAA can compete. Thus, as the District Court found, many telecasts that would occur in a competitive market are foreclosed by the NCAA's plan.

Petitioner argues, however, that its television plan can have no significant anticompetitive effect since the record indicates that it has no market power—no ability to alter the interaction of supply and demand in the market.[38] We must reject this argument for two reasons, one legal, one factual.

As a matter of law, the absence of proof of market power does not justify a naked restriction on price or output. To the contrary, when there is an agreement not to compete in terms of price or output, "no elaborate industry analysis is required to demonstrate the anticompetitive character of such an agreement." *Professional Engineers*, 435 U.S., at 692, 98 S.Ct., at 1365. Petitioner does not quarrel with the District Court's finding that price and output are not responsive

28. In this connection, it is not without significance that Congress felt the need to grant professional sports an exemption from the antitrust laws for joint marketing of television rights. See 15 U.S.C. §§ 1291-1295. The legislative history of this exemption demonstrates Congress' recognition that agreements among league members to sell television rights in a cooperative fashion could run afoul of the Sherman Act.

38. Market power is the ability to raise prices above those that would be charged in a competitive market.

to demand. Thus the plan is inconsistent with the Sherman Act's command that price and supply be responsive to consumer preference. We have never required proof of market power in such a case. This naked restraint on price and output requires some competitive justification even in the absence of a detailed market analysis.

As a factual matter, it is evident that petitioner does possess market power. The District Court employed the correct test for determining whether college football broadcasts constitute a separate market—whether there are other products that are reasonably substitutable for televised NCAA football games. Petitioner's argument that it cannot obtain supracompetitive prices from broadcasters since advertisers, and hence broadcasters, can switch from college football to other types of programming simply ignores the findings of the District Court. It found that intercollegiate football telecasts generate an audience uniquely attractive to advertisers and that competitors are unable to offer programming that can attract a similar audience. These findings amply support its conclusion that the NCAA possesses market power. . . .

Thus, the NCAA television plan on its face constitutes a restraint upon the operation of a free market, and the findings of the District Court establish that it has operated to raise prices and reduce output. Under the Rule of Reason, these hallmarks of anticompetitive behavior place upon petitioner a heavy burden of establishing an affirmative defense which competitively justifies this apparent deviation from the operations of a free market. We turn now to the NCAA's proffered justifications. . . .

V

Throughout the history of its regulation of intercollegiate football telecasts, the NCAA has indicated its concern with protecting live attendance. This concern, it should be noted, is not with protecting live attendance at games which are shown on television; that type of interest is not at issue in this case. Rather, the concern is that fan interest in a televised game may adversely affect ticket sales for games that will not appear on television. Although the NORC studies in the 1950's provided some support for the thesis that live attendance would suffer if unlimited television were permitted, the District Court found that there was no evidence to support that theory in today's market. Moreover, as the District Court found, the television plan has evolved in a manner inconsistent with its original design to protect gate attendance. Under the current plan, games are shown on television during all hours that college football games are played. The plan simply does not protect live attendance by ensuring that games will not be shown on television at the same time as live events.

There is, however, a more fundamental reason for rejecting this defense. The NCAA's argument that its television plan is necessary to protect live attendance is not based on a desire to maintain the integrity of college football as a distinct and attractive product, but rather on a fear that the product will not prove sufficiently attractive to draw live attendance when faced with competition from televised games. At bottom the NCAA's position is that ticket sales for most college games are unable to compete in a free market. The television plan protects ticket sales by limiting output—just as any monopolist increases revenues by reducing output. By seeking to insulate live ticket sales from the full spectrum of competition because of its assumption that the product itself is insufficiently attractive to consumers, petitioner forwards a justification that is inconsistent with the basic policy of the Sherman Act. "[T]he Rule of Reason does not support a defense based on the assumption that competition itself is unreasonable."

VI

Petitioner argues that the interest in maintaining a competitive balance among amateur athletic teams is legitimate and important and that it justifies the regulations challenged in this case. We agree with the first part of the argument but not the second.

Our decision not to apply a per se rule to this case rests in large part on our recognition that a certain degree of cooperation is necessary if the type of competition that petitioner and its member institutions seek to market is to be preserved. It is reasonable to assume that most of the regulatory controls of the NCAA are justifiable means of fostering competition among amateur athletic teams and therefore procompetitive because they enhance public interest in intercollegiate athletics. The specific restraints on football telecasts that are challenged in this case do not, however, fit into the same mold as do rules defining the conditions of the contest, the eligibility of participants, or the manner in which members of a joint enterprise shall share the responsibilities and the benefits of the total venture.

The NCAA does not claim that its television plan has equalized or is intended to equalize competition within any one league. The plan is nationwide in scope and there is no single league or tournament in which all college football teams compete. There is no evidence of any intent to equalize the strength of teams in Division I-A with those in Division II or Division III, and not even a colorable basis for giving colleges that have no football program at all a voice in the management of the revenues generated by the football programs at other schools.

The interest in maintaining a competitive balance that is asserted by the NCAA as a justification for regulating all television of intercollegiate football is not related to any neutral standard or to any readily identifiable group of competitors.

The television plan is not even arguably tailored to serve such an interest. It does not regulate the amount of money that any college may spend on its football program, nor the way in which the colleges may use the revenues that are generated by their football programs, whether derived from the sale of television rights, the sale of tickets, or the sale of concessions or program advertising. The plan simply imposes a restriction on one source of revenue that is more important to some colleges than to others. There is no evidence that this restriction produces any greater measure of equality throughout the NCAA than would a restriction on alumni donations, tuition rates, or any other revenue-producing activity. At the same time, as the District Court found, the NCAA imposes a variety of other restrictions designed to preserve amateurism which are much better tailored to the goal of competitive balance than is the television plan, and which are "clearly sufficient" to preserve competitive balance to the extent it is within the NCAA's power to do so. And much more than speculation supported the District Court's findings on this score. No other NCAA sport employs a similar plan, and in particular the court found that in the most closely analogous sport, college basketball, competitive balance has been maintained without resort to a restrictive television plan.

Perhaps the most important reason for rejecting the argument that the interest in competitive balance is served by the television plan is the District Court's unambiguous and well-supported finding that many more games would be televised in a free market than under the NCAA plan. The hypothesis that legitimates the maintenance of competitive balance as a procompetitive justification under the Rule of Reason is that equal competition will maximize consumer demand for the product. The finding that consumption will materially increase if the controls are removed is a compelling demonstration that they do not in fact serve any such legitimate purpose.

VII

The NCAA plays a critical role in the maintenance of a revered tradition of amateurism in college sports. There can be no question but that it needs ample latitude to play that role, or that the preservation of the student-athlete in higher education adds richness and diversity to intercollegiate athletics and is entirely consistent with the goals of the Sherman Act. But consistent with the Sherman Act, the role of the NCAA must be to preserve a tradition that might otherwise die; rules that restrict output are hardly consistent with this role. Today we hold only that the record supports the District Court's conclusion that by curtailing output and blunting the ability of member institutions to respond to consumer preference, the NCAA has restricted rather than enhanced the place of intercollegiate athletics in the Nation's life. Accordingly, the judgment of the Court of Appeals is

Affirmed.   H

Justice WHITE, with whom Justice REHNQUIST joins, dissenting.

Although some of the NCAA's activities, viewed in isolation, bear a resemblance to those undertaken by professional sports leagues and associations, the Court errs in treating intercollegiate athletics under the NCAA's control as a purely commercial venture in which colleges and universities participate solely, or even primarily, in the pursuit of profits. Accordingly, I dissent. . . .

The NCAA, in short, "exist[s] primarily to enhance the contribution made by amateur athletic competition to the process of higher education as distinguished from realizing maximum return on it as an entertainment commodity." *Association for Intercollegiate Athletics for Women v. NCAA*, 558 F. Supp. 487, 494 (DC 1983), *aff'd*, 236 U.S.App.D.C. 311, 735 F.2d 577 (1984). In pursuing this goal, the organization and its members seek to provide a public good—a viable system of amateur athletics—that most likely could not be provided in a perfectly competitive market. See *Hennessey v. NCAA*, 564 F.2d 1136, 1153 (CA5 1977). "Without regulation, the desire of member institutions to remain athletically competitive would lead them to engage in activities that deny amateurism to the public. No single institution could confidently enforce its own standards since it could not trust its competitors to do the same." Note, *Antitrust and Nonprofit Entities*, 94 Harv. L. Rev. 802, 817-818 (1981). The history of intercollegiate athletics prior to the advent of the NCAA provides ample support for this conclusion. By mitigating what appears to be a clear failure of the free market to serve the ends and goals of higher education, the NCAA ensures the continued availability of a unique and valuable product, the very existence of which might well be threatened by unbridled competition in the economic sphere.

good point

In pursuit of its fundamental goal and others related to it, the NCAA imposes numerous controls on intercollegiate athletic competition among its members, many of which "are similar to those which are summarily condemned when undertaken in a more traditional business setting." [citation omitted.] Thus, the NCAA has promulgated and enforced rules limiting both the compensation of student-athletes and the number of coaches a school may hire for its football and basketball programs; it also has prohibited athletes who formerly have been compensated for playing from participating in intercollegiate competition, restricted the number of athletic scholarships its members may award, and established minimum academic standards for recipients of those scholarships; and it has pervasively regulated the recruitment process, student eligibility, practice schedules, squad size, the number of games played, and many other aspects of intercollegiate athletics. One clear effect of most, if not all, of these regulations is to prevent institutions with competitively and economically successful programs from taking advantage of their success by expanding their programs, improving the quality of the product they offer, and increasing their sports revenues. Yet each of these regulations represents a desirable and legitimate attempt "to keep university athletics from becoming professionalized to the extent that profit making objectives would overshadow educational objectives." *Kupec v. Atlantic Coast Conference*, 399 F. Supp. 1377, 1380 (MDNC 1975). Significantly, neither the Court of Appeals nor this Court questions the validity of these regulations under the Rule of Reason.

Notwithstanding the contrary conclusion of the District Court and the majority, . . . I do not believe that the restraint under consideration in this case—the NCAA's television plan—differs fundamentally for antitrust purposes from the other seemingly anti-competitive aspects of the organization's broader program of self-regulation. The television plan, like many of the NCAA's actions, furthers several complementary ends. Specifically, the plan is designed "to reduce, insofar as possible, the adverse effects of live television . . . upon football game attendance and, in turn, upon the athletic and related educational programs dependent upon the proceeds therefrom; to spread football television participation among as many colleges as practicable; to reflect properly the image of universities as educational institutions; to promote college football through the use of television; to advance the overall interests of intercollegiate athletics; and to provide college football television to the public to the extent compatible with these other objectives." More generally, in my view, the television plan reflects the NCAA's fundamental policy of preserving amateurism and integrating athletics and education. . . .

[handwritten margin note: But even if it reflects the NCAA's objectives, can't it still restrain trade?]

IV

Finally, I return to the point with which I began—the essentially noneconomic nature of the NCAA's program of self-regulation. Like Judge Barrett, who dissented in the Court of Appeals, I believe that the lower courts "erred by subjugating the NCAA's educational goals (and, incidentally, those which Oklahoma and Georgia insist must be maintained in any event) to the purely competitive commercialism of [an] 'every school for itself' approach to television contract bargaining." . . .

For all of these reasons, I would reverse the judgment of the Court of Appeals.

NOTES AND QUESTIONS   *Read carefully!*

1. *Commercial or Noncommercial Restraint?* The Supreme Court's majority characterizes the NCAA's restrictions on televised college football games as commercial activity subject to Sherman Act scrutiny. They conclude that NCAA members "compete against each other to attract television revenues, not to mention fans and athletes," and therefore are economic competitors in some instances. By contrast, the dissenting justices, in an opinion written by Justice White (who played college football as a student at the University of Colorado and finished second in the 1937 Heisman Trophy balloting) emphasizes the "essentially non-economic nature of the NCAA's program of self regulation" and asserts that the majority erroneously treats intercollegiate athletics "as a purely commercial venture in which . . . universities participate solely, or even primarily, in the pursuit of profits." They suggest that, unlike the conduct of professional sports leagues, the antitrust laws should not be applied to NCAA regulation of intercollegiate athletics. Do the differences between professional sports and intercollegiate athletics justify subjecting the former to antitrust scrutiny but not the latter? *Latter = exempt* *Dissent*

2. *Concerted Action Requirement.* The collective adoption and enforcement of NCAA rules by its member universities is considered concerted action for purposes of §1 of the Sherman Act. As the Tenth Circuit observed, "The NCAA is essentially an integration of the rulemaking and rule-enforcing activities of its member institutions." *NCAA v. Bd. of Regents,* 707 F.2d 1147, 1153 (10th Cir. 1983). As a result, virtually all NCAA rules and conduct are potentially subject to antitrust challenge.

   Although all NCAA member schools individually may be sued as co-conspirators for an alleged violation of §1, the NCAA itself generally is named as the sole defendant. Such pleading is justifiable because it is permissible to sue but one of several alleged co-conspirators. See *Hennessey v. NCAA,* 564 F.2d 1136, 1147 (5th Cir. 1977). As a result, any antitrust judgment against the NCAA, such as the approximately $67 million treble damages award in *Law v. NCAA, infra,* is collectable only against the association itself. The issue of whether individual schools would be legally liable for paying the judgment if the NCAA's assets are insufficient to do so is a matter of state law. John C. Weistart, *Antitrust Issues in the Regulation of College Sports,* 5 J. C. & Univ. L. 77, 91 n.44 (1977). NCAA members that are public universities and colleges may be entitled to Eleventh Amendment immunity from private damage actions in federal court. *University of Texas at Austin v. Vratil,* 96 F.3d 1337 (10th Cir. 1996); *Bowers v. NCAA,* 9 F. Supp. 2d 460, 498 n.15 (D. N.J. 1998). *11th Amend.*

3. *Per se Illegality Versus Rule of Reason.* To determine whether an agreement unreasonably restrains trade, courts historically have applied either per se or rule-of-reason analysis. The objective of either standard is "to form a judgment about the competitive significance of the restraint," although the respective application of these tests is quite different. Restraints deemed to be predominantly anticompetitive, as a matter of law or fact, are found to be unreasonable and thus illegal under the antitrust laws. Under the per se rule, certain restraints are conclusively presumed to be illegal as a matter of law because of their significant adverse effects on competition and lack of redeeming procompetitive virtues. Under the rule of reason, the anticompetitive effects of the challenged restraint are *Rule of Reason v. Per se*

balanced against its procompetitive effects on a case-by-case basis, considering the specific facts introduced into evidence by the parties. Although the Supreme Court notes that agreements among industry competitors to fix prices and limit output generally are illegal per se, why does it analyze the legality of the NCAA's television plan (which was found to be an output restriction raising the price networks paid for television rights) under the rule of reason? *Why?*

4. *Application of the Rule of Reason.* The plaintiff has the burden of proving the challenged restraint has actual or potential significant anticompetitive effects. How did the plaintiffs do this in the *Board of Regents* case? Why didn't they have to prove the NCAA possessed "market power"?

After plaintiffs proved the requisite anticompetitive effects of the television plan, the NCAA had "a heavy burden of establishing an affirmative defense" to justify this agreement. Which procompetitive justifications offered by the NCAA in defense of its television plan were recognized by the Court as valid? Did the NCAA's television plan further any of these valid justifications as a matter of fact? Even if it did, consider whether there are any viable alternative means for the NCAA to accomplish those objectives without imposing significant anticompetitive effects.

On the other hand, do you agree with the dissent's view that "the television plan reflects the NCAA's fundamental policy of preserving amateurism and integrating athletics and education"? *kind of* Should these "primarily noneconomic values pursued by educational institutions" justify restraints that would be illegal in other industries—namely, professional sports?

5. *Effect on Consumer Welfare.* The Supreme Court observes that "Congress designed the Sherman Act as a 'consumer welfare prescription.'" In other words, the federal antitrust laws are intended to ensure that consumers *there is no comp. market* receive the benefits of a competitive marketplace. What implications does this have for applying the antitrust laws to NCAA regulation of intercollegiate athletics? Have college football fans benefited from judicial invalidation of the NCAA's television plan? *can't charge outrageous amounts*

6. *Post*–Board of Regents *Commentary.* Tom McMillen, a former All-American college basketball player at the University of Maryland and congressman as well as a member of the Knight Foundation, argues that *Board of Regents* was wrongly decided because "the NCAA's loss of monopoly broadcast power [has led] to an escalating competition for money among schools." McMillen supports Justice White's dissent, arguing that "the NCAA monopoly 'fosters the goal of amateurism by spreading revenues among various schools and reducing the financial incentives towards professionalism.'" Tom McMillen, Opinion, *"Whizzer" White Had It Right When It Came to TV Money*, NCAA News, May 27, 2002, at 4.

Do you agree with McMillen's view that judicial validation of the NCAA's college football television plan would have alleviated some of the current influence of money on college sports?

7. *College Sports Television Contracts Today.* Although *Board of Regents* determined that the NCAA may not limit the total number of televised college football games or fix the price of broadcasting rights, it did not rule that groups of NCAA universities are prohibited from jointly selling television or other media rights to college football games or other athletic events. Today, college sports television contracts generally are negotiated and entered into by athletic conferences on behalf of their member universities with network

television (e.g., ABC, CBS, NBC, or Fox) or cable television broadcasters (e.g., ESPN). In *Association of Independent Television Stations, Inc. v. College Football Association*, 637 F. Supp. 1289 (W.D. Okla. 1984), the court rejected a television broadcaster's contention that a series of contracts conveying exclusive rights to televise Big Eight Conference football games to other broadcasters is per se illegal because it limited the number of available games that the plaintiff could televise. The court noted that these contracts have potential procompetitive efficiencies: "In the marketing of television rights, just as in the management of the live contest itself, some cooperation is necessary if the product, live college football television, is to be available at all." *Id.* at 1297. The court found that the conference television package creates a new product — namely, a "national series of games" — that creates more effective competition in the live college football television market. In addition, the marketing of exclusive television rights may provide incentives to broadcasters to promote and develop programs fully (which they might not otherwise do), thereby increasing the number of available television broadcasts to consumers, a collective business practice that generally does not violate the antitrust laws.

Broadcaster argument

8. *NCAA Limits on College Basketball Tournament Participation.* In *Worldwide Basketball and Sport Tours, Inc. v. NCAA*, 388 F.3d 955 (6th Cir. 2004), the promoters of certified college basketball tournaments alleged that the NCAA's "Two in Four Rule" violates the antitrust laws. This rule allows a university to participate in only one certified basketball tournament per academic year and no more than two every four years. The NCAA adopted this rule to prevent the more "powerful" basketball schools from disproportionately participating in these events, thereby achieving a competitive advantage. The promoters contended that the rule limits their ability to have the best and most famous teams play in their tournaments, which reduces their revenues. Although it found the challenged rule has a commercial impact and is subject to antitrust scrutiny, the Sixth Circuit concluded that its anticompetitive effects are not readily apparent. Because the plaintiffs failed to define the relevant market within which the rule adversely affected competition, their antitrust claims were dismissed.

restraining top ranked teams from competing in tourneys = not enough for antitrust

Five New York area colleges and universities that sponsored the Postseason National Invitational Tournament (NIT) claimed that NCAA rules requiring its member schools, if invited, to participate in the NCAA basketball tournament basketball violate the antitrust laws. The NCAA also prohibits an institution from participating in more than one postseason college basketball tournament. A federal district court held that plaintiffs "raised a genuine issue of fact in support of its claim that the NCAA possesses monopoly power in the market of Division I men's college basketball postseason tournaments and maintains this monopoly through exclusionary means." *Metropolitan Intercollegiate Basketball Assn. v. NCAA*, 339 F. Supp. 2d 545 (S.D.N.Y. 2004). Pursuant to an August 2005 settlement, the NCAA bought both the NIT preseason and postseason basketball tournaments for $40.5 million and paid $16 million to settle the litigation. The Metropolitan Intercollegiate Basketball Association, consisting of the five New York City universities (Fordham, Manhattan, St. John's, Wagner, and NYU) that sponsored the NIT tournaments, disbanded as a basketball entity. Given your evaluation of the merits of the case, was this a good settlement from the NCAA's perspective?

Now NCAA runs both and controls both?

STOP for WED.

b. Input Market

Board of Regents considered the validity of NCAA rules that restrain the intercollegiate athletics output market (e.g., a limit on the total number of televised college football games), whose adverse effects on consumer welfare are readily apparent. Next we will consider the validity of NCAA rules limiting competition among universities in the input market for the resources necessary to produce intercollegiate sports such as the services of coaches and student-athletes, which effects on consumer welfare are more difficult to determine.

i. Coaches' Salaries

LAW v. NCAA

134 F.3d 1010 (10th Cir. 1998)

EBEL, Circuit Judge.

Defendant-Appellant the National Collegiate Athletic Association ("NCAA") promulgated a rule limiting annual compensation of certain Division I entry-level coaches to $16,000. Basketball coaches affected by the rule filed a class action challenging the restriction under Section 1 of the Sherman Antitrust Act. . . .

I. BACKGROUND

. . . During the 1980s, the NCAA became concerned over the steadily rising costs of maintaining competitive athletic programs, especially in light of the requirements imposed by Title IX of the 1972 Education Amendments Act to increase support for women's athletic programs. The NCAA observed that some college presidents had to close academic departments, fire tenured faculty, and reduce the number of sports offered to students due to economic constraints. At the same time, many institutions felt pressure to "keep up with the Joneses" by increasing spending on recruiting talented players and coaches and on other aspects of their sports programs in order to remain competitive with rival schools. In addition, a report commissioned by the NCAA known as the "Raiborn Report" found that in 1985, 42% of NCAA Division I schools reported deficits in their overall athletic program budgets, with the deficit averaging $824,000 per school. The Raiborn Report noted that athletic expenses at all Division I institutions rose more than 100% over the eight-year period from 1978 to 1985. Finally, the Report stated that 51% of Division I schools responding to NCAA inquiries on the subject suffered a net loss in their basketball programs alone that averaged $145,000 per school.

Part of the problem identified by the NCAA involved the costs associated with part-time assistant coaches. The NCAA allowed Division I basketball teams to employ three full-time coaches, including one head coach and two assistant coaches, and two part-time coaches. The part-time positions could be filled by part-time assistants, graduate assistants, or volunteer coaches. The NCAA imposed salary restrictions on all of the part-time positions. . . . The NCAA limited compensation to part-time assistants to the value of full grant-in-aid compensation based on the value of out-of-state graduate studies.

Despite the salary caps, many of these part-time coaches earned $60,000 or $70,000 per year. Athletic departments circumvented the compensation limits by employing these part-time coaches in lucrative summer jobs at profitable sports camps run by the school or by hiring them for part-time jobs in the physical education department in addition to the coaching position. Further, many of these positions were filled with seasoned and experienced coaches, not the type of student assistant envisioned by the rule.

In January of 1989, the NCAA established a Cost Reduction Committee (the "Committee") to consider means and strategies for reducing the costs of intercollegiate athletics "without disturbing the competitive balance" among NCAA member institutions. . . . In his initial letter to Committee members, the Chairman of the Committee thanked participants for joining "this gigantic attempt to save intercollegiate athletics from itself." It was felt that only a collaborative effort could reduce costs effectively while maintaining a level playing field because individual schools could not afford to make unilateral spending cuts in sports programs for fear that doing so would unduly hamstring that school's ability to compete against other institutions that spent more money on athletics. . . . It became the consensus of the Committee that reducing the total number of coaching positions would reduce the cost of intercollegiate athletic programs.

The Committee proposed an array of recommendations to amend the NCAA's bylaws, including proposed Bylaw 11.6.4 that would limit Division I basketball coaching staffs to four members—one head coach, two assistant coaches, and one entry-level coach called a "restricted-earnings coach." The restricted-earnings coach category was created to replace the positions of part-time assistant, graduate assistant, and volunteer coach. The Committee believed that doing so would resolve the inequity that existed between those schools with graduate programs that could hire graduate assistant coaches and those who could not while reducing the overall amount spent on coaching salaries.

A second proposed rule, Bylaw 11.02.3, restricted compensation of restricted-earnings coaches in all Division I sports other than football to a total of $12,000 for the academic year and $4,000 for the summer months (the "REC Rule" for restricted-earnings coaches). The Committee determined that the $16,000 per year total figure approximated the cost of out-of-state tuition for graduate schools at public institutions and the average graduate school tuition at private institutions, and was thus roughly equivalent to the salaries previously paid to part-time graduate assistant coaches. . . . The REC Rule did not prevent member institutions from using savings gained by reducing the number and salary of basketball coaches to increase expenditures on other aspects of their athletic programs. . . .

The NCAA adopted the proposed rules, including the REC Rule, by majority vote in January of 1991, and the rules became effective on August 1, 1992.[5] The rules bind all Division I members of the NCAA that employ basketball coaches.

5. Other cost-saving measures were adopted that, *inter alia*, limited:

- the number of coaches who could recruit off campus.
- off-campus contacts with prospective student-athletes.
- visits by prospective student-athletes.
- printed recruiting materials.
- the number of practices before the first scheduled game.
- the number of games and duration of seasons.
- team travel and training table meals.
- financial aid grants to student-athletes.

The schools normally compete with each other in the labor market for coaching services. . . .

III. Rule of Reason Analysis

. . . The NCAA does not dispute that the REC Rule resulted from an agreement among its members. However, the NCAA does contest the district court's finding that on the record before it, there was no genuine dispute of fact that the REC Rule is an unreasonable restraint of trade.

Two analytical approaches are used to determine whether a defendant's conduct unreasonably restrains trade: the *per se* rule and the rule of reason. The *per se* rule condemns practices that "are entirely void of redeeming competitive rationales." Once a practice is identified as illegal *per se*, a court need not examine the practice's impact on the market or the procompetitive justifications for the practice advanced by a defendant before finding a violation of antitrust law. Rule of reason analysis, on the other hand, requires an analysis of the restraint's effect on competition. A rule of reason analysis first requires a determination of whether the challenged restraint has a substantially adverse effect on competition. The inquiry then shifts to an evaluation of whether the procompetitive virtues of the alleged wrongful conduct justifies the otherwise anticompetitive impacts. The district court applied the rule of reason standard to its analysis of the REC Rule.

Horizontal price-fixing is normally a practice condemned as illegal *per se*. . . . By agreeing to limit the price which NCAA members may pay for the services of restricted-earnings coaches, the REC Rule fixes the cost of one of the component items used by NCAA members to produce the product of Division I basketball. As a result, the REC Rule constitutes the type of naked horizontal agreement among competitive purchasers to fix prices usually found to be illegal *per se*. . . . [T]he Supreme Court in *NCAA v. Board of Regents* departed from the general treatment given to horizontal price-fixing agreements by refusing to apply a *per se* rule and instead adopting a rule of reason approach in reviewing an NCAA plan for televising college football that involved both limits on output and price-fixing. . . . *Rather, what is critical is that this case involves an industry in which horizontal restraints on competition are essential if the product is to be available at all.*

The "product" made available by the NCAA in this case is college basketball; the horizontal restraints necessary for the product to exist include rules such as those forbidding payments to athletes and those requiring that athletes attend class, etc. Because some horizontal restraints serve the procompetitive purpose of making college sports available, the Supreme Court subjected even the price and output restrictions at issue in *Board of Regents* to a rule of reason analysis. . . .

The coaches also argue that *Board of Regents* is distinguishable because the agreement in that case went to marketing the product itself—college sports—and because that agreement was closer to a joint venture because it involved a "joint selling arrangement." By contrast, they contend (1) that the hiring of coaches involves the market for coaching services, an input, rather than college sports, the output. . . . [This] point is similarly unpersuasive. *Board of Regents* does not turn on whether the agreement in question is based on input components or output products. Rather, *Board of Regents* more generally concluded that because horizontal agreements are necessary for sports competition, all horizontal agreements among NCAA members, even those as egregious as price-fixing, should be subject to a rule of reason analysis. . . .

Courts have imposed a consistent structure on rule of reason analysis by casting it in terms of shifting burdens of proof. Under this approach, the plaintiff bears the initial burden of showing that an agreement had a substantially adverse effect on competition. If the plaintiff meets this burden, the burden shifts to the defendant to come forward with evidence of the procompetitive virtues of the alleged wrongful conduct. If the defendant is able to demonstrate procompetitive effects, the plaintiff then must prove that the challenged conduct is not reasonably necessary to achieve the legitimate objectives or that those objectives can be achieved in a substantially less restrictive manner. Ultimately, if these steps are met, the harms and benefits must be weighed against each other in order to judge whether the challenged behavior is, on balance, reasonable.

A. ANTICOMPETITIVE EFFECT

We first review whether the coaches in this case demonstrated anticompetitive effect so conclusively that summary judgment on the issue was appropriate. A plaintiff may establish anticompetitive effect indirectly by proving that the defendant possessed the requisite market power within a defined market or directly by showing actual anticompetitive effects, such as control over output or price. A naked, effective restraint on market price or volume can establish anticompetitive effect under a truncated rule of reason analysis.

The NCAA argues that the district court erred by failing to define the relevant market and by failing to find that the NCAA possesses power in that market. The NCAA urges that the relevant market in this case is the entire market for men's basketball coaching services,[12] and it presented evidence demonstrating that positions as restricted-earnings basketball coaches make up, at most, 8% of that market. Thus, the NCAA argues it has at least created a genuine issue of material fact about whether it possesses market power and that summary judgment was therefore inappropriate.

The NCAA misapprehends the purpose in antitrust law of market definition, which is not an end unto itself but rather exists to illuminate a practice's effect on competition. In *Board of Regents*, the Court rejected a nearly identical argument from the NCAA that a plan to sell television rights could not be condemned under the antitrust laws absent proof that the NCAA had power in the market for television programming. "As a matter of law, the absence of proof of market power does not justify a naked restriction on price or output. To the contrary, when there is an agreement not to compete in terms of price or output, 'no elaborate industry analysis is required to demonstrate the anticompetitive character of such an agreement.'" No "proof of market power" is required where the very purpose and effect of a horizontal agreement is to fix prices so as to make them unresponsive to a competitive marketplace. Thus, where a practice has obvious anticompetitive effects—as does price-fixing—there is no need to prove that the defendant possesses market power. Rather, the court is justified in proceeding directly to the question of whether the procompetitive

---

12. According to the NCAA, the relevant market would include, in addition to coaching positions in Division I schools, coaching positions in Division II and III schools, junior colleges, high schools, and professional teams.

justifications advanced for the restraint outweigh the anticompetitive effects under a "quick look" rule of reason.

We find it appropriate to adopt such a quick look rule of reason in this case. Under a quick look rule of reason analysis, anticompetitive effect is established, even without a determination of the relevant market, where the plaintiff shows that a horizontal agreement to fix prices exists, that the agreement is effective, and that the price set by such an agreement is more favorable to the defendant than otherwise would have resulted from the operation of market forces. Under this standard, the undisputed evidence supports a finding of anticompetitive effect. The NCAA adopted the REC Rule to reduce the high cost of part-time coaches' salaries, over $60,000 annually in some cases, by limiting compensation to entry-level coaches to $16,000 per year. The NCAA does not dispute that the cost-reduction has effectively reduced restricted-earnings coaches' salaries. Because the REC Rule was successful in artificially lowering the price of coaching services, no further evidence or analysis is required to find market power to set prices. Thus, in the case at bar, the district court did not need to resolve issues of fact pertaining to the definition of the relevant market in order to support its decision on summary judgment that the REC Rule is a naked price restraint. . . .

B.   PROCOMPETITIVE RATIONALES

Under a rule of reason analysis, an agreement to restrain trade may still survive scrutiny under section 1 if the procompetitive benefits of the restraint justify the anticompetitive effects. Justifications offered under the rule of reason may be considered only to the extent that they tend to show that, on balance, "the challenged restraint enhances competition." *Board of Regents*, 468 U.S. at 104, 104 S.Ct. at 2961.

In *Board of Regents* the Supreme Court recognized that certain horizontal restraints, such as the conditions of the contest and the eligibility of participants, are justifiable under the antitrust laws because they are necessary to create the product of competitive college sports. Thus, the only legitimate rationales that we will recognize in support of the REC Rule are those necessary to produce competitive intercollegiate sports. The NCAA advanced three justifications for the salary limits: retaining entry-level coaching positions; reducing costs; and maintaining competitive equity. We address each of them in turn.

1.   *Retention of Entry-Level Positions*

The NCAA argues that the plan serves the procompetitive goal of retaining an entry-level coaching position. The NCAA asserts that the plan will allow younger, less experienced coaches entry into Division I coaching positions. While opening up coaching positions for younger people may have social value apart from its affect [*sic*] on competition, we may not consider such values unless they impact upon competition. . . .[14]

The NCAA also contends that limiting one of the four available coaching positions on a Division I basketball team to an entry-level position will create

---

14. Similarly, the NCAA cannot be heard to argue that the REC Rule fosters the amateurism that serves as the hallmark of NCAA competition. While courts should afford the NCAA plenty of room under the antitrust laws to preserve the amateur character of intercollegiate athletics, courts have only legitimized rules designed to ensure the amateur status of student athletes, not coaches.

more balanced competition by barring some teams from hiring four experienced coaches instead of three. However, the REC Rule contained no restrictions other than salary designed to insure that the position would be filled by entry-level applicants; it could be filled with experienced applicants. . . . In fact, the evidence in the record tends to demonstrate that at least some schools designated persons with many years of experience as the restricted-earnings coach. The NCAA did not present any evidence showing that restricted-earnings positions have been filled by entry-level applicants or that the rules will be effective over time in accomplishing this goal. Nothing in the record suggests that the salary limits for restricted-earnings coaches will be effective at creating entry-level positions. Thus, the NCAA failed to present a triable issue of fact as to whether preserving entry-level positions served a legitimate procompetitive end of balancing competition.

2.   *Cost Reduction*

The NCAA next advances the justification that the plan will cut costs. However, cost-cutting by itself is not a valid procompetitive justification. If it were, any group of competing buyers could agree on maximum prices. Lower prices cannot justify a cartel's control of prices charged by suppliers, because the cartel ultimately robs the suppliers of the normal fruits of their enterprises. Further, setting maximum prices reduces the incentive among suppliers to improve their products. Likewise, in our case, coaches have less incentive to improve their performance if their salaries are capped. . . .

The NCAA adopted the REC Rule because without it competition would lead to higher prices. The REC Rule was proposed as a way to prevent Division I schools from engaging in behavior the association termed "keeping up with the Joneses," *i.e.*, competing. However, the NCAA cannot argue that competition for coaches is an evil because the Sherman Act "precludes inquiry into the question whether competition is good or bad."

While increasing output, creating operating efficiencies, making a new product available, enhancing product or service quality, and widening consumer choice have been accepted by courts as justifications for otherwise anticompetitive agreements, mere profitability or cost savings have not qualified as a defense under the antitrust laws. . . . The NCAA's cost containment justification is illegitimate because . . . [r]educing costs for member institutions, without more, does not justify the anticompetitive effects of the REC Rule.

The NCAA argues that reducing costs can be considered a procompetitive justification because doing so is necessary to maintain the existence of competitive intercollegiate sports. . . .

We are dubious that the goal of cost reductions can serve as a legally sufficient justification for a buyers' agreement to fix prices even if such cost reductions are necessary to save inefficient or unsuccessful competitors from failure. Nevertheless, we need not consider whether cost reductions may have been required to "save" intercollegiate athletics and whether such an objective served as a legitimate procompetitive end because the NCAA presents no evidence that limits on restricted-earning coaches' salaries would be successful in reducing deficits, let alone that such reductions were necessary to save college basketball. Moreover, the REC Rule does not equalize the overall amount of money Division I schools are permitted to spend on their basketball programs. There is no reason to think that the money saved by a school on the salary of a restricted-earnings coach will not be put into another aspect of the school's basketball *good point !*

program, such as equipment or even another coach's salary, thereby increasing inequity in that area. . . .

NCAA

3. *Maintaining Competitiveness*

We note that the NCAA must be able to ensure some competitive equity between member institutions in order to produce a marketable product: a "team must try to establish itself as a winner, but it must not win so often and so convincingly that the outcome will never be in doubt, or else there will be no marketable 'competition.'" Michael Jay Kaplan, Annotation, *Application of Federal Antitrust Laws to Professional Sports*, 18 A.L.R. Fed. 489 § 2(a) (1974). The NCAA asserts that the REC Rule will help to maintain competitive equity by *NCAA* preventing wealthier schools from placing a more experienced, higher-priced coach in the position of restricted-earnings coach. . . .

While the REC Rule will equalize the salaries paid to entry-level coaches in Division I schools, it is not clear that the REC Rule will equalize the experience level of such coaches.[15] Nowhere does the NCAA prove that the salary restrictions enhance competition, level an uneven playing field, or reduce coaching inequities. Rather, the NCAA only presented evidence that the cost reductions would be achieved in such a way so as to maintain without "significantly altering," "adversely affecting," or "disturbing" the existing competitive balance. The undisputed record reveals that the REC Rule is nothing more than a cost-cutting measure and shows that the only consideration the NCAA gave to competitive balance was simply to structure the rule so as not to exacerbate competitive imbalance. Thus, on its face, the REC Rule is not directed towards competitive *terrible evidence!* balance nor is the nexus between the rule and a compelling need to maintain competitive balance sufficiently clear on this record to withstand a motion for summary judgment.[16]

Affirmed. *(In favor of the coaches)*

NOTES AND QUESTIONS

1. *Standard for Analyzing Input Market Restraints.* The *Law* court recognized that coaching services are a necessary input to produce intercollegiate athletic competition and analyzed the legality of fixed maximum salaries for restricted-earnings basketball coaches (the "REC Rule") under the same antitrust standard used by *Board of Regents* to invalidate restraints on the sale of output (e.g., television rights) by NCAA members. Is this appropriate? Do NCAA restrictions affecting the output market or input market present the most significant antitrust concerns from the perspective of consumers?

2. *Full Rule of Reason.* In Part III of its opinion, the Tenth Circuit's explains the parties' respective burdens of proof in a rule of reason case. The plaintiff

15. For example, some more-experienced coaches may take restricted-earnings coach positions with programs such as those at Duke or North Carolina, despite the lower salary, because of the national prominence of those programs. In fact, absent the REC Rule, the market might produce greater equity in coaching talent, because a school with a less-prominent basketball program might be able to entice a more-experienced coach away from a prominent program by offering a higher salary.

16. Because we hold that the NCAA did not establish evidence of sufficient procompetitive benefits, we need not address question of whether the plaintiffs were able to show that comparable procompetitive benefits could be achieved through viable, less anticompetitive means.

must prove that the challenged restraint has anticompetitive effects. If it does so, the burden shifts to the defendant to prove that the restraint has procompetitive effects. If so, the plaintiff has the burden of producing sufficient evidence establishing that the challenged restraint is not reasonably necessary to achieve these procompetitive objectives or that they can be achieved in a substantially less restrictive manner. If the parties meet their respective burdens of proof, the fact finder must determine whether the competitive effects of the restraint are, on balance, anticompetitive (and unreasonable) or procompetitive (and reasonable). Relatively few cases reach this stage because an antitrust claim is resolved by the court as a matter of law if adverse to the party that fails to satisfy its required burden of proof.

3. *Application of "Quick Look" Rule of Reason.* In *Law*, the Tenth Circuit affirmed the trial court's grant of summary judgment in favor of the plaintiff basketball coaches. Applying the "quick look" rule of reason rather than the per se rule (why?), both courts concluded that capping the salaries of restricted-earnings coaches is illegal as a matter of law. Why wasn't it necessary to have the jury balance the anticompetitive effects of fixing these coaches' salaries with the NCAA's claimed procompetitive justifications, which occurs when the full rule of reason is applied? To answer these questions, carefully review part III of *Law*, particularly the Tenth Circuit's explanation of the parties' respective burdens of proof.

4. *NCAA's Justifications.* Why does the court reject the NCAA's argument that the REC Rule is a legitimate means of preventing a "keep up with the Joneses" type of spending in its members' athletic programs? Is the rule necessary to ensure competitive balance among NCAA members, to preserve the amateur nature of NCAA sports, or to maintain academic integrity?

5. *REC Rule Damages Award and Settlement.* Coaches whose economic interests were adversely affected by the NCAA's REC Rule (including those coaching sports other than basketball) ultimately won a jury verdict of $22.3 million, which, with mandatory trebling, resulted in a total award of $66.9 million from the NCAA. The trial court also awarded them an additional $5.026 million as a net present value adjustment. Thereafter, the NCAA agreed to pay $54.5 million as part of a settlement to resolve all damage claims, and the court awarded approximately $20 million in attorney fees and costs to the plaintiffs' attorneys. See *Law v. NCAA*, 108 F. Supp. 2d 1193 (D. Kan. 2000) (approving revised settlement plan as fair, reasonable, and adequate).

6. *Permissible NCAA Cost Containment?* In the 1970s, courts held that NCAA limits on the size of coaching staffs do not violate the antitrust laws. See *Hennessey v. NCAA*, 564 F.2d 1136 (5th Cir. 1977); *Board of Regents of the Univ. of Oklahoma v. NCAA*, 561 P.2d 499 (Okla. 1977). They found that reducing Division I football coaching staffs was a legitimate cost-cutting measure that promoted competitive balance by preventing more successful and economically powerful universities from expanding their football programs to the detriment of intercollegiate athletics. (This may have been why the *Law* plaintiffs did not challenge the NCAA's reduction in the size of basketball coaching staffs.) Not surprisingly, the NCAA cited *Hennessey* in defense of the REC Rule. *Law*, however, distinguished *Hennessey* because it involved a restriction on the maximum number of assistant coaches, not their salary; the Tenth Circuit also concluded that *Hennessey* is inconsistent with *Board of Regents*. Do you agree that this distinction is relevant for antitrust purposes,

or that an NCAA-mandated reduction of coaches in a particular sport would be an antitrust violation under current law?

Review the other NCAA cost-saving measures described in footnote 5 of the *Law* case that were not challenged by the plaintiffs and consider which ones would survive antitrust scrutiny under the rule of reason. Would NCAA-mandated cost-cutting or caps on total expenditures in some men's sports (e.g., football) in an effort to comply with Title IX gender equity requirements violate the antitrust laws? See John C. Weistart, *Can Gender Equity Find a Place in Commercialized College Sports?*, 3 Duke J. Gender L. & Pol'y 191 (1995). If not, why hasn't the NCAA adopted such rules?

7. *NCAA Limits on Revenue Streams.* If NCAA limits on costs (e.g., part-time coaches' salaries) violate the antitrust laws, are NCAA limits on its members' potential sources of revenue (e.g., advertising rights) an antitrust violation?

Adidas America, Inc., a leading sporting goods manufacturer, alleged that an NCAA bylaw limiting the size of trademarks on player uniforms and equipment illegally restrains the sale of advertising and promotional rights by NCAA universities. In denying Adidas's requested injunctive relief against NCAA enforcement of the bylaw, the federal district court found this to be noncommercial regulation not subject to the antitrust laws. It concluded that *Law* did not require the challenged advertising restrictions to be characterized as commercial activity within the scope of the Sherman Act. Finding the bylaw's purpose to be protecting student-athletes from commercial exploitation and avoiding excessive advertising that could potentially interfere with the basic function of player uniforms, the court explained that the bylaw "is an incidental by-product of the NCAA's legitimate attempt to maintain the amateurism and integrity of college sports, and it does not economically benefit the NCAA or its member institutions." See *Adidas America, Inc. v. NCAA*, 40 F. Supp. 2d 1275 (D. Kan. 1999).

ii. Athlete Eligibility Rules

PROBLEM 3-9

In *Bloom v. NCAA, supra,* Jeremy Bloom alleged that NCAA bylaws prohibiting student-athletes from being paid for advertisements and endorsements restrain trade and violate the antitrust laws. As you read the following materials, consider (1) the arguments you would make on Bloom's behalf, (2) the arguments you would make on the NCAA's behalf in defending this claim, and (3) how a court is likely to resolve the merits of Bloom's antitrust claim.

SMITH v. NCAA
139 F.3d 180 (3d Cir. 1998)

GREENBERG, Circuit Judge.

[EDS. Renee M. Smith, a pro se litigant, appealed the district court's order dismissing her complaint for failure to state a claim and denying her motion for leave to amend her complaint. She alleged that the NCAA's promulgation and enforcement of a bylaw prohibiting a student-athlete from participating in intercollegiate athletics while enrolled in a graduate program at an institution other than the student-athlete's undergraduate institution violated §1 of the Sherman Act. Her unsuccessful claim that this conduct violated Title IX is discussed *infra*. NCAA Bylaw 14.1.9.1 now permits student-athletes who graduate before their four years of eligibility is exhausted to participate in intercollegiate athletics at another institution as a graduate student.]

II. FACTS AND PROCEDURAL HISTORY

Smith graduated from high school in the spring of 1991 and enrolled in St. Bonaventure University the following fall, where she participated in Division I athletics. Smith played intercollegiate' volleyball for St. Bonaventure during the 1991-92 and 1992-93 athletic seasons. By her choice, Smith did not participate in intercollegiate volleyball for St. Bonaventure during the 1993-94 season.

Smith graduated from St. Bonaventure in two and one half years. Thereafter, she enrolled in a postbaccalaureate program at Hofstra University, and then in 1995 she enrolled in a second postbaccalaureate program at the University of Pittsburgh. St. Bonaventure did not offer either of these postbaccalaureate programs.

The NCAA is an unincorporated association comprised of public and private colleges and universities and is responsible for promulgating rules governing all aspects of intercollegiate athletics, including recruiting, eligibility of student-athletes, and academic standards. The member institutions agree to abide by and enforce these rules. The NCAA denied Smith eligibility to compete for Hofstra and the University of Pittsburgh in the 1994-95 and 1995-96 athletic seasons, respectively, based upon Bylaw 14.1.8.2 in the NCAA Manual (the "Postbaccalaureate Bylaw"). The Postbaccalaureate Bylaw provides that a student-athlete may not participate in intercollegiate athletics at a postgraduate institution other than the institution from which the student earned her undergraduate degree. Both Hofstra and the University of Pittsburgh applied to the NCAA for a waiver of the bylaw with respect to Smith, but the NCAA denied both requests. Smith was, however, in good academic standing and in compliance with all other NCAA eligibility requirements for the 1994-95 and 1995-96 athletic seasons.

III. DISCUSSION

A. SHERMAN ACT CLAIM

Count I of Smith's complaint alleges that the NCAA, in promulgating and enforcing the Postbaccalaureate Bylaw, violated section 1 of the Sherman Act because the bylaw unreasonably restrains trade and has an adverse anticompetitive effect. As we have indicated, the district court dismissed this claim for failure to state a claim upon which relief could be granted, holding that "the actions of the NCAA in refusing to waive the Postbaccalaureate Bylaw and allow the Plaintiff to participate in intercollegiate athletics is not the type of action to which the Sherman Act was meant to be applied." Smith argues that the district court erred in limiting the application of the Sherman Act to the NCAA's commercial and business activities. We disagree. . . .

The Supreme Court addressed the applicability of the Sherman Act to the NCAA in [*Board of Regents*], holding that the NCAA's plan to restrict television coverage of intercollegiate football games violated section 1. The Court discussed the procompetitive nature of the NCAA's activities such as establishing eligibility requirements as opposed to the anticompetitive nature of the television plan. Yet, while the Court distinguished the NCAA's television plan from its rule making, it did not comment directly on whether the Sherman Act would apply to the latter.

Although insofar as we are aware no court of appeals expressly has addressed the issue of whether antitrust laws apply to the NCAA's promulgation of eligibility rules, *cf. McCormack v. National Collegiate Athletic Assn*, 845 F.2d 1338, 1343 (5th Cir. 1988) (assuming without deciding that the NCAA's eligibility rules were subject to antitrust scrutiny and holding that the "no-draft" and "no-agent" rules do not have an anticompetitive effect), many district courts have held that the Sherman Act does not apply to the NCAA's promulgation and enforcement of eligibility requirements. *See Gaines v. National Collegiate Athletic Assn*, 746 F. Supp. 738, 744-46 (M.D. Tenn. 1990) (holding that antitrust law cannot be used to invalidate NCAA eligibility rules, but noting in dicta that the "no-agent" and "no-draft" rules have primarily procompetitive effects); *Jones v. National Collegiate Athletic Assn*, 392 F. Supp. 295, 303 (D. Mass. 1975) (holding that antitrust law does not apply to NCAA eligibility rules); *College Athletic Placement Service, Inc. v. National Collegiate Athletic Assn*, 1975-1 Trade Cas. (CCH) T 60,117, available in 1974 WL 998, *2, *3 (D.N.J. 1974) (holding that the NCAA's adoption of a rule furthering its noncommercial objectives, such as preserving the educational standards of its members, is not within the purview of antitrust law), *aff'd*, 506 F.2d 1050 (3d Cir. 1974) (table).

We agree with these courts that the eligibility rules are not related to the NCAA's commercial or business activities. Rather than intending to provide the NCAA with a commercial advantage, the eligibility rules primarily seek to ensure fair competition in intercollegiate athletics. Based upon the Supreme Court's recognition that the Sherman Act primarily was intended to prevent unreasonable restraints in "business and commercial transactions," and therefore has only limited applicability to organizations which have principally noncommercial objectives, we find that the Sherman Act does not apply to the NCAA's promulgation of eligibility requirements.[5] . . .

For the foregoing reasons, we will affirm the district court's dismissal of appellant's Sherman Act claim. . . .

NOTE AND QUESTIONS

1. *Commercial Versus Noncommercial Restraints Revisited. Smith* and the cases cited therein have characterized NCAA student-athlete eligibility rules as noncommercial activity not subject to antitrust scrutiny. See also *Bassett v. NCAA*,

---

5. The recent decision of the Court of Appeals for the Tenth Circuit in *Law v. National Collegiate Athletic Assn*, 134 F.3d 1010 (10th Cir. 1998), does not alter our result. At issue in Law was the NCAA's bylaw restricting entry-level coaches' annual compensation. . . . The bylaw at issue in *Law* concerned a restriction on the business activities of the institutions, whereas the Postbaccalaureate Bylaw does not. Because our analysis regarding the applicability of the Sherman Act focuses on the distinction between commercial and noncommercial activities, *Law* is inapposite. . . .

528 F.3d 426 (6th Cir. 2008) (dismissing antitrust challenge to sanctions imposed on coach stemming from NCAA enforcement of rules governing recruiting, improper benefits to athletes, and academic fraud because "not within purview of antitrust law as it is not related to NCAA's commercial or business activities); *Pocono Invitational Sports Camp, Inc. v. NCAA*, 2004 WL 1000012 (E.D. Pa.) (NCAA restrictions regarding college coaches' activities at youth basketball camps hosted by organizations other than NCAA institutions are immune from antitrust scrutiny because the rules relate to noncommercial matters). However, in *Board of Regents*, the Supreme Court observed that NCAA schools compete against each other to attract student-athletes to their intercollegiate athletic programs. Because uniform eligibility rules both define and limit the nature and scope of competition among NCAA members for student-athletes' services, some legal scholars contend that these rules should be characterized as commercial activity with their respective net competitive effects individually analyzed under the rule of reason. See, e.g., Daniel E. Lazaroff, *The NCAA in Its Second Century: Defender of Amateurism or Antitrust Recidivist?*, 83 Or. L. Rev. 329 (2007); Matthew J. Mitten, *University Price Competition for Elite Students and Athletes: Illusions and Realities*, 36 S. Tex. L. Rev. 59 (1995). Do you agree with the view of courts or these scholars?

In January 2013 the Commonwealth of Pennsylvania filed an antitrust suit against the NCAA, which alleged that the unprecedented disciplinary sanctions imposed against Penn State University (see the Consent Decree, *supra*) for the role of former university administrators and football coaches in a child molestation scandal constitute arbitrary and capricious punishment that is not reasonably related to the NCAA's legitimate objectives of maintaining the fairness and integrity of intercollegiate athletics competition. Rather, the sanctions are intended to debilitate Penn State's football program, thereby "boosting the competing football programs of certain member colleges and universities by removing from competition one of the leading competitors," which has irreparably harmed the university as well as Pennsylvania's general economy and citizens, in violation of §1 of the Sherman Act. See *Commonwealth of Pennsylvania v. NCAA* (M.D. Pa., filed Jan. 2, 2013). Is the NCAA's disciplinary action noncommercial regulation or a commercial restraint?

2. *Per se Legality of Student-Athlete Eligibility Requirements.* Consistent with *Smith*, courts have uniformly upheld, as a matter of law, the validity of NCAA and athletic conference eligibility rules that athletes must satisfy to participate in intercollegiate athletics. Without any detailed legal or factual analysis, such rules are deemed necessary to preserve amateurism, academic values, and competitive balance in intercollegiate athletics. Courts have held that rules prohibiting the marketing of high school students' athletic prowess to universities, *College Athletic Placement Service, Inc. v. NCAA*, 1974 WL 998 (D.N.J. 1974), *aff'd*, 506 F.2d 1050 (3d Cir. 1974), and a college athlete's receipt of any compensation or extra benefits exceeding the value of an athletics scholarship, *Justice v. NCAA*, 577 F. Supp. 356 (D. Ariz. 1983), are legal under the antitrust laws. Rules declaring that athletes who have previously been paid to play a sport, *Jones v. NCAA*, 392 F. Supp. 295 (D. Mass. 1975), or who have hired agents or entered a professional league's draft, *Banks v. NCAA*, 977 F.2d 1081 (7th Cir. 1992), *Gaines v. NCAA*, 746 F. Supp. 738 (M.D. Tenn. 1990), are ineligible in participate in NCAA sports have been upheld. Rules

defining athletic eligibility for transfer students also have survived antitrust challenge. *Tanaka v. University of S. Cal.*, 252 F.3d 1059 (9th Cir. 2001); *Smith v. NCAA*, 139 F.3d 180 (3d Cir. 1998). Courts also have ruled that NCAA or athletic conference sanctions against member institutions for violating such rules do not violate the antitrust laws. *McCormack v. NCAA*, 845 F.2d 1338 (5th Cir. 1988); *Hairston v. Pac.-10 Conference*, 101 F.3d 1315 (9th Cir. 1995).

For example, in *Banks v. NCAA*, 977 F.2d 1081 (7th Cir.), *cert. denied*, 508 U.S. 908 (1992), Braxton Banks, a former University of Notre Dame football player, alleged that two NCAA rules causing the loss of eligibility to participate in collegiate sports if a student-athlete chooses to enter a professional draft or agrees to be represented by an agent in that sport violated the antitrust laws. Rule 12.2.4.2, the "no-draft" rule, at that time provided without exception that "[a]n individual loses amateur status in a particular sport when the individual asks to be placed on the draft list or supplemental draft list of a professional league in that sport." Rule 12.3.1, the "no-agent" rule, stated, "An individual shall be ineligible for participation in an intercollegiate sport if he or she ever has agreed (orally or in writing) to be represented by an agent for the purpose of marketing his or her athletics ability or reputation in that sport." Rejecting Banks's claim, the court explained:

> The no-draft rule has no more impact on the market for college football players than other NCAA eligibility requirements such as grades, semester hours carried, or requiring a high school diploma. They all constitute eligibility requirements essential to participation in NCAA sponsored amateur athletic competition. Banks might just as well have alleged that only permitting a student five calendar years in which to participate in four seasons of intercollegiate athletics restrains trade. Banks' allegation that the no-draft rule restrains trade is absurd. None of the NCAA rules affecting college football eligibility restrain trade in the market for college players because the NCAA does not exist as a minor league training ground for future NFL players but rather to provide an opportunity for competition among amateur students pursuing a collegiate education. Because the no-draft rule represents a desirable and legitimate attempt "to keep university athletics from becoming professionalized to the extent that profit making objectives would overshadow educational objectives," the no-draft rule and other like NCAA regulations preserve the bright line of demarcation between college and "play for pay" football. We consider college football players as student-athletes simultaneously pursuing academic degrees that will prepare them to enter the employment market in non-athletic occupations, and hold that the regulations of the NCAA are designed to preserve the honesty and integrity of intercollegiate athletics and foster fair competition among the participating amateur college students.

Id. at 1089-1090.

In a vigorous dissent, Judge Flaum expressed a very different view:

> It is hardly a revelation that colleges fiercely compete for the most promising high school football players—the players who, incidentally, are most likely to feel constrained by the challenged rules two or three years down the line. If the no-draft rule were scuttled, colleges that promised their athletes the opportunity to test the waters in the NFL draft before their eligibility expired, and return if things didn't work out, would be more attractive to athletes than colleges that declined to offer the same opportunity. The no-draft rule eliminates this potential element of competition among colleges, the purchasers

of labor in the college football labor market. It categorically rules out a term of employment that players, the suppliers of labor in that market, would find advantageous. . . .

I add here a caveat to avert any potential misunderstandings. My point is only that Banks has properly alleged an anticompetitive effect in a relevant market and has demonstrated antitrust injury, and hence that his damages action should survive the NCAA's motion to dismiss. But this is, of course, only the first step. To ultimately prevail, Banks also must demonstrate, under the rule of reason, that the no-agent and no-draft rules, despite their anticompetitive effects, are not "justifiable means of fostering competition among amateur athletic teams and therefore procompetitive" on the whole. It may very well be that the no-draft and no-agent rules are essential to the survival of college football as a distinct and viable product, in which case Banks would lose. A lively debate has arisen among those who have already considered this matter. I opt not to join the fray here, for I think it unwise to weigh pro- and anti-competitive effects under the rule of reason on a motion to dismiss. . . .

why?

Id. at 1095-1098. Which view is correct?

3. In *Agnew v. NCAA*, 683 F.3d. 328 (7th Cir. 2012), the Seventh Circuit distinguished between NCAA student-athlete eligibility rules and other forms of NCAA regulation such as limiting the duration of athletic scholarships to one year and the total number of scholarships a university may award for a particular sport, which have adverse commercial effects on student-athletes and may be challenged as a violation of §1 of the Sherman Act. The court explained:

The Bylaws at issue, especially the prohibition against multi-year scholarships, seem to be aimed at containing university costs, not preserving the product of college football, though evidence presented at a later stage could prove that the Bylaws are, in fact, key to the survival of the student-athlete and amateurism.

It is true that the prohibition against multi-year scholarships is, in a sense, a rule concerning the amount of payment a player receives for his labor, and thus may seem to implicate the split between amateur and pay-for-play sports. After all, student-athletes are paid, but their payment is limited to reimbursement for costs attendant to receiving an education. For the purposes of college sports, and in the name of amateurism, we consider players who receive nothing more than educational costs in return for their services to be "unpaid athletes." It is for this reason, though, that the prohibition against multi-year scholarships does not implicate the preservation of amateurism, for whether or not a player receives four years of educational expenses or one year of educational expenses, he is still an amateur. It is not until payment above and beyond educational costs is received that a player is considered a "paid athlete." . . .

The NCAA's limitation on athlete compensation *beyond* educational expenses . . . directly advances the goal of maintaining a "clear line of demarcation between intercollegiate athletics and professional sports," and thus is best categorized as an eligibility rule aimed at preserving the existence of amateurism and the student-athlete. The Bylaws at issue in this case, on the other hand, are not directly related to the separation of amateur athletics from pay-for-play athletics, as explained in the preceding paragraphs. Nor do they help preserve the existence of the student-athlete (as a facial matter, anyway), since they actually limit the number of athletes awarded financial aid and the amount of financial aid that an athlete can be awarded. Thus, financial aid rules do not always assist in the preservation of amateurism or the existence of student-athletes, so the regulations at issue cannot be presumptively procompetitive simply because they relate to financial aid.

Id. at 344-345. While this case was pending, but before it was decided by the Seventh Circuit, NCAA bylaws were amended to permit Division I universities to award multiyear athletic scholarships. See Michelle Brutlag Hosick, *Multiyear Scholarships to Be Allowed,* NCAA.com, Feb. 17, 2012, http://www.ncaa.com/news/ncaa/article/2012-02-17/multiyear-scholarships-be-allowed.

4.   *Amateurism Defense.* Courts readily accept preservation of amateurism as a justification for NCAA rules limiting competition among its member institutions for the services of athletes, which reduces the cost of an essential input necessary to produce intercollegiate athletics. However, if cost reduction is not a valid justification for fixing the price of coaches' salaries, why is it an accepted justification for limiting the compensation for student-athletes' services?

NCAA rules permit student-athletes to be professionals in one sport (e.g., baseball) without losing one's amateur status and intercollegiate eligibility to participate in another sport (e.g., football). From the perspective of fans, is the fact that student-athletes only receive the value of room, board, tuition, books, and educational fees what distinguishes college sports from pro sports? Is "amateurism" an essential feature of intercollegiate athletics? See *Board of Regents v. NCAA,* 546 F. Supp. 1276, 1299 (W.D. Okla. 1982) ("NCAA football is a unique product because of its history and tradition, the color and pageantry of the event, and the interest of college alumni in the football success of their alma mater").

Contrary to the prevailing judicial view, several commentators have argued that prohibiting price competition among NCAA member institutions for the services of college athletes (under the guise of preserving amateurism) may violate the antitrust laws. See, e.g., Walter Byers, Unsportsmanlike Conduct—Exploiting College Athletes, 374-384 (Univ. of Michigan Press 1995); Daniel E. Lazaroff, *The NCAA in Its Second Century: Defender of Amateurism or Antitrust Recidivist?*, 83 Or. L. Rev. 329 (2007); C. Peter Goplerud III, *Pay for Play for College Athletes: Now, More Than Ever*, 38 So. Tex. L. Rev. 1081 (1997); Gary R. Roberts, *The NCAA, Antitrust, and Consumer Welfare*, 79 Tul. L. Rev. 2631 (1996); Matthew J. Mitten, *University Price Competition for Elite Students and Athletes: Illusions and Realities*, 36 S. Tex. L. Rev. 59, 77-78 (1995); Lee Goldman, *Sports and Antitrust: Should College Students Be Paid to Play?*, 65 Notre Dame L. Rev. 206, 207-208 (1990); James V. Koch, *The Economic Realities of Amateur Sports Organization*, 61 Ind. L.J. 9, 12 (1986). But scholars are not unanimous in their belief that the NCAA's amateurism rules violate the antitrust laws. See, e.g., Peter C. Carstensen and Paul Olszowski, *Antitrust Law, Student-Athletes, and the NCAA: Limiting the Scope and Conduct of Private Economic Regulation*, 1995 Wis. L. Rev. 545; Richard B. McKenzie and E. Thomas Sullivan, *Does the NCAA Exploit Colleges? An Economics and Legal Reinterpretation*, 32 Antitrust Bull. 373 (1987).

The historically prevalent practice of under-the-table payments to athletes suggests that athletes do not receive fair market value for their playing services from their respective universities. In dicta, in a case involving the criminal prosecution of an agent for making prohibited payments to student-athletes, the Seventh Circuit observed, "The NCAA depresses athletes' income—restricting payments to the value of tuition, room, board, while receiving services of substantially greater worth. The NCAA treats this as desirable preservation of amateur sports; a more jaundiced eye would see it as the use of monopsony power to obtain athlete's services for less than the competitive market price." *U.S. v. Walters*, 997 F.2d 1219, 1225 (7th Cir. 1993).

Effective August 1, 2001, Division II changed its amateurism rules to allow prospective student-athletes, prior to initial full-time enrollment, to (1) accept prize money based on finish for competition in open athletics events; (2) sign a contract with a professional athletics team; (3) enter a professional draft and be drafted; (4) receive compensation for athletics participation, although compensation must end when the student-athlete enters college; and (5) compete with professionals on a professional team. Division II Bylaw 12.1.2.

These allowances are subject to a "seasons of competition rule," which requires that "[a]n individual who does not enroll in a collegiate institution as a full-time student during the regular academic term that is immediately after the date that the individual's high-school class normally graduates from high school . . . shall use a season of intercollegiate competition for each calendar year or sports season (after that date) in which the individual has participated in activities . . . in Bylaw 14.2.4.2.3." Division II Bylaw 14.2.4.2. Such activities include any team competition or training in which compensation is provided to any of the participants, any competition or training in which the individual receives compensation, any competition based on an athletics contract, any competition in relation to a professional draft, any competition organized by a professional organization, "any competition funded by a representative of an institution's athletics interest that is not an open event," and "any practice with a professional athletics team."

Division III deregulation, effective August 1, 2002, is similar to Division II's reforms in that it allows prospective student-athletes to accept prize money based on finish, sign a contract with a professional team, enter a draft and be drafted, and compete on a team with professionals. Student-athletes cannot remain under contract while competing at a Division III institution, and a student-athlete who signs a contract prior to enrollment must end the relationship with the professional team and sever all terms of the contract before enrolling at the Division III level. Unlike Division II, however, pre-enrolled student-athletes cannot have received "pay to play." Division III Bylaw 12.1.3. This is considered money above actual and necessary expenses for participation in athletics, and is different from the acceptance of prize money based on finish. NCAA Regional Rules Compliance Seminar, Division III Amateurism. Division III also adheres to the "season of competition" rule, which is triggered by activities including participation in team competition or training where any participant receives more than actual and necessary expenses, individual competition where money is received based on place finish, competition based on signing of a contract or entrance in a draft, and competition funded by a representative of a school's athletic interests that is not an open event.

In April 2002, the Division I Management Council considered, but rejected, similar amateurism reforms. Specifically, it rejected proposals that would have permitted student-athletes to enter professional drafts and compete as professionals and retain limited eligibility to compete at the intercollegiate level.

How does Division II and Division III deregulation of amateurism impact the legal validity of the NCAA's antitrust defense that its rules are necessary to preserve the distinction between amateur and professional sports?

5. *Competitive Balance Defense.* In defending NCAA rules limiting competition for student-athletes' services, the need to preserve on-field competitive balance among universities that regularly compete against each other in intercollegiate athletics is a stronger justification than maintaining "amateurism." "Competitive balance" has the dual meaning of "parity" (i.e., the extent to which all teams playing at the same level are able to play close and exciting games during a season of competition) and "potential to change" (i.e., teams' ability to improve their relative performance in terms of on-field success vis-à-vis other teams over time). Gary R. Roberts, *The NCAA, Antitrust, and Consumer Welfare*, 79 Tul. L. Rev. 2631, 2664-2665. (1996). Does preservation of competitive balance in intercollegiate athletics require uniform limits on student-athlete compensation for all levels of competition (Division I, II, and III)? Or are uniform limits within each NCAA division (or subgroup within a particular division) a less restrictive means of maintaining competitive balance?

6. *Antitrust Injury Requirement.* An antitrust plaintiff must prove that its economic loss was caused by the anticompetitive effects of the challenged restraint. Because the antitrust laws are intended to protect competition rather than individual competitors, the "antitrust injury" requirement precludes recovery for NCAA rules and conduct that are predominantly procompetitive, even if particular parties' economic interests are injured. See, e.g., *Warrior Sports, Inc. v. NCAA*, 623 F.3d 281 (6th Cir. 2010) (dismissing lacrosse stick manufacturer's antitrust claims because NCAA regulation of lacrosse equipment increases rather than reduces competition and permits plaintiff to "compete in the market on the same footing as all other participants"); *Association for Intercollegiate Athletics for Women v. NCAA*, 735 F.2d 577 (D.C. Cir. 1984) (dismissing women's intercollegiate athletics governing body claim that NCAA sponsorship of women's intercollegiate sports championships violates antitrust laws; universities chose to participate in NCAA women's championships because they are a "superior product," demonstrating legal competition on the merits); *In re Baseball Bat Antitrust Litigation*, 75 F. Supp. 2d 1189 (D. Kan. 1999) (rejecting wooden bat manufacturer's claim that NCAA's failure to establish baseball bat performance standards is antitrust violation because its nonregulation stimulated rather than restricted competition among baseball bat manufacturers).

7. *Antitrust Immunity?* Would you favor adoption of a federal statute immunizing the NCAA and its member institutions from Sherman Act §1 antitrust liability conditioned on certain requirements they must satisfy to ensure that commercialized intercollegiate athletics are primarily an educational endeavor and that student-athletes receive valuable educational benefits in exchange for their playing services? See Matthew J. Mitten, James L. Musselman, and Bruce W. Burton, *Targeted Reform of Commercialized Intercollegiate Athletics*, 47 San Diego L. Rev. 779, 843 (2010) ("Congressional antitrust immunity from section 1 of the Sherman Act would enable the NCAA and its member universities to pursue important socially desirable objectives, some of which

otherwise would violate the antitrust laws. . . . Given the shield of antitrust immunity, the NCAA could adopt legislation to curb the existing athletic arms race by imposing annual or multiyear per sport aggregate spending caps or limits on certain expenditures—coaches' salaries—for the different levels of intercollegiate athletics competition. In turn, these cost savings could be used to maintain or increase intercollegiate athletics participation opportunities in women's sports and men's nonrevenue sports").

PROBLEM 3-10

After a tryout, Talented Freshman (TF) was selected to be a "walk-on" member of the Big University football team. TF was not a heavily recruited high school football player, and he was not offered a scholarship to play football at any NCAA Football Bowl Subdivision (formerly Division I-A) university. TF was offered a partial athletic scholarship to play football by two NCAA Division II universities. NCAA Division III colleges and universities do not offer any athletic scholarships. Big University's head football coach wants to offer TF a full scholarship to play football during his freshman year. However, he cannot do so because Big University already has awarded 85 football scholarships, which is the maximum number that NCAA rules permit Division I FBS universities to award each year. TF feels he has earned a football scholarship and is very upset that Big University cannot give him one. He files an antitrust suit alleging that the NCAA's scholarship limit is an illegal output restriction designed to reduce the costs of producing Division I FBS football, which violates §1 of the Sherman Act. Does TF have a valid antitrust claim?

PROBLEM 3-11

In *White v. NCAA*, CV06-0999 (C.D. Cal., filed Feb. 17, 2006), a group of former Division I-A football and Division I basketball players asserted that an NCAA rule limiting the maximum value of their football and basketball scholarships to the value of tuition, fees, room and board, and books (which is approximately $2,500 to $3,000 less than the full annual cost of attending college) violates §1 of the Sherman Act. This case was settled before trial, but the plaintiffs sought damages and an injunction "restraining the NCAA from enforcing its unlawful and anticompetitive agreement to cap the amount of financial aid available to student-athletes at an amount that does not cover the full cost of attendance." Is this an antitrust violation?

CHAPTER
4

Regulating Olympic and International Athletics

A. INTRODUCTION

Olympic and international sports competition demonstrates that sport is a universal cultural phenomenon, which is tremendously popular and a significant part of the world's twenty-first-century global economy. It also gives rise to numerous important national and international legal issues. This chapter initially provides an overview of the Olympic Games and describes how Olympic sports are structured and governed pursuant to an international hierarchy. It then discusses how Olympic sports are internally governed within the United States and regulated by a federal statute, the Ted Stevens Olympic and Amateur Sports Act. After considering the general reluctance of courts to use U.S. law to regulate Olympic and international sports competitions, this chapter describes the jurisdiction and role of the Court of Arbitration for Sport in resolving Olympic and international sports disputes (e.g., athlete misconduct, challenged competition results, and doping violations and sanctions).

1. Origin, History, and Objectives of the Olympic Games

The Olympic Games have been held during two distinct historical time periods. The Ancient Olympics began in 776 B.C. in Elis, Greece, in the valley of Olympia, to honor the mythical Greek god Zeus. The Olympics likely were not the first athletic competitions in Greece, but represented the dawn of organized athletic activity for the Western world.

The first Olympic Games consisted of one event—a 200-meter footrace—and were subsequently expanded to include boxing, wrestling, chariot racing, and the pentathlon. Competitors included local residents in addition to those who lived outside the Greek city-states. Because of the highly competitive nature of the ancient Greeks, a victory at the Games was considered one of the greatest athletic accomplishments. The prize for winning was a simple olive tree branch, which the Greeks believed would transfer its sacred vitality to the recipient. This simple prize demonstrated the magnitude of the honor of an Olympic victory and emphasized the importance of athletics and competition in Greek life. As the Ancient Olympics grew in importance, athletes evolved from amateurs to professionals and began to train for their sports year-round and to receive substantial gifts and money from their home cities and others. The purpose of the Ancient Olympics, which is the same for the Modern Games (if not as easily recognizable today), was to promote goodwill and unity among competing nations. To facilitate this objective, a peace agreement, called "ekecheiria," or "sacred truce," was established, and provided for a three-month truce on fighting surrounding the time of the Games, which were held every four years. From their inception, the Ancient Games continued for almost 1,200 years without interruption. They were even held in 480 B.C. during the Persian War and, despite Roman control of Greece, beginning in 146 B.C. The Games embodied the Greek ideal of transforming violent urges into playful athletic competition and provided a forum for Greeks from all city-states to gather for attempted unification through athletic competition and religious ceremonies. However, in 393 A.D., the Ancient Olympics were abolished by the Christian Byzantine emperor Theodosius I because they were perceived to be a pagan festival. *Brief History of the Olympic Games*, available at http://www.nostos.com/olympics (last visited April 22, 2012).

After ending in 393 A.D., the Olympic Games were not held again until Baron Pierre de Courbetin of France announced the reestablishment of the Olympic Games in 1892. At the Congress of Paris in 1894, 13 nations met to create the Modern Games. The International Olympic Committee (IOC) was created, and the Modern Games (initially consisting of only traditional Summer Olympic events) were scheduled to be held every fourth year. Returning to their country of origin, the first Modern Games were held in Athens, Greece, in 1896 and consisted of 300 athletes from 13 countries participating in events in ten sports.

Courbetin chose the Latin words "Citius, altius, fortius" as the motto of the modern Olympic Movement. This motto connotes not only athletic achievement but also moral and educational development—"Citius: fast not only in the race, but with a quick and vibrant mind as well. Altius: higher, not only toward a coveted goal, but also toward the uplifting of an individual. Fortius: not only more courageous in the struggles on the field of play, but in life, also." Pierre de Courbetin, Olympism—Selected Writings at 585 (International Olympic Committee 2000).

In 1914 Courbetin designed the now widely recognized Olympic rings, consisting of five interlocking rings of blue, yellow, black, green, and red with a white background. He explained that they "represent the five parts of the world now won over to Olympism, ready to accept its fruitful rivalries. In addition, the six colors combined in this way reproduce the colors of every country without exception." *Id.* at 594.

The Olympic Winter Games began in 1924 and were held in the same years as the Summer Games until 1986, when the IOC decided to schedule Summer and Winter Olympic competitions in different years two years apart. The Games were canceled in 1916, 1940, and 1944 because of World Wars I and II. In modern times, the Ancient Games' Olympic truce has been renewed by the IOC with the "view to protecting, as far as possible, the interests of the athletes and sport in general, and to encourage searching for peaceful and diplomatic solutions to the conflicts around the world." *Olympic Truce*, available at http://www.olympic.org/content/the-ioc/commissions/international-relations-/olympic-truce/ (last visited August 13, 2012).

2. Organization, Governance, and Structure of the Olympic Movement

The modern Olympic Movement "is the concerted, organised, universal and permanent action, carried out under the supreme authority of the IOC, of all individuals and entities who are inspired by the values of Olympism." "Olympism is a philosophy of life, exalting and combining in a balanced whole the qualities of body, will and mind. Blending sport with culture and education, Olympism seeks to create a way of life based on the joy of effort, the educational value of good example, social responsibility and respect for universal fundamental ethical principles." International Olympic Committee, Olympic Charter, at 10, http://www.olympic.org/Documents/olympic_charter_en.pdf (last visited Jan. 8, 2013). Numerous organizations and persons are part of the Olympic Movement, including the International Olympic Committee (IOC); international sports federations (IFs), the international governing bodies for each Olympic sport; National Olympic Committees (NOCs), such as the United States Olympic Committee (USOC); national governing bodies (NGBs) for each Olympic sport in each NOC; the World Anti-Doping Agency (WADA); Court of Arbitration for Sport (CAS); and the Olympic Museum, as well as thousands of individual athletes, judges, and coaches.

The Olympic Charter governs the Olympic Movement, which codifies the fundamental principles, rules, and bylaws adopted by the IOC, and establishes rules for the production and operation of the Olympic Games. See Olympic Charter, *supra*. The goal of Olympism "is to place sport at the service of the harmonious development of man with a view to promoting the preservation of human dignity." *Id.* at 10. The goal of the Olympic Movement itself is to "contribute to building a peaceful and better world by educating youth through sport practised in accordance with Olympism and its values." *Id.*, Chap. 1, Rule 1(1). The IOC "opposes any political or commercial abuse of sport and athletes." *Id.*, Chap. 1, Rule 2(10).

The Olympic Charter states that the IOC is the "supreme authority" of the Olympic Movement, and all members are bound by its provisions and the IOC's decisions regarding its application or interpretation. *Id.*, Chap. 1, Rule 1(1). The IOC is an "international non-governmental not-for-profit organization" domiciled in Lausanne, Switzerland, and recognized by the Swiss Federal Council. *Id.*, Chap. 2, Rule 15(1). The IOC is the "authority of last resort on any question concerning the Olympic Games" (*Id.*, Chap. 1, Rule 6(3)), although those adversely affected by its decision may submit the dispute to final and binding arbitration before the Court of Arbitration for Sport. Despite its plenary governing authority, the IOC must rely on the agreement of the IFs and NOCs—and the willingness of national governments—to enforce its decisions and those of the CAS.

Emblematic of its international authority, the IOC has 106 elected individuals who serve as its representatives in their respective home countries (see International Olympic Committee, *Factsheet: IOC Members*, July 2, 2012, http://www.olympic.org/Documents/Reference_documents_Factsheets/IOC_Members.pdf); however, these individuals are not representatives of their respective countries of residence or their country's delegates to the IOC. These persons are chosen and elected by the IOC's nominations committee, and they serve for renewable eight-year terms. See generally James A.R. Nafziger, International Sports Law (2d ed.) 17-26 (Transnational Publishers, Inc. 2004).

The IOC's organizational structure consists of an executive board, its individual members, and an administrative staff. The executive board comprises the IOC president, four vice-presidents, and ten other members, all of whom are elected by secret ballot for an eight-year term. The current IOC president is Jacques Rogge of Belgium, who began his first term on July 16, 2001, and was reelected in October 2009.

Like the IOC, the IFs are nongovernmental organizations. Each IF is recognized by the IOC as the worldwide governing body for a particular sport or group of sports and encompasses the NGBs that serve as affiliates for the subject sport(s) in each country. Its statutes, practices, and activities must conform to the Olympic Charter and be approved by the IOC Executive Board. The IFs establish and enforce the rules for their respective sports; establish eligibility criteria for Olympic sports competition (subject to IOC approval); select referees, judges, or umpires for competitions; establish and provide an internal dispute resolution process; and are responsible for the technical control and direction of their sports during the Olympic Games. There are 64 recognized IFs, including members of the Association of Summer Olympic International Federations (ASOIF), the Association of International Olympic Winter Sports Federations (AIOWF), the Association of the IOC Recognised International Sports Federations (ARISF), and the General Association of International Sports Federations (GAISF), ranging from the well-known International Amateur Athletic Federation (IAAF) for track and field to the lesser-known IFs such as the International Canoe Federation (ICF).

The more than 200 NOCs develop and protect the Olympic Movement within their respective countries. Most of them are from nations, although the IOC does recognize independent territories, commonwealths, protectorates, and geographical areas as national governing bodies for Olympic sports. The NOCs are responsible for encouraging the development of high-performance sport and sports opportunities for all their citizens; recognizing NGBs for Olympic sports; taking action against discrimination and violence in sport; and fighting against the use of substances and doping procedures banned by the IOC or IFs. Each NOC has exclusive authority regarding the representation of its country at the Olympic Games and selects its Olympic teams and athletes, usually based on the recommendations of the NGB for the particular sport. The NOCs also have the authority to designate which cities may apply to host the Olympics within their respective countries.

In carrying out their responsibilities, NOCs frequently cooperate with government agencies and other nongovernmental bodies to promote sports. However, they must preserve their autonomy and resist all pressures, including those of a political, religious, or economic nature, to do anything contrary to the Olympic Charter. The NOCs are subject to the laws of their respective nations as well as the provisions of the Olympic Charter and the governing authority of the IOC. For example, the United States Olympic Committee (USOC) must comply with the Ted Stevens Olympic and Amateur Sports Act, 36 USC §§220501 et seq., and other applicable federal and state laws.

An NGB is the national governing authority for a particular sport that is affiliated with the appropriate IF and is recognized by the country's NOC. NGBs must comply with the Olympic Charter and IF rules as well as "exercise a specific and real sports activity." Olympic Charter, *supra*, Chap. 4, Rule 33. The NGBs serve a function at the national level similar to that of the IFs at the international level of athletic competition. Each NGB recognized by the USOC (e.g.,

USA Track & Field) serves as the United States' member representative in the IF for its particular sport (e.g., IAAF). Like NOCs, NGBs also are subject to applicable domestic laws within their respective countries.

In summary, the following diagram illustrates that a series of hierarchical contractual relationships defines the Olympic Movement's governing structure.

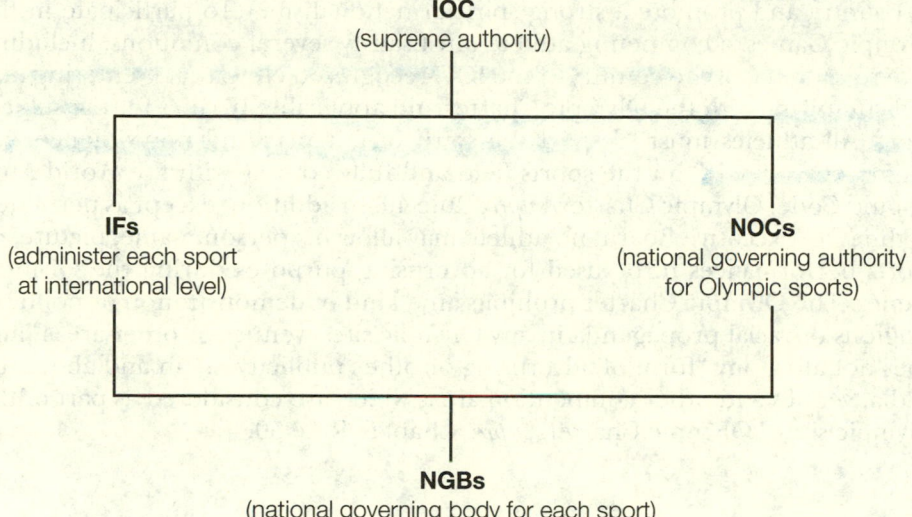

IOC
(supreme authority)

IFs
(administer each sport
at international level)

NOCs
(national governing authority
for Olympic sports)

NGBs
(national governing body for each sport)

The IOC is responsible for ensuring the regular celebration of the Summer and Winter Olympic Games and exclusively owns all rights relating thereto. There are 28 summer sports and 7 winter sports on the Olympic Program, constituting nearly 400 events. See *35 Sports*, available at http://www.olympic.org/sports (last visited Aug. 13, 2012).

The IOC selects a host city for each Olympic Games, which is entrusted with responsibility for organizing the Games along with the country's NOC, which forms an Organizing Committee for the Olympic Games (OCOG) to fulfill all responsibilities connected with the organization and hosting of the Olympic Games. The IOC collects revenues from the exploitation of commercial rights relating to the Olympic Games, some of which are distributed to the IFs, NOCs, and OCOG hosting the Games. All profits from the Games must be "applied to the development of the Olympic Movement and of sport." Olympic Charter, *supra*, Chap. 5, Rule 33(5).

The OCOG must fully comply with its contract with the IOC, NOC, and host city as well as the Olympic Charter and the IOC Executive Board's instructions. All financial responsibility for staging the Olympic Games is assumed jointly and severally by the OCOG and the host city. OCOGs have evolved into huge administrative entities, which are seemingly necessary to carry out the significant multiyear commitments necessary to successfully host the Olympic Games. An OCOG's governing body includes the IOC member(s) of the host country, the president and secretary general of the NOC, at least one representative of the host city, and various public authorities. In organizing the Olympic Games, an OCOG must treat every sport equally; abide by the IFs' rules of competition; ensure that no political demonstrations disrupt the Games; construct the necessary venues, stadiums, and other facilities; provide food and lodging for all athletes and officials; provide medical services; and accommodate the media. In addition, in light of recent world events, OCOGs now face the daunting task of ensuring the security of those competing in and attending the Games.

The Olympic Charter states that "[t]he Olympic Games are competitions between athletes in individual or team events, and not between countries." Olympic Charter, *supra*, Chap. 1, Rule 6(1). (In reality, is this an accurate characterization? Is this objective furthered when the sports media list medal counts by country and promote a strong spirit of nationalism?) To participate in the Olympic Games, a competing athlete must satisfy several conditions, including being a national of the country of the IOC-recognized NOC that is entering him and complying with the Olympic Charter and applicable IF rules for the subject sport. All athletes must "respect the spirit of fair play and non-violence and behave accordingly" on the sports field and fully comply with the World Anti-Doping Code. Olympic Charter, *supra*, Rule 40. In addition, except as permitted by the IOC Executive Board, no athlete may allow his person, name, picture, or sports performances to be used for advertising purposes during the Olympic Games. The Olympic Charter prohibits any "kind of demonstration or political, religious or racial propaganda in any Olympic sites, venues or other areas" and does not allow any "form of advertising or other publicity . . . in and above the stadia, venues and other competition areas which are considered as part of the Olympic sites." Olympic Charter, *supra*, Chap. 5, Rule 50.

B.   REGULATION OF OLYMPIC SPORTS WITHIN THE UNITED STATES

1. *Basis of Governing Body Authority and Legal Limits Thereon*

DEFRANTZ v. U.S. OLYMPIC COMMITTEE
492 F. Supp. 1181 (D.D.C. 1980)

PRATT, District Judge.

Plaintiffs, 25 athletes and one member of the Executive Board of defendant United States Olympic Committee (USOC), have moved for an injunction barring defendant USOC from carrying out a resolution, adopted by the USOC House of Delegates on April 12, 1980, not to send an American team to participate in the Games of the XXIInd Olympiad to be held in Moscow in the summer of 1980. Plaintiffs allege that in preventing American athletes from competing in the Summer Olympics, defendant has exceeded its statutory powers and has abridged plaintiffs' constitutional rights.

For the reasons discussed below, we find that plaintiffs have failed to state a claim upon which relief can be granted. Accordingly, we deny plaintiffs' claim for injunctive and declaratory relief and dismiss the action.

THE FACTS

In essence, the action before us involves a dispute between athletes who wish to compete in the Olympic Games to be held in Moscow this summer and the United States Olympic Committee, which has denied them that opportunity in the wake of the invasion and continued occupation of Afghanistan by Soviet military forces. Because this dispute confronts us with questions concerning the statutory authority of the USOC, its place and appropriate role in the international Olympic movement, and its relationship to the United States Government and with certain United States officials, we begin with a brief discussion of the organizational structure of the Olympic Games and the facts which have brought this action before us. These facts are not in dispute.

According to its Rules and By-laws, the International Olympic Committee (IOC) governs the Olympic movement and owns the rights of the Olympic games. IOC Rules provide that National Olympic Committees (NOC) may be established "as the sole authorities responsible for the representation of the respective countries at the Olympic Games," so long as the NOC's rules and regulations are approved by the IOC. The USOC is one such National Olympic Committee.

The USOC is a corporation created and granted a federal charter by Congress in 1950. Pub L. No. 81-805, 64 Stat. 899. This charter was revised by the Amateur Sports Act of 1978 Pub. L. No. 95-606, 92 Stat. 3045, 36 U.S.C. §§ 371 et seq. Under this statute, defendant USOC has "exclusive jurisdiction" and authority over participation and representation of the United States in the Olympic Games.

The routine procedure initiating the participation of a national team in Olympic competition is the acceptance by the NOC of an invitation from the Olympic Organizing Committee for the particular games. In accordance with this routine procedure under IOC Rules, the Moscow Olympic Organizing Committee extended an invitation to the USOC to participate in the summer games. Recent international and domestic events, however, have made acceptance of this invitation, which must come on or before May 24, 1980, anything but routine.

On December 27, 1979, the Soviet Union launched an invasion of its neighbor, Afghanistan. That country's ruler was deposed and killed and a new government was installed. . . .

President Carter termed the invasion a threat to the security of the Persian Gulf area as well as a threat to world peace and stability and he moved to take direct sanctions against the Soviet Union. . . .

As the affidavit of then Acting Secretary of State Warren Christopher makes clear, the Administration was concerned that "[t]he presence of American competitors would be taken by the Soviets as evidence that their invasion had faded from memory or was not a matter of great consequence or concern to this nation." The Administration's concern was sharpened because "[t]he Soviet Union has made clear that it intends the Games to serve important national political ends. For the U.S.S.R., international sports competition is an instrument of government policy and a means to advance foreign policy goals."

With these concerns in mind, the Administration strenuously urged a boycott of the Moscow games. On January 20, 1980, President Carter wrote the President of the United States Olympic Committee to urge that the USOC propose to the IOC that the 1980 summer games be transferred from Moscow, postponed, or cancelled if the Soviet forces were not withdrawn within a month. On January 23, 1980, the President delivered his State of the Union Message, in which he said that he would not support sending American athletes to Moscow while Soviet military forces remained in Afghanistan.

Following these statements, the United States House of Representatives passed, by a vote of 386 to 12, a Concurrent Resolution opposing participation by United States athletes in the Moscow Games unless Soviet troops were withdrawn from Afghanistan by February 20th. The Senate passed a similar resolution by a vote of 88 to 4. . . .

After what USOC President Kane describes in his affidavit as "full, open, complete and orderly debate by advocates of each motion," the House of Delegates, on a secret ballot, passed by a vote of 1,604 to 798, a resolution [not to enter a U.S. team in the Moscow Olympics]. . . .

Plaintiffs describe these attempts by the Administration to persuade the USOC to vote not to send an American team to Moscow as "a campaign to coerce defendant USOC into compliance with the President's demand for a boycott of the Olympic Games." In addition, plaintiffs' complaint alleges that the President and other Executive Branch officials threatened to terminate federal funding of the USOC and that they raised the possibility of revoking the federal income tax exemption of the USOC if the USOC did not support the President's decision to boycott the 1980 Games. The complaint also alleges that these officials state that the Federal government would provide increased funding to the USOC if the USOC supported a boycott. . . .

Plaintiffs allege that unredressed, these violations will result in great and irreparable injury to the athletes. "Many would lose a once-in-a-lifetime opportunity to participate in the Olympic Games, and the honor and prestige that such participation affords. Most of the class members are at or near their physical peaks at the present time and will not physically be capable of reaching the same or higher levels at a later period of their lives."

In summary, plaintiffs ask this court to declare the April 12, 1980 resolution of the USOC House of Delegates null and void because it violated statutory authority and constitutional provisions and to permanently enjoin the USOC from carrying out that resolution. . . .

ANALYSIS

1.   THE AMATEUR SPORTS ACT OF 1978

Plaintiffs allege in their complaint that by its decision not to send an American team to compete in the summer Olympic Games in Moscow, defendant USOC has violated the Amateur Sports Act of 1978. . . . Reduced to their essentials, these allegations are that the Act does not give, and that Congress intended to deny, the USOC the authority to decide not to enter an American team in the Olympics, except perhaps for sports-related reasons, and that the Act guarantees to certain athletes a right to compete in the Olympic Games which defendant denied them. . . .

(a)   The USOC's Authority Not to Send a Team to Moscow

The United States Olympic Committee was first incorporated and granted a federal charter in 1950. However, predecessors to the now federally-chartered USOC have existed since 1896, and since that time, they have exercised the authority granted by the International Olympic Committee to represent the United States as its National Olympic Committee in matters pertaining to participation in Olympic games. It is unquestioned by plaintiffs that under the International Olympic Committees Rules and By-laws, the National Olympic Committees have the right to determine their nation's participation in the Olympics. IOC Rule 24B provides that "NOCs shall be the sole authorities responsible for the representation of the respective countries at the Olympic Games . . ." and Chapter 5, paragraph 7 of the By-laws to Rule 24 provides that "*[r]epresentation* covers the decision to participate. . . ." (emphasis supplied). Nothing in the IOC Charter, Rules or By-laws requires a NOC, such as the USOC, to accept an invitation to participate in any particular Olympic contest and the President of the IOC has said that participation in the Olympic games is entirely voluntary. As defendant has argued, an invitation to participate is just that, an invitation which may be accepted or declined.

Because defendant USOC clearly has the power under IOC Rules to decide not to enter an American team in Olympic competition, the question then becomes whether the Amateur Sports Act of 1978, which rewrote the USOC's charter, denies the USOC that power. . . .

Plaintiffs' argument is simple and straightforward: The Act by its terms does not expressly confer on the USOC the power to decline to participate in the Olympic Games, and if any such power can be inferred from the statute, the power must be exercised for sports-related reasons. Defendant and the Government respond that the Act gives the USOC broad powers, including the authority to decide not to accept an invitation to send an American team to the Olympics.

The principal substantive powers of the USOC are found in § 375(a) of the Act. In determining whether the USOC's authority under the Act encompasses the right to decide not to participate in an Olympic contest, we must read these provisions in the context in which they were written. In writing this legislation, Congress did not create a new relationship between the USOC and the IOC. Rather, it recognized an already long-existing relationship between the two and statutorily legitimized that relationship with a federal charter and federal incorporation. The legislative history demonstrates Congressional awareness that the USOC and its predecessors, as the National Olympic Committee for the United States, have had a continuing relationship with the IOC since 1896. Congress was necessarily aware that a National Olympic Committee is a creation and a creature of the International Olympic Committee, to whose rules and regulations it must conform. The NOC gets its power and its authority from the IOC, the sole proprietor and owner of the Olympic Games.

In view of Congress' obvious awareness of these facts, we would expect that if Congress intended to limit or deny to the USOC powers it already enjoyed as a National Olympic Committee, such limitation or denial would be clear and explicit. No such language appears in the statute. . . . [W]e find a compatibility and not a conflict between the Act and the IOC Rules on the issue of the authority of the USOC to decide whether or not to accept an invitation to field an American team at the Olympics. The language of the statute is broad enough to confer this authority, and we find that Congress must have intended that the USOC exercise that authority in this area, which it already enjoyed because of its long-standing relationship with the IOC. We accordingly conclude that the USOC has the authority to decide not to send an American team to the Olympics.

Plaintiffs next argue that if the USOC does have the authority to decide not to accept an invitation to send an American team to the Moscow Olympics, that decision must be based on "sports-related considerations." . . .

The provision on which plaintiffs place reliance by analogy is specifically concerned with eliminating the feuding between various amateur athletic organizations and national governing bodies which for so long characterized amateur athletics. As all parties recognize, this friction, such as the well-publicized power struggles between the NCAA and the AAU, was a major reason for passage of the Act, and the provisions plaintiffs cite, among others, are aimed at eliminating this senseless strife, which the Senate and House Committee reports indicate had dramatically harmed the ability of the United States to compete effectively in international competition. In order to eliminate this internecine squabbling, the Act elevated the USOC to a supervisory role over the various amateur athletic organizations, and provided that the USOC establish procedures for the swift and equitable settlement of these disputes. As indicated above, it also directed that the national governing bodies of the various sports could only withhold their approvals of international competition for sports-related reasons. Previously, many of these bodies had withheld their sanction of certain athletic competitions in order to further their own interests at the expense of other groups and to the detriment of athletes wishing to participate.

In brief, this sports-related limitation is intimately tied to the specific purpose of curbing the arbitrary and unrestrained power of various athletic organizations subordinate to the USOC not to allow athletes to compete in international competition below the level of the Olympic Games and the Pan American Games. This purpose has nothing to do with a decision by the USOC to exercise authority granted by the IOC to decide not to participate in an Olympic competition. . . .

We therefore conclude that the USOC not only had the authority to decide not to send an American team to the summer Olympics, but also that it could do so for reasons not directly related to sports considerations.

(b)   Athletes' Statutory Right to Compete in the Olympics

Plaintiffs argue that the Act provides, "in express terms" an "Athlete's Bill of Rights," pointing to the following provisions in the Act's "objects and purposes" section, which directs that the USOC shall:

> provide for the swift resolution of conflicts and disputes involving amateur athletes, national governing bodies, and amateur sports organizations, and protect the opportunity of any amateur athlete, coach, trainer, manager, administrator, or official to participate in amateur athletic competition. (emphasis supplied).

36 U.S.C. § 374(8) . . .

The Senate Report makes clear that the language relied on by plaintiffs is not designed to provide any substantive guarantees, let alone a Bill of Rights. Further, to the extent that any guarantees of a right to compete are included in the USOC Constitution as a result of this provision, they do not include a right that amateur athletes may compete in the Olympic Games despite a decision by the USOC House of Delegates not to accept an invitation to enter an American team in the competition. This provision simply was not designed to extend so far. Rather, it was designed to remedy the jurisdictional disputes among amateur athletic bodies, not disputes between athletes and the USOC itself over the exercise of the USOC's discretion not to participate in the Olympics.

(c)   Statutory Cause of Action

Plaintiffs argue that they have a private cause of action under the Amateur Sports Act of 1978 to maintain an action to enforce their rights under that Act.

This argument assumes (1) the existence of a right and (2) the capability of enforcing that right by a private cause of action. As the foregoing discussion establishes, we have found that the statute does not guarantee plaintiffs a right to compete in the Olympics if the USOC decides not to send an American team to the Olympic Games and we have found that defendant has violated no provision of the Act. Thus, the "right" the plaintiffs seek to enforce under the Act simply does not exist. (Plaintiffs have pointed to no express private right of action in the statute, and none exists). Under these circumstances, we cannot find that plaintiffs have an implied private right of action under the Amateur Sports Act to enforce a right which does not exist. . . .

[W]e find that plaintiffs have no implied private right of action under the Amateur Sports Act of 1978 to maintain this suit.

2.   CONSTITUTIONAL CLAIMS

Plaintiffs have alleged that the decision of the USOC not to enter an American team in the summer Olympics has violated certain rights guaranteed to plaintiffs under the First, Fifth and Ninth Amendments to the United States Constitution. This presents us with two questions: (1) whether the USOC's decision was "governmental action" (state action), and, assuming state action is found, (2) whether the USOC's decision abridged any constitutionally protected rights.

(a)   *State Action*

Although federally chartered, defendant is a private organization. Because the Due Process Clause of the Fifth Amendment, on which plaintiffs place great reliance, applies only to actions by the federal government, plaintiffs must show that the USOC vote is a "governmental act," i.e., state action. . . .

Plaintiffs clearly recognize this, but they argue that by the actions of certain federal officials, the federal government initiated, encouraged, and approved of the result reached (i.e., the vote of the USOC not to send an American team to the summer Olympics). Plaintiffs advance a novel theory. Essentially, their argument is that the campaign of governmental persuasion, personally led by President Carter, crossed the line from "governmental recommendation," which plaintiffs find acceptable and presumably necessary to the operation of our form of government, into the area of "affirmative pressure that effectively places the government's prestige behind the challenged action," and thus, results in state action. We cannot agree. . . .

Here there is no such control. The USOC is an independent body, and nothing in its chartering statute gives the federal government the right to control that body or its officers. Furthermore, the facts here do not indicate that the federal government was able to exercise any type of "de facto" control over the USOC. The USOC decided by a secret ballot of its House of Delegates. The federal government may have had the power to prevent the athletes from participating in the Olympics even if the USOC had voted to allow them to participate, but it did not have the power to make them vote in a certain way. All it had was the power of persuasion. We cannot equate this with control. To do so in cases of this type would be to open the door and usher the courts into what we believe is a largely nonjusticiable realm, where they would find themselves in the untenable position of determining whether a certain level, intensity, or type of "Presidential" or "Administration" or "political" pressure amounts to sufficient control over a private entity so as to invoke federal jurisdiction.

no state action! (margin note)

We accordingly find that the decision of the USOC not to send an American team to the summer Olympics was not state action, and therefore, does not give rise to an actionable claim for the infringements of the constitutional rights alleged.

(b)   Constitutionally Protected Rights

if SA... (margin note)

Assuming arguendo that the vote of the USOC constituted state action, we turn briefly to plaintiffs' contention that by this action they have been deprived of their constitutional rights to liberty, to self-expression, to travel, and to pursue their chosen occupation of athletic endeavor. Were we to find state action in this case, we would conclude that defendant USOC has violated no constitutionally protected right of plaintiffs. . . .

Plaintiffs have been unable to draw our attention to any court decision which finds that the rights allegedly violated here enjoy constitutional protection, and we can find none. Plaintiffs would expand the constitutionally-protected scope of liberty and self-expression to include the denial of an amateur athlete's right to compete in an Olympic contest when that denial was the result of a decision by a supervisory athletic organization acting well within the limits of its authority. Defendant has not denied plaintiffs the right to engage in every amateur athletic competition. Defendant has not denied plaintiffs the right to engage in their chosen occupation. Defendant has not even denied plaintiffs the right to travel, only the right to travel for one specific purpose. We can find no justification and no authority for the expansive reading of the Constitution which plaintiffs urge. To find as plaintiffs recommend would be to open the floodgates to a torrent of lawsuits. The courts have correctly recognized that many of life's disappointments, even major ones, do not enjoy constitutional protection. This is one such instance.

At this point, we find it appropriate to note that we have respect and admiration for the discipline, sacrifice, and perseverance which earns young men and women the opportunity to compete in the Olympic Games. Ordinarily, talent alone has determined whether an American would have the privilege of participating in the Olympics. This year, unexpectedly, things are different. We express no view on the merits of the decision made. We do express our understanding of the deep disappointment and frustrations felt by thousands of American athletes. In doing so, we also recognize that the responsibilities of citizenship often fall more heavily on some than on others. Some are called to military duty. Others never serve. Some return from military service unscathed. Others never return. These are the simple, although harsh, facts of life, and they are immutable.

NOTES AND QUESTIONS

1. *USOC's Contractual and Legal Obligations.* As the *DeFrantz* court observed, the USOC is authorized by the International Olympic Committee to represent the United States in all matters relating to participation in the Olympic Games. The USOC is bound by contract to follow the IOC's Charter, rules and regulations, and executive board decisions. Did the USOC comply with its obligation to resist political pressure not to do anything contrary to the Olympic Charter? If the USOC violated the Olympic Charter, would the *DeFrantz* plaintiffs have a valid legal basis for obtaining effective relief from a

U.S. court? For background information and an in-depth analysis of the U.S. boycott of the 1980 Olympic Games, see James A. R. Nafziger, International Sports Law (2d. ed.) at 260-264 (Transnational Publishers, Inc. 2004). In addition to the United States, more than 60 other countries, including Japan, West Germany, China, the Philippines, Argentina, and Canada, were part of this boycott. In response, 14 Eastern Bloc countries including the Soviet Union, Cuba, and East Germany (but not Romania) boycotted the *retaliated* 1984 Olympic Games in Los Angeles.

As a federally chartered corporation, the USOC also must comply with the provisions of the Amateur Sports Act (ASA), which was amended in 1998 by the Ted Stevens Olympic and Amateur Sports Act, 36 U.S.C. §220501 et seq. What if the USOC has conflicting obligations under IOC rules and federal law? For example, the IOC requires that a majority of the members of a NOC's governing body must be affiliated with the Olympic Movement, but Congress enacted legislation requiring that a majority of the USOC's board of directors be independent. During June 2003 congressional hearings regarding this legislation, Senator John McCain asked why "a corporation chartered by the U.S. Congress has to comply with the IOC." Vicki Michaelis, *McCain Seeks Swift USOC Fix*, USA Today, June 25, 2003, at 8C. See *Michels v. USOC*, 741 F.2d 155, 159 (7th Cir. 1984) (J. Posner, concurring) (observing that the international sports governing body "can thumb its collective nose at the U.S. Olympic Committee" for disregarding its rules and that the IOC could disqualify an American team); *Akiyama v. U.S. Judo Inc.*, 181 F. Supp. 2d 1179, 1188 (W.D. Wash. 2002) (American court's invalidation of athletic governing body's rule on ground that it violates federal law prohibiting religious discrimination "would have no force over international organizations who are not parties to this litigation or in international competitions such as the Olympics and World Championships").

2. *USOC's Governing Authority.* As the *DeFrantz* court noted, the ASA empowered the USOC to serve as the coordinating body within the United States for international amateur athletic competition, including the Olympics, Paralympics, and the Pan-American Games. Pursuant to this authority, the USOC recognizes a single U.S. amateur sports organization as the national governing body for each Olympic sport. The Amateur Sports Act establishes arbitration as the procedure for finally resolving disputes regarding which organization is entitled to be the national governing body for a particular sport, and the USOC is bound to accept a judicially confirmed arbitration award. *United States Wrestling Federation v. Wrestling Division of the AAU, Inc.*, 545 F. Supp. 1053 (N.D. Ohio 1982).

3. *Olympic Sports Governing Bodies Not State Actors.* The Supreme Court has confirmed that the USOC is a private entity, not a state actor, whose conduct is not subject to the constraints of the federal constitution. In *San Francisco Arts & Athletics, Inc. v. United States Olympic Committee*, 483 U.S. 522, 543-44 (1987), the Court explained, "The fact that Congress granted it a corporate charter does not render the USOC a [g]overnment agent. All corporations act under charters granted by a government, usually by a State. They do not thereby lose their essentially private character. . . . Moreover, the intent on the part of Congress to help the USOC obtain funding does not change the analysis. The Government may subsidize private entities without assuming constitutional responsibility for their actions." Although the USOC's

activities serve a national interest, the Court concluded that the coordination of amateur sports is not a traditional governmental function and found no evidence that the federal government coerced or significantly encouraged the USOC's exercise of its exclusive control over the Olympic marks.

For similar reasons, lower courts have held that the U.S. NGBs for Olympic sports also are not "state actors;" therefore, their rules and conduct are not subject to the constraints of the federal constitution. *Behagen v. Amateur Basketball Assn. of the United States*, 884 F.2d 524 (10th Cir. 1989); *Harding v. United States Figure Skating Assn.*, 851 F. Supp. 1476 (D. Ore. 1994), *vacated on other grounds*, 879 F. Supp. 1053 (1995).

4. *No Private Right of Action Under ASA.* Courts generally follow *DeFrantz*'s holding that athletes have no express or implied private right of action under the ASA and do not recognize claims against the USOC or NGBs seeking injunctive relief or judicial orders regarding their eligibility to compete in protected competitions. See, e.g., *Slaney v. International Amateur Athletic Federation*, 244 F.3d 580 (7th Cir. 2001); *Martinez v. USOC*, 802 F.2d 1275 (10th Cir. 1986); *Oldfield v. Athletic Congress*, 779 F.2d 505 (9th Cir. 1985); *Michels v. USOC*, 741 F.2d 155 (7th Cir. 1984); *Walton-Floyd v. USOC*, 965 S.W.2d 35 (Tex. Ct. App. 1998); *Cantrell v. United States Soccer Federation*, 924 P.2d 789 (Okla. App. 1996); *Dolan v. United States Equestrian Team*, 257 N.J. Super. 314 (N.J. App. 1992). But see *Sternberg v. USA Nat'l Karate-Do Federation, Inc.*, 123 F. Supp. 2d 659 (E.D.N.Y. 2000) (athlete allegedly excluded from competing in a protected competition because of her gender has an implied right of action for damages against an NGB for violating the ASA's prohibition against gender discrimination).

2. *Legal Framework for Resolving Domestic Athlete Eligibility Disputes*

The USOC typically grants the recognized NGB for each sport the authority to select U.S. athletes to participate in the Olympics and other international athletic competitions. To be eligible to be recognized by the USOC as the NGB for an Olympic sport, a sports organization must provide all athletes with an equal opportunity to participate "without discrimination on the basis of race, color, religion, sex, age, or national origin." 36 U.S.C. §220522(a)(8). Each NGB has an affirmative duty to encourage and support athletic participation opportunities for women and those with disabilities. 36 U.S.C. §220524(6)-(7). An NGB's eligibility and participation criteria for U.S. athletes to participate in the Olympic, Paralympic, and Pan American Games must be consistent with those of the IF for its sport. 36 U.S.C. §220522(a)(14).

The Amateur Sports Act (ASA) requires the USOC to establish a procedure for investigating and resolving complaints by athletes alleging that an NGB has violated these requirements, which adversely affects his or her eligibility to compete. 36 U.S.C. §220509 (a). The ASA mandates that the USOC establish a procedure for "swift and equitable resolution" of disputes "relating to the opportunity of an amateur athlete . . . to participate" in the Olympics, Paralympics, Pan-American Games, and world championship competitions ("protected competitions"). *Id.* The USOC is required to hire an athlete ombudsman to provide independent advice to athletes (free of charge) regarding resolution of disputes regarding his or her eligibility to participate in these competitions.

Section 9 (formerly Article IX) of the USOC's Bylaws creates some important procedural and substantive rights for an "amateur athlete" (defined as "any athlete who meets the eligibility standards established by the [NGB] or Paralympic Sports Organization for the sport in which the athlete competes"), which also protects professional athletes who are eligible to participate in the Olympic Games and other international sports competitions. No NGB, "may deny or threaten to deny any amateur athlete the opportunity to participate" in a protected competition. An athlete may file a complaint with the USOC against an NGB that declares him or her ineligible to participate in a protected competition. Pursuant to Section 9, the USOC is required "by all reasonable means at its disposal" to "protect the right of an amateur athlete to participate if selected (or to attempt to qualify for selection to participate) as an athlete representing the United States" in any protected competition. The USOC must "seek information from the parties" if an athlete files a complaint and attempt to resolve the matter. The ASA gives an athlete the right to submit an eligibility dispute with an NGB to final and binding arbitration in accordance with the Commercial Rules of the American Arbitration Association (AAA) if it is not resolved by the USOC to his or her satisfaction. Section 9 arbitration awards are published and available at http://www2.teamusa.org/About-the-USOC/Organization/Legal/Arbitration-and-Hearing-Panel-Cases/Section-9 .aspx.

As illustrated by the following case, the Amateur Sports Act generally preempts state law claims by U.S. athletes arising out of eligibility disputes regarding protected competitions except for a breach of contract action to require the USOC or an NGB to follow their own rules and fairly apply them.

SLANEY v. INTERNATIONAL AMATEUR ATHLETIC FEDERATION

244 F.3d 580 (7th Cir.), *cert. denied*, 534 U.S. 828 (2001)

FLAUM, Chief Judge.

Former Olympic runner Mary Decker Slaney ("Slaney") brought suit against the International Amateur Athletic Federation ("IAAF") and the United States Olympic Committee ("USOC") shortly after an IAAF arbitration panel determined that Slaney had committed a doping offense. Slaney's complaint raised a litany of state-law claims [arising out of her positive test for the banned substance testosterone based on an elevated T/E ratio and suspension by the IAAF, the international governing federation for track and field]. . . .

I.   BACKGROUND

In the course of her storied career, middle-distance runner Mary Decker Slaney has captured a multitude of United States and world records. She is considered by many to be one of the most celebrated female athletes of the past century, as well as one of the greatest runners of all-time. . . .

. . . In June of 1996, she competed in the 5000- and 1500-meter races in the national trials for the Atlanta Olympics. Following her 5000-meter race, Slaney provided the USOC with a urine sample, which was tested for prohibited substances including exogenous testosterone.

Because current technology cannot detect the presence of prohibited testosterone in the body, testing programs measure the ratio of testosterone to epitestosterone ("T/E") in the body. This test, referred to as the T/E test, assumes that an ordinary T/E ratio in humans is one to one, and thus any ratio of above six to one is consistent with "blood doping." The ratio was established at six to one in order to account for non-doping factors that might cause elevated ratios in female athletes. Factors which may influence the T/E ratio include an individual changing birth control pills, age, menstrual cycle, bacterial contamination of the urine sample, and alcohol use.

Slaney's test . . . revealed that Slaney's T/E ratio was elevated significantly beyond the permitted six to one ratio.[1] . . . The IAAF's investigating doctor analyzed Slaney's samples, her past test results, and two additional samples. Slaney claimed that her elevated level was the result of (1) her menstrual cycle, and (2) her changing of birth control pills. Furthermore, Slaney posited that there was no scientific validity to the hypothesis that a T/E ratio above six to one was not normal for female athletes. Nonetheless, on February 5, 1997, the IAAF adopted the investigating doctor's recommendation and found Slaney's specimen positive for the prohibited substance testosterone.

As a result of the IAAF's decision, IAAF and USOC rules required the [United States Track & Field Association ("USATF")] to hold a hearing to determine whether Slaney had committed a doping offense. . . .

Slaney received her hearing before the USATF Doping Hearing Board on September 14, 1997. The Hearing Board, unpersuaded by the testimony of the IAAF's investigating doctor, unanimously determined that no doping violation had occurred. . . .

The IAAF was unsatisfied with the USATF Hearing Board's findings, and invoked arbitration of the USATF's decision. Slaney and the USATF opposed arbitration, but both were represented before the IAAF Arbitral Panel ("the Tribunal"). In late January 1999, the Tribunal issued an interlocutory decision upholding the IAAF's interpretation of how to adjudicate a testosterone doping offense, and found that the rules were neither vague nor inconsistent. Thus, once the IAAF showed that Slaney had a T/E ratio greater than six to one, Slaney had to come forth and show by clear and convincing evidence that the elevated ratio was attributable to a pathological or physiological condition. Believing that it was scientifically impossible to prove by clear and convincing evidence that her high T/E ratio was due to pathological or physiological factors, Slaney withdrew from the arbitration, followed by the USATF. Ultimately, the Tribunal ruled that Slaney had committed a doping offense. . . .

B.   STATE-LAW CLAIMS AGAINST THE USOC

. . . Slaney's complaint alleges state-law violations against the USOC. . . . The district court granted USOC's motion to dismiss after determining that the Amateur Sports Act preempted Slaney's state-law claims against the [USOC],

---

1. Specifically, Slaney's samples tested at ratios of 9.5:1 to 11.6:1.

and that the Act did not provide for a private right of action under which Slaney could seek to have those claims addressed by the district court. Slaney challenges the decision of the district court, arguing that the preemption doctrine does not apply in this arena, such that the Amateur Sports Act poses no jurisdictional barrier to the adjudication of Slaney's state-law claims against the USOC. . . .

We begin by noting that Slaney does not challenge the district court's statement that the Amateur Sports Act creates no private right of action. . . . Thus, we concentrate our inquiry on the issue of whether the Amateur Sports Act precludes the court from examining Slaney's state-law claims.

According to the Amateur Sports Act, one of the purposes of the USOC is to exercise exclusive jurisdiction over all matters pertaining to United States participation in the Olympic Games. *See* 36 U.S.C. § 220503(3). The Act also states that the USOC is designed "to provide swift resolution of conflicts and disputes involving amateur athletes, national governing bodies, and amateur sports organizations," and "to encourage and provide assistance to amateur athletic activities for women." *Id.* at §§ 220503(8), 220503(12).

Beginning with the often quoted language from the concurrence in *Michels v. United States Olympic Committee*, the district court reiterated that "there can be few less suitable bodies than the federal courts for determining the eligibility, or procedures for determining the eligibility, of athletes to participate in the Olympic Games." 741 F.2d 155, 159 (7th Cir. 1984) (Posner, J., concurring). From there, the court cited numerous cases which have adopted the principle that eligibility decisions fall within the USOC's exclusive jurisdiction over all matters pertaining to United States participation in the Olympic Games. For example, in *Dolan v. United States Equestrian Team, Inc.*, 257 N.J. Super. 314, 608 A.2d 434, 437 (App. Div. 1992), the court focused on the need for uniformity in determining questions of eligibility, and held "that it would be inappropriate to attribute different or unique meanings to [the Amateur Sports Act's] provisions in New Jersey and thus create a jurisdictional sanctuary from the Congressional determination that these types of disputes should be resolved outside the judicial processes." Similarly, in *Walton-Floyd v. United States Olympic Committee*, 965 S.W.2d 35, 40 (Tex. Ct. App. 1998), the court noted that "[t]he interest of maintaining consistent interpretations among jurisdictions requires the Act to preempt claims asserted under state tort law. To hold a common law duty exists outside the scope of the Act, thereby enabling an individual athlete to bring suit, threatens to override legislative intent and opens the door to inconsistent interpretations of the Act." We agree with the district court and the courts in *Dolan* and *Walton-Floyd* that strict questions of athletes' eligibility are preempted by the Amateur Sports Act's grant of exclusive jurisdiction to the USOC over all matters pertaining to United States participation in the Olympic Games. However, that conclusion does not end our analysis.

Despite the fact that the district court specifically noted its ruling was not based on a finding that the Amateur Sports Act was a complete preemption to all state-law claims, Slaney devotes an ample portion of her brief to arguing that the complete preemption doctrine should not be applied in this context. There is no disagreement that state-law causes of action can be brought against the USOC. However, when it comes to challenging the eligibility determination of the USOC, only a very specific claim will avoid the impediment to subject matter jurisdiction that § 220503(3) poses.

In *Foschi v. United States Swimming Inc.*, 916 F. Supp. 232 (E.D.N.Y. 1996) — a case relied upon by Slaney for the proposition that the Amateur Sports Act does not create complete preemption — the court addressed issues of federal juris-diction in the context of state-law claims against the USOC, and other amateur athletic organizations. While the district court did not dismiss those claims as being preempted by the Amateur Sports Act, that decision can be understood by examining the claims alleged. There, the plaintiff alleged that her contrac-tual due process right was violated when United States Swimming, among other things, contravened its own rules. While there is no dispute that the USOC has exclusive jurisdiction when it comes to eligibility determinations, the courts can still play a role in ensuring that the organization follows its rules for determining eligibility. The extent of the courts' powers in this area was previously examined by way of a suit brought by an athlete who captured the world's attention for rea-sons other than her competitive achievements. In *Harding v. United States Figure Skating Ass'n*, 851 F. Supp. 1476, 1479 (D. Or. 1994), *vacated on other grounds*, 879 F. Supp. 1053 (D. Or. 1995), the court defined (we believe correctly) the limited role that federal courts should play in eligibility determinations. There, the court cautioned that "courts should rightly hesitate before intervening in disciplinary hearings held by private associations. . . . Intervention is appropri-ate only in the most extraordinary circumstances, where the association has clearly breached its own rules, that breach will imminently result in *serious* and irreparable harm to the plaintiff, and the plaintiff has exhausted all internal remedies." Yet, while carving out this limited exception to the preemption cre-ated by the Amateur Sports Act, the opinion forewarned that while examining whether internal rules had been complied with, the courts "should not inter-vene in the merits of the underlying dispute."

With this understanding of the limits of preemption, we turn to Slaney's claims against the USOC. Slaney suggests that nothing in the Act precludes her from bringing her state-law claims regarding the USOC's administration of its drug testing program, and specifically "the unlawful manner in which the USOC conducts its doping program." Based on our analysis above, we disagree. An inspection of the state-law claims that Slaney brings against the USOC reveals that, despite her best efforts to suggest to the contrary, Slaney is challenging the method by which the USOC determines eligibility of its athletes. Slaney's first state-law cause of action against the USOC is a breach of contract claim. Slaney suggests that the USOC violated its contractual obligations to Slaney by which she suffered damages. While Slaney attempts to skirt the issue, what she is actu-ally alleging is that she was injured by the USOC's determination that she was ineligible to compete. Similarly, Slaney's negligence claim against the USOC posits that the USOC breached a duty to Slaney by using the T/E ratio as a proxy for doping, and that as a result Slaney was damaged. Slaney's other state-law claims are no different. Examination of any of those claims would require an Article III court to examine as an underlying issue the validity of the T/E test, an endeavor we cannot partake in.

. . . Slaney cannot escape the fact that her state-law claims, whether framed as breach of contract, negligence, breach of fiduciary duty, fraud, constructive fraud, or negligent misrepresentation, are actually challenges to the method by which the USOC determines eligibility of athletes. Slaney does not suggest that the organization contravened its own guidelines, and as Slaney freely admits, the Amateur Sports Act creates no private cause of action. Thus, the district court was correct in determining that it lacked subject matter jurisdiction over Slaney's state-law claims against the USOC. . . .

District court lacked jurisdiction!

1. *Preemption of State Law Claims by ASA.* If an athlete has no private right of action under the Stevens Act, why did the court hold that Mary Slaney's state-law claims against the USOC are preempted?

In *Lee v. United States Taekwondo Union*, 331 F. Supp. 2d 1252 (D. Haw. 2004), the plaintiff alleged that he was removed as coach of the 2004 U.S. Olympic tae kwon do team because of his Korean ancestry. Consistent with *Slaney*, the court held that his state-law claims challenging the national governing body's eligibility requirements and seeking reinstatement as coach of the team are preempted by the Amateur Sports Act. However, it ruled that the ASA does not supersede or nullify federal antidiscrimination laws and permitted plaintiff to assert his race discrimination claim under 42 U.S.C. §1981. Although the plaintiff could recover money damages for successfully proving his claim at trial, the court refused to grant preliminary injunctive relief ordering the coach's reinstatement because doing so would interfere with the USOC's exclusive authority to establish a process for resolving Olympic participation disputes pursuant to the ASA. As *Slaney* notes, state law breach of contract claims against an NGB are not preempted. Courts have recognized and enforced an athlete's contractual right to require a governing body to follow its own rules, provide appropriate due process, and take action consistent with its rules and adjudicatory findings. See, e.g., *Schulz v. United States Boxing Assn.*, 105 F.3d 127 (3d Cir. 1997) (athlete possesses a contractual right to have governing body follow own rules and disqualify a competitor for positive drug test); *Gahan v. U.S. Amateur Confederation of Roller Skating*, 382 F. Supp. 2d 1127 (D. Neb. 2005) (preliminary injunction denied because no evidence sport's governing body will infringe athlete's contractual due process rights); *Lindemann v. American Horse Shows Assn., Inc.*, 624 N.Y.S.2d 723, 734 (N.Y. Sup. Ct. 1994) (holding that athletes' suspensions were "arbitrary and capricious and imposed without a meaningful hearing and in the absence of substantial evidence").

In *Harding v. U.S. Figure Skating*, 851 F. Supp. 1476 (D. Or. 1994), *vacated on other grounds*, 879 F. Supp. 1053 (D. Or. 1995), the court preliminarily enjoined the United States Figure Skating Association (USFSA) from conducting a disciplinary proceeding against Tonya Harding until she had sufficient time to prepare a defense to its charges against her. Figure skater Nancy Kerrigan's knee was clubbed outside a Detroit ice rink by Harding's associates. As a result of her injury, Kerrigan was forced to withdraw from the U.S. Figure Skating Championship, which was won by Harding. This victory earned her a performance-based spot on the U.S. Olympic team. Thereafter, USFSA instituted a disciplinary proceeding against Harding for alleged unethical conduct. The then-existing USOC Code of Conduct required that all members of the U.S. Olympic team conduct themselves "in conformity with traditions of the Olympic Games." This incident also led to a criminal investigation that sought to determine Harding's knowledge of, or involvement in, the attack on Kerrigan.

The court found that USFSA violated its bylaws, which required a disciplinary proceeding to be held on a date "reasonably convenient for all parties." Observing that "[w]hen one party to a contract is given discretion in the performance of some aspect of the contract, that discretion must be exercised in good faith," it concluded that the date unilaterally set by USFSA "was arbitrary and manifestly unreasonable, and would severely prejudice plaintiff's chances of obtaining a fair hearing." *Id.* at 1479. It explained:

> This is one of those rare cases where judicial intervention was appropriate. It appeared at the time that had defendant not been enjoined from holding the hearing on March 10, plaintiff would have suffered serious irreparable harm. Defendant argued that the matter was not ripe because the outcome of the hearing was unknown. If the only issue was whether plaintiff should have been allowed to skate in the World Championships in Japan later that month, defendant's point might have been well taken, since injunctive relief could still be sought at the conclusion of the disciplinary hearing. In this particular case, however, merely holding the hearing on March 10 would have caused plaintiff to suffer irreparable harm. In order to maintain her right to contest the decision of the Hearing Panel, plaintiff would have been obliged to appear before the panel and prematurely present her defense without having adequate time to prepare for that hearing. If the Hearing Panel found her guilty as charged, the resultant publicity could have severely prejudiced her chances for a fair trial in any future criminal case. Plaintiff would also have been obliged to decide upon and publicly disclose a defense strategy for both the civil and criminal matters before she had time to conduct full discovery and interview witnesses. Finally, the entire testimony, including information that has heretofore not been made public, would inevitably have been leaked to the media, despite defendant's best intentions to maintain the confidentiality of the proceedings, thereby further poisoning plaintiff's chance of obtaining a fair trial in the criminal proceeding. Under the circumstances, plaintiff's attorneys might well have advised their client not to attend the hearing. In that case, plaintiff would likely have forfeited any right to contest the results of the hearing. Her failure to contest the charges would have also resulted in her being found guilty in the court of public opinion.

Id. at 1479. The court "merely ordered defendant to comply with the requirement in its own bylaws that the hearing be set at a time reasonably convenient for all parties" (but rejected plaintiff's request that the disciplinary hearing be postponed until after resolution of the criminal charges against her) and refused to "take any position upon the merits of the disciplinary proceeding." *Id.* at 1480.

Despite being forced to withdraw from the U.S. Figure Skating Championship because of her injury, Nancy Kerrigan was awarded a spot on the U.S. Olympic team and won a silver medal. Tonya Harding skated at the 1994 Olympics but fell during her routine and did not medal.

2. *Implied Antitrust Immunity.* Courts have held that the Amateur Sports Act creates implied immunity for antitrust claims arising out of an athlete's ineligibility to participate in a sport. *Behagen v. Amateur Basketball Assn. of the United States*, 884 F.2d 524, 529 (10th Cir. 1989). See also *JES Properties v. USA Equestrian*, 458 F.3d 1224 (11th Cir. 2006) (national governing body rule that minimizes event scheduling conflicts and furthers congressional intent regarding governance of amateur athletics is immune from antitrust scrutiny). But see *Minnesota Made Hockey, Inc. v. Minnesota Hockey, Inc.*, 789 F. Supp. 2d 1133 (D. Minn. 2011) (although NGB has implied exemption from antitrust liability for promulgation of athlete eligibility rules, exemption does not immunize state association or one district of state association from antitrust liability for its eligibility rules that reduce competition with

another local amateur sports league); *Championsworld LLC v. United States Soccer Federation, Inc.*, 726 F. Supp. 2d 961 (N.D. Ill. 2010) (holding that because "USSF has no clear mandate from Congress to govern the whole of professional soccer in the U.S.," it "is not entitled to an exemption from the antitrust laws regarding professional soccer, except to the extent necessary for USSF to oversee Olympic and related events"); *TYR Sport Inc. v. Warnaco Swimwear Inc.*, 679 F. Supp. 2d 1120 (C.D. Cal. 2009) (USA Swimming has no implied antitrust immunity from claim it conspired with Speedo, a corporate sponsor, to exclusively promote, to disparage a competing manufacturer's high-end competitive swimwear, and to persuade Olympic-caliber swimmers to switch to Speedo's "LZR Racer" suit).

Courts will not resolve the merits of an eligibility dispute with the USOC or an NGB because the Amateur Sports Act gives an aggrieved U.S. athlete the right to submit the dispute to final and binding arbitration under the auspices of the American Arbitration Association. The following case illustrates the role of U.S. courts in the post-arbitration process and the need for all affected parties to have the opportunity to be heard. It also raises questions regarding which substantive issues should be within the arbitrators' authority to decide on the merits.

LINDLAND v. U.S. WRESTLING ASSOCIATION, INC.

227 F.3d 1000 (7th Cir. 2000)

EASTERBROOK, Circuit Judge.

Readers of our prior opinions (or the sports pages) know that Keith Sieracki and Matt Lindland both believe that they are entitled to be the U.S. entrant in the 76 kilogram weight class of Greco-Roman wrestling at the 2000 Olympic Games. They have met twice in championship bouts where the Olympic spot was the victor's reward: Sieracki won the first by a score of 2-1; Lindland won the second by a score of 8-0. Each claims that his victory entitles him to the slot in Sydney. Lindland protested the result of the first match through the hierarchy of USA Wrestling, the national governing body for amateur wrestling. After USA Wrestling rejected his protests, Lindland commenced arbitration, which was his right under the Ted Stevens Olympic and Amateur Sports Act. See 36 U.S.C. § 220529(a). Arbitrator Burns ordered the rematch, which Lindland won. USA Wrestling was unwilling to accept this outcome; instead of sending Lindland's name to the United States Olympic Committee (USOC) as its nominee for the Games, it told the USOC to send Sieracki and listed Lindland only as a person eligible to compete in the event of injury. Lindland then sought confirmation of the Burns Award under § 9 of the Federal Arbitration Act, 9 U.S.C. § 9, and in an opinion issued on August 24 we held that Lindland is entitled to that relief—which, we pointedly added, means that he is entitled to be USA Wrestling's nominee to the USOC.

Later that day, USA Wrestling informed the USOC that Sieracki remained its nominee. Its explanation for this defiance was that a second arbitrator, in a proceeding initiated by Sieracki, had disagreed with Arbitrator Burns and directed USA Wrestling to make Sieracki its nominee on the basis of his victory in the first match. USA Wrestling had no excuse for following Arbitrator Campbell's unreviewed award rather than a decision of a federal court confirming Arbitrator Burns's award, and on August 25 we issued a writ of mandamus requiring the district court to ensure that USA Wrestling implemented the Burns Award "immediately and unconditionally." On August 26 USA Wrestling finally complied, but the USOC then refused to accept Lindland as a member of the team, asserting that USA Wrestling's nomination of Lindland was untimely because Sieracki's name already had been sent to the International Olympic Committee (IOC) in Lausanne, Switzerland.

Lindland then returned to the district court, asking it to compel the USOC to send his name to the IOC. Sieracki fought back by asking a different district court (in Denver, Colorado) to confirm the Campbell Award. The district judge in Denver sensibly transferred that request to the Northern District of Illinois under 28 U.S.C. § 1404, consolidating all proceedings arising out of the dispute. The Northern District ordered the USOC to request the IOC to substitute Lindland for Sieracki. The USOC has done so, and the IOC has made the substitution. The Northern District also denied Sieracki's petition to confirm the Campbell Award. . . .

Lindland had argued to Arbitrator Burns that USA Wrestling's grievance proceedings were flawed. Arbitrator Burns agreed and ordered the rematch as a remedy in lieu of directing USA Wrestling to reconsider Lindland's protest to the judging of his match with Sieracki. Arbitrator Campbell went over the same ground, disagreed with Arbitrator Burns about the adequacy of USA Wrestling's processes and added that in his view the result of the first match (which everyone calls "Bout #244") had not been affected by any errors in applying the scoring rules for Greco-Roman Wrestling. It is not a surprising view for Arbitrator Campbell to have taken, because the proceedings began amicably. Sieracki initiated the arbitration to defend his initial victory, and USA Wrestling, the respondent, likewise defended both the scoring of the match and the conduct of its internal appeals. (Lindland intervened to defend the Burns Award, but, having already won the rematch, was more interested in preserving that victory than in litigating from scratch.) What *is* surprising was that Arbitrator Campbell not only approved the result of the original Bout #244 and the adequacy of USA Wrestling's grievance procedures but also directed it to ignore the result of the rematch—that is, Arbitrator Campbell directed USA Wrestling not to implement the Burns Award.

Sieracki argues that the Campbell Award is no less confirmable under the standards of the Federal Arbitration Act than was the Burns Award, see 9 U.S.C. § 10, and if he is entitled to confirmation of the Campbell Award then we should set aside the confirmation of the Burns Award (because relief from the BurnsAward is *part* of the Campbell Award). Certainly there is no evidence that the Campbell Award is the result of "corruption," "fraud," "evident partiality," or any similar bar to confirmation. The district court refused to enforce the Campbell Award because the Burns Award had been enforced already, and it read *Consolidation Coal Co. v. United Mine Workers*, 213 F.3d 404 (7th Cir. 2000), as precluding enforcement of incompatible awards. Only one of these athletes can be on the Olympic Team, and the district judge thought that federal courts should not order the USOC to send both. . . .

Definitive resolution of the right way to handle conflicting awards, after one has been confirmed, may await another day. The Campbell Award could not be confirmed even if it were the sole award. It is doubly flawed: first, the entire proceeding appears to have been *ultra vires;* second, the award violates the Commercial Rules of the American Arbitration Association, under which the proceeding was conducted. 36 U.S.C. § 220529(b)(2). Because Arbitrator Campbell exceeded his powers, his award cannot be confirmed. 9 U.S.C. § 10(a)(4).

Sieracki initiated an arbitration not to contest a final decision by USA Wrestling but to protest the Burns Award. Sieracki filed his demand for arbitration on August 11, two days after the Burns Award and three days before his rematch with Lindland (and thus before any issues associated with that bout could have arisen). The Stevens Act does not authorize arbitration about the propriety of another arbitrator's decision. . . .

What is arbitrable is "a determination of . . . the USOC, though some of its powers have been delegated to national governing bodies such as USA Wrestling. . . . Lindland exhausted his remedies within USA Wrestling and obtained "a determination of the corporation [i.e., USOC] under section 220527 . . . of this title," and thus was entitled to arbitrate his grievance. Sieracki, by contrast, did not initiate any proceedings within the scope of § 220527. . . . No other provision of which we are aware supports arbitration whose *sole* subject is the decision of a prior arbitrator. The Stevens Act would be self-destructive if it authorized such proceedings, which would lead to enduring turmoil (as happened here) and defeat the statute's function of facilitating final resolution of disputes, see § 220529(d).

Even if the second arbitration had been authorized, however, the outcome would have been forbidden by the rules under which it was conducted. Rule 48 of the AAA's Commercial Rules provides that an "arbitrator is not empowered to redetermine the merits of any claim already decided." . . . Arbitrators are not ombudsmen; they are authorized to resolve disputes under contracts and rules, not to declare how the world should work in the large. Arbitrator Campbell did not misinterpret Rule 48; he decided to ignore it utterly. The whole point of the Campbell proceeding was to redecide the issues that had been before Arbitrator Burns, and the Campbell Award directs USA Wrestling to disregard the Burns Award. Campbell observed, correctly, that Sieracki was not a party to the Burns proceedings, but the other participants in the proceedings before Arbitrator Campbell *were* parties to the Burns proceedings. By the time Campbell acted, the Burns Award had "already decided" that the nomination to the Olympic team would depend on a rematch between Sieracki and Lindland. Whatever powers Campbell possessed *vis-a-vis* Sieracki, he lacked the power to order USA Wrestling to nominate anyone other than the winner of the rematch. The Campbell Award therefore is not entitled to confirmation. . . .

For completeness, we add that none of the parties' arguments persuades us that the order confirming the Burns Award should be reconsidered. Sieracki, USA Wrestling, and the USOC continue to assert that the Burns proceedings were flawed because Sieracki was not a party to them. These submissions ignore the language of the Stevens Act, which provides for arbitration between an aggrieved athlete and the national governing body, not for arbitration among athletes. In arbitration the national governing body, by defending its decision (as USA Wrestling vigorously did), also defends the interests of the winning athlete. Doubtless the constitution or bylaws of the USOC or USA Wrestling could designate as additional parties those athletes potentially affected by the proceedings, but they do not do so. Arbitrator Campbell himself remarked that "customarily in a USOC Article IX arbitration . . . the competing athlete who does not initiate the arbitration . . . is not a participant and is not considered a necessary party by the USOC." If the USOC now favors a different approach, it should change its own rules rather than ask a federal court to disregard an award that was reached following normal procedures. . . .

. . . One of [the USOC's] rules specifies that the winner of Bout #244 would be USA Wrestling's nominee in the 76 kilogram classification. Lindland is the winner of Bout #244 and the recipient of USA Wrestling's (belated) nomination. Under the USOC's own rules, therefore, Lindland is entitled to the position on the Olympic Team. . . .

Affirmed.

Lindland won!

NOTES AND QUESTIONS

1. Although there is no private right of action under the Amateur Sports Act, *Lindland* illustrates that the Federal Arbitration Act, 9 U.S.C. §§1 et seq., enables an athlete (such as Matt Lindland, who won a silver medal at the Sydney Olympics) to judicially confirm and enforce an arbitration award if an NGB or the USOC refuses to comply with it. But see *USOC v. Ruckman*, 2010 WL 2179527 (D. N.J.) (remanding U.S Rowing's suit to confirm arbitration award resolving dispute regarding selection of Olympic team athletes in its favor to state court and denying athlete's petition for removal because Federal Arbitration Act does not create independent federal question jurisdiction to confirm arbitration award). In *Gault v. United States Bobsled and Skeleton Federation*, 578 N.Y.S.2d 683, 685 (N.Y. App. Div. 1992), a New York appellate court explained, "Although we also may disagree with the arbitrator's award and find most unfortunate the increasing frequency with which sporting events are resolved in the courtroom, we have no authority to upset it when the arbitrator did not exceed his authority." However, a court will vacate or refuse to confirm an arbitration award that is "the result of 'corruption,' 'fraud,' 'evident partiality,' or any similar bar to confirmation." *Lindland*, 227 F.3d at 1003.

2. *Lindland* illustrates the need for disputes to be resolved by an independent tribunal before whom all affected parties have a fair opportunity to be heard. If you were Sieracki's counsel, what would have been your advice when Lindland instituted an arbitration proceeding?

like everyone was notified in Hyatt v. US Judo

After *Lindland*, the USOC's Bylaws were amended to provide that an athlete submitting a dispute to AAA arbitration as well as the USOC member against which the arbitration has been filed must provide to AAA a list of all individuals they believe may be adversely affected by the arbitration. The AAA is responsible for providing notice to those individuals, who may choose to participate in the arbitration as a party. An individual who receives notice is bound by the arbitration decision even if he or she chooses not to participate in the arbitration. USOC Bylaw 9.8.

Regarding disputed competition results, USOC Bylaw 9.12 provides:

The final decision of a referee during a competition regarding a field of play decision (a matter set forth in the rules of the competition to be within the discretion of the referee) shall not be reviewable through or the subject of these complaint procedures unless the decision is (i) outside the authority of the referee to make or (ii) the product of fraud, corruption, partiality or other misconduct of the referee. For purposes of this Section, the term 'referee' shall include any individual with discretion to make field of play decisions.

The Amateur Sports Act provides:

In any lawsuit relating to the resolution of a dispute involving the opportunity of an amateur athlete to participate in the Olympic Games, the Paralympic Games, or the Pan-American Games, a court shall not grant injunctive relief against [the USOC] within 21 days before the beginning of such games if [the USOC], after consultation with the chair of the Athletes' Advisory Council, has provided a sworn statement in writing . . . to such court that its constitution and bylaws cannot provide for the resolution of such dispute prior to the beginning of such games.

36 U.S.C. §220509(a). The *Lindland* court observed that this statutory provision "is designed to prevent a court from usurping the USOC's powers when time is too short for its own dispute-resolution machinery to do its work." 227 F.3d at 1007. However, the Seventh Circuit held this provision did not preclude judicial authority to order the USOC to comply with the Burns arbitration award because it was both issued and confirmed outside the 21-day window.

PROBLEM 4-1

After failing to qualify as a member of the 2002 United States Olympic 1,000-meter team, Tommy O'Hare alleged that Apolo Ohno and Rusty Smith conspired to enable Shani Davis to win the final qualifying race for this event and a spot on the Olympic team. The U.S. Speedskating Code of Conduct required fair play and responsible conduct on the part of all athletes competing in events. In an arbitration proceeding, Ohno, who had already qualified for a spot on the United States Olympic team for that event, testified he held back during the race to prevent injury. Three other U.S. speed skaters retracted their initial claim of hearing Ohno and Smith discuss conspiring to ensure that Davis won the qualifying event. The race referee and official timer stated their belief that Ohno had not skated to the best of his ability, but did not violate any racing rule. Three assistant race referees testified it was a clean race. As an arbitrator, how would you resolve this dispute? If you found the race had been "fixed," what relief would you order?

C. LIMITS ON USE OF NATIONAL LAW TO REGULATE OLYMPIC AND INTERNATIONAL ATHLETIC COMPETITION

A U.S. court has no personal jurisdiction (i.e., valid authority to render a legally binding judgment against the defendant) over a nonresident international athletics governing body such as an International Federation (IF) or the IOC unless an athlete's claims arise out of its activities within both the United States and forum state. For example, in *Reynolds v. Int'l Amateur Athletic Federation*, 23 F.3d 1110 (6th Cir. 1994), the Sixth Circuit held that an Ohio court had no jurisdiction to hear American world-class sprinter Butch Reynolds' state law claims against the IAAF (then based in London, England), which alleged his positive drug test was erroneous (his urine sample was collected at an event in Monaco and tested in Paris, France). The merits of Reynolds's legal claims were resolved adversely to him in an IAAF arbitration proceeding that was held in London. See also *Shepherd v. USOC*, 94 F. Supp. 2d 1136 (D. Col. 2000) (U.S. court has no personal jurisdiction over the IOC merely because it requires the USOC, which is not an IOC member, to act in accordance with Olympic Charter). Should an IF be subject to an American court's jurisdiction based solely on its U.S. NGB's domestic activities, such as sanctioning competitions for the sport within the United States and enforcing athlete eligibility determinations? In other words, does personal jurisdiction exist if the NGB functions as the IF's agent in the United States? See *Behagen v. Amateur Basketball Assn. of United States of America*, 744 F.2d 731, 732-734 (10th Cir. 1984) (record shows IF "is its members" and governs sport through its member organizations in each country, which raises a question of fact whether German-based IF is subject to U.S. court's jurisdiction).

Even if there is personal jurisdiction over an international athletics governing body, U.S. courts are very reluctant to apply the constraints of U.S. federal or state law to IOC or IF rules, which are the product of a private international agreement intended to provide for uniform, worldwide governance of sport. In *Martin v. IOC*, 740 F.2d 670 (9th Cir. 1984), the Ninth Circuit affirmed the denial of a preliminary injunction to require the organizers of the 1984 Los Angeles Summer Olympic Games to include 5,000- and 10,000-meter track events for women as existed for men. The court rejected plaintiffs' claims that the failure to include these events constituted illegal gender discrimination, even though "the women runners made a strong showing that the early history of the modern Olympic Games was marred by blatant discrimination against women." *Id.* at 673. The majority explained, "[W]e find persuasive the argument that a court should be wary of applying a state statute to alter the content of the Olympic Games. The Olympic Games are organized and conducted under the terms of an international agreement—the Olympic Charter. We are extremely hesitant to undertake the application of one state's statute to alter an event that is staged with competitors from the entire world under the terms of that agreement." *Id.* at 677. See also *Sagen v. Vancouver Organizing Committee for the 2010 Olympic & Paralympic Games*, 98 B.C.L.R. 4th 141 (Can. B.C.), (British Columbia Court of Appeal rejects similar gender discrimination claim and rules that IOC's decision not to include women's ski jumping as an event in the Vancouver Olympic Games, while including men's ski jumping events, does not violate Canadian Charter of Rights and Freedoms).

The *Martin* dissenting judge argued:

The IOC made concessions to the widespread popularity of women's track and field by adding two distance races this year. The IOC refused, however, to grant women athletes equal status by including all events in which women compete internationally. In so doing, the IOC postpones indefinitely the equality of athletic opportunity that it could easily achieve this year in Los Angeles. When the Olympics move to other countries, some without America's commitment to human rights, the opportunity to tip the scales of justice in favor of equality may slip away. Meanwhile, the Olympic flame—which should be a symbol of harmony, equality, and justice—will burn less brightly over the Los Angeles Olympic Games.

Id. at 683.

American courts also have rejected state discrimination law claims by foreign athletes seeking to march in opening ceremonies in Olympic Games held in the United States under flags of countries not recognized by the IOC. See, e.g., *Spindulys v. Los Angeles Olympic Organizing Comm.*, 175 Cal. App. 3d 206, 220 Cal. Rptr. 565 (Cal. App. 1985); *Ren-Guey v. Lake Placid 1980 Olympic Games*, 72 A.D.2d 439, 424 N.Y.S.2d 533, *aff'd*, 49 N.Y.2d 771, 429 N.Y.S.2d 473 (1980).

Is it appropriate for courts to refuse to apply laws prohibiting discrimination to Olympic and other international sports events held in the United States?

By comparison, although English courts will require a domestic IF to comply with its own rules, *Reel v. Holder*, 3 All ER 321, 1 WLR 1226 (Court of Appeal, Civil Division 1981), British judges are equally reluctant to use national law to regulate international sports governing bodies. See *Gasser v. Stinson* (Queens Bench Division 1988) (although English restraint of trade laws applied to the IAAF, which was then based in London, court refused to interfere with "honest decisions of bodies exercising jurisdiction over sporting and other activities which those bodies exercising jurisdiction are far better fitted to judge than courts" and upheld an athlete's doping sanction); *Cowley v. Heatley* (Chancery Div., July 24, 1986) (unreported case) ("The concepts of natural justice and the duty to be fair must not be allowed to discredit themselves by making unreasonable requirements and imposing undue burdens" on a sports organization's internal governance decisions).

PROBLEM 4-2   — For Class

Andy is a junior at Aquatic State University and the NCAA champion in the 100-meter butterfly swimming event. In the recently completed Olympic Trials conducted under the auspices of United States Swimming, Inc. (USS), he finished fourth in this event, only 0.01 second behind the third-place finisher. He failed to make the United States Olympic team because only the top three finishers qualify for this event. Andy believes that the winner of this event used an "illegal kick" during the race and should have been disqualified. He promptly filed a complaint with the USS race officials overseeing this event, which was rejected within one hour after the race ended. The USS's executive committee denied his appeal. Andy wants to sue USS, the USOC, and the International Olympic Committee and obtain a court order enabling him to participate in the Olympic 100-meter butterfly swimming event that will be held in the United States in three weeks. What would you advise him to do?   *No, there will be no jurisdiction.*

As previously discussed, a U.S. athlete's dispute with the USOC or an NGB is resolved by domestic arbitration under the auspices of the American Arbitration Association. By comparison, a U.S. athlete's dispute with the IOC or an IF generally will be resolved before a foreign or international arbitration panel such as the Court of Arbitration for Sport. In accordance with an international treaty, the United Nations Convention on the Recognition and Enforcement of Foreign Arbitral Awards ("New York Convention"), 9 U.S.C. §201, to which the United States is a party, U.S. courts will recognize and confirm foreign arbitration awards resolving the merits of international sports disputes affecting U.S. athletes. The following case illustrates that U.S. courts generally will recognize and confirm foreign arbitration awards resolving international sports disputes, which precludes the losing party from re-litigating issues under national or state laws.

SLANEY v. INTERNATIONAL AMATEUR ATHLETIC FEDERATION

244 F.3d 580 (7th Cir.), *cert. denied*, 534 U.S. 828 (2001)

FLAUM, Chief Judge.

Former Olympic runner Mary Decker Slaney ("Slaney") brought suit against the International Amateur Athletic Federation ("IAAF") and the United States Olympic Committee ("USOC") shortly after an IAAF arbitration panel determined that Slaney had committed a doping offense. . . . [The facts giving rise to this case are set forth *supra*.]

. . . [T]he district court held that the United Nations Convention on the Recognition and Enforcement of Foreign Arbitral Awards, 9 U.S.C. § 201 ("New York Convention"), barred Slaney's claims against the IAAF, as those claims had been the subject of a valid arbitration decision. . . .

A.   STATE-LAW CLAIMS AGAINST THE IAAF

. . . Slaney challenges the district court's decision dismissing her IAAF claims, arguing that (1) Slaney is not subject to the New York Convention, in that she has never agreed—in writing or by actions—to arbitrate all disputes with the IAAF; (2) the claims raised in Slaney's complaint are separate and distinct from the matter decided by the IAAF; and (3) she has defenses under the New York Convention that preclude enforcement of the IAAF arbitration award against her.

. . . According to 9 U.S.C. § 201, the Convention on the Recognition and Enforcement of Foreign Arbitral Awards (New York Convention) shall be enforced in the United States courts. Article II of the Convention speaks to the requirements of states that have signed on to the Convention. Specifically, the section states that "[e]ach Contracting State shall recognize an agreement in writing under which the parties undertake to submit to arbitration all or any differences which have arisen or which may arise between them in respect of a defined legal relationship, whether contractual or not, concerning a subject matter capable of settlement by arbitration."

. . . If an award has been rendered, that award must be enforced unless the party against whom enforcement is sought presents evidence that one of the limited defenses enumerated under Article V of the Convention is applicable. For purposes of this appeal, we note that both the United States and Monaco are signatories to the Convention, such that the United States is bound to enforce arbitral awards validly rendered in that country.

In analyzing the merits of Slaney's appeal, we proceed in a systematic fashion. First, we must examine the decision rendered by the IAAF arbitration panel and determine the specific findings made by that Tribunal. Second, we shall examine the state-law causes of action that Slaney now brings against the IAAF in her complaint to the district court, and determine whether in fact those claims seek relitigation of an issue determined by the arbitration. If we determine that adjudication of Slaney's present claims would necessitate a reexamination of matters decided by the arbitration decision, we must resolve whether the arbitration decision, which took place on foreign soil, should be recognized by the courts, and thus deprive us of subject-matter jurisdiction over the present claims. Finally, assuming that we are theoretically obligated to recognize the decision of the Tribunal, we must inquire whether any defense to enforcement is applicable.

1.   Decision of the Tribunal

. . . [T]he Tribunal notes that the initial burden of proof rests with the IAAF to show that an athlete has a T/E ratio greater than the 6:1 established limit. If the IAAF can do so, according to the Tribunal, the Federation has provided sufficient evidence for the sample to be deemed positive. At that point, the burden is shifted to the athlete, who must prove by clear and convincing evidence that the elevated T/E ratio was due to pathological or physiological conditions. In making this analysis, the Tribunal drew from the IAAF rules on testing for testosterone.

With the evidentiary procedure established, the Tribunal continued to consider whether Slaney had committed a doping offense. The Tribunal noted that the IAAF had established that both of Slaney's specimens had been analyzed as having T/E ratios significantly higher than 6:1. The tribunal also observed that Slaney's longitudinal study revealed a previous T/E ratio high of 3:1; meaning that her present ratio, by the most modest of calculations, was more than three times greater than she had ever previously tested. Thus the burden was shifted to Slaney to produce a valid explanation for the findings. The Tribunal noted that Slaney had produced no evidence, let alone that of a clear and convincing nature, to prove that her elevated ratio was the result of pathological or physiological factors. Since Slaney had withdrawn from the proceedings, and refused to tender her medical records to the Tribunal, the panel was forced to conclude under the burden-shifting procedure it had outlined that Slaney was guilty of a doping offense on June 17, 1996.

2.   Slaney's Present Complaint and Its Relationship to the Tribunal's Decision

Keeping in mind the orbit of the Tribunal's decision, we now turn to examine Slaney's present state-law causes of action against the IAAF. Slaney raises six such claims: breach of contract, negligence, breach of fiduciary duty of good faith and fair dealing, fraud, constructive fraud, and negligent misrepresentation. . . . [W]e note that her complaints center around the claim that the IAAF violated its obligations to Slaney by "using the T/E ratio as a proxy for doping in women." Thus, she alleges that the Federation failed to properly investigate her urine sample. Though Slaney does not specify how she was damaged by the implementation of the T/E test . . . the answer is apparent. The implementation by the IAAF of a burden-shifting approach to proving ingestion of testosterone damaged Slaney in that, as a result, she was unable to disprove that she had committed the offense — resulting in her suspension.[1]

---

1. We note that Slaney walks a tightrope throughout this portion of her appellate argument. On the one hand, in order to raise many of the causes of action she alleges, Slaney must establish that there is a contractual relationship between her and the IAAF. However, in order to maintain the action as a whole against the IAAF, Slaney must avoid any suggestion that she has a contractual relationship with the IAAF whereby she has agreed to abide by their rules, including those which compel arbitration of all disputes.

We conclude that Slaney's present complaint seeks to address issues decided by the Tribunal. During the course of the IAAF arbitration, Slaney presented two positions: (1) that the IAAF's T/E ratio test for determining ingestion of exogenous testosterone was invalid, and (2) that it could not be proven that Slaney had committed a doping violation. . . . As our inquiry above made transparent, Slaney's state-law claims against the IAAF seek deliberation on the identical issues. For example, in order to adjudicate whether Slaney's Fifth Count (negligence against the IAAF) is a valid claim, the court would be required to delve into whether the cause of action makes the *prima facie* case. That probing would require that the court assess whether the IAAF in fact breached its obligations to Slaney. Slaney claims that the IAAF had a duty to properly test her for drug use. Since Slaney asserts that the IAAF breached this duty by employing the T/E test, the court would *de facto* be required to determine whether the implementation of that test constituted a breach of the duty to properly test athletes. Of course, the court could not reach that decision without addressing the validity of the test itself. Likewise, any examination of damages would require an assessment of whether Slaney was properly found guilty of a doping offense. Thus, we accept the district court's finding that allowing Slaney's current action would undermine or nullify the Tribunal's decision.

3.   *Application of the New York Convention*

[W]e now turn to the critical issue of whether we are required to acknowledge the foreign arbitration decision. If we are, then unless Slaney can present a defense to enforcement, we cannot exercise subject-matter jurisdiction over her present claims, as that would require prohibited relitigation of previously decided issues.

Slaney's primary contention in this regard is that the arbitration between herself and the IAAF need not be enforced by federal courts in that it did not satisfy the requirements of the New York Convention. First, Slaney points out that there is no agreement in writing between her and the IAAF in which she agreed to submit her claims to arbitration. . . . The IAAF counters that Slaney, by becoming a member of the USATF, agreed to abide by all IAAF rules. Included within those rules is the requirement that she arbitrate all disputes with the IAAF. . . . Additionally, because the IAAF suggests that Slaney participated in the IAAF arbitration, she cannot now raise the procedural defense of lack of an arbitration agreement.

Whether Slaney's written agreement to follow the rules of the USATF would satisfy the requirement of an agreement in writing for purposes of enforcing an arbitration agreement with the IAAF is a question we need not resolve. Instead, we direct our inquiry to whether Slaney was a party to the IAAF arbitration, and what results flow from that fact. An examination of Slaney's actions following the IAAF's submission of the matter to the Tribunal leads to only one conclusion: Slaney was a participant in the arbitration. During the arbitration, Slaney's counsel appeared before and presented arguments to the Tribunal. Her counsel called an expert witness to testify on Slaney's behalf, filed a motion to dismiss, and a motion for summary judgment. Furthermore, Slaney's counsel moved for an interlocutory ruling regarding the burden of proof the Tribunal would apply. Given this level of participation, the district court was correct to reject Slaney's contention that she was merely an interested athlete in the proceedings. . . .

We see no reason why, even in the absence of a writing, ordinary rules of contract law should not apply. . . . Non-signatories to an arbitration agreement may nevertheless be bound according to ordinary principles of contract and agency, including estoppel. Our judicial system is not meant to provide a second bite at the apple for those who have sought adjudication of their disputes in other forums and are not content with the resolution they have received. Slaney had the opportunity to show that she had never agreed to arbitrate the dispute when she was notified of the arbitration, but she let that opportunity pass. Slaney could not "sit back and allow the arbitration to go forward, and only after it was all done . . . say: oh by the way, we never agreed to the arbitration clause. That is a tactic that the law of arbitration, with its commitment to speed, will not tolerate."

. . . Thus, we find that the Tribunal's decision must be recognized by this court, and unless a defense is present, must bar her present claims.

4. New York Convention Defenses

Slaney alternatively suggests that even if we are to determine that she is bound by the arbitration panel's decision, the New York Convention provides exceptions in which a court need not enforce a foreign arbitral decision, and that those defenses to enforcement are applicable to the Tribunal's decision.

The first such defense raised by Slaney is that the Tribunal's decision should not be enforced because she was denied the opportunity to present her case. Slaney contends that under the IAAF rules, the IAAF has the burden of proving beyond a reasonable doubt that a doping offense has occurred. Her defense, she puts forth, was that the IAAF could not scientifically prove beyond a reasonable doubt that any prohibited substance was in her urine. Thus, when the Tribunal concluded it was bound by the IAAF's position — that upon a showing that an athlete had a T/E ratio greater than 6:1 the burden shifted to the athlete to show by clear and convincing evidence that the elevated ratio was due to a pathological or physiological condition — the Tribunal in effect denied Slaney a meaningful opportunity to present her case.

Article V(1)(b) of the New York Convention states that recognition and enforcement of an award may be refused if the party against whom it is invoked furnishes proof that it "was not given proper notice of the appointment of the arbitrator or of the arbitration proceedings or *was otherwise unable to present his case.*" (Emphasis added.) . . . As we have noted, in order to comport with the requirement that a party to a foreign arbitration be able to present her case, we require that the arbitrator provide a fundamentally fair hearing. A fundamentally fair hearing is one that "meets the minimal requirements of fairness — adequate notice, a hearing on the evidence, and an impartial decision by the arbitrator." Nevertheless, parties that have chosen to remedy their disputes through arbitration rather than litigation should not expect the same procedures they would find in the judicial arena. . . .

. . . Our examination of these cases leads us to conclude that Slaney's allegation has no merit. This defense to enforcement of a foreign arbitration need not apply when a panel employs a burden-shifting test in a fair manner. Slaney was not denied an opportunity to present her evidence. Rather, the arbitrator's decision merely maintained the same standard of proof the IAAF had always been guided by. As such, Slaney's complaint does not truly attack the procedure implemented by the arbitration panel, but rather an underlying evidentiary decision of the panel. . . .

Slaney's final submission on this issue is that "presuming she had committed a doping offense based on a test that is scientifically invalid and discriminatory towards female athletes violated the 'most basic notions of morality and justice.'" Slaney further postulates that "eliminating the presumption of [her] innocence based upon her elevated T/E ratio also violates . . . explicit public policy that is well defined and dominant and is ascertained by reference to the laws and legal precedents and not from general considerations of supposed public interests."

According to Article V(2)(b) of the New York Convention, "Recognition and enforcement of an arbitral award may also be refused if the competent authority in the country where recognition and enforcement is sought finds that: . . . [t]he recognition or enforcement of the award would be contrary to the public policy of that country." . . . In *Fotochrome, Inc. v. Copal Co.*, 517 F.2d 512, 516 (2d Cir. 1975), the Second Circuit noted that the public policy defense is exceedingly narrow. While Slaney states that the Tribunal's decision meets the stringent requirements of that case and others, in that the Tribunal's decision violated the "most basic notions of morality and justice," and that enforcement would entail a violation of a paramount legal principle that is "ascertained by reference to the laws and legal precedents and from general considerations of supposed public interests," *Industrial Risk Insurers v. M.A.N. Gutehoffnungshutte GmbH*, 141 F.3d 1434, 1445 (11th Cir. 1998), she provides little support for her contention.

Reduced to its essence, Slaney contends that the burden-shifting approach adopted by the IAAF violates United States public policy. We disagree. According to the parties, proving the presence of exogenous testosterone in the body by scientific tests is not possible at the present time. Therefore, the IAAF has adopted the rebuttable presumption of ingestion from a high T/E ratio in an athlete's urine, as detailed throughout this opinion. Were the IAAF not to make use of the rebuttable presumption, it would be nearly impossible, absent eyewitness proof, to ever find that an athlete had ingested testosterone. . . . We hope that at some juncture, science will develop a means for detecting exogenous testosterone in athletes, such that an athlete's T/E ratio of 11.6:1 can be discounted if it is based on innocent factors. However, until that point in time, we are confident that requiring an athlete to prove by clear and convincing evidence that her elevated ratio was due to pathological or physiological factors does not invoke a violation of United States public policy as federal case law has required in order for a court to refuse to enforce a foreign arbitral award.

Thus, having found that (1) Slaney participated in the IAAF arbitration, (2) her present state-law complaint seeks to relitigate issues decided by the IAAF Tribunal, (3) the New York Convention mandates enforcement of the arbitrator's decision, and (4) there is no defense that should bar enforcement of the arbitration decision, we find that the district court did not err in dismissing Slaney's state-law claims against the IAAF. . . .

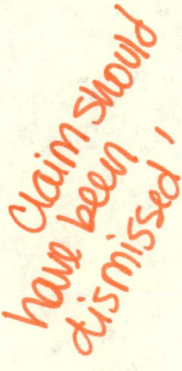

Claim should have been dismissed !

NOTES AND QUESTIONS

1. The *Lindland* case, *supra*, illustrates the offensive use of an arbitral award to obtain judicial enforcement of the prevailing party's rights. On the other hand, *Slaney* illustrates the defensive use of an arbitral award by the prevailing party in arbitration to preclude re-litigation of the same claims by the losing party in a judicial forum. This dual approach is consistent with the prevailing judicial preference that Olympic and international sports-related disputes be resolved by arbitration. See generally James A.R. Nafziger,

Arbitration of Rights and Obligations in the International Sports Arena, 35 Val. U. L. Rev. 357 (2001).

2. The New York Convention treaty requires national courts of signatory countries to enforce valid arbitration awards if the parties agreed in writing to arbitrate their dispute. What defenses to judicial enforcement of foreign arbitration awards are established by the New York Convention? Do you agree that requiring Slaney "to prove by clear and convincing evidence that her elevated T/E ratio was due to pathological or physiological factors" does not violate United States public policy? Would an athletics governing body's violation of its own rules satisfy the "exceedingly narrow" grounds for invalidating an arbitration award on the ground it violates public policy? If the Seventh Circuit had refused to recognize and enforce the IAAF arbitration award, would this provide Slaney with an effective legal remedy for her alleged harm?

STOP

D.   COURT OF ARBITRATION FOR SPORT

1.   *Historical Perspective*

The materials in the previous section illustrate the inherent problems of adjudication of Olympic and international sports disputes by self-interested sports governing authorities and judicial review by national courts. Courts generally do not provide an ideal forum for resolving such disputes. There are potential jurisdictional and conflicts-of-law problems as well as inherent difficulties attempting to apply a specific country's laws to the rules and enforcement activities of international sports organizations whose governing authority is exercised worldwide. Courts are understandably reluctant to regulate Olympic and international sports competition by judicial decree, but the rising tide of disputes generated the need for an independent international tribunal with final and binding authority to resolve them.

In 1983, the International Olympic Committee established the Court of Arbitration for Sport (CAS), which is based in Lausanne, Switzerland, and subject to Swiss law. The CAS was formed to resolve legal disputes in sports quickly and inexpensively. Its creation recognizes the need for international sport's governance to be uniform and protective of the integrity of athletics competition, while also safeguarding all athletes' legitimate rights and adhering to fundamental principles of natural justice. Tricia Kavanagh, *The Doping Cases and the Need for the International Court of Arbitration for Sport (CAS)*, 22 Univ. New S. Wales L.J. 721 (1999). The CAS "provides a forum for the world's athletes and sports federations to resolve their disputes through a single, independent and accomplished sports adjudication body that is capable of consistently applying the rules of different sports organizations." Richard H. McLaren, *The Court of Arbitration for Sport: An Independent Arena for the World's Sports Disputes*, 35 Val. U. L. Rev. 379, 381 (2001). It is "a unifying institution that can help deliver sport back to its origins . . . [and] ensures fairness and integrity in sport through sound legal control and the administration of diverse laws and philosophies." *Id.*

Despite its designation as a "court," the CAS is actually an arbitral tribunal. CAS arbitrators have legal training and recognized competence in the field of sport and international arbitration. The working languages of the CAS are French and English. Like other arbitral bodies, the CAS's jurisdiction is dependent on the parties' written agreement to submit their dispute to the CAS for final adjudication. Courts will enforce a written agreement to arbitrate before the CAS, which bars litigation arising out of the subject dispute in a judicial forum. *N. v. Federation Equestre Internationale* (Swiss Federal Tribunal 1996) in Digest of CAS Awards 1986-1998 at 585 (Reeb, ed. 1998); *Raguz v. Sullivan*, 2000 NSW LEXIS 265 (Sup. Ct. NSW, Ct. of Appeal 2000). Accord *Slaney v IAAF*, 244 F.3d 580, 590-591 (7th Cir. 2001) (observing that valid written agreement to arbitrate before foreign arbitral tribunal enforceable under New York Convention treaty). The IOC and all Olympic IFs have agreed to CAS jurisdiction; the only major world sports that have not yet done so are rugby and cricket. By rule, the IFs require their respective member NGBs and athletes to submit all disputes with the IF to CAS arbitration. Interested third parties, such as athletes whose interests may be affected, may intervene in CAS proceedings, which avoids the problem of conflicting arbitration awards raised by the *Lindland* case, *supra*.

Prior to 1994 the IOC established the CAS's rules and procedures by statute and paid its operating costs, and the IOC's president appointed some members of the CAS. Under the pre-1994 statute and regulations, there was a single type of CAS adversarial proceeding regardless of the nature of the parties' sports-related dispute. See generally Matthieu Reeb, *The Court of Arbitration for Sport: History and Operation*, Digest of CAS Awards II 1998-2000 at xxiii (2002).

In *Gundel's Case*, the Swiss Federal Tribunal, Switzerland's highest court, rejected a horse rider's challenge to the validity of a CAS award affirming the International Equestrian Federation's finding of a doping violation and imposition of a disciplinary sanction. *G. v. Federation Equestre Internationale* (Swiss Federal Tribunal 1993) in Digest of CAS Awards 1986-1998 at 561 (Reeb, ed. 1998). He contended that the CAS was not sufficiently independent and impartial to be considered a valid arbitral authority whose decisions should be given binding legal effect. Finding that "the CAS is a true arbitral tribunal independent of the parties, which freely exercises complete juridical control over the decisions of the associations which are brought before it," the Swiss court ruled that "the CAS offers the guarantees of independence upon which Swiss law makes conditional the valid exclusion of ordinary judicial recourse." *Id.* at 568-569. Observing that the IOC established the CAS's rules, appointed its members, and paid its operating costs, the court limited its holding to "proceedings conducted before the CAS in which the IOC does not appear as a party." *Id.* at 569.

In 1994, in response to the Swiss Federal Tribunal's admonition, the structure and operation of the CAS were modified in several major respects to make it independent from the IOC and more efficient. On June 22, 1994, in Paris, France, the presidents of the IOC, the Association of Summer Olympic International Federations, the Association of International Winter Sports Federations, and the Association of National Olympic Committees, signed the "Agreement Concerning the Constitution of the International Council of Arbitration for Sport," known as the "Paris Agreement." The International Council of Arbitration and Sport (ICAS), a group of 20 high-level jurists, was created to oversee the CAS and appoint its members, thereby removing these roles from the IOC's auspices. The IOC and other international sports organizations continue to fund the operations of ICAS and the CAS, but they do not govern or administer either organization. The ICAS administers the basic operations of the CAS and manages its funds, and its president also serves as the

CAS president. Members of the ICAS cannot serve as a CAS arbitrator or represent a party in a case before the CAS.

In May 2003, the Swiss Federal Tribunal ruled that the CAS is sufficiently independent from the IOC for its arbitration decisions "to be considered true awards, equivalent to the judgments of State courts." *A. ___ and B. ___ v. IOC* (Swiss Federal Tribunal 2003). The court rejected the plaintiffs' contention that the CAS is not impartial when it decides a dispute between an athlete and the IOC.

2.   *Composition, Operation, and Jurisprudence*

As of August 15, 2012, there are 288 CAS arbitrators representative of the world's continents, including 30 of U.S. nationality, who are appointed by the ICAS for four-year renewable terms. CAS arbitrators must have legal training and knowledge of sport, be objective and independent in their decisions, and adhere to a duty of confidentiality.

The Code of Sports-Related Arbitration governs the organization, operations, and procedures of the ICAS and the CAS. See the website of the Court of Arbitration for Sport at http://www.tas-cas.org/en/infogenerales.asp/4-3-236-1011-4-1-1/5-0-1011-3-0-0. In any CAS proceeding, the parties may be represented by counsel and must follow the code's procedural rules and time limits for bringing claims. The code establishes three distinct procedures for resolving sports-related disputes: (1) the ordinary arbitration procedure, (2) the appeals arbitration procedure, and (3) the mediation procedure.

The CAS ordinary arbitration procedure is used to resolve disputes relating to legal relations between the parties such as sports-related sponsorship contracts, television rights to sports event, and contracts between athletes and their agents. These proceedings are conducted before a single arbitrator or a panel of three arbitrators, usually are confidential and private, and do not result in publication of an opinion by the CAS. The dispute is resolved according to the law chosen by the parties, or Swiss law if none has been chosen. Rule 45, Code of Sports-Related Arbitration (2012).

The CAS appeals arbitration procedure is used to resolve appeals from final decisions of sports federations (requiring the exhaustion of all available internal administrative remedies) involving matters such as doping, discipline for misconduct, athlete eligibility issues, or competition results. These proceedings usually are before a three-person arbitration tribunal; each party selects one arbitrator, and the President of the Appeals Arbitration Procedure appoints the third arbitrator who serves as the president of the panel. The applicable substantive law generally is the relevant sport governing body rules (e.g., IOC or IF rules) and the law of the country in which it is domiciled (the IOC and most IFs are based in Switzerland), although the CAS panel has authority to resolve the dispute according to the "rules of law" it deems appropriate. Rule 58, Code of Sports-Related Arbitration (2012). CAS rules provide for these cases brought pursuant to this procedure to be decided within four months from the filing of an appeal, and they generally result in a published opinion.

The CAS operates the Ad Hoc Division at the site of each Olympic Games (which effectively operates as an appeals arbitration procedure) to provide for expedited resolution of all disputes arising during the Games or during a period of ten days preceding the Games Opening Ceremony (e.g., nationality requirements, doping violations). Pursuant to Article 74 of the Olympic Charter and a clause contained in the Olympic Athlete Entry Form, all members of the Olympic Movement are subject to CAS jurisdiction for any dispute in connection with the Olympic Games. All disputes are resolved by a panel of three arbitrators from a pool of CAS arbitrators specifically chosen by the ICAS for the Olympic Games. The applicable substantive law is the Olympic Charter and the general principles and rules of law that the arbitration panel deems appropriate. Article 17, Arbitration Rules for the Olympic Games (July 10, 2012). The arbitration award, which must be written and provide reasons, generally must be rendered within 24 hours of the filing of a request for CAS adjudication unless extended by the president of the CAS Ad Hoc Division for exceptional circumstances. For excellent summaries of Ad Hoc Division procedures and arbitration awards, see generally Gabrielle Kaufman-Kohler, Arbitration at the Olympics: Issues of Fast-Track Dispute Resolution and Sports Law (Kluwer Law Int'l 2001); Richard H. McLaren, *Introducing the Court of Arbitration for Sport: The Ad Hoc Division at the Olympic Games*, 12 Marq. Sports L. Rev. 517 (2001).

In both appeals arbitration and Ad Hoc Division proceedings, the CAS provides *de novo* review of a sports governing body's interpretation or application of rules affecting an athlete's eligibility to compete. As a result, even if the athlete was denied due process in the sport governing body's internal proceeding, this violation is remedied by providing a full and fair opportunity to be heard during the CAS arbitration.

The CAS currently has branches in New York City and Sydney, Australia. Regardless of its physical location, the "seat" of all CAS adjudication is always considered to be Lausanne, Switzerland, and Swiss law governs all CAS proceedings. This ensures uniform procedural rules for all CAS arbitrations, which provides a stable legal framework and facilitates efficient dispute resolution in locations convenient for the parties.

As an Australian appellate court explained:

> There are three main reasons for the choice of a sole seat, regardless of the actual place of arbitration. First, that choice provides a uniform procedural regime for all CAS arbitrations, not only in terms of applicable rules under the Code, but also with respect to the arbitration law governing the proceedings. The Games move around, but the legal framework is stable.
>
> Second, conducting the arbitration at the site of the Games is intended to make arbitration as convenient as possible for the parties and to resolve disputes as expeditiously as possible. It is not meant to have any legal significance.
>
> Third, the equal treatment so achieved is consistent with the equal standards that govern the activities giving rise to disputes, i.e., sports competition. A time on a stopwatch is the same wherever the race takes place. It is further consistent—which may be of even greater significance here—with the choice of substantive law governing sports disputes. . . .
>
> All these sets of rules . . . are transnational, universal, global. Their application is not dependent on a territorial nexus, nor is it restricted territorially. This global substantive law is matched by a uniform procedural law thanks to the choice of a sole seat for all CAS arbitrations.

Raguz v. Sullivan, 2000 NSW LEXIS 265, *47-*49 (Sup. Ct. NSW, Ct. of Appeal 2000).

A CAS arbitration award resolves the subject dispute, orders appropriate relief (including damages and allocation of costs), and is final and binding on the parties. CAS panels frequently cite and rely on prior awards. See *International Assn. of Athletics Federations v. USA Track & Field and Jerome Young*, Arbitration CAS 2004/A/628, award of June 28, 2004 ("In CAS jurisprudence there is no principle of binding precedent, or *stare decisis*. However, a CAS Panel will obviously try, if the evidence permits, to come to the same conclusion on matters of law as a previous CAS Panel. Whether that is considered a matter of comity, or an attempt to build a coherent corpus of law, matters not."); *Anderson, et al. v. IOC*, Arbitration CAS 2008/A/1545, award of July 16, 2010 ("although a CAS panel in principle might end up deciding differently from a previous panel, it must accord to previous CAS awards a substantial precedential value and it is up to the party advocating a jurisprudential change to submit persuasive arguments and evidence to that effect").

3. *Judicial Review*

CAS arbitration awards are creating a body of Olympic and international sports law, a so-called *lex sportiva*. See generally James A.R. Nafziger, International Sports Law (2d ed.) at 48-61 (Transnational Publishers, Inc. 2004) (observing that CAS awards "provide guidance in later cases, strongly influence later awards, and often function as precedent," which reinforce and help elaborate "established rules and principles of international sports law"); Allan Erbsen, *The Substance and Illusion of* Lex Sportiva, in The Court of Arbitration for Sport 1984-2004 at 452 (I.S. Blackshaw, R.C.R. Siekmann, and J.W. Soek, eds. 2006) ("the gradual accretion of CAS precedent that is often labeled as Lex Sportiva can more helpfully be understood as comprising several distinct approaches to legal analysis that rely on diverse sources of governing principles"). Matthieu Reeb, the CAS secretary general, publishes digests of CAS Ad Hoc Division and appeals arbitration awards, and there is an index and database of CAS awards on the CAS website at http://www.tas-cas.org.

A CAS award is a Swiss arbitration award that may be judicially confirmed and enforced by a court in a country that is a signatory to the New York Convention on the Uniform Enforcement of Foreign Arbitration Awards. Because the seat of all CAS arbitration is Lausanne, Switzerland (regardless of where it actually takes place), a CAS award may be challenged before the Swiss Federal Tribunal. Article 190(2) of the Swiss Federal Code on Private International Law of December 18, 1987, specifies only very limited grounds for judicially challenging a CAS award such as if there was incompetence or irregularity in the arbitration panel, if the award is outside the CAS's jurisdiction or did not decide a claim, if the parties' rights to be heard and treated equally were violated, or if the award is incompatible with Swiss public policy. See *Matuzalem v. FIFA*, 4A_558/2011(1st Civil Court, March 27, 2012) at 6 (CAS "substantive adjudication of a dispute violates public policy only when it disregards some fundamental legal principles and consequently becomes completely inconsistent with the important, generally recognized values, which according to dominant opinions in Switzerland should be the basis of any legal order."); *Raducan v. International Olympic Committee*, 5P.427/2000 (2nd Civil Court, Dec. 4, 2000) (Swiss public policy requires international sports governing bodies to act in good faith and treat all athletes equally).

In *Canas v. ATP Tour*, 4P.172/2006, (1st Civ. Law Ct., March 22, 2007), the Swiss Federal Tribunal refused to enforce a contractual waiver of an athlete's right to appeal a CAS award, which was a condition of participating in any events organized or sponsored by the Association of Tennis Professionals Tour. The athlete's agreement to arbitrate a doping dispute before the CAS is enforceable because it "promotes the swift settlement of [sports] disputes . . . by specialized arbitral tribunals that offer sufficient guarantees of independence and impartiality." However, the Tribunal observed that it is important to ensure that "the parties, especially professional athletes, do not give up lightly their right to appeal awards issued by a last instance arbitral body before the supreme judicial authority of the state in which the arbitral tribunal is domiciled." The Tribunal explained this apparent contradiction by stating "this logic is based on the continuing possibility of an appeal acting as a counterbalance to the 'benevolence' with which it is necessary to examine the consensual nature of recourse to arbitration where sporting matters are concerned."

The following cases are illustrative examples of CAS appeals arbitration and Ad Hoc Division jurisprudence in the context of governing body disciplinary action against athletes for misconduct or corruption, disputed competition results, and doping violations and sanctions.

4.   *Governing Body Disciplinary Action*

D'ARCY v. AUSTRALIAN OLYMPIC COMMITTEE

Arbitration CAS 2008/A11574
Award of 11 June 2008

Panel: Mr. Malcolm Holmes (Australia), President; Mr. David Grace (Australia); Mr. Alan Sullivan (Australia)

[Eds. On February 28, 2008, Mr. Nicholas D'Arcy (Mr. D'Arcy) entered into an agreement with the Australian Olympic Committee Inc. (the AOC), which governed the conditions by which Mr. D'Arcy was to participate, if selected, as a member of the 2008 Australian Olympic Team and his continued membership on the team (the Membership Agreement). Under the terms of Clause 2(8) of the Membership Agreement, Mr. D'Arcy agreed to observe the provisions of the AOC Ethical Behaviour Bylaw, and in particular Clause 2.2(6) of the bylaw, which provided that he "must not, by [his] acts or omissions, engage or participate in . . . conduct which, if publicly known, would be likely to bring [him] into disrepute or censure." On March 29, 2008, Mr. D'Arcy was selected as a member of the 2008 Australian Olympic swimming team. In the early hours of March 30, 2008, in a public establishment known as the Loft bar in Sydney, Mr. D'Arcy struck Simon Cowley in the face with his elbow and inflicted serious injuries on him, which conduct resulted in criminal charges against Mr. D'Arcy.

After considering a letter from Mr. D'Arcy regarding his account of this incident, Mr. John Coates, the President of the AOC, removed him from the Olympic team. The first CAS panel considering Mr. D'Arcy's appeal determined that he breached Clause 2.2(6) of the AOC Ethical Behaviour Bylaw and did not satisfy Clause 2(8) of the Membership Agreement with the AOC. However, it set aside the AOC President's decision to terminate Mr. D'Arcy's membership of the Olympic team because the proper termination procedure established by the Membership Agreement had not been followed. The panel ordered that the matter be submitted to the members of the AOC Executive, the body having the requisite authority and discretion to remove Mr. D'Arcy from the Olympic team.

The AOC Executive resolved unanimously "that Nicholas D'Arcy's membership of the 2008 Olympic Team be terminated." Following the meeting a statement was issued on behalf of the AOC that said:

> We have approached this matter based on the standards of behaviour expected of a member of the Australian Olympic Team, drawing our many years of collective experience. The effect that Nicholas D'Arcy's conduct had on his reputation, as found by the President and confirmed by the CAS, was the basis for the decision by the AOC Executive. The matter of criminal proceedings is entirely separate from today's decision. The Australian Olympic Committee is proud of the excellent standards and conduct of past and present Olympians and in the eyes of the Australian public we have an obligation to protect that reputation. To terminate the membership of an athlete on the Australian Olympic Team is a very serious matter. After careful consideration we have reached a decision based on that responsibility.

For purposes of the present appeal, Mr. D'Arcy accepted the first CAS panel's determination that he breached his Membership Agreement with the AOC, but he appealed the AOC Executive's decision to terminate his membership on the 2008 Australian Olympic team.]

The first issue raised by the parties concerned the powers available to the Panel on the hearing of this "Appeal." The AOC [which is based in Sydney, New South Wales] submitted that as the applicable law for the review is the law of New South Wales the Panel was required *"to limit its review to whether the decision appealed against was obviously or self-evidently so unreasonable or perverse that it could be said to be irrational."* This is commonly known as "Wednesbury unreasonableness" so named after the decision in *Associated Provincial Picture House Ltd. v. Wednesbury Corporation,* [1948] 1 KB 223. In response, Mr D'Arcy submitted that there was no such limitation on the powers of this Panel. It was submitted that this particular limitation which was imposed by the law of New South Wales in particular circumstances on the jurisdiction of a court of law did not apply to this arbitration tribunal which was acting pursuant to the parties' agreement in terms of the special provisions of the CAS Code applicable to the Appeal Arbitration Procedure and in particular Article R.57 by which the parties agreed that the appeal panel has "full power to review the facts and the law." In the alternative Mr D'Arcy submitted that even if the Panel's powers were limited to a consideration of whether the decision appealed against was obviously or self evidently so unreasonable or perverse that it could be said to be irrational, this was nevertheless such a case and one where the decision could and should be set aside.

The Panel, by a majority, is of the view that it is not limited in the manner described above in its powers to review the decision. Nevertheless, whichever view is taken of the powers of the Panel on this Appeal, it is the unanimous view of the Panel that in the particular circumstances of this case the Appeal should be dismissed. . . .

. . . [P]rivate parties cannot confer by agreement jurisdiction on a court which the court does not have. On the other hand private parties can by their agreement agree on a process such as arbitration by which a matter in dispute between them can be reviewed and determined by an award. The parties by their agreement may also include an appellate arbitration process. And they can agree on the powers which the independent arbitrators involved in the agreed appellate process can exercise in determining such an "appeal." . . .

. . . [T]he parties have agreed to have their dispute arbitrated according to the Appeals Arbitration Procedure of the CAS Code. . . .

. . . [T]he parties' agreement in Article R.57 that [states] . . . the Appeal Arbitration Procedure "shall have full power to review the facts and the law" must be considered.

This procedure whereby the appeal procedure is initiated strongly suggests that each party has a right to advance a completely fresh case on the facts. This procedure does not imply that the party appealing is required to show any error on the facts presented to the initial decision maker or arbitration panel. It suggests the contrary. It suggests that the issue is being heard afresh with both parties able to lead such evidence (whether old or new it does not matter) and to make such submissions relating to the dispute and not the decision, as it chooses. The facts are not limited to the facts as found by the initial arbitration panel. The parties agreement expressly confers on the appeal panel "full" power to "review" the "facts" and the "law." Each of these elements combines to reinforce the view that objectively, the parties intended a complete rehearing of their dispute. The wording used by the parties is "full power" and this must be given effect. The wording contradicts any suggestion that there is a narrow power of review. There is nothing which suggests that the appeal arbitration panel is limited in any way in its review of both the facts and law.

The type of decision which an appeal panel may make is described in the second sentence of Article R.57 which states that the appeal panel "may issue a new decision which replaces the decision challenged or annul the decision and refer the case back to the previous instance." This description does not seek to limit the powers of the appeal panel or that it can only act if it finds error in the initial decision or award. . . .

It is also significant that there is no requirement in the provisions applicable to the Appeal Arbitration Procedure to establish any particular grounds of the appeal. The jurisdiction of the Appeal Panel is not "an error-based jurisdiction." The provisions address the "facts" and the legal arguments and submissions giving rise to the appeal and the parties are not required to identify, assret or address any error in the initial decision or in the initial arbitration award. Further it is significant that the requirement is to provide a "copy of the decision appealed against" and not a statement of the reasons for that decision. . . .

When the issue relating to Article R.57 was most recently considered by an arbitral panel under the CAS Code, the panel stated that "*it* is *the duty* of *the* [appeal panel] *to make its independent determination* of *whether the Appellant's contentions are correct, not to limit itself to assessing the correctness* of the "award or decision from which the appeal was brought. . . .

Under the Code, the CAS has a list of arbitrators who are required under S.14 of the Code to be "personalities with full legal training, recognised competence with regard to sports law and/or international arbitration, a good knowledge of sport in general and a good command of at least CAS working language." Where the parties adopt the CAS Code they are required to have their dispute arbitrated by persons with a particular background and knowledge which they can properly bring to bear in the resolution of their dispute. They are not bound by the rules of evidence. The panel is "*entitled to draw upon its own expert resources* . . ." although it must not "*derogate from evidence of the* [parties] *without putting* [the Panel's] *knowledge to them and giving them the chance of answering it.*" . . . Again, this use of a panel of arbitrators with specialised knowledge for the appeal arbitration procedure rather than a court of law which is bound to apply the strict rules of evidence and which has "a *strictly limited*" ability to intervene, supports the construction of this agreement that where there is an Appeal Arbitration Procedure under the Code, the parties have agreed that it is to be a completely fresh rehearing of the dispute and not one narrowly focussed on finding error in the original decision. . . .

The First Panel found that the President of the AOC, Mr. John Coates, was entitled to find that the Appellant's conduct was likely to and did bring himself into disrepute. . . .

In his Application to this Panel, the Appellant contended that the decision of the AOC to terminate his membership for the team was not fair and reasonable in the circumstances and did not place adequate or due weight upon the consequences of termination of membership for the Appellant. It was further contended that the decision to terminate was in the circumstances manifestly excessive as a sanction and disproportionate to the Appellant's breach of the Membership Agreement. . . .

. . . Clause 2(2) of the Membership Agreement triggers the exercise of discretion when a finding is made that the team member "was *likely to and did bring himself into disrepute.*" The fact that conceivably there could be more grave forms of conduct which would bring the sport, the AOC and the team into disrepute may well be accepted, but the fact that the Appellant's conduct has brought himself into disrepute is clearly sufficient to trigger the exercise of discretion adversely to him.

[T]his Panel has approached the matter on the basis that it is a hearing *de novo*, and on the material before it, the Panel finds that it would have reached the same conclusion in the exercise of its discretion as the AOC Executive. We have reached this conclusion after taking into account in the Appellant's favour all the relevant matters that have and could be put on his behalf.

The conduct of the Appellant on the night in question, putting to one side the allegations of criminal misbehaviour, was serious misconduct. The grossly excessive consumption of alcohol resulting in intoxication, culminating in his involvement in a fracas, was conduct that could form an ample basis for the exercise of discretion to terminate the Appellant's membership of the team.

The decision relates to whether or not he should be part of a large group of athletes, young and old, travelling overseas as a united body of representatives of his country and living together during periods when they are under the pressure of competition and periods when the competition has finished. The likely impact of his serious misconduct on the problems and responsibilities faced by other athletes in the team and on those involved in the management and organization of such a large group of diverse athletes in varying and unusual circumstances, is a matter particularly within the knowledge and experience of the members of the AOC Executive. Their unanimous view must be given great weight.

Nevertheless, as has been recognised, whilst this panel "can *use the rationale and wisdom* of *the lower panel* as a *guide*" ultimately the Panel must make its "*independent determination* of the matter" and this it has done.

The extent of the disrepute that the Appellant's behaviour has brought himself is highlighted by the voluminous number of media reports that have accompanied his misconduct. Many of these reports were provided to the Panel and the Panel has considered their contents whilst noting that many of the allegations contained within the media reports are unproven and sensationalist. There are, however, a considerable number of statements in the media reports that are substantiated by the admitted facts and amplify the conclusion of the first CAS Panel that the media reports "*could not help but be likely to bring him into disrepute.*"

Further in the alternative, given the accepted finding of the First Panel that the Appellant's conduct was likely to and did bring himself into disrepute and the acceptance therefore that there had been a breach by the Appellant of the Membership Agreement, the exercise of the discretion was triggered. It could not be said that the decision of the AOC Executive was perverse or irrational, or aberrant in the "*Wednesbury*" sense. It could not be said that the AOC Executive could not honestly and reasonably have come to the decision it did.

The Appellant's submissions either taking singly or in combination do not give rise to a conclusion that the decision of the AOC Executive is so aberrant that it cannot be classed as rational. The sanction was not disproportionate, nor manifestly excessive so as to give rise to a finding of "*irrationality.*" . . .

Accordingly, the Panel finds that none of the Appellant's contentions have been made out and the appeal must be dismissed. [EDS. In November 2008 Mr. D'Arcy pled guilty to assault in the criminal prosecution arising out of this incident. He competed in the 2012 London Olympics as a member of the Australian swimming team.]

SAMOA NOC AND SPORTS FEDERATION, INC. v. INTERNATIONAL WEIGHTLIFTING FEDERATION (IWF)

**Arbitration CAS ad hoc Division (O.G. Sydney 2000) 042
Award of September 12, 2000**

Panel: The Hon. Michael Beloff (England), President; The Hon. Justice Tricia Kavanagh (Australia); Prof. Richard McLaren (Canada)

This is an appeal by the Claimant, the Samoan NOC ("NOC"), against a decision of the Respondent ("IWF") to support the suspension of Ofisa Junior Ofisa ("Ofisa"), ordered by the Samoan Weightlifting Federation ("SWF"), preventing him from participating in the Olympic Games in the 85.0-kg class. At issue, then, is the ability of Ofisa to participate in such competition. . . .

In May 2000, Ofisa competed in Oceania-Commonwealth and South Pacific Weightlifting Championships in Nauru. He won three gold medals and was selected to represent Samoa by the Samoan NOC as appears from a form for confirmation of participation signed by the NOC dated 18 May 2000.

Thereafter allegations were made that Ofisa had sex with a female minor in Nauru. There has been no charge, no arrest, no extradition proceedings . . . and Ofisa has denied the allegations in affidavit form.

By letter dated 23rd May 2000, the Samoan Weightlifting Federation informed IWF that Ofisa was suspended as a member of SWF until 7th June 2001 "due to serious misconduct at the recent Oceania Weightlifting Championships." We do not have a copy of the relevant constitution or rules of the SWF, but it is accepted that the SWF enjoyed powers to suspend a weightlifter for misconduct at the material time.

On 1st September 2000, Dr. Ajan, Secretary General of the IWF, circulated a document to, *inter alia*, NOC that IWF had, in accordance with its constitution, adopted SWF's decision of Ofisa's suspension and [endorsed] it to the Sydney Olympics. . . .

By a further letter dated 6th September 2000, IWF repeated the substance of its letter of 1st September 2000.

On 7th September 2000, Ofisa instituted injunction proceedings in Samoa against JJW Wallwork (the President of SWF) and SWF, both of whom were subject to its jurisdiction, seeking an order in effect lifting the suspension on grounds of misconstruction of the SWF constitution, taking into account irrelevant matters (the suggestion being that Ofisa was penalized because he did not support Wallwork in elections to the NOC), breach of both the main rules of natural justice, malice and disproportionate penalty. . . .

On 8th September 2000, the Samoan Supreme Court [enjoined Wallwork and SWF from continuing to suspend Ofisa and attempting to enforce the suspension to prevent him from competing in international weight lifting competitions and the Sydney Olympic Games] ("the interim order"). . . .

On 8th September 2000, NOC appealed to CAS stating that: "Since Court order has lifted the suspension of [Ofisa], the only cause of action that IWF [can take] is likewise to lift its endorsement of said suspension of Ofisa." . . .

The IWF adheres to its earlier decision.

In Law . . .

The IWF decision expressly assumed the validity of the SWF decision to suspend: the letters of 1st September and 6th September both refer to the adoption of the SWF decision.

On the evidence before us there were and are arguable grounds to challenge the validity of the SWF decision. A failure to accord Ofisa any kind of hearing as well as apparent bias on the part of the effective decision maker, if established, makes it fatally flawed.

It is, however, unnecessary for us to form a concluded view about either the way in which the SWF decision was reached or the legal consequence thereof. The Supreme Court of Samoa has set the suspension aside until further order. There is no reason for us not to accept the interim order at face value. It was for that reason that we rejected an application on behalf of the IWF to adduce evidence said to be relevant to the allegations against Ofisa. To have entertained such evidence would necessarily have involved going behind the order of the Samoan Court (in this instance the Chief Justice). It is the Samoan Court to which such evidence should have been (or should be) addressed.

Although the Samoan Court order does not bind the IWF directly, it indirectly affects it, since if the SWF decision is set aside, the foundations of the IWF decision are removed. The IWF decision required the SWF decision to be valid: the Samoan Court has held that it is not to be treated as valid. That decision which the IWF purported to adopt (and to continue to adopt) no longer has any weight in law.

The IWF decision is not supported on any other ground. Therefore we find that the decision of the IWF must be set aside. The IWF have made no independent examination of the allegations against Ofisa or come to any conclusion about them independently of the SWF.

For the avoidance of doubt, our decision is not to be taken as any precedent should an athlete be validly suspended by an IF: nor should it be read as confirming that an athlete may participate in the Olympic Games where he/she is guilty of serious sexual or other offences. However Ofisa is entitled, until trial, to the presumption of innocence. Other Tribunals than CAS may have to decide in accordance with the appropriate rules and principles which govern their jurisdiction, whether the allegations against him have substance or not.

The CAS ad hoc Division rules: The decision of the IWF that Ofisa Jr. Ofisa cannot participate in the Sydney Olympic Games is no longer effective and is therefore set aside.

NOTES AND QUESTIONS

1. *CAS* De Novo *Review and Applicable Laws.* When resolving athlete eligibility disputes pursuant to its appeals arbitration jurisdiction, *D'Arcy* illustrates that the CAS panel's review is *de novo.* How does the nature and scope of CAS review differ from judicial review of a domestic sports governing body's athlete eligibility determination? Does CAS *de novo* review effectively counterbalance the monolithic authority of Olympic and international sports governing bodies?

    In construing the parties' agreement to submit their dispute to CAS arbitration, *D'Arcy* applied domestic law (i.e., New South Wales law) because the Australian Olympic Committee is headquartered in Sydney. (Note that, in Australia, domestic Olympic sports disputes are resolved by CAS rather than a national arbitral tribunal like the AAA, which is used to resolve domestic Olympic sports disputes in the United States.) *Samoa NOC* also illustrates that the CAS must consider applicable transnational, national, and local laws when deciding the merits of athletic eligibility disputes. See *Canas v. ATP Tour*, 4P.172/2006 (1st Civ. Law Ct., March 22, 2007) (the Swiss Federal Tribunal vacates CAS award because it violated the athlete's right to a fair hearing by not providing a reasoned decision for rejecting arguments that his doping sanction violated Delaware, U.S., and European Union law).

2. *Match Fixing and Corruption Legal Issues.* Illegal betting and match fixing pose an increasing threat to the integrity of Olympic and international sports competition, and recent high-profile scandals have occurred in cricket and soccer. In July 2011, IOC president Jacques Rogge stated, "I can't open my newspapers without finding an article on the prevalence of cheating and match fixing. In Germany, Italy, Belgium, Hungary, Turkey, Greece. In China, in South Korea, in Singapore. It is a world problem and it is a very pernicious problem. With the introduction of broadband, you can bet worldwide. The danger is that from illegal betting comes match fixing and you see more and more attempts to manipulate matches. It is as dangerous as doping for the credibility of sport. It's only the beginning of a huge battle." Owen Gibson, *London's Olympic Preparations Best of Any Games, Says IOC President*, Guardian, July 25, 2011, http://www.guardian.co.uk/sport/2011/jul/25/london-olympics-preparations-ioc-president.

    In *Kollerer v. Association of Tennis Professionals, Women's Tennis Assn., International Tennis Federation & Grand Slam Committee*, Arbitration CAS 2011/A/2490 (award of March 23, 2012), the CAS upheld a lifetime ban of Daniel Kollerer, an Austrian professional tennis player, for attempting to fix matches three times during 2009 and 2010 based on the findings of the Tennis Integrity Unit, an initiative formed by four international tennis governing bodies, to investigate breaches of the Uniform Tennis Anti-Corruption Program (UTACP) and to impose appropriate penalties. The CAS ruled that the UTACP's standard of proof requiring that a corruption offense be proved by a preponderance of evidence was contractually agreed to by Kollerer and does not violate Florida law (which the UTACP expressly states it is subject thereto). Rejecting Kollerer's contention that a higher standard such as proof of corruption to its comfortable satisfaction (i.e., clear and convincing evidence), the panel concluded there "is no universal (minimum) standard of proof for match-fixing offences" and "does not consider that applying the standard of proof provided for by the UTACP would violate any rules of national and/or international public policy." Acknowledging that "consistency across different associations may be desirable, in the absence of any overarching regulation (such as the WADA Code for doping cases), each association can decide for itself which standard of proof to apply, subject to national and/or international public policy." The CAS determined that the preponderance of evidence is not void on the ground of unconscionability, even though Kollerer was required to agree to it as a condition of participating in ATP tennis tournaments, because the ATP's Player Council did not object to it.

Given the seriousness of match-fixing allegations and potential adverse effects on an accused athlete's career and reputation, does the preponderance of evidence standard provide an adequate level of due process? See Mike Morgan, *Assessment of Evidence in Sporting Fraud Cases*, Jusletter, July 16, 2012, http://www.jusletter.ch (observing that "it cannot be ruled out that imposing a particularly severe sanction on the basis of balance of probabilities for an offence akin to a crime would fail to be considered a matter of public policy in certain states," which may apply "the criminal standard of proof, or at least a standard higher than that applied in mere civil proceedings").

5. *Disputed Competition Results*

During the 2004 Athens Olympics, American Paul Hamm came from twelfth place to win the gold medal in men's all-around gymnastics when he earned scores of 9.837 in both the parallel bars and the high bar, the competition's final two events. However, judges incorrectly deducted one-tenth of a point from the start value of South Korean gymnast Yang Tae-Young's parallel bars routine. Because of this error, Yang received a lower score for his routine. Yang's final overall score was 0.049 point behind Hamm, which resulted in his winning the bronze medal rather than the gold medal.

The Korean Olympic Committee (KOC) protested the start value attributed to Yang's parallel bars routine because it was lower than he had previously received for the same routine in the gymnastics team and qualifying competitions. Acknowledging this error, the International Gymnastics Federation (FIG) suspended the three judges responsible for incorrectly determining the start value of Yang's routine.

The IOC refused to issue duplicate gold medals to both Hamm and Yang as proposed by KOC and the USOC. However, IOC president Jacques Rogge stated that the IOC would respect a request by FIG to correct the error in Yang's score and to reallocate the medals for the men's all-around gymnastics competition. FIG, however, refused to change the competition results or award a duplicate gold medal to Yang because a timely protest on his behalf had not been made to the appropriate official in charge of the competition's judging.

FIG subsequently attempted to send a letter to Hamm stating that Yang was the "true winner" of this event because of the judges' scoring error. FIG's letter suggested that Hamm's voluntary decision to return his gold medal would be regarded "as the ultimate demonstration of fair play by the whole world." The USOC rejected FIG's proposal and refused to forward the letter to Hamm.

Yang and the KOC petitioned the CAS to correct the judging error and to rule that Yang was entitled to receive the gold medal in the men's all-around gymnastics competition.

YANG TAE YOUNG v. INTERNATIONAL GYMNASTICS FEDERATION

Arbitration CAS 2004/A/704
Award of October 21, 2004

Panel: The Hon. Michael Beloff (England); Mr. Dirk-Reiner Martens (Germany); Mr. Sharad Rao (Kenya).

[EDS. In gymnastics, an individual competitor's score is awarded by a combination of start values based on the degree of difficulty in a particular routine and on execution as determined by FIG's Code of Points. The primary purpose of this Code is to provide an objective means of evaluating gymnastics exercises, and each gymnast "has the right [t]o have his performance judged correctly, fairly, and in accordance with the stipulations of the Code of Points."

Unlike sports such as diving, an evaluation of the start value of a gymnastics routine is not made before its performance because gymnasts will frequently modify a planned routine in response to competitive circumstances, or will fail to execute a planned element. The judges' assessment of start values is in part subjective and in part objective. Elements that make up start values such as a Belle or a Morisue are objectively identified. Whether any element has been fully performed is a matter of subjective judgment. In this case, the three judges responsible for determining the start value of Yang's parallel bars routine erroneously characterized a Belle as a Morisue, giving him a start value of 9.9 rather than 10. Video analysis confirmed that Yang's start value should have been 10.]

. . . [A]s was conceded on behalf of Yang and KOC, the protest even *if* made *before* the Medal Ceremony was certainly made *after* the competition had ended with the conclusion of the sixth rotation [for the high bar]. . . .

There is no doubt that a mechanism exists for reversing judging errors, although there did not appear to be universal familiarity with it even among those responsible for its operation. . . . The Chair of the Apparatus Jury has the power, with the approval of the Chair of the Competition Jury, to change "*an extremely incorrect score*" . . . [T]he Code provides also for the Superior Jury, on which the same person also sits, to supervise the competition where there is a grave error of judgment on the part of one or several judges to take such action as they consider necessary— (words large enough to embrace reversing marks as well as disciplining judges) —and continually to review the marks awarded by judges.

It is, however, notable that all the provisions we have recited refer to the role of the persons/bodies *vis a vis a competition.* . . . We consider that this sufficiently identifies that any appeal must be dealt with during, not after a competition. After a competition, the person/body is effectively functus officio. This interpretation conforms with the natural expectation of both participants, spectators and the public at large that at the close of a competition in any sport, gymnastics included, the identity of the winner should be known, and not subject to alteration thereafter save where exceptionally, for example, the purported winner is proved to have failed a drug test and so been disqualified. . . .

The extent to which, if at all, a Court including CAS can interfere with an official's decision is not wholly clear. An absolute refusal to recognize such a decision as justiciable and to designate the field of play as "*a domain into which the King's writ does not seek to run*" in Lord Atkin's famous phrase would have a defensible purpose and philosophy. It would recognize that there are areas of human activity which elude the grasp of the law, and where the solution to disputes is better found, if at all, by agreement. It would contribute to finality. It would uphold, critically, the authority of the umpire, judge or referee, whose power to control competition, already eroded by the growing use of technology such as video replays, would be fatally undermined if every decision taken could be judicially reviewed. And, to the extent that the matter is capable of analysis in conventional legal terms, it could rest on the premise that any contract that the player has made in entering into a competition is that he or she should have the benefit of honest "field of play" decisions, not necessarily correct ones.

Sports law does not, however, have a policy of complete abstention. In *Mendy v. AIBA* where the challenge was to a referee's decision to disqualify a boxer for a low blow (CAS OG 96/06), the CAS ad hoc Panel accepted jurisdiction, even over a game rule, but considered it inappropriate to exercise it. It said . . .

> [T]he referee's decision, is a purely technical one pertaining to the rules which are the responsibility of the federation concerned. It is not for the ad hoc Panel to review the application of these rules. This restraint is all the more necessary since, far from where the action took place, the ad hoc Panel is less well-placed to decide than the referee in the ring or the ring judges. The above-mentioned restraint must be limited to technical decisions or standards; it does not apply when such decisions are taken in violation of the law, social rules, or general principles of law, which is not the case in this particular instance. . . .

In short courts may interfere only if an official's field of play decision is tainted by fraud or arbitrariness or corruption; otherwise although a Court may have jurisdiction it will abstain as a matter of policy from exercising it. . . .

[EDs. The CAS rejected Yang's claim that the judges' scoring decision was arbitrary because one judge's head was lowered at the start of his routine, causing him to not observe a second of Yang's initial sequence. Quoting *KOC v. ISU*, *infra*, the arbitrators explained that "arbitrary" or "bad faith" means "more than that the decision is wrong or one that no sensible person could have reached. If it were otherwise, every field of play decision would be open to review on the merits. . . . [E]ach of those phrases means there must be some evidence of preference for, or prejudice against, a particular team or individual."]

While in this instance we are being asked, not to second guess an official but rather to consider the consequences of an admitted error by an official so that the "field of play" jurisprudence is not directly engaged, we consider that we should nonetheless abstain from correcting the results by reliance of an admitted error. An error identified with the benefit of hindsight, whether admitted or not, cannot be a ground for reversing a result of a competition. We can all recall occasions where a video replay of a football match, studied at leisure, can show that a goal was given, when it should have been disallowed (the Germans may still hold that view about England's critical third goal in the World Cup Final in 1966), or vice versa, or where in a tennis match a critical line call was mistaken. However, quite apart from the consideration, which we develop below, that no one can be certain how the competition in question would have turned out had the official's decision been different, for a Court to change the result would on this basis still involve interfering with a field of play decision. Each sport may have within it a mechanism for utilising modern technology to ensure a correct decision is made in the first place (e.g., cricket with run-outs) or for immediately subjecting a controversial decision to a process of review (e.g., gymnastics) but the solution for error, either way, lies within the framework of the sport's own rules; it does not licence judicial or arbitral interference thereafter. If this represents an extension of the field of play doctrine, we tolerate it with equanimity. Finality is in this area all important: rough justice may be all that sport can tolerate. As the CAS Panel said in *KOC v. IOC*:

> There is a more fundamental reason for not permitting trial, by television or otherwise, of technical, judgmental decisions by referees. Every participant in a sport in which referees have to make decisions about events on the field of play must accept that the referee sees an incident from a particular position, and makes his decision on the basis of what he or she sees. Sometimes mistakes are made by referees, as they are players. That is an inevitable fact of life and one that all participants in sporting events must accept. But not every mistake can be reviewed. It is for that reason that CAS jurisprudence makes it clear that it is not open to a player to complain about a "field of play" decision simply because he or she disagrees with that decision.

There is another and powerful consideration, well articulated on behalf of Hamm. Had the competition been on one apparatus only, i.e., the parallel bars, then the conclusion that the judging error led to a disarray in the medal positions would follow as night follows day. (We put on one side the contention . . . that Yang had the benefit of the error—a failure by AB Judges to deduct points for a gymnastic fault exceeding the stipulated number of pauses during his exercise. . . .) But the event was not a single apparatus event, but an all around one.

After the parallel bars there was one more apparatus on which the competitors had to perform, i.e., the high bar. We have no means of knowing how Yang would have reacted had he concluded the competition in this apparatus as the points leader rather than in third position. He might have risen to the occasion; he might have frozen (his marks on the high bar were in fact below expectation and speculation is inappropriate.) So it needs to be clearly stated that while the error *may* have cost Yang a gold medal, it did not necessarily do so. . . .

There are two victims of this unusual sequence of events, Hamm and Yang. Hamm because, as he eloquently explained, a shadow of doubt has been cast over his achievement in winning the sport's most prestigious prize. Yang because he may have been deprived of an opportunity of winning it. Both Hamm and Yang are superb athletes at the pinnacle of their sport: neither was in any way responsible for the Judge's error: each has comported himself with dignity which this controversy has subsisted. Nonetheless the Court of Arbitration is not Solomon: nor can it mediate a solution acceptable to both gymnasts or their respective NOCs. CAS must give a verdict based on its findings of fact viewed in the context of the relevant law.

For the reasons set out above, we dismiss this appeal.

NOTES AND QUESTIONS

1. *Scope of CAS Jurisdiction to Resolve Disputes Regarding Competition Results.* Even if rules provide that athletics governing body's final determination of competition results is not appealable, "CAS will always have jurisdiction to overrule the Rules of any sport federation if its decision making bodies conduct themselves with a lack of good faith or not in accordance with due process." Arbitration CAS Ad Hoc Division (O.G. Athens 2004) 009, *Hellenic Olympic Committee and Nikolaos Kaklamanakis v. International Sailing Federation*, award of August 24, 2004. The CAS has ruled that a sports governing body must comply with and consistently apply objective criteria established by its rules such as time or points earned by competition results when selecting athletes for a team or event. Arbitration CAS 2000/A/284, *Sullivan v. The Judo Federation of Australia, Inc., the Judo Federation of Australia, Inc. Appeal Tribunal, and Raguz*, award of August 14, 2000, in Digest of CAS Awards II 1998-2000, at 542.

In Arbitration CAS Ad Hoc Division (O.G. Sydney 2000) 012, *Rumyana Dimitrova Neykova v. International Rowing Federation (FISA) and International Olympic Committee (IOC)*, Award of 29 September, 2000, in Digest of CAS Awards II 1998-2000, at 674, the applicant claimed that television video called into question the accuracy of the official finish of the 2002 Olympics women's single sculls event and indicated the possibility of mechanical error in the photo finish depicted by the official race camera. Because of the 0.0012-second difference between the first- and second-place finishers and the videotape evidence, applicant asked the CAS to declare the race a dead heat and award two gold medals. Rejecting this claim, the CAS stated:

> The issue presented here, however, is somewhat different to that of a typical official's field of play decision, in that it is the accuracy of the technical equipment used that is being challenged and not the judgment of any official. Be this as it may, it is not necessary for this panel to determine to what extent a challenge of a field of play decision based on faulty equipment may be reopened by CAS. Indeed, the Applicant, who has the burden of proof, has not proved that the technical equipment was deficient. Therefore, even if *arguendo* the decision could be reopened, the Application would have to be dismissed for lack of proof.

If the applicant had proven that the official race equipment was defective, how should the CAS have resolved this case?

2. *Other Recent Controversies Regarding Olympic Sports Competition Results.* During the 2002 Salt Lake City Olympics, American speed skater Apolo Ohno won a silver medal in the 1,000 meters despite suffering a minor injury from falling in a chain-reaction, multiskater collision while jostling for position with Chinese skater Li Jiajun, who was disqualified by officials. Subsequently, Ohno was awarded the gold medal in the 1,500 meters after Kim Dong-

Sung, a Korean skater, was disqualified by International Skating Union (ISU) judges for illegally blocking him during the race. This controversial decision resulted in an unsuccessful appeal of Kim's disqualification to the CAS, which the *Yang* CAS panel relied on in its decision allowing Paul Hamm to retain his gold medal despite an acknowledged judging error. Months later, at the 2002 soccer World Cup, several South Korean players pantomimed like they were speed skating when their team scored a tying goal on the U.S. team.

During the 2002 Olympics, by a 5-4 judges' decision, a Russian pairs figure-skating team won the gold medal despite making a few technical errors, while the silver medalist Canadian team skated flawlessly. Shortly thereafter, the French competition judge claimed the French skating federation president had pressured her to vote for the Russians. Based on a recommendation from the ISU, the IOC's executive board voted to also award gold medals to the Canadian team. Because there was no evidence of any Russian involvement in the matter, the Russian team was permitted to keep its gold medals. If the IOC had allowed the initial competition results to stand, would the Canadian team have prevailed in an appeal to the CAS? Although the French judge later recanted her accusation, the ISU suspended her and the French federation president for three years plus the 2006 Olympics. This scandal led the ISU to change its methods of judging skaters' performances. After Keith Sieracki lost an arbitrator-ordered rematch with Matt Lindland and unsuccessfully sought relief from American courts (see *Lindland v. USA Wrestling, supra*), he filed a petition with the CAS challenging the IOC's decision to withdraw him as a member of the United States Greco-Roman wrestling team for the 2000 Sydney Olympics. However, faced with a federal court order restraining him from pursuing this claim under threat of contempt sanctions, he withdrew his appeal before the CAS heard his case. Is it likely that the CAS would have ruled in his favor?

In *NOC of Sweden and Ara Abrahamian v IOC*, Arbitration CAS 2008/A/1647, award of February 12, 2009, the CAS upheld the IOC's decision to strip a Greco-Roman wrestler of his bronze medal, which he rejected during the medal ceremony to protest his disqualification during a semifinal bout in violation of international wrestling federation rules that allegedly denied his right to a fair competition. The CAS reasoned, "The Athlete chose to reject his medal. That is a course of conduct, the consequence of which he should, and must, live with and is not to be disturbed by action of this Panel. The manner by which he rejected his medal caused him to violate the Olympic Charter. His own actions preclude making a determination that the sanction was not proportional to his conduct. The IOC's decision did nothing more than affirm the state of affairs created by the Athlete himself."

PROBLEM 4-3

During the Olympics in Athens with only seconds left in a game in which the Ruritanian team led 3-2, a Ruritanian soccer player elbowed a Slobovian soccer player in the head. This injury ultimately caused him to lose the sight in his right eye. At the time of this incident, the Slobovian player was ten feet directly in front of the Ruritanian goal (within the Ruritanian penalty area) and was preparing to kick the ball toward the net. However, the force of the blow caused him to lose control of the ball. Although he clearly observed this incident, the Coste Pobre referee did not call this a foul or award a penalty kick to the Slobovian team. If the Slobovian team had made the penalty kick, it would have tied the game and advanced to the medal round of the competition rather than the Coste Pobre soccer team.

The "laws of the game" for soccer, promulgated by the International Association Football Federation (FIFA), the sport's governing body, provide as follows: The referee will send a player off the field and show him the red card for being guilty of "serious foul play" or "violent conduct." The opposing team will be awarded a penalty kick if, inside his own penalty area, a player "strikes or attempts to strike an opponent in a manner considered by the referee to be too careless, reckless or using excessive force." "The decisions of a referee regarding facts connected with a play are final."

After the soccer match ended, FIFA's Match Protest Committee reviewed a videotape of the incident, but rejected the Slobovian team's challenge to the referee's refusal to call a foul and its request for a penalty kick. As a result, the Ruritanian team was declared the winner of the match. This decision was upheld by FIFA's Executive Board later the same day.

Discuss how the CAS is likely to resolve the Slobovian soccer team's appeal of FIFA's decision.

6.   *Doping Violations and Sanctions*

a.   **Strict Liability Standard, Clear Notice Requirements, and Proportionate and Authorized Sanctions**

As a policy matter, the CAS has upheld a sport's governing body's adoption and use of a strict liability standard (i.e., liability without any personal fault) for doping offenses. In *USA Shooting and Q. v. Int'l Shooting Union* (*Quigley*), Arbitration CAS 94/129, Award of May 23, 1995, in Matthieu Reeb, Digest of CAS Awards 1986-1998 (1998) at 187, the CAS stated:

> It is true that a strict liability test is likely in some sense to be unfair in an individual case, such as that of Q., where the athlete may have taken medication as the result of mislabelling or faulty advice for which he or she is not responsible—particularly in the circumstances of sudden illness in a foreign country. But it is also in some sense "unfair" for an athlete to get food poisoning on the eve of an important competition. Yet in neither case will the rules of the competition be altered to undo the unfairness. Just as the competition will not be postponed to await the athlete's recovery, so the prohibition of banned substances will not be lifted in recognition of its accidental absorption. The vicissitudes of competition, like those of life generally, may create many types of unfairness, whether by accident or the negligence of unaccountable persons, which the law cannot repair.
>
> Furthermore, it appears to be a laudable policy objective not to repair an accidental unfairness to an individual by creating an intentional unfairness to the whole body of other competitors. This is what would happen if banned performance-enhancing substances were tolerated when absorbed inadvertently. Moreover, it is likely that even intentional abuse would in many cases escape sanction for lack of proof of guilty intent. And it is certain that a requirement of intent would invite costly litigation that may well cripple federations—particularly those run on modest budgets—in their fight against doping.

In *Quigley*, the CAS stated that doping rules must provide clear notice to protect athletes' legitimate expectations. It explained that if a strict liability test is adopted, "it becomes even more important that the rules for the testing procedure are crystal clear, that they are designed for reliability, and that it may be shown that they have been followed." Moreover, "as a general matter, if breaches of specific requirements laid down by a federation for the testing procedure are sufficiently material as to call into question the validity and correctness of the positive result, any athlete would be entitled to have that federation's decision overturned." The CAS panel ruled that the athlete, who tested positive for a banned stimulant in medication prescribed by a physician for bronchitis while competing in a skeet shooting competition in Egypt, did not commit a doping violation because the IF rule defined doping as the use of a banned substance "with the aim of attaining an increase in performance." The language of this rule did not clearly articulate a strict liability standard for doping offenses.

Applying these principles, the CAS Ad Hoc Division for the 1998 Nagano Winter Olympics overturned the IOC's decision to strip the winner of the giant slalom event of his gold medal for a positive marijuana test. The CAS ruled that the IOC's sanction lacked a valid basis because neither its rules nor those of the international skiing federation clearly banned the usage of marijuana. Olympic athletes were tested for marijuana solely to compile a database for determining whether its usage is a sports-related problem justifying its ban. Arbitration CAS Ad Hoc Division (O.G. Nagano 1998) 002, *R. v. International Olympic Committee (IOC)* (*Rebagliati*), award of February 12, 1998, in Digest of CAS Awards 1986-1998 at 419 (Reeb, ed. 1998).

NOTES AND QUESTIONS

1. *Strict Liability Standard.* Why does the CAS uphold strict liability for a doping violation? Does this standard appropriately balance all parties' interests?

   Consistent with *Quigley*, the CAS Ad Hoc Division for the Sydney Summer Olympics upheld clearly defined IOC strict liability doping rules requiring Romanian gymnast Andreea Raducan to forfeit her gold medal in the women's individual all-around competition in artistic gymnastics. She tested positive for pseudoephedrine, a banned substance, after taking a cold and flu tablet prescribed by the Romanian gymnastics team doctor on the day she competed in this event. The CAS ruled that this doping violation justified the stripping of her gold medal "as a matter of fairness to all other athletes." Raducan did not challenge the identity or integrity of her urine sample or the validity of its analysis, but pointed out a discrepancy between the recorded total volume of her collected urine sample (62 mL) and that which arrived at the laboratory (80 mL in the A sample, and 20 mL in the B sample). The CAS ruled that "the minor irregularity revealed in the record showing the volume of urine taken cannot reasonably be considered to have affected the results of what is a valid test." It also rejected her claimed defenses that pseudoephedrine impaired (rather than enhanced) her athletic performance, that heavier athletes would not produce positive test results if taking the same dosage of the drug as she did, and that she is a 16-year-old minor who should not be found guilty of doping under these circumstances. Arbitration CAS Ad Hoc Division (O.S. Sydney 2000) 011, *Andreea Raducan v. International Olympic Committee (IOC)*, award of 28

September, 2000, in CAS Awards-Sydney: The Decisions Delivered by the ad hoc Division of the Court of Arbitration for Sport During the 2000 Olympic Games in Sydney (2000) at 111.

Do you agree with the CAS panel's decision? (Note that Olympic athletes have the ability to seek prior approval to take a particular medication from the IOC's medical authority, a process not utilized by Raducan.)

Raducan unsuccessfully appealed the CAS's decision to the Swiss Federal Tribunal. (Why didn't she appeal to an Australian court in Sydney?) Recognizing there should be "a very special rigor in the scrupulous application of the testing procedures issued by [a] sporting body," the Swiss court found that the recorded sample volume discrepancy did not impact the positive results of the sample analysis. Because Raducan admitted taking cold medication containing a prohibited substance, it upheld the CAS's finding of a doping violation because the relevant IOC rule defined it to include "evidence of the use thereof." The court noted that "in the context of anti-doping testing, the athlete is in a precarious situation, since the simple presence of a prohibited substance in his or her urine triggers a legal presumption of doping, which the athlete can rebut only by proving a malevolent act by a third party or an erroneous analysis result." *Raducan v. International Olympic Committee*, 5P.427/2000 (2d Civil Court, Dec. 4, 2000).

2. *Proportionate and Authorized Sanctions.* In *Chagnaud v. FINA*, Arbitration CAS 95/141, Award of April 22, 1996, the CAS concluded, "[T]he system of strict liability of the athlete must prevail when sporting fairness is at stake. This means that, once a banned substance is discovered in the urine or blood of an athlete, he must automatically be disqualified from the competition in question, without any possibility for him to rebut this presumption of guilt (irrebuttable presumption). It would indeed be shocking to include in a ranking an athlete who had not competed using the same means as his opponents, for whatever reasons." However, it ruled that sports governing bodies "should make allowance for an appreciation of the subjective elements in each case" in order to determine "a just and equitable sanction." Rather than a fixed minimum sanction for all doping offenses (e.g., a two-year suspension), the CAS panel expressed its preference for "a sliding scale of suspension periods depending on the degree of fault of the athlete." Applying this principle of proportionality, it reduced a swimmer's suspension from the two-year period provided by FINA's rules to approximately 13½ months because her coach mistakenly gave her a tablet that she did not know contained a banned substance shortly before an event.

In *USOC v. IOC & IAAF*, Arbitration CAS 2004/A/725, award of July 20, 2005, the CAS reversed the IAAF's decision to disqualify the United States 1,600-meter relay team (which won the gold medal in the 2000 Sydney Games) because of Jerome Young's 1999 positive drug test. In June 2004, the CAS found that Young, who competed in a preliminary round as a member of the American 1,600-meter Olympic relay team, committed a 1999 doping offense and that he was ineligible to participate in the 2000 Sydney Games (which resulted in the loss of his gold medal). In July 2004, the IAAF determined that the United States team's first-place finish in the 1,600-meter relay should be annulled because of Young's ineligibility to compete in the 2000 Olympics.

The CAS found that the IAAF's rules in effect in 2000 concerned only the disqualification, ineligibility, and annulment of an individual athlete's performance results; it was not until their amendment in 2004-2005 that the rules expressly required disqualification of the result of any relay team for which an ineligible athlete competed. The CAS arbitration panel explained:

> To take a rule that plainly concerns individual ineligibility and the annulment of individual results, and then to stretch and complement and construe it in order that it may be said to govern the results achieved by teams, is the sort of legal abracadabra that lawyers and partisans in the fight against doping in sport can love, but in which athletes should not be required to engage in order to understand the meaning of the rules to which they are subject. . . . The rationale for requiring clarity of rules extends beyond enabling athletes in given cases to determine their conduct in such cases by reference to understandable rules. As argued by the Appellants at the hearing, clarity and predictability are required so that the entire sport community are informed of the normative system in which they live, work and compete, which requires at the very least that they be able to understand the meaning of rules and the circumstances in which those rules apply.

See also *Anderson, et al. v. IOC*, Arbitration CAS 2008/A/1545, award of July 16, 2010 (ruling that U.S. teams that competed in women's 4 × 100 meters and 4 × 400 meters relay events in 2000 Sydney Games should not be disqualified and seven U.S. female team members may keep medals won, although Marion Jones ran in both medal-winning final relays and subsequently admitted to a doping offense during the Games resulting in her individual disqualification and return of medals; "the Panel concurs with the convincing analysis of the CAS 2004/A/725 panel and sees no reason to reach a different conclusion" regarding applicable IAAF rule in effect in 2000); *Tzagaev v. Int'l Weightlifting Federation*, Arbitration CAS Ad Hoc Division 010 (O.G. Sydney 2000) (award of September 25, 2000) (annulling International Weightlifting Federation's decision to prohibit all Bulgarian weightlifters from further participation in the Sydney Olympics after three of them tested positive for banned substances because "suspension of an entire federation from participation in the Olympic Games, including innocent athletes who have not committed a doping offence or any other violation of the applicable rules, at least requires an explicit, and unambiguous legal basis").

b.   Interpretation and Application of the World Anti-Doping Code

On November 10, 1999, the World Anti-Doping Agency (WADA), an international collaborative effort between governments and sports organizations to combat doping in sport, was established in Lausanne, Switzerland. Its purpose is to promote harmonization and equity for athlete drug testing as well as to establish common and effective minimum standards for doping controls, especially for out-of-competition tests, and uniform sanctions for doping.

On March 5, 2003, at the World Conference on Doping in Sport held in Copenhagen, Denmark, almost 80 national governments and all of the major international sports federations approved the first World Anti-Doping Code

(WADA Code).[2] The code seeks to harmonize regulations regarding anti-doping across all sports and all countries of the world. It is described as "a core document that will provide a framework for anti-doping policies, rules and regulations within sport organizations and among public authorities."

The WADA Code seeks to protect all athletes' "fundamental right to participate in doping-free sport and thus promote health, fairness and equality" worldwide. According to the code, "Anti-doping rules, like *Competition* rules, are sports rules governing the conditions under which sport is played. All *Athletes* or other *Persons* accept these rules as a condition of participation and shall be bound" by them. The code states that WADA will consider including a substance or method on its banned list if it meets any two of three criteria: (1) medical or scientific evidence or pharmacological effect or experience demonstrates that it, alone or in combination, "has the potential to enhance or enhances sport performance; (2) medical or scientific evidence or pharmacological effect or experience demonstrates that its usage represents an actual or potential health risk to an athlete; or (3) WADA has determined that its usage "violates the spirit of sport." It establishes a uniform system of drug-testing procedures and fixes sanctions for violations, which may be reduced in "exceptional circumstances" if the athlete bears "no fault or no negligence" or "no significant fault or no significant negligence." Virtually all international sports federations now have adopted and implemented the code, which applies to their respective NGBs and athletes.

A revised World Anti-Doping Code, which became effective on January 1, 2009, was adopted by the WADA Foundation Board at a November 2007 conference in Madrid, Spain. See http://www.wada-ama.org/Documents/World_Anti-Doping_Program/WADP-The-Code/WADA_Anti-Doping_CODE_2009_EN.pdf. It provides the CAS with more flexibility in reducing or decreasing the standard two-year suspension for a first doping offense, but still does not permit consideration of an individual athlete's personal circumstances. An athlete's immediate admission or cooperation with a doping violation may reduce his sanction; conversely, it may be increased if there are aggravating circumstances. The entire team may be sanctioned if more than two of its members commit a doping violation. The WADA Code currently is being reviewed, and a new edition will be issued in 2013.

In July 2008, the U.S. Senate ratified the International Convention Against Doping in Sport adopted by the United Nations Educational, Scientific, and Cultural Organization on October 19, 2005, which is based on the WADA Code. On August 4, 2008, shortly before the Beijing Olympics began, President Bush signed the treaty's instrument of ratification.[3]

---

2. For two independent legal opinions that the WADA Code complies with Swiss law and commonly accepted principles of international law, see http://www.wada-ama.org/en/World-Anti-Doping-Program/Legal-articles-case-law-and-national-laws/Advisory-and-Legal-Opinions-on-the-Code/.

3. The National Collegiate Athletic Association and U.S. professional sports leagues and their respective athletes, which are not members of an international sports federation or currently directly regulated by the federal government, are not automatically subject to the WADA Code. In accordance with federal labor law, doping regimens for unionized professional sports leagues are established by collective bargaining. See Chapter 7. However, it is important to note that all U.S. college and professional athletes must agree to comply with the WADA Code as a condition of competing in the Olympic Games.

The following case provides an example of how the CAS has interpreted and applied the WADA Code.

GUILLERMO CANAS v. ATP TOUR
Arbitration CAS 2005/A/951
Revised Award of 23 May 2007

Panel: Ms Maidie Oliveau (USA); Mr Christopher Campbell (USA); Mr Yves Fortier (Canada)

[EDS. Guillermo Canas is a professional tennis player from Argentina who has been a member of the ATP Tour since 1995 and a member of the ATP's Player Council since 2004. The Respondent, ATP Tour, is a not-for-profit membership organization composed of male professional tennis players and tournament organizations. The ATP sanctions tennis tournaments and provides league governance and support to its member tournaments and players.]

In relevant part, the ATP's anti-doping rules, which are largely patterned after the World Anti-Doping Code (WADC) and applicable to all ATP players, are as follows:

C.   DOPING OFFENSES

Doping is defined as the occurrence of one or more of the following (each, a "Doping Offense"):

1. The presence of a Prohibited Substance or its Metabolites or Markers in a Player's Specimen, unless the Player establishes that the presence is pursuant to a therapeutic use exemption. . . .

a) It is each Player's personal duty to ensure that no Prohibited Substance enters his body. A Player is responsible for any Prohibited Substance or its Metabolites or Markers found to be present in his Specimen. Accordingly, it is not necessary that intent, fault, negligence or knowing Use on the Player's part be demonstrated in order to establish a Doping Offense under Article C.1; nor is the Player's lack of intent, fault, negligence or knowledge a defense to a charge that a Doping Offense has been committed under Article C.1. . . .

K.   DUE PROCESS . . .

3. Burdens and Standards of Proof

a) The ATP . . . shall have the burden of establishing that a Doping Offense has been committed. The standard of proof shall be whether the ATP has established the commission of the alleged Doping Offense to the comfortable satisfaction of the Anti-Doping Tribunal, bearing in mind the seriousness of the allegation that is made. This standard of proof in all cases is greater than a mere balance of probability but less than proof beyond a reasonable doubt.

b) Where this Program places the burden of proof upon the Participant alleged to have committed a Doping Offense to rebut a presumption or establish specified facts or circumstances, the standard of proof shall be by a balance of probability.

L.   Automatic Disqualification of Individual Results

1. A Doping Offense committed by a Player in connection with or arising out of an In-Competition test automatically leads to Disqualification of the individual result obtained by the Player involved in that Competition with all resulting consequences, including forfeiture of any medals, titles, computer ranking points and prize money (without deduction for tax) obtained in that Competition.

M. Sanctions on Individuals . . .

2. *Imposition of Ineligibility for Prohibited Substances and Prohibited Methods.* . . . [T]the period of ineligibility imposed for a violation of Article C.1 . . . shall be: First offense: Two (2) years' Ineligibility. Second offense: Lifetime Ineligibility. However, the Participant shall have the opportunity in each case, before a period of ineligibility is imposed, to establish the basis for eliminating or reducing this sanction as provided in Article M.5. . . .

5. *Elimination or Reduction of Period of Ineligibility Based on Exceptional Circumstances.*

a) If the Player establishes in an individual case involving a Doping Offense under Article C.1 (presence of Prohibited Substance or its Metabolites or Markers) or Article C.2 (Use of a Prohibited Substance or Prohibited Method) that he bears *No Fault or Negligence* for the offense, the otherwise applicable period of ineligibility shall be eliminated. When the case involves a Doping Offense under Article C.1 (presence of a Prohibited Substance or its Metabolites or Markers), the Player must also establish how the Prohibited Substance entered his or her system in order to have the period of Ineligibility eliminated. . . .

b) This Article M.5.b applies only to Doping Offenses involving Article C.1. . . .

If a Player establishes in an individual case involving such offenses that he bears *No Significant Fault or Negligence,* then the period of Ineligibility may be reduced, but the reduced period of Ineligibility may not be less than one-half of the minimum period of Ineligibility otherwise applicable. . . . When the Doping Offense involves Article C.1 (presence of Prohibited Substance or its Markers or Metabolites), the Player must also establish how the Prohibited Substance entered his or her system in order to have the period of Ineligibility reduced.

DEFINITIONS

No Fault or Negligence. The Player establishing that he did not know or suspect, and could not reasonably have known or suspected even with the exercise of utmost caution, that he had Used or been administered the Prohibited Substance or Prohibited Method.

No Significant Fault or Negligence. The Player establishing that his or her fault or negligence, when viewed in the totality of the circumstances and taking into account the criteria for No Fault or Negligence, was not significant in relationship to the Doping Offense.

Canas provided a urine specimen during an ATP sanctioned tournament, the "Abierto Mexicano de Tenis" in Acapulco, Mexico, on February 21, 2005.

The Appellant's case is next reviewed under the provisions of ATP Rules M.5.b (which allows Player to establish *No Significant Fault or Negligence*). . . .

It is the degree of negligence which is at issue pursuant to the criteria established in the ATP Rules. The definition of *No Significant Fault or Negligence* requires the Panel to look at "the totality of the circumstances."

The following factors weigh in the Appellant's favor: Appellant was at a Tournament sanctioned by the Respondent, where as a star player, he had every expectation that his visit to the Tournament doctor . . . would be the safest possible way for him to obtain medical treatment for his condition. There was no use of this or any other Prohibited Substance in any competition other than the one in respect of which the specimen was obtained. The reason for Player's ingestion of the substance was clearly medical. A mistake in the delivery of the medication was made not by Appellant or anyone working for him, but rather by the Tournament employees. . . .

Taking into account these factors, the Panel believes that the present case is substantially different from the typical doping case and qualifies as "exceptional." Appellant has established that he bears *No Significant Fault or Negligence*, allowing for the period of *Ineligibility* to be reduced by no less than one-half of the minimum period of *Ineligibility* otherwise applicable (ATP Rules M.5.b.), which in this instance is two years. . . .

Based on the provisions of ATP Rules M.5.b., the Panel must determine the actual period of ineligibility to be imposed on Appellant. . . . [T]he period of ineligibility can range between one and two years. In deciding how this wide range is to be applied in a particular case, one must closely examine and evaluate the athlete's level of fault or negligence. . . .

The following factors weigh against the Player in determining his level of fault or negligence: He did not list the medications on the doping control form he completed during the Tournament. He took the medication he received with no review whatsoever of the contents of the box, even though he knew that the medication had been through several hands before being delivered to him. At the hearing held before the Tribunal, Player was unable to recall whether he took pills or liquid but he now recognizes Rofucal as the medication he took. He is an experienced professional tennis player, active on the Player Council and aware of the risks inherent in the ingestion of unknown substances.

Under the circumstances, he could have at least made the effort to double check the prescription he was given against the medication he received or at least paid attention to the medications he was taking and read the label. . . .

Weighing all of the factors in favor of and against the Appellant identified above, the previous CAS decisions with respect to medical prescriptions and the totality of the circumstances, the Panel is unable to give the Player the maximum reduction in the period of ineligibility. Thus, the Panel determines that Player's period of ineligibility will be reduced by nine months, from two years to fifteen months. . . .

In accordance with ATP Rules L.1., Appellant's results obtained at the Tournament shall be disqualified, including forfeiture of any medals, titles, computer ranking points and prize money. . . .

NOTES AND QUESTIONS

1. *Legality of WADA Code Sanctions.* Pursuant to the WADA Code, which was incorporated into the ATP's anti-doping rules, what are the consequences

of an athlete's doping violation? What defenses did Guillermo Canas raise in response to the ATP's doping allegations, and how did the CAS panel resolve these issues?

Canas also asserted that, because his doping violation was unintentional, the standards for reducing his period of ineligibility are "too strict," "fall short of the proportionality doctrine," and "do not provide the Panel with sufficient discretion to consider all relevant factors and, as a result of such consideration, arrive at a result that meets the justice of the overall case" in violation of Delaware, U.S., and European law. In response, the ATP relied on a 2003 independent legal opinion obtained by WADA concluding that a fixed two-year period of ineligibility regardless of the seriousness of the doping offense does not conflict with fundamental principles of law because of the need for uniform doping sanctions for all sports. See Gabrielle Kaufmann-Kohler, Antonio Rigozzi, and Giorgio Malinverni, *Legal Opinion on the Conformity of Certain Provisions of the Draft World Anti-Doping Code with Commonly Accepted Principles of International Law*, Feb. 26, 2003, http://www.wada-ama.org/Documents/World_Anti-Doping_Program/ WADP-Legal_Library/Advisory_and_Legal_Opinions/kaufmann-kohler-full.pdf. It also argued that flexibility as to the appropriate sanction should be narrowly circumscribed and based only on the degree of Canas's fault or negligence.

The CAS panel determined that no applicable national or transnational laws were violated and concluded:

> [T]he ATP Rules give enough latitude to allow for a sanction proportionate to the fault or negligence committed to be imposed on the Player. The Panel did exercise such latitude by establishing that the Appellant bears *No Significant Fault or Negligence*, allowing for the period of ineligibility to be reduced. Respondent adopted the ATP Rules in furtherance of a legitimate objective taking into account the difficulty of determining the intent of any player and the effect on his performance when taking a particular substance. Such Rules are reasonably aimed to foster the proper organization of professional tennis.

2. *"Exceptional Circumstances."* The existence of "exceptional circumstances" under the WADA Code establishing "no fault or negligence" or "no significant fault or negligence" for a doping violation is necessarily a fact-specific inquiry to determine the reasonableness of an athlete's action (or inaction) to ensure that he or she does not ingest or use a banned substance.

As illustrated by *Canas*, it is very difficult (but not impossible) for an athlete be able to prove "no fault or negligence" for a doping offense. In *Pobyedonostev v. IIHF*, CAS 2005/A/990 (2005), the CAS panel found that an ice hockey player's positive test for norandrosterone was caused by emergency hospital treatment in Europe following his on-ice injury. Unknown to him, while unconscious in the hospital, he was treated for a heart condition with a steroid called retabolil. He left the hospital 24 hours after receiving treatment, resumed training soon afterward, and did not discover he had been treated for his heart condition until long after his positive test. The panel determined he was without fault or negligence because, under the circumstances, he had no reason to suspect he was being treated with any medication for a heart condition.

In *ITF and WADA v. Richard Gasquet,* Arbitration CAS 2009/A/1926 & 1930, award of December 17, 2009, the CAS determined that a professional tennis player's positive urine test for a small amount of cocaine more likely than not resulted from kissing a previously unknown woman in a nightclub multiple times. The panel concluded: "under the given circumstances, even if the Player exercised the utmost caution, he could not have been aware of the consequences of kissing a girl who he had met in a totally unsuspicious environment. It was simply impossible for the Player, even when exercising the utmost caution, to know that in kissing Pamela, he could be contaminated with cocaine. The Player therefore acted without fault or negligence." It observed that "the [ITF Anti-doping] Programme cannot impose an obligation on an athlete never to go out to any restaurant or nightclub where he might meet an attractive stranger whom he might later be tempted to kiss. This would be an unrealistic and impractical expectation that should not be imposed on athletes by sanctioning bodies in their endeavors to defeat doping."

By comparison, in *IRB v. Keyter,* Arbitration CAS 2006/A/1067, award of October 13, 2006, the CAS found no "exceptional circumstances" justifying reduction of a two-year suspension for a positive cocaine test because athlete's alleged ingestion through "'spiked drink' is only a speculative guess"; even if supported by plausible evidence, the athlete was significantly negligent by "getting drunk, and possibly not realizing and/or remembering what was going on." See also *Galabin Boevski v. IWF,* Arbitration CAS 2004/A/607, award of December 6, 2004 (finding doping violation and rejecting weightlifter's claim that his urine sample was sabotaged with urine free of any prohibited substance because, without evidence indicating any manipulation by a third party, "it is beyond a reasonable doubt that manipulation occurred through something the athlete did or condoned").

In *UCI & WADA v. Contador & RFEC,* CAS 2011/A/2384 and CAS 2011/A/2386, award of February 6, 2012, the CAS rejected the contention of Alberto Contador, a Spanish cyclist who won the 2012 Tour de France, that his positive test for a very small amount of the banned substance clenbuterol resulted from eating contaminated meat both the day before and the day of his sample collection, thereby negating any negligent behavior on his part. The CAS panel found that "if the meat he ate was contaminated with clenbuterol, it is possible that this caused the presence of 50 pg/mL clenbuterol in [his] urine doping sample." However, it found "no established facts that would elevate the possibility of meat contamination to an event that could have occurred on a balance of probabilities," which Contador was required to prove. The panel concluded, "[I]n light of all the evidence on record, the Athlete's positive test for clenbuterol is more likely to have been caused by the ingestion of a contaminated food supplement," which Contador would bear complete responsibility for taking. Contador was found guilty of a doping violation, which resulted in the loss of his Tour de France title and a two-year ban from competition. Note that the Comments to Article 10.5 of the 2009 WADA Code state, "[A] sanction could not be completely eliminated on the basis of No Fault or Negligence" for "a positive test resulting from a mislabeled or contaminated vitamin or nutritional supplement" because "[a]thletes are responsible for what they ingest and have been warned against the possibility of supplement contamination."

An athlete also may have difficulty proving "no significant fault or negligence" for a doping violation, which is necessary to justify a reduced sanction from the fixed minimum. In Arbitration CAS Ad Hoc Division (O.G. Athens 2004) 003, *Torri Edwards v. International Assn. of Athletics Federations and USA Track & Field*, award of August 17, 2004, the CAS upheld an American female sprinter's two-year suspension for testing positive for the banned stimulant nikethamide, which prevented her from competing in the 2004 Athens Olympics. Edwards's chiropractor gave her a package of Coramine Glucose tablets purchased in Martinique (where the event was being held) that contained nikethamide, which she ingested. Edwards claimed that "exceptional circumstances" justified reducing or eliminating her two-year suspension pursuant to IAAF rules. Rejecting Edwards's appeal, the CAS ruled:

> [T]he Appellant's chiropractor had access to the box of "Coramine Glucose" which stated the substances contained in the tablet (including nikethamide) and to the leaflet which even contained a warning for athletes. . . . To ignore these facts was at a minimum negligence on the part of the chiropractor and such negligence must be attributed to the athlete who uses him in supplying the athlete either a food source or a supplement. It would put an end to any meaningful fight against doping if an athlete was able to shift his/her responsibility with respect to substances which enter the body to someone else and avoid being sanctioned because the athlete himself/herself did not know of that substance.

Is there any discernible consistency among the foregoing CAS awards, or are different CAS panels applying the same standard differently without any apparent consistency?

3. *Doping Violation Based on Analysis of Athlete's Blood Profile.* In a case of first impression, the CAS, relying on WADA Code Article 3.2, which permits a doping violation to be established "by any reasonably reliable means," held that the International Skating Union (ISU) could use a blood profiling program that measured hemoglobin and hematocrit levels and the percentage of reticulocytes ("%retics") in an athlete's blood to prove she committed a doping violation. *Claudia Pechstein and Deutsche Eisschnelllauf Gemeinschaft e. V. v. ISU*, Arbitration CAS 2009/A/1912 & 1913, award of November 25, 2009. To do so, the CAS panel stated the ISU must prove that "i) the blood samples used to acquire the Athlete's hematological values and portray her profile were properly taken, ii) there was a reliable chain of custody of the blood samples from the place of collection to the laboratory, iii) the machine used to analyse the blood samples . . . was a reliable equipment to record accurate hematological values, iv) the transmission of those values to, and storage in, the ISU data base was reliable, and v) the hematological values of Ms Pechstein are reliable evidence of her use of a prohibited method in violation of Article 2.2 of the ISU ADR."

Claudia Pechstein, an elite German speed skater who participated in five Olympic Games from 1992 to 2006 and won five gold and two bronze medals, provided numerous blood and urine samples as part of the ISU's anti-doping program from February 2, 2000 to April 30, 2009. None of them tested positive for a banned substance. During this same period the ISU collected more than 90 blood samples from her as part of its blood profiling program. The ISU charged Pechstein with a doping offense based on high %retics values in her blood of 3.49 on February 6, 2009, and 3.54 and 3.38

on February 7, 2009, along with a February 18, 2009, value of 1.37. Normal %retics values fall within a range of 0.4-2.4.

After considering complex scientific evidence and expert testimony, the CAS concluded that Pechstein committed a doping violation: "[T]he ISU has discharged its burden of proving to the comfortable satisfaction of the Panel that the abnormal values of %retics recorded by Ms Pechstein in Hamar on 6 and 7 February 2009, and the subsequent sharp drop recorded on 18 February 2009, cannot be reasonably explained by any congenital or subsequently developed abnormality. The Panel finds that they must, there-fore, derive from the Athlete's illicit manipulation of her own blood, which remains the only reasonable alternative source of such abnormal values."

4. *"Specified Substances."* The 2009 WADA Code provides that the range of sanctions for use of a "specified substance" is a minimum of a reprimand and a maximum two-year period of ineligibility if the athlete proves (1) how the substance entered his or her body, and (2) that it was not intended to enhance sport performance or mask the use of a performance-enhancing substance. The code defines "specified substances" as all prohibited sub-stances except anabolic agents and hormones and certain stimulants and hormones. WADC, Art. 4.2.2. To justify any elimination or reduction of the two-year period of ineligibility, the athlete must produce corroborating evidence establishing "the absence of an intent to enhance sport perfor-mance or mask the Use of a performance-enhancing substance." WADC, Art. 10.4. For this provision to apply, Article 10.4 requires proof that use of a "specified substance" was not intended to enhance sport performance, but for purposes of determining whether an athlete qualifies for a reduced sanction, it is unclear whether "the absence of an intent to enhance sport performance" requires proof of a general lack of intent to enhance sport performance, or no intent to enhance performance through usage of the particular specified substance. If a case with substantially similar facts to those in *Canas* (which applied the 2003 WADA Code) arose under the 2009 WADA Code, would Art. 4.2.2 and 10.4 apply? If so, what would be an appro-priate sanction?

5. *Exclusivity of WADA Code Sanctions.* The CAS has determined that sports gov-erning bodies that are signatories to the WADA Code are prohibited by contract from imposing sanctions for doping violations in addition to those prescribed by the code. *USOC v. IOC,* CAS 2011/O/2422 (2011) (invalidat-ing IOC rule precluding any person sanctioned with a suspension of more than six months for a doping violation on or after July 1, 2008, from par-ticipating in the next Olympic Games after expiration of the suspension); *British Olympic Association (BOA) v. WADA,* CAS 2011/A/2658 (2011) (invali-dating BOA bylaw declaring any British athlete previously found guilty of a doping offense to be permanently ineligible to represent Great Britain in the Olympic Games).

6. *Post-CAS Award Litigation.* In *Meca-Medina and Majcen v. Comm'n of European Communities,* [2006] 5 C.M.L.R. 18 (ECJ 3d Chamber 2006), the European Court of Justice (ECJ) ruled that two professional swimmers could chal-lenge their doping sanctions in litigation under European Union law, spe-cifically the Treaty of Rome's competition and freedom to provide services provisions, after unsuccessful CAS arbitration. After the swimmers tested positive for nandrolone, FINA, the Swiss-based international federation for swimming, suspended them from competition for four years. Although

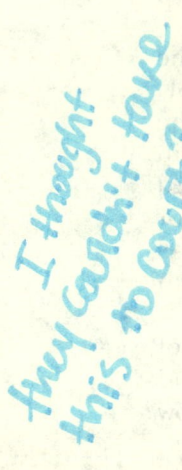

the CAS reduced the length of their suspension to two years, the athletes filed suit claiming their doping sanctions violated the Treaty, rather than appealing to the Swiss Federal Tribunal. The ECJ ruled the Treaty provisions applied because the challenged doping rules, although "purely sporting in nature," have the requisite effect on economic activity by banning applicants from professional swimming. Acknowledging that doping rules have legitimate objectives (including ensuring healthy rivalry among athletes), the ECJ ruled that "the restrictions thus imposed by those rules must be limited to what is necessary to ensure the proper conduct of competitive sport." Although these athletes' doping sanctions met this standard and were upheld by the ECJ, is it appropriate to allow CAS awards to be judicially reviewed on legal grounds other than those set forth in the Swiss Federal Code on Private International Law or the New York Convention? Cf. *Gatlin v. U.S. Anti-Doping Agency, Inc.*, 2008 WL 2567657 (N.D. Fla. 2008) at *1 ("Pursuant to the United Nations Convention on the Recognition and Enforcement of Foreign Arbitral Awards, ('New York Convention'), claims that have been properly submitted to arbitration and ruled upon by entities such as CAS are barred from relitigation in this forum").

c.   United States Anti-Doping Agency

The U.S. Anti-Doping Agency (USADA) was formed in 2000 and is an independent anti-doping agency for Olympic sports in the United States. USADA, which is not subject to the control of the USOC, currently provides drug education, conducts drug testing of U.S. athletes, investigates positive results, and recommends charges and sanctions for violations. Its website is http://www.usantidoping.org. See generally Travis T. Tygart, *Winners Never Dope and Finally, Dopers Never Win: USADA Takes Over Drug Testing of United States Olympic Athletes*, 1 DePaul J. Sports L. & Contemp. Probs. 124 (2003).

Under the former system in the United States, the USOC conducted drug testing for Olympic athletes, and the national governing bodies acted as the disciplinary and adjudicatory authority for their respective sports. USADA now handles the initial adjudication procedure that an IF requires its member NGB to undertake when a U.S. athlete tests positive for a banned substance.

Applying the IF's rules, a USADA review board considers written submissions to determine whether there is sufficient evidence of doping to warrant a hearing. If so, USADA proposes doping charges and sanctions that are consistent with the IF's rules for the athlete. WADA or an IF may challenge USADA's disposition of a doping matter by appealing to the CAS. See *WADA v. USADA, USBSF, and Zachery Lund*, CAS OG 06/001 (February 10, 2006) (upholding WADA's contention that USADA erroneously concluded that Zachery Lund, a member of the American skeleton race team who failed to check the IF website, which clearly listed the banned substance for which he tested positive, had "no fault or negligence" for his doping violation).

If the athlete does not accept USADA's proposed sanction, he or she may request a hearing before an American Arbitration Association (AAA) panel (a right provided by the Stevens Act), whose members are also U.S. CAS arbitrators. Special AAA Supplementary Procedures apply to USADA doping arbitrations, including rules that provide the panel with broad discretion to "determine the admissibility, relevance, and materiality of evidence offered (Rule R-28) and that permit the panel to "consider the evidence of witnesses by declaration or affidavit, but shall give it only such weight as [it] deems it entitled to after consideration of any objection made to its admission" (Rule R-29). See *Jacobs v. USA Track & Field,* 374 F.3d 85 (2d Cir. 2004) (rejecting athlete's petition to compel arbitration pursuant to AAA Commercial Rules). In the arbitration proceeding, USADA and the athlete are adverse parties. The IF may observe the proceeding or participate as a party.

Externalizing this process through USADA and using U.S. CAS arbitrators to resolve USADA doping proceedings seemingly has enhanced the credibility of the United States' anti-doping efforts within the international community and has resulted in the disposition of doping cases in a manner more acceptable to all concerned parties. See generally Anne Benedetti and Jim Bunting, *There's a New Sheriff in Town: A Review of the United States Anti-Doping Agency,* [2003] I.S.L.R. 19 (concluding that "USADA has laid a strong foundation to combat doping at the national level" and "is achieving international and national respect for its commitment to eradicate doping among U.S. athletes").

Armstrong v. Tygart, 2012 WL 3569682 (W.D. Tex.), arose out of USADA's July 2012 charges that Lance Armstrong, although he had not tested positive for a banned substance, had committed several anti-doping rule violations including use or attempted use of EPO, blood transfusions, testosterone, corticosteroids, and masking agents. USADA also alleged that Armstrong possessed banned substances, engaged in their trafficking, and had been involved in a doping conspiracy with five others beginning in January 1998 and continuing until he retired from cycling in 2009. It sought to invalidate all of his competition results from August 1, 1998 (including his seven Tour de France cycling titles) to the present and to impose a lifetime period of ineligibility for future competitions sanctioned by sports governing bodies that are signatories to the WADA Code.

Armstrong alleged that the USADA arbitration procedures violated his federal constitutional due process rights:

> Specifically, he complains of the following alleged procedural deficiencies: (1) he was not provided an adequate charging document; (2) he has no guarantee of a hearing by the appellate arbitral panel; (3) he has no right to cross-examine or confront witnesses against him; (4) he has no right to an impartial arbitration panel; (5) he has no right to disclosure of exculpatory evidence; (6) he has no right to disclosure of cooperation agreements or inducements provided by USADA; (7) he has no right to obtain investigative witness statements; (8) he has no right to obtain full disclosure of laboratory analyses or an impartial assessment of their accuracy; and (9) he has no right to judicial review of the arbitrators' decision by a United States court.

Id. at *6.

Acknowledging that "it is very possible" that USADA is not a state actor, the court concluded that "the USADA arbitration rules, which largely follow those of the American Arbitration Association (AAA), are sufficiently robust to satisfy the requirements of due process." It also stated:

> The Supreme Court has already rejected challenges to arbitration based on speculation of bias by arbitration panels (challenge 4, above), the relatively narrow discovery available in arbitration as compared to judicial proceedings (challenges 5, 6, 7, and 8), and limited judicial review options (challenge 9). *See Gilmer v. Interstate/Johnson Lane Corp.,* 500 U.S. 20, 30-32 & n.4 (1991). This Court does likewise, and also rejects Armstrong's other challenges.

Like the Supreme Court, this Court declines to assume either the pool of potential arbitrators, or the ultimate arbitral panel itself, will be unwilling or unable to render a conscientious decision based on the evidence before it. Further, Armstrong has ample appellate avenues open to him, first to the Court of Arbitration for Sport (CAS), where he is entitled to de novo review, and then to the courts of Switzerland, as permitted by Swiss law, if he so elects. Further, the record shows CAS routinely grants hearings in cases such as Armstrong's, and this Court declines to presume it will break with tradition in this particular instance. Thus, the Court rejects challenges (2), (4), and (9). With respect to challenges (5), (6), and (7), as Armstrong admits, such disclosures are only applicable to criminal matters, and there is no reason to believe they would be required under UCI's rules (which Armstrong argues are applicable and, presumably, valid), much less the Federal Rules of Civil Procedure. Challenge (8) again asks this Court to predict what may occur at arbitration, and to assume the arbitration panel will give undue weight to adverse laboratory findings, both of which the Court declines to do. Though USADA's woefully inadequate charging letter makes it difficult to say with certainty, it appears USADA's evidence will revolve more around eyewitness testimony than lab results. In any case, Armstrong's lawyers will have the opportunity to question the reliability of any adverse test results at arbitration, and the Court must presume the arbitration panel will discount the weight of those results to the extent it finds them unreliable or unpersuasive. Similarly, Armstrong will be able to call into question the reliability of any witness testimony, by affidavit or otherwise, that was not subject to cross-examination, and the panel may discount the weight of that evidence accordingly. The Court thus rejects challenges (3) and (8).

Id. at *8.

Observing that "Armstrong is asking a court of the United States to decide matters which are designed to be resolved by, and with direct input from, members of the international community," the court ruled that it lacked subject matter jurisdiction over Armstrong's state common law due process and tortious interference with contract claims:

> The Court agrees with the reasoning of *Slaney* and *Harding*, that federal courts should not interfere with an amateur sports organization's disciplinary procedures unless the organization shows wanton disregard for its rules, to the immediate and irreparable harm of a plaintiff, where the plaintiff has no other available remedy. To hold otherwise would be to turn federal judges into referees for a game in which they have no place, and about which they know little.

Id. at *10. See also *Graham v. USADA*, 2011 WL 1261321 (E.D. N.C.) (court lacks jurisdiction over coach's claims against USADA challenging his lifetime suspension from coaching Olympic athletes in amateur sports).

Thereafter, Armstrong refused to participate in the USADA arbitration process. Was this what you would have advised him to do? On October 10, 2012, USADA published its 200-page "reasoned decision" with numerous exhibits, including testimony from 11 of Armstrong's former U.S. Postal Service cycling teammates, detailing its evidence that Armstrong was the central figure in the "most sophisticated, professionalized and successful doping program that sport has ever seen" and imposed the foregoing sanctions. After reviewing USADA's report, the Union Cycliste Internationale (UCI), the international governing body for cycling, recognized these sanctions rather than appealing to the CAS. The UCI's president Pat McQuaid stated, "I was sickened by what I read in the USADA report," and "Lance Armstrong deserves to be forgotten in cycling."

Article 3.2 of the 2009 World Anti-Doping Code provides that "anti-doping rule violations may be established by any reliable means." As the following case illustrates, USADA has adopted an aggressive stance in its efforts to combat doping by U.S. athletes, as evidenced by its proceedings against athletes, including Lance Armstrong, for doping offenses based on circumstantial evidence of usage of banned substances (i.e., nonanalytical positives).

UNITED STATES ANTI-DOPING AGENCY
v. KIRK O'BEE

AAA No.77 190 00515 09 JENF
Award of October 1, 2010

Panel: Christopher L. Campbell, Matthew J. Mitten, James M. Murphy

INTRODUCTION

In this case, the United States Anti-Doping Agency ("USADA") seeks a lifetime period of ineligibility for cyclist Kirk O'Bee's second anti-doping violation based on his alleged use or attempted use, possession, trafficking or attempted trafficking, and administration or attempted administration of prohibited substances, including recombinant human erythropoietin ("rhEPO"), testosterone, and human growth hormone ("HGH"). USADA also seeks disqualification of Mr. O'Bee's cycling competition results from July 15, 2003 or when its nonanalytical positive evidence establishes Mr. O'Bee committed a second doping violation, which USADA contends occurred prior to his May 20, 2009 positive test for rhEPO.

Mr. O'Bee asserts that the evidence in this case does not prove he committed his second anti-doping violation prior to May 12, 2009, which is the date he admitted using rhEPO for the first time. He asserts that the appropriate sanction for his second anti-doping violation is an eight-year period of ineligibility and that there should be no invalidation of his cycling competition results prior to May 12, 2009.

[handwritten margin note: what O'Bee wants]

For the reasons described in this Award, the Panel finds that USADA has proven to the comfortable satisfaction of the Panel, while bearing in mind the seriousness of the allegations made, that the evidence establishes that Mr. O'Bee used or attempted to use rhEPO on or at least as early as October 3, 2005, thereby committing his second anti-doping violation in violation of Article 21.2 of the International Cycling Union Anti-Doping Rules ("UCI ADR") (Article 2.2 of World Anti-Doping Code ("WADA Code")), which is substantially similar in relevant part in both the 2003 and 2009 versions. The Panel imposes a lifetime suspension on Mr. O'Bee and disqualifies his cycling competition results from October 3, 2005 through July 29, 2009, the date Mr. O'Bee accepted a provisional suspension. . . .

USADA's Non-Analytical Positive Evidence of Mr. O'Bee's Doping Violations . . .

Email Correspondence Between Mr. O'Bee and Others and Other Documents Forensically Retrieved from Mr. O'Bee's Computer Hard Drive

A substantial component of the non-analytical positive evidence USADA relies on to prove Mr. O'Bee's second doping violation prior to his May 20, 2009 positive test for rhEPO is forensically retrieved email correspondence between Mr. O'Bee and others (USADA Exhibit 103, pp. 1-94) and other documents (USADA Exhibits 30 and 31) copied from the hard drive of the desktop computer jointly owned and used by Mr. O'Bee and Ms. Johnson, which she provided to USADA in late October or early November 2008. Mr. O'Bee's counsel stipulated that the computer disks received by USADA from Ms. Johnson were not changed or altered in any fashion by USADA. . . .

All of the September 16-December 25, 2005 email correspondence in USADA's Exhibit 103 between Mr. O'Bee and five different parties (e.g., Team Life Research, a supplier of Growth Hormone Releasing Peptide Sermorelin Acetate; Ellis Toussier, a Mexican internet supplier of rhEPO and HGH; Nathan O'Neil, a fellow cyclist; Kirk Detterich, a fellow cyclist; and Marty Nothstein) were sent or received by kirkobee@telus.net, an email address Mr. O'Bee acknowledged using from January 2005 through end of 2008. This is the email address Mr. O'Bee provided to USADA in his whereabouts form for the time period from October to December 2005. Mr. O'Bee and Ms. Johnson lived together and shared access to a jointly owned computer during this period of time, so it can be fairly inferred that this email correspondence came from the hard drive of this computer.

There was no testimony from any witness who saw Mr. O'Bee type or send any of these emails, and there was no testimony from any of the recipients or senders of this email correspondence. However, Mr. O'Bee's assertion that Ms. Johnson may have either used his kirkobee@telus.net account without his authorization to send emails purporting to be from him, or fabricated or altered any emails he originally sent from this account is convincingly rebutted by the uncontradicted testimony of USADA's two expert witnesses, whom Mr. O'Bee's counsel stipulated are experts in their respective fields. . . .

Findings

The Panel finds that USADA has proven to the comfortable satisfaction of the Panel, while bearing in mind the seriousness of the allegations made, that Mr. O'Bee committed his second anti-doping violation prior to May 12, 2009, the date he contends he used rhEPO for the first time. The following evidence establishes Mr. O'Bee's usage or attempted usage of rhEPO on multiple occasions beginning on or at least as early as October 3, 2005:

Mr. O'Bee's May 20, 2009 urine sample tested positive for rhEPO.

In a July 2009 telephone conversation, Mr. O'Bee told Glen Mitchell, the general manager of his Bissell racing team, that his "A" sample tested positive and admitted taking rhEPO. Mr. O'Bee admitted using rhEPO "in the past for specific races here and there, and that it was kind of in his mind that it was needed to perform against the—against, you know, the bigger venue that we were racing against." Mr. O'Bee testified he was unaware Mr. Mitchell "had anything against him," and the Panel finds Mr. Mitchell's testimony to be credible.

During an August 13, 2009 telephone call with Dr. Daniel Eichner and Bill Bock to further USADA's knowledge regarding his doping protocols, Mr. O'Bee admitted he started to use rhEPO in 2001 and continued to do so until "he was caught." Dr. Eichner testified that Mr. O'Bee said "he would use EPO for two to three weeks leading to major races. Two to three times a year he would take a dose of EPO two to three weeks up to those events." Dr. Eichner testified Mr. O'Bee said he monitored his hematocrit levels "with his little hemoglobin kit." This admission is corroborated by a May 31, 2007 email from riomedical to kirkobee@telus.net to "bluevanrider," a name Mr. O'Bee admitted to using to purchase items on eBay, regarding 1 Box of HemoCue Hb201, which is used in connection with a hemoglobin meter and February 23, 2008 email correspondence from "bluevanrider" using kirkobee@telus.net regarding the proposed purchase of a microhematocrit centrifuge on eBay. According to Dr. Eichner, there is no legitimate personal use of either a hemoglobin meter, which may be possessed by someone using rhEPO to ensure his blood is not too concentrated, or a centrifuge, which is used by rhEPO users to measure their hematocrit levels.

During the hearing Mr. O'Bee admitted using rhEPO on May 12, 2009 by injecting himself while alone at his home in North Vancouver, British Columbia, which he claimed was the first time he ever used rhEPO. The Panel does not find Mr. O'Bee's testimony to be credible based on the following corroborating evidence that he was using or attempting to use rhEPO prior to this time. Moreover, it appears very unlikely that, after competing in a cycling race in Arkansas on May 7-10, 2009, he returned home before competing in another cycling race in Delaware that began on or around May 16, 2009, which would require multiple cross country flights of several hours.

In an October 3, 2005 email to Ellis Toussier, Mr. O'Bee wrote "I've worked out the kinks in getting products across the border so I'd like to inquire about an order of GH and EPO. How much does a box of 6 × 4,000 units EPO cost? Is it possible to get a box of 6 × 10,000 units?

On October 5, 2005, Ellis Toussier responded that a box of 6 × 4,000 units EPO cost "$650 + $35" and that it is not possible to get a box of 6 × 10,000 units because "4000 iu is the highest it comes in."

In email correspondence with Nathan O'Neill from November 8-December 26, 2005, Mr. O'Bee discussed the purchase and use of EPO and the degree to which it is detectable by anti-doping agencies. In a November 15, 2005 email, Mr. O'Bee informed Mr. O'Neill he could get "vit.e," a term used to refer to EPO, from Ellis (presumably Ellis Toussier). In a December 22, 2005 email, Mr. O'Bee told Mr. O'Neill that "My vit.e arrived today at my friends place."

In a December 25, 2005 email to Kirk Ditterich, Mr. O'Bee stated "I pretty much just confirmed from my own research that the amount of vit.e I bought was only 6,000 iu. Not 60,000 iu like I thought." . . .

After June 10, 2001 through May 19, 2009 anti-doping authorities tested Mr. O'Bee at least 22 times, which results were all negative for the presence of banned performance-enhancing substances. However, these negative tests do not necessarily prove Mr. O'Bee was not using rhEPO, HGH, or testosterone during this time period. An athlete could be using one or more of these substances (as well as others), and its presence in his bodily fluids may not be sufficiently high to be detected by laboratory analysis at the time of sample collection and testing, or it may be detectable in the sample given (e.g., HGH currently can be detected only in blood, not urine).

Evidence

LEGAL ANALYSIS

Although not squarely on point factually, several Court of Arbitration for Sport and American Arbitration Association/North American Court of Arbitration for Sport Panels have found that non-analytical positive evidence such as an athlete's uncontroverted admission of a doping violation or a corroborated admission establishes his use or attempted use of a prohibited substance. See, e.g., *Australian Sports Anti-Doping Agency v. Wyper*, CAS A4/2007; *USADA v. Montgomery*, CAS 2004/O/645; *USADA v. Gaines*, CAS 2004/O/649; *USADA v. Leogrande*, AAA No. 77 190 00111 08; *USADA v. Collins*, AAA No. 30 190 00658 04.

In *Montgomery* and *Gaines*, the panel ruled that an athlete's single uncontroverted verbal admission to one other athlete has been found sufficient to prove use of a prohibited substance and commission of a doping offense. For example, in *Gaines*, the panel determined that the following uncontroverted admission, which it found to be "clear and compelling," is "sufficient in and of itself to find Respondent guilty of doping." (¶52) The incriminating testimony was: "Ms. White testified that Ms. Gaines called her 'not long after' her own (Ms. Gaines') appearance before the Grand Jury (the exact date of this conversation was not provided). The evidence is that during that conversation, Ms. Gaines said that 'they asked her whether or not she used it. And she said, Yeah but it made me gain weight so I stopped using it.' . . . As regards what 'it' meant, Ms. White was unequivocal: it meant 'the Clear.'" (¶49)

Similarly, Mr. O'Bee's written admissions in his December 22, 2005 email to Nathan O'Neill ("My vit.e arrived today at my friends place.") and his December 25, 2005 email to Kirk Ditterich ("I pretty much just confirmed from my own research that the amount of vit.e I bought was only 6,000 iu.") constitute "clear and compelling" evidence that of his use or attempted use of rhEPO. Although Mr. O'Bee disputes Dr. Eichner's testimony that he admitted using rhEPO since 2001 and Glen Mitchell's testimony that he used rhEPO "in the past for specific races here and there," Mr. O'Bee's email correspondence with Ellis Toussier, Nathan O'Neill, Kirk Ditterich and others corroborates their testimony and rebuts Respondent's denials.

In *Collins*, the panel found that email correspondence in which an athlete admitted her usage of banned substances or techniques proved that she committed a doping violation. The panel ruled that these email admissions along with the athlete's corroborating blood and urine test results "independently and collectively prove [her] use of prohibited substances and techniques beyond a reasonable doubt." (¶4.2)

In *Wyper*, the panel concluded that an athlete's on-line communications, investigation, research, ordering, and paying for hGH and rhEPO, including email correspondence regarding the benefits of and inquiries regarding how to obtain these banned substances, constitute "a series of acts which were purposely engaged in" and taken together establish attempted use of performance-enhancing banned substances. (¶38) Although Australian customs officials seized the hGH and rhEPO ordered by the athlete before it was delivered to him, the panel ruled that his actual possession of banned substances not required "before he could take a substantial step in a course of conduct planned to culminate in the commission of an Anti-Doping Rule violation." (¶36)

In *Leogrande*, the panel found a doping violation based on the athlete's admitted use of EPO to the director of his cycling team and another employee (both of which he later denied making), corroborating scientific evidence showing that his protein patterns are very atypical and show suppression of human production of EPO consistent with taking rhEPO, and other circumstantial evidence. The panel concluded that the athlete's denials were not credible in light of circumstantial evidence of his use of rhEPO, including photos of him holding vials of rhEPO and his signature on a UPS receipt for rhEPO. Because he had admitted using a prohibited substance, confirming laboratory results were not required to establish the athlete's doping violation.

Based on its comparison of the totality of the evidence in this case with the evidence in *Montgomery, Gaines, Collins, Wyper,* and *Leogrande,* the Panel determines that USADA has proven Mr. O'Bee's use or attempted use of rhEPO on or at least as early as October 3, 2005 to its comfortable satisfaction bearing in mind the seriousness of the allegation which is made. This is his second anti-doping violation; he committed his first doping violation on June 10, 2001 when his in-competition urine sample tested positive for synthetic testosterone. The Panel is not comfortably satisfied USADA has established Mr. O'Bee's use or attempted use of rhEPO prior to October 3, 2005 based solely on Dr. Eichner's testimony, which is disputed by Mr. O'Bee and is not independently corroborated.

In accordance with Article 10.2 of the 2003 WADA Code, the Panel imposes a lifetime suspension on Mr. O'Bee for his second doping violation. Because Mr. O'Bee used or attempted to use rhEPO, a prohibited substance that is administered by injection and used intentionally to gain a competitive advantage, the Panel concludes there is no basis for finding Mr. O'Bee has "no fault or negligence" or "no significant fault or negligence" for his second doping violation under Article 10.5 of the 2003 WADA Code, thereby justifying any reduction of his suspension. Moreover, at no time during the hearing did Mr. O'Bee express any remorse for his doping violations.

In accordance with Article 10.7 of the 2003 WADA Code, which is substantially the same as Article 10.8 of the 2009 WADA Code and provides that "competitive results obtained from the date . . . doping violation occurred . . . shall, unless fairness requires otherwise, be Disqualified," the Panel disqualifies Mr. O'Bee's cycling competition results from October 3, 2005 through July 29, 2009. See *Leogrande,* supra (disqualifying athlete's race results from the date of corroborated admission of rhEPO use). Respondent disputes Dr. Eichner's testimony that he admitted using rhEPO since 2001, but there is substantial corroborating evidence that Respondent used or attempted to use rhEPO on or at least as early as October 3, 2005. See *Montgomery,* supra at ¶62 and *Gaines,* supra at ¶65 (ordering retroactive invalidation of race results under the 2003 WADA Code based on non-analytical positive evidence establishing an athlete's doping violations).

DECISION AND AWARD

Based on the foregoing facts and legal analysis, the Panel renders the following decision and award: Mr. O'Bee has committed doping violations under Articles 21.1 and 21.2 of the UCI ADR (Articles 2.1 and 2.2 of WADA Code, which are substantially similar in relevant part in both the 2003 and 2009 versions). The following sanctions shall be imposed on Mr. O'Bee: Pursuant to Articles 10.2 and 10.8 of the 2003 WADA Code, a lifetime period of ineligibility from the date of this award, including his ineligibility from participating in and having access to the training facilities of the United States Olympic Committee Training Centers or other programs and activities of the USOC including, but not limited to, any grants, awards, or employment. Pursuant to Article 10.7 of the 2003 WADA Code, invalidation of all of Mr. O'Bee's cycling competition results from October 3, 2005 through July 29, 2009.

NOTES AND QUESTIONS

1. *Nonanalytical Positive Doping Violations.* What is the requisite standard of proof that USADA had to satisfy to establish Mr. O'Bee's doping violation? Do you agree with the arbitration panel's conclusion that USADA's evidence established that Mr. O'Bee committed a doping violation? For scholarly commentary analyzing the developing body of jurisprudence regarding proof of doping violations by evidence other than positive laboratory test results, see Richard H. McLaren, *An Overview of Non-Analytical Positive & Circumstantial Evidence Cases in Sports,* 16 Marq. Sports L. Rev. 193 (2006); Michael Straubel, *Enhancing the Performance of the Doping Court: How the Court of Arbitration for Sport Can Do Its Job Better,* 36 Loy. U. Chi. L.J. 1203, 1266-1270 (2005).

2. *CAS Review of AAA/U.S. CAS Doping Awards.* The athlete, the IF, or WADA may appeal the AAA arbitration award to the CAS, whose decision is final and binding. (This is a unique procedure that applies only to AAA doping awards because an arbitration award generally cannot be appealed to and reconsidered by another panel of different arbitrators.) For example, in a widely publicized case, a majority of the three-person AAA panel upheld a USADA doping charge against Floyd Landis, the winner of the 2006 Tour de France bicycle race, based on a French laboratory's finding of exogenous testosterone in his urine. Although Landis proved that the French lab deviated from the international standards for laboratory analysis, USADA proved to the comfortable satisfaction of the panel that the lab's departure from the standards did not cause the positive test results. *USADA v. Landis,* AAA 30 190 00847 06 (Sept. 20, 2007). In its *de novo* review of the AAA award based on Landis's appeal, a CAS panel unanimously agreed with the majority's ruling. It awarded USADA $100,000 in costs, to be paid by Landis, because, *inter alia,* all he proved were "some minor procedural imperfections" by the French lab and all his multiple defenses were "unfounded" and "barely arguable." *Landis v. USADA,* CAS 2007/A/1394, award of June 30, 2008.

PROBLEM 4-4

Popeye, an American weightlifter, won the gold medal during the most recent Olympic Games held in the United States with a world record lift for the super-heavyweight class. The same day he tested positive for nandrolone, a performance-enhancing steroid metabolite, and the International Olympic Committee (IOC) stripped him of his gold medal. The International Weightlifting Federation (IWF) suspended him from participating in any future weightlifting competitions for two years.

The WADA Code provides that the presence of a prohibited substance in an athlete's bodily specimen is an anti-doping violation. It provides that an anti-doping violation automatically leads to invalidation of individual competition results obtained (including forfeiture of any medal won), and suspension of the athlete from any future competition for a minimum period of two years for testing positive for any steroid metabolite. However, the code provides for the possible reduction or elimination of the period of ineligibility based on "exceptional circumstances" (i.e., if an athlete can establish "No Fault or Negligence" or "No Significant Fault or Negligence" in connection with the doping violation).

Popeye filed a timely appeal with the CAS Ad Hoc Division. At the hearing, a Canadian weightlifting coach testified he saw a Bulgarian weightlifter (who ultimately won the silver medal) spike Popeye's Gatorade with an unidentified liquid on the day before the competition. Popeye did not see this happen because he left his bottle of Gatorade unattended in the gym while he went to the bathroom. The U.S. Olympic team physician testified that nandrolone is a clear liquid that is tasteless and odorless, which readily mixes with other liquids. In his opinion, ingesting nandrolone one day before a competition would not enhance a weightlifter's performance. Both the A and B samples of Popeye's urine were tested by an IOC-accredited lab and contained small amounts of nandrolone. The seal for both samples was intact. However, rather than signing the accompanying form as required by the WADA Code, the person who monitored the collection of Popeye's urine sample initialed it.

Consider how the CAS Ad Hoc Division is likely to resolve Popeye's appeal of the action taken by the IOC and IWF.

No fault, no negligence!

CHAPTER
5

Coaches' Contracts and Related Issues

A. INTRODUCTION

It was once common for coaches to negotiate contracts with professional teams or educational institutions without the assistance of lawyers or agents. In fact, more than a few coaching contracts were sealed with a handshake. Although many coaches (particularly those outside the sports of football, basketball, and baseball) continue to be employed without a written contract, it is no longer uncommon for coaches to have written contracts with their institutions. The changing landscape of sports and the coaching profession has transformed the manner in which coaching contracts are consummated. The past several years have been marked by escalating salaries paid to football and men's basketball coaches. Increased compensation has been accompanied, however, by expanded duties and increased pressure on these coaches to win. The end result is a profession notable for high visibility and job stress but low job security. Consequently, the terms that regulate the rights and duties of parties to coaching contracts take on more significance than perhaps in the past. Notes one author, coaching contracts are "sophisticated endeavors—no standard forms, no two that look the same, no union protecting their interests, and no data bank that correctly reports the intricacies of their packages." Martin J. Greenberg, *College Coaching Contracts Revisited: A Practical Perspective*, 12 Marq. Sports L. Rev. 127, 127 (2001). Given these and other dynamics, coaches require the assistance of agents or lawyers in drafting and negotiating contracts that adequately protect the interests of both parties.

Those who represent coaches in contract negotiations must be prepared to address a myriad of issues, including the scope of a coach's responsibilities, the duration of a contract, reassignment to noncoaching positions, termination of the relationship for cause and without cause, entitlement to perquisites and fringe benefits, and buyout provisions. The materials that follow are intended to provide a glimpse at clauses that increasingly find their way into coaching contracts and provide the source of disputes. The following discussion also briefly examines other issues that confront those who enter into the coaching profession. (Issues involving coaches are also discussed in other chapters, including Chapters 9 and 10, which examine racial equity and gender equity.)

B. IS THERE A PROPERTY INTEREST IN A COACHING POSITION?

KISH v. IOWA CENTRAL COMMUNITY COLLEGE

142 F. Supp. 2d 1084 (N.D. Iowa 2001)

BENNETT, Chief Judge.

I. INTRODUCTION

A. FACTUAL BACKGROUND

Plaintiff Charles R. (Chad) Kish entered into a written "Extracurricular Contract With Coach" with defendant Iowa Central Community College (Iowa Central) on September 14, 1999. Iowa Central is a community college in Fort Dodge, Iowa, which is organized pursuant to IOWA CODE CH. 260C. Under the Extracurricular Contract With Coach, Kish was to perform the duties of Women's Basketball Coach from September 7, 1999, for a period of nine months and eighteen days, and such other time as might be assigned to coach post-season or other related duties. The contract provided, among other things, as follows: "This contract is not continuing in nature and may be terminated at the pleasure of the Board [of Iowa Central]." . . . On September 14, 1999, Vice President of Financial Affairs Charles D. Peterson . . . advised Kish in writing that his employment as Retention Coordinator for the remainder of the 1999-2000 college year had been authorized, presumably by Iowa Central's Board of Trustees. . . . The particulars of this position, as stated in Vice President Peterson's letter, included the following:

> The period of your employment shall begin on September 7, 1999, and continue through June 30, 2000. Your employment, however, may be terminated at any time if there is a need to reduce staff because of the uncertainties of funding, reduction in enrollment, discontinuance of programs or services, or for other just cause.

Id. Kish accepted this position as well as the head coaching job. Kish's combined salary for both positions was approximately $31,000. Kish worked approximately thirty hours per week at the Retention Coordinator job and that position provided almost two-thirds of his salary and benefits.

Kish's coaching career at Iowa Central apparently did not begin smoothly. Dr. Paxton, the President of Iowa Central, first raised concerns with Kish's coaching during a meeting with Kish on September 23, 1999. Complaints and comments critical of the women's basketball program, Kish's coaching, and practice schedules continued during the fall of 1999. . . . Eventually, on Thursday, November 4, 1999, Kish contends that he was terminated from *all duties* at Iowa Central during a meeting with [Tom Beneke, the Vice President of Iowa Central] and Dennis Pilcher, the Athletic Director for Iowa Central. . . . (emphasis added).

II. LEGAL ANALYSIS

[EDS. The court concluded that Kish failed to "meet his burden to generate a genuine issue of material fact on the essential element that Iowa Central breached a term of either of his contracts of employment." It therefore granted defendant summary judgment on Kish's breach of contract and wrongful discharge claims.]

B.   DUE PROCESS

1.   Arguments of the Parties

Iowa Central . . . contends that Kish has no property right in his employment as a coach, where his coaching contract stated that it was not "continuing" in nature and that he served "at the pleasure" of the Board. Furthermore, Iowa Central contends that Kish has not been deprived of any such property right, if it existed, where he was suspended *with pay* from the coaching job and told to continue in his job as Retention Coordinator. Finally, Iowa Central contends that Kish never requested a post-deprivation hearing and did not take advantage of opportunities he was given by Iowa Central to review his suspension as head women's basketball coach.

Kish . . . contends that both of his contracts were sufficient to create cognizable property rights entitled to due process protection. He contends further that he was not suspended, but terminated, as women's basketball coach, which impinged upon that property right. He also contends that he requested due process review via the letter from his counsel to the Equity Coordinator of Iowa Central, but that his request was ignored.

2.   Due Process and Property Interests

Kish's due process claim . . . fails as a matter of law. Due process claims are generally subjected to a two-part analysis: (1) is the asserted interest protected by the due process clause; and if so, (2) what process is due? [Citations omitted]. As this court has previously explained,

> When a public employee asserts a protected property interest in his or her employment, the public employee must show that the protected property interest is derived from a source such as state law, which requires a showing that the employee could have been fired only for good cause. . . . While a public employee with a protected property interest in continued employment is entitled to due process before termination, [Citations omitted], where the claimant can show only that he or she was an at-will employee, the claimant lacks the necessary property interest in his or her employment. . . .

Randall v. Buena Vista County Hosp., 75 F. Supp. 2d 946, 953-54 (N.D. Iowa 1999). Similarly, the Eighth Circuit Court of Appeals recently explained,

> To succeed on a procedural due process claim, [a public employee] must establish that he had a constitutionally protected property interest, that is, a "legitimate claim of entitlement" to continued employment by the [public entity]. [Citation omitted]. If a public employee may not be terminated except for good cause, that is a property interest entitled to due process protection. [Citation omitted]. On the other hand, an at-will probationary employee does not have a protected property interest in continued public employment. [Citation omitted].

Somers v. City of Minneapolis, 245 F.3d 782, 785 (8th Cir. 2001). Recognizing these same standards, the Eighth Circuit Court of Appeals has concluded that language providing that a public employee serves "at the pleasure" of an administrative board or executive is "inconsistent with the . . . conclusion that [the employee] could only be removed for cause," and thus the employee had no protected property interest. [Citation omitted].

3. Analysis of the Record

Under these standards, as a matter of law, Kish had no cognizable property interest in his coaching contract. The contract expressly states, "This contract is not continuing in nature and may be terminated at the pleasure of the Board [of Iowa Central]. . . ." Nor are the authorities cited by Kish to the contrary. He cites *Buchanan v. Little Rock School District of Pulaski County*, 84 F.3d 1035, 1038 (8th Cir. 1996), for the broad proposition that a contract may create a property interest, and that, because he had a contract, he had a claim of entitlement to his coaching position, giving rise to a property interest in that position. However, in *Buchanan*, the court held that a school principal had no property interest in assignment as a principal at a particular school, even though her contract designated her "primary duty" as serving as principal of that school, where the contract also provided that she was to "perform services as assigned by Superintendent or Principal," and Arkansas law permitted school boards and superintendents to determine assignments for principals and teachers. *See Buchanan*, 84 F.3d at 1038-39. Thus, *Buchanan* does not stand for the proposition that any public employment contract creates a property interest subject to due process protection. . . .

In *Winegar* [*v. Des Moines Independent Community School District*, 20 F.3d 895 (8th Cir.), *cert. denied*, 513 U.S. 964, 115 S.Ct. 426, 130 L.Ed.2d 340 (1994)], the court explained the circumstances under which such a property interest arises, as follows:

> Typically, this interest arises from contractual or statutory limitations on the employer's ability to terminate an employee. [Citation omitted.] A property interest in employment can also be created by implied contract, arising out of customs, practices, and de facto policies. [Citation omitted.]

Winegar, 20 F.3d at 899. Whatever the parties may have agreed about the teacher's property interest in his employment in *Winegar*, it is clear that Kish has not demonstrated any contractual or statutory limitations on Iowa Central's ability to terminate his coaching contract, nor has he demonstrated that a protectible property interest arose from any implied contract arising out of customs, practices, or de facto policies. . . . Instead, Kish's coaching contract expressly provided to the contrary, by stating, "This contract is not continuing in nature and may be terminated at the pleasure of the Board [of Iowa Central]."

Because Kish has failed to generate a genuine issue of material fact on the essential element of his due process claim that he had a protectible property interest in his employment as Women's Basketball Coach at Iowa Central . . . Iowa Central is entitled to summary judgment on Kish's due process claim as to that position. Iowa Central apparently concedes that Kish had a property interest in his retention coordinator position, and the court notes that, unlike Kish's coaching contract, the retention coordinator position could not be terminated, except under specified conditions, including a "just cause" requirement. . . . However, Kish cannot maintain his claim of a due process violation as to this position, because he was reinstated to it, with full pay and benefits, agreed to the reinstatement, and worked for two days after reinstatement, then abandoned the position. In other words, Kish received all the process he was due with regard to his termination from his retention coordinator position, because he was promptly reinstated with full pay and benefits. A due process hearing could not have provided him with more. Therefore, Iowa Central is entitled to summary judgment on Kish's due process claim in its entirety. . . .

Therefore, Iowa Central's motion for summary judgment is granted. Judgment in favor of Iowa Central shall enter on all claims.

IT IS SO ORDERED.

NOTES AND QUESTIONS

1. *Analysis of* Kish. In *Kish,* the district court rejected the plaintiff's argument that the mere existence of a contract gave rise to a property interest that required that he be afforded due process. In reaching this conclusion, the court found that Kish possessed no claim of entitlement to his position as coach. How did the court characterize Kish's contract with Iowa Central? Was this characterization a predicate to finding that Kish possessed no property interest in his coaching position?

2. *Due Process. Kish* aligns with cases in which courts have addressed whether a coach should be afforded due process prior to being terminated. See e.g., *Jones v. Washington Interscholastic Athletic Assn.*, 2008 WL 351013 (W.D. Wash. Feb. 6, 2008) (there is no fundamental right to coach an interscholastic or high school football team); *Ott v. Edinburgh Community School Corp.*, 2005 WL 2886212 (S.D. Ind. Oct. 31, 2005) (absent an express promise or a representation from which a right to continued employment could reasonably be inferred, coach was not deprived of property right when his employment was terminated). In *Price v. Univ. of Alabama*, 318 F. Supp. 2d 1084 (N.D. Ala. 2003), the University of Alabama terminated its head football coach, Mike Price, for indiscretions relating to his attendance at a charity golf tournament. Subsequent to his firing, Price filed suit alleging, *inter alia*, that his termination violated his Fifth and Fourteenth Amendment rights because the university failed to give him notice of the charges and refused to allow him to present evidence at a hearing before his termination. At the time Price was fired, he had not signed a contract with the university. The court concluded that Price possessed no property interest in his coaching position at the university because of his failure to accept the terms of the employment contract offered by the university and because any agreement he had with the university was not in writing.

A terminated coach may, under limited circumstances, be entitled to due process protections even though he or she is employed under a contract of indefinite duration. The contours of a plaintiff's right to due process were explored in *Kingsford v. Salt Lake City School District*, 247 F.3d 1123 (10th Cir. 2001). There the court held that because the coach did not sign an employment contract for a definite term, his employment was presumed to be at will, and he possessed no property interest in his position. It noted, however, that the plaintiff might possess a claim to entitlement to continued employment as a football coach if he could establish an implied-in-fact promise that "he would not be terminated as football coach except for cause." *Id.* at 1132. "An implied-in-fact promise to terminate only for cause can be demonstrated by 'conduct of the parties, announced personnel policies, practices of that particular trade or industry, or other circumstances which show the existence of such a promise.'" *Id.* See *Jacobeit v. Rich Twp. High Sch. Dist. 227*, 673 F. Supp. 2d 653 (N.D. Ill. 2009) (even though coach and school had not entered into an express written contract, property interest gave rise to due process right where a form of de facto tenure existed since the school district's established practice was to retain coaches unless certain specified acts occurred); *Ridpath v. Board of Governors Marshall Univ.*, 447 F.3d 292 (4th Cir. 2006) (university's labeling as "corrective action" its reassignment of athletic director to position outside athletic department created a charge of a serious character defect which in turn gave rise to a liberty interest and entitled plaintiff to Fourteenth Amendment due process protections); but see *Patria v. East Hartford Bd. of Educ.*, 2009 WL 840667 (D. Conn. March 31, 2009) (where school board followed statutory requirements for terminating or not renewing a coach's contract, there was no procedural due process violation; substantive due process violation arises when discipline is "brutal or offensive to human dignity"); *Williams v. Board of Regents of the Univ. of Minnesota*, 763 N.W.2d 646 (Ct. App. Minn. 2009) (coach's failure to comply with university's grievance procedures precluded his due process property interest claim premised on an alleged contract between him and university).

Statements that defame a coach's reputation potentially may infringe on his or her liberty interest. See *Campanelli v. Bockrath*, 100 F.3d 1476 (9th Cir. 1996) (statements by public officials charging that coach abused players verbally and psychologically presented question of fact as to whether such statements placed a stigma on coach's "good name, reputation, honor and integrity" so as to foreclose his freedom to take advantage of employment opportunities as a college basketball coach and thereby infringed on his liberty interest); *Babi v. Colorado High Sch. Activities Assn.*, 77 P.3d 916 (Colo. App. Ct. 2003) ("[A] liberty interest exists in a plaintiff's good name and reputation as it affects his or her protected property interest in continued employment." To be actionable statements must: impugn the reputation, good name, or integrity of the employee; be false; be published; and occur in the course of terminating the employee, or they must foreclose other employment opportunities); but see *Sanchez v. Dubois*, 291 Fed. Appx. 187 (10th Cir. 2008) (cross country coach whose contract was terminated following a history of poor performance, including a failure to follow NCAA practice reporting guidelines, failed to establish violation of liberty interest where institution's reporting of secondary violation to the NCAA was confidential and therefore was never published).

PROBLEM 5-1

William Barr was the head coach of the Richmond football team on a yearly basis for ten years. His contract term was August 11, 2008, to August 10, 2011. During a football game, a local sports reporter informed Mr. Reynolds, Richmond's principal, that Barr had shouted a racial epithet at a player on the opposing team. At some point after this game, the principal met with the school district's superintendent and discussed the renewal of Barr's coaching contract. In January 2010, at the conclusion of the football season, Reynolds informed Barr that he would be fully compensated for the entire term of his coaching contract, but that all of Barr's duties as coach would cease immediately. (Barr received the total amount due under his coaching contract.) Reynolds provided no reasons for terminating Barr and did not afford Barr a hearing to contest his termination. The school denied Barr's request that he be permitted to present evidence at a hearing as to why his contract should be renewed. Mr. Reynolds announced to the local newspaper that "Coach Barr's contract will not be renewed." He made no comments as to the reasons why the contract would not be renewed. Following his termination, Barr sent out applications for several head football coaching positions but received no job offers.

Barr has filed suit alleging breach of contract and that he has been deprived of his fundamental rights to continued employment and to the protection of his reputation. Consider the preceding materials in determining whether Barr is likely to prevail on his claims. Also see *Puchalski v. Sch. Dist. of Springfield*, 161 F. Supp. 2d 395 (E.D. Penn. 2001).

C. COMPENSATION ISSUES

In the event that a coach is justifiably terminated pursuant to one of the circumstances set forth in his or her contract, the institution is not liable to the coach for any damages other than those that may be specified in the contract between the parties. Coaches, however, often are terminated prior to the lapse of the contract term because of the poor performance of the team or other matters such as conflicts between a coach and a team owner or university administrators. Assuming the termination is unjustified (i.e., without cause), the coach is entitled to compensation for the duration of the contract term of employment. Therefore, if a coach with a three-year contract is unjustifiably terminated after the second year of his or her contract with a team, the coach generally would be entitled to compensation for the third year of the three-year contract term. In these circumstances, it is not unusual for the coach and institution to disagree over what compensation the coach is owed. These issues are addressed in the following case.

1. *What Constitutes Compensation?*

RODGERS v. GEORGIA TECH ATHLETIC ASSN.

303 S.E.2d 467 (Ga. App. 1983)

Pope, Judge.

Franklin C. "Pepper" Rodgers brought this breach of contract action against the Georgia Tech Athletic Association to recover the value of certain perquisites which had been made available to him as the head coach of football at the Georgia Institute of Technology. Both parties moved for summary judgment, Rodgers' motion encompassing only the issue of liability under his contract of employment with the Association. The trial court granted the Association's motion and denied Rodgers' motion. The issue presented for resolution by this appeal is whether Rodgers is entitled to recover the value of certain perquisites or "fringe benefits" of his position as head coach of football under the terms of his contract of employment with the Association.

Rodgers was removed from his coaching position by vote of the Association's Board of Trustees on December 18, 1979, notwithstanding a written contract of employment through December 31, 1981. In addition to an annual salary, the contract provided that Rodgers, as an employee of the Association, would be entitled "to various insurance and pension benefits and perquisites" as he became eligible therefore. Rodgers makes no claim for base salary, health insurance and pension plan benefits, all of which were provided voluntarily by the Association through December 31, 1981, the expiration date of the contract. Rather, his claim is solely for the value of the aforesaid "perquisites," to which he claims entitlement under this employment contract.

Rodgers lists some 29 separate items as such perquisites. In support of his motion for summary judgment, Rodgers categorized these items into two groups: A. Items provided directly to him by the Association but discontinued when Rodgers was relieved of his duties, and B. Items provided by sources other than the Association by virtue of his position as head coach of football. These items are listed in the Appendix to this opinion.

The subject contract was in the form of a letter from the Association dated April 20, 1977 offering Rodgers the position of head coach of football for three years at an annual salary plus certain benefits and perquisites. This contract provided that Rodgers could be terminated for illness or other incapacity continuing for three months, death, or "any conduct or activity involving moral turpitude or which in the opinion of [the Board of Trustees] would constitute an embarrassment to the school." Rodgers accepted this contract on April 25, 1977. This contract was extended until January 1, 1982 by a subsequent letter agreement between the parties. At its December 18, 1979 meeting, the Association's Board of Trustees determined that a change should be made in the position of head coach of football. The following statement was approved and released to the press: "The Board of Trustees of the Georgia Tech Athletic Association met at its regular December meeting this morning. After full discussion, the Board determined that in the best interest of Georgia Tech, with full respect for Coach Pepper Rodgers, a change should be made in the position of Head Coach of Football. The Board stated that it would, of course, honor the financial contractual obligation to Coach Rodgers and that Doug Weaver, the Athletic Director, had been directed to immediately pursue the obtaining of a new head coach."

Rodgers contends that he was terminated or fired from his employment by the Association. However, the evidence of record supports the Association's view that Rodgers was merely relieved of his duties as the head coach of football yet remained an employee of the Association, albeit without any function or duties, for the duration of his contract. In either event, this disassociation of Rodgers from his position and duties was not "for cause" pursuant to the terms of the contract. Therefore, the Association was obligated to pay Rodgers that part of the amount set forth in the contract "which he himself was entitled to receive as compensation for his services." *Southern Cotton Oil Co. v. Yarborough*, 26 Ga. App. 766, 770, 107 S.E. 366 (1921).

In addition to a salary, health insurance and pension benefits, the contract provided that Rodgers, as an employee of the Association, was entitled to "perquisites" as he became eligible therefor. The term "perquisites" is defined as "[e]moluments or incidental profits attaching to an office or official position, beyond the salary or regular fees." Black's Law Dictionary 1299 (4th ed. 1968). The term is also defined as "a privilege, gain, or profit incidental to an employment in addition to regular salary or wages; *esp:* one expected or promised [e.g.,] the [perquisites] of the college president include a home and car. . . ." Webster's Third New International Dictionary 1685 (1981). Thus, Rodgers was entitled to the perquisites (or their value) for which he was eligible during the duration of his contract. The problem presented here for resolution is to determine whether any of the items listed in the Appendix were indeed perquisites to which Rodgers was entitled pursuant to his contract.

First, we must determine the intention of the parties as to the scope of the perquisites to which Rodgers was entitled under the contract. See Code Ann. § 20-702 (now OCGA § 13-2-3). The pertinent language of the contract provides: "You, as Head Coach of Football, will devote your time, attention, skill, and efforts to the performance of your duties as Head Coach under the policies established by the Athletic Board and the Athletic Director, and you will receive compensation at [an] annual rate of $35,175.00 payable in equal monthly installments. In addition, as an employee of the Association, you will be entitled to various . . . perquisites as you become eligible therefore." The Association contends that the language "as an employee of the Association" limited Rodgers' eligibility for perquisites to those items common to all Association employees. Rodgers argues that he was not only entitled to those perquisites common to all Association employees, but that he was also entitled to additional perquisites for which he became eligible as the head coach of football. Since the contract is susceptible to either construction, it is ambiguous. This ambiguity may be resolved by applying the appropriate rules of construction.

"If a contract is so framed as to be susceptible of two constructions, that interpretation which is least favorable to the author . . . should generally be accepted. [Cits.] 'When it is possible to do so without contravening any rule of law, the courts will construe a contract as binding on both the parties, where, from the language of the contract, the conduct of the parties, and all the attendant circumstances, it appears that the intention of the parties was that both should be bound [thereby], and substantial justice requires that the contract be given effect. [Cits.]'" *Bridges v. Home Guano Co.*, 33 Ga. App. 305, 309, 125 S.E. 872 (1924). . . . The subject contract was drafted by the Association. Moreover, the record discloses that Rodgers, during his tenure as head coach of football, did receive perquisites in addition to those received by other Association employees. Accordingly, we conclude that the parties intended that Rodgers would receive perquisites, as he became eligible therefore, based upon his position as head coach of football and not merely as an employee of the Association.

We must next determine the nature of the items for which Rodgers seeks damages, i.e., whether the items listed in the Appendix are perquisites vel non. We will first address ourselves to those items listed in Section A of the Appendix and address separately those items listed in Section B. (a) The Association asserts that Rodgers was not entitled to any of the items listed in Section A because they were expense account items—"tools" to enable him to more effectively execute his duties as head coach of football. Rodgers counters that those items were an integral part of the total compensation package that he received as head coach of football and constituted consideration for his contract of employment. We certainly agree with the Association that Rodgers would be entitled to recover only "compensatory damages that he suffered by reason of the breach of his contract; in other words, that the proper measure of damages arising from the breach of the contract of employment was actual loss sustained by the breach, and not the gross amount of [his] wages and expenses [under the contract]." *Southern Cotton Oil Co. v. Yarborough, supra,* 26 Ga. App. at 770, 107 S.E. 366. . . . However, the evidence offered as to the nature of the items in Section A was in considerable dispute. The fact that these items were not reported as taxable income by Rodgers is not conclusive as to their nature . . . nor is the fact that Rodgers reimbursed the Association for occasional "personal" expenses which it had paid. Thus, with three exceptions, we cannot say as a matter of law either that Rodgers was entitled to the items listed in Section A as perquisites of his employment, or that he was not.

The three exceptions to this finding are the services of a secretary, the services of an administrative assistant, and the cost of trips to football conventions, clinics, etc. The undisputed purpose of the services of the secretary and administrative assistant was to assist Rodgers in fulfilling his duties under the contract. Since Rodgers had been relieved of his duties as head coach of football, and, thus, had no responsibilities under the contract, he had no need for these support services. This is true even though the secretary and administrative assistant may have occasionally provided personal services to Rodgers beyond their duties to him as head coach of football since, as Rodgers admits, their primary functions were to provide services to the head coach of football. Also, since Rodgers had been relieved of his coaching duties, the Association was not obligated to pay his expenses for trips to various football-related activities, these costs clearly being business-related and not in the nature of compensation. . . .

(b) We turn our attention finally to those items in Section B of the Appendix—items which Rodgers asserts were perquisites he received from sources other than the Association by virtue of his position as head coach of football at Georgia Tech. . . . [W]e must now determine whether Rodgers may recover the items in Section B under his breach of contract theory.

"[T]he consideration of a contract need not flow directly from the promis[or] [here, the Association], but may be the promise or undertaking of one or more third persons." *Bing v. Bank of Kingston,* 5 Ga. App. 578, 580, 63 S.E. 652 (1908). "Damages growing out of a breach of contract, in order to form the basis of a recovery, must be such as can be traced solely to the breach, must be capable of exact computation, must have arisen naturally and according to the usual course of things from such breach, and must be such as the parties contemplated as a probable result of the breach." *Sanford-Brown Co. v. Patent Scaffolding Co.,* 199 Ga. 41, 33 S.E.2d 422 (1945). "As a general rule, a party is entitled to recover profits that would have resulted from a breach of a contract into which he has entered, where the breach is the result of the other party's fault. And while a breach of the original contract will not ordinarily entitle a plaintiff to recover as damages the profits of collateral enterprises or subcontracts, yet where the knowledge of the subcontract [or collateral enterprise] is within the contemplation of the parties when the original contract is made, and is known to have been made with reference thereto, anticipated profits shown to be certain, fixed in amount, and the direct fruit of the contract, are recoverable. Profits are excluded only when there are no criteria, definite and certain, upon which an adjudication can be based. They then become speculative and imaginary." *Carolina Portland Cement Co. v. Columbia Improvement Co.,* 3 Ga.App. 483(2), 60 S.E. 279 (1908).

We will apply the foregoing legal principles to the facts of record. Can Rodgers' loss of the items in Section B be traced solely to the Association's breach of the contract? Rodgers testified that he received these perquisites as a result of his being head coach of football at Georgia Tech. The record discloses, however, that the items relating to housing and the cost of premiums on a life insurance policy were discontinued several years prior to the Association's breach of contract and were, in fact, not related to the breach. Thus, these items were properly excluded by the trial court. The remaining items were discontinued as the direct result of Rodgers being relieved of his duties as head coach of football.

Are the remaining items in Section B capable of exact computation? A "gift" is defined as "[a] voluntary transfer of personal property without consideration." Black's Law Dictionary 817 (4th ed. 1968). A gift, then, being a *voluntary* transaction and *without consideration*, can not form an enforceable part of the consideration of a contract. Although Rodgers may have received gifts of money and personalty during his tenure as head coach of football, such voluntary contributions to his financial well-being are totally incapable of exact computation, for a gift made in one year is no assurance of a similar gift in the next. In fact, Rodgers concedes that he did not receive these gifts each year. Thus, the item which listed various financial gifts was properly excluded from recovery. The items now remaining are sufficiently capable of computation. *See generally Hoffman v. Louis L. Battey Post etc. Am. Legion*, 74 Ga.App. 403, 410-1, 39 S.E.2d 889 (1946).

Did these remaining items arise naturally and according to the usual course of things, and were they such as the parties contemplated as a probable result of a breach? There is no evidence of record showing that the Association had any knowledge of Rodgers' free lodging at certain Holiday Inns or of his membership in Terminus International Tennis Club. Thus, the loss of these items could not be such as was contemplated as a probable result of a breach of the contract. The evidence was in dispute as to the remaining items — profits from his television and radio shows and from his summer football camp plus the loss of use of a new automobile and tickets to professional sporting events — i.e., whether such items were contemplated by the parties at the time the contract was executed as perquisites or fringe benefits to which Rodgers would be entitled as the result of his position as head coach of football at Georgia Tech. These items are of the type commonly provided to head coaches at major colleges and universities. There was some evidence that the Association knew that Rodgers would receive (and, in fact, did receive) these benefits as the result of his head coaching position and that his removal from that position would result in the loss of these benefits. In fact, some members of the Association assisted Rodgers in obtaining many of these items. Also, there was at least some evidence by which the amount of these items could be fixed. Therefore, summary judgment in favor of the Association as to these items was inappropriate. . . . . For these same reasons, summary judgment in favor of Rodgers was properly denied.

In summary, a question of fact remains as to whether Rodgers is entitled to recover those items listed in Section A of the Appendix not excluded in this opinion and also those items in Section B not heretofore excluded, any recovery being subject to proof of the amount of his damages as set forth in this opinion. All items which have been excluded are denoted by asterisks in the Appendix.

Judgment affirmed in part; reversed in part.

DEEN, P.J., and SOGNIER, J., concur.

APPENDIX

A. Benefits and Perquisites Received by Rodgers Directly from the Georgia Tech Athletic Association.

    (1)   gas, oil, maintenance, repairs, other automobile expenses;

    (2)   automobile liability and collision insurance;

    (3)   general expense money;

    (4)   meals available at the Georgia Tech training table;

    (5)   eight season tickets to Georgia Tech home football games during fall of 1980 and 1981;

    (6)   two reserved booths, consisting of approximately 40 seats at Georgia Tech home football games during fall of 1980 and 1981;

    (7)   six season tickets to Georgia Tech home basketball games for 1980 and 1981;

    (8)   four season tickets to Atlanta Falcon home football games for 1980 and 1981;

    (9)   four game tickets to each out-of-town Georgia Tech football game during fall of 1980 and 1981;

    (10)   pocket money at each home football game during fall of 1980 and 1981;

    (11)   pocket money at each out-of-town Georgia Tech football game during fall of 1980 and 1981;

    (12)   parking privileges at all Georgia Tech home sporting events;

    *(13)   the services of a secretary;

    *(14)   the services of an administrative assistant;

    (15)   the cost of admission to Georgia Tech home baseball games during spring of 1980 and 1981;

    *(16)   the cost of trips to football coaches' conventions, clinics, and meetings and to observe football practice sessions of professional and college football teams;

    (17)   initiation fee, dues, monthly bills, and cost of membership at the Capital City Club;

    (18)   initiation fee, dues, monthly bills, and cost of membership at the Cherokee Country Club;

    (19)   initiation fee and dues at the East Lake Country Club.

B. Benefits and Perquisites Received by Rodgers from Sources Other Than the Georgia Tech Athletic Association by Virtue of Being Head Coach of Football.

    (1)   profits from Rodgers' television football show, "The Pepper Rodgers Show," on Station WSB-TV in Atlanta for the fall of 1980 and 1981;

    (2)   profits from Rodgers' radio football show on Station WGST in Atlanta for the fall of 1980 and 1981;

    (3)   use of a new Cadillac automobile during 1980 and 1981;

    (4)   profits from Rodgers' summer football camp, known as the "Pepper Rodgers Football School," for June, 1980 and June, 1981;

    *(5)   financial gifts from alumni and supporters of Georgia Tech for 1980 and 1981;

    *(6)   lodging at any of the Holiday Inns owned by Topeka Inn Management, Inc. of Topeka, Kansas, for the time period from December 18, 1979 through December 31, 1981;

*(7) the cost of membership in Terminus International Tennis Club in Atlanta for 1980 and 1981;

(8) individual game tickets to Hawk basketball and Braves baseball games during 1980 and 1981 seasons;

*(9) housing for Rodgers and his family in Atlanta for the period from December 18, 1979 through December 31, 1981;

*(10) the cost of premiums of a $400,000.00 policy on the life of Rodgers for the time period from December 18, 1979 through December 31, 1981.

NOTES AND QUESTIONS

1. *Compensation of College Coaches.* A major component of what has been characterized as the athletics arms race in big-time intercollegiate athletics is escalating salaries paid to coaches. As of January 2004, 23 college football coaches earned at least $1 million. Mary Jo Sylvester and Tom Witosky, *Athletic Spending Grows as Academic Funds Dry Up,* USA Today, Feb. 18, 2004, at 1A. In 2011, the average compensation for major-college football coaches was $1.4 million, a 55 percent increase over the average pay in 2006. Erik Brady, Jodi Upton, and Steve Berkowitz, *Salaries for College Football Coaches Back on Rise,* USA Today, Nov. 11, 2011, http://www.usatoday.com/sports/college/football/story/2011-11-17/cover-college-football-coaches-salaries-rise/51242232/1. In 2011, 64 major-college football coaches had annual salaries in excess of $1 million, 32 had compensation in excess of $2 million, 9 had compensation in excess of $3 million, and 3 had compensation in excess of $4 million. *Id.* The year 2012 also witnessed further escalation in coaches' salaries. In 2012, 66 major-college football coaches had annual salaries in excess of $1 million, 42 had compensation in excess of $2 million, 13 had compensation in excess of $3 million, 4 had compensation in excess of $4 million, and 2 had compensation in excess of $5 million. Erik Brady, Steve Berkowitz, and Jodi Upton, *College Football Coaches Continue to See Salary Explosion,* USA Today, Nov. 20, 2012, http://www.usatoday.com/story/sports/ncaaf/2012/11/19/college-football-coaches-contracts-analysis-pay-increase/1715435/. An interactive database of coaches' salaries in 2012 is available at http://www.usatoday.com/story/sports/ncaaf/2012/11/19/ncaa-college-football-head-coaches-salary-database/1715543/. In 2012, the average pay for Football Bowl Subdivisions head football coaches was $1.64 million, which represents a 12 percent increase over 2011 and a 70 percent increase over 2006. Brady et al., Nov. 20, 2012, *supra.*

Factors that have fueled the dramatic rise in the salaries of college football coaches are the proliferation of money from football bowl games and television contracts. Another factor has been the substantial rise since the mid-1990s in agents representing coaches in their contract negotiations. Increased competition for coaches fueled by the willingness of NFL teams to hire college coaches and colleges to hire NFL coaches has also contributed to rising salaries. For an insightful article discussing the economics of college coaching contracts see Richard T. Karcher, *The Coaching Carousel in Big-Time Intercollegiate Athletics: Economic Implications and Legal Considerations,* 20 Fordham Intell. Prop. Media & Ent. L.J. 1 (2009). Acknowledging the foregoing factors, Professor Karcher identifies several additional factors that have contributed to the dramatic increase in coaches' salaries, including "the desire to win and the prospects of generating more revenue, the granting of contract extensions to keep winning coaches from being poached . . . , the payment of huge buyouts when coaches do not win, and the tremendous leverage that coaches have over schools in the hiring and contract negotiation process." *Id.* at 4. He also attributes the increase to the refusal of colleges to pay the student-athletes a portion of the income generated in football and men's basketball. *Id.* at 44-45.

Examples of the approximate annual compensation (which includes university- and nonuniversity-based compensation, excluding bonuses) earned by coaches include:

- Nick Saban (football coach at University of Alabama): $5.47 million
- Bob Stoops (football coach at University of Oklahoma): $4.5 million
- Mack Brown (football coach at University of Texas): $5.35 million
- John Calipari (men's basketball coach at University of Kentucky): $5.4 million
- Urban Meyer (football coach at Ohio State University): $4.3 million in annual compensation
- Tom Izzo (men's basketball coach at Michigan State University): $3.6 million
- Billy Donovan (men's basketball coach at University of Florida): $3.6 million
- Rick Pitino (men's basketball coach at University of Louisville): $3 million
- Tubby Smith (men's basketball coach at University of Minnesota): $1.8 million

USA Today Sports College Football Coaches Salaries Database, http://www.usa today.com/story/sports/ncaaf/2012/11/19/ncaa-college-football-head-coaches-salary-database/1715543/; *USA Today–NSLI Coaches' Salary Database Salaries,* USA Today, March 30, 2011, http://www.usatoday.com/sports/college/mensbasketball/2011-coaches-salary-database.htm.

2. *Bonuses and Perquisites.* As *Rodgers* indicates, perquisites and various performance incentives continue to represent significant components of college coaches' salaries. When Bobby Knight became head men's basketball coach at Texas Tech University, he refused a base salary of $250,000 but still received $650,000 in the form of perquisites and bonuses from the university. Rion A. Scott, *Competing at the Division I Level,* Press & Sun-Bulletin, Feb. 29, 2004, at 1A. A *New York Times* review of the contracts of 40 major college coaches revealed that most of coaches' compensation is derived not from an annual base salary but from sources such as media appearances and endorsement revenue. James K. Gentry and Raquel M. Alexander, *From the Sideline to the Bottom Line,* N.Y. Times, Jan. 1, 2012. Noted the article, "[A]greements that once seemed simple and straightforward have morphed into an ever more intricate combination of guaranteed salary increases, lucrative bonuses and desirable perks that cover everything from country-club membership to free travel in private jets." *Id.*

The contract of Les Miles, head football coach at Louisiana State University, helps to further elucidate the intricacies of college coaching contracts. For the 2011-2012 season, Miles was to receive compensation totaling $4.2 million in excess of his $300,000 annual-base salary. His compensation package included $2.9 million for radio, television, and Internet appearances; an annual retention bonus of $550,000; a maximum of $200,000 for various academic accomplishments; an additional $500,000 for other performance-related achievements; and a courtesy vehicle allowance of $7,200 annually. Additionally, Coach Miles's contract included remuneration for various athletic achievements, the most notable of which would provide an increase in his salary to $1,000 above the then highest Southeastern Conference (SEC) salary pending a Bowl Championship Series (BCS) title win. *Id.*

Is the compensation paid to Division I-A coaches justified?

3. *Compensation and Athlete Academic Performance.* Should the contracts of college coaches include financial incentives and disincentives related to the academic performance and off-campus conduct of student-athletes? Professor Linda Greene's analysis of the contracts of head football coaches revealed the following:

> [T]his review of head football coach contracts revealed a trend toward explicit head football coach responsibility for student-athlete academic performance as either a term of the contract or a factor in bonus determination. . . . In contrast, fewer contracts impose a duty of responsibility for athlete misbehavior or penalize or reward the coach for improper or unlawful conduct of their student-athletes. . . . The . . . trend of contracts without explicit coach responsibility for athlete misconduct seems counterintuitive. . . .

Linda S. Greene, *Football Coach Contracts: What Does the Student-Athlete Have to Do With It?*, 76 UMKC L. Rev. 665, 688-689 (2008).

4. *Required Public Disclosure.* In *University System of Maryland v. Baltimore Sun Co.*, 847 A.2d 427 (Md. Ct. App. 2004), a newspaper sought disclosure, under Maryland's Public Information Act (MPIA), of income and compensation information concerning two University of Maryland head coaches, football coach Ralph Friedgen and basketball coach Gary Williams. Based on its interpretation of the MPIA, the Maryland Court of Appeals held that the "employment contracts and any amendments thereto, side letters or documents reflecting the total compensation of monies paid directly by the University" to the coaches must be disclosed. *Id.* at 441. It reasoned that disclosure was essential to the public obtaining an understanding of the salaries paid to coaches. With respect to outside income, the case was remanded for a determination of whether this "income is intimately connected to [Williams's] activities as coach of [University of Maryland, College Park] UMCP." If so, such income is "part of his compensation and subject to disclosure." *Id.* at 443. In providing guidance to the trial court, the court also stated:

> [I]f after reviewing the contract terms, the court is convinced that the payments the coach is receiving from the third party company, although prompted by his position as an NCAA coach, and the University's coach in particular, are not so connected with or related to his activities as coach of UMCP as to render the contract proceeds a part of his official compensation, the contract is not subject to disclosure under the MPIA.

Id. at 443. Should documents relating to coaches' third-party income be disclosed to the public? What is the public's interest in such disclosure?

5. *Memorandum of Understanding.* Increasingly, colleges and coaches will enter into a memorandum of understanding (MOU) before executing a formal

contract. The MOU will typically outline the elements of the terms that will eventually appear in the formal contract. James K. Gentry, *In Coaching Contracts, Deals Within the Deal*, N.Y. Times, Jan. 1, 2012. The MOU can often play a key role in disputes between colleges and coaches. On October 13, 2009, the University of Kentucky entered into a settlement in which it agreed to pay $3 million to its former head men's basketball coach, Billy Gillispie. Gillispie, who was hired in 2007 and compiled a two-season record of 40-27, never signed a formal contract and coached under a memorandum of understanding. The university fired Gillispie citing "incompatibility," which allegedly stemmed, in part, from his refusal to sign a formal contract. Thereafter, Gillispie filed suit asserting breach of contract and seeking $6 million. The university defended that it owed Gillispie nothing because the memorandum was not an enforceable contract.

2.   Termination and Breach

As the following materials reveal, whether an institution or a club has grounds for justifiably terminating a coach turns principally on the terms of the parties' contract. As the Leach case demonstrates, however, other legal principles influence the legal relationship between the parties.

LEACH v. TEXAS TECH UNIVERSITY

335 S.W.3d 386 (Tex. Ct. App.-Amarillo 2011)
(review denied, Feb. 17, 2012)

BRIAN QUINN, Chief Justice.

[EDS. On December 30, 2009, Texas Tech University fired its highly successful head football coach, Mike Leach, who compiled a 10-season record of 84-43. The for-cause termination was based on allegations that the coach had improperly treated a player who had suffered a concussion. On January 10, 2010, Leach, who had signed a five-year contract extension on January 1, 2009, filed a lawsuit against Texas Tech alleging wrongful termination and defamation. Leach alleged the university fired him to avoid making an $800,000 bonus payment due to Leach on December 31, 2009. In 2010, a judge rejected Texas Tech's sovereign immunity defense and allowed Leach's breach of contract claim to move forward. The university appealed the ruling. The appellate court ruling demonstrates the significance of contract law in disputes between coaches and their teams. It also shows, however, that other factors may ultimately determine an institution's liability to a terminated coach.]

The issues before us today implicate the above quoted section of our state constitution. We have been asked to determine whether the common law doctrine of sovereign immunity barred the suit of Mike Leach against Texas Tech University (the University), its Chancellor Kent Hance, its regents Jerry Turner and Larry Anders, its president Guy Bailey, its athletic director Gerald Myers, and its employee/attorney Charlotte Bingham. Applying the doctrine via a plea to the court's jurisdiction, the trial court dismissed all but one cause of action averred by Leach. The one remaining encompassed the allegation of breached contract. The trial court refused to dismiss it because the University "by and through its conduct . . . waived [its] immunity from suit. . . ." We affirm in part, reverse in part, and render in part the trial court's order. . . .

THE LAW OF SOVEREIGN IMMUNITY

We wish not to mislead. It is clear that sovereign immunity is alive and well in Texas. As it now exists, it provides a double shield to the entities it protects. They are insulated from both liability and suit. *Tex. A & M University–Kingsville v. Lawson*, 87 S.W.3d at 520-21; *Federal Sign v. Texas S. Univ.*, 951 S.W.2d 401, 405 (Tex.1997). That is, one can neither sue for payment nor compel payment from the State without legislative consent. *Federal Sign v. Texas S. Univ.*, 951 S.W.2d at 405. Given this double shield, defeating one still meant the other stood. Take, for instance, the subject of contracts. In Texas, when the State executes such an obligation it loses its immunity from liability. *Id.* at 405-06. Yet, it remains protected from being forced into litigation via suit. *Id.* So, while it must perform and, like any other party to a contract, is responsible for its failure to do so, it cannot be sued for damages without its permission if it opts to forego performance. In other situations, the converse is also true; the State may grant someone permission to sue it but retain its insulation from being forced to pay. *Id.*; *Ben Bolt-Palito Blanco Consol. Indep. Sch. Dist. v. Tex. Political Subdivisions Prop./ Cas. Joint Self-Insurance Fund*, 212 S.W.3d 320, 323-24 (Tex.2006) (explaining the nature of the immunity). The logic behind that circumstance is not ours to debate for that is the law as declared by our Supreme Court.

That sovereign immunity extends to state universities is similarly clear. *Ben Bolt-Palito Blanco Consol. Indep. Sch. Dist. v. Tex. Political Subdivisions Prop./Cas. Ins. Joint Self-Insurance Fund*, 212 S.W.3d at 324. Of less clarity, however, is the manner by which a university or the State, for that matter, waives immunity.

Admittedly, our Supreme Court has declared that it has "consistently deferred to the Legislature" to effectuate waiver. *Id.* at 326, quoting *Tex. Natural Res. Comm'n v. IT-Davy*, 74 S.W.3d 849, 854 (Tex.2002). That is, we have been told that only the legislature can remove the insulation. *Id.* . . .

If one invokes a statute as basis for defeating immunity, that statute must clearly and unambiguously abrogate the shield. Tex. Gov't Code Ann. § 311.034 (Vernon Supp.2010). On the other hand, if the purported waiver is founded upon non-statutory grounds, then we must search precedent to determine whether the factual situation has already been addressed by the Supreme Court. *E.g., Federal Sign v. Texas S. Univ.*, *supra* (wherein the court clearly held that executing a contract waives immunity from liability). If that court has not, then we defer to the legislature's general authority to act on the matter, except when the circumstances compel the judiciary to intervene, if ever. With that said, we turn to the issues posed to us by the parties.

APPLICATION OF SOVEREIGN IMMUNITY — LEACH ISSUES

A.   WAIVER BY OPERATING PROCEDURE

We first address Leach's argument that the University's immunity was waived by statute. The statute in question is § 109.001(c) of the Texas Education Code. Through it, the legislature wrote:

> The governance, control, jurisdiction, organization, and management of the Texas Tech University System is hereby vested in the present board of regents of Texas Tech University, which will hereinafter be known and designated as the board of regents of the Texas Tech University System. The board by rule may delegate a power or duty of the board to an officer, employee, or other agent of the board.

Tex. Educ.Code Ann. § 109.001(c) (Vernon 2002). Per that grant, the University enacted specific "operating policy and procedures" allowing an employee to "elect to remove such issues of grievance or complaint from further consideration through . . ." the school's administrative process if the employee "files substantially the same issues . . . with any external agency or court. . . ." Leach reads this as consent from the University to sue it in state court. We disagree for several reasons.

First, and assuming arguendo that any state-supported university has the power to waive its immunity, such a waiver is not explicit in the "operating policy and procedures" at issue. Recognizing that an employee may end an internal grievance proceeding if the same complaint is encompassed within a later suit speaks to whether the person must exhaust internal administrative remedies before suing. It does not speak to the matter of waiving immunity. Indeed, nothing in the procedure even mentions immunity, much less its waiver. . . .

Finally, and to the extent Leach argues that the University's operating procedures are comparable to state statutes, we abide by the legislature's unambiguous directive regarding the waiver of immunity. Again, per that directive, a statute "shall not be construed" as waiving immunity unless the "waiver is effected by clear and unambiguous language." Tex. Gov't Code Ann. § 311.034 (Vernon Supp.2010). Those words plainly mean that any waiver one attempts to derive from a statute must be clear and unambiguous. And, the statute underlying Leach's claim of waiver is § 109.001(c). According to him, it purports to vest the University's regents with the power to do most anything they want, including the power to waive immunity. Yet, nothing in it expressly addresses immunity or its waiver.

B.   WHISTLEBLOWER CLAIM

Next, Leach argues that the trial court erred in dismissing his whistleblower claim. We again disagree and overrule the issue.

It is true that suits upon claims arising under what we know as the Texas Whistleblower's Act, Tex. Gov't Code Ann. § 554.001 et seq. (Vernon 2004) are not barred by sovereign immunity. Id. § 554.0035. Nonetheless, to enjoy that freedom to sue, the complainant must plead facts establishing jurisdiction. In other words, he must allege facts in his original petition satisfying the elements of the cause of action for which immunity has been waived. See *State v. Lueck*, 290 S.W.3d 876, 883-85 (Tex.2009) (holding that the elements of § 554.002(a) can be considered to determine both jurisdiction and liability). That did not happen here. Nor do we think his petition is capable of being amended to meet the requirement given the facts involved.

The Whistleblower Act forbids a "state or local governmental entity . . . [from] suspend[ing] or terminat[ing] the employment of, or tak[ing] other adverse personnel action against, a public employee who in good faith reports a violation of law by the employing governmental entity or another public employee to an appropriate law enforcement authority." Tex. Gov't Code Ann. § 554.002(a) (Vernon 2004). Furthermore, a "report is made to an appropriate law enforcement authority if the authority" receiving the report "is a part of a state or local governmental entity . . . that the employee in good faith believes is authorized to . . . regulate under or enforce the law alleged to be violated . . . or . . . investigate or prosecute a violation of criminal law." *Id.* § 554.002(b). Here, the alleged report consisted of Leach filing suit against the University, among others, in the district court. . . .

Simply put, the factual allegations contained in Leach's petition, the context in which the word "report" appears, and the traditional purpose of the judiciary lead us to conclude, as a matter of law, that filing a lawsuit against the University and others failed to satisfy the mandate of § 554.002(a). . . . [F]iling suit to redress claims of breached contract and constitutional deprivation arising from the termination of the complainant's job is not such a circumstance. . . .

C. CONSTITUTIONAL CLAIMS

We next address the argument that the trial court erred in dismissing Leach's [state] constitutional claims. The claims in question involve the purported taking without compensation of Leach's property and his termination without due process. We overrule the issues in part.

1. Takings Claim

With regard to the takings claim, we find the Supreme Court's decision in *General Servs. Comm'n v. Little-Tex Insulation Co.*, 39 S.W.3d 591 (Tex.2001) dispositive. According to the Supreme Court in *Little-Tex*, to establish a takings claim, the complainant must prove 1) that the State intentionally performed certain acts, 2) that the acts resulted in a "taking" of property, and 3) that the property was taken for public use. *Id.* at 598. These elements are not satisfied when the State withholds property in a contractual dispute. This is apparently so because the party demanding compensation after performing his contractual duty to provide goods or services actually provided those goods or services voluntarily as opposed to being forced to do so via the State's power of eminent domain. *Id.* at 598-99, quoting *State v. Steck Co.*, 236 S.W.2d 866 (Tex.Civ.App.-Austin 1951, writ ref'd). So, when the State withholds property under color of a contractual right, such as when it believes the contract was not properly performed, it is not acting as a sovereign invoking powers of eminent domain, but rather as a private party to a contract invoking rights expressed or implicit in the contract. *Id.* at 599. Thus, the takings clause appearing under Texas Constitution art. I, § 17 does not apply to contractual disputes. . . .

The compensation sought by and allegedly due Leach is that which the University contracted to pay him in return for his performance of services as the head football coach. The University purports to withhold that compensation because Leach failed to abide by the terms of their accord. Thus, what we have here is nothing other than a contractual dispute described in *Little-Tex* and which falls outside the takings clause.

2. Denial of Due Course of Law

As for the dispute regarding due process, Leach argues that he was denied constitutionally protected interests without due course of law. The property rights at issue were to 1) continue employment for a term of years (except when terminated for cause) and 2) specific compensation accruing while so employed. And because he tendered sufficient evidence establishing the constitutional claim, it allegedly was error for the trial court to use the doctrine of sovereign immunity to dismiss it. We sustain the issue for several reasons.

Sovereign immunity bars a trial court from adjudicating lawsuits through which a complainant seeks money damages from the State. *Tex. Natural Res. & Conservation Comm'n v. IT-Davy*, 74 S.W.3d 849, 853 (Tex.2002). It does not pretermit legal actions against a governmental entity seeking equitable relief to redress violations of the Texas Constitution. *City of Elsa v. M.A.L.*,

He tested positive for hydrochlorothiazide (HCT), which is identified in the ATP Rules under "S5. Diuretics and Other Masking Agents as a Prohibited Substance." The ATP Anti-Doping Tribunal determined that Canas committed a "Doping Offense" by having HCT present in his body and imposed a two-year period of ineligibility on him.

The Appellant claims that he ingested Rofucal, a medication containing HCT, which he received from Tournament personnel after requesting that a prescription from the Tournament doctor to treat congestion be filled and Appellant instead received a prescription intended for the coach of another participant in the Tournament, Mr Carvallo. He claims that the HCT was present in his urine as a result of taking the medication intended for Mr Carvallo. As a result, Appellant bears no fault or negligence. . . .

The Respondent contends that, if the Appellant's version of the circumstances leading up to the Appellant's positive specimen is accepted, Appellant has met his burden under ATP Rules M.5.b to demonstrate how the prohibited substance entered his system. However, Respondent points out that the Appellant did not read the label on the medication he received. He did not ask the physician from whom he received the prescription what medication was being prescribed. He did not compare the label (which clearly identified the ingredient in Rofucal as the prohibited substance HCT) to the wallet card which the Player testified he always carried with him. Therefore, the Appellant was at fault. . . .

Under the ATP Rules, since a Prohibited Substance was present in the Player's specimen, there is a Doping Offense. The only issue to be determined is what are the *Consequences* based on this Doping Offense.

The burden of proof shifts to the [Canas] under ATP Rules, K.3.b. to establish by a balance of probability: first how the prohibited substance entered his system; and second, that he bears *No Fault or Negligence,* or in the alternative *No Significant Fault or Negligence,* for the Doping Offense in order for the two years period of ineligibility to be eliminated or reduced.

With respect to the first requirement of how the Prohibited Substance entered his system, Appellant established that he ingested Rofucal delivered to him by Tournament staff. . . .

Once the Panel accepts that Appellant has met his burden of proving how the Prohibited Substance entered his system, the question of his level of fault or negligence needs to be determined.

Appellant is responsible for the presence of the Prohibited Substance in his specimen. He is an experienced professional athlete, active in the ATP Player Council and fully aware of the risks of doping, as evidenced by his testimony and the fact that he carries the ATP wallet card with the list of Prohibited Substances with him.

He took the medication he received with no review whatsoever of the contents of the box, even though he knew that the medication had been through several hands before being delivered to him. . . .

Appellant relied blindly on the system set up to take care of him at the Tournament site, assuming that it was foolproof. This is clearly negligent. The Player has a duty of utmost caution after visiting the Tournament doctor, when actually ingesting medications. It would have been normal for him to rely on the trustworthiness and knowledge of the Tournament doctor if the doctor had handed the medications to him but any professional athlete these days has to be wary when, as in this case, he receives medications which, he knows, have gone through several hands. Thus, ATP Rules M.5.a (which allows Player to establish *No Fault or Negligence)* is not applicable to the Appellant's case. . . .

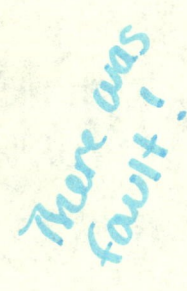

226 S.W.3d 390, 392 (Tex.2007). . . . One means of determining whether constitutional violations have occurred that survive the invocation of sovereign
immunity is through prosecuting a declaratory action. . . . Leach requested
such declaratory relief here when seeking a declaration of whether he was
denied a constitutionally protected interest by the University without due
course of the law. See Tex. Const. art. I, § 19 (stating that "[n]o citizen of
this State shall be deprived of life, liberty, property, privileges or immunities,
or in any manner disfranchised, except by the due course of the law of the
land"). Admittedly, he cannot avoid the shield of sovereign immunity by simply morphing a demand for monetary relief into one for declaratory relief,
City of El Paso v. Heinrich, 284 S.W.3d at 370–71, and that is what the University
contended he did here. That is, it argued through its plea to the court's jurisdiction that his pleadings regarding the due course of law violations were "a
disguised attempt to obtain money damages under the 2009 Contract recast
as a declaratory judgment claim." Yet, whether Leach had a constitutionally
protected interest (property or liberty) that was denied him without due process is quite distinct from whether the University breached the employment
contract. It is possible for there to be a due process violation without a breach
of contract or a breach of contract without a due process violation. So, simply because both types of claims may be included in the same petition does
not ipso facto mean that the constitutional allegation is a mere "disguised
attempt to obtain money damages" for a breach of contract. Examining the
nature of the relief sought is determinative for one may invoke the jurisdiction of Texas courts via a declaratory action to redress, through equitable
remedies, unconstitutional acts. *City of Elsa v. M.A.L., supra.* So, the trial court
had jurisdiction to declare whether Leach was denied due course of law even
though it cannot adjudicate the attempt to recover damages for breach of
contract. The same may be true for other choses-in-action that he may assert
and which are independent of his breach of contract claim; they must be
assessed on an individual basis. . . .

[EDS. The court's discussion of the trial court's dismissal of Leach's complaint
against university officials is omitted.]

THE UNIVERSITY'S APPELLATE ISSUES

A.   BREACH OF CONTRACT

Through its sole issue, the University argues that the trial court erred in refusing
to dismiss Leach's breach of contract allegation. Again, the trial court refused
to do so because it reasoned that the University "waived its immunity from
suit . . . by and through its conduct." We sustain the issue.

As previously mentioned, the Supreme Court left open, in *Federal Sign*, the
question of whether the state entity may waive its immunity through its conduct.
Yet, whether the idea of waiving immunity through conduct extends to choses-
in-action sounding in breach of contract is not an open question. In *General
Servs. Comm'n. v. Little-Tex Insulation Co.*, Little-Tex sued Texas A & M for breach
of contract and argued that the school waived its immunity by accepting the
benefits of the contract. The proposition was rejected by the Supreme Court
after acknowledging that it had left open "the question of whether the State's
conduct may waive its immunity from suit." *General Servs. Comm'n v. Little-Tex
Insulation Co.*, 39 S.W.3d at 595. The Court rather clearly stated that "there is but

one route to the courthouse for breach-of-contract claims against the State, and that route is through the Legislature." *Id.* at 597. . . .

Admittedly, the factual circumstances in *Little-Tex* differ from those before us. And, because of that Leach argues that the holding does not control the outcome here. Though the circumstances may differ between the two suits, the Supreme Court in *Little-Tex* actually focused not upon the facts underlying the cause of action but rather upon the cause of action itself, that is, the claim of breached contract. Nor did it simply say that a governmental entity retains its immunity even though it accepted contractual benefits. Rather, it told us that there was only one way the State could be sued for breach of contract and that involved first garnering the legislature's approval via chapter 107 of the Texas Civil Practice and Remedies Code. . . .

We also recognize that our opinion contradicts that in *Texas Southern University v. State Street Bank & Trust Co.*, 212 S.W.3d 893 (Tex.App.-Houston [1st Dist.] 2007, pet. denied). In that breach of contract case, the intermediate court of appeals held that the University's conduct resulted in the waiver of its immunity. That decision, however, contradicts the Supreme Court's statements in *Little-Tex*, *IT-Davy*, and *E.E. Lowrey Realty, Ltd.* about the only avenue for redress being through the Texas Legislature. If the highest civil court in Texas truly means what it said, then the holding in *State Street* simply is wrong. If, on the other hand, there may still be instances akin to those in *State Street* warranting the application of waiver by conduct, then the Supreme Court's utterances about the legislature having the exclusive authority to waive sovereign immunity are inaccurate. In either case, it is a matter for the Supreme Court (or Texas Legislature) to resolve, and we have no choice but to abide by their decision.

In sum, we reverse those portions of the trial court's order 1) dismissing, for want of jurisdiction, Leach's due course of law claim and request for non-monetary declaratory and equitable relief founded upon it and 2) concluding that Texas Tech University waived its sovereign immunity from the breach of contract claim due to its conduct. We next dismiss, for want of jurisdiction, the appellate issue involving whether Bailey, Myers, and Bingham were properly dismissed by the trial court, render judgment dismissing Leach's claim of breached contract against the University, and affirm the remainder of the order granting the pleas to the trial court's jurisdiction.

NOTES AND QUESTIONS

1. *Termination for "Cause" Defined.* A wide array of events may give an institution or team a right to terminate a coach for cause. At the collegiate level, contracts typically contain provisions allowing an institution the right to terminate a coach if the coach has committed serious violations of NCAA rules and regulations. Similarly, a contract may include a provision that grants the institution the discretion to terminate a coach if a member of his or her coaching staff committed an NCAA rules violation if such violation was under the control or direction of the head coach. Among the more common provisions in coaching contracts at both the collegiate and professional levels are those that permit termination for cause if a coach (1) refuses or is unable (e.g., because of death or incapacity) to perform duties either stipulated in the contract or reasonably associated with the position of coach, (2) is convicted of a serious criminal offense, (3) engages in fraud or dishonesty

in the performance of his or her duties, and (4) participates or encourages participation in gambling or betting involving sports. Finally, coaching contracts typically give colleges or professional clubs the right to terminate a coach if he or she engages in conduct that is detrimental to the best interests of the institution or club. For a detailed discussion of termination provisions, see Adam Epstein, *An Explanation of Interesting Clauses in Sports*, 21 J. Legal Aspects of Sport 5, 17-22 (2011) (discussing the evolution of termination provisions in sports); Richard T. Karcher, *The Coaching Carousel in Big-Time Intercollegiate Athletics: Economic Implications and Legal Considerations*, 20 Fordham Intell. Prop. Media & Ent. L.J. 1 (2009) (discussing termination provisions in coaching contracts); Martin J. Greenberg, *Termination of College Coaching Contracts: When Does Adequate Cause to Terminate Exist and Who Determines Its Existence?*, 17 Marq. Sports L. Rev. 197 (2006) (discussing what constitutes just cause); Robert H. Lattinville and Robert A. Boland, *Coaching in the National Football League: A Market Survey and Legal Review*, 17 Marq. Sports L. Rev. 109 (2006) (discussing termination provisions included in NFL coaching contracts).

In *Cole v. Valley Ice Garden, L.L.C.*, 113 P.3d 275 (Mont. 2005), a five-year employment contract between a coach and a professional hockey team provided the coach could be terminated for cause. The agreement failed to define cause. After the team terminated the coach because of his poor performance, he filed suit for breach of contract alleging he was wrongfully terminated. The coach argued that because the contract failed to expressly require that he maintain a specific win/loss ratio, the court could not imply such a term into the agreement. He further argued that since coaches are commonly terminated for failing to maintain a winning record, the team was obligated to pay off the remainder of the compensation due to him under the contract. Relying on definitions from other contexts to lend meaning to the term "cause," the court ruled in favor of the team, finding that "discharging the coach of a professional sports team which is performing poorly, despite management's good faith efforts, is a discretionary decision related to the legitimate needs of the business and constitutes 'cause.'" *Id.* at 280. See *Chang v. University of Rhode Island*, 606 F. Supp. 1161, 1256 (D. R.I. 1985) (identifying a won-lost record as an objective measure for evaluating a coach).

2. *Termination for Rules Violations and Non-Sports-Related Indiscretions.* Institutions and teams have terminated coaches for exercises of poor judgment that range from abusive conduct toward players to violating NCAA rules to off-the-field indiscretions. In 2012, Bobby Petrino, the successful former head football coach at the University of Arkansas, was terminated following revelations of an affair with a female staff employee and misleading statements he made to university officials. See Tom Weir, *Petrino Dumped by Arkansas*, USA Today, April 11, 2012. In December 2012, Petrino was appointed head football coach at Western Kentucky University. Moving back in time, in 2003, the number and severity of incidents involving alleged and established improper conduct by coaches in intercollegiate basketball reached such a level that, in a move characterized as unprecedented, the National Association of Basketball Coaches convened a mandatory ethics summit for all NCAA Division I men's head coaches. One of the more notorious incidents, which also provided a major catalyst for the coaching summit, involved Dave Bliss, former head men's basketball

coach at Baylor University. Bliss was forced to resign following an investigation that revealed that Bliss lied to school officials who were investigating the death of Baylor basketball player Patrick Dennehy; that Bliss instructed coaches and players to lie to those investigators and to portray Dennehy as a drug dealer; and that Bliss improperly paid the tuition for players on the basketball team. See Jeff Caplan, *Baylor's Situation Catalyst for Summit*, Star-Telegram, Sept. 5, 2003.

Other incidents involving poor judgment and indiscretions by coaches occurring in 2003 alone included the following:

- Mike Price's termination as the University of Alabama's head coach for conduct that included a visit to a topless bar and reports that a young woman charged $1,000 for room service at a hotel at which Price stayed (in December 2003, the University of Texas at El Paso hired Price as its head football coach)
- University of Washington's firing of head football coach Rick Neuheisel after he admitted that he bet more than $6,000 on the NCAA Division I men's basketball tournament (in December 2007, Neuheisel was named head football coach of the UCLA Bruins until November 2011 when the university fired him)
- Alabama State University's firing of head football coach L.C. Cole in 2002 in the aftermath of allegations of improper academic support for players and players being entertained by strippers
- Jan van Breda Kolff's termination as St. Bonaventure head men's basketball coach in connection with the use of an academically ineligible player who was admitted to the university with a welding certificate instead of an associate's degree from a junior college
- Larry Eustachy's resignation as Iowa State University's head men's basketball coach after the release of a photograph showing him surrounded by and kissing younger women and drinking a beer at a college party following a basketball game (in March 2004, Eustachy was named head basketball coach at the University of Southern Mississippi; in April 2012, Eustachy became the head coach at Colorado State)
- The now deceased Nolan Richardson III's termination as head men's basketball coach at Tennessee State University after he pulled a gun on an assistant coach

Craig Bennett et al., *One Year Later: A Look Back at College Scandals, the People Involved and Where They Stand*, USA Today, June 15, 2004, at C3; Welch Suggs, *A Hard Year in College Sports*, Chron. Higher Educ., Dec. 19, 2003, at A37; John L. Pulley and Welch Suggs, *Coaches Will Be Coaches?*, Chron. Higher Educ., May 16, 2003, at A40.

The termination or forced resignations of coaches for conduct such as that noted above raises questions of whether coaches are being held to standards that are too high, particularly if the indiscretion does not involve rules violations or matters related to the athletics program. What interest does a university have in regulating the personal behavior of coaches? Which clause or clauses within a coach's contract is an institution likely to contend justify its termination of a coach for cause for nonathletic-related behavior? See generally Greenberg, *Termination of College Coaching Contracts*, *supra*.

Two cases provide good illustrations of the issues involved when a court must determine whether NCAA rules violations constitute grounds for a good-cause termination. In *O'Brien v. The Ohio State Univ.*, 2007 WL 2729077 (Ohio App. 10 Dist. 2007), the former head coach of Ohio State's men's basketball team was terminated for violating NCAA rules prohibiting institutional representatives from providing extra benefits to players (giving a loan to a student-athlete). Plaintiff filed a breach of contract action alleging wrongful termination. The dispositive issue was whether the coach's violations of NCAA rules constituted a material breach of contract so as to discharge the university's obligations and allow it to terminate O'Brien without having to pay him. In concluding that O'Brien's failure to comply with NCAA rules did not constitute a material breach, the court found that compliance with NCAA rules represented only one of the coach's duties stipulated in the contract. In addition, the court pointed to contract language providing that the contracting party's failure to perform in each instance would not necessarily justify termination for cause. Since O'Brien's violation of NCAA rules and his failure to promptly report his violations were not so fundamental that they defeated "the essential purpose of the contract" and "thus rendered performance by defendant impossible," the court held that plaintiff's breach was not material and defendant did not have cause to terminate his employment. The court also upheld the trial court's damages award of approximately $2.49 million.

In *Harrick v. NCAA*, 454 F. Supp. 2d 1255 (N.D. Ga. 2006), the head coach subsequently resigned and an assistant coach's contract was not renewed as the result of an NCAA investigation concerning rules violations while coaching at [the University of Georgia]. Plaintiffs Jim Harrick, Sr., and Jim Harrick, Jr., asserted that the NCAA had tortiously interfered with their contracts with the university. In analyzing this claim, the court found that plaintiffs had failed to establish an essential element—"the defendant is a 'third party' i.e., a 'stranger' to the contract with which the defendant allegedly interfered." *Id.* at 1260. The court found NCAA member schools require their employees to sign documents in which they agree to abide by NCAA legislation. According to the court, both plaintiffs signed their employment contracts and certified that they understood they were subject to NCAA guidelines. "The NCAA was 'an essential entity' in the employment relationships at issue. . . . Therefore, the NCAA is not a stranger to the contracts, and thus, cannot be liable for tortious interference with those contracts." *Id.* See also *Bassett v. NCAA*, 528 F.3d 426 (6th Cir. 2008) (Coach who resigned his position as assistant football coach at the University of Kentucky amid allegations of NCAA rules infractions failed to establish cognizable fraud claim since it would have been unreasonable for him to rely on alleged misrepresentation of athletic director that coach's infractions would not be investigated. In addition, any alleged agreement between the coach and athletic director that they would ignore their respective obligations to report infractions was unenforceable as against public policy.).

3. *Termination for Abusive Conduct.* When a coach crosses the thin line that separates appropriate tough discipline from abuse, institutions are justified in terminating a coach for cause. Throughout his coaching career, former Texas Tech and Indiana University men's basketball coach Bobby Knight fended off criticism that he verbally and physically abused his players. In 2002, Knight sued Indiana University for breach of contract and defamation

following his termination for violating a "zero tolerance" behavior policy when he grabbed a student by the arm. He alleged the termination caused him to lose more than $2 million in media and clothing contracts, endorsements, and camp fees. In October 2003, a judge dismissed Knight's lawsuit. The state judge noted that Knight's contract contained a provision that allowed IU to terminate him at will and that IU was not required to give Knight another chance.

In *Campanelli v. Bockrath*, 100 F.3d 1476 (9th Cir. 1996), Louis Campanelli was fired as head coach of the men's basketball team at the University of California at Berkeley. Newspaper accounts attributed Campanelli's firing to his conduct toward players. A *Washington Post* article described Campanelli as "an abusive bully" who "perpetuate[d] a cycle of abuse" and psychologically attacked his players. Tony Kornheiser, *When the Boot Fits*, Washington Post, Feb. 17, 1993, at C1. In another matter, Winston Bennett pled guilty to fourth-degree assault. Bennett was suspended and later fired from his position as head men's basketball coach at Kentucky State University after he struck a player in the face. The player later filed assault charges that ended in the plea bargain. Bennett was ordered to complete 200 hours of community service and to obtain anger management counseling or serve 90 days in jail. *Finish Line*, Rocky Mountain News, Feb. 27, 2004, at 22C.

The Iowa Supreme Court has ruled that evidence showing that a coach engaged in threatening and intimidating treatment of student-athletes is sufficient to support a good-cause termination. *Board of Directors of Ames Cmty. Sch. Dist. v. Cullinan*, 745 N.W. 2d 487 (Iowa 2008).

Other cases involving alleged coach abuse of players include *Leach*, discussed *supra*. Another involved Jim Leavitt. On March 15, 2010, former University of South Florida head football coach Jim Leavitt sued the university alleging wrongful termination of his contract. The university terminated Leavitt for cause following allegations that Leavitt had mistreated a walk-on running back. The coach disputed allegations that he had grabbed a player by his throat and struck him during halftime of a game and filed a wrongful termination suit against the university. On January 11, 2011, the University of South Florida and Leavitt reached a settlement that paid Leavitt $2.75 million. Specifically the settlement included $2 million for "salary and benefits" and also $750,000 for Leavitt's contributions to building USF's "nationally respected" football program. *Jim Leavitt Gets $2.75M in Settlement*, ESPN, Jan. 11, 2011, http://sports.espn.go.com/ncf/news/story?id=6013605.

4. *Illegal Discrimination Claims*. In contesting their terminations, coaches are asserting with increased frequency (thus far generally unsuccessfully) that their terminations violated constitutional and statutory prohibitions against age, gender, or racial discrimination. See, e.g., *Jackson v. Univ. of New Haven*, 228 F. Supp. 2d 156 (2002) (African American applicant for head football coach position unsuccessful in claiming disparate impact and treatment amounted to racial discrimination); *Ranieri v. Highlands Falls-Fort Montgomery Sch. Dist.*, 198 F. Supp. 2d 542 (2002) (football coach established prima facie case of age discrimination under the Age Discrimination in Employment Act but failed to show that employer's nondiscriminatory reason for declining to rehire him was pretextual); *Lamb-Bowman v. Delaware State Univ.*, 152 F. Supp. 2d 553 (D. Del. 2001) (women's basketball coach unsuccessful in establishing she was wrongfully terminated and retaliated against in violation of Titles VII and IX); *Maddox v. Univ. of Tennessee*, 62 F.3d 843 (6th

Cir. 1995) (university not liable under Americans with Disabilities Act and Rehabilitation Act of 1973 because its discharge of coach was not based solely on his disability—alcoholism).

5. *Tort Liability.* Two recent developments raise questions of the potential tort liability of an institution that hires a coach from another institution before his contract term has ended at the institution. On June 30, 2010, a New York trial court granted a default judgment in favor of Marist College in its lawsuit against the state of Virginia and James Madison University. Plaintiff Marist alleged tortious interference with its contract with former head basketball coach, Matt Brady. The contract between Marist and Brady contained a clause pursuant to which Brady agreed not to contact, without the consent of Marist, players he had previously recruited on behalf of Marist if Brady took a job with another institution. The court found that this clause combined with allegations that Brady took the head coaching position at JMU and, with the knowledge of JMU, contacted former players he had recruited to attend Marist were sufficient to support plaintiff's claim that JMU intentionally induced Brady to breach fiduciary duties arising from his contract with Marist. *Marist College v. Brady, Commonwealth of Virginia, JMU,* Sup. Ct. of NY Index No. 2009-5006:d.

6. *Tortious Interference.* On July 26, 2010, the NFL's Tennessee Titans filed a tortious interference of contract claims against USC and its head football coach Lane Kiffin. The Titans claim it had an enforceable contract with Kennedy Paola to serve as its running-backs coach from February 1, 2010, through February 14, 2011. The contract allegedly contained provisions giving the Titans the exclusive right to Paola's services and preventing Paola from discussing or entertaining other employment prospects without the Titans' written consent. Although he never obtained the written consent of the Titans, on July 24, 2010, Paola agreed to become the offensive coordinator at USC after being solicited by Lane Kiffin for the position.

7. *Negligent Misrepresentation. Williams v. Smith,* 820 N.W.2d 807 (Minn. 2012), demonstrates the need for coaches to exercise caution in representations made to prospective employees. James Williams, an assistant basketball coach at Oklahoma State University, was contacted by Tubby Smith, head men's basketball coach at the University of Minnesota, about an assistant basketball coach position at Minnesota. Following several communications during which salary and other terms were discussed, Smith orally offered Williams the position, which Williams orally accepted. Thereafter, athletic administrators expressed concerns to Smith regarding the commissions of NCAA rules infractions by Williams. Following further communications between Smith and Williams, and after Williams had submitted his resignation to OSU, Williams was officially informed that Minnesota would not hire him because of his previous major NCAA rules infractions.

A jury awarded over $1 million in damages based on Williams's negligent misrepresentation claim. In affirming the jury verdict, the court of appeals found that Smith owed a duty of care to Williams during the hiring negotiations and there was evidence sufficient to support the jury's finding that Williams reasonably relied on Smith's representations regarding his authority to hire Williams. *Id.* at 4. The Minnesota Supreme Court reversed, explaining:

> We conclude that the legal relationship between Williams and Smith is not the type of relationship entitled to legal protection, and therefore no duty

of care against negligent misrepresentation is owed. . . . First, their relationship in negotiating potential employment was not a professional, fiduciary,
or special relationship in which one party had superior knowledge or expertise. . . . Second, the nature of the relationship between Williams and Smith
does not support a duty of care in this case. The relationship between Williams
and Smith in their discussions of Williams' prospective employment as an
assistant basketball coach was that of two sophisticated business people, both
watching out for their individual interests while negotiating at arm's length.

> *Id.* at 10-11.

3.   Liquidated Damages

It is not uncommon for coaches to attempt to move up to a more prestigious
college or university. For this reason, institutions increasingly seek some form
of compensation when a coach leaves an institution prior to the expiration of
the term of his or her contract. When the coach quits before his or her contract
has expired, that coach has committed a breach of contract. The options theoretically available to an institution are to seek negative injunctive relief (affirmative injunctive relief is unavailable), to sue for damages, or simply to cancel
the contract and allow the coach to leave. Institutions will most likely resort
to an increasingly popular additional option: seek compensation under a buyout or liquidated-damages provision. The amounts due to institutions under
such provisions are often paid by the breaching coaches' new institutions. The
DiNardo case discusses the validity of liquidated damages provisions in coaching
contracts.

VANDERBILT UNIVERSITY v. DINARDO
174 F.3d 751 (6th Cir. 1999)

GIBSON, Circuit Judge.

Gerry DiNardo resigned as Vanderbilt's head football coach to become
the head football coach for Louisiana State University. As a result, Vanderbilt
University brought this breach of contract action. The district court entered
summary judgment for Vanderbilt, awarding $281,886.43 pursuant to a damage
provision in DiNardo's employment contract with Vanderbilt. DiNardo appeals,
arguing that the district court erred in concluding: (1) that the contract provision was an enforceable liquidated damage provision and not an unlawful
penalty under Tennessee law; (2) that Vanderbilt did not waive its right to liquidated damages. . . . We affirm the district court's ruling that the employment
contract contained an enforceable liquidated damage provision and the award
of liquidated damages under the original contract. . . .

On December 3, 1990, Vanderbilt and DiNardo executed an employment
contract hiring DiNardo to be Vanderbilt's head football coach. Section one of
the contract provided:

> The University hereby agrees to hire Mr. DiNardo for a period of five (5) years
> from the date hereof with Mr. DiNardo's assurance that he will serve the entire
> term of this Contract, a long-term commitment by Mr. DiNardo being important
> to the University's desire for a stable intercollegiate football program. . . .

The contract also contained reciprocal liquidated damage provisions. Vanderbilt agreed to pay DiNardo his remaining salary should Vanderbilt replace him as football coach, and DiNardo agreed to reimburse Vanderbilt should he leave before his contract expired. Section eight of the contract stated:

> Mr. DiNardo recognizes that his promise to work for the University for the entire term of this 5-year Contract is of the essence of this Contract to the University. Mr. DiNardo also recognizes that the University is making a highly valuable investment in his continued employment by entering into this Contract and its investment would be lost were he to resign or otherwise terminate his employment as Head Football Coach with the University prior to the expiration of this Contract. Accordingly, Mr. DiNardo agrees that in the event he resigns or otherwise terminates his employment as Head Football Coach (as opposed to his resignation or termination from another position at the University to which he may have been reassigned), prior to the expiration of this Contract, and is employed or performing services for a person or institution other than the University, he will pay to the University as liquidated damages an amount equal to his Base Salary, less amounts that would otherwise be deducted or withheld from his Base Salary for income and social security tax purposes, multiplied by the number of years (or portion(s) thereof) remaining on the Contract.

During contract negotiations, section eight was modified at DiNardo's request so that damages would be calculated based on net, rather than gross, salary.

Vanderbilt initially set DiNardo's salary at $100,000 per year. DiNardo received salary increases in 1992, 1993, and 1994. . . .

[EDS. The facts relating to an Addendum under which DiNardo allegedly agreed to extend the term of his contract with Vanderbilt for an additional two years are omitted.]

In November 1994, Louisiana State University contacted Vanderbilt in hopes of speaking with DiNardo about becoming the head football coach for L.S.U. [Paul] Hoolahan, [Vanderbilt's athletic director] gave DiNardo permission to speak to L.S.U. about the position. On December 12, 1994, DiNardo announced that he was accepting the L.S.U. position.

Vanderbilt sent a demand letter to DiNardo seeking payment of liquidated damages under section eight of the contract. Vanderbilt believed that DiNardo was liable for three years of his net salary: one year under the original contract and two years under the Addendum. DiNardo did not respond to Vanderbilt's demand for payment.

Vanderbilt brought this action against DiNardo for breach of contract. . . .

I

DiNardo first claims that section eight of the contract is an unenforceable penalty under Tennessee law. DiNardo argues that the provision is not a liquidated damage provision but a "thinly disguised, overly broad non-compete provision," unenforceable under Tennessee law. . . .

Contracting parties may agree to the payment of liquidated damages in the event of a breach. . . . The term "liquidated damages" refers to an amount determined by the parties to be just compensation for damages should a breach occur. . . . Courts will not enforce such a provision, however, if the stipulated amount constitutes a penalty. . . . A penalty is designed to coerce performance by punishing default. . . . In Tennessee, a provision will be considered one for liquidated damages, rather than a penalty, if it is reasonable in relation to the anticipated damages for breach, measured prospectively at the time the contract was entered into, and not grossly disproportionate to the actual damages. . . . When these conditions are met, particularly the first, the parties probably intended the provision to be for liquidated damages. However, any doubt as to the character of the contract provision will be resolved in favor of finding it a penalty. . . .

The district court held that the use of a formula based on DiNardo's salary to calculate liquidated damages was reasonable "given the nature of the unquantifiable damages in the case." The court held that parties to a contract may include consequential damages and even damages not usually awarded by law in a liquidated damage provision provided that they were contemplated by the parties. . . . The court explained:

> The potential damage to [Vanderbilt] extends far beyond the cost of merely hiring a new head football coach. It is this uncertain potentiality that the parties sought to address by providing for a sum certain to apply towards anticipated expenses and losses. It is impossible to estimate how the loss of a head football coach will affect alumni relations, public support, football ticket sales, contributions, etc. . . . As such, to require a precise formula for calculating damages resulting from the breach of contract by a college head football coach would be tantamount to barring the parties from stipulating to liquidated damages evidence in advance.

Id. at 642.

DiNardo contends that there is no evidence that the parties contemplated that the potential damage from DiNardo's resignation would go beyond the cost of hiring a replacement coach. He argues that his salary has no relationship to Vanderbilt's damages and that the liquidated damage amount is unreasonable and shows that the parties did not intend the provision to be for liquidated damages.

DiNardo's theory of the parties' intent, however, does not square with the record. The contract language establishes that Vanderbilt wanted the five-year contract because "a long-term commitment" by DiNardo was "important to the University's desire for a stable intercollegiate football program," and that this commitment was of "essence" to the contract. Vanderbilt offered the two-year contract extension to DiNardo well over a year before his original contract expired. Both parties understood that the extension was to provide stability to the program, which helped in recruiting players and retaining assistant coaches. Thus, undisputed evidence, and reasonable inferences therefrom, establish that both parties understood and agreed that DiNardo's resignation would result in Vanderbilt suffering damage beyond the cost of hiring a replacement coach.

This evidence also refutes DiNardo's argument that the district court erred in presuming that DiNardo's resignation would necessarily cause damage to the University. That the University may actually benefit from a coaching change (as DiNardo suggests) matters little, as we measure the reasonableness of the liquidated damage provision at the time the parties entered the contract, not when the breach occurred, *Kimbrough & Co.*, 939 S.W.2d at 108, and we hardly think the parties entered the contract anticipating that DiNardo's resignation would benefit Vanderbilt.

The stipulated damage amount is reasonable in relation to the amount of damages that could be expected to result from the breach. As we stated, the parties understood that Vanderbilt would suffer damage should DiNardo prematurely terminate his contract, and that these actual damages would be difficult to measure. *See Kimbrough & Co.*, 939 S.W.2d at 108. . . .

Vanderbilt hired DiNardo for a unique and specialized position, and the parties understood that the amount of damages could not be easily ascertained should a breach occur. Contrary to DiNardo's suggestion, Vanderbilt did not need to undertake an analysis to determine actual damages, and using the number of years left on the contract multiplied by the salary per year was a reasonable way to calculate damages considering the difficulty of ascertaining damages with certainty. *See Kimbrough & Co.*, 939 S.W.2d at 108. The fact that liquidated damages declined each year DiNardo remained under contract, is directly tied to the parties' express understanding of the importance of a long-term commitment from DiNardo. Furthermore, the liquidated damages provision was reciprocal and the result of negotiations between two parties, each of whom was represented by counsel.

We also reject DiNardo's argument that a question of fact remains as to whether the parties intended section eight to be a "reasonable estimate" of damages. The liquidated damages are in line with Vanderbilt's estimate of its actual damages. . . . Vanderbilt presented evidence that it incurred expenses associated with recruiting a new head coach of $27,000.00; moving expenses for the new coaching staff of $86,840; and a compensation difference between the coaching staffs of $184,311. The stipulated damages clause is reasonable under the circumstances, and we affirm the district court's conclusion that the liquidated damages clause is enforceable under Tennessee law.

[EDS. The court's discussion of whether Vanderbilt waived its right to liquidated damages when it granted DiNardo permission to discuss a coaching position with L.S.U., the enforceability of an addendum to the parties' contract, and the duration of DiNardo's contract if the addendum was deemed to be enforceable is omitted.]

Accordingly, we affirm the district court's judgment that the contract contained an enforceable liquidated damage provision, and we affirm the portion of the judgment reflecting damages calculated under the original five-year contract. We reverse the district court's judgment concluding that the Addendum was enforceable as a matter of law. We remand for a resolution of the factual issues as to whether Larry DiNardo's approval was a condition precedent to the enforceability of the Addendum and, if so, whether the condition was satisfied by Larry DiNardo's failure to object.

DAVID A. NELSON, Circuit Judge, concurring in part and dissenting in part.

It seems to me that [section 8 of the contract] was designed to function as a penalty, not as a liquidation of the university's damages. Insofar as the court holds otherwise, I am constrained to dissent. In all other respects, I concur in Judge Gibson's opinion and in the judgment entered pursuant to it.

My principal reasons for viewing section eight as a penalty are these: (1) although the damages flowing from a premature resignation would normally be the same whether or not Coach DiNardo took a job elsewhere, section eight does not purport to impose liability for liquidated damages unless the coach accepts another job; (2) the section eight formula incorporates other variables that bear little or no relation to any reasonable approximation of anticipated damages; and (3) there is no evidence that the parties were attempting, in section eight, to come up with a reasonable estimate of the university's probable loss if the coach left. I shall offer a few words of explanation on each of these points.

Section eight does not make Coach DiNardo liable for any liquidated damages at all, interestingly enough, unless, during the unexpired term of his contract, he "is employed or performing services for a person or institution other than the University. . . ." But how the coach spends his post-resignation time could not reasonably be expected to affect the university's damages; should the coach choose to quit in order to lie on a beach somewhere, the university would presumably suffer the same damages that it would suffer if he quit to coach for another school. The logical inference, therefore, would seem to be that section eight was intended to penalize the coach for taking another job, and was not intended to make the university whole by liquidating any damages suffered as a result of being left in the lurch.

This inference is strengthened, as I see it, by a couple of other anomalies in the stipulated damages formula. First, I am aware of no reason to believe that damages arising from the need to replace a prematurely departing coach could reasonably be expected to vary in direct proportion to the number of years left on the coach's contract. Section eight, however, provides that for every additional year remaining on the contract, the stipulated damages will go up by the full amount of the annual take-home pay contemplated under the contract. Like the "other employment" proviso, this makes the formula look more like a penalty than anything else.

Second, the use of a "take-home pay" measuring stick suggests that the function of the stick was to rap the coach's knuckles and not to measure the university's loss. Such factors as the number of tax exemptions claimed by the coach, or the percentage of his pay that he might elect to shelter in a 401(k) plan, would obviously bear no relation at all to the university's anticipated damages.

Finally, the record before us contains no evidence that the contracting parties gave any serious thought to attempting to measure the actual effect that a premature departure could be expected to have on the university's bottom line. On the contrary, the record affirmatively shows that the university did not attempt to determine whether the section eight formula would yield a result reasonably approximating anticipated damages. The record shows that the university could not explain how its anticipated damages might be affected by the coach's obtaining employment elsewhere, this being a subject that the draftsman of the contract testified he had never thought about. And the record shows that the question of why the number of years remaining on the contract would have any bearing on the amount of the university's damages was never analyzed either.

In truth and in fact, in my opinion, any correspondence between the result produced by the section eight formula and a reasonable approximation of anticipated damages would be purely coincidental. What section eight prescribes is a penalty, pure and simple, and a penalty may not be enforced under Tennessee law. . . .

NOTES AND QUESTIONS

1. *Analysis of* DiNardo. What is the likely practical effect of buyout clauses such as that in *DiNardo*? Are liquidated damages clauses such as in *DiNardo* intended primarily to deter a coach from leaving an institution or to compensate an institution for the damages attributable to the loss of a coach's services? Do you agree or disagree with the concurring/dissenting judge's argument that Section 8 constituted an unenforceable penalty? In the

absence of a liquidated-damages provision, how might an institution calculate the damages caused by the departure of a successful football or basketball coach? Are damages resulting from a coach's breach too uncertain to quantify? See Richard T. Karcher, *The Coaching Carousel in Big-Time Intercollegiate Athletics: Economic Implications and Legal Considerations,* 20 Fordham Intell. Prop. Media & Ent. L.J. 1 (2009) (discussing the validity of liquidated-damages provisions in coaching contracts).

Shortly after the trial began, DiNardo settled the dispute by agreeing to pay Vanderbilt an undisclosed sum. As an attorney representing DiNardo, what would be your strategy during settlement negotiations? What would be your strategy as counsel representing Vanderbilt?

2. University of West Virginia v. Rodriguez. The validity of a $4 million liquidated-damages provision was at issue in a lawsuit filed by the University of West Virginia against its former head football coach Rich Rodriguez, who left the school in 2007 to assume the same position at the University of Michigan. The disputed $4 million liquidated-damages provision was included in the Rodriguez/West Virginia contract after the coach had received an offer from another school. Rodriguez argued: He was induced by fraud and improper pressure to sign the agreement; the disputed clause was an unenforceable penalty provision; and West Virginia breached the contract by failing to abide by an oral commitment to reduce the agreed-on damage amount in the event he resigned before the end of his contract term. The university argued the clause was valid and entered into in good faith. In July 2008, Rodriguez agreed to a $4 million settlement pursuant to which Rodriguez and Michigan paid $1.5 million and $2.5 million, respectively, to West Virginia. Rodriguez's employer also paid his attorney fees incurred in the litigation. Rodriguez's new contract with Michigan included a $4 million liquidated-damages provision. Vicki Smith, *Rodriguez, Michigan to Pay WVU $4 Million,* Pittsburgh Trib., Jul. 10, 2008. In November 2011, Rodriguez was hired as the head coach at the University of Arizona.

3. *Exclusivity of Liquidated Damages and Availability of Injunctive Relief.* The question before a state superior court judge in Massachusetts was whether a liquidated-damages provision constituted the sole remedy available to the university in *Northeastern University v. Brown,* 2004 WL 616225 (Mass. Super. March 11, 2004). In July 2003, Northeastern University entered into a contract to have Donald Brown serve as its head football coach through the end of the 2007-2008 football season. The contract provided in part as follows:

> Coach [Brown] agrees to devote full time and effort to the University and agrees not to seek, discuss, negotiate for, or accept other employment during the term of this Agreement without first obtaining the written consent of the President of the University. Such consent shall not be unreasonably withheld.

Id. at *1. The contract also provided that in the event that Brown left Northeastern prior to the end of the contract term, he would pay the university $25,000. Six months after he signed the contract, Brown accepted an offer to coach the University of Massachusetts football team. Northeastern thereupon sought an injunction to prevent Brown from coaching at the University of Massachusetts.

The Massachusetts superior court judge first considered whether the liquidated-damages provision constituted Northeastern's exclusive remedy.

In concluding that, when specific performance is sought, a liquidated-damages provision is not the exclusive remedy, the judge emphasized the general applicability of rules of contract law to the sports context. Citing to section 361 of the Restatement (Second) of Contracts, the court stated, "Specific performance or an injunction may be granted to enforce a duty even though there is a provision for liquidated damages for breach of that duty." *Id.* at *3.

Initially granting Northeastern's request for negative injunctive relief, the court focused on the irreparable harm that Northeastern's football team would sustain.

> Brown knows the program, the plays, and the set procedures used at Northeastern, and he will be able to use his knowledge of same against Northeastern. Northeastern and U. Mass. compete to recruit the same student athletes and compete with each other on a regional basis for television coverage for their games. As noted, U. Mass. and Northeastern are members of the same football conference, and they play each other each year.

Id. Within a month of granting the interim injunction, the judge reversed himself, lifted the injunction and instructed the parties to settle. Eventually the parties worked out a settlement under which the University of Massachusetts agreed to pay Northeastern $150,000 and to suspend Brown from coaching the first three games of the 2004-2005 season. Mark Blaudschun, *Settlement Is Reached on Brown UMass, NU End Coach Saga*, Boston Globe, May 13, 2004, at E1.

Applying general rules of contract law, did the judge reach the right decision in lifting the injunction?

4. Sexual Harassment of Student-Athletes by Coaches

Chapter 3's discussion of the sanctions imposed by the NCAA on Penn State University's athletics program addressed a former assistant coach's sexual harassment of children. This comment examines the sexual harassment of female student-athletes by male coaches.

One of the more celebrated cases involved allegations made by two female soccer players against the male coach of the University of North Carolina women's soccer team. The players alleged, among other things, that the coach made inappropriate sexual comments to them and uninvited sexual advances toward them. One of the two soccer players settled with the university for $70,000 and an agreement that the coach would undergo sensitivity training. *UNC Will Pay Settlement in Dorrance Case*, Charlotte Observer, March 24, 2004, at 6C.

In subsequently dismissing the remaining player's action, a federal district court noted that the plaintiff's complaint revolved around sexually related comments and statements made by her soccer coach that allegedly amounted to "hostile environment" sexual harassment in violation of Title IX. *Jennings v. University of North Carolina at Chapel Hill*, 2004 WL 2414536 (M.D.N.C.). The court adopted the following standard as controlling whether such a claim is actionable under Title IX: "[T]he sexual harassment must be 'so severe, pervasive, and objectively offensive that it can be said to deprive the victims of access to the educational opportunities or benefits provided by the school.'" *Id.* at

*5 (quoting *Davis v. Monroe Cty. Sch. Bd. of Educ.*, 526 U.S. 629, 650 (1999)). Applying this standard, the court dismissed the plaintiff's Title IX claim.

> While inappropriate in some respects and quite possibly offensive to her, the conduct that she alleges occurred was not "severe, pervasive and objectively offensive" to the point of depriving her of educational opportunities. The comments Ms. Jennings claims to have found offensive occurred less than weekly. When comments were made, they were not severe, especially when the social context is considered. . . . The players were teasing and joking amongst themselves on these occasions. Mr. Dorrance did not initiate these discussions or steer the players' conversation in the direction of sex. The comments were only "mere utterances," and were not physically threatening. There is no evidence, beyond Ms. Jennings' own vague assertion, that the atmosphere at practice interfered with her performance on the field or in the classroom. . . .
>
> As for the inquiries Mr. Dorrance allegedly made directly to Ms. Jennings, one of these occurred in a group setting and was only mildly related to any sort of sexual topic. In the setting of an athletic practice where players are discussing their social activities, a coach inquiring about a player's weekend, or about whether a certain person is her boyfriend, is not harassment. . . .

Id.

A three-judge panel of the Fourth Circuit affirmed the district court ruling. *Jennings v. University of North Carolina at Chapel Hill*, 444 F.3d 255 (4th Cir. 2006). It stated a cognizable hostile environment claim arises under Title IX if a plaintiff establishes "(1) that she belongs to a protected group (e.g., a student at an institution covered by Title IX); (2) that she was subjected to harassment based on her sex; (3) that the harassment was sufficiently severe or pervasive to create an abusive educational environment; and (4) a cognizable basis for imputing institutional liability under Title IX." *Id.* at 267-268. The court concluded that no reasonable jury could find that Coach Dorrance's "remarks during Jennings' two-year tenure on the team were sufficiently severe or pervasive to create a sexually hostile educational environment." *Id.* at 275. After considering the case en banc, however, the court ruled that the plaintiff alleged sufficient facts for a jury to find that Dorrance subjected Jennings to sexual harassment. *Jennings v. University of North Carolina*, 482 F.3d 686 (4th Cir. 2007). It found that a jury could reasonably find that Dorrance's persistent harassment was sufficiently degrading to young women to create a hostile or abusive environment.

In *Simpson v. University of Colorado*, 500 F.3d 1170 (10th Cir. 2007), the plaintiffs alleged they were sexually assaulted at a party by football players and recruits. According to the plaintiffs, the university had an official policy that paired recruits with "female ambassadors" to ensure that the recruits would be shown a good time. In determining the viability of the plaintiffs' Title IX claim, the court framed the central issue as whether a risk existed that a sexual assault might occur during a recruiting visit. The court found evidence sufficient to establish such a risk, including the head football coach's general knowledge of the serious risk of sexual assault during recruiting visits, the coach's specific knowledge that assaults had occurred during recruiting visits at CU, the coach's maintenance of an unsupervised player-host program notwithstanding this knowledge, the inadequacy of steps taken by CU to reduce the risk of sexual assaults during recruiting visits, and conduct by the head coach in resisting recruiting reforms.

In settlement of the plaintiffs' claims, CU agreed to pay them a total of $2.5 million. The settlement terms also required CU to hire an external Title IX monitor to focus on the university's sexual harassment and gender discrimination issues and to add staff to its victims' assistance center. Allison Sherry, *$2.85 Million CU Settles Case Stemming from Recruit Scandal*, Denver Post, Dec. 6, 2007, at A01.

For examples of other cases in which male coaches have been accused of sexually harassing female athletes, see *Bostic v. Smyrna Sch. Dist.*, 418 F.3d 355 (2d Cir. 2005) (although acknowledging that a teacher's harassment of a student falls within the ambit of Title IX, the court refused to hold the school liable because there was no proof that the school had actual knowledge of a sexual relationship between a 15-year-old student and her track coach); *Doe v. Rains County Indep. Sch. Dist.*, 76 F.3d 666 (5th Cir. 1996); *Ericson v. Syracuse Univ.*, 35 F. Supp. 2d 326 (S.D.N.Y. 1999); *Maier ex rel. B.T. v. Canon McMillian Sch. Dist.*, 2009 WL 2591098 at*10 (W.D. Pa. Aug. 20, 2009); *K.P. v. Corsey*, 228 F. Supp. 2d 547 (D. N.J. 2002), *rev'd in part and remanded*, 77 Fed. Appx. 611 (3d Cir. 2003). See generally Deborah L. Brake, *Going Outside of Title IX to Keep Coach-Athlete Relationships in Bounds*, 22 Marq. Sports L. Rev. 395 (2012); Caitlin M. Cullitan, *"I'm His Coach, Not His Father:" A Title IX Analysis of Sexual Harassment in College Sports*, 12 Tex. Rev. Ent. & Sports L. 53 (2010); Diane Heckman, *Title IX and Sexual Harassment Claims Involving Educational Athletic Department Employees and Student-Athletes in the Twenty-First Century*, 8 Va. Sports & Ent. L.J. 223 (2009); Wes R. McCart, *Simpson v. University of Colorado: Title IX Crashes the Party in College Athletic Recruiting*, 58 DePaul L. Rev. 153 (2008); Michael E. Buchwald, Comment, *Sexual Harassment in Education and Student Athletics: A Case for Why Title IX Sexual Harassment Jurisprudence Should Develop Independently of Title VII*, 67 Md. L. Rev. 672 (2008).

What factors may contribute to cases of sexual harassment by male coaches against female student-athletes? Are there unique aspects of college sports that warrant a careful balancing of preventing potential sexual harassment claims against those unique features? Two commentators have identified the following three factors as creating special opportunities for sexual harassment: (1) the coach/student-athlete relationship, which is marked by the immense authority and power coaches exercise over student-athletes, and the one-on-one contact coaches have with student-athletes; (2) the physical nature of sports, in which coaches often apply a hands-on approach to instructing athletes, and frequent physical contact between coaches and athletes in the form of a congratulatory pat on the back; and (3) focus on the athlete's body, around which daily discussions between coach and student-athlete revolve. See Nancy Hogshead-Makar and Sheldon E. Steinbach, *Intercollegiate Athletics' Unique Environment for Sexual Harassment Claims: Balancing the Realities of Athletics with Preventing Potential Claims*, 13 Marq. Sports L. Rev. 173 (2003). See also Jesse Mendelson, *Sexual Harassment in Intercollegiate Athletics by Male Coaches of Female Athletes: What It Is, What It Means for the Future, and What the NCAA Should Do*, 9 Cardozo Women's L.J. 597 (2003).

PROBLEM 5-2

Coach entered into a five-year contract with University at an annual base salary of $250,000, not including perquisites, which contained the following provision:

NOTICE OF APPOINTMENT AND CONTRACT: During the term of Coach's contract, Coach shall hold the appointment, title, and duties of Head Coach in the University's men's basketball program, except that at any time during the Appointment Term with 30 days' notice, the appointment, title, and duties of Head Coach may be terminated and another title and duties assigned. The University's termination of Coach's appointment, title, and duties as Head Coach of the men's basketball program, and its reassignment of Coach to other appointment, title, and duties within the University, shall be within the discretion of University and may be exercised with or without cause.

During the first two years of his contract, the basketball team had a losing record of 8 wins and 45 losses. University, which previously had a highly regarded men's basketball program, lost money on its men's basketball program and attendance was down during these two years. In a letter to Coach dated March 15, University's athletic director stated:

University hereby notifies you that your appointment as Head Coach of University's men's basketball team, and all duties associated with your title as Head Coach, will terminate as of April 16. University hereby offers to reassign you to the position of compliance coordinator for NCAA rules and regulations. A change in leadership of the basketball team is required and this reassignment is for the good of the athletic department. If you accept University's offer of reassignment, it will take effect April 16. You will continue to receive your annual base salary of $250,000 for each of the remaining three years of your contract, except you will not be entitled to receive perquisites that are normally associated with the position of head basketball coach.

Coach is very upset and believes University's reassignment of him constitutes an effort to get him to resign. He is also concerned that accepting a noncoaching position will detrimentally affect his ability to secure another coaching position. Coach would like nothing better than to sue University and comes to you for advice. What advice would you offer to Coach? What are the legal and professional consequences of Coach accepting the reassignment and of Coach rejecting the reassignment? What type of compromise might Coach consider? In advising Coach, consider the following materials: *Monson v. Oregon*, 901 P.2d 904 (Or. Ct. App. 1995); Martin J. Greenberg and James T. Gray, 1 Sports Law Practice 585-587 (2d ed. 1998); see also *Dennison v. Murray State Univ.*, 465 F. Supp. 2d 733 (W.D. Ky. 2006) (even though athletic director's contract stated that the university could only reassign him to job with responsibilities consistent with the duties of an athletic director, university acted properly in reassigning plaintiff to position of director of corporate giving since contract also included a provision providing it was subject to all university policies, which included its transfer/reassignment policy).

D.   CONTRACT NEGOTIATION EXERCISE

You are an attorney who represents Coach Reynolds, who is widely regarded as an up-and-coming head college football coach. He began his head football coaching career at Midwest U, a poorly regarded Division I university. Prior to his arrival at Midwest U, the school's football team had suffered through eight consecutive losing seasons. After Reynolds assumed the head coaching position, he immediately turned around Midwest U's football program. During the second through fifth years of his five-year contract at Midwest U, the team qualified for postseason play. Moreover, his student-athletes graduated at a rate far above the average graduation rate for football players. He runs what is considered a very clean program.

Reynolds has been approached by his alma mater, Southeastern U, to become its head coach because of the resignation of its longtime successful coach. After extensive negotiations, Reynolds tentatively agrees to become the head coach of Southeastern U, subject to finalizing the details of the contract. Southeastern U has a strong program in a moderately strong conference, but not one of the elite conferences. The general counsel for Southeastern U is concerned that Reynolds will use the institution as a steppingstone to a school with an elite conference. Reynolds, on the other hand, wants to retain the flexibility to leave Southeastern U before his contract term ends if such an offer becomes available. Reynolds is also interested in making certain that he obtains the types of incentives and bonuses that he believes he deserves given his past success. Coach Reynolds, who is 45, is also interested in securing the future of his family. Reynolds is married and has four children, ages 8, 10, 13, and 17. The 17-year-old will enter college a year from now.

Set forth below is a sample contract. Analyze the sample contract from the perspectives of the general counsel for Southeastern U and the agent representing Coach Reynolds. Discuss terms that should be modified, deleted, or added. In addition to the sample contract, the following resources may assist you in developing your negotiation points.

1.   Summaries of Coaches' Contracts

The following summaries provide select compensation information that may assist you in developing a negotiation strategy.

UNIVERSITY OF OKLAHOMA

Coach: Bob Stoops[1]
Term: Six years—Jan. 1, 2009, through Dec. 31, 2015
Total annual compensation: $4,075,000
Base salary: $250,000
TV/radio/personal services: $2.1 million (increased by $200,000 annually)
Perks and other terms: $600,000 annually for appearance and speaking engagements on behalf of OU unrelated to athletics; two cars and a housing allowance; up to 45 hours annually of private airplane availability; membership and monthly dues at a golf course; 20 football tickets.
Termination/liquidated damages: University will pay coach $3 million per year remaining on contract if terminated without cause.

---

1. Salary information for Coach Stoops was obtained from the following: *USA Today Sports College Football Coaches Salaries Database*, http://www.usatoday.com/story/sports/ncaaf/2012/11/19/ncaa-college-football-head-coaches-salary-database/1715543/; *Salaries and Contracts*, Coaches Hot Seat, Jan. 12, 2013, http://www.coacheshotseat.com/SalariesContracts.htm; *Contract of Employment*, http://www.coacheshotseat.com/CHSOklahoma.pdf.

PERFORMANCE BONUSES

Big 12 championship game participation: $66,000
Big 12 championship game victory: $88,000
BCS bowl game participation: $110,000
BCS national championship game participation: $165,000
National championship victory: $275,000
Top 10 in final BCS national rankings: $82,500
Graduation rate of 75% or better: $55,000
Big 12 coach of the year: $33,000
AP national coach of year: $66,000

THE OHIO STATE UNIVERSITY

Coach: Urban Meyer[2]
Term: Seven years—Nov. 28, 2011, through Jan. 31, 2018
Total annual compensation: $4,000,000
Base salary: $700,000
TV/radio/personal services: $1,850,000
Perks and other terms: $500,000 one-time signing bonus payable upon execution of contract; $1,400,000 Nike equipment/apparel; use of private aircraft on recruiting and university business—jet aircraft on trips at least 200 miles from Columbus and 35 hours of personal use of a jet aircraft; 12 tickets to each home football game and two tickets to each home basketball game; $10,000 for one annual appearance on behalf of Coca-Cola; membership and monthly dues at a golf course; two cars and housing allowance.
Termination/liquidated damages: Coach can request to leave the job and receive $1.5 M per year over the life of the six-year deal if more major NCAA violations predating his arrival are found. Contract may be terminated by the school if Coach or his staff fails to report known or suspected NCAA violations.

PERFORMANCE BONUSES

Graduation rates: $100,000 for 70%-79.99%; $150,000 for 80% or higher
Team's participation in #1 v. #2 BCS championship game: $250,000

BOWLING GREEN UNIVERSITY

Coach: Dave Clawson[3]
Term: Six years—Dec. 11, 2008, through June 30, 2015

---

2. Salary information for Coach Meyer was obtained from the following: Brian Bennett, *Urban Meyer's Full Contract Details Released*, ESPN.com, June 18, 2012, http://espn.go.com/blog/ncf nation/post/_/id/62151/urban-meyers-full-contract-details-released; Doug Lesmerises, *Urban Meyer's Full Ohio State Contract Released, with More Details on Bowl Bonuses, NCAA Violations*, Plain Dealer, June 18, 2012, http://www.cleveland.com/osu/index.ssf/2012/06/post_96.html; *Head Football Coach—Terms of Employment*, http://media.cleveland.com/osu_impact/other/meyer-contract-osu-june19.pdf.

3. Salary information for Coach Clawson was obtained from the following: *USA Today Sports College Football Coaches Salaries Database*, http://www.usatoday.com/story/sports/ncaaf/2012/11/19/ncaa-college-football-head-coaches-salary-database/1715543/; *Salaries and Contracts, Coaches Hot Seat*, Jan. 12, 2013, http://www.coacheshotseat.com/SalariesContracts.htm; *Bowling Green State University Employment Contract for Head Coach of Intercollegiate Football*, http://www.coacheshotseat.com/CHSBowlingGreen.pdf.

Total annual compensation: $364,200
Base salary: $200,000 (2008-2011); $205,000 (2011-2012); $210,000 (2012-2013); $215,000 (2013-2014); $220,000 (2014-2015)
TV/radio/personal services: N/A
Perks and other terms: Provided an automobile and golf privileges and is given 12 season tickets for home games.
Termination/liquidated damages: University will pay coach $300,000 if he is terminated without cause; if he resigns for another job, coach owes $100,000 if he accepts another college coaching position or $250,000 if he accepts an NFL coaching position.

PERFORMANCE BONUSES

MAC championship: $20,000 if team wins MAC Conference Championship; $10,000 per year if the Team plays a regular season game against a team from the BCS conference and the University is guaranteed and actually receives $400,000 for such game; $5,000 if team participates in any bowl game.
MAC coach of the year: $2,000
Graduation rate: $5,000 for graduation rate of 77% or higher
Attendance: $5,000 for home attendance ten (10) to fourteen (14) percent above the baseline attendance figure; $8,000 for home attendance fifteen (15) to nineteen (19) percent above the baseline attendance figure; $12,000 for home attendance twenty plus (20+) percent above the baseline attendance figure.

2. *Helpful Resource Materials*

Students may wish to refer to the following materials in developing a negotiating strategy:

- Michael L. Buckner, *Structuring College Coaches' Employment Agreements: Important Clauses and Issues in Agreements—Part One*, 3 Holland & Knight LLP Newsletter, no. 2 (Second Quarter 2000), at 1.
- Michael L. Buckner, *Structuring College Coaches' Employment Agreements: Important Clauses and Issues in Agreements—Part Two*, 3 Holland & Knight LLP Newsletter, no. 3 (Third Quarter 2000), at 1.
- Canadian Professional Coaches Association, A Guide to Employment Contracts for Coaches, Section 3: The Coaching Contract: Basic Elements (2000).
- Martin J. Greenberg, *A Study of Division I Assistant Football and Men's Basketball Coaches' Contracts*, 18 Marq. Sports L. Rev. 25 (2007).
- Martin J. Greenberg, *Termination of College Coaching Contracts: When Does Adequate Cause to Terminate Exist and Who Determines Its Existence?*, 17 Marq. Sports L.J. 197 (2006).
- Martin J. Greenberg, *College Coaching Contracts Revisited: A Practical Perspective*, 17 Marq. Sports L. Rev. 197 (2001).
- Martin J. Greenberg, *College Coaching Contracts: A Practical Perspective*, 1 Marq. Sports L.J. 207 (1991).
- Michael Smith, *Coach's Contracts Have Clauses with Some Claws*, Courier-Journal Louisville, 2003 WLNR 17830068 (May 8, 2003).
- Edward Stoner, II, and Arlie Nogay, *The Model University Coaching Contract ("MCC"): A Better Starting Point for Your Next Negotiation*, 16 J.C. & U.L. 43 (1989).

3. Sample Contract

EMPLOYMENT CONTRACT
STATE OF TEXAS
COUNTY OF LUBBOCK

This Employment Contract (the "Agreement") is made and entered into effective the 23rd day of March, 2001, by and between Texas Tech University, herein called "University" and Robert M. Knight, herein called "Coach."

I. Term

Both parties hereby mutually agree that for and in consideration of the mutual benefits and consideration received or to be received by the parties that Coach shall be employed as Head Men's Basketball Coach at the University for a term of five years beginning the 23rd day of March, 2001, and ending on the 31st day of May, 2006. Coach shall have a ten-month appointment for each Contract Year of this Agreement. For purposes of this Agreement the term "Contract Year" shall mean June 1 through May 31 of each year of this Agreement. Coach shall be employed upon the terms, conditions, stipulations, covenants, and agreements as set forth herein:

II. Primary Duty Assignment

Coach shall be employed as Head Men's Basketball Coach at University during the period of this Agreement.

III. Compensation and Benefits

A. Base Salary

Coach shall be paid the following annual base salary during the period of this Agreement.

March 23, 2001–May 31, 2002	$15,000
June 1, 2002–May 31, 2003	$250,000
June 1, 2003–May 31, 2004	$250,000
June 1, 2004–May 31, 2005	$250,000
June 1, 2005–May 31, 2006	$250,000

Payment shall be in accordance with the payroll policies of the University and subject to such deductions as may be required by applicable state and federal laws and regulations.

B. Health, Retirement, Vacation and Other Leave

Coach will be eligible to participate in the benefits as all other University employees. Such benefits shall be governed by University policies and the laws of the State of Texas.

C. Perquisites

1. Courtesy Automobiles: Coach shall receive two (2) courtesy automobiles.

2. Complimentary Tickets: During each year of this Agreement, Coach shall receive four (4) complimentary seats in the football press box during all Texas

Tech home football games; Coach shall receive twenty-four (24) season tickets for home men's basketball games.

3. Camps: Coach, acting as an individual or a private legal entity, may offer a camp using University facilities after first receiving written approval by the Director of Intercollegiate Athletics. It is understood that Coach or other University personnel involved will use personal vacation time when preparing for and conducting a private camp and that University facilities, equipment and resources may be used according to the terms and conditions of a separate facility use agreement. Such facility agreement must be in writing and signed by both parties before commencement of a camp. Coach shall have permission to use the terms "Texas Tech University" and "Red Raider Basketball" in the description and identification of any basketball camp conducted by the Coach, upon approval by the Director of Intercollegiate Athletics.

4. Guarantee of Outside Athletics-Related Personal Income: If the annual Outside Athletics-Related Personal Income of Coach does not reach $500,000 annually, the University agrees to make up any shortfall up to that amount. If the annual Outside Athletics-Related Personal Income of Coach exceeds $500,000, Coach shall be entitled to retain such excess income. It is agreed that the Outside Athletics-Related Personal Income of Coach shall include but not be limited to the following income arranged through University.

a. Uniform/clothing contracts
b. Shoe/equipment contracts
c. Apparel contracts, e.g., sweaters
d. Television coaches' shows
e. Pregame, postgame and other radio shows
f. Sports camps
g. Speaking engagements arranged through University
h. Merchandising contracts
i. Other income received by Coach resulting from being the Head Men's Basketball Coach at University

The following types of income arranged through International Management Group ("IMG") shall be excluded from the determination of annual Outside Athletics-Related Personal Income.

a. National speaking engagements arranged through IMG
b. Television commercial contracts
c. Book contracts
d. Other income arranged by IMG not related to serving as Men's Basketball Coach at University

This guarantee is provided to Coach based on an anticipated increase in ticket sales.

A report of such income, with supporting documentation, shall be presented by Coach to the University by June 30 of each year of this agreement for the annual period from June 1 through May 31. University will pay such shortfall to Coach by August 1 of each year.

5. Deferred Compensation: University shall establish an account for the following amounts of deferred compensation during the term of this Agreement.

University will deposit funds into the account during the term of this Agreement as follows:

Date	Amount
September 1, 2001	$225,833
March 1, 2002	$225,833
September 1, 2002	$150,000
March 1, 2003	$75,000
September 1, 2003	$75,000
January 1, 2004	$75,000
July 1, 2004	$75,000
January 1, 2005	$75,000
July 1, 2005	$75,000

University's obligations to provide funding for this account shall cease upon termination of this Agreement. The account shall remain the sole property of University at all times during the term of this Agreement.

Beginning June 1, after termination of this Agreement, Coach or his estate shall be paid deferred compensation, including any accrued interest, over a period of ten (10) years, with 1/10th of the current balance being paid in the first year, 1/9th of the remaining balance in the second year, 1/8th in the third year, 1/7th in the fourth year, 1/6th in the fifth year, 1/5th in the sixth year, 1/4th in the seventh year, 1/3rd in the eighth year, 1/2 in the ninth year, and the remainder in the tenth year.

Notwithstanding other remedies provided under Section V.F., Non-Compete Consideration, the above deferred compensation shall be forfeited if Coach should accept a position in any coaching capacity with another Big 12 Conference institution, or any other institution in a conference in which the university is a member or any other NCAA Division I institution located within the State of Texas.

IV.   PERFORMANCE

In the performance of his duties, Coach shall be directly responsible to and under the supervision of the Director of Intercollegiate Athletics. Without limitation of the foregoing, Coach, in the performance of his duties, shall conduct himself at all times in a manner consistent with his position as an instructor of students. The parties agree that, although this Agreement is sports related, the primary purpose of the University and this Agreement is to support the University's educational mission. Thus, the educational purposes of the University shall have priority in the various provisions of this agreement. Coach will follow all applicable University policies and procedures. Coach shall not, either directly or indirectly, breach or countenance the breach of any player or coach subject to his control or supervision of any of the rules and standards of the Big 12 Conference, the NCAA, youth, collegiate, and the master's amateur athletics as well as other associations or agencies to which Texas Tech University adheres. In this connection, Coach agrees to devote his entire time, labor, effort and attention, in good faith, to conduct and perform the duties commensurate with the position as Head Men's Basketball Coach. Breach of such rules and standards, whether willful or through negligence, may be subject to disciplinary action and penalties ranging from termination, public or private reprimand to monetary fines or adjustments in compensation as determined by the University President following consultation and review with the Director of Intercollegiate Athletics. The provision of this paragraph shall be without prejudice to any right the University may have under Section V of this Agreement.

V. TERMINATION

A. FOR CAUSE

The University specifically reserves the right to terminate this Agreement without further obligations at any time for good cause, such as the following: failure or refusal to perform assigned duties; actions detrimental to the University, its employees, or students; including a major violation or violations of the governing policies, rules, regulations, and procedures of the University, any athletic conference of which the University is a member, or the NCAA; violations of local, state, or federal laws; or actions involving moral turpitude by Coach.

B. INABILITY TO PERFORM

In the event of the inability of Coach to continue to perform his obligations under this Agreement by reason of illness or some other occurrence beyond the control of either party hereto, and such inability to perform has continued or will continue beyond a reasonable period of time, this Agreement shall thereupon terminate and all future obligations between the parties hereto shall cease. The parties further agree that in the event that Coach is unable to continue to perform his obligations under this Agreement and the contract is terminated pursuant to this section, Coach shall not be entitled to, nor shall University be required to pay any portion of the perquisites as defined in Section III of this Agreement, with the exception of deferred compensation as set out in Section III.C.6.

C. RESIGNATION OF COACH

In the event Coach terminates his employment to coach at another NCAA Division 1-A institution or at a professional level, during the term of this Agreement as defined herein, Coach shall pay to University, within thirty (30) days of resignation as liquidated damages, in lieu of any and all other legal remedies or equitable relief, the remaining base salary for the remaining period of this Agreement.

D. TERMINATION WITHOUT CAUSE

In addition to the provision set forth above, there is also reserved to the University the right to terminate this Agreement without cause at any time. The parties agree that in the event this right to terminate is exercised, the University will pay remaining annual base salaries to Coach in monthly installments as set forth in Section III of this Agreement. In addition, the University will pay to Coach the existing balance of the Deferred Compensation as set out in Section III.C.5 above. In such event, the University shall not be liable to Coach for any other University benefits, perquisites, or any collateral business opportunities, outside income revenues, or other benefits associated with Coach's position as coach. For purposes of this paragraph, salary shall be limited to compensation as defined as Base Salary in Section III above.

E.   MUTUAL AGREEMENT

The parties reserve the right to terminate this Agreement by mutual agreement. In the event the right to terminate pursuant to this paragraph is exercised, all liabilities of the parties shall cease effective the date of termination.

F.   NON-COMPETE CONSIDERATION

Coach acknowledges that during the term of employment by University, he will gain confidential information concerning the University athletic program and that the use of this confidential information by a Conference opponent would place the University's athletic program at a serious competitive disadvantage. Accordingly, Coach expressly promises and agrees not to engage in employment with another Big 12 Conference school or any other Conference in which University is a member in any coaching capacity during the period of this Agreement. In the event Coach breaches this Agreement by accepting coaching-related employment with any Conference school during the term of this Agreement, Coach agrees that the liquidated damages, as defined in Section V.C., shall not be considered sufficient to mitigate against loss. Coach further agrees that because the services Coach is to render under this contract are of a special, unique, unusual, extraordinary, and intellectual character that gives those services peculiar value, the loss to the University of which cannot be reasonably or adequately compensated in damages in an action of law, and because said breach would place University at significant competitive disadvantage, the University shall have the right to obtain from any court such equitable, injunctive, or other relief as may be appropriate, including a decree enjoining Coach from performing coaching-related services for any Conference school.

VI.   OUTSIDE INCOME

Coach shall receive written approval from the University President prior to entering into any agreement for all athletically related income and benefits from sources outside the University.

Coach shall annually report in writing all athletically related income and benefits from sources outside the University (including but not limited to income from annuities; sports camps; housing benefits; automobile benefits; television and radio programs; and endorsements or consultation contracts with athletic shoes, apparel, or equipment manufacturers) through the Director of Intercollegiate Athletics to the University President.

VII.   PUBLIC APPEARANCES

Coach shall make no public appearance, either in person or by means of radio or television, or willingly allow the use of his name in connection with his relationship to the University when any such appearance or use of name will result in unfavorable reflection upon the University. Coach will neither participate in, nor allow his name to be used in connection with, any particular athletic equipment and/or commercial activity wherein Coach will receive remuneration for such participation or use unless Coach first shall have received written consent therefore from the Director of Intercollegiate Athletics. Endorsement or consultation contracts with athletics shoe, apparel, or equipment manufacturers must be reviewed and approved by the Director of Intercollegiate Athletics before Coach can execute such an agreement.

VIII.   Representations

It is mutually understood that this Agreement contains all of the terms and conditions to which the parties have agreed and that no other understandings or representations, either oral or written, unless referenced in the preceding paragraphs, regarding the subject matter of this Agreement shall be deemed to exist or to bind the parties hereto and that any modification, amendment, or addendum to this Agreement shall only be by written instrument signed by each party hereto.

IX.   Interpretation

No provision or part of this Agreement which shall prove to be invalid, void, or illegal shall in anyway affect, impair, or invalidate any other provision or part, and such other provision and parts shall remain in full force and effect.

X.   Applicable Law

This Agreement is made and entered in Lubbock County in the State of Texas, the law of Texas shall govern its validity and interpretation and the performance by the parties of their respective duties and obligations under this Agreement.

Coach has been advised to have this Agreement reviewed by counsel familiar with employment agreements before agreeing to the terms and conditions contained herein.

IN WITNESS WHEREFOF, the parties hereto shall consider this Agreement to be effective on the 23rd day of March, 2001.

_____   Date
ROBERT M. KNIGHT
Head Men's Basketball Coach

_____   Date
GERALD MYERS
Director of Intercollegiate Athletics

_____   Date
DR. DAVID J. SCHMIDLY
President

CHAPTER
6

Professional Sports League Governance and Legal Regulation

A. INTRODUCTION

This chapter begins our exploration of the regulation of legal and business relationships within professional sports in the United States. Greatest emphasis is on league sports, particularly the so-called major leagues exemplified by the National Football League (NFL), National Basketball Association (NBA), Major League Baseball (MLB), and National Hockey League (NHL). Other leagues (e.g., Major League Soccer) and individual-performer sports (e.g., golf and tennis) also deserve and receive scrutiny. In Chapters 3 and 4 we observe that, to a certain extent, aspects of professionalism have descended onto big-time college athletics and events such as the Olympics and other international competitions. To label these sports activities as strictly "amateur" and to attempt to contrast them as standing distinctly apart from professional sports leagues is a dichotomy that simply does not withstand serious examination. Even so, we can say that our earlier considerations are "significantly" different from what we now confront. The professional sports leagues and other associations we now examine have a bottom line that is overwhelmingly driven by economics and that in turn determines most of the decision making and creates most of the legal issues.

The first section of this chapter examines the development of the American professional sports industries (particularly team sports), their unique features, and their primary components. We then turn to the structure, operation, and internal governance of professional sports leagues consisting of independently owned and operated clubs with a league commissioner generally vested with broad "best interest" of the game authority. As proven time after time, club owners do not always agree among themselves, or with the commissioner, on various matters of league governance, and these disputes often find their way into the courts.

Finally, we explore antitrust law and its implications in the professional sports context, ranging from litigation arising out of the proposed ownership or movement of a club to litigation brought by a new sports league claiming that the established league has engaged in anticompetitive conduct to bring about its demise.

B.   ORIGIN AND EVOLUTION OF MODERN PROFESSIONAL SPORTS INDUSTRIES

The origins of today's most popular American individual and team professional sports are to a large degree shrouded in mystery. The so-called great American pastime of baseball may not be American in origin at all. Some claim it is a derivative of the English game of rounders. Of course, the well-known and honorable American claim for decades was that baseball started with Abner Doubleday in Cooperstown, New York. We even had a major league commission that investigated the matter over 100 years ago and verified that Doubleday was indeed the creator. That finding has been debunked and a better estimate is that baseball, at least as we know it, may have started on the Elysian Fields in New Jersey in 1848.

Football, the American version, has equally obscure beginnings. Most would attribute its modern origin to games at Harvard in 1871, when the rules were altered to allow players to scoop up the round ball and run with it. At that point, football became played with more than feet. We do know that in the early 1900s, it had reached sufficient levels of mayhem to be condemned by the old Rough Rider himself, Theodore Roosevelt.

We are not at all certain of even the origin of the word *hockey*. Some of the theories are certainly amusing. It may have come from the French word *hoquet*, meaning "shepherd's crook." A more fanciful theory is that French explorers in North America observed Iroquois Indians playing a version of the game, striking a hard ball with sticks, and yelling "Hogee!" or "It hurts!" What is known is that something resembling the modern version was played in Canada as early as the 1830s.

The one sport that seems uncontroversial concerning its origins is basketball. Dr. James Naismith did nail a peach basket to a wall in the Springfield, Massachusetts YMCA's gymnasium during the winter of 1891 in order to provide the youth with an indoor sport to play when snow and wind thwarted outdoor activity. Dr. Naismith first instructed his charges to play soccer (undisputedly of British origin) in the gym, but their lack of ball control resulted in broken windows, leading Dr. Naismith to concoct a game in which players used their hands rather than their feet to control the ball. Basketball became a popular sport almost immediately. Indeed, there are reports that even young ladies embraced the sport within a couple of years. The first collegiate game between women was played at Smith College in 1893, and women at Stanford and the University of California at Berkeley introduced a female-rules version of the game in 1895. Both the appeal and potential for the sport were established almost from the date of its founding.

None of these sports, in their present form, can equal the foundations of golf and its journey to the modern day. It was so popular that in 1457 the king of Scotland had his parliament ban it, lest it detract from more serious pursuits such as archery. But this ban was largely ignored and was completely overturned when King James IV of Scotland took up the game in the early sixteenth century. His granddaughter Mary, Queen of Scots, was a great devotee of the sport and took the game with her to France. She was attended by a host of young male admirers, known as *cadets*, who followed her over the meadows. They eventually were called *caddies*. Most caddies today probably are unaware of their noble lineage.

This brief history simply underscores the unique appeal that sports have always had, and these are but summary examinations of only a few of the sports that might be explored. It is small wonder that sports have evolved, in our modern age, into overriding obsessions and commercial successes.

1.   Evolution of Sports into a Business and Profession

Sports as activities, diversions, and cohesive societal events have been with us for centuries, but sports as professions, businesses, and industries are of more recent vintage. Along with the industrial revolution in the 1800s, a sports revolution occurred as well. This was no coincidence. Activity became a business, and business evolved into industry. For sports, the roots were perhaps not as obvious as the invention of steam locomotion or electricity harnessed into light, but sports took advantage of emerging industrial technologies just as surely as the wings of birds inspired the flight of man.

Each new step in the advancement of technology led to increased opportunities for sports exposure and thus expansion. Transportation was the first crucial ingredient. Communications was the second. The two have been powerful concomitants—necessary elements to allow sports to transcend the confines of the ballpark or arena and to enter the homes of millions of sports fans. Although the movers and shakers in early professional sports ventures could not have recognized fully the enormous commercial potential within their grasp, such is not true today. The preeminent sports business entrepreneurs are those with the greatest vision and ability to exploit this vast potential. Sports as commercial successes owe much to technological advances and to deepened understanding of business and marketing techniques. There is still the game itself, with winners and losers, but there is a driving force—economic success—that is equally influential in just how, when, and where a game is played and who ultimately plays it.

In the United States, the sport of baseball was the pioneer for professional players, teams, and leagues. The Cincinnati Red Stockings are generally acknowledged as the first truly professional team, touring the country in 1869 and taking on all challengers. The National League, which still exists today, was founded in 1876. Some would take issue with it being designated as the first professional sports league. However, though it bears perhaps small resemblance to its current structure within Major League Baseball (MLB), it was a significant start on the road to professionalization.

As baseball wended its uncertain way in developing the professional sports model, the sports of football, hockey, and basketball proceeded along even more tenuous paths. Their efforts were often greeted by apathy or even antipathy. Even so, although decades later than baseball, the other professional sports leagues eventually emerged. The National Football League (NFL) began in 1919, 1920, or 1921. In 1919, it called itself the American Professional Football Conference and boasted of teams far removed in many respects from today's clubs. The league's struggles led to its near demise in 1920 and restart in 1921. So when it actually began can be debated. By whatever definition, however, the NFL's ultimate astounding success and popularity are beyond dispute.

The National Hockey League (NHL) actually predated the NFL by two years, starting in 1918 in the aftermath of a one-year wonder, the National Hockey Association. The "national" designation, however, signified Canada, not the

United States. The first U.S. team, the Boston Bruins, did not join the league until 1924. Today the number of American clubs significantly exceeds that of Canadian clubs. When the league took a more permanent form, four of the six clubs were located in the United States, with this trend continuing as the NHL expanded. However, until relatively recently, NHL players were almost exclusively Canadian; but this changed as hockey developed in the United States, leading to more American NHL players. Additionally, the NHL increasingly looks to Europe for an infusion of talent. This grand mixture, with global implications, is in full force today.

The history of professional basketball has been circuitous. An appellation for players used to be *cagers*. This referred to the wire netting surrounding the court to keep the players from hurtling into the stands near the sidelines. This makeshift, precarious nature of the court was a fitting description for the business of basketball as well. There were teams who played for money, and there were leagues here and there. Through the 1920s and 1930s, the sport gained popularity but headed in directions both unknown and uncharted. The end of World War II caused a new beginning for sports in the United States, enabling the American public to seek new diversions. Professional basketball rode this wave. The National Basketball Association (NBA) owes its foundations to the Basketball Association of America (BAA) in 1946.

Soccer, known to the rest of the world as "football," is truly global in its nature and fan appeal, more so than any other American team sport. Its World Cup is the premier worldwide team sports event (with apologies to the NFL's Super Bowl). And yet it is decidedly a minor sport in the United States, at least at the professional level. Although Major League Soccer has a throng of hardcore supporters, it is still several steps below the other sports leagues both economically and in terms of general fan interest in the United States.

Two individual-performer sports, among many, deserve mention. Tennis and golf have carved out special niches both in the United States and globally. But their movements from merely recreational activities to businesses have also been slow and often tested. There is the lure of the star player, but there is the lack of local or regional identification because there is no "home team" to cheer or to jeer. Tennis and golf are more truly global than team sports because the top players in both sports come from all parts of the world. American players currently do not dominate competition in these sports, and at times take a distinct backseat to foreign players. Despite loyal and avid followings, the overall depth of support for these individual-performer sports pales in comparison to team sports, at least in the United States.

Tennis had its professionals dating at least from the 1920s, but the main action was in the amateur tournaments. The pros were reduced to barnstorming, with the prevailing champion taking on the latest challenger from the amateur ranks. The big tournaments were closed to professionals. Only with the arrival of the *open* tennis era in 1968 did professional tennis truly emerge. Golf also had its share of early professionals, with the U.S. Open dating from 1895 and later with Walter Hagen's winning the first Professional Golfers' Association Championship in 1921. However, it was not until after World War II that the professionals came to dominate the sport of golf.

Auto racing currently is one of the country's most popular professional spectator sports, although some might be reluctant to characterize it as a sport. The first Indianapolis 500 Mile Race was held in 1911. The National Association of Stock Car Auto Racing (NASCAR) has been in existence since 1951. NASCAR and IndyCar each sponsor an annual series of auto races at tracks throughout the nation.

2. Unique Features of Professional Team Sports

Competitions involving individual sports sometimes take on a team format, such as when golfers come together as a team for the Ryder Cup or tennis players do battle in the Davis Cup competitions, but the heart of these athletic exploits is of an individual nature. And even though the individual sporting context certainly presents legal issues, team sports, which garner the major attention and dollars in the United States, have unique features that permeate their foundations and influence greatly how they operate. In turn, the legal consequences of these unique qualities raise ever-changing and complex challenges.

In team sports, a team, of course, must have other teams to play. It is best if this is done on a continuing basis from one year to the next. Thus, there has to be competition in the playing of the games. But to sustain interest, at least theoretically, the competition cannot be too one-sided in favor of any single team from year to year. Team owners, players, and ultimately consumers tire of being perennial losers (although a few teams have a knack for doing so).

Without any agreed-on limitations, there is nothing to prevent teams from being economic competitors. Meaningful on-field competition economically benefits all league teams, but too much off-field economic competition can be harmful. The league's viability and the economic health of all teams necessitate some reasonable limits on economic competition among its member clubs.

Economic competition does exist among various sports leagues, either those that offer games in the same sport or those that offer different sports. Again, in the case of different sports, there are certain mutual advantages in not having too much economic competition. Teams in different sports located in the same city may peacefully coexist. On the other hand, each team needs a fan base for its sport and must appeal to a group of potential consumers who may transfer their interest from one sport to another as the fortunes of the various local teams ebb and flow. For example, professional hockey and basketball franchises in the same city, whose playing seasons largely overlap, often experience the whims of fair-weather fans.

Add to this mix the fact that professional sports leagues, while in existence in some form for well over a century, are relatively new as multibillion-dollar national and even international business operations. Even as we enter the twenty-first century, teams and their owners, as well as their respective leagues, are still to a degree in an embryonic phase. Part of this results from the unique nature of professional team sports. There are no analogous models in other industries. The strong desire to compete successfully on the playing field versus the simultaneous need to limit economic competition among league clubs to some degree presents significant challenges to businesspeople accustomed to ruthless competition in other industries. To work both competitively and cooperatively can be very difficult.

If one adds players to this mix, business and legal issues multiply in their complexity. Highly skilled players are essential to the game's attractiveness to consumers and economic success. Sports leagues, as commercial vehicles, thrive on the special talents of players, their celebrity status, and their resulting marketability. Major league professional athletes have unique talents and playing abilities, but they also must fit into the business and legal structures of the various sports.

The following section explores in greater depth how the respective roles of teams, leagues, players, and other important components of the sports industries interact and often conflict. This interplay illustrates the need for legal regulation of this complex web of relationships.

3.   The Principal "Players" in the Professional Sports Industries

The old cliché "you can't tell the players without a scorecard" aptly describes why we cannot appreciate the dimensions of sports business and legal problems unless we understand what interests are involved and how these interests both intersect and conflict. The following discussion concerning the principal players uses the team-sports model; with only minor adjustments, it might also apply to individual-performer sports.

In general, the league, its commissioner, and the teams are aligned on one side; the players, their union, and player-agents are on the other. However, there are a host of related entities that play integral roles in a sports league's operations. Television and other media, advertisers and corporate sponsors, insurance companies, governmental entities, and financial institutions are just a few of the heavyweights that influence the professional team sports and individual-performer sports industries. Each of these components adds a layer of complexity and raises corresponding legal issues.

a.   Leagues

American professional sports leagues have existed since baseball's National League was founded in 1876. It was only a short time, because of various circumstances, until rival leagues formed. Most of them existed only briefly, but they helped shape the development of modern professional sports. These early rivals to the National League, such as the Union Association (1882), the American Association (1882), and the Players League (1890), challenged the established order. This produced competition—both legal and allegedly illegal. In essence, a sports league is a group of team owners that join together in a formal association to produce, market, and sell their product—organized athletic competition.

b.   Clubs or Teams

The terms *clubs* and *teams* are used interchangeably in the professional sports context. Each league has several member clubs located throughout the United States (or Canada), which are expanded (or contracted) from time to time. Indeed, the growth in the popularity of professional sports is often tracked by the expansion in a league's number of teams. By the same token, a decline in interest is often marked by a reduction in teams and perhaps the demise of an entire league.

Clubs are at times referred to as *franchises*, which denotes in part a club's legal relationship to a league. A club as a franchise is an accurate description only in part. Normally, in other industries, a corporation exists first and later awards franchises. In the case of most major professional sports leagues, this is only partly true. Clubs are formed, then band together as a league. Other clubs are formed later by the league, making them more truly franchises.

The legal nature and character of the interrelationship between a league and its member clubs are important from a legal standpoint, particularly for purposes of the antitrust laws. Even within a particular league, all clubs are not on equal footing. There is substantial variation in their approaches to the business in which they are engaged. A club's geographical location usually determines its potential consumer (fan) and economic base. Another important factor is the club's ownership, which in turn determines who operates and manages the club, thereby undoubtedly influencing who plays for the team and its performance level.

c.   Commissioners

The concept of a league commissioner with broad governing authority came to fruition when MLB club owners appointed their first commissioner, Judge Kenesaw Mountain Landis, to his throne in 1921. This bold act was done to ensure that baseball would not witness another scandal such as befell the Chicago White Sox in the 1919 World Series. Commissioner Landis was ceded sweeping powers to act "in the best interests of baseball." He and his successors have not been hesitant to use those powers, though some baseball commissioners, such as Fay Vincent, have not been able to sustain their power over obstreperous owners.

The other American major professional sports leagues — the NBA, NFL, and NHL — have followed baseball's example by adopting a league commissioner model of governance, and each league currently has a commissioner unafraid to flex his broad powers. David Stern has long controlled most significant moves made by owners in the NBA, and Roger Goodell, the NFL commissioner since 2006, has developed a reputation for doling out fierce discipline (in the form of both suspensions and monetary fines) when he believes coaches, players, or team executives have engaged in conduct detrimental to the league. The NHL adopted the commissioner model of governance long after the other major professional sports leagues. For the bulk of the NHL's existence, the league's top executive was titled its president, but the establishment of the commissioner's office in 1993 symbolized a new, enhanced central authority that would determine many of the vital questions in the league's dealings with the players association and outside interests. Gary Bettman became the NHL's first commissioner, and he quickly established his broad authority over league matters.

The existence of a commissioner with broad powers is an invitation to legal conflict. In this regard, there has been no shortage of disputes regarding a league commissioner's exercise of his plenary authority in a wide variety of situations, as explored later in this chapter.

d.   Players

One of the greatest anomalies in sports is the professional athlete, who often has folk hero status that can be commercially exploited. Some exceptional athletes remain folk heroes for life, but this stature is accorded only to a few. For most, it is an early grave as to fame and fortune. They have but a few brief years, if that, to capture the minds of the populace and garner long-term wealth as a reward for their athletic talents. This leads to a standard best exemplified by such phrases as "show me the money" and "grab the money and run." An athlete who fails to do so may find his or her day has passed and cannot be recovered.

The professional athlete, therefore, must be savvy enough to get needed advice and counsel from business professionals. He or she also must be cognizant of the cold realities of the business. If necessary, an athlete must be willing to fight for his or her legal rights. In some situations, these rights may not be absolutely clear. And a player may be thrust into litigation or arbitration to determine just who has what duties and who has what rights. When playing careers and the economic rewards of those careers are greatly affected, legal conflicts may be unavoidable. In the professional sports context, the legal issues involving players are widespread and are fully explored throughout this text.

e.   Players Associations

In most team sports, players associations typically are certified labor unions. Players are employees of the club (and arguably of the league as well). As employees, players have the right to organize as a union under federal labor law. However, professional sports players associations are not the usual labor union and thus give rise to special types of labor relations not typically found in other industrial settings.

The role of players associations is not easily explained. Though attempts to organize players have occurred throughout much of the history of professional sports, the modern beginnings that have led to players associations becoming permanent fixtures date only to the 1950s with the formation of the Major League Baseball Players Association. In its early days, this organization was not a true union. Indeed, its founders emphasized that it was not a labor union. But that soon changed.

By the 1960s, players associations in baseball, basketball, and football were all seeking recognition as labor unions and were striving to advance their members' economic interests through collective bargaining. Hockey players were somewhat behind in their union organization efforts, but eventually also unionized. The first collective bargaining agreements between players unions and leagues were negotiated in 1968 and 1969.

The basic dilemma for a players association is that it must fairly represent all players, although their playing abilities and economic values vary (often considerably). There are many marginal players and relatively few truly elite players—all of whom must somehow fit under the same union umbrella. (Chapter 7 examines in detail the even greater problems faced by players associations in dealing with their own members, with management, with those who want to be part of the union, and with individual player-agents.)

f.   Agents

Those who represent athletes in contract negotiations are usually called agents. They generally are lawyers and trained professionals, but this is not always the case. The term *agent* itself is not a misnomer, because clearly there is established a principal-agent relationship that imposes fiduciary obligations on the agent. The athlete is the principal, and the agent is his or her representative. At times, however, agents act as if they are the principal figures in the relationship, which ultimately causes problems.

Agents arrived on the sports scene at roughly the same time as players associations. Although agents in some form or other had been around for several years prior to the 1960s, these individuals functioned as promoters rather than strictly agents. The best known of these early pioneers in promoting professional players' interests was a person known as "Cash 'n' Carry Pyle." He organized a national tour for the French tennis star Suzanne Leglen in 1926, and that same year obtained unprecedented salary and bonuses for Illinois running back Red Grange as an NFL player. Grange's entry into the NFL helped ensure the league's existence, and he was well worth his price.

It was not until the 1960s that agents began to proliferate and enter the professional sports scene in notable fashion. Before then, players were largely on their own and at the mercy of the owners. However, as rival leagues were formed to compete with the established major professional leagues, salaries escalated. Agents descended on the scene to ensure this happened, happily taking a cut of the action in the process.

Several problems and abuses to the detriment of players surfaced with the appearance of agents. Agents who represent athletes in team sports, at least at the major league level, are now regulated to a certain extent by players associations. As noted in Chapter 8, there are other regulatory authorities as well.

g.   Other Industries Integral to Modern Professional Sports

Several interests are vitally affected by the operation of professional sports leagues and associations. Some have become so involved with the sports industries that at times they seem almost inseparable. A prime example is the media, particularly television.

Society today is much more deeply connected to sports, because sports events and news have entered the living room through television, radio, print media, and the Internet. Pervasive media coverage of sports means greater immersion at all levels and, in turn, has set related industries into the development of strategies as to how to benefit from this explosion. In particular, as television has developed from over-the-air to cable, increased dollars have flowed into the coffers of both sports and the other industries. The latest development is the Internet. From depictions of live sports events and news about them have come new ways to present sports, including up-to-the-minute information about everything happening—all conveyed at a price, of course.

Financial and insurance institutions, even governments, provide the wherewithal for the presentation and security measures needed for big-dollar events. Corporations provide huge sums for advertising, sponsorships, and other accoutrements. Sports interests outside the leagues are affected by what happens and attempt to exert their influence accordingly.

Each of the above-listed stakeholders play roles in today's professional sports industries, but the leagues and associations that produce the organized professional athletic competition are at the industries' core. They are the entities around which the industries swirl and on which they rely.

C. INTERNAL LEAGUE GOVERNANCE AND COMMISSIONER AUTHORITY

Leagues and associations generally have a constitution and bylaws. A central system of governance is identified, and there is a strong likelihood that one particular individual is given substantial authority to oversee the general operation of the organization. This individual is often designated as the commissioner of that particular league or association. The constitution and bylaws are considered to be the primary authority for the governance of the league or association. Because it is a private contract between the parties, only rarely can its terms and provisions be legally challenged in a successful manner—a circumstance more fully detailed in the paragraphs that follow.

Team sports have an additional complication. The players on the teams are considered to be employees. The same is often true for other actors in the mix—in particular, umpires and referees. As employees, they are entitled to organize collectively as a union and avail themselves of the protections of our nation's labor laws. If they are successful in their organizational efforts, as discussed in Chapter 7, the product of their efforts may supersede a league's constitution and bylaws. For example, if professional athletes form a labor union and engage in collective bargaining with the owners, the resulting labor agreement takes precedence over the league's internal rules as to most labor-management issues and relations.

The individual player-team contracts also must be considered. In theory, they are at the bottom of the hierarchy of documents defining the parties' relationship. Both the collective bargaining agreement and the league constitution and bylaws take precedence over the individual contract provisions. However, in recent years, most player contracts have been standardized, and most are incorporated into the collective bargaining agreement and are a part thereof. Thus, the standardized player contract terms, when incorporated into the collective bargaining agreement, take precedence over the league constitution and bylaws.

In the discussion that follows, primary attention is on internal league governance issues that do not venture into the area of labor law and labor relations. The following material focuses on relations and disputes between the league and its member clubs and their owners. To an extent, it also considers the nature and scope of regulatory authority of associations formed to govern individual-performer sports. Because the athletes in these sports are not employees who can unionize and collectively bargain, labor law issues generally are not implicated, and contract law governs.

1. Scope of Judicial Review of Internal League Governance

American professional sports leagues and associations are private entities that are not subject to the constraints of the United States Constitution. *Long v. National Football League*, 870 F. Supp. 101 (W.D. Pa. 1994), *aff'd*, 66 F.3d 311 (3d Cir. 1994). The league or association constitution, bylaws, and rules create binding contractual rights and responsibilities if they are reasonable and do not infringe on other parties' rights. Thus, the legal relationships among member clubs or individuals of professional sports leagues are primarily governed by contract law and the law of private associations. The federal antitrust laws also play a significant role in circumscribing the governing activities of professional leagues and associations.

Courts recognize that private associations must be accorded considerable latitude in rule making and enforcement in order to accomplish their legitimate objectives. See, e.g., *Mayfield v. NASCAR*, 674 F.3d 369 (4th Cir. 2012) (enforcing disciplinary suspension imposed on professional race car driver for breaching contractual obligation to comply with NASCAR's Substance Abuse Policy and release of liability and covenant not to sue NASCAR for any claims arising out of implementation of its policy). They generally permit professional sports leagues and associations to establish their respective systems of self-governance and are reluctant to interfere with or second-guess their internal decision making. Their members generally are bound by the terms of the sports league or association's constitution, bylaws, and other governing documents unless there is a breach of fiduciary duty, a conflict of interest, bad faith, or violation of applicable laws such as, for example, federal antitrust law. But otherwise there is broad discretion accorded to a sports league or association to interpret its own rules without judicial intervention, as illustrated by the following cases.

In *Koszela v. National Association of Stock Car Auto Racing, Inc.*, 646 F.2d 749 (2d Cir. 1981), the Second Circuit rejected the claims of a stock car owner and driver that NASCAR misapplied its rules in determining that another car and driver were the winners of two races. The court found that the plaintiffs' membership contract with NASCAR did not provide for an administrative appeal or judicial review of official decisions regarding race procedures or determination of car positions. The court concluded that the plaintiffs had been given an opportunity to be heard by NASCAR officials and had exhausted all available rights. The court affirmed the dismissal of the plaintiffs' claims and held that NASCAR was not in violation of any contractual duties owed to the plaintiffs.

A similar result was reached in *Crouch v. National Association of Stock Car Auto Racing, Inc.*, 845 F.2d 397 (2d Cir. 1988). At issue was whether NASCAR violated its own procedures in determining the winner of a stock car race. The court initially drew a distinction between reviewing the decisions made by private organizations and reviewing the procedures used in reaching those decisions. The court recognized the appropriateness of intervening if there were inadequate procedures to safeguard a member's rights, but the plaintiffs did not make any such assertions. Nor was there any allegation that NASCAR violated its own rules or that NASCAR officials acted in bad faith in reviewing the plaintiffs' challenge to the race results. The Second Circuit held that the lower court erred in delving into NASCAR's rulebook and conducting basically an inquiry *de novo*. Instead, the proper approach was to defer to an association's interpretation of its own rules absent a showing of bad faith or violation of any state or federal laws.

Despite a general judicial reluctance to oversee a professional sports organization's affairs to avoid becoming mired down in areas outside their expertise, courts will nevertheless provide a forum for resolution of internal governance disputes. At least at the major league level, a professional sports league is often without direct competition from another league. Because of the for-profit and monopolistic nature of major professional sports leagues and associations, there is a recognized need for some limited judicial oversight to prevent exploitation and blatant unfairness toward any of the organization's members or participants. As the *Koszela* court observed, when a sports organization has such a "'strangle-hold'" that all teams or individuals desiring to participate in a sport must join it, "rigid adherence to a 'hands off' policy is inappropriate." 646 F.2d at 754.

A sports governing body has a legal obligation to follow its own rules and bylaws; its failure to do so may give rise to a breach of contract claim by an aggrieved member whose interests are harmed. Courts will review the actions of professional sports organizations "(1) where the rules, regulations or judgments of the association are in contravention to the laws of the land or in disregard of the charter or bylaws of the association and (2) where the association has failed to follow the basic rudiments of due process of law." *Charles O. Finley & Co. v. Kuhn*, 569 F.2d 527, 544 (7th Cir. 1978). In addition, courts will intervene if an association's decision-making process is arbitrary or capricious, or is tainted by malice or bad faith. This will occur even if the aggrieved party, prior to the dispute in question, expressly waived its right to judicial recourse.

Gilder v. PGA Tour, Inc., 727 F. Supp. 1333 (D. Ariz. 1989), *aff'd*, 936 F.2d 417 (9th Cir. 1991), illustrates the potential for conflicts of interest that may require judicial intervention when individuals with vested interests make rules and policy for the association as a whole. Nine members of the Professional Golfers' Association (PGA) Tour sued the PGA for amending its tournament regulations to prohibit the use of golf clubs with U-shaped grooves. The PGA's then-existing bylaws permitted these rules to be amended only by an affirmative vote of a majority of its ten-member board (including at least three of the four directors who were professional golfers playing on the PGA Tour) at a regular meeting attended by a quorum. At a meeting of the board attended by all ten members, the ban on U-shaped grooved irons was passed when three members who were not touring professionals voted in favor of the amendment and the other seven board members abstained because of possible conflicts of interest. Four of the abstaining members were touring professionals in competition with those using the U-shaped grooved clubs, and three others were officers of the PGA.

After the plaintiffs, a group of professional golfers who wanted to use clubs with U-shaped grooves, complained about this voting procedure, the board unanimously voted to permit amendments to the PGA's tournament regulations by a majority vote of present board members who actually voted. The same three PGA board members again voted to ban the U-shaped irons, and the other seven members once again abstained from voting.

Observing that the effect of the PGA board's amended voting requirement and the abstentions by seven directors was to ban U-shaped irons, the district court issued a preliminary injunction against this prohibition based on the board's failure to follow its own rules. The Ninth Circuit affirmed and held that the touring professional golfers serving on the PGA's board owe a fiduciary duty to act in the best interests of the association and are prohibited from using their position for potential personal gain (each of them had endorsement deals with manufacturers of V-shaped grooved irons). Their vote to amend the bylaws' voting procedures, which resulted in U-shaped irons being banned, breached this fiduciary duty. See also *Blalock v. Ladies Professional Golf Assn.*, 359 F. Supp. 1260 (N.D. Ga. 1973) (suspension of professional golfer for alleged rules violations by governing board that included competing tour players infringes her right to fair disciplinary hearing in violation of federal antitrust laws; her competitors, sitting in judgment of her, unlawfully had authority to exercise unfettered, subjective discretion to discipline her for their own potential financial benefit).

Courts have also imposed implied covenants of good faith and fair dealing in contracts governing the internal affairs of professional sports leagues. For example, in a case arising out of the Oakland Raiders' initial move to Los Angeles in the early 1980s, the Ninth Circuit applied California law in ruling that league teams owed each other a reciprocal duty "to refrain from doing anything to injure the right of the other to receive the benefits of the agreement . . . [and] the duty to do everything that the contract presupposes that he will do to accomplish the purpose." *Los Angeles Memorial Coliseum Commission v. National Football League (Raiders II)*, 791 F.2d 1356, 1361 (9th Cir. 1986). Concerning franchise relocation, the court held that each league member must exercise its contractual right of approval or disapproval or its discretionary power over the interests of others in good faith.

In summary, these cases illustrate that courts generally are reluctant to interfere with the internal affairs of a professional sports league or association unless specific breaches of contract, breach of fiduciary duties, failure to provide due process, bad faith conduct, or violations of state or federal law occur.

2. *League Commissioner "Best Interests" Power*

The major professional sports leagues in the United States have all adopted a model of organization and governance that places an independent commissioner in control of internal affairs. This official is certainly more powerful than a chairperson of the board of a corporation, and probably wields more power than a typical president of a company. Although selected by and answerable to the league owners and their governing body, a sports league commissioner traditionally has been accorded certain powers and attendant enforcement rights that create a special role.

The first commissioner in any sport was Judge Kenesaw Mountain Landis, who assumed that position in baseball in 1920 to ensure that the infamous Black Sox scandal arising out of the 1919 World Series would not recur. Reportedly, at his insistence, Judge Landis was accorded the authority to do whatever was necessary to protect the "best interests" of baseball. That same sweeping power—to act in the best interests of the sport—is found in similar phraseology in the description of powers and duties vested in all commissioners of the American major professional sports leagues. To that end, the commissioner is delegated disciplinary powers, dispute resolution authority, and decision-making responsibility. Although an employee of the league, the commissioner is granted virtual autonomous authority to govern a great extent of a league's affairs without direct supervision or control by the member clubs. The commissioner is hired by the owners and can be fired; however, while in office, the commissioner cannot easily be challenged successfully.

A league's commissioner is an integral part of the league's governance structure whose role often consists of the following functions:

1. To create a fair and impartial internal authority to resolve disputes within the league and to enforce independently a disciplinary process—these being essential to maintain the game's integrity and provide rudimentary due process protections necessary to avoid judicial oversight of league affairs.
2. To take action when needed to restrain the unwarranted exercise of power by the league's owners to the detriment of fans and others, again to avoid judicial intervention.
3. To serve as a centralized administrative authority to facilitate efficient decision making and league governance.

4.   To be a skillful mediator when owners cannot agree.
5.   To be the lead negotiator for league-wide contracts, such as the all-important television deals.
6.   At times, to become involved in labor disputes between the owners and the players—in fact, in some leagues, the commissioner is the lead negotiator on behalf of the owners. (Such is the case today in the NBA and the NHL.)

For a general overview of a league's organizational structure, commissioner's governing authority, and objectives, see Gregor Lentze, *The Legal Concept of Professional Sports Leagues: The Commissioner and an Alternative Approach from a Corporate Perspective*, 6 Marq. Sports L.J. 65 (1995).

Despite having the above powers, it must be emphasized that a league commissioner does not have unfettered independence or authority. And, at times, he or she must walk a tightrope to avoid undermining or losing his or her authority. The commissioner, for example, has certain disciplinary authority over the league's club owners and can make decisions adverse to some or even all of them and their interests. Even so, the commissioner's job security is subject to the will of these owners, and a commissioner may be put in the middle of disputes that pose threats to his position. A commissioner may feel compelled to compromise to avoid alienating owners, which could possibly reduce his or her authority or possibly jeopardize his or her continued employment. For example, MLB commissioner Fay Vincent resigned in August 1992 under pressure from MLB club owners after making a series of controversial decisions.

A sports league commissioner's authority is contractual in nature and derived from the league's constitution, bylaws, and operating rules. The most sweeping power that a league commissioner is typically granted is the ability to take action deemed necessary to further the best interests of the sport. Although interpretation of the nature and scope of the commissioner's contractual authority ultimately is a question for judicial resolution, courts usually provide substantial deference to the commissioner's judgment and carefully consider the customs and usages under which the current commissioner and his or her predecessors have operated. However, a court will require a league commissioner to have valid authority to act, to comply with rudimentary notions of due process, to not act in bad faith, and to not contravene any state or federal laws.

The following cases provide illustrations of challenges to a league commissioner's exercise of his "best interests" of the game authority that have shaped the law in this area.

CHARLES O. FINLEY & CO., INC. v. KUHN
569 F.2d 527 (7th Cir.), *cert. denied*, 439 U.S. 876 (1978)

SPRECHER, Circuit Judge.

The two important questions raised by this appeal are whether the Commissioner of baseball is contractually authorized to disapprove player assignments which he finds to be "not in the best interests of baseball" where neither moral turpitude nor violation of a Major League Rule is involved, and whether the provision in the Major League Agreement whereby the parties agree to waive recourse to the courts is valid and enforceable.

The defendant Bowie K. Kuhn is the Commissioner of baseball (Commissioner), having held that position since 1969. On June 18, 1976, the Commissioner disapproved the assignments of the contracts of [Joe] Rudi, [Rollie] Fingers and [Vida] Blue to the Red Sox and Yankees "as inconsistent with the best interests of baseball, the integrity of the game and the maintenance of public confidence in it." The Commissioner expressed his concern for (1) the debilitation of the Oakland club, (2) the lessening of the competitive balance of professional baseball through the buying of success by the more affluent clubs, and (3) "the present unsettled circumstances of baseball's reserve system." . . .

II

Basic to the underlying suit brought by Oakland and to this appeal is whether the Commissioner of baseball is vested by contract with the authority to disapprove player assignments which he finds to be "not in the best interests of baseball." In assessing the measure and extent of the Commissioner's power and authority, consideration must be given to the circumstances attending the creation of the office of Commissioner, the language employed by the parties in drafting their contractual understanding, changes and amendments adopted from time to time, and the interpretation given by the parties to their contractual language throughout the period of its existence. . . .

In November, 1920, the major league club owners unanimously elected federal Judge Kenesaw Mountain Landis as the sole Commissioner of baseball and appointed a committee of owners to draft a charter setting forth the Commissioner's authority. In one of the drafting sessions an attempt was made to place limitations on the Commissioner's authority. Judge Landis responded by refusing to accept the office of Commissioner.

On January 12, 1921, Landis told a meeting of club owners that he had agreed to accept the position upon the clear understanding that the owners had sought "an authority . . . outside of your own business, and that a part of that authority would be a control over whatever and whoever had to do with baseball." Thereupon, the owners voted unanimously to reject the proposed limitation upon the Commissioner's authority, they all signed what they called the Major League Agreement, and Judge Landis assumed the position of Commissioner. Oakland has been a signatory to the Major League Agreement continuously since 1960. The agreement, a contract between the constituent clubs of the National and American Leagues, is the basic charter under which major league baseball operates.

The Major League Agreement provides that "[t]he functions of the Commissioner shall be . . . to investigate . . . any act, transaction or practice . . . not in the best interests of the national game of Baseball" and "to determine . . . what preventive, remedial or punitive action is appropriate in the premises, and to take such action. . . ." Art. I, Sec. 2(a) and (b).

The Major League Rules, which govern many aspects of the game of baseball, are promulgated by vote of major league club owners. Major League Rule 12(a) provides that "no . . . (assignment of players) shall be recognized as valid unless . . . approved by the Commissioner."

The Major Leagues and their constituent clubs severally agreed to be bound by the decisions of the Commissioner and by the discipline imposed by him. They further agreed to "waive such right of recourse to the courts as would otherwise have existed in their favor." Major League Agreement, Art. VII, Sec. 2.

Upon Judge Landis' death in 1944, the Major League Agreement was amended in two respects to limit the Commissioner's authority. First, the parties deleted the provision by which they had agreed to waive their right of recourse to the courts to challenge actions of the Commissioner. Second, the parties added the following language to Article I, Section 3:

> No Major League Rule or other joint action of the two Major Leagues, and no action or procedure taken in compliance with any such Major League Rule or joint action of the two Major Leagues shall be considered or construed to be detrimental to Baseball.

The district court found that this addition had the effect of precluding the Commissioner from finding an act that complied with the Major League Rules to be detrimental to the best interests of baseball.

The two 1944 amendments to the Major League Agreement remained in effect during the terms of the next two Commissioners, A. B. "Happy" Chandler and Ford Frick. Upon Frick's retirement in 1964 and in accordance with his recommendation, the parties adopted three amendments to the Major League Agreement: (1) the language added in 1944 preventing the Commissioner from finding any act or practice "taken in compliance" with a Major League Rule to be "detrimental to baseball" was removed; (2) the provision deleted in 1944 waiving any rights of recourse to the courts to challenge a Commissioner's decision was restored; and (3) in places where the language "detrimental to the best interests of the national game of baseball" or "detrimental to baseball" appeared those words were changed to "not in the best interests of the national game of Baseball" or "not in the best interests of Baseball."

The nature of the power lodged in the Commissioner by the Major League Agreement is further exemplified "(i)n the case of conduct by organizations not parties to this Agreement, or by individuals not connected with any of the parties hereto, which is deemed by the Commissioner not to be in the best interests of Baseball" whereupon "the Commissioner may pursue appropriate legal remedies, advocate remedial legislation and take such other steps as he may deem necessary and proper in the interests of the morale of the players and the honor of the game." Art. I, Sec. 4.

The Commissioner has been given broad power in unambiguous language to investigate any act, transaction or practice not in the best interests of baseball, to determine what preventive, remedial or punitive action is appropriate in the premises, and to take that action. He has also been given the express power to approve or disapprove the assignments of players. In regard to non-parties to the agreement, he may take such other steps as he deems necessary and proper in the interests of the morale of the players and the honor of the game. Further, indicative of the nature of the Commissioner's authority is the provision whereby the parties agree to be bound by his decisions and discipline imposed and to waive recourse to the courts. . . .

III

Despite the Commissioner's broad authority to prevent any act, transaction or practice not in the best interests of baseball, Oakland has attacked the Commissioner's disapproval of the Rudi-Fingers-Blue transactions on a variety of theories which seem to express a similar thrust in differing language.

The complaint alleged that the "action of Kuhn was arbitrary, capricious, unreasonable, discriminatory, directly contrary to historical precedent, baseball tradition, and prior rulings and actions of the Commissioner." In pre-trial answers to interrogatories, Oakland acknowledged that the Commissioner could set aside a proposed assignment of a player's contract "in an appropriate case of violation of (Major League) Rules or immoral or unethical conduct." . . .

The plaintiff has argued that it is a fundamental rule of law that the decisions of the head of a private association must be procedurally fair. Plaintiff then argued that it was "procedurally unfair" for the Commissioner to fail to warn the plaintiff that he would "disapprove large cash assignments of star players even if they complied with the Major League Rules."

In the first place it must be recalled that prior to the assignments involved here drastic changes had commenced to occur in the reserve system and in the creation of free agents. In his opinion disapproving the Rudi, Fingers and Blue assignments, the Commissioner said that "while I am of course aware that there have been cash sales of player contracts in the past, there has been no instance in my judgment which had the potential for harm to our game as do these assignments, particularly in the present unsettled circumstances of baseball's reserve system and in the highly competitive circumstances we find in today's sports and entertainment world."

Absent the radical changes in the reserve system, the Commissioner's action would have postponed Oakland's realization of value for these players. Given those changes, the relative fortunes of all major league clubs became subject to a host of intangible speculations. No one could predict then or now with certainty that Oakland would fare better or worse relative to other clubs through the vagaries of the revised reserve system occurring entirely apart from any action by the Commissioner.

In the second place, baseball cannot be analogized to any other business or even to any other sport or entertainment. Baseball's relation to the federal antitrust laws has been characterized by the Supreme Court as an "exception," an "anomaly" and an "aberration." Baseball's management through a commissioner is equally an exception, anomaly and aberration, as outlined in Part II hereof. In no other sport or business is there quite the same system, created for quite the same reasons and with quite the same underlying policies. Standards such as the best interests of baseball, the interests of the morale of the players and the honor of the game, or "sportsmanship which accepts the umpire's decision without complaint," are not necessarily familiar to courts and obviously require some expertise in their application. While it is true that professional baseball selected as its first Commissioner a federal judge, it intended only him and not the judiciary as a whole to be its umpire and governor.

. . . [T]he Commissioner was vested with broad authority and that authority was not to be limited in its exercise to situations where Major League Rules or moral turpitude was involved. When professional baseball intended to place limitations upon the Commissioner's powers, it knew how to do so. In fact, it did so during the 20-year period from 1944 to 1964.

The district court found and concluded that the Rudi-Fingers-Blue transactions were not, as Oakland had alleged in its complaint, "directly contrary to historical precedent, baseball tradition, and prior rulings." During his almost 25 years as Commissioner, Judge Landis found many acts, transactions and practices to be detrimental to the best interests of baseball in situations where neither moral turpitude nor a Major League Rule violation was involved, and he disapproved several player assignments.

On numerous occasions since he became Commissioner of baseball in February 1969, Kuhn has exercised broad authority under the best interests clause of the Major League Agreement. Many of the actions taken by him have been in response to acts, transactions or practices that involved neither the violation of a Major League Rule nor any gambling, game-throwing or other conduct associated with moral turpitude. Moreover, on several occasions Commissioner Kuhn has taken broad preventive or remedial action with respect to assignments of player contracts. . . .

We conclude that the evidence fully supports, and we agree with, the district court's finding that "(t)he history of the adoption of the Major League Agreement in 1921 and the operation of baseball for more than 50 years under it, including: the circumstances preceding and precipitating the adoption of the Agreement; the numerous exercises of broad authority under the best interests clause by Judge Landis and . . . Commissioner Kuhn; the amendments to the Agreement in 1964 restoring and broadening the authority of the Commissioner; . . . and most important the express language of the Agreement itself are all to the effect that the Commissioner has the authority to determine whether any act, transaction or practice is 'not in the best interests of baseball,' and upon such determination, to take whatever preventive or remedial action he deems appropriate, whether or not the act, transaction or practice complies with the Major League Rules or involves moral turpitude." Any other conclusion would involve the courts in not only interpreting often complex rules of baseball to determine if they were violated but also, as noted in the Landis case, the "intent of the (baseball) code," an even more complicated and subjective task.

We conclude that the evidence fully supports, and we agree with, the district court's finding and conclusion that the Commissioner "acted in good faith, after investigation, consultation and deliberation, in a manner which he determined to be in the best interests of baseball" and that "(w)hether he was right or wrong is beyond the competence and the jurisdiction of this court to decide." . . .

V

Following the bench trial, the district court reached its decision in favor of the Commissioner without considering the impact of Article VII, Section 2 of the Major League Agreement, wherein the major league baseball clubs agreed to be bound by the Commissioner's decisions and discipline and to waive recourse to the courts. . . .

Even in the absence of a waiver of recourse provision in an association charter, "[i]t is generally held that courts . . . will not intervene in questions involving the enforcement of bylaws and matters of discipline in voluntary associations." . . .

. . . This clause can be upheld as coinciding with the common law standard disallowing court interference. We view its inclusion in the Major League Agreement merely as a manifestation of the intent of the contracting parties to insulate from review decisions made by the Commissioner concerning the subject matter of actions taken in accordance with his grant of powers. . . .

Even if the waiver of recourse clause is divorced from its setting in the charter of a private, voluntary association . . . we think that it is valid under the circumstances here involved. Oakland claims that such clauses are invalid as against public policy. This is true, however, only under circumstances where the waiver of rights is not voluntary, knowing or intelligent, or was not freely negotiated by parties occupying equal bargaining positions. The trend of cases in many states and in the federal courts supports the conclusion of the district court under the circumstances presented here that "informed parties, freely contracting, may waive their recourse to the court." . . .

Although the waiver of recourse clause is generally valid . . . we do not believe that it forecloses access to the courts under all circumstances. Thus, the general rule of nonreviewability which governs the actions of private associations is subject to exceptions (1) where the rules, regulations or judgments of the association are in contravention to the laws of the land or in disregard of the charter or bylaws of the association and (2) where the association has failed to follow the basic rudiments of due process of law. . . . We therefore hold that, absent the applicability of one of these narrow exceptions, the waiver of recourse clause contained in the Major League Agreement is valid and binding on the parties and the courts.

We affirm the district court's judgments. . . .

NOTES AND QUESTIONS

1. In the wake of the Messersmith-McNally arbitration, discussed in Chapter 7, MLB clubs in 1976 entered a new era when free agency of players became a reality. How clubs were to deal with this was uncertain. In anticipation of potential problems, Commissioner Bowie Kuhn issued warnings to clubs that tampering rules would be enforced. In particular, a club was not to have direct or indirect dealings with a potential free agent prior to the end of the season. The commissioner stated that violation of these strictures could result in "fines, loss of rights under (amateur free agent) and re-entry drafts and suspension of those responsible."

    The general manager of the Atlanta Braves, John Alevizos, and later the owner, Ted Turner, were charged with improper contacts and public remarks concerning Gary Matthews, who at the time played for the San Francisco Giants. In the first instance, after a hearing, Commissioner Kuhn held that Alevizos had violated the anti-tampering rules on two occasions and fined the Braves club $5,000 for each violation. In addition, the club lost its first-round selection in the next amateur player draft. This disciplinary action was accepted by the Braves. Subsequently, at a cocktail party, owner Ted Turner informed the Giants co-owner, Robert Lurie, that the Braves would do anything necessary to sign Matthews after the season officially ended. These comments were overheard by several witnesses and reported in San Francisco newspapers. Lurie and the Giants filed a complaint with the commissioner. After a second hearing, the commissioner ruled that Turner's statements "were in clear violation of the prohibitions of the directives. . . . These statements clearly had the effect of subverting the collective bargaining agreement and the re-entry draft procedures adopted pursuant to it."

    The commissioner declined to nullify Matthews's new contract with the Braves because Matthews had not engaged in any misconduct. The punishment levied was to suspend Turner from baseball for one year and to order a forfeiture of the Braves' first-round selection in the amateur draft, which was to follow the one in which Atlanta had already forfeited its first-round choice.

The Braves and Turner brought suit to overturn these rulings. See *Atlanta National Baseball Club v. Kuhn*, 432 F. Supp. 1213 (N.D. Ga. 1977). The questions before the court revolved around the explicit powers accorded the commissioner in these situations. The commissioner argued that he had broad powers to act in the best interest of baseball and impose appropriate discipline at his sole discretion, whereas the Braves asserted he was given explicit powers to deal with the current situation and could act only as specifically authorized. The court concluded that the commissioner had proper discretionary authority to suspend Turner for one year, but not to strip the Braves club of a draft choice because this sanction "is simply not among the penalties authorized for this offense."

Similarly, in *Riko Enterprises, Inc. v. Seattle Supersonics Corp.*, 357 F. Supp. 521 (S.D.N.Y. 1973), the court ruled that NBA commissioner Kennedy lacked valid authority to fine and require a league team to forfeit a draft choice for negotiating with a player who was on another club's draft list. It found that, pursuant to the NBA's constitution, only the league's board of governors has such authority.

2. Both *Finley* and *Atlanta National Baseball Club* upheld the MLB commissioner's exercise of his "best interests" of the game authority. Read together, what judicial precedent is established by these two cases? Do these decisions establish and further sound public policy? Should courts provide similar deference to a league commissioner's decisions that adversely affect third parties, such as local communities in which league franchises are located or fans in general?

3. Although a court will not second-guess a league commissioner's exercise of discretionary judgment, as *Atlanta National Baseball Club* illustrates, it will require that the commissioner have valid authority to take any challenged action.

In an unpublished opinion that was subsequently vacated, a federal district court held that the MLB commissioner could not order involuntary realignment of the teams in the National League pursuant to his "best interests" of the game authority. In *Chicago National League Ball Club, Inc. v. Vincent*, 1992 WL 179208 (N.D. Ill. 1992), the Chicago Cubs successfully challenged Commissioner Vincent's authority to transfer the club to the Western Division of the National League. In 1992, ten National League clubs voted to realign their two divisions so that the Cubs and St. Louis Cardinals would move to the Western Division, and the Atlanta Braves and Cincinnati Reds would move to the Eastern Division. The Cubs and New York Mets voted against the proposed realignment. The National League Constitution required approval by three-fourths of the league's clubs for divisional realignment but provided that no club could be transferred to a different division without its consent. Nevertheless, acting on the request of several National League clubs to intervene, Commissioner Vincent ordered the proposed realignment in accordance with his "best interests" power.

The court preliminarily enjoined the commissioner's order from taking effect based on its finding that he exceeded his authority and impaired the Cubs' contract rights under the National League Constitution. Although the Major League Agreement empowered the commissioner to resolve disputes among member clubs and conferred broad "best interests" power, this authority did not extend to disputes whose resolution is otherwise expressly provided for in the constitution of either Major League. Relying on the statutory construction principle that the specific governs the general, the court held that the commissioner could not use his general "best interests" authority to unilaterally abrogate the Cubs' express right under the National League Constitution not to be moved to another division without its consent.

4. When exercising disciplinary authority, courts require that a league commissioner provide due process to the party subject to sanctions. *Finley*, 569 F.2d at 544 and n.65 ("the procedure must not be a sham designed merely to give colorable propriety to an inadequate process"). A party is entitled to notice of the alleged misconduct and a fair opportunity to be heard. *American League Baseball Club of New York v. Johnson*, 179 N.Y. Supp. 498, 506 (N.Y. Sup. Ct. 1919), *aff'd*, 179 N.Y.S. 898 (1920). The league's constitution generally establishes procedural safeguards or enables the commissioner to formulate rules necessary to satisfy the minimum requirements of due process in connection with a disciplinary proceeding. *Rose v. Giamatti*, 721 F. Supp. 906, 916 (S.D. Ohio 1989) (observing that under Major League Agreement, "Commissioner is given virtually unlimited authority to formulate his own rules of procedure for conducting ['not in the best interests' of baseball] investigations, the only limitations being that whatever rules he adopts must recognize the right of any party in interest to appear before him and be heard").

One court found a league commissioner did not provide due process to the involved parties under the following circumstances:

> No notice of any hearing to be held at a specified time and place was given either orally or in writing; there is no indication that the Commissioner apprised the plaintiff of the nature of the charges; and he certainly did not apprise plaintiff of the basis for his authority to act. There could have been "no meaningful" hearing, for the parties had no opportunity to present witnesses, documents or other relevant information; nor could the informal discussions in the rooms and hallways of hotels be considered a fair and full hearing.

Professional Sports, Ltd. v. Va. Squires Basketball Club Ltd. Partnership, 373 F. Supp. 946, 951 (W.D. Tex. 1974).

A league commissioner must follow established procedural rules when exercising disciplinary authority and act in an impartial and fair manner without prejudging the disciplinary matter before him. In *Rose v. Giamatti*, No. A8905178, 1989 WL 111447 (Ct. Com. Pl. Ohio, Hamilton Co. June 26, 1989), a state trial judge temporarily enjoined MLB commissioner Bart Giamatti from holding a disciplinary hearing to determine whether Pete Rose placed bets on MLB games. The court relied on affidavit testimony alleging that Rose was being denied his right to a fair hearing before the commissioner. After reviewing a report prepared by his special investigator that he intended to rely on, the commissioner wrote a letter to a federal judge on behalf of Ron Peters, a convicted drug dealer who was awaiting sentencing. The letter stated that Peters had provided sworn testimony concerning allegations that Rose had bet on MLB, and that the commissioner was satisfied that Peters had told the truth to his special investigator. Commissioner Giamatti and Rose ultimately entered into a settlement agreement pursuant to which Rose accepted a lifetime suspension from baseball. See generally Matthew B. Pachman, Note, *Limits on the Discretionary Powers of Professional Sports Commissioners: A Historical and Legal Analysis of Issues Raised by the Pete Rose Controversy*, 76 Va. L. Rev. 1409 (1990).

OAKLAND RAIDERS v. NATIONAL FOOTBALL LEAGUE
131 Cal. App. 4th 621, 32 Cal. Rptr. 3d 266 (Cal. App. 2005)

PREMO, J.

The Oakland Raiders (Raiders), a member club of an unincorporated association known as the National Football League (NFL or League), sued the NFL and its commissioner, Paul Tagliabue. The Raiders alleged that the NFL and Tagliabue (collectively, defendants) took various actions that were discriminatory towards the Raiders and placed it at a competitive disadvantage vis-à-vis other member clubs. One legal theory that the Raiders advanced was breach of fiduciary duty. . . .

Broadly speaking, the complaint alleged that the Raiders was discriminated against and treated unfavorably as compared with the other member clubs. The alleged breaches of fiduciary duty included: "singling the Raiders out" from other clubs and "treating the Raiders disparately and adversely"; permitting other member clubs to violate NFL rules, thereby giving them a competitive advantage over the Raiders; requiring that the Raiders (over its objection) participate with other member clubs in the European football league known as the "World League of American Football"; concealing information from the Raiders and excluding its participation in a lawsuit involving the former owner of the New England Patriots, William H. Sullivan, Jr.; and denying Al Davis (former Raiders' managing general partner) and his family permission to buy the Oakland Athletics baseball team, notwithstanding that defendants permitted violations of the League's "Cross-ownership Rule" by other club owners. In addition, the Raiders alleged that Tagliabue committed further breaches of fiduciary duty: by removing Davis from the Management Council Executive Committee in September 1995; by removing Raiders' representatives from NFL committees, and by excluding the Raiders from participating in significant NFL committees, thereby placing the Raiders at a competitive disadvantage; and by concealing from the Raiders certain rules violations by other member clubs. . . .

[Granting defendants' motion for summary judgment, the trial court held] that (1) defendants owed no fiduciary duties to the Raiders, and (2) even were the breach of fiduciary duty claim legally viable, the court was required to abstain from deciding it. . . .

III.   WHETHER DEFENDANTS OWED FIDUCIARY DUTIES TO THE RAIDERS

We first examine whether there was a fiduciary relationship between defendants and the Raiders as a matter of law. . . .

As the Ninth Circuit Court of Appeals has previously recognized, "[t]he NFL is [a] unique business organization." (*Los Angeles Memorial Coliseum Com'n v. N.F.L.* (9th Cir.1984) 726 F.2d 1381, 1401.) It is perhaps for this reason that there is no authority cited by the parties—or known by this court to exist—that is definitive on the question of whether the NFL or its commissioner owes fiduciary duties to one of the NFL's member clubs (in this case, the Raiders). . . .

The Raiders relies extensively on *Jones v. H.F. Ahmanson & Co.*, 1 Cal.3d 93, 81 Cal.Rptr. 592, 460 P.2d 464 (Cal. 1969), in support of its assertion that defendants owed the Raiders fiduciary duties. For a number of reasons, *Jones* is inapposite. In *Jones*, the Supreme Court held definitively that majority shareholders owe fiduciary duties to the corporation and its minority shareholders "to use their ability to control the corporation in a fair, just, and equitable manner." Thus, under the circumstances presented in that case, the court concluded that "when, as here, no market [for the corporation's stock] exists, the controlling shareholders may not use their power to control the corporation for the purpose of promoting a marketing scheme that benefits themselves alone to the detriment of the minority."

Most notably, the discussion of fiduciary duties in *Jones* was premised on the existence of a *corporation, controlling shareholders, and minority shareholders.* No such organizational structure is presented in the instant appeal. To the contrary, it is without dispute that the NFL is *an unincorporated not-for-profit association* of 31 (now 32) member clubs. Indeed, we acknowledged this organizational status in a prior appeal by the Raiders. (See *Oakland Raiders, supra,* 93 Cal.App.4th 572, 578, 113 Cal.Rptr.2d 255.) As such, neither the NFL nor its member clubs fit the *Jones* model of fiduciary duties owed by majority shareholders to their corporation and to minority shareholders. . . .

The Raiders has cited no cases—and we are aware of none—in which it has been held as a blanket proposition that a voluntary unincorporated association and/or its leadership owes fiduciary duties to its members. A voluntary association, although it has some attributes of a legal entity, is not the equivalent of a corporation. . . .

Finally, we reject the Raiders' intimation that a fiduciary relationship exists between it and the defendants because of an alleged joint venture. A joint venture, of necessity, "requires an agreement under which the parties have (1) a joint interest in a common business, (2) an understanding that profits and losses will be shared, and (3) a right to joint control. [Citations.]" Here, there is no sharing of profits and losses by member clubs indicative of a joint venture. As one federal district court concluded, specifically with respect to the NFL: "Strictly speaking, the NFL teams are not engaged in a joint venture. 'A joint venture is a joint business undertaking of two or more parties who share the risks as well as the profits of the business.' [Citation.] Though the NFL teams share revenues, they do not share profits or losses." (*Los Angeles Memorial Coliseum v. N.F.L.* (S.D.Cal.1979) 468 F.Supp. 154, 162, fn. 9; see also *Los Angeles Memorial Coliseum Com'n v. N.F.L.,* *supra,* 726 F.2d 1381, 1390 [NFL clubs do not share "profits and losses . . . a feature common to partnerships"].) There is thus no merit to the Raiders' claim for breach of fiduciary duty arising out of a joint venture.

We conclude therefore that the relationship between the Raiders, on the one hand, and the NFL and Tagliabue, on the other hand, is not one under which a fiduciary relationship exists as a matter of law. . . .

IV. APPLICABILITY OF ABSTENTION DOCTRINE UNDER CALIFORNIA DENTAL

The Raiders contends that the trial court also erred by concluding that it was required to abstain from this intra-association dispute under *California Dental.* . . .

. . . From our careful review of *California Dental,* we conclude that the abstention doctrine described by the Supreme Court was one that applies broadly to intra-association disputes, irrespective of whether the particular dispute concerns a claimed breach of association bylaws.

This conclusion is consistent with other cases that have followed *California Dental.* (See *Berke v. TRI Realtors* (1989) 208 Cal.App.3d 463, 469, 257 Cal. Rptr. 738 [abstention doctrine means that "[c]ourts must guard against unduly interfering with an organization's autonomy by substituting judicial judgment" for the organization's]; *California Trial Lawyers Assn. v. Superior Court* (1986) 187 Cal. App.3d 575, 580, 231 Cal.Rptr. 725 (*California Trial Lawyers*).) In *California Trial Lawyers,* the court found that the *California Dental* "policy of judicial restraint control[led]" to preclude judicial intervention in interpreting the bylaws of a voluntary association of attorneys that impacted the election of the association's president. In so holding, the court explained that "[t]his reluctance to intervene in internecine controversies, the resolution of which requires that an association's constitution, bylaws, or rules be construed, is premised on the principle that the judiciary should generally accede to any interpretation by an independent voluntary organization of its own rules which is not unreasonable or arbitrary."

In this instance, the trial court properly held that it was barred by the abstention doctrine from resolving the dispute between the Raiders and defendants. Ignoring for the moment that the Raiders' breach of fiduciary duty claim is not viable as a matter of law, the underlying basis for the claim is not one for an asserted breach of the NFL constitution. The court correctly concluded—after a discussion in its order of each alleged act that the Raiders claimed constituted breaches of fiduciary duty—that the Raiders had not shown any evidence of a violation of a clear and unambiguous provision of the NFL constitution. . . .

In short, the court correctly construed and applied the abstention doctrine of *California Dental.* We observe that the rationale of abstention from intra-association disputes applies with particular force in this instance. Given the unique and specialized nature of this association's business—the operation of a professional football league—there is significant danger that judicial intervention in such disputes will have the undesired and unintended effect of interfering with the League's autonomy in matters where the NFL and its commissioner have much greater competence and understanding than the courts. . . .

[The court affirmed the granting of summary judgment for defendants.]

NOTES AND QUESTIONS

1. If the court had ruled that the NFL commissioner owed the Raiders a fiduciary duty, what would this mean? Would it facilitate or inhibit effective league governance? Does the court's ruling that the California state law abstention doctrine applies totally preclude a court from intervening in league internal governance disputes? As you read *Raiders I, infra,* note that federal antitrust law may provide an aggrieved league club with legal relief unavailable under state law.

   Another California appellate court previously characterized the legal duty clubs owe to each other in connection with league business affairs as fiduciary in nature. For example, in *Professional Hockey Corp. v. World Hockey Assn.,* 191 Cal. Rptr. 773, 777 (Cal. Ct. App. 1983), the court ruled that each club's representative "owes the league as a whole the traditional fiduciary duties in this commonly shared corporate purpose." It explained, "The law requires, irrespective of the competitive personal feelings of the various owners of teams may have towards each other, when they or their representatives sit on the board of directors of WHA to the extent they have common corporate goals, they have a duty to make decisions for the benefit of the corporation, the hockey league as a whole." Is this holding consistent with *Oakland Raiders*?

2. *Finley v. Kuhn* and *Oakland Raiders v. NFL* both involved a league club challenging commissioner authority, but in some instances (e.g., the *Rose v. Giamatti* matter discussed previously) league *players* challenge commissioner authority. NFL Commissioner Roger Goodell's handling of the New Orleans Saints "bounty scandal" in 2012 sparked such a challenge. Having concluded that Saints coaches and players created and effectuated a system of financial incentives for injuring opposing players, Goodell suspended the Saints' general manager, multiple Saints coaches, and several Saints players for various lengths of time. The NFLPA, on behalf of three of the suspended players — Scott Fujita, Will Smith, and Anthony Hargrove — sued Goodell, charging that he was "incurably and evidently biased" against them. Another of the suspended players, Jonathan Vilma, sued separately, and the cases were eventually consolidated into one. See Albert Breer, *Jonathan Vilma, NFLPA Suits vs. NFL to Be Consolidated*, NFL.com, July 6, 2012, http://www.nfl.com/news/story/09000d5d82a5de93/article/jonathan-vilma-nflpa-suits-vs-nfl-to-be-consolidated?module=HP11_headline_stack.

   Goodell, who has been called "a dictator" and "judge, jury, and executioner" by league players, has been a stern disciplinarian throughout his tenure as commissioner, and the central issue in the "bounty scandal" case was the appropriate scope of Goodell's disciplinary power and the manner in which he exercised it. Under the NFL collective bargaining agreement (CBA), Goodell has power both to issue suspensions and to serve as arbitrator in hearing the suspension appeals, which Goodell did in this case, denying the players' appeals. While the players did not challenge the text of the CBA, they argued that the CBA did not "grant[] the Commissioner, when serving as an arbitrator, the authority to disregard the essence of the parties' agreement, to conduct proceedings that are fundamentally unfair, and to act with evident bias." *NFLPA v. NFL*, Case 2:12-cv-01744, *2 (E.D. La, 2012).

   The dispute (further addressed in Chapter 7) raises many questions. Why would a players union assent in a CBA to such a disciplinary structure? Is it appropriate (even if permitted under a CBA) for a league commissioner to both make disciplinary decisions and serve as the arbitrator of appeals from those decisions? Might this structure ultimately call in to question the legitimacy of the commissioner's office?

3. What happens when a commissioner's exercise of "best interests" authority creates a conflict of interest? In 2010, the NBA purchased the floundering New Orleans Hornets, giving Commissioner David Stern supervisory authority over a particular team in a league over which he had general supervisory authority. A year later, Hornets general manager Dell Demps engineered a three-way trade with the Houston Rockets and Los Angeles Lakers, which involved sending the Hornets' All-Star point guard Chris Paul to the Lakers.

Before the trade was finalized, however, Stern vetoed it, raising questions as to whether he was doing so in the best interests of the Hornets, in the best interests of the NBA, or for other reasons. Stern publicly justified his decision as being in the "best interests" of the Hornets. Many in the NBA community, however, viewed the proposed trade (which reportedly would have given the Hornets several players and a 2012 first round draft pick) as advantageous to the Hornets and believed that, in actuality, Stern was pressured to quash the deal by a group of owners of other teams who were leery that it would too greatly benefit the Lakers. Demps was angered by Stern's decision and considered quitting, and Paul—before later being dealt to the Los Angeles Clippers—contemplated suit under an anti-collusion clause in the CBA that prevents the league from conspiring with teams regarding player transactions. See Sam Amick, *Lakers, Hornets, Rockets, Resubmit Paul Trade for League Approval,* Sports Illustrated, Dec. 10, 2011, http://sports illustrated.cnn.com/2011/writers/sam_amick/12/10/chris.paul/index .html; Mitch Lawrence, *Paul Eyes Court Assist,* N.Y. Daily News, Dec. 13, 2011, at 68.

Stern's refusal to permit the trade raises a host of questions. Is it possible to act both in the "best interests" of a particular team and in the "best interests" of a league in all instances? If not, in the event that a league owns a team in the league, should the league appoint an independent party to have ultimate supervisory authority over that team? Assume, as many believe, that other teams' owners influenced Stern's thinking on the matter and further assume that Stern publicly justified his decision as being in the best interests of the game rather than in the best interests of the Hornets. Can a commissioner's action taken at the urging of a subset of a league's owners be appropriately justified by "best interests" authority? If so, should there be any recourse for owners opposed to the action? Does your answer depend on whether the owners opposed to the action constitute a minority or a majority of the league's owners?

PROBLEM 6-1

Stars Candy Company has asked Stan Tallace of the Portland Flyers to advertise its candy by prominently displaying a tattoo of its company logo on his upper arm during the World Basketball League (WBL) play-offs. WBL rules do not prohibit players from having visible tattoos. Stars hopes that fans watching Flyers games in person and on national television will see its logo on Tallace's arm, and that this advertising will significantly increase its candy sales. Stars has offered to pay Tallace a substantial undisclosed amount of money (depending on how far the Flyers advance in the play-offs) for displaying the Stars tattoo, which is temporary and will wash off in a few months.

After learning about Stars's proposed advertising deal with Tallace, WBL commissioner Don Bern announced that no player would be permitted to display a tattoo of any company's logo on his body during a WBL game. He stated that any WBL player doing so would be suspended indefinitely and fined $250,000.00. Bern is concerned that Stars's proposal will disrupt the league's business relationship with Westle, which has paid the WBL a $7.5 million sponsorship fee to be advertised as the "WBL's Official Candy" during nationally televised WBL regular season and play-off games for the next three years.

The WBL Uniform Player Contract (UPC) does not prohibit players from having tattoos, but does prohibit players from "sponsoring commercial products without the consent of the WBL and his club, which shall not be withheld except to protect the reasonable interests of the WBL and player's club." The UPC also provides, "Player agrees that the Commissioner has the right to fine Player a reasonable amount and/or suspend Player for a period certain or indefinitely for conduct judged by Commissioner to be detrimental to the WBL or professional basketball."

Neither Stars nor Westle has a sponsorship agreement with the Flyers, but the club sells both Stars and Westle candy at concession stands in its playing facility in Portland. The Flyers' sale of Stars candy to their fans does not violate any WBL rules or regulations. The Flyers have no objections to Stars's proposed advertising deal with Tallace.

Tallace believes he has a First Amendment right to display expressive material, including the Stars logo, on his skin in the form of a tattoo. He points out that Bern took no action against Philadelphia 99ers' player Andy McPherson for producing a rap album with lyrics offensive to gays and women, although McPherson is earning a lot of money from sales of the album.

Does Bern have the authority to prohibit Tallace from displaying a Stars logo tattoo during WBL play-off games?

D.   ANTITRUST LAW LIMITS ON LEAGUE GOVERNANCE AND RULES

The federal antitrust laws are one of the primary bodies of public law used to regulate professional sports. Courts, however, were initially reluctant to apply antitrust law to the professional sports industry. It was more than 60 years after the passage of the Sherman Antitrust Act in 1890 before courts ruled that most professional sports are covered by the Sherman Act, although MLB has broad common law antitrust immunity. In the following materials we consider the objectives of antitrust law and the unique business aspects of professional sports, MLB's common law antitrust immunity and congressional limits along with other sports-specific antitrust exemptions, and the judicial application of antitrust law to professional sports league rules and governance decisions.

1.   Nature and Purposes of Antitrust Law

The federal antitrust laws prohibit agreements and collective action that unreasonably restrain trade under §1 of the Sherman Act (15 U.S.C. §1) and monopolization and attempted monopolization under §2 (15 U.S.C. §2). The purpose of the antitrust laws is to preserve a competitive marketplace and protect consumer welfare. Competition is hurt when conduct harms the market's ability to achieve lower prices, better products, and more efficient methods of production—all of which benefit consumers. *Sullivan v. NFL*, 34 F.3d 1091, 1097 (1st Cir. 1994), *cert. denied*, 513 U.S. 1190 (1995).

Professional sports leagues and organizations are commercial enterprises that compete against other available entertainment options for consumer economic support. Because of the unique nature of professional sports (particularly team sports), it is very difficult for courts to apply the antitrust laws in a principled and consistent fashion to challenged rules and collective decisions. Traditional antitrust law jurisprudence does not provide a simple means of accurately measuring whether a particular practice enhances or harms consumer welfare as represented by the interests of sports fans.

Like any other business enterprise, the member clubs of a professional sports league collectively seek to maximize sales of product and profits. However, unlike members of other industries that sell the same product and compete among themselves for consumer support (for example, McDonald's, Wendy's, and Burger King), a professional sports league's member clubs do not have an economic self-interest in driving each other out of business. To the contrary, league clubs have an inherent economic interdependence. As one court explained:

> Professional teams in a league, however, must not compete too well with each other, in a business way. On the playing field, of course, they must compete as hard as they can all the time. But it is not necessary and indeed it is unwise for all the teams to compete as hard as they can against each other in a business way. . . . [If this happened,] not only would the weaker teams fail, but eventually the whole league, both the weaker and the stronger teams, would fail, because without a league no team can operate profitably.

United States v. NFL, 116 F. Supp. 319, 323 (E.D. Pa. 1953).

To further league members' collective economic interests, it is essential that competitive balance exist within the league and that the outcome of games be relatively uncertain to maintain fan interest in the league's product. Courts have recognized:

> For maximum customer receptivity and profit it is in the best interest of any club that its opponents not generally be viewed by the public as totally incompetent and utterly unable to compete effectively. For if the latter occurs, thousands of customers will not spend their dollars for tickets to view hundreds of games when the contest seems to present no more of a challenge than an ant confronting an elephant.

Philadelphia World Hockey Club, Inc. v. Philadelphia Hockey Club, Inc., 351 F. Supp. 462, 504 (E.D. Pa. 1972).

League clubs do not share profits like the members of a typical business partnership, and they do not subsidize an individual franchise's economic losses. However, to maintain the financial integrity of all member clubs, protect economically weaker teams from stronger ones, and further all clubs' collective interests in producing competitive games, professional sports leagues have rules mandating the sharing of certain revenues as well as limiting the degree of economic competition among its teams. Substantial economic disparities may have the undesirable effect of adversely impacting competition among league clubs on the playing field. As one court observed:

> Teams with impressive records tend to show bigger revenues than teams in the cellar. On the very most basic level, going to the playoffs means more games, and therefore more gate receipts, and more fan following and therefore higher rights fees from local broadcasting (which belong 100% to the teams) — in other words, more money. . . .

In addition, and to complete the circle, more money means a better chance at making the playoffs again. The richest teams enjoy competitive advantages on the court over the poorest teams—in the ability to bid for free agents or to pay to keep their own players who opt for free agency, and so field a strong team; in the ability to charter flights for away games, and so field an alert team; in the ability to hire top notch staffs, and so field a well-coached team, and more.

Chicago Prof. Sports Ltd. Partnership v. NBA, 754 F. Supp. 1336, 1341-1342 (N.D. Ill. 1991).

As one noted sports antitrust law expert explains:

> Sports leagues present special challenges for those interested in a sound, consumer-oriented approach to antitrust enforcement. As the Supreme Court has recognized, sports leagues operate in an industry where some agreements among competitors—perhaps even all the competitors—is necessary for there to be a product at all. In addition to the need for joint action to produce a product, sports leagues have perhaps a unique interest in maintaining a significant degree of competitive balance among the teams within their venture. In conventional markets, both society and individual consumers prefer that firms strive independently (or in rival joint ventures) to produce the best possible product, and are willing to reward the most successful firm with the lion's share of the market; in network markets, consumers are primarily interested in patronizing the seller with the dominant market share. In contrast, courts seem to accept the economic premise that consumers as a whole are better off, and will show it through greater patronage of a sports league's product, when a championship race is characterized by real competition and each fan's team has a reasonable shot at contention.

Stephen F. Ross, *Antitrust Options to Redress Anticompetitive Restraints and Monopolistic Practices by Professional Sports Leagues*, 52 Case W. Res. L. Rev. 133, 134 (2001).

Thus, it is ironic that league limits on clubs' economic competition among themselves may be necessary to preserve and enhance on-field competition between league clubs that is attractive to the sport's fans. On the other hand, in the United States, currently there is only one major professional league for sports such as football, basketball, hockey, and soccer (with the American League and National League effectively operating as a single league under the auspices of Major League Baseball). As is more fully discussed later in this chapter, a sports league may have either monopoly power or a significant degree of market power that may enable it and/or its member clubs to engage in conduct with predominantly anticompetitive effects that harm existing or prospective clubs and their owners, local communities, other sports leagues and franchises, and ultimately, sports fans.

2.   MLB's Antitrust Law Immunity and Other Exemptions

In 1890, Congress enacted the Sherman Act pursuant to its authority to regulate interstate commerce. To be subject to scrutiny under the federal antitrust laws, the defendant's business activities or the allegedly anticompetitive conduct must have the requisite nexus to interstate commerce. *Summit Health, Ltd. v. Pinhas*, 500 U.S. 322 (1991).

In 1922, the Supreme Court decided its first antitrust case involving professional sports, deciding specifically the issue of whether organized professional baseball is subject to the Sherman Act. A former Federal League baseball club filed an antitrust suit alleging that the American League and National League conspired to monopolize professional baseball by acquiring all seven other Federal League clubs, leaving the plaintiff without a league in which to play. In *Federal Baseball Club of Baltimore, Inc. v. National League of Professional Baseball Clubs*, 259 U.S. 200 (1922), the Court ruled that professional baseball is a business (i.e., it constitutes "trade or commerce") but that it is not interstate in nature as required to be regulated by the Sherman Act:

> The business is giving exhibitions of baseball, which are purely state affairs. It is true that, in order to attain for these exhibitions the great popularity that they have achieved, competitions must be arranged between clubs from different cities and States. But the fact that in order to give the exhibitions the Leagues must induce free persons to cross state lines and must arrange and pay for their doing so is not enough to change the character of the business. According to the distinction insisted upon in *Hooper v. California*, 155 U.S. 648, 655 . . . the transport is a mere incident, not the essential thing. That to which it is incident, the exhibition, although made for money would not be called trade or commerce in the commonly accepted use of those words. As it is put by the defendants, personal effort, not related to production, is not a subject of commerce. That which in its consummation is not commerce does not become commerce among the States because the transportation . . . takes place. To repeat the illustrations given by the Court below, a firm of lawyers sending out a member to argue a case . . . does not engage in such commerce because the lawyer . . . goes to another State.

In a 1953 case, *Toolson v. New York Yankees*, 346 U.S. 356 (1953), the Supreme Court reaffirmed *Federal Baseball Club*. In a per curiam opinion, the Court reasoned that baseball had been allowed to develop for more than 30 years without being subject to the antitrust laws. The Court also observed that Congress did not eliminate baseball's antitrust exemption, thereby evidencing its intention that organized baseball not be covered by the antitrust laws. In dissent, Justices Burton and Reed vigorously argued that professional baseball is interstate in nature and that Congress has not expressly exempted baseball from the Sherman Act.

On the other hand, after *Toolson*, the Supreme Court held that other professional sports such as football (*Radovich v. National Football League*, 352 U.S. 445 (1957)); basketball (*Haywood v. NBA*, 401 U.S. 1204 (1971)); and boxing (*United States v. International Boxing Club of N.Y., Inc.*, 348 U.S. 236 (1955)) are subject to the antitrust laws because their respective business activities occur in interstate commerce. As to baseball, however, court decisions continued to follow *Toolson* and held that professional baseball retained its immunity from the federal antitrust laws. See, e.g., *Salerno v. American League of Prof'l Baseball Clubs*, 429 F.2d 1003 (2d Cir. 1970); *Portland Baseball Club, Inc. v. Baltimore Baseball Club, Inc.*, 282 F.2d 680 (9th Cir. 1960).

This background set the stage for the Supreme Court's 1972 reconsideration of whether professional baseball is subject to federal antitrust law.

FLOOD v. KUHN
407 U.S. 258 (1972)

Mr. Justice BLACKMUN delivered the opinion of the Court.

For the third time in 50 years the Court is asked specifically to rule that professional baseball's reserve system is within the reach of the federal antitrust laws. . . .

[EDS. Curt Flood rose to fame as a center fielder with the Cardinals during the years 1958-1969 and distinguished himself as a star player. But at the age of 31, in October 1969, Flood was traded to the Philadelphia Phillies of the National League in a multiplayer transaction. He was not consulted about the trade. He was informed by telephone and received formal notice only after the deal had been consummated. In December he complained to the commissioner of baseball and asked that he be made a free agent and be placed at liberty to strike his own bargain with any other major league team. His request was denied. Thereafter, he filed an antitrust challenge to baseball's reserve system, which effectively precluded him from contracting with the major league baseball club of his choice. Flood declined to play for Philadelphia in 1970, despite a $100,000 salary offer, and he sat out the year. After the season was concluded, Philadelphia sold its rights to Flood to the Washington Senators. Washington and the petitioner were able to come to terms for 1971 at a salary of $110,000. Flood started the season but apparently because he was dissatisfied with his performance, he left the Washington club on April 27, early in the campaign. At the time of his suit, he had not played baseball since then. Relying on *Federal Baseball Club* and *Toolson*, the Second Circuit affirmed the district court's dismissal of Flood's suit.]

. . . It seems appropriate now to say that:

1. Professional baseball is a business and it is engaged in interstate commerce.
2. With its reserve system enjoying exemption from the federal antitrust laws, baseball is, in a very distinct sense, an exception and an anomaly. *Federal Baseball* and *Toolson* have become an aberration confined to baseball.
3. Even though others might regard this as "unrealistic, inconsistent, or illogical," the aberration is an established one, and one that has been recognized not only in Federal Baseball and *Toolson*, but in *Shubert, International Boxing*, and *Radovich*, as well, a total of five consecutive cases in this Court. . . . It is an aberration that has been with us now for half a century, one heretofore deemed fully entitled to the benefit of stare decisis, and one that has survived the Court's expanding concept of interstate commerce. It rests on a recognition and an acceptance of baseball's unique characteristics and needs.
4. Other professional sports operating interstate—football, boxing, basketball, and, presumably, hockey and golf—are not so exempt.
5. The advent of radio and television, with their consequent increased coverage and additional revenues, has not occasioned an overruling of *Federal Baseball* and *Toolson*.
6. The Court has emphasized that since 1922 baseball, with full and continuing congressional awareness, has been allowed to develop and to expand unhindered by federal legislative action. Remedial legislation has been introduced repeatedly in Congress but none has ever been enacted. The Court, accordingly, has concluded that Congress as yet has had no intention to subject baseball's reserve system to the reach of the antitrust statutes. This, obviously, has been deemed to be something other than mere congressional silence and passivity.
7. The Court has expressed concern about the confusion and the retroactivity problems that inevitably would result with a judicial overturning of *Federal Baseball*. It has voiced a preference that if any change is to be made, it come by legislative action that, by its nature, is only prospective in operation.

8. The Court noted in *Radovich*, 352 U.S., at 452, 77 S.Ct., at 394, that the slate
    with respect to baseball is not clean. Indeed, it has not been clean for half a
    century.

This emphasis and this concern are still with us. We continue to be loath, 50
years after *Federal Baseball* and almost two decades after *Toolson*, to overturn
those cases judicially when Congress, by its positive inaction, has allowed those
decisions to stand for so long and, far beyond mere inference and implication,
has clearly evinced a desire not to disapprove them legislatively.

Accordingly, we adhere once again to *Federal Baseball* and *Toolson* and to their
application to professional baseball. We adhere also to *International Boxing* and
Radovich and to their respective applications to professional boxing and professional football. If there is any inconsistency or illogic in all this, it is an inconsistency and illogic of long standing that is to be remedied by the Congress and
not by this Court. If we were to act otherwise, we would be withdrawing from the
conclusion as to congressional intent made in *Toolson* and from the concerns as
to retrospectivity therein expressed. Under these circumstances, there is merit
in consistency even though some might claim that beneath that consistency is a
layer of inconsistency. . . .

The judgment of the Court of Appeals is affirmed. . . .

Mr. Justice MARSHALL, with whom Mr. Justice BRENNAN joins, dissenting.

. . . The importance of the antitrust laws to every citizen must not be minimized. They are as important to baseball players as they are to football players,
lawyers, doctors, or members of any other class of workers. Baseball players cannot be denied the benefits of competition merely because club owners view
other economic interests as being more important, unless Congress says so.

Has Congress acquiesced in our decisions in *Federal Baseball Club* and *Toolson*?
I think not. Had the Court been consistent and treated all sports in the same
way baseball was treated, Congress might have become concerned enough to
take action. But, the Court was inconsistent, and baseball was isolated and distinguished from all other sports. In *Toolson* the Court refused to act because
Congress had been silent. But the Court may have read too much into this legislative inaction.

Americans love baseball as they love all sports. Perhaps we become so enam-
ored of athletics that we assume that they are foremost in the minds of legislators as well as fans. We must not forget, however, that there are only some 600
major league baseball players. Whatever muscle they might have been able to
muster by combining forces with other athletes has been greatly impaired by
the manner in which this Court has isolated them. It is this Court that has made
them impotent, and this Court should correct its error.

We do not lightly overrule our prior constructions of federal statutes, but
when our errors deny substantial federal rights, like the right to compete freely
and effectively to the best of one's ability as guaranteed by the antitrust laws, we
must admit our error and correct it. We have done so before and we should do
so again here. (citations omitted.)

To the extent that there is concern over any reliance interests that club owners may assert, they can be satisfied by making our decision prospective only.
Baseball should be covered by the antitrust laws beginning with this case and
henceforth, unless Congress decides otherwise.

NOTES AND QUESTIONS

1. *The Supreme Court's Decision in* Flood. If all other professional sports leagues, organizations, and governing bodies are subject to the federal antitrust laws, why should baseball have a common law antitrust immunity? What are "baseball's unique characteristics and needs" that the Supreme Court relies on to justify its antitrust exemption? If you were a member of Congress, would you vote to take away baseball's antitrust exemption?

    In *Flood*, the Supreme Court majority waxed nostalgic:

> Then there are the many names, celebrated for one reason or another, that have sparked the diamond and its environs and that have provided tinder for recaptured thrills, for reminiscence and comparisons, and for conversation and anticipation in-season and off-season: Ty Cobb, Babe Ruth, Tris Speaker, Walter Johnson, Henry Chadwick, Eddie Collins, Lou Gehrig, Grover Cleveland Alexander, Rogers Hornsby, Harry Hooper, Goose Goslin, Jackie Robinson, Honus Wagner, Joe McCarthy, John McGraw, Deacon Phillippe, Rube Marquard, Christy Mathewson, Tommy Leach, Big Ed Delahanty, Davy Jones, Germany Schaefer, King Kelly, Big Dan Brouthers, Wahoo Sam Crawford, Wee Willie Keeler, Big Ed Walsh, Jimmy Austin, Fred Snodgrass, Satchel Paige, Hugh Jennings, Fred Merkle, Iron Man McGinnity, Three-Finger Brown, Harry and Stan Coveleski, Connie Mack, Al Bridwell, Red Ruffing, Amos Rusie, Cy Young, Smokey Joe Wood, Chief Meyers, Chief Bender, Bill Klem, Hans Lobert, Johnny Evers, Joe Tinker, Roy Campanella, Miller Huggins, Rube Bressler, Dazzy Vance, Edd Roush, Bill Wambsganss, Clark Griffith, Branch Rickey, Frank Chance, Cap Anson, Nap Lajoie, Sad Sam Jones, Bob O'Farrell, Lefty O'Doul, Bobby Veach, Willie Kamm, Heinie Groh, Lloyd and Paul Waner, Stuffy McInnis, Charles Comiskey, Roger Bresnahan, Bill Dickey, Zack Wheat, George Sisler, Charlie Gehringer, Eppa Rixey, Harry Heilmann, Fred Clarke, Dizzy Dean, Hank Greenberg, Pie Traynor, Rube Waddell, Bill Terry, Carl Hubbell, Old Hoss Radbourne, Moe Berg, Rabbit Maranville, Jimmie Foxx, Lefty Grove.

407 U.S. at 263. One scholar asserts that "[Justice] Blackmun's list is worthy of attention. The list lies at the heart of his curious and quite exceptional celebration of [baseball] in what was a critical sports law decision." Roger I. Abrams, *Blackmun's List*, 6 Va. Sports & Ent. L.J. 181, 189 (2007). He notes that "[a]lthough Blackmun took considerable time in his opinion to celebrate the national game, he could not have considered how the reserve system, which the Court's opinion upheld, affected the lives of the men he memorialized." *Id.* at 192.

   Flood has generated significant scholarly commentary, with most of it criticizing the Supreme Court's decision as an unprincipled judicial aberration. See, e.g., Edmund P. Edmonds, *Over Forty Years in the On-Deck Circle: Congress and the Baseball Antitrust Exemption*, 19 T. Marshall L. Rev. 627 (1994); Connie Mack and Richard M. Blau, *The Need for Fair Play: Repealing the Federal Baseball Antitrust Exemption*, 45 Fla. L. Rev. 201 (1993); Robert G. Berger, *After the Strikes: A Reexamination of Professional Baseball's Exemption From the Antitrust Laws*, 45 U. Pitt. L. Rev. 209 (1983). Nevertheless, some scholars argue that its congressional or judicial repeal more than 50 years later would potentially do more harm than good. Nathaniel Grow, *In Defense of Baseball's Antitrust Exemption*, 49 Am. Bus. L.J. 211, 215 (2012) ("Congress has obtained considerable leverage over baseball throughout the years by threatening to revoke the sport's antitrust exemption. Congress has used this power to help extract various procompetitive concessions from MLB, benefits that would not have been directly obtained via antitrust litigation alone"); Gary Roberts, *On the Scope and Effect of Baseball's Antitrust Exclusion*, 4 Seton Hall J. Sport L. 321, 323 (1994) ("while it is in theory unjustified to treat baseball differently from other sports and, while problems exist in baseball which concern both the public and Congress, trying to abolish the exclusion would be politically futile and unlikely to further the public interest").

2. *Lower Courts' Interpretation of* Flood. Most courts have broadly construed *Flood* to exempt all aspects of the "business of baseball," rather than merely player-management labor relations, from the federal antitrust laws. These courts have extended baseball's antitrust immunity to disputes concerning compensation of minor league franchises for harm to their assigned territories (*Portland Baseball Club, Inc. v. Kuhn*, 491 F. Supp. 1101 (9th Cir. 1974)); exercise of the Commissioner's "best interests of baseball authority" (*Charles O. Finley & Co., Inc. v. Kuhn*, 569 F.2d 527 (7th Cir. 1978)); the minor league player assignment system, franchise location system, and scheduling rules (*Professional Baseball Schools and Clubs, Inc. v. Kuhn*, 693 F.2d 1085 (11th Cir. 1982)); major league club owners' alleged unfair labor practices during a players' strike (*McCoy v. Major League Baseball*, 911 F. Supp. 454 (W.D. Wash. 1995)); and a state attorney general's investigation of a proposed sale and relocation of a baseball franchise (*Major League Baseball v. Crist*, 331 F.3d 1177 (11th Cir. 2003); *Minnesota Twins Partnership v. Hatch*, 592 N.W.2d 847 (Minn. 1999)).

Other courts have attempted to distinguish *Flood* and narrowly limit the scope of its antitrust immunity to the reserve clause and matters integral to baseball's structure. See, e.g., *Postema v. National League of Professional Baseball Clubs*, 799 F. Supp. 1475 (S.D.N.Y. 1992) (no antitrust immunity for a common law restraint of trade claim concerning baseball's employment relations with its umpires because *Flood* limits exemption to baseball's "unique characteristics and needs"). One federal district court, *Piazza v. Major League Baseball*, 831 F. Supp. 420 (E.D. Pa. 1993), and Florida state courts have ruled that baseball's antitrust exemption does not extend to decisions involving the sale and location of baseball franchises. *Butterworth v. National League of Professional Baseball Clubs*, 644 So. 2d 1021 (Fla. 1994); *Morsani v. Major League Baseball*, 663 So. 2d 653 (Fla. Dist. App. Ct. 1995). What are the policy reasons in favor of construing baseball's antitrust exemption broadly? Narrowly? What is the appropriate judicial view of this common law antitrust immunity?

3. *Curt Flood Act of 1998.* In 1998, Congress modified the Sherman Act to provide MLB players with the same antitrust remedies as other professional athletes such as football and basketball players. 15 U.S.C. §26b. This legislation is the product of a joint lobbying effort by the MLB players union and major league club owners pursuant to a provision in their 1994 CBA to do so. The act's standing provision gives MLB players the same right to sue under the antitrust laws concerning MLB employment terms as other professional athletes have in their sports. 15 U.S.C. §27b(c). This legislation is not intended to affect judicial construction and application of the nonstatutory labor exemption (which is discussed in great detail in Chapter

7) to baseball players' antitrust claims brought against professional baseball organizations. 15 U.S.C. §26b(d)(4). In other words, unionized MLB players will still not have any antitrust remedies for certain terms and conditions of their employment arising out of the collective bargaining process.

The act expressly permits antitrust challenges only to conduct or agreements by those persons "in the business of organized professional major league baseball directly relating to or affecting employment of major league baseball players to play baseball at the major league level." 15 U.S.C. §26b(a). The act does not provide a basis for challenging conduct or agreements relating to employment as a minor league baseball player, the amateur or first-year player draft, or any reserve clause applied to minor league players. 15 U.S.C. §26b(b)(1). Its legislative history evidences that the act cannot be used to attack any conduct or agreements affecting minor league baseball employment. The act is not intended to affect the applicability or inapplicability of the antitrust laws to any areas other than MLB labor relations issues. It has no prospective or retroactive effect on judicial construction of the scope of baseball's antitrust exemption on any other matters. Rejecting an argument that the act is a congressional endorsement of baseball's antitrust exemption, one court explained: "I take Congress at its word and resolve this case without reliance on the Curt Flood Act as affecting the outcome one way or the other. I conclude that the business of baseball *is* exempt; the exemption was well established long prior to adoption of the Curt Flood Act and certainly was not *repealed* by that Act." *Major League Baseball v. Butterworth*, 181 F. Supp. 2d 1316, 1331 n.16 (N.D. Fla. 2001), *aff'd on other grounds, Major League Baseball v. Crist*, 331 F.3d 1177 (11th Cir. 2003).

MLB franchise ownership, location, or expansion issues, as well as matters between the commissioner's office and clubs, are unaffected by the act for antitrust purposes. Marketing or sales, intellectual property licensing, and broadcasting issues affecting organized professional baseball are similarly unaffected by this legislation.

4. *Sports Broadcasting Act (SBA) of 1961*. This act, codified at 15 U.S.C. §1291, et seq., expressly permits professional sports league clubs to pool and sell or transfer "all or any part of the rights of such league's member clubs in the sponsored telecasting of the games." Legislative history indicates that the SBA is intended to "enable the member clubs . . . to pool their separate rights in the sponsored broadcasting of their games and to permit the league to sell the resulting package of pooled rights to a purchaser, such as a television network, without violating the antitrust laws." S. Rep. No. 1087, 87th Cong. at 1 (1961), reprinted in 1961 U.S.C.C.A.N. 3042, 3042.

As one court observed, "The purpose of the SBA, as opposed to the purpose of the Sherman Act itself, was not to promote competition. It was to establish the legality of a practice which tends to restrain competition, package sales to the networks." *Chicago Prof'l Sports Limited Partnership v. NBA* (*Bulls I*), 754 F. Supp. 1336, 1352 (N.D. Ill. 1991), *aff'd*, 961 F.2d 667 (7th Cir. 1992). Congress provided professional sports leagues with this limited antitrust exemption to protect their home game ticket sales, especially those of the weaker clubs, and to facilitate the sharing of television broadcast revenues among clubs, thereby preserving the league's competitive balance, product integrity, and existence.

The SBA does not define "sponsored telecasting." Its legislative history evidences Congress's intent to exclude league-pooled television rights packages with games shown on closed circuit and subscription television from antitrust immunity. Telecasting of Professional Sports Contests: Hearing Before the Antitrust Committee of the House Committee on the Judiciary on H.R. 8757, 87th Cong. 1st Sess. at 5 (1961).

For several years after the SBA was enacted in 1961, professional sports league games were telecast exclusively on national broadcast networks or local over-the-air network television. Today, with advances in technology, many league games are also shown on cable television or superstations (which are independent, over-the-air television stations that are broadcast in their local market areas and also carried by satellite to cable systems in other parts of the country).

This has given rise to litigation concerning the types of broadcasts encompassed within the meaning of "sponsored telecasting," which has been narrowly construed by courts. See *Shaw v. Dallas Cowboys Football Club, Inc.*, 172 F.3d 299, 300 (3d Cir. 1999) (package sale of television broadcast rights to satellite distributor not "sponsored telecasting" immune from antitrust scrutiny); *Chicago Prof'l Sports Ltd. Partnership v. NBA* (*Bulls III*), 808 F. Supp. 646, 650 (N.D. Ill. 1992) ("sponsored telecasting" encompasses only "free television," such as "national network and local over-the-air broadcasting provided at no direct cost to viewers," not league's pooled television rights contract with cable television programming service).

The SBA does not confer an antitrust exemption for any joint agreement that prohibits a purchaser of a league's pooled television rights from telecasting the games in a particular area "except within the home territory of a member club of the league on a day when such club is playing a game at home." 15 U.S.C. §1292. Thus, prohibiting telecasts of other league games into a club's home territory when it has a home game does not violate the antitrust laws, whereas any other collective limits on the territorial scope of broadcasts of league games may be an antitrust violation.

In recognition of the unique nature of a professional sports league and the economic interdependence of its members, a league's pooled rights telecasting contracts are exempt from antitrust scrutiny to enable all clubs to receive an equal share of these collectively generated revenues. Local telecasting blackouts of other league games are permitted to protect professional clubs' home attendance. In both instances, the economic viability of all league members is enhanced, thereby at least theoretically facilitating league-wide competitive balance and production of a desirable entertainment product.

Courts, however, will not construe the SBA in a manner that enables a professional sports league's telecasting agreements to harm consumers' interests. The SBA's limitation of antitrust immunity to "sponsored telecasting" has been narrowly interpreted to ensure the continuing availability of free national and local over-the-air telecasting of league games.

5. *State Antitrust Law.* In *Flood*, the Supreme Court held that the Supremacy and dormant Commerce Clauses of the United States Constitution bar state antitrust regulation of organized baseball in light of its exemption from federal antitrust law. The Court observed that national uniformity is necessary in connection with baseball's reserve system, and that state antitrust regulation would conflict with national antitrust policy.

Regarding sports other than baseball that are subject to federal antitrust regulation, courts generally hold that applying state antitrust laws to a professional sports league's interstate activities, such as labor disputes and franchise location issues, violates the Commerce Clause. In *Partee v. San Diego Chargers Football Co.*, 668 P.2d 674, 678 (Cal. 1983), the California Supreme Court explained:

> Professional football is a nationwide business. . . . The necessity of a nationwide league structure for the benefit of both teams and players for effective competition is evident as is the need for a nationally uniform set of rules governing the league structure. Fragmentation of the league structure on the basis of state lines would adversely affect the success of the competitive business enterprise, and differing state antitrust decisions if applied to the enterprise would likely compel all member teams to comply with the laws of the strictest state.

In light of these concerns, is any state regulation of professional sports appropriate? Consider that many businesses are national, even global, in their operations. Should they also be exempt from state regulation, or are professional sports leagues different from other industries? Does the rationale of the court overly protect professional sports leagues from state regulation?

3.   Application of Sherman Act §1

a.   Concerted Action Requirement

The express language of Sherman Act §1 broadly prohibits "[e]very contract, combination in the form of trust or otherwise, or conspiracy" that restrains trade, which literally encompasses virtually all professional sports league rules (which are the product of the agreement among league clubs) and collective governance decisions by league clubs. Nevertheless, as a defense to Sherman Act §1 claims, professional sports leagues (particularly the NFL) have argued that the league and its member clubs collectively produce a single product (e.g., NFL football) that no individual club is capable of producing. Therefore, a professional sports league's rules and member clubs' collective decisions should not be subject to §1 because they are not economic competitors who produce separate products.

In 1974, the single-entity defense was first judicially addressed in *San Francisco Seals, Ltd. v. National Hockey*, 379 F. Supp. 966 (C.D. Cal. 1974), in which a federal district held that the member clubs of the NHL are not legally capable of conspiring to restrain trade in the alleged relevant market. The owner of the San Francisco Seals club asserted that league members' refusal to permit the team to relocate to Vancouver, British Columbia, violated §1 of the Sherman Act. The court found the relevant market to be "the production of professional hockey games before live audiences . . . [in] the United States and Canada." *Id.* at 969. Finding that "the plaintiff and defendants are acting together as one single business enterprise, competing against other similarly organized professional leagues," the court concluded, "they are not competitors in the economic sense in this relevant market." *Id.* at 969-970. Because the parties cooperated in producing hockey games, the court held that the league's refusal to permit the plaintiff's relocation was not a conspiracy to restrain trade as a matter of law.

Most federal appellate courts, however, historically rejected this "single economic entity" defense. For example, in *Los Angeles Memorial Coliseum Comm'n v. NFL (Raiders I)*, 726 F.2d 1381 (9th Cir.), *cert. denied*, 469 U.S. 990 (1984), the Ninth Circuit rejected the NFL's claim that the league is in essence a single economic entity, like a partnership that shares profits and losses, precluding application of §1, which prohibits only agreements among business entities with economically separate interests that restrain trade:

> Our inquiry discloses an association of teams sufficiently independent and competitive with one another to warrant rule of reason scrutiny under § 1 of the Sherman Act. The NFL clubs are, in the words of the district court, "separate business entities whose products have an independent value." The member clubs are all independently owned. Most are corporations, some are partnerships, and apparently a few are sole proprietorships. Although a large portion of League revenue, approximately 90%, is divided equally among the teams, profits and losses are not shared, a feature common to partnerships or other "single entities." In fact, profits vary widely despite the sharing of revenue. The disparity in profits can be attributed to independent management policies regarding coaches, players, management personnel, ticket prices, concessions, luxury box seats, as well as franchise location, all of which contribute to fan support and other income sources.
>
> In addition to being independent business entities, the NFL clubs do compete with one another off the field as well as on to acquire players, coaches, and management personnel. In certain areas of the country where two teams operate in close proximity, there is also competition for fan support, local television and local radio revenues, and media space.

Id. at 1389-1390. See also *North American Soccer League v. National Football League*, 670 F.2d 1249, 1252 (2d Cir. 1981), *cert. denied*, 459 U.S. 1074 (1982) (NFL teams are "separate economic entities engaged in a joint venture" whose joint conduct is subject to scrutiny under §1).

Subsequent to *Raiders I*, in *Copperweld Corp. v. Independence Tube Corp.*, 467 U.S. 752 (1984), the Supreme Court held that legally separate business entities with a "complete unity of interest," such as a parent corporation and its wholly owned subsidiary, are not subject to §1 of the Sherman Act. It reasoned that this business arrangement is "like a multiple team of horses drawing a vehicle under the control of a single driver"; therefore, there is no sudden joining of previously diverse economic forces raising the prospect of collusive anticompetitive conduct. The court observed that internal coordination within a single business enterprise is often necessary for effective competition and that a business entity's internal organizational structure is irrelevant to the resulting anticompetitive consequences. The Court explained that the Sherman Act contains a "basic distinction between concerted and independent action," with the result that anticompetitive independent conduct by a single entity does not violate §1. Although there is no complete unity of interest between professional sports league teams like there is between a corporate parent and wholly owned subsidiary or among the members of a partnership, some of *Copperweld*'s reasoning suggests a professional sports league and its member clubs should be treated as a single economic entity for antitrust purposes.

Thereafter, in *Brown v. Pro Football, Inc.*, 518 US 231, 248 (1996), the Supreme Court observed "that the clubs that make up a professional sports league are not completely independent economic competitors, as they depend upon a degree of cooperation for economic survival." However, the Court did not specifically consider whether league clubs are separate economic entities whose collective action is subject to §1, or whether a sports league and its members are an economically integrated single business enterprise whose conduct is not covered by §1.

Most lower courts refused to construe *Copperweld* and *Brown* as requiring the conclusion that a professional sports league and its member clubs are a single entity as a matter of law. See *Sullivan v. National Football League*, 34 F.3d 1091 (1st Cir. 1994); *Shaw v. Dallas Cowboys Football Club, Ltd.*, 1998 WL 419765 (E.D. Pa. 1998), *aff'd on other grounds*, 172 F.3d 299 (3d Cir. 1999). Some courts have reasoned that league clubs do not satisfy *Copperweld*'s "complete unity of interest" standard because they often act in furtherance of their own individual economic interests rather than the league's collective economic interests. *Sullivan v. NFL*, 34 F.2d 1091, 1099 (1st Cir. 1994), *cert. denied*, 513 U.S. 1190 (1995).

By contrast, in *Chicago Professional Sports Limited Partnership v. National Basketball Association*, 95 F.3d 593 (7th Cir. 1996), the Seventh Circuit suggested the single entity defense should not be rejected based simply on how professional sports leagues are structured and governed. The court proposed that a functional approach, which analyzes whether league clubs are economic competitors in the alleged relevant market that is restrained (as *San Francisco Seals* did), be used to determine the appropriateness of applying §1 on a case-by-case basis. In other words, whether the particular challenged conduct has the requisite degree of economic integration to be considered that of a single economic entity requires facet-by-facet analysis of each league's operations.

Judge Easterbrook observed that the NBA is closer to a single firm than a group of independent firms when acting in the broadcast market:

> Whether the NBA itself is more like a single firm, which would be analyzed only under § 2 of the Sherman Act [which prohibits monopolization or attempted monopolization], or like a joint venture, which would be subject to the Rule of Reason under § 1, is a tough question under Copperweld. It has characteristics of both. Unlike the colleges and universities that belong to the National Collegiate Athletic Association . . . the NBA has no existence independent of sports. It makes professional basketball; only it can make "NBA Basketball" games . . . From the perspective of fans and advertisers (who use sports telecasts to reach fans), "NBA Basketball" is one product from a single source even though the Chicago Bulls and Seattle Supersonics [two of the NBA's clubs] are highly distinguishable.

Id. at 599.

Relying on *Chicago Professional Sports*, in *American Needle, Inc. v. New Orleans La. Saints*, 496 F. Supp. 2d 941 (N.D. Ill. 2007), the NFL argued that its member clubs function as a single economic entity in jointly producing NFL football and collectively licensing their intellectual property (e.g., trademarked merchandise), which does not constitute the requisite concerted action under §1. The district court agreed and held that "with regard to the facet of their operations respecting exploitation of intellectual property rights, the NFL and its 32 teams are, in the jargon of antitrust law, acting as a single entity." *Id.* at 943. The Seventh Circuit affirmed, concluding that "the record amply establishes that since 1963, the NFL teams have acted as one source of economic power—under the auspices of NFL Properties—to license their intellectual property collectively and to promote NFL football." *American Needle, Inc., v. National Football League*, 538 F.3d 736, 744 (7th Cir. 2008).

Because the Seventh Circuit's ruling conflicted with the precedent from other circuits, American Needle petitioned the Supreme Court for a writ of certiorari. Although it had prevailed in the lower courts, the NFL also petitioned the Supreme Court for review, hoping it would accept the "single entity" defense and effectively provide professional sports leagues with immunity from Sherman Act §1.

AMERICAN NEEDLE, INC. v. NATIONAL FOOTBALL LEAGUE
130 S. Ct. 2201 (2010)

STEVENS, Justice.

. . . Originally organized in 1920, the NFL is an unincorporated association that now includes 32 separately owned professional football teams. Each team has its own name, colors, and logo, and owns related intellectual property. Like each of the other teams in the league, the New Orleans Saints and the Indianapolis Colts, for example, have their own distinctive names, colors, and marks that are well known to millions of sports fans.

Prior to 1963, the teams made their own arrangements for licensing their intellectual property and marketing trademarked items such as caps and jerseys. In 1963, the teams formed National Football League Properties (NFLP) to develop, license, and market their intellectual property. Most, but not all, of the substantial revenues generated by NFLP have either been given to charity or shared equally among the teams. However, the teams are able to and have at times sought to withdraw from this arrangement.

Between 1963 and 2000, NFLP granted nonexclusive licenses to a number of vendors, permitting them to manufacture and sell apparel bearing team insignias. Petitioner, American Needle, Inc., was one of those licensees. In December 2000, the teams voted to authorize NFLP to grant exclusive licenses, and NFLP granted Reebok International Ltd. an exclusive 10-year license to manufacture and sell trademarked headwear for all 32 teams. It thereafter declined to renew American Needle's nonexclusive license.

American Needle filed this action in the Northern District of Illinois, alleging that the agreements between the NFL, its teams, NFLP, and Reebok violated §§ 1 and 2 of the Sherman Act. In their answer to the complaint, the defendants averred that the teams, NFL, and NFLP were incapable of conspiring within the meaning of § 1 "because they are a single economic enterprise, at least with respect to the conduct challenged." . . .

As the case comes to us, we have only a narrow issue to decide: whether the NFL respondents are capable of engaging in a "contract, combination . . . , or conspiracy" as defined by § 1 of the Sherman Act, 15 U.S.C. § 1, or, as we have sometimes phrased it, whether the alleged activity by the NFL respondents "must be viewed as that of a single enterprise for purposes of § 1." *Copperweld Corp. v. Independence Tube Corp.*, 467 U.S. 752, 771, 104 S.Ct. 2731, 81 L.Ed.2d 628 (1984). . . .

The meaning of the term "contract, combination . . . or conspiracy" is informed by the "'basic distinction'" in the Sherman Act "'between concerted and independent action'" that distinguishes § 1 of the Sherman Act from § 2. *Copperweld*, 467 U.S., at 767. Section 1 applies only to concerted action that restrains trade. Section 2, by contrast, covers both concerted and independent action, but only if that action "monopolize[s]," 15 U.S.C. § 2, or "threatens actual monopolization," *Copperweld*, 467 U.S. at 767, a category that is narrower than restraint of trade. Monopoly power may be equally harmful whether it is the product of joint action or individual action.

Congress used this distinction between concerted and independent action to deter anticompetitive conduct and compensate its victims, without chilling vigorous competition through ordinary business operations. The distinction also avoids judicial scrutiny of routine, internal business decisions. . . .

As *Copperweld* exemplifies, "substance, not form, should determine whether a[n] . . . entity is capable of conspiring under § 1." 467 U.S., at 773, n. 21. This inquiry is sometimes described as asking whether the alleged conspirators are a single entity. That is perhaps a misdescription, however, because the question is not whether the defendant is a legally single entity or has a single name; nor is the question whether the parties involved "seem" like one firm or multiple firms in any metaphysical sense. The key is whether the alleged "contract, combination . . . , or conspiracy" is concerted action-that is, whether it joins together separate decisionmakers. The relevant inquiry, therefore, is whether there is a "contract, combination . . . or conspiracy" amongst "separate economic actors pursuing separate economic interests," *id.*, at 769, such that the agreement "deprives the marketplace of independent centers of decisionmaking," *ibid.*, and therefore of "diversity of entrepreneurial interests," *Fraser v. Major League Soccer, L.L. C.,* 284 F.3d 47, 57 (C.A.1 2002) (Boudin, C. J.), and thus of actual or potential competition. . . .

The NFL teams do not possess either the unitary decisionmaking quality or the single aggregation of economic power characteristic of independent action. Each of the teams is a substantial, independently owned, and independently managed business. . . . The teams compete with one another, not only on the playing field, but to attract fans, for gate receipts and for contracts with managerial and playing personnel.

Directly relevant to this case, the teams compete in the market for intellectual property. To a firm making hats, the Saints and the Colts are two potentially competing suppliers of valuable trademarks. When each NFL team licenses its intellectual property, it is not pursuing the "common interests of the whole" league but is instead pursuing interests of each "corporation itself," *Copperweld*, 467 U.S., at 770, teams are acting as "separate economic actors pursuing separate economic interests," and each team therefore is a potential "independent cente[r] of decisionmaking," *id.*, at 769. Decisions by NFL teams to license their separately owned trademarks collectively and to only one vendor are decisions that "depriv[e] the marketplace of independent centers of decisionmaking," *ibid.*, and therefore of actual or potential competition. See *NCAA,* 468 U.S., at 109, n. 39.

In defense, respondents argue that by forming NFLP, they have formed a single entity, akin to a merger, and market their NFL brands through a single outlet. But it is not dispositive that the teams have organized and own a legally separate entity that centralizes the management of their intellectual property. An ongoing § 1 violation cannot evade § 1 scrutiny simply by giving the ongoing violation a name and label. . . .

The NFL respondents may be similar in some sense to a single enterprise that owns several pieces of intellectual property and licenses them jointly, but they are not similar in the relevant functional sense. Although NFL teams have common interests such as promoting the NFL brand, they are still separate, profit-maximizing entities, and their interests in licensing team trademarks are not necessarily aligned. Common interests in the NFL brand "*partially* unit[e] the economic interests of the parent firms," Broadley, Joint Ventures and Antitrust Policy, 95 Harv. L. Rev. 1521, 1526 (1982) (emphasis added), but the teams still have distinct, potentially competing interests.

It may be, as respondents argue, that NFLP "has served as the 'single driver'" of the teams' "promotional vehicle," "'pursu[ing] the common interests of the whole.'" But illegal restraints often are in the common interests of the parties to the restraint, at the expense of those who are not parties. It is true, as respondents describe, that they have for some time marketed their trademarks jointly. But a history of concerted activity does not immunize conduct from § 1 scrutiny. . . .

Respondents argue that nonetheless, as the Court of Appeals held, they constitute a single entity because without their cooperation, there would be no NFL football. It is true that "the clubs that make up a professional sports league are not completely independent economic competitors, as they depend upon a degree of cooperation for economic survival." *Brown,* 518 U.S., at 248. But the Court of Appeals' reasoning is unpersuasive.

The justification for cooperation is not relevant to whether that cooperation is concerted or independent action. A "contract, combination . . . or conspiracy," § 1, that is necessary or useful to a joint venture is still a "contract, combination . . . or conspiracy" if it "deprives the marketplace of independent centers of decisionmaking," *Copperweld,* 467 U.S., at 769. See *NCAA,* 468 U.S., at 113 ("[J]oint ventures have no immunity from antitrust laws"). Any joint venture involves multiple sources of economic power cooperating to produce a product. And for many such ventures, the participation of others is necessary. But that does not mean that necessity of cooperation transforms concerted action into independent action; a nut and a bolt can only operate together, but an agreement between nut and bolt manufacturers is still subject to § 1 analysis. Nor does it mean that once a group of firms agree to produce a joint product, cooperation amongst those firms must be treated as independent conduct. The mere fact that the teams operate jointly in some sense does not mean that they are immune.

The question whether NFLP decisions can constitute concerted activity covered by § 1 is closer than whether decisions made directly by the 32 teams are covered by § 1. This is so both because NFLP is a separate corporation with its own management and because the record indicates that most of the revenues generated by NFLP are shared by the teams on an equal basis. Nevertheless we think it clear that for the same reasons the 32 teams' conduct is covered by § 1, NFLP's actions also are subject to § 1, at least with regards to its marketing of property owned by the separate teams. NFLP's licensing decisions are made by the 32 potential competitors, and each of them actually owns its share of the jointly managed assets. Apart from their agreement to cooperate in exploiting those assets, including their decisions as the NFLP, there would be nothing to prevent each of the teams from making its own market decisions relating to purchases of apparel and headwear, to the sale of such items, and to the granting of licenses to use its trademarks.

We generally treat agreements within a single firm as independent action on the presumption that the components of the firm will act to maximize the firm's profits. But in rare cases, that presumption does not hold. Agreements made within a firm can constitute concerted action covered by § 1 when the parties to the agreement act on interests separate from those of the firm itself, and the intrafirm agreements may simply be a formalistic shell for ongoing concerted action.

For that reason, decisions by the NFLP regarding the teams' separately owned intellectual property constitute concerted action. Thirty-two teams operating independently through the vehicle of the NFLP are not like the components of a single firm that act to maximize the firm's profits. The teams remain separately controlled, potential competitors with economic interests that are distinct from NFLP's financial well-being. Unlike typical decisions by corporate shareholders, NFLP licensing decisions effectively require the assent of more than a mere majority of shareholders. And each team's decision reflects not only an interest in NFLP's profits but also an interest in the team's individual profits. The 32 teams capture individual economic benefits separate and apart from NFLP profits as a result of the decisions they make for the NFLP. NFLP's decisions thus affect each team's profits from licensing its own intellectual property. "Although the business interests of" the teams "will *often* coincide with those of the" NFLP "as an entity in itself, that commonality of interest exists in every cartel." *Los Angeles Memorial Coliseum Comm'n v. NFL,* 726 F.2d 1381, 1389 (C.A.9 1984) (emphasis added). In making the relevant licensing decisions, NFLP is therefore "an instrumentality" of the teams. . . .

Football teams that need to cooperate are not trapped by antitrust law. "[T]he special characteristics of this industry may provide a justification" for many kinds of agreements. *Brown,* 518 U.S., at 252, 116 S.Ct. 2116 (Stevens, J., dissenting). The fact that NFL teams share an interest in making the entire league successful and profitable, and that they must cooperate in the production and scheduling of games, provides a perfectly sensible justification for making a host of collective decisions. But the conduct at issue in this case is still concerted activity under the Sherman Act that is subject to § 1 analysis.

When "restraints on competition are essential if the product is to be available at all," *per se* rules of illegality are inapplicable, and instead the restraint must be judged according to the flexible Rule of Reason. *NCAA,* 468 U.S., at 101; see *id.,* at 117, ("Our decision not to apply a *per se* rule to this case rests in large part on our recognition that a certain degree of cooperation is necessary if the type of competition that petitioner and its member institutions seek to market is to be preserved"); see also *Dagher,* 547 U.S., at 6. In such instances, the agreement is likely to survive the Rule of Reason. See *Broadcast Music, Inc. v. Columbia Broadcasting System, Inc.,* 441 U.S. 1, 23, 99 S.Ct. 1551, 60 L.Ed.2d 1 (1979) ("Joint ventures and other cooperative arrangements are also not usually unlawful . . . where the agreement . . . is necessary to market the product at all"). And depending upon the concerted activity in question, the Rule of Reason may not require a detailed analysis; it "can sometimes be applied in the twinkling of an eye." *NCAA,* 468 U.S., at 109, n. 39.

Other features of the NFL may also save agreements amongst the teams. We have recognized, for example, "that the interest in maintaining a competitive balance" among "athletic teams is legitimate and important," *NCAA,* 468 U.S., at 117. While that same interest applies to the teams in the NFL, it does not justify treating them as a single entity for § 1 purposes when it comes to the marketing of the teams' individually owned intellectual property. It is, however, unquestionably an interest that may well justify a variety of collective decisions made by the teams. What role it properly plays in applying the Rule of Reason to the allegations in this case is a matter to be considered on remand.

Accordingly, the judgment of the Court of Appeals is reversed, and the case is remanded for further proceedings consistent with this opinion.

NOTES AND QUESTIONS

1. Do you agree with the Supreme Court's rejection of the single entity defense and its reasoning? Should all league rules and agreements among league clubs (e.g., rules of the game, scheduling of games, the number of teams qualifying for the play-offs, selection of a commissioner) be subject to judicial scrutiny under §1? Does *American Needle* inhibit the ability of a league and its member clubs to adopt rules and to make joint decisions that enhance the league's ability to compete in the U.S. entertainment market?

2. *Post*–American Needle *Cases and Scholarly Debate.* Construing *American Needle* soon after it was decided by the Supreme Court, in *Deutscher Tennis Bund v. ATP Tour, Inc.*, 610 F.3d 820, 835-837 (3d Cir. 2010), the Third Circuit suggested an agreement among the Association of Tennis Professionals' member tournaments regarding the stratification of ATP tennis tournaments is not immune from §1 scrutiny. The court stated:

> At trial, ATP contended it constitutes a single enterprise, and under *Copperweld*, its internal decisions cannot violate § 1 of the Sherman Act. It asserted each of its tournament members is dependent on the others to produce a common product-a marketable annual professional tennis tour that competes with other forms of entertainment, within and without the sports arena. ATP maintained its members do not compete but instead cooperate to produce the Tour, and its adoption of the Brave New World plan was the core activity of producing this product. For their part, the Federations contended ATP operates in the market for top tier men's professional tennis players, and individual tournaments compete to attract top players. They asserted the Brave New World plan was an agreement unreasonably restraining trade in this alleged market. . . .
>
> [T]he agreement among the ATP's tournament members in the Brave New World Plan might have deprived the marketplace of potential competition. Professional sports teams or tournaments always have an interest in obtaining the best players possible. *Brown v. Pro Football, Inc.*, 518 U.S. 231, 116 S.Ct. 2116, 135 L.Ed.2d 521 (1996). The record in this case indicates that the individual tennis tournaments traditionally compete for player talent. An agreement restricting this competition should not necessarily be immune from § 1 scrutiny merely because the tournaments cooperate in various aspects of producing the ATP Tour. "The justification for cooperation is not relevant to whether that cooperation is concerted or independent action." *Am. Needle*, 130 S.Ct. 2201, 2214 (2010). The necessity of cooperation does not "transform[ ] concerted action into independent action. The mere fact that the teams operate jointly in some sense does not mean that they are immune." *Id.*

In contrast, in *Minnesota Made Hockey, Inc. v. Minnesota Hockey, Inc.*, 789 F. Supp. 2d 1133 (D. Minn. 2011), a federal district court ruled that a state-wide amateur hockey governing body and its local associations and their respective directors constitute a single economic entity under *Copperweld*, whose joint conduct is not subject to §1 of the Sherman Act. Although the court did not cite *American Needle* in its opinion (presumably because the operative facts were dissimilar), its ruling is consistent with this Supreme Court precedent.

In *Washington v. National Football League*, Civil No. 11-3354 (PAM/AJB) (D. Minn., June 13, 2012) (unpublished opinion), a Minnesota federal district court rejected a group of former NFL players' allegations that the NFL's refusal to pay them royalties for the use of their images in game films for promotional purposes violated §1. Distinguishing *American Needle*'s facts, the court explained, "Here, unlike in *American Needle*, the intellectual property involved is historical football game footage, something that the individual teams do not separately own, and never have separately owned. Rather, the NFL owns the game footage, either alone or in conjunction with the teams involved in the game being filmed." It rejected the plaintiffs' assertion that *American Needle* "determined that the NFL and its teams can 'act in concert for the purpose of marketing their collective intellectual property.'" The court concluded that the "NFL and its teams can conspire to market each teams' individually owned property, but not property the teams and NFL can only collectively own."

Scholarly commentary regarding the post–*American Needle* application of the single entity defense to the joint conduct of U.S professional sports league clubs outside the context of intellectual property licensing and other restrictions is divided. One commentator has stated that "because differences do exist between the various leagues' structures, *American Needle* should not be read to automatically foreclose the possibility that another league could assert a colorable case for single entity status." Nathaniel Grow, *American Needle and the Future of the Single Entity Defense Under Section One of the Sherman Act*, 48 Am. Bus. L.J. 449, 497 (2011). Another one has observed, "*American Needle* is unclear . . . whether a court should treat a league pooling all of the teams' revenues and costs as single economic entity or as a cartel. By stressing the potential for competition, American Needle suggests treatment as a cartel, but by focusing on incentives to maximize league profits, the decision suggests single-entity treatment." Gregory J. Werden, American Needle *and the Application of the Sherman Act to Professional Sports Leagues*, 18 Vill. Sports & Ent. L.J. 395, 404-406 (2011). Another has suggested *American Needle* leaves open the possibility that any "core activity" of a professional sports league (e.g., the rules of the game; equipment, club ownership, club relocation, and broadcast restrictions; player restraints) may be effectively immune from §1 scrutiny. James A. Keyte, American Needle: *A New Quick Look for Joint Ventures*, 25 Antitrust 48, 51-52 (2010). Others, however, assert that *American Needle* "put[s] an end to the argument that a sports league [as currently structured] is a single entity immune from antitrust scrutiny" and "reinforces the need to view skeptically any argument purporting to define a zone of conduct as automatically lawful without regard to its competitive effects." Meir Feder, *Is There Life After Death for Sports League Immunity?* American Needle *and Beyond*, 18 Vill. Sports & Ent. L.J. 407, 428 (2011).

3. Consider how a professional sports league might be restructured to have the requisite complete unity of economic interest under *American Needle* and *Copperweld* to justify characterizing it as a single economic entity. It could be governed by a separate economic entity that wholly owns and controls all of its member clubs. *Fraser v. Major League Soccer, LLC*, 284 F.3d 47, 56 (1st Cir. 2002), *cert. denied*, 537 U.S. 885 (2002) ("If ordinary investors decided to set up a company that would own and manage all of the teams in a league, it is hard to see why this arrangement would fall outside *Copperweld*'s safe harbor"). See also Gregory J. Werden, American Needle *and the Application*

of the Sherman Act to Professional Sports Leagues, 18 Vill. Sports & Ent. L.J. 395, 403 (2011) ("A professional sports league entirely owned and operated by a single person undoubtedly would be treated as a single economic entity, even though the teams compete on the field of play, and even though the teams have separate identities and fan loyalties"). Alternatively, the league could be an independent company with separate ownership and control from its clubs similar to the National Association for Stock Car Auto Racing's business model. See generally Stefan Szymanski and Stephen F. Ross, Fans of the World, Unite! A (Capitalist) Manifesto for Sports Consumers 70-107 (2008).

b.   Unreasonable Restraint of Trade

The production of professional sports athletic competition requires many aspects of cooperation, and professional leagues and their member clubs are economically interdependent. One team cannot survive without other league teams as on-field competitors. To offer an attractive product desirable to consumers (e.g., close and exciting games), a professional sports league must maintain on-field competitive balance among its member teams and preserve the long-term financial viability of each club. In an effort to achieve these objectives, league rules may either prohibit certain conduct by an individual club owner or require its approval by a majority of other member clubs to avoid harming the league's collective economic interests. League rules or its member clubs' collective decisions may limit an individual club owner's ability to sell or relocate the club, contract with third parties in an effort to maximize the team's revenues, or take other desired action. Thus, league rules and internal agreements precluding or limiting economic competition among league clubs are not irrefutably presumed to be anticompetitive and per se illegal.

It is well settled law that the rule of reason, which involves a complicated case-by-case analysis is the applicable standard for evaluating the competitive effects of collective action by professional sports league members or organizations under §1 of the Sherman Act. *American Needle, Inc. v. NFL,* — U.S. —, 130 S. Ct. 2201 (2010); *National Collegiate Athletic Assn. v. Board of Regents of the Univ. of Oklahoma,* 468 U.S. 85 (1984). Virtually all professional sports industry restraints that allegedly violate §1 require detailed consideration of both their anticompetitive effects and procompetitive benefits to determine their net competitive consequences and effect on consumer welfare. If the restraint has predominately anticompetitive effects, it is unreasonable and illegal. Conversely, if it has predominately procompetitive effects, it is reasonable and legal.

Regarding application of the rule of reason to restraints in the sports industry, in *Law v. NCAA,* 134 F.3d 1010, 1019 (10th Cir. 1998), the Tenth Circuit explained:

> [T]he plaintiff bears the initial burden of showing that an agreement had a substantially adverse effect on competition. . . . If the plaintiff meets this burden, the burden shifts to the defendant to come forward with evidence of the procompetitive virtues of the alleged wrongful conduct. . . . If the defendant is able to demonstrate procompetitive effects, the plaintiff then must prove that the challenged conduct is not reasonably necessary to achieve the legitimate objectives or that those objectives can be achieved in a substantially less restrictive manner. . . .

Ultimately, if these steps are met, the harms and benefits must be weighed against each other in order to judge whether the challenged behavior is, on balance, reasonable.

The following materials analyze claims by a prospective club owner denied entry into a league, or by an existing club owner whose individual revenue-generating capacity has allegedly been harmed by league rules as well as anti-trust claims asserted by third parties. Legal redress is accordingly sought against a league and its member clubs, generally under §1 of the Sherman Act, which prohibits concerted action that causes anticompetitive economic effects. The range of circumstances giving rise to antitrust claims are considerable and include acquisition, ownership, and sale of franchises; franchise relocations; and league restrictions on an individual club's sale or licensing of intellectual property rights to third parties.[1]

i. Acquisition, Ownership, and Sale of a Franchise

LEVIN v. NBA
385 F. Supp. 149 (S.D.N.Y. 1974)

OWEN, District Judge.

The plaintiffs, two businessmen, in 1972 had an agreement to buy the Boston Celtics basketball team, one of the 17-member National Basketball Association.

The N.B.A., as its constitution recites, is a joint venture "organized to operate a league consisting of professional basketball teams each of which shall be operated by a member of the Association." It has been in existence since 1946. Each of its joint venturers holds a franchise to operate a team. While the teams compete vigorously on the basketball court, the joint venturers are dependent upon one another as partners in the league format to make it possible. N.B.A. operates through its Board of Governors which consists of one governor designated by each member. Action by the Board on a transfer of membership requires the affirmative vote of three-quarters of the members of the Board. [EDS. When the plaintiffs applied to become owners of the Celtics franchise, only two votes were cast favorable to their application, thirteen were opposed, and one club owner was not present.]

Plaintiffs immediately demanded and were granted a personal hearing before the Board. Following the presentation of their case a second vote was taken. It was, however, to identical effect.

There is a sharp dispute on the reason for the rejection. Plaintiffs contend that they were rejected because of their friendship and business associations with one Sam Schulman, owner of the Seattle SuperSonics, who was an anathema to the other members of the league. . . .

---

1. Although the following materials focus on antitrust issues relating to the internal governance of team sports, the internal regulation of individual-performer sports also raises antitrust concerns. For example, restrictions on the use of playing equipment (*Gunter Harz Sports v. United States Tennis Assn.*, 511 F. Supp. 1103 (D. Neb. 1981)) and race car tires (*Race Tires America, Inc. v. Hoosier Racing Tire Corp.*, 614 F.3d 57 (3d Cir. 2010)), player eligibility (*Toscano v. PGA Tour, Inc.*, 201 F. Supp. 2d 1106 (E.D. Cal. 2002)), and player discipline (*Blalock v. LPGA*, 359 F. Supp. 1260 (N.D. Ga. 1973)) have been challenged on antitrust grounds.

On the other hand, the reason given by the N.B.A. for the rejection was that the business association between the plaintiffs and Schulman violated the "conflict of interest" provision of the N.B.A. constitution. That provision reads: A member shall not exercise control, directly or indirectly, over any other member of the Association. . . . This provision is necessary, N.B.A. claims, in order that the league may enjoy public support because there is in fact, and the public believes there is, intense competition in the league framework between the teams operated by the N.B.A. members.

In any event plaintiffs, rejected, sold their rights in the Celtics elsewhere and commenced this action.

In order to survive defendants' motion for summary judgment, plaintiffs must demonstrate that the conduct complained of is a violation of the antitrust laws. While it is true that the antitrust laws apply to a professional athletic league, and that joint action by members of a league can have antitrust implications, this is not such a case. Here the plaintiffs wanted to join with those unwilling to accept them, not to compete with them, but to be partners in the operation of a sports league for plaintiffs' profit. Further, no matter which reason one credits for the rejection, it was not an anti-competitive reason. Finally, regardless of the financial impact of this rejection upon the plaintiffs, if any, the exclusion of the plaintiffs from membership in the league did not have an anticompetitive effect nor an effect upon the public interest. The Celtics continue as an operating club, and indeed are this year's champion. . . .

Since there was no exclusion of plaintiffs from competition with the alleged excluders, nor anti-competitive acts by them and no public injury occasioned thereby, the defendants' acts did not constitute a violation of the antitrust laws and defendants' motion for summary judgment is granted.

MID-SOUTH GRIZZLIES v. NFL

720 F.2d 772 (3d Cir. 1983)

GIBBONS, Circuit Judge.

. . . The suit concerns the defendants' refusal to grant the plaintiffs a football franchise. . . .

I. BACKGROUND

In 1974 and 1975 the Grizzlies participated in the World Football League from a home team location in Memphis, Tennessee. The members of that league could be found to have been competitors of the members of the NFL in the national market for network television revenue. The World Football League disbanded, however, halfway through the 1975 football season. The NFL had no franchise at Memphis, and a home team designation for that location would not infringe upon the home territory of any NFL member. Upon the demise of the World Football League the Grizzlies applied to the NFL for admission to the league with a designated home territory at Memphis.

At meetings with the NFL Expansion Committee, and with the full NFL membership, the Grizzlies urged that it had in place at Memphis an established, functioning professional football enterprise. The application was rejected. . . .

II. The complaint

The Grizzlies' complaint . . . does not charge that the provisions of the NFL's Constitution and By-Laws reserving to its members franchise exclusivity for designated home territories violates the antitrust laws. Indeed, the Grizzlies sought such an exclusive franchise for themselves. Thus this case does not present any issue of possible antitrust violation from the exclusion of potential competitors in the designated exclusive home territories. . . .

. . . The complaint alleges that Memphis is a highly desirable submarket for major league professional football, that the refusal to consider it as a home territory for a franchise was made pursuant to an agreement or understanding or conspiracy among NFL members, the NFL and the Commissioner, that no valid basis for rejection of the Grizzlies was articulated or formulated by the defendants, and that the rejection amounted to an unreasonable restraint of trade, or a group boycott. One motive for that conspiracy is alleged to have been a desire to punish, intimidate and restrain plaintiffs from participation in major league professional football because they had entered into competition with NFL members by participating in the World Football League. The exclusion, so motivated, and having the effects alleged, is said to be a violation of Section 1 of the Sherman Act. . . .

IV. The Merits

A. SHERMAN ACT SECTION 1

Public Law 89-800 establishes as a matter of law that the merger which produced the NFL from two formerly competing leagues did not violate the antitrust laws. Public Law 87-331 establishes as a matter of law that the members may lawfully pool revenues from the sale of television rights. The parties agree that in other respects a rule of reason analysis is appropriate. . . .

. . . In this case there is no dispute about the requisite concert of action among the defendants. The defendants do deny injury to competition in any relevant market from their rejection of the Grizzlies' application. They urge that any limitations on actual or potential competition in any relevant market were insulated from antitrust scrutiny by the 1961 and 1966 statutes referred to, or, are reasonable as a matter of law. They also urge that as a matter of law there was no competition among league members or between league members and non-members in other markets to which the Grizzlies point.

The Grizzlies identify as the relevant product market major-league professional football, and as the relevant geographic market the United States. The trial court found these markets to be relevant. The court observed as well that "[t]here is no doubt that the NFL currently has a monopoly in the United States in major league football." The Grizzlies pose as the question on this appeal "whether it can be said as a matter of law that defendants neither acquired nor maintained monopoly power over any relevant market in an unlawful manner."

As to the acquisition of dominant position and monopoly power, the facts are undisputed. Long before the Grizzlies and the World Football League came into existence, Congress authorized the merger of the two major football leagues extant in 1966, and granted to the merged league the power to pool television revenues. That congressional decision conferred on the NFL the market power which it holds in the market for professional football. Congress could not have been unaware that necessary effect of the television revenue sharing scheme which it approved for the NFL would be that all members of that league would be strengthened in their ability to bid for the best available playing and coaching personnel, to the potential disadvantage of new entrants. . . .

But, the Grizzlies urge, the 1966 statute did not confer the authority to abuse the market power, even though it may have authorized its acquisition. Rather, the merger was approved only "if such agreement increases rather than decreases the number of professional clubs so operating." 15 U.S.C. § 1291. Paraphrasing their argument, it is the Grizzlies' contention that the statute which authorized NFL acquisition of monopoly power in the professional football market required not only that the league members refrain from abusing that power against potential competitors, but that it take affirmative steps to share its market power with others.

. . . The only basis on which the Grizzlies seek recovery . . . is that they were denied admission to the monopoly, and thus were deprived of a share of the NFL's monopoly power. No claim is made that abuse of NFL market power led to the demise of the World Football League, and no issue is before us concerning activities of the NFL, since that demise, which may have inhibited the development of competition by another football league. The NFL structure as a barrier to entry to the market by another football league is relevant in this case only to the extent that it bears on the obligation to permit entry to the NFL.

There are two possible sources of any NFL obligation to permit entry to its shared market power; the 1966 statute, and the Sherman Act. Each will be considered separately.

The provision in the 1966 statute that "such agreement increases rather than decreases the number of professional football clubs so operating" cannot reasonably be construed as addressing competition, the preservation of which is the object of the Sherman Act. The basic thrust of the 1966 statute is to authorize an arrangement which eliminated competition among the only two viable competitors then in the professional football market. The reference to an increase in the number of professional football teams "so operating" is a reference to professional teams operating under the antitrust exemption for television revenue sharing provided in the 1961 statute. Thus what the 1966 statute suggests is that more home team territories would be added, not to increase competition in professional football, but to permit geographic enlargement of the NFL's market power. . . .

Since the 1966 statute is not directed at preservation of competition in the market for professional football, and cannot be construed as conferring any economic benefit on the class to which the Grizzlies belong, we conclude that it does not oblige the NFL to permit entry by any particular applicant to the NFL shared market power.

We turn, therefore, to the Sherman Act. As noted above, Sherman Act liability requires an injury to competition. In this case the competition inquiry is a narrow one, because the Grizzlies are not seeking recovery as potential competitors *outside* the NFL. They identify as the antitrust violation the league's negative vote on their application for membership. . . .

The NFL's stated reasons for rejecting the Grizzlies' application included scheduling difficulties created by the presence of an odd number of teams, a long-running collective bargaining dispute with league players, several pending antitrust lawsuits, and league concern over legislation prohibiting television blackouts in home team territories, all of which allegedly made consideration of expansion unpropitious. The Grizzlies contend that there are material issues of disputed fact as to the accuracy of these reasons. They contend that at trial they could prove that the motivation for their rejection was to punish them for having attempted in the past to compete with the NFL in the World Football League, or to reserve the Memphis location for friends of present league team owners.

Assuming, without deciding, that the summary judgment record presents disputed fact issues with respect to the actual motivation of the NFL members, those disputed facts are not material, under Section 1 of the Sherman Act, if the action complained of produced no injury to competition.

As to competition with NFL members in the professional football market, including the market for sale of television rights, the exclusion was patently pro-competitive, since it left the Memphis area, with a large stadium and a significant metropolitan area population, available as a site for another league's franchise, and it left the Grizzlies' organization as a potential competitor in such a league. If there was any injury to competition, actual or potential, therefore, it must have been to intra-league competition. . . .

. . . The Grizzlies do not challenge the legality of the NFL's revenue sharing arrangements, and seek to participate in them. The Grizzlies emphasize that there nevertheless remains a not insignificant amount of intra-league non-athletic competition. We need not, in order to affirm the summary judgment, accept entirely the NFL's position that there is no intra-league competition. Conceivably within certain geographic submarkets two league members compete with one another for ticket buyers, for local broadcast revenue, and for sale of the concession items like food and beverages and team paraphernalia. Thus rejection of a franchise application in the New York metropolitan area, for example, might require a different antitrust analysis than is suggested by this record. But the Grizzlies were obliged, when faced with the NFL denial of the existence of competition among NFL members and a potential franchisee at Memphis, to show some more than minimal level of potential competition, in the product markets in which league members might compete. They made no such showing. The record establishes that the NFL franchise nearest to Memphis is at St. Louis, Mo., over 280 miles away. There is no record evidence that professional football teams located in Memphis and in St. Louis would compete for the same ticket purchasers, for the same local broadcast outlets, in the sale of team paraphernalia, or in any other manner.

. . . Relying on the essential facilities doctrine . . . [the Grizzlies] urge that because the NFL is a practical monopoly it had an obligation to admit members on fair, reasonable, and equal terms, absent some procompetitive justification for their exclusion. This Grizzlies argument suffers from the same defect as the others. The essential facilities doctrine is predicated on the assumption that admission of the excluded applicant would result in additional competition, in an economic rather than athletic sense. The Grizzlies have simply failed to show how competition in any arguably relevant market would be improved if they were given a share of the NFL's monopoly power.

Since on the record before us the Grizzlies have shown no actual or potential injury to competition resulting from the rejection of their application for an NFL franchise, they cannot succeed on their section 1 Sherman Act claim. . . .

NOTES AND QUESTIONS

1. *Anticompetitive Effects?* The rejection of a prospective purchaser of an existing franchise does not reduce the number of league clubs, which remains the same as before denial of the proposed transfer of franchise ownership. As the *Levin* court observed, all this does is preclude a particular party from owning a league franchise. See also *Fishman v. Estate of Wirtz*, 807 F.2d 520, 542-544 (7th Cir. 1986) (league's mere selection of one prospective franchise owner over another is not anticompetitive). Do you agree that league members' disapproval of a proposed franchise sale (regardless of the reasons therefore) is not anticompetitive as a matter of law?

    Other courts have held that a league's denial of a prospective owner's bid to acquire an existing franchise may have an anticompetitive effect on the market for the purchase and sale of clubs. In *Piazza v. Major League Baseball*, 831 F. Supp. 420 (E.D. Pa. 1993), the court refused to dismiss the plaintiffs' antitrust claims alleging that a conspiracy among MLB club owners interfered with their efforts to acquire the San Francisco Giants franchise and relocate the team to Florida. The plaintiffs' complaint alleged injury to competition in the market for ownership of major league professional baseball teams, particularly the market for ownership of the Giants team. They averred that they were competing with other potential bidders to acquire ownership of the Giants franchise and that defendants directly and substantially interfered with competition in this market. The court ruled that the plaintiffs sufficiently alleged an injury to competition in a relevant product market.

    Piazza distinguished *Levin* on the ground that it did not involve an alleged reduction of competition among bidders for an existing franchise. MLB club owners rejected the *Piazza* plaintiffs' $115 million bid for the Giants, which was higher than the eventual sales price of $100 million to another group of investors. Is this anticompetitive? Even if so, it is difficult for a disappointed bidder to prevail on the merits of an antitrust claim. If the rejection of a prospective owner is based on adequate evidence of a lack of the minimally necessary financial capital, character and fitness, or business skills to successfully operate a league franchise, it is a justifiable means of enhancing interbrand competition. See *National Basketball Assn. v. Minnesota Professional Basketball Limited Partnership*, 56 F.3d 866 (8th Cir. 1995) (affirming preliminary injunction against sale of NBA club without league approval and denial of prospective owner based on inadequate financial resources).

2. *Sullivan v. NFL.* One court has suggested that a league rule banning a club owner's sale of a minority interest in a franchise to the public may violate the antitrust laws. In *Sullivan v. National Football League*, 34 F.3d 1091 (1st Cir. 1994), the First Circuit held that an NFL policy prohibiting the sale of an ownership interest in a league club through a public stock offering raises a fact question regarding whether it is anticompetitive. The former owner of the New England Patriots franchise claimed he was precluded from selling 49 percent of his team to the public and thereby forced to sell the club at a depressed price to private buyers. He asserted that, absent the NFL's policy, he would have been able to retain a majority interest in the Patriots and earn future profits from continued ownership of the club.

    The court observed that the league's public ownership policy "compromises the entire process by which competition for club ownership occurs," rather than merely preventing transfers of club ownership, which do not adversely affect competition. *Id.* at 1099. The jury found the relevant market to be the "nationwide market for the sale and purchase of ownership interests in the National Football League member clubs, in general, and in the New England Patriots, in particular." *Id.* at 1097. The court rejected the NFL's contention that, as a matter of law, its clubs do not compete against each other for the sale of their ownership interests and ruled that whether NFL teams are economic competitors in this market is a fact question. The court found sufficient evidence to support the jury's determination that the NFL's policy against public ownership of franchises is anticompetitive because it interferes with consumer demand for ownership interests in NFL teams and prevents ownership by a class of persons that may be more efficient operators of teams than private owners.

On the other hand, the First Circuit recognized that the NFL's public ownership policy has a legitimate procompetitive objective. It contributes to the league's ability to effectively function by preventing a potential detrimental conflict of interest between team shareholders' short-term dividend interests and the league's long-term interest in maintaining each club's financial integrity and competitiveness. The court observed, however, that modifying the NFL's policy to permit a club's sale of minority, nonvoting shares of team stock to the public with limits on the size of an individual's holdings might accomplish this objective in a substantially less restrictive manner. It ultimately reversed the jury's verdict in the plaintiff's favor because erroneous jury instructions had been given and remanded the case for a new trial. The retrial of the case resulted in a hung jury, and the parties settled before it was tried for the third time. Is antitrust law the best means of resolving disputes regarding the purchase and sale of professional sports franchises? And is consumer welfare furthered by doing so?

3. *Interbrand Versus Intrabrand Economic Competition.* Why were the Memphis Grizzlies' antitrust claims dismissed as a matter of law? Although the NFL was found to have a monopoly over major league professional football in the United States, the Memphis Grizzlies did not allege the NFL's conduct caused the demise of the WFL or inhibited the development of a rival professional football league. Thus, the denial of the Grizzlies' application for an NFL franchise did not reduce competition in the *interbrand* market (i.e., among competing professional football leagues or other forms of consumer entertainment). See also *Seattle Totems Hockey Club, Inc. v. National Hockey League,* 783 F.2d 1347 (9th Cir. 1986) (finding no §2 violation).

Do you agree with the court's conclusion that this conduct was "patently procompetitive"? In other words, did the NFL's decision benefit consumers? See Thomas A. Piraino, Jr., *The Antitrust Rationale for the Expansion of Professional Sports Leagues,* 57 Ohio St. L.J. 1677, 1677-1678 (1996) (arguing that "owners refusal to expand their leagues to meet demand for additional franchises . . . has the effect of reducing the importance of consumer preference in setting price and output [and] is not consistent with this fundamental goal of antitrust law").

Why did the court reject the Grizzlies' claim that its exclusion reduced *intrabrand* economic competition among NFL clubs? Given the fact that the NFL's Tennessee Titans currently play in Nashville, would the NFL's refusal to place a team in Memphis today be an antitrust violation? See Stephen

F. Ross, *Antitrust Options to Redress Anticompetitive Restraints and Monopolistic Practices by Professional Sports Leagues*, 52 Case W. Res. L. Rev. 133, 150-151 (2001) (noting "considerable conceptual and remedial problems with any finding that a sports league's refusal to expand to permit a *particular* franchise to enter its joint venture constitutes an unreasonable restraint of trade").

The Supreme Court has observed that a reduction in intrabrand competition among sellers of the same branded product may have the procompetitive effect of preserving or enhancing interbrand competition among sellers of similar competing products. *Continental T.V., Inc. v. GTE Sylvania, Inc.*, 433 U.S. 36 (1977). Does limiting intrabrand economic competition among NFL clubs in the same geographical market further the league's collective ability to compete economically with other forms of entertainment in the interbrand market?

4. *Implications for Contraction.* After the conclusion of the 2001 season and expiration of the collective bargaining agreement with the MLB Players Association, MLB announced its intention to contract two teams prior to the 2002 season. However, after entering into a new collective bargaining agreement, MLB ultimately agreed not to contract any teams at least through the 2006 season. Under what circumstances, if any, would a professional sports league's unilateral decision to contract one of its clubs potentially violate the antitrust laws?

ii.   Franchise Relocation

In recent years, local communities, including mid-major cities such as Nashville, Memphis, Charlotte, and Oklahoma City, have provided multimillion-dollar public subsidies for playing facilities to attract major league professional sports franchises. Many other communities have made similar investments of public funds to keep their local sports franchises and prevent them from relocating elsewhere. Courts generally rule that these arrangements are a legitimate use of state and local tax dollars to promote the public good, although these significant public expenditures combined with favorable lease terms provide substantial economic benefits to privately owned professional sports clubs.

Depending on the specific circumstances, a sports league's refusal to permit one of its clubs to relocate to another city may violate the antitrust laws. Former Oakland Raiders' owner Al Davis' antitrust litigation against the NFL provides an example of a successful case arising out of the league's initial rejection of his 1980 request to move the Raiders from Oakland to Los Angeles.

LOS ANGELES MEMORIAL COLISEUM COMMISSION v. NFL (RAIDERS I)

726 F.2d 1381 (9th Cir.), *cert. denied*, 469 U.S. 990 (1984)

ANDERSON, Circuit Judge:

These appeals involve the hotly contested move by the Oakland Raiders, Ltd. professional football team from Oakland, California, to Los Angeles, California. . . .

I. Facts

In 1978, the owner of the Los Angeles Rams, the late Carroll Rosenbloom, decided to locate his team in a new stadium, the "Big A," in Anaheim, California. That left the Los Angeles Coliseum without a major tenant. Officials of the Coliseum then began the search for a new National Football League occupant. They inquired of the League Commissioner, Pete Rozelle, whether an expansion franchise might be located there but were told that at the time it was not possible. They also negotiated with existing teams in the hope that one might leave its home and move to Los Angeles. . . .

[Eds. The L.A. Coliseum ran into a major obstacle in its attempts to convince a team to move because it was located in the home territory of the Rams franchise. The obstacle was Rule 4.3 of Article IV of the NFL Constitution, which as amended, stated, "The League shall have exclusive control of the exhibition of football games by member clubs within the home territory of each member. No member club shall have the right to transfer its franchise or playing site to a different city, either within or outside its home territory, without prior approval by the affirmative vote of three-fourths of the existing member clubs of the League."

After the Oakland Raiders' lease with the Oakland Coliseum expired in 1978, Al Davis, the club's managing general partner, and L.A. Coliseum officials signed a March 1, 1980, "memorandum of agreement" outlining the terms of the Raiders' proposed relocation to Los Angeles. At an NFL meeting on March 3, 1980, Davis announced his intentions. Over Davis's objection that Rule 4.3 was illegal under the antitrust laws, the NFL teams voted 22-0 against the move on March 10, 1980, with five teams abstaining. That vote did not meet Rule 4.3's requirement of three-quarters approval.

An antitrust action against the NFL and its member clubs brought by the Raiders in Los Angeles federal court resulted in a verdict in favor of the Raiders, and the jury awarded the Raiders $11.55 million in damages, which was automatically trebled as a prevailing party in an antitrust suit.] . . .

B. RULE OF REASON

. . . In a quite general sense, the case presents the competing considerations of whether a group of businessmen can enforce an agreement with one of their co-contractors to the detriment of that co-contractor's right to do business where he pleases. More specifically, this lawsuit requires us to engage in the difficult task of analyzing the negative and positive effects of a business practice in an industry which does not readily fit into the antitrust context. Section 1 of the Sherman Act was designed to prevent agreements among competitors which eliminate or reduce competition and thereby harm consumers. Yet, as we discussed in the context of the single entity issue, the NFL teams are not true competitors, nor can they be.

The NFL's structure has both horizontal and vertical attributes. On the one hand, it can be viewed simply as an organization of 28 competitors, an example of a simple horizontal arrangement. On the other, and to the extent the NFL can be considered an entity separate from the team owners, a vertical relationship is disclosed. In this sense the owners are distributors of the NFL product, each with its own territorial division. In this context it is clear that the owners have a legitimate interest in protecting the integrity of the League itself. Collective action in areas such as League divisions, scheduling and rules must be allowed, as should other activity that aids in producing the most marketable product attainable. Nevertheless, legitimate collective action should not be construed to allow the owners to extract excess profits. In such a situation the owners would be acting as a classic cartel. Agreements among competitors, i.e., cartels, to fix prices or divide market territories are presumed illegal under § 1 because they give competitors the ability to charge unreasonable and arbitrary prices instead of setting prices by virtue of free market forces.

On its face, Rule 4.3 divides markets among the 28 teams, a practice presumed illegal, but, as we have noted, the unique structure of the NFL precludes application of the per se rule. Instead, we must examine Rule 4.3 to determine whether it reasonably serves the legitimate collective concerns of the owners or instead permits them to reap excess profits at the expense of the consuming public.

1. Relevant Market

The NFL contends it is entitled to judgment because plaintiffs failed to prove an adverse impact on competition in a relevant market. . . .

In the antitrust context, the relevant market has two components: the product market and the geographic market. Product market definition involves the process of describing those groups of producers which, because of the similarity of their products, have the ability—actual or potential—to take significant amounts of business away from each other. A market definition must look at all relevant sources of supply, either actual rivals or eager potential entrants to the market. . . .

. . . The Raiders attempted to prove the relevant market consists of NFL football (the product market) in the Southern California area (the geographic market). The NFL argues it competes with all forms of entertainment within the United States, not just Southern California. . . .

That NFL football has limited substitutes from a consumer standpoint is seen from evidence that the Oakland Coliseum sold out for 10 consecutive years despite having some of the highest ticket prices in the League. A similar conclusion can be drawn from the extraordinary number of television viewers—over 100 million people—that watched the 1982 Super Bowl, the ultimate NFL product. NFL football's importance to the television networks is evidenced by the approximately $2 billion they agreed to pay the League for the right to televise the games from 1982-1986. . . .

To some extent, the NFL itself narrowly defined the relevant market by emphasizing that NFL football is a unique product which can be produced only through the joint efforts of the 28 teams. Don Shula, coach of the Miami Dolphins, underscored this point when he stated that NFL football has a different set of fans than college football.

The evidence from which the jury could have found a narrow pro football product market was balanced, however, with other evidence which tended to show the NFL competes in the first instance with other professional sports, especially those with seasons that overlap with the NFL's. On a broader level, witnesses such as Pete Rozelle and Georgia Frontierre (owner of the L.A. Rams) testified that NFL football competes with other television offerings for network business, as well as other local entertainment for attendance at the games.

In terms of the relevant geographic market, witnesses testified, in particular Al Davis, that NFL teams compete with one another off the field for fan support in those areas where teams operate in close proximity such as New York City-New Jersey, Washington, D.C.-Baltimore, and formerly San Francisco-Oakland. Davis, of course, had firsthand knowledge of this when his team was located in Oakland. Also, the San Francisco Forty-Niners and the New York Giants were paid $18 million because of the potential for harm from competing with the Oakland Raiders and the New York Jets, respectively, once those teams joined the NFL as a result of the merger with the American Football League. Al Davis also testified at length regarding the potential for competition for fan support between the Raiders and the Los Angeles Rams once his team relocated in Los Angeles. . . .

. . . We find that this evidence taken as a whole provided the jury with an adequate basis on which to judge the reasonableness of Rule 4.3 both as it affected competition among NFL teams and among stadia.

. . . In fact, because of the exceptional structure of the League, it was not necessary for the jury to accept absolutely either the NFL's or the plaintiff's market definitions. Instead, the critical question is whether the jury could have determined that Rule 4.3 reasonably served the NFL's interest in producing and promoting its product, i.e., competing in the entertainment market, or whether Rule 4.3 harmed competition among the 28 teams to such an extent that any benefits to the League as a whole were outweighed. As we find below, there was ample evidence for the jury to reach the latter conclusion.

2. The History and Purpose of Rule 4.3

The NFL has awarded franchises exclusive territories since the 1930s. In the early days of professional football, numerous franchises failed and many changed location in the hope of achieving economic success. League members saw exclusive territories as a means to aid stability, ensuring the owner who was attempting to establish an NFL team in a particular city that another would not move into the same area, potentially ruining them both.

Rule 4.3 is the result of that concern. Prior to its amendment in 1978, it required unanimous League approval for a move into another team's home territory. That, of course, gave each owner an exclusive territory and he could vote against a move into his territory solely because he was afraid the competition might reduce his revenue. Notably, however, the League constitution required only three-quarters approval for all other moves. The 1978 amendment removed the double-standard, and currently three-quarters approval is required for all moves.

That the purpose of Rule 4.3 was to restrain competition among the 28 teams may seem obvious and it is not surprising the NFL admitted as much at trial. It instead argues that Rule 4.3 serves a variety of legitimate League needs, including ensuring franchise stability. We must keep in mind, however, that the Supreme Court has long rejected the notion that "ruinous competition" can be a defense to a restraint of trade. . . .

3. Ancillary Restraints and the Reasonableness of Rule 4.3

. . . We assume, with no reason to doubt, that the agreement creating the NFL is valid and the territorial divisions therein are ancillary to its main purpose of producing NFL football. The ancillary restraint must then be tested under the rule of reason, *id.*, the relevance of ancillarity being it "increases the probability that the restraint will be found reasonable." As we have already noted, the rule of reason inquiry requires us to consider the harms and benefits to competition caused by the restraint and whether the putative benefits can be achieved by less restrictive means.

The competitive harms of Rule 4.3 are plain. Exclusive territories insulate each team from competition within the NFL market, in essence allowing them to set monopoly prices to the detriment of the consuming public. . . . The harm from Rule 4.3 is especially acute in this case because it prevents a move by a team into another existing team's market. If the transfer is upheld, direct competition between the Rams and Raiders would presumably ensue to the benefit of all who consume the NFL product in the Los Angeles area.

The NFL argues, however, that territorial allocations are *inherent* in an agreement among joint venturers to produce a product. This inherent nature, the NFL asserts, flows from the need to protect each joint venturer in the "legitimate fruits of the contract, or to protect him from the dangers of an unjust use of those fruits by the other party." We agree that the nature of NFL football requires some territorial restrictions in order both to encourage participation in the venture and to secure each venturer the legitimate fruits of that participation.

Rule 4.3 aids the League, the NFL claims, in determining its overall geographical scope, regional balance and coverage of major and minor markets. Exclusive territories aid new franchises in achieving financial stability, which protects the large initial investment an owner must make to start up a football team. Stability arguably helps ensure no one team has an undue advantage on the field. Territories foster fan loyalty which in turn promotes traditional rivalries between teams, each contributing to attendance at games and television viewing.

Joint marketing decisions are surely legitimate because of the importance of television. [15 U.S.C. §1291] grants the NFL an exemption from antitrust liability, if any, that might arise out of its collective negotiation of television rights with the networks. To effectuate this right, the League must be allowed to have some control over the placement of teams to ensure NFL football is popular in a diverse group of markets.

Last, there is some legitimacy to the NFL's argument that it has an interest in preventing transfers from areas before local governments, which have made a substantial investment in stadia and other facilities, can recover their expenditures. In such a situation, local confidence in the NFL is eroded, possibly resulting in a decline in interest. All these factors considered, we nevertheless are not persuaded the jury should have concluded that Rule 4.3 is a reasonable restraint of trade. The same goals can be achieved in a variety of ways which are less harmful to competition.

As noted by Justice Rehnquist, a factor in determining the reasonableness of an ancillary restraint is the "possibility of less restrictive alternatives" which could serve the same purpose. Here, the district court correctly instructed the jury to take into account the existence of less restrictive alternatives when determining the reasonableness of Rule 4.3's territorial restraint. . . .

The NFL argues that the requirement of Rule 4.3 that three-quarters of the owners approve a franchise move is reasonable because it deters unwise team transfers. While the rule does indeed protect an owner's investment in a football franchise, no standards or durational limits are incorporated into the voting requirement to make sure that concern is satisfied. Nor are factors such as fan loyalty and team rivalries necessarily considered.

The NFL claims that its marketing and other objectives are indirectly accounted for in the voting process because the team owners vote to maximize their profits.

Since the owners are guided by the desire to increase profits, they will necessarily make reasonable decisions, the NFL asserts, on such issues of whether the new location can support two teams, whether marketing needs will be adversely affected, etc. Under the present Rule 4.3, however, an owner need muster only seven friendly votes to prevent three-quarters approval for the sole reason of preventing another team from entering its market, regardless of whether the market could sustain two franchises. A basic premise of the Sherman Act is that regulation of private profit is best left to the marketplace rather than private agreement. The present case is in fact a good example of how the market itself will deter unwise moves, since a team will not lightly give up an established base of support to confront another team in its home market.

The NFL's professed interest in ensuring that cities and other local governments secure a return on their investment in stadia is undercut in two ways. First, the local governments ought to be able to protect their investment through the leases they negotiate with the teams for the use of their stadia. Second, the NFL's interest on this point may not be as important as it would have us believe because the League has in the past allowed teams to threaten a transfer to another location in order to give the team leverage in lease negotiations.

Finally, the NFL made no showing that the transfer of the Raiders to Los Angeles would have any harmful effect on the League. Los Angeles is a market large enough for the successful operation of two teams, there would be no scheduling difficulties, facilities at the L.A. Coliseum are more than adequate, and no loss of future television revenue was foreseen. Also, the NFL offered no evidence that its interest in maintaining regional balance would be adversely affected by a move of a northern California team to southern California.

It is true, as the NFL claims, that the antitrust laws are primarily concerned with the promotion of *interbrand* competition. . . . To the extent the NFL is a product which competes with other forms of entertainment, including other sports, its rules governing territorial division can be said to promote interbrand competition. Under this analysis, the territorial allocations most directly suppress intrabrand, that is, NFL team versus NFL team, competition. A more direct impact on intrabrand competition does not mean, however, the restraint is reasonable. The finder of fact must still balance the gain to interbrand competition against the loss of intrabrand competition. Here, the jury could have found that the rules restricting team movement do not sufficiently promote interbrand competition to justify the negative impact on intrabrand competition.

To withstand antitrust scrutiny, restrictions on team movement should be more closely tailored to serve the needs inherent in producing the NFL "product" and competing with other forms of entertainment. An express recognition and consideration of those objective factors espoused by the NFL as important, such as population, economic projections, facilities, regional balance, etc., would be well advised. *See* L. Kurlantzick, *Thoughts on Professional Sports and the Antitrust Laws*, 15 Conn. L.R. 183, 206 (1983). Fan loyalty and location continuity could also be considered. *Id.* at 206-207. Al Davis in fact testified that in 1978 he proposed that the League adopt a set of objective guidelines to govern team relocation rather than continuing to utilize a subjective voting procedure.

Some sort of procedural mechanism to ensure consideration of all the above factors may also be necessary, including an opportunity for the team proposing the move to present its case. . . . In the present case, for example, testimony indicated that some owners, as well as Commissioner Rozelle, dislike Al Davis and consider him a maverick. Their vote against the Raiders' move could have been motivated by animosity rather than business judgment.

Substantial evidence existed for the jury to find the restraint imposed by Rule 4.3 was not reasonably necessary to the production and sale of the NFL product. Therefore, the NFL is not entitled to judgment notwithstanding the verdict. . . .

V.   CONCLUSION

The NFL is an unique business organization to which it is difficult to apply antitrust rules which were developed in the context of arrangements between actual competitors. . . .

We believe antitrust principles are sufficiently flexible to account for the NFL's structure. To the extent the NFL finds the law inadequate, it must look to Congress for relief.

The judgment finding the NFL liable to . . . the Raiders, and enjoining the NFL from preventing the Raiders from relocating in Los Angeles is Affirmed.

NOTES AND QUESTIONS

1. *Determination of Anticompetitive Effect.* Why was the NFL's refusal to allow the Raiders to move to Los Angeles anticompetitive? Note that the Raiders' proposed 1980 relocation to Los Angeles would result in a shared market with the Rams, while leaving the San Francisco Forty-Niners as the only NFL club in the Bay area. How do you accurately measure the net impact on *intrabrand competition* as a result of an increased number of NFL teams in Los Angeles with a corresponding reduction of NFL clubs in the Bay area?

2. *League Procompetitive Justifications for Territorial Restrictions.* The NFL argued that its rules concerning franchise relocation are necessary to promote *interbrand* competition with other forms of entertainment. Why were none of the NFL's proffered defenses successful, especially since the Supreme Court has stated that preserving interbrand competition among sellers of different brands of competing products is the primary objective of antitrust law? See *Continental TV, Inc. v. GTE Sylvania, Inc.*, 433 U.S. 36 (1977) (a nonsports case holding that vertical territorial restrictions are to be analyzed under the rule of reason because of their economic potential for facilitating interbrand competition).

3. *Calculation of Damages and Offset.* In *Los Angeles Memorial Coliseum Comm'n v. National Football League* (*Raiders II*), 791 F.2d 1356 (9th Cir. 1986), the Ninth Circuit affirmed the jury's finding that the Raiders' gross lost profits from the two-year delay in moving to Los Angeles until 1982 as a result of the NFL's vote against this move amounted to $11,554,382. However, the NFL's relocation rule is not per se illegal. Because the rule was invalid only as applied to the Raiders' proposed move to Los Angeles, the club could recover only those damages caused by the NFL's antitrust violation.

The court initially observed that, prior to 1980, when the Raiders sought to relocate to Los Angeles, the NFL as a whole owned the right to expand into the Los Angeles area and the corresponding value of this expansion opportunity. When the Raiders subsequently moved into this market without league approval, the club appropriated this expansion value for itself, which increased its value by approximately $25 million. Its move out of Oakland created a potential expansion opportunity for the NFL, but the Los Angeles market was a significantly more lucrative venue. Therefore, "the accumulated value of that business opportunity is not something to which the Raiders became entitled as a result of the liability verdict. As a result, the injunction permitting the Raiders to play NFL football in Los Angeles provided them with a windfall benefit beyond the scope of the anti-trust verdict." *Id.* at 1372.

The Ninth Circuit reasoned:

> Thus, by taking possession of the Los Angeles expansion opportunity from the NFL, the Raiders reaped a windfall benefit beyond the scope of the anti-trust verdict. For this reason, and also because the NFL, in the absence of its antitrust violation, would have been justified in requiring the Raiders to compensate the NFL for the excess value represented by the Los Angeles expansion opportunity, that excess value should have been offset against the Raiders' lost profits from the two years they were precluded from moving to Los Angeles. . . . On remand, the scope of the offset should be broadened to include the full value of the Los Angeles opportunity that had accrued prior to 1980, less the value of the "Oakland opportunity" that was returned to the NFL.

Id. at 1373. Is *Raiders II* consistent with *Raiders I*?

4. After the *Raiders* litigation, in *National Basketball Assn. v. SDC Basketball Club, Inc.*, 815 F.2d 562, 567 (9th Cir. 1987), the Ninth Circuit held that league rules regarding franchise relocation, including requiring a club to seek league approval before moving, are not per se illegal; rather "rule of reason analysis governed a professional sports league's efforts to restrict franchise movement." The court explained:

> The Clippers assert that the rule "is illegal as applied . . . [but that under *Raiders I*], a professional sports league's club relocation rule must at least be 'closely tailored' and incorporate objective standards and criteria such as population, economic projections, playing facilities, regional balance, and television revenues." . . . The Clippers' confusion, and that of a number of commentators, may derive from the *Raiders I* panel's painstaking efforts to guide sports leagues toward procedures that might, in all cases, withstand anti-trust analysis. The objective factors and procedures recounted by the Clippers are "well advised," and might be sufficient to demonstrate procompetitive purposes that would save the restriction from the rule of reason. They are not, however, necessary conditions to the legality of franchise relocation rules.

Id. at 567-568.

In *In re Dewey Ranch Hockey, LLC*, 414 B.R. 577 (D. Ariz. 2009), a bankruptcy court rejected the efforts of a prospective purchaser of the Phoenix Coyotes NHL club to use the federal bankruptcy laws to avoid required NHL approval to purchase and relocate the club to Hamilton, Ontario, in Canada. Relying on Section 363(e) of the bankruptcy code, "which requires that [a] court 'shall prohibit' any sale, where the interests sought to be removed by the proposed sale free and clear of such interests, cannot be adequately protected," the court ruled it "cannot find or conclude that the interests of the NHL can be adequately protected if the Coyotes are moved to Hamilton without first having a final decision regarding the claimed rights of the NHL and the claims of the debtors and PSE." *Id.* at 591.

What advice would you give to a league commissioner and its clubs regarding the antitrust validity of franchise relocation rules under current law?

5. *Policy Considerations.* What is the ultimate effect on consumer welfare if antitrust law is used to regulate internal governance of a professional sports league, especially if the challenged conduct does not adversely affect *interbrand* competition? How much confidence do you have that the market will prevent a sports league from engaging in conduct that will harm consumers? Would you favor federal legislation providing professional sports leagues with antitrust immunity in franchise location matters? Who should be the ultimate arbiter of disputes among league clubs regarding internal governance matters such as franchise ownership or location—the league commissioner, majority vote of the clubs, courts, an independent arbitrator, or legislators?

North American professional sports leagues are "closed," which means that current league members must approve a new club's admission to the league, usually by supermajority vote. As two scholars have observed:

> This is fundamentally different than the structure of team sports in the rest of the world. Elsewhere, sports leagues are usually open: membership in the league is contingent on success. Professional sports leagues in soccer, rugby, basketball, and cricket are organized in ascending tiers (generally called divisions), and every year the teams with the worst record are relegated to a lower division and replaced by the most successful teams from that lower division.

Stephen F. Ross and Stephan Szymanski, *Open Competition in League Sports,* 2002 Wis. L. Rev. 625, 62. Consider the pros and cons of their following proposal:

> A system of promotion and relegation places a significant limit on the monopoly power of sports leagues. The system preserves the integrity of the league itself and indeed allows leagues to legitimately expand or contract to most effectively market the product. At the same time, a club's threat to relocate without tax subsidies is diluted by the possibility that the team itself may be relegated and, more importantly, by the creation of alternative entry routes for cities that do not possess a major league team. In other words, both the expected benefit of the subsidy for the municipality and the expected benefit to the team of its other option (relocation) are diminished. As a result, the ability of teams to extract subsidies is either reduced or eliminated altogether.
>
> Given its advantages, would a system of promotion and relegation ever be adopted in North America? We think it unlikely that clubs themselves would voluntarily introduce such a system. Thus, some form of government intervention is probably necessary to achieve this result. Promotion and relegation is in fact an ideal structure for surgical intervention to promote entry, since it involves replacing the least efficient incumbent (in terms of wins) with the most efficient entrant. Moreover, entry is only conditional on continuing success, so that a relegated incumbent has an opportunity to recapture its position the following season.

Id. at 629.

6. *Possible Alternatives to Antitrust Law in Regulating Internal League Governance.* Would the public interest be better served by applying state contract or

fiduciary duty law to disputes among a league's clubs on internal governance issues rather than federal antitrust law?

Some courts have held that the various agreements among member clubs of a sports league contain an implied reciprocal covenant of good faith and fair dealing. In *Raiders II*, applying California law, the Ninth Circuit explained, "This covenant not only 'requires each contracting party to refrain from doing anything to injure the right of the other to receive the benefits of the agreement,' . . . 'but also [imposes] the duty to do everything that the contract presupposes that he will do to accomplish its purpose.'" 791 F.2d at 1361. The court held that the Oakland Raiders club could not prevail on this claim despite the jury's verdict that the other NFL clubs acted in bad faith by refusing to approve its relocation to Los Angeles. The Raiders' unilateral decision to relocate and deliberate efforts to circumvent NFL rules for approving franchise moves also constituted a failure to act in good faith. The court ruled that "mutual breaches of the implied good faith obligation extinguish one another." *Id.* at 1362.

In *Professional Hockey Corp. v. World Hockey Assn.*, 191 Cal. Rptr. 773, 777 (Cal. Ct. App. 1983), the court held, "The law requires, irrespective of the competitive personal feelings of the various owners of teams may have towards each other, when they or their representatives sit on the board of directors of WHA to the extent they have common corporate goals, they have a duty to make decisions for the benefit of the corporation, the hockey league as a whole." The court ruled that each club's representative "owes the league as a whole the traditional fiduciary duties in this commonly shared corporate purpose." *Id.* The court, however, found no breach of any fiduciary duty arising out of the specific facts relating to the league-approved sale of a franchise. See generally Timothy D. Watson, Note, *What's "Love" Got To Do With It? Potential Fiduciary Duties Among Professional Sports Teams*, 9 Sports Law. J. 153 (2002).

7. *Community Cost of Acquiring a Franchise.* As mentioned previously, local communities, particularly mid-major cities such as Nashville, Memphis, and Charlotte, recently have provided multimillion-dollar public subsidies for playing facilities to attract major league sports franchises. Many other communities have made similar investments of public funds to keep their local sports franchises and prevent them from relocating elsewhere. Although these significant public expenditures combined with favorable lease terms provide substantial economic benefits to privately owned professional sports clubs, courts generally rule that these arrangements are a legitimate use of state and local tax dollars to promote the public good. See, e.g., *King County v. Taxpayers of King County*, 949 P.2d 1260 (Wash. 1997), *cert. denied*, 522 U.S. 1076 (1998); *Libertarian Party of Wisconsin v. State*, 199 Wis. 2d 791 (1996); *Lifteau v. Metropolitan Sports Facility Commission*, 270 N.W.2d 749 (1978); *Bazell v. City of Cincinnati*, 13 Ohio St. 2d 63 (1968); *New Jersey Sports & Exposition Authority v. McCrane*, 61 N.J. 1 (1972).

In *St. Louis Convention & Visitors Commission v. National Football League*, 154 F.3d 851 (8th Cir. 1998), the Eighth Circuit affirmed the dismissal of the St. Louis Convention & Visitors Commission's (CVC) antitrust claims against the NFL arising out of the Rams franchise's relocation to St. Louis and lease to play its games in the Trans World Dome. NFL club owners approved the Rams' move only after its owner agreed to pay the NFL a $29 million relocation fee, $20 million of which CVC agreed to reimburse to the Rams' owner.

CVC contended that the application of the NFL's relocation rules and the league's imposition of an unreasonably high relocation fee discouraged other NFL teams from moving and bidding on the Trans World Dome lease. This allegedly forced CVC to give the Rams more favorable lease terms than it would have in a competitive market, which caused CVC damage in an amount between $77 million and $122 million.

The Eighth Circuit found that CVC had not proved the existence of a conspiracy among NFL clubs to prevent competitive bidding on the Trans World Dome lease, or that the NFL's alleged anticompetitive acts caused its economic harm. There was no explicit NFL rule or policy that banned or limited NFL clubs from engaging in competitive bidding for available stadium leases. There was no evidence that the NFL's relocation rules had precluded league clubs other than the Rams from bidding on the Trans World Dome lease. CVC did not solicit other NFL teams to move to St. Louis. It also did not prove that other NFL clubs failed to bid because of the league's relocation rules. CVC also did not present evidence excluding the possibility that NFL owners were not bidding on the Trans World Dome lease because of independent business reasons, such as satisfaction with their current leases or loyalty to their present host cities.

In *Warnock v. NFL*, 356 F. Supp. 2d 535 (W.D. Pa. 2005), *aff'd*, 154 Fed. Appx. 291 (3d Cir. 2005), *cert. denied*, 547 U.S. 1021 (2006), the plaintiff, a Pittsburgh municipal taxpayer, alleged that by limiting the number of teams, the NFL forced cities to either build new stadiums or to enter into leases with onerous terms in order to keep an NFL franchise in a particular market. The court ruled that he lacked standing to sue the NFL and its member clubs for allegedly violating the antitrust laws by acting in concert to force league's cities, including Pittsburgh, to build new football stadiums. See also *Hamilton County Bd. of County Comm'rs v. NFL*, 491 F.3d 310 (6th Cir. 2007) (dismissing local government's antitrust claim against NFL after agreeing to "highly favorable" lease terms to prevent Bengals franchise from relocating, because "county officials knew—or should have known—the NFL was a monopoly during lease negotiations 10 years ago," which is outside applicable statute of limitations).

8. *Legal Remedies for Community Loss of Franchise.* The relocation of professional sports franchises causes great upset among the local populace and has spawned litigation against club owners by their respective host cities, states, or local governing bodies. Such litigation is motivated by the potential loss of economic benefits to a city and its local businesses, outstanding bond indebtedness to finance the departing club's playing facility, and wounded community pride resulting from the loss of a major league professional sports franchise. These lawsuits seek to prevent loss of the franchise, to keep the local team from moving before its stadium lease expires and without an opportunity to retain the franchise, or to require the league to provide a replacement franchise. See generally Matthew J. Mitten and Bruce W. Burton, *Professional Sports Franchise Relocations from Private Law and Public Law Perspectives: Balancing Marketplace Competition, League Autonomy, and the Need for a Level Playing Field*, 56 Md. L. Rev. 57 (1997).

The following legal theories have been asserted in an effort to achieve one or more of the foregoing objectives:

a. *Eminent Domain.* In an unsuccessful effort to prevent the Raiders from moving to Los Angeles, the City of Oakland attempted to "take" the franchise pursuant to its eminent domain authority. In *City of Oakland v. Oakland Raiders,* 183 Cal. Rptr. 673 (Cal. 1982), the California Supreme Court held that state law permitted the taking of intangible property such as a professional sports franchise, and that doing so could be shown to constitute a valid public purpose. Although the court concluded that "the acquisition and, indeed, the operation of a sports franchise may be an appropriate municipal function," it cautioned, "we are not concerned with the economic or governmental wisdom of City's acquisition or management of the Raiders' franchise, but only with the legal propriety of the condemnation action." *Id.* at 681. The dissent asserted that it is "dangerous and heavy-handed for the government to take over a business, including all of its intangible assets, for the sole purpose of preventing its relocation." *Id.* at 684.

However, a California court of appeals subsequently ruled that the use of eminent domain to prevent the Raiders from relocating to Los Angeles would violate the Dormant Commerce Clause, even though this was an intrastate move the NFL clubs had unanimously voted against. *City of Oakland v. Oakland Raiders,* 220 Cal. Rptr. 153 (Cal. Ct. App. 1985). Observing that eminent domain could be used to "bar indefinitely defendant's business from relocating out of Oakland," the court concluded, "This is the precise brand of parochial meddling with the national economy that the commerce clause was designed to prohibit." *Id.* at 157.

Does the court's perceived need for uniform national regulation of league affairs outweigh the local community's interest in promoting public recreation and its citizens' social welfare? Even if eminent domain could be legally exercised by a governmental entity to acquire a sports franchise, how should "just compensation" for this taking be calculated? For example, should it be based on the club's fair market value in its current community or the one in which the club seeks to relocate?

b. *Antitrust Law.* In *State v. Milwaukee Braves, Inc.,* 1966 Trade Cas. (CCH) P 71,738 (Wis. Cir. Ct.), *rev'd on other grounds,* 144 N.W.2d 1 (Wis. 1966), the State of Wisconsin alleged that the National League and its member baseball clubs violated state antitrust law by allowing the Milwaukee Braves to move to Atlanta and by refusing to provide a replacement team in Milwaukee.

The trial court issued an injunction barring the Braves from relocating unless the league granted a franchise to a group that sought to operate an MLB team in Milwaukee. The trial court made the following fact findings: (1) the National League and the American League and their respective member teams collectively have monopoly power over major league professional baseball, thereby giving them "unlimited power and discretion to determine the location of franchises"; (2) expansion by the National League was feasible; (3) the Braves franchise had been profitable in Milwaukee; (4) Milwaukee had the economic and population bases needed to support an MLB team; (5) the National League had no objective standards for evaluating the propriety of franchise relocations or any procedure to enable cities faced with the loss of a team an opportunity to be heard; and (6) the move of the Braves to Atlanta would cause a substantial economic loss to Milwaukee's metropolitan area.

The trial court heard testimony that MLB "is an operation in a sense quasi public in nature," and the court cited the league's "persistent refusal to expand." The court also heard testimony that, from the perspective of a host community, the loss of a baseball franchise "would be a detriment where there was a benefit before." The court held that the defendants unreasonably exercised monopolistic control over MLB and engaged in a concerted refusal to deal with a consumer in violation of state antitrust law.

As an alternative to facilitating competition by dissolving the league, the trial court permitted the league to continue its monopoly status, but required the league "to respond in a responsible and reasonable manner in matters pertaining to the transfer and allocation of franchises." The court awarded the plaintiff $5,000 in damages and ordered the National League to place a baseball franchise in Milwaukee. On appeal, the Wisconsin Supreme Court reversed the trial court's judgment because the use of state law to require the National League to expand the number of its franchises conflicts with the Supremacy and Commerce Clauses of the United States Constitution. (See discussion of MLB's common law antitrust exemption and judicial reluctance to permit use of state antitrust law to regulate league affairs, *supra.*)

To protect a host community's legitimate interests, should antitrust law impose a fairness requirement on a professional sports league when making franchise relocation decisions? Should antitrust law be used to resolve disputes involving conflicting claims to the same team by different communities within the United States? Would doing so further antitrust law's primary objective of enhancing consumer welfare by prohibiting anticompetitive conduct?

c. *Contract Law.* A well-drafted stadium lease is the most effective means of protecting a host community's public investment in the playing facility that houses a local team and ensuring that the local populace receives the full benefit of its contractual bargain. See Bruce W. Burton and Matthew J. Mitten, *New Remedies for Breach of Sports Facility Use Agreements: Time for Marketplace Realism,* 88 Iowa L. Rev. 811 (2003). For example, requiring a club to pay agreed liquidated damages of several million dollars for breach of a playing facility lease may be an effective means of protecting a host community's interests.

Finding that damages are not an adequate remedy for breach of a playing facility lease and that the premature relocation of a team causes irreparable harm to a city and its fans, some courts have enjoined teams from scheduling and playing home games outside their host cities prior to the lease's expiration. See, e.g., *City of New York v. New York Yankees,* 458 N.Y.S.2d 486 (N.Y. Sup. Ct. 1983); *City of New York v. New York Jets Football Club, Inc.,* 394 N.Y.S.2d 799 (N.Y. Sup. Ct. 1977). In *New York Yankees,* the court stated:

> Much more is at stake than merely the loss of direct and indirect revenue to the City. The Yankee pin stripes belong to New York like Central Park, like the Statue of Liberty, like the Metropolitan Museum of Art, like the Metropolitan Opera, like the Stock Exchange, like the lights of Broadway, etc. Collectively they are "The Big Apple." Any loss represents

a diminution of the quality of life here, a blow to the City's standing at
the top, however narcissistic that perception may be.

458 N.Y.S.2d at 489-490.

In *Metropolitan Sports Facilities Comm'n v. Minnesota Twins Partnership*,
638 N.W.2d 214, 224 (Minn. Ct. App. 2002), the court rejected the contention that money damages are adequate to compensate a public stadium authority for the breach of a playing facility lease if MLB contracted
by eliminating the Minnesota Twins franchise prior to the 2002 season:
"In addition, legal commentators have recognized that money damages
are not sufficient to compensate for the harm suffered by a community for the loss of a professional sports team." *Id.* See, e.g., Matthew
J. Mitten and Bruce W. Burton, *Professional Sports Franchise Relocations
From Private Law Public Law Perspectives: Balancing Marketplace Competition,
League Autonomy, and the Need for Level Playing Field*, 56 Md. L. Rev. 57,
70-71 (1997). According to these commentators, "Merely allowing a city
to recover contract damages for the premature loss of a team does not
provide adequate compensation for the city's lost benefit of the bargain
in providing the public, financial inducements necessary to attract or
retain a sports franchise. . . . The city's real benefits of the bargain are
the highly valued, intangible benefits. . . . The value of such benefits is
virtually impossible to quantify and, therefore, is not recoverable for a
team owner's breach of contract."

Finding that the Twins club does not pay rent for using the Metrodome
to play its home games, the court observed that "the use agreement
at issue here is not a typical commercial lease." *Id.* at 222. The court
explained, "[T]he benefit of the bargain that the commission received
was the Twins promise to play their home games at the Metrodome for
the duration of their lease. Indeed, the stated purpose for building and
operating the stadium was to attract major league sport franchises to play
at the stadium for the enjoyment of fans." *Id.* at 223. The trial court's
injunction requiring the Twins club to play its 2002 home games in the
Metrodome and prohibiting MLB from interfering with this contractual
obligation was affirmed.

PROBLEM 6-2

The NFL owners voted to deny the Raiders' request to move from Oakland
to Los Angeles for the season after the club's stadium lease in Oakland expires.
The Raiders moved from Oakland to Los Angeles in 1982, and then moved
back to Oakland in 1995. Both the Raiders and San Francisco Forty-Niners currently play their home games in the Oakland-San Francisco Bay Area. Although
the Raiders club is profitable in Oakland, the club's current owner claims the
team generates the league's third-lowest stadium revenues (which revenues are
not shared with other NFL clubs) and that the team is at a competitive disadvantage in attracting NFL free agent players to Oakland. He believes the club's
stadium revenues will substantially increase by playing in the newly renovated
Los Angeles Coliseum. Since 1995, there has not been an NFL team in Los
Angeles; the former Los Angeles Rams NFL club moved to St. Louis that year.
Currently, the closest NFL club is the San Diego Chargers franchise, which plays

its games in a stadium 135 miles south of Los Angeles. Rather than allowing an existing NFL franchise to relocate, NFL club owners want to place one or two expansion teams in Los Angeles whenever a new football stadium is built in the Los Angeles area. It is anticipated that the future owner(s) of the Los Angeles expansion team(s) will pay at least a $1 billion franchise fee that will be divided equally among the NFL's existing 32 clubs. NFL club owners also are tired of the Raiders club's historical game of "franchise musical chairs" and are concerned that allowing the team to relocate yet again will harm the league's efforts to foster fan loyalty.

What is your opinion regarding the likely success of an antitrust challenge to the NFL club owners' refusal to allow the Raiders to move to Los Angeles.

iii.   *Restrictions on Intellectual Property Rights Licensing and Sales*

The four major North American professional sports leagues (NFL, MLB, NBA, and NHL) are geographically dispersed throughout the United States and Canada. Their respective clubs are located in cities with vastly different populations and economic bases; for example, large-market metropolitan areas such as New York City, Los Angeles, and Chicago, as well as much smaller markets like Kansas City, Milwaukee, and Pittsburgh. Thus, league clubs' respective revenue-generating potential from ticket sales (including personal seat licenses), concessions, parking fees, sponsorships, merchandising rights, and game broadcasts within differing local markets varies considerably.

As a means of preventing significant disparities in local revenue streams from inhibiting or destroying on-field competitive balance and fan interest in league games, the NFL, MLB, NBA, and NHL have implemented varying degrees of revenue sharing among their member clubs. In each league, national television and broadcasting rights revenues are shared equally among league clubs. Individual clubs' trademarks and logos are collectively licensed by a central league authority, with revenues distributed to league clubs on a pro rata basis. A recent trend is for leagues to require their clubs' Internet rights to be consolidated and centrally licensed (rather than, or with limits on, an individual club's exploitation) with revenues shared among league clubs. Gate receipts from individual ticket sales frequently are also shared between the home and visiting teams in an agreed percentage.

The NFL currently has the most significant degree of revenue sharing among its member clubs, which provides the Green Bay Packers, located in a metropolitan area of approximately 100,000 people, with the financial resources to compete effectively on the field with large market clubs such as the Chicago Bears. Except for designated local advertising and facility-related revenues, NFL clubs share virtually all other revenues in an effort to jointly produce exciting games between closely matched teams that attracts fan interest.

In the words of George Halas, former Chicago Bears owner and one of the NFL's founders:

> [O]ur league for me was then—and still is—best exemplified as a wheel. . . . In 1920 [before the NFL was formed], we were 12 independent spokes. But spokes, if they are to serve a useful purpose and make a contribution, must have a rim. A spoke may weaken, even break, but the rim prevents collapse. Our league was and is our rim. The credo of sharing became the foundation of our league. On

this foundation, professional football was built. This sharing concept was unprecedented in sport.

Chris Harry, *NFL Owners in a League of Their Own*, Orlando Sentinel, Mar. 17, 2002, at C1. In testimony before Congress, former NFL commissioner Pete Rozelle stated that "revenue sharing is the key to maintaining geographic and competitive balance in professional football . . . and ensure[s] that each club, irrespective of the size of its community, stadium, or television market, has a comparable opportunity to field a championship team." See William J. Hoffman, Comment, *Dallas' Head Cowboy Emerges Victorious in a Licensing Showdown with the NFL*: National Football League Properties v. Dallas Cowboys Football Club, 7 Seton Hall J. Sport L. 255, 262 (1997).

The exclusive licensing or sale of pooled intellectual property rights by a central league marketing arm, along with corresponding restrictions on individual clubs, is designed to (and often does) maximize their aggregate economic value and total revenues generated by the league. However, the pro rata revenue shares received by the most popular individual league clubs or those in the largest markets may be significantly less than the percentage of league revenues generated by the intellectual property associated with those clubs. Such conduct may force the league to bring breach of contract and trademark infringement litigation to protect its clubs' collective economic interests and exclusive sponsorship agreements with third parties from being harmed. *NFL Properties, Inc. v. Dallas Cowboys Football Club, Ltd.*, 922 F. Supp. 849 (S.D.N.Y. 1996) (alleging that Dallas Cowboys used NFL and club marks without authorization to solicit sponsorship agreements with Dr. Pepper, Pepsi, and Nike, which were competitors of official NFL sponsors, in violation of federal Lanham Act, which prohibits unauthorized use of another's trademark that creates a likelihood of confusion, as well as state contract, misappropriation, and tortious interference with contract laws).

In response, league-imposed restrictions on a club's sale of sponsorship and merchandising rights have been challenged on antitrust grounds. *Dallas Cowboys Football Club, Ltd. v. NFL Trust*, 1996 WL 601705 (S.D.N.Y. 1996) (alleging that NFL Trust and Licensing Agreements create price-fixing cartel that precludes free competition in pro football sponsorship and merchandising markets). See also, e.g., Complaint, *New York Yankees Partnership v. Major League Baseball Enterprises, Inc*, 97-1153-CIV-T-2513 (M.D. Fla. Filed May 19, 1997) (asserting that MLB Properties is a "cartel organized at the behest of a large group of the less successful Major League Clubs" that illegally restrains trade). Both cases settled before being judicially resolved on the merits, but the following case squarely addressed similar antitrust claims by a third party against Major League Baseball.

MAJOR LEAGUE BASEBALL PROPERTIES, INC. v. SALVINO, INC.

542 F.3d 290 (2d Cir. 2008)

KEARSE, Circuit Judge.

[EDS. Defendant Salvino, Inc., which was sued for trademark infringement because of its unauthorized use of Major League Baseball clubs' trademarks, alleged that the collective trademark licensing arrangement of Major League Baseball Properties, Inc. (MLBP) violates §1 of the Sherman Act. MLBP is the worldwide exclusive licensing agent for all 30 MLB clubs' trademarks on retail products and acts as their agent for quality control and trademark protection. It charged "a standard royalty percentage" license for products bearing or incorporating an MLB club's trademarks "irrespective of variations in the Clubs' popularity as reflected by their respective fan bases." The dollar amount of royalties that each licensee pays to MLBP varies with its sales rather than being uniform. Each club receives a pro rata share of the profits from licensing royalties regardless of the amount of revenues generated by the licensing of its trademarks. A prospective licensee can request and obtain from MLBP a license to use the trademarks of one, some, or all MLB clubs. MLBP did not limit the number of products it would license or the number of companies to which it granted licenses for any particular products. The defendant was licensed by MLBP to use MLB clubs' trademarks on several products, but it did not have a license to use those marks in connection with a line of plush, bean-filled bears that it called "Bammers."]

II.   Discussion

On appeal, Salvino contends that the district court erred in ruling that the centralization in MLBP of the licensing of MLB Intellectual Property for use on retail products is to be analyzed under the rule of reason. Salvino principally adheres to the contention on which it relied in the district court, *i.e.,* that MLBP's operations should be evaluated only under a stricter standard-either the *per se* standard or the "quick-look" standard-and that under those stricter standards, summary judgment was inappropriate. In support of this contention, it characterizes the Clubs' agreement to make MLBP their exclusive licensor as "naked horizontal price and output restrictions [that] traditionally fall within the per se proscriptions." . . .

B.   MODES OF ANALYSIS UNDER THE SHERMAN ACT

By its terms, § 1 of the Sherman Act prohibits "[e]very contract, combination in the form of trust or otherwise, or conspiracy, in restraint of trade or commerce among the several States." 15 U.S.C. § 1. The Supreme "Court has not taken a literal approach to this language, however," but instead "has long recognized that Congress intended to outlaw only *unreasonable* restraints." *Texaco Inc. v. Dagher,* 547 U.S. 1, 5, 126 S.Ct. 1276, 164 L.Ed.2d 1 (2006) ("*Dagher*") (internal quotation marks omitted) (emphasis in *Dagher*). Thus, "th[e] Court presumptively applies rule of reason analysis, under which antitrust plaintiffs must demonstrate that a particular contract or combination is in fact unreasonable and anticompetitive before it will be found unlawful." *Id.*

There are, however, "certain agreements or practices which because of their pernicious effect on competition and lack of any redeeming virtue are conclusively presumed to be unreasonable and therefore illegal without elaborate inquiry as to the precise harm they have caused or the business excuse for their use." [citations omitted] Among the practices that have been held to be *per se* illegal are geographic division of markets . . . and horizontal price fixing. . . .

Per se treatment is not appropriate, however, where the economic and competitive effects of the challenged practice are unclear. "To justify a *per se* prohibition a restraint must have manifestly anticompetitive effects, . . . and lack . . . any redeeming virtue. . . ." [citation omitted]. Accordingly, the Supreme

Court has repeatedly "expressed reluctance to adopt *per se* rules . . . "where the economic impact of certain practices is not immediately obvious."" [citations omitted]. . . .

In a few cases, the Supreme Court has ruled that the challenged practice should neither be held a *per se* violation of the Sherman Act nor be subjected to full-blown rule-of-reason analysis, but rather should be held illegal on the basis of an "abbreviated or 'quick-look' [rule-of-reason] analysis" because "the great likelihood of anticompetitive effects can easily be ascertained." *California Dental Ass'n v. FTC,* 526 U.S. 756, 770, 119 S.Ct. 1604, 143 L.Ed.2d 935 (1999) ("*California Dental*"). Thus, in *National Society of Professional Engineers,* the Court, faced with the society's absolute ban on competitive bidding, ruled that "no elaborate industry analysis [wa]s required to demonstrate the anticompetitive character of such an agreement." 435 U.S. at 692, 98 S.Ct. 1355. The Court reached the same conclusion with respect to a plan that expressly limited the number of college football games that could be televised and fixed a minimum price for those games, *see National Collegiate Athletic Ass'n v. Board of Regents of the University of Oklahoma,* 468 U.S. 85, 109-10, 104 S.Ct. 2948, 82 L.Ed.2d 70 (1984) ("*NCAA*"), and with respect to a horizontal agreement among dentists to "withhold from their customers a particular service that they desire[d]," *Indiana Federation of Dentists,* 476 U.S. at 459, 106 S.Ct. 2009. The *California Dental* Court noted that

> [i]n each of these cases, which have formed the basis for what has come to be called abbreviated or "quick-look" analysis under the rule of reason, an observer with even a rudimentary understanding of economics could conclude that the arrangements in question would have an anticompetitive effect on customers and markets.

The Court has applied quick-look analysis only "to business activities that are so plainly anticompetitive that courts need undertake only a cursory examination before imposing antitrust liability." . . .

C. THE RECORD IN THE PRESENT CASE

Salvino contends that . . . "[t]he conduct at issue here [constitutes] naked horizontal price and output restrictions [that] traditionally fall [ ] within the per se proscriptions." . . .

. . . [T]he record in this case does not show any reduction in the licensing of the Clubs' intellectual property; rather MLBP presented evidence that there were sizeable increases. According to this evidence, when MLBP became the Clubs' exclusive licensor in 1987, there were approximately 100 licensees; in the first year thereafter, the number of licensees more than doubled. And in the years since, the number has continued to grow, with MLBP having, at the time of its summary judgment motion in this case, more than 300 licenses outstanding for some 4,000 products in the United States, along with licenses to some 170 licensees for sales of products outside of the United States. . . .

In sum, Salvino has pointed to no evidence in the record to support its contention that there has been a horizontal agreement to limit "output," and the only evidence of record-which Salvino has not genuinely disputed-is that output has greatly increased. We turn now to Salvino's contention that there has been a horizontal agreement on "price."

2. *The Nature of the "Price" Agreement Challenged by Salvino*

While Salvino contends that its challenge concerns "naked . . . price restrictions," it is important to focus on precisely what conduct Salvino characterizes as "price" restrictions. Although price usually refers to the amount of money a seller charges a buyer for the product, Salvino has made no assertions that there is an agreement as to the fees that the licensees of the MLB Intellectual Property are required to pay MLBP. Instead, throughout this litigation, the conduct that Salvino has contended is *per se* illegal price fixing is the Clubs' agreement to share equally in the profits from MLBP's licensing of the Clubs' intellectual property. . . .

With the recognition that what Salvino calls a "price" restriction is in actuality an agreement for profit sharing, and bearing in mind that, as discussed in the preceding section, there is no genuine dispute that "output" since MLBP became the Clubs' exclusive licensing agent with respect to all retail products bearing Club intellectual property has increased rather than decreased, we turn to Salvino's contention that the district court erred in finding this case similar to *Broadcast Music*, instead of finding the present arrangement *per se* illegal, or illegal after a quick look, based on *NCAA*. . . .

3. *The* Broadcast Music *Comparison*

In *Broadcast Music*, the Supreme Court considered antitrust claims by Columbia Broadcasting System, Inc. ("CBS"), against Broadcast Music, Inc., and the American Society of Composers, Authors and Publishers (collectively the "organizations"), with respect to the organizations' respective issuance of blanket performance licenses to the CBS television network, *i.e.,* licenses to perform any, some, or all of the copyrighted musical compositions owned by that organization's members or affiliates. CBS asserted that the issuance of blanket licenses in exchange for fees negotiated by the respective organizations was price fixing, and hence *per se* illegal. . . . The Supreme Court stated:

> The blanket license, as we see it, is not a "naked restrain[t] of trade with no purpose except stifling of competition," . . . but rather accompanies the integration of sales, monitoring, and enforcement against unauthorized copyright use. . . . [The organizations] and the blanket license developed together out of the practical situation in the marketplace: thousands of users, thousands of copyright owners, and millions of compositions. Most users want unplanned, rapid, and indemnified access to any and all of the repertory of compositions, and the owners want a reliable method of collecting for the use of their copyrights. Individual sales transactions in this industry are quite expensive, as would be individual monitoring and enforcement, especially in light of the resources of single composers. Indeed, as both the Court of Appeals and CBS recognize, the costs are prohibitive for licenses with individual radio stations, nightclubs, and restaurants, . . . and it was in that milieu that the blanket license arose.
>
> A middleman with a blanket license was an obvious necessity if the thousands of individual negotiations, a virtual impossibility, were to be avoided. Also, individual fees for the use of individual compositions would presuppose an intricate schedule of fees and uses, as well as a difficult and expensive reporting problem for the user and policing task for the copyright owner.

. . . MLBP can offer a license that covers all of the intellectual property of all of the MLB Clubs; no one Club could offer such a license, for no Club has the right to license the intellectual property of any other. Accordingly, even if direct licensing for retail products were available from each Club, any purveyor of memorabilia who wanted to offer products bearing the intellectual property of more than one Club could not obtain the necessary authorization from a single Club. Only MLBP can offer licenses to use the intellectual property of more than one Club, and it can grant a license to use any, some, or all of the Clubs' intellectual property. Accordingly, MLBP offers a large number of products that the individual intellectual property owners cannot match.

. . . [I]t is true, as Salvino argues, that the rights of the individual MLB Clubs to license their own respective intellectual property are more limited than the unfettered direct licensing rights of the copyright owners in *Broadcast Music*. We conclude that this distinction is insignificant, however, in light of the fact that the MLB Clubs exist as members of a sports league, and their interests are interdependent. That interdependence and Major League Baseball's need for competitive balance among the Clubs distinguish the Clubs from the individual composers and publishers of music who were the subject of *Broadcast Music;* those factors are not characteristic of the music industry. And those factors, among others, . . . plainly foreclose the imposition of *per se* or quick-look liability.

4. The NCAA Comparison

Salvino contends that "*NCAA* . . . is . . . the yardstick that should have been used by the court to evaluate the arrangement at issue" in the present case. We disagree, as we find the circumstances in *NCAA* to be different from those here in every meaningful respect.

In *NCAA,* the Supreme Court considered rules of the National Collegiate Athletic Association ("NCAA") with respect to the televising of college football games. The NCAA had entered into contracts with American Broadcasting Companies ("ABC") and CBS, permitting those networks to broadcast such games, and had entered into a contract with Turner Broadcasting System, Inc. ("TBS"), for the cablecasting of such games. The NCAA did not license any other network, and the NCAA plan forbade its member colleges to enter into agreements for the televising of their games on any other network or any local station.

The NCAA plan set an absolute maximum on the number of games that could be broadcast. It also contained "appearance limitations" with respect to each two-year period covered by the network contracts. The number of times that a given college could have its football games televised was limited to six, of which no more than four could be televised nationally. Thus, the NCAA plan limited both the total amount of televised intercollegiate football and the number of games that could be televised for any one team.

The per-telecast prices paid by the networks to the NCAA were fixed. For example, the ABC television network paid fees of $600,000 for each of the 12 national games it telecast during the 1981 regular fall season, and $426,779 for each of the 46 regional telecasts in 1980. *Id.* at 93 n. 10, 104 S.Ct. 2948. Except for the price differences between national and regional telecasts, the colleges whose games were televised received equal payments for those telecasts. . . .

The Supreme Court found that the NCAA plan was anticompetitive under rule-of-reason analysis because, *inter alia,* that plan deprived the individual colleges of their freedom to compete for television appearances. . . .

. . . [W]hereas the NCAA plan "create[d] a limitation on output" by limiting the total number of televised games and the number of times any one college's games could be televised, Salvino has not adduced any evidence of a limitation on the number of Club intellectual property licenses available here. MLBP does not limit the number of products that may be licensed (although it would doubtless refuse to license a product that it believed would reflect badly on Major League Baseball); indeed, MLBP presented evidence that it works with existing and prospective licensees to attempt to develop new products that would use MLB Intellectual Property. Salvino has not adduced any evidence that there is any agreement to limit the number of products that can be licensed or the number of entities to which licenses may be granted. . . .

The *NCAA* Court also noted that output was reduced by the NCAA plan because "only those broadcasters able to bid on television rights covering the entire NCAA can compete." In effect, the NCAA offered only bulk licenses. That fact has no analogy here. Here, a prospective licensee can request and obtain from MLBP a license to use the intellectual property of some or all of the Clubs, or of any single Club. . . .

The NCAA price controls and lack of responsiveness to demand find no parallels in the present record. First, a license to use MLB Intellectual Property is not sold "for a sum certain"; the licensing agreements call for licensees to pay MLBP a percentage of the moneys they receive from the sale of their products bearing MLB Intellectual Property. Thus, although the royalty percentages for various types of products may be standardized, the dollar amounts to be paid to MLBP by the licensees are not uniform but instead vary with the licensees' sales.

Second, Salvino has presented no evidence to suggest that the licensing of MLB Intellectual Property is not entirely responsive to demand. MLBP does not issue licenses that are not requested; there is no evidence that an entity that wishes to obtain a license for particular intellectual property is required to accept or pay for a license that encompasses other intellectual property as well.

Moreover, it may be presumed that a prospective licensee, acting in its own economic self-interest, requests licenses only with respect to products that it believes will be purchased. Thus, MLBP grants licenses that are responsive to the licensees' anticipation of consumer demand.

Further, a licensee's actual sales of products bearing MLB Intellectual Property are, by definition, responsive to consumer demand. Assuming that the licensees assess consumer demand correctly, they will sell more products bearing logos of a Club that is more popular-more popular either because of its success on the playing field or because of a dedicated fan base-than products bearing logos of a less popular Club. Accordingly, because the license requires the licensee to pay a percentage of its sales prices, the licensee will pay MLBP higher dollar amounts with respect to the intellectual property of the more popular Clubs. Thus, the dollar amounts of the license fees received by MLBP with respect to the intellectual property of the various Clubs are not uniform from Club to Club, but instead are plainly responsive both to the relative quality of the various Major League Baseball teams and to the preferences of the buyers. Indeed, the fact that MLBP receives proportionately higher revenues with respect to some Clubs than others is the cornerstone of what Salvino complains of as "price" restrictions, *i.e.*, the Clubs' agreement to share the profits equally.

Finally, MLBP-licensed products that are not desired by the consumer are not purchased. And because the licenses granted by MLBP require payments of percentages of the licensee's sales, products left behind by the consumer do not result in payments to MLBP or to the Clubs.

In sum, unlike the "sum[s] certain" payable in *NCAA*, the dollar sums payable for licenses to use the Clubs' intellectual property are not uniform and are entirely responsive to the preferences of licensees and retail product consumers.

c. Procompetitive Efficiencies

. . . In the present case, the record shows that, similarly to the blanket licensing at issue in *Broadcast Music*, centralization of the licensing and protection of MLB Intellectual Property has produced many cost-savings and efficiencies. And, in contrast to the effect of the NCAA plan, since the Clubs made MLBP their exclusive licensing agent for all retail products bearing MLB Intellectual Property, the number of licenses and licensees has multiplied. . . .

. . . Major League Baseball is a highly integrated professional sports entity comprising two Leagues, in which all of the Clubs compete. Each season constitutes a single tournament, leading to playoffs among the League leaders, and ultimately to the World Series. [T]here is no dispute that competitive balance is a necessary ingredient in the continuing popularity of the MLB Entertainment Product. And unlike the NCAA restrictions on televising games, which were "not even arguably tailored to serve" an interest in competitive balance, the Clubs' agreement that MLBP's profits from licensing MLB Intellectual Property will be distributed equally among the 30 Clubs is a precisely tailored attempt to achieve, or at least increase, competitive balance. . . .

In sum, unlike . . . *NCAA*, this case involves an integrated professional sports league in which the competitors are not independent but interdependent, competitive balance among the teams is essential to both the viability of the Clubs and public interest in the sport, and profit sharing is a legitimate means-approved by both of the economists in this case-of maintaining some measure of competitive balance. . . .

5. Professional Sports Ventures

In the present case, the district court observed that antitrust challenges to the operations of sports leagues have generally been analyzed by the courts under the rule of reason, rather than being held illegal *per se*, because competition among the teams in their fields of play is to an extent dependent upon the teams' cooperation with each other in various other respects. . . .

[T]he MLB Entertainment Product comprises some 2,400 interrelated regular-season Major League Baseball games played each year, followed by playoff games for the American and National League championships, and culminating in the World Series. The production of this entertainment requires the joint efforts of the 30 Clubs; it cannot be produced by any one Club individually or even by a few Clubs. In creating the MLB Entertainment Product, the Clubs plainly do not operate separately or independently but rather are interdependent entities in an organization that is highly integrated.

It is undisputed that the production and value of the MLB Entertainment Product affect the value of MLB Intellectual Property. For example, when the Major League Baseball players were on strike in 1994 and 1995, sales of products bearing MLB Intellectual Property decreased; when the strike ended, sales of those products increased. Further, the value of the intellectual property of a particular Club is dependent in part on that Club's membership in MLB . . . (and in part on the Club's popularity. Although every Club no doubt has a core of die-hard fans, a Club's popularity is affected principally by its success on the baseball field and by how the play of each game relates to the season as a whole.

Moreover, it cannot be disputed that the performance aspect of a Club's popularity is related to the Clubs' interdependence. Obviously, a team cannot win games or championships unless it has opponents. Thus, even Clubs that fail to achieve winning records, and that have only small steadfast fan bases, contribute to the popularity of the more successful Clubs. . . . Direct licensing by the Clubs . . . would result in the more popular Clubs granting more licenses and receiving more income for their intellectual property than the less popular Clubs would grant and receive. This inequality in licensing income, however, would "over-compensat[e] the popular team for the joint efforts of all Clubs." (Fisher Report ¶ 81.)

Further, the disproportionate distribution of licensing income would foster a competitive imbalance among the Clubs. The concept of "competitive balance" reflects the expected equality of opportunity to compete and prevail on the field. Competitive balance also relates to the fans' expectations that each team is a potential champion-i.e. that each Club has a reasonable opportunity to win each game and also to compete for a championship. . . .

There is no genuine dispute here that maintaining the value of the MLB Entertainment Product requires competitive balance among the Clubs. Fisher calls "competitive balance . . . critical to the success of MLB." And Salvino acknowledges that *MLB teams,* like all teams in sports leagues, *need to cooperate in terms of* scheduling, rulemaking, league format, *competitive balance* and both the live performance and televising of games, in order to create and market the product, which is baseball games. Accordingly, Fisher opined that "*all* the Clubs must be rewarded in order to ensure continued league-wide efforts as well as to foster competitive balance." . . .

D.   RULE OF REASON

Finally, given the present record, we see no error in the district court's analysis of Salvino's claim under the rule of reason. The court noted that Salvino had proffered no evidence that the centralization of licensing in MLBP caused any actual injury to competition or any evidence that MLBP possessed power in the relevant market.

CONCLUSION

. . . The judgment of the district court is affirmed.

NOTES AND QUESTIONS

1.   One legal scholar has observed:

> League collective trademark licensing offers several procompetitive benefits with the potential for enhancing consumer welfare. In addition to reduced cost-savings and increased efficiencies (e.g., lower transaction and trademark rights enforcement costs) recognized by both the *Salvino* majority and concurrence, its provision of one-stop shopping for licensees facilitates the production of merchandise incorporating multi-club logos such as video games

featuring league clubs and player trading cards. On the other hand, there is no readily available empirical evidence that cost savings from centralized league licensing lowers retail prices for trademarked merchandise. Even if exclusive league licensing is necessary to prevent free-riding by individual clubs and/or to achieve other substantial economic efficiencies, it is uncertain whether pro rata distribution of the profits to each club actually results in enhanced league-wide competitive balance or that it is positively correlated to increased revenue sharing.

Considering the difficulty proving that collective exclusive trademark licensing, a standard royalty based on a licensee's percentage of sales, and pro rata profit-sharing (individually or in combination) significantly reduce intrabrand competition along with the probability that a sports league's trademarked products face significant interbrand competition in the licensee and retail markets trademarked merchandise as well as the existence of several potential procompetitive benefits, it appears these restrictions are legal under the rule of reason. As long as a centralized league trademark licensing entity does not limit the number of companies to which it will grant licenses for particular categories of products and prospective licensee may obtain a license to use the trademarks of one, some, or all league clubs, it is arguable that collective exclusive licensing of professional sports club trademarks is virtually per se legal.

Matthew J. Mitten, *From* Dallas Cap *to* American Needle *and Beyond: Antitrust Law's Limited Capacity to Stitch Consumer Harm From Professional Sports Club Trademark Monopolies*, 86 Tul. L. Rev. 901, 926-927 (2012).

2. In contrast to *Salvino*, the challenged conduct at issue in *American Needle*, *supra*, is the validity of a league trademark licensor's granting of product category exclusivity to a single licensee for a fixed, up-front licensing fee. Plaintiff alleges that NFLP's grant of an exclusive license to manufacture apparel and headwear bearing the trademarks of the NFL and its individual clubs resulted in termination of its nonexclusive license to design, manufacture, and sell headwear bearing NFL clubs' trademarks, which had been in effect for more than 20 years when it expired and was not renewed. It alleges that this agreement reduces competition in the wholesale market for the distribution and sale of apparel and headwear products bearing the trademarks of NFL clubs, which violates §1.

As one scholar points out:

[T]here are two important differences between the NFL's licensing arrangement in American Needle and Major League Baseball's licensing arrangement in Salvino. First, one feature of the NFL's licensing arrangement in American Needle that is absent from Major League Baseball's ("MLB") arrangement in Salvino is category exclusivity. Thus, while the MLB arrangement maintains some level of competition among licensees to sell MLB licensed items, the NFL arrangement does not allow multiple licensees to compete against each other to sell NFL teams' apparel and headwear.

Additionally, while the MLB arrangement allows licensees "to pay a percentage of [their] sales prices," the NFL arrangement requires licensees instead to make a fixed, up-front payment. Thus, while the MLB "percentage of . . . sales" arrangement allows individual licensees to pay only for selling merchandise of specific teams, the NFL arrangement ties together the licenses for all thirty-two NFL marks. As a result, many smaller apparel companies that only have the capital to bid on one or a few NFL team marks are precluded from competing for any licensing rights.

Marc Edelman, *Upon Further Review: Will the NFL's Trademark Licensing Practices Survive Full Antitrust Scrutiny? The Remand of* American Needle v. Nat'l Football League, 16 Stan. J.L. Bus. & Fin. 183, 219 (2011).

On remand, should the district court apply the full or "quick look" rule of reason (an issue not resolved by the Supreme Court)? In answering this question, consider then-Judge Sotomayor's concurring opinion in *Salvino*, in which she agreed it was proper to apply the full rule of reason and to grant summary judgment for MLBP but applied the doctrine of ancillary restraints rather than the majority's legal framework to reach this conclusion. She observed that "under the doctrine of ancillary restraints, when a challenged restraint is not reasonably necessary to achieve any of the efficiency-enhancing purposes of a joint venture, it will be evaluated apart from the rest of the venture" and "a *per se* or quick-look approach may apply" if it "serves only as naked restraint against competition." *Id.* at 338. She disagreed with the majority's view that MLBP's collective trademark licensing is not price fixing, observing that MLB clubs "have agreed through the exclusivity and profit-sharing clauses in the MLBP agreement not to compete with each other on the sale of trademark licenses." 542 F.3d at 335. However, because a collective league trademark licensing joint venture "offers substantial efficiency-enhancing benefits that the individual Clubs could not offer on their own," Judge Sotomayor agreed that MLBP's ancillary exclusivity and profit-sharing provisions should be analyzed under the rule of reason because their competitive effects "are intertwined with the effects of the remainder of the venture." *Id.* at 337-338. She concluded that these provisions "are reasonably necessary to achieve MLBP's efficiency-enhancing purposes because they eliminate several potential externalities that may otherwise distort the incentives of individual Clubs and limit the potential efficiency gains of MLBP." *Id.* at 340. By comparison, is exclusive product licensing a restraint with direct anticompetitive effects not reasonably necessary to achieve the recognized procompetitive benefits of collective trademark licensing by league clubs (e.g., lower transaction and trademark rights enforcement costs, enhanced competitive balance among league clubs) that should be invalidated under the quick-look rule of reason? See Mitten, *supra*, at 931-932 ("The procompetitive justifications for collective exclusive trademark licensing clearly could be achieved in a substantially less restrictive manner other than by granting one licensee the exclusive rights to use league clubs' trademarks in connection with particular products. For example, offering licenses with the same terms (including appropriate quality control provisions) to two or more competing companies to produce and sell merchandise bearing or incorporating league clubs' trademarks").

3. Consistent with *Salvino*, in *Madison Square Garden, L.P. v. NHL*, 270 Fed. Appx. 56, 2008 WL 746524 (2d Cir.), the Second Circuit ruled that requiring the New York Rangers NHL club to migrate its website to a common technology platform managed by the NHL, rather than allowing its independent operation, is not clearly anticompetitive conduct that violates §1 under the "quick look" rule of reason. It affirmed the lower court's finding that the NHL's challenged conduct has several plausible procompetitive effects, including a standardized website layout to attract national sponsors and advertisers interested in uniform exposure across the NHL.com network, which is a key element of the NHL's strategy to enhance its national brand to better compete against other sports and entertainment products.

Other courts have expressed a similar reluctance to invalidate league restrictions on member clubs' individual sale of intellectual property rights such as television broadcasting rights under the "quick look" rule of reason. In *Chicago Professional Sports Ltd. Partnership v. NBA*, 95 F.3d 593 (7th Cir. 1996), the Seventh Circuit held that the NBA's limit on the number of games a club may televise on a superstation (e.g., WGN) and a league-imposed tax on televised games must be evaluated under a full rule of reason analysis, which would require proof that the NBA has market power from the perspective of television viewers or advertisers. In other words, to establish the requisite anticompetitive effects of the restrictions, a plaintiff challenging such restrictions must show there are no reasonable entertainment substitutes for NBA games from the perspective of television viewers (or no alternative means for companies to advertise their products to consumers with the same demographic characteristics). Consider whether the NBA's tax on superstation games should be any different for antitrust purposes than the NFL's relocation fee upheld by the Ninth Circuit in *Raiders II*, supra.

4. Sherman Act §2 Limits on Dominant Sports League's Responses to Formation of a Rival League

This section considers antitrust issues arising out of the formation of a new league that challenges an established league's dominance of a major professional league sport. An established league would not be receptive to a newcomer that threatens its popularity and profitability. Whether the threat is actual or simply potential, the established league may be tempted to react in ways that are anticompetitive and raise antitrust concerns.

Our focus here is on challenged restraints affecting interbrand competition between professional sports leagues or clubs that sell competing products within the U.S. sports industry. Similar issues may arise in connection with competition between promoters of individual performer sports. See, e.g., *Deutscher Tennis Bund v. ATP Tour, Inc.*, 610 F.3d 820 (3d Cir. 2010); *Kentucky Speedway, LLC v. National Assn. of Stock Car Auto Racing, Inc.*, 588 F.3d 908 (6th Cir. 2009); *Volvo N. Am. Corp. v. Men's Int'l Prof'l Tennis Council*, 857 F.2d 55 (2d Cir. 1988). Interbrand competition exists among sellers of different brands of products that are reasonable substitutes from the perspective of consumers. For example, this encompasses competition between professional leagues in the same sports (e.g., NFL and USFL football) or other sports with overlapping seasons (e.g., soccer and football), as well as competition between clubs in a different sport within the same geographical area (e.g., Chicago Bulls NBA team and Chicago Blackhawks NHL team).

Most antitrust challenges to restraints on interbrand competition have been brought under §2 of the Sherman Act, which prohibits monopolization or attempted monopolization. Unlike §1, which governs only concerted action, §2 applies to unilateral conduct. Monopolization requires proof that (1) the defendant possesses monopoly power in the relevant market; and (2) the defendant has willfully acquired or maintained that power rather than having grown or developed power as a consequence of a superior product, business acumen, or historical accident. *United States v. Grinnell Corp.*, 384 U.S. 563, 570-571 (1966). Attempted monopolization requires proof "(1) that the defendant has engaged in predatory or anticompetitive conduct with (2) a specific intent to monopolize and (3) a dangerous probability of achieving monopoly power." *Spectrum Sports, Inc. v. McQuillan*, 506 U.S. 447, 456 (1993). Although the elements of monopolization and attempted monopolization are different, both require analysis of the defendant's degree of control over the relevant market and a determination of whether its conduct is legal, fair competition on the merits or is illegal exclusionary conduct with anticompetitive market effects.

Determining whether a professional sports league has monopoly power for Sherman Act §2 purposes requires definition of both the relevant product and geographical markets and calculation of the defendant(s)' market share in order to evaluate the actual or potential anticompetitive effects of the challenged league rules or conduct. Although courts generally require at least a 70 percent market share to justify a finding of monopoly power, no rigid mathematical approach is used in §2 sports antitrust cases. Rather, the dispositive issue is whether the relevant market is appropriately defined, which determines whether the league has monopoly power and the corresponding ability to exclude rivals and prevent economic competition.

For example, in *American Football League v. National Football League*, 323 F.2d 124 (4th Cir. 1963), the Fourth Circuit ruled that the NFL did not have sufficient control of the market to prevent a newly formed rival from competing with it:

> The relevant market is nationwide, though the fact that there are a limited number of desirable sites for team locations bears upon the question of [the NFL]'s power to monopolize the national market. The District Court's finding that [the NFL] did not have the power to monopolize the relevant market appears plainly correct. In 1959, it occupied eleven of the thirty-one apparently desirable sites for team locations, but its occupancy of some of them as New York and San Francisco-Oakland was not exclusive, for those metropolitan areas were capable of supporting more than one team. Twenty of the thirty-one potentially desirable sites were entirely open to American. Indeed, the fact that the American League was successfully launched, could stage a full schedule of games in 1960, has competed very successfully for outstanding players, and has obtained advantageous contracts for national television coverage strongly supports the District Court's finding that [the NFL] did not have the power to prevent, or impede, the formation of the new league. Indeed, at the close of the 1960 season, representatives of the American League declared that the League's success was unprecedented.

There has been a historical tendency toward a single American major professional league for the most popular North American team sports of baseball, football, basketball, and hockey. Throughout the twentieth century, competition among rival leagues in the same sport has never continued for any appreciable period of time. See generally Paul Weiler, Leveling the Playing Field: How the Law Can Make Sports Better for Fans, 324-328 (2001) (analyzing history and economic reasons for this phenomenon). Most recently, two competing women's professional basketball leagues, the American Basketball League (ABL) and the Women's National Basketball Association (WNBA), began play in the late 1990s. The ABL, despite having some of the best women's basketball players on its clubs' rosters, ceased operations after only a few years of existence because of its inability to market its product and finance its operations as well as the WNBA, many of whose clubs are owned and operated by the NBA teams in their respective locations.

There may be certain inherent conditions in the professional sports industries that predispose each sport to dominance by one league at the major league level; the mere fact there is only a single major league for a particular sport does not violate §2 of the Sherman Act. One potential reason for this phenomenon is that fans may prefer a single champion for the highest level of competition within the sport. If so, over time, fans will prefer the product of one league over that of another, thereby leading to the demise of the disfavored league. There is no §2 violation if a league's market dominance results from winning the off-field competitive economic struggle by providing a superior entertainment product that is most desirable to sports fans. In *American Football League, supra*, the court held that the NFL could expand its business operations in response to increasing consumer demand for its product and compete with the AFL for the best available remaining geographical areas in which to place a professional football franchise, which is legal, fair competition on the merits.

On the other hand, this phenomenon may be the result of an established league's efforts to unfairly exclude a rival league, which reduces interbrand competition and harms consumers by reducing available entertainment options and increasing their cost. See generally Stephen F. Ross, *Antitrust Options to Redress Anticompetitive Restraints and Monopolistic Practices by Professional Sports Leagues*, 52 Case W. L. Rev. 133, 158-165 (2001) (providing historical description of dominant leagues' successful predatory practices to achieve and maintain monopoly power).

To be economically viable, a major professional sports league needs several resources, including (1) franchise owners with the financing and business acumen to successfully operate its member clubs, (2) teams in several large cities throughout the country with the population and economic base to support them, (3) access to adequate playing facilities, (4) major league–quality players, and (5) a national television broadcasting contract. Even if a new league is able to satisfy these minimum requirements, its long-term survival as a profitable independent entity is not ensured. Upstart leagues often fold after a relatively short period of existence because of financial problems or improper management and strategic business decisions. Or fans may choose to support an established league and its clubs rather than a new league and its members.

The following cases provides illustrative examples of a successful Sherman Act §2 suit against an established league for allegedly restricting access to essential inputs that a rival league needs to engage in competition.

PHILADELPHIA WORLD HOCKEY CLUB, INC. v. PHILADELPHIA HOCKEY CLUB, INC.

351 F. Supp. 462 (E.D. Pa. 1972)

HIGGINBOTHAM, District Judge.

I.   INTRODUCTION

. . . [F]rom what in 1917 was a relatively minor sports attraction, the National Hockey League has skated into the 1970's to a position of substantial wealth, power, broad spectator interest, international recognition and many superstars, all crescendoing into huge profits for both its owners and players. . . .

Since 1971, the World Hockey Association (hereinafter referred to as WHA) has attempted to enter major league professional hockey to become a real competitor in this field where the National Hockey League (hereinafter referred to as NHL) has for so long held a total monopolistic position as the sole supplier of major league hockey competition. The basic issue is whether through their reserve clause, affiliation agreements, and market power dominance, the National Hockey League has violated the federal antitrust laws and if such a violation is found, whether the WHA is entitled to relief at this preliminary injunction stage. . . .

II.   FINDINGS OF FACT

[EDS. The presence of qualified players of major league professional caliber is essential to the successful conduct of major league professional ice hockey competition. Unlike professional football and basketball, which can draw on an ample supply of talented players developed in competition at the college level in the United States at no cost to the member clubs of the professional leagues, the NHL has never had such a ready-made source of talent. It has invested millions of dollars to help support a system of amateur league and minor league hockey in Canada and the United States that gives youngsters an opportunity to play hockey and to develop their skills, and also provides a source of potential players of major league caliber.

There are more than 50,000 amateur hockey players in Canada and the United States, but very few have sufficiently developed skills to play immediately in the NHL. In 1972, approximately 7,000 Canadian players attained the age of 20 and were eligible for the NHL draft; only 152 were drafted by NHL clubs. Any and all of these 50,000 amateur players, including those subject to the NHL draft or actually drafted by an NHL club, but not successfully signed, are available to play in the WHA or any other hockey league.

Prior to the formation of the WHA in 1971, the NHL was the only major league professional hockey association in North America. In addition to the NHL, there are three other professional hockey leagues in North America. These are the American Hockey League (AHL), the Western Hockey League (WHL), and the Central Hockey League, formerly the Central Professional Hockey League (CHL), with a total of 24 teams. The best players are found in the NHL, the next best in the American and Western Hockey Leagues, and the lowest level of professional players is in the Central Hockey League. The International and Eastern Hockey Leagues are amateur or at best semiprofessional leagues; their players are generally less talented than those in the minor professional leagues.

NHL clubs have invested large sums for the development and support of professional minor league hockey clubs in Canada and the United States, many of which could not continue to operate without the subsidies provided by the NHL clubs. The NHL requires that each of its member teams must have an affiliation with a "player development team." Thus, at least 16 of the 24 professional minor league teams are owned or operated by or affiliated with NHL teams. All of the teams in the CHL are owned by NHL teams. In addition to the teams owned by NHL members, "there are almost an unlimited number of affiliations and loaning arrangements of various kinds."

The willingness of the NHL clubs to invest so heavily in the development of hockey players in the amateur and minor leagues is based in large part on their belief that if a player developed through this system signs a standard contract with an NHL club, that club will, because of the "reserve" clause, have the perpetual right to his services as a professional hockey player. NHL club owners have been insistent on the continuation of the reserve clause basically in its present form, and after unionizing, the NHL players have been consistently against this type of reserve clause.

In 1971, a special and highly confidential NHL Presidential Study Committee, which had representatives from six NHL clubs, was established to make recommendations with regard to several problems faced by the NHL in the light of the formation of the WHA. In May 1972, the NHL Board of Governors established a Legal Committee to develop and implement a policy with regard to players who had signed contracts with the WHA. It promptly employed a law firm to aid in this task. NHL president Campbell subsequently suggested that NHL clubs send a form letter to all players, particularly those who had signed with the WHA, reminding them of the club's contract rights and threatening litigation to enforce the reserve clause. NHL clubs sent such letters to particular players and instituted legal actions against 11 NHL players who had signed contracts with WHA teams to seek enforcement of the league's reserve clause. The targets of the suits included several well-known players, such as Bobby Hull, Derek Sanderson, and Gerry Cheevers.

More than 200 of the 345 of the players signed by WHA teams for the 1972-1973 playing season were subject to reserve clauses in their 1971-1972 contracts with the NHL, AHL, CHL, and WHL. Approximately 58 to 60 of them played for an NHL team during the past season. The remainder (more than 140 players) played with a minor league team last year. Of the 345 players who signed WHA contracts, four or five were enjoined from playing with their WHA teams as a result of the enforcement of the NHL's reserve clause.]

III. THE LABOR EXEMPTIONS OF THE SHERMAN ACT

[EDS. The court held that the nonstatutory labor exemption, which is considered in Chapter 7, does not immunize the NHL's reserve clause from antitrust scrutiny.]

IV. THE RELEVANT MARKET

A. RELEVANT PRODUCT MARKET

. . . In the leading case discussing relevant product market, *United States v. E. I. DuPont De Nemours & Co.*, 351 U.S. 377, 76 S.Ct. 994, 100 L.Ed. 1264 (1956), the Supreme Court stated:

> The varying circumstances of each case determine the result. In considering what is the relevant market for determining the control of price and competition, no more definite rule can be declared than that commodities reasonably interchangeable by consumers for the same purposes make up that "part of the trade or commerce," monopolization of which may be illegal.

351 U.S. at 395, 76 S.Ct. at 1007.

. . . The NHL argues that the relevant market for anti-trust purposes should include at a minimum both major league professional hockey and minor league professional hockey. Further, the NHL urges that from a realistic view of hockey the relevant market should be expanded beyond the professional and semi-professional leagues to include also the amateur leagues. In contrast, the WHA asserts that the relevant market is only major league professional hockey, namely the hockey played today in the National Hockey League. I find that the relevant market is major league professional hockey.

The rationale of *International Boxing Club v. United States*, 358 U.S. 242, 249-250, 79 S.Ct. 245, 250, 3 L.Ed.2d 270 (1959), is decisive here. From the vastness of innumerable boxing contests, the Court isolated as a relevant market championship boxing contests. They noted the common denominators of all boxing contests, whether championship or not, were: one ring, two boxers, and a fight under a similar set of rules, before a greater or lesser number of spectators. But, in spite of the apparent "physical identity of the product," the determinative difference in championship bouts was money: more revenue from (1) more spectators, (2) television rights, (3) movie rights, and (4) higher ticket prices.

Similarly, any hockey match whether in the NHL, the minor professional hockey leagues, or in the amateur leagues always includes one hockey rink, 12 hockey players, two referees, and a similar set of rules, before a greater or lesser number of spectators. That major league professional hockey is the relevant product here is substantiated by . . . higher ticket prices, increased television revenues, and greater players' *skill* and *salaries.*

Of course, the consumer is no longer king in sports; he has lost the unilateral power to demand and always get high quality competition. Yet, though his voice is weak, he is not totally impotent. He can withdraw his support when the level of performance becomes so outrageously low that he feels the admission price does not justify the quality of performance observed. There is a point where even avid fans will not support minor league performances for major league prices. This residuum of discretion in the sports fan to refrain from paying high prices for low performance is an additional factor in separating the minor leagues from the major professional league market.

A review of the record convinces me that above all else, the NHL owners are probably more shrewd as businessmen than they are as enthusiasts of sports. It is inconceivable that they would pay much larger salaries to major league players for any reason other than the fact that these players are more skillful, generally have more professional hockey experience, and as a group at least in the profits returned to the owners are worth the salaries paid. This profit pattern of payment to the players conclusively establishes that major and minor league hockey players are not interchangeable products. . . . I find the relevant product market to be major league professional hockey as it is currently played in the NHL.

B.   RELEVANT GEOGRAPHIC MARKET

In *Brown Shoe Co. v. United States*, 370 U.S. 294, 336-337, 82 S.Ct. 1502, 1530, 8 L.Ed.2d 510 (1962), the Supreme Court articulated the requirements for selecting the appropriate and relevant geographic market. The Court noted as follows:

> . . . The geographic market selected must, therefore, both "correspond to the commercial realities" (footnote omitted) of the industry and be economically significant. Thus, although the geographic market in some instances may encompass the entire Nation, under other circumstances it may be as small as a single metropolitan area. . . .

The record establishes that almost all of the hockey players currently playing in the NHL, began their skating careers in either Canadian or United States amateur hockey. The typical players' journey to the "big league" carried them through at least one of the five semi-professional leagues which play throughout the United States and Canada. Further, the NHL and WHA have teams at the present solely in the United States and Canada. Against this factual background presented by the plaintiffs, the defendants urge that the plaintiffs have available a potentially large source of supply of European players. However, in order to be guilty of monopolization under § 2 of the Sherman Act, 15 U.S.C. § 2, the WHA need not prove that the NHL has an international monopoly in the hockey players' market. The language of the Sherman Act itself does not require a monopolization of *all* the trade or commerce, but rather *any part* of the trade or commerce among the several states or with foreign nations.

. . . I find that the relevant geographic market here is the United States and Canada. . . .

VI. THE SHERMAN ACT § 2

. . . The WHA charges that the NHL has through a series of agreements and other concerted actions monopolized, conspired to monopolize, and attempted to monopolize major league professional hockey by (1) controlling the pool of players capable and available to play major league professional hockey, and (2) expanding the NHL so as to exclude the WHA from participation in major league professional hockey. . . .

. . . I hold that in the circumstances of this case, the three year restraint following the expiration of a current contract (considering this factor along with the other numerous interlocking agreements NHL has fashioned and shaped over the years to monopolize a hockey player's professional career) is unreasonable, and in violation of Section 2 of the Sherman Act. . . .

B. MONOPOLY POWER

. . . Here, through the use, *inter alia,* of (1) Standard Players' Contracts, including the "reserve clause" in paragraph 17 of that contract, (2) the agreements between the NHL and three of the major semi-professional leagues, and (3) the agreements between the professional and semi-professional leagues and the amateur leagues, it is clear that the NHL overwhelmingly controls the supply of players who are capable and available for play in a new league where the level of internal competitions fairly approaches the levels currently existing in the NHL. In an attempt to minimize the NHL's extraordinary degree of control over the players, the NHL asserts that there are many other available players who will shortly be able to play major league professional hockey. However, the relevant market place is the market place of *today*, not the market place of 1980 or even the market place of 1975. A monopolist may not today excuse his present predatory practices because someday in the future his total domination of the market place may be lessened.

The NHL's monopoly power is their power to control overwhelmingly the supply of hockey players who are today available for play in any major professional league. It is that total control by the NHL which I hold is proscribed by § 2 of the Sherman Act. One who builds the most modern steel mill cannot operate without an adequate supply of iron ore. The 50,000 amateur hockey players allegedly available to the WHA are not the "iron ore" from which viable competition can be built. If the WHA is to compete effectively for attendance and television rights with commensurate payments, the WHA must have a "show" which is equal or nearly equal to that of the NHL today. Since the WHA is a newcomer, the quality of play need not instantly equal that of the NHL, but there must be a prospect that the product will be nearly equal in a relatively short period of time.

. . . I find that the NHL possesses monopoly power in the relevant market. . . .

C. WILLFULNESS & INTENT

The mere possession of monopoly power in the relevant market does not alone constitute a violation of section 2 of the Sherman Act. There must also be "(2) the willful acquisition or maintenance of that power as distinguished from growth or development as a consequence of a superior product, business acumen, or historic accident." *United States v. Grinnell*, 384 U.S. 563, 86 S.Ct. 1698, 1704, 16 L.Ed.2d 778 (1966). The activities of the NHL go beyond mere possession of monopoly power in the relevant market to breach these aforementioned prohibitions articulated in *United States v. Grinnell, supra.*

The NHL has willfully acquired and maintained its monopoly power through the use of the many agreements. . . . Its continuing and overriding goal is to maintain a monopoly over the supply of major league professional hockey players.

The NHL employs devices such as reserve clauses, Standard Player Contracts, an NHL semi-professional league Joint-Affiliation Agreement, and control over the amateurs through the Pro-Am Agreement in which the amateurs agreed to recognize the NHL as the "sole and exclusive governing body of professional hockey." If the NHL reserve clause were valid for those players whose contracts terminated in September, 1972, then the NHL would have the power, directly or indirectly, to prevent any player under "contract" to the NHL or one of its affiliated minor professional leagues from playing with any other team or league outside the NHL System.

Upon reading the self-serving tributes for its expenditure of millions of dollars to develop amateur and minor league hockey, one might infer that the millions were spent solely for the honor and glory of amateur and minor league hockey. The NHL's motives were not quite so noble; these expenditures to develop the amateur and minor professional leagues were essential to maintain the NHL's monopolistic position. . . .

Keeping in mind both the many agreements employed by National Hockey League and its continuing expansion, it is apparent that the National Hockey League's intent is and was the willful acquisition and maintenance of a position as the only major professional hockey league in the United States and Canada. . . .

VII. PRELIMINARY INJUNCTIVE RELIEF

. . . Here, the injunction restraining the NHL from enforcing or attempting to enforce its reserve clause is not a contest involving just one superstar. Rather, it is a dispute of a substantially larger magnitude. The superstars in issue are many,

Bobby Hull, Derek Sanderson, Gerry Cheevers, John McKenzie, to name just a few of the players whose former NHL clubs will be precluded from enjoying their services as a result of this injunction. However, the players directly affected include more than 200 players who but for the formation of the WHA and the issuance of this preliminary injunctive relief would still be obligated to play with the NHL if the reserve clause is valid. . . .

The NHL is no shaky institution which will collapse if it loses a few superstars or even many average players during the pendency of this preliminary injunction. The NHL is merely sustaining the fate which monopolists must face when they can no longer continue their prior total dominance of the market. For the reality of today is that the federal antitrust laws preclude the continued implementation of NHL President Campbell's fondest dream that it remains "the *only* major professional hockey league operating from coast-to-coast in the United States [and] Canada." (Emphasis added.) . . .

The WHA and its member teams have demonstrated that they will be immediately irreparably injured by the enforcement of the reserve clause in that they will be deprived of the services of professional caliber players vital to the existence of a major professional league. . . .

For the foregoing reasons, the Preliminary Injunction should be granted. . . .

NOTES AND QUESTIONS

1. *Relevant Market for Players.* Why did the court find that "major and minor league hockey players are not interchangeable products"? Under what circumstances, if any, would it be appropriate to include college and minor league players in the same product market as major league players? Note that the current relevant geographical market for players (i.e., source of supply) in sports such as baseball, basketball, soccer, and hockey extends beyond the United States or North America, given the large number of foreign-born players playing in U.S. sports leagues. *Fraser v. Major League Soccer, L.L.C.*, 284 F.3d 47 (2002) (upholding jury's finding of a worldwide geographical market for elite soccer players).

2. *Fair Competition for Players Versus Illegal Exclusionary Conduct.* Although the *Philadelphia World Hockey Club* court recognized the need for "some type of intraleague reserve system," why were the NHL's player restraints found to violate §2? What relief did the court order to remedy this antitrust violation?

   A dominant league's clubs are free to compete fairly with a rival league's clubs for the services of the best available players, *American Football League v. National Football League*, 205 F. Supp. 60, 77 (D. Md. 1962), *aff'd*, 323 F.2d 124 (4th Cir. 1963), and enforce valid, existing player contracts, thereby preventing their players from switching leagues before their respective contracts expire. See, e.g., *Winnipeg Rugby Football Club, Ltd. v. Freeman*, 140 F. Supp. 365 (N.D. Ohio 1955); *Philadelphia Ball Club v. Lajoie*, 51 A. 973 (Pa. 1902). As one court explained, "Nobody has ever thought, so far as we can find, that in the absence of some monopolistic purpose every one had not the right to offer better terms to another's employee so long as the latter is free to leave." *Washington Capitols Basketball Club, Inc. v. Barry*, 419 F.2d 472, 478 (9th Cir. 1969).

UNITED STATES FOOTBALL LEAGUE v. NFL

842 F.2d 1335 (2d Cir. 1988)

WINTER, Circuit Judge.

This appeal follows a highly publicized trial and jury verdict of $1.00. The plaintiff is a now-defunct professional football league that began play in this decade; the defendant is a football league founded nearly seventy years ago. The older of the two leagues, the National Football League, is a highly successful entertainment product. . . . After three seasons and losses in the neighborhood of $200 million, the USFL played its last game in July 1985. Meanwhile, in October, 1984, blaming its older competitor for its difficulties, the USFL instituted this litigation. Plans to play in the fall of 1986 were abandoned after the jury's verdict that is the principal subject of this appeal. . . .

. . . The jury's finding of illegal monopolization of a market of major-league professional football was based upon evidence of NFL attempts to co-opt USFL owners, an NFL Supplemental Draft of USFL players, an NFL roster increase, and NFL conduct directed at particular USFL franchises. These activities, however, were hardly of sufficient impact to support a large damages verdict or to justify sweeping injunctive relief. For that reason, the USFL candidly admits that "at the heart of this case" are its claims that the NFL, by contracting with the three major networks and by acting coercively toward them, prevented the USFL from acquiring a network television contract indispensable to its survival. The jury expressly rejected the television claims. . . .

In 1970, the NFL entered into a contract with ABC to televise a game nationally on Monday nights. Since then, all three major television networks have broadcast NFL games, and the NFL's annual revenues from television have increased by more than 800 percent. . . .

The ABC, CBS and NBC contracts from 1970 onward have given each network rights of first negotiation and first refusal to decide whether to continue its NFL contract for subsequent years. The NFL's 1982-86 contracts were nonexclusive and did not forbid a network from televising another football league's games at any time when it was not broadcasting NFL games. NBC was thus legally free to televise to a particular city another league's games on Sunday afternoons directly opposite NFL games on CBS when there was no NFL game scheduled for NBC to be televised to that city. CBS had a similar option. ABC was legally free to televise another league's games all afternoon each Sunday. All three networks were legally free to telecast another league's games in prime time. Because the NFL was forbidden by its network contracts to televise games on cable, cable television contracts were open to a competing league, although such contracts are less lucrative than network contracts. When the NFL's network contracts expired in 1981 and 1986, the networks were free to contract with a competing league's games for all time slots.

The NFL's three-network "tie-up" was a central issue at trial. The USFL claimed that the NFL intentionally set out to tie up the three networks as a means of excluding competitors. In support of its theory, the USFL introduced a memorandum from NFL general counsel Jay Moyer written during the NFL's 1973 network contract negotiations stating that "an open network may well be an open invitation to formation of a new league." Commissioner Rozelle testified, however, that in 1970, before contacting ABC and signing the Monday night football contract with it, he unsuccessfully approached CBS and NBC, both of which already televised NFL games, about their interest in prime-time football. . . .

The USFL also sought to show that the NFL had placed unlawful pressure on the networks to prevent the broadcast of USFL games. Much of this evidence consisted of statements by USFL representatives and hearsay and speculation by third parties. Officials from the three networks and one cable network testified that the NFL had not exerted any pressure on them regarding the broadcast of USFL games. Several network officials did testify, however, that they feared that televising the USFL in the fall might jeopardize their NFL relationships. . . . Executives from all three major networks also testified that by 1986, after the USFL had left several large television markets and was encountering financial and other difficulties, the USFL was not an attractive entertainment product. . . .

6. MANAGEMENT OF THE USFL

The USFL was conceived and organized in 1981 to play in the spring rather than the fall. Its founders believed that public demand for football was not satisfied by the NFL's and the colleges' fall seasons; that cable television, which could not televise NFL games under the existing NFL-network contracts, would offer unique opportunities for television revenues and exposure; that a spring football league would face limited competition; that there was a sufficient supply of football players for two leagues; and that a spring league could draft college players and put them on the field even before the NFL draft.

The USFL's founders placed a high priority on the fans' perception of the quality of play. They intended to use major stadiums and to hire well-known coaches. At the same time, they wanted the league to control costs. For its first season, therefore, the USFL established budget guidelines for player salaries of between $1.3 and $1.5 million per team.

The USFL's founders did not seek to obtain a television contract for fall play. Before fielding a team, however, the USFL received bids for a spring television contract from ABC and NBC and from two cable networks, ESPN and the Turner Broadcasting System. The league entered a four-year contract with ABC, and a two-year contract with ESPN. . . . The USFL began with eight of its twelve teams in the nation's top ten television markets. The ABC contract required the USFL to field teams in the three largest television markets (New York, Los Angeles, and Chicago) and in at least four of the five other top-ten television markets in which teams were originally located (Philadelphia, Boston, Detroit, San Francisco/Oakland and Washington).

The USFL's first year of play, 1983, was a mixed success. The league received extensive media exposure when it signed Heisman Trophy winner Herschel Walker to a three-year, $3,250,000 contract. The Nielsen television rating for the first week of games was 14.2, a figure comparable to NFL ratings. As the season went on, however, the USFL's television ratings declined. . . . Average attendance for the year was approximately 25,000. Nevertheless, these figures were consistent with the league's and networks' preseason projections.

On the financial side, the picture was not as bright. The USFL lost a total of almost $40 million, or an average of $3.3 million per team. The league had projected losses of only about $2 million per year for each team over the first three years. The unanticipated financial losses were chiefly the result of the failure to stay within the original salary guidelines. . . .

The USFL's second year was marked by change. Four teams shifted locations. For example, the owner of the Chicago franchise exchanged that franchise for the Phoenix franchise, taking his winning Chicago coach and players while the original Phoenix team moved to Chicago under a new owner. The league, over the objection of some owners, expanded from twelve teams to eighteen. Five of the original owners left the league. Some of the new owners, notably Donald Trump of the New Jersey Generals, believed that the USFL ought to play in the fall. Thereafter, the issue of when to play became divisive, and several owners came to believe that Trump was trying to bring about a merger with the NFL that would include only some USFL teams.

The NFL introduced extensive evidence designed to prove that the USFL followed Trump's merger strategy, and that this strategy ultimately caused the USFL's downfall. The merger strategy, the NFL argued, involved escalating financial competition for players as a means of putting pressure on NFL expenses, playing in the fall to impair NFL television revenues, shifting USFL franchises out of cities where NFL teams played into cities thought to be logical expansion (through merger) cities for the NFL, and, finally, bringing the antitrust litigation now before us.

Throughout the second half of 1983 and early 1984, several USFL owners escalated spending on player salaries. . . . The USFL's spending on players greatly outpaced its revenues. The owner of the Los Angeles team, for example, committed the team to $13.1 million in salaries and bonuses for just one season. He even entered into a multiyear, $40 million contract with just one player, Steve Young of Brigham Young University.

By the end of the 1984 season, USFL franchises in two of the top three television markets, Chicago and Los Angeles, had failed, and only four of the original owners remained in the league. The league was not a failure as entertainment, however. Despite a decline in the USFL's television ratings . . . ABC exercised its option to carry the USFL in the spring of 1985 at $14 million and offered a new contract worth $175 million for four years in the spring beginning in 1986. ESPN offered a contract worth $70 million over three years.

Nevertheless, during an August 1984 owners' meeting, the USFL decided to move to the fall in 1986. This decision was made despite: (i) ABC's warning that such a move would breach its contract for the spring of 1985 and 1986; (ii) the contrary recommendations of a management consulting firm, McKinsey & Company, which the USFL had retained for $600,000 to consider the advisability of a fall season; and (iii) the contrary recommendations of the USFL's directors of operations and marketing.

Moreover, Eddie Einhorn, a USFL owner who was to represent the USFL in negotiations to secure a network contract for the fall, warned that moving from large television markets to "merger" cities too quickly might preclude the securing of a network contract. Nevertheless, in the ensuing months, the USFL withdrew from Chicago, Detroit, Philadelphia, Pittsburgh and Washington, D.C.—each a large television market with an NFL team—and moved into Baltimore (which had lost its NFL team in 1984) and Orlando (which had no NFL team). Through mergers, the USFL bolstered franchises in Oakland (which had lost the NFL Raiders to Los Angeles) and Phoenix (which had been discussed as a possible NFL expansion city). The decision to move to the fall damaged the USFL's relations with ABC and ESPN. The former withheld a significant portion of the USFL's rights fees for the 1985 season, while the latter demanded a renegotiation of its proposed 1985-87 USFL contract. . . .

... The USFL's 1985 "lame-duck" spring season appears to have been affected adversely by the now publicly announced move to the fall. The league's television ratings declined to 4.1 on ABC and 2.0 on ESPN. By the end of the season, several owners had withdrawn financial support for their teams, and a number of clubs were no longer meeting their payrolls and other bills. The USFL scheduled eight teams for its fall 1986 season, which was ultimately cancelled after the verdict in this case. Only one team (New Jersey), was in a top-ten television market. One other team (Tampa Bay), was in a top-twenty market. Three teams were located in Florida (Jacksonville, Orlando and Tampa Bay) but only one was west of the Mississippi River (Phoenix). In three years, USFL teams had left fourteen of the twenty-two cities in which they had played. ...

DISCUSSION

On appeal, the USFL raises a host of claims with respect to the NFL's liability, the district court's evidentiary rulings, damages charge, and denial of injunctive relief.

1.   LIABILITY

a.   The Sports Broadcasting Act

The USFL contends that the Sports Broadcasting Act of 1961 limits the antitrust exemption for pooled-rights contracts to a single contract with one network. ...

In any event, the passage of the 1966 NFL-AFL merger statute provides conclusive evidence that Congress did not intend the 1961 Act to prohibit NFL contracts with more than one network. When considering this legislation, Congress was explicitly informed that the merged league would continue to broadcast its games on "at least 2 networks," and no concern whatsoever was expressed in Congress that such conduct was either undesirable or would go beyond the scope of the 1961 Act's exemption. ... The lack of a "one network" limitation in the 1966 merger bill thus dooms the USFL's claims. Accordingly, we hold that the mere existence of the NFL contracts with the three networks does not violate the antitrust laws. ...

h.   Essential-Facilities Charge

Finally, the USFL contends that it was held to an improperly high standard of proof on its "essential-facilities" claim. We set out the pertinent charge:

> Plaintiffs allege that defendants violated Sections [1] and [2] of the Sherman Act by conspiring to and in fact denying plaintiffs access to a satisfactory national broadcast television contract for future seasons, with any one of the three networks. The legal basis for this particular claim by plaintiffs is that a network contract is an essential facility which the USFL or any other professional football league needs in order to compete in major league professional football. ...

In order to prove their essential "facilities" claim, plaintiffs must prove all of the following elements by a preponderance of the evidence:

> First: That a national broadcast television contract with at least one of the three networks, CBS, NBC or ABC is essential to the ability of a professional football league to compete successfully in the United States;

Second: that potential competitors of the NFL cannot as a practical matter, duplicate the benefits of a network contract;

Third: That the defendants control access to each of the three networks, that is, the defendants themselves have the ability by their actions to deny actual or potential competitors, such as the USFL, access to national broadcast television—access to a national broadcast television contract;

Fourth: That the defendants through their actions have exercised their ability to deny actual or potential competitors access to a national broadcast television contract by denying the USFL such access;

Fifth: That a national broadcast television contract between one or more of the networks and a professional football league other than the NFL would not interfere with any of the defendants' lawful dealings with those networks.

The USFL argues first that this charge erred in failing to distinguish between a network television contract in the spring and one in the fall. The charge did, however, address the USFL's denial of "access to a *satisfactory* national broadcast contract for future seasons" (emphasis added). The jury was well aware of the USFL's claim that a spring contract was unsatisfactory as an "inferior facility" or "minor league." It thus either rejected that characterization of spring football or rejected the USFL's claim that the NFL could deny the USFL access to a network in the fall. . . .

3.   THE DISTRICT COURT'S DAMAGES INSTRUCTIONS

. . . The jury was given the following nominal damages instruction:

> Just because you have found the fact of some damage resulting from a given unlawful act, that does not mean that you are required to award a dollar amount of damages resulting from that act. You may find, for example, that you are unable to compute the monetary damages resulting from the wrongful act, except by engaging in speculation or guessing, or you find that you cannot separate out the amount of the losses caused by the wrongful act from the amount caused by other factors, including perfectly lawful competitive acts and including business decisions made by the plaintiffs or the plaintiffs' own mismanagement. Or you may find that plaintiffs failed to prove an amount of damages.
>
> You may decline to award damages under such circumstances, or you may award a nominal amount, say $1.

The jury's $1.00 award was consistent with this instruction. The NFL offered much evidence of self-destructive USFL decisions, and the jury's nominal award suggests that it credited this proof, as it was free to do. . . .

4.   THE DISTRICT COURT'S DENIAL OF INJUNCTIVE RELIEF

Finally, the USFL claims that the district court should have granted sweeping injunctive relief under Section 16 of the Clayton Act, 15 U.S.C. § 26 (1982). In particular, the USFL requested membership in the NFL, separation of the NFL into two leagues, each league being limited to one network, or a prohibition on the NFL from broadcasting its games in more than one afternoon time slot on Sunday. Judge Leisure held that the requested relief was unrelated to the monopolization of the market for major-league professional football verdict and not justified by the record as a whole.

The USFL contends that the jury's monopolization verdict compelled the district court to "pry open to competition [the] market that has been closed by defendants' illegal restraints." However, this argument simply glosses over the critical fact that the jury did not find the NFL liable on any of the USFL's television-related claims. With regard to the findings implied by the monopolization verdict that the NFL engaged in predatory conduct through attempts to co-opt USFL owners, creation of a Supplemental Draft, or expansion in roster size, Judge Leisure denied relief on the ground that the USFL provided no evidence that such conduct was likely to continue or recur. The USFL has not asked us to overturn that denial of relief.

Instead, the USFL seeks sweeping injunctive relief on the ground that the NFL's single-league structure, in conjunction with television contracts with the three networks, creates an impenetrable barrier to entry by a competing league into the market of professional football. No matter what the jury found, however, such relief would not have been appropriate. First, Congress has authorized the NFL's single-league structure and its joint economic operations. Second, at the time the district court denied the relief, the NFL's contracts with the networks had expired. . . . There was only free competition between the NFL's product and the USFL's product. Of course, the district court also properly rejected this claim in view of the jury's outright rejection of all of the USFL's television-related claims.

What the USFL seeks is essentially a judicial restructuring of major-league professional football to allow it to enter. Because of the explicit congressional authorization in 1966 for the NFL-AFL merger and single-league operation, the USFL does not attack the league structure directly. Instead, the USFL asks us to prevent networks from broadcasting, and fans from watching, NFL games in the hope that they will turn to the USFL. Absent a showing of an unlawful barrier to entry, however, new sports leagues must be prepared to make the investment of time, effort and money that develops interest and fan loyalty and results in an attractive product for the media. The jury in the present case obviously found that patient development of a loyal following among fans and an adherence to an original plan that offered long-run gains were lacking in the USFL. Instead, the USFL quickly changed to a strategy of competition with the NFL in the fall, hoping thereby to force a merger of a few USFL teams into the NFL. That led to a movement of USFL teams out of large television markets and a resultant reduction in value of USFL games to television. As USFL owner and negotiator Einhorn predicted, abandoning major television markets precluded the possibility of obtaining a network contract. The USFL hoped, however, that if a merger did not occur, a jury verdict in the instant litigation followed by a decree effectively forcing a network to televise its product would save the day. Instead, the jury found that the failure of the USFL was not the result of the NFL's television contracts but of its own decision to seek entry into the NFL on the cheap.

CONCLUSION

For the foregoing reasons, we affirm the jury's verdict and the judgments entered thereon. . . .

NOTES AND QUESTIONS

1. *Appropriate Relief.* Why did the jury award the USFL only $1 in damages (which is automatically trebled under the antitrust laws)? Note that the USFL, by proving the NFL was guilty of monopolization, was awarded approximately $5.5 million in attorney fees as a prevailing party. What, if any, specific exclusionary conduct should be enjoined to remedy the NFL's illegal conduct and create a competitive market in the United States professional football market?

    The Second Circuit refused to grant the USFL's proposed "sweeping injunctive relief" that it characterized as "essentially a judicial restructuring of major league professional football to allow it to enter." Specifically, what did the USFL ask to court to do, and why were these proposals rejected?

2. *Policy Considerations.* As a policy matter, what form of judicial relief for a §2 antitrust violation—simply enjoining specific exclusionary practices, or requiring a league to restructure its business operations or divest certain aspects—is in sports fans' best interests?

    Some commentators argue that the historical pattern of anticompetitive practices by the dominant major professional sports leagues justify breaking the existing monopoly leagues into two or more independent competing leagues. James Quirk and Rodney Fort, Hard Ball—The Abuse of Power in Pro Team Sports, 171-186 (1999); Stephen Ross, *Monopoly Sports Leagues*, 73 Minn. L. Rev. 643 (1989). Professors Quirk and Fort explain:

    > We don't want the courts or regulatory bodies to be micromanaging the sports industry—instead, we want owners and general managers of teams to make the same kinds of decisions they make today, but in a competitive market environment, not in the present monopoly setup. If there is one thing about which economists are in agreement, it is that decentralized decision making in a competitive market environment leads to outcomes that are in the best interests of consumers, and that is all we are proposing here.

    Id. at 177-178. They continue:

    > Our proposal does not involve the creation of a regulatory authority nor the intervention of courts into the day-to-day decision making in pro team sports. Instead, under our solution, the role of the government and the courts in pro team sports would be what it is in every other industry, as a corrective to monopolistic abuses if they arise again in the future.

    Id. at 182.

    However, others question whether forced divestiture ultimately would be an effective remedy: "A once-and-for-all intervention to break up each current league monopoly into three or four competing leagues would provide the ideal solution . . . [but] there remains the crucial practical question of whether competition among major leagues can endure over the longer run." Paul Weiler, Leveling the Playing Field: How the Law Can Make Sports Better for Fans 333 (2000).

PROBLEM 6-3

Since the American Basketball League (ABL) ceased operations, the WNBA has been the only women's professional basketball league in the United States. It has 12 teams, primarily in cities in which NBA teams play. It is a summer league that plays its games from May through September (when the NBA is not playing). Each WNBA team has a roster of 11 players and plays 32 regular season games. ESPN2 nationally televises a regular season "game of the week" and all of the league's play-off games. The WNBA currently is negotiating with both ESPN and ESPN2 to televise more games in the future.

Because of the increasing popularity of women's professional basketball, a group of wealthy investors is seeking to resurrect the ABL as an eight-team league with franchises in different American cities than the WNBA's clubs. They plan to play a 24-game regular season, with each club having a roster of ten players. The ABL's season will run from October through December.

The WNBA's commissioner is considering whether the league should increase its regular season to 36 games and allow six teams (rather than the current four teams) to participate in the WNBA play-offs. This would extend the WNBA's season into late October. She also is pondering whether to recommend that the league go forward with its plan to expand into Boston and Dallas, two cities in which ABL franchises will be located. She also is concerned about the enforceability of a provision in the WNBA standard player contract that prohibits a player from playing professional basketball for anyone other than her current team while the contract is in effect.

Advise the WNBA commissioner regarding any possible antitrust problems and how to minimize any potential liability.

CHAPTER
7

Labor Relations in Professional Sports

A. INTRODUCTION

Contract, labor, and antitrust law historically have been the most important areas of law regulating labor relations between professional athletes and professional sports clubs and leagues, or the organizers of individual performer sports events. The chronology of professional sports leagues reveals a corresponding chronology regarding the prevailing legal principles that have helped shape the development of the professional sports industries during particular periods of time. Contract law was the first guiding light. Antitrust law concerns did not play a major role until the 1950s. Labor relations and labor law weighed in heavily, at least as to team sports, in the late 1960s. From the 1970s to the present day, the combination of contracts, antitrust, and labor law has significantly influenced the development of professional sports leagues in the United States. Together, these three areas of law are of great importance in understanding why professional sports leagues and associations are what they are today and how they will conduct business in the future.

This chapter begins by exploring the basic application of contract law in professional sports and then turns to labor law with an analysis of five important, interrelated labor law areas that have substantially affected professional sports. These five areas are (1) the collective bargaining process, collective bargaining agreements, and uniform player contracts; (2) professional team sports drug testing regimes; (3) the activities of either a league and its clubs or the players union that constitute unfair labor practices under the NLRA; (4) the duty of a players union to represent all of its constituents fairly; and (5) the labor arbitration process established to resolve disputes between players and the league or their clubs. This chapter then explores the complex intersection between labor and antitrust law, including the statutory and non-statutory labor exemptions and the application of antitrust law to professional sports industry labor market restraints. Finally, because there is a global labor market for many professional sports (e.g., soccer, basketball, hockey, and baseball), this chapter briefly explores some European and other international labor relations issues.

For a more extensive general analysis of labor relations in the professional sports industries, see Robert C. Berry, William B. Gould IV, and Paul D.

Staudohar, Labor Relations in Professional Sports (1986); Robert C. Berry and William B. Gould IV, *A Long Deep Drive to Collective Bargaining: Of Players, Owners, Brawls and Strikes*, 31 Case Western Reserve L. Rev. 685-813 (Summer 1981). For a history of baseball's early labor problems, see Lee Lowenfish and T. Lupien, The Imperfect Diamond (1980). See also Marvin Miller, A Whole Different Ballgame: The Sport and Business of Baseball (1991) and Bowie Kuhn, Hardball: The Education of a Baseball Commissioner (1987). For an informative general introduction to labor law and labor relations, see William B. Gould IV, A Primer on American Labor Law (4th ed. 2004) and Douglas E. Ray, Calvin W. Sharpe, and Robert N. Strassfeld, Understanding Labor Law (3d ed. 2011).

B. CONTRACT LAW

Owners of the first professional sports teams encountered player contract problems almost from the outset of their business operations. When an outstanding player was contractually bound to play for a particular club, but another club desired his services, legal problems ensued.

1. *The Early Cases*

One of the first player contract disputes involved Samuel Washington Wise, who in 1882 refused to honor his contract with the Cincinnati club of the newly formed American Association. In 1884, Tony Mullane, one of the better-known pitchers in that era, was sued by the short-lived Union Association as a result of a contract dispute. Little is known of the results of those cases, although the Union Association lasted so briefly that one can safely predict that Mullane was soon free to play for whomever he wished.

In 1890, the Players League was formed—ill-fated on the playing fields but notable for the litigation its creation produced. The question raised in two early cases was whether star ballplayers, Buck Ewing and John Montgomery Ward, could escape being bound by their contracts with the National League's New York club or, to the contrary, be enjoined from jumping to the nascent Players League. In both cases the players prevailed. See *Metropolitan Exhibition Co. v. Ewing*, 42 F. 198 (C.C.S.D.N.Y. 1890); *Metropolitan Exhibition Co. v. Ward*, 9 N.Y.S. 779 (N.Y. Sup. Ct. 1890).

The *Ewing* court recognized the availability of a negative injunction in appropriate circumstances. If granted, a player in breach of an existing contract would be prohibited from playing for another club. The court, however, held that the subject player contract was not sufficiently definite to warrant a negative injunction. The club's right to retain rights to the player at the end of the contract was not adequately defined, and there was insufficient evidence of general custom and usage in the trade to define the contract's terms.

The *Ward* court also recognized the appropriateness of granting injunctive relief in some cases, focusing on the requirement that there be a likelihood that the club would succeed at trial on the merits on its breach of contract claim against the player. The court expressed concern about the player contract's indefinite terms and its lack of mutuality. As to the latter point, which was at issue in many of these early cases, the court emphasized that the club could terminate the contract almost at will while the player was potentially bound to play for the club as long as it wanted him. The court concluded that this situation evidenced a lack of required mutuality of contractual obligations sufficient to deny injunctive relief.

The leading early case emanated from conflicts associated with the formation of the American League in 1900, which motivated National League star Napoleon Lajoie's efforts to leave the league's Philadelphia club and join its crosstown rival in the new American League.

PHILADELPHIA BALL CLUB, LTD. v. LAJOIE
51 A. 973 (Pa. 1902)

POTTER, J.

The defendant in this case contracted to serve the plaintiff as a baseball player for a stipulated time. During that period he was not to play for any other club. He violated his agreement, however, during the term of his engagement, and, in disregard of his contract, arranged to play for another and a rival organization. The plaintiff, by means of this bill, sought to restrain him during the period covered by the contract. The court below refused an injunction, holding that to warrant the interference prayed for "the defendant's services must be unique, extraordinary, and of such a character as to render it impossible to replace him; so that his breach of contract would result in irreparable loss to the plaintiff." In the view of the court, the defendant's qualifications did not measure up to this high standard. The trial court was also of opinion that the contract was lacking in mutuality, for the reason that it gave plaintiff an option to discharge defendant on 10 days' notice, without a reciprocal right on the part of defendant.

. . . We think, however, that in refusing relief unless the defendant's services were shown to be of such a character as to render it impossible to replace him he has taken extreme ground. It seems to us that a more just and equitable rule is . . ." [w]here one person agrees to render personal services to another, which require and presuppose a special knowledge, skill, and ability in the employée, so that in case of a default the same service could not easily be obtained from others, although the affirmative specific performance of the contract is beyond the power of the court, its performance will be negatively enforced by enjoining its breach. . . . The damages for breach of such contract cannot be estimated with any certainty, and the employer cannot, by means of any damages, purchase the same service in the labor market." We have not found any case going to the length of requiring, as a condition of relief, proof of the impossibility of obtaining equivalent service. It is true that the injury must be irreparable; but, as observed by Mr. Justice Lowrie in *Com. v. Pittsburgh & C. R. Co.*, 24 Pa. 160, 62 Am. Dec. 372: "The argument that there is no 'irreparable damage' would not be so often used by wrongdoers if they would take the trouble to discover that the word 'irreparable' is a very unhappily chosen one, used in expressing the rule that an injunction may issue to prevent wrongs of a repeated and continuing character, or which occasion damages which are estimated only by conjecture, and not by any accurate standard." We are therefore within the term whenever it is shown that no certain pecuniary standard exists for the measurement of the damages. . . .

The court below finds from the testimony that "the defendant is an expert baseball player in any position; that he has a great reputation as a second baseman; that his place would be hard to fill with as good a player; that his withdrawal from the team would weaken it, as would the withdrawal of any good player, and would probably make a difference in the size of the audiences attending the game." We think that, in thus stating it, he puts it very mildly, and that the evidence would warrant a stronger finding as to the ability of the defendant as an expert ball player. He has been for several years in the service of the plaintiff club, and has been re-engaged from season to season at a constantly increasing salary. He has become thoroughly familiar with the action and methods of the other players in the club, and his own work is peculiarly meritorious as an integral part of the team work which is so essential. In addition to these features which render his services of peculiar and special value to the plaintiff, and not easily replaced, Lajoie is well known, and has great reputation among the patrons of the sport, for ability in the position which he filled, and was thus a most attractive drawing card for the public. He may not be the sun in the baseball firmament, but he is certainly a bright particular star. We feel, therefore, that the evidence in this case justifies the conclusion that the services of the defendant are of such a unique character, and display such a special knowledge, skill, and ability, as renders them of peculiar value to the plaintiff, and so difficult of substitution that their loss will produce "irreparable injury," in the legal significance of that term, to the plaintiff. . . .

But the court below was also of the opinion that the contract was lacking in mutuality of remedy, and considered that as a controlling reason for the refusal of an injunction. The opinion quotes the nineteenth paragraph of the contract, which gives to the plaintiff a right of renewal for the period of six months, beginning April 15, 1901, and for a similar period in two successive years thereafter. The seventeenth paragraph also provides for the termination of the contract upon 10 days' notice by the plaintiff. But the eighteenth paragraph is also of importance, and should not be overlooked. It provides as follows: "(18) In consideration of the faithful performance of the conditions, covenants, undertakings, and promises herein by the said party of the second part, inclusive of the concession of the options of release and renewal prescribed in the seventeenth and nineteenth paragraphs, the said party of the first part, for itself and its assigns, hereby agrees to pay to him for his services for said term the sum of twenty-four hundred dollars, payable as follows," etc. And, turning to the fifth paragraph, we find that it provides expressly for proceedings, either in law or equity, "to enforce the specific performance by the said party of the second part, or to enjoin said party of the second part from performing services for any other person or organization during the period of service herein contracted for; and nothing herein contained shall be construed to prevent such remedy in the courts, in case of any breach of this agreement by said party of the second part, as said party of the first part, or its assigns, may elect to invoke."

We have, then, at the outset, the fact that the paragraphs now criticised and relied upon in defense were deliberately accepted by the defendant, and that such acceptance was made part of the inducement for the plaintiff to enter into the contract. We have the further fact that the contract has been partially executed by services rendered, and payment made therefor, so that the situation is not now the same as when the contract was wholly executory. The relation between the parties has been so far changed as to give to the plaintiff an equity, arising out of the part performance, to insist upon the completion of the agreement according to its terms by the defendant. This equity may be distinguished from the original right under the contract itself, and it might well be questioned whether the court would not be justified in giving effect to it by injunction, without regard to the mutuality or nonmutuality in the original contract. The plaintiff has so far performed its part of the contract in entire good faith, in every detail, and it would therefore be inequitable to permit the defendant to withdraw from the agreement at this late day. . . .

. . . In the contract now before us the defendant agreed to furnish his skilled professional services to the plaintiff for a period which might be extended over three years by proper notice given before the close of each current year. Upon the other hand, the plaintiff retained the right to terminate the contract upon 10 days' notice and the payment of salary for that time and the expenses of defendant in getting to his home. But the fact of this concession to the plaintiff is distinctly pointed out as part of the consideration for the large salary paid to the defendant, and is emphasized as such; and owing to the peculiar nature of the services demanded by the business, and the high degree of efficiency which must be maintained, the stipulation is not unreasonable. Particularly is this true when it is remembered that the plaintiff has played for years under substantially the same regulations.

We are not persuaded that the terms of this contract manifest any lack of mutuality in remedy. Each party has the possibility of enforcing all the rights stipulated for in the agreement. It is true that the terms make it possible for the plaintiff to put an end to the contract in a space of time much less than the period during which the defendant has agreed to supply his personal services; but mere difference in the rights stipulated for does not destroy mutuality of remedy. Freedom of contract covers a wide range of obligation and duty as between the parties, and it may not be impaired, so long as the bounds of reasonableness and fairness are not transgressed. . . .

. . . The defendant sold to the plaintiff, for a valuable consideration, the exclusive right to his professional services for a stipulated period, unless sooner surrendered by the plaintiff, which could only be after due and reasonable notice and payment of salary and expenses until the expiration. Why should not a court of equity protect such an agreement until it is terminated? The court cannot compel the defendant to play for the plaintiff, but it can restrain him from playing for another club in violation of his agreement. No reason is given why this should not be done, except that presented by the argument, that the right given to the plaintiff to terminate the contract upon 10 days' notice destroys the mutuality of the remedy. But to this it may be answered that, as already stated, the defendant has the possibility of enforcing all the rights for which he stipulated in the agreement, which is all that he can reasonably ask. Furthermore, owing to the peculiar nature and circumstances of the business, the reservation upon the part of the plaintiff to terminate upon short notice does not make the whole contract inequitable.

In this connection another observation may be made, which is that the plaintiff, by the act of bringing this suit, has disavowed any intention of exercising the right to terminate the contract on its own part. This is a necessary inference from its action in asking the court to exercise its equity power to enforce the agreement made by the defendant not to give his services to any other club. Besides, the remedy by injunction is elastic and adaptable, and is wholly within the control of the court. If granted now, it can be easily dissolved whenever a change in the circumstances or in the attitude of the plaintiff should seem to require it. The granting or refusal of an injunction or its continuance is never a matter of strict right, but is always a question of discretion, to be determined by the court in view of the particular circumstances.

Upon a careful consideration of the whole case, we are of opinion that the provisions of the contract are reasonable, and that the consideration is fully adequate. The evidence shows no indications of any attempt at overreaching or unfairness. Substantial justice between the parties requires that the court should restrain the defendant from playing for any other club during the term of his contract with the plaintiff. . . .

The specifications of error are sustained, and the decree of the court below is reversed, and the bill is reinstated; and it is ordered that the record be remitted to the court below for further proceedings in accordance with this opinion.

NOTES AND QUESTIONS

1. *Negative Injunction.* Although the relevant contractual language was essentially the same, the *Lajoie* court (unlike the *Ewing* and *Ward* courts) held that the subject contract was sufficiently definite and mutual to be enforceable. Which of these differing judicial views is most persuasive? Why? For the past century, *Lajoie* has represented the prevailing judicial view regarding the availability of equitable relief to remedy a professional athlete's breach of contract. Pursuant to the so-called negative injunction, a player is not ordered to perform for his former club, but is instead ordered not to perform for his new club or elsewhere. A negative injunction may be granted if the court concludes that damages alone (which may be uncertain and very difficult to ascertain) are not an adequate legal remedy for loss of a player's services. How would a club's damages for a player's nonperformance because of his breach of contract be calculated? (Hint: The standard measure of damages for breach of contract is to award the nonbreaching party the "benefit of the bargain," otherwise termed the expectation interest.) What is the appropriate nature and scope of injunctive relief?

2. *Affirmative Injunction.* Because of the Thirteenth Amendment prohibition of involuntary servitude and judicial reluctance to police compliance with the terms of an employment contract, courts generally do not order a player to honor his contract. Is it ever appropriate for a court to order a player under contract to play for his current club? See Geoff Rapp, *Affirmative Injunctions in Athletic Employment Contracts: Rethinking the Place of the Lumley Rule in American Sports Law*, 16 Marq. Sports L. Rev. 261 (2006) (arguing in favor of specific performance enforceable by affirmative injunction as a remedy for player's holdout in breach of his employment contract).

3. The legal victory by the Philadelphia National League club was largely illusory. After the Pennsylvania court's decision, Lajoie was traded by the Philadelphia American League club to its American League counterpart in Cleveland. The National League attempted to enforce its Pennsylvania decree in Ohio but was rebuffed. See *Philadelphia Baseball Club v. Lajoie*, 13 Ohio Dec. 504 (1902). Thus, Lajoie never returned to the National League. The only practical effect of the Pennsylvania decision was that Lajoie did not risk contempt of court by playing in that state until the National and American Leagues reached an agreement in 1903 that allowed players such as Lajoie to remain with their chosen ball clubs.

4. Lajoie, known as the "Big Frenchman," achieved several notable milestones in his long baseball career. His .422 batting average in 1901 is still the American League single-season high mark, topped in the post-1900 era only by Rogers Hornsby's .424 record in 1924 for the St. Louis Cardinals. Lajoie's playing career spanned 21 seasons. He had 9,589 official at bats, 3,251 hits, and compiled a career batting average of .339. He was elected to baseball's Hall of Fame in the second year of its existence. The only players selected ahead of him were Babe Ruth, Walter Johnson, Ty Cobb, Christy Mathewson, and Honus Wagner. Lajoie is also noted for the fact that when he managed the Cleveland club late in his career, the team became known as the Cleveland Naps.

2.   *Modern Judicial View*

By and large, cases such as *Lajoie* have arisen when a rival league is formed and players are enticed to abandon their present teams, lured by more lucrative contracts offered by new clubs. Such was the situation not only in *Lajoie* but also in the *Ward* and *Ewing* cases. During the twentieth century, several new professional leagues were created, particularly after World War II. The inspiration for new leagues was the result of a combination of factors. The sport's increased popularity was the primary factor, aided in great part by the developing technologies of radio and television. As an established league's revenues increased, so did the economic incentives for new rival leagues to form.

Baseball's National League, after being challenged by the upstart American League at the beginning of the twentieth century, joined with the American League in 1903 to create Major League Baseball. But the combined leagues then had to fight off the Federal League (founded in 1914) and later the Mexican League (1946). In 1949 the National Basketball Association (formed in 1946 as the Basketball Association of America) renamed itself after absorbing teams from the original National Basketball League, then faced challenges from the American Basketball League (1961) and the American Basketball Association (1967). The National Football League, as it became increasingly popular, dealt with a myriad of rivals, notably the All America Football Conference (1946), the American Football League (AFL) (1960), the World Football League (1973), and the United States Football League (1983). The World Hockey Association (1972) lasted a few tenuous years in competition with the National Hockey League, with the WHA finally succumbing as four of its clubs were absorbed by the established league. Some rival leagues lasted only a year, while others persevered longer. Some new leagues were sufficient nuisances that a few of their teams were permitted to join the established league. The most successful rival league, in addition to baseball's American League, that developed in the twentieth century was the AFL, which was allowed to merge in its entirety with the NFL through an act of Congress (which is discussed in *Mid-South Grizzlies v. NFL*, set forth in Chapter 6).

The formation of rival leagues led to vast amounts of litigation. Clubs in established leagues brought breach of contract suits and sought negative injunctions against players seeking to jump to clubs in new leagues. (As discussed in Chapter 6, the upstart league frequently responded by asserting antitrust law claims against the established league and its clubs.)

Two issues typically raised in breach of contract require close scrutiny: (1) whether a negative injunction is necessary to prevent imminent and irreparable harm to the breaching player's former club and (2) whether the requested injunction is reasonable in its duration and scope. Although other issues such as mutuality of obligation frequently were raised in the early cases, these two issues historically have been most important.

a.   Imminent and Irreparable Harm

The *Lajoie* court concluded that a professional player of Lajoie's status was sufficiently special to merit injunctive relief to prevent his breach of contract. The court focused on the irreparable harm to Lajoie's club if it lost a player of his ability prior to the expiration of his contract, observing that "[h]e may not be the sun in the baseball firmament, but he is certainly a bright particular star." 51 A. at 974.

More recently, courts have not required that a player be irreplaceable, only that it be shown that he has unique skills not *easily* replaced, and in evaluating whether a professional athlete has "unique" skills, courts have reached different conclusions using variant measures. In *Winnipeg Rugby Football Club v. Freeman*, 140 F. Supp. 365 (N.D. Ohio 1955), a federal court opined that even if the player was not unique by simply being a "good" NFL player, he might be unique in the Canadian Football League, where the quality of play might be lower. Thus, the player, who was in breach, was enjoined from playing for an NFL club. In *Dallas Cowboys Football Club, Inc. v. Harris*, 348 S.W.2d 37 (Tex. Civ. App. 1961), the court ruled that a player who played for only one year with minimal success could be found not "unique," but the subject player had not proved his "nonunique" status. Based on these cases and others, even if a court considers evidence that a player is not unique, the player has a substantial burden to prove this factually. Today, it is probably a safe assumption that those who make the major leagues in any sport are almost certain to be characterized as "unique."

The standard player contracts in all major leagues have a provision stating that the player acknowledges he is unique and that a negative injunction can be obtained against him if he refuses to perform. Although this is not necessarily conclusive and a court or arbitrator might refuse to enforce this provision, this is highly unlikely. Thus, the odds are increased that a major league professional athlete will be found to have unique skills.

b.   Duration and Scope of the Injunction

The greatest hurdle to obtaining a negative injunction relates to its scope and duration. If a court finds the requested injunction will create an unreasonable hardship to the party sought to be restrained, the injunction will be denied or its scope may be limited. What constitutes unreasonableness, or undue harshness, varies with the particular circumstances. Factors considered by a court may include the length of the requested injunction, its geographical reach, the types of employment or activities prohibited under the injunction, and its potential effects in preventing employment or other opportunities for the restrained party. However, these factors are balanced against the resulting damage to the plaintiff if an injunction is not granted.

In the absence of an express agreement, an injunction normally will not be imposed beyond the time period specified in the contract. For example, when basketball star Rick Barry decided to abandon the NBA for the ABA, he had an option year remaining on his NBA contract. Faced with an injunction barring his immediate move to the ABA, Barry simply sat out his option year and did not play for anyone. After that year, when he did join the ABA, his old NBA club sought a further injunction preventing him from playing in the ABA until he fulfilled his option year obligation. However, the court ruled that the duration of his contract had lapsed and that an injunction would not be granted for any additional length of time. See *Lemat Corp. v. Barry*, 275 Cal. App. 2d 671 (1969).

The granting of an injunction becomes more complicated when it becomes international in scope. In *Winnipeg Football Club v. Freeman, supra,* a U.S. court upheld a Canadian contract and enforced a negative injunction that enjoined the breaching player from playing in the NFL while his CFL contract was in effect. Today, contracts may be entered into and performed on a global basis. Traditionally, courts have hesitated to order an injunction with extraterritorial effect that requires enforcement abroad. However, *Boston Celtics v. Shaw*, discussed at length later in this chapter, illustrates that U.S. courts may no longer be reluctant to do so. A U.S. court confirmed an arbitration award ordering Brian Shaw to honor a valid contract with the Boston Celtics and not to continue playing basketball with an Italian basketball team. The duration and scope of an injunction may present complex issues when the activity contemplated in the contract is a single event, such as a tennis or golf tournament or exhibition, or a boxing match. The following case raises several important issues related to the appropriateness of a negative injunction in such circumstances. A critical analysis of the court's reasoning should produce arguments both for and against the court's final disposition of the matter.

LEWIS v. RAHMAN
147 F. Supp. 2d 225 (S.D.N.Y. 2001)

CEDARBAUM, District Judge.

[EDS. In one of two related contract disputes, Lennox Lewis, the then-former heavyweight champion of the world, claimed a contractual right to fight a rematch against Hasim Rahman, the then-current heavyweight champion of the world, within 150 days of an April 21, 2001, bout in which Rahman defeated Lewis. A Provision of Services Agreement (PSA) obligated the boxers to a boxing match on April 21, 2001. The agreement included a provision entitling Lewis to a rematch bout within 150 days after the April 21, 2001, match in the event that Rahman won the bout. A subsequent amendment to the PSA (hereinafter "Addendum") stated as follows:

> [I]f Fighter [Rahman] is declared the winner of the bout by the applicable boxing commission, he agrees to participate in a rematch within 150 days of the date of the bout upon the terms and conditions that may be negotiated by promoter.

Although Lewis was the favorite, he was defeated in the bout by Rahman, who thereby became the World Boxing Council, International Boxing Federation, and International Boxing Organization and linear heavyweight champion (linear is a "term used in the industry to describe the boxer whose championship can be traced back in a straight line to a single, undisputed champion"). Thereafter, the representatives of Lewis and Rahman negotiated a deal for a rematch that would have granted HBO exclusive rights, but the deal fell through when HBO failed to present a check for $3 million signing bonus to Rahman as had been negotiated.]

On the evening of May 9, 2001, Rahman and Hoffman [Rahman's manager] met with [boxing promoter Don] King in King's hotel room in New York. King offered Rahman an Exclusive Promotional Agreement (the "King agreement"). The King agreement promised a signing bonus to Rahman of $5 million. It also provided that Rahman's first bout would be against Brian Nielsen on August 4, 2001, and that his second bout would be a "unification bout" against the [World Boxing Association] WBA champion. The winner of that bout would hold the heavyweight title of all four sanctioning organizations. Rahman signed the King agreement, and King gave him $200,000 in cash and a check for $4.8 million. After Rahman signed the King agreement, his opponent in the August 4, 2001 bout was changed from Nielsen to David Izon. Rahman has not yet signed a Bout Agreement to fight Izon.

Lennox Lewis was an extremely credible witness. He testified that he has been a boxer since the age of 12. He fought in over 300 amateur fights before turning professional at age 23. He represented Canada in the 1984 and 1988 Olympic Games. In 1998, he won the Olympic gold medal for boxing. He has fought 36 professional bouts. Prior to the loss to Rahman, Lewis had lost only one professional fight. Lewis described the rigorous training program he undertakes to prepare for each fight, as well as the physical risks he assumes when he boxes. He testified that it was a material condition of his bout with Rahman that Rahman agree to a prompt rematch if he won the bout. Lewis wants an immediate rematch both because of his age and because he fears that other boxers will try to freeze him out of title contention. He will be 36 years old this fall.

Emmanuel Steward, Lewis' manager and trainer, was also a very credible witness. He testified that Lewis is reaching the age at which a boxer's skills begin to diminish. Steward testified that Lewis has fought longer and more often than most heavyweight boxers, especially champions, and has suffered even more wear and tear than other boxers his age. He further testified that Lewis needs to fight three or four times a year to maintain his weight and keep his skills sharp. Because of his age and the relatively large number of fights he has fought in his amateur and professional careers, Lewis plans to retire in two years.

I find that Lewis would suffer irreparable harm were he denied the opportunity to regain his championship title. It is undisputed that the heavyweight championship is the most prestigious title in professional boxing. The opportunity to fight for the heavyweight championship, and especially the opportunity to regain the championship, cannot be measured in money. Because of his age, Lewis has only a limited time to regain his title and restore his reputation. Rahman, in contrast, is only 28 years old. Even if he chose not to box for 18 months, he would still have several productive years left in his career. Rahman concedes that he has a contractual obligation to fight Lewis in a rematch eventually, although he prefers to fight an interim bout. When asked if he wished to fight Lewis immediately, he said, "I don't have a problem with it." . . .

DISCUSSION

Lewis has a right to a rematch on August 18, 2001. . . . By signing the Addendum, Rahman expressly agreed to fight Lewis in a rematch within 150 days. . . .

Defendants' fraudulent inducement defense fails. A contract may be voided if it is induced by fraud, as where "one party possesses superior knowledge, not readily available to the other, and knows the other is acting on the basis of mistaken knowledge." *Brass v. American Film Tech., Inc.*, 987 F.2d 142, 150 (2d Cir. 1993). There is no evidence that the terms of the rematch provision were not readily available to Hoffman and Rahman. It is clear on the face of the Addendum that Rahman was agreeing to 1) a rematch within 150 days, 2) the terms of the PSA and 3) the grant of certain future rights to Lion [Lewis' promotion company]. Rahman's and Hoffman's failure to ask Kushner [Rahman's former promoter] questions about paragraphs 5 and 7 of the Addendum, even if believed, does not show fraud on the part of CKP [Kushner's promotion company] or Lion [Lewis promotion company].

Defendants' other argument . . .—that the WBC rule against immediate rematches . . .—[is] equally without merit. Violation of the WBC's rule may cause the WBC to refuse to sanction the Lewis-Rahman rematch. WBC sanction, however, is not required by the PSA . . . or the Addendum. Moreover, only Lewis, and not Rahman, can be harmed by the withholding of the WBC sanction. Whether or not the bout is sanctioned, if Rahman should win the rematch, he would keep all the titles; if he should lose, he would lose all the titles. . . .

Neither the Addendum nor the PSA contains an express negative covenant pursuant to which Rahman agreed not to fight anyone else before he fights the rematch. But, under New York law, a negative covenant will be implied where the party from whom performance is sought is a unique and extraordinary talent. *Harry Rogers Theatrical Enterprises, Inc. v. Comstock*, 225 A.D. 34, 232 N.Y.S. 1, 4 (1st Dep't 1928). Rahman holds the heavyweight championship title. He is therefore both unique and extraordinary.

INJUNCTIVE RELIEF

Several courts have granted equitable relief to enforce negative covenants where, as here, the party to be enjoined is a unique and extraordinary boxing talent. *Madison Square Garden Corp. v. Carnera*, 52 F.2d 47 (2d Cir. 1931); *Madison Square Garden Boxing, Inc. v. Shavers*, 434 F. Supp. 449 (S.D.N.Y. 1977); *Arias v. Solis*, 754 F. Supp. 290 (S.D.N.Y. 1991); but see *Machen v. Johansson*, 174 F. Supp. 522 (S.D.N.Y. 1959).

"The basic requirements to obtain injunctive relief have always been a showing of irreparable injury and the inadequacy of legal remedies." *Ticor Title Insurance Co. v. Cohen*, 173 F.3d 63, 68 (2d Cir.1999). Lewis would be irreparably harmed if he were denied the opportunity to regain the championship. The value of the opportunity to regain the heavyweight championship while he still has the ability to do so cannot be measured or compensated for in money damages.

In contrast, an injunction will not impose a significant burden on Rahman. Rahman concedes that he has an obligation to fight a rematch with Lewis eventually, and he testified that he does not have a problem fighting the rematch first. Moreover, the evidence at trial demonstrates that Rahman will earn several million dollars in a rematch bout. The potential harm to Lewis should injunctive relief be denied greatly outweighs the relatively minor burden the injunction imposes on Rahman.

Defendants, in their post-trial submissions, now argue that lack of mutuality precludes injunctive relief. See *Lawrence v. Dixey*, 119 A.D. 295, 104 N.Y.S. 516

(1st Dep't 1907). This argument is unavailing. Lion has exercised its option under the rematch provision, binding itself and Lewis to fight the rematch on the terms described in the PSA and to negotiate in good faith for a purse that exceeds the stipulated minimum. The Lawrence doctrine is, therefore, inapplicable.

A preponderance of the credible evidence shows that Lewis will not be able to fight for more than the next two years. Even during the next two years, his boxing abilities may diminish. An injunction for 18 months provides an effective remedy for Lewis' irreparable harm and does not unfairly impede Rahman. Cf. *Machen*, 174 F. Supp. at 529-531 (denying injunctive relief based on the finding that a limited injunction would be ineffective and an indefinite injunction would unduly burden the defendant).[6] If I were to limit the injunction to 150 days, as Rahman urges, I would be permitting Rahman to escape his obligation by letting a short period of time elapse. As soon as Rahman complies with his obligation, he will be free to fight other bouts. The power to end the restriction is in his hands.

CONCLUSION

The foregoing Opinion constitutes my findings of fact and conclusions of law pursuant to Fed.R.Civ.P. 52(a). Defendant Hasim Rahman is hereby enjoined from engaging in any heavyweight bout for the next 18 months unless and until he complies with his contractual obligation to fight a rematch with Lennox Lewis under the terms and conditions of the Provision of Services Agreement. . . .

NOTE AND QUESTIONS

The *Lewis* court references *Machen v. Johansson*, 174 F. Supp. 522 (S.D.N.Y. 1959), and adds an interesting comment in footnote 6 of its opinion. Clearly, *Lewis* is a departure from the rationale in *Machen*. Thus, it is instructive to note the main core of the *Machen* decision. As in *Lewis*, heavyweight boxers were central parties to the litigation after Eddie Machen lost a fight to Ingemar Johansson. Instead of honoring a "return bout" clause in the contract leading to that fight, Johansson stated his intention to fight Floyd Patterson. Machen sought to enjoin him from doing so. Consider the following language central to the *Machen* court's refusal to grant the injunction:

THE INJUNCTIVE RELIEF SOUGHT

However, even were I to conclude that the parties intended to restrict Johansson's right to fight indefinitely and until such time as he would agree to engage Machen in a return fight, I would not enforce such a covenant by injunction. . . .

---

6. *Machen* did not involve a right to fight to regain the heavyweight championship. Accordingly, Eddie Machen's interest in fighting a rematch with the defendant, and the harm resulting from the loss of that opportunity, were not comparable to Lewis's injury.

. . . I find that the instant covenant . . . is not enforceable by injunction for two reasons:

1. It is not reasonable in its terms;
2. The granting of an injunction would inflict serious injury on the defendant, while not providing the plaintiff with the protection he seeks.

(A)   REASONABLENESS OF THE TERMS OF THE COVENANT

Injunctive relief is an extraordinary remedy to be granted sparingly. . . . The instant covenant is extremely broad geographically. It prevents Johansson from fighting anyone in the United States and from fighting Floyd Patterson anywhere in the world. If such a restriction is imposed upon Johansson for an indefinite period of time it would be tantamount to denying him the right to advance himself within his trade or to fight in the United States which, it was testified to, offers the most fertile field for fights. I find that this would constitute an unreasonable restraint.

(B)   THE INEFFECTIVENESS OF THE REMEDY SOUGHT

Finally there is no way that an injunction could be framed to secure for plaintiff the results he seeks without at the same time placing Johansson under an intolerable restriction. . . .

A restriction running for only a limited period would be ineffective. Let us explore this further. Were I to restrain Johansson from fighting Patterson or fighting anyone in the United States for, let us say, one year, he might well return to Sweden, engage in several contests in Europe during the year, and then, upon the expiration of the injunction, again contract to meet Patterson. This would neither safeguard Machen's reputation nor secure for him a return match.

Nor would a longer term injunction be satisfactory. Were I to restrain Johansson from fighting for two or three years the damage to him would be very great. He would be unable to advance his position by fighting in the United States during a period that might well represent a relatively large portion of his effective ring career. Yet the benefit to plaintiff from such a restriction would be small. Machen would undoubtedly engage in bouts with other fighters during the period when Johansson was under the restriction. Indeed, he has already engaged in one such fight since his defeat by Johansson on September 14, 1958. Each time Machen fought, the outcome would have an impact, for good or ill, upon his standing as a fighter. These subsequent fights, and not any activity upon Johansson's part, would form the basis of the sports world's evaluation of Machen's abilities. Thus, while it may be argued that at this moment Johansson in effect carries Machen's reputation into the ring with him, this is a situation which will be of but short duration.

In summary, I find that plaintiff has failed on a number of grounds to demonstrate his right to the extraordinary relief he seeks. . . .

Machen, 174 F. Supp. at 529-531.

Why is the "remedy sought" more effective in *Lewis* than in *Machen*? Assuming as the court does that the injury is more severe in *Lewis* (because a title fight was at stake) than in *Machen*, is this a persuasive factor in granting a negative injunction in *Lewis* but not in *Machen*?

PROBLEM 7-1

Driver Johnny Joe Milton has compiled an enviable record on the NASCAR circuit since joining the Il Penseroso racing team two years ago. In fact, he has been so successful that he has attracted the attention of other race team owners, including Claude Forsooth. Despite the fact that Johnny has a year remaining on his three-year contract with Il Penseroso, not to mention two one-year options exercisable by Il Penseroso, Johnny agrees to leave that group and join Forsooth and his Formula One racing team. Though Johnny regrets leaving the NASCAR circuit, he looks forward to the new challenges of Formula One. He will race mainly in Europe in Grand Prix events, but will also be in the United States for such races as the Indy 500 and two or three other similar events.

Il Penseroso's owner, Alfonse Allegro, is not about to allow Johnny to leave his team that easily. He points to wording in his written contract with Johnny whereby Johnny promises to render "his race driving services *exclusively*" to Il Penseroso for the term of the contract. Allegro files suit against Johnny for breach of contract and seeks a worldwide injunction to restrain him from racing for Forsooth for the three-year remaining duration of his contract.

Considering the arguments likely to be raised by the parties, how should the court rule?

C. LABOR LAW

1. *Historical Overview*

Our nation's labor laws have become predominant influences in the structure and operations of professional sports leagues in the United States. If sports leagues engage in interstate commerce, which almost all do, they come under the aegis of our national labor laws. Players are employees of teams; when players organize into groups to voice and advance their interests collectively, they become labor unions. The federal labor laws have had a profound impact on the development of professional sports leagues, particularly those at the major league level, for more than 40 years. To understand these effects more fully, we first need to consider the general role of the National Labor Relations Act, and then analyze its application to professional sports industries.

The National Labor Relations Act (NLRA), 29 U.S.C. §§151 et seq., was enacted by Congress in 1935. The NLRA, which is known as the Wagner Act, and its numerous amendments (in particular the Taft-Hartley Act of 1947 and the Landrum-Griffin Act of 1959) provide the basic legal structure governing management-worker relations in the United States. Section 7 of the NLRA provides three basic rights for workers: (1) the right to form, join, and assist labor organizations; (2) the right to bargain collectively through representatives chosen by the workers; and (3) the right to engage in "concerted activities" such as picketing and strikes to advance and protect their interests. 29 U.S.C. §157.

Section 8(a) of the NLRA details prohibited employer conduct, including interference with employees' rights to organize and bargain collectively, domination or interference with the formation or administration of a labor union, discrimination against employees to discourage union membership, retaliation against employees for exercising their rights, and refusing to bargain in good faith. 29 U.S.C. §158(a). All of these prohibited employer actions may constitute unfair labor practices. The NLRA also prohibits unfair labor practices by a labor union; for example, a refusal to bargain collectively in good faith. 29 U.S.C. §158(b).

The oversight and enforcement of these rights comes under the jurisdiction of the National Labor Relations Board (NLRB) and the federal courts. The NLRB enforces the federal labor laws by adjudicating claims of "unfair labor practices" allegedly committed by either management or labor. The NLRB also administers the machinery that determines appropriate units or groups of employees qualified to vote in a union representation election, and that conducts such elections to determine which, if any, union will represent all employees who are part of that unit.

The NLRB also determines which issues are subject to negotiation under the labor laws, delving into questions concerning the required scope of bargaining. Under the NLRA, *scope of bargaining* includes all issues relating to wages, hours, and terms and conditions of employment. 29 U.S.C. §158(d). Wages include pay, fringe benefits, and bonus payments; hours encompass time spent on the job; and working conditions cover factors influencing the work environment, such as work rules, seniority, and safety. Most important, these three areas—wages, hours, and working conditions—are considered *mandatory* subjects of bargaining. If either labor or management requests bargaining on issues that are mandatory under the labor laws, the other side must bargain over these in good faith. A failure to do so is an unfair labor practice that violates §8 of the NLRA. However, what actually constitutes an issue of wages, hours, or conditions of employment is not always crystal clear. In particular, it is not uncommon for labor and management to disagree regarding what is a condition of employment. Such disputes must be resolved by the NLRB.

If an issue is not a *mandatory* subject of bargaining, it is either a *permissive* or *illegal* subject. See *NLRB v. Wooster Div. of Borg-Warner Corp.*, 356 U.S. 342 (1958). It is permissive if it is a nonmandatory lawful subject of bargaining. It is an *illegal* subject of bargaining if one or more laws prohibit it from being implemented (e.g., discriminatory treatment of certain employees based on their race), even if it were successfully negotiated. If a subject is permissive, management may negotiate with a union on that issue, but is not required to do so. If the subject is illegal, neither side has either the duty or freedom to bargain about such issues.

For purposes of the NLRA, there are two additional important factors to consider. First, a union that is duly certified by the NLRB pursuant to the prescribed procedures becomes the exclusive bargaining agent for all employees within the unit. As a practical matter, all active players in a U.S. professional sports league come under the aegis of the union that has been chosen to represent them. A player is not required to become a member of the union that the NLRB recognizes for his or her league. The player is bound, however, by the union's actions and the terms of any collective bargaining agreements that it negotiates with the league and its member clubs.

The second factor is equally important. Those who are not currently active players in the league (as defined by the bargaining unit) are *not* members of the union and, as such, have no vote and little voice in union affairs. Even so, to a large extent, the actions of the union may affect their rights. For example, college players who want to play professionally usually find that their eligibility to do so is determined by the collective bargaining agreement between the league and the players union. The same may be true for foreign players and others such as high school graduates seeking the opportunity to play in an American professional league that is unionized. The extent to which management and labor, by their agreement, can effectively control prospective players outside the bargaining unit has been the subject of extensive litigation and is explored later in this chapter.

Until 1969, the NLRB expressed its reluctance to assert jurisdiction over labor relations in the context of professional sports. For example, it had declined to do so for the thoroughbred horse-racing industry, which was deemed to be merely a local activity. See *Walter A. Kelley*, 139 N.L.R.B. 744 (1962); *Los Angeles Turf Club, Inc.*, 90 N.L.R.B. 20 (1950). However, in its landmark ruling in *American League of Professional Baseball Clubs and Association of National Baseball League Umpires*, 180 N.L.R.B. 190 (1969), the NLRB recognized the interstate nature of professional sports and the appropriateness of having federal labor law govern the relationships between league clubs and their players.

THE AMERICAN LEAGUE OF PROFESSIONAL BASEBALL CLUBS AND ASSN. OF NATIONAL BASEBALL LEAGUE UMPIRES

180 N.L.R.B. 190 (1969)

Upon the entire record in this case, including the briefs, the National Labor Relations Board finds:

1. The Petitioner seeks an election in a unit of umpires employed by the American League of Professional Baseball Clubs (hereinafter called the Employer or the League). The Employer, while conceding the Board's constitutional and statutory power to exercise jurisdiction herein, nevertheless urges the Board, as a matter of policy, not to assert jurisdiction pursuant to Section 14(c) of the Act.

The Employer is a nonprofit membership association consisting of 12 member clubs located in 10 states and the District of Columbia. Operating pursuant to a constitution adopted and executed by the 12 member clubs, the Employer is engaged in the business of staging baseball exhibitions and, with its counterpart the National League of Professional Baseball Clubs, constitutes what is commonly known as "major league baseball." The Employer currently employs, among other persons, the 24 umpires requested herein, and one umpire-in-chief. . . .

The Board's jurisdiction under the Act is based upon the commerce clause of the Constitution, and is coextensive with the reach of that clause. In 1922 the Supreme Court in *Federal Baseball Club of Baltimore v. National League of Professional Baseball Clubs*, 259 U.S. 200, although characterizing baseball as a "business," ruled that it was not interstate in nature, and therefore was beyond the reach of the nation's antitrust laws. However, subsequent Supreme Court decisions appear to proceed on the assumption that baseball, like the other major professional sports, is now an industry in or affecting interstate commerce, and that baseball's current antitrust exemption has been preserved merely as a matter of judicial *stare decisis*. Thus, in both the *Toolson* and *Radovich* decisions the Supreme Court specifically stated that baseball's antitrust status was a matter for Congress to resolve, implying thereby that Congress has the power under the commerce clause to regulate the baseball industry. Since professional football and boxing have been held to be in interstate commerce and thus subject to the antitrust laws, it can no longer be seriously contended that the Court still considers baseball alone to be outside of interstate commerce. Congressional deliberations regarding the relationship of baseball and other professional team sports to the antitrust laws likewise reflect a Congressional assumption that such sports are subject to regulation under the commerce clause. It is, incidentally, noteworthy that these deliberations reveal Congressional concern for the rights of employees such as players to bargain collectively and engage in concerted activities. Additionally, legal scholars have agreed, and neither the parties nor those participating as *amici* dispute, that professional sports are in or affect interstate commerce, and as such are subject to the Board's jurisdiction. Therefore, on the basis of the above, we find that professional baseball is an industry in or affecting commerce, and as such is subject to Board jurisdiction under the Act.

Section 14(c)(1) of the National Labor Relations Act, as amended, permits the Board to decline jurisdiction over labor disputes involving any "class or category of employers, where, in the opinion of the Board, the effect of such labor dispute on commerce is not sufficiently substantial to warrant the exercise of its jurisdiction. . . ." The Employer and other employers contend that because of baseball's internal self-regulation, a labor dispute involving The American League of Professional Baseball Clubs is not likely to have any substantial effect on interstate commerce; and that application of the National Labor Relations Act to this Employer is contrary to national labor policy because Congress has sanctioned baseball's internal self-regulation. The Employer also contends that effective and uniform regulations of baseball's labor relations problems is not possible through Board processes because of the sport's international aspects.

The Petitioner and other employee representatives contend, on the other hand, that Section 14(c) precludes the Board from declining jurisdiction, as any labor dispute arising in this industry will potentially affect millions of dollars of interstate commerce and have nationwide impact. They assert that baseball's self-regulation is controlled entirely by employers, and therefore has not and will not prevent labor disputes from occurring in this industry. Additionally, it is submitted that Congressional intent does not preclude, and national labor policy requires, Board jurisdiction—for without a national forum for uniform resolution of disputes, the industry might be subject to many different labor laws depending upon the State in which any particular dispute arises.

We have carefully considered the positions of the parties, and the *amicus* briefs, and we find that it will best effectuate the mandates of the Act, as well as national labor policy, to assert jurisdiction over this Employer. We reach this decision for the following reasons:

Baseball's system for internal self-regulation of disputes involving umpires is made up of the Uniform Umpires Contract, the Major League Agreement, and the Major League Rules, which provide, among other things, for final resolution of disputes through arbitration by the Commissioner. The system appears to have been designed almost entirely by employers and owners, and the final arbiter of internal disputes does not appear to be a neutral third party freely chosen by both sides, but rather an individual appointed solely by the member club owners themselves. We do not believe that such a system is likely either to prevent labor disputes from arising in the future, or, having once arisen, to resolve them in a manner susceptible or conductive to voluntary compliance by all parties involved. Moreover, it is patently contrary to the letter and spirit of the Act for the Board to defer its undoubted jurisdiction to decide unfair labor practices to a disputes settlement system established unilaterally by an employer or group of employers. Finally, although the instant case involves only umpires employed by the League, professional baseball clubs employ, in addition to players, clubhouse attendants, bat boys, watchmen, scouts, ticket sellers, ushers, gatemen, trainers, janitors, office clericals, batting practice pitchers, stilemen, publicity, and advertising men, grounds keepers and maintenance men. . . . As to these other categories, there is no "self-regulation" at all. This consideration is of all the more consequence for those employees in professional baseball whose interests are likely to call the Board's processes into play, the great majority are in the latter-named classifications.

We can find, neither in the statute nor in its legislative history, any expression of a Congressional intent that disputes between employers and employees in this industry should be removed from the scheme of the National Labor Relations Act. . . .

There is persuasive reason to believe that future labor disputes — should they arise in this industry — will be national in scope, radiating their impact far beyond individual State boundaries. As stated above, the Employer and its members are located and conduct business in 10 States and the District of Columbia. The stipulated commerce data establishes that millions of dollars of interstate commerce are involved in its normal business operations. The nature of the industry is such that great reliance is placed upon interstate travel. Necessarily, then, we are not here confronted with the sort of small, primarily intrastate employer over which the Board declines jurisdiction because of failure to meet its prevailing monetary standards. Moreover, it is apparent that the Employer, whose operations are so clearly national in scope, ought not have its labor relations problems subject to diverse state labor laws.

The Employer's final contention, that Board processes are unsuited to regulate effectively baseball's international aspects, clearly lacks merit, as many if not most of the industries subject to the Act have similar international features.

Accordingly, we find that the effect on interstate commerce of a labor dispute involving professional baseball is not so insubstantial as to require withholding assertion of the Board's jurisdiction, under Section 14(c) of the Act, over Employers in that industry, as a class. As the annual gross revenues of this Employer are in excess of all of our prevailing monetary standards, we find that the Employer is engaged in an industry affecting commerce, and that it will effectuate the policies of the Act to assert jurisdiction herein. . . .

Accordingly, we find that the umpires are not supervisors, and thus the Employer's motion to dismiss on this ground is hereby denied. We further find that the following employees of the Employer constitute a unit appropriate for the purposes of collective bargaining within the meaning of Section 9(b) of the Act: All persons employed as umpires in the American League of Professional Baseball Clubs, but excluding all other employees, office clerical employees, guards, professional employees and supervisors as defined in the Act. . . .

NOTE

Shortly after *American League of Professional Baseball Clubs* was decided, the first collective bargaining agreements were entered in the major professional sports leagues. Labor and management reached rudimentary (by today's standards) but significant agreements. Within months of each other, the National Basketball Association (NBA), the National Football League (NFL), and Major League Baseball (MLB) all reached formal agreements with the players unions in their respective leagues. The National Hockey League (NHL) also reached a series of less formal agreements with the National Hockey League Players Association. Professional sports league labor relations have been significantly more complex and governed primarily by federal labor law since then.

2. Collective Bargaining in the Professional Sports Industries

The primary basis for determining legal relationships between owners and players in professional sports is the collective bargaining agreement (CBA) reached between the players association and the owners' multiemployer bargaining unit. The collective bargaining agreement under our nation's labor laws is the predominant legal source and prevails over a league's enunciated rules or the individual agreements reached between a player and a league. This also applies to other employee unions, such as umpires and referees.

The primary focus of bargaining between players and owners has shifted over the past decades since the first agreements in the late 1960s. Those first agreements largely concentrated on job security for the players and focused on pension plans, minimum salaries, and fringe benefits such as health and life insurance. These are still important considerations, but as the economics of sports have changed, so has much of the emphasis of collective bargaining. Two general areas, driven by economics, have dictated a shift in focus on collective bargaining.

The first of these areas are concerns of the players and center around the so-called player mobility issues — those relating to initial allocation of players through a draft and the later restraints on player movement through free agency. The second arises from a league's concern that free agency has strained the player market by greatly increasing player salaries and other benefits. Thus, the response has been to seek restrictions on spending by team owners. Because owners have seemingly been unable to control themselves, probably fearing that other owners would not be similarly inclined, owners through their leagues have sought such constraints as salary caps, luxury or competitive balance taxes, and other devices aimed to discourage excessive spending.

These two areas have a direct impact on players' wages and conditions of employment and thus are mandatory subjects of bargaining, so much so that they have often been central issues of contention. More than one strike or lockout has been triggered in the various leagues over issues relating to player mobility and salary caps.

a. Salary Caps and Competitive Balance Taxes

The NBA was the first league to institute anything approaching a comprehensive cap on salaries. This occurred in 1983, at a time when the NBA was clearly struggling financially. In an unprecedented move, the league opened its books for inspection. The picture was bleak. The players association (NBPA) reluctantly acquiesced to a cap on player salaries, although it was months after the "agreement" was reached before full details were formulated and the new collective bargaining agreement signed. Even then, the cap was fraught with vagueness. No one had contemplated the many ways in which its provisions could be circumvented. But restraints came into existence under what later became known as a "soft cap." The "soft" was a reference to the many ways by which a team could exceed the cap and still be within its provisions.

The chief exception, often used, was to pay salaries to a team's own veteran players that sent the overall team salary far beyond the official league team limit. This became known as the "Larry Bird Exception," because the famous Celtics Hall of Famer was completing the final year of his first contract when the new collective bargaining agreement was to take effect. When the league and the union fashioned a method by which veterans were not penalized by the cap if their old team was willing to pay their asking price, Bird was the prime example of the largesse accorded the league's superstars. It is also true that representatives of Bird had worked behind the scenes to ensure that he was not injured by the new cap. In one fashion or another, an exception was carved that has provided millions for the many top players in the NBA since 1983. Also of note is that, since its first inception, the NBA cap has gone through several revisions, including more explicit limits on both veteran and rookie salaries, but it still remains, in most respects, a "soft" cap approach. (For the most recent specifics of the NBA salary cap, see 2011 NBA CBA, Article VII. See also the WNBA formulation of its cap at 2008 WNBA CBA, Article VII.)

Ten years later, the NFL instituted its salary cap. The notable difference from the NBA efforts was that the NFL got its players to agree to a "hard cap." Under this, a team maximum salary is determined each year based on prior and projected team revenues. Every team has to fit its total salaries into that maximum figure, with no give at the top. This sounds fairly simple. It is not. It has led to multiple schemes to restructure player contracts to free up room under the salary cap in a particular year. By this device, players enter into new contracts wherein their immediate salary is low, but a new signing bonus gives them most of the monies that would have been received under the old contract. The signing bonus, however, is then allocated equally over the years of the new contract, thus reducing the club's immediate cap obligations. Another device to change a club's cap obligations is to have the player sacrifice immediate income provided in the old contract for even greater future rewards in a new agreement struck between the parties.

However, the cap has also led to clubs being careful about guaranteed income, leaving a player vulnerable to later release with the big salary suddenly evaporating. The large salaries reported in the newspapers, in other words, are often highly illusory. Even so, despite the cap's obvious difficulties, the NFL has used the cap to maintain its position as the most prosperous organization in professional sports. Overall, player salaries continue to rise on average each year, team revenues increase annually, and the owners benefit by sharp increases in the values of their franchises. (For the latest formulations of the NFL cap, see 2011 NFL CBA, Article XIV.)

The economics of Major League Baseball breeds revenue imbalance among large and small market clubs, even though national broadcast, trademark licensing, and Internet income are equally shared, and Commissioner Selig has broad authority to distribute central fund revenues created by each club's payment of a fixed percentage of its locally generated revenues. In MLB, complaints by teams from smaller markets have created the impression that baseball has its "haves" and its potential "have nots," which has given rise to attempts to curtail some teams' profligate spending by requiring them to pay some type of tax if their spending on player salaries exceeds certain amounts. The first attempt was a so-called "luxury tax," which expired under the terms of the collective bargaining agreement provision that created it and was not subsequently revived in its original form. The 2002 agreement, reached just in time to avert a late-season strike, created a "competitive balance tax." This is similar to the earlier tax, in that it requires that teams above a certain aggregate player salary level pay a tax into the league coffers for distribution to lower-income clubs. The "competitive balance tax" is also used to help finance an Industry Growth Fund, established in 1997, to "promote the growth of baseball in the United States and Canada, as well as throughout the world." In addition, revenue sharing provisions were instituted to aid clubs in smaller, less lucrative markets. These provisions were by and large retained in the latest collective bargaining agreement. (In general, see 2012 MLB CBA, Articles XXIII and XXIV.) In an effort to maintain competitive balance among league clubs, the current MLB CBA requires clubs above a certain level ($178 million for the 2012 and 2013 seasons, and $189 million for the 2014, 2015, and 2016 seasons) to pay a competitive balance tax to the league for distribution to lower-income clubs. In fact, on-field competitive balance seems to be improving. As an example, the two teams in the 2010 World Series ranked tenth (San Francisco Giants) and twenty-seventh (Texas Rangers) in terms of average player salaries. As a comparison, the Giants, at $3.49 million, and the Rangers, at $1.9 million, were not even in the same ballpark as the New York Yankees' average of $8.25 million.

The NHL had no salary cap or competitive balance tax through 2004, and the players had long staunchly opposed the imposition of any such salary controls. When the NHL CBA expired at the end of the 2004 season, however, the owners refused to enter a new CBA without a salary cap, which triggered a collective bargaining stalemate and led to the cancellation of the 2004-2005 season. Only after a ten-month lockout did the NHL and NHLPA agree to a salary cap, the basic contours of which are discussed in section c.iv, below.

For various perspectives on efforts by leagues to impose constraints and limits on player salaries, see Zachary Golden, Note, *Is This Heaven? No, It's I.O.U.: Why Major League Baseball Must Modify Its Current Revenue-Sharing and Luxury-Tax Procedures*, 45 Suffolk U. L. Rev. 125 (2011); Justin Hunt, *Why Single Is Better: The Implications of a Multi-Entity Ruling on Revenue Sharing and the NFL Salary Cap*, 10 Va. Sports & Ent. L.J. 17 (2010); William B. Gould, *Labor Issues in Professional Sports: Reflections on Baseball, Labor and Antitrust Law*, 15 Stan. L. & Pol'y Rev. 61 (2004); Richard A. Kaplan, Note, *The NBA Luxury Tax Model: A Misguided Regulatory Regime*, 104 Colum. L. Rev. 1615 (2004); Bappa Mukherji, *The New NBA Collective Bargaining Agreement: The Changing Role of Agents in Professional Basketball*, 2 Vand. J. Ent. L. & Prac. 96 (2000); Dan Messeloff, Note, *The NBA Deal with the Devil: The Antitrust Implications of the 1999 NBA-NBPA Collective Bargaining Agreement*, 10 Fordham Intell. Prop. Media & Ent. L.J. 521 (2000).

b. Collective Bargaining Provisions on Player Mobility

Beginning in the 1890s with the National League, major professional leagues and their clubs unilaterally established rules tying players to a particular team through a draft of players initially entering the league, a "reserve clause" that purportedly gave a club perpetual rights to a player even after his contract expired, and other restrictions on player movement to other teams. Only a trade of the player allowed him to move to a new team—at least within the league in which he currently played. In some instances, as discussed *infra*, NFL, NBA, and NHL players successfully challenged free agency restrictions on antitrust grounds, a means of legal recourse not available to MLB players because of baseball's broad common law antitrust immunity. However, MLB players gained free agency through a 1976 landmark labor arbitration decision, *National & American League Professional Baseball Clubs v. Major League Baseball Players Association*, discussed *infra*. In modern times, the nature and scope of restrictions on player mobility usually are a contentious part of collective bargaining negotiations in all of the major professional leagues that are unionized.

The main existing restraints are summarized as follows:

The Draft. All four major sports leagues (NFL, NBA, MLB, and NHL) hold one or more drafts per year to divide rights to new players among their member clubs. Although a player draft (depending on its number of rounds and other factors) may violate the antitrust laws, the players associations in each of these leagues, for diverse reasons, have agreed to some form of a draft. In most instances, the number of rounds in the draft has been reduced, most notably in the NBA and NFL. But the bottom line is that the best players are drafted and have little initial choice where they will play. Player eligibility for the draft has also changed over the years. MLB continues to allow players right out of high school to be drafted, as well as those who go to college and become eligible again at a later date. The NFL has relaxed its eligibility rules somewhat, but most players are not eligible to be drafted and play in the league until they are three years out of high school. The NBA tightened its rules by making players ineligible who are not out of high school for a full year. The NHL allows 18- and 19-year-olds to be drafted in certain early rounds of its draft, but not in the later rounds. A veritable montage of differing league rules provide (or do not provide) for the drafting of foreign players.

If all of this sounds confusing, do not be alarmed. It is. The end result is that along with issues of free agency, trades, and related topics, discussed below, those who represent athletes or teams need to have thorough knowledge of the collective bargaining provisions, as well as league rules, that have a significant effect on how one does business in the sports industries.

Uniform Player Contract. By whatever name it is called, "uniform" or "standard" or something else, it is a contract signed by every player in a league, as well as those seeking to enter the league and join a team's preseason training camp. In all major sports leagues, at least in the United States, the uniform player contract is an important part of the collective bargaining agreement, with its terms and legal effects governed by U.S. labor laws. It is referenced here because many of its terms incorporate several of the restraints on player mobility. As an illustration of its overriding importance, we consider one example (the NBA Uniform Player Contract) later in this chapter.

Free Agency. Over the years, free agency has been a major battleground. For decades, the players lost the battles. As noted previously, this changed with the legal victories via antitrust lawsuits and arbitration in the 1970s. Even so, a player is not entirely free to play for the club of his choice, because the players associations for each league have agreed to some type of restrictions on free agency. Arguably the most stringent is MLB, where a player must have six full major league seasons to be eligible for free agency, which is earned by credited time on a major league roster. Each day is counted, so that a player who is shuttled back and forth between the major and minor leagues by his club may need more than six seasons to earn six years of credited service. Only an MLB player's right to salary arbitration after three full years of credited service softens the impact. (See the discussion of salary arbitration, *infra*.)

The NBA's approach to free agency concentrates on the top players entering the league (i.e., those taken in the first round of the draft). Basically, they are now tied to a potential five-year contract—an initial three-year guaranteed deal, a fourth year at the team's option to renew, and a fifth year during which the club retains a right of first refusal and can match the offer made by any other club.

The NFL has a somewhat similar scheme in that the player's rights may be retained by his initial club (or one to which he is traded) for four years (or, in the case of first round draft picks, for five years).

The NHL uses a complicated set of criteria to determine if a player is a restricted or unrestricted free agent, which depends on either the player's length of service or age.

In all four major sports leagues, the player's current contract must expire before he may become a free agent. For example, even if a MLB player fulfills the six years of credited service, he is not a free agent if he is contractually bound to his current club (e.g., if he signed a three-year contract at the end of his fifth year).

In summary, though free agency is much easier for a player to achieve now than a few years ago, there are still strings attached through the draft, free agency eligibility requirements and conditions, current club's rights of first refusal, free agent compensation systems, and other mechanisms pursuant to the league CBA and uniform player contracts. (General references to the above include 2011 NBA CBA, Article X *Draft* and Article XI *Free Agency*; 2011 NFL CBA, Article VI *College Draft* and Articles VIII, IX, and X, various types of free agency; 2012 MLB CBA, Article XX *Reserve System*; and 2005 NHL CBA, Article 8 *Entry Draft* and Article 10 *Free Agency*.)

c. Key Provisions of the NBA, NFL, MLB, and NHL CBAs as of January 2013

i. *NBA Collective Bargaining Agreement, 2011-2022*

After the CBA expired on June 30, 2011, the NBA and its member clubs imposed a player lockout. Claiming that 22 of its 30 teams were losing money in an aggregate sum of more than $300 million per year, the NBA was seeking a 10-year deal establishing a new economic model that, among other things, guaranteed the players at least $2 billion annually in salary and benefits but reduced their overall share of league revenues, imposed a "flex" salary cap that placed more restrictions on club spending than the "soft cap" in place since 1983, reduced the maximum length of player contracts, and eliminated "sign and trade" player transactions. See Andrew Brandt, *What Owners, Players Want in New CBA*, ESPN.com, June 29, 2011, http://sports.espn.go.com/nba/news/story?page=labor-110629.

The NBA labor dispute resulted in litigation raising many of the same legal issues as the litigation arising out of the NFL labor dispute (see *Brady v. NFL, infra*). In March 2010 the NBPA filed an unfair labor practices complaint with the NLRB alleging that the NBA was engaging in impermissible "surface bargaining" only as a prelude to its planned lockout when the CBA expired. Although the NBPA had not disclaimed its authority to represent the players, the NBA filed suit in a New York federal district court seeking a declaratory judgment that its ongoing lockout did not violate the antitrust laws and that the Norris-LaGuardia Act precluded federal courts from enjoining the lockout regardless of whether the NBPA disclaims its authority to represent the players. See *NBA v. NBPA, et al.* (S.D.N.Y., filed Aug. 2, 2011). The NBA also filed unfair labor practice charges with the NLRB alleging that any purported disclaimer by the NBPA would be ineffective and violate federal labor law.

The NBA and the NBPA concluded negotiations for a new collective bargaining agreement in December 2011, which, unless either of the parties exercises an option to terminate after six years, will run until 2022. The new CBA resolved the foregoing litigation and ended a 161-day lockout, which had prevented the 2011-2012 season from starting on time in the beginning of November. Instead it began on Christmas day, December 25. The late start to the season reduced the number of regular season games from 82 to 66.

Central features of the agreement are:

- The new agreement provides for a 50-50 split of revenues between the owners and players (which would provide approximately $2 billion for each side based on current revenues), with the possibility players may receive as much as 51 percent or as little as 49 percent, depending on whether revenue projections are met.
- There is now an "Amnesty Provision," allowing a team to waive one player before the season without that player's salary impacting the team's salary cap as long as the player being waived was signed under the previous CBA.
- Exceeding the cap by a large margin will be costly. During the first two years of the agreement, a team will have to pay $1 for every $1 it is above the salary cap. Moreover, in subsequent years, for every $5 million a team is over the cap, the team will have to pay an additional incrementally increasing amount per dollar over (i.e., if $5 million over the cap, the tax will be $1.50 per dollar over, if $10 million over the cap, the tax will be $1.75 per dollar over, if $15 million over the cap, the tax will be $2.50 per dollar over, etc.).
- The minimum team salary for the 2011-2012 and 2012-2013 seasons is 85 percent of the salary cap. After these two seasons, it will increase to 90 percent of the salary cap.
- The longest contract a player may sign with his current team was reduced from six years to five, with maximum yearly increases lowered from 10.5 percent to 7.5 percent.
- The owners capped the amount withheld from players' checks at 10 percent to ensure that aggregate players' salaries do not exceed 50 percent of league revenues.
- The minimum age of eligibility for players entering the draft remained the same. A U.S. player must be at least 19 years old and one year removed from the graduation date of his high school class. A foreign player must be 19 years old during the calendar year of the draft.
- Veteran players are subject to four random drug tests per year. Players cannot be tested on game nights.
- Players with less than four years of NBA service may be assigned to the NBA's minor league, the National Basketball Development League.
- Players can appeal to arbitration suspensions of any length for any on-court conduct. The previous CBA only allowed arbitration for suspensions longer

than 12 games for on-court conduct. (See discussion of the *Jermaine O'Neal* case, *infra*.)

ii.   *NFL Collective Bargaining Agreement, 2011-2020*

After months of negotiation and a lockout by the owners that began in March 2011 and extended through much of the summer, the NFL and NFLPA came together to forge a new collective bargaining agreement with only one pre-season game lost.[1]

Central features of the agreement are:

- The ten-year agreement will be in existence through the 2020 season. There will be no opt-out provision allowing either side to terminate the agreement before that date. This differs from the 2006 CBA that allowed the owners to end the agreement two years before its scheduled date and led to early and extended labor strife. Although the NFL had sought to expand the regular schedule to 18 games per team, the season will remain at 16 games pending further discussions.
- The new CBA includes new provisions to protect player health and safety, including reduced mandatory off-season workouts and fewer contact practices during the season, along with enhanced injury protection benefits. Retired NFL players will receive $1 billion in additional health insurance and disability benefits.
- A good number of contentious issues dealt with division of money and the salary cap. Both sides received something in the compromise that ensued. The players' share of league-wide revenue is reduced from 50 percent to 47 percent, but revenue is defined to be more inclusive as to sources of income that are included.
- The salary cap and bonus cap for 2012 was set at $125 million. Importantly, in addition to a revised and expanded definition of "revenue," each team must spend at least 89 percent of the salary cap but the league as a whole must spend 99 percent of the cap during the next two years, a significant advance for the players.
- There is a rookie wage scale and all players taken in the regular draft must sign four-year contracts, with first-round picks also giving their club an option to extend their contracts for a fifth year.
- Veteran players whose contracts have expired will be unrestricted free agents if they have four years of league service.
- Disputes concerning the terms of the CBA will be resolved by arbitration, rather than judicial oversight by a federal court as has been provided by Judge David Doty since 1993.

---

1. Fifteen months after the NFL locked out its players, it locked out its game day officials. Like the NFL's dispute with the NFLPA, its dispute with the National Football League Referees Association (NFLRA) revolved around financial issues, with the NFLRA demanding increased salaries and enhanced pension benefits for officials. Throughout the 2012 NFL preseason and for the first three weeks of the regular season, replacement officials officiated games, but following weeks of criticism regarding missed calls and poor game management—highlighted by an outcry over an officiating error that gave the Seattle Seahawks a last-second win over the Green Bay Packers during the season's third week—a new eight-year CBA was reached on September 27, 2012.

- The *Brady v. NFL* lawsuit, see *infra*, was settled as part of the agreement. Also settled was another pending suit in Minnesota federal district court before Judge Doty in which the NFL was found to have breached its duty to obtain maximum value for its television contracts by accepting a lower amount in exchange for guaranteed payments even if no football was played during the 2012 season.[2]

iii. MLB Collective Bargaining Agreement, 2012-2016

In November 2011, MLB clubs and players reached agreement on a new CBA through the 2016 season. Unlike the contentious labor relations that have resulted in NHL, NFL, and NBA lockouts in recent years, MLB clubs and players have resolved their labor issues peacefully since 1995. Much of the new agreement tracks the previous one. Revenue sharing remains, but is slightly modified. The competitive balance tax is still in place, although with modifications. Significantly, MLB remains the only major U.S. professional sports league not to have a salary cap.

Central features of the agreement are:

- The new CBA does not impose a salary cap, but it limits the amount of money clubs can pay for drafted players and international players not subject to the draft; a team that exceeds the limit is subject to a tax and the loss of future draft picks.
- More players with two-plus years of MLB experience are eligible for salary arbitration, and the instances in which clubs will receive compensation for the loss of a free agent are reduced.
- The minimum salary for major league players will go up from $414,000 in 2011 to $500,000 in 2014.
- Regarding the luxury tax, the limit of $178 million will remain the same in 2012 and 2013 but it will go up to $189 million in 2014, 2015, and 2016. The tax rate will be 17.5 percent for first-time offenders, 30 percent for second-time offenders, 40 percent for the third time, and 50 percent for the fourth time.
- Players are required to participate in the All-Star Game if selected unless they are injured or receive an exception from the Commissioner.
- MLB's drug testing program has been expanded to include blood testing for human growth hormone.
- There will be realignment into three five-team divisions in both the American and National Leagues (the Houston Astros join the AL West in 2013), which will result in more interleague games, and an additional wild-card team in each league that will have a one-game play-off.
- During day-night double headers, teams will be allowed to expand their rosters to 26 players.
- Small-market and low-revenue teams will be able to obtain additional supplemental draft picks through a specially designed lottery system.
- The 15 largest markets will be eliminated from revenue sharing by 2016.

---

2. For a thorough exploration of the NFL CBA and the process that produced it, see Chris Deubert, *All Four Quarters: A Retrospective and Analysis of the 2011 Collective Bargaining Process and Agreement in the National Football League*, 19 UCLA Ent. L. Rev. 1 (2012).

iv.   NHL Collective Bargaining Agreement, 2013-2022

In 2012, the NHL experienced its second work stoppage in eight years. As noted in section C.2.a above, the first work stoppage caused the cancellation of an entire season and created a widespread sense that the league might not survive. The NHL and the NHLPA, however, eventually reached a collective bargaining agreement that included, among other provisions, a salary cap tied to revenues (something the NHLPA initially vowed it would never accept) and an immediate rollback of 24 percent on all existing contracts (e.g., a contract that paid a player $1 million in 2005-2006 was reduced to $760,000), and as a result, the league not only survived; it thrived. Revenues increased, and as they did, so too did the salary cap. Indeed, the salary cap for the 2012-2013 season was set to be $70.2 million, $31.2 million higher than when the cap was initially instituted in 2005.

When the 2005 CBA neared expiration in September 2012, renewal discussions began, but as in 2004 the NHL and NHLPA negotiated to a stalemate, and a month before the 2012-2013 season was scheduled to begin, the 2005 CBA expired with no new agreement, sparking another lockout. Negotiations dragged on through the fall of 2012 and resulted in the cancellation of hundreds of games before the parties signed a Memorandum of Understanding reflecting the terms of a new, ten-year CBA on Saturday, January 12, 2013. This new CBA has an opt-out clause for both the NHL and the NHLPA. The owners have the first option to terminate on September 1, 2019.

Central features of the agreement are:

- The salary cap for the first full season under the agreement will be $64 million. For all subsequent seasons the salary cap will be determined by a complex formula that considers hockey-related revenues from the previous season, the cost of preliminary benefits (e.g., pension funding, group insurance programs, and individual bonuses), and the number of teams then playing in the league.
- The new agreement provides a 50-50 split of hockey related revenues between owners and players. This provision represents a substantial concession for players, who under the previous CBA received a 57 percent share of such revenues.
- Individual player contracts are limited to seven years, with an exception (permitting eight-year contracts) for players who re-sign with their current clubs.
- The minimum player salary for the 2012-2013 season is $525,000. By the start of the 2021-2022 season, that figure will have risen to $750,000.
- A player's on-ice infractions can result in fines in an amount up to 50 percent of the player's salary and non-performance-based bonuses divided by the number of days in the regular season. Fines, however, cannot exceed $10,000 for the first infraction and $15,000 for each subsequent infraction. More egregious offenses may result in suspension.
- Random drug testing of players will occur during the preseason, the regular season, the play-offs, and the off-season. Notably, the agreement modifies the Prohibited Substances List to include amphetamines and other stimulants. The agreement also considers the creation of a committee to study the issue of human growth hormone (HGH) testing and to make recommendations on whether an HGH testing program should be established in the NHL.

- Each NHL club will be required—upon the NHL's request—to participate in at least one international trip during the term of the CBA, and the NHL and NHLPA will work together to develop and pursue other international opportunities involving NHL players.
- Any NHL club not generating regular-season gate revenues equaling 75 percent or more of the league-wide gate revenue average will be subject to oversight from the league's Revenue Sharing Oversight Committee and may be eligible for financial assistance from the league's new Industry Growth Fund. Clubs seeking such assistance must submit business plans explaining the steps they will take to improve business performance.
- A newly created Owner-Player Relations Committee will meet twice a year to discuss matters of mutual interest and will ensure that there exists consistent communication between players and owners as to how to best grow the game for their mutual benefit and that of the fans.

NOTE

As illustrated by provisions in the NBA and NFL collective bargaining agreements, a player's current club may have a right of first refusal before a so-called restricted free agent can move to a new club. These first refusal rights often create a basis for hard feelings between clubs and frustrate players and their agents, who feel that first refusal rights diminish a player's market value. They also may cause problems, as illustrated by the situation involving NFL All-Pro guard Steve Hutchinson. When the Seattle Seahawks made him their transition player in February 2006, this meant he could negotiate with other clubs, but the Seahawks retained a right of first refusal. The Minnesota Vikings offered him a seven-year, $49 million contract, with only $16 million guaranteed. However, there was a proviso that if Hutchinson was not the highest-paid offensive lineman on the team, the entire amount would be guaranteed. This was of small concern to the Vikings, because their highest-paid offensive lineman was paid $4.2 million per year. With the Seahawks, it was entirely different, because offensive tackle Walter Jones was averaging $7.5 million annually during his seven-year contract. The Seahawks protested and sought relief in a complaint filed with Special Master Stephen Burbank, whose jurisdiction arose from the 1994 Reggie White antitrust litigation because it dealt with matters related to the salary cap, free agency, and other issues before the federal district court in which the litigation had occurred.

Special Master Burbank rejected the Seahawks' contention that it needed only to match the Vikings contract's financial terms, not its guarantee, to retain rights to Hutchinson. In addition, the Seahawks' attempt to restructure Walter Jones's contract to reduce its value below that offered Hutchinson was unsuccessful because Burbank ruled that the Vikings offer referred to salaries in effect at the time of the offer or any time thereafter.

d. Uniform Player Contracts

The *uniform* or *standard* player contract is a staple in the world of professional team sports. Although the contract terms for each league may vary slightly, they are remarkably similar. As leagues experienced legal challenges to various provisions in their respective agreements, new language was unilaterally adopted to protect against further problems. In the past, leagues often simply looked at each other's standard agreements and refined their own accordingly. More recently, each league's players association came to play a role in refining provisions in the standard agreement. Today, as a result, the standard contract is incorporated into and is thus an integral part of the league's collective bargaining agreement.

The standard contract has obtained a status that places it above a league's constitution and bylaws and the individually negotiated terms of the contract between a player and his club. Often, the uniform player contract mentions, and thus incorporates, other collective bargaining provisions. Thus, one cannot adequately represent a team or player in a contract negotiation without knowing applicable collective bargaining provisions as well as the terms of the uniform player contract. This is the key to proper representation and why this section sets forth illustrative examples to provide familiarity with the multiple issues relevant to the employment relationship between the player and his club.

The form reproduced *infra* is an edited version of the one used by the NBA, and is incorporated as Exhibit A to the current collective bargaining agreement. Each provision should be studied, with attention to possible complications raised by other collective bargaining provisions. One must also study the Uniform Player Contract to determine what amendments or additions to its terms are possible and potentially desirable.

In general, depending on the status of the particular player, several of the following terms are considered negotiable:

1. Basic salary and length of contract
2. Bonuses—signing, roster, performance (individual and team)
3. Guaranteed income (with details when this is applicable)
4. Trade provisions (assignment of contract) and possible limitations
5. Special benefits
6. Added injury protection
7. Personal conduct provisions

Not all of these provisions are negotiated in every contract. Some may be precluded by a league's collective bargaining agreement. Others may be unobtainable because of a particular club's unwillingness to negotiate and the player's lack of bargaining leverage (which usually depends on his level of talent). But all should be considered.

Set forth at the end of this section is the NBA Uniform Player Contract, which is similar to its NFL, MLB, and the NHL counterparts. However, one should not assume the provisions of each league's Uniform Player Contract are identical, and care should always be taken to consider a contract for its exact provisions.

The NBA's Uniform Player Contract is incomplete in two respects. First, it does not reference all NBA collective bargaining provisions applicable to the interpretation and operation of the uniform player contract. To understand the full consequences of dealings between players and teams, one must know and understand all applicable terms of the collective bargaining agreement. Second, it does not explicitly state which of its terms may be amended or changed by new terms, although the NBA's CBA is fairly explicit in stating which uniform player contract provisions may be amended or supplemented. (This created some problems for the Boston Celtics in the *Brian Shaw* case, *infra*, which the Celtics were able to overcome.) This is not necessarily true of the CBAs in the other leagues. Under these circumstances, the amendable provisions are based more on business practices and customs within the league, or on parameters established and followed by the particular team involved in the negotiations. Thus, one must know the league and the team involved to appreciate what is possible.

PROBLEM 7-2

Prior to examining the NBA Uniform Player Contract, review the questions set forth below. They will assist in directing your attention to particular provisions. The questions also inform you of the multiple variables that parties must consider during contract negotiation.

a. The term of the contract is obviously of great importance. This is a negotiable item for veteran players, but rookies drafted in the first round are now subject to a variety of provisions that limit the negotiability as to length. The NBA collective bargaining agreement prescribes three-year contracts for first-round rookie draftees, with restricted free agent status thereafter. In general, if the team and player are not restricted as to the term of years (other than the five-year veteran maximum), what considerations go into the determination of the length of the contract? Identify general factors as well as those that may be specific to an individual player and his team.

b. Provision 5, which relates to matters of conduct, makes several references to applicable CBA provisions and to Article 35 of the NBA Constitution (attached to the Uniform Player Contract as an addendum). Other provisions may also be applicable. If a player objects to discipline levied against him, what legal recourse does he have?

c. Provision 7 provides that if a player is not in good physical condition, he may be suspended by the team. What if an NBA player is suspended under this rationale and then signs with a European club? May his NBA team enjoin him from playing in Europe? Consider cases discussed earlier in this chapter on negative injunctions, as well as the *Shaw* case set forth in section C.6, *infra*.

d. Provision 9 states that the player recognizes he possesses unique skills and thus can be enjoined if he is in breach of contract. What is the legal effect of this language? Can a judge or arbitrator decide that, despite this declaration, the player in fact does not have unique skills? On this point, is this to be decided exclusively by arbitration? Or does the team (or player) have the right to have this decided by a court? See Provision 17.

e. Provision 10 addresses the assignment of a player's contract. After the assignment (or trade), suppose the team that acquires the player fails to pay the player all that is owed under the contract. Does the player have recourse against his old club, as well as his current employer? Does Provision 10 provide a definitive answer to this question? Is the general law on assignments of contracts relevant?

f. Under Provision 12, which prohibits the player from certain athletic activities, the player agrees not to "engage in . . . sports endangering his health or safety." As a matter of interpretation, does this prohibition extend only to such activities when the player engages in them as a professional? Is the prohibition more expansive?

g. Provision 13 allows the league and clubs to use a player's image for "publicity and promotional activities." Does this cause potential problems in the definition of "publicity and promotion"? Should a player's attorney or agent seek to define more precisely what these words mean? Would a player's refusal to engage in such activities provide a club with grounds for terminating his contract?

h. Provision 13 also includes the requirement that players get written consent to engage in any endorsement activity. This has created problems because clubs increasingly depend on advertising and sponsorships from companies that may be competitors of those who may seek player endorsements. If a player seeks permission from a club to endorse a particular product, and the club denies this, what recourse does player have? What happens if a player endorses a product without seeking the club's permission, or does so after the club has denied player's request? What recourse does the club have?

i. The termination provisions in Provision 16 must be studied with great care, particularly section (a)(iii) as to a player's failure to exhibit sufficient skill. This provision embodies what was traditionally termed the right of a club to "cut" a player. That term, for good reason, has largely been discarded. Essentially, however, this provision allows a team to terminate the contract of a player if the club, for whatever reason, feels the player does not have sufficient skills to make the team. If there are no other safeguards in the contract, the player is paid to the date of termination, he or she is released under the procedures applicable in the league (generally through the so-called waiver system), and the contract is terminated with no further obligations owed by player or club. The question is whether there can ever be any bases for a player to contest the club's use of this provision? (Hint: What if a player claims he was injured when he was released? What if he claims he cursed at the coach and incurred the personal enmity of the coach? In section C.6, on labor arbitrations, *infra*, examine the cases for other possible examples.)

j. Provision 17 stipulates that arbitration is the proper method for resolution of disputes arising from the player-team contract. It excludes Provision 9 from the purview of interpretation by an arbitrator. What does this mean?

k. Provision 20 on its face appears to be simply an iteration of the boilerplate merger clause that appears in many contracts. However, in the sports context, it may have particular significance, particularly in leagues such as the NBA that have a salary cap. Why is this? Should leagues have special provisions to guard against "side deals"? Or are decisions such as that reached in the Elvin Bethea arbitration, *infra*, sufficient to safeguard against surreptitious deals?

l. What provisions often found in individual contracts between a player and a team are not included in the Uniform Player Contract? How does one introduce these into the player-team negotiations? Where does one go to find out whether any such limitations exist?

NBA UNIFORM PLAYER CONTRACT [FORMER CBA]

THIS AGREEMENT made this _____ day of _____ is by and between (here-inafter called the "Team"), a member of the National Basketball Association (hereinafter called the "NBA" or "League") and an individual whose address is shown below (hereinafter called the "Player"). In consideration of the mutual prom-ises hereinafter contained, the parties hereto promise and agree as follows:

1. TERM.

The Team hereby employs the Player as a skilled basketball player for a term of _____ year(s) from the 1st day of September.

2. SERVICES.

The services to be rendered by the Player pursuant to this Contract shall include: (a) training camp, (b) practices, meetings, and conditioning ses-sions conducted by the Team during the Season, (c) games scheduled for the Team during any Regular Season, (d) Exhibition games scheduled by the Team or the League during and prior to any Regular Season, (e) the NBA's All-Star Game (including the Rookie Game) and every event conducted in association with such All-Star Game . . .

3. COMPENSATION.

(a) Subject to paragraph 3(b) below, the Team agrees to pay the Player for rendering the services and performing the obligations described herein the Compensation described in Exhibit 1 or Exhibit lA hereto (less all amounts required to be withheld by federal, state, and local authorities, and exclusive of any amount(s) which the Player shall be entitled to receive from the Player Playoff Pool). Unless otherwise provided in Exhibit 1, such Compensation shall be paid in twelve (12) equal semi-monthly payments beginning with the first of said payments on November 15th of each year covered by the Contract and continuing with such payments on the first and fifteenth of each month until said Compensation is paid in full.

(b) The Team agrees to pay the Player $1,500 per week, pro rata, less all amounts required to be withheld by federal, state, and local authorities, for each week (up to a maximum of four (4) weeks for veterans and up to a maxi-mum of five (5) weeks for Rookies) prior to the Team's first Regular Season game that the Player is in attendance at training camp or Exhibition games; provided, however, that no such payments shall be made if, prior to the date on which he is required to attend training camp, the Player has been paid $10,000 or more in compensation with respect to the NBA Season scheduled to commence immediately following such training camp. Any Compensation paid by the Team pursuant to this subparagraph shall be considered an advance against any Compensation owed to the Player pursuant to paragraph 3(a) above, and the first scheduled payment of such Compensation (or such subsequent payments, if the first scheduled payment is not sufficient) shall be reduced by the amount of such advance.

(c) The Team will not pay and the Player will not accept any bonus or any-thing of value on account of the Team's winning any particular NBA game or series of games or attaining a certain position in the standings of the League as of a certain date, other than the final standing of the Team.

4. EXPENSES.

The Team agrees to pay all proper and necessary expenses of the Player, including the reasonable lodging expenses of the Player while playing for the Team "on the road" and during the training camp period (defined for this paragraph only to mean the period from the first day of training camp through the day of the Team's first Exhibition game) for as long as the Player is not then living at home. . . .

5. CONDUCT.

(a) The Player agrees to observe and comply with all Team rules, as maintained or promulgated in accordance with the CBA, at all times whether on or off the playing floor. Subject to the provisions of the CBA, such rules shall be part of this Contract as fully as if herein written and shall be binding upon the Player.

(b) The Player agrees (i) to give his best services, as well as his loyalty, to the Team, and to play basketball only for the Team and its assignees; (ii) to be neatly and fully attired in public; (iii) to conduct himself on and off the court according to the highest standards of honesty, citizenship, and sportsmanship; and (iv) not to do anything that is materially detrimental or materially prejudicial to the best interests of the Team or the League.

(c) For any violation of Team rules, any breach of any provision of this Contract, or for any conduct impairing the faithful and thorough discharge of the duties incumbent upon the Player, the Team may reasonably impose fines and/or suspensions on the Player in accordance with the terms of the NBA/NBPA Collective Bargaining Agreement.

(d) The Player agrees to be bound by Article 35 of the NBA Constitution, a copy of which, as in effect on the date of this Contract, is attached hereto. The Player acknowledges that the Commissioner is empowered to impose fines upon and/or suspend the Player for causes and in the manner provided in such Article, provided that such fines and/or suspensions are consistent with the terms of the NBA/NBPA Collective Bargaining Agreement.

(e) The Player agrees that if the Commissioner, in his sole judgment, shall find that the Player has bet, or has offered or attempted to bet, money or anything of value on the outcome of any game participated in by any team which is a member of the NBA, the Commissioner shall have the power in his sole discretion to suspend the Player indefinitely or to expel him as a player for any member of the NBA, and the Commissioner's finding and decision shall be final, binding, conclusive, and unappealable.

(f) The Player agrees that he will not, during the term of this Contract, directly or indirectly, entice, induce, or persuade, or attempt to entice, induce, or persuade, any player or coach who is under contract to any NBA team to enter into negotiations for or relating to his services as a basketball player or coach, nor shall he negotiate for or contract for such services, except with the prior written consent of such team. Breach of this subparagraph, in addition to the remedies available to the Team, shall be punishable by fine and/or suspension to be imposed by the Commissioner.

(g) When the Player is fined and/or suspended by the Team or the NBA, he shall be given notice in writing (with a copy to the Players Association), stating the amount of the fine or the duration of the suspension and the reasons therefore.

6. WITHHOLDING.

(a) In the event the Player is fined and/or suspended by the Team or the NBA, the Team shall withhold the amount of the fine or, in the case of a suspension, the amount provided in Article VI of the CBA from any Current Cash Compensation due or to become due to the Player with respect to the contract year in which the conduct resulting in the fine and/or the suspension occurred (or a subsequent contract year if the Player has received all Current Cash Compensation due to him for the then current contract year). . . .

7. PHYSICAL CONDITION.

(a) The Player agrees to report at the time and place fixed by the Team in good physical condition and to keep himself throughout each NBA Season in good physical condition.

(b) If the Player, in the judgment of the Team's physician, is not in good physical condition at the date of his first scheduled game for the Team, or if, at the beginning of or during any Season, he fails to remain in good physical condition (unless such condition results directly from an injury sustained by the Player as a direct result of participating in any basketball practice or game played for the Team during such Season), so as to render the Player, in the judgment of the Team's physician, unfit to play skilled basketball, the Team shall have the right to suspend such Player until such time as, in the judgment of the Team's physician, the Player is in sufficiently good physical condition to play skilled basketball. In the event of such suspension, the Compensation (excluding any signing bonus or Incentive Compensation) payable to the Player for any Season during such suspension shall be reduced in the same proportion as the length of the period during which, in the judgment of the Team's physician, the Player is unfit to play skilled basketball, bears to the length of such Season.

(c) If, during the term of this Contract, the Player is injured as a direct result of participating in any basketball practice or game played for the Team, the Team will pay the Player's reasonable hospitalization and medical expenses (including doctor's bills), provided that the hospital and doctor are selected by the Team, and provided further that the Team shall be obligated to pay only those expenses incurred as a direct result of medical treatment caused solely by and relating directly to the injury sustained by the Player. . . .

(d) The Player agrees to provide to the Team's coach, trainer, or physician prompt notice of any injury, illness, or medical condition suffered by him that is likely to affect adversely the Player's ability to render the services required under this Contract, including the time, place, cause, and nature of such injury, illness, or condition. . . .

(e) Should the Player suffer an injury, illness, or medical condition as provided in this paragraph 7, he will submit himself to a medical examination and appropriate medical treatment by a physician designated by the Team. Such examination when made at the request of the Team shall be at its expense, unless made necessary by some act or conduct of the Player contrary to the terms of this Contract. . . .

8. PROHIBITED SUBSTANCES.

The Player acknowledges that this Contract may be terminated in accordance with the express provisions of Article XXXIII (Anti-Drug Program) of the NBA/NBPA Collective Bargaining Agreement, and that any such termination will result in the Player's immediate dismissal and disqualification from any employment by the NBA and any of its teams. Notwithstanding any terms or provisions of this Contract (including any amendments hereto), in the event of such termination, all obligations of the Team, including obligations to pay Compensation, shall cease, except the obligation of the Team to pay the Player's earned Compensation (whether Current or Deferred) to the date of termination.

9. UNIQUE SKILLS.

The Player represents and agrees that he has extraordinary and unique skill and ability as a basketball player, that the services to be rendered by him hereunder cannot be replaced or the loss thereof adequately compensated for in money damages, and that any breach by the Player of this Contract will cause irreparable injury to the Team, and to its assignees. Therefore, it is agreed that in the event it is alleged by the Team that the Player is playing, attempting or threatening to play, or negotiating for the purpose of playing, during the term of this Contract, for any other person, firm, corporation, or organization, the Team and its assignees (in addition to any other remedies that may be available to them judicially or by way of arbitration) shall have the right to obtain from any court or arbitrator having jurisdiction such equitable relief as may be appropriate, including a decree enjoining the Player from any further such breach of this Contract, and enjoining the Player from playing basketball for any other person, firm, corporation, or organization during the term of this Contract. The Player agrees that the Team may at any time assign such right to the NBA for the enforcement thereof. In any suit, action, or arbitration proceeding brought to obtain such equitable relief, the Player does hereby waive his right, if any, to trial by jury, and does hereby waive his right, if any, to interpose any counterclaim or set-off for any cause whatever.

10. ASSIGNMENT.

(a) The Team shall have the right to assign this Contract to any other NBA team and the Player agrees to accept such assignment and to faithfully perform and carry out this contract with the same force and effect as if it had been entered into by the Player with the assignee team instead of with the Team.

(b) In the event that this Contract is assigned to any other NBA team, all reasonable expenses incurred by the Player in moving himself and his family to the home territory of the team to which such assignment is made, as a result thereof, shall be paid by the assignee team. . . .

(c) If the Player, without a reasonable excuse, does not report to the team to which this Contract has been assigned within the time provided in subsection (c) above, then, (i) upon consummation of the assignment, the player may be suspended by the assignee team or, if the assignment is not consummated or is voided as a result of the Player's failure to so report by the assignor Team, and (ii) such conduct shall constitute conduct prejudicial to the NBA under Article 35(d) of the NBA Constitution, and shall therefore subject the Player to discipline from the NBA in accordance with such Article.

11. VALIDITY AND FILING.

(a) This Contract shall be valid and binding upon the Team and the Player immediately upon its execution.

(b) The Team agrees to file a copy of this Contract, and/or any amendment(s) thereto, with the Commissioner of the NBA as soon as practicable by facsimile and overnight mail, but in no event may such filing be made more than forty-eight (48) hours after the execution of this Contract and/or amendment(s).

(c) If pursuant to the NBA Constitution and By-Laws or the NBA/NBPA Collective Bargaining Agreement, the Commissioner disapproves this Contract (or amendment) within ten (10) days after the receipt thereof in his office by overnight mail, this Contract (or amendment) shall thereupon terminate and be of no further force or effect and the Team and the Player shall thereupon be relieved of their respective rights and liabilities there-under. If the Commissioner's disapproval is subsequently overturned in any proceeding brought under the arbitration provisions of the CBA (including any appeals), the Contract shall again be valid and binding upon the Team and the Player, and the Commissioner shall be afforded another ten-day period to disapprove the Contract (based on the Team's Room at the time the Commissioner's disapproval is overturned) as set forth in the foregoing sentence. The NBA will promptly inform the Players Association if the Commissioner disapproves this Contract.

12. OTHER ATHLETIC ACTIVITIES.

The Player and the Team acknowledge and agree that the Player's participation in other sports may impair or destroy his ability and skill as a basketball player, and the Player's participation in basketball out of season may result in injury to him. Accordingly, the Player agrees that he will not, without the written consent of the Team, engage in any activity that a reasonable person would recognize as involving or exposing the participant to a substantial risk of bodily injury including, but not limited to: (i) sky-diving, hang gliding, snow skiing, rock or mountain climbing (as distinguished from hiking), rappelling and bungee jumping; (ii) any fighting, boxing or wrestling; (iii) driving or riding on a motorcycle or moped; (iv) riding in or on any motorized vehicle in any kind of race or racing contest; (v) operating an aircraft of any kind; (vi) engaging in any activity excluded or prohibited by or under any insurance policy which the Team procures against the injury, illness or disability to or of the Player, or the death of the Player, for which the Player has received written notice from the Team prior to the execution of this Contract; or (vii) engaging in any game or exhibition of basketball, football, baseball, hockey lacrosse or other team sport or competition. If the Player violates this Paragraph 12, he shall be subject to discipline imposed by the Team and/or the Commissioner of the NBA. Nothing contained herein shall be intended to require the Player to obtain the written consent of the Team in order to enable the Player to participate in, as an amateur, the sports of golf, tennis, handball, swimming, hiking, softball, or volleyball, and other similar sports that a reasonable person would not recognize as involving or exposing the participant to a substantial risk of bodily injury.

13. PROMOTIONAL ACTIVITIES.

(a) The Player agrees to allow the Team or the League to take pictures of the Player, alone or together with others, for still photographs, motion pictures, or television, at such times as the Team or the League may designate. No matter by whom taken, such pictures may be used in any manner desired by either the Team or the League for publicity or promotional purposes. The rights in any such pictures taken by the Team or by the League shall belong to the Team or to the League, as their interests may appear.

(b) The Player agrees that, during any year of this Contract, he will not make public appearances, participate in radio or television programs, permit his picture to be taken, write or sponsor newspaper or magazine articles, or sponsor commercial products without the written consent of the Team, which shall not be withheld except in the reasonable interests of the Team or the NBA. The foregoing shall be interpreted in accordance with the decision in Portland Trail Blazers v. Darnell Valentine and Jim Paxson, Decision 86-2 (August, 13, 1986).

(c) Upon request, the Player shall consent to and make himself available for interviews by representatives of the media conducted at reasonable times.

(d) In addition to the foregoing, and subject to the conditions and limitations set forth in Article II, Section 8 of the CBA, the Player agrees to participate, upon request, in all other reasonable promotional activities of the Team and the NBA. For each such promotional appearance made on behalf of a commercial sponsor of the Team, the Team agrees to pay the Player $2500 or, if the Team agrees, such higher amount that is consistent with the Team's past practice and not otherwise unreasonable.

14. GROUP LICENSE.

(a) The Player hereby grants to NBA Properties, Inc. the exclusive rights to use the Player's Player Attributes as such term is defined and for such group licensing purposes as are set forth in the Agreement between NBA Properties, Inc. and the National Basketball Players Association, made as of September 18, 1995 and amended January 20, 1999 and July 29, 2005 (the "Group License"), a copy of which will, upon his request, be furnished the Player; and the Player agrees to make the appearances called for by such Agreement. . . .

15. TEAM DEFAULT.

In the event of an alleged default by the Team in the payments to the Player provided for by this Contract, or in the event of an alleged failure by the Team to perform any other material obligation that it has agreed to perform hereunder, the Player shall notify both the Team and the League in writing of the facts constituting such alleged default or alleged failure. If neither the Team nor the League shall cause such alleged default or alleged failure to be remedied within five (5) days after receipt of such written notice, the National Basketball Players Association shall, on behalf of the Player, have the right to request that the dispute concerning such alleged default or alleged failure be referred immediately to the Grievance Arbitrator in accordance with the provisions of the NBA/NBPA Collective Bargaining Agreement. If, as a result of such arbitration, an award issues in favor of the Player, and if neither the Team nor the League complies with such award within ten (10) days after the service thereof, the Player shall have the right, by a further written notice to the Team and the League, to terminate this Contract.

16. TERMINATION.

(a) The Team may terminate this Contract upon written notice to the Player if the Player shall:

(i) at any time, fail, refuse, or neglect to conform his personal conduct to standards of good citizenship, good moral character (defined here to mean not engaging in acts of moral turpitude, whether or not such acts would constitute a crime), and good sportsmanship, to keep himself in first class physical condition, or to obey the Team's training rules; or

(ii) at any time commit a significant and inexcusable physical attack against any official or employee of the Team or the NBA (other than another player), or any person in attendance at any NBA game or event, considering the totality of the circumstances, including (but not limited to) the degree of provocation (if any) that may have led to the attack, the nature and scope of the attack, the player's state of mind at the time of the attack, and the extent of any injury resulting from the attack; or

(iii) at any time, fail, in the sole opinion of the Team's management, to exhibit sufficient skill or competitive ability to qualify to continue as a member of the Team; provided, however, (A) that if this Contract is terminated by the Team, in accordance with the provisions of this subparagraph, prior to January 10 of any Regular Season, and the Player, at the time of such termination, is unfit to play skilled basketball as the result of an injury resulting directly from his playing for the Team, the Player shall (subject to the provisions set forth in Exhibit 3) continue to receive his full Compensation, less all workers' compensation benefits (which, to the extent permitted by law, and if not deducted from the Player's Compensation by the Team, the Player hereby assigns to the Team) and any insurance provided for by the Team paid or payable to the Player by reason of said injury, until such time as the Player is fit to play skilled basketball, but not beyond the Season during which such termination occurred; and provided, further, (B) that if this Contract is terminated by the Team, in accordance with the provisions of this subparagraph, during the period from the January 10 of any Regular Season through the end of such Regular Season, the Player shall be entitled to receive his full Compensation for said Season; or

(iv) at any time, fail, refuse, or neglect to render his services hereunder or in any other manner materially breach this Contract.

(b) If this Contract is terminated by the Team by reason of the Player's failure to render his services hereunder due to disability caused by an injury to the Player resulting directly from his playing for the Team and rendering him unfit to play skilled basketball, and notice of such injury is given by the Player as provided herein, the Player shall (subject to the provisions set forth in Exhibit 3) be entitled to receive his full Compensation for the Season in which the injury was sustained, less all workers' compensation benefits (which, to the extent permitted by law, and if not deducted from the Player's Compensation by the Team, the Player hereby assigns to the Team) and any insurance provided for by the Team paid or payable to the Player by reason of said injury.

(c) Notwithstanding the provisions of subparagraph 16(b) above, if this Contract is terminated by the Team prior to the first game of a Regular Season by reason of the Player's failure to render his services hereunder due to an injury or condition sustained or suffered during a preceding Season, or after such Season but prior to the Player's participation in any basketball practice or game played for the Team, payment by the Team of any Compensation earned through the date of termination under paragraph 3(b) above, payment of the Player's board, lodging, and expense allowance during the training camp period, payment of the reasonable traveling expenses of the Player to his home city, and the expert training and coaching provided by the Team to the Player during the training season shall be full payment to the Player.

(d) If this Contract is terminated by the Team during the period designated by the Team for attendance at training camp, payment by the Team of any Compensation earned through the date of termination under paragraph 3(b) above, payment of the Player's board, lodging, and expense allowance during such period to the date of termination, payment of the reasonable traveling expenses of the Player to his home city, and the expert training and coaching provided by the Team to the Player during the training season shall be full payment to the Player.

(e) If this Contract is terminated by the Team after the first game of a Regular Season, except in the case provided for in subparagraphs (a)(iii) and (b) of this paragraph 16, the Player shall be entitled to receive as full payment hereunder a sum of money which, when added to the salary which he has already received during such Season, will represent the same proportionate amount of the annual sum set forth in Exhibit 1 hereto as the number of days of such Regular Season then past bears to the total number of days of such Regular Season, plus the reasonable traveling expenses of the Player to his home.

(f) If the Team proposes to terminate this Contract in accordance with subparagraph (a) of this paragraph 16, it must first comply with the following waiver procedure:

(i) The Team shall request the NBA Commissioner to request waivers from all other clubs. Such waiver request may not be withdrawn.

(ii) Upon receipt of the waiver request, any other team may claim assignment of this Contract at such waiver price as may be fixed by the League, the priority of claims to be determined in accordance with the NBA Constitution and By-Laws.

(iii) If this Contract is so claimed, the Team agrees that it shall, upon the assignment of this Contract to the claiming team, notify the Player of such assignment as provided in paragraph 10(c) hereof, and the Player agrees he shall report to the assignee team as provided in said paragraph 10(c).

(iv) If the Contract is not claimed prior to the expiration of the waiver period, it shall terminate and the Team shall promptly deliver written notice of termination to the Player.

(v) The NBA shall promptly notify the Players Association of the disposition of any waiver request.

(vi) To the extent not inconsistent with the foregoing provisions of this subparagraph (f), the waiver procedures set forth in the NBA Constitution and By-Laws, a copy of which, as in effect on the date of this Contract, is attached hereto, shall govern.

(g) Upon any termination of this Contract by the Player, all obligations of the Team to pay Compensation shall cease on the date of termination, except the obligation of the Team to pay the Player's Compensation to said date.

17. DISPUTES.

In the event of any dispute arising between the Player and the Team relating to any matter arising under this Contract, or concerning the performance or interpretation thereof (except for a dispute arising under paragraph 9 hereof), such dispute shall be resolved in accordance with the Grievance and Arbitration Procedure set forth in the CBA.

18. PLAYER NOT A MEMBER.

Nothing contained in this Contract or in any provision of the NBA Constitution and By-Laws shall be construed to constitute the Player a member of the NBA or to confer upon him any of the rights or privileges of a member thereof.

19. RELEASE.

The Player hereby releases and waives every claim he may have against the NBA and its related entities and every member of the NBA, and against every director, officer, owner, stockholder, trustee, partner, and employee of the NBA and its related entities and/or any member of the NBA and their related entities (excluding persons employed as players by any such member), and against any person retained by the NBA and/or the Players Association in connection with the NBA/NBPA Anti-Drug Program, the Grievance Arbitrator, the System Arbitrator, and any other arbitrator or expert retained by the NBA and/or the Players Association under the terms of the NBA/NBPA Collective Bargaining Agreement, arising out of or in connection with (i) any injury that is subject to the provisions of paragraph 7, (ii) any fighting or other form of violent and/or unsportsmanlike conduct occurring during the course of any practice and/or any Exhibition, Regular Season, and/or Playoff game (on or adjacent to the playing floor or in or adjacent to any facility used for practices or games), (iii) the testing procedures or the imposition of any penalties set forth in paragraph 8 hereof and in the NBA/NBPA Anti-Drug Program, or (iv) any injury suffered in the course of his employment as to which he has or would have a claim for workers' compensation benefits. The foregoing shall not apply to any claim of medical malpractice against a Team-affiliated physician or other medical personnel.

20. ENTIRE AGREEMENT.

This Contract (including any Exhibits hereto) contains the entire agreement between the parties and sets forth all components of the Player's Compensation from the Team or any Team Affiliate, and there are no other agreements or transactions of any kind (whether disclosed or undisclosed to the NBA) express or implied, oral or written. . . .

**EXAMINE THIS CONTRACT CAREFULLY
BEFORE SIGNING IT.**

THIS CONTRACT INCLUDES EXHIBITS _____, WHICH ARE ATTACHED HERETO AND MADE A PART HEREOF. . . .

EXCERPT FROM NBA CONSTITUTION

MISCONDUCT

35. The provisions of this Article 35 shall govern all Players in the Association, hereinafter referred to as "Players."

(a) Each Member shall provide and require in every contract with any of its Players that they shall be bound and governed by the provisions of this Article. Each Member, at the direction of the Board of Governors or the Commissioner, as the case may be, shall take such action as the Board or the Commissioner may direct in order to effectuate the purposes of this Article.

(b) The Commissioner shall direct the dismissal and perpetual disqualification from any further association with the Association or any of its Members, of any Player found by the Commissioner after a hearing to have been guilty of offering, agreeing, conspiring, aiding or attempting to cause any game of basketball to result otherwise than on its merits.

(c) Any Player who gives, makes, issues, authorizes or endorses any statement having, or designed to have, an effect prejudicial or detrimental to the best interests of basketball or of the Association or of a Member or its Team, shall be liable to a fine not exceeding $25,000, to be imposed by the Commissioner. The Member whose Player has been so fined shall pay the amount of the fine should such Player fail to do so within ten (10) days of its imposition.

(d) If in the opinion of the Commissioner any other act or conduct of a Player at or during an Exhibition, Regular Season, or Playoff game has been prejudicial to or against the best interests of the Association or the game of basketball, the Commissioner shall impose upon such Player a fine not exceeding $35,000, or may order for a time the suspension of any such Player from any connection or duties with Exhibition, Regular Season, or Playoff games, or he may order both such fine and suspension.

(e) The Commissioner shall have the power to suspend for a definite or indefinite period, or to impose a fine not exceeding $35,000, or inflict both such suspension and fine upon any Player who, in his opinion, shall have been guilty of conduct that does not conform to standards of morality or fair play, that does not comply at all times with all federal, state, and local laws, or that is prejudicial or detrimental to the Association.

(f) Any Player who, directly or indirectly, entices, induces, persuades or attempts to entice, induce, or persuade any Player, Coach, Trainer, General Manager or any other person who is under contract to any other Member of the Association to enter into negotiations for or relating to his services or negotiates or contracts for such services shall, on being charged with such tampering, be given an opportunity to answer such charges after due notice and the Commissioner shall have the power to decide whether or not the charges have been sustained; in the event his decision is that the charges have been sustained, then the Commissioner shall have the power to suspend such Player for a definite or indefinite period, or to impose a fine not exceeding $35,000, or inflict both such suspension and fine upon any such Player.

(g) Any Player who, directly or indirectly, wagers money or anything of value on the outcome of any game played by a Team in the league operated by the Association shall, on being charged with such wagering, be given an opportunity to answer such charges after due notice, and the decision of the Commissioner shall be final, binding and conclusive and unappealable. The penalty for such offense shall be within the absolute and sole discretion of the Commissioner and may include a fine, suspension, expulsion and/or perpetual disqualification from further association with the Association or any of its Members.

(h) Except for a penalty imposed under Paragraph (g) of this Article 35, any challenge by a Team to the decisions and acts of the Commissioner pursuant to Article 35 shall be appealable to the Board of Governors who shall determine such appeals in accordance with such rules and regulations as may be adopted by the Board in its absolute and sole discretion. Any such challenge by a player shall be resolved by the Grievance Arbitrator in accordance with the grievance and arbitration procedures of the collective bargaining agreement then in effect.

NOTE

Provision 7, "Physical Condition," is discussed in Problem 7-2, *supra*. What is far from clear is the extent to which a club can demand that a player submit to new types of physical examinations and tests to determine whether the player is in good physical condition. As medical technology advances, these questions need to be addressed through collective bargaining negotiations. An example of such a problem is illustrated by the dispute between the NBA's Chicago Bulls and its center, Eddy Curry. Before the start of the 2005-2006 season, the Bulls requested that Curry submit to DNA testing to determine if he had a genetic predisposition for a condition that might lead to a fatal heart attack. Curry had experienced an irregular heartbeat toward the end of the prior season that caused him to miss the Bulls' final 17 games. Deaths by other players, including the Celtics' Reggie Lewis, from this condition led the Bulls to insist on this examination. Curry refused, the union backed him, and the dispute seemed headed to arbitration. However, Curry was traded to the Knicks, which did not require this testing before signing him to a multiyear, multimillion-dollar guaranteed contract. The issue thus became moot. Even so, the underlying question as to how far clubs may go to protect their interests through medical tests is an important one that likely will be considered in future CBA negotiations.

3. Professional Team Sports Drug Testing Programs

Two types of drug problems have plagued professional sports in recent years. One is performance-enhancing drugs such as anabolic steroids, which are taken to help the athlete perform better despite their associated health risks. The use of these banned drugs constitutes a form of cheating that provides an unfair competitive advantage over clean athletes not using these substances. The other is the widespread use of "recreational" or "street" drugs such as marijuana and cocaine. Various questions are posed by the regulation of either type of drug by a professional sports league. One is whether sports club owners and leagues have any legitimate reason to interfere with the private decisions made by individual athletes, at least in instances when their on-field athletic performances are not impaired and no threat is posed to the safety of others. Second, because the usage and possession of these drugs for other than legitimate medical reasons is illegal in most United States jurisdictions, does the damage done to the image of sports outweigh an individual's freedom to choose?

Three major issues differentiate the legal framework governing drug testing in professional sports as contrasted with interscholastic, intercollegiate, and Olympic sports, which is discussed in other chapters. First, professional sports leagues are private in nature. There are no public professional sports leagues, in contrast to the thousands of public universities and public high school systems. Thus, the U.S. Constitution rarely supports any legal challenge to drug testing programs in the professional ranks because no governmental or "state" action, which is required to assert federal constitutional law claims, is involved. Thus, players such as Terry Long of the Pittsburgh Steelers, who tested positive for anabolic steroids, have been unable to show a sufficient nexus between a professional sports league's drug policies and the actions of government officials or state actors to assert any federal constitutional claims. *Long v. National Football League*, 66 F.3d 311 (3d Cir. 1994).

Second, despite the lack of federal constitutional law oversight, professional sports leagues are in many respects more constrained in their ability to implement drug testing programs than are universities or other educational institutions. Professional team sport athletes are usually employees either of a club, the league, or both. When athletes agree to have a union represent them, they gain the protections of the National Labor Relations Act, pursuant to which drug testing programs are mandatory subjects of collective bargaining. Consequently, in

most major league professional team sports, leagues and teams cannot unilaterally institute drug programs that must be implemented through collective bargaining with the agreement of the players union. Although one would expect
a players union to consent to a drug testing program because drug usage has
adverse health effects on players, its nature and scope as well as sanctions for violations often are the subject of considerable debate and negotiation. Individual
athlete privacy concerns, the validity of testing measures for specific substances,
and the consequences of proven drug usage have caused player unions to have
significant trepidation about wide-ranging testing procedures and the penalties
for impermissible drug use. As new drugs enter the scene, and new pressures
arise, problems multiply.

Third, a strong reason for union hesitancy to agree to stringent drug testing
programs is pressure from athletes and their agents. A great deal is at stake
for professional athletes, arguably more so than for amateur athletes at the
interscholastic and intercollegiate levels or even Olympic athletes. Professional
careers may end prematurely through noncompliance with league drug testing and treatment programs. Salaries, bonuses, and endorsement opportunities may be lost, often costing a professional athlete thousands, even millions,
of dollars. Economically, the stakes are high. Consequently, both the players
union and clubs' multiemployer bargaining unit must scramble to reach reasonable solutions, with common ground and compromise frequently difficult
to achieve.

In general, two overriding concerns need to be addressed and resolved in
collective bargaining agreements if adequate drug testing programs are to be
implemented. One is protection of privacy of the individual players, to the
maximum extent possible. Second, there must be a clear and definite articulation of the program's purposes, procedures, and sanctions. See generally
E. Tim Walker, Comment, *Missing the Target: How Performance-Enhancing Drugs
Go Unnoticed and Endanger the Lives of Athletes*, 10 Vill. Sports & Ent. L.J. 181
(2003) (comparing drug testing policies of various sports leagues and organizations); Mark M. Rabuano, *An Examination of Drug-Testing as a Mandatory
Subject of Collective Bargaining in Major League Baseball*, 4 U. Pa. J. Lab. & Emp.
L. 439 (2002); Jason M. Pollack, Note, *Take My Arbitrator, Please: Commissioner
"Best Interests" Disciplinary Authority in Professional Sports*, 67 Fordham L. Rev. 1645
(1999) (discussing authority of commissioner to discipline players for conduct,
including drug-related offenses, that may not be in the "best interest" of professional sports leagues); Thomas J. Arkell, *National Hockey League Jurisprudence:
Past, Present and Future*, 8 Seton Hall J. Sport L. 135 (1998) (discussing scope of
authority of NHL commissioner in league decision making, dispute resolution,
and discipline, including drugs).

In 2005, Congress held hearings regarding drug use by professional athletes.
See generally Matthew J. Mitten, *Drug Testing of Athletes—An Internal, Not External,
Matter*, 40 New Eng. L. Rev. 797 (2006). The commissioners of the four major
team sports leagues all appeared before Congress, as did several athletes, such
as former MLB player Mark McGuire. Two proposed pieces of legislation should
be noted, even though neither was ultimately enacted. The first is the Clean
Sports Act of 2005, introduced by Senator John McCain and Representatives
Tom Davis and Henry Waxman. The proposed legislation was intended to eliminate performance-enhancing drugs in professional sports and to reduce usage
by others. Technically, the legislation would apply only to the NFL, NBA, NHL,
MLB, and the United States Boxing Commission. It would require the leagues

and the commission to develop drug testing policies at least as stringent as those developed by the United States Anti-Doping Agency (USADA), an independent entity that oversees the drug testing program for U.S. Olympic athletes. In the bill, it is strongly suggested that this would include testing at least five times yearly, with a mandatory two-year suspension for a first offense and a lifetime ban for a second offense.

A second bill introduced was the Drug Free Sports Act, which would cover Major League Soccer and the Arena Football League, in addition to the four major team sports leagues. Random drug testing would be performed at least five times yearly. Penalties would be a half-season suspension for a first offense, a full year for a second offense, and lifetime ban for a third offense. It would allow possible reduced penalties for mitigating circumstances. A professional sports league could be fined $5 million for failing to adopt testing policies promulgated under regulations of the Secretary of Commerce.

Other proposals were also being developed by members of Congress. For example, a bill introduced by Senators Jim Bunning and John McCain in November 2005 proposed a half-season suspension for a professional athlete's first positive drug test, which is a compromise intended to facilitate passage of a federal drug testing program applicable to the NFL, NBA, NHL, MLB, and minor league baseball. It also had a provision urging professional sports leagues to erase player records achieved with the assistance of performance-enhancing drugs.

As a result of this proposed stringent federal legislation, three leagues reached new collective bargaining agreements (the NHL, NBA, and NFL), and one league (MLB) developed new, more stringent drug testing measures with the players associations' approval. Current suspensions for a first drug testing violation are 4 games for NFL players, 10 games for NBA players, and 20 games for NHL players, which increase significantly for subsequent offenses. For example, in the NHL, a second offense for use of a performance-enhancing drug triggers a 60-game suspension, and a third offense triggers a permanent suspension (although one can apply for reinstatement after two years).

In response to the legislation proposed by Senators Bunning and McCain, MLB clubs and the players union agreed to a comprehensive system of enhanced penalties for steroid and methamphetamines usage. First-time offenders face a 50-game suspension for testing positive for the use of steroids, which is significantly more severe than the previous sanction of a 10-day suspension for MLB players. This rises to a 100-game suspension for a second positive test, and a lifetime ban (which can later be lifted after two years) for a third. The sanctions are even more severe for a criminal conviction for possession of steroids or a conviction for steroids distribution. The sanctions are somewhat less as they relate to positive tests for methamphetamines, but are nonetheless significant. Even so, though the length of suspensions appears more severe than for other sports, Major League Baseball's current 50-game suspension for a player's first positive test for steroids, for example, is proportionately similar to the corresponding NFL and NHL sanctions based on the length of their respective regular seasons.

A monumental development in the MLB drug saga was completion of the December 2007 Mitchell Report, a 409-page tome that traces the use of steroids and human growth hormones by present and former MLB players. In this report, 85 individuals were named as having used at least one type of drug. Probably most notable among the names was Roger Clemens, because he had not previously been identified as a likely steroids user and, until this report, was clearly headed for the Baseball Hall of Fame. As with Barry Bonds, also named in the report, that honor is now in serious doubt. Former Senator George Mitchell spent almost two years and an estimated $20 million investigating allegations from various sources. He interviewed extensively, but without the power of subpoena, he had to rely on persons appearing voluntarily. Many individuals who were summoned declined Mitchell's request.

The report itself did not result in any punishments being levied against current players. It did, however, raise consciousness as to the degree of performance-enhancing drug usage in the sport of baseball, still considered by many to be the flagship of professional sports leagues in the United States. In addition, the report contained three significant recommendations. First, Major League Baseball should create a department solely to investigate drug use allegations that should have the authority to investigate circumstantial evidence of drug usage, such as drug shipment records. Second, MLB should expand education efforts to increase players' awareness of the dangers of taking performance-enhancing steroids. Third, MLB should establish an independent drug testing program, under which neither teams nor players would have any advance notice of testing.

A brief history and summary of the major professional sports leagues' respective drug testing policies follows.

a. NBA Drug Policy

The initial steps taken in the NBA were tentative, even though assertions were made that drug usage, particularly cocaine, was at epidemic proportions in the early 1980s. The drug issue was confronted by the league and players association in the negotiations leading to the landmark 1983 collective bargaining agreement, but the league faced an uphill battle in gaining major concessions from the players on the drug issue. The league clearly was in financial difficulty and, for the first time for any league, opened its books for inspection by the players association. This led to the implementation of a salary cap for the first time in any league as well. In light of this momentous concession by the players, it is significant and somewhat surprising that the league also secured a drug testing program.

The 1983 version provided for testing only when there was reasonable cause and not the mandatory testing of all players sought by the league. However, it did provide for graduated sanctions and for possible permanent disqualification. In 1988, rookies were added to the list of players to be tested. Prior to this, in 1986, the Celtics first-round draft pick, Len Bias of the University of Maryland, died of a drug overdose one day after the draft. Not only was the death of this number-two overall pick in the draft a great human tragedy, it was one more smear on the state of professional and amateur athletics alike. His death also dealt a devastating blow to the Celtics' long-term plans to rebuild its team gradually as stars such as Larry Bird, Kevin McHale, Robert Parish, Dennis Johnson, and others approached retirement. Even so, the 1988 agreement did not provide random testing for veteran players, and marijuana was not on the list of prohibited drugs.

The 2005 CBA included several new provisions. Article XXXIII, some 30 pages in length, details the procedures. In summary, the following highlights should be noted:

- Prohibited drugs include marijuana, steroids, amphetamines, cocaine, opiates (such as heroin, codeine, and morphine), and PCP.
- Sanctions vary depending on the drug detected in the tests. Steroids and marijuana are separated from the others. In general, the NBA is tougher on "recreational" or "street" drugs than on "performance-enhancing" drugs such as steroids. Marijuana has the lightest penalties, starting with no penalty on the first offense and increasing to five-game suspensions. Steroid use carries a minimum ten-game suspension. Use of steroids and other prohibited substances can result eventually in permanent disqualification, which means at least two years for veterans and one year for rookies, with reinstatement granted only by approval of both the league and the players association.
- Testing procedures provide safeguards through a two-sample testing protocol.
- Veteran players are subject to four random drug tests per year. The prior provision allowed only one test during training camp and additional tests if reasonable cause existed. Rookies are subject to unlimited testing. (See 2005 NBA CBA, Article XXXIII, "Drug Testing.")

The 2011 CBA incorporates these same basic provisions and also specifies that players cannot be tested on days during which they have games.

b. WNBA Drug Policy

The Women's National Basketball Association (WNBA) also has a drug testing, treatment, and sanctions program. It is a part of the collective bargaining agreement between the league and the NBPA, which represents both male and female players of the two leagues. The approaches are very similar, however in the WNBA use of steroids is subject to significant fines and penalties, including a $1,000-per-day fine if a player enters the WNBA Steroid Program and fails to comply with its dictates. Suspensions for steroid use begin with a five-game suspension, then ten games, then one year. If a player has run the gamut of those suspensions, the next step is disqualification for a period of not less than two years, and the player's contract shall be voided. Reinstatement is discretionary after the mandatory two-year suspension. (See 2008 WNBA CBA, Article XXI and Exhibit 2, "Anti-Drug Program.")

c. NFL Drug Policy

In 1982, the NFL implemented a drug testing program through its collective bargaining agreement. The drug testing provisions were limited in their scope, however, and Commissioner Rozelle became dissatisfied with their effectiveness. This led to his unilateral announcement of additional prohibitions, which were challenged by the NFLPA in 1986. Arbitrator Sam Kagel agreed with Rozelle that he had authority to implement drug policies, because the overall problem posed threats to the "integrity of the game," but he held that the commissioner's policies could not contradict provisions in the collective bargaining agreement. As a result, if specific issues were not covered in the CBA, Rozelle could address them pursuant to his power to protect the "integrity of the game." At the time, the NFL CBA included provisions regarding what drugs were on the prohibited list, issues of drug treatment, and the severity of the sanctions to be imposed. However, his attempts to institute random mandatory testing were held to contradict the CBA and therefore were nullified.

Since that time, the NFL commissioner has continued to be active in establishing key elements of the league's drug policies. Gradually, however, more and more issues have been settled through the collective bargaining process. For example, an addendum to the 1994 CBA changed some of the basic approaches to drug testing, sanctions, and treatment. At present, the major aspects of the NFL's drug program can be summarized as follows:

1. Steroids are dealt with severely. A first-time offense results in a four-game suspension. This drug category was expanded to include ephedra, a dietary supplement, after the death of Korey Stringer in 2001. For steroids, the sanction is six games for a second offense and one year or more for subsequent violations. Recreational drugs (such as marijuana, opiates, PCP, and amphetamines) are dealt with more leniently, with no penalty until the third offense (four-game suspension) and at least a one-year suspension thereafter.

2. There are also sanctions for alcohol abuse and for drug offenses discovered through criminal prosecutions that result in either a guilty or no-contest verdict or plea by a player. The penalties for drug use discovered by criminal violations are more severe than those discovered through testing.

3. The commissioner has reserved the right to impose more stringent sanctions when drug trafficking is involved. The player effectively agrees to be subject to enhanced discipline by signing the standard NFL Player Contract, which stipulates that the commissioner has the right "to suspend Player for a period certain or indefinitely; and/or to terminate this contract" if the player "uses or provides other players with stimulants or other drugs for the purpose of attempting to enhance on-field performance."

4. The latest NFL collective bargaining agreement, entered in 2011, continues the earlier testing procedures. (See 2011 NFL CBA, Article 39 Section 7, "Substance Abuse.")

In August 2008, Kevin Williams (Vikings), Pat Williams (Vikings), Charles Grant (Saints), Deuce McAllister (Saints), and Will Smith (Saints) were notified they had tested positive for bumetanide, initiating perhaps the most drawn-out drug-related litigation in NFL history. Bumetanide is a prescription diuretic banned because it may mask the presence of steroids. This violation of the NFL's drug testing policy subjected each player to a four-game suspension. At an appeals proceeding/arbitration before Jeffrey Pash, the NFL's chief legal officer, the players established that they unknowingly ingested bumetanide as an unlisted ingredient in weight-loss pills (StarCaps). The players argued that their violations should be excused on grounds that both NFL personnel and Dr. John Lombardo, the "Independent Administrator" of the NFL's drug testing policy, knew as early as 2006 that StarCaps might contain bumetanide and that they failed to advise NFL players and team doctors accordingly. On December 2, 2008, Pash upheld the suspensions and reaffirmed the NFL's commitment to strict liability for banned substance violations.

On December 3, 2008, a federal district judge preliminarily enjoined the NFL from suspending the five players and invalidated the Pash arbitration award because the NFL breached a fiduciary duty owed to the players by not specifically disclosing that StarCaps contained bumetanide. *NFLPA v. NFL*, 598 F. Supp. 2d 971 (D. Minn. 2008).

On May 22, 2009, in considering the parties' respective summary judgment motions, the district court dismissed the players' federal claims under §301 of the Labor Management Relations Act (LMRA) and confirmed the Pash arbitration award on the ground that NFL players are strictly liable for violations of the NFL's collectively bargained drug policy. Although it found the NFL's failure to inform players about the presence of bumetanide in StarCaps was "baffling," this failure did not breach any NFL legal duty to the players. The court remanded to Minnesota state court the claims of Vikings players Kevin Williams and Pat Williams that the NFL's drug testing policy and four-game suspensions violated Minnesota's Drug and Alcohol Testing in the Workplace Act (DATWA) and its Consumable Products Act (CPA), which impose limits on employer drug testing and prohibitions on employee discipline for using a legal substance offsite during nonworking hours. *National Football League Players Assn. v. National Football League*, 654 F. Supp. 2d 960 (D. Minn. 2009). In early June 2009, a Minnesota state trial court granted a temporary restraining order preventing the NFL from suspending Kevin Williams and Pat Williams or subjecting them to reasonable cause testing under the drug policy pending resolution of their Minnesota statutory claims on the merits.

In September 2009, the Eighth Circuit affirmed the district court's confirmation of the Pash arbitration award and its ruling that the LMRA preempted the players' state common law claims because their resolution requires interpretation or construction of a collective bargaining agreement. However, it held that their DATWA and CPA claims were not preempted. *Williams v. NFL*, 582 F.3d 863 (8th Cir. 2009). The court rejected the NFL's argument that, although its drug testing procedures do not strictly comply with DATWA, the players were tested pursuant to a collectively bargained policy providing them with protections equal to or greater than those of DATWA, which preempted their DATWA claim because its resolution required comparison to this policy. Noting that "DATWA does not state that an employee who is a party to such a CBA cannot bring a claim," the Eighth Circuit concluded that "a court would have no need to consult the Policy in order to resolve the Players' DATWA claim. Rather, it would compare the facts and the procedure that the NFL actually followed with respect to its drug testing of the Players with DATWA's requirements for determining if the Players are entitled to prevail. Such a claim is not preempted." *Id.* at 876. The court also held that the players' CPA claim was not preempted because it creates employee rights independent of the NFL collective bargaining agreement. On November 8, 2010, the Supreme Court denied the NFL's petition for certiorari.

The Eighth Circuit's decision inhibits the uniform application of a professional sports league drug testing program to all players. What are potential solutions to this problem? If you were a member of Congress, would you vote in favor of the proposed Clean Sports Protection Act, which was introduced by Senator Byron Dorgan (D-N.D.) in 2010 to permit collectively bargained drug testing programs to preempt state laws if they are "more likely to detect performance-enhancing drugs"?

On May 6, 2010, a Minnesota state trial court ruled that the NFL violated DATWA by not giving the players timely notice of their failed drug tests, but held they could not recover for the NFL's violation because they admittedly did not suffer any harm from the delayed notice. The court stayed their suspensions during the case's appeal. In *Williams v. NFL*, 794 N.W.2d 391, 2011 WL 382747 (Minn. App.), a Minnesota appellate court ruled that DATWA does not apply to bumetanide, which is not listed as a controlled substance under the act. However, the court stated that its ruling "is limited to the specific facts of this case and should not be read to excuse the NFL from complying with DATWA when applicable," observing that DATWA's requirements apply to testing for anabolic steroids. The Minnesota Supreme Court subsequently declined to review the appellate court's decision, thereby ending this lengthy federal and state court litigation and permitting the NFL to impose the original four-game suspensions on the players for violating its drug testing policy. In May 2011, legislation was enacted in Minnesota that effectively precludes Minnesota's employer drug testing laws from interfering with a collectively bargained professional sports league's drug testing program.[3] In September 2011, the NFL imposed two-game suspensions on the four players to be served once the season commenced.

In a more recent if less elongated NFL drug use–related litigation, Genos Derwin "D.J." Williams, a player for the Denver Broncos, was suspended for six games for attempting to manipulate a urine specimen taken in conjunction with the NFL's drug policy. *Williams v. National Football League*, 2012 WL 2366636, at *1 (D. Colo. June 21, 2012). Williams appealed his suspension arguing that a gap in the chain of custody of the specimen and a failure to collect and handle the specimen in accordance with established protocol violated the integrity of the test, but the league arbitrator upheld the suspension noting that in two previous cases Williams's collected specimens were determined to not be human urine and that all told there existed with respect to Williams's drug tests a "compelling picture of deceit and evasion." *Id.* at *3.

Undaunted, Williams sued to have the arbitrator's decision vacated; arguing principally that the arbitrator disregarded the law concerning the chain of custody of his urine specimen. In doing so, he referenced the 2011 arbitral overturning of MLB player Ryan Braun's suspension for performance-enhancing drug use. In that case, Braun was suspended for 50 games as a result of a drug test revealing he had a testosterone-to-epitestosterone ratio seven times higher than the acceptable threshold. Braun, however, appealed, and although he did not challenge the accuracy of the test or argue that the urine sample was tampered with, he won his appeal because MLB drug testing protocol was not followed. Williams claimed that the handling of his specimen was more flawed than the handling of Braun's and noted that the NFL even acknowledged "'troubling' gaps in the chain of custody and 'an environment of haste, rushing, confusion and short cuts'" with respect to urine specimen collection. *Id.* at *3. Ultimately, though, the district court hearing the case rejected Williams's argument and found for the NFL. And on appeal, the Tenth Circuit, reiterating that "a court's role in these types of arbitration cases is simply to determine whether the arbitrator strayed from the collective-bargaining agreement" upheld the district court's judgment. *Williams v. National Football League*, 2012 WL 3642839 (10th Cir. Aug. 27, 2012).

---

3. The provision states that no aspect of DATWA shall "be construed to interfere with the operation of a drug and alcohol testing program if: (1) the drug and alcohol testing program is permitted under a contract between the employer and employees; and (2) the covered employees are employed as professional athletes." Minn. Stat. §181.955(3).

In an even more recent NFL drug testing dispute, the Seattle Seahawks's Richard Sherman successfully challenged his four-game suspension for violating the league's performance-enhancing drug policy during the NFL's 2012 season. Like Williams, Sherman appealed to the league arbitrator citing a failure to collect and handle the specimen in accordance with established protocol. Sherman alleged that as his urine sample was taken, "several errors and departures from the Policy occurred," including the use of a second collection cup because of a leak in the first. See National Football League Management Council, Richard Sherman Arbitration (Dec. 27, 2012) (Wallace, Arb.). The arbitrator ultimately sided with Sherman and overturned the suspension on the basis of the irregularities involved in sample collection. *Id.*

While Sherman's appeal was successful, most such appeals, including of course D.J. Williams's, have not been. Indeed, the 2011 NFL CBA specifically set out to strengthen player drug testing protocols, and most notably includes a provision regarding the difficult-to-detect HGH. Unfortunately, because there is currently no reliable urine test for HGH, and blood testing would therefore be necessary, the NFL and NFLPA have not reached an agreement on the specifics of the testing, so HGH testing has not yet been implemented.

d.   MLB Drug Policy

Several commissioners of baseball have dealt with the drug problems in their sport without agreement by the MLB Players Association. Time and again, a strong players union has asserted that concerns for privacy of its members, and fears about the unreliability of widespread testing make it reluctant to agree to broad drug testing and treatment provisions. However, the MLB commissioner has unilaterally instituted drug programs for minor leaguers (who are not unionized) and for league personnel such as managers and coaches. But drug testing programs applicable to major league players have historically been minimal unless based on voluntary acquiescence.

This has not prevented commissioners from taking action and imposing discipline pursuant to their "best interests" of the game authority when player drug use was discovered through outside legal actions, such as occurred with Ferguson Jenkins, Willie Wilson, Jerry Martin, and Pascual Perez, among others. There was also the Steven Howe series of incidents, which led to supervised testing under a "just cause" rationale. However, there was no broad drug testing program applicable to all MLB players until the 2002 collective bargaining agreement, which was entered into after several contentious months of negotiation over a variety of issues. As to drug testing, the players association agreed to allow random testing for steroids in 2003. Subsequently, in part because of pressures applied by Congress, increased testing was implemented and much harsher suspensions and other penalties were employed.

In its new CBA, MLB expanded its drug testing program to include testing for HGH. MLB previously had unilaterally implemented random blood testing to detect HGH usage by *minor* league baseball players, but under the new CBA, beginning with the 2012 season, all major league players were to be tested for HGH during spring training and were otherwise subject to testing "for reasonable cause" throughout the year. Beginning with the off-season following the 2012 season, all major league players are to be subject to random, unannounced testing.

e. NHL Drug Policy

The NHL has experienced basically the same union and player reactions to drug testing proposals as have occurred in MLB. In 1986, reports of widespread cocaine use by NHL players caused then-NHL president John Ziegler and Alan Eagleson, head of the NHLPA, to announce a mandatory drug testing program. This was subsequently rejected by the players and was never instituted.

However, concessions were obtained from players in 1996. A four-step drug testing program was instituted that begins with in-patient treatment for a first offense and escalates after each subsequent offense to a fourth stage that involves a minimum one-year suspension with no guarantee of reinstatement. In these initial efforts, few details on the actual operation of the programs were released by either the league or players association out of concern for the privacy of the players, and details did not appear in the actual collective bargaining agreement. Rather, the disclosure of drug use came from outside sources. This occurred with NHL players Grant Fuhr in connection with his divorce proceedings, and Kevin Stephens after his arrest on cocaine charges, resulting in a suspension for Fuhr and a mandatory enrollment in a drug treatment program for Stevens.

This approach was substantially changed by the 2005 CBA. The agreement describes in detail the NHL drug testing program, penalties, and procedures (see 2005 NHL CBA, Article 47, "Performance Enhancing Substances Program"), and these provisions were largely reaffirmed in the 2012 CBA. For a first positive test, a player is suspended for 20 games without pay. For a second positive test, the suspension is 60 games without pay. There is also a mandatory referral to the NHL substance abuse program for both a first and second offense. For a third positive test, there is a "permanent" suspension without pay, although the player can reapply for reinstatement after a minimum period of two years. The player's reinstatement is a discretionary decision to be made by a special committee.

NOTES AND QUESTIONS

1. In 2011, MLB superstar Barry Bonds was tried for perjury and obstruction of justice in relation to a governmental investigation of steroid use in MLB. Several years earlier, federal authorities had seized drug testing information for approximately 100 MLB players who tested positive for performance-enhancing drugs in 2003, reportedly including Bonds, David Ortiz, Manny Ramirez, Alex Rodriguez, and Sammy Sosa. The Ninth Circuit held that the seizure violated the players' federal constitutional rights, see *U.S. v. Comprehensive Drug Testing, Inc.*, 621 F.3d 1162 (9th Cir. 2010), and as a result, federal authorities were ordered to return the seized information to the MLBPA for destruction. The government, however, was permitted to retain Bonds's positive test results, and those results were presented at his 2011 trial as evidence that his performance-enhancing drug use denials were false.

    Ultimately, a San Francisco jury convicted Bonds of obstruction of justice, but it failed to reach a verdict on the perjury charges. Although Bonds was found guilty of obstructing justice, he never admitted knowingly using performance-enhancing drugs, received no jail time, and is appealing the verdict. Roger Clemens was also pursued by federal prosecutors for perjury and obstruction of justice. Indeed, he was prosecuted twice. The first case against Clemens, brought in 2011, ended in a mistrial on the second day of testimony because of a prosecutorial blunder. Prosecutors tried again in 2011, and Clemens was acquitted of all charges. Both before and after the Bonds and Clemens prosecutions, wide swaths of the public and the media believed that justice was not served — that Bonds and Clemens knowingly used performance-enhancing drugs and perjured themselves when denying it. During the months between Clemens's two trials, National League MVP Ryan Braun was, as noted previously, suspended for 50 games because of a drug test revealing that he had an extremely and unacceptably high testosterone-to-epitestosterone ratio, but his suspension was overturned because MLB drug testing protocol was not followed.

The outcomes of the Bonds and Clemens trials and the Braun case have convinced some observers that high-profile MLB players accused of performance-enhancing drug usage are — whether because of technicalities or expensive lawyers — more likely than not to "get off" and that the investigations are a waste of resources. See, e.g., Jerome Solomon, *Bonds Able to Coax His Biggest Walk*, Hous. Chron., April 14, 2011, at 1 (addressing Bonds's and Clemens's prosecutions). Other observers argue that performance-enhancing drug development tends to outpace performance-enhancing drug detection technology, resulting in the continuous creation of undetectable performance-enhancing drugs. Indeed, although the decade-long inquiry that prompted the United States Anti-Doping Agency's August 2012 lifetime ban of renowned cyclist Lance Armstrong was widely hailed as a victory for the anti-doping establishment, it starkly revealed (1) the myriad means by which athletes can manipulate drug testing procedures (Armstrong passed over 500 drug tests during his career, never failed one, and was ultimately sanctioned only on the strength of circumstantial evidence and extensive testimony from fellow cyclists before finally admitting his doping history in a televised interview with Oprah Winfrey), and (2) the exorbitant costs involved in such investigations. See Alexander Wolff and David Epstein, *A Massive Fraud Now More Fully Exposed*, Sports Illustrated, Oct. 22, 2012, at 40.

If performance-enhancing drug detection is challenging and in some cases impossible, and if users will rarely be held accountable (and in those cases only if exorbitant investigatory resources are expended), might it make sense to simply permit performance-enhancing drug use in professional sports? Consider the following opinion column excerpt:

> Athletes should be permitted to use performance enhancers, so long as the users are monitored for safety.... [T]he sporting world must ultimately accept that the distinctions between doping and nutritional supplements, illegal enhancements and scientific training, no longer exist. Elite sports are already thoroughly enmeshed in a laboratory world of pharmaceuticals, medicine, and high tech nutrition. Any athlete who wants a banned drug can get it. And as we've seen repeatedly, designer drugs co-evolve with tests, staying one step ahead of authorities and allowing savvy athletes to juice unnoticed.
>
> Imagine a world where performance enhancement was open and regulated. Instead of forcing athletes to sneak through back alleys to stay competitive, sports authorities should admit that drugs are essential — then help athletes cope with the side effects. Once legalized, drug use would still have limits, but they would be established by physicians and athletes — based on their ability

to handle performance enhancers. Bad outcomes would be far less frequent if players were not forced to rely on quacks. . . . Innovation in performance enhancers would accelerate in the light of day.

Could Doping Be Effectively Legalized, Regulated?, Bus. Pundit, May 20, 2010, http://www.businesspundit.com/?s=Could+Doping+Be+Effectively+Legalized. Do you agree that "the distinctions between doping and nutritional supplements, illegal enhancements and scientific training, no longer exist"? Whether or not you agree with this statement, do you agree with the author's ultimate point? What negative consequences might flow (in the sporting world and in society generally) from the author's proposed regimen?

2. A player who tests positive for drugs or who is caught in violation of drug laws may find that the consequences are far more extensive than the enforcement of a league's or association's drug policies. In addition to potential criminal prosecution, as discussed previously, contracts entered into by the player with a professional team and product endorsement deals may be compromised or even terminated. All this may occur based on a single act, or it may even be based on nothing but rumors. In any event, possible consequences must be foreseen and dealt with in advance. In this light, please consider the following problem.

PROBLEM 7-3

a. *Loss of Signing Bonus.* Traditionally, the typical signing bonus provision contained language such as:

> It is expressly understood that no part of the bonus herein provided is part of any salary in the contract specified above . . . and that such obligations of Club are not terminable if such contract is terminated pursuant to the League's waiver system.
>
> In the event Player, in any of the years specified above, fails or refuses to report to Club, fails or refuses to practice or play with Club, or leaves Club without its consent, then, upon demand by Club, Player will return to Club the proportionate amount of the total bonus not having been earned at the time of Player's default.

Suppose that NFL Player received a $4 million signing bonus when he entered into a four-year contract with Club. He played for one year, but tested positive for a prohibited substance in training camp before the start of the second year of his contract. He received a four-game suspension for this offense pursuant to the applicable collective bargaining agreement. Club now requests that Player return a proportionate amount of his bonus money. This amounts to one-quarter of a year (four games, for NFL players) or one-sixteenth of the total bonus calculated on a four-year basis.

Player argues he has not failed or refused to report or to practice and thus is not in breach of his contract. He argues that his bonus was earned when he received it. What would be the result? Does Player have to return the money?

Is the preceding contract language adequate to address situations such as Player's foregoing conduct? Can better contract language be drafted to clarify the duties of both Club and Player and to prevent this dispute from arising with other players in the future?

b.   *Endorsement Contracts.* Suppose Player, a professional tennis star, entered an endorsement contract with Nibok Shoes. Through base guarantees and bonuses based on Player's performance on the professional tennis circuit, Player had the potential to earn sums in excess of $2 million over the term of the contract. The endorsement agreement, however, contained the following provision:

> 14.   TERMINATION BY COMPANY
>
> Company shall have the right to terminate this Agreement on fifteen days prior written notice to Player or his legal representative in the event of the occurrence of any of the following contingencies:
>
> . . . (c) If Player has engaged in illegal or immoral conduct resulting in a felony conviction, or if he has otherwise conducted himself in a manner which is not reasonably in keeping with the standards of professional athletics.

Player was stopped for speeding, and when he got out of the car to talk to the arresting officer, the officer noted something lying on the driver's seat. The officer retrieved it and found it was a small amount of marijuana. Player was charged with speeding and the illegal possession of a "prohibited substance." Both charges are misdemeanors. Company, for what is suspected to be multiple reasons, immediately announced it was terminating Player's endorsement contract. The announcement stated that the Company expected its product endorsers to maintain the highest standards of personal conduct.

In the meantime, Player has pled guilty to the speeding charge and not guilty to the illegal drug possession charge. Company is adamant regarding its decision to terminate the contract.

Please discuss the respective legal positions of both Company and Player. What better language might have been drafted from the perspective of Player? What language would have been better from the perspective of Company?

4.   *Unfair Labor Practices*

Section 8(d) of the National Labor Relations Act (NLRA) imposes a mutual obligation on representatives of both management and labor "to meet at reasonable times and confer in good faith with respect to wages, hours, and other terms and conditions of employment," so-called mandatory subjects of collective bargaining. 29 U.S.C. §158(d). Either side's failure to do so constitutes an unfair labor practice. However, this obligation "does not compel either party to agree to a proposal or require the making of a concession." *Id.* Labor disputes are to be resolved by collective bargaining or resort to economic coercion in the form of a strike by players or a lockout by league clubs.

The NLRB enforces the requirements of the NLRA and polices the unionization and collective bargaining processes. After an administrative hearing, the NLRB is empowered to order either labor or management to cease and desist from engaging in any unfair labor practice. 29 U.S.C. §160(a). The NLRB may petition the appropriate federal circuit court for judicial enforcement of its orders. 29 U.S.C. §160(e). Upon issuance of an administrative complaint alleging that a party has committed an unfair labor practice, the NLRB may petition a federal district court for appropriate interlocutory relief as warranted by the alleged illegal conduct. 29 U.S.C. §160(j). Failure to comply with an injunction may result in contempt sanctions.

In the context of professional sports, allegations of unfair labor practices have arisen in a variety of circumstances. A refusal by the league's multiemployer bargaining unit to bargain over a mandatory subject of collective bargaining is a relatively common allegation, which is explored more fully later. Other illustrative examples of alleged unfair labor practices arising in the professional sports industries are discussed in the following sections.

a.   League Interference with Players' Rights to Unionize

Section 8(a) prohibits an employer from attempting to interfere with the rights of employees freely to choose which union represents them or from discriminating against any employee to encourage or discourage union membership. 29 U.S.C. §158(a)(1) and (2).

In September 2000, the NLRB filed unfair labor practice charges against the AFL alleging that its club owners both threatened players and illegally promised them benefits to coerce them to accept AFLPOC as their union. Two AFL players alleged that players had been illegally pressured to select AFLPOC as their union, which was unduly sympathetic to league management and had been formed primarily at the club owners' behest to immunize them from antitrust liability (the statutory and nonstatutory labor exemptions that protect a professional sports league and its member clubs from antitrust liability if the players have unionized are discussed *infra*). The NLRB found evidence that an uncoerced majority of players did not support AFLPOC.

After the NLRB's complaint was filed, the AFL reached a settlement that resolved both the unfair labor practice claims and the pending antitrust litigation. The net effect of the settlement was that players received $5 million in damages, the AFL withdrew its recognition of AFLPOC as the players' collective bargaining representative, players regained the right to choose which union was to represent them, and players gained free agency concessions.

b.   League Refusal to Recognize Players Union as Exclusive Bargaining Representative

Player associations in professional sports date as far back as the 1880s, but effective associations were not formed until the 1950s and 1960s. It was several years before these associations, functioning as unions, were able to obtain the first collective bargaining agreements with the various major professional sports leagues. A difficult threshold task was to obtain full recognition as the players' exclusive bargaining representative, especially by a newly formed league. This was particularly true in the case of the now-defunct North American Soccer League (NASL). Two cases underscore the difficulties that a newly formed union faced in its initial efforts to collectively bargain with NASL club owners. The legal principles developed in these cases have general application to labor relations involving professional team sports.

In *North American Soccer League v. National Labor Relations Board*, 613 F.2d 1379 (5th Cir. 1980), the NASL disputed the NLRB's certification of "all NASL players of clubs based in the United States" as the appropriate collective bargaining unit, which was requested by the players union. The Fifth Circuit upheld the NLRB's determination that there is a "joint employer relationship" among the NASL and its member clubs:

> The League exercises a significant degree of control over essential aspects of the clubs' labor relations, including but not limited to the selection, retention, and termination of the players, the terms of individual player contracts, dispute resolution and player discipline. Furthermore, each club granted the NASL authority over not only its own labor relations but also, on its behalf, authority over the labor relations of the other member clubs.

Id. at 1382.

The court then concluded that a "leaguewide unit of players" for purposes of collective bargaining is appropriate:

> Notwithstanding the substantial financial autonomy of the clubs, the Board found they form, through the League, an integrated group with common labor problems and a high degree of centralized control over labor relations. In these circumstances the Board's designation of a leaguewide bargaining unit as appropriate is reasonable, not arbitrary or capricious.

Id. at 1383. This effectively required the NASL's member clubs to function as a multiemployer collective bargaining unit in labor relations issues with the players. See also *Brown v. Pro Football, Inc.*, 518 U.S. 231 (1996) (recognizing need for multiemployer collective bargaining in professional team sports).

Once certified, the union is the exclusive bargaining representative of the league's players. 29 U.S.C. §159(a). In *Morio v. North American Soccer League*, 501 F. Supp. 633 (S.D.N.Y. 1980), the court enjoined the NASL from refusing to collectively bargain with the players union and continuing to negotiate contracts with individual players. To avoid undermining the union's authority, the league's "duty to bargain with the exclusive representative carries with it the negative duty not to bargain with individual employees." *Id.* at 639. The court required the NASL to maintain the present terms of player contracts, except for its illegal unilaterally imposed changes, until an agreement or impasse is reached pursuant to good faith bargaining with the players union.

A decision by the British Columbia Labour Relations Board demonstrates that issues pertaining to the determination of the appropriate bargaining unit in the sports labor context are still being contested. During the prolonged NHL lockout of 2004-2005, Vancouver Canucks players sought certification as a separate union under British Columbia Labour Law. (Labor law in Canada is controlled by the laws of each province rather than on a national basis.) The National Hockey League and the owners of the Canucks, the Orca Bay Hockey Limited Partnership, resisted this effort. The initial decision by a British Columbia labor panel favored the establishment of a separate bargaining unit of Canucks players, which was overturned by the British Columbia Labour Relations Board. See *Orca Bay Hockey Limited Partnership (Orca Bay) and National Hockey League (NHL) and British Columbia Chapter of the National Hockey League Players Association (BC-NHLPA)*, Case number 55143, July 31, 2007.

The Board noted that despite the earlier decision favoring the Canucks players' application, the NHLPA continued bargaining on a league-wide basis with the NHL on behalf of all NHL players, including Canucks players. Even after a new collective bargaining agreement was entered into between the NHLPA and NHL, the BC-NHLPA, acting on behalf of the Canucks players, pursued its application for British Columbia certification as a separate bargaining unit.

In a lengthy decision, the Board concluded:

> Orca Bay is the employer, but Orca Bay itself is an integral part of the NHL, just as the BC-NHLPA is an integral part of the NHLPA, and the Canucks players, as a team, are an integral part of the hockey league within which they play. All three elements . . . are well served by their current league-wide bargaining structure. This is a crucial factor in our finding that the applied for bargaining unit is inappropriate. If this circumstance were to change, . . . it may be we would have to revisit our decision. However, in light of the present circumstances, we find that the bargaining unit applied for is inappropriate.

Similarly, in a publicly available legal opinion provided in connection with the 2012 NHL lockout, Professor William Gould, a former chair of the National Labor Relations Board, stated:

> It is my opinion that collective bargaining for North American sports leagues has to be conducted on a league-wide basis to meet the interests of the parties, labor and management, as well as the public. Public policy and labor law have promoted leaguewide bargaining under the laws of the United States. This is the way that it has been treated under the laws of the United States, and it is my view that it would be contrary to U.S. labor law and the requirements of sound collective bargaining between the parties for the existing league-wide bargaining unit involving the parties, the National Hockey League and the National Hockey League Players' Association, to be fragmented by the creation of separate bargaining units for the Canadian teams, as well as separate rules governing the right to engage in strikes and lockouts which would balkanize the bargaining unit and disrupt the orderly collective bargaining process. . . .
>
> The law relating to NLRB assertion of jurisdiction over conduct engaged in outside the United States has particular significance for professional sports. This is because so many sports, like baseball and basketball, as well as hockey, possess both American and Canadian franchises and thus give rise to litigation involving relationships between organized labor and multi-employer entities in so-called "mixed territory" cases. The fact that professional sports are *sui generis* and involve player movement, scheduling, roster arrangements, and the like, between different employers in the multi-employer association requires the involvement of the administrative process in the territory which possesses the majority of franchises. In professional sports, including hockey, the overwhelming majority are to be found in the United States, where the National Labor Relations Board possesses exclusive jurisdiction, which is why in my opinion the NLRB has the jurisdiction to intervene in the "mixed territory" relationship between the NHL and the NHLPA.

Letter from William B. Gould, IV, to Heenan Blaikie, LLP, re Colby Armstrong, et al. and The National Hockey League Players Association v. Club de Hockey Canadien Inc. and the National Hockey League, November 30, 2012.

c.   Retaliation Against Union Activists

Section 8(a)(3) prohibits an employer from discriminating against any employee to encourage or discourage union membership. 29 U.S.C. §158(a)(3).

The release of a player because of his union activities, if proved, is an unfair labor practice.

In *Nordstrom d/b/a Seattle Seahawks*, 292 NLRB 899 (1989), Sam McCullum asserted that the Seattle Seahawks NFL club cut him from the team's final roster in violation of §8(a)(3). McCullum started as a wide receiver for the Seahawks during the 1976-1981 seasons. In 1981 his teammates selected him to be their union player representative. McCullum's union activities incurred head coach Jack Patera's ire, particularly for his orchestration of a "solidarity handshake" between his teammates and players on the opposing team prior to the first 1982 preseason game. Despite starting all of the Seahawks 1982 preseason games, McCullum was cut shortly after the club acquired Roger Carr, another wide receiver.

McCullum and the NFL Players Association claimed that his union activities were a "motivating factor" in the termination of his employment with the Seahawks. The club asserted that he would have been cut even without his participation in union activities based on his relative skills in comparison to the team's other wide receivers. The Seahawks claimed a stronger team need for Carr's services and the inability to keep McCullum as a fifth wide receiver without harming the need for players at other positions.

In a divided opinion, the NLRB affirmed the administrative law judge's ruling that McCullum's termination was illegal discrimination based on his role "as a fairly aggressive union spokesman." Patera's attempted heavy fines for team players' participation in the solidarity handshake evidenced his animus toward union activity for which McCullum was the focal point. Patera also had the final authority regarding player cuts, and there was some evidence that Carr was acquired to enable McCullum's release because of his union activities. A dissenting NLRB member concluded that McCullum's release was a valid exercise of team management's business judgment regarding its personnel needs, which decision would have been made absent any antiunion motivation.

The effectiveness of available administrative remedies can be questioned, however, because it may be a lengthy period of time before an NLRB proceeding and appeals are concluded. See *Nordstrom v. NLRB*, 984 F.2d 479 (D.C. Cir. 1993) (affirming $301,000 award of back pay to McCullum for period he would have been employed by the Seahawks but for his unlawful termination, 11 years after his 1982 release).

This case illustrates the difficulty of determining why a player active in union activities was cut by a team. Does federal labor law potentially interfere with a club's efforts to field its best possible team? As a player agent, what is your advice to a marginal veteran player who is interested in serving as the team's union representative? As the club's general counsel, what is your advice to team management regarding cutting a player serving as the team's union representative?

d.   Breach of Duty to Bargain in Good Faith and to Provide Relevant Information Concerning Mandatory Subjects of Collective Bargaining

As noted previously, both the league's labor representatives and the players union have a duty to collectively bargain over wages, hours, and other terms and conditions of employment. The players union generally wants to bargain over a wide range of issues, but league clubs may be reluctant to do so. The following cases consider what constitutes mandatory subjects of collective bargaining in the context of professional sports labor relations as well as the parties' mutual obligation to provide relevant information concerning these subjects to the other side.

SILVERMAN v. MAJOR LEAGUE BASEBALL PLAYER RELATIONS COMMITTEE, INC. (SILVERMAN I)

516 F. Supp 588 (S.D.N.Y. 1981)

WERKER, District Judge.

. . . Since 1966 the Major League baseball players have been represented by the Players Association. During this time the respondent [Major League Baseball Player Relations Committee, Inc. (PRC)] has been the exclusive collective bargaining agent of twenty-six Major League clubs. The Board of Directors of the PRC is empowered to formulate labor policy for the clubs and direct all negotiations with the Players Association. C. Raymond Grebey, Director of Player Relations of PRC, has been designated by the PRC Board as the official spokesman for the PRC in all collective bargaining matters. . . .

The Players Association and the PRC bargain to establish an agreement on pensions, allowances, and a variety of rules governing players' employment. Except as to a base salary, under the various agreements negotiated by the parties, the Players Association has waived its right to bargain with the PRC about individual player salaries. Thus, above a minimum salary, the subject has been left to each individual player to negotiate with his club.

Prior to 1975, when a Major League baseball player's employment contract expired, he was precluded from negotiating for employment with any other team except his own. In December 1975, as the result of grievances filed by the Players Association on behalf of John Messersmith and David McNally, an arbitrator found that Major League clubs could not reserve a player for more than one year ("option year") past the expiration of his contract. A player who completes the option year without signing a renewal contract with his team becomes a "free agent" who is able to negotiate with other clubs.

In 1976 the Players Association and the PRC entered into a collective bargaining agreement, effective January 1, 1976 through December 31, 1979, which provided, *inter alia*, for "free agency" as established by the Messersmith-McNally decision. Pursuant to this agreement, however, a player was required to serve six years in the Major Leagues before becoming a "free agent." The agreement also provided for "compensation" in the form of an amateur player draft choice to each club which lost a "free agent" player selected by more than two clubs for negotiation rights. After four years of experimenting with this new system, the Players Association and the PRC commenced negotiations for a new collective bargaining agreement on November 11, 1979.

On January 16, 1980, the PRC presented a proposal which recognized the difference in quality, as measured by skill and ability, among the various players choosing to become "free agents." Under this proposal, as finally offered on May 12, 1980, a team losing a "free agent" selected by less than four clubs will not be afforded replacement player "compensation." If a player is selected for negotiation rights by four to seven clubs, the club signing a contract with the player must compensate the player's former club with an amateur draft choice, as before. However, if a player is selected by eight or more clubs, and meets certain minimum performance standards, the signing club must compensate the former club with not only an amateur draft choice, but also a professional player of the former club's choice from a list of unprotected players under contract with the signing club. In this third category, the player is referred to as a "ranking free agent" or "premium" player. Each club may retain 40 players under the contract. Depending upon the performance level of the "free agent" signed, the signing team may protect from 15 to 18 of its 40 players.

The Players Association adamantly opposed this proposal as having a negative impact on player salaries. Since the proposal requires a club signing a "ranking free agent" to give up a professional player as well as an amateur draft choice, the Association predicts that the number of clubs willing to bid for a "premium" player and the salaries they would offer would be limited by the knowledge that they would be required to forfeit a player of perhaps comparable quality. Correspondingly, the player's present club could then offer him less to insure his remaining with the team.

As negotiations progressed, various matters were being resolved, but it became apparent that the issue of additional replacement player "compensation" was a significant impediment to settlement. . . . On December 8, 1980, Bowie Kuhn, Commissioner of Baseball, delivered a speech at the Annual Convention of Professional Baseball. Commenting on the financial difficulties facing the industry, Commissioner Kuhn expressed concern about escalating player salaries brought about by "free agency." He cited the companion problem of "compensation" as a threat to competitive balance in baseball and thus expressed a concern about adequate replacement talent for the loss of a "free agent." Sounding a clarion call to owners and players alike to recognize the need to correct the system of "free agency" which has given rise to these problems, he predicted further financial loss without cooperation between the two groups. . . .

By letter of February 27, 1981, the Players Association requested the PRC to provide certain financial information for all member clubs. The Players Association premised the appropriateness of its request on Commissioner Kuhn's December 1980 speech which the Association interpreted as an affirmation of its belief that the "compensation" proposal was motivated by financial concerns.

Mr. Miller explained that the requested financial data was "necessary for the Players Association to properly discharge its duties and responsibilities . . . as the exclusive collective bargaining representative of all major league players, for purposes of preparation for and conduct of the ongoing negotiations."

On March 13, 1981, the PRC, through Mr. Grebey, refused to comply with the Association's request, repeating the PRC's position that its bargaining stance regarding "compensation" was not based on "economic incapacity or inability." . . .

. . . Grebey [subsequently] stated that the PRC had "never advanced the position nor taken refuge in argumentation which either directly or indirectly claims an inability to pay as a defense for (its) position in collective bargaining." Rather, the objective of the PRC in proposing the plan for "compensation," explained Mr. Grebey, "is to enhance player balance between clubs losing a quality free agent over the long term by providing replacement personnel that will: (1) compensate for the loss of a player; (2) compensate for the general inability of clubs to overcome this added turn-over on a club roster through additions from the Minor Leagues; and (3) provide equity balance in compensation, reflecting the different levels of skill and ability of players who chose to become free agents as evidenced by our experience of the past four years."

Meanwhile, during this second round of negotiations, various statements by club owners appeared in the media. These statements all reflect an expression of concern about the financial well-being of the baseball industry and/or the level of player salaries. . . .

Believing that the PRC's bargaining position on the issue of player "compensation" was based at least in part on the financial difficulties of certain member clubs, on May 7, 1981, the Players Association filed an unfair labor practice charge with the Board alleging respondents' failure to bargain in good faith by refusing to comply with the Players Association's request for financial disclosure in violation of Sections 8(a)(1) and (5) of the Act, 29 U.S.C. §§ 158(a) (1) and (5).

Following investigation and pursuant to Section 10(b) of the Act, 29 U.S.C. § 160(b), the Board filed a complaint charging respondents with violating Sections 8(a)(1) and (5) of the Act. A hearing on this complaint before an administrative law judge of the Board is scheduled to commence on June 15, 1981.

The temporary injunctive relief sought by petitioner requires respondents to rescind their February 19, 1981, action by which they exercised their right under the 1980 basic agreement and unilaterally implemented their bargaining proposal regarding "compensation." This relief, if granted, would thus preclude the Players Association, under the terms of the basic agreement, from commencing a strike. Petitioner argues that if its request for relief is not granted, the Players Association and the baseball player-employees it represents will be forced to strike within forty-eight hours after this Court rules, or be bound through the end of 1983 by the PRC's proposal. Petitioner emphasizes that obvious irreparable harm to the players, owners and fans would flow from a decision by the Players Association to strike.

The Association contends that if petitioner should prevail in the proceedings presently before the administrative law judge, the Board would be unable to adequately remedy the PRC's alleged unfair labor practice by ordering the clubs to disclose the financial information which the Association seeks, since the Board cannot undo the effects of a strike which would ensue as a result of the denial of petitioner's instant request for relief.

Respondents vigorously oppose petitioner's application as a tactic by the Players Association to avoid the consequences of a contract freely bargained for and entered into by it. . . .

The Board alleges in its petition that the public statements by club owners regarding claims of financial difficulties created a reasonable belief on the part of the Players Association that respondents' bargaining position during this second round of negotiations was based, "at least in part, on the present or prospective financial difficulties of certain of Respondents' member clubs." Although Marvin Miller has expressed some doubt as to club owners' inability to pay rising player salaries, he nevertheless takes the position that the Players Association must have the financial information it requests if it is to fulfill its duty of fair representation. If deprived of that information, the Association claims that it must blindly decide whether to press its demands and risk the loss of jobs for its members if the clubs cannot survive under the "compensation" terms proposed by the Association, or to recede from it position and accept the

PRC's proposal without verifying owners' claims of financial distress caused by "free agency." Thus, the Association brought an unfair labor practice charge against the PRC for its failure to disclose the requested financial data after the clubs allegedly put into issue their inability to pay.

In *N. L. R. B. v. Truitt Manufacturing Co.*, 351 U.S. 149, 76 S.Ct. 753, 100 L.Ed. 1027 (1956), the Supreme Court laid to rest the question of whether an employer, bound by the National Labor Relations Act to bargain in good faith, could claim that it was financially unable to pay higher wages and then refuse a union's request to produce financial data to substantiate the claim. Holding that such conduct supported a finding of failure to bargain in good faith, in violation of Section 8(a)(5) of the Act, 29 U.S.C. § 158(a)(5), the Court explained:

> Good-faith bargaining necessarily requires that claims made by either bargainer should be honest claims. This is true about an asserted inability to pay an increase in wages. If such an argument is important enough to present in the give and take of bargaining, it is important enough to require some sort of proof of its accuracy.

However, *Truitt's* progeny have held that an employer is required to disclose its financial condition only when the employer claims an inability to pay, however phrased, during the course of bargaining. . . . Petitioner admits that at no time during bargaining sessions have respondents made a claim of inability to pay. Nevertheless, petitioner urges the Court to find that public statements made by several club owners as well as the Commissioner of Baseball about the financial condition of the industry are sufficient to support a finding of reasonable cause to believe that respondents have injected the inability to pay into the negotiations.

The cases cited by petitioner in support of its position are simply inapposite. In each case, inability to pay was put in issue at the bargaining table. . . .

Thus, Petitioner concedes, as it must, that the Board and courts have never found that an employer has injected financial condition into negotiations, absent statements or conduct by the employer at the bargaining table. Nevertheless, it urges this Court to find, on the basis of statements by Commissioner Kuhn and various owners, that the financial issue has become relevant to the negotiations regarding "compensation" because of the unique nature of collective bargaining in baseball. Mindful that this Court must be "hospitable" to the views of the Regional Director, however novel, . . . I am nevertheless convinced that the Board's position is wrong, and thus will not "defer to the statutory construction urged by (it)."

It is the PRC Board of Directors which is charged with the exclusive authority to formulate the collective bargaining position of the clubs and to negotiate agreements with the Players Association. Indeed, Grebey, the official spokesman for the PRC in collective bargaining matters, has consistently denied that the clubs' financial status is at issue in the current negotiations.

Commissioner Kuhn's remarks in December 1980 at the convention cannot be imputed to the PRC as a statement of its bargaining position. First, petitioner's attempt to establish an agency relationship between the Commissioner and the PRC is unavailing. As Commissioner of Baseball, Kuhn presides at the regular joint meetings of the Major Leagues, but does not request nor preside at special meetings called by the PRC. Moreover, while Kuhn is responsible for disciplining players who may then file grievances against him in his capacity as

Commissioner, he has likewise ordered the clubs to cease certain action when the interests of baseball warranted his intercession, as when he directed the clubs to open their training camps in the spring of 1976. . . .

In a multi-employer bargaining unit as large and publicly visible as the Major League Baseball Clubs, it is inevitable that extraneous statements will be made by individuals affiliated in some way with the group which are inconsistent with the official position of the unit. This only underscores the necessity, recognized by the PRC, for centralized bargaining responsibility and authority. Clearly, individual expressions of opinion cannot serve to bind the entire bargaining unit in the absence of authority to speak for the group. . . .

The Act has provided for collective bargaining between the parties through their authorized representatives. If this Court were to find that the several public statements by club officials and the Commissioner were sufficient to support a finding that the PRC and its negotiating team view the respondents' "compensation" proposal as related to the financial condition of the clubs, it would do violence to the intent and purpose of the Act which limits the jurisdiction of this Court. . . .

To accept petitioner's argument would permit disgruntled employers in a multi-employer unit who disagreed with the negotiation policies of their representatives to force negotiation issues into the courts, thereby "conducting labor management relations by way of an injunction," a result clearly contrary to the purpose of the Act. . . .

Thus, I cannot find that the comments by several club officials and the Commissioner, relied upon by petitioner, are statements of policy on behalf of the PRC which would support a claim of inability to pay.

Moreover, the issue of salary, above a minimum rate, is not a subject of collective bargaining between the Players Association and the PRC. Rather, individual players negotiate independently with the clubs as to their salary. Indeed, it is the high player salaries which have resulted from the negotiation of individual contracts by players and clubs which Commissioner Kuhn addressed in his 1980 speech. Noting that player salaries are increasing at a more rapid rate than revenues, he opined that bargaining of individual contracts has led to this problem. . . .

The court is mindful that a strike may result from its denial of petitioner's request for a 10(j) injunction. Indeed, the industry has suffered a strike in the past. Nevertheless, in struggling with a temptation and even compulsion to prevent a strike in the public interest, I am bound by the law. The possibility of a strike, although a fact of life in labor relations, offers no occasion for this Court to distort the principles of law and equity. The resolution of the "compensation" issue is left to the parties through the negotiation process.

PLAY BALL!!!

SO ORDERED.

NOTES AND QUESTIONS

1. Unfortunately for MLB and its fans, the judge's "order" to "play ball" was a wish, not a command enforceable by contempt sanctions. On June 10, 1981, he declined to grant the NLRB's request to enjoin the PRC from unilaterally implementing its bargaining proposal regarding "compensation" for lost free agents. The players went on strike two days later. The strike

lasted 50 days, eliminating much of the season and resulting in a "split season" that left all parties dissatisfied. It is hard to determine what would have happened if the judge had granted the injunction. In all likelihood, the strike would have been postponed at least until after the 1981 season. In the interim, perhaps the PRC and MLBPA would have found compromise and reached a new collective bargaining agreement, possibly averting a strike altogether.

The *Silverman I* judge was following well-established legal precedent in denying the injunction based on the circumstances. It generally takes more than a few outsider comments, even by owners, about potential economic hardship to require the clubs to open their books. In general, league clubs prefer not to disclose information about their finances. However, there have been some instances in which disclosure of league financial information has occurred. In 1982, the NFLPA filed a successful unfair labor practices claim, pursuant to which the NFL was required to divulge the terms of its television contracts to allow the players association to evaluate its fair share of such proceeds. In 1982-1983, the National Basketball Association voluntarily opened its books to demonstrate to players the tenuous state of its finances, thus leading to the first professional sports collective bargaining agreement with an aggregate player salary cap.

2. One tactic used by MLB club owners in 1981 foreshadowed what has become a common practice. The club owners built a "war chest" in anticipation of the strike, primarily strike insurance costing the insurers millions of dollars. Since then, insurance companies have been reluctant to assume such risks even for the payment of hefty premiums. Instead, both sides regularly accumulate funds received from their respective constituents (i.e., club owners or players) or third-party sources (e.g., media contracts or intellectual property licensing royalties) for economic protection against a protracted strike.

In 2008, anticipating that the 2011 NFL CBA expiration would trigger a work stoppage, NFL owners appeared to begin building a "war chest" of their own. Rather than relying on insurance, however, they negotiated television contract extensions that would produce revenue during the 2011 season even if no games were played. These extensions created for the NFL a $4 billion cushion, and recognizing the economic leverage that money created for the NFL owners, the NFLPA sued to prevent them from accessing it. See *White v. National Football League*, 766 F. Supp. 2d 941, 948 (D. Minn. 2011). In the suit, the NFLPA alleged that the NFL brokered a relatively weak deal for pre–work stoppage revenues, which were shared with players, in exchange for the robust $4 billion deal, which would not be shared with players if a work stoppage were to occur. The court decided in the NFLPA's favor, finding that "the NFL renegotiated the broadcast contracts to benefit its exclusive interest at the expense of, and contrary to, the joint interests of the NFL and the Players[,] which constitutes 'a design . . . to seek an unconscionable advantage' and is inconsistent with good faith." *White*, 766 F. Supp. 2d at 951 (internal citations omitted).

3. Players unions, for their part, tend to systematically prepare for potential labor stoppages as well. For instance, as it became increasingly clear that a 2011 NFL work stoppage was likely, the NFLPA tried to brace players economically through raising their financial awareness and encouraging them to save at least three game checks in case of a work stoppage. In addition,

the NFLPA took out a secret insurance policy sufficient to pay each player $200,000 in the event the lockout extended into the season. In fact, the insurance fund may have helped turned the tide in the CBA negotiations: when the players revealed its existence during what had devolved into a stalemate, it "got the [owners'] attention," signaling that the players might not break solidarity for fear of financial hardship as quickly as was previously assumed. Jim Trotter, *Players' Secret Lockout Insurance Could Have Sparked Talks*, Sports Illustrated, July 15, 2011, http://sportsillustrated.cnn.com/2011/writers/jim_trotter/07/15/secret-lockout-fund/index.html.

Similarly, about 200 NBA players bought lockout insurance prior to the 2011 NBA lockout to ensure income flow despite the work stoppage. Moreover, some NBA players chose to ensure income flow by playing basketball in foreign leagues during the lockout under contracts that allowed them to return to the NBA mid-season in the event labor peace was achieved.

Both sides must negotiate in good faith over wages, hours, and other terms and conditions of player employment. The league cannot unilaterally implement new terms relating to mandatory subjects of collective bargaining until the parties have reached an impasse in collective bargaining negotiations. It is an unfair labor practice to violate either of these requirements.

Soon after the NFL's first collective bargaining agreement was reached, NFL club owners, at the league commissioner's behest, unilaterally adopted a rule imposing an automatic $200 fine on all players leaving the bench and going onto the field of play during altercations transpiring in the heat of battle. The NFLPA alleged that this unilateral conduct constituted a refusal to bargain with the union in violation of §8(a)(5). The owners contended that the commissioner promulgated this rule pursuant to his authority under the collective bargaining agreement to fine a player for conduct detrimental to the NFL. The Eighth Circuit affirmed the NLRB's determination that the rule was promulgated by the NFL club owners rather than the commissioner. Because the rule, which establishes a term or condition of employment, is a mandatory subject of bargaining, its unilateral implementation is an unfair labor practice. See *National Football League Players Assn. v. National Labor Relations Bd.*, 503 F.2d 12 (8th Cir. 1974).

The following case, which arose out of the 1994 MLB players strike, considers the important distinction between mandatory and permissive subjects of collective bargaining.

SILVERMAN V. MAJOR LEAGUE BASEBALL PLAYER RELATIONS COMMITTEE, INC. (SILVERMAN II)

880 F. Supp. 246 (S.D.N.Y. 1995)

SOTOMAYOR, District Judge.

. . . On March 15, 1995, on the basis of charges filed by [the Major League Baseball Players Association (the "Players")], the [NLRB] issued a Complaint and Notice of Hearing alleging, *inter alia*, that [the Major League Baseball Player Relations Committee, Inc. (the PRC)] had violated Sections 8(a)(1) and (5) of the Act by unilaterally eliminating, before an impasse had been reached, salary arbitration for certain reserve players, competitive bargaining for certain free agents, and the anti-collusion provision of their collective bargaining agreement, Article XX(F). After the Board concluded that there was reasonable cause to believe that a violation of the Act had occurred and that injunctive relief was just and proper, it filed this Petition on March 27, 1995. . . .

The most recent Basic Agreement between the parties extended from January 1990 through December 1993. The Agreement covered a multitude of employment terms and conditions. The pertinent provisions of the Agreement to the issues before me involve the Agreement's reserve and free agency systems. Essentially, the free agency system permits players who have completed six major-league playing seasons to set their wages with individual owner clubs. . . . The anti-collusion provision of the Basic Agreement, Subsection F of Article XX, provides, in relevant part, that the wage process between the free agent individual player and club owner is an individual matter to be determined solely by each Player and each Club for his or its own benefit. Players shall not act in concert with other Players and the Clubs shall not act in concert with other Clubs. . . .

In the matter before me, the NLRB has charged the Owners with violating §§ 8(a)(1) & (5) of the Act, that is, of violating the duty to bargain collectively in good faith with the Players. . . .

The potential subject matter of parties engaged in collective bargaining has been divided by the Supreme Court into two categories: mandatory and permissive subjects of bargaining. . . . Mandatory subjects are those encompassed in Section 8(d) in the phrase "wages, hours, and other terms and conditions of employment," while permissive subjects are all other matters. The distinction between mandatory and permissive subjects of bargaining is crucial in labor disputes, because it determines to what extent one party may compel the other to bargain over a given proposal: mandatory subjects require the parties to bargain in good faith, whereas no such requirement adheres to permissive subjects. It is not always obvious whether or not a provision relates to "wages, hours, and other terms and conditions of employment," and the mandatory/permissive distinction is the subject of much case law.

The distinction between mandatory and permissive subjects of bargaining is also important upon expiration of a collective bargaining agreement, in the period before the parties have instituted a successor agreement. During the interim between agreements, the Supreme Court has held, the parties must honor the terms and conditions of the expired contract that involve mandatory subjects of bargaining, at least until the parties reach a good faith impasse. . . . A unilateral change of an expired provision on a mandatory topic, such as one involving wages, is an unfair labor practice, as it violates the duty to bargain collectively in good faith. The provision of the expired agreement survives only until the parties reach a new agreement or until the parties bargain in good faith to impasse. The policy behind the rule retaining the mandatory terms of the expired agreement is that it will be more effective in promoting peaceful negotiations than a rule allowing a change in the status quo during the critical bargaining period. . . .

In the matter before me, the Owners do not deny that they changed provisions in the expired contract; specifically, that they revoked the salary arbitration clause and eliminated section XX(F), the free agency anti-collusive provision. The Owners assert, however, that their changes were allowed because the provisions concerned a statutorily permissive topic, i.e., who would collectively bargain for them over free agent and reserve player salaries. The NLRB maintains that the Owners' changes involved mandatory subjects, and the Owners thereby committed an unfair labor practice by undermining the collective bargaining process. . . .

Collective bargaining in the context of professional sports presents issues different from most other contexts. On the one hand, the talent of an individual athlete can provide him with extraordinary bargaining power, but on the other hand, a player may sell his talent only to a circumscribed group of owners, who have something akin to monopoly power in the sport at issue. These circumstances in professional sports have given rise to the development of the reserve/free agency system, which, perhaps not surprisingly, is quite different from other models of collective bargaining in less specialized and unique industries.

To look for guidance, then, in deciding whether the Board had reasonable cause for making its determination that the provisions changed by the Owners were mandatory, I find most helpful precedent that involves professional sports. *Accord, Wood v. Nat'l Basketball Ass'n*, 809 F.2d 954, 961 (2d Cir.1987) (collective bargaining between athletes and their leagues "raise[s] numerous problems with little or no precedent in standard industrial relations"). And in the sports context, courts have overwhelmingly held that the constituent parts of reserve/free agency systems are mandatory, not permissive, subjects of bargaining.

For example, this Circuit held in *Wood* that the agreement between professional basketball players and team owners "is a unique bundle of compromises," and matters such as salary caps, minimum individual salaries, fringe benefits, minimum aggregate team salaries, guaranteed revenue sharing, and first refusal provisions are all mandatory subjects of bargaining, as "[e]ach of them is intimately related to 'wages, hours, and other terms and conditions of employment.'" . . . Likewise, in *Mackey v. Nat'l Football League*, 543 F.2d 606, 615 (8th Cir.1976), *cert. dismissed*, 434 U.S. 801, 98 S.Ct. 28, 54 L.Ed.2d 59 (1977), the Eighth Circuit held that the Rozelle Rule, even though it does not on its face deal with wages, hours, and other terms and conditions of employment, is a mandatory subject of bargaining because it "operates to restrict a player's ability to move from one team to another and depresses player salaries." *See also, Powell v. Nat'l Football League*, 930 F.2d 1293, 1298-99 (8th Cir.1989) (agreements establishing first refusal and compensation system are mandatory subjects).

I recognize that these precedents, which address the question of whether wage topics trump the antitrust laws, do not deal with the issue before me, i.e., the continuation of reserve and free agency systems in which individual owners competitively bid for players after the expiration of a collective bargaining agreement and pending the completion by Player and Owner representatives of negotiations over a successor agreement. The owners argue that the right to bid competitively or collectively must be a permissive topic of bargaining, because if it were a mandatory topic, the Owners would be forced to give up their statutory right to bargain collectively.

Courts in addressing the antitrust area of law have easily recognized, however, that the essence of collective bargaining in professional sports is the establishment and maintenance of reserve and free agency systems in which owners agree to bid competitively for some players and collectively for others. The Owners' argument has a superficial appeal in its attempt to harken back to the unionizing cry of employees when they banded together to create this nation's labor laws. What the Owners have missed here, and the NLRB has not, is that the statutory right to join collective bargaining units belongs to employees, not to employers. The NLRA gives only employees the section 7 right to bargain collectively through an elected representative. The only reciprocal statutory right the Act imposes on employers and employees is that they bargain with the other in good faith. In other words, the term "employer union" for collective bargaining purposes is not meaningful.

The extent of statutory protection for an employer is that it may select a representative for the purpose of bargaining free of coercion from a labor union. . . . This right is not a statutory right for a group of employers to bargain collectively through one representative. In fact, while many multi-employer bargaining units, like the PRC, have been formed, the NLRB and the union must consent to the such formation. *See, e.g., NLRB v. Johnson Sheet Metal, Inc.*, 442 F.2d 1056, 1059 (10th Cir.1971) ("[t]he basic test of the appropriateness of a multi-employer bargaining unit is whether it was created with the approval, express or implied, of the parties"). . . .

Maintaining the reserve/free agency systems in the interim between collective bargaining agreements does not alter the rights of Owners to have the PRC represent them for purposes of negotiating a successor agreement or to continue to oppose the inclusion of the systems in any successor agreement. The Owners can, if they successfully bargain, end the free agency and salary arbitration systems, exclude the anti-collusion provision, and create an entirely new system. What they cannot do is alter particular individual's wages until the system is changed by agreement or until the parties negotiate to impasse. That is the nub of all wage negotiations which are inherently mandatory subjects of bargaining. It must be remembered that many employers are forced to continue sometimes onerous and debilitating wage obligations until the collective bargaining process runs its course, just as many employees may earn less than they would in a system that more closely duplicates the free market. Having freely entered into the free agency and reserve systems in their Basic Agreement, the Owners are bound to that system until they bargain in good faith to an impasse.

In view of the abundant case law in the professional sports context that has found that constituent parts of the reserve/free agency system are mandatory subjects of collective bargaining, I find that the Board had substantial reasonable cause to conclude, and a substantial likelihood of success ultimately in establishing, that the unilateral changes made by the Owners to the free agency system before impasse violated the rule against changes to mandatory subjects of bargaining. In summary, the Board has clearly met its injunctive remedy standard in demonstrating that the Owners committed an unfair labor practice by their unilateral abrogation of Article XX(F) and the free agency system.

For substantially similar reasons, I find that salary arbitration for reserve players is also a mandatory part of the collective bargaining process between the Players and the Owners. . . .

I find injunctive relief here warranted for several reasons. An important public interest in the process of collective bargaining will be irreparably harmed if an injunction does not issue. This strike has captivated the public's attention, given the popularity of the sport as well as the protracted nature and well-documented bitterness of the strike. Thus, this strike is about more than just whether the Players and Owners will resolve their differences. It is also about how the principles embodied by federal labor law operate. In a very real and immediate way, this strike has placed the entire concept of collective bargaining on trial. It is critical, therefore, that the Board ensure that the spirit and letter of federal labor law be scrupulously followed. If the Board is unable to enforce the NLRA, public confidence in the collective bargaining process will be permanently and severely undermined. . . . Issuing the injunction before Opening Day is important to ensure that the symbolic value of that day is not tainted by an unfair labor practice and the NLRB's inability to take effective steps against its perpetuation.

Although this public interest alone justifies the issuance of an injunction, I also find that returning the parties to the status quo will permit them to salvage some of the important bargaining equality that existed before the February 6 unfair labor practices were committed. Before February 6, the Players had the right to attempt to salvage the upcoming season and avoid the continuing damage to their short professional careers by offering to return to work under the terms of the Basic Agreement before replacement players were used in the regular season. . . .

Finally, the Owners argue that even if there is reasonable cause to believe that they committed unfair labor practices, the resulting injury to the Players is merely lost wages which can be compensated through damages. The Owners' argument is flawed because there is more than money involved in the systems at issue here and because there is no adequate way to reconstruct the systems to fully recompense the losses of free agents or reserve players.

Salary is just one factor a free agent considers when seeking and accepting offers. A free agent may wish to join a team because of personal reasons such as family considerations, or because of promises of more playing time. Likewise, a free agent may select a team that pays less money but whose coaching staff and team roster make it a World Series contender. . . .

The protections of the NLRA extend to non-monetary bargaining topics that are "terms and conditions of employment." . . . In professional baseball, whether to leave a team, where to go and why are of "deep concern" to the affected players and the loss of those choices in the terms and conditions of employment cannot be adequately recompensed by money. The only adequate remedy to protect these important personal rights, rights which the NLRB is empowered to protect, is to issue an injunction and thereby restore the status quo. . . .

Similarly, to the extent the salary arbitration system is intimately intertwined with the choice for both owners and players between free agency or arbitration, it is nearly impossible to reconstruct retrospectively the factors that would have influenced each side's decision at the time of election. Hence, even though it is easier later to reconstruct the actual process of salary arbitration and more precisely determine a lost wage from that process, monetary damages are insufficient to recompense for the harm caused in eliminating the salary arbitration process as a choice in the integrated reserve/free agency systems.

Free agency, salary arbitration, and the reserve systems are three aspects of the professional baseball wage structure which are inexorably linked. . . .

Thus, a poisoning of the free agency bargaining process will also affect the wage negotiations of reserve and salary arbitration players. Conversely, the loss of salary arbitration in the reserve system skews the choice of free agency rights. The unusual wage structure in this monopoly industry makes it extraordinarily difficult if not nearly impossible to reconstruct past market conditions for purposes of retroactive damage calculations. Where "monetary damages are difficult to ascertain or are inadequate," an injunction is appropriate. In short, in balancing the equities, I find that the harm to the public, the players, and the NLRB compels the issuance of a Section 10(j) injunction in this case.

. . . This injunction is to remain in effect until either (1) the Players and Owners enter into a new collective bargaining agreement that replaces the expired Basic Agreement, or (2) the final disposition of the matters pending before the National Labor Relations Board . . . or (3) a finding of this court, upon petition of the Players or Respondents . . . demonstrating that an impasse in good faith bargaining has occurred despite a reasonable passage of time negotiating in good faith the full mandatory bargaining terms of the expired Basic Agreement. . . .

NOTES AND QUESTIONS

1. William Gould was Chairman of the NLRB when the foregoing matter came before the Board. In his book, Labored Relations: Law, Politics and the NLRB—A Memoir (2000), Professor Gould discusses his experiences in being confirmed by the U.S. Senate after his nomination by President Clinton and his tenure on the NLRB. He devotes a chapter to an analysis of the MLB labor conflict and strike in 1994-1995 and the Board's role in those matters.

    In 1995, he also discussed these matters in the Cambridge Lectures at Queen's College, University of Cambridge, England. In unpublished remarks, he stated:

> Labor law has become a dominant element in the resolution of professional sports disputes. . . . The National Labor Relations Act of 1935, as amended, provides for a secret ballot method of resolving disputes about union recognition and representation, as well as a balanced system of unfair labor practice prohibitions applicable to both management and labor. But it does not provide a mechanism for resolving contract negotiations issues except for requiring the parties to bargain in good faith.
>
> The baseball dispute has involved the unfair labor practices portions of the Board's jurisdiction. On March 26 of this year, the Board determined to seek injunctive relief against unilateral changes in free agency and salary arbitration procedures which had been instituted by the owners prior to that time. The relevant portions of the duty to bargain obligation require that both sides bargain in "good faith"—that is, with a good faith intent to consummate a collective bargaining agreement (entering into an agreement is not required under the statute) until the point of impasse or deadlock on all mandatory subjects of bargaining. . . .
>
> Notwithstanding the Curt Flood decision's adherence to the doctrine of stare decisis, the fact of the matter is that labor law, whatever its deficiencies, has played a significant role in the world of baseball and in other professional sports. The statutory support for collective bargaining has been facilitated by virtue of the Board's assertion of jurisdiction. Arbitration awards creating free agency were enforced in the federal courts under the standards of deference accorded arbitration awards by the United States Supreme Court for the past 35 years. And, perhaps most important of all, the 1995 baseball season has been played because of the Board's March 26 decision to intervene in federal district court to obtain an injunction. This injunction prompted the players to agree to go back to work. The owners then agreed to accept them without a lockout. . . .
>
> The Board has no authority to oblige the parties to continue the 1995 season—or to fashion an agreement for them. Under our system of voluntary collective bargaining, that process is for the parties themselves. The Board's only role is to insure adherence to the proper procedures, to rid the process of unlawful impediments, and to provide for an appropriate framework for future collective bargaining.

2. Shortly after *Silverman II* was decided, MLB players ended their strike and began playing the 1995 season, even though its start date was delayed. Why did the owners not declare a lockout at this point to exert economic pressure on the players in an effort to obtain their agreement to the disputed terms of employment? Why doesn't the NLRB or courts review the reasonableness of the parties' respective collective bargaining positions on the merits?

3. The foregoing cases and Professor Gould's observations return to a continuing inquiry—what are (and what are not) mandatory subjects of bargaining in the professional sports industries? By the express terms of §8(d), this means "wages, hours, and other terms and conditions of employment." But what does this terminology mean as applied to both the business surrounding a sport and to the sport itself? Consider which of the following examples are mandatory subjects of bargaining:

   a. Whether players can be fined for leaving the bench and going onto the field when there is an altercation among other players.
   b. The placement (distance from the basket) of the three-point line in basketball.
   c. The height of the pitcher's mound. (It was lowered in the late 1960s to reduce the perceived advantage given to pitchers.)
   d. The dimensions of the hockey rink or a baseball field.
   e. The addition (in the National League) or elimination (in the American League) of baseball's designated hitter rule.
   f. The expansion or contraction of the number of teams in a league.
   g. The movement of a franchise (in any sport) from one city to another.
   h. The determination of whether foreign players are eligible for a league's draft.

e. Discrimination Against Striking Players

Players have a statutory right to strike, which is an important aspect of our national labor laws designed to facilitate peaceful and productive collective bargaining relations. If the players strike, league clubs may hire replacement players for the duration of their strike as the NFL did during the 1987 three-week strike by its players. In the alternative, a professional sports league may choose to cease operations and lock out its players as the NHL did in 2004 and 2012 and as the NFL and NBA did in 2011. In each of the major professional sports leagues, do club owners or players have the greater economic leverage to exercise in a labor dispute? Whatever the case, as illustrated below, a league and its member clubs are prohibited from retaliating against striking players.

NFL MANAGEMENT COUNCIL
309 N.L.R.B. 78 (1992)

By Chairman Stephens and Members Devaney and Oviatt.

The parties began negotiations for a successor to the 1982-1987 agreement early in 1987. These negotiations were unsuccessful and, on September 21, 1987, after the second week of regular season play, the players went out on strike. The

Respondents immediately began hiring temporary replacements for the striking players. Because certain Clubs were unable to assemble complete teams in time for the games scheduled for September 27-28, 1987, the Respondents canceled those games.

The Respondents also substantially modified the NFL's complex personnel rules governing the hiring of players and their eligibility to play in a game. . . .

Only players on a Club's Active list were eligible to play in a game. The Respondents' rules usually provide that, for games played on a Saturday or Sunday, each Club must establish its Active list for the game by 2 p.m. New York time the day prior to that game. For Monday night games, the deadline is 2 p.m. New York time the day of the game.

In response to the strike, the Respondents substantially modified these rules. On September 29, 1987, the NFL Management Council Executive Committee (CEC) eliminated roster limits until 4 p.m. New York time on October 3, 1987. Clubs were permitted an unlimited number of players on their Inactive lists with a 45-player Active list limit for participating in the games on October 4-5. The deadline for establishing the Active lists was set at 4 p.m. New York time on October 3, and a deadline of 12 p.m. noon local time on Friday (October 2) was established for signing nonroster players. The CEC also established a deadline of 12 p.m. noon local time on October 2 for strikers to report in order to be eligible to play in the Sunday or Monday games.

On October 1, the above rules were modified to establish a 3 p.m. Friday New York time deadline for strikers to report in order to be eligible for that weekend's games or for Clubs to sign nonroster players.

On October 5, the CEC further modified its eligibility rules for returning strikers. The deadline for signing nonroster players was moved back to 4 p.m. New York time Saturday for teams playing on Sunday, and to 4 p.m. New York time on Monday for teams playing that night. For strikers, however, the reporting deadline was set at 1 p.m. New York time on Wednesdays. Strikers reporting after that time were not eligible to play in the following weekend's game, could not be paid for that game, and were exempt from counting against the Club's Active or Inactive list until 4 p.m. New York time on the day following that game. This rule was in effect on Thursday October 15, when the Union advised the Respondents that the strike was over; on the basis of this rule all strikers who had not reported prior to the deadline were declared ineligible to play in the games scheduled for October 18-19 and were not paid for that game. . . .

The judge found, and we agree, that the Union unconditionally offered to return to work on Thursday October 15. For the reasons that follow, we find that the Respondents unlawfully discriminated against the strikers by maintaining and enforcing the Wednesday eligibility deadline to preclude their participation in or payment for the games played on October 18-19.

The Supreme Court has recognized that "there are some practices which are inherently so prejudicial to union interests and so devoid of significant economic justification . . . that the employer's conduct carries with it an inference of unlawful intent so compelling that it is justifiable to disbelieve the employer's protestations of innocent purpose." *American Ship Building Co. v. NLRB*, 380 U.S. 300 (1965). If an employer's conduct falls within this category, "the Board can find an unfair labor practice even if the employer introduces evidence that the conduct was motivated by business considerations." *NLRB v. Great Dane Trailers*, 388 U.S. 26, 34 (1967).

On the other hand, if the impact on employee rights of the discriminatory conduct is comparatively slight, an antiunion motivation must be proved to sustain the charge if the employer has come forward with evidence of legitimate and substantial business justifications for the conduct. Thus, in either situation, once it has been proved that the employer engaged in discriminatory conduct which could have adversely affected employee rights to some extent, the burden is upon the employer to establish that it was motivated by legitimate objectives since proof of motivation is most accessible to him.

Applying these principles to this case, we find as an initial matter that the Wednesday deadline rule clearly constitutes discriminatory conduct which adversely affects employee rights. On its face, the rule discriminates against strikers by applying different, and more stringent, standards for eligibility to participate in NFL games (and to be paid for such participation). Moreover, the rule also adversely affects one of the most significant rights protected by the Act—the right to strike. The Board and the courts, applying the principles of *Great Dane*, have long recognized that the right to strike includes the right to full and complete reinstatement upon unconditional application to return. . . .

As in *Laidlaw*, the Respondents—in reliance on their Wednesday reporting deadline—offered the striking employees who reported for work on October 15 "less than the rights accorded by full reinstatement" (i.e., the right to participate in the games scheduled for October 18-19 and to be paid for those games). . . . Thus, the Wednesday deadline adversely affected the striking employees in the exercise of their right to strike or to cease participating in the strike, by prohibiting the full and complete reinstatement, for the October 18-19 games, of those employees who chose to return to work after the Respondents' deadline had passed.

We need not decide whether, as the General Counsel contends, the Respondents' conduct was inherently destructive of employee rights. Even assuming that the impact on employee rights of the Wednesday deadline rule for strikers was "comparatively slight," the burden still rests with the Respondents to establish "legitimate and substantial business justifications" for the rule. For the reasons that follow, we find that the Respondents have not made the required showing.

The Respondents assert that the Wednesday deadline was justified by the Clubs' need for sufficient time to prepare returning players for game conditions. In this regard, the Respondents presented evidence that the strikers' physical condition would be expected to deteriorate as the strike progressed. In addition, NFL Management Council official Eddie LeBaron testified that players could not maintain their "football condition" without participating in practices involving physical contact. The Respondents also assert that they particularly did not wish to risk injuries to so-called franchise players.

The Respondents also assert that the rule is justified by their goal of ensuring that each Club operates from the same competitive position. Thus, the Wednesday deadline would give each Club the same amount of preparation time with returning players, prevent situations in which a replacement squad was "mismatched" against a squad composed of veterans who had reported late in the week, and ensure that Clubs could prepare for specific players during the Wednesday and Thursday practices when game plans were typically practiced.

Finally, the Respondents assert that the Wednesday deadline was justified in light of substantial administrative difficulties allegedly posed if strikers returned at a late date in the week. These alleged difficulties included the question of how to merge replacement squads and strikers, as well as the logistics of practicing and evaluating two squads of players at the same time and arranging transportation to away games for late-reporting players.

In evaluating the Respondents' justifications, we initially note the unprecedented nature of the Wednesday deadline and the absence of any evidence that the Respondents have imposed a deadline of this type on employees outside of a strike setting. In particular, the record shows that players who withheld their services in pursuit of individual goals (i.e., players holding out for a more lucrative contract) are not subject to comparable restraints on their status on their return. Rather, such players are eligible to play immediately so long as they are included in the Club's active roster. . . .

It is undisputed that the Wednesday deadline was only applicable to striking players. The Respondents could and did sign nonstrikers to contracts subsequent to the date the strikers were declared ineligible. . . .

Under these circumstances, we find that the Respondents have not established legitimate and substantial justifications for the deadline rule. While it may be true that some striking employees' physical conditioning declined during the strike, the same considerations were present in the case of holdouts and of replacement players. . . .

We also find that the Respondents' asserted competitiveness concerns are unpersuasive. Although the Respondents were entitled to ensure that all clubs operated under the same rules, adopting a deadline which discriminated against strikers was unnecessary to the achievement of this goal. The Respondents' argument that Clubs needed the practice time provided by the Wednesday deadline to prepare the strikers to play (and, for the purpose of those practices, needed to know who would be playing for its opponent) is contradicted by their willingness to allow nonstrikers with substantially less preparation time to play in those games. . . .

The Respondents also provide no explanation for the fact that the initial deadline for returning strikers, 12 noon on Friday (later modified to 3 p.m. New York time), would have provided the Clubs with less time to accomplish the reinstatement of returning strikers than they actually had when the strikers reported on October 15. . . .

In sum, the Respondents' Wednesday deadline prohibited employees who returned from the strike on October 15 from playing in the following weekend's games and prohibited their Club from paying them for that game on the basis of their absence from the Club during the strike. The only players subject to such restrictions were those who chose to participate in the strike, a concerted activity protected by the Act. Players absent from their Club for other reasons were not subject to any similar restriction on their eligibility to participate in games; players ineligible to play for other reasons were nevertheless still entitled to be paid. Accordingly, for the reasons stated above, we find that the Respondents' maintenance and enforcement of its Wednesday deadline rule violated Section 8(a)(1) and (3) of the Act. . . .

To remedy the unfair labor practices which we have found, we shall order the Respondents to cease and desist, and to take certain affirmative action necessary to effectuate the purposes of the Act. Specifically, we shall order the Respondents to make whole all employees who were denied wages and declared ineligible for the games played on October 18 and 19, 1987, on the basis of the Respondents' Wednesday eligibility rule for strikers, with interest computed in the manner set forth in the judge's decision. The Respondents shall also make whole those injured players denied compensation on account of their participation in the strike in the manner set forth in the judge's decision. . . .

5.   Union's Duty of Fair Representation

Unlike most other unions, a labor union representing professional athletes faces unique challenges. It must represent the diverse interests of several hundred extremely talented athletes who have overcome difficult odds to rise to the top of a very elite profession. The small number of athletes who ever get the chance to play their sport at a major league level for even a brief period are far outnumbered by those who would seek to invade their ranks. Even within their membership ranks are telling divisions within a spectrum including a relatively few superstars, several very good players, numerous marginal players, and some perennial benchwarmers.

The career of a major league professional athlete is, on average, very short in relation to most other professional careers, although their egos often are much bigger. Thus, the substantial economic rewards that may be gained in the brief time allotted to a professional athlete must be grasped eagerly. That is why professional athletes have turned to agents, attorneys, accountants, marketing specialists, and others in an effort to maximize their earning potential. It is also why the task of the labor union representing them is a difficult one.

The NLRA grants to a union exclusive negotiating and other rights to act on behalf of all members of the collective bargaining unit. As a result, the union sometimes has the ability to sacrifice particular individuals' rights to further the collective good. In 1944, the Supreme Court held that the NLRA implicitly required a union to fairly represent all members of the collective bargaining unit. *Steele v. Louisville & Nashville Railroads*, 323 U.S. 192 (1944). Under the "hiring hall" concept, this duty has been extended to include incoming rookie players (e.g., Leon Wood, discussed *infra*) and even those at the time ineligible to play in the league (e.g., Maurice Clarett, discussed *infra*). The NLRB has determined that a union's breach of its duty of fair representation is an unfair labor practice. *Miranda Fuel Co.*, 140 N.L.R.B. 181 (1962).

Because the nonstatutory labor exemption precludes any antitrust challenge to the terms of the collective bargaining agreement, the union's duty to fairly represent all current and prospective players' interests becomes particularly significant. In truth, however, breach of this duty has seldom been alleged in the sports context. The following case illustrates the difficulty proving that a players association has breached its duty of fair representation.

PETERSON v. KENNEDY
771 F.2d 1244 (9th Cir. 1985)

REINHARDT, Circuit Judge.

[EDS. James Peterson brought suit against the National Football League Players Association and two of its attorneys. He claimed that the union, through its attorneys, had furnished him with inaccurate advice on which he detrimentally relied in pursuing a grievance against his former ball club, the Tampa Bay Buccaneers. The district court granted a judgment notwithstanding the verdict for defendants after the jury had decided in Peterson's favor. Peterson appealed the JNOV as well as summary judgment and directed verdict rulings in favor of the union attorneys. The following excerpts relate to the granting of the JNOV.]

Peterson's breach of duty claim is based principally on allegations that the union, through its representatives, erroneously advised him to file an injury grievance and that the union failed to rectify its error while there still was time to do so. We assume *arguendo* that the advice was in fact erroneous, although it is not entirely clear that such was the case. Viewed in a light most favorable to Peterson, the evidence presented at trial established, *inter alia*, that: Kennedy, after being informed that Peterson's 1977 contract contained an "injury protection" clause, advised Peterson's agent to file an injury grievance against Tampa Bay; based on Kennedy's advice, Peterson designated his claim as an injury grievance; the union failed to recognize its error within the 60 day period in which a non-injury grievance could have timely been filed; union representatives assured Peterson on many occasions during this 60 day period that the union was handling his grievance for him; as a result of the union's assurances, Peterson failed to file a non-injury grievance within the 60 day period.

The district court concluded that the evidence presented was legally insufficient to sustain the jury's verdict that the union breached its duty of fair representation. We agree. After reviewing all of the evidence in the light most favorable to Peterson, we conclude that the union did not breach its duty of fair representation; the record is devoid of evidence that the union acted in an arbitrary, discriminatory, or bad faith manner.

The duty of fair representation is a judicially established rule imposed on labor organizations because of their status as the exclusive bargaining representative for all of the employees in a given bargaining unit. The Supreme Court recently explained the basis and scope of the duty:

> The duty of fair representation exists because it is the policy of the National Labor Relations Act to allow a single labor organization to represent collectively the interests of all employees within a unit, thereby depriving individuals in the unit of the ability to bargain individually or to select a minority union as their representative. In such a system, if individual employees are not to be deprived of all effective means of protecting their own interests, it must be the duty of the representative organization to "serve the interests of all members without hostility or discrimination toward any, to exercise its discretion with complete good faith and honesty, and to avoid arbitrary conduct." . . .

A union breaches its duty of fair representation only when its conduct toward a member of the collective bargaining unit is "arbitrary, discriminatory, or in bad faith." *Vaca v. Sipes*, 386 U.S. at 190, 87 S.Ct. at 916. The duty is designed to ensure that unions represent fairly the interests of all of their members without exercising hostility or bad faith toward any. It stands "as a bulwark to prevent arbitrary union conduct against individuals stripped of traditional forms of redress by the provisions of federal labor law." . . .

The Supreme Court has long recognized that unions must retain wide discretion to act in what they perceive to be their members' best interests. . . . To that end, we have "stressed the importance of preserving union discretion by narrowly construing the unfair representation doctrine." . . . We have emphasized that, because a union balances many collective and individual interests in deciding whether and to what extent it will pursue a particular grievance, courts should "accord substantial deference" to a union's decisions regarding such matters.

A union's representation of its members "need not be error free." . . . We have concluded repeatedly that mere negligent conduct on the part of a union does not constitute a breach of the union's duty of fair representation. . . .

Peterson recognizes and does not challenge the established principle that a union's negligence cannot give rise to a suit for breach of the duty of fair representation. Furthermore, he does not contend that the NFLPA or any of its representatives acted toward him or his grievance in a discriminatory or bad faith manner. Rather, Peterson claims that the union breached its duty to represent him fairly because its mishandling of his grievance was so egregious as to constitute "arbitrary" conduct.

Whether in a particular case a union's conduct is "negligent," and therefore non-actionable, or so egregious as to be "arbitrary," and hence sufficient to give rise to a breach of duty claim, is a question that is not always easily answered. A union acts "arbitrarily" when it simply ignores a meritorious grievance or handles it in a perfunctory manner, . . . for example, by failing to conduct a "minimal investigation" of a grievance that is brought to its attention. . . . We have said that a union's conduct is "arbitrary" if it is "without rational basis," . . . or is "egregious, unfair and unrelated to legitimate union interests." . . . In *Robesky v. Qantas Empire Airways Ltd.*, 573 F.2d 1082, 1089-90 (9th Cir.1978), we held that a union's unintentional mistake is "arbitrary" if it reflects a "reckless disregard" for the rights of the individual employee, but not if it represents only "simple negligence violating the tort standard of due care." In *Dutrisac v. Caterpillar Tractor Co.*, 749 F.2d 1270, 1274 (9th Cir.1983), we concluded that unintentional union conduct may constitute a breach of the duty of fair representation in situations where "the individual interest at stake is strong and the union's failure to perform a ministerial act completely extinguishes the employee's right to pursue his claim."

There are some significant general principles that emerge from our previous decisions. In all cases in which we found a breach of the duty of fair representation based on a union's arbitrary conduct, it is clear that the union failed to perform a procedural or ministerial act, that the act in question did not require the exercise of judgment and that there was no rational and proper basis for the union's conduct. For example, we found a union acted arbitrarily where it failed to: (1) disclose to an employee its decision not to submit her grievance to arbitration when the employee was attempting to determine whether to accept or reject a settlement offer from her employer, . . . (2) file a timely grievance *after* it had decided that the grievance was meritorious and should be filed, . . . (3) consider individually the grievances of particular employees where the factual and legal differences among them were significant, . . . or (4) permit employees to explain the events which led to their discharge before deciding not to submit their grievances to arbitration. . . .

We have never held that a union has acted in an arbitrary manner where the challenged conduct involved the union's judgment as to how best to handle a grievance. To the contrary, we have held consistently that unions are not liable for good faith, non-discriminatory errors of judgment made in the processing of grievances. . . . We have said that a union's conduct may not be deemed arbitrary simply because of an error in evaluating the merits of a grievance, in interpreting particular provisions of a collective bargaining agreement, or in presenting the grievance at an arbitration hearing. . . . In short, we do not attempt to second-guess a union's judgment when a good faith, non-discriminatory judgment has in fact been made. It is for the union, not the courts, to decide whether and in what manner a particular grievance should be pursued. We reaffirm that principle here.

Sound policy reasons militate against imposing liability on unions for errors of judgment made while representing their members in the collective bargaining process. In *Dutrisac*, we recognized that holding unions liable for such errors would serve ultimately to "defeat the employees' collective bargaining interest in having a strong and effective union." . . . If unions were subject to liability for "judgment calls," it would necessarily undermine their discretion to act on behalf of their members and ultimately weaken their effectiveness. In the long run, the cost of recognizing such liability would be borne not by the unions but by their memberships. Not only would the direct costs of adverse judgments be passed on to the members in the form of increased dues, but, more importantly, unions would become increasingly reluctant to provide guidance to their members in collective bargaining disputes. Such a result would be inconsistent with our oft-repeated commitment to construe narrowly the scope of the duty of fair representation in order to preserve the unions' discretion to decide how best to balance the collective and individual interests that they represent.

Freeing a union from liability for ordinary acts of negligence in the performance of its representational responsibilities requiring judgment on its part, reflects a balance of the union's organizational interest against the individual interests of its members. Our cases, and those of the Supreme Court, tip the balance in favor of the union, and accept the consequence of uncompensated loss sustained by an individual union member. Whether liability for a loss occasioned by ordinary negligence of the union might be spread more equitably among the membership as a whole, rather than be borne by the individual member who is harmed, is no longer an open question.

In applying the foregoing principles to the case at hand, we conclude, as a matter of law, that Peterson failed to establish that the NFLPA breached its duty of fair representation. As mentioned, Peterson does not contend that the union acted in a discriminatory or bad faith manner toward either him or his grievance. He relies exclusively on his claim that the union's error was so egregious as to be "arbitrary." We disagree. The alleged error was one of judgment. Viewing the evidence in the light most favorable to Peterson, the most that can be said is that the union provided him with incorrect advice and did not alter its judgment until it was too late to rectify the error. In this case, deciding whether to file an injury or a non-injury grievance was not a purely mechanical function; the union attorneys were required to construe the scope and meaning of the injury and non-injury grievance provisions of the collective bargaining agreement and to determine which of the two grievance procedures was more appropriate. As we have indicated earlier, the answer was not as simple as a literal reading of the two contract sections might indicate.

Peterson also contends that the union failed adequately to investigate the facts and circumstances of his claim before advising him to file an injury grievance. Peterson does not specify exactly what the union neglected to do; however, his only possible claim appears to be that the union failed to examine copies of his contracts with Tampa Bay before rendering its advice. We find this contention insufficient as a matter of law. Both Peterson and his agent testified that they informed Kennedy of the inclusion of the "injury protection" clause in Peterson's 1977 contract and described its substance to him. We do not believe that a further examination of that provision, or of any other provision in Peterson's contracts, would have better enabled Kennedy to advise Peterson as to which form of grievance to file. It was the grievance and arbitration provisions of the standard collective bargaining agreement, rather than the "injury protection" clause of Peterson's contract, that the union was required to construe in order to determine which grievance procedure was applicable to Peterson's claim. Examining the text of the injury protection clause would not have materially influenced the union's judgment in that regard.

Although the union's representatives may have erred in initially advising Peterson to file an injury grievance and in failing to recognize its mistake in time to file a non-injury grievance in its stead, we are unwilling to subject unions to liability for such errors in judgment. Accordingly, we affirm the district court's conclusion that the evidence presented was insufficient, as a matter of law, to support the jury's verdict against the union. . . .

NOTES AND QUESTIONS

1. The *Peterson* case clarifies the nature of the duty of fair representation that the union owes to its members. What is the standard adopted by the court and its underlying policy justification?

    It bears noting, though, that this case involves a unique, narrow set of circumstances. As previously discussed, other player union actions affect, perhaps adversely and unfairly, not only its members but also others brought within the overall sway of professional sports labor relations. Regarding the NFL's current draft eligibility rules, could Maurice Clarett (who did not meet the age eligibility threshold when he attempted to enter the draft) have successfully asserted that the NFLPA did not fairly represent him and others in negotiations with the NFL regarding initial player eligibility requirements? See generally Matthew J. Mitten and Timothy Davis, *Athlete Eligibility Requirements and Legal Protection of Sports Participation Opportunities*, 8 Va. Sports & Ent. L.J. 71, 107 (2009) ("Under existing law a minimum age eligibility rule (or a *de facto* equivalent) for professional athletes is not a form of prohibited discrimination that breaches a players union's duty of fair representation").

2. As is more fully considered in section C.6 of this chapter, arbitration is the predominate method of resolving disputes in the professional sports industries. Thus, it is important to note the impact of *Vaca v. Sipes*, 386 U.S. 171 (1967), in which the Supreme Court held that a union has the authority to control whether an employee's grievance proceeds to arbitration. In other words, an aggrieved player has no "absolute right" to arbitration if the player's claim is subject to the union's control. However, a player can successfully assert that the union failed to represent his or her interests fairly by proving that the union's actions were arbitrary, discriminatory, or in bad faith. As *Peterson* illustrates, this is a high standard to meet. Additional cases that illustrate the application of the legal principles previously discussed to the professional sports industries include *Sharpe v. NFLPA*, 941 F. Supp. 8 (D.D.C. 1996) and *Chuy v. NFLPA*, 495 F. Supp. 137 (E.D. Pa. 1980). In *Sharpe*, the player brought suit against the union while his injury grievance arbitration with his former club, the Green Bay Packers, was still pending. The court

dismissed the player's complaint, alleging that the union mishandled his grievance because his lawsuit, which is "inextricably interdependent" with the pending arbitration, was premature. At a minimum, the player must receive an adverse decision in arbitration before asserting breach of the union's duty of fair representation in litigation. In *Chuy*, the court held that a player could recover his attorney fees incurred in prosecuting a successful breach of contract claim against his club if the union's failure to process his arbitration grievance was arbitrary, discriminatory, or in bad faith. The player would not have incurred this cost in litigation against his team absent the union's breach of its duty of fair representation.

3. *Eller v. NFLPA*, 2012 WL 1933746 (D. Minn. May 29, 2012), which grew out of the 2011 NFL lockout and the *Brady v. NFL* case that the lockout spurred (discussed in section D.2, *infra*), explores the scope of a union's duty to represent retired players in collective bargaining negotiations. When the NFL and NFLPA agreed to a new ten-year CBA, ending the lockout, a group of retired players who alleged their interests were not represented in the negotiations that produced the CBA, sued the NFLPA, Tom Brady, and others for breach of fiduciary duty and intentional interference with prospective economic advantage, arguing that the defendants "had no authority to negotiate with the League the terms of pension, retirement, and disability benefits with respect to the class of retired NFL players." *Id.* at *3. These retired players, led by Carl Eller, had sued the NFL two weeks after the *Brady* plaintiffs had sued the NFL at the start of the lockout, because they believed the *Brady* plaintiffs would not adequately represent retired players' interests. The United States District Court for the District of Minnesota consolidated the two cases against the NFL and moved forward with the *Eller* plaintiffs representing retired players and the *Brady* plaintiffs representing current and prospective players. As the case proceeded, however, the NFL and the *Brady* plaintiffs held negotiation sessions from which the *Eller* plaintiffs claimed they were excluded, and when the *Brady* plaintiffs and the NFL neared ultimate settlement, the *Eller* plaintiffs were allegedly told that "the NFL would not negotiate retiree issues directly with [them] and that the League's resolution of the dispute with the *Brady* Defendants would include increased benefits for the retired players." *Id.* at *2.

When the retired players then sued the NFLPA et al. for breach of fiduciary duty and intentional interference with prospective economic advantage, the defendants moved for 12(b)(6) dismissal, and the court granted their motion, finding that the NFLPA had done nothing to "assume any legally enforceable fiduciary duty towards the retired players" and that any harm to the retired players resulting from the NFLPA's good faith negotiations with the NFL could not be attributed to improper interference. *Id.* at *8. The court also seemed to doubt whether any harm was actually caused, noting that "a better package of benefits was in fact obtained for the retired players in the 2011 CBA as compared to those in the former CBA." *Id.* at *9.

In coming to its decision, the *Eller* court distinguished *Parrish v. NFLPA*, 2009 WL 88484 (N.D. Cal. Jan. 19, 2009), a class action suit regarding the licensing of retired players' images, in which the NFLPA assumed a fiduciary duty it did not assume in the events precipitating the *Eller* case. In *Parrish*, retired players who had signed a "Retired Player Group License Agreement" with the NFLPA alleged that the NFLPA breached its duty to market their names and likenesses. The court agreed, finding that the NFLPA not only failed to market the retired players, but also actively worked against their interests by devoting a grossly disproportionate measure of its marketing efforts to promoting active, and therefore more profitable, NFL players. In awarding the class $7.1 million in compensatory damages and $21 million in exemplary damages, the court stressed that the NFLPA held itself out to the retired players as a "marketing agent," which assumed an affirmative duty to promote the retired players' names and licenses. *Id.* at *2.

While the district court's judgment in *Parrish* was pending appeal, the retired players and the NFLPA settled the dispute, resulting in a $26.25 million payment to the retired players.

6. *Labor Arbitration*

Labor arbitration's impact on the professional sports industries has been substantial and long lasting. When the first collective bargaining agreements were reached in most of the leagues in the late 1960s, basic provisions for arbitration of many types of grievances were included in these agreements. Often it was designated that the commissioner of the league would be the arbitrator. This was later deemed unsatisfactory by the players, because they felt the commissioner was in reality a representative of the league and the owners. Consequently, the players union and league generally agreed that more types of grievances would be decided by an independent and impartial arbitrator or panel of arbitrators or by a panel consisting of a representative of each side that was chaired by an impartial arbitrator who was usually the deciding vote. To a certain degree, all these models continue in various configurations today.

Except for certain player disciplinary matters that are resolved exclusively by the league commissioner, most disputes between a player and the league or club are resolved by some form of impartial arbitration. There are three general types of disputes that are resolved by arbitration; examples of each are provided and analyzed in the following materials.

The first are matters deemed by management or the players association to be significant far beyond the bounds of that particular arbitration; for example, the following 1976 arbitration involving baseball players Dave McNally and Andy Messersmith. Although this arbitration technically involved only those two individuals, the decision by arbitrator Peter Seitz effectively laid the groundwork for a free agency system benefiting all MLB players. Consequently, the decision should be studied for its long-term effects as well as its immediate resolution. It effectively forced the MLB club owners to collectively bargain with the players over significant modifications to the "reserve system" that had existed in baseball almost from the inception of the National League in 1876. This arbitration proceeding was also significant because the players had recently failed in their antitrust law challenge to the reserve system, because the Supreme Court affirmed the continuing validity of baseball's common law antitrust immunity in its 1972 *Flood v. Kuhn* decision. Thus, the result the MLB players could not accomplish in court through antitrust law was obtained under the auspices of labor law by an arbitrator who gave them a favorable interpretation as to what the "reserve clause" actually meant.

This arbitration decision is joined by others that have far-reaching implications. Baseball's collusion arbitrations in the 1980s show that an arbitrator, by enforcing collective bargaining provisions, can effectively require the owners to adhere to the system of free agency established by the CBA. In a series of three arbitrations MLB players were awarded in excess of $280 million for the collusive actions of the club owners that violated the CBA.

A second type of arbitration has been instituted through collective bargaining to establish a league-wide system for dealing with specific disputes unable to be resolved by individual negotiations between a team and a player. A notable example of this is MLB and NHL player salary arbitration. For various reasons, both leagues have recognized that several factors may coalesce to thwart successful bargaining that determines an individual player's salary. Therefore, in carefully defined circumstances, players and owners may arbitrate a player's salary for the ensuing season.

The third category of matters that generally are submitted to arbitration are grievances arising out of a contract dispute between a player and his club. These are numerous, with multiple grievances filed in every league on a yearly basis. It is harder to see the broader effects of these arbitration decisions, which, strictly speaking, do not create binding precedent with the same legal effect as court decisions. However, it is evident that arbitrators pay close attention to earlier arbitration decisions resolving similar disputes, particularly those involving parties in the same league as the current dispute.

a.   Wide Impact Arbitration

The *McNally-Messersmith* arbitration is a leading example of arbitration in the sports industries that has significantly altered the way a league conducts its business with players.

NATIONAL & AMERICAN LEAGUE PROFESSIONAL BASEBALL CLUBS v. MAJOR LEAGUE BASEBALL PLAYERS ASSN.

66 Labor Arbitration 101 (1976)

SEITZ, Arbitrator.

. . . The Chairman understands the dispute in arbitration to be as follows: The Association claims that the terms of the Uniform Player Contracts of [Andy] Messersmith and [Dave] McNally, respectively, having expired, the two players are at liberty to negotiate contract relationships with any of the other clubs in the leagues and that they are not to be regarded as having been "reserved" by the Los Angeles and Montreal clubs, respectively, in such manner as to inhibit clubs from dealing with them.

The leagues and the clubs assert that the terms of the contracts of these players have not expired; that they are still under contract; and that, in any event, the grievants have been duly "reserved" by their respective clubs; and, accordingly, they are not free to deal with other clubs for the performance of services for the 1976 season; nor are such other clubs free to deal with them for that season excepting under circumstances and conditions not here obtaining. . . .

[EDS. Arbitrator Seitz then proceeded to explain there were two general issues before him. The first was a jurisdictional question—that is, whether these matters were properly the subject of arbitration. The second was the issues on the merits, which of course would be reached only if the arbitrator ruled that he had jurisdiction to hear the dispute.

On the first issue, Seitz held that the case was properly before him. He did so despite language in Article XV of the MLB collective bargaining agreement that specified "*this Agreement does not deal with the reserve system.*" Despite this language, Seitz found that time and again questions arose in other aspects of the Agreement that necessitated interpretations of the reserve system in order to clarify these other provisions. Consequently, he found that he did have jurisdiction to hear the dispute and thus proceeded to the merits. A fuller discussion of the jurisdiction issue is in *Kansas City Royals v. Major League Baseball Players Association*, 532 F.2d 615 (8th Cir. 1976), *infra*.]

. . . I have reached the conclusion that, as a matter of contract construction, the position of the Players Association in the dispute has merit and deserves to be sustained. . . .

No one challenges the rights of a Club to renew a Player's contract with or without his consent under § 10(a) [of the MLB Uniform Player Contract], "for the period of one [renewal] year." I read the record, however, as containing a contention by the leagues that when a Club renews a Player's contract for the renewal year, the contract in force during that year contains the "right of renewal" clause as one of its terms, entitling the Club to renew the contract in successive years, to perpetuity, perhaps, so long as the Player is alive and the Club has duly discharged all conditions required of it. This is challenged by the Players Association whose position it is that the contractual relationship between the Club and the Player terminates at the end of the first renewal year. Thus, it claims that there was no longer any contractual bond between Messersmith and the Los Angeles Club [after the renewal year.]

The league's argument is based on the language in § 10(a) of the Player's Contract that the Club "may renew this contract for the period of one year *on the same terms*" (emphasis supplied); and that among those "terms" is the right to further contract renewal.

In the law of contract construction, as I know it, there is nothing to prevent parties from agreeing to successive renewals of the terms of their bargain (even to what has been described as "perpetuity"), provided the contract expresses that intention with explicit clarity and the right of subsequent renewals does not have to be implied. . . .

There is nothing in Section 10(a) which, explicitly, expresses agreement that the Players Contract can be renewed for any period beyond the first renewal year. The point the leagues present must be based upon the implication or assumption, that if the renewed contract is "on the same terms" as the contract for the preceding year (with the exception of the amount of compensation) the right to additional renewals must have been an integral part of the renewed contract. I find great difficulties, in so implying or assuming, in respect of a contract providing for the rendition of personal services in which one would expect a more explicit expression of intention. . . .

We now turn to the Major League Rules, as to which it has already been stated that, by virtue of § 9(a) of the Uniform Players Contract and Article XIII of the Basic Agreement, they are a part of the agreements of the parties if not inconsistent with the provisions of the Basic Agreement and the Players Contract.

The parties are in sharp conflict on this. The leagues claim that there is exclusive reservation of a player's services under Rule 4-A(a) regardless of the continued existence of any contractual relationship between the Club and the Player. Thus, Counsel for the National League asserted that:

> The club may continue the pattern of career-long control over the player and that this pattern of career-long control is not essentially dependent upon the renewal clause (Section 10-A) at all.

The Players Association, on the other hand, asserts that in the absence of a nexus or linkage of contract between the Player and the Club, there can be no exclusive reservation of the right to his future services. . . .

These provisions and others in the very Rules which, allegedly, establish the kind of reservation of services for which the leagues contend, all subsume the existence of a *contractual relation*. The leagues would have it that it is only when there is a release or assignment that a contract must have been in existence; but even if there were no contract in existence (the players' contract having expired) a Club, by placing the name of a player on a list, can reserve exclusive rights to his services from year to year for an unstated and indefinite period in the future. I find this unpersuasive. It is like the claims of some nations that persons once its citizens, wherever they live and regardless of the passage of time, the swearing of other allegiances and other circumstances, are still its own nationals and subject to the obligations that citizenship in the nation imposes. This "status" theory is incompatible with the doctrine or policy of freedom of contract in the economic and political society in which we live and of which the professional sport of baseball ("the national game") is a part. . . .

Finally, on this point, it is evident that traditionally, the leagues have regarded the existence of a contract as a basis for the reservation of players. In Club's Exhibit No. 15 there is set forth the Cincinnati Peace Compact of the National and American Leagues, signed January 10, 1903 — probably the most important step in the evolution and development of the present Reserve System. In that document it provided:

> Second—A *reserve rule* shall be recognized, by which each and every club may reserve *players under contract*, and that a uniform contract for the use of each league shall be adopted. (Emphasis supplied.)

This emphasis on the existence of a contract for reservation of a player to be effective was perpetuated in the Major League Rules to some of which I have referred. It is even found in Rule 3(g) in which, however, it is referred to disjunctively along with acceptance of terms "or by which he was reserved." However, *even in Rule 3(g)*, reading it analytically and construing it syntactically, one may reasonably reach the conclusion — *no contract, no reservation*. The provision says there shall be no dealings between a player and a club other than the one "with which he is under *contract*, or acceptance of terms, *or by which he is reserved.*" (Emphasis supplied.) . . .

Thus, I reach the conclusion that, absent a contractual connection between Messersmith and the Los Angeles Club after September 28, 1975, the Club's action in reserving his services for the ensuing year by placing him on its reserve list was unavailing and ineffectual in prohibiting him from dealing with other clubs in the league and to prohibit such clubs from dealing with him.

In the case of McNally whom the Montreal Club had placed on its disqualified list, a similar conclusion has been reached. . . .

I am not unmindful of the testimony of the Commissioner of Baseball and the Presidents of the National and American League given at the hearings as to the importance of maintaining the integrity of the Reserve System. It was represented to me that any decision of the Arbitration Panel sustaining the Messersmith and McNally grievances would have dire results, wreak great harm to the Reserve System and do serious damage to the sport of baseball.

Thus, for example, it was stated that a decision favoring these grievants would encourage many other players to elect to become free agents at the end of the renewal years; that this would encourage clubs with the largest monetary resources to engage free agents, thus unsettling the competitive balance between clubs, so essential to the sport; that it would increase enormously the already high costs of training and seasoning young players to achieve the level of skills required in professional baseball and such investments would be sacrificed if they became free agents at the end of a renewal year; that driven by the compulsion to win, owners of franchises would over-extend themselves financially and improvident bidding for players in an economic climate in which, today, some clubs are strained, financially; that investors will be discouraged from putting money in franchises in which several of the star players on the club team will become free agents at the end of a renewal year and no continuing control over the players' services can be exercised; and that even the integrity of the sport may be placed in hazard under certain circumstances.

I do not purport to appraise these apprehensions. They are all based on speculations as to what may ensue. Some of the fears may be imaginary or exaggerated; but some may be reasonable, realistic and sound. After all, they were voiced by distinguished baseball officials with long experience in the sport and a background for judgment in such matters much superior to my own. However, as stated above, at length, it is not for the Panel (and especially the writer) to determine what, if anything, is good or bad about the reserve system. The Panel's sole duty is to interpret and apply the agreements and undertakings of the parties. If any of the expressed apprehensions and fears are soundly based, I am confident that the dislocations and damage to the reserve system can be avoided or minimized through good faith collective bargaining between the parties. There are numerous expedients available and arrangements that can be made that will soften the blow—if this decision, indeed, should be regarded as a blow. This decision is not the end of the line by any means. The parties, jointly, are free to agree to disregard it and compose their differences as to the reserve system in any way they see fit. . . .

However strong my conviction that the basic dispute should be determined by the parties, in collective bargaining rather than by an Arbitration Panel, that Panel could not justify any further delay, and the accompanying Award, accordingly, is being rendered. The parties are still in negotiation, however, and continue to have an opportunity to reach agreement on measures that will give assurance of a reserve system that will meet the needs of the clubs and protect them from the damage they fear this decision will cause, and, at the same time, meet the needs of the players. . . .

Grievance upheld.

NOTES AND QUESTIONS

1. Do you agree with Arbitrator Seitz's conclusion that the parties' dispute was an arbitrable matter? Was Arbitrator Seitz remiss in his failure to discuss

business custom and usage in his opinion? Or does he indirectly address past business practices? How might arguments on these issues have been framed?

2. The baseball owners were given advance notice of the probable outcome of the Messersmith and McNally grievances. Rather than immediately forging ahead to reach a new agreement with the players, the owners appealed the decision to the federal courts. In many respects, this was not the wisest tactic, because successful appeals of arbitration decisions occur only under very narrow circumstances; for example, when the arbitrator's decision is permeated by bad faith or malice toward one of the parties. The grounds pursuant to which an arbitration award may be vacated are explored in *National Baseball League Players Association v. Garvey*, 532 U.S. 504 (2001), and *Kansas City Royals v. Major League Baseball Players Association*, 532 F.2d 615 (8th Cir. 1976), *infra*. In *Kansas City Royals*, the court upheld the *Messersmith-McNally* arbitration decision. A detailed examination of the *Messersmith-McNally* decision and its subsequent appeal to the courts is found in Charles P. Korr, The End of Baseball As We Knew It: The Players Union, 1960-81, 149-67 (2002); Robert C. Berry and William B. Gould IV, *A Long Deep Drive to Collective Bargaining: Of Players, Owners, Brawls and Strikes*, 31 Case Western L. Rev. 685, 749-53 (1981).

3. After going through a period of readjustment, in which every major league player currently in the league was given one opportunity to be a free agent, the owners and players entered a new CBA providing that a player can earn free agent status after six years of credited major league service. This basic threshold is still the standard today, as was explored in the foregoing MLB provisions on free agency detailed in section C.2.b, *supra*. Why would the players agree to a six-year standard? Is this an unduly lengthy period of time? Are there good reasons why baseball has a higher threshold than other professional team sports?

b. Defining the Scope of Judicial Review

In this section, we focus on two principal cases that establish the contours of judicial review of arbitration decisions. Both cases coincidentally arise in the context of baseball. As you review these decisions, consider the breadth of judicial deference that is afforded arbitrators, the reasons for it, and whether it is appropriate.

KANSAS CITY ROYALS v. MAJOR LEAGUE BASEBALL PLAYERS ASSN.

532 F.2d 615 (8th Cir. 1976)

HEANEY, Circuit Judge.

The owners of the twenty-four Major League Baseball Clubs seek reversal of a judgment of the District Court for the Western District of Missouri. The court refused to set aside and enforced an arbitration panel's award rendered in favor of the Major League Baseball Players Association. The arbitration panel was established pursuant to a collective bargaining agreement between the Club Owners and the Players Association. The award relieved pitcher Andy Messersmith of any contractual obligation to the Los Angeles Dodgers, and pitcher Dave McNally of any similar obligation to the Montreal Expos. It directed the Dodgers and Expos to remove Messersmith and McNally, respectively, from their reserve or disqualified lists. It ordered the American and National Leagues to inform and instruct their member clubs that the provisions of Major League Rule 4-A (reserve list rule) and Rule 3(g) (no-tampering rule) do not inhibit, prohibit or prevent such clubs from negotiating or dealing with Messersmith and McNally with respect to employment.

We hold that the arbitration panel had jurisdiction to resolve the dispute, that its award drew its essence from the collective bargaining agreement, and that the relief fashioned by the District Court was appropriate. Accordingly, we affirm the judgment of the District Court. . . .

II

The Supreme Court articulated the legal principles applicable to the arbitration of labor disputes in the Steelworkers trilogy,[6] and recently reaffirmed them in *Gateway Coal Co. v. United Mine Workers of America*, 414 U.S. 368, 94 S.Ct. 629, 38 L.Ed.2d 583 (1974).

A party may be compelled to arbitrate a grievance only if it has agreed to do so. *Gateway Coal Co. v. United Mine Workers of America, supra.* . . . The question of arbitrability is thus one of contract construction and is for the courts to decide. . . .

In resolving questions of arbitrability, the courts are guided by Congress's declaration of policy that arbitration is the desirable method for settling labor disputes. See § 203 of the Labor-Management Relations Act, 29 U.S.C. § 173(d). Accordingly, a grievance arising under a collective bargaining agreement providing for arbitration must be deemed arbitrable "unless it may be said with positive assurance that the arbitration clause is not susceptible of an interpretation that covers the asserted dispute. Doubts should be resolved in favor of coverage." *United Steelworkers of America v. Warrior & Gulf Navigation Co., supra,* 363 U.S. at 582-583, 80 S.Ct. at 1353, 4 L.Ed.2d at 1417. . . . Consistent with these principles, a broad arbitration provision may be deemed to exclude a particular grievance in only two instances: (1) where the collective bargaining agreement contains an express provision clearly excluding the grievance involved from arbitration; or (2) where the agreement contains an ambiguous exclusionary provision and the record evinces the most forceful evidence of a purpose to exclude the grievance from arbitration. . . .

If it is determined that the arbitrator had jurisdiction, judicial review of his award is limited to the question of whether it "draws its essence from the collective bargaining agreement." *United Steelworkers of America v. Enterprise Wheel & Car Corp.*, 363 U.S. 593, 597, 80 S.Ct. 1358, 1361, 4 L.Ed.2d 1424, 1428 (1960). . . . We do not sit as an appellate tribunal to review the merits of the arbitrator's decision. . . .

6. *United Steelworkers of America v. American Mfg. Co.*, 363 U.S. 564, 80 S.Ct. 1343, 4 L.Ed.2d 1403 (1960). . . .

III

We begin with the proposition that the language of Article X of the 1973 agreement [which gives the Arbitration Panel "jurisdiction and authority . . . to interpret, apply or determine compliance with the provisions of agreements between the [Players] Association and the Clubs or any of them, and agreements between individual Players and Clubs"] is sufficiently broad to require arbitration of the Messersmith-McNally grievances. We think this is clear because the disputes involve the interpretation of the provisions of agreements between a player or the Players Association and a club or the Club Owners. . . .

IV

We cannot say, on the basis of the evidence discussed above, that the record evinces the most forceful evidence of a purpose to exclude the grievances here involved from arbitration.

(a) The 1968 agreement clearly permitted the arbitration of grievances relating to the reserve system. It, therefore, cannot be said that the Club Owners never consented to the arbitration of such grievances. The Club Owners might have argued that they agreed to arbitrate such grievances because the Commissioner of Baseball was designated as the arbitrator, and that he, recognizing the importance of the reserve system to baseball, would interpret the disputed provisions to allow perpetual control by a Club Owner over its players. That argument, however, was not advanced before either the arbitration panel, the District Court or this Court. Moreover, the argument would not be particularly flattering to any Commissioner of Baseball.[19]

(b) Article XIV, the predecessor to Article XV, was suggested by the Players Association for rather specific purposes and the Club Owners clearly did what they could to preserve their right to argue that the reserve system remained a part of the collective bargaining agreement. Indeed, if the Club Owners' counterproposals with respect to Article XIV had been accepted, the reserve system would clearly have remained subject to arbitration.

Article XV was clearly designed to accomplish the same purposes as Article XIV. If in accomplishing these purposes the players had clearly agreed to exclude disputes arising out of the operation of the reserve system from arbitration, the Messersmith-McNally grievances would not be arbitrable. For the reasons discussed in this opinion, however, no such agreement can be found.

(c) From 1970 to 1973, a number of grievances concerning the reserve system were submitted to arbitration. The Club Owners raised no jurisdictional objections. While this fact alone is not of controlling significance, because the grievances submitted did not go to what the Club Owners regard as the "core" or "heart" of the reserve system, the submission of grievances relating to the

19. Mr. Bowie Kuhn, the present Commissioner of Baseball, testified, in substance, that he felt that Article X of the 1973 agreement gave him the power to withdraw a grievance from arbitration if he felt that the grievance involved the "preservation of the integrity of, or the maintenance of public confidence in, the game of baseball." He testified further that he did not withdraw these grievances from arbitration because he didn't want to do anything to adversely affect the collective bargaining process: he respected the reputation of Mr. Seitz, the impartial arbitrator, and he respected the arbitration process.

reserve system is certainly a fact that detracts from the Club Owners' contention that the parties clearly understood Article XIV to mean that grievances relating to the reserve system would not be subject to arbitration.

(d) The fact that Marvin Miller may have given assurances, during the 1970 negotiations, that the players would not grieve over house rules cannot be viewed as the most forceful evidence of a purpose to exclude the Messersmith-McNally grievances from arbitration. First, there is some dispute in the record as to whether Miller made such a statement. Second, assuming he did, the term "house rules" is ambiguous. Third, and we think most important, the weight of the evidence, when viewed as a whole, does not support the conclusion that Article XV was intended to preclude arbitration of any grievances otherwise arbitrable.

The essence of the Club Owners' arguments on the question of arbitrability was perhaps best articulated in the testimony of Larry McPhail, President of the American League, in which he stated: "Isn't it fair to say that our strong feelings on the importance of the core of the reserve system would indicate that we wouldn't permit the reserve system to be within the jurisdiction of the arbitration procedure?" The weaknesses in this argument have been previously discussed in paragraphs (a), (b) and (c) above. We add only that what a reasonable party might be expected to do cannot take precedence over what the parties actually provided for in their collective bargaining agreement.

V

The Club Owners contend that even if the arbitration panel had jurisdiction, the award must be vacated. They argue that the award exceeded the scope of the panel's authority by "fundamentally altering and destroying the Reserve System as it historically existed and had been acquiesced in by the Association."

As we have previously noted, our review of the merits of an arbitration panel's award is limited. The award must be sustained so long as it "draws its essence from the collective bargaining agreement." *United Steelworkers of America v. Enterprise Wheel & Car Corp., supra,* 363 U.S. at 597, 80 S.Ct. at 1361, 4 L.Ed.2d at 1428. . . .

The nub of the Club Owners' argument is that both they and the Players Association understood the reserve system to enable a club to perpetually control a player, that this understanding was reflected in the 1973 agreement, and that the arbitration panel was without authority to alter the agreed upon operation of the reserve system.

We cannot agree that the 1973 collective bargaining agreement embodied an understanding by the parties that the reserve system enabled a club to perpetually control a player. First, the agreement contained no express provision to that effect. Second, while there is evidence that the reserve system operated in such a manner in recent years,[21] the record discloses that various Players Association representatives viewed the system as allowing a player to become a free agent by playing under a renewed contract for one year.

---

21. In *Flood v. Kuhn,* . . . both the majority opinion and Mr. Justice Marshall's dissent viewed the reserve system as involving perpetual player control, although that issue was not squarely before the Court. 407 U.S. at 259 n. 1, 289, 92 S.Ct. at 2100, 32 L.Ed. 2d at 731.

Moreover, it can be argued that the arbitration panel's award did not "alter" the reserve system. To the extent that the reserve system did enable a club to perpetually control a player, it was not necessarily by virtue of successive invocations of the renewal clause . . . or application of the reserve list and no-tampering rules . . . in the absence of a contractual obligation. Other provisions operate to deter a player from "playing out his option," as is evidenced by the fact that few players have done so. . . . On this basis, it may be said that the arbitration panel's decision did not change the reserve system, but merely interpreted various elements thereof under circumstances which had not previously arisen.

The 1973 agreement empowered the arbitration panel to "interpret, apply or determine compliance with the provisions of agreements" between the players and the clubs. . . . We find that the arbitration panel did nothing more than to interpret certain provisions of the Uniform Player's Contract and the Major League Rules. We cannot say that those provisions are not susceptible of the construction given them by the panel. Accordingly, the award must be sustained. . . .

CONCLUSION

We hold that the arbitration panel had jurisdiction to hear and decide the Messersmith-McNally grievances, that the panel's award drew its essence from the collective bargaining agreement, and that the relief fashioned by the District Court was appropriate. Accordingly, the award of the arbitration panel must be sustained, and the District Court's judgment affirmed. In so holding, we intimate no views on the merits of the reserve system. We note, however, that Club Owners and the Players Association's representatives agree that some form of a reserve system is needed if the integrity of the game is to be preserved and if public confidence in baseball is to be maintained. The disagreement lies over the degree of control necessary if these goals are to be achieved. Certainly, the parties are in a better position to negotiate their differences than to have them decided in a series of arbitrations and court decisions. We commend them to that process and suggest that the time for obfuscation has passed and that the time for plain talk and clear language has arrived. Baseball fans everywhere expect nothing less. . . .

NOTE

Consider the Ilya Kovalchuk matter, in which the parties to a CBA responded to an arbitrator's decision by altering their agreement. On August 9, 2010, Richard Bloch, the NHL's system arbitrator, ruled that the NHL had valid authority to reject the New Jersey Devils' 17-year, $102 million contract with Ilya Kovalchuk. At the time of his signing, Kovalchuk was 27 years old, and the contract would cover his service with the club until he was 43. His $102 million salary was to be paid as follows: $6 million in 2010-2011, $6 million in 2011-2012, $11.5 million in 2012-2013, $11.5 million in 2013-2014, $11.5 million in 2014-2015, $11.5 million in 2015-2016, $11.5 million in 2016-2017, $10.5 million in 2017-2018, $8.5 million in 2018-2019, $6.5 million in 2019-2020, $3.5 million in 2020-2021, $750,000 in 2021-2022, $500,000 in 2022-2023, $500,000 in 2023-2024, $500,000 in 2024-2025, $500,000 in 2025-2026, and $500,000 in 2026-2027. His contract also included a "No Move" clause until June 30, 2017, followed by a "No Trade" clause through the end of the contract. The NHL claimed the contract's last six years were illusory and that "one cannot reasonably conclude this is an agreement that will be, or was intended to be, fulfilled." Rather, it was intended to and has the effect of artificially reducing the averaged amount attributable to each year of Kovalchuk's contract on the Devils' annual salary cap, in circumvention of the maximum team salary cap established by the NHL CBA, which threatens competitive balance among league clubs.

Although none of the contract's individual terms were prohibited by the CBA, the arbitrator determined the contract "is intended to or has the effect of defeating or circumventing" the NHL's team salary cap:

> The elements of this Agreement are unique. They include the age of the Player, the dramatic diveback [decreased payments during the final years] after 11 years, the notable frontloading of the compensation, the relatively minimal payment during the 6-year tail of the contract and the clear incentives and ability of the team to move the Player out and likely rid itself of the continuing salary cap burden during the out years of the contract. All of this supports the League's conclusion that it is reasonably unlikely the last years of this contract will be performed.

After the arbitrator's ruling, the NHL and NHLPA agreed to implement new rules governing the parameters of contracts five years or longer and to provide the NHL with unilateral, exclusive authority to determine any discipline for clubs violating these rules. The NHL subsequently approved Kovalchuk's new 15-year, $100 million contract with the Devils, but it fined the club $3 million and required it to forfeit two future draft picks because his original contract was an effort to circumvent the salary cap (which discipline was permissible under the NHL-NHLPA agreement).

MAJOR LEAGUE BASEBALL PLAYERS ASSN. v. GARVEY
532 U.S. 504 (2001)

PER CURIAM.

The Court of Appeals for the Ninth Circuit here rejected an arbitrator's factual findings and then resolved the merits of the parties' dispute instead of remanding the case for further arbitration proceedings. . . .

In the late 1980's, petitioner Major League Baseball Players Association (Association) filed grievances against the Major League Baseball Clubs (Clubs), claiming the Clubs had colluded in the market for free-agent services after the 1985, 1986 and 1987 baseball seasons, in violation of the industry's collective-bargaining agreement. A free agent is a player who may contract with any Club, rather than one whose right to contract is restricted to a particular Club. In a series of decisions, arbitrators found collusion by the Clubs and damage to the players. The Association and Clubs subsequently entered into a Global Settlement Agreement (Agreement), pursuant to which the Clubs established a $280 million fund to be distributed to injured players. The Association also designed a "Framework" to evaluate the individual player's claims, and, applying that Framework, recommended distribution plans for claims relating to a particular season or seasons.

The Framework provided that players could seek an arbitrator's review of the distribution plan. The arbitrator would determine "only whether the approved Framework and the criteria set forth therein have been properly applied in the proposed Distribution Plan." (*Garvey I*). The Framework set forth factors to be considered in evaluating players' claims, as well as specific requirements for lost contract-extension claims. Such claims were cognizable "'only in those cases where evidence exists that a specific offer of an extension was made by a club prior to collusion only to thereafter be withdrawn when the collusion scheme was initiated.'"

Respondent Steve Garvey, a retired, highly regarded first baseman, submitted a claim for damages of approximately $3 million. He alleged that his contract with the San Diego Padres was not extended to the 1988 and 1989 seasons due to collusion. The Association rejected Garvey's claim in February 1996, because he presented no evidence that the Padres actually offered to extend his contract. Garvey objected, and an arbitration hearing was held. He testified that the Padres offered to extend his contract for the 1988 and 1989 seasons and then withdrew the offer after they began colluding with other teams. He presented a June 1996 letter from Ballard Smith, Padres' President and CEO from 1979 to 1987, stating that, before the end of the 1985 season, Smith offered to extend Garvey's contract through the 1989 season, but that the Padres refused to negotiate with Garvey thereafter due to collusion.

The arbitrator denied Garvey's claim, after seeking additional documentation from the parties. In his award, he explained that "'there exists . . . substantial doubt as to the credibility of the statements in the Smith letter.'" He noted the "stark contradictions" between the 1996 letter and Smith's testimony in the earlier arbitration proceedings regarding collusion, where Smith, like other owners, denied collusion and stated that the Padres simply were not interested in extending Garvey's contract. The arbitrator determined that, due to these contradictions, he "'must reject [Smith's] more recent assertion that Garvey did not receive [a contract] extension'" due to collusion, and found that Garvey had not shown a specific offer of extension. He concluded that:

> The shadow cast over the credibility of the Smith testimony coupled with the absence of any other corroboration of the claim submitted by Garvey compels a finding that the Padres declined to extend his contract not because of the constraints of the collusion effort of the clubs but rather as a baseball judgment founded upon [Garvey's] age and recent injury history.

Garvey moved in Federal District Court to vacate the arbitrator's award, alleging that the arbitrator violated the Framework by denying his claim. The District Court denied the motion. The Court of Appeals for the Ninth Circuit reversed by a divided vote. The court acknowledged that judicial review of an arbitrator's decision in a labor dispute is extremely limited. But it held that review of the merits of the arbitrator's award was warranted in this case, because the arbitrator "'dispensed his own brand of industrial justice.'" The court recognized that Smith's prior testimony with respect to collusion conflicted with the statements in his 1996 letter. But in the court's view, the arbitrator's refusal to credit Smith's letter was "inexplicable" and "bordered on the irrational," because a panel of arbitrators, chaired by the arbitrator involved here, had previously concluded that the owners' prior testimony was false. The court rejected the arbitrator's reliance on the absence of other corroborating evidence, attributing that fact to Smith and Garvey's direct negotiations. The court also found that the record provided "strong support" for the truthfulness of Smith's 1996 letter. The Court of Appeals reversed and remanded with directions to vacate the award.

The District Court then remanded the case to the arbitration panel for further hearings, and Garvey appealed. The Court of Appeals, again by a divided vote, explained that *Garvey I* established that "the conclusion that Smith made Garvey an offer and subsequently withdrew it because of the collusion scheme was the only conclusion that the arbitrator could draw from the record in the proceedings." (*Garvey II*). Noting that its prior instructions might have been unclear, the Court clarified that *Garvey I* "left only one possible result—the result our holding contemplated—an award in Garvey's favor." The Court of Appeals reversed the District Court and directed that it remand the case to the arbitration panel with instructions to enter an award for Garvey in the amount he claimed.

The parties do not dispute that this case arises under § 301 of the Labor Management Relations Act, 1947, as the controversy involves an assertion of rights under an agreement between an employer and a labor organization. Although Garvey's specific allegation is that the arbitrator violated the Framework for resolving players' claims for damages, that Framework was designed to facilitate payments to remedy the Clubs' breach of the collective-bargaining agreement. Garvey's right to be made whole is founded on that agreement.

Judicial review of a labor-arbitration decision pursuant to such an agreement is very limited. Courts are not authorized to review the arbitrator's decision on the merits despite allegations that the decision rests on factual errors or misinterprets the parties' agreement. We recently reiterated that if an "'arbitrator is even arguably construing or applying the contract and acting within the scope of his authority,' the fact that 'a court is convinced he committed serious error does not suffice to overturn his decision.'" It is only when the arbitrator strays from interpretation and application of the agreement and effectively "dispenses his own brand of industrial justice" that his decision may be unenforceable. When an arbitrator resolves disputes regarding the application of a contract, and no dishonesty is alleged, the arbitrator's "improvident, even silly, factfinding" does not provide a basis for a reviewing court to refuse to enforce the award.

In discussing the courts' limited role in reviewing the merits of arbitration awards, we have stated that "'courts . . . have no business weighing the merits of the grievance [or] considering whether there is equity in a particular claim.'" When the judiciary does so, "it usurps a function which . . . is entrusted to the arbitration tribunal." Consistent with this limited role, we said in *Misco* that "even in the very rare instances when an arbitrator's procedural aberrations rise to the level of affirmative misconduct, as a rule the court must not foreclose further proceedings by settling the merits according to its own judgment of the appropriate result." That step, we explained, "would improperly substitute a judicial determination for the arbitrator's decision that the parties bargained for" in their agreement. Instead, the court should "simply vacate the award, thus leaving open the possibility of further proceedings if they are permitted under the terms of the agreement."

To be sure, the Court of Appeals here recited these principles, but its application of them is nothing short of baffling. The substance of the Court's discussion reveals that it overturned the arbitrator's decision because it disagreed with the arbitrator's factual findings, particularly those with respect to credibility.

The Court of Appeals, it appears, would have credited Smith's 1996 letter, and found the arbitrator's refusal to do so at worst "irrational" and at best "bizarre." But even "serious error" on the arbitrator's part does not justify overturning his decision, where, as here, he is construing a contract and acting within the scope of his authority.

In *Garvey II*, the court clarified that *Garvey I* both rejected the arbitrator's findings and went further, resolving the merits of the parties' dispute based on the court's assessment of the record before the arbitrator. For that reason, the court found further arbitration proceedings inappropriate. But again, established law ordinarily precludes a court from resolving the merits of the parties' dispute on the basis of its own factual determinations, no matter how erroneous the arbitrator's decision. Even when the arbitrator's award may properly be vacated, the appropriate remedy is to remand the case for further arbitration proceedings. The dissent suggests that the remedy described in *Misco* is limited to cases where the arbitrator's errors are procedural. *Misco* did involve procedural issues, but our discussion regarding the appropriate remedy was not so limited. If a remand is appropriate *even* when the arbitrator's award has been set aside for "procedural aberrations" that constitute "affirmative misconduct," it follows that a remand ordinarily will be appropriate when the arbitrator simply made factual findings that the reviewing court perceives as "irrational." The Court of Appeals usurped the arbitrator's role by resolving the dispute and barring further proceedings, a result at odds with this governing law.

For the foregoing reasons, the Court of Appeals erred in reversing the order of the District Court denying the motion to vacate the arbitrator's award, and it erred further in directing that judgment be entered in Garvey's favor. The judgment of the Court of Appeals is reversed, and the case is remanded for further proceedings consistent with this opinion.

Justice STEVENS, dissenting.

It is well settled that an arbitrator "does not sit to dispense his own brand of industrial justice." We have also said fairly definitively, albeit in dicta, that a court should remedy an arbitrator's "procedural aberrations" by vacating the award and remanding for further proceedings. Our cases, however, do not provide significant guidance as to what standards a federal court should use in assessing whether an arbitrator's behavior is so untethered to either the agreement of the parties or the factual record so as to constitute an attempt to "dispense his own brand of industrial justice." Nor, more importantly, do they tell us how, having made such a finding, courts should deal with "the extraordinary circumstance in which the arbitrator's own rulings make clear that, more than being simply erroneous, his finding is completely inexplicable and borders on the irrational." *Garvey* v. *Roberts*, 203 F.3d 580 (CA9 2000). Because our caselaw is not sufficiently clear to allow me to conclude that the case below was wrongly decided—let alone to conclude that the decision was so wrong as to require the extraordinary remedy of a summary reversal—I dissent from the Court's disposition of this petition.

Without the benefit of briefing or argument, today the Court resolves two difficult questions. First, it decides that even if the Court of Appeals' appraisal of the merits is correct—that is to say, even if the arbitrator did dispense his own brand of justice untethered to the agreement of the parties, and even if the correct disposition of the matter is perfectly clear—the only course open to a reviewing court is to remand the matter for another arbitration. That conclusion is not compelled by any of our cases, nor by any analysis offered by the Court. As the issue is subject to serious arguments on both sides, the Court should have set this case for argument if it wanted to answer this remedial question.

Second, without reviewing the record or soliciting briefing, the Court concludes that, in any event, "no serious error on the arbitrator's part is apparent in this case." At this stage in the proceedings, I simply cannot endorse that conclusion. After examining the record, obtaining briefing, and hearing oral argument, the Court of Appeals offered a reasoned explanation of its conclusion. Whether or not I would ultimately agree with the Ninth Circuit's analysis, I find the Court's willingness to reverse a fact bound determination of the Court of Appeals without engaging that court's reasoning troubling.

NOTES AND QUESTIONS

1.   What standard does *Garvey* adopt for determining when an arbitrator's award will be judicially vacated? Does this provide sufficient guidance to lower courts regarding the appropriate level of deference to be afforded an arbitrator's decision? What concern is expressed by the dissent in *Garvey*? See generally Jaime D. Byrnes and Alison B. Prout, Major League Baseball Players Association v. Garvey: *Revisiting the Standard for Arbitral Review*, 7 Harv. Negot. L. Rev. 389 (2004); Emily Huitsing, *Retaining Bargained-For Finality and Judicial Review in Labor Arbitration Decisions: Dual Interests Preserved in Major League Baseball*, 2002 J. Disp. Resol. 453.

2.   *Scope of Judicial Review.* For further discussions of the limited scope of judicial review of arbitration awards and the ability of aggrieved employees to circumvent the arbitration process, see Martin J. Greenberg and James T. Gray, Sports Law Practice §2.03 (2d ed. 2002) (arbitration awards will be vacated by courts in a limited range of circumstances including when the award was procured by fraud or corruption, when partiality on the part of the arbitrator was obvious, or when an arbitrator exceeds his or her power); *National Football League Players Assn. v. Pro-Football, Inc.*, 857 F. Supp. 71, 75-76 (D.C. 1994) (although arbitration decisions should be afforded deference even if arbitrator makes errors of fact and law, an award will not be upheld if it compels violation of law or conduct contrary to well-established public policy); *Morris v. New York Football Giants, Inc.*, 150 Misc. 2d 271, 575 N.Y.S.2d 1013, 1017 (1991) (refusing to compel arbitration where circumstances made it clear that arbitrator was deprived of the requisite neutrality); *Dryer v. Los Angeles Rams*, 709 P.2d 826, 830 (Cal. 1985) ("Normally a claim that the grievance procedures are unfair or inadequate cannot be asserted until the aggrieved party has attempted to implement the procedures and found them to be unfair").

c.   Salary Arbitration

Both MLB and the NHL use arbitration to resolve salary disputes between teams and individual players; arbitration is available only in limited situations but has far-reaching effects on player salaries within the league. The MLB CBA salary arbitration provisions apply to players who have between three (or in some cases slightly less) and six years of credited major league service. Other

CBA provisions provide for compulsory arbitration in limited circumstances, such as to a veteran free agent who moved to a new club and whose contract has expired before a certain time period has passed. However, most salary arbitration involves players with three to six years of credited MLB service.

Under normal circumstances, the saga begins when the club and player attempt to negotiate a new contract. This negotiation process may continue for months, even after there is a filing for arbitration and, indeed, up to the time of the arbitration itself. But if negotiations fail, arbitration is the alternative. On an annual basis, approximately 90 to 100 players head toward arbitration. Ten to 15 may have hearings scheduled. Perhaps only seven or eight actually go through the full arbitration process. Even so, the mere possibility that a salary dispute will be arbitrated looms large for both the club and the player, and it is a widespread consensus that the entire process influences the overall market value placed on players' services.

One of the most notable aspects of baseball salary arbitration is that it utilizes "final offer arbitration." This means that, without knowing what the other side will submit as a salary figure, the team and the player each submit an amount for a one-year contract. This requires substantial thought by both parties, because the arbitration panel must select one figure or the other. There can be no compromise. Thus, if the matter is decided by arbitration, the end result will be a one-year, nonguaranteed contract (with no bonuses) at a salary submitted by the club or the player. The club may release its rights to the player at any time consistent with the then-applicable collective bargaining agreement.

NOTES AND QUESTIONS

1. *Assessing Final Offer Arbitration.* What are the advantages and disadvantages of final offer arbitration? Does it result in greater leverage for clubs, players, or neither? Commentators have noted that despite owners' expressed dislike for final offer arbitration, they have done well in this forum. In a study of 417 baseball salary arbitrations between 1974 and 1999, clubs prevailed in 236 cases and players prevailed in 181 cases. Roger I. Abram, *Inside Baseball's Salary Arbitration Process*, 6 U. Chi. L. Sch. Roundtable 55, 64 (1999) (also providing historical and practical overviews of the final offer arbitration process).

   The authors of an empirical study of baseball's final offer arbitration concluded:

   > Aggressive offers by players trigger arbitration and that more aggressive offers are associated with inferior outcomes in arbitration. Overall, clubs appear to outperform players in arbitration. Unexpectedly high or low offers are less common for players who have previously been through arbitration, which suggests that learning occurs. Our results are inconsistent with simple one-sided asymmetric-information models of arbitration. The results are more consistent with an optimism model or a model in which players are risk-loving.

   Amy Farmer, Paul Pecorino and Victor Stango, *The Causes of Bargaining Failure: Evidence from Major League Baseball*, 47 J.L. & Econ. 543, 543 (2004). For other scholarly discussions of baseball salary arbitration, see William

B. Gould, *Labor Issues in Professional Sports: Reflections on Baseball, Labor and Antitrust Law*, 15 Stan. L. & Pol'y Rev. 61 (2004) (addressing development of salary arbitration); Stuart J. Riemer, *Albert Pujols: Major League Baseball Salary Arbitration from a Unique Perspective*, 22 Cardozo Arts & Ent. L.J. 219 (2004); Brien M. Wassner, *Major League Baseball's Answer to Salary Disputes and the Strike Final Offer Arbitration: A Negotiation Tool Facilitating Adversary Agreement*, 6 Vand. J. Ent. L. & Prac. 5 (2003); Jonathan M. Conti, *The Effect of Salary Arbitration on Major League Baseball*, 5 Sports Law. J. 221 (1998); David J. Faurot and Stephen McAllister, *Salary Arbitrations and Pre-Arbitration Negotiation in Major League Baseball*, 45 Indus. & Lab. Rel. Rev. 697 (1992).

2. *NHL Salary Arbitration.* Unlike MLB's final offer arbitration, the NHL's salary arbitration system is premised on a conventional arbitration model. Like MLB's system, the NHL's salary arbitration system contains eligibility requirements that must be met in order for players to seek salary arbitration; procedures are in place for selecting arbitrators, and limitations are imposed on the factors the arbitrator can consider in determining a player's compensation. Because it is based on a conventional arbitration model, the salary determined by the arbitrator can "be either one of the two offers made by the parties or an amount ranging anywhere between the two." Melanie Aubut, *When Negotiations Fail: An Analysis of Salary Arbitration and Salary Cap Systems*, 10 Sports Law. J. 189, 205 (2003). Another notable difference is the binding effect of the arbitrator's award. Generally, the arbitrator's decision is final and binding on the player and club. As a result of a compromise agreed to by the NHL and NHLPA in 1995 during a period of considerable player/management conflict, owners have a limited right to reject a salary award (a walk-away right). "Each club can exercise the right up to three times in two continuous years and not more than twice in the same year." *Id.* at 206. When this right is exercised, the player becomes a free agent. "If the player is unable to obtain a better offer from another team, he can then return to his previous team and accept the offer that was last on the table prior to his becoming a free agent." *Id.* See also Stephen J. Barlett, *Contract Negotiations and Salary Arbitration in the NHL: An Agent's View*, 4 Marq. Sports L.J. 1 (1993). The current provisions are set forth in 2012 NHL CBA, Article 12.

d. Contract Dispute Arbitration

The third major category of arbitration relates to disputes arising out of team-player contracts. It runs the gamut from whether the contract was properly formed, the consequences for a material breach of a contract, rights of a club (as well as the league) to discipline a player, contract renegotiations and renewals, guaranteed salaries, bonus provisions, and side deals to the standard player contract. The following materials provide some examples of the myriad issues that have been raised through arbitration in the professional sports leagues.

One general question can be posed at this point: If more attention had been paid to the drafting of language in the original contract, would the problems leading to the arbitration have been avoided or alleviated? Often the answer will be "yes." If so, consider alternative provisions to gain a fuller appreciation of the rewards of good "preventive" contract drafting.

i.   Failure to Honor Contract and Remedies for Enforcement

The negative injunction cases considered earlier in this chapter illustrate some of the legal problems that confronted sports leagues when rival leagues were formed. However, modern times have given new meaning to what is meant by rival leagues, which may be in foreign countries. Do the old rules developed more than a century ago when U.S. professional sports leagues were primarily regional still apply? To complicate matters more, pursuant to applicable CBAs, these issues may be required to be resolved by arbitration.

The following case is one of the more important ones involving a player/team conflict in recent years. It tested the ability of arbitrators and judges to use U.S. law and procedures to decide player/team contract disputes with international dimensions. This case relies on basic legal principles enunciated over 100 years ago in landmark cases such as *Ward, Ewing,* and *Lajoie* (discussed earlier in this chapter) and provides an opportunity to reexamine them. As you read this case, consider whether domestic arbitration provides an effective means of resolving disputes with international implications.

BOSTON CELTICS LIMITED PARTNERSHIP v. BRIAN SHAW
908 F.2d 1041 (lst Cir. 1990)

BREYER, Chief Judge.

I.   BACKGROUND

A.   FACTS

The basic facts, which are not in dispute, include the following:

(a) In 1988, soon after Shaw graduated from college, he signed a one-year contract to play for the Celtics.

(b) In 1989, Shaw signed a two-year contract to play with the Italian team Il Messaggero Roma ("Il Messaggero"). The team agreed to pay him $800,000 for the first year and $900,000 for the second year. The contract contains a clause permitting Shaw to cancel the second year (1990-91). It says that Shaw has the right to rescind the second year of this Agreement . . . [if he] returns to the United States to play with the NBA . . . by delivering a registered letter to [Il Messaggero] . . . between June 20, 1990 and July 20, 1990.

(c) At the end of January 1990 Shaw signed a five-year "Uniform Player Contract" with the Celtics. The contract contains standard clauses negotiated by the National Basketball Association ("NBA") franchise owners and the National Basketball Players Association (the "Players Association"). It adopts by cross-reference arbitration provisions contained in the NBA-Players Association Collective Bargaining Agreement. In the contract, the Celtics promise Shaw a $450,000 signing bonus and more than $1 million per year in compensation. In return, Shaw promises the Celtics, among other things, that he will cancel his second year with Il Messaggero. The contract says that the "Player [*i.e.,* Shaw] and Club [*i.e.,* the Celtics] acknowledge that Player is currently under contract with Il Messaggero Roma (the 'Messaggero Contract') for the 1989-90 & 1990-91 playing seasons. The Player represents that in accordance with the terms of the Messaggero Contract, the Player has the right to rescind that contract prior to the 1990-91 season *and the player hereby agrees to exercise such right of rescission* in the manner and at the time called for by the Messaggero Contract." (Emphasis added.)

(d) On June 6, 1990, Shaw told the Celtics that he had decided to play for Il Messaggero during the 1990-91 season and that he would not exercise his right of rescission.

B. PROCEDURAL HISTORY

On June 11, 1990, the Celtics invoked their right under the Collective Bargaining Agreement (cross-referenced in the Contract) to an "expedited" arbitration proceeding. The arbitrator held a two-day hearing on June 13 and 14. He found that Shaw's refusal to rescind the Il Messaggero contract violated Shaw's contract with the Celtics. He ordered Shaw to rescind the Il Messaggero contract (on June 20) and not to play for any team other than the Celtics during the term of his Celtics contract. On June 15, Shaw said he still did not intend to rescind the Il Messaggero contract.

The Celtics responded immediately by asking the federal district court to use its authority under § 301 of the Labor Management Relations Act, 29 U.S.C. § 185, to enforce the award . . . The Celtics asked the court for "expedited enforcement" of the award and for a preliminary injunction. After receiving Shaw's response (in the form of an opposition, a motion to dismiss, a brief, and supporting affidavits), and after holding an oral hearing, on June 26, the court granted the Celtics' motion to expedite, ordered Shaw to cancel the Il Messaggero agreement "forthwith," and "enforced" the award. Shaw now appeals this district court decision, attacking both the preliminary injunction and the order enforcing the arbitration award.

II. THE LEGAL MERITS

Shaw makes two basic categories of argument in his effort to show that the district court lacked the legal power to enter its order. First, he says that the arbitration award was itself unlawful. Second, he says that regardless of the lawfulness of the award, the district court followed improper procedures. We shall address these arguments in turn and explain why we find each not persuasive.

A. THE ARBITRATOR'S DECISION

Shaw says that the district court should not have enforced the arbitrator's award because that award was itself unlawful, for any of five separate reasons.

1. The termination promise. Shaw argues that the arbitrator could not reasonably find that he broke a contractual promise to the Celtics because, he says, the Celtics had previously agreed with the Players Association that contracts with individual players such as Shaw would not contain promises of the sort here at issue, namely, a promise to cancel a contract to play with a different team. Shaw says that this previous agreement between the Celtics and the Players Association renders his promise to terminate Il Messaggero "null and void." To support this argument, he points to Article I, § 2 of

the Collective Bargaining Agreement, which Shaw and the Celtics, through cross-reference, made part of their individual agreement. Section 2 says, "Any amendment to a Uniform Player Contract [of the type Shaw and the Celtics used], other than those permitted by this [Collective Bargaining] Agreement, shall be null and void." The Agreement permits amendments (a) "in . . . respect to the compensation . . . to be paid the player," (b) "in respect to specialized compensation arrangements," (c) in respect to a "compensation payment schedule," and (d) in respect to "protect[ion]" of compensation in the event of contract termination. Shaw says that his promise to cancel the Il Messaggero agreement was an amendment to the Uniform Players Contract that does not concern compensation, specialized compensation, compensation schedules, or compensation protection; therefore, it is "null and void." . . .

Shaw's argument, while logical, fails to show that the arbitrator's contrary finding is unlawful. The reasons it fails are fairly straightforward. First, the argument concerns the proper interpretation of a contract negotiated pursuant to a collective bargaining agreement. Second, federal labor law gives arbitrators, not judges, the power to interpret such contracts. The Supreme Court, noting the strong federal policy favoring the voluntary settlement of labor disputes, has written that a labor arbitration award is valid so long as it "draws its essence" from the labor contract. . . .

Third, one can find "plausible arguments" favoring the arbitrator's construction. Shaw's "rescission" promise defines the beginning of the compensation relationship. It also plausibly determines, at the very least, whether Shaw's compensation will begin at $1.1 million (and continue for three years) or whether it will begin at $1.2 million (and continue for only two years). . . . More importantly, and also quite plausibly, Shaw's overall compensation might have been much different had he declined to promise to play for the Celtics in 1990-91, thereby forcing the Celtics, perhaps, to obtain the services of a replacement for that year. The NBA Commissioner, who reviews all player contracts, found that the term was related to "compensation," as did the arbitrator. We cannot say that their findings lack any "plausible" basis . . .

In sum, we find the arbitration award lawful. . . .

B. THE DISTRICT COURT PROCEEDINGS

The district court, as we have pointed out, issued a preliminary injunction requiring Shaw to rescind "forthwith" his contract with Il Messaggero and forbidding him to play basketball for any team other than the Celtics during the term of his Celtics contract. The court also "enforced" an arbitration award containing essentially the same terms. Shaw argues that both the preliminary injunction and the enforcement order are unlawful. Since the district court correctly upheld the award's validity, Shaw's only remaining arguments are that the district court lacked discretion to award preliminary injunctive relief and that it mismanaged the proceedings below. We discuss both points briefly.

1. *The preliminary injunction.* . . .

The only legal question before us, therefore, is whether the district court acted outside its broad equitable powers when it issued the preliminary injunction. That is to say, did the court improperly answer the four questions judges in this Circuit must ask when deciding whether to issue a preliminary injunction.

They are: (1) have the Celtics shown a likelihood of success on the merits? (2) have they shown that failure to issue the injunction would cause the Celtics "irreparable harm?" (3) does the "balance of harms" favor Shaw or the Celtics? and (4) will granting the injunction harm the "public interest?" Our examination of the record has convinced us that the court acted well within the scope of its lawful powers. . . .

To begin with, the Celtics have shown a clear likelihood of success on the merits. As we pointed out in section "A," the arbitration award is lawful, and courts have authority to enforce lawful arbitration awards. The Celtics also have demonstrated irreparable harm. Without speedy relief, they will likely lose the services of a star athlete next year, . . . and, unless they know fairly soon whether Shaw will, or will not play for them, they will find it difficult to plan intelligently for next season. Indeed, in his contract Shaw expressly represents and agrees that he has extraordinary and unique skill and ability as a basketball player, . . . and that any breach by the Player of this contract will cause irreparable injury to the Club.

Further, the court could reasonably find that the "balance of harms" favors the Celtics. Of course, a preliminary injunction, if ultimately shown wrong on the merits, could cause Shaw harm. He might lose the chance to play in the country, and for the team, that he prefers. On the other hand, this harm is somewhat offset by the fact that ultimate success on the merits — *i.e.*, a finding that Shaw was not obligated to terminate Il Messaggero after all — would likely result in the following scenario: Shaw might still be able to sign with Il Messaggero and, if not, he would always have the Celtics contract of over $5 million to fall back upon. At the same time, the court's failure to issue the injunction, if the merits ultimately favored the Celtics, could cause them serious harm of the sort just mentioned (*i.e.*, significantly increased difficulty in planning their team for next season). Given the very small likelihood that Shaw would ultimately prevail on the merits, and the "comparative" harms at stake, the district court could properly decide that the overall "balance" favored the Celtics, not Shaw.

Finally, the court could properly find that issuing a preliminary injunction would not harm the public interest. Indeed, as we have pointed out, the public interest favors court action that "effectuate[s]" the parties' intent to resolve their disputes informally through arbitration. . . . Where the dispute involves a professional basketball player's obligation to play for a particular team, one could reasonably consider expeditious, informal and effective dispute-resolution methods to be essential, and, if so, the public interest favoring court action to "effectuate" those methods of dispute-resolution would seem at least as strong as it is in respect to work-related disputes typically arising under collective bargaining agreements. . . .

Shaw makes an additional argument. He notes that courts will not provide equitable relief such as an injunction to a party with "unclean hands," and he argues that the Celtics' hands are not clean. To support this argument, he has submitted an affidavit saying, in effect, that he signed the contract in a weak moment. His trip to Italy had made him "homesick"; he was "depressed" by what he viewed as undeserved and "negative criticism" in the Italian press; he was not represented by an agent; the Celtics had been urging him to sign up; he read the contract only for about 20 minutes while he was driving around Rome with a Celtics official; and no one ever explained to him that if he did not sign and played with Il Messaggero for another year, he would become a "free agent," able to bargain thereafter with any American team, perhaps for an even greater salary than the Celtics were willing to pay him.

Other evidence in the record, however, which Shaw does not deny, shows that he is a college graduate; that he has played under contract with the Celtics before; that the contract is a standard form contract except for a few, fairly simple, rather clear, additions, . . . that he had bargained with the Celtics for an offer that increased from $3.4 million (in December) to $5.4 million (less than one month later); that he looked over the contract before signing it; that he told the American consul in Rome (as he signed it) that he had read and understood it; and that he did not complain about the contract until he told the Celtics in June that he would not honor it.

Given this state of the record, the district court could easily, and properly, conclude that the Celtics' hands were not "unclean." . . .

In sum, issuance of the preliminary injunction was legally proper. For these reasons, the order of the district court is *Affirmed*.

NOTES AND QUESTIONS

1. Although it could not require Shaw to play for the Celtics, the U.S. court imposed a daily fine on Shaw for contempt of court, one that would mount exponentially until he returned to the United States and honored his Celtics contract. Shaw thus faced a dilemma—stay abroad indefinitely or comply with the import of the negative injunction by returning to play for the Celtics. He ultimately chose the latter option.

2. The NBA collective bargaining agreement is more explicit than most in detailing the negotiable items that are allowed either to change language in the Uniform Player Contract or to add new provisions. In this instance, the Celtics persuaded Shaw to agree to send a letter to his Italian club, *Il Messagero*, stating that Shaw was exercising his option to terminate the second year of his contract. Did the arbitrator properly rule that this did not contravene the collective bargaining provisions on allowable amendments? Or, perhaps more to the point, does it appear that the First Circuit agreed or disagreed with the arbitrator's finding? If the court simply disagreed, would it be appropriate to vacate the arbitrator's award?

3. The arbitrator and the courts here considered the issuance of a negative injunction prohibiting Shaw from playing for *Il Messaggero*. How was it to be enforced? Should it be honored by a court in Italy?

4. *Shaw* illustrates the deference U.S. courts provide to properly initiated arbitration decisions (with the grounds for successful appeal being very limited). In considering whether an Italian court would enforce a U.S. arbitration award enjoining Shaw from playing for Il Messaggero, note that national courts generally enforce foreign arbitration awards if the parties that it binds had a valid written arbitration agreement, there were no procedural defects in the arbitration process, and the award does not violate the country's public policy pursuant to the Convention on the Recognition and Enforcement of Foreign Arbitral Awards (New York Convention), a 1958 treaty entered into by the United States. However, in *Dynamo v. Ovechkin,* 412 F. Supp. 2d 24 (D.D.C. 2006), a federal district court refused to enforce the decision of a Russian arbitrator that Alexander Ovechkin, who was playing for the NHL's Washington Capitals, had a contractual obligation to play

during the 2005-2006 season for a Russian hockey team, Dynamo Moscow. Because neither the Capitals nor Ovechkin were parties to the Russian arbitration, the court held they were not bound by the arbitration award and it was not enforceable in the United States under the New York Convention. *Dynamo* and *Shaw* illustrate the growing complexity of sports labor issues as a global market for the services of professional players continues to develop.

ii.   Club and League Power to Discipline

We now shift our focus to the authority of clubs and leagues to discipline players. Player disciplinary matters are a major source of arbitration disputes in professional sports. As you examine the following materials, note the standard employed by the arbitrator to determine whether the club had a legitimate basis for disciplining a player.

NATIONAL BASKETBALL PLAYERS ASSOCIATION ON BEHALF OF PLAYER LATRELL SPREWELL AND WARRIORS BASKETBALL CLUB AND NBA

(May 4, 1998)

JOHN D. FEERICK, Grievance Arbitrator

SUMMATION OF EVENTS

Latrell Sprewell has been playing for the Golden State Warriors since he entered the NBA in 1992. The three-time all-star had been involved in two fights previous to the December 1, 1997 incident. The first fight occurred during his 1992, rookie, season with Byron Houston during a practice. The two were and have remained close friends since the incident. A few years later Jerome Kersee and Sprewell fought during a scrimmage. Sprewell was not fined or disciplined by the league or the Warriors for either incident.

P.J. Carlesimo was hired in the summer of 1997. . . . The two's relationship began amicably but after a disappointing pre-season in October, it soon deteriorated. Carlesimo testified that Sprewell was "selectively defiant" towards him. Sprewell believed that he was being singled out by the coach and was subject to a scrutiny that other players did endure.

Carlesimo is a "screamer" type coach, who is prone towards profanity and harping on players that he believes are capable and expected to perform at another level. Donyell Marshall and Sprewell were often the focus of Carlesimo's attention. During the month of November, Carlesimo viewed Sprewell's behavior as incidents of unsportsman like conduct, resulting in the player being fined a thousand dollars, not allowed to start for one game, and being benched during several others. . . .

The inability of the player and the coach to work with each other reached its zenith on December 1, 1997. The team was conducting three-man, two-ball shooting drills during a practice. Carlesimo was supervising Sprewell, Muggsy Bogues, and Mark Grabow at an end of the gym while the three performed the drill. During the drill, one man shoots, one rebounds, and another passes to the shooter. After 55 seconds, the players rotate positions. Bogues was shooting, Grabow was rebounding, and Sprewell was passing to Bogues. Carlesimo was not satisfied with the amount of shots that Bogues was taking and said "get Muggsy some more shots, Spree." Carlesimo believed that Sprewell was not responding and repeated himself. Sprewell thought that Carlesimo was singling him out again and snapped. Sprewell slammed the ball down and said to Carlesimo "What the f*** do you want me to do?" Carlesimo responded, "Get the f*** out of here."

Sprewell became even more infuriated and grabbed Carlesimo around the neck and began to apply pressure. Carlesimo reacted by saying something to the effect "Go ahead" or "I'm here." Sprewell's hold on Carlesimo controlled the coach's movement and the player's nails scratched into Carlesimo's skin.

Bimbo Coles saw the altercation and at first did not realize that Sprewell was attacking Carlesimo. He turned back to the basket and took another shot. He then turned back to Sprewell and Carlesimo. It was then he realized the seriousness of the incident. Grabow, Warrior's trainer Tom Abdenour, and Coles pulled Sprewell away from Carlesimo. After being pulled off Carlesimo, Sprewell was heard saying something to the effect of "I'll kill you."

Sprewell was lead out of the gym by Abdenour and later joined by Coles and Higgens. Once in the hallway, Sprewell was left alone and went to the locker room. He showered and changed into his street clothes. While there, Sprewell dwelled on all the negative incidents that had occurred in the past month.

He then returned to gym about 10-20 minutes later. Seeing that Sprewell was walking towards Carlesimo, Stank and Higgens both tried, unsuccessfully, to stop him. When Sprewell came closer to Carlesimo, several players and coaches tried to restrain him, while Westhead attempted to pull Carlesimo from the melee.

The testimony concerning this part of the altercation is conflicting but coach Westhead and Assistant General Manager Alvin Attles both saw Sprewell direct and land at least one punch on Carlesimo. . . . The other players were eventually able to push him towards the exit. Sprewell contends that he was struggling to free himself from the players holding him, and while he was flailing, he may have hit Carlesimo.

Upon leaving, he demanded the he be traded, and said "get me the f*** out of here" and "I'll kill you." He immediately went to the office of the General Manager, Garry St. Jean. St. Jean was on the phone with Sprewell's agent Arm Tellem at the time he entered. After expressing in an emotional manner his desire to be traded, St. Jean handed the phone over to Sprewell so that he may speak with his agent. Sprewell left the office after a short conversation with Tellem.

After learning of the first incident, St. Jean informed Red Thorn, head of basketball operations for the NBA. St. Jean then informed the team's counsel, Kenneth Baggett, the team owner and Tellem. He then went to speak to the team about the incident. He asked them not to leak anything to the press, that the team wanted to decide how to deal with this, and mentioned how Sprewell was a friend and would be treated as such.

The Warriors management, including St. Jean and Baggett, then spent the rest of the day discussing the events and creating the proper punishment. After speaking with counsel for the NBA and taking into account previous suspensions for violence, the Warriors decided on a minimum ten game suspension and to further review the situation. The decision was announced at a press conference that night.

Baggett did not interview any of the players because he had been informed that the NBA would be conducting its own investigation. However, he spoke with Attles, Abdenour, and the coaching staff about the incident. Baggett was convinced by the morning of December 3, that Sprewell's contract should be terminated, and that the team should not attempt to trade him. After conferring with the Warriors' owner and management, it was decided that Sprewell's contract was to be terminated.

On December 2, Commissioner Stern had been informed of the altercations. Horace Balmer, NBA Security vice-president, and his team were dispatched to conduct an investigation. The next day, they conducted several player interviews, typed a report from the information obtained from the interviews, and submitted it to the commissioner on the evening of December 3. The commissioner eventually decided to suspend Sprewell for a year. . . .

THE DECISION

A. LEGAL FRAMEWORK

. . . Arbitrators apply progressive discipline, take account of mitigating factors, and look to see whether discipline is consistent with prior penalties for comparable acts. Variations in penalties are appropriate depending on the circumstances and context surrounding the act in question. . . . [W]here "the nature of the offense is the same, but other circumstances . . . vary, variations in the discipline imposed must be nevertheless be reasonably appropriate to the variations in the other circumstances. . . . [P]revious lax discipline on the part of an employer will not require similar treatment of subsequent misconduct where clear notice is given that such behavior would warrant greater discipline. . . .

Another aspect of fairness is the notion of industrial due process. It is, however, a less exacting standard than its constitutional counterpart. . . . "[E]mployers and unions meet in bargaining on approximately equal terms, and their contracts speak of 'just cause' rather than 'due process.'" . . . The essential question for an arbitrator is not whether disciplinary action was totally free from procedural error, but rather whether the process was fundamentally fair. . . .

. . . Thus, arbitrators at times will refuse to uphold a grievance in the face of flawed procedures that do not prejudice the grievant. . . .

B. THE ARGUMENTS MADE BY THE PARTIES

1. Whether the Standard of Review of the Commissioner's One-Year Suspension Is Just Cause or Arbitrary and Capricious

The parties disagree on whether just cause or an arbitrary and capricious standard is applicable in reviewing the Commissioner's one-year suspension of the Grevant. To determine which is applicable, one must interpret the CBA. [The Arbitrator quotes from Sections 5(c) and 14(c) of the CBA.]

The language of Section 5(c) of Article XXXI is broad in nature. To be sure, "integrity" and "public confidence" are directly related to the public perception that what occurs on the basketball court is full-fledged competition. That perception, if undermined, would certainly lead to decline for both the game of basketball and the National Basketball Association. . . . Conduct that would implicate public perceptions of the competition include gambling, acts affecting the outcome of a game other than by its merits, and the use of performance-enhancing drugs. . . . When the Commissioner determines that such action has taken place he is instructed by the Constitution to impose dismissal and perpetual disqualification. . . . Section 5(c) . . . seems to be written too broadly to include only drug offenses that result in suspensions. Section 5(c) appears to involve at least a suspension since fines by the Commissioner under Article 35 do not exceed $25,000, except perhaps for gambling. Section 5(c) . . . is written in such a way that encompasses more conduct than merely offenses involving the outcome of games, gambling and certain drug offenses. . . .

It is difficult to fashion a bright line rule for determining conduct that implicates the integrity of or public confidence in the game of basketball. . . . [S]uch conduct would include . . . a well-publicized violent subversion of the most fundamental authority relationship in the game, that between the player and coach. An attack on a head coach puts in jeopardy the entire structure and organization of a team, affecting its morale and the sport at large. The witnesses who testified said that they have never seen an incident before of a player attacking a head coach. Westhead put tellingly: ". . . this it is not something that is good for a team. . . . [I]t kind of cut right to the core of the team, you know player/coach, coach/player."

With respect to a review based on an arbitrary and capricious standard, The New York Court of Appeals has stated, in an administrative context, that it chiefly relates to whether a particular action should have been taken or is justified and whether the action is without foundation. . . . Under this standard, courts consider whether the determination is based on a consideration of the relevant factors and whether a clear error of judgment has been committed. . . .

Arbitrators have followed a similar application of arbitrary and capricious. . . . "The only circumstances under which a penalty imposed by management can be rightfully set aside are those where discrimination, unfairness, or capricious and arbitrary are proved—in other words, where there has been abuse of discretion." *Stockham Pipe Fittings Co.*, 1 LA 160, 162 (1945). . . .

. . . Although the arbitrary and capricious standard is applicable to this proceeding, I find that is should be read together what the just cause standard of Article XXXI, Section 14(c), which provides that "in grievances regarding discipline, the issue to be resolved *shall be* whether there has been just cause for the penalty imposed." (emphasis mine). . . .

5.   *Whether a Just Cause Standard of Review Is Applicable to the Termination of Grievant's Player Contract by the Warriors*

The record establishes beyond dispute that the termination of Grievant's contract was issued as additional punishment for the incidents of December 1. . . . [T]he Warriors made a decision to terminate Grievant's contract, so as not to reward him . . . [which] would have been the case if he were traded. The record is beyond dispute that the termination was done to punish Grievant for what he had done on December 1. Since the disciplinary nature of this action is plain, a just cause standard of review under Section 14(c) of Article XXXI of the CBA is applicable. . . .

As for the standard of just cause . . .

> . . . [N]o clear standards exist to aid an Arbitrator in finding a conclusive answer to such a question and, therefore, perhaps the best he can do is to decide what reasonable man, mindful of the habits and customs of industrial life and of the standards of justice and fair dealing prevalent in the community, ought to have

done under similar circumstances and in that light to decide whether the conduct of the discharged employee was defensible and the disciplinary penalty just.

Riker Stoker Corp., 7 LA 764, 767 (Platt and Lavery, 1947). . . .
. . . The burden of proof is with the employer and I have determined to apply a clear and convincing standard regarding material issues of dispute given the nature of the conduct and the discipline involved in this proceeding. . . .

3. Whether the CBA Allows Discipline to Be Imposed Jointly by the Commissioner and Warriors with Respect to the Same Conduct

. . . [Section 14(c) of the CBA] provides:

> The parties recognize that a player may be subjected to disciplinary action for just cause by his Team or by the Commissioner (or his designee). Therefore, in Grievances regarding discipline, the issue to be resolved shall be whether there has been just cause for the penalty imposed.

. . . I do not read the provision as dealing with the issue of multiple discipline one way or another except emphasizing the imperative of just cause in reviewing matters of discipline. . . . [O]ne would have expected some expressions in the CBA as to which has primacy. No such provision is to be found and I interpret the CBA as allowing for both with respect to the same conduct, provided the discipline is otherwise appropriate. . . .

4. Whether the Actions Taken by the Commissioner and Warriors Violate Double Jeopardy Principles of Labor Law

The Supreme Court has noted that at common law, and under the Constitution, the protection against double jeopardy is designed to prohibit a second punishment and trial for the same offense. . . . [I]t is also the rule that both the state and federal government . . . may prosecute and punish the same person for the same act. . . .

. . . It is reasonably well accepted in the employment context . . . that once a penalty has been assessed and accepted, it cannot be increased without the discovery of new additional facts that were not readily available to an employer at the time of the original punishment. On the other hand, the Warriors are correct in contending that double jeopardy is inapplicable where the first punishment cannot reasonably considered final. . . .

. . . [B]ased on the letter the Warriors sent to the Grievant on December 1 announcing the suspension as a "minimum of 10 games" and reserving any right with respect to the subject of termination, the Grievant and NBPA could not reasonably have considered the subject closed with respect to the Team. The letter explicitly reserved the right to impose future punishment. . . . I conclude that the Grievant could not have considered the initial punishment final and thus the doctrine of double jeopardy is not available for his protection in this proceeding. . . .

5. Whether the Actions Taken by the Commissioner and Warriors Are Appropriate

. . . [T]he investigation conducted by the NBA was done in good faith and was fair and adequate under the exigencies of the well-publicized situation with which it was then confronted. . . . [T]he NBA complied with the standard of industrial due process. . . .

. . . [T]he investigation by the Warriors, I find it was both helped and hampered by the concurrent investigation conducted by the NBA. . . . [T]he NBA's investigation gave it added reason not to speak to its own players, who easily could have been interviewed in person rather than briefly by telephone. . . .

The telephone interview conducted by the NBA with the Grievant . . . was insufficient for the Team's investigation given the conversations that had taken place between Tellem and St. Jean and my findings that Tellem had conveyed a request to meet. . . .

I do not find it necessary to make a final judgment on the investigation conducted by the Team with respect to the standard of the industrial due process. I considered the residual interest of the team after its ten game suspension of December 1 to have been effectively absorbed by or merged into the NBA's treatment of the matter. . . .

. . . [T]he investigations by the Team and the NBA became, in reality, one after December 1, requiring from a fairness standpoint that any disciplinary actions be treated jointly and not as entirely separate events. . . . [E]ach closely shared information with the other through their lawyers, with the Warriors relying totally on the NBA's office to conduct interviews with the players. . . . [W]hen the Warriors made its termination decision . . . the NBA's investigation was still in the process. . . .

There has never been a case of contract termination in the history of the NBA for a physical assault or a one-year suspension for such conduct, or . . . in the sports of baseball and football. In the case of the NFL, joint action by a team and the League is prohibited as a matter of contract. . . . [T]he evidence indicates that there is no history of both the League and a team imposing discipline for the same violent conduct, on or off the court. . . . Given the magnitude of the Warriors' earlier discipline of the Grievant . . . and the NBA having become dominant in the investigatory process after that, I am unable to sustain the termination of the Grievant's contract as meeting a standard of just cause. I also find that the conduct in question was born of anger and passion and did not constitute an act of moral turpitude, which is at the core of the Team's action. . . .

In approaching my responsibility in the instant matter, I considered whether I should apply to the Commissioner's decision a level of review that asked and answered whether the NBA conducted a fair and adequate investigation and rendered a fair and reasonable judgment based on what was before it as a result of that investigation. Applying such a standard, I would sustain the decision of the one-year suspension of the Grievant.

. . . [T]he conduct of the Grievant . . . which was grievous in nature, was not the result of premeditation and deliberation. . . . I do not consider the time spent by him in the locker room, to have been a sufficient and adequate cooling off period under all the circumstances. . . . [T]he anger, if not rage, that erupted in the first incident fed on itself during the period he spent in the locker room between the incidents, continuing the fury of the first and connecting the two incidents and making them actually one. . . . This finding . . . does not justify his misconduct but is a factor to be considered in rending fair and just determination. . . .

. . . While the violence inflicted by the Grievant on his head Coach is to be condemned, the form of the condemnation in terms of discipline must be tempered by the principles of fairness, as the Commissioner recognized at the hearings. Confidence in the game of basketball is dependent not only on appropriate punishment for misconduct but also on the fairness of proceedings where that punishment is reviewed. . . .

. . . I have determined to uphold the discipline imposed by the NBA, but to limit it to the 1997/98 season. In justice and fairness to the Grievant should be allowed to start the 1998/99 season with this tragic event behind him instead of having it extend into the next season. . . . [A] suspension for the 1997/98 season involves the loss of 68 games and $6.4 million. It is many times the aggregate suspensions imposed on the other players for acts of physical violence, exceeding the total of all suspensions imposed on all players for physical altercations during the 1995/96 and 1996/97 seasons combined, and all suspensions imposed for acts of altercations during the 1992/3, 1993/4, 1994/5 seasons combined.

I find that a penalty of 68 games is commensurate with the severity of the misconduct, addresses the wrong done to the Head Coach, the Grievant's Team, and the NBA and conveys a message that violence in the NBA will be dealt with severely but always with due regard to principles of fairness. . . . [A] greater penalty would be unreasonable and disproportionate to the circumstances involved in this proceeding. As for a penalty of $6.4 million against a history of lesser penalties for misconduct not involving a Coach, I find it justified by virtue of the singularity of the misconduct and the emphasis placed on combating violence by both the NBA and NBPA. . . .

NOTE AND QUESTIONS

What standard did the arbitrator employ in determining whether the disciplined imposed on Sprewell was proper? On what grounds did the arbitrator reduce the severity of the sanctions imposed on Sprewell? Do you agree?

SPREWELL v. GOLDEN STATE WARRIORS
266 F.3d 979 (9th 2001)

TROTT, Circuit Judge. . . .

Judicial scrutiny of an arbitrator's decision in a labor dispute "is extremely limited." The Supreme Court has instructed that "as long as the arbitrator is even arguably construing or applying the contract and acting within the scope of his authority, that a court is convinced he committed serious error does not suffice to overturn his decision." *United Paperworkers Int'l Union v. Misco, Inc.*, 484 U.S. 29, 38, 108 S.Ct. 364, 98 L.Ed.2d 286 (1987). . . .

Notwithstanding the foregoing, we have identified four instances in which the vacatur of an arbitration award under section 301 is warranted: (1) when the award does not draw its essence from the collective bargaining agreement; (2) when the arbitrator exceeds the scope of the issues submitted; (3) when the award runs counter to public policy; and (4) when the award is procured by fraud. . . .

1.   THE ARBITRATION AWARD DRAWS ITS ESSENCE FROM THE CBA

Sprewell contends that the arbitrator's approval of Sprewell's "multiple punishments"—the disciplinary actions taken by *both* the NBA *and* the Warriors in response to Sprewell's misconduct—did not draw its essence from the CBA. The thrust of Sprewell's argument is that the arbitrator improperly ascribed a conjunctive meaning to the word "or" in the CBA provision that subjects players "to disciplinary action for just cause by his Team or by the Commissioner." Sprewell alleges that by failing to read the word "or" in the disjunctive, the arbitrator not only discarded the "plain and unambiguous" language of the CBA, but actually rewrote it. Sprewell additionally argues that the arbitrator's award does not draw its essence from the CBA because "the Arbitrator relied upon the [National Football League's] collective bargaining agreement, which uses different language, *i.e.*, the word 'and' instead of 'or.'" Sprewell's claims are legally untenable.

We have held that an arbitration award will only be set aside for failing to draw its essence from the contract in "those egregious cases in which a court determines that the arbitrator's award ignored the plain language of the contract." *Stead Motors of Walnut Creek v. Automotive Machinists Lodge No. 1173*, 886 F.2d 1200, 1205-06 n. 6 (9th Cir.1989). This is not such a case. In the arbitration award, the arbitrator explained in detail the logic underlying his conclusion, including why he read the word "or" in the conjunctive rather than the disjunctive. Specifically, the arbitrator found that: (1) the CBA provision upon which Sprewell relies was not intended to deal with the issue of multiple disciplines, but rather was designed to emphasize "the imperative of just cause in reviewing the matters of discipline"—thus illustrating that the word "or" was likely chosen without careful consideration of its implications; (2) the CBA does not include the word "either," which would have supported the conclusion that the penalties were intended to be mutually exclusive; and (3) as demonstrated by the NFL's CBA, "[h]ad the parties here intended by contract to limit discipline with respect to the same matter to a team or the Commissioner, but not both, one would have expected some expression in the CBA as to which has primacy." Regardless of whether we would reach the same conclusion advanced by the arbitrator, we must defer to the arbitrator's decision on the grounds that he was, at the very least, "arguably construing or applying the contract." *Misco*, 484 U.S. at 38, 108 S.Ct. 364.

2.   THE ARBITRATOR DID NOT EXCEED THE SCOPE OF HIS AUTHORITY

Sprewell argues that the arbitrator "exceeded the scope of his authority" because he was required either to uphold or to reject the suspension in its entirety. Sprewell does not, however, attempt to cite language—nor is there any—in the CBA supporting this conclusion. The Supreme Court has held that an arbitrator should be given substantial latitude in fashioning a remedy under a CBA. *See Enterprise Wheel, 363 U.S. at 596-97, 80 S.Ct. 1358.* Sprewell has failed to demonstrate why the above rule should not be applied with full vigor in the instant case. Accordingly, we reject Sprewell's contention that the arbitrator exceeded the scope of his authority by fashioning an originative remedy.

3.   THE AWARD DOES NOT RUN COUNTER TO PUBLIC POLICY

Sprewell alleges that the arbitration award should be vacated on the ground that it contravenes California's public policy against race-discrimination. The crux of Sprewell's argument is that by upholding the dual punishments issued by the NBA and the Warriors, the arbitrator simultaneously spread the virus of racial animus plaguing those penalties. "To vacate an arbitration award on public policy grounds, we must (1) find that 'an explicit, well defined and dominant policy' exists here and (2) that 'the policy is one that specifically militates against the relief ordered by the arbitrator.'" *United Food & Commercial Workers Int'l Union, Local 588 v. Foster Poultry Farms,* 74 F.3d 169, 174 (9th Cir.1995) (citation omitted). The latter element is dispositive of Sprewell's claim. The arbitrator held that Sprewell's punishments were wholly justified by the language of the CBA and by virtue of the uniquely egregious nature of Sprewell's misconduct. Therefore, Sprewell has failed to demonstrate that the public policy of California militates against the enforcement of the arbitration award.

4. The Arbitration Award Was Not Procured by Fraud

Finally, Sprewell claims that the NBA and the Warriors tainted the arbitral process by introducing false statements and doctored pictures of Carlesimo's injuries, thus requiring that the award be vacated on account of fraud. This claim can be summarily dismissed under the rule that "where the fraud or undue means is not only discoverable, but discovered and brought to the attention of the arbitrators, a disappointed party will not be given a second bite at the apple." *A.G. Edwards & Sons, Inc. v. McCollough,* 967 F.2d 1401, 1403 (9th Cir.1992). Sprewell's fraud claim was presented in its entirely to, and ruled upon by, the arbitrator. Thus, we do not find it necessary to revisit this issue. . . .

NOTES AND QUESTIONS

1. Is the Ninth Circuit's opinion consistent with the view expressed in *Major League Baseball Players Association v. Garvey,* 121 S. Ct. 1724 (2001), *supra,* regarding the deference courts should afford arbitrators' decisions? Does *Sprewell* provide guidance as to "when the arbitrator strays from interpretation and application of the agreement and effectively 'dispense[s] his own brand of industrial justice'" so as to provide grounds for overturning an arbitrator's decision?

2. Much like Latrell Sprewell, the NFL's Terrell Owens was a controversial player off the field. Prior to the 2005 season, Owens, then a wide receiver for the Philadelphia Eagles, wanted to have his contract restructured because he felt that he "outperformed his contract." When the Eagles did not restructure the contract, Owens became a distraction to the team by consistently criticizing teammates and disrupting practices. As a result, Eagles management decided to suspend Owens for four games (which was the maximum discipline allowable under the CBA) and announced that although they would pay him for the remainder of the season, he would not be permitted to practice or play with the team. The NFLPA filed a protest on Owens's behalf arguing that the suspension was not warranted and that the Eagles violated the maximum discipline policy in the CBA by excluding Owens from playing for the rest of the year. Arbitrator Richard I. Bloch found that the suspension was, indeed, warranted and that the responsibility of determining who will and who will not play in games is

appropriately left to a team's coach. *Owens v. Phila. Eagles*, NFL Arbitration (2005) (Bloch, Arb.).

A 2004 incident ranking among the NBA's ugliest moments produced another landmark disciplinary case, this one favoring the players union. On November 19, 2004, NBA Commissioner David Stern suspended Indiana Pacers forward Ron Artest for the remainder of the season, guard Stephen Jackson for 30 games, forward Jermaine O'Neal for 25 games, and guard Anthony Johnson for 5 games in response to their involvement in a fight during a game against the Detroit Pistons that spilled into the stands and involved fans. Following the suspensions, the NBPA filed an appeal to the grievance arbitrator, stating that the suspensions were inconsistent with the terms of the NBA CBA, and the grievance arbitrator reduced Jermaine O'Neal's suspension from 25 to 15 games. The NBA then sued, arguing that the grievance arbitrator did not have jurisdiction to hear the appeal since it involved an issue of substantive arbitrability rather than procedural arbitrability. The court, however, disagreed and upheld the arbitrator's decision to reduce the suspension, giving the NBPA a victory in its effort to check the Commissioner's disciplinary authority. *National Basketball Assn. v. National Basketball Players Assn.*, 2005 WL 22869 (S.D.N.Y Jan. 3, 2005).

3.   *The New Orleans Saints Bounty Scandal.* As discussed briefly in Chapter 6, beginning in 2010 the NFL suspected that the New Orleans Saints were financially incentivizing their defensive players to injure opposing players. After investigating the matter and concluding that the alleged bounty system existed, NFL Commissioner Roger Goodell stripped the Saints of two future second round draft picks, fined the Saints $500,000, and suspended the Saints general manager Mickey Loomis, multiple Saints coaches, and several Saints players for various lengths of time. These actions spawned one of the most intense and complex disputes over disciplinary authority in American sports history.

Loomis, Head Coach Sean Payton, and Assistant Head Coach Joe Vitt all appealed their suspensions, but Commissioner Goodell, who, as noted above, imposed the initial punishments, heard the appeals and denied them. The NFLPA, on behalf of the suspended players—Scott Fujita, Will Smith, Anthony Hargrove, and Jonathan Vilma—also appealed to the Commissioner.

In addition, however, the NFLPA sought to have the dispute resolved along an alternative adjudicatory track by initiating a separate proceeding before an Independent System Arbitrator, pursuant to Article 15 of the NFL CBA, arguing that the System Arbitrator rather than the Commissioner had jurisdiction over the bounty system allegations because they constituted an allegedly impermissible "undisclosed agreement" (over which the System Arbitrator would have jurisdiction) rather than alleged "conduct detrimental to the league" (over which Commissioner Goodell would have jurisdiction). See *Compl.*, ¶51, *NFLPA v. NFL Mgmt. Council*, No. 2:12-cv-01744 (E.D. La. 2012).

The System Arbitrator, in a decision issued in June 2012, deferred jurisdiction to Commissioner Goodell, asserting that the allegations, if proved, would not constitute an impermissible "undisclosed agreement" and that they would, therefore, be more appropriately analyzed as alleged "conduct detrimental to the league." *Id.* ¶53. The NFLPA promptly appealed the

System Arbitration Award to an Appeals Panel provided for in the CBA. *Id.* ¶ 55.

While the NFLPA's appeal from the System Arbitrator's decision was pending, Commissioner Goodell rejected the NFLPA's original appeal to him, and the NFLPA responded by suing the NFL on behalf of Fujita, Smith, and Hargrove, claiming the Commissioner acted with evident partiality in hearing the appeal and, in any event, lacked jurisdiction to dispense punishment in, or arbitrate, the matter in the first place. See *NFLPA v. NFL Mgmt. Council*, No. 2:12-cv-01744 (E.D. La. 2012). The fourth suspended player, Jonathan Vilma, sued Commissioner Goodell separately, alleging that Commissioner Goodell made defamatory statements about him that caused permanent harm to his reputation. See *Vilma v. Goodell*, No. 2:12-cv-01283 (E.D. La. 2012). The NFL then countered with a grievance against the NFLPA alleging that Vilma's defamation suit violated the CBA.

Vilma filed an additional suit as well, this time against the NFL, arguing that Commissioner Goodell failed to serve as a neutral arbiter and that he failed to issue a timely decision on the appeal in accordance with the CBA. See *Vilma v. NFL*, No. 2:12-cv-01718 (E.D. La. 2012). In this suit, Vilma sought injunctive relief to vacate the suspension and allow him to participate in team activities.

As the parties awaited decisions in these cases, the Appeals Panel considering the appeal from the System Arbitration Award issued a summary[4] of its decision on September 7, 2012, in which it found that the "alleged bounty program was both an undisclosed agreement to provide compensation to players and an agreement to cause or attempt to cause injury to players (conduct detrimental to the league)," and thus, both the System Arbitrator and the Commissioner would have exclusive jurisdiction to impose punishments under their respective powers. *CBA Appeals Panel Summary Decision* at 3. But because the record did not reveal whether Commissioner Goodell issued the punishments under the "conduct detrimental" clause (for which he would have authority) or the "undisclosed agreement" clause (for which he would not have authority), the Appeals Panel vacated the System Arbitration Award and remanded the matter to Commissioner Goodell for redetermination. *Id.* at 4.

Roughly a month later, on October 9, 2012, after meetings with the players and their attorneys, Commissioner Goodell reissued his decision to punish the players, explaining that the "players confirmed many of the key facts disclosed in [the] investigation" and clearly stating that the punishments were for *conduct detrimental* to the league. NFL Communications, *Discipline Reaffirmed for Four Players Suspended for Participation in Saints' Bounty Program*, press release, Oct. 9, 2012. In reissuing the decision, however, Commissioner Goodell reduced the lengths of the suspensions for two of the players: Scott Fujita and Anthony Hargrove (the punishments for Smith and Vilma remained the same). *Id.*

Three days following Goodell's reissued decision, all four players appealed and requested that this time Goodell recuse himself and therefore

---

4. The decision was issued in summary form because of a joint request from the NFLPA and the NFL for a decision to be issued prior to the start of the regular season. See *Summary of CBA Appeals Panel Decision* at 4. A full decision was to be issued at a later date. *Id.*

not handle the appeal of his own decision. Goodell agreed to recusal and appointed former NFL Commissioner Paul Tagliabue to hear the appeals.

On December 11, 2012, over seven months after Goodell initially doled out the players' suspensions, Tagliabue vacated them. In doing so, he did not dispute the essence of what Goodell's investigation uncovered. Indeed, he generally affirmed Goodell's factual findings. He insisted, though, that "[u]nlike [the] Saints' broad organizational misconduct, player appeals involve sharply focused issues of alleged individual player misconduct in several different aspects, [and in this instance] this entire case had been contaminated by the coaches and others in the Saints' organization." Jesse Reed, *Reviewing the Entire Timeline of Saints, Bountygate Scandal,* Bleacher Report, Dec. 11, 2012, http://bleacherreport.com/articles/1441646-reviewing-the-complete-timeline-of-nfl-saints-bountygate-scandal.

Therefore, Tagliabue did not find the suspensions appropriate, and in vacating them he dealt both Goodell (renowned as among the most fiercely disciplinarian commissioners in recent professional sports history) and the concept of broad league commissioner authority a rare defeat.

For differing perspectives on disciplining players in professional sports, see Michael R. Wilson, *Why So Stern?: The Growing Power of the NBA Commissioner,* 7 DePaul J. Sports L. Contemp. Probs. 45 (2010); Janine Young Kim and Matthew J. Parlow, *Off-Court Misbehavior: Sports Leagues and Private Punishment,* 99 J. Crim. L. & Criminology 573 (2009); Colin J. Daniels and Aaron Brooks, *From the Black Sox to the Sky Box: The Evolution and Mechanics of Commissioner Authority,* 10 Tex. Rev. Ent. & Sports L. 23 (2008); Robert L. Bard and Lewis Kurlantzick, *Knicks-Heat and the Appropriateness of Sanctions in Sport,* 20 Cardozo Arts & Ent. L.J. 507 (2002); Jeffrey A. Mishkin, *Dispute Resolution in the NBA: The Allocation of Decision Making Among the Commissioner, Impartial Arbitrator, System Arbitrator, and the Courts,* 35 Val. U. L. Rev. 449 (2001); Roger A. Javier, *"You Can't Choke Your Boss & Hold Your Job Unless You Play in the NBA": The Latrell Sprewell Incident Undermines Disciplinary Authority in the NBA,* 7 Vill. Sports & Ent. L.J. 209 (2000); Jason M. Pollack, Note, *Take My Arbitrator, Please: Commissioner "Best Interests" Disciplinary Authority in Professional Sports,* 67 Fordham L. Rev. 1645 (1999) (discussing authority of commissioner to discipline players for conduct that may not be in the "best interest" of professional sports leagues); Gene Orza, *The Perception and Reality of Discipline in Sports,* 17 Hofstra Lab. & Emp. L.J. 139 (1999); Jan Stiglitz, *Player Discipline in Team Sports,* 5 Marq. Sports L.J. 167 (1995) (discussing authority of league commissioners to discipline players).

4. *Preemption of State Claims.* In *Sprewell,* the Ninth Circuit observed:

> The Supreme Court has held that federal law exclusively governs suits for breach of a CBA, while concomitantly preempting state law claims predicated on such agreements. *See Allis-Chalmers Corp. v. Lueck,* 471 U.S. 202, 210, 105 S.Ct. 1904, 85 L.Ed. 2d 206 (1985). The Court has expanded the preemptive reach of section 301 beyond contract claims, holding that section 301 "also preempts tort claims which, 'as applied, would frustrate the federal labor-contract scheme established in § 301.'" . . . A state law claim is preempted by section 301 when it is "substantially dependent" on analysis of a CBA. . . . Stated alternatively, "[i]f the plaintiff's claim cannot be resolved without interpreting the applicable CBA . . . it is preempted." . . . "[T]he bare fact that a collective bargaining agreement will be consulted in the course of state-law litigation," however, does not require that the state-claim be extinguished. . . . Nor is a

state-law claim preempted merely because the defendant has raised a defense based on the terms of a CBA.

266 F.3d at 990. The court ruled that Sprewell's state claim alleging unfair business practices was preempted by Section 301 of the Labor Relations Act because it "requires an interpretation of the disciplinary provisions of the CBA." *Id.* at 992.

However, the court held that Sprewell's state claims alleging that his team and the league interfered with his contracts with third parties by making defamatory media reports were not preempted. The Ninth Circuit ruled these claims arose under California law independent of the terms of the collective bargaining agreement.

In the years following *Sprewell*, courts have continued to struggle with the preemption issue. For instance, in *Atwater v. NFLPA*, 2009 WL 1020848 (N.D. Ga. March 27, 2009), six former NFL players and their spouses sued the NFL and the NFLPA alleging that the NFLPA breached its duty to them by negligently performing background checks on certain financial advisors who participated in the NFLPA's Financial Advisors Program. The NFLPA filed a motion for summary judgment asserting that Section 301 preempted all of plaintiffs' state claims. In addressing the issue, the federal district court—using a slightly different formulation than that used in *Sprewell*, but one also endorsed by the Supreme Court—stated that a tort action is governed by federal law if it is "inextricably intertwined" with a collective bargaining agreement. *Id.* at *4. Finding that the plaintiffs' state claims fell within the parameters of this standard and that resolution of those claims would therefore require an interpretation of the CBA, the court granted defendants motion for summary judgment regarding preemption of plaintiffs' state claims.

A similar result was reached in *Givens v. Tennessee Football, Inc.*, 684 F. Supp. 2d 985 (M.D. Tenn. 2010), in which the court held that the state law claims were preempted by Section 301 because they were not sufficiently independent of the terms of the CBA. Noting that the Supreme Court has interpreted the language of Section 301 to require preemption of state law claims when those claims are "inextricably intertwined" with or "substantially dependent" on consideration of the terms of the labor contract, the defendant's motion to dismiss was granted. *Id.* at 989.

In *Duerson v. National Football League*, 2012 WL 1658353 (N.D. Ill. May 11, 2012), a case in which the family of deceased former Chicago Bears safety Dave Duerson sued the NFL for wrongful death under the theory that Duerson's suicide resulted from brain damage he suffered while playing in the league, the court commented on the factually intensive nature of Section 301 preemption questions: "As one would expect in case-by-case analysis, in some situations preemption is found and in others it is not." *Id.* at *5. The court went on to find that the Duersons' claims were preempted because they were "substantially dependant on the interpretation of CBA provisions" but noted numerous other suits brought against the NFL and NFL teams involving health and safety in which state claims were not preempted. *Id.* at *5-6. See, e.g., *Jurevicius v. Cleveland Browns Football Co.*, No. 1:09 CV 1803, 2010 WL 846120, at *12-13 (N.D. Ohio Mar. 31, 2010) (holding that a player's negligence claim filed after he contracted a serious infection from using the Cleveland Brown's training facility was not preempted because CBA provisions bearing on player health and safety governed players' physical condition rather than training facility management); *McPherson v. Tenn. Football Inc.*, No. 3:07-0002, 2007 U.S. Dist. LEXIS 39595, 2007 WL 5445124, *16 (M.D. Tenn. May 31, 2007) (holding that a player's negligence claim against the NFL's Tennessee Titans related to a mascot running into him with a golf cart during halftime was not preempted because the CBA contained no provisions "concerning . . . mascots or field safety for halftime activities"); *Brown v. National Football League*, 219 F. Supp. 2d 372, 387 (S.D.N.Y. 2002) (holding that a player's negligence claim against the NFL for failing to appropriately monitor a referee who threw a penalty flag into his eye was not preempted because the NFL rules he cited regarding the scope of the league's duty to train referees were not part of the CBA).

iii. *Bonus Provision Arbitrations*

In professional sports contracts, bonus provisions are often important additions to standard terms. In some NFL and MLB contracts, for example, performance bonus provisions may run four or five pages. Some players may actually earn more in bonuses than in base salary. These are exceptional cases, but they do occur.

This suggests two cautionary warnings. First, great care must be taken in the consideration of when bonus provisions should be used and what types are realistically available and desirable. Second, equally great care should be employed in the drafting of these provisions. To engage in sloppy drafting, as illustrated in the following arbitrations, is to invite the contract provisions to give rise to future litigation.

ARBITRATION BETWEEN MAJOR LEAGUE BASEBALL CLUBS (CLEVELAND INDIANS) AND MAJOR LEAGUE BASEBALL PLAYERS ASSOCIATION (JAMES B. BIBBY)

April 3, 1978

PORTER, Impartial Arbitrator.

. . . On March 9, 1977, Player Bibby and the Cleveland Club entered into a two-year contract for the 1977 and 1978 playing seasons, consisting of the Uniform Player Contract and certain Special Covenants. One of the Special Covenants provided that Bibby, a pitcher, would receive an additional ("bonus") sum of Five Thousand Dollars ($5,000.00), if he started 20 games or pitched 180 innings during a season, and would receive a further Five Thousand Dollars ($5,000.00) bonus (*i.e.*, a total of $10,000.00), if he started 30 games during a season. . . . Finally, the Special Covenant provided: "All payments earned pursuant to the above provisions *will be paid at the end* of *the respective seasons* (emphasis added)."

Bibby did, in fact, start 30 games in the 1977 season, thereby earning the $10,000.00 bonus. The Club's season ended on October 1 or 2, 1977. The Club did not pay the bonus at the end of the season. . . .

The Club argues that the contract's requirement of payment "at the end of the season" did not establish a specific date and, hence, "the past practice of the parties must be the basis for determining the obligation of the Club with respect to that bonus." Since Bibby had had a similar "end of the season" bonus provision in his 1976 contract and was paid that bonus on December 15, 1976, the payment of his 1977 bonus on December 22, 1977 is said to have been consistent with the payment practice followed under the prior year's contract. Thus, in the Club's view, it was not in default.

The Panel majority cannot accept the Club's argument that "the end of the season" standard lacks sufficient specificity to establish a date on which payment was due under the contract. To be sure, the Club's season could arguably be said to end upon the completion of the regular scheduled season of 162 games; upon the Club's elimination from the playoffs, if it had qualified for them; or upon the end of the World Series, if Cleveland had reached the Series. However, the term "season" or "playing season" is used to determine all manner of rights and obligations of the parties under the Uniform Player's Contract, including salary payments under Paragraph 2, and the parties themselves obviously consider the commencement and end of the season to be clearly definable events.

There is no dispute herein that Cleveland's season ended with the last game played by the Club in Toronto, the game on which Bibby made his 30th start. No one at the hearing could recall with certainty whether this game was played on October 1 or 2, but there is no doubt the season ended for Cleveland when that last game had been played.

There is also no dispute that Bibby earned the $10,000.00 bonus and that, under the contract, the bonus was due to be paid at the end of the season. When it was not paid to him, the Club was clearly in default under the terms of the Agreement. . . .

The grievance is sustained. James B. Bibby's Contract for services to be performed during the 1978 season no longer binds him and he is a free agent.

NOTES AND QUESTIONS

1.   Was there any reason for the parties involved in the *Bibby* case not to name a date certain by which the bonus was to be paid? What about the time of payment for other bonuses?

2.   Another illustrative bonus arbitration case is *Arbitration Between National Football League Players Association and Russ Bolinger v. Detroit Lions* (1977). The arbitrator ruled that a contract provision providing a player is entitled to a bonus if he was named to the official All-Rookie Team by either the AP, UPI, or NEA news services in 1976 did not require payment of the bonus when the player was named to the All-Rookie Second Team by the Pro-Football Writer's Association. The player was, however, entitled to his bonus for starting seven regular season games on offense, because playing on goal-line offense was a special circumstance not considered a part of "special team" play.

3.   *Repayment of Bonus.* Ricky Williams, a former running back for the NFL's Miami Dolphins, signed a contract with the team that covered 2002-2005. In 2004, just before the beginning of preseason training camp, Williams notified the Dolphins that he was retiring from football. Thereafter, Miami notified Williams that his actions constituted a breach of contract and demanded that he repay a portion of his signing bonus. In the *Matter of Arbitration Between Miami Dolphins and National Football League Management Council v. Ricky Williams and the National Football Player Association* (Oct. 5,

2004), the club argued that relevant provisions of the CBA and its contract with Williams mandated repayment of the bonuses paid to Williams. Williams argued that the bonus payments had been made by his previous team, the New Orleans Saints; consequently, Miami sought to recover sums it had not paid to him. Williams also argued that Miami's demand for repayment was a disguised liquidated damages provision that bore no relationship to any loss the club suffered as a result of his decision to retire.

Arbitrator Richard I. Bloch agreed with the club. He found that the relevant terms of Williams's contract with the Saints applied to his contract with Miami. According to Bloch, when Williams was traded from New Orleans to Miami, his contract with the Saints was assigned to Miami. Although the Saints renegotiated Williams's contract with respect to salary and bonus provisions, the Miami contract "covered the same terms as the New Orleans contract and, indeed, incorporated by reference and physically attached" the bonus payment and default provisions of the New Orleans contract. *Id.* at 5. Bloch concluded that several contract provisions read as a whole required Williams to repay a proportionate amount of the bonus payment made to him because of his default, which was defined to include a failure or refusal of the player to report to the club.

Characterizing the question of liquidated damages as a matter of first impression, Bloch ruled that "the clauses in these agreements are not liquidated damage provisions; they are, instead terms that highlight, with precision, those circumstances in which bonus monies will be given and those in which they will be taken away." *Id.* at 11. He further concluded:

> [T]here is no real question that what was bargained here was a comprehensive incentive and default mechanism. At stake was not solely a series of individual field performance goals and rewards for the player but also a long-term arrangement that figured prominently in the Club's overall plan. . . . These were not simply surrogate methods of estimating damages in event the bargain went sour; rather, they were the essence of the bargain themselves.

Id.

The Miami Dolphins and the NFL then filed a motion for confirmation of the award in federal district court. Ricky Williams and the NFLPA filed a cross-motion to vacate the arbitration award. The court ruled in favor of the Dolphins. See *Miami Dolphins and NFL v. Williams and NFLPA*, 356 F. Supp. 2d 1301 (S.D. Fla. 2005). The court noted the substantial deference accorded arbitration awards and that this deference is even greater "in the context of collective bargaining agreements and labor-management disputes." *Id.* at 1303. Even if a court feels an arbitrator committed serious error in construing a contract, the court will not overturn the decision. Here, then, the question was whether the arbitrator acted in manifest disregard of Florida law or if enforcement of the award would be contrary to public policy. The court concluded that neither had occurred but opined:

> The public policy argument of Williams has some merit. It is true that under Florida law, agreement between parties to apply liquidated damages upon default can be deemed unenforceable as penalty provisions by a court. . . . This Court recognizes that the default provisions of the Dolphins-Williams contract could be construed as valid liquidated damages or as an unenforceable penalty. However, the Court finds that the arbitrator in this case was well

within the scope of his authority in interpreting the default provisions of the contract in the context of the NFL's CBA and Florida law. The fact that the arbitrator construed the contract in a manner that avoided consideration of whether the actual damages were proportional to the default provisions does not render his decision in manifest disregard or against the public policy of Florida.

Id. at 1305.

Williams returned to play for the Miami Dolphins in 2005 after serving a suspension imposed by the NFL for violation of the league's drug testing policy. He played for several years with the Dolphins and then for a year with the Baltimore Ravens before retiring for good in 2012.

In a different case involving an NFL player, the NFLPA filed a complaint on February 9, 2009, alleging the New York Giants breached its contract with receiver Plaxico Burress by suspending him without pay for four games and by withholding $1 million from his signing bonus. The Giants did so following Burress's arrest for illegally carrying a gun with which he accidentally shot himself in a Manhattan nightclub. On April 6, 2009, the Special Master Stephen Burbank ruled in favor of Burress. Essentially, Burbank sided with the union in stating that "[a]nything that's earned prior to [the] conduct is the player's to keep." He further ruled that Burress could be docked 25 percent only if he "willfully" hurt his chances of playing again. See Tony Grossi, *Rulings Could Be Bonus for Stallworth,* Cleveland Plain Dealer, April 12, 2009, at 2009 WLNR 6486748.

The same day, pursuant to similar reasoning, Special Master Burbank ruled on the NFLPA's grievance on behalf of Kansas City Chiefs running back Larry Johnson, who was financially penalized by his team after incidents at nightclubs that led to his arrest and conviction for disturbing the peace. Burbank explained that "money earned by a player, such as a signing bonus, cannot be forfeited even if the player subsequently gets into trouble" and determined that Johnson was therefore allowed to retain the money he had earned up to that point. Burbank found that the Chiefs acted properly, however, in terminating Johnson's contract and not paying him $3.5 million guaranteed for the 2009 and 2010 seasons. See *Burress Can Keep Money; Chiefs' RB Johnson's Pay Not Guaranteed,* NFL.com, April 6, 2009, http://www.nfl.com/news/story?id=09000d5d80fa20db&template=with-video-with-comments&confirm=true.

4. *Interpretation of CBA Provisions.* The National Football League Management Council (NFLMC) sought a declaration that the Atlanta Falcons could recover money already paid to its quarterback, Michael Vick, after he pled guilty to federal criminal charges and was suspended indefinitely without pay by the NFL. The Falcons immediately demanded that Vick repay most of the bonus monies paid him in 2004, 2005, and 2006. At issue was the interpretation of CBA, Article XIV, §9(c). A special master determined that the Falcons could seek forfeiture, but the district court disagreed. It found that a forfeiture of the 2004 and 2005 monies based on Roster, Reporting, and Playing bonuses would violate §9(c) because of its language concerning "years already performed." When the criminal charges were brought against Vick, those years were in the past, and he had earned the monies. Forfeiture was not allowed. As to the 2006 bonuses, the Falcons' unchallenged recovery of this sum did not violate §9(c). Finally, the court agreed

with the special master's finding that the Falcons were precluded from pursuing state law claims to recover the bonuses. Relief through the special master and the district court was the exclusive remedy for the parties. See *White v. NFL*, 533 F. Supp. 2d 929 (D. Minn. 2008).

PROBLEM 7-4

NBA player signs a two-year guaranteed contract that contains the following bonus provision:

One Year		Two Years
1,800 minutes: $50,000	—or—	3,600 minutes: $100,000
2,200 minutes: $75,000		4,400 minutes: $150,000

Player plays 2,431 minutes in first year of contract. He is released after the first year. What does the club owe him for his minutes played in his first contract year? Is he owed anything, since the contract is guaranteed, for the excess 231 minutes accumulated toward the two-year totals?

Assume the contract had reversed the totals, with the following provisions:

One Year		Two Years
1,800 minutes: $75,000	—or—	3,600 minutes: $150,000
2,200 minutes: $50,000		4,400 minutes: $100,000

If Player is released after the first year, what is he owed under *this* contract? Are your answers to the two scenarios consistent? Are there other facts about Player's performance history that should be evaluated before you can give a final answer?

iv. Side Deals and Undisclosed Agreements

All agreements between a club and player are generally required to be filed with the league. If there are side deals, they are not recognized by the league if not disclosed. This does not necessarily mean side deals are unenforceable in a court of law, but they may be prohibited by league rules or a collective bargaining agreement. With the prevalence of league salary caps and other restrictive devices that limit player salaries, the temptation to use side deals has increased. The response by leagues has been to impose sanctions on the involved parties, so both clubs and players must hesitate before exploring prohibited or undisclosed means of compensation.

For example, in *Arbitration Between National Football League Players Association (Elvin Bethea) and NFL Management Council (Houston Oilers)* (April 17, 1978), Elvin Bethea, a defensive lineman for the Houston Oilers, agreed to a lower salary after he was encouraged by the Oilers owner, head coach, and general manager to participate in a cattle-feeding partnership from which he expected to receive 10 percent of the profits. The operation was a failure, and the partnership was dissolved. Bethea demanded that the Oilers pay him the yearly profit he expected to receive over the term of his three-year contract. In protest, Bethea skipped training camp for six to eight days and was fined. Bethea initiated a noninjury grievance, claiming that the club was liable to him for $20,000, $40,000, and $60,000 for 1977, 1978, and 1979. He also sought immediate payment of all salary monies previously deferred.

Arbitrator Searce concluded that "[t]he partnership was established over a month before his player contracts and not as a package deal. The agreement did not set forth as a condition that Bethea would have to sign his player contracts. Also, neither the agreement nor the parties' conversations contained an express guarantee of returns from the partnership. Thus, Searce found that the partnership agreement was not part of the NFL Player Contract and the club was not in breach of contract or in violation of Article XIX."

As a more recent example, *In the Matter of National Basketball Association Minnesota Timberwolves, Joe Smith and Eric Fleisher* (Nov. 9, 2000), an arbitrator found that Joseph Smith, a Minnesota Timberwolves player, and the club entered into an undisclosed letter agreement dated January 22, 1999. Apparently, the letter agreement provided for a series of contracts that would be signed in the future requiring the Timberwolves pay Smith a total of $84 million. The end result of this agreement was to make Smith a "Larry Bird" player. The NBA argued that the "the undisclosed agreement kept other teams from enticing Smith away because Smith had figuratively in his pocket the promise of many millions in the future, a promise that other teams could not make consistently with the CBA." The letter agreement constituted a violation of Article XIII, §2, which prohibits undisclosed agreements.

It was clear that the NBA commissioner possessed the power to void Smith's contract for the upcoming season. The narrow issue before the arbitrator was the commissioner's authority to void any player contract Smith and the Timberwolves might enter into in the future. After reviewing the CBA, arbitrator Kenneth M. Dam wrote, "I conclude that the Commissioner does have the authority to void contracts not yet entered into at the time of the violation. . . . If the Commissioner, having voided the existing contract, simply voids the same contract when resubmitted (with new signatures and a new signature date), he is still voiding "upon a violation of Section 2. . . . Surely the word 'void' means that the contract remains null and void." The arbitrator also noted the matter before him extended beyond the imposition of a penalty on Smith, but also involved the need to maintain competitive balance and the integrity of the league's salary cap, which are primary objectives that the rule against undisclosed agreements is designed to further. See Jeffrey A. Mishkin, *Dispute Resolution in the NBA: The Allocation of Decision Making Among the Commissioner, Impartial Arbitrator, System Arbitrator, and the Courts*, 35 Val. U. L. Rev. 449, 456-57 (2001) (discussing the Smith matter).

D.   THE INTERSECTION OF ANTITRUST AND LABOR LAW

One of the more perplexing aspects of labor relations in professional sports is the intersection of antitrust law and labor law. It is important to understand the inherent tension between these two bodies of federal law. Labor law permits employees and employers to engage in joint conduct among themselves, and with each other, that otherwise may violate the antitrust laws.

The objective of antitrust law is to promote competition among buyers and sellers of goods and services. Section 1 of the Sherman Act prohibits agreements that unreasonably restrain interstate trade or commerce. 15 U.S.C. §1. Applied literally, §1 prohibits both employees and employers from engaging in joint activity or making agreements that unreasonably restrain the labor market. Section 1 requires employers in an industry (e.g., league clubs) to compete independently for employee (e.g., player) services. Similarly, employees must individually compete for employment. Theoretically, consumers will benefit because the operation of free market forces in the labor market will result in the most efficient allocation of human resources.

On the other hand, labor law permits employees to unionize and collectively bargain, which is an allowable form of anticompetitive behavior. Multiemployer bargaining within an industry, which is similarly anticompetitive, is legal under labor law. Such concerted action among otherwise competing groups of employees (e.g., players) and employers (e.g., league clubs) squarely conflicts with §1 of the Sherman Act.

In the early 1900s employers outside the professional sports industries successfully used §1 of the Sherman Act (which was enacted in 1890) to thwart employees' efforts to unionize. See *Loewe v. Lawlor*, 208 U.S. 274 (1908). In 1914, Congress responded by enacting §6 of the Clayton Act, which provides in relevant part:

> The labor of a human being is not a commodity or article of commerce. Nothing contained in the antitrust laws shall be construed to forbid the existence and operation of labor . . . organizations, instituted for the purposes of mutual help . . . or to forbid or restrain individual members of such organizations from lawfully carrying out the legitimate objects thereof; nor shall such organizations, or the members thereof, be held or construed to be illegal combinations or conspiracies in restraint of trade, under the antitrust laws.

15 U.S.C. §17.

In 1934, Congress enacted the Norris-LaGuardia Act, 29 U.S.C. §§101-115, because courts were narrowly construing the scope of union activities immunized from antitrust liability under §6 of the Clayton Act. The combined effect of these laws is to create a *statutory labor exemption*, which provides a labor union with immunity from antitrust liability for its unilateral efforts to further its members' economic interests. Thus, in general, union collective bargaining activities over issues of wages, hours, and conditions of employment as well as strikes, picketing, and boycotts of employers do not violate the antitrust laws. *United States v. Hutcheson*, 312 U.S. 219 (1941). To facilitate the collective bargaining process, courts have held that the activities of multiemployer bargaining units to further their members' common interests, such as collective strike insurance and lockouts, also are protected by the statutory exemption. *Kennedy v. Long Island Rail Road Co.*, 319 F.2d 366 (2d Cir. 1963), *cert. denied*, 375 U.S. 830 (1963).

In the 1970s players sought to use antitrust law (in addition to labor law) to advance their economic interests by challenging league-imposed labor market restraints such as player drafts and free agency restrictions. In defense, professional leagues and clubs asserted that the statutory labor exemption bars these antitrust claims (an ironic assertion given that the exemption primarily is intended to shield union activity from antitrust immunity). However, courts have uniformly rejected this argument. *Smith v. Pro Football, Inc.*, 593 F.2d 1173,

1175 n.2 (D.C. Cir. 1978) ("athletes have standing to challenge player restrictions in professional sports since the restraints operate directly on, and to the detriment of, the employee"); *Mackey v. National Football League*, 543 F.2d 606, 618 (8th Cir. 1976) ("restraints on competition within the market for players' services fall within the ambit of the Sherman Act"); *McNeil v. National Football League*, 790 F. Supp. 871, 881 (D. Minn. 1992) (rejecting league's contention that "restraints that operate solely in a labor market are outside the scope of the antitrust laws").

In *Brown v. Pro Football, Inc.*, 1992 WL 88039 at *4 (D.D.C 1992), *rev'd on other grounds*, 50 F.3d 1041 (D.C. Cir. 1995), the court explained:

> Contrary to defendants' assertion, wage-fixing restraints which affect the labor market are considered price-fixing restraints subject to the antitrust laws. Section 6 of the Clayton Act does not exempt such restraints from antitrust liability: "It is readily apparent that Congress, in enacting § 6, was concerned with the right of labor and similar organizations to continue engaging in [activities which otherwise would be considered antitrust violations], including the right to strike, not with the right of employers to band together for joint action in fixing the wages to be paid by each employer."

Throughout the 1970s, NFL players successfully challenged the then-existing 16-round draft and certain free agency restrictions on antitrust grounds. See, e.g., *Smith v. Pro Football, Inc.*, 593 F.2d 1173 (D.C. Cir. 1978); *Kapp v. National Football League*, 586 F.2d 644 (9th Cir. 1978); *Mackey v. National Football League*, 543 F.2d 606 (8th Cir. 1976). Antitrust litigation challenging similar restraints that had been unilaterally implemented by the NBA and NHL also was successful. *Robertson v. National Basketball Assn.*, 389 F. Supp. 867 (D.D.N.Y. 1975); *Philadelphia World Hockey Club, Inc. v. Philadelphia Hockey Club, Inc.*, 351 F. Supp. 462 (E.D. Pa. 1972). From the players' perspective, the antitrust laws became powerful weapons for effectuating changes in how sports leagues conduct business vis-à-vis the players. However, MLB's unique antitrust exemption barred professional baseball players' antitrust claims. *Flood v. Kuhn*, 407 U.S. 258 (1972).

Although federal antitrust law may be used by players to invalidate league rules that effectively limit their salaries or ability to play for the club of one's choosing, it is only prohibitory rather than remedial in nature. In other words, although antitrust law prohibits league clubs from unreasonably restraining the market for player services, it does not require them to agree to or implement any particular terms and conditions of employment. Thus, courts that struck down various restraints observed that the collective bargaining process governed by labor law, rather than antitrust litigation, should resolve labor disputes between players and clubs. *Smith v. Pro Football, Inc.*, 593 F.2d 1173, 1188 (D.C. Cir. 1978) ("We are not required in this case to design a draft that would pass muster under the antitrust laws"); *Mackey v. National Football League*, 543 F.2d 606, 623 (8th Cir. 1976) ("The parties are far better situated to agreeably resolve what rules governing player transfers are best suited for their mutual interests than the courts"). See also *Philadelphia World Hockey Club, Inc. v. Philadelphia Hockey Club, Inc.*, 351 F. Supp. 462 (E.D. Pa. 1972); *Flood v. Kuhn*, 316 F. Supp. 271 (S.D.N.Y. 1970). As a result, leagues and their member clubs attempted to reinstate player restraints (usually in modified form) through collective bargaining with player unions. However, the statutory labor exemption, which applies only to unilateral union conduct, does not immunize the terms of collective bargaining agreements with employers from antitrust challenge. See *Connell Construction Co. v. Plumbers, Local 100*, 421 U.S. 616 (1975); *Mackey v. National Football League*, 543 F.2d 606, 611 (8th Cir. 1976) (this exemption "does not extend to concerted action or agreements between unions and non-labor groups"). *Connell Construction*, though, recognized the need for a *nonstatutory labor exemption* to further "the strong labor policy favoring the association of employees to eliminate competition over wages and working conditions" through collective bargaining. 421 U.S. at 622.

The following cases explore the contours of the nonstatutory labor exemption in the context of collective bargaining between league clubs and players unions as well as whether nonimmunized player restraints violate the antitrust laws. While reading and analyzing these cases, consider the following questions: (1) Does the nonstatutory labor exemption immunize the terms of an existing collective bargaining agreement from antitrust challenge? If so, why and under what conditions? (2) If the collective bargaining agreement has expired, are its provisions still protected by this exemption, and if so, for how long? (3) After a collective bargaining agreement expires, can league clubs unilaterally implement new terms and practices that are permissible under labor law without incurring antitrust liability? (4) If the nonstatutory labor exemption is not applicable, when do player restraints (e.g., player draft, limits on player salaries, and veteran-free restrictions) violate the antitrust laws? As a matter of policy, also consider whether courts are appropriately balancing the competing objectives of antitrust law and labor law regarding labor relations in professional sports.

1.   Initial Judicial Development and Application of the Nonstatutory Labor Exemption

Mackey v. NFL, 543 F.2d 606 (8th Cir. 1976), is an early case considering the intersection of antitrust and labor law in the context of collective bargaining between a professional sports league and a players union. It is important because it was decided a few years after the first collective bargaining agreements were reached in professional team sports. It established a starting point for analyzing the scope of the nonstatutory labor exemption and an early view regarding the antitrust law framework for analyzing player restraints not protected by this exemption. Perhaps more important, this case has significantly influenced the course of labor relations in professional team sports from the mid-1970s to the present.

Mackey considered the validity of the NFL's Rozelle Rule, so named because it was fashioned and applied by then-commissioner Pete Rozelle from 1963 until it was successfully challenged on antitrust grounds by a group of NFL players. The "rule" was twofold. First, if a club signed a free agent player who had previously played for another club, the signing club owed the other club "compensation." Second, if the two clubs could not agree what the "compensation" should be, Commissioner Rozelle made that determination. This compensation, either agreed to by the clubs or ordered by the commissioner, could be in the form of draft choices, players, cash, or a combination thereof.

The NFL players union challenged this rule on the basis that it illegally depressed the market for players' services and free agent players' salaries. It also contended that the rule had the anticompetitive effect of adversely affecting player mobility. Free agent players faced difficulties finding new opportunities with other clubs and felt forced to sign contracts with their old clubs for less than their current full market value.

MACKEY v. NFL

543 F.2d 606 (8th Cir. 1976)

LAY, Circuit Judge.

This is an appeal by the National Football League (NFL), twenty-six of its member clubs, and its Commissioner, Alvin Ray "Pete" Rozelle, from a district court judgment holding the "Rozelle Rule" to be violative of § 1 of the Sherman Act, and enjoining its enforcement. This action was initiated by a group of present and former NFL players . . . alleg[ing] that the defendants' enforcement of the Rozelle Rule constituted an illegal combination and conspiracy in restraint of trade denying professional football players the right to freely contract for their services. Plaintiffs sought injunctive relief and treble damages. . . .

The district court held that the defendants' enforcement of the Rozelle Rule constituted a concerted refusal to deal and a group boycott, and was therefore a per se violation of the Sherman Act. Alternatively, finding that the evidence offered in support of the clubs' contention that the Rozelle Rule is necessary to the successful operation of the NFL insufficient to justify the restrictive effects of the Rule, the court concluded that the Rozelle Rule was invalid under the Rule of Reason standard. Finally, the court rejected the clubs' argument that the Rozelle Rule was immune from attack under the Sherman Act because it had been the subject of a collective bargaining agreement between the club owners and the National Football League Players Association (NFLPA).

The defendants raise two basic issues on this appeal: (1) whether the so-called labor exemption to the antitrust laws immunizes the NFL's enforcement of the Rozelle Rule from antitrust liability; and (2) if not, whether the Rozelle Rule and the manner in which it has been enforced violate the antitrust laws. . . .

HISTORY

. . . For a number of years, the NFL has operated under a reserve system whereby every player who signs a contract with an NFL club is bound to play for that club, and no other, for the term of the contract plus one additional year at the option of the club. . . . Once a player signs a Standard Player Contract, he is bound to his team for at least two years. He may, however, become a free agent at the end of the option year by playing that season under a renewed contract rather than signing a new one. A player "playing out his option" is subject to a 10% salary cut during the option year.

Prior to 1963, a team which signed a free agent who had previously been under contract to another club was not obligated to compensate the player's former club. In 1963, after R.C. Owens played out his option with the San Francisco 49ers and signed a contract with the Baltimore Colts, the member clubs of the NFL unilaterally adopted the following provision, now known as the Rozelle Rule, as an amendment to the League's Constitution and Bylaws:

Whenever a player, becoming a free agent in such manner, thereafter signed a contract with a different club in the League, then, unless mutually satisfactory arrangements have been concluded between the two League clubs, the Commissioner may name and then award to the former club one or more players, from the Active, Reserve, or Selection List (including future selection choices) of the acquiring club as the Commissioner in his sole discretion deems fair and equitable; any such decision by the Commissioner shall be final and conclusive.

. . . During the period from 1963 through 1974, 176 players played out their options. Of that number, 34 signed with other teams. In three of those cases, the former club waived compensation. In 27 cases, the clubs involved mutually agreed upon compensation. Commissioner Rozelle awarded compensation in the four remaining cases. . . .

THE LABOR EXEMPTION ISSUE

. . . To determine the applicability of the nonstatutory exemption we must first decide whether there has been any agreement between the parties concerning the Rozelle Rule. . . .

GOVERNING PRINCIPLES

Under the general principles surrounding the labor exemption, the availability of the nonstatutory exemption for a particular agreement turns upon whether the relevant federal labor policy is deserving of pre-eminence over federal antitrust policy under the circumstances of the particular case. . . .

We find the proper accommodation to be: First, the labor policy favoring collective bargaining may potentially be given pre-eminence over the antitrust laws where the restraint on trade primarily affects only the parties to the collective bargaining relationship. . . . Second, federal labor policy is implicated sufficiently to prevail only where the agreement sought to be exempted concerns a mandatory subject of collective bargaining. . . . Finally, the policy favoring collective bargaining is furthered to the degree necessary to override the antitrust laws only where the agreement sought to be exempted is the product of bona fide arm's-length bargaining. . . .

APPLICATION

Applying these principles to the facts presented here, we think it clear that the alleged restraint on trade effected by the Rozelle Rule affects only the parties to the agreements sought to be exempted. Accordingly, we must inquire as to the other two principles: whether the Rozelle Rule is a mandatory subject of collective bargaining, and whether the agreements thereon were the product of bona fide arm's-length negotiation. . . .

MANDATORY SUBJECT OF BARGAINING

Under § 8(d) of the National Labor Relations Act, 29 U.S.C. § 158(d), mandatory subjects of bargaining pertain to "wages, hours, and other terms and conditions of employment . . ." See *NLRB v. Borg-Warner Corp.*, 356 U.S. 342, 78 S.Ct. 718, 2 L.Ed. 2d. 823 (1958). Whether an agreement concerns a mandatory subject depends not on its form but on its practical effect. . . .

On its face, the Rozelle Rule does not deal with "wages, hours and other terms or conditions of employment" but with inter-team compensation when a player's contractual obligation to one team expires and he is signed by another. Viewed as such, it would not constitute a mandatory subject of collective bargaining. The district court found, however, that the Rule operates to restrict a player's ability to move from one team to another and depresses player salaries. There is substantial evidence in the record to support these findings. Accordingly, we hold that the Rozelle Rule constitutes a mandatory bargaining subject within the meaning of the National Labor Relations Act.

Bona Fide Bargaining

The district court found that the parties' collective bargaining history reflected nothing which could be legitimately characterized as bargaining over the Rozelle Rule; that, in part due to its recent formation and inadequate finances, the NFLPA, at least prior to 1974, stood in a relatively weak bargaining position vis-a-vis the clubs; and that "the Rozelle Rule was unilaterally imposed by the NFL and member club defendants upon the players in 1963 and has been imposed on the players from 1963 through the present date."

On the basis of our independent review of the record, including the parties' bargaining history as set forth above, we find substantial evidence to support the finding that there was no bona fide arm's-length bargaining over the Rozelle Rule preceding the execution of the 1968 and 1970 agreements. The Rule imposes significant restrictions on players, and its form has remained unchanged since it was unilaterally promulgated by the clubs in 1963. The provisions of the collective bargaining agreements which operated to continue the Rozelle Rule do not in and of themselves inure to the benefit of the players or their union. . . .

In view of the foregoing, we hold that the agreements between the clubs and the players embodying the Rozelle Rule do not qualify for the labor exemption. . . .

NOTES AND QUESTIONS

1. In the context of player restraints, the *Mackey* case recognized that the non-statutory labor exemption may immunize a professional league and its member clubs from antitrust liability. According to *Mackey*, what are the elements of the nonstatutory labor exemption? Why was it found to be inapplicable in this case?

2. In a related case, the Eighth Circuit strongly suggested that the bargained-for terms of a collective bargaining agreement are not subject to antitrust scrutiny. In *Reynolds v. National Football League*, 584 F.2d 280 (8th Cir. 1978), the precise question before the court was the fairness of a settlement of the *Mackey* antitrust litigation. This settlement resulted in a new collective bargaining agreement between the NFL Management Council for the owners and the National Football League Players Association. Several NFL players

objected to the settlement terms and corresponding provisions in the new collective bargaining agreement. The court held that the overall settlement was fair and denied the players' protests.

After *Mackey*, other federal appellate courts held that the terms of existing collective bargaining agreements were not subject to antitrust attack, thereby providing an effective means of resolving labor disputes between league clubs and their players union. In *McCourt v. California Sports, Inc.*, 600 F.2d 1193 (6th Cir. 1979), the Sixth Circuit rejected an antitrust challenge to the NHL's "equalization payment" compensation system. At issue was the compensation that a club signing a free agent must pay to his former club. An NHL bylaw establishing the procedure for determining this compensation had been incorporated into the league collective bargaining agreement. Pursuant to this procedure, an arbitrator ordered that Dale McCourt be transferred from the Detroit Red Wings to the Los Angeles Kings as compensation for the former club's free agency acquisition of Rogatien Vachon. McCourt asserted that the bylaw violated the antitrust laws. The court found that the nonstatutory labor exemption barred McCourt's antitrust claims because all three elements of the *Mackey* test were satisfied. The court concluded "that the inclusion of the reserve system in the collective bargaining agreement was the product of good faith, arm's length bargaining." *Id.* at 1203.

In *Wood v. National Basketball Assn.*, 809 F.2d 954 (2d Cir. 1987), the Second Circuit held that even players such as draft-eligible rookies who are not yet playing in the league are barred from challenging the terms of an existing collective bargaining agreement on antitrust grounds. Despite being the Philadelphia 76ers' first-round draft choice, the club offered Leon Wood only a one-year $75,000 contract. Because the 76ers' player payroll exceeded the amount permitted by the NBA's salary cap, this was the maximum amount that the club could offer to Wood pursuant to the league's collective bargaining agreement. Wood claimed that the NBA salary cap and college draft violated the antitrust laws by reducing competition among league clubs for the services of college basketball players.

The Second Circuit initially observed that antitrust law should not be used "to subvert fundamental principles of our federal labor policy," which encourages collective bargaining by workers. *Id.* at 959. Refusing to address the merits of Wood's antitrust claims, the court explained:

> Freedom of contract is an important cornerstone of national labor policy for two reasons. First, it allows an employer and a union to agree upon those arrangements that best suit their particular interests. . . . Courts cannot hope to fashion contract terms more efficient than those arrived at by the parties who are to be governed by them. Second, freedom of contract furthers the goal of labor peace. To the extent that courts prohibit particular solutions for particular problems, they reduce the number and quality of compromises available to unions and employers for resolving their differences.
>
> Freedom of contract is particularly important in the context of collective bargaining between professional athletes and their leagues. Such bargaining relationships raise numerous problems with little or no precedent in standard industrial relations. As a result, leagues and player unions may reach seemingly unfamiliar or strange agreements. If courts were to intrude and to outlaw such solutions, leagues and their player unions would have to arrange their affairs in a less efficient way. It would also increase the chances of strikes by reducing the number and quality of possible compromises.

Id. at 960.

Relying on labor law policy that "allows employees to seek the best deal for the greatest number" through union collective bargaining on their behalf, the court held that "Wood's [antitrust] claim is beyond peradventure one that implicates the labor market and subverts federal labor policy." *Id.* at 959 and 963. Thus, Wood's only potentially viable claim for harm to his individual economic interests was against the NBA players union for breaching its duty of fair representation.

2. *Judicial Extension of the Scope of the Nonstatutory Labor Exemption*

The 1980s saw unprecedented labor strife in the NFL, which forced courts to further interpret and apply the nonstatutory labor exemption. The following materials examine the duration and scope of the exemption as well as its underlying policy justifications. Although the NFL has been a party to most litigation concerning the applicability of this exemption, the legal principles developed in these cases apply throughout the professional sports industries.

In 1982, with the previous CBA (negotiated in 1977) coming to an end and with league revenues steadily increasingly, the NFL and the NFLPA entered into negotiations over a new CBA. The NFLPA sought a much more beneficial deal including a guarantee that players be paid 55 percent of league-wide revenues, but the owners balked. The players then voted to go on strike, and the owners responded by barring all players from team facilities. After a two-month standoff that shortened and nearly doomed the 1982 season, the two sides entered a new five-year CBA incorporating among other things a first refusal/compensation system, which existed in the 1977 CBA and which allowed a team to keep its free agent players if it exercised a right of first refusal and matched any other team's offer.

When the 1982 CBA neared expiration in 1987, the two sides began negotiations to renew the CBA, but talks broke down and the players again voted to strike. This time, team owners, after canceling one week of games, hired replacement players—pejoratively called "scabs"—and went on with the season. After three games featuring primarily replacement players, the striking players voted to end the strike and return to their teams. That same day, however, Marvin Powell along with eight other NFL players and the NFLPA (the Players) sued the NFL for violating the antitrust laws. They argued that when the two sides reached an "impasse" in negotiating a new CBA, the nonstatutory labor exemption that protected league policies such as the first refusal/compensation system from antitrust scrutiny ceased to exist. In *Charles D. Bonanno Linen Service, Inc. v. NLRB*, 454 U.S. 404, 412, the Supreme Court defined "impasse" as "a temporary deadlock or hiatus in negotiations 'which in almost all cases is eventually broken, through either a change of mind or the application of economic force'" and observed that an impasse may be "brought about intentionally by one or both parties as a device to further, rather than destroy, the bargaining process."

The district court found for the Players, holding that "once the parties reach impasse concerning player restraint provisions those provisions will lose their immunity and further imposition of those conditions may result in antitrust liability." See *Powell v. National Football League*, 678 F. Supp. 777, 788-789 (D.

Minn. 1988) *rev'd*, 930 F.2d 1293 (8th Cir. 1989). The league, however, promptly appealed to the Eighth Circuit, arguing that the "district court's standard [provides the Players] with undue motivation to generate impasse in order to pursue an antitrust suit for treble damages." *Powell v. National Football League*, 930 F.2d 1293, 1299 (8th Cir. 1989).

In a 2-1 decision, the Eighth Circuit reversed the district court and found in favor of the league, holding that "the nonstatutory labor exemption protects agreements conceived in an ongoing collective bargaining relationship from challenges under the antitrust laws . . . and extends beyond impasse." *Id.* at 1303. The majority explained:

> Both relevant case law and the more persuasive commentators establish that labor law provides a comprehensive array of remedies to management and union, even after impasse. After a collective bargaining agreement has expired, an employer is under an obligation to bargain with the union before it may permissibly make any unilateral change in terms and conditions of employment which constitute mandatory subjects of collective bargaining. (citation omitted.) After impasse, an employer may make unilateral changes that are reasonably comprehended within its pre-impasse proposals. We are influenced by those commentators who suggest that, given the array of remedies available to management and unions after impasse, a dispute such as the one before us "ought to be resolved free of intervention by the courts" where "the union has had a sufficient impact in shaping the content of the employer's offers" and where the challenged restraint is "clothed with union approval."

Id. at 1302.

The dissent observed: "The majority purports to reject the owners' argument that the labor exemption in this case continues indefinitely. The practical effect of the majority's opinion, however, is just that—because the labor exemption will continue until the bargaining relationship is terminated either by a NLRB decertification proceeding or by abandonment of bargaining rights by the union." *Id.* at 1305.

The NFLPA interpreted the *Powell* decision to mean that as long as the union remained intact, players would have no recourse under antitrust law, and so to preserve their antitrust rights, the NFLPA disclaimed its authority to represent the players as a labor union, and player representatives from the league's 24 clubs unanimously voted to end the NFLPA's status as the players' collective bargaining representative and to restructure the organization as a voluntary professional association. The NFLPA filed a labor organization termination notice with the U.S. Department of Labor and discontinued collective bargaining on behalf of NFL players.

Thereafter, Freeman McNeil and other NFL players filed suit challenging the league's Plan B free agency restrictions on antitrust grounds. Those restrictions allowed clubs to retain limited rights to 37 players each season, therefore substantially hampering those players' ability to sign with other clubs. A threshold issue in the case was whether the NFLPA was continuing to function as the players union and whether its disclaimer to the contrary was a sham as the NFL asserted. The trial court held that the NFLPA's actions were sufficient to terminate the nonstatutory labor exemption. The court explicitly rejected the NFL's contention that the NFLPA must decertify as a labor union, which would require a determination by the National Labor Relations Board that its certification as a union is no longer operative. *Powell v. NFL*, 764 F. Supp. 1351 (D. Minn. 1991). See also *McNeil v. National Football League*, 790 F. Supp. 871, 885 (D. Minn. 1992).

The *McNeil* plaintiffs ultimately prevailed on the merits of their antitrust claims. Applying the rule of reason, the jury found that certain aspects of the NFL's Plan B first refusal/compensation system for veteran players violated §1 of the Sherman Act. See *McNeil*, 790 F. Supp. 871, 896-897. Under Plan B, each NFL club had various first refusal and compensation rights for 37 designated players, including those whose contracts with their clubs had expired. All players then under contract were bound to their existing clubs. For those who were not, the current club had a right of first refusal if the player received a contract offer from another club. If the club chose not to exercise its first refusal rights, it was entitled to compensation from the new club for the loss of that player. Four of the plaintiffs were awarded substantial damages. *Id.* at 897.

After the *McNeil* jury verdict, another group of NFL players filed a class action suit seeking damages resulting from the free agency restrictions invalidated on antitrust grounds in that case. The NFL ultimately settled all antitrust litigation challenging the validity of the player restraints and paid a $115 million settlement. See *White v. NFL*, 41 F.3d 402 (8th Cir. 1994). The NFLPA then recertified as a union and negotiated a new collective bargaining agreement with the NFL.

The *Powell* case, which broadly construed the scope of the nonstatutory labor exemption, illustrates that labor law rather than antitrust law generally regulates labor relations in the professional sports industries. This governing principle is reaffirmed and expanded by the Supreme Court's decision in *Brown v. Pro Football, Inc.*, 518 U.S. 231 (1996). As you read *Brown*, consider the facts giving rise to this litigation. The NFL clubs unilaterally established a maximum weekly salary for developmental squad players who were not members of the NFLPA. The trial court found this to be illegal price fixing of nonunionized employee wages by a group of employers. See *Brown v. Pro Football, Inc.*, 1992 WL 88039 (D.D.C. 1992), *rev'd on other grounds*, 50 F.3d 1041 (D.C. Cir. 1995). It should be underscored that in *Brown* the Court is confronted with the question of determining whether new terms of employment that were not in the expired collective bargaining agreement can be implemented by management without fear of antitrust liability.

BROWN v. PRO FOOTBALL, INC.

518 U.S. 231 (1996)

BREYER, Justice.

The question in this case arises at the intersection of the Nation's labor and antitrust laws. A group of professional football players brought this antitrust suit against football club owners. The club owners had bargained with the players' union over a wage issue until they reached impasse. The owners then had agreed among themselves (but not with the union) to implement the terms of their own last best bargaining offer. The question before us is whether federal labor laws shield such an agreement from antitrust attack. . . .

I

We can state the relevant facts briefly. In 1987, a collective-bargaining agreement between the National Football League (NFL or League), a group of football clubs, and the NFL Players Association, a labor union, expired. The NFL and the Players Association began to negotiate a new contract. In March 1989, during the negotiations, the NFL adopted Resolution G-2, a plan that would permit each club to establish a "developmental squad" of up to six rookie or "first-year" players who, as free agents, had failed to secure a position on a regular player roster. . . . Squad members would play in practice games and sometimes in regular games as substitutes for injured players. Resolution G-2 provided that the club owners would pay all squad members the same weekly salary.

The next month, April, the NFL presented the developmental squad plan to the Players Association. The NFL proposed a squad player salary of $1,000 per week. The Players Association disagreed. It insisted that the club owners give developmental squad players benefits and protections similar to those provided regular players, and that they leave individual squad members free to negotiate their own salaries.

Two months later, in June, negotiations on the issue of developmental squad salaries reached an impasse. The NFL then unilaterally implemented the developmental squad program by distributing to the clubs a uniform contract that embodied the terms of Resolution G-2 and the $1,000 proposed weekly salary. The League advised club owners that paying developmental squad players more or less than $1,000 per week would result in disciplinary action, including the loss of draft choices.

In May 1990, 235 developmental squad players brought this antitrust suit against the League and its member clubs. The players claimed that their employers' agreement to pay them a $1,000 weekly salary violated the Sherman Act. See 15 U.S.C. § 1 (forbidding agreements in restraint of trade). The Federal District Court denied the employers' claim of exemption from the antitrust laws; it permitted the case to reach the jury; and it subsequently entered judgment on a jury treble-damages award that exceeded $30 million. . . .

The Court of Appeals (by a split 2-to-1 vote) reversed. The majority interpreted the labor laws as "waiv[ing] antitrust liability for restraints on competition imposed through the collective-bargaining process, so long as such restraints operate primarily in a labor market characterized by collective bargaining." (citation omitted.) The court held, consequently, that the club owners were immune from antitrust liability. . . . Although we do not interpret the exemption as broadly as did the Appeals Court, we nonetheless find the exemption applicable, and we affirm that court's immunity conclusion.

The immunity before us rests upon what this Court has called the "nonstatutory" labor exemption from the antitrust laws. *Connell Constr. Co. v. Plumbers*, 421 U.S. 616, 622, 95 S.Ct. 1830, 1835, 44 L.Ed.2d 418 (1975). . . . The Court has implied this exemption from federal labor statutes, which set forth a national labor policy favoring free and private collective bargaining. . . .

As a matter of logic, it would be difficult, if not impossible, to require groups of employers and employees to bargain together, but at the same time to forbid them to make among themselves or with each other *any* of the competition-restricting agreements potentially necessary to make the process work or its results mutually acceptable. Thus, the implicit exemption recognizes that, to give effect to federal labor laws and policies and to allow meaningful collective bargaining to take place, some restraints on competition imposed through the bargaining process must be shielded from antitrust sanctions. . . .

The petitioners and their supporters concede, as they must, the legal existence of the exemption we have described. They also concede that, where its application is necessary to make the statutorily authorized collective-bargaining process work as Congress intended, the exemption must apply both to employers and to employees. . . . Consequently, the question before us is one of determining the exemption's scope: Does it apply to an agreement among several employers bargaining together to implement after impasse the terms of their last best good-faith wage offer? We assume that such conduct, as practiced in this case, is unobjectionable as a matter of labor law and policy. On that assumption, we conclude that the exemption applies.

Labor law itself regulates directly, and considerably, the kind of behavior here at issue — the postimpasse imposition of a proposed employment term concerning a mandatory subject of bargaining. Both the Board and the courts have held that, after impasse, labor law permits employers unilaterally to implement changes in pre-existing conditions, but only insofar as the new terms meet carefully circumscribed conditions. For example, the new terms must be "reasonably comprehended" within the employer's preimpasse proposals (typically the last rejected proposals), lest by imposing more or less favorable terms, the employer unfairly undermined the union's status. . . . The collective-bargaining proceeding itself must be free of any unfair labor practice, such as an employer's failure to have bargained in good faith. . . .

Although the case law we have cited focuses upon bargaining by a single employer, no one here has argued that labor law does, or should, treat multiemployer bargaining differently in this respect. Indeed, Board and court decisions suggest that the joint implementation of proposed terms after impasse is a familiar practice in the context of multiemployer bargaining. . . . We proceed on that assumption. . . .

In these circumstances, to subject the practice to antitrust law is to require antitrust courts to answer a host of important practical questions about how collective bargaining over wages, hours, and working conditions is to proceed — the very result that the implicit labor exemption seeks to avoid. And it is to place in jeopardy some of the potentially beneficial labor-related effects that multi-employer bargaining can achieve. That is because unlike labor law, which sometimes welcomes anticompetitive agreements conducive to industrial harmony, antitrust law forbids all agreements among competitors (such as competing employers) that unreasonably lessen competition among or between them in virtually any respect whatsoever. . . .

If the antitrust laws apply, what are employers to do once impasse is reached? If all impose terms similar to their last joint offer, they invite an antitrust action premised upon identical behavior (along with prior or accompanying conversations) as tending to show a common understanding or agreement. If any, or all, of them individually impose terms that differ significantly from that offer, they invite an unfair labor practice charge. Indeed, how can employers safely discuss their offers together even before a bargaining impasse occurs? A pre-impasse discussion about, say, the practical advantages or disadvantages of a particular proposal invites a later antitrust claim that they agreed to limit the kinds of action each would later take should an impasse occur. The same is true of postimpasse discussions aimed at renewed negotiations with the union. Nor would adherence to the terms of an expired collective-bargaining agreement eliminate a potentially plausible antitrust claim charging that they had "conspired" or tacitly "agreed" to do so, particularly if maintaining the status quo were not in the immediate economic self-interest of some. (citation omitted.) All this is to say that to permit antitrust liability here threatens to introduce instability and uncertainty into the collective-bargaining process, for antitrust law often forbids or discourages the kinds of joint discussions and behavior that the collective bargaining process invites or requires.

We do not see any obvious answer to this problem. We recognize, as the Government suggests, that, in principle, antitrust courts might themselves try to evaluate particular kinds of employer understandings, finding them "reasonable" (hence lawful) where justified by collective-bargaining necessity. But any such evaluation means a web of detailed rules spun by many different nonexpert antitrust judges and juries, not a set of labor rules enforced by a single expert administrative body, namely the Board. The labor laws give the Board, not antitrust courts, primary responsibility for policing the collective-bargaining process. And one of their objectives was to take from antitrust courts the authority to determine, through application of the antitrust laws, what is socially or economically desirable collective-bargaining policy. . . .

III

A

Petitioners claim that the implicit exemption applies only to labor-management *agreements*—a limitation that they deduce from case-law language. . . . The language, however, reflects only the fact that the cases previously before the Court involved collective-bargaining agreements. . . . The language does not reflect the exemption's rationale. . . .

Nor do we see how an exemption limited by petitioners' principle of labor-management consent could work. One cannot mean the principle literally—that the exemption applies only to understandings embodied in a collective-bargaining agreement—for the collective-bargaining process may take place before the making of any agreement or after an agreement has expired. Yet a multiemployer bargaining process itself necessarily involves many procedural and substantive understandings among participating employers as well as with the union. Petitioners cannot rescue their principle by claiming that the exemption applies only insofar as *both* labor and management consent to those understandings. Often labor will not (and should not) consent to certain common bargaining positions that employers intend to maintain. . . .

B

The Solicitor General argues that the exemption should terminate at the point of impasse. After impasse, it says, "employers no longer have a duty under the labor laws to maintain the status quo," and "are free as a matter of labor law to negotiate individual arrangements on an interim basis with the union."

Employers, however, are not completely free at impasse to act independently. The multiemployer bargaining unit ordinarily remains intact; individual employers cannot withdraw. . . . The duty to bargain survives; employers must stand ready to resume collective bargaining. . . . And individual employers can negotiate individual interim agreements with the union only insofar as those agreements are consistent with "the duty to abide by the results of group bargaining." . . .

The problem is aggravated by the fact that "impasse" is often temporary . . . and it may occur several times during the course of a single labor dispute, since the bargaining process is not over when the first impasse is reached. . . . Employers who erroneously concluded that impasse had *not* been reached would risk antitrust liability were they collectively to maintain the status quo, while employers who erroneously concluded that impasse *had* occurred would risk unfair labor practice charges for prematurely suspending multiemployer negotiations.

The Solicitor General responds with suggestions for softening an "impasse" rule by extending the exemption after impasse "for such time as would be reasonable in the circumstances" for employers to consult with counsel, confirm that impasse has occurred, and adjust their business operations. . . . But even as so modified, the impasse-related rule creates an exemption that can evaporate in the middle of the bargaining process, leaving later antitrust courts free to second-guess the parties' bargaining decisions and consequently forcing them to choose their collective-bargaining responses in light of what they predict or fear that antitrust courts, not labor law administrators, will eventually decide. . . .

C

Petitioners and their supporters argue in the alternative for a rule that would exempt postimpasse agreement about bargaining "tactics," but not postimpasse agreement about substantive "terms," from the reach of antitrust. . . . They recognize, however, that both the Board and the courts have said that employers can, and often do, employ the imposition of "terms" as a bargaining "tactic." . . . This concession as to joint "tactical" implementation would turn the presence of an antitrust exemption upon a determination of the employers' primary purpose or motive. . . . But to ask antitrust courts, insulated from the bargaining process, to investigate an employer group's subjective motive is to ask them to conduct an inquiry often more amorphous than those we have previously discussed. And, in our view, a labor/antitrust line drawn on such a basis would too often raise the same related (previously discussed) problems. . . .

D

. . . Petitioners also say that irrespective of how the labor exemption applies elsewhere to multiemployer collective bargaining, professional sports is "special." We can understand how professional sports may be special in terms of, say, interest, excitement, or concern. But we do not understand how they are special in respect to labor law's antitrust exemption. We concede that the clubs that make up a professional sports league are not completely independent economic competitors, as they depend upon a degree of cooperation for economic survival. . . . In the present context, however, that circumstance makes the league more like a single bargaining employer, which analogy seems irrelevant to the legal issue before us.

We also concede that football players often have special individual talents, and, unlike many unionized workers, they often negotiate their pay individually with their employers. . . . But this characteristic seems simply a feature, like so many others, that might give employees (or employers) more (or less) bargaining power, that might lead some (or all) of them to favor a particular kind of bargaining, or that might lead to certain demands at the bargaining table. We do not see how it could make a critical legal difference in determining the underlying framework in which bargaining is to take place. . . . Indeed, it would be odd to fashion an antitrust exemption that gave additional advantages to professional football players (by virtue of their superior bargaining power) that transport workers, coal miners, or meat packers would not enjoy. . . .

For these reasons, we hold that the implicit ("nonstatutory") antitrust exemption applies to the employer conduct at issue here. That conduct took place during and immediately after a collective-bargaining negotiation. It grew out of, and was directly related to, the lawful operation of the bargaining process. It involved a matter that the parties were required to negotiate collectively. And it concerned only the parties to the collective-bargaining relationship.

Our holding is not intended to insulate from antitrust review every joint imposition of terms by employers, for an agreement among employers could be sufficiently distant in time and in circumstances from the collective-bargaining process that a rule permitting antitrust intervention would not significantly interfere with that process. *See, e.g.,* 50 F.3d. at 1057 (suggesting that exemption lasts until collapse of the collective-bargaining relationship, as evidenced by decertification of the union); *El Cerrito Mill & Lumber Co.,* 316 N.L.R.B., at 1006-1007 (suggesting that "extremely long" impasse, accompanied by "instability" or "defunctness" of multiemployer unit, might justify union withdrawal from group bargaining). We need not decide in this case whether, or where, within these extreme outer boundaries to draw that line. Nor would it be appropriate for us to do so without the detailed views of the Board, to whose "specialized judgment" Congress "intended to leave" many of the "inevitable questions concerning multi-employer bargaining bound to arise in the future." . . .

The judgment of the Court of Appeals is affirmed.

Justice STEVENS, Dissenting.

. . . The statutory labor exemption protects the right of workers to act collectively to seek better wages, but does not "exempt concerted action or agreements between unions and nonlabor parties." *Connell Constr. Co. v. Plumbers,* 421 U.S. 616, 621-22, 95 S.Ct. 1830, 1834-1835, 44 L.Ed.2d 418 (1975). It is the judicially crafted, nonstatutory labor exemption that serves to accommodate the conflicting policies of the antitrust and labor statutes in the context of action between employers and unions. . . .

Consistent with basic labor law policies, I agree with the Court that the judicially crafted labor exemption must also cover some collective action that employers take in response to a collective-bargaining agent's demands for higher wages. Immunizing such action from antitrust scrutiny may facilitate collective bargaining over labor demands. . . .

In my view, however, neither the policies underlying the two separate statutory schemes, nor the narrower focus on the purpose of the nonstatutory exemption, provides a justification for exempting from antitrust scrutiny collective action initiated by employers to depress wages below the level that would be produced in a free market. Nor do those policies support a rule that would allow employers to suppress wages by implementing noncompetitive agreements among themselves on matters that have not previously been the subject of either an agreement with labor or even a demand by labor for inclusion in the bargaining process. That, however, is what is at stake in this litigation.

II

In light of the accommodation that has been struck between antitrust and labor law policy, it would be most ironic to extend an exemption crafted to protect collective action by employees to protect employers acting jointly to deny employees the opportunity to negotiate their salaries individually in a competitive market. Perhaps aware of the irony, the Court chooses to analyze this case as though it represented a typical impasse in an unexceptional multiemployer bargaining process. In so doing, it glosses over three unique features of the case that are critical to the inquiry into whether the policies of the labor laws require extension of the nonstatutory labor exemption to this atypical case.

First, in this market, unlike any other area of labor law implicated in the cases cited by the Court, player salaries are individually negotiated. The practice of individually negotiating player salaries prevailed even prior to collective bargaining. The players did not challenge the prevailing practice because, unlike employees in most industries, they want their compensation to be determined by the forces of the free market rather than by the process of collective bargaining. Thus, although the majority professes an inability to understand anything special about professional sports that should affect the framework of labor negotiations . . . in this business it is the employers, not the employees, who seek to impose a noncompetitive uniform wage on a segment of the market and to put an end to competitive wage negotiations.

Second, respondents concede that the employers imposed the wage restraint to force owners to comply with league-wide rules that limit the number of players that may serve on a team, not to facilitate a stalled bargaining process, or to revisit any issue previously subjected to bargaining. The employers could have confronted the culprits directly by stepping up enforcement of roster limits. They instead chose to address the problem by unilaterally preventing players from individually competing in the labor market.

Third, although the majority asserts that the "club owners had bargained with the players' union over a wage issue until they reached impasse," . . . that hardly constitutes a complete description of what transpired. When the employers' representative advised the union that they proposed to pay the players a uniform wage determined by the owners, the union promptly and unequivocally responded that their proposal was inconsistent with the "principle" of individual salary negotiation that had been accepted in the past and that predated collective bargaining. The so-called "bargaining" that followed amounted to nothing more than the employers' notice to the union that they had decided to implement a decision to replace individual salary negotiations with a uniform wage level for a specific group of players.

Given these features of the case, I do not see why the employers should be entitled to a judicially crafted exemption from antitrust liability. We have explained that "[t]he nonstatutory exemption has its source in the strong labor policy favoring the association of employees to eliminate competition over wages and working conditions." (citation omitted.) I know of no similarly strong labor policy that favors the association of employers to eliminate a competitive method of negotiating wages that predates collective bargaining and that labor would prefer to preserve.

Even if some collective action by employers may justify an exemption because it is necessary to maintain the "integrity of the multiemployer bargaining unit," . . . no such justification exists here. The employers imposed a fixed wage even though there was no dispute over the pre-existing principle that player salaries should be individually negotiated. They sought only to prevent certain owners from evading roster limits and thereby gaining an unfair advantage. . . .

The point of identifying the unique features of this case is not, as the Court suggests, to make the case that professional football players, alone among workers, should be entitled to enforce the antitrust laws against anticompetitive collective employer action. . . . Other employees, no less than well-paid athletes, are entitled to the protections of the antitrust laws when their employers unite to undertake anticompetitive action that causes them direct harm and alters the state of employer-employee relations that existed prior to unionization. Here that alteration occurred because the wage terms that the employers unilaterally imposed directly conflict with a pre-existing principle of agreement between the bargaining parties. In other contexts, the alteration may take other similarly anticompetitive and unjustifiable forms. . . .

IV

Congress is free to act to exempt the anticompetitive employer conduct that we review today. In the absence of such action, I do not believe it is for us to stretch the limited exemption that we have fashioned to facilitate the express statutory exemption created for labor's benefit so that unions must strike in order to restore a prior practice of individually negotiating salaries. I therefore agree with the position that the District Court adopted below.

"Because the developmental squad salary provisions were a new concept and not a change in terms of the expired collective bargaining agreement, the policy behind continuing the nonstatutory labor exemption for the terms of a collective bargaining agreement after expiration (to foster an atmosphere conducive to the negotiation of a new collective bargaining agreement) does not apply. To hold that the nonstatutory labor exemption extends to shield the NFL from antitrust liability for imposing restraints never before agreed to by the union would not only infringe on the union's freedom to contract . . . but would also contradict the very purpose of the antitrust exemption by not promoting execution of a collective bargaining agreement with terms mutually acceptable to employer and labor union alike. Labor unions would be unlikely to sign collective bargaining agreements with employers if they believed that they would be forced to accept terms to which they never agreed." [Citation omitted.]

Accordingly, I respectfully dissent.

NOTES AND QUESTIONS

1. At a minimum, the *Brown* majority's broad construction of the nonstatutory labor exemption expands the parameters of allowable actions by management after the collective bargaining agreement has expired without fear of antitrust liability. In the long run, does this foster or impede the settlement of labor disputes between league clubs and their players? Are the parties' respective economic power and available labor law remedies sufficient to enable the fair and efficient resolution of disputes concerning mandatory subjects of collective bargaining? Consider that neither side has an antitrust remedy as long as there is an ongoing collective bargaining process.

The *Brown* majority focuses on what is necessary to make the collective bargaining process work and concludes that a multiemployer bargaining unit should not be liable for conduct that is lawful under the labor laws. By contrast, the dissenting justice concludes that allowing a union to use antitrust law furthers the labor law policy goal of achieving higher wages for workers. Do you favor the majority's process-oriented approach or the dissent's results-oriented view?

Congress enacted the federal labor laws, which permit unionization and collective bargaining, because of concern that the disparity of bargaining power between individual workers and large employers would result in employee wage levels that are too low for the good of our national economy. Although players in the NFL, NBA, MLB, and NHL have unionized, they generally want free market competition for their services among league clubs to determine their individual salaries. Unlike employees in other industries, major league professional athletes have unique talents and skills that generally are not fungible or readily interchangeable. Each player's individual market value varies based on the nature of his or her respective talents and skills relative to those of other league players. Do these distinctions justify a special legal rule regarding the nature and scope of the nonstatutory labor exemption's application to professional sports?

2. According to *Brown*, when does the nonstatutory labor exemption end? If the multiemployer bargaining unit for a league's clubs commits an unfair labor practice, does the players union also have an antitrust remedy?

In an effort to circumvent *Brown*'s broad construction of the nonstatutory labor exemption, professional soccer players chose not to unionize and engage in collective bargaining with Major League Soccer (MLS) when the league was initially formed. Instead, they unsuccessfully claimed the league and the operator/investors of its member clubs violated the antitrust laws by conspiring to eliminate competition for their services. *Fraser v. Major League Soccer*, 284 F.3d 47 (1st Cir. 2002). Although this issue was not raised in the *Fraser* litigation, does *Brown* allow players to deprive a league of the antitrust immunity conferred by the nonstatutory labor exemption by not unionizing?

3. Because professional baseball has a broad common law antitrust exemption, MLB players historically have not been able to use antitrust law to challenge league rules restricting their ability to become free agents. *Flood v. Kuhn*, 407 U.S. 258 (1972). In 1998, Congress modified the Sherman Act to provide MLB players with the same right to sue under the antitrust laws concerning their employment terms as other professional athletes have in their sports. 15 U.S.C. §27b(c). What is the practical effect of this statutory provision regarding the ability of MLB players to assert antitrust claims arising out of labor disputes?

4. For scholarly commentary concerning *Brown*, see John C. Tvras, Comment, *Players Versus Owners: Collective Bargaining and Antitrust After* Brown v. Pro Football, Inc., 1 U. Pa. J. Lab. & Emp. L. 297 (1998); Robert A. McCormack, *Labor or Antitrust? Let the Players Choose*, 4 Vill. Sports & Ent. L.J. 39 (1997); Brian T. Coolidge, *Form over Function: The Goals of Labor and Antitrust Laws Sacrificed upon a Collective Bargaining Impasse*, Brown v. Pro Football, Inc., 38 So. Tex. L. Rev. 841 (1997); Steven D. Buchholz, Comment, *Run, Kick, and (Im)Passe: An Expanding Employers' Ability to Unilaterally Impose Conditions*

of Employment After Impasse in Brown v. Pro Football, 81 Minn. L. Rev. 1201 (1997).

From the time that the NFLPA recertified and negotiated a new CBA with the NFL in 1993 through 2011, the NFL enjoyed relative labor peace, again and again renewing the CBA with some modifications. In the spring of 2011, however, the then-governing CBA expired before the NFL and the NFLPA were able to come to terms over an extension, leading to the NFL's lockout of the players, which set the stage for the following precedent-setting litigation.

BRADY v. NATIONAL FOOTBALL LEAGUE

644 F.3d 661 (8th Cir. 2011)

COLLOTON, Circuit Judge.

This appeal arises from an action filed by nine professional football players and one prospective football player ("the Players") against the National Football League and its thirty-two separately-owned clubs, more commonly known as football teams (collectively, "the NFL" or "the League"). On March 11, 2011, a collective bargaining agreement between the League and a union representing professional football players expired. The League had made known that if a new agreement was not reached before the expiration date, then it would implement a lockout of players, during which the athletes would not be paid or permitted to use club facilities. The League viewed a lockout as a legitimate tactic under the labor laws to bring economic pressure to bear on the players as part of the bargaining process. *See Am. Ship Bldg. Co. v. NLRB*, 380 U.S. 300, 301-02, 318 (1965).

The players, aware of the League's strategy, opted to terminate the union's status as their collective bargaining agent as of 4:00 p.m. on March 11, just before the agreement expired. Later that day, the Players filed an action in the district court alleging that the lockout planned by the League would constitute a group boycott and price-fixing agreement that would violate § 1 of the Sherman Antitrust Act. The complaint explained that "the players in the NFL have determined that it is not in their interest to remain unionized if the existence of such a union would serve to allow the NFL to impose anticompetitive restrictions with impunity." The plaintiffs also alleged other violations of the antitrust laws and state common law.

The League proceeded with its planned lockout on March 12, 2011. The Players moved for a preliminary injunction in the district court, urging the court to enjoin the lockout as an unlawful group boycott that was causing irreparable harm to the Players. The district court granted a preliminary injunction, and the League appealed. We conclude that the injunction did not conform to the provisions of the Norris–LaGuardia Act, 29 U.S.C. § 101 *et seq.*, and we therefore vacate the district court's order. . . .

B.

Since 1993, the players and the League have operated under [the *White v. NFL* Stipulation and Settlement Agreement (SSA), which resolved the *McNeil v. NFL* antitrust litigation and led to a new collective bargaining agreement (CBA) between the NFL and the National Football League Players Assocation (NFLPA) shortly thereafter], and the district court has continued to oversee the settlement by resolving numerous disputes over the terms of the SSA and CBA. *White v. NFL*, 585 F.3d 1129, 1133 (8th Cir.2009). Whenever the NFL and the NFLPA have agreed to change a provision in the CBA, a conforming change has also been made to the SSA. *Id.* at 1134. The SSA has been amended several times over the past eighteen years, most recently in 2006, when the NFL and the NFLPA reached an agreement on a new CBA that would last through the 2012-2013 football season. The 2006 SSA and CBA gave both sides the right to opt out of the final two years of each agreement upon written notice.

In May 2008, the NFL opted out of the final two years of the SSA and CBA, citing concerns about operating costs and other elements of the agreements. As a result, the SSA and CBA were scheduled to expire in early March 2011. Although the NFL and the NFLPA engaged in more than two years of negotiations toward a new CBA, the League and the players were unable to reach an agreement. The League filed an unfair labor practice charge with the NLRB in February 2011, asserting that the union failed to confer in good faith. The Players say that the charge is meritless.

As the deadline approached, a substantial majority of NFL players voted to end the NFLPA's status as their collective bargaining representative. On March 11, 2011—the expiration date of the SSA and CBA—the NFLPA notified the NFL that it disclaimed interest in continuing to serve as the players' collective bargaining representative, effective at 4:00 p.m. The NFLPA also amended its bylaws to prohibit collective bargaining with the League or its agents, filed a labor organization termination notice with the Department of Labor, asked the Internal Revenue Service to reclassify the NFLPA as a professional association rather than a labor organization, and notified the NFL that it would no longer represent players bringing grievances against the League.

The League filed an amended unfair labor practice charge on March 11, alleging that the NFLPA's disclaimer was a "sham" and that the combination of a disclaimer by the union and subsequent antitrust litigation was "a ploy and an unlawful subversion of the collective bargaining process." The Players dispute the charge, citing an advice memorandum of an associate general counsel of the NLRB in *Pittsburgh Steelers, Inc.*, No. 6-CA-23143, 1991 WL 144468 (NLRB G.C. June 26, 1991). The memorandum concluded that the NLFPA's 1989 disclaimer was valid, and that it was "irrelevant" whether the disclaimer was motivated by "litigation strategy," so long as the disclaimer was "otherwise unequivocal and adhered to." *Id.* at *2 & n. 8.

The Players, funded by the NFLPA, commenced this action on the same day as the disclaimer, March 11, 2011. Four of the plaintiffs are under contract with an NFL club; five are free agents, and one is a prospective player who had entered the 2011 NFL draft and was ultimately selected in that draft. The Players brought this action on behalf of themselves and a putative class consisting of players who are under contract with any NFL club, free agents seeking employment with any NFL club, and college or other players who have not previously been under contract with any NFL club and who are eligible to play as a rookies for any club. As the case comes to us, no class has been certified.

The Players explained in their complaint that "[t]he players . . . have ended the role of the NFLPA as their collective bargaining representative and no longer have a collective bargaining relationship with the NFL defendants." They asserted, based on the Supreme Court's language in [*Brown v. Pro Football*], that the nonstatutory labor exemption therefore no longer protects the League from antitrust liability. The complaint alleged that the NFL's planned lockout was an illegal group boycott and price-fixing arrangement that violated § 1 of the Sherman Act. . . .

The complaint further alleged that the League planned to institute or to continue several anticompetitive practices that would violate § 1 of the Sherman Act, including a limitation on the amount of compensation that can be paid to recently drafted first-year "rookie" players, a cap on salaries for current players, and "franchise player" and "transition player" designations that restrict the ability of free agents to join a team other than their former team. The Players requested damages and declaratory and injunctive relief regarding these practices, including an injunction prohibiting the League from implementing or continuing the lockout. . . .

On April 25, 2011, the district court granted the Players' motion to enjoin the lockout, rejecting the League's assertions that the court lacked jurisdiction to enter the injunction, that the court should defer to the primary jurisdiction of the NLRB, and that the League is in any event immune from antitrust liability under the nonstatutory labor exemption. *See Brady v. NFL*, No. 11-639, 2011 WL 1535240, at *37 (D.Minn. Apr. 25, 2011) [hereinafter *Brady I*]. . . .

The League appealed, challenging the district court's application of the Norris–LaGuardia Act, the doctrine of primary jurisdiction, and the nonstatutory labor exemption. This court granted the NFL's motion to expedite the appeal and its motion for a stay of the district court's order pending appeal. We now consider the merits of the appeal.

II.

We consider first the League's contention that the Norris-LaGuardia Act deprived the district court of jurisdiction to enter the injunction. The NLGA, enacted in 1932, curtails the authority of a district court to issue injunctions in a labor dispute. "Congress was intent upon taking the federal courts out of the labor injunction business except in the very limited circumstances left open for federal jurisdiction under the Norris-LaGuardia Act." *Marine Cooks & Stewards v. Pan. S.S. Co.*, 362 U.S. 365, 369 (1960). . . .

To determine whether the NLGA forbids or places conditions on the issuance of an injunction here, we begin with the text of the statute. Section 1 provides that "[n]o court of the United States . . . shall have jurisdiction to issue any . . . temporary or permanent injunction in a case involving or growing out of a labor dispute, except in strict conformity with the provisions of this chapter." 29 U.S.C. § 101. As noted, the district court concluded that the Act is inapplicable to this action, because the case is not one "involving or growing out of a labor dispute."

Section 13(c) of the Act states that "[t]he term 'labor dispute' includes *any controversy concerning terms or conditions of employment*, or concerning the association or representation of persons in negotiating, fixing, maintaining, changing, or seeking to arrange terms or conditions of employment, regardless of whether or not the disputants stand in the proximate relation of employer and employee." 29 U.S.C. § 113(c) (emphasis added). This lawsuit is a controversy concerning terms or conditions of employment. The Players seek broad relief that would affect the terms or conditions of employment for the entire industry of professional football. In particular, they urge the court to declare unlawful and to enjoin several features of the relationship between the League and the players, including the limit on compensation that can be paid to rookies, the salary cap, the "franchise player" designation, and the "transition player" designation, all of which the Players assert are anticompetitive restrictions that violate § 1 of the Sherman Act. . . .

The Act also states expressly that "[a] case shall be held to involve or grow out of a labor dispute when the case involves persons who are engaged in the same industry, trade, craft, or occupation." 29 U.S.C. § 113(a). This case, of course, involves persons engaged in the "same industry," namely, professional football. The statute continues that such a case "shall be held to involve or grow out of a labor dispute" when "such dispute is . . . between one or more employers or associations of employers and one or more employees or associations of employees." *Id.* This dispute is between one or more employers or associations of employers (the League and the NFL teams) and one or more employees (the Players under contract). By the plain terms of the Act, this case "shall be held to involve or grow out of a labor dispute."

The district court reached a contrary conclusion by departing from the text of § 13(a). The court thought the phrase "one or more employees or associations of employees" did not encompass the Players in this dispute, because "one or more employees" means "individual *unionized* employee or employees." *Brady I,* 2011 WL 1535240, at 24 n. 43 (emphasis added). We see no warrant for adding a requirement of unionization to the text.

A similar argument did not persuade the Supreme Court in *New Negro Alliance v. Sanitary Grocery Co.,* 303 U.S. 552 (1938). There, a company sought an injunction against the New Negro Alliance, which the Supreme Court described as "a corporation composed of colored persons, organized for the mutual improvement of its members and the promotion of civic, educational, benevolent, and charitable enterprises." *Id.* at 555. The Alliance allegedly had conspired to picket and boycott one of the company's grocery stores to pressure the store to employ African-American clerks. *Id.* at 555-56. The company claimed, among other things, that the Alliance's acts were "unlawful, [and] constitute[d] a conspiracy in restraint of trade." . . .

. . . Although no labor organization was involved in the dispute, and the company argued that "a recognized labor union or unions or individual members thereof were involved" in all but one of the "labor dispute" precedents cited by the Alliance, Brief for Respondent at 24, *New Negro Alliance,* 303 U.S. 552 (No. 511), the Court ruled that the definitions in the Act "plainly embrace the controversy which gave rise to the instant suit and classify it as one arising out of a dispute defined as a labor dispute." *New Negro Alliance,* 303 U.S. at 560. The Court observed that § 13(a) provides that a case shall be held to involve or grow out of a labor dispute "when the case involves any conflicting or competing interests in a 'labor dispute' . . . of 'persons participating or interested' therein," and ruled that the Alliance and its individual members were "persons interested in the dispute." *Id.* (internal quotation omitted). If § 13(a) were limited to controversies involving unions or unionized employees, then the Court could not have reached this conclusion. . . .

The text of the Norris-LaGuardia Act and the cases interpreting the term "labor dispute" do not require the present existence of a union to establish a labor dispute. Whatever the precise limits of the phrase "involving or growing out of a labor dispute," this case does not press the outer boundary. The League and the players' union were parties to a collective bargaining agreement for almost eighteen years prior to March 2011. They were engaged in collective bargaining over terms and conditions of employment for approximately two years through March 11, 2011. At that point, the parties were involved in a classic "labor dispute" by the Players' own definition. Then, on a single day, just hours before the CBA's expiration, the union discontinued collective bargaining and disclaimed its status, and the Players filed this action seeking relief concerning industry-wide terms and conditions of employment. Whatever the effect of the union's disclaimer on the League's immunity from antitrust liability, the labor dispute did not suddenly disappear just because the Players elected to pursue the dispute through antitrust litigation rather than collective bargaining.

III.

The Players argue alternatively that even if this case does involve or grow out of a labor dispute, the district court's injunction conforms to the provisions of the NLGA, and should be affirmed on this alternative ground. The League counters that § 4 of the Act includes a flat prohibition on injunctions against a lockout, and, alternatively, that even if the court has authority to enjoin a lockout under certain circumstances, the district court did not comply with the procedural requirements set forth in § 7 of the Act.

A.

Section 4 of the NLGA, 29 U.S.C. § 104, is entitled, "Enumeration of specific acts not subject to restraining orders or injunctions." It provides:

> No court of the United States shall have jurisdiction to issue any restraining order or temporary or permanent injunction in any case involving or growing out of any labor dispute to prohibit any person or persons participating or interested in such dispute . . . from doing, whether singly or in concert, any of the following acts:
>   (a) Ceasing or refusing to perform any work or to remain in any relation of employment. . . .

The League relies on § 4(a). It argues that this subsection forbids an injunction to prohibit a lockout. There is no uniform definition of the term "lockout," but one "practical definition" used by this court is "a refusal by [an employer] to furnish available work to its regular employees." *Laclede Gas Co. v. NLRB*, 421 F.2d 610, 615 & n. 9 (8th Cir.1970); *see also* 2 *The Developing Labor Law* 1639-40 (John E. Higgins, Jr. et al. eds., 5th ed. 2006) ("As used by the Board and the courts, . . . a lockout is most simply and completely defined as the withholding of employment by an employer from its employees for the purpose of either resisting their demands or gaining a concession from them."). The League maintains that by locking out all professional football players, it is "[r]efusing to . . . remain in any relation of employment," and is thus doing one of the acts that cannot be enjoined according to § 4. . . .

The Players respond that § 4(a) does not apply to employer injunctions at all. . . .

. . . The introductory clause of § 4 forbids a court to issue an injunction to prohibit "*any person or persons* participating or interested" in a labor dispute from doing any of the acts set forth below, including those in § 4(a). Employers, of course, are among the persons participating in a labor dispute. The introductory clause thus plainly encompasses employers. If language in a particular subsection is applicable on its face to employees and employers alike (or to employers alone), then there is no need for a specific mention of employers. . . .

The disputed language in § 4(a) — "remain in any relation of employment" — may apply to an employer. Section 3 of the Act makes clear that both employers and employees can be in a "relation of employment." Section 3(b) contemplates that either party to a labor agreement can agree to "withdraw from an employment relation." 29 U.S.C. § 103(b). . . .

Aside from the text and structure of § 4, the Players argue that the policy of the NLGA and the legislative history support their position that § 4(a) offers no protection to employers. To be sure, the policy stated in § 2 is that the individual unorganized worker should be free from the interference, restraint, or coercion of employers in the designation of representatives, self-organization, or other concerted activities. But it does not follow that a prohibition on injunctions against employer lockouts is contrary to the policy of the Act. The Supreme Court has observed that while the Act was designed to protect workingmen, the broader purpose was "to prevent the injunctions of the federal courts from *upsetting the natural interplay of the competing economic forces of labor and capital*." *Bhd. of R.R. Trainmen v. Chi. River & Ind. R.R. Co.*, 353 U.S. 30, 40 (1957) (emphasis added). An employer's lockout is part of this interplay; it is not the equivalent of a judicial injunction that interferes with the ability of workers to exercise organized economic power. . . .

. . . A one-way interpretation of § 4(a) — prohibiting injunctions against strikes but not against lockouts — would be in tension with the purposes of the Norris-LaGuardia Act to allow free play of economic forces and "to withdraw federal courts from a type of controversy for which many believed they were ill-suited and from participation in which, it was feared, judicial prestige might suffer." *Marine Cooks & Stewards*, 362 U.S. at 369 n. 7. We are not convinced that the policy of the Act counsels against our textual analysis of § 4(a). . . .

[W]e conclude that § 4(a) of the Norris-LaGuardia Act deprives a federal court of power to issue an injunction prohibiting a party to a labor dispute from implementing a lockout of its employees. This conclusion accords with the few decisions that have addressed the specific question. *Clune v. Publishers' Ass'n of N.Y.C.*, 214 F.Supp. 520, 528-29 (S.D.N.Y.), *aff'd*, 314 F.2d 343, 344 (2d Cir.1963) (per curiam); *Plumbers & Steamfitters Local 598 v. Morris*, 511 F.Supp. 1298, 1311 (E.D.Wash.1981); *Stone & Webster Eng'g Corp.*, 163 F.Supp. at 896. Because the Norris-LaGuardia Act prohibits the district court from issuing an injunction against the League's lockout of employees, the court's order cannot stand.

B.

Another portion of the injunction is not foreclosed by § 4(a). The district court enjoined not only the League's lockout of employees, *i.e.*, players under contract, but also the League's refusal to deal with non-employees, *i.e.*, free agents and prospective players or "rookies." As to these latter groups of players, § 4(a) does not apply. The refusal of the League and NFL clubs to deal with free agents and rookies is not a refusal "to remain in any relation of employment," for there is no existing employment relationship in which "to remain."

An injunction with respect to the League's actions toward free agents and rookies, however, cannot be issued except in strict conformity with § 7 of the

NLGA, 29 U.S.C. § 107, because this is "a case involving or growing out of a labor dispute." *Id.* §§ 101, 107. The present injunction does not conform to § 7. . . .

Section 7 provides that a court has no authority to issue an injunction "except after hearing the testimony of witnesses in open court (with opportunity for cross-examination) in support of the allegations of a complaint made under oath, and testimony in opposition thereto." 29 U.S.C. § 107. Although a hearing is not required where the party enjoined does not contest on appeal that the relevant facts are undisputed, *Kansas City S. Transp. Co. v. Teamsters Local Union No. 41*, 126 F.3d 1059, 1067-68 (8th Cir.1997), the League does contest the facts in this case, and it is entitled to test the credibility of the Players' evidence by cross-examination. Section 7(c) requires the court to evaluate the relative harms to the parties, and the court's calculus with respect to free agents and rookies undoubtedly was affected by its view that the entire lockout could be enjoined. Whether to enter an injunction requiring the League to deal with free agents and rookies, only to have these players locked out as soon as they enter into any new contract of employment, was not considered. . . . We therefore conclude that the injunction as a whole must be vacated.

IV.

Given our conclusion that the preliminary injunction did not conform to the provisions of the Norris-LaGuardia Act, we need not reach the other points raised by the League on appeal. In particular, we express no view on whether the League's nonstatutory labor exemption from the antitrust laws continues after the union's disclaimer. The parties agree that the Act's restrictions on equitable relief are not necessarily coextensive with the substantive rules of antitrust law, and we reach our decision on that understanding. . . .

BYE, Circuit Judge, dissenting.

. . . Despite the repeated efforts of the legislative branch to come to the rescue of organized labor, today's opinion puts the power of the Act in the service of employers, to be used against non-unionized employees who can no longer avail themselves of protections of labor laws. Because I cannot countenance such interpretation of the Act, I must and hereby dissent. . . .

. . . I must take issue with the majority's conclusion as to this case not representing the outer boundary of the phrase "involving or growing out of a labor dispute." Like the nonstatutory labor exemption, statutory exemption from antitrust liability, which rests in part on the Norris-LaGuardia Act, *Connell Construction Co.*, 421 U.S. at 621-22, lies at the intersection between labor and antitrust laws. . . . "While the Norris-LaGuardia Act's bar of federal-court labor injunctions is not explicitly phrased as an exemption from the antitrust laws, it has been interpreted broadly as a statement of congressional policy that the courts must not use the antitrust laws as a vehicle to interfere in labor disputes." *H.A. Artists & Associates, Inc.*, 451 U.S. at 714. The scope of the two exemptions differs somewhat—"the statutory exemption allows unions to accomplish some restraints by acting unilaterally, [whereas] the nonstatutory exemption offers no similar protection when a union and a nonlabor party agree to restrain competition in a business market," *see Connell Construction Co.*, 421 U.S. at 622,—but there is no place for the application of either at the time labor laws no longer govern and labor policy is no longer implicated.

The Supreme Court recognized as much when it explained that nonstatutory immunity from antitrust review is no longer necessary when "an agreement among employers [is] sufficiently distant in time and in circumstances from the collective-bargaining process that a rule permitting antitrust intervention would not significantly interfere with that process." *Brown*, 518 U.S. at 250. As an example of such endpoint, the Court cited "collapse of the collective-bargaining relationship, as evidenced by decertification of the union." *Id.* (quoting *Brown v. Pro Football, Inc.*, 50 F.3d 1041, 1057 (D.C.Cir.1995)). With the players having voted to end the NFLPA's status as their collective bargaining representative and the NFLPA likewise having disclaimed its status as the players' representative, this case has reached that endpoint. *See Brady v. NFL*, 640 F.3d 785, 798-99 (8th Cir.2011) (Bye, J., dissenting) (elaborating on the reasons why the union disclaimer should end the protection against antitrust liability). . . .

NOTES AND QUESTIONS

1. Is the *Brady* majority's opinion consistent with *Brown*'s guidance regarding whether (and when) federal antitrust or labor law should govern professional sports industry labor disputes? Note that the majority held only that the Norris-LaGuardia Act barred an injunction against the NFL lockout; it did not rule whether the nonstatutory labor exemption precluded plaintiffs' antitrust claims, resolve the merits of these claims, or consider the issue of whether potential plaintiffs other than players (e.g., consumers, coaches, stadium vendors) have standing to recover damages for antitrust violations arising out of a lockout. How should each of these issues be judicially resolved?

2. The NFL's owners and players came to terms on a new CBA in July 2011,[5] and *Brady v. NFL* was therefore settled before the court had a chance to address one of the NFL's primary contentions: that the NFLPA's disclaimer was a sham initiated to pave the way for the players' antitrust suit and to subvert the collective bargaining process. Just days after the case settled, the NFLPA resumed operations as the players union (following the same strategy it adopted in 1989 in connection with the *Powell* and *McNeil* litigations, *supra*), seemingly lending credence to the sham theory. If the *Brady* court were to have reached the sham disclaimer question, how should it have ruled?

3. Unions can be dissolved in two ways: (1) by decertification or (2) by a disclaimer of interest (as was done in the *Brady* and *McNeil* cases). Although the two methods are often confused, decertification is a more formal and time-consuming process involving the National Labor Relations Board, which ultimately requires that at least 50 percent of the members of the players association vote to decertify the union in an NLRB-supervised election. See generally Catherine Meeker, *Defining "Ministerial Aid": Union Decertification Under the National Labor Relations Act*, 66 U. Chi. L. Rev. 999, 1000-1001 (1999). If a majority of the players vote to decertify the union, they cannot vote to re-unionize (and engage in collective bargaining with the league) before the lapse of a 12-month period. 29 U.S.C. §159. In contrast, a disclaimer of

5. Although hopes were high that the agreement would improve the rocky relationship between the NFL and the NFLPA, which was made worse during the lockout and the *Brady* litigation, the two sides were soon at odds again, with the NFLPA alleging in federal court that NFL teams colluded to institute a secret unauthorized salary cap during the 2010 season. In December 2012, U.S. District Court Judge David Doty dismissed the complaint, noting that "the NFLPA released the claims it attempts to assert" when the parties reached agreement in the *Brady* case and entered the CBA. The NFLPA appealed the case to the U.S. Court of Appeals for the Eighth Circuit, where it is pending at the time of this writing. Mark Maske, *NFL Players' Collusion Complaint Against League Is Dismissed*, Wash. Post, Dec. 31, 2012.

interest is an informal procedure pursuant to which the union leadership disclaims authority to represent the players based on at least 50 percent of them indicating they do not desire such representation. *Powell v. NFL*, 764 F. Supp. 1351 (D. Minn. 1991). A majority of the players can reauthorize the union to represent them at any time, creating the possibility of stepping into and out of a collective bargaining relationship as desired based on the circumstances. In light of the differences between decertification and a disclaimer of interest, should the method used to dissolve a union's collective bargaining authority determine whether the dissolution is effective for purposes of the applicability of the Norris LaGuardia Act's anti-injunction provision or the nonstatutory labor exemption?

4. For an electronic discussion of the legal and public policy issues raised by the 2011 NFL lockout among a group of sports law professors as it was ongoing, see *A Roundtable Discussion for the Digital Age*, 29 Ent. & Sports Law. 1 (American Bar Association, Summer 2011) (Jeremy Davis, ed.). For an exploration of the manner in which the 2011 NFL and NBA lockouts and the legal disputes they spawned will impact collective bargaining and the application of labor law in professional sports going forward, see Gabriel Feldman, *Antitrust Versus Labor Law in Professional Sports: Balancing the Scales After* Brady v. NFL *and* Anthony v. NBA, 45 U.C. Davis L. Rev. 1221 (2012).

In *Brown v. Pro Football, Inc., supra,* the players affected by the wage limitations imposed by the league were not presently eligible for membership in the NFLPA. A central question, therefore, is whether these players' terms and conditions of employment are an aspect of the collective bargaining process even if they are not part of the unionized bargaining unit.[6] This raises the concept of the "hiring hall" in labor relations, pursuant to which a union can enter into agreements that affect prospective future employees outside the bargaining unit. See, e.g., *Wood v. National Basketball Assn.*, 809 F.2d 954 (2d Cir. 1987) (nonstatutory labor exemption precludes antitrust challenge to CBA terms by a drafted player who is not yet a union member). In contrast to *Wood*, which involved an NBA first-round draft choice who was eligible to join the players union as soon as he signed a contract with the club that drafted him, the following case involves an athlete's claim that a professional sports league's eligibility rules, which have the *imprimatur* of the players union, exclude him from league employment in violation of antitrust law.

CLARETT v. NFL

369 F.3d 124 (2d Cir. 2004), *cert. denied*, 544 U.S. 961 (2005)

SOTOMAYOR, Circuit Judge.

[EDS. Maurice Clarett wanted to play in the National Football League despite his inability to comply with a league rule limiting eligibility to players three

---

6. The *Brady* case raised this issue, which was left unresolved when this litigation was settled. Although nine of the ten named plaintiffs in the class action were NFL players, the tenth, Von Miller, was a prospective NFL player who at the time of suit was a senior at Texas A&M University. Miller was included as a plaintiff to represent the interests of members of the incoming rookie class in order to challenge the NFL's proposed establishment of a rookie wage scale on antitrust grounds.

seasons removed from their high school graduation. Clarett was a star freshman football player while attending Ohio State University (OSU) and was in his sophomore year at the time he filed this lawsuit. He claimed he was ready, willing, and able to play in the NFL and that his exclusion violated the antitrust laws.

In his short collegiate career, Clarett's credentials as a football player were impressive. In the 2002-2003 collegiate season, Clarett—the first freshman starter at running back for OSU since 1943—led his team to an undefeated (14-0) season that was capped by a 31-24 double-overtime victory over University of Miami in the Fiesta Bowl, OSU's first national championship in 34 years. As a result of his resounding freshman-year success, Clarett was named the Big Ten Freshman of the Year and voted the best running back in college football by *The Sporting News.*

Ohio State suspended Clarett for the entire 2003 college football season because of concerns that he violated NCAA amateurism rules. When this suit was filed there was some question whether the NCAA would permit him to play during the 2004 season, and the NFL may have been his only real option for playing football the next year.

The current CBA took effect on May 6, 1993, and was to expire in 2007. That CBA, along with the League's Constitution and Bylaws, comprehensively outlines the relationship between the players and the League, covering the operation of the League, player salary and the player draft, including detailed rules by which the teams select new players. Two provisions of that CBA are at issue here. Article III, section 1, provides:

> This Agreement represents the complete understanding of the parties on all subjects covered herein, and there will be no change in the terms and conditions of this Agreement without mutual consent. . . . [T]he NFLPA and the Management Council *waive all rights to bargain with one another concerning any subject covered or not covered in this Agreement* for the duration of this Agreement, *including the provisions of the NFL Constitution and Bylaws.* . . .

Article IV, section 2, entitled "No Suit," provides:

> [N]either the NFLPA nor any of its members, agents acting on its behalf, nor any members of its bargaining unit will sue, or support financially or administratively any suit against, the NFL or any Club relating to the presently existing provisions of the Constitution and Bylaws of the NFL as they are currently operative and administered. . . .

Clarett and the NFL disagree on whether these two provisions establish that the NFL and the players union actually bargained over the terms of the Constitution and Bylaws (which contained the eligibility rule at issue), or merely bargained away the NFLPA's ability to bargain over or challenge the Bylaws' provisions.

With respect to the 2004 draft, the Commissioner issued a release that included the following iteration of the Rule:

> *SPECIAL ELIGIBILITY.* . . . Any applications for special eligibility must be in the Commissioner's office no later than Thursday, January 15, 2004, if the player is to be considered for inclusion in the League's principal draft scheduled for April 24-25, 2004. Applications will be accepted only for college players for whom at least three full *college seasons* have elapsed since their high school graduation. . . .]

. . . Clarett argues that the NFL clubs are horizontal competitors for the labor of professional football players and thus may not agree that a player will be hired only after three full football seasons have elapsed following that player's high school graduation. That characterization, however, neglects that the labor market for NFL players is organized around a collective bargaining relationship that is provided for and promoted by federal labor law, and that the NFL clubs, as a multi-employer bargaining unit, can act jointly in setting the terms and conditions of players' employment and the rules of the sport without risking antitrust liability. For those reasons, the NFL argues that federal labor law favoring and governing the collective bargaining process precludes the application of the antitrust laws to its eligibility rules. . . .

Relying on *Mackey*, the district court below held that the nonstatutory exemption provides no protection to the NFL's draft eligibility rules, because the eligibility rules fail to satisfy any of the three *Mackey* factors. . . .

We, however, have never regarded the Eighth Circuit's test in *Mackey* as defining the appropriate limits of the nonstatutory exemption. . . .

Clarett does not contend that the NFL's draft eligibility rules work to the disadvantage of the NFL's competitors in the market for professional football or in some manner protect the NFL's dominance in that market. *Compare N. Am. Soccer League v. Nat'l Football League*, 670 F.2d 1249 (2d Cir. 1982). He challenges the eligibility rules only on the ground that they are an unreasonable restraint upon the market for players' services. . . . Thus, we need not decide here whether the *Mackey* factors aptly characterize the limits of the exemption in cases in which employers use agreements with their unions to disadvantage their competitors in the product or business market, because our cases have counseled a decidedly different approach where, as here, the plaintiff complains of a restraint upon a unionized labor market characterized by a collective bargaining relationship with a multi-employer bargaining unit. . . .

Our decisions in *Caldwell*, *Williams*, and *Wood* all involved players' claims that the concerted action of a professional sports league imposed a restraint upon the labor market for players' services and thus violated the antitrust laws. In each case, however, we held that the nonstatutory labor exemption defeated the players' claims. Our analysis in each case was rooted in the observation that the relationships among the defendant sports leagues and their players were governed by collective bargaining agreements and thus were subject to the carefully structured regime established by federal labor laws. We reasoned that to permit antitrust suits against sports leagues on the ground that their concerted action imposed a restraint upon the labor market would seriously undermine many of the policies embodied by these labor laws, including the congressional policy favoring collective bargaining, the bargaining parties' freedom of contract, and the widespread use of multi-employer bargaining units. Subsequent to our decisions in this area, similar reasoning led the Supreme Court in *Brown v. Pro Football, Inc.*, 518 U.S. 231, 135 L. Ed. 2d 521, 116 S. Ct. 2116 (1996), to hold that the nonstatutory exemption protected the NFL's unilateral implementation of new salary caps for developmental squad players after its collective bargaining agreement with the NFL players union had expired and negotiations with the union over that proposal reached an impasse. . . .

Clarett argues that his case differs in material respects from *Brown*, but he does not argue, nor do we find, that the Supreme Court's treatment of the nonstatutory exemption in that case gives reason to doubt the authority of our prior decisions in *Caldwell*, *Williams*, and *Wood*. Because we find that our prior decisions in this area fully comport—in approach and result—with the Supreme Court's decision in *Brown*, we regard them as controlling authority. . . .

Clarett argues that he is physically qualified to play professional football and that the antitrust laws preclude the NFL teams from agreeing amongst themselves that they will refuse to deal with him simply because he is less than three full football seasons out of high school. Such an arbitrary condition, he argues, imposes an unreasonable restraint upon the competitive market for professional football players' services, and, because it excludes him from entering that market altogether, constitutes a *per se* antitrust violation. The issue we must decide is whether subjecting the NFL's eligibility rules to antitrust scrutiny would "subvert fundamental principles of our federal labor policy." . . . For the reasons that follow, we hold that it would and that the nonstatutory exemption therefore applies.

Although the NFL has maintained draft eligibility rules in one form or another for much of its history, the "inception of a collective bargaining relationship" between the NFL and its players union some thirty years ago "irrevocably alter[ed] the governing legal regime." . . . Our prior cases highlight a number of consequences resulting from the advent of this collective bargaining relationship that are relevant to Clarett's litigation. For one, prospective players no longer have the right to negotiate directly with the NFL teams over the terms and conditions of their employment. That responsibility is instead committed to the NFL and the players union to accomplish through the collective bargaining process, and throughout that process the NFL and the players union are to have the freedom to craft creative solutions to their differences in light of the economic imperatives of their industry. Furthermore, the NFL teams are permitted to engage in joint conduct with respect to the terms and conditions of players' employment as a multi-employer bargaining unit without risking antitrust liability. The arguments Clarett advances in support of his antitrust claim, however, run counter to each of these basic principles of federal labor law.

Because the NFL players have unionized and have selected the NFLPA as its exclusive bargaining representative, labor law prohibits Clarett from negotiating directly the terms and conditions of his employment with any NFL club, . . . and an NFL club would commit an unfair labor practice were it to bargain with Clarett individually without the union's consent, . . . The terms and conditions of Clarett's employment are instead committed to the collective bargaining table and are reserved to the NFL and the players union's selected representative to negotiate. . . .

The players union's representative possesses "powers comparable to those possessed by a legislative body both to create and restrict the rights of those whom it represents." . . . In seeking the best deal for NFL players overall, the representative has the ability to advantage certain categories of players over others, subject of course to the representative's duty of fair representation. (citation omitted.) The union representative may, for example, favor veteran players over rookies . . . and can seek to preserve jobs for current players to the detriment of new employees and the exclusion of outsiders. (citations omitted.) This authority and exclusive responsibility is vested in the players' representative "once a mandatory collective bargaining relationship is established and continues throughout the relationship." (citation omitted.) For the duration of that relationship, federal labor law then establishes a "'soup-to-nuts array' of rules, tribunals and remedies to govern [the collective bargaining] process." . . .

Clarett's argument that antitrust law should permit him to circumvent this scheme established by federal labor law starts with the contention that the eligibility rules do not constitute a mandatory subject of collective bargaining and thus cannot fall within the protection of the non-statutory exemption. Contrary to the district court, however, we find that the eligibility rules are mandatory bargaining subjects. Though tailored to the unique circumstance of a professional sports league, the eligibility rules for the draft represent a quite literal condition for initial employment and for that reason alone might constitute a mandatory bargaining subject.

. . . Similarly, the complex scheme by which individual salaries in the NFL are set, which involves, *inter alia*, the NFL draft, league-wide salary pools for rookies, team salary caps, and free agency, was built around the longstanding restraint on the market for entering players imposed by the eligibility rules and the related expectations about the average career length of NFL players. The eligibility rules in other words cannot be viewed in isolation, because their elimination might well alter certain assumptions underlying the collective bargaining agreement between the NFL and its players union. . . .

Clarett, however, argues that the eligibility rules are an impermissible bargaining subject because they affect players outside of the union. But simply because the eligibility rules work a hardship on prospective rather than current employees does not render them impermissible. (citation omitted.) The eligibility rules in this respect are not dissimilar to union demands for hiring hall arrangements that have long been recognized as mandatory subjects of bargaining. (citation omitted.) In such hiring hall arrangements, the criteria for employment are set by the rules of the hiring hall rather than the employer alone. . . . Nevertheless, such an arrangement constitutes a permissible, mandatory subject of bargaining despite the fact that it concerns prospective rather than current employees. . . .

As a permissible, mandatory subject of bargaining, the conditions under which a prospective player, like Clarett, will be considered for employment as an NFL player are for the union representative and the NFL to determine. Clarett, however, stresses that the eligibility rules are arbitrary and that requiring him to wait another football season has nothing to do with whether he is in fact qualified for professional play. But Clarett is in this respect no different from the typical worker who is confident that he or she has the skills to fill a job vacancy but does not possess the qualifications or meet the requisite criteria that have been set. In the context of this collective bargaining relationship, the NFL and its players' union can agree that an employee will not be hired or considered for employment for nearly any reason whatsoever so long as they do not violate federal laws such as those prohibiting unfair labor practices, 29 U.S.C. § 201 *et seq.*, or discrimination. . . .

Even accepting that an individual club could refuse to consider him for employment because he is less than three full seasons out of high school, Clarett contends that the NFL clubs invited antitrust liability when they agreed amongst themselves to impose that same criteria on every prospective player. As a consequence of the NFL's unique position in the professional football market, of course, such joint action deprives Clarett of the opportunity to pursue, at least for the time being, the kind of high-paying, high-profile career he desires. In the context of collective bargaining, however, federal labor policy permits the NFL teams to act collectively as a multi-employer bargaining unit in structuring the rules of play and setting the criteria for player employment. Such concerted action is encouraged as a matter of labor policy and tolerated as a matter of antitrust law. . . .

The threat to the operation of federal labor law posed by Clarett's antitrust claims is in no way diminished by Clarett's contention that the rules were not bargained over during the negotiations that preceded the current collective bargaining agreement. The eligibility rules, along with the host of other NFL rules and policies affecting the terms and conditions of NFL players included in the NFL's Constitution and Bylaws, were well known to the union, and a copy of the Constitution and Bylaws was presented to the union during negotiations. Given that the eligibility rules are a mandatory bargaining subject for the reasons set out above, the union or the NFL could have forced the other to the bargaining table if either felt that a change was warranted. . . .

. . . [T]he collective bargaining agreement itself makes clear that the union and the NFL reached an agreement with respect to how the eligibility rules would be handled. In the collective bargaining agreement, the union agreed to waive any challenge to the Constitution and Bylaws and thereby acquiesced in the continuing operation of the eligibility rules contained therein — at least for the duration of the agreement. . . . The value of such a clause to the NFL is obvious, as control over any changes to the eligibility rules is left in the hands of management at least until the expiration of the collective bargaining agreement. Although it is entirely possible that the players union might not have agreed entirely with the eligibility rules, the union representative might not have regarded any difference of opinion with respect to the eligibility rules as sufficient to warrant the expenditure of precious time at the bargaining table in light of other important issues.

Clarett would have us hold that by reaching this arrangement rather than fixing the eligibility rules in the text of the collective bargaining agreement or in failing to wrangle over the eligibility rules at the bargaining table, the NFL left itself open to antitrust liability. Such a holding, however, would completely contradict prior decisions recognizing that the labor law policies that warrant withholding antitrust scrutiny are not limited to protecting only terms contained in collective bargaining agreements. . . . The reach of those policies, rather, extends as far as is necessary to ensure the successful operation of the collective bargaining *process* and to safeguard the "unique bundle of compromises" reached by the NFL and the players' union as a means of settling their differences. It would disregard those policies completely to hold that some "particular *quid pro quo* must be proven to avoid antitrust liability" . . . or to allow Clarett to undo what we assume the NFL and its players' union regarded as the most appropriate or expedient means of settling their differences. . . .

[Eds. The Second Circuit reversed the district court's ruling regarding the applicability of the nonstatutory labor exemption and vacated its order that Clarett be made eligible for the 2004 NFL draft.]

NOTES AND QUESTIONS

1. In its opinion, the Second Circuit asserts that a broad construction of the nonstatutory labor exemption promotes compromises by unions and

employers to resolve their differences. Do you agree with this statement? Might its ruling have the opposite effect if league clubs know they can propose new player restraints, bargain to impasse, and then implement these terms unilaterally while preparing for a strike or lockout?

2. Although Maurice Clarett could not use antitrust law to challenge his exclusion from the NFL draft, did he have an effective labor law remedy?

3. *Maurice Clarett Postscript.* After losing his suit and his chance to play in the NFL, Clarett's life took a sharp downward spiral. In February 2006, Clarett was indicted and charged with two counts of aggravated robbery and four lesser robbery charges for taking property from two people at gunpoint in an alley behind a bar in Columbus, Ohio. Several months later, while charges were still pending in that matter, Clarett was arrested after he refused to pull over after a traffic violation, was pursued by police, and was eventually found to have three handguns and an AK-47 assault rifle in the vehicle. In September 2006, Clarett pled guilty to aggravated robbery and carrying a concealed weapon and was sentenced to 7½ years in prison (with release possible after 3½ years) as well as 5 years of probation. He was released from prison in April 2010 for good behavior and, after his release, reenrolled in classes at Ohio State and played professional football with the Omaha Nighthawks of the United Football League.

4. In *National Hockey League Players' Assn. v. Plymouth Whalers*, 419 F.3d 462, 474 (6th Cir. 2005), the Sixth Circuit ruled that "any anti-competitive effect of a properly bargained collective bargaining agreement is excluded from antitrust scrutiny by [the] non-statutory antitrust exemption." Does the continuing broad judicial construction of the nonstatutory labor exemption by the Supreme Court and federal circuit courts distort Congress's original reasons for enacting the statutory labor exemption? Is judicial extension of statutory antitrust immunity for players unions to a nonstatutory antitrust immunity that effectively allows clubs to unilaterally implement new restrictions on the terms and conditions of player employment that the union has *never* agreed to justified?

5. The NFL is not the only American professional sports league with an age eligibility rule. With narrow exceptions, the NBA limits eligibility to players who are 19 years old and one year removed from their high school graduation and the WNBA limits eligibility to players who are 22 years old and four years removed from their high school graduation. MLB and the NHL have lower age eligibility thresholds than the NFL, NBA, or WNBA, while MLS, the PGA, the LPGA, and the USTA have no age eligibility requirements at all. What accounts for the differences in age eligibility criteria among the various leagues and associations? In *Clarett v. National Football League*, 306 F. Supp. 2d 379, 408 (S.D.N.Y. 2004) *judgment rev'd in part, vacated in part*, 369 F.3d 124 (2d Cir. 2004), the NFL argued that its age eligibility rules are necessary to protect "younger and/or less experienced players—that is, players who are less mature physically and psychologically—from heightened risks of injury in NFL games," but if this is so, wouldn't a similar age eligibility rule be prudent in hockey, which, like football, is a physically punishing game? If you believe that different sports' particular physical demands adequately explain the variety of age eligibility requirements, consider the basketball context: although the rules governing play in the NBA and WNBA are no different with regard to physical contact, a player must be roughly three

years older to play in the WNBA than in the NBA. This means women basketball players face a three-year delay in earning salaries and endorsements as compared with their male counterparts. Because the WNBA is a partially owned subsidiary of the NBA in that some WNBA clubs are owned and operated by NBA clubs, might the different age eligibility thresholds make the NBA vulnerable to a sex discrimination claim? It bears noting that the NBA and WNBA age eligibility rules discussed in this paragraph do not apply to international players. What justifies international basketball players facing less stringent age eligibility criteria than American basketball players?

3. Continued Viability of Antitrust Litigation in Player-Management Conflicts

In light of the seemingly ever-increasing expansion of the parameters of the nonstatutory labor exemption, it appears there is little room for professional athletes to assert successful antitrust claims arising out of labor relations disputes. However, there are still some instances in which courts will consider the merits of antitrust challenges to player eligibility rules and other limits on the terms and conditions of professional athletes' employment. As previously discussed, players in team sports can choose not to unionize or may decertify their union, thereby preventing or discontinuing the collective bargaining process and the applicability of the nonstatutory labor exemption.

Courts generally hold that the nonstatutory labor exemption does not bar an antitrust challenge by nonparties to collective bargaining agreement terms that have anticompetitive effects outside the labor market for players' services. In *Philadelphia World Hockey Club, Inc. v. Philadelphia Hockey Club, Inc.*, 351 F. Supp. 462 (E.D. Pa. 1972), the court ruled that this exemption does not preclude a rival league's claim that the NHL's reserve clause violates the antitrust laws. The World Hockey Association (WHA) prevailed on its antitrust claim by proving that the reserve clause in the NHL's collective bargaining agreement deprived it from competing for the services of players with the ability to play major league professional hockey. The WHA needed access to such players in order to produce major league professional ice hockey in competition with the NHL.

The nonstatutory labor exemption has not been applied to individual-performer sports, such as tennis, golf, boxing, and others. See, e.g., *Blalock v. Ladies Prof'l Golfers Assn.*, 359 F. Supp. 1260 (N.D. Ga. 1973) (finding that golfer's one-year suspension imposed by LPGA with "completely unfettered, subjective discretion" by a group of her competitors violates the antitrust laws). Professional players in the individual-performer sports generally are not unionized employees who engage in collective bargaining activities. Even if athletes in the sport form a players association and enter into agreements with event promoters or organizers, this generally does not constitute collective bargaining under the federal labor laws or make the nonstatutory labor exemption applicable.

Consequently, there are several instances in which antitrust litigation is not barred by the nonstatutory labor exemption. Thus, there is need to examine the developing framework of antitrust analysis applicable to challenged labor market restraints. Some early cases held that restraints that preclude or reduce competition among league clubs for player services are per se illegal. See, e.g.,

Smith v. Pro-Football Inc., 420 F. Supp. 738 (D.D.C. 1976), *aff'd in part and rev'd in part*, 593 F.2d 1173 (D.C. Cir. 1978); *Denver Rockets v. All-Pro Management*, 325 F. Supp. 1049 (C.D. Cal. 1971). Under the per se rule, certain concerted practices among economic competitors are conclusively presumed to be illegal because of their significant anticompetitive effects and are deemed incapable of justification.

On the other hand, the Supreme Court has recognized that the unique features of the sports industry require some uniform rules and agreements among competing teams in order to produce on-field competition that is appealing to consumers, which requires application of the rule of reason. *American Needle, Inc. v. NFL*, 130 S. Ct. 2201, 2216 (2010) ("When 'restraints on competition are essential if the product is to be available at all,' *per se* rules of illegality are inapplicable, and instead the restraint must be judged according to the flexible Rule of Reason"); *National Collegiate Athletic Assn. v. Board of Regents of the Univ. of Okla.*, 468 U.S. 85, 101 (1984) ("refusing to apply *per se* rule to sports industry because some horizontal restraints are necessary 'if product to be available at all'"). Thus, courts generally have applied the more flexible *rule of reason* on a case-by-case basis to determine whether particular restraints affecting the market for player services violate the antitrust laws. See, e.g., *Smith v. Pro Football Inc.*, 593 F.2d 1173, 1182 (D.C. Cir. 1978) ("legality of NFL draft should not be governed by *per se* rule . . . legality of player restriction in professional sports should be governed by the rule of reason"); *Mackey v. NFL*, 543 F.2d 606, 619 (8th Cir. 1976) ("unique nature of the business of professional football renders it inappropriate to mechanically apply *per se* illegality rules" to challenged league free agency restrictions). See also *National Hockey League Players' Assn. v. Plymouth Whalers Hockey Club*, 325 F.3d 712 (6th Cir. 2003); *McNeil v. NFL*, 790 F. Supp. 871 (D. Minn. 1992).

However, applying the rule of reason to player restraints requires complicated analysis and balancing of several different factors and their economic effects. Considering the validity of the NBA's then-current draft eligibility rules, one court observed:

> The primary disadvantages of the "rule of reason" are that it requires difficult and lengthy factual inquiries and very subjective policy decisions which are in many ways essentially legislative and ill-suited to the judicial process. For instance, in the present case, a complex economic inquiry would be required to determine the economic necessity of action of this type. In addition, the court would be required to determine a standard which could be used to weigh the various public policy goals which might be alleged as justification by the NBA. The court would further be forced to determine whether the boycott was genuinely motivated by the purposes given or by other reasons. Frequently, these motives are closely intertwined.

See *Denver Rockets v. All-Pro Management*, 325 F. Supp. 1049, 1063 (C.D. Cal. 1971).

There are few recent cases in which courts have addressed whether professional sports league labor market restraints violate the federal antitrust laws. Although it is an older case, the Eighth Circuit's application of the rule of reason to the Rozelle Rule in *Mackey* provides an illustration of how courts have applied Sherman Act §1 to labor market restraints.

MACKEY v. NFL

543 F.2d 606 (8th Cir. 1976)

Lay, Circuit Judge.

. . . Antitrust Issues

We turn, then, to the question of whether the Rozelle Rule, as implemented, violates § 1 of the Sherman Act, which declares illegal "every contract, combination . . . or conspiracy, in restraint of trade or commerce among the several States." 15 U.S.C. § 1. . . .

Rule of Reason

The focus of an inquiry under the Rule of Reason is whether the restraint imposed is justified by legitimate business purposes, and is no more restrictive than necessary. . . .

In defining the restraint on competition for players' services, the district court found that the Rozelle Rule significantly deters clubs from negotiating with and signing free agents; that it acts as a substantial deterrent to players playing out their options and becoming free agents; that it significantly decreases players' bargaining power in contract negotiations; that players are thus denied the right to sell their services in a free and open market; that as a result, the salaries paid by each club are lower than if competitive bidding were allowed to prevail; and that absent the Rozelle Rule, there would be increased movement in interstate commerce of players from one club to another.

We find substantial evidence in the record to support these findings. Witnesses for both sides testified that there would be increased player movement absent the Rozelle Rule. . . .

In support of their contention that the restraints effected by the Rozelle Rule are not unreasonable, the defendants asserted a number of justifications. First, they argued that without the Rozelle Rule, star players would flock to cities having natural advantages such as larger economic bases, winning teams, warmer climates, and greater media opportunities; that competitive balance throughout the League would thus be destroyed; and that the destruction of competitive balance would ultimately lead to diminished spectator interest, franchise failures, and perhaps the demise of the NFL, at least as it operates today. Second, the defendants contended that the Rozelle Rule is necessary to protect the clubs' investment in scouting expenses and player development costs. Third, they asserted that players must work together for a substantial period of time in order to function effectively as a team; that elimination of the Rozelle Rule would lead to increased player movement and a concomitant reduction in player continuity; and that the quality of play in the NFL would thus suffer, leading to reduced spectator interest, and financial detriment both to the clubs and the players. Conflicting evidence was adduced at trial by both sides with respect to the validity of these asserted justifications.

The district court held the defendants' asserted justifications unavailing. . . . The court further concluded that elimination of the Rozelle Rule would have no significant disruptive effects, either immediate or long term, on professional football. In conclusion the court held that the Rozelle Rule was unreasonable in that it was overly broad, unlimited in duration, unaccompanied by procedural safeguards, and employed in conjunction with other anticompetitive practices such as the draft, Standard Player Contract, option clause, and the no-tampering rules.

We agree that the asserted need to recoup player development costs cannot justify the restraints of the Rozelle Rule. That expense is an ordinary cost of doing business and is not peculiar to professional football. Moreover, because of its unlimited duration, the Rozelle Rule is far more restrictive than necessary to fulfill that need.

We agree, in view of the evidence adduced at trial with respect to existing players' turnover by way of trades, retirements and new players entering the League, that the club owners' arguments respecting player continuity cannot justify the Rozelle Rule. . . .

In sum, we hold that the Rozelle Rule, as enforced, unreasonably restrains trade in violation of § 1 of the Sherman Act. . . .

NOTES AND QUESTIONS

1. As a threshold matter, an antitrust plaintiff must prove actual or threatened economic loss caused by the anticompetitive effects of the defendant's challenged conduct. This "antitrust injury" requirement is relatively easily satisfied by players challenging labor market restraints that reduce their potential income. If an antitrust violation is proved, a player's damages generally are based on the difference between his actual compensation and the value of his services in a free market. See *Smith v. Pro Football, Inc.*, 593 F.2d 1173, 1189-1191 (D.C. Cir. 1979).

2. *Single-Entity Defense.* Most litigation seeking to invalidate player restraints involves claimed violations of §1 of the Sherman Act, which requires concerted anticompetitive conduct. Courts previously rejected the argument that a professional sports league and its member clubs function as a single economic entity whose labor market rules are not subject to challenge under §1, which seems correct given the Supreme Court's rejection of the single entity defense in *American Needle, Inc. v. NFL, supra.*

    In *McNeil v. NFL*, 790 F. Supp. 871 (D. Minn. 1992), the court held that agreements among league clubs to reduce competition for player services are subject to §1. See also *Chicago Professional Sports Ltd. Partnership v. NBA* (*Bulls IV*), 95 F.3d 593, 599 (7th Cir. 1996) ("[F]rom the perspective of college basketball players who seek to sell their skills, the teams are distinct, and because the human capital of players is not readily transferable to other sports (as even Michael Jordan learned) the league looks more like a group of firms acting as a monopsony").

3. *Anticompetitive Effects.* Under the rule of reason, a player must prove that the challenged restraint reduces economic competition among the defendants for player services. *National Hockey League Players' Assn. v. Plymouth Whalers*, 419 F.3d 462, 474 (6th Cir. 2005) (dismissing antitrust claims because mere "diminished quality of athletic competition" is not "an anti-competitive effect within the meaning of the antitrust laws"). For example, agreements among league clubs to fix players' wages, which thereby eliminate individual salary negotiations, have clear anticompetitive effects. *McNeil v. NFL*, 790 F. Supp. 871, 877 (D. Minn. 1992).

Because their adverse economic effects are not as direct and less clear, other labor market restraints such as player drafts, free agency restrictions, and other forms of allocating players among league clubs may require detailed market analysis to determine their effects on economic competition. In such cases, the plaintiff must prove the relevant market for the services of players and that the defendant league and its clubs have a sufficiently large market share to adversely affect competition. The relevant market has both a product and geographical component. The product market includes all prospective purchasers of player services that are reasonable substitutes from the players' perspective in terms of earning potential, prestige, and other economic factors. *Smith v. Pro Football, Inc.*, 593 F.2d 1173, 1185 n.48 (D.C. Cir. 1979) (finding that employment in Canadian Football League is not reasonable substitute for employment with an NFL team). The geographical market is the geographical area "to which players can turn, as a practical matter, for alternate opportunities for employment" as professional athletes. *Fraser v. Major League Soccer, LLC*, 284 F.3d 47, 63 (1st Cir. 2002), *cert. denied*, 537 U.S. 885 (2002) (upholding jury finding of an international market for the services of professional soccer players).

4. *Legitimate Procompetitive Justifications.* Some early cases held that the anticompetitive effects of labor market restraints cannot be justified by procompetitive effects in a different market. As one court explained:

> The draft is "procompetitive," if at all, in a very different sense from that in which it is anticompetitive. The draft is anticompetitive in its effect on the market for players' services, because it virtually eliminates economic competition among buyers for the services of sellers. The draft is allegedly "procompetitive" in its effect on the playing field; but the NFL teams are not economic competitors on the playing field, and the draft, while it may heighten athletic competition and thus improve the entertainment product offered to the public, does not increase competition in the economic sense of encouraging others to enter the market and to offer the product at lower cost. Because the draft's "anticompetitive" and "procompetitive" effects are not comparable, it is impossible to "net them out" in the usual rule-of-reason balancing. The draft's "anticompetitive evils," in other words, cannot be balanced against its "procompetitive virtues," and the draft be upheld if the latter outweigh the former. In strict economic terms, the draft's demonstrated procompetitive effects are nil.

Smith v. Pro Football, Inc., 593 F.2d 1173, 1186 (D.C. Cir. 1979).

More recently, other courts have ruled that procompetitive effects in a closely related market (i.e., those that enhance a professional sports league's ability to more effectively compete with other forms of entertainment) should be balanced against a restraint's anticompetitive effects. *Sullivan v. NFL*, 34 F.3d 1091, 1111-1113 (1st Cir. 1994). In *American Needle, Inc. v. NFL*, 130 S. Ct. 2201, 2217, the Supreme Court recognized that a professional sports league's interest in maintaining competitive balance among its member clubs is "legitimate and important," which is "unquestionably an interest that may well justify a variety of collective decisions made by the teams." *American Needle* strongly suggests that a sports league can justify labor market restraints by proving that they promote competitive balance and playing-field equality among its member clubs, thereby producing better entertainment for consumers, thereby effectively overruling or at least casting substantial doubt on the continuing validity of cases such as *Smith*.

5. *Less Restrictive Alternatives.* A labor market restraint may be invalidated if there is a less restrictive means of achieving the league's procompetitive objective. *Smith v. Pro Football, Inc.*, 593 F.2d 1173, 118 (D.C. Cir. 1979) (holding that the NFL's 16-round draft violated §1 because "significantly less anticompetitive alternatives" exist). How strictly should a court apply this standard?

PROBLEM 7-5

An 18-year-old soccer player from England moves with his parents to the United States. He believes he has the kicking skills necessary to play in the NFL and applies for admission to the NFL draft. In the meantime, he also is being courted by several universities interested in luring him into the college ranks. The NFL Commissioner rules that foreign nationals are not eligible for the NFL draft and, in addition, that, as a U.S. resident, the player must adhere to the same regulations that apply to other prospective players. Thus, the Commissioner informs the player he will not be eligible until three college seasons have passed since his graduation from the equivalent of a U.S. high school. What is the player's likelihood of success if he files an antitrust lawsuit? Does the nonstatutory labor exemption bar his antitrust claim?

E.   DEVELOPING INTERNATIONAL LABOR ISSUES

Professional sports leagues and associations around the globe must grapple with an increasing array of business and legal issues that transcend national borders, so far related in large part to the movement of professional athletes from one country to another. Although the internationalization of professional team sports has not yet occurred, domestic major professional leagues may expand outside the United States and Canada in the future. For example, Commissioner David Stern has expressed interest in having a league associated with the NBA in Europe. And the NFL is considering the possibility of having a club based in London, England. Thus, it is not too early to consider briefly some of the legal ramifications arising from the movement of athletes across national borders.

The following case, decided by the European Court of Justice, is an excellent example of some of these legal issues. It deserves study not just for the specific issue it addresses under European Union law but also as an illustration of the complex intersection of the competing interests of players, domestic professional sports clubs, national federations, and international sports governing bodies.

UNION ROYALE BELGE DES SOCIÉTÉS DE FOOTBALL ASSOCIATION, ROYAL CLUB LIÉGOIS, AND UNION DES ASSOCIATIONS EUROPÉENNES DE FOOTBALL (UEFA) v. JEAN-MARC BOSMAN (BOSMAN)

Case C-415/93, (European Court of Justice, 15 December 1995)

***

THE RULES GOVERNING THE ORGANIZATION OF FOOTBALL

Association football, commonly known as "football," professional or amateur, is practised as an organized sport in clubs which belong to national associations or federations in each of the Member States.

The national associations are members of the Fédération Internationale de Football Association ("FIFA"), an association governed by Swiss law, which organizes football at world level. FIFA is divided into confederations for each continent, whose regulations require its approval. . . .

TRANSFER RULES

[EDS. FIFA and UEFA regulations, which are incorporated into the rules of the European national associations, govern the movement of football players between clubs. These regulations are applicable to player transfers between clubs in different European Union countries or clubs belonging to the same national association within a European Union country. Pursuant to these regulations, when a player is transferred between clubs, his new club is required to pay his former club a transfer fee to compensate for the former club's development and training of the player. If the two clubs disagree as to the amount of the transfer fee, it is to be determined by a UEFA board of experts based on a predetermined formula. A transfer fee was required to be paid even if the player's contract with his former club had expired. The former club's national association must issue an international clearance certificate before a player is eligible to play for his new club.]

NATIONALITY CLAUSES

[EDS. Many UEFA national football associations have nationality clauses restricting the extent to which foreign players can be recruited or fielded in a match. For the purposes of these clauses, nationality is defined in relation to whether the player can be qualified to play in a country's national or representative team. After collaboration with the European Commission (which is charged with enforcing the European Union's competition laws), UEFA removed the limitations on the number of contracts entered into by each football club with players from other European Union countries and set the number of such players who may participate in any one match at two, this limit not being applicable to players established for over five years in the member country in question. UEFA subsequently adopted the "3 + 2" rule, permitting each national association to limit to three the number of foreign players a club may field in any first division match in their national championships, plus two players who have played in the country of the relevant national association for an uninterrupted period of five years, including three years as a junior. The same limitation also applies to UEFA matches in competitions for club teams.]

REVELANT FACTS AND BOSMAN'S CLAIMS

[EDS. Mr. Bosman, a professional footballer of Belgian nationality, was employed from 1988 by RC Liège, a Belgian first division club, under a contract expiring on June 30, 1990, which assured him an average monthly salary of BFR (Belgian francs) 120,000, including bonuses. On April 21, 1990, RC Liège offered Mr. Bosman a new contract for one season, reducing his pay to BFR 30,000, the minimum permitted by the URBSFA (the Royal Belgian Football Association) federal rules. Mr. Bosman refused to sign and was put on the transfer list. The compensation fee for training was set, in accordance with the said rules, at BFR 11,743,000. Since no club showed an interest in a compulsory transfer, Mr. Bosman made contact with US Dunkerque, a club in the French second division, which led to his being engaged for a monthly salary in the region of BFR 100,000 plus a signing-on bonus of some BFR 900,000. On July 27, 1990, a contract was also concluded between RC Liège and US Dunkerque for the temporary transfer of Mr. Bosman for one year, against payment by US Dunkerque to RC Liège of a compensation fee of BFR 1,200,000 payable on receipt by the Fédération Française de Football (FFF) of the transfer certificate issued by URBSFA. The contract also gave US Dunkerque an irrevocable option for full transfer of the player for BFR 4,800,000. Both contracts between US Dunkerque and RC Liège and between US Dunkerque and Mr. Bosman were, however, subject to the condition that the transfer certificate must be sent by URBSFA to FFF in time for the first match of the season, which was to be held on August 2, 1990. RC Liège, which had doubts as to US Dunkerque's solvency, did not ask URBSFA to send the certificate to FFF. As a result, neither contract took effect. On July 31, 1990, RC Liège also suspended Mr. Bosman, thereby preventing him from playing for the entire season.

In a suit against RC Liège, URBSFA, and UEFA in a Belgium court, Bosman alleged that the transfer rules and nationality clauses were illegal and sought damages for lost earnings caused by the result of the application of the transfer rules. The Cour d'Appel, Liège, a Belgian appellate court, referred the following questions to the European Court of Justice for resolution.]

Are Articles 48, 85 and 86 of the Treaty of Rome of 25 March 1957 to be interpreted as:

(i)   prohibiting a football club from requiring and receiving payment of a sum of money upon the engagement of one of its players who has come to the end of his contract by a new employing club;
(ii) prohibiting the national and international sporting associations or federations from including in their respective regulations provisions restricting access of foreign players from the European Community to the competitions which they organize?

[EDS. The court at length declined to discuss Articles 85 and 86, the European Union competitions laws, relying instead on its interpretations of Article 48's prohibited restrictions on worker's freedom of movement among European Union countries.]

APPLICATION OF ARTICLE 48 TO RULES LAID DOWN BY SPORTING ASSOCIATIONS

. . . UEFA argued, inter alia, that the Community authorities have always respected the autonomy of sport, that it is extremely difficult to distinguish between the economic and the sporting aspects of football and that a decision of the Court concerning the situation of professional players might call in question the organization of football as a whole. For that reason, even if Article 48 of the Treaty were to apply to professional players, a degree of flexibility would be essential because of the particular nature of the sport.

. . . [I]t is to be remembered that, having regard to the objectives of the Community, sport is subject to Community law only in so far as it constitutes an economic activity within the meaning of Article 2 of the Treaty. . . .

. . . [F]or the purposes of the application of the Community provisions on freedom of movement for workers . . . all that is required is the existence of, or the intention to create, an employment relationship.

Application of Article 48 of the Treaty is not precluded by the fact that the transfer rules govern the business relationships between clubs rather than the employment relationships between clubs and players. The fact that the employing clubs must pay fees on recruiting a player from another club affects the players' opportunities for finding employment and the terms under which such employment is offered.

. . . [T]he freedom of movement of workers guaranteed by Article 48 . . . is a fundamental freedom in the Community system. . . .

Whether the Situation Envisaged by the National Court Is of a Purely Internal Nature

UEFA considers that the disputes pending before the national court concern a purely internal Belgian situation which falls outside the ambit of Article 48 of the Treaty. They concern a Belgian player whose transfer fell through because of the conduct of a Belgian club and a Belgian association.

It is true that . . . the provisions of the Treaty concerning the free movement of workers, and particularly Article 48, cannot be applied to situations which are wholly internal to a Member State. . . . However, it is clear from the findings of fact made by the national court that Mr. Bosman had entered into a contract of employment with a club in another Member State with a view to exercising gainful employment in that State. By so doing, as he has rightly pointed out, he accepted an offer of employment actually made, within the meaning of Article 48(3)(a).

Since the situation in issue in the main proceedings cannot be classified as purely internal, the argument put forward by UEFA must be dismissed.

Existence of an Obstacle to Freedom of Movement for Workers

It is thus necessary to consider whether the transfer rules form an obstacle to freedom of movement for workers prohibited by Article 48 of the Treaty. . . .

The Court has also held that the provisions of the Treaty relating to freedom of movement for persons are intended to facilitate the pursuit by Community citizens of occupational activities of all kinds throughout the Community, and preclude measures which might place Community citizens at a disadvantage when they wish to pursue an economic activity in the territory of another Member State. . . .

In that context, nationals of Member States have in particular the right, which they derive directly from the Treaty, to leave their country of origin to enter the territory of another Member State and reside there in order to pursue an economic activity. . . .

Provisions which preclude or deter a national of a Member State from leaving his country of origin in order to exercise his right to freedom of movement therefore constitute an obstacle to that freedom even if they apply without regard to the nationality of the workers concerned. . . .

Since they provide that a professional footballer may not pursue his activity with a new club established in another Member State unless it has paid his former club a transfer fee agreed upon between the two clubs or determined in accordance with the regulations of the sporting associations, the said rules constitute an obstacle to freedom of movement for workers.

EXISTENCE OF JUSTIFICATIONS

First, URBSFA, UEFA and the French and Italian Governments have submitted that the transfer rules are justified by the need to maintain a financial and competitive balance between clubs and to support the search for talent and the training of young players. . . .

As regards the first of those aims, Mr. Bosman has rightly pointed out that the application of the transfer rules is not an adequate means of maintaining financial and competitive balance in the world of football. Those rules neither preclude the richest clubs from securing the services of the best players nor prevent the availability of financial resources from being a decisive factor in competitive sport, thus considerably altering the balance between clubs.

As regards the second aim, it must be accepted that the prospect of receiving transfer, development or training fees is indeed likely to encourage football clubs to seek new talent and train young players.

However, because it is impossible to predict the sporting future of young players with any certainty and because only a limited number of such players go on to play professionally, those fees are by nature contingent and uncertain and are in any event unrelated to the actual cost borne by clubs of training both future professional players and those who will never play professionally. The prospect of receiving such fees cannot, therefore, be either a decisive factor in encouraging recruitment and training of young players or an adequate means of financing such activities, particularly in the case of smaller clubs. Furthermore, as the Advocate General has pointed out, the same aims can be achieved at least as efficiently by other means which do not impede freedom of movement for workers. . . .

Finally, the argument that the rules in question are necessary to compensate clubs for the expenses which they have had to incur in paying fees on recruiting their players cannot be accepted, since it seeks to justify the maintenance of obstacles to freedom of movement for workers simply on the ground that such obstacles were able to exist in the past.

The answer to the first question must therefore be that Article 48 of the Treaty precludes the application of rules laid down by sporting associations, under which a professional footballer who is a national of one Member State may not, on the expiry of his contract with a club, be employed by a club of another Member State unless the latter club has paid to the former club a transfer, training or development fee.

INTERPRETATION OF ARTICLE 48 OF THE TREATY WITH REGARD TO THE NATIONALITY CLAUSES

By its second question, the national court seeks in substance to ascertain whether Article 48 of the Treaty precludes the application of rules laid down by sporting associations, under which, in matches in competitions which they organize, football clubs may field only a limited number of professional players who are nationals of other Member States.

EXISTENCE OF AN OBSTACLE TO FREEDOM OF MOVEMENT FOR WORKERS

As the Court has held . . . above, Article 48 of the Treaty applies to rules laid down by sporting associations which determine the conditions under which professional sports players may engage in gainful employment. It must therefore be considered whether the nationality clauses constitute an obstacle to freedom of movement for workers, prohibited by Article 48.

Article 48(2) expressly provides that freedom of movement for workers entails the abolition of any discrimination based on nationality between workers of the Member States as regards employment, remuneration and conditions of work and employment. . . .

[This] principle applies to clauses contained in the regulations of sporting associations which restrict the right of nationals of other Member States to take part, as professional players, in football matches . . .

The fact that those clauses concern not the employment of such players, on which there is no restriction, but the extent to which their clubs may field them in official matches is irrelevant. In so far as participation in such matches is the essential purpose of a professional player's activity, a rule which restricts that participation obviously also restricts the chances of employment of the player concerned.

EXISTENCE OF JUSTIFICATIONS

The existence of an obstacle having thus been established, it must be considered whether that obstacle may be justified in the light of Article 48 of the Treaty.

URBSFA, UEFA and the German, French and Italian Governments argued that the nationality clauses are justified on non-economic grounds, concerning only the sport as such. . . .

It must be recalled that in . . . its judgment in *Donà*, the Court held that the Treaty provisions concerning freedom of movement for persons do not prevent the adoption of rules or practices excluding foreign players from certain matches for reasons which are not of an economic nature, which relate to the particular nature and context of such matches and are thus of sporting interest only, such as, for example, matches between national teams from different countries. It stressed, however, that that restriction on the scope of the provisions in question must remain limited to its proper objective.

Here, the nationality clauses do not concern specific matches between teams representing their countries but apply to all official matches between clubs and thus to the essence of the activity of professional players.

In those circumstances, the nationality clauses cannot be deemed to be in accordance with Article 48 of the Treaty, otherwise that article would be deprived of its practical effect and the fundamental right of free access to employment which the Treaty confers individually on each worker in the Community rendered nugatory . . . None of the arguments put forward by the sporting associations and by the governments which have submitted observations detracts from that conclusion.

It follows . . . that Article 48 of the Treaty precludes the application of rules laid down by sporting associations under which, in matches in competitions which they organize, football clubs may field only a limited number of professional players who are nationals of other Member States. . . .

NOTES AND QUESTIONS

1. *U.S. Leagues in Foreign Countries.* At present, U.S. professional sports leagues such as the NHL, NBA, MLB, and Major League Soccer have clubs only in the United States and Canada. In addition to cultural differences in business practices and currency valuation, there is a host of complex legal issues to consider if a sports league operates in multiple countries. For example, as mentioned previously, Canadian labor law is largely provincial rather than national like in the United States. Considering the European Court of Justice's *Bosman* ruling, how would its labor issues become more complicated if a U.S. professional league established a division or satellite league in two or more countries that are part of the European Union?

2. *U.S. League Agreements with Foreign Governing Bodies and Professional Leagues.* The NBA and MLB have agreements with foreign leagues or organizations that seek to stablilize the process by which players move from a club in one country to one in another country. The NBA's agreement with the international governing federation for basketball (FIBA) requires recognition by all concerned parties that an existing player contract will be respected and not interfered with during its term. Note the implications of this agreement in connection with the dispute giving rise to *Boston Celtics v. Shaw, supra.*

   A central agreement for MLB is a U.S.-Japanese Player Contract Agreement, although dealings with several other countries, most notably South American countries, Mexico, and Caribbean countries, are important as well. The U.S.-Japanese contract provides, among other things, the following:
   - U.S. players not under present contractual restrictions in the United States can be contacted by a Japanese club and signed to a contract after clearance by the office of the U.S. commissioner. However, if the player, though not bound by an actual contract, is on the reserve, military, voluntarily retired, restricted, disqualified, suspended, or ineligible list of any club, then approval to sign the player must be obtained through the office of the commissioner.
   - The issue is more complicated for U.S. clubs wishing to sign a Japanese player. The list of those players who are free to negotiate is more restrictive, under interpretations of the Japanese office of the commissioner. In addition, the more likely process in recent years has been that a Japanese club may decide to market a player who desires to play in the United States. The club notifies the Commissioner of Major League Baseball of its willingness to market the player. If there is interest in the United States, a bidding process ensues. The highest bid is ultimately submitted to the Japanese club, which may accept or reject the bid. If it is accepted, the U.S. club must then negotiate with the player. If the negotiations are successful, the U.S. club gets the player and pays the Japanese club. If the negotiations are not successful, the Japanese club is owed nothing, and the process cannot be renewed until the following

year. Several high-profile Japanese players have entered MLB through this procedure.

See *United States-Japanese Player Contract Agreement*, December 15, 1998. For a description and legal analysis of this agreement, see William B. Gould IV, *Globalization in Collective Bargaining, Baseball, and Matsuzaka: Labor and Antitrust Law on the Diamond*, 28 Comp. Lab. Law & Pol'y J. 287 (2007).

3. *NHL Agreements with European Hockey Leagues and Federations.* After the NHL and NHLPA resolved the 2004-2005 lockout through enacting their 2005 CBA, the NHL signed a new player transfer agreement with the International Ice Hockey Federation (IIHF), the governing body for international ice hockey for all national federations, later that same year. The agreement established regulations for the transfer of European players to the NHL, however, the Russian Federation declined to enter into the agreement, and its players were therefore subject to different rules when negotiating with NHL clubs. The player transfer agreement with the IIHF expired following the 2006-2007 season, and although a new agreement was reached for the 2007-2008 season, it was terminated after one year.

Since the 2009-2010 season, the NHL has executed player transfer agreements on an individualized country-by-country basis instead of an overarching agreement with the IIHF. The NHL currently has agreements in place with countries such as Sweden, Finland, Slovakia, and Germany. These player transfer agreements require the NHL to pay a development fee to the individual federations for the right to sign their players while under contract, approximately $225,000 per player.

The NHL does not have a player transfer agreement with Russia. However, the NHL and Russia's Kontinental Hockey League agreed for the 2011-2012 and 2012-2013 seasons that they will cooperate regarding disputed player contracts. Russian players (and players coming from other countries not subject to a player transfer agreement) are subject to the defected status provisions of the CBA. Essentially, these provisions permit an NHL club to extend its negotiation rights indefinitely for an NHL drafted player whose rights reside with that NHL club. In contrast, a club's negotiation rights for a player subject to a player transfer agreement would expire after two years.

4. *Anticipating International Play and Expansion.* Some U.S. leagues have already addressed the possibility of international play and possible international expansion by negotiating with their players association some of the ground rules by which this may occur. Consider, for example, the following provisions in the latest MLB collective bargaining agreement:

- [I]f a Major League franchise is awarded to a city outside the United States and Canada, then championship season, All-Star, Division Series, League Championship Series and World Series games played in that city by such franchise shall not be considered international play.
- In furtherance of joint efforts to develop the sport internationally, the [MLBPA] and the Office of the Commissioner, on behalf of the Clubs, agree to (i) meet regularly to ensure continued collaboration and cooperation and (ii) keep the other informed regarding all contemplated or planned International Play.

See 2012 MLB CBA, Article XV, Section K.

CHAPTER
8

Regulating Agents

A. INTRODUCTION

As discussed in Chapter 6, the use of agents by professional athletes can be traced back to as early as the mid-1920s, when Charles Pyle negotiated a football contract and endorsement and movie deals for NFL player Harold "Red" Grange. The proliferation in the number and use of agents by athletes did not occur until the 1960s and 1970s, as a result of the demise of reserve and option clauses in standard-form contracts between players and clubs; competition for players between rival leagues (e.g., National Football League (NFL) and American Football League (AFL)); the growing strength of labor unions and their positive impact on players' salaries; the increased income of athletes that necessitated advice on matters ranging from taxes to estates; and the increase in players' opportunities to generate outside income through endorsement contracts.

As alluded to in the previous paragraph, the proliferation in the use of agents has been accompanied by an expansion in the range of services that they perform. The role of agents extends beyond the commonly held belief that their job is to negotiate a player's contract with his or her club. The functions performed by agents include the following:

> Contract negotiations, tax planning, financial planning, money management, investments, estate planning, income tax preparation, incorporating the client, endorsements, sports medicine consultations, physical health consultations, post-career development, career and personal development counseling, legal consultations and insurance matters.

Walter T. Champion, Jr., *Attorneys Qua Sports Agents: An Ethical Conundrum*, 7 Marq. Sports L.J. 349, 351-352 (1997).

The range of services that athletes' agents perform is indicative of the breadth of substantive expertise required in order for agents to effectively represent athletes. The problem is that few people have either the ability or expertise to perform all the tasks listed above. All too often perhaps out of ignorance or perhaps out of greed, agents take on more than they can competently handle. Unless they are part of a company, with individuals of diverse professional expertise ready to assist, agents may well overreach and perform at levels approaching negligence. Despite the useful functions provided by agents, other inappropriate agent conduct that is detrimental to athletes is also a pervasive part of the relationship. This chapter examines mechanisms that regulate the agent-athlete relationship and seek to enhance the likelihood that agents and athletes will fulfill their respective obligations. These mechanisms consist of a web of common law rules, state and federal legislation, and regulations promulgated by players associations. Our examination begins with an analysis of common law principles, derived principally from the law of agency and contract, which are instrumental in regulating the agent-athlete relationship.

B.   THE NATURE OF THE RELATIONSHIP

1.   Basic Duties

This section examines the legal duties agents owe to their athlete clients and the standard of care adopted by courts to determine if those duties are competently performed. The following excerpt provides the legal framework within which to consider these cases.

THE LEGAL BASIS OF THE RELATIONSHIP[1]

A great deal of criticism was directed toward Leland Hardy, the agent who negotiated the contract between then-top draft pick and NFL running back Ricky Williams and the New Orleans Saints. Critics assailed the length and the incentive-laden nature of the contract that resulted in Williams making a base salary far less than a player of his caliber could demand. In defending Hardy against criticism that questioned the agent's competence and negotiation skills, Williams stated as follows:

> I'm first and last when it comes to my decisions. . . . I don't work for my agent. My agent works for me. This was my decision and my decision alone. . . . When I got drafted, I told Leland I was going to get the deal done in the next two weeks. So we waited a little while longer . . . and after the course of negotiations [with Saints salary cap expert Terry O'Neil], Leland called and said, "I'm going to give you some options on contracts to look at," and when I told him what kind of a deal I wanted, he told me I shouldn't do it.

Williams reportedly told Hardy to reject a deal that would have paid him a guaranteed salary of $25.6 million over seven years. Instead, Williams signed a contract that paid him an upfront signing bonus of $8.8 million and required him to meet certain performance objectives in order to earn more than the yearly base salaries. . . .

---

1. Originally published in Kenneth L. Shropshire and Timothy Davis, The Business of Sports Agents (2d ed. 2008). Reprinted with permission of the University of Pennsylvania Press.

Williams's statement is instructive for two reasons. First, Williams demonstrates an appreciation for the most fundamental principle of the agent's relationship with his principal: ultimate decision making authority rests with the principal. In addition, Williams's statement illustrates that the relationship between sports agents and the athletes whom they represent are governed by the same core concepts that govern other principal/agent relationships. . . .

The agency relationship is defined as "the fiduciary relationship which results from the manifestation of consent by one person to another that the other shall act in his behalf and subject to his contract, and consent by the other so to act." The Restatement (Second) of the Law of Agency also provides definitions of agent and principal. The principal is "the one for whom action is to be taken." In the sports context, the athlete is the principal. The agent is "the one who is to act" for the principal. "The essential nature and character of the agency relationship is that the principal authorizes his agent to contract on his behalf with one or more third parties."

These definitions tell us that the agency relationship is consensual—typically expressed in a contract. This is certainly the case in the sports context in which the major sports leagues have developed model contracts for the agent-principal relationship. For example, the National Football League Players Association (NFLPA) has developed a "Standard Representation Agreement" for mandatory use by agents and their football-player clients. In addition to provisions governing the fees to which an agent is entitled, the NFLPA agreement sets forth general principles including the concept that the "Contract Advisor" acts "in a fiduciary capacity." The Uniform Athlete Agents Act provides the following definition: "'Agency contract' means an agreement in which a student-athlete authorizes a person to negotiate or solicit on behalf of the student-athlete a professional-sports-services contract or an endorsement contract."

The above definitions relating to agency also inform us that the most basic obligations that agents owe to their principals are defined not only by contract, but by the fiduciary characteristics of the relationship. A fiduciary is defined as "one who acts primarily for the benefit of another." Consequently, the essence of the principal/agent relationship spawns a fundamental obligation that the "agent owes his principal the fiduciary duty of undivided loyalty and the duty to act in good faith at all times. This fiduciary relationship is imposed by law upon the agent because the very nature of the agency relationship involves the principal entrusting his fortune, reputation, and legal rights and responsibilities to his agent whose actions, for better or worse, vitally affect the economic well-being and reputation of the principal."

As alluded to above, Ricky Williams's statement also reflects the basic notion that it is an agent's duty to carry out the desires of its principal. This certainly makes sense, as the agent acts not to carry on its own business affairs, but those of the principal. Thus it is the agent's duty to act in accordance with his or her principal's instructions even if the agent believes they are unwise. As stated by two commentators, "[a]n agent has the duty to obey all of his principal's lawful instructions no matter how arbitrary or capricious any of those instructions seem to the agent or anyone else. . . . By contrast, if the principal's instructions are illegal, immoral, unethical, or opposed to public policy, as where the principal instructs his agent to bribe another to obtain business for his principal, the agent has no duty to obey." Moreover, by acting on its principal's behalf, the agent assumes a duty that it "possesses a degree of skill commensurate with the job to be done and that he will use such skill with diligence." In exercising this duty of reasonable care and skill, it is important to emphasize that the agent does not guarantee or ensure that he or she will achieve the result desired by the client unless the agent has expressly agreed to do so. Rather the agent has fulfilled his or her duty by acting with the care and skill employed by a reasonable person under the same circumstances. . . .

Another basic duty of the agent to the principal seems particularly relevant in the sports context. The agent must account to its principal for all of the principal's funds that come into the agent's possession as a part of the agency relationship. Other basic duties that the agent owes to the principal include the duty to comply with the law, the duty to notify the principal of all matters that may affect the principal's interests, and the duty not to delegate their performance to another without the consent of the principal.

Finally, the agent owes a duty of loyalty and good faith to its principal. This duty precludes an agent from acting on behalf of parties adverse to his or her principal. Courts have attempted to incorporate these core concepts into rulings addressing matters ranging from agent malpractice to conflict of interest.

2.   *The Standard of Care*

ZINN v. PARRISH
644 F.2d 360 (7th Cir. 1981)

BARTELS, Judge.

This is an appeal in a diversity action by Leo Zinn from a judgment of the District Court for the Northern District of Illinois, Eastern Division, wherein he sought to recover agent fees due him under a personal management contract between him and the defendant Lemar Parrish. . . .

FACTS

For over two decades the appellant Zinn had been engaged in the business of managing professional athletes. He stated that he was a pioneer in bringing to the attention of various pro-football teams the availability of talented players at small black colleges in the South. In the Spring of 1970, Parrish's coach at Lincoln University approached Zinn and informed him that Parrish had been picked by the Cincinnati Bengals in the annual National Football League draft of college seniors, and asked him if he would help Parrish in negotiating the contract. After Zinn contacted Parrish, the latter signed a one-year "Professional Management Contract" with Zinn in the Spring of 1970, pursuant to which Zinn helped Parrish negotiate the terms of his rookie contract with the Bengals, receiving as his commission 10% of Parrish's $16,500 salary. On April 10, 1971 Parrish signed the contract at issue in this case, which differed from the 1970 contract only insofar as it was automatically renewed from year to year unless one of the parties terminated it by 30 days' written notice to the other party. There were no other restrictions placed on the power of either party to terminate the contract.

Under the 1971 contract, Zinn obligated himself to use "reasonable efforts" to procure pro-football employment for Parrish, and, at Parrish's request, to "act" in furtherance of Parrish's interest by: (a) negotiating job contracts; (b) furnishing advice on business investments; (c) securing professional tax advice at no added cost; and (d) obtaining endorsement contracts. It was further provided that Zinn's services would include, "at my request efforts to secure for me gainful off-season employment," for which Zinn would receive no additional compensation, "unless such employment (was) in the line of endorsements, marketing and the like," in which case Zinn would receive a 10% commission on the gross amount. If Parrish failed to pay Zinn amounts due under the contract, Parrish authorized "the club or clubs that are obligated to pay me to pay to you instead all monies and other considerations due me from which you can deduct your 10% and any other monies due you. . . ."

Over the course of Parrish's tenure with the Bengals, Zinn negotiated base salaries for him of $18,500 in 1971; $27,000 in 1972; $35,000 in 1973 (plus a $6,500 signing bonus); and a $250,000 series of contracts covering the four seasons commencing in 1974 (plus a $30,000 signing bonus). The 1974-77 contracts with the Bengals were signed at a time when efforts were being made by the newly-formed World Football League to persuade players in the NFL to "jump" to the WFL to play on one of its teams. By the end of [the] 1973 season Parrish had become recognized as one of the more valuable players in the NFL. He was twice selected for the Pro Bowl game, and named by Sporting News as one of the best cornerbacks in the league. Towards the end of the 1973 season, the Bengals approached Parrish with an offer of better contract terms than he had earlier been receiving. By way of exploring alternatives in the WFL, Zinn entered into preliminary discussions with the Jacksonville Sharks in early 1974, but decided not to pursue the matter once he ascertained that the Sharks were in a shaky financial position. In retrospect, Zinn's and Parrish's decision to continue negotiating and finally sign with the Bengals was a sound one, for the Sharks and the rest of the WFL with them folded in 1975 due to a lack of funds.

Shortly after signing the 1974 series of contracts, Parrish informed Zinn by telephone that he "no longer needed his services." By letter dated October 16, 1975 Parrish reiterated this position, and added that he had no intention of paying Zinn a 10% commission on those contracts. In view of its disposition of the case, the district court made no specific fact finding as to the amounts Parrish earned during the 1974-77 seasons. Zinn claims that the total was at least $304,500 including bonus and performance clauses. The 1971 contract by its terms entitled Zinn to 10% of the total amount as each installment was paid, and Zinn claims that he has only received $4,300 of the amounts due him. Accordingly, this suit was filed to recover the balance, plus interest at the rate of 5% per annum for vexatious delay in payment, pursuant to Ill.Rev.Stat., ch. 74, § 2.

In addition to negotiating the Bengals contracts, Zinn performed a number of other services at Parrish's request. In 1972 he assisted him in purchasing a residence as well as a four-unit apartment building to be used for rental income; he also helped to manage the apartment building. That same year Zinn negotiated an endorsement contract for Parrish with All-Pro Graphics, Inc., under which Parrish received a percentage from the sales of "Lemar Parrish" t-shirts, sweatshirts, beach towels, key chains, etc. The record shows that Zinn made a number of unsuccessful efforts at obtaining similar endorsement income from stores with which Parrish did business in Ohio. He also tried, unsuccessfully, to obtain an appearance for Parrish on the Mike Douglas Show. Zinn arranged for Parrish's taxes to be prepared each year by H & R Block.[2]

The evidence showed that, despite his efforts, Zinn was unable to obtain off-season employment for Parrish. In this connection, however, it was Zinn's advice to Parrish that he return to school during the off-season months in order to finish his college degree, against the time when he would no longer be able to play football. With respect to Zinn's obligation to provide Parrish with advice on "business investments," he complied first, by assisting in the purchase of the apartment building; and second, by forwarding to Parrish the stock purchase recommendations of certain other individuals, after screening the suggestions himself. There was no evidence that Zinn ever forwarded such recommendations to any of his other clients; he testified that he only did so for Parrish. In summing up Zinn's performance under the contract, Parrish testified as follows:

Did you ever ask Zinn to do anything for you, to your knowledge, that he didn't try to do?

I shall say not, no.

DISCUSSION

I

We turn, first, to the district court's decision that Zinn's contract was void under the 1940 Act. The Act makes void any contract for investment advice made by an unregistered adviser. 15 U.S.C. § 80b-15(b). . . . [EDS. The court concluded that Zinn had not provided services that brought him within the scope of the act and the contract was not void for his failure to be registered under the act. The court found that Zinn had not held himself out as an investment adviser. Moreover, acts that included Zinn giving Parrish advice regarding a home and an apartment building that Parrish purchased, Zinn engaging in certain managerial tasks at Parrish's request regarding the apartment building, and Parrish sending Zinn $1,500 to invest in Zinn's company did not bring Zinn within the scope of the act. The court concluded that Zinn provided ordinary business advice rather than securities advice. According to the court, "[I]solated transactions with a client as an incident to the main purpose of his management contract to negotiate football contracts do not constitute engaging in the business of advising others on investment securities."]

II

We consider next the district court's judgment that Zinn failed to perform the terms and conditions of his contract. . . . [T]he court concluded that Zinn "was unable to and did not provide the services which he was obligated to provide by the contract under which he sues." We address the findings seriatim.

Employment Procurement

Zinn's obligation under the 1971 Management Contract to procure employment for Parrish as a pro football player was limited to the use of "reasonable

---

2. Once Zinn secured the services of H&R Block for Parrish, his obligation ended. Parrish's contention on appeal that Zinn was at fault for a dispute he later had with the IRS requiring the payment of additional taxes is unfounded.

efforts." At the time the contract was signed, Parrish was already under contract with the Cincinnati Bengals for the 1970-71 season, with a one-year option clause for the 1971-72 season exercisable by the Bengals. Parrish could not, without being in breach of his Bengals contract, enter into negotiations with other teams for the 1971-72 season. The NFL's own rules prevented one team from negotiating with another team's player who had not yet attained the status of a "free agent." At no time relevant to this litigation did Parrish become a free agent. Thus, unless he decided to contract for future services for the year following the term of the option clause with the Canadian or World Football League, Parrish's only sensible course of action throughout the time Zinn managed him was to negotiate with the Bengals.

Parrish had no objection to Zinn's performance under the professional management contract for the first three years up to 1973, during which time Zinn negotiated football contracts for Parrish. A drastic change, however, took place in 1974 when a four-season contract was negotiated with the Bengals for a total of $250,000 plus a substantial signing bonus. At that time, the new World Football League came into existence and its teams, as well as the teams of the Canadian Football League, were offering good terms to professional football players as an inducement to jump over to their leagues from the NFL. In order to persuade Parrish to remain with the team, the Bengals club itself first initiated the renegotiation of Parrish's contract with an offer of substantially increased compensation. This was not surprising.

Parrish claims, however, that Zinn should have obtained offers from the World Football League that would have placed him in a stronger negotiating position with the Bengals. This is a rather late claim. It was not mentioned in Parrish's letter of termination, and is entirely speculative. Given what Zinn accurately perceived as the unreliability of any offers he might have obtained from the WFL, his representation of Parrish during this period was more than reasonable. As the district court properly noted, prior to the signing of the 1974-77 series of football contracts the needs of the defendant, the services of the plaintiff, and the fees paid by the defendant for those services were all "relatively modest." We conclude that up to that point it is impossible to fault Zinn in the performance of his contract, nor can we find any basis for Parrish to complain of Zinn's efforts in 1974 with respect to procuring employment for him as a pro-football player.

Other Obligations

We focus next on the other obligations, all incidental to the main purpose of the contract. The first of these refers to "negotiating employment contracts with professional athletic organizations and others." Unless this is with respect to a professional football contract, it is difficult to understand to what "professional athletic organizations and others" refers. At all events, there is no claim that there was a failure to negotiate employment contracts with other athletic organizations. And the evidence clearly shows that Zinn performed substantial services in negotiating with the Bengals by letter, telephone, and in person when he and Parrish were flown at the Bengals' expense to Cincinnati for the final stage of negotiations on the 1974-77 series of contracts.

Zinn was further obligated to act in Parrish's professional interest by providing advice on tax and business matters, by "seek[ing] . . . endorsement contracts," and by making "efforts" to obtain for Parrish gainful off-season employment. Each of these obligations was subject to an implied promise to make "good faith" efforts to obtain what he sought. . . . Under Illinois law, such efforts constitute full performance of the obligations. . . . *Id.* Until Parrish terminated the contract, the evidence was clear that Zinn made consistent, good faith efforts to obtain off-season employment and endorsement contracts. Indeed the district court found that Zinn at all times acted in good faith, with a willingness "to provide assistance within his ability." The district court confused success with good faith efforts in concluding that Zinn's failure to obtain in many cases jobs or contracts for Parrish was a failure to perform. Moreover, Zinn did give business advice to Parrish on his real estate purchases, and he did secure tax advice for him.

Parrish fully accepted Zinn's performance for the years 1970, 1971, 1972, and 1973 by remitting the 10% due Zinn under the contract. Parrish was at all times free to discharge Zinn as his agent before a new season began. Instead, he waited until Zinn had negotiated a series of contracts worth a quarter of a million dollars for him before letting Zinn know over the phone that his services were no longer required. That call, coupled with Parrish's failure to make the 10% commission payments as they came due, was a breach of the 1971 contract. [Citation omitted.] The district court was in error in considering Zinn's performance or non-performance during the period following that call, for Parrish by his own breach excused Zinn from any further duties under the contract. . . . Zinn had no obligations thereafter, and Parrish was estopped from asserting Zinn's non-performance as a defense to the suit on the commission fees due him. . . . Therefore Zinn has a right to recover a 10% commission on all amounts earned by Parrish under the 1974, 1975, 1976, and 1977 Bengals contracts.

We must disagree with the district court's interpretation of the terms of the contract, and Zinn's obligations thereunder, and also with its findings and conclusions concerning Zinn's performance. Insofar as the district court made any findings of fact which are inconsistent with the foregoing, we find them to be clearly erroneous. Consequently, judgment should be entered for Zinn. The decision of the district court is REVERSED, and the case REMANDED for further proceedings consistent with this opinion, including the calculation of damages and interest, if any, due Zinn.

WILLIAMS v. CWI, INC.

777 F. Supp. 1006 (D.D.C. 1991)

SPORKIN, District Judge.

This claim was brought by a young professional basketball player and his wife — Reginald and Kathy Williams — against a financial advisor and his associated companies to recover $50,000 that the Williams had entrusted to the defendant, Waymon Hunt through one of his affiliated companies. Plaintiffs also seek to recover certain costs and expenses that they incurred as a result of Mr. Hunt's actions. Plaintiffs have also prayed for punitive damages. . . .

I.   FINDINGS OF FACT

The facts clearly show that Reginald Williams, a gifted young professional basketball player, and his wife, Kathy, were unsophisticated in matters of finance and business. In the late 1980's, upon his graduation from Georgetown University where he had a distinguished career as a star basketball player, Mr. Williams signed a million-dollar-a-year contract with the Los Angeles Clippers, a National Basketball Association team. As a result of this lucrative contract, Mr. Williams and his wife were looking for opportunities to invest part of Mr. Williams substantial earnings.[1] He was directed to Waymon Hunt, a financial planner, and his company, CWI, Inc., by his wife's parents who had met Mr. Hunt through Clara Neeley who had previously worked in a local bank near Mrs. Williams' parents' home. Ms. Neeley was working for Mr. Hunt by the time the Williams were introduced to him.

The Williams first met Mr. Hunt in June of 1988. At that time, they agreed that Mr. Hunt would provide the Williams with financial and tax advice, including preparation of the Williams' tax returns. At approximately that time, Mr. Hunt brought to the Williams' attention an opportunity for investment involving the purchase of a product styled atmospheric reverse refrigeration heating units (hereinafter referred to as "units").[2] Because of how these units were supposed to perform, they were represented as being capable of producing an investment return and tax benefits.

The Williams agreed to buy $1 million worth of these units through a Hunt affiliated company, Success Through Association ("STA"). In September of 1988, before the Williams decided to make the investment, STA had only $301.50 in its bank account. . . . The Williams did not know this at the time nor were they aware that STA was a Hunt operated and controlled company. The Williams agreed to purchase the reverse refrigeration units under the following terms:

(a) The Williams would buy $1 million worth of units at a price of $10,000 each.

(b) The deal would be financed by a $50,000 down payment from the Williams and a loan to be arranged by STA for $950,000.

(c) STA was to serve as "non-exclusive agent for the purpose of leasing" the units.

(d) As agent, STA would "arrange for [the Williams] to receive confirmation of the purchase, financing and leases . . . of the units. . . ."

(e) In the event that the purchase could not be made, STA was to "return [the Williams] deposit in full within one week of [STA's] determination that [the Williams'] criteria cannot be met, but in no event later than December 16, 1988."

---

1. Like many young professional athletes, Mr. Williams was earning a considerable salary but had no experience in making investments or managing his money. He needed reliable expert advice and did not find any readily available. Because Mr. Williams' predicament appears to be a recurring problem for basketball players and other athletes who suddenly receive large disposable incomes, it seems that it would be appropriate for either the NBA, or the players' team, or the players' organization to develop a three-pronged program to assist these young people. First, they could offer at least some rudimentary education in business and finance. Second, they could assemble a package of low-risk blue chip investments for young players that will provide for their futures, as well as a system for referring them to wise and ethical professionals who can advise them on managing money. Third, they might offer a financial incentive for players to place a portion of their funds in a deferred investment program. Perhaps the League and the players' association could even establish their own high-grade, low-risk investment fund. In this way, young athletes would be protected from highly speculative ventures like the one involved in this case.

2. Now that there doesn't appear to be any current market for the Brooklyn Bridge and the supply of swampland in Florida has been depleted, it appears that atmospheric reverse refrigeration heating units are the wave of the future in get-rich-quick schemes and tax dodges, if anyone can figure out what they do.

Waymon Hunt agreed to arrange for the $950,000 in financing. The Williams signed a purchase agreement and forwarded $50,000 to STA, but no money was ever remitted to the purported manufacturer and seller of the units. Immediately upon STA's receipt of the $50,000, Hunt appropriated the money for his own use. Hunt did not obtain the $950,000 of financing.

Around the time of this transaction, there was an internal battle among the owners of the company that manufactured and sold the units, and the company was placed in receivership. While it later turned out that Mr. Hunt was able to contact a second seller and manufacturer, no purchase of the units ever came to pass. The parties have stipulated that the $50,000 sent to Mr. Hunt's company, STA, was never used to purchase reverse refrigeration units from any entity.

Mr. Hunt has attempted to deviate from the agreement he provided to the Williams, an agreement he drafted, by stating that he was entitled to the $50,000 as a finder's fee for locating financing for the project. He has produced two cashier's checks to show that he spent $68,000 on a fee he paid to a Georgia company, Aslanien Ltd., to obtain financing. He claims he did this on the Williams' behalf, but his testimony is not credible. While this Court cannot deny that Mr. Hunt may have discussed some financing for the purchase of the so-called reverse refrigeration units, it was clear he did not have the Williams in mind when he sent the first check for $34,000 to Aslanien, Ltd. since he wrote that check before the Williams ever signed a contract or purchase order for the units. It is not even clear that they knew about the investment opportunity before Hunt sent the check to Aslanien. Hunt admitted that the second check for $34,000 sent in November of 1988 was sent on behalf of other clients and not the Williams. It is clear that the $50,000 sent to STA by the Williams was to be a down payment on the units. It was not a finder's fee or any other kind of advance fee. Indeed Mr. Hunt conceded in his testimony before the Court that he owes the Williams the $50,000 they sent to him. Although he testified that he does not have the funds to pay the Williams now, he clearly acknowledges that under his agreement with them, he owes them the money.

The Williams are entitled to a judgment against Mr. Hunt on both contract and fraud theories. The contract provided that the money be repaid "if for any reason [STA] cannot fulfill [the Williams] request. . . ." It is also clear that Mr. Hunt's actions with respect to the Williams prove that Mr. Hunt defrauded the Williams. Hunt flat out misappropriated the money given to him. He dissembled when the Williams periodically asked about their investment and its status. He said "things were going fine" when they were not. He never told them that the $50,000 had not been sent to the manufacturer, nor did he inform them that he had not obtained financing. Hunt misrepresented the status of the arrangement when he prepared the Williams' tax returns on which Hunt took certain deductions and credits that could only be taken if a transaction had in fact been consummated. The Williams incurred significant expenses because of Mr. Hunt's violation of the contract and fraudulent conduct. They are entitled to recover the following sums from Hunt:

(a) $50,000, the amount of the down payment that was not returned;
(b) $2,500, the amount paid to Mr. Christopher Moss to prepare amended tax returns for the Williams;
(c) $3,000, the amount paid to Mr. Gary Lu to prepare amended California state tax returns;

(d) $21,000 for the penalties and interest owed to the IRS as a result of the improper tax returns filed by Mr. Hunt;

(e) $4,300 for the penalties and interest owed to the California state government as a result of the improper tax returns prepared by Mr. Hunt;

(f) $3,000 in attorney's fees incurred by the Williams to address the problems created by Mr. Hunt's activities;

(g) $500 for Mr. Moss's expert witness fee; and

(h) $3,000 for the costs of this litigation.

The Williams may not collect tax savings they claim they might have enjoyed had they received legitimate financial advice. It would be too speculative to assume post hoc what investments they might have chosen and what savings they might have received. . . .

Finally, plaintiffs seek punitive damages. The Court finds that they are warranted in this case. Mr. Hunt's egregious behavior was utterly unworthy of someone who calls himself a professional. His fraudulent conduct put the plaintiffs at risk of committing tax fraud. In recognition of these facts, the Court will award $50,000 in punitive damages, an amount that reflects the $50,000 down payment that was misappropriated and that was the basis for the grievous errors made on the Williams tax returns and caused them to incur substantial costs and expenses. . . .

II. CONCLUSIONS OF LAW

1. The defendant, Mr. Hunt, breached his contract with the plaintiffs. He should have returned their $50,000 and did not.

2. The defendant has defrauded the plaintiff in that he
   a) took money under false pretenses;
   b) misappropriated the money; and
   c) prepared improper tax returns. The defendant, Mr. Hunt, is liable to the plaintiffs who are entitled to the return of their $50,000.

3. The preparation of the improper and illegal tax returns was a direct and proximate cause of substantial expenses and costs incurred by the Williams in the sum of $37,300.

4. Defendant Hunt's conduct toward the Williams was intentional, willful, and egregious therefore the plaintiffs are entitled to punitive damages in the amount of $50,000. . . .

Judgment shall be entered for plaintiffs in the amount of $137,300.

NOTES AND QUESTIONS

1. *Analysis of* Zinn. In *Zinn*, Parrish argued, *inter alia*, that he was not obligated to pay his agent because the latter had failed to provide competent services. Parrish's position is one commonly asserted by athletes who have been sued for fees by their agents. In addition to arguing that agents have provided substandard care, athletes assert that agents breached other basic obligations owed to them or engaged in some form of illegal conduct.

In *Zinn*, what standard does the court employ in rejecting Parrish's defense? What was the source of the standard adopted by the court? What is the role of good faith in determining whether an agent has competently performed his or her duties?

2. *Agent and Athlete Compensation Disputes.* Players will not always prevail in lawsuits against their agents. Agents have argued successfully that they properly performed the services rendered. Moreover, an agent will argue that an athlete's financial plight is the result of the athlete's poor handling of his financial resources rather than the agent's mishandling. In one case, an agent successfully argued that the athlete's assets had been depleted because the athlete "wasted his assets by making exorbitant purchases, transferring large sums of money to his family members and friends, and refusing to save for the future or consider the consequences if he were injured or unable to continue playing football." *Clark v. Weisberg*, 1999 WL 543191, at *2 (N.D. Ill July 23, 1999).

Note also that a dispute between an agent and athlete may be subject to mandatory arbitration if the representation agreement includes such a clause. In a recent dispute, a court denied an athlete's attempt to defeat an agency's motion to compel arbitration. The court found that the contract language was sufficiently broad to require arbitration of the athlete's challenge to the enforceability of the parties' agreement. *Hicks v. HSInternational Sports Mgmt., Inc.*, 2009 WL 3698132 (D. Or. Oct. 27, 2009). See also *Adams v. Barnes*, 2010 WL 2484251 (N.D. Tex. June 17, 2010) (upholding arbitrator's award granting agent percentage of athlete's compensation earned over an eight-year period notwithstanding athlete's allegations that arbitrator was biased and engaged in misconduct); *Octagon, Inc. v. Richards*, 2010 WL 3932272 (E.D. Va. Oct. 5, 2010) (upholding arbitration award of $279,836.50 in favor of agency against athlete and rejecting track athlete's attempt to vacate the award); *Wasserman Media Group, Inc. v. Bender*, 2011 WL 1886460 (S.D.N.Y. May 16, 2011) (confirming arbitration award in favor of agency against basketball player).

3. *Analysis of* Williams. *Williams* illustrates that athletes can prevail in suits against agents and the substantive theories to which athletes will resort when suing their agents for alleged mismanagement of the athlete's financial affairs. Athletes have sued for breach of contract and negligence. They have also asserted fraud and breach of fiduciary duty claims as a means of potentially recovering punitive damages. See, e.g., *Jones v. Childers*, 18 F.3d 899 (11th Cir. 1994) (court holds agent committed fraud and RICO violations in relation to an investment scheme in which plaintiff and other investors participated); *Hilliard v. Black*, 125 F. Supp. 2d 1071 (N.D. Fla. 2000) (athletes asserted claims sounding in breach of fiduciary duty, breach of contract, conversion, negligence, and civil conspiracy in contending that Tank Black and his company improperly induced them to invest millions in investment schemes); see also *Gordon v. Vitalis Partners, LLC*, 2010 WL 381119 (N.D. Ill Jan. 27, 2010) (financial advisor owed fiduciary duty to client, a professional basketball player); *Terrell v. Childers*, 920 F. Supp. 854 (N.D. Ill. 1996); *Kendricks v. Grant Thornton Int'l*, 973 S.W.2d 348 (Tex. App. 1999); *Blatt v. Farley*, 276 Cal. Rptr. 612 (Cal. App. 1990).

The *Williams* court also identified several factors that render athletes particularly vulnerable to unscrupulous agents and financial managers. Do you agree with the court? What additional factors prompt athletes to place what often approaches blind trust in agents and financial managers to manage their financial affairs? A Securities and Exchange Commission (SEC) lawyer involved in the Tank Black matter, discussed in note 4, *infra*, commented, "Professional athletes are prime candidates for financial fraud. Many are unsophisticated in financial matters and suddenly find themselves with a six- or seven-figure salary. They're young, they're trusting, and they've been taken care of most of their lives." L. Jon Wertheim, *Web of Deceit*, Sports Illustrated, May 29, 2000, at 80.

4. *Financial Improprieties.* One of the more notorious cases of financial mismanagement and illegal conduct involved William "Tank" Black, who rose to fame as a successful agent of clients including Sterling Sharp, Vince Carter, Fred Taylor, and Ike Hilliard. An investigation resulted in allegations that Black not only made under-the-table payments to players, he also fraudulently involved athletes in a pyramid scheme and he laundered money. Black and his general counsel eventually pled guilty to federal charges that they laundered the money of drug traffickers. Black received a federal sentence of six years and ten months, followed by three years of supervised probation. In a separate lawsuit, a Florida jury convicted Black of conspiring to commit mail and wire fraud.

As illustrated by the Black matter, both criminal and civil actions may be initiated against agents and financial advisors for alleged financial irregularities. Corey Jenkins, a first-round draft pick of the Boston Red Sox, allegedly handed the $575,000 signing bonus he received from the team to Summit Management Company to pay bills, including his house and car payments. Summit allegedly failed to make the payments as promised. Based on these and other alleged improprieties, the U.S. Attorney in South Carolina issued a criminal indictment charging Summit with mail, bank, and wire fraud and money laundering. Former baseball player Mookie Wilson was awarded $450,000 in damages, which included $50,000 in punitive damages, in a civil action against Summit Management for the company's failure to pay his mortgage and other financial obligations, and the company's improper use of his credit card and power of attorney. As is often true in cases of financial mismanagement, however, it is highly questionable to what extent Summit will be able to pay the damages awarded against it. Similarly, former NBA star Scottie Pippen won an $11.8 million judgment against a financial advisor for financial improprieties, but it is unlikely Pippen will be able to recover any of the judgment.

On occasion, the SEC has taken an aggressive stance toward agents. For example, it filed a complaint alleging that financial adviser Donald Lukens "violated federal securities laws by systematically defrauding at least 100 (and perhaps more than 200) clients and brokerage customers collectively of tens of millions of dollars in a series of investment schemes during at least the mid-to-late 1990s." Lukens is said to have represented over 40 athletes at various times. In another case of financial impropriety, Howard J. Golub, the financial manager for athletes including Lance Parrish and Rich Karlis, was sentenced in 1989 to serve 10 to 12 years in prison and ordered to pay restitution of $163,600 to his clients following Golub's guilty plea to fraud and theft charges.

5. *Financial Advisors Regulations.* In footnote 1 of *Williams*, the district court admonished the NBA to implement reforms to protect athletes such as Mr. Williams. In 2002, the NFLPA became the first professional sports union

to attempt to curb the abuse of financial advisors with its promulgation of the NFLPA Regulations and Code of Conduct Governing Registered Player Financial Advisors. The regulations represent the NFLPA's response to incidents involving mismanagement of players' financial affairs. Those financial advisors who agree to participate, by applying to become registered in the voluntary program, are given "unique information on NFL players, their benefits, and compensation structure." *Introduction*, NFLPA Regulations and Code of Conduct Governing Registered Player Financial Advisors 3 (2002, as amended 2012). Notwithstanding language indicating that the NFLPA does not endorse a registered financial advisor, participating advisors will be perceived as having received the union's blessing. For a discussion of the NFLPA's Financial Advisor Regulations, see Shropshire and Davis, *supra*, at 140-143.

In 2006, then current and former NFL players, including Steve Atwater and Ray Crockett, sued the NFLPA alleging it had negligently performed background checks on Kirk Wright, a financial advisor, who defrauded investors, including the athletes, out of more than $100 million. (In May 2008, a federal jury convicted Wright of 467 counts of mail fraud, securities fraud, and money laundering. A few days later, Wright hung himself in his jail cell.) In 2007, a federal district court refused to dismiss the athletes' lawsuit, notwithstanding exculpatory language in the Financial Advisors Regulations, which states the NFLPA does not endorse any particular advisor and disclaims responsibility or liability for the acts of financial advisors who participate in its program. In 2010, the Eleventh Circuit Court of Appeals dismissed the former players' contract and tort claims after finding that they were subject to preemption under §301 of the National Labor Relations Act. *Atwater v. National Football League Players Assn.*, 626 F.3d 1170 (11th Cir. 2010).

6. *An International Perspective.* Internationally, agents perform the broad range of functions that agents perform in the United States. These include contract negotiation; "management and services in matters such as housing, taxes, social security, permits and licenses, financial planning, legal advice, career development and health . . . [;] and organization of sports activities and events." Robert Parrish, *Regulating Players' Agents: A Global Perspective*, in Players' Agents Worldwide: Legal Aspects (Robert C.R. Siekmann et al. eds., 2007). Similar to the conceptualization of agents in the United States, from an international perspective, the term agent refers to a person who acts as "an intermediary between a sports man or woman and other parties, for example between a football player (employee or potential employee) and a club (employer or potential employer)." *Id.*

> Not surprisingly, the problems that have beset the athlete agent industry in the United States arise internationally. Noting the high number of licensed agents in countries such as Spain, Italy and England, one commentator articulates that regulation of agents is necessary "'to introduce professionalism and morality to the occupation of players' agent in order to protect players whose careers are short.' Rephrased, the absence of player agent regulation will result in a lack of professionalism, immorality and a lack of protection for players."

Id. at 4.

This author goes on to describe *bungs*, tapping-up, and dual representation as examples of improper agent conduct that demonstrate the need for agent regulation:

> Bungs refer to illegal payments paid by and to agents (and others) in order to facilitate the transfer of a player. . . .
>
> Another FIFA and association rule . . . was the common practice of "tapping-up" which refers to a process, often facilitated by agents, whereby players are offered for sale to other clubs without the knowledge and consent of the club with whom the player is registered. . . . FIFA Players' Agents Regulations state that a licensed players' agent must never "approach a player who is under contract with a club with the aim of persuading him to terminate his contract prematurely or to flout the rights and duties stipulated in the contract. . . ."
>
> The third issue reaching prominence in the UK in the summer of 2006, . . . was the issue of dual representation. This refers to an agent who represents both a club and a player in negotiations. This is prohibited by . . . FIFA Players' Agents Regulations which state that a licensed players' agent is required "to represent only one party when negotiating a transfer."

Id. at 6.

As to the representation of a U.S. athlete wishing to play abroad, the agent faces a series of challenges. In all likelihood, the client is not at a skill level to play in the major league of his sport in the United States. The options are narrow as to where he can play abroad. The number of foreign (including U.S.) players per team may well be limited. While agents are not bound by union regulations, such as those in the United States, they may find other strictures in effect. These restrictions may vary among foreign leagues, and learning what they are can be challenging. Thus, obtaining the basic knowledge of business practices in other countries can be much more difficult than in the United States. Even the question as to whether there is something approaching a standard form contract may not be known. The drafting and negotiation of devices to protect the athlete if things go awry in a foreign country are no simple matter. For example, does an agent really want to have to seek enforcement of contractual obligations in the courts of a foreign country? If not, what are the alternatives? Added to this mix is the need to understand the complexities of the U.S. tax laws and the possible foreign immigration laws. As to immigration, the foreign club may be of assistance. As to tax, the agent advising the athlete is probably on his or her own. See Carole C. Berry, *Taxation of U.S. Athletes Playing in Foreign Countries*, 13 Marq. Sports L. Rev. 1 (2002).

PROBLEM 8-1

William Wills, a professional football player, hired Terry Davis as his sports agent. Davis, an attorney, is registered as a player representative with the NFLPA. Wills and Davis entered into the NFLPA's standard representation agreement between a player and contract advisor. From 2008 to 2012, with Wills's authorization, Davis received most of Wills's income. Davis gave Wills an allowance for living expenses and occasionally gave Wills advances against his salary when Wills asked for them. In addition to his salary, Wills was paid $20,000 a year to be invested in an annuity on his behalf. Davis was supposed to invest these amounts each year in an annuity for Wills but did not do so. Between 2008 and 2012, Davis used much of Wills's income to cover Davis's business and personal expenses. In 2011, Wills began to suspect that Davis was misappropriating his income and requested an accounting, which Davis said was forthcoming but never provided. Wills became certain that something was wrong when in early 2012 he was informed by the Internal Revenue Service (IRS) that he had not paid his tax deficiencies for years 2010 to 2012. Davis had told Wills that he was paying his taxes at the time he filed Wills's tax returns. The tax returns, which were signed by Wills, were filed by Davis, who had not paid the tax deficiencies. Wills has a tax liability of over $240,000 as a result of the actions taken by Davis. What causes of action may Wills assert in a lawsuit against Davis? See *Willoughby v. Commissioner of Internal Revenue*, 1994 WL 444427 (Tax Ct. 1994).

3.   Conflicts of Interest

One of an agent's fundamental obligations is not to compromise the interests of his or her principal. The requirement that an agent avoid conflicts of interest is derived from the duties of undivided loyalty and good faith that agents owe to their principals. In the sports context, numerous factual scenarios present real or potential conflicts of interest. Historically, the paradigmatic case of a conflict of interest has involved "nondisclosure by an agent of a financial interest that conflicts with that of the athlete client." Shropshire and Davis, *supra*, at 88. As the following discussion reveals, however, nondisclosure represents only one of the factual scenarios in which conflicts arise in the sports representation business. Nevertheless, we begin our discussion with an example that presents the paradigmatic conflict of interest.

PROBLEM 8-2

Determine whether a conflict of interest exists in the following scenarios and, if so, what mechanisms might be instituted to avoid a conflict.

a.   An agent represents players from different teams in the same sport.
b.   The situation in (a) applies, and the athletes play in the same position.
c.   An agent represents two players on different teams. After a trade, the two players end up on the same team. One player is considerably more valuable than the other player. The league has imposed a salary cap on the total amount of monies that an individual team can allocate to salaries.
d.   An agent encourages an 18-year-old female athlete, who has aspirations to become a sports commentator after her athletic career ends, to accept an offer to pose in a promiscuous photo for a liquor advertisement. The agent is aware that the athlete's parents are opposed to her accepting the offer, that other athletes who have followed this route later regretted having done so and have encountered difficulty moving from sport into television commentary, and that both the agent and athlete will make a great deal of money if she accepts the offer.
e.   An agent represents a player and a coach on the same team.
f.   A large sports management firm that represents players also enters into a sponsorship sales agreement with a professional league.

g. A large sports management firm represents a superstar basketball player while he is a member of the league. After the player retires and becomes co-owner of a professional basketball team, the sports management firm continues to represent him.

h. A sports management firm that represents baseball players is purchased by a large media conglomerate, which also owns an MLB franchise.

In responding to the preceding scenarios, discuss what additional facts would assist you in determining whether a conflict of interest exists. Also consider the *Argovitz* case and the following: Shropshire and Davis, *supra*, at 88-96; Melissa Neiman, *Fair Game: Ethical Considerations in Negotiation by Sports Agents*, 9 Tex. Rev. Ent. & Sports L. 123 (2007); Jamie E. Brown, *The Battle the Fans Never See: Conflicts of Interest for Sports Lawyers*, 7 Geo. J. Legal Ethics 813, 816 (1994); MLBPA Regulations Governing Player Agents (October 1, 2010), Section 5(B)(13); NFLPA Regulations Governing Contract Advisors, Section 3, *infra* at 694-695; NBPA Regulations Governing Contract Advisors, Section 3, *infra* at 699.

THE DETROIT LIONS, INC. v. ARGOVITZ

580 F. Supp. 542 (D. Mich. 1984)

DeMascio, District Judge.

The plot for this Saturday afternoon serial began when Billy Sims, having signed a contract with the Houston Gamblers on July 1, 1983, signed a second contract with the Detroit Lions on December 16, 1983. On December 18, 1983, the Detroit Lions, Inc. (Lions) and Billy R. Sims filed a complaint in the Oakland County Circuit Court seeking a judicial determination that the July 1, 1983, contract between Sims and the Houston Gamblers, Inc. (Gamblers) is invalid because the defendant Jerry Argovitz (Argovitz) breached his fiduciary duty when negotiating the Gamblers' contract and because the contract was otherwise tainted by fraud and misrepresentation. Defendants promptly removed the action to this court based on our diversity of citizenship jurisdiction. . . .

For the reasons that follow, we have concluded that Argovitz's breach of his fiduciary duty during negotiations for the Gamblers' contract was so pronounced, so egregious, that to deny rescission would be unconscionable.

Sometime in February or March 1983, Argovitz told Sims that he had applied for a Houston franchise in the newly formed United States Football League (USFL). In May 1983, Sims attended a press conference in Houston at which Argovitz announced that his application for a franchise had been approved. The evidence persuades us that Sims did not know the extent of Argovitz's interest in the Gamblers. He did not know the amount of Argovitz's original investment, or that Argovitz was obligated for 29 percent of a $1.5 million letter of credit, or that Argovitz was the president of the Gamblers' Corporation at an annual salary of $275,000 and 5 percent [of] the yearly cash flow. The defendants could not justifiably expect Sims to comprehend the ramifications of Argovitz's interest in the Gamblers or the manner in which that interest would create an untenable conflict of interest, a conflict that would inevitably breach Argovitz's fiduciary duty to Sims. Argovitz knew, or should have known, that he could not act as Sims' agent under any circumstances when dealing with the Gamblers. Even the USFL Constitution itself prohibits a holder of any interest in a member club from acting "as the contracting agent or representative for any player."

Pending the approval of his application for a USFL franchise in Houston, Argovitz continued his negotiations with the Lions on behalf of Sims. On April 5, 1983, Argovitz offered Sims' services to the Lions for $6 million over a four-year period. The offer included a demand for a $1 million interest-free loan to be repaid over 10 years, and for skill and injury guarantees for three years. The Lions quickly responded with a counter offer on April 7, 1983, in the face amount of $1.5 million over a five-year period with additional incentives not relevant here. The negotiating process was working. The Lions were trying to determine what Argovitz really believed the market value for Sims really was. On May 3, 1983, with his Gamblers franchise assured, Argovitz significantly reduced his offer to the Lions. He now offered Sims to the Lions for $3 million over a four-year period, one-half of the amount of his April 5, 1983, offer. Argovitz's May 3rd offer included a demand for $50,000 to permit Sims to purchase an annuity. Argovitz also dropped his previous demand for skill guarantees. The May 10, 1983 offer submitted by the Lions brought the parties much closer.

On May 30, 1983, Argovitz asked for $3.5 million over a five-year period. This offer included an interest-free loan and injury protection insurance but made no demand for skill guarantees. The May 30 offer now requested $400,000 to allow Sims to purchase an annuity. On June 1, 1983, Argovitz and the Lions were only $500,000 apart. We find that the negotiations between the Lions and Argovitz were progressing normally, not laterally as Argovitz represented to Sims. The Lions were not "dragging their feet." Throughout the entire month of June 1983, Mr. Frederick Nash, the Lions' skilled negotiator and a fastidious lawyer, was involved in investigating the possibility of providing an attractive annuity for Sims and at the same time doing his best to avoid the granting of either skill or injury guarantees. The evidence establishes that on June 22, 1983, the Lions and Argovitz were very close to reaching an agreement on the value of Sims' services.

Apparently, in the midst of his negotiations with the Lions and with his Gamblers franchise in hand, Argovitz decided that he would seek an offer from the Gamblers. Mr. Bernard Lerner, one of Argovitz's partners in the Gamblers agreed to negotiate a contract with Sims. Since Lerner admitted that he had no knowledge whatsoever about football, we must infer that Argovitz at the very least told Lerner the amount of money required to sign Sims and further pressed upon Lerner the Gamblers' absolute need to obtain Sims' services. In the Gamblers' organization, only Argovitz knew the value of Sims' services and how critical it was for the Gamblers to obtain Sims. In Argovitz's words, Sims would make the Gamblers' franchise.

On June 29, 1983, at Lerner's behest, Sims and his wife went to Houston to negotiate with a team that was partially owned by his own agent. When Sims arrived in Houston, he believed that the Lions organization was not negotiating in good faith; that it was not really interested in his services. His ego was bruised and his emotional outlook toward the Lions was visible to Burrough and Argovitz. Clearly, virtually all the information that Sims had up to that date came from Argovitz. Sims and the Gamblers did not discuss a future contract on the night of June 29th. The negotiations began on the morning of June 30, 1983, and ended that afternoon. At the morning meeting, Lerner offered Sims a $3.5 million five-year contract, which included three years of skill and injury guarantees. The offer included a $500,000 loan at an interest rate of 1 percent over prime. It was from this loan that Argovitz planned to receive the $100,000 balance of his fee for acting as an agent in negotiating a contract with his own team. Burrough testified that Sims would have accepted that offer on the spot because he was finally receiving the guarantee that he had been requesting from the Lions, guarantees that Argovitz dropped without too much quarrel. Argovitz and Burrough took Sims and his wife into another room to discuss the offer. Argovitz did tell Sims that he thought the Lions would match the Gamblers financial package and asked Sims whether he (Argovitz) should telephone the Lions. But, it is clear from the evidence that neither Sims nor Burrough believed that the Lions would match the offer. We find that Sims told Argovitz not to call the Lions for purely emotional reasons. As we have noted, Sims believed that the Lions' organization was not that interested in him and his pride was wounded. Burrough clearly admitted that he was aware of the emotional basis for Sims' decision not to have Argovitz phone the Lions, and we must conclude from the extremely close relationship between Argovitz and Sims that Argovitz knew it as well. When Sims went back to Lerner's office, he agreed to become a Gambler on the terms offered. At that moment, Argovitz irreparably breached his fiduciary duty. As agent for Sims he had the duty to telephone the Lions, receive its final offer, and present the terms of both offers to Sims. Then and only then could it be said that Sims made an intelligent and knowing decision to accept the Gamblers' offer.

During these negotiations at the Gamblers' office, Mr. Nash of the Lions telephoned Argovitz, but even though Argovitz was at his office, he declined to accept the telephone call. Argovitz tried to return Nash's call after Sims had accepted the Gamblers' offer, but it was after 5 p.m. and Nash had left for the July 4th weekend. When he declined to accept Mr. Nash's call, Argovitz's breach of his fiduciary duty became even more pronounced. Following Nash's example, Argovitz left for his weekend trip, leaving his principal to sign the contracts with the Gamblers the next day, July 1, 1983. The defendants, in their supplemental trial brief, assert that neither Argovitz nor Burrough can be held responsible for following Sims' instruction not to contact the Lions on June 30, 1983. Although it is generally true that an agent is not liable for losses occurring as a result of following his principal's instructions, the rule of law is not applicable when the agent has placed himself in a position adverse to that of his principal.

During the evening of June 30, 1983, Burrough struggled with the fact that they had not presented the Gamblers' offer to the Lions. He knew, as does the court, that Argovitz now had the wedge that he needed to bring finality to the Lions' negotiations. Burrough was acutely aware of the fact that Sims' actions were emotionally motivated and realized that the responsibility for Sims' future rested with him. We view with some disdain the fact that Argovitz had, in effect, delegated his entire fiduciary responsibility on the eve of his principal's most important career decision. On July 1, 1983, it was Lerner who gave lip service to Argovitz's conspicuous conflict of interest. It was Lerner, not Argovitz, who advised Sims that Argovitz's position with the Gamblers presented a conflict of interest and that Sims could, if he wished, obtain an attorney or another agent. Argovitz, upon whom Sims had relied for the past four years, was not even there. Burrough, conscious of Sims' emotional responses, never advised Sims to wait until he had talked with the Lions before making a final decision. Argovitz's conflict of interest and self dealing put him in the position where he would not even use the wedge he now had to negotiate with the Lions, a wedge that is the dream of every agent. Two expert witnesses testified that an agent should telephone a team that he has been negotiating with once he has an offer in hand. Mr. Woolf, plaintiff's expert, testified that an offer from another team is probably the most important factor in negotiations. Mr. Lustig, defendant's expert, believed that it was prudent for him to telephone the Buffalo Bills and inform that organization of the Gamblers' offer to Jim Kelly, despite the fact that he believed the Bills had already made its best offer to his principal. The evidence here convinces us that Argovitz's negotiations with the Lions were ongoing and it had not made its final offer. Argovitz did not follow the common practice described by both expert witnesses. He did not do this because he knew that the Lions would not leave Sims without a contract and he further knew that if he made that type of call Sims would be lost to the Gamblers, a team he owned.

On November 12, 1983, when Sims was in Houston for the Lions game with the Houston Oilers, Argovitz asked Sims to come to his home and sign certain papers. He represented to Sims that certain papers of his contract had been mistakenly overlooked and now needed to be signed. Included among those papers he asked Sims to sign was a waiver of any claim that Sims might have against Argovitz for his blatant breach of his fiduciary duty brought on by his glaring conflict of interest. Sims did not receive independent advice with regard to the wisdom of signing such a waiver. Despite having sold his agency business in September, Argovitz did not even tell Sims' new agent of his intention to have Sims sign a waiver. Nevertheless, Sims, an unsophisticated young man, signed the waiver. This is another example of the questionable conduct on the part of Argovitz who still had business management obligations to Sims. In spite of his fiduciary relationship he had Sims sign a waiver without advising him to obtain independent counseling.

Argovitz's negotiations with Lustig, Jim Kelly's agent, illustrates the difficulties that develop when an agent negotiates a contract where his personal interests conflict with those of his principal. Lustig, an independent agent, ignored Argovitz's admonishment not to "shop" the Gamblers' offer to Kelly. Lustig called the NFL team that he had been negotiating with because it was the "prudent" thing to do. The Gamblers agreed to pay Kelly, an untested rookie quarterback $3.2 million for five years. His compensation was $60,000 less than Sims', a former Heisman Trophy winner and a proven star in the NFL. Lustig also obtained a number of favorable clauses from Argovitz; the most impressive one being that Kelly was assured of being one of the three top paid quarterbacks in the USFL if he performed as well as expected. If Argovitz had been free from conflicting interests he would have demanded similar benefits for Sims. Argovitz claimed that the nondisclosure clause in Kelly's contract prevented him from mentioning the Kelly contract to Sims. We view this contention as frivolous. Requesting these benefits for Sims did not require disclosure of Kelly's contract. Moreover, Argovitz's failure to obtain personal guarantees for Sims without adequately warning Sims about the risks and uncertainties of a new league constituted a clear breach of his fiduciary duty.

One cannot help but wonder whether Argovitz took his fiduciary duty seriously. For example, after investing approximately $76,000 of Sims' money, Argovitz, with or without the prior knowledge of his principal, received a finder's fee. Despite the fact that Sims paid Argovitz a 2 percent fee, Argovitz accepted $3,800 from a person with whom he invested Sims' money. In March 1983, Argovitz had all of his veteran players, including Sims, sign a new agency contract with less favorable payment terms for the players even though they already had an ongoing agency agreement with him. He did this after he sold his entire agency business to Career Sports. Finally, Argovitz was prepared to take the remainder of his 5 percent agency fee for negotiating Sims' contract with the Gamblers from monies the Gamblers loaned to Sims at an interest rate of 1 percent over prime. . . . We find this circumstantial evidence useful only insofar as it has aided the court in understanding the manner in which these parties conducted business.

We are mindful that Sims was less than forthright when testifying before the court. However, we agree with plaintiff's counsel that the facts as presented through the testimony of other witnesses are so unappealing that we can disregard Sims' testimony entirely. We remain persuaded that on balance, Argovitz's breach of his fiduciary duty was so egregious that a court of equity cannot permit him to benefit by his own wrongful breach. We conclude that Argovitz's conduct in negotiating Sims' contract with the Gamblers rendered it invalid.

Conclusions of Law . . .

3.   The relationship between a principal and agent is fiduciary in nature, and as such imposes a duty of loyalty, good faith, and fair and honest dealing on the agent. . . .
4.   A fiduciary relationship arises not only from a formal principal-agent relationship, but also from informal relationships of trust and confidence. . . .
5.   In light of the express agency agreement, and the relationship between Sims and Argovitz, Argovitz clearly owed Sims the fiduciary duties of an agent at all times relevant to this lawsuit.
6.   An agent's duty of loyalty requires that he not have a personal stake that conflicts with the principal's interest in a transaction in which he represents his principal. As stated in *Burleson v. Earnest*, 153 S.W.2d 869 (Tex. Civ. App. 1941):

> [T]he principal is entitled to the best efforts and unbiased judgment of his agent. . . . [T]he law denies the right of an agent to assume any relationship that is antagonistic to his duty to his principal, and it has many times been held that the agent cannot be both buyer and seller at the same time nor connect his own interests with property involved in his dealings as an agent for another.

Id. at 874.

7.   A fiduciary violates the prohibition against self-dealing not only by dealing with himself on his principal's behalf, but also by dealing on his principal's behalf with a third party in which he has an interest, such as a partnership in which he is a member. . . .
8.   Where an agent has an interest adverse to that of his principal in a transaction in which he purports to act on behalf of his principal, the transaction is voidable by the principal unless the agent disclosed all material facts within the agent's knowledge that might affect the principal's judgment. *Burleson v. Earnest*, 153 S.W.2d at 874-75.

9.   The mere fact that the contract is fair to the principal does not deny the principal the right to rescind the contract when it was negotiated by an agent in violation of the prohibition against self-dealing. As stated in *Burleson*:

> The question, therefore, does not relate to the *mala fides* of the agent nor to whether or not a greater sum might have been procured for the property, nor even to whether or not the vendor received full value therefor. The self-interest of the agent is considered a vice which renders the transaction voidable at the election of the principal without looking into the matter further than to ascertain that the interest of the agent exists.

10. Once it has been shown that an agent had an interest in a transaction involving his principal antagonistic to the principal's interest, fraud on the part of the agent is presumed. The burden of proof then rests upon the agent to show that: his principal had full knowledge, not only of the fact that the agent was interested, but also of every material fact known to the agent that might affect the principal and that, having such knowledge, the principal freely consented to the transaction.

11. It is not sufficient for the agent merely to inform the principal that he has an interest that conflicts with the principal's interest. Rather, he must inform the principal "of all facts that come to his knowledge that are or may be material or which might affect his principal's rights or interests or influence the action he takes." *Anderson v. Griffith*, 501 S.W.2d 695, 700 (Tex. Civ. App. 1973).

12. Argovitz clearly had a personal interest in signing Sims with the Gamblers that was adverse to Sims' interest—he had an ownership interest in the Gamblers and thus would profit if the Gamblers were profitable, and would incur substantial personal liabilities should the Gamblers not be financially successful. Since this showing has been made, fraud on Argovitz's part is presumed, and the Gamblers' contract must be rescinded unless Argovitz has shown by a preponderance of the evidence that he informed Sims of every material fact that might have influenced Sims' decision whether or not to sign the Gamblers' contract.

13. We conclude that Argovitz has failed to show by a preponderance of the evidence either: (1) that he informed Sims of the following facts, or (2) that these facts would not have influenced Sims' decision whether to sign the Gamblers' contract
     a.   The relative values of the Gamblers' contract and the Lions' offer that Argovitz knew could be obtained.
     b.   That there was significant financial differences between the USFL and the NFL not only in terms of the relative financial stability of the Leagues, but also in terms of the fringe benefits available to Sims.
     c.   Argovitz's 29 percent ownership in the Gamblers; Argovitz's $275,000 annual salary with the Gamblers; Argovitz's five percent interest in the cash flow of the Gamblers.
     d.   That both Argovitz and Burrough failed to even attempt to obtain for Sims valuable contract clauses which they had given to Kelly on behalf of the Gamblers.
     e.   That Sims had great leverage, and Argovitz was not encouraging a bidding war that could have advantageous results for Sims.

14. Under Texas law, a nonbinding prior act cannot be ratified, and the right to seek rescission cannot be waived, unless the party against whom these defenses are asserted had full knowledge of all material facts at the time the acts of ratification or waiver are alleged to have occurred.

15. At no time prior to December 1, 1983, was Sims aware of the material non-disclosures outlined above; accordingly, the defenses of ratification and waiver must be rejected.

16. Defendants asserted defenses of estoppel and latches are also without merit.

17. As a court sitting in equity, we conclude that rescission is the appropriate remedy. We are dismayed by Argovitz's egregious conduct. The careless fashion in which Argovitz went about ascertaining the highest price for Sims' service convinces us of the wisdom of the maxim: no man can faithfully serve two masters whose interests are in conflict.

Judgment will be entered for the plaintiffs rescinding the Gamblers' contract with Sims.

IT IS SO ORDERED.

NOTE AND QUESTIONS

Analysis of Argovitz. Describe how Argovitz violated his duties of undivided loyalty, good faith, and fair dealing. Will an athlete's knowledge of a conflict or a potential conflict necessarily absolve an agent of liability for a conflict of interest? In *Argovitz* the court concluded that knowledge by Sims of Argovitz's ownership of the Gamblers franchise or approval of the application failed to absolve the agent of responsibility. Why? For another example involving alleged conflicts of interest, see *Mandich v. Watters*, 970 F.2d 462 (8th Cir. 1992) (discussing alleged conflict of interest resulting from a secret side deal negotiated between player's agent and team that deprived player of post-retirement salaries).

PROBLEM 8-3

Agent represents basketball players Williams and Smith, who play for different teams in the same NBA conference. Williams, who is considered by many to be the greatest basketball player of all time, is also the highest-paid athlete (salary and endorsements) in the world. One of Williams's teammates complains about the aggressive play of Smith, who is a solid player but is not a superstar. Williams takes these complaints to Agent, who is currently in the midst of negotiating Smith's contract with his current team, Team A. Team B has also expressed an interest in Smith. Agent rejects Team A's offer of $8.1 million for three years and secures for Smith a $9.6 million deal with Team B, which plays in another conference. Under his contract with Team B, Smith will receive only $6.4 million in his first three years. Agent says that the deal with Team B is better because it will pay Smith $3.2 million ($1.5 million of which is guaranteed) in his fourth year and has less deferred money. Team A's president says that Team A was willing to compromise on the issue of deferred money. What, if any, conflicts or potential conflicts are present here?

4.   *Competition for Clients: Conflicts Between Agents*

The underlying source of conflicts between agents is the fierce competition for clients. Factors that contribute to the intense competition that breeds conflict among agents include the significant fees that are potentially available if an agent signs an athlete; the increase in the number of agents between 1960 and 2000; the relatively stable pool of potential athlete-clients; and the ease with which provisions in standard agent representation agreements allow athletes to terminate their contracts with agents. As of June 2012, 112 of the 345 registered agents in the NBA had athlete clients. Records on file at the National Basketball Players Association (NBPA) show that eight of the certified NBPA agents represent 17 or more NBA players by themselves or with another agent. The same records also indicate that 27 of the certified NBPA agents represent at least 5 NBA players by themselves or with another agent. Fewer than 50 percent of the estimated 800 to 1,000 certified NFL agents had clients. An NFLPA-commissioned study reported that in 2003, "a small percentage of agents represent the majority of players; just over 100 agents—barely more than 10 percent of all agents—represent three of every four players on an active roster. And nearly 90 percent of agent fees are at the 3 percent maximum." M.J. Duberstein, *Agents and Players: An NFL Overview*, NFLPA, Sept. 2003.

The wave of consolidations that proliferated during the 1990s and resulted in what were then the four major sports representation firms—IMG, SFX, Octagon, and Assante—intensified the competition for clients. Consolidation increased the competition for clients among smaller firms and individual agents who lack the resources to compete effectively against larger firms. In addition, agents within larger sports representation firms often employ aggressive tactics in recruiting athletes; some of these tactics are products of resources that give larger athlete representation firms a competitive edge. For a discussion of industry consolidation and the demise of large representation firms such as SFX and Assante, and the emergence of new firms such as Create Artists Agency (CAA) and the Wasserman Group (WMG), see Shropshire and Davis, *supra* at 37-52.

A representative example of a termination provision in a standard player-agent contract follows.

NFLPA STANDARD REPRESENTATION AGREEMENT[3]

12.   Term

The term of this Agreement shall begin on the date hereof and shall remain in effect until such time that it is terminated by either party in which case termination of this Agreement shall be effective five (5) days after written notice of termination is given to the other party. Notice shall be effective for purposes of this paragraph if sent by confirmed facsimile or overnight delivery to the appropriate address contained in this Agreement. Notwithstanding the above, if this Standard Representation agreement is being signed by a prospective rookie

---

3. The complete NFLPA Standard Representation Agreement (as amended through March 2012) can be found in Appendix D of NFLPA Regulations Governing Contract Advisors (2012), available at http://images.nflplayers.com/mediaResources/files/PDFs/SCAA/2012_NFLPA_Regulations_Contract_Advisors.pdf.

player (a "rookie" shall be defined as a person who has never signed an NFL Player Contract) prior to the date which is thirty (30) days before the NFL Draft, then this Agreement shall not be terminable by Player until at least 30 days after it has been signed by Player.

If termination pursuant to the above provision occurs prior to the completion of negotiations for an NFL player contract(s) acceptable to Player and signed by Player, Contract Advisor shall be entitled to compensation for the reasonable value of services performed in the attempted negotiation of such contract(s) provided such services and time spent thereon are adequately documented by Contract Advisor. If termination pursuant to the above provision occurs after Player has signed an NFL player contract negotiated by Contract Advisor, Contract Advisor shall be entitled to fee prescribed in Paragraph 4 above for negotiation of such contract(s). . . .

If the Contract Advisor's Certification is suspended or revoked by the NFLPA or the Contract Advisor is otherwise prohibited by the NFLPA from performing the services he/she has agreed to perform herein, this Agreement shall automatically terminate, effective as of the date of such suspension or termination.

The following case, *Speakers*, illustrates the fierce competition for clients and the standards employed by courts in determining when competition exceeds what is permissible.

SPEAKERS OF SPORT, INC. v. PROSERV, INC.

178 F.3d 862 (7th Cir. 1999)

POSNER, Chief Judge.

The plaintiff, Speakers of Sport, appeals from the grant of summary judgment to the defendant, ProServ, in a diversity suit in which one sports agency has charged another with tortious interference with a business relationship and related violations of Illinois law. The essential facts, construed as favorably to the plaintiff as the record will permit, are as follows. Ivan Rodriguez, a highly successful catcher with the Texas Rangers baseball team, in 1991 signed the first of several one-year contracts making Speakers his agent. ProServ wanted to expand its representation of baseball players and to this end invited Rodriguez to its office in Washington and there promised that it would get him between $2 and $4 million in endorsements if he signed with ProServ—which he did, terminating his contract (which was terminable at will) with Speakers. This was in 1995. ProServ failed to obtain significant endorsement for Rodriguez and after just one year he switched to another agent who the following year landed him a five-year $42 million contract with the Rangers. Speakers brought this suit a few months later, charging that the promise of endorsements that ProServ had made to Rodriguez was fraudulent and had induced him to terminate his contract with Speakers.

The parties agree that the substantive issues in this diversity suit are governed by Illinois law, and we do not look behind such agreements so long as they are reasonable, . . . as this one is. . . .

Speakers could not sue Rodriguez for breach of contract, because he had not broken their contract, which was, as we said, terminable at will. Nor, therefore, could it accuse ProServ of inducing a breach of contract. . . . But Speakers did have a contract with Rodriguez, and inducing the termination of a contract, even when the termination is not a breach because the contract is terminable at will, can still be actionable under the tort law of Illinois, either as an interference with prospective economic advantage . . . (citations omitted), or as an interference with the contract at will itself. . . . Nothing turns on the difference in characterization.

There is in general nothing wrong with one sports agent trying to take a client from another if this can be done without precipitating a breach of contract. That is the process known as competition, which though painful, fierce, frequently ruthless, sometimes Darwinian in its pitilessness, is the cornerstone of our highly successful economic system. Competition is not a tort, . . . but on the contrary provides a defense (the "competitor's privilege") to the tort of improper interference. . . . It does not privilege inducing a breach of contract, *Soderlund Bros., Inc. v. Carrier Corp., supra*, 215 Ill.Dec. 251, 663 N.E.2d at 8—conduct usefully regarded as a separate tort from interfering with a business relationship without precipitating an actual breach of contract—but it does privilege inducing the lawful termination of a contract that is terminable at will. . . . Restatement, *supra*, § 768 comment i. Sellers (including agents, who are sellers of services) do not "own" their customers, at least not without a contract with them that is not terminable at will. . . .

There would be few more effective inhibitors of the competitive process than making it a tort for an agent to promise the client of another agent to do better by him, *Triangle Film Corp. v. Artcraft Pictures Corp.*, 250 F. 981 (2d Cir.1918) (L. Hand, J.)—which is pretty much what this case comes down to. It is true that Speakers argues only that the competitor may not make a promise that he knows he cannot fulfill, may not, that is, compete by fraud. Because the competitor's privilege does not include a right to get business from a competitor by means of fraud, it is hard to quarrel with this position in the abstract, but the practicalities are different. If the argument were accepted and the new agent made a promise that was not fulfilled, the old agent would have a shot at convincing a jury that the new agent had known from the start that he couldn't deliver on the promise. Once a case gets to the jury, all bets are off. The practical consequence of Speakers' approach, therefore, would be that a sports agent who lured away the client of another agent with a promise to do better by him would be running a grave legal risk.

This threat to the competitive process is blocked by the principle of Illinois law that promissory fraud is not actionable unless it is part of a scheme to defraud, that is, unless it is one element of a pattern of fraudulent acts. . . . By requiring that the plaintiff show a pattern, by thus not letting him rest on proving a single promise, the law reduces the likelihood of a spurious suit; for a series of unfulfilled promises is better (though of course not conclusive) evidence of fraud than a single unfulfilled promise.

Criticized for vagueness, . . . and rejected in most states, . . . the Illinois rule yet makes sense in a case like this, if only as a filter against efforts to use the legal process to stifle competition. Consider in this connection the characterization by Speakers' own chairman of ProServ's promise to Rodriguez as "pure fantasy and gross exaggeration"—in other words, as puffing. Puffing in the usual sense signifies meaningless superlatives that no reasonable person would take seriously, and so it is not actionable as fraud. . . . Rodriguez thus could not have sued ProServ (and has not attempted to) in respect of the promise of $2-$4 million in endorsements. If Rodriguez thus was not wronged, we do not understand on what theory Speakers can complain that ProServ competed with it unfairly.

The promise of endorsements was puffing not in the most common sense of a cascade of extravagant adjectives but in the equally valid sense of a sales pitch that is intended, and that a reasonable person in the position of the "promisee" would understand, to be aspirational rather than enforceable—an expression of hope rather than a commitment. It is not as if ProServ proposed to employ Rodriguez and pay him $2 million a year. That would be the kind of promise that could found an enforceable obligation. ProServ proposed merely to get him endorsements of at least that amount. They would of course be paid by the companies whose products Rodriguez endorsed, rather than by ProServ. ProServ could not force them to pay Rodriguez, and it is not contended that he understood ProServ to be warranting a minimum level of endorsements in the sense that if they were not forthcoming ProServ would be legally obligated to make up the difference to him.

It is possible to make a binding promise of something over which one has no control; such a promise is called a warranty. . . . But it is not plausible that this is what ProServ was doing—that it was guaranteeing Rodriguez a minimum of $2 million a year in outside earnings if he signed with it. The only reasonable meaning to attach to ProServ's so-called promise is that ProServ would try to get as many endorsements as possible for Rodriguez and that it was optimistic that it could get him at least $2 million worth of them. So understood, the "promise" was not a promise at all. But even if it was a promise (or a warranty), it cannot be the basis for a finding of fraud because it was not part of a scheme to defraud evidenced by more than the allegedly fraudulent promise itself.

It can be argued, however, that competition can be tortious even if it does not involve an actionable fraud (which in Illinois would not include a fraudulent promise) or other independently tortious act, such as defamation, or trademark or patent infringement, or a theft of a trade secret; that competitors should not be allowed to use "unfair" tactics; and that a promise known by the promisor when made to be unfulfillable is such a tactic, especially when used on a relatively unsophisticated, albeit very well to do, baseball player. Considerable support for this view can be found in the case law. . . . But the Illinois courts have not as yet embraced the doctrine, and we are not alone in thinking it pernicious. . . . The doctrine's conception of wrongful competition is vague—"wrongful by reason of . . . an established standard of a trade or profession," *Yoakum v. Hartford Fire Ins. Co., supra*, 923 P.2d at 423, or "a violation of recognized ethical rules or established customs or practices in the business community," *RTL Distributing, Inc. v. Double S Batteries, Inc., supra*, 545 N.W.2d at 591, or "improper because they [the challenged competitive tactics] violate an established standard of a trade or profession, or involve unethical conduct, . . . sharp dealing[, or] over-reaching." *Duggin v. Adams, supra*, 360 S.E.2d at 837. Worse, the established standards of a trade or profession in regard to competition, and its ideas of unethical competitive conduct, are likely to reflect a desire to limit competition for reasons related to the self-interest of the trade or profession rather than to the welfare of its customers or clients. We agree with Professor Perlman that the tort of interference with business relationships should be confined to cases in which the defendant employed unlawful means to stiff a competitor, Harvey S. Perlman, *Interference with Contract and Other Economic Expectancies: A Clash of Tort and Contract Doctrine*, 49 U. Chi. L. Rev. 61 (1982), and we are reassured by the conclusion of his careful analysis that the case law is generally consistent with this position as a matter of outcomes as distinct from articulation.

Invoking the concept of "wrongful by reason of . . . an established standard of a trade or profession," Speakers points to a rule of major league baseball forbidding players' agents to compete by means of misrepresentations. The rule is designed to protect the players, rather than their agents, so that even if it established a norm enforceable by law Speakers would not be entitled to invoke it; it is not a rule designed for Speakers' protection. In any event its violation would not be the kind of "wrongful" conduct that should trigger the tort of intentional interference; it would not be a violation of law. . . .

We add that even if Speakers could establish liability under . . . common law of torts . . . , its suit would fail because it cannot possibly establish, as it seeks to do, a damages entitlement (the only relief it seeks) to the agent's fee on Rodriguez's $42 million contract. That contract was negotiated years after he left Speakers, and by another agent. Since Rodriguez had only a year-to-year contract with Speakers—terminable at will, moreover—and since obviously he was dissatisfied with Speakers at least to the extent of switching to ProServ and then when he became disillusioned with ProServ of *not* returning to Speakers' fold, the likelihood that Speakers would have retained him had ProServ not lured him away is too slight to ground an award of such damages. . . . Such an award would be the best example yet of puffing in the pie-in-the-sky sense.

AFFIRMED.

NOTES AND QUESTIONS

1. *Analysis of* Speakers. In affirming the district court's summary judgment on behalf of the defendant, the court in *Speakers* acknowledged the competitive nature of the agent business as reflective of our business system. Consistent with this underlying premise, the court adopted the notion of the competitor's privilege, which validates a broad range of activities in which an agent can engage in attempting to lure clients away from a competitor. Nevertheless, the court circumscribed the parameters of the competitor's privilege. What limitation did the court impose on an agent's permissible conduct in attempting to recruit clients in an established relationship with an agent?

   In *Wright v. Bonds*, 117 F.3d 1427 (9th Cir. 1999) (unpublished opinion), the Ninth Circuit adopted a similar approach. It ruled that in order for Barry Bonds's former agent to establish interference with prospective economic advantage he had to establish that Bonds's new agent "engaged in some wrongful conduct beyond mere interference." The court found that plaintiff came nowhere close to carrying its burden of proof by introducing evidence that Bonds's new agent attempted to hide the fact that it had contacted the player; Bonds made false claims against his former agent after talking with his new agent; and Bonds's new agent had a history of contacting athletes under contract with other agents. See also *Roundball Enterprise, Inc. v. Richardson*, 616 F. Supp. 1537 (S.D.N.Y. 1985) (involving allegations that an agent improperly persuaded basketball player Michael Richardson to terminate relationship with his former agent). *Luchs v. Pro Tect Management Corp.*, 2009 WL 1364434 (Cal. App. 2 Dist. May 18, 2009) (providing a good description of the dissolution of the business relationship between agents);

see *IMG Worldwide, Inc. v. Baldwin*, 2010 WL 3211686 (N.D. Ohio Aug. 11, 2010) (describing confidentiality provision in agreement between representation firm and employee).

Is the range of permissible competitive behavior validated in *Speakers* and *Wright* too broad? One critic of the results reached in these cases argues that although these cases "appear legally accurate, they provide a broad spectrum of competition that borders on interference thereby tolerating unfair and corrupt dealing." Bryan Couch, Comment, *How Agent Competition and Corruption Affects Sports and the Athlete-Agent Relationship and What Can Be Done to Control It*, 10 Seton Hall J. Sport L. 111, 119 (2000). Other discussions of the competitiveness of the agent industry may be found in William Rothstein, *The Business of Sports Representation: Agent Evolution in the "Industry,"* 9 Va. Sports & Ent. L.J. 19 (2009); Timothy Davis, *Regulating the Athlete-Agent Industry: Intended and Unintended Consequences*, 42 Willamette L. Rev. 781 (2006); Lloyd Z. Remick and Christopher J. Cabott, *Keeping Out the Little Guy: An Older Contract Advisor's Concern, A Younger Contract Advisor's Lament*, 12 Vill. Sports & Ent. L.J. 1 (2005); R. Alexander Payne, *Rebuilding the Prevent Defense: Why Unethical Agents Continue to Score and What Can Be Done to Change the Game*, 13 Vand. J. Ent. & Tech. L. 657 (2011).

2. *Disparagement.* In the fierce competition for clients, agents try to convince athletes to sign with them by both expressing the virtues of their organization and by disparaging the competition. All sorts of negative information may be communicated regarding a competing agent. Experienced agents believe that the corruption in the industry has reached an all-time high. This has resulted in agents filing "an unprecedented number of lawsuits, charging one another with stealing clients, fraud, extortion and slander." Liz Mullen, *Sleaze Factor Off the Charts, Agents Allege*, Sports Bus. J. (June 24-30, 2002) at 1 & 30. A recent trend that may have contributed to the increase in suits alleging tampering was described as follows: "In the past, while agents competed against each other as aggressively as anyone could imagine, once the client came to an agreement with an agent, everybody in essence backed off. . . . That was the end of the game. What is going on now is once an agent signs a client, the second game begins." *Id.*

Bauer v. The Interpublic Group of Companies, Inc., 255 F. Supp. 2d 1086 (N.D. Cal. 2003), represents a fairly realistic depiction of the recruiting techniques employed by agents.

Asserting claims, *inter alia*, of intentional interference with contract, an agent, Frank Bauer, contended rival agents acted improperly in persuading a NFL rookie quarterback, David Carr, to terminate his representation agreement with plaintiff and to sign with them. Bauer alleged that Carr's decision to terminate their contractual relationship was a consequence of negative information concerning Bauer that was disseminated by defendants. In rejecting the plaintiff's claims, the court stated, in pertinent part, as follows:

> Bauer's first claim is for intentional interference with contract. "The elements which a plaintiff must plead to state the cause of action for intentional interference with contractual relations are (1) a valid contract between plaintiff and a third party; (2) defendant's knowledge of this contract; (3) defendant's intentional acts designed to induce a breach or disruption of the contractual relationship; (4) actual breach or disruption of the contractual relationship;

and (5) resulting damage." *Quelimane Co., Inc. v. Stewart Title Guaranty Co.,* 19 Cal. 4th 26, 55, 77 Cal. Rptr. 2d 709, 726, 960 P.2d 513 (1998). . . .

Bauer has presented no evidence from which a jury could reasonably conclude that any of the defendants committed acts designed to induce a breach or disruption of his contract with Carr. Although there is conflicting evidence as to whether Carr received an anonymous letter containing negative information about Bauer, there is no evidence that defendants sent the letter. Further, the evidence is undisputed that Carr regularly received anonymous letters containing negative information about other agents before he even signed with Bauer. Thus, even if the Court assumes that Carr did receive such a letter about Bauer, as it must in considering defendants' motion for summary judgment, there is no evidence tying that letter to any of the defendants or their agents. There is no evidence that any of the defendants ever made any disparaging comments about Bauer to Carr. There is no evidence that any of the defendants even spoke to Carr during the time he was under contract to Bauer and before he notified Bauer that he was terminating their contract. It would be mere speculation to conclude that the letter must have been sent by the defendants.

In a suit for intentional interference with contract, the plaintiff must show that "the act complained of was the proximate cause of the injury." *Augustine v. Trucco,* 124 Cal. App. 2d 229, 246, 268 P.2d 780 (1954). Bauer has no evidence that any acts by the defendants caused Carr to terminate his contract with Bauer. Carr was the one who initiated contact with the defendants *after* he decided to terminate his contract with Bauer. The National Football League Players Association Regulations Governing Contract Advisors permits agents to speak with players who are under contract with another agent if the player is the one who initiates the communication. The evidence is undisputed that defendants began negotiating with Carr at his request after he had already made his decision to terminate his contract with Bauer. Although there is a dispute of fact as to whether Carr signed a contract with defendants on January 17 or January 22, that dispute is irrelevant because Carr's decision to terminate Bauer occurred before either of those dates.

No reasonable jury could find that defendants induced Carr to terminate his contract with Bauer. Accordingly, summary judgment is granted for defendants on Bauer's claim for intentional interference with contract.

Id. at 1093-1095.

In the aftermath of the dispute in *Bauer,* the NFLPA changed the termination provisions of its Standard Representation Agreement. Generally, either the agent or athlete may terminate the relationship effective five days after written notice is given to the other party. However, an agreement between an agent and a rookie (a player who has never signed an NFL player contract) cannot be terminated by the rookie until 30 days after the player signed the representation agreement.

3. *The Issue of Race.* In an interesting situation with racial implications, Lamont Smith, an African American NFL sports agent, filed a federal lawsuit against IMG agent Tom Condon. Smith's suit alleged that Condon, who is white, "may have told other current or perspective NFL players . . . that they should not become clients of plaintiff Smith because Smith had alienated general managers of NFL clubs by 'playing the race card.'" Liz Mullen, *Lawsuit Targets IMG Football Chief Condon,* Sports Bus. J. (Sept. 8-14, 2003). According to Smith, Condon made his statements when they competed to sign clients during the 2001-2003 NFL drafts and with the alleged intent of blackballing.

"It leads a player to think you are not accepted in NFL circles, which could not be further from the truth." *Id.*

Assuming that Condon made the comments asserted in Smith's complaint, would they exceed the bounds of what is considered permissible competition? For discussions of race and sports agents, see Shropshire and Davis, *supra*, at 55-58; James G. Sammataro, *Business and Brotherhood, Can They Coincide? A Search into Why Black Athletes Do Not Hire Black Agents*, 42 Howard L.J. 535 (1999).

Despite the barriers many African American sports agents believe they encounter, some have developed impressive rosters of clients. In June 2004, *Sports Illustrated* listed the 101 most influential minorities in sports. Richard Deitsch et al., *Same Game, New Players*, Sports Illustrated, June 28, 2004, at 80. Among the agents included on the list and notable clients they represented at the time the article was published were Aaron Goodwin (clients: LeBron James, Chris Webber, and Dwight Howard); Bill Duffy (clients: Yao Ming and Carmelo Anthony); Eugene Parker (clients: Larry Fitzgerald, Ahmad Carroll, and Chris Perry); Bill Strickland and his partner, Mason Ashe (clients: Rasheed Wallace, Allan Houston, and Daunte Culpepper); Lamont Smith (clients: Eddie George, Jerome Bettis, Samari Rolle, and Trevor Pryce); James Tanner, Jr. (clients: Tim Duncan and Shane Battier); and brothers Carl and Kevin Poston (clients: Kellen Winslow, Jr., Chris Gamble, Reggie Williams, Ty Law, Charles Woodson, and Charles Rogers).

Carl and Kevin Poston attracted considerable attention because of their negotiating style and their success in signing high-profile African American athletes. Professor Kenneth Shropshire describes the brothers' style as "almost a take-no-prisoners approach . . . that can work to a client's advantage." Mark Hyman, *Playing as Rough as Linebackers: The Controversial Poston Brothers Are Rewriting the Rules on NFL Salaries*, Bus. Week, Sept. 27, 2004. On the other hand, some agents accused the Postons of being too confrontational. It was reported that some NFL executives avoided clients represented by the Postons because of the agents' approach to negotiation. *Id.*

4. *Consolidation and Conflict.* The consolidations of the 1990s have shown fault lines in the new millennium. Many agents who helped to create larger firms during the 1990s have since departed to create smaller representation firms or have been absorbed by emerging firms such as CAA. Unfortunately, these departures often have been accompanied by allegations of client stealing. A paradigmatic example is the dispute between David Dunn and Leigh Steinberg. Dunn, a partner in what was then Steinberg, Moorad & Dunn (a division of Assante), departed to start his own firm. His new firm represented several clients of his previous firm. This led to a lawsuit in which the Steinberg firm alleged that Dunn's new firm conspired to lure clients away from it and that Dunn violated a noncompete covenant. A Los Angeles jury awarded Steinberg $44.66 million in damages after it decided Dunn had breached his contract, engaged in unfair competition, and had acted with fraud and malice. In 2003 Steinberg repurchased the remnants of his firm from Assante and formed a new firm.

In 2005, a California appellate court vacated the $44.66 million jury award. *Steinberg Moorad & Dunn Inc. v. Dunn*, 136 Fed. Appx. 6 (9th Cir. 2005). Among the grounds relied on by the appellate court was the trial court's failure to instruct the jury that the noncompete clause was invalid under California law. The court pointed to a state statute that it interpreted as "establishing that non-competition clauses in an employment agreement are unenforceable to the extent that they limit the employee's ability to compete after leaving, whether or not the employee is at-will and whether or not his term of employment has ended." *Id.* at *5.

The NFLPA's suspension of Dunn was held in abeyance after Dunn filed for personal Chapter 11 bankruptcy in response to the $44 million judgment. On March 1, 2006, however, a federal district court judge agreed with the NFLPA's argument that Dunn lost the right to retain his certification without the union's permission after he entered bankruptcy. Liz Mullen, *NFL Union Wins a Round in Fight to Discipline Agent Dunn*, Sports Bus. J., March 13, 2006, at 14. The court also ruled, however, that it was within the jurisdiction of the bankruptcy court judge to determine whether and when to lift the stay so as to allow the NFLPA to proceed with disciplinary action against Dunn. *Id.* In 2006, the NFLPA and Dunn reached a settlement that allowed the union to proceed with disciplinary action against him. Liz Mullen, *NFLPA Set to Resume Disciplinary Action Against Agent Dunn*, Sports Bus. J., May, 15, 2006, at 14.

In November 2006, Dunn agreed with the NFLPA to accept an 18-month suspension. *Dunn and NFLPA Agree Suspension Will Last 18 Months*, Sports Bus. J., Nov. 27, 2006. The settlement between Dunn and the NFLPA occurred just before Dunn's appeal was to be heard by an arbitrator.

In a case involving a similar fact scenario, Eric Fleisher sued his former protégé, Andy Miller. Following Miller's departure from the firm to establish his own agent firm, Fleisher sued, alleging Miller improperly signed clients, including NBA star Kevin Garnett. Fleisher alleged that Miller secretly signed clients while still employed at the firm. In October 2002, a jury agreed with Fleisher and awarded him $4.6 million in damages.

C.   REGULATIONS AND LEGISLATION

Problems within the agent industry that we have thus far examined in this chapter have hastened the call for better solutions. The materials in this section explore the various efforts that have been and are being made to sanction inappropriate conduct by sports agents. Incidents occurring in 2009 and 2010 underscored the need to regulate the industry but also revealed that regulatory efforts will not completely solve problems within the industry.

On June 10, 2010, an NCAA investigation and subsequent report revealed that former University of Southern California running back, Reggie Bush, had received impermissible benefits from two men attempting to form a sports agency in conjunction with Bush and his family. According to the NCAA, the improper benefits included cash, merchandise, an automobile, housing, hotel lodging and airline transportation. That same NCAA investigative report revealed that former University of Southern California guard O.J. Mayo had also received impermissible benefits from a representative of a sports agency while playing at the school. The violations caused both Bush and Mayo to be permanently disassociated from USC and resulted in Bush voluntarily relinquishing his Heisman trophy award. Also in 2010 it was found that during the recruitment of eventual Heisman trophy winning Auburn quarterback, Cam Newton, a man said to be representing Newton attempted to secure a six-figure sum in exchange for Newton signing a National Letter of Intent (NLI) to attend Mississippi State University. The investigation resulted in findings of improper dealings on the part of Kenny Rodgers and Cecil Newton, Cam Newton's father. Erick Smith, *NCAA Rules Auburn's Newton Eligible for Now After Rules Violation*, USA Today, Dec. 1, 2010, http://content.usatoday .com/communities/campusrivalry/post/2010/12/auburn-cam-newton-ncaa-eligible/1.

On October 11, 2010, the NCAA ruled two University of North Carolina football players permanently ineligible for taking improper benefits from agents. The two players, Greg Little and Robert Quinn, were found to have accepted benefits totaling $4,952 and $5,642, respectively. The gifts provided by the agents included travel accommodations to various locations, diamond earrings, and black diamond watches. Erick Smith, *Marvin Austin, Greg Little, Robert Quinn All Will Not Play Again for North Carolina*, USA Today, Oct. 11, 2010, http://con tent.usatoday.com/communities/campusrivalry/post/2010/10/marvin-aus tin-greg-little-robert-quinn-all-will-not-play-again-for-north-carolina/1. A third University of North Carolina football player, Marvin Austin, was dismissed from the team after it was revealed that he had accepted over $10,000 in improper benefits. The fallout from the UNC scandal led to long-time NFL agent, the late Gary Wichard, receiving a nine-month suspension from the NFLPA for having impermissible contact with Austin. *Gary Wichard Suspended 9 Months*, ESPN.com, Dec. 3, 2010, http://sports.espn.go.com/nfl/news/story?id=5880708. See also Timothy G. Nelson, *Flag on the Play: The Ineffectiveness of Athlete-Agent Laws — and How North Carolina Can Take Advantage of a Scandal to Be a Model for Reform*, 90 N.C. L. Rev. 800 (2012) (discussing evolution of sports agent's role in America's athletics and agent regulations and how the UNC case presents an opportunity to affect change on a national scale).

The NCAA possesses no authority to regulate sports agents. The NCAA attempts, however, to stymie what it considers inappropriate agent conduct through a set of rules intended to regulate the interaction between student-athletes and agents. For example, NCAA rules prohibit student-athletes from receiving benefits from agents. Therefore, a student-athlete who receives money or other benefits from an agent risks losing his or her amateur status and being deemed, by the NCAA, ineligible to participate in intercollegiate competition. See 2012-13 NCAA Division I Manual, Bylaw 12.3.

1. Federal Regulation

a. The Sports Agent Responsibility Trust Act

In September 2004, President George W. Bush signed into law the Sports Agent Responsibility Trust Act (SPARTA), the first federal legislation that specifically regulates sports agents. P.L. (Public Law) 108-304. SPARTA is modeled after key provisions of the Uniform Athlete Agents Act (UAAA), which numerous states have adopted and is discussed *infra*. SPARTA does not preempt but rather supplements state requirements imposed by the UAAA. Indeed, SPARTA states that it is the "sense of Congress that States should enact the Uniform

Athletes Agents Act . . . to protect student athletes and the integrity of amateur sports from unscrupulous sports agents." *Id.*

Like the UAAA, SPARTA prohibits agents from using improper inducements (e.g., cash payments and gifts) and misleading information to recruit student-athletes. In this regard, SPARTA makes it unlawful for an athlete agent to:

(1) directly or indirectly recruit or solicit a student athlete to enter into an agency contract, by
    (A) giving any false or misleading information or making a false promise or representation; or
    (B) providing anything of value to a student athlete or anyone [including family and friends] associated with the student athlete before the student athlete enters into an agency contract, including any consideration in the form of a loan, or acting in the capacity of a guarantor or co-guarantor for any debt;
(2) enter into an agency contract with a student athlete without providing the student athlete with the disclosure document described in subsection (b); or
(3) predate or postdate an agency contract.

Id. at 2.

The disclosure document, referred to in (2) above, must conspicuously notify student-athletes, and parents or guardians of athletes under the age of 18, of the potential loss of eligibility to compete as an amateur if he or she signs an agency agreement. Within 72 hours of signing an agency contract or before the next athletic event in which the athlete is eligible to participate, both the student-athlete and agent "by whom you are agreeing to be represented must notify the athletic director of the educational institution at which you are enrolled, or other individual responsible for athletic programs at such educational institution, that you have entered into an agency contract." *Id.* at 2, 3. Violations of SPARTA constitute unfair and deceptive acts or practices under the Federal Trade Commission Act and will be enforced by the FTC. Under 15 U.S.C. §§41 et seq., which SPARTA incorporates by reference, such acts are punishable by fines up to $10,000 per incident. 15 U.S.C. §45(l) and (m).

Upon proper notification to the FTC, SPARTA specifically authorizes state attorney generals to bring civil actions in federal court if a

> "State has reason to believe that an interest of the residents of that State has been or is threatened or adversely affected" by a violation of the SPARTA. States may seek the following relief in these civil actions:
> (A) enjoin the practice;
> (B) enforce compliance with this Act; or
> (C) obtain damages, restitution, or other compensation on behalf of residents of the State.

P.L. 108-304 at 3. If the FTC has instituted an action against a defendant, a state may not institute an action against the named defendant during the pendency of the FTC complaint. SPARTA also permits individuals to seek "remedies available under existing Federal or State law or equity." *Id.* at 4.

b.   Non-Agent-Specific Federal Legislation

Prior to the enactment of SPARTA, despite calls for it, no federal legislation existed that specifically regulated sports agents. Nevertheless, from time to time, federal criminal laws have been used to address improper conduct by agents. For example, prosecutors employed the Racketeer Influenced and Corrupt Organizations Act (RICO) and mail fraud statutes in *U.S. v. Bloom*, 997 F.2d 1219 (7th Cir. 1993), 913 F.2d 388 (7th Cir. 1990). Norby Walters, a former nightclub owner, and Lloyd Bloom, who served as his runner, enticed 58 student-athletes, while they had remaining collegiate eligibility, to sign exclusive representation agreements with them. The secret agreements were postdated to be effective after the expiration of the athletes' collegiate athletic eligibility. The athletes submitted false information to their universities regarding any restrictions on their eligibility. Facts providing the predicate for the alleged RICO violation included alleged extortion, mail fraud, and wire fraud. The mail fraud allegedly was committed against the NCAA and occurred when the athletes had their institutions send written documents to the NCAA indicating that the athletes were eligible for intercollegiate competition. The matter became a mail fraud case after prosecutors agreed to dismiss the RICO violations as a part of a plea bargain. A failure of the prosecutors to prove the elements of mail fraud resulted in the Seventh Circuit's dismissal of the claim against Walters. *U.S. v. Bloom*, 997 F.2d 1219 (7th Cir. 1993).

Despite the setback to the U.S. Attorney's office in *Bloom*, federal prosecutors have not only relied on RICO and mail fraud laws, but also on SEC regulations and federal laws prohibiting money laundering as grounds for asserting federal criminal charges against agents who have inappropriately handled their athlete-clients' assets. The cases involving Tank Black and Summit Management Company illustrate the use of non-agent-specific federal criminal laws to prosecute agents. These and other cases are discussed *supra*.

The use of non-agent-specific statutes and the implications of improper payments to student-athletes are demonstrated in *United States v. Piggie*, 303 F.3d 923 (8th Cir. 2002). Myron Piggie developed a scheme whereby he paid elite high school players to compete for his Amateur Athletic Union (AAU) summer basketball team. "The payments were designed to retain top athletes on his team, gain access to sports agents, obtain profitable sponsorship contracts, and forge ongoing relationships with players to his benefit when the athletes joined the National Basketball Association (NBA)." *Id.* at 924. Between 1995 and 1998, Piggie realized at least $677,760 in income from his scheme. He also anticipated receiving a percentage of the compensation his players would earn after they signed contracts with NBA teams.

The court described the consequences of Piggie's scheme as follows:

After accepting Piggie's payments to play AAU basketball, Jaron Rush, Maggette, Kareem Rush, and Williams submitted false and fraudulent Student-Athlete Statements to the universities where they were to play intercollegiate basketball.[3] These four athletes falsely certified that they had not previously received payments to play basketball. The athletes delivered through the U.S. Postal Service signed letters of intent asserting their eligibility. Based upon the false assertions that these athletes were eligible amateurs, the University of California, Los Angeles (UCLA);

---

3. Young signed a contract in 1998, directly out of high school, to play for the NBA Detroit Pistons, and did not play intercollegiate basketball.

Duke University (Duke); the University of Missouri-Columbia (Missouri); and Oklahoma State University (OSU) (collectively Universities) awarded scholarships to these athletes, enrolled them in classes, and allowed them to play on NCAA basketball teams.

NCAA regulations permit universities to award only thirteen basketball scholarships per year. When Piggie's payments to these players were discovered, the Universities became subject to NCAA penalties. Each school lost the use of one of the thirteen scholarships and lost the value of each player's participation due to the player's NCAA-required suspension. The scholarships were forfeited, and the Universities lost the opportunity to award the scholarships to other top amateur athletes, who had actual eligibility to play intercollegiate basketball. In 1999 and 2000, UCLA lost the benefit of playing Jaron Rush, the $44,862.88 scholarship awarded to him, and also forfeited $42,339 in tournament revenue; Missouri lost the benefit of playing Kareem Rush, and the $9,388.92 scholarship awarded to him; and OSU lost the benefit of playing Williams and the $12,180 scholarship awarded to him. Duke provided Maggette with a $32,696 scholarship for the 1998-1999 season based upon the false assertion that he was an eligible amateur. As a result of the ineligible athlete's participation, the validity of Duke's entire 1998-1999 season was called into question.[4]

NCAA regulations also required each of the four Universities involved to conduct costly internal investigations after Piggie's scheme was discovered. UCLA spent $59,225.36 on the NCAA-mandated investigation of Jaron Rush, Duke spent $12,704.39 on the NCAA-mandated investigation of Maggette, Missouri spent $10,609 on the NCAA-mandated investigation of Kareem Rush, and OSU spent $21,877.24 on the NCAA-mandated investigation of Williams. The total monetary loss to the Universities was $245,882.79. The scandal following the disclosure of Piggie's scheme caused further intangible harms to the Universities including adverse publicity, diminished alumni support, merchandise sales losses, and other revenue losses.

Pembroke Hill High School (Pembroke), where Jaron and Kareem Rush played high school basketball, sustained a loss of $10,733.89 in investigative costs and forfeiture of property as a result of the conspiracy. Pembroke was placed on probation by the State of Missouri after the violations of Jaron and Kareem Rush were discovered and a mandatory investigation of the matter was concluded. . . .

Id. at 925-926.

Federal prosecutors charged Piggie with violations of non-agent-specific statutes. He pled guilty to conspiracy to commit mail and wire fraud in violation of 18 U.S.C. §371 and failure to file an income tax return in violation of 26 U.S.C. §7203. Thereafter, Piggie received a 37-month prison term and was ordered to pay $324,279.87 in restitution. On appeal, Piggie argued the court miscalculated the amount of loss to the various institutions in enhancing his base offense levels under federal sentencing guidelines. In rejecting his appeal, the court found that the loss was appropriately calculated given the tangible and intangible harm to both the institutions and athletes who were impacted by Piggie's scheme.

2.   *State Regulation: The Uniform Athlete Agents Act*

Two bodies of state law may be available to regulate the agent profession. One level consists of non-agent-specific civil and criminal laws that might be invoked to penalize agents for improprieties. The other level consists of agent-specific

---

4. Maggette played the full 1998-1999 season for Duke before Piggie's scheme was uncovered.

legislation. Prior to the year 2000, agent-specific legislation was in effect in 28 states (the state of Washington had adopted such legislation, but repealed it in 1999). States achieved a modicum of success in prosecuting agents under these statutes. For example, in 1994 agent Nate Cebrun received 30 days in jail and was fined $2,255 for conduct related to making improper payments to a Florida State football player and for failing to register in the state as a sports agent. See Shropshire and Davis, *supra*, at 142-143 (discussing the Cebrun matter and other instances in which states have sanctioned athletes pursuant to agent-specific statutes).

In 2000, the National Conference of Commissioners on Uniform State Laws finished drafting the UAAA and presented it to the states for adoption. From a regulatory perspective, the primary goal of the UAAA is to protect the interests of student-athletes and academic institutions by regulating the activities of sports agents. The UAAA's other critical goal is to achieve uniformity. Commenting on the need for uniformity, the Prefatory Note to the UAAA states:

> The statutes differ greatly. About two-thirds of the statutes impose registration requirements. There are substantial differences in the registration procedures, disclosure required, and requirements relating to record maintenance, reporting, renewal, notice, warning and security. The term of the registration is one year in thirteen States, two years in four states, and two States do not specify a term. Most States require notification to States or educational institutions and athletes of certain matters, but the matters vary widely. Conscientious agents operating in more than a single State must have nightmares caused by the lack of uniformity in the existing statutes, and the difficulties in compliance and the severity of penalties which may be imposed for violations.

Uniform Athlete Agents Act (2000), at 1.

For informative discussions of state regulation of sports agents see Shropshire and Davis, *supra*, at 148-164; Phillip J. Closius, *Hell Hath No Fury Like a Fan Scorned: State Regulation of Sports Agents*, 30 U. Tol. L. Rev. 511 (1999); Robert N. Davis, *Exploring the Contours of Agent Regulation: The Uniform Athlete Agent Act*, 8 Vill. Sports & Ent. L.J. 1 (2001); Rob Remis and Diane Sudia, *Statutory Regulation of Agent Gifts to Athletes*, 10 Seton Hall J. Sport L. 265 (2000); Jan Stiglitz, *A Modest Proposal: Agent Deregulation*, 7 Marq. Sports L.J. 361 (1997); Diane Sudia and Rob Remis, *The History Behind Athlete Agent Regulation and the "Slam Dunking" of Statutory Hurdles*, 8 Vill. Sports & Ent. L.J. 67 (2001); Michael L. Martin, *It's Not a Foul Unless the Ref Blows the Whistle: How to Step Up Enforcement of the UAAA and SPARTA*, 19 Sports Law. J. 209 (2012).

A short note should also be added to underscore the impact that the machinations, legal entanglements, and ultimate downfall of Norby Walters and Lloyd Bloom had on the sports agent business. By boldly bragging of their disregard for NCAA and other rules regarding payments to athletes still playing college sports, they soon incurred the wrath of federal and state authorities. When the legal dust had cleared, they had been dragged through lengthy proceedings in the federal district and appellate courts, the courts of Alabama on both criminal and civil charges (brought by the University of Alabama), numerous lawsuits involving ex-clients (see, e.g., *Walters v. Fullwood* and *Walters v. Harmon, infra*), and threatened actions in other quarters. Before the Walters and Bloom scandal, only one state, California, had legislation directly regulating sports agents, which was patterned after California statutes dealing with agents in the entertainment industries. After Walters and Bloom, state after state enacted legislation, creating a crazy quilt of legislation that created great problems for the honest agent. Finally, along came the Uniform Athletes Agent Act, discussed *infra*.

Although the questionable actions of other agents also surfaced during the 1980s, with at least a couple doing prison time for improper payments to athletes and other defalcations, the undoubted catalysts were Walters and Bloom. In the end, the various pressures and lawsuits left Norby Walters reportedly bankrupt. In 1993, Lloyd Bloom, age 36, was found shot to death in a Malibu residence. No weapon was found. No arrests were ever made. The mob was suspected. See Washington Post Obituaries, Aug. 28, 1993. To gain some sense of the scope of the public reactions to the Walters and Bloom controversies, see the following in-depth *Sports Illustrated* articles, obtainable at http://sportsillustrated.cnn.com/vault: Craig Neff, *Agents of Turmoil*, Aug. 3, 1987; Jill Lieber, *A Sad Goodbye to Columbus*, Aug. 3, 1987; Craig Neff, *Agents: What's the Deal?*, Oct. 19, 1987 (multiple articles about a variety of sports agents); and Bruce Selcraig, *The Deal Went Sour*, Sept. 5, 1988 (Walters and Bloom indicted for racketeering and extortion). See also Chris Mortensen, Playing for Keeps: How One Man Kept the Mob from Sinking Its Hooks into Pro Football (1991).

UNIFORM ATHLETE AGENTS ACT (2000)[4]

SECTION 2. DEFINITIONS. In this [Act]:

(1) "Agency contract" means an agreement in which a student-athlete authorizes a person to negotiate or solicit on behalf of the student-athlete a professional-sports-services contract or an endorsement contract.

(2) "Athlete agent" means an individual who enters into an agency contract with a student-athlete or, directly or indirectly, recruits or solicits a student-athlete to enter into an agency contract. The term includes an individual who represents to the public that the individual is an athlete agent. The term does not include a spouse, parent, sibling, [or] grandparent, [or] guardian of the student-athlete or an individual acting solely on behalf of a professional sports team or professional sports organization. . . .

(4) "Contact" means a communication, direct or indirect, between an athlete agent and a student-athlete, to recruit or solicit the student-athlete to enter into an agency contract.

(5) "Endorsement contract" means an agreement under which a student-athlete is employed or receives consideration to use on behalf of the other party any value that the student-athlete may have because of publicity, reputation, following, or fame obtained because of athletic ability or performance. . . .

(8) "Professional-sports-services contract" means an agreement under which an individual is employed, or agrees to render services, as a player on a professional sports team, with a professional sports organization, or as a professional athlete. . . .

---

4. As of February 2013, UAAA had been adopted in over 40 states and two territories. For a listing of states, see http://www.uniformlaws.org/LegislativeFactSheet.aspx?title=Athlete Agents Act. The UAAA can be found in its entirety at http://www.uniformlaws.org/Shared/Docs/Finals_NC/UAAA_Final_NC.wpd.

(12) "Student-athlete" means an individual who engages in, is eligible to engage in, or may be eligible in the future to engage in, any intercollegiate sport. If an individual is permanently ineligible to participate in a particular intercollegiate sport, the individual is not a student-athlete for purposes of that sport. . . .

SECTION 4. ATHLETE AGENTS: REGISTRATION REQUIRED; VOID CONTRACTS.

(a) Except as otherwise provided in subsection (b), an individual may not act as an athlete agent in this State without holding a certificate of registration under Section 6 or 8.

(b) Before being issued a certificate of registration, an individual may act as an athlete agent in this State for all purposes except signing an agency contract, if:

(1) a student-athlete or another person acting on behalf of the student-athlete initiates communication with the individual; and

(2) within seven days after an initial act as an athlete agent, the individual submits an application for registration as an athlete agent in this State.

(c) An agency contract resulting from conduct in violation of this section is void and the athlete agent shall return any consideration received under the contract. . . .

SECTION 6. CERTIFICATE OF REGISTRATION; ISSUANCE OR DENIAL; RENEWAL.

(a) Except as otherwise provided in subsection (b), the [Secretary of State] shall issue a certificate of registration to an individual who complies with Section 5(a) or whose application has been accepted under Section 5(b).

(b) The [Secretary of State] may refuse to issue a certificate of registration if the [Secretary of State] determines that the applicant has engaged in conduct that has a significant adverse effect on the applicant's fitness to act as an athlete agent. In making the determination, the [Secretary of State] may consider whether the applicant has:

(1) been convicted of a crime that, if committed in this State, would be a crime involving moral turpitude or a felony;

(2) made a materially false, misleading, deceptive, or fraudulent representation in the application or as an athlete agent;

(3) engaged in conduct that would disqualify the applicant from serving in a fiduciary capacity;

(4) engaged in conduct prohibited by Section 14;

(5) had a registration or licensure as an athlete agent suspended, revoked, or denied or been refused renewal of registration or licensure as an athlete agent in any State;

(6) engaged in conduct the consequence of which was that a sanction, suspension, or declaration of ineligibility to participate in an interscholastic or intercollegiate athletic event was imposed on a student-athlete or educational institution; or

(7) engaged in conduct that significantly adversely reflects on the applicant's credibility, honesty, or integrity.

(c) In making a determination under subsection (b), the [Secretary of State] shall consider:

(1) how recently the conduct occurred;

(2) the nature of the conduct and the context in which it occurred; and

(3) any other relevant conduct of the applicant. . . .

(e) An individual who has submitted an application for renewal of registration or licensure in another State, in lieu of submitting an application for renewal in the form prescribed pursuant to subsection (d), may file a copy of the application for renewal and a valid certificate of registration or licensure from the other State. The [Secretary of State] shall accept the application for renewal from the other State as an application for renewal in this State if the application to the other State:

(1) was submitted in the other State within six months next preceding the filing in this State and the applicant certifies the information contained in the application for renewal is current;

(2) contains information substantially similar to or more comprehensive than that required in an application for renewal submitted in this State; and

(3) was signed by the applicant under penalty of perjury.

(f) A certificate of registration or a renewal of a registration is valid for [two] years. . . .

SECTION 10. REQUIRED FORM OF CONTRACT.

(a) An agency contract must be in a record, signed or otherwise authenticated by the parties.

(b) An agency contract must state or contain:

(1) the amount and method of calculating the consideration to be paid by the student-athlete for services to be provided by the athlete agent under the contract and any other consideration the athlete agent has received or will receive from any other source for entering into the contract or for providing the services;

(2) the name of any person not listed in the application for registration or renewal of registration who will be compensated because the student-athlete signed the agency contract;

(3) a description of any expenses that the student-athlete agrees to reimburse;

(4) a description of the services to be provided to the student-athlete;

(5) the duration of the contract; and

(6) the date of execution.

(c) An agency contract must contain, in close proximity to the signature of the student-athlete, a conspicuous notice in boldface type in capital letters stating:

WARNING TO STUDENT-ATHLETE

IF YOU SIGN THIS CONTRACT:

(1) YOU MAY LOSE YOUR ELIGIBILITY TO COMPETE AS A STUDENT-ATHLETE IN YOUR SPORT;

(2) IF YOU HAVE AN ATHLETIC DIRECTOR, WITHIN 72 HOURS AFTER ENTERING INTO THIS CONTRACT, BOTH YOU AND YOUR ATHLETE AGENT MUST NOTIFY YOUR ATHLETIC DIRECTOR; AND

(3) YOU MAY CANCEL THIS CONTRACT WITHIN 14 DAYS AFTER SIGNING IT. CANCELLATION OF THIS CONTRACT MAY NOT REINSTATE YOUR ELIGIBILITY.

(d) An agency contract that does not conform to this section is voidable by the student-athlete. If a student-athlete voids an agency contract, the student-athlete is not required to pay any consideration under the contract or to return any consideration received from the athlete agent to induce the student-athlete to enter into the contract.

(e) The athlete agent shall give a record of the signed or otherwise authenticated agency contract to the student-athlete at the time of execution. . . .

SECTION 11. NOTICE TO EDUCATIONAL INSTITUTION.

(a) Within 72 hours after entering into an agency contract or before the next scheduled athletic event in which the student-athlete may participate, whichever occurs first, the athlete agent shall give notice in a record of the existence of the contract to the athletic director of the educational institution at which the student-athlete is enrolled or the athlete agent has reasonable grounds to believe the student-athlete intends to enroll.

(b) Within 72 hours after entering into an agency contract or before the next athletic event in which the student-athlete may participate, whichever occurs first, the student-athlete shall inform the athletic director of the educational institution at which the student-athlete is enrolled that he or she has entered into an agency contract. . . .

SECTION 12. STUDENT-ATHLETE'S RIGHT TO CANCEL.

(a) A student-athlete may cancel an agency contract by giving notice of the cancellation to the athlete agent in a record within 14 days after the contract is signed.

(b) A student-athlete may not waive the right to cancel an agency contract.

(c) If a student-athlete cancels an agency contract, the student-athlete is not required to pay any consideration under the contract or to return any consideration received from the athlete agent to induce the student-athlete to enter into the contract. . . .

SECTION 14. PROHIBITED CONDUCT.

(a) An athlete agent, with the intent to induce a student-athlete to enter into an agency contract, may not:

(1) give any materially false or misleading information or make a materially false promise or representation;

(2) furnish anything of value to a student-athlete before the student-athlete enters into the agency contract; or

(3) furnish anything of value to any individual other than the student-athlete or another registered athlete agent.

(b) An athlete agent may not intentionally:

(1) initiate contact with a student-athlete unless registered under this [Act];

(2) refuse or fail to retain or permit inspection of the records required to be retained by Section 13;

(3) fail to register when required by Section 4;

(4) provide materially false or misleading information in an application for registration or renewal of registration;

(5) predate or postdate an agency contract; or

(6) fail to notify a student-athlete before the student-athlete signs or otherwise authenticates an agency contract for a particular sport that the signing or authentication may make the student-athlete ineligible to participate as a student-athlete in that sport. . . .

SECTION 15. CRIMINAL PENALTIES. An athlete agent who violates Section 14 is guilty of a [misdemeanor] [felony] and, upon conviction, is punishable by [ ]. . . .

SECTION 16. CIVIL REMEDIES.

(a) An educational institution has a right of action against an athlete agent or a former student-athlete for damages caused by a violation of this [Act]. In an action under this section, the court may award to the prevailing party costs and reasonable attorney's fees.

(b) Damages of an educational institution under subsection (a) include losses and expenses incurred because, as a result of the conduct of an athlete agent or former student-athlete, the educational institution was injured by a violation of this [Act] or was penalized, disqualified, or suspended from participation in athletics by a national association for the promotion and regulation of athletics, by an athletic conference, or by reasonable self-imposed disciplinary action taken to mitigate sanctions likely to be imposed by such an organization.

(c) A right of action under this section does not accrue until the educational institution discovers or by the exercise of reasonable diligence would have discovered the violation by the athlete agent or former student-athlete.

(d) Any liability of the athlete agent or the former student-athlete under this section is several and not joint.

(e) This [Act] does not restrict rights, remedies, or defenses of any person under law or equity. . . .

SECTION 17. ADMINISTRATIVE PENALTY. The [Secretary of State] may assess a civil penalty against an athlete agent not to exceed [$25,000] for a violation of this [Act].

NOTE AND QUESTION

UAAA Prosecutions. In one of the first indictments brought pursuant to the UAAA, on October 13, 2006, a grand jury in Baton Rouge, Louisiana, charged Charles Taplin with two counts of violating Louisiana's athlete-agent statute, the UAAA. Taplin allegedly violated the UAAA's registration and notification provisions when he sent text messages to two Louisiana State University football players on behalf of an agent. Taplin was not a registered agent and allegedly failed to notify LSU within seven days of contacting the players. Adrian Angelette, *"Runner" Indicted in Sports Agent Case*, Baton Rouge Advocate, Aug. 15, 2007. While investigating Taplin, information was allegedly uncovered that led to the arrest of Travelle Gaines, a former assistant strength coach at LSU. Gaines was booked on a felony count of engaging in activities prohibited by Louisiana's UAAA—allegedly inviting players to his home where they came into contact with a California-based agent, C.J. Laboy. Adrian Angelette, *La. Law Allows Agent-Athlete Contact Within Rules*, Baton Rouge Advocate, Oct. 26, 2006, at A1. Gaines's attorney denied that his client had done anything illegal.

In October 2008, a Virginia-based and NFLPA-certified contract advisor, Raymond L. Savage, Jr., was indicted for allegedly violating the UAAA. Savage was charged with failing to register under Alabama's UAAA and for initiating contact with a student-athlete. One of Savage's former employee's, Jason Goggins, allegedly contacted Tyrone Prothro, a University of Alabama wide receiver, while the athlete was in the hospital recovering from a broken leg. The indictment of Savage alleges that in 2006 the agent instructed Goggins to visit the player and paid for Goggins's plane fare to Alabama. Goggins's alleged conduct led to his indictment in 2006 for the same alleged violations of Alabama's UAAA. In Alabama, failure to register under the UAAA is a felony and carries a maximum sentence of ten years in prison and a fine of up to $5,000. Liz Mullen, *State of Alabama Say Agent Ran Afoul of Tough Recruiting Laws*, Sports Bus. J., Nov. 10, 2008, at 13; Peter Dujardin, *Sports Agent Denies He Violated Alabama Law*, Daily Press (Newport News, VA), Oct. 15, 2008, at A11. In 2006, the state of Florida exacted a $2,500 fine against agent Jason Paul Wood for failing to notify the University of Miami after meeting with two of its baseball players, and for not registering as an agent in the state. Alan S. Zagler, *US Sports Agents*, Associated Press, Aug. 17, 2010.

Notwithstanding the foregoing prosecutions, a 2010 study conducted by the Associated Press revealed that over half of the 42 states that have enacted the UAAA had "yet to revoke or suspend a single license, or invoke penalties of any sort." Zagler, *supra.* According to the Associated Press review, "[t]wenty four-states reported taking no disciplinary or criminal actions against sports agents, and were unable to determine if state or local prosecutors had pursued such cases. Others described the laws as being enforced a few times, or rarely, an indication of what a low priority they are." *Id.* Texas was reportedly one of the few states that consistently enforced the UAAA. The review found between 2008 and 2010, Texas had disciplined 31 agents and levied fines totaling $17,500. *Id.*

What reasons may underlie the underenforcement of the UAAA?

PROBLEM 8-4

Bruce Reynolds, a football player, met Mr. Fritz of Complete Sports Management, Inc., when Reynolds was a football player at Allstate University. Fritz is an NFLPA-certified contract advisor. On January 3, 2009, Reynolds met Fritz at the latter's car dealership. To enable Reynolds to purchase a car without paying anything, Fritz advanced Reynolds credit on a "house note." On January 18, 2009, Reynolds signed an undated, standard-form NFLPA representation agreement with Complete. Fritz told Reynolds not to send the agreement to the NFLPA as provided for in the union's regulations. Sometime thereafter, a coach advised Reynolds to sign with another agent, which the athlete did. Reynolds informed Fritz that he had signed with another agent and that he would return the automobile to Fritz. Reynolds also informed Fritz that he would reimburse him for the more than $2,900 in checks and goods that Fritz had extended to Reynolds since January 18. Reynolds was drafted by the Atlanta Falcons and signed contracts for the years 2009-2012 that provided a total compensation of $4.1 million and other incentive bonuses.

Considering the UAAA and following materials, answer these questions:

a. Did Fritz violate any rules, regulations, or laws? If so, what are the consequences of any such rules violation?
b. Is Complete entitled to compensation based on the contracts negotiated by Reynolds's new agent? In responding consider the following:

In the context of professional sports, the player's breach of an agency agreement does not necessarily entitle the agent to commission. . . . Technically, the agent is only entitled to damages for breach of contract, i.e., the value of the promised performance reduced by any expenses saved. In addition, the agent is entitled to his commission only if he can show that, had he been permitted to continue performance, he would have been able to consummate the contracts upon which he claims commission.

Total Economic Athletic Management of America, Inc. v. Pickens, 898 S.W.2d 98 (Mo. App. 1995). Also consider the materials below and NFLPA Regulations Governing Contract Advisors, Section 1, *infra,* and 2012-13 NCAA Manual, Articles 12.02.1 and 12.1.2(g), *supra.*

In *Walters v. Fullwood,* 675 F. Supp. 155 (S.D. NY 1987), Brent Fullwood, a running back on Auburn University's football team, signed an agreement with a sports agency firm that was postdated for the last game of Fullwood's college football career. As an enticement for Fullwood to enter into the contract, the firm paid Fullwood $4,000.00, which was secured by the athlete's future football earnings. The agreement violated NCAA and NFLPA regulations. In dismissing the agents' claims, the court stated that an "agreement may be unenforceable . . . as contrary to public policy even in the absence of a direct violation of a criminal statute, if the sovereign has expressed a concern for the values underlying the policy implicated. . . . Even in the context of a non-criminal contract, 'a prime and long-settled public policy closes the doors on our courts to those who sue to collect the rewards of corruption.'" *Id.* at 161. The court also refused to enforce an arbitration agreement on public policy grounds. But see *Walters v. Harmon,* 516 N.Y.S.2d 874 (N.Y. Sup. 1987) (denying motion to stay arbitration in case involving similar facts. An arbitrator subsequently voided the contract in violation of NFLPA rules, but the NCAA rules violation did not factor into his decision. The arbitrator awarded plaintiffs a quantum meruit recovery of $3,153.75, a small fraction of the six-figure amount sought by plaintiffs.). See also *Chiappeparelli v. Henderson,* 2005 WL 1847221 (Cal. Ct. App. Aug. 5, 2005) (unpublished) (the court found that a plaintiff agent, who failed to obtain a license as required by the applicable state agent regulations, could not collect a percentage of the compensation the defendant had earned from martial arts contests because the representation contract between the agent and defendant was illegal and unenforceable).

3. *Players Associations*

a. **Authority to Regulate**

As noted in Chapter 6, in team sports, players associations are unions. These unions represent a principal component of the web of regulation that affects the athlete-agent relationship.

The following excerpt describes the genesis of players associations and how these entities fit into the larger scheme of labor relations law that regulates the representation of employees once they have entered into a collective bargaining agreement with employers.

The sports unions' power to regulate and certify agents represents a departure from the ways in which employees' unions typically operate. In most industries, unions (pursuant to collective bargaining agreements with employers) negotiate terms and conditions of employment as well as all union member salaries. Professional sports unions, also pursuant to collective bargaining agreements, possess the exclusive authority to negotiate individual player salaries and other terms and conditions of employment such as minimum salaries, pension benefits, health insurance, playing conditions, travel accommodations, the ability of a player to move from one team to another, medical treatment, and grievance and arbitration procedures. However, unlike other unions, sports unions have delegated their exclusive authority to negotiate individual player salaries. Thus, players are free to select representatives to negotiate the individual terms of their contract compensation packages within the framework established by the collective bargaining agreements.

In 1983, the NFLPA asserted that it possessed the inherent authority to regulate agents who represented football players in contract negotiations with teams. Pursuant to its asserted authority, the NFLPA mandated that those agents who desired to represent its members be certified by the union. Similarly, in 1986, in response to complaints by players of abuse by agents, the NBPA established a comprehensive system of agent certification. . . .

The MLBPA asserts its authority in the MLBPA regulations by citing the NLRA and emphasizing that it is "the exclusive representative for all the employees in such unit." It then cites its collective bargaining agreement with management, noting that players may negotiate contracts with teams "in accordance with the provisions set forth in this Agreement." The certification requirement also appears in the Major League Baseball Collective Bargaining Agreement (effective December 20, 2006), which states that a player may use an agent for negotiations "provided such agent has been certified to the Clubs by the Association [MLBPA] as authorized to act as a Player's Agent for such purposes."

Shropshire and Davis, *supra*, at 135-137.

In *Collins v. National Basketball Players Association*, 850 F. Supp. 1468 (D. Colo. 1991), the court described the abuses that prompted players unions to legislate the agent-athlete relationship as follows:

> Specifically, players complained that the agents imposed high and non-uniform fees for negotiation services, insisted on execution of open-ended powers of attorney giving the agents broad powers over players' professional and financial decisions, failed to keep players apprised of the status of negotiations with NBA teams, failed to submit itemized bills for fees and services, and, in some cases had conflicts of interest arising out of representing coaches and/or general managers of NBA teams as well as players. Many players believed that they were bound by contract not to dismiss their agents regardless of dissatisfaction with their services and fees, because the agents had insisted on the execution of long-term agreements. Some agents offered money and other inducements to players, their families, and coaches to obtain player clients.

Collins, 850 F. Supp. at 1471

In *Collins v. National Basketball Players Association*, 976 F.2d 740 (10th Cir. 1992), a federal appellate court upheld the authority of a players union to refuse to recertify an agent. Former NBA superstar Kareem Abdul-Jabbar filed a lawsuit accusing his agent of financial improprieties. Prior to a settlement of Abdul-Jabbar's lawsuit against Collins, the agent had been decertified by the NBPA. After his application for recertification was denied, Collins sued the NBPA. The court rejected Collins's claims stating as follows:

Before the district court, Collins claimed that the NBPA certification process violates the antitrust laws because it amounts to a group boycott. We agree with the district court's analysis of the labor and antitrust statutes and its conclusion that the statutory labor exemption from the Sherman Act permits the NBPA to establish a certification procedure for player agents. Specifically, we hold that the Regulations meet both prongs of the test established in *United States v. Hutcheson*, 312 U.S. 219 (1941), in which the Supreme Court held that labor unions acting in their self-interest and not in combination with nonlabor groups are statutorily exempt from Sherman Act liability.

On appeal, Collins now acknowledges that the NBPA has the statutory authority to establish player agent regulations. [Collins] maintains his attack on the Committee's decision to deny his certification because it was based in part on its finding that he had breached his fiduciary duty as an investment agent and money manager. He argues that his conduct outside of negotiations between players and their teams is not a legitimate interest of the union because it has no bearing on the union's interest in the wage scale and working conditions of its members. . . . The NBPA established the Regulations to deal with agent abuses, including agents' violations of their fiduciary duties as labor negotiators. It was entirely fair for the Committee to conclude that a man who had neglected his fiduciary duties as an investment agent and money manager could not be trusted to fulfill his fiduciary duties as a negotiator. The integrity of a prospective negotiating agent is well within the NBPA's legitimate interest in maintaining the wage scale and working conditions of its members.

Collins, 976 F.2d at *2. The court affirmed the district court's grant of summary judgment in favor of the NBPA.

NOTES AND QUESTIONS

1. *Union Regulatory Authority. Collins* is viewed as standing for the proposition that players associations have the right to regulate agents. The authority of the NFLPA to police agents was impliedly affirmed in *White v. NFL*, 92 F. Supp. 2d 918 (D. Minn. 2000). The NFL charged that the San Francisco Forty-Niners and certain agents violated the NFL's collective bargaining agreement (CBA) and a stipulation and settlement in the named case by entering into undisclosed agreements concerning player compensation. The NFL sought discovery against certain agents for purposes of the underlying litigation. The agents, Leigh Steinberg, Jeffrey Moorad, and Gary Wichard, resisted on grounds that they were "not signatories to the CBA and SSA [stipulation and settlement agreement] and were not subject to any penalty scheme provided in those agreements." *Id.* at 920. A special master dismissed the agents from the underlying proceeding. The master also ruled, however, that if the court were to find that the agents were bound by the CBA and SSA, the agents could be subject to penalties thereof. The court concluded that the CBA and SSA bind agents, even though they have not signed them. It reasoned that agents give implied consent to be bound by the CBA when they accept the Players Association's permission to negotiate player contracts; "player agents enjoy significant and ongoing economic benefits" that result directly from the CBA; and "agents have expressly agreed to be bound by NFLPA agent regulations which include specific provisions (1) requiring each certified player agent to become familiar with 'applicable Collective

Bargaining Agreements and other governing documents,' and (2) prohibiting certified agents from 'negotiating and/or agreeing to any provision in any agreement involving a player which directly or indirectly violates any stated policies or rules established by the NFLPA.'" *Id.* at 924-925.

In *Black v. NFLPA*, 87 F. Supp. 2d 1 (D. D.C. 2000), Tank Black asserted novel theories in attempting to undermine the authority of the NFLPA to revoke his agent certification. In July 1999, the NFLPA's Disciplinary Committee issued a proposed ruling that called for a three-year revocation of agent Tank Black's contract advisor certification. Black asserted that three white agents who had been subjected to discipline by the NFLPA had been treated more favorably than he had. According to Black, this constituted unlawful racial discrimination in violation 42 U.S.C. §1982. Black also asserted that by "means of its racially discriminatory and defamatory comments, the NFLPA had tortiously interfered with his existing and prospective contracts." *Id.* at 4. Rejecting Black's contentions, the court found that the NFLPA regulations established arbitration before an NFLPA-selected arbitrator as the mechanism available for Mr. Black to challenge the proposed ruling. *Id.* at 5-6. See Richard T. Karcher, *Fundamental Fairness in Union Regulation of Sports Agents*, 40 Conn. L. Rev. 355 (2007) (discussing the fairness of player association disciplinary processes).

2. *Suspension and Decertification.* Perhaps the most severe sanctions that a players association can impose on an agent are suspension and decertification. Section 6 of the NFLPA Regulations Governing Contract Advisors provides that discipline may include one or more of the following:

(3) Suspension of a Contract Advisor's Certification for a specified period of time during which Contract Advisor shall be prohibited from representing any NFL player in individual contract negotiations with an NFL club or assisting in or advising with respect to such negotiations. During such suspension Contract Advisor shall also be prohibited from engaging either directly or indirectly in any "recruiting activities." The term "recruiting activities" shall be deemed to include recruiting of any NFL players or prospective NFL players on behalf of himself/herself or any representation firm with which the suspended Contract Advisor is associated, and/or recruiting on behalf of any other Contract Advisor or representation firm. During such suspension Contract Advisor may, at the discretion of the Committee on Agent Regulation and Discipline, be prohibited from collecting fees that he/she would otherwise have been entitled to receive pursuant to any Standard Representation Agreement;

(4) Revocation of the Contract Advisor's Certification hereunder. . . .

(6) Imposition of a fine payable within thirty (30) days of the imposition of such fine, with one-half (1/2) of such fine payable to the Players Assistance Trust (PAT) and one-half (1/2) payable to the NFL Players Charities.

Article 6 of the NBPA Regulations Governing Player Agents includes similar sanctions. An agent who is suspended may resume work as a certified athlete agent as soon as the suspension ends. An agent who is decertified cannot work as an agent for a minimum of three years and must apply to the union for reinstatement before he or she can resume representing players.

An important instance in which an agent's conduct was deemed sufficiently egregious to warrant suspension or decertification includes the matters involving William "Tank" Black, discussed *supra*. Also in early 2003, a Texas District Court judge confirmed an arbitrator's $550,000 judgment entered against Sean Jones, a sports agent and former NFL player, in favor of former NFL player Cris Dishman. Dishman alleged that Jones, while handling his investments, engaged in unauthorized trading and churning. Jones was decertified by the NFLPA following allegations by a NFL player who submitted a sworn declaration that Jones had fraudulently induced him to participate in a $1 million loan on which Jones defaulted. The NFLPA's disciplinary committee decertified Jones. In December 2003, an arbitrator reduced the decertification to a two-year suspension. In November 2003, the NFL decertified Ajili Hodari, "finding that the agent took his entire fee out of a signing bonus paid to former client, Carolina Panthers wide receiver Mushin Muhammad, and also finding that Hodari offered an Ohio State football player a payment to sign with him." Liz Mullen, *NFLPA Decertifies Hodari, Issues Complaints Against 2*, Sports Bus. J., Nov. 17-23, 2003, at 6. For a discussion of cases involving income mismanagement, see Shropshire and Davis, *supra*, at 64-78; Edward T. Pound and Douglas Pasternak, *Money Player: How Some of the NFL's Biggest Stars Got Taken for Millions*, U.S. News & World Rep., Feb. 11, 2002, at 30.

In March 2006, the NFLPA's Committee on Agent Regulation voted to suspend NFL certified agent Carl Poston for "allegedly signing an important contract for a client without fully reading it first." Liz Mullen, *Source: NFLPA Files Complaint Against Arrington's Agent*, Sports Bus. J., Jan. 23, 2006, at 14. The contract omitted a $6.5 million bonus Poston believed he had negotiated for his client, former NFL linebacker LaVar Arrington. In July 2006, the NFLPA announced it would immediately institute the suspension. This was an unusual move because the union, at that time, had typically permitted agents to continue to represent clients in contract negotiations until an arbitrator ruled on sanctions imposed by the union. In December 2007, following a three-day hearing, arbitrator Roger Kaplan upheld the NFLPA's suspension of Poston. Liz Mullen, *Arbitrator Upholds NFLPA's Two-Year Suspension of Poston*, Sports Bus. J., Dec. 10, 2007, at 13. On November 9, 2008, the National Basketball Players Association (NBPA) decertified agent Josh Nochimson for, among other things, stealing approximately $500,000 from clients including Richard Hamilton of the Detroit Pistons. K.C. Johnson, *Deng's Old Agent Faces Allegations*, Chi. Trib., Aug. 6, 2008, 2008 WLNR 14671511. Finally, on August 26, 2008, the NBPA suspended agent Calvin Andrews for one year for conduct involving the recruitment of then University of Southern California and current NBA player O.J. Mayo. The NBPA's disciplinary committee found that Andrews, a vice president of Bill Duffy Associates Sports Management, was an intermediary in funneling $30,000 to Mayo. Ben Bolch, *Mayo's Former Agent Suspended*, L.A. Times, Aug. 30, 2008, 2008 WLNR 16411352.

3. *NFLPA Amended Regulations.* In attempting to confront problems aggressively in the agent industry, the NFLPA has enacted several amendments to its agent regulations. In 2002, the NFLPA adopted the one-in-three rule. NFLPA-certified agents are required to negotiate at least one contract during a three-year period in order to retain their certification. In 2004, the NFLPA amended its regulations to require agents to disclose, in writing, payments they make to runners. In May 2005, the NFLPA amended its regulations to impose a heightened educational requirement. In order to be

eligible for certification, prospective agents must have received a postgraduate degree from a college or university or demonstrate sufficient negotiation experience. In 2005, the NLFPA amended its regulations to require agents to obtain malpractice insurance. As with the NFLPA's one-in-three rule, a consequence of this amendment is likely to be a decrease in the number of certified NFL agents. In February 2006, the NFLPA decided not to proceed with a proposed amendment that would have reduced the maximum fee that agents can charge from 3 percent to 2 percent. The maximum fee agents can charge for franchise and transition players is, however, reduced under certain circumstances.

In 2007, the NFLPA adopted a new regulation that prohibits suspended agents from directly or indirectly recruiting players during the period of his or her suspension. NFLPA, 2007 Amendments to the NFLPA Regulations Governing Contract Advisors (April 4, 2007). This amendment responded to agent complaints that agent David Dunn, who was suspended for 18 months in November 2006, recruited clients during his suspension. Responding to complaints by college coaches that agents are jeopardizing the intercollegiate eligibility of student-athletes and encouraging juniors to jump to the NFL before they were ready, the NFLPA in 2007 enacted the "junior rule." This rule prohibits agents from contacting college players prior to mid-January of their third year, or "true" junior year, when players become eligible to declare for the NFL draft. *Id.* In 2007, the NFLPA also adopted a regulation requiring an agent to disclose to player clients the identity of the coaches, including college coaches, the agent represents. *Id.* On March 17, 2009, the NFLPA Board of Player Representatives voted to modify its "junior rule." The modification allows agents to contact college underclassmen after the latest of either the athlete's last regular season game or conference championship game or after December 1.

4. *MLBPA Regulations.* In 2010, the Major League Baseball Players Association adopted the first major substantive overhaul of its agent regulations since they were initially enacted in 1988. The 2010 regulations include provisions relating to client stealing, solicitation and inducements, runners, and arbitration. See MLBPA Regulations Governing Player Agents, available at http://reg.mlbpaagent.org/Documents/AgentForms/Agent%20Regulations.pdf. For a descriptive overview and a critical analysis of MLBPA's new agent regulations, see Darren A. Heitner and Jason B. Wolf, *In Baseball's Best Interest? A Discussion of the October 10, 2010 MLBPA Regulations Governing Player Agents,* 10 Va. Sports & Ent. L.J. 249 (2011).

5. *An International Perspective.* In the United States, agents are potentially subject to several layers of direct and indirect regulation: state agent regulations, federal regulations, players association regulations, state bar association regulations for agents who are attorneys, and the NCAA (although the NCAA has no authority to regulate agents, agents are indirectly affected by NCAA rules in that players, in order not to violate NCAA rules, avoid engaging in behaviors often encouraged by agents). Internationally, player agents are also subject to levels of regulations. In Europe, one level of regulation is the International Labour Law Organisation Convention on Private Employment Agencies, which allows for private employment agencies to operate, but also seeks to protect workers who use the services of such agencies. At the national level, countries such as France, Portugal, and Italy have promulgated statutes that regulate player agents and require that

such persons be licensed. In such countries, agents must be licensed even though the agent may have also obtained a license from the sporting federation. The third tier of regulation consists of FIFA and national association agent regulations. The following excerpt describes this tier of regulation and some of the problems that arise with respect to it:

> FIFA's Licensed Players' Agent Regulations require national associations [to] make to their own Regulations for Players' Agents based on the guidelines provided by FIFA, and such guidelines must be approved by the FIFA Players' Status Committee. The FIFA Regulations have received a wide airing . . . and these regulations have in turn been transposed onto national association law. Nevertheless, the pattern of transposition has been varied, and conflicts and inconsistencies remain. For some states, the interventionist nature of state involvement in sport (such as in Greece) can pose problems for national associations obliged to follow national law whilst also being required to pay heed to FIFA regulations. In other cases, some national associations have adopted more detailed and restrictive rules than FIFA requires (as in England), whilst others have simply incorporated the FIFA principles into their registration procedures.

Robert Parrish, *Regulating Players' Agents: A Global Perspective*, in Players' Agents Worldwide: Legal Aspects 12 (Robert C.R. Siekmann et al. eds., 2007).

The bottom line is that the degree of regulation of agents in foreign countries is largely dictated by the sport and by the country. As to U.S. players performing abroad, largely in basketball, hockey, and baseball, the agent may encounter little regulation. However, the aspiring agent needs to check carefully to ascertain what restrictions apply in dealing with the client's sport and the country in which he wishes to play.

b.   Fees

BROWN v. WOOLF
554 F. Supp. 1206 (S.D. Ind. 1983)

Steckler, District Judge.

This matter comes before the Court on the motions of defendant, Robert G. Woolf, for partial summary judgment and for summary judgment. . . .

The complaint in this diversity action seeks compensatory and punitive damages and the imposition of a trust on a fee defendant allegedly received, all stemming from defendant's alleged constructive fraud and breach of fiduciary duty in the negotiation of a contract for the 1974-75 hockey season for plaintiff who was a professional hockey player. Plaintiff alleges that prior to the 1973-74 season he had engaged the services of defendant, a well known sports attorney and agent, who represents many professional athletes, has authored a book, and has appeared in the media in connection with such representation, to negotiate a contract for him with the Pittsburgh Penguins of the National Hockey League. Plaintiff had a professionally successful season that year under the contract defendant negotiated for him and accordingly again engaged defendant's services prior to the 1974-75 season. During the negotiations in July 1974, the Penguins offered plaintiff a two-year contract at $80,000.00 per year but plaintiff rejected the offer allegedly because defendant asserted that he could obtain a better, long-term, no-cut contract with a deferred compensation feature with the Indianapolis Racers, which at the time was a new team in a new league. On July 31, 1974, plaintiff signed a five-year contract with the Racers. Thereafter, it is alleged the Racers began having financial difficulties. Plaintiff avers that Woolf continued to represent plaintiff and negotiated two reductions in plaintiff's compensation including the loss of a retirement fund at the same time defendant was attempting to get his own fee payment from the Racers. Ultimately the Racers' assets were seized and the organizers defaulted on their obligations to plaintiff. He avers that he received only $185,000.00 of the total $800,000.00 compensation under the Racer contract but that defendant received his full $40,000.00 fee (5% of the contract) from the Racers.

Plaintiff alleges that defendant made numerous material misrepresentations upon which he relied both during the negotiation of the Racer contract and at the time of the subsequent modifications. Plaintiff further avers that defendant breached his fiduciary duty to plaintiff by failing to conduct any investigation into the financial stability of the Racers, failing to investigate possible consequences of the deferred compensation package in the Racers' contract, failing to obtain guarantees or collateral, and by negotiating reductions in plaintiff's compensation from the Racers while insisting on receiving all of his own. Plaintiff theorizes that such conduct amounts to a prima facie case of constructive fraud for which he should receive compensatory and punitive damages and have a trust impressed on the $40,000.00 fee defendant received from the Racers.

Defendant's motion for partial summary judgment attacks plaintiff's claim for punitive damages, contending that plaintiff has no evidence to support such an award and should not be allowed to rest on the allegations of his complaint. Further, he claims that punitive damages are unavailable as a matter of law in a constructive fraud case because no proof of fraudulent intent is required. By his motion for summary judgment, defendant attacks several aspects of plaintiff's claims against him. He argues (1) that plaintiff cannot recover on a breach of contract theory because Robert G. Woolf, the individual, was acting merely as the agent and employee of Robert Woolf Associates, Inc. (RWA), (2) that defendant's conduct could not amount to constructive fraud because (a) plaintiff alleges only negligent acts, (b) there is no evidence defendant deceived plaintiff or violated a position of trust, (c) there is no showing of harm to the public interest, and (d) there is no evidence that defendant obtained an unconscionable advantage at plaintiff's expense.

The Court concludes that Indiana courts would not adopt a per se rule prohibiting such damages in a constructive fraud action, but would rather consider the facts and circumstances of each case. If elements of recklessness, or oppressive conduct are demonstrated, punitive damages could be awarded. . . .

Indiana cases contain several formulizations of the tort of constructive fraud. Generally it is characterized as acts or a course of conduct from which an unconscionable advantage is or may be derived, . . . or a breach of confidence coupled with an unjust enrichment which shocks the conscience, . . . or a breach of duty, including mistake, duress or undue influence, which the law declares fraudulent because of a tendency to deceive, injure the public interest or violate the public or private confidence. . . . Another formulization found in the cases involves the making of a false statement, by the dominant party in a confidential or fiduciary relationship or by one who holds himself out as an expert, upon which the plaintiff reasonably relies to his detriment. The defendant need not know the statement is false nor make the false statement with fraudulent intent. . . .

The Court believes that both formulizations are rife with questions of fact, *inter alia*, the existence or nonexistence of a confidential or fiduciary relationship, . . . and the question of reliance on false representations, . . . as well as questions of credibility.

Defendant argues that despite the customary existence of such fact questions in a constructive fraud case, judgment is appropriate in this instance because plaintiff has produced nothing to demonstrate the existence of fact questions. He makes a similar argument in the motion for partial summary judgment on the punitive damages issue. . . .

In this case, defendant has offered affidavits, excerpts of depositions, and photocopies of various documents to support his motions. He contends that such materials demonstrate that reasonable minds could not conclude that defendant did the acts with which the complaint charges him. In response, plaintiff rather belatedly offered portions of plaintiff's depositions as well as arguing that issues such as those raised by a complaint based on constructive fraud are inherently unsuited to resolution on a motion for summary judgment.

Having carefully considered the motions and briefs and having examined the evidentiary materials submitted, the Court concludes that summary judgment would not be appropriate in this action. The Court is not persuaded that there are no fact questions remaining unresolved in this controversy such that defendant is entitled to judgment as a matter of law. As movant for summary judgment, defendant bears the "heavy burden" of clearly demonstrating the absence of any genuine issue of a material fact. . . .

By reason of the foregoing, defendant's motions for partial summary judgment and for summary judgment are hereby DENIED.

NOTES AND QUESTIONS

1. *Fee Maximums.* The matter addressed in *Woolf*, excessive fees charged by agents, is not as troublesome today, given limitations imposed by union regulation of agents. For example, NFLPA agent regulations restrict the maximum amount of fees an agent can charge for negotiating a player contract with a team. An agent can receive a maximum fee of 3 percent of the compensation that a player receives during the playing season covered by the contract the agent negotiates. Compensation is defined broadly to include salaries, signing bonuses, roster bonuses, and other monies earned by a player. (For an example of player association regulations governing agents, see NFLPA Section 4(B), "Contract Advisors Compensation," *infra*.) Note that agents are allowed to charge less than the maximum. Are endorsement deals that an agent negotiates for an NFL player subject to the 3 percent maximum?

   The NBPA allows fees of up to 4 percent. MLB allows the market to control and sets no maximum on the size of fee an agent can earn for negotiating a player/team contract. Larger representation firms will often waive the fee the NBPA regulations allow in negotiating the first contract between an NBA team and draft picks. Such a firm is willing to forgo the fee as an incentive for the player to sign a representation agreement in anticipation of collecting a larger fee when the player signs a more lucrative contract three or four years later.

2. *Time of Payment.* At what point in time was the fee paid in *Woolf?* Do the NFLPA regulations effectively resolve when an agent is to be paid his fee?

3. *The Legal Effects of* Brown v. Woolf. The actual legal impact of the case is something of an enigma. The reported opinion only denies summary relief to the defendant. It proffers a theory of constructive fraud, which should serve as a wake-up call to agents, but it does not fully explain the circumstances under which ill-fated reliance on an agent's advice is actionable. The case was settled before it went to trial; thus, the theory is left hanging in a never-never land, evidently not adopted in other jurisdictions and ill-defined in Indiana. Nevertheless, it is important to examine the opinion for what it portends for the theory of constructive fraud and for agents who perhaps overreach in taking fees up front. Though this latter practice has been curtailed in leagues with union regulations restricting the practice, what about other leagues and individual performer sports? What about players performing in foreign countries? Indeed, in some instances, the foreign club pays the agent directly. Is this a conflict of interest?

NFLPA REGULATIONS GOVERNING CONTRACT ADVISORS[5]

(as amended through June 2012)

SECTION 1 — SCOPE OF REGULATIONS

A. PERSONS SUBJECT TO REGULATIONS

No person (other than a player representing himself) shall be permitted to conduct individual contract negotiations on behalf of a player* and/or assist in or advise with respect to such negotiations with NFL Clubs after the effective date of these Regulations unless he/she is (1) currently certified as a Contract Advisor pursuant to these Regulations; (2) signs a Standard Representation Agreement with the player (See Section 4; Appendix D); and (3) files a fully executed copy of the Standard Representation Agreement with the NFLPA, along with any contract(s) between the player and the Contract Advisor for other services to be provided.

B. ACTIVITIES COVERED

The activities of Contract Advisors which are governed by these Regulations include: the providing of advice, counsel, information or assistance to players with respect to negotiating their individual contracts with Clubs and/or thereafter in enforcing those contracts; the conduct of individual compensation negotiations with the Clubs on behalf of players; and any other activity or conduct which directly bears upon the Contract Advisor's integrity, competence or ability to properly represent individual NFL players and the NFLPA in individual contract negotiations, including the handling of player funds, providing tax counseling and preparation services, and providing financial advice and investment services to individual players. . . .

---

5. The complete NFLPA Regulations Governing Contract Advisors (as amended through June 2012) can be found at http://images.nflplayers.com/mediaResources/files/PDFs/SCAA/2012_ NFLPA_Regulations_Contract_Advisors.pdf.

Section 2 — Certification

After the effective date of these Regulations, any person who wishes to perform the functions of a Contract Advisor as described in Section 1 above must be certified by the NFLPA. . . .

C.   Grounds for Denial of Certification

Grounds for denial of Certification shall include, but not be limited to, the following:

- The applicant has made false or misleading statements of a material nature in his/her application;
- The applicant has misappropriated funds, or engaged in other specific acts such as embezzlement, theft or fraud, which would render him/her unfit to serve in a fiduciary capacity on behalf of players;
- The applicant has engaged in any other conduct that significantly impacts adversely on his/her credibility, integrity or competence to serve in a fiduciary capacity on behalf of players;
- The applicant is unwilling to swear or affirm that he/she will comply with these Regulations and any amendments hereto and/or that he/she will abide by the fee structure contained in the Standard Representation Agreement incorporated into these Regulations;
- The applicant has been denied certification by another professional sports players association;
- The applicant directly or indirectly solicited a player for representation as a Contract Advisor during the period of time between the filing of his/her Application for Certification and Certification by the NFLPA;
- The applicant has not received a degree from an accredited four year college/university and a postgraduate degree from an accredited college/university, unless excepted from this requirement pursuant to Section 2(A). . . .

Section 3 — Standard of Conduct For Contract Advisors . . .

A.   General Requirements

A Contract Advisor shall be required to:

(1) Disclose on his/her Application and thereafter upon request of the NFLPA all information relevant to his/her qualifications to serve as a Contract Advisor, including, but not limited to, background, special training, experience in negotiations, past representation of professional athletes, and relevant business associations or memberships in professional organizations;

(2) Pay an application fee pursuant to Section 2 above unless waived;

(3) Pay the annual fee in a timely manner as established by the Board of Player Representatives . . . ;

(4) Attend an NFLPA seminar on individual contract negotiations each year;

(5) Comply with the maximum fee schedule and all other provisions of these Regulations and any amendments thereto;

(6) Execute and abide by the printed Standard Representation Agreement with all players represented and file with the NFLPA a copy of that fully

executed agreement along with any other agreement(s) for additional services that the Contract Advisor has executed with the player. . . .

(9) Provide on or before May 1 each year, to every player who he/she represents, with a copy to the NFLPA, an itemized statement covering the period beginning March 1 of the prior year through February 28 or 29 of that year, which separately sets forth both the fee charged to the player for, and any expenses incurred in connection with, the performance of the following services:

    (a)   individual player salary negotiations,

    (b)   management of the player's assets,

    (c)   financial, investment, legal, tax and/or other advice to the player, and

    (d)   any other miscellaneous services . . . ;

(14) Fully comply with applicable state and federal laws . . . ;

(16) Disclose in an addendum (in the form attached as Appendix G) attached to the Standard Representation Agreement between the Contract Advisor and player, the names and current positions of any NFL management personnel or coaches whom Contract Advisor represents or has represented in matters pertaining to their employment by or association with any NFL club;

(17) Act at all times in a fiduciary capacity on behalf of players.

(18) Comply with and abide by all of the stated policies of the NFLPA.

(19) In connection with payments for assistance in recruiting any player:

    (a)   Prepare a typewritten SRA Disclosure Form (attached as Appendix E) disclosing any other Contract Advisor(s) to whom the Contract Advisor has paid or has promised to pay money or any other thing of value (excluding any other Contract Advisor(s) whose name appears on the Standard Representation Agreement) in return for recruiting or helping to recruit a player to sign a Standard Representation Agreement;

    (b)   Provide a copy of that SRA Disclosure Form to the player in advance of signing that player to a Standard Representation Agreement so as to allow the player adequate time to consider the information before the player signs the Standard Representation Agreement; [and]

    (c)   Have the player sign that SRA Disclosure Form acknowledging that he is aware of the payments and that he approves of them. . . .

(20) Educate player-clients as to their benefits, rights and obligations pursuant to the Collective Bargaining Agreement; and to advise and assist those player-clients in taking maximum advantage of those benefits and rights. . . .

B. PROHIBITED CONDUCT

Contract Advisors are prohibited from:

(1) Representing any player in individual contract negotiations with any Club unless he/she (i) is an NFLPA Certified Contract Advisor; (ii) has signed the Standard Representation Agreement with such player; and (iii) has filed a copy of the Standard Representation Agreement with the NFLPA along with any other contract(s) or agreement(s) between the player and the Contract Advisor;

(2) Providing or offering money or any other thing of value to any player or prospective player to induce or encourage that player to utilize his/her services;

(3) Providing or offering money or any other thing of value to a member of the player's or prospective player's family or any other person for the purpose of inducing or encouraging that person to recommend the services of the Contract Advisor;

(4) Providing materially false or misleading information to any player or prospective player in the context of recruiting the player as a client or in the course of representing that player as his Contract Advisor;

(5) Representing or suggesting to any player or prospective player that his/her NFLPA Certification is an endorsement or recommendation by the NFLPA of the Contract Advisor or the Contract Advisor's qualifications or services;

(6) Directly or indirectly borrowing money from any player (whether or not the player is a client), either by receiving the funds directly from the player or by the player providing collateral for or agreeing to guarantee a loan to the Contract Advisor by another party;

(7) Holding or seeking to hold, either directly or indirectly, a financial interest in any professional football club or in any other business entity when such investment could create an actual conflict of interest or the appearance of a conflict of interest in the representation of NFL players;

(8) Engaging in any other activity which creates an actual or potential conflict of interest with the effective representation of NFL players;

(9) Soliciting or accepting money or anything of value from any NFL Club in a way that would create an actual or apparent conflict with the interests of any player that the Contract Advisor represents;

(10) Negotiating and/or agreeing to any provision in a player contract which deprives or purports to deprive that player of any benefit contained in any collectively bargained agreement between the NFL and the NFLPA or any other provision of any applicable documents which protect the working conditions of NFL players;

(11) Negotiating and/or agreeing to any provision in any agreement involving a player which directly or indirectly violates any stated policies or rules established by the NFLPA;

(12) Concealing material facts from any player whom the Contract Advisor is representing which relate to the subject of the player's individual contract negotiation;

(13) Failing to advise the player and to report to the NFLPA any known violations by an NFL Club of a player's individual contract;

(14) Engaging in unlawful conduct and/or conduct involving dishonesty, fraud, deceit, misrepresentation, or other activity which reflects adversely on his/her fitness as a Contract Advisor or jeopardizes his/her effective representation of NFL players;

(15) Failure to comply with the maximum fee provisions contained in Section 4 of these Regulations;

(16) Circumventing the maximum fee provisions contained in Section 4 of these Regulations by knowingly and intentionally increasing the fees that Contract Advisor charges or otherwise would have charged the player for other services including, but not limited to, financial consultation, money management, and/or negotiating player endorsement agreements . . . ;

(18) Filing any lawsuit or other proceedings against a player for any matter which is subject to the exclusive arbitration provisions contained in Section 5 of these Regulations . . . ;

(21) (a) Initiating any communication, directly or indirectly, with a player who has entered into a Standard Representation Agreement with another Contract Advisor and such Standard Representation Agreement is on file with the NFLPA if the communication concerns a matter relating to the:

    (i)   Player's current Contract Advisor;

    (ii) Player's current Standard Representation Agreement;

    (iii) Player's contract status with any NFL Club(s); or

    (iv) Services to be provided by prospective Contract Advisor either through a Standard Representation Agreement or otherwise.

   (b) If a player, already a party to a Standard Representation Agreement, initiates communication with a Contract Advisor relating to any of the subject matters listed in Section 3(B)(21)(a) the Contract Advisor may continue communications with the Player regarding any of those matters.

   (c) Section 3(B)(21) shall not apply to any player who has less than sixty (60) days remaining before his NFL Player Contract expires, and he has not yet signed a new Standard Representation Agreement with a Contract Advisor within the sixty (60) day period.

   (d) Section 3(B)(21) shall not prohibit a Contract Advisor from sending a player written materials which may be reasonably interpreted as advertising directed at players in general and not targeted at a specific player. . . .

(26) Directly or indirectly soliciting a prospective rookie player for representation as a Contract Advisor (A "rookie" shall be defined as a person who has never signed an NFL Player Contract) if that player has signed a Standard Representation Agreement prior to a date which is thirty (30) days before the NFL Draft and if thirty (30) days have not elapsed since the Agreement was signed and filed with the NFLPA . . . ;

(31) Violating any other provision of these Regulations;

(32) Using, associating with, employing or entering into any business relationship with any individual in the recruitment of prospective player-clients who is not Certified and in good standing as a Contract Advisor pursuant to these Regulations;

A Contract Advisor who engages in any prohibited conduct as defined above shall be subject to discipline in accordance with the procedures of Section 6 of these Regulations. [The sanctions listed in Section 6 include the payment of fines, suspension of certification, and decertification.]

SECTION 4 — AGREEMENTS BETWEEN CONTRACT ADVISORS AND PLAYERS; MAXIMUM FEES . . .

B.   CONTRACT ADVISOR'S COMPENSATION

(1) The maximum fee which may be charged or collected by a Contract Advisor shall be three percent (3%) of the "compensation" (as defined within this

Section) received by the player in each playing season covered by the contract negotiated by the Contract Advisor, except as follows:

(a)   The maximum fee which may be charged or collected by a Contract Advisor shall be:

   (i)   Two percent (2%) for a player who signs a one (1) year tender while subject to a Franchise or Transition designation, or as a Restricted Free Agent.

   (ii)   One-and-one half percent (1.5%) for a player who signs a one (1) year tender while subject to a Franchise or Transition designation for the second time he is tagged; and

   (iii) One percent (1%) for player who signs a one (1) year tender while subject to a Franchise or Transition designation for the third time he is tagged.

(2) The Contract Advisor and player may agree to any fee which is less than the maximum fee set forth in (1) above.

(3) As used in this Section 4(B), the term "compensation" shall be deemed to include only salaries, signing bonuses, reporting bonuses, roster bonuses, Practice Squad salary in excess of the minimum Practice Squad salary specified in Article 33 of the Collective Bargaining Agreement, and any performance incentives earned by the player during the term of the contract (including any option year) negotiated by the Contract Advisor. For example, and without limitation, the term compensation shall not include any "honor" incentive bonuses (e.g. ALL PRO, PRO BOWL, Rookie of the Year), or any collectively bargained benefits or other payments provided for in the player's individual contract.

(4) A Contract Advisor is prohibited from receiving any fee for his/her services until and unless the player receives the compensation upon which the fee is based. However, these Regulations recognize that in certain circumstances a player may decide that it is in his best interest to pay his Contract Advisor's fee in advance of the receipt of any deferred compensation from his NFL club. Accordingly, a player may enter into an agreement with a Contract Advisor to pay the Contract Advisor a fee advance on deferred compensation due and payable to the player. Such fee advance may only be collected by the Contract Advisor after the player has performed the services necessary under his contract to entitle him to the deferred compensation. Further, such an agreement between a Contract Advisor and a player must be in writing, with a copy sent by the Contract Advisor to the NFLPA.

   For purposes of determining the fee advance, the compensation shall be determined to be an amount equal to the present value of the deferred player compensation. The rate used to determine the present value of the deferred compensation shall be the rate at which the term "Interest" is defined under Article 1 of the 2011 CBA.

(5) A Contract Advisor who is found to have violated Section 3(B)(2) or (3) of these Regulations shall not be entitled to a fee for services provided to a player who was the subject of an improper inducement under Section 3(B) (2) or (3). In the event that the Contract Advisor collects any fees from the player before a finding of such violation, he/she shall be required to reimburse the player for such fees. . . .

NBPA REGULATIONS GOVERNING PLAYER AGENTS

(as amended June 1991)

Section 3: Standard of Conduct For Player Agents In Providing Services Governed By These Regulations. . . .

B.   PROHIBITED CONDUCT SUBJECT TO DISCIPLINE

To further effectuate the objectives of these Regulations players agents are prohibited from:

(e) Holding or seeking to hold, either directly or indirectly, a financial interest in any professional basketball team or in any other business venture that would create an actual conflict of interest or the appearance of a conflict of interest between the individual player and his agent;

(f) Representing the General Manager or coach of any NBA team (or any other management representative who participates in the team's deliberations or decision concerning what compensation is to be offered individual players) in matters pertaining to his employment or any other matters in which he has any financial stake or by association with any NBA team;

(g) Engaging in any other activity which creates an actual or potential conflict of interest with the effective representation of NBA players; provided that the representation of two or more players on any one club shall not itself be deemed to be prohibited by this provision;

(h) Soliciting or accepting money or anything of value from any NBA club in circumstances where to do so would create a conflict or an apparent conflict with the interests of any player he represents . . . ;

(k) Concealing material facts from any player whom the agent is representing which relate to the subject of the individual's contract negotiations. . . .

A player agent who engages in any prohibited conduct defined above shall be subject to discipline in accordance with the procedures of Section 6 of these Regulations.

NCAA BYLAW, ARTICLE 12

12.3   USE OF AGENTS

12.3.1 General Rule. An individual shall be ineligible for participation in an intercollegiate sport if he or she ever has agreed (orally or in writing) to be represented by an agent for the purpose of marketing his or her athletics ability or reputation in that sport. Further, an agency contract not specifically limited in writing to a sport or particular sports shall be deemed applicable to all sports, and the individual shall be ineligible to participate in any sport. . . .

12.3.1.1 Representation for Future Negotiation. An individual shall be ineligible per Bylaw 12.3.1 if he or she enters into a verbal or written agreement with an agent for representation in future professional sports negotiations that are to take place after the individual has completed his or her eligibility in that sport.

12.3.1.2 Benefits from Prospective Agents. An individual shall be ineligible per Bylaw 12.3.1 if he or she (or his or her relatives or friends) accepts transportation or other benefits from:

(a) Any person who represents any individual in the marketing of his or her athletics ability. The receipt of such expenses constitutes compensation based on athletics skill and is an extra benefit not available to the student body in general; or

(b) An agent, even if the agent has indicated that he or she has no interest in representing the student-athlete in the marketing of his or her athletics ability or reputation and does not represent individuals in the student-athlete's sport.

12.3.2 Legal Counsel. Securing advice from a lawyer concerning a proposed professional sports contract shall not be considered contracting for representation by an agent under this rule, unless the lawyer also represents the individual in negotiations for such a contract. . . .

PROBLEM 8-5

For purposes of this question, assume that Wisconsin adopted the UAAA in its entirety without any modifications, and that it was in effect during Will Cheatham's dealings with Bill Jammer.

Will Cheatham was licensed to practice law in both Wisconsin and Illinois, and maintained his business office in Chicago. He was not registered as an athlete agent with the Wisconsin Secretary of State's office. Through a mutual acquaintance, Cheatham induced Bill Jammer, University of Wisconsin-Madison's (UW) star basketball player, to secretly sign an agent representation agreement on December 1 of Jammer's senior year. This agreement was postdated to April 15 of the following year, which was after the college basketball season ended.

The day after UW was selected for the NCAA basketball tournament, the NCAA declared Jammer ineligible for NCAA tournament competition after discovering he entered into the agent representation agreement with Cheatham last December. The NCAA required UW to forfeit 20 games that Jammer played in after signing this agreement, and the university's resulting losing record caused it to be dropped from the NCAA tournament. UW lost $100,000 in revenues it would have received for participating in a first-round NCAA tournament game, and potentially more revenue it could have earned by advancing to subsequent rounds of the tournament.

Although he was a projected second-round pick in this year's NBA draft if he performed well in the NCAA tournament, Jammer was not drafted by any NBA team. Jammer signed as a free agent with the Orlando Magic, but did not receive a signing bonus. The last player selected in this year's draft received a $350,000 signing bonus. Jammer signed a contract for the upcoming NBA season, but only received the minimum annual player salary of $250,000. Cheatham negotiated Jammer's contract, but did not request that the Magic pay him a bonus or a higher salary than the NBA minimum. Cheatham was concerned that the Magic's payment of more money to Jammer would leave the club with less available money under the NBA salary cap to pay Michael Swisher, Cheatham's prized client who was seeking a lucrative free agent deal with the Magic.

a. Discuss Jammer's potential claims against Cheatham.
b. Discuss UW's potential claims against Cheatham.
c. Discuss whether Cheatham has violated the Uniform Athlete Agent Act and any potential consequences.

D. ETHICAL ISSUES

Given that attorneys must comply with state-imposed professional codes of conduct, the violation of which may result in disciplinary action, it is not surprising that some attorney agents have claimed that the representation of athlete clients does not involve legal work. Thus, they argue that they should not be subject to professional codes with respect to such services. Attorney agents, attempting to disavow their attorney status in this context, find justification in the fact that nonattorney agents who provide competent services on behalf of their athlete clients are not subject to the same requirements. Most fundamentally, these attorney agents argue that it is unfair to impose standards on them to which nonattorney agents are not bound. As noted by one analyst:

> Some sports lawyers argue that based on the nature of the representation industry, . . . if they enter the industry and holdout themselves as a sports agent, they avoid application of the ethical rules of the legal profession.
>   One problem with the argument lies in the nature of the services provided by agents. A principal service provided by the athlete agent is the negotiation of the athlete's contract with his or her team. . . .
>   There can be little doubt that the general service of negotiation is an area of traditional legal representation. On the other hand, athlete agents provide services that do not fall within the scope of what is typically considered legal representation. Many of these services related to the athlete's business affairs for which legal training is not required, such as advice on personal and financial matters.

Shropshire and Davis, *supra*, at 100-101. For recent discussions of the ethical dimensions of the athlete representation industry, see Jonathan J. Amoona, *Top Pick: Why a Licensed Attorney Acting As a Sports Agent Is a "Can't Miss" Prospect*, 21 Geo. J. Legal Ethics 599 (2008); Jeremy J. Geisel, Comment, *Disbarring Jerry Maguire: How Broadly Defining "Unauthorized Practice of Law" Could Take the "Lawyer" Out of "Lawyer-Agent" Despite the Current State of Athlete Agent Legislation*, 18 Marq. Sports L. Rev. 225 (2007).

ETHICS OPINION
Ala. State Bar Disciplinary Comm., Opin. 85-73 (1985)

QUESTION

"A part of my law practice involves sports law, and in addition, I will be teaching the course of Sports Law as an Adjunct Professor of Law at . . . School of Law beginning the fall term of 1985.

My question relates to certain 'agents' who represent athletes and whether or not under the particular fact circumstances set forth in this letter their actions could be construed as the unauthorized practice of law. The fact circumstances consist of the following:

(1)   Individuals represent athletes as 'agents' who have graduated from law school with law degrees but are not members of the state bar association or any local bar association in which they are located; and

(2)   These individuals state that the reason they have no license to practice law, even though they have a law degree, is that it is unethical for attorneys to solicit business, and in order to obtain athletes as clients, one must solicit.

(3)   These agents may belong to or be members of certain organizations involving or relating to sports law. In the biographical section of such organization's or membership's roster, the agents will list immediately following their names or in the biographical sections the following: 'attorney.'

For purposes of this letter, any reference to 'agents' shall include only those individuals who meet the three requirements stated above.

It is obvious that 'agents' have and will be able to continue representing athletes in negotiating contracts for athletes. Furthermore, a person with a law degree does not have to be an attorney and can be an 'agent.' In addition, the listing of these agents' degrees, including law degrees, either publicly or in biographical sections or other matters of writing, is permissible.

The two questions, based on the facts above, for these agents (as defined above) are as follows: (1) Are such agents by listing themselves as 'attorneys' practicing law without a license? (2) Since such agents solicit business, are they violating the Canons of Ethics of the Alabama Bar Association?"

Answer

If a law school graduate who is not a member of the Alabama State Bar or of any local bar association describes himself as "attorney" on the membership roster of any organization or any other publication he would "assume to act or hold himself out to the public as a person qualified to practice or carry on the calling of a lawyer" in violation of § 34-3-1, Code of Alabama, 1975, and would be guilty of a misdemeanor as described in the statute.

A law school graduate could not circumvent the statutes prohibiting the unauthorized practice of law by merely failing to become a member of the State Bar or any local bar association nor could he thus circumvent the rules against solicitation, DR 2-103 and DR 2-104. Furthermore, a lawyer shall not permit any person who recommends, employs, or pays him to render legal services for another to direct or regulate his professional judgment in rendering such legal services.

Discussion

Disciplinary Rule 2-103 (A)(1) provides:

(A) A lawyer shall not:
(1) Solicit his employment or professional engagement or the professional employment or engagement of another whose partner he is, or from whose employment there is an expectation of profit or benefit, directly or indirectly, to himself.

Disciplinary Rule 2-104 (A) provides:

> A lawyer shall not recommend employment, as a private practitioner, of himself, his partner, or associate to a non-lawyer who has not sought his advice regarding employment of a lawyer.

Disciplinary Rule 5-107 (B) provides:

> A lawyer shall not permit a person who recommends, employs, or pays him to render legal services for another to direct or regulate his professional judgment in rendering such legal services.

An opinion of the Ethics Committee of the Kentucky Bar Association addresses a question closely analogous to that which you pose in your request for opinion.

We adopt as the opinion of the Disciplinary Commission Opinion KBA E-89 of the Ethics Committee of the Kentucky Bar Association and attach the same hereto as Exhibit "A."

ISBA ADVISORY OPINION ON PROFESSIONAL CONDUCT

Opinion No. 700 1980 WL 130464 (Ill. St. Bar. Assn.), Nov. 4, 1980

Attorney has a "sports law" practice and represents athletes in contract negotiations. The athletes he represents are handled through his law office from which he conducts a private law practice. . . .

The second question presented deals with whether an attorney may handle "player representation" from the same office in which he engages in the general practice of law. It would appear, therefore, that the attorney making this inquiry questions whether the representation of athletes is actually the practice of law in that it may include a wide range of business counseling, as well as contract negotiation. This doubt could be prompted by the fact that nonlawyers frequently engage in these activities.

The committee is of the opinion that, when an attorney engaged in the private practice of law represents a client in contract negotiations and general business counseling, these activities constitute the practice of law and it would be professionally proper to handle them from the same office in which he engages in the general practice of law.

NOTES AND QUESTIONS

1. *Dual Capacity Cases.* In *In re Clinton A. Jackson*, 650 A.2d 675 (D.C. App. 1994), the court held that "a lawyer is held to a high standard of honesty, no matter what role the lawyer is filling: acting as lawyer, testifying as a witness in a proceeding, handling fiduciary responsibilities, or conducting the private affairs of everyday life." In two reported opinions, the courts assumed, without discussion, that lawyers who acted as sports agents were subject to the rules of their respective bar associations. *In the Matter of Frederick J. Henley*, 478 S.E.2d 134 (Ga. 1996); *Cuyahoga County Bar Assn. v. Glenn*, 649 N.E.2d 1213 (Ohio 1995). The conclusion reached in these cases is consistent with the result courts tend to reach in cases outside the attorney agent context.

In re Dwight, 573 P.2d 481 (Ariz. 1977), is illustrative of the approach that courts take in these "dual capacity" cases (i.e., instances in which legal and nonlegal advice is provided to a client). In addition to legal services, the attorney therein provided financial advice. The court held, "as long as a lawyer is engaged in the practice of law, he is bound by ethical requirements of that profession, and he may not defend his actions by contending that he was engaged in some other kind of professional activity." *Id.* at 484.

For helpful discussions of the foregoing issues, see Shropshire and Davis, *supra*, at 88-98; Chris J. Evanoff, *Show Me the Money: How the ABA Model Rules of Professional Conduct Can Deter NCAA Rules Violations Involving Sports Agents and College Athletes*, 8 DePaul J. Sports L. & Contemp. Probs. 63 (2011); David S. Caudill, *Sports and Entertainment Agents and Agent-Attorneys: Discourses and Conventions Concerning Crossing Jurisdictional and Professional Borders*, 43 Akron L. Rev. 697 (2010); Tamara L. Barner, *Show Me the . . . Ethics? The Implications of the Model Rules of Ethics on Attorneys in the Sports Industry*, 16 Geo. J. Legal Ethics 519 (2003); Mark Domain, *Attorneys As Athlete-Agents: Reconciling the ABA Rules of Professional Conduct with the Practice of Athlete Representation*, 5 Tex. Rev. Ent. & Sports L. 37 (2003); Robert E. Fraley and F. Russell Harwell, *Sports Law and the "Evils" of Solicitation*, 9 Loy. Ent. L.J. 21 (1989).

2. *Solicitation.* The Model Rules of Professional Conduct provide in part that an attorney "shall not, by in-person or live telephone or real-time electronic contact solicit professional employment from a prospective client when a significant motive for the lawyer's doing so is the lawyer's pecuniary gain unless the person contacted: (1) is a lawyer, or (2) has a family, close personal, or prior relationship with the lawyer." American Bar Association, Model Rules of Professional Conduct, 7th ed., Rule 7.3 (2011). Given this rule, to what extent are attorneys, who also act as sports agents, allowed to directly solicit the business of athletes? Do the limitations imposed on attorney solicitation of clients place attorney agents at a disadvantage when competing for clients against nonattorney agents? Would strict adherence to the nonsolicitation rule disadvantage some attorney agents more than others? Do the model rules that govern attorneys make it more difficult for attorneys, who may be better able to effectively serve athlete clients, to gain entry into the agent industry?

PROBLEM 8-6

Robert Williams was admitted to practice and became a licensed member of the bar of North Carolina in 2008. Beginning in 2011, Williams provided services for professional athletes, coaches, and a couple of sports-related entities. With respect to his athlete clients, Williams negotiated player-team contracts, negotiated endorsement deals, and provided a range of other services, such as assisting his athlete clients in managing their financial affairs. He provided similar services to his coach clients. Williams calls himself a sports agent and disavows that he is a practicing attorney, even though he continues to be licensed and notes on his business cards that he is an attorney. Williams is certified as a player representative by both the NFLPA and the NBPA.

Last year, Williams took out several loans on behalf of one of his sports entity clients, the government of St. Timothy. Williams was representing St. Timothy in the island's bid for entry into the Olympic Summer Games. Williams defaulted on the loans procured on behalf of St. Timothy and commingled his assets with those of his governmental client. Following a hearing, the grievance committee of the state in which Williams is licensed as an attorney disbarred him. Williams filed a court action challenging his disbarment on grounds that he was acting as a sports agent rather than as an attorney.

a.   Assess whether Williams is likely to succeed in having his disbarment set aside on grounds that the services he provided were as an agent and not as an attorney.
b.   Assume that Williams is disbarred because he mismanages monies of one of his athlete clients. Also assume that Williams's only clients are professional athletes. Also assume that over the past five years, Williams has not held himself out as an attorney. He neither identified himself as an attorney on his business cards nor published materials that he usually sends out to prospective athlete clients. What is the likelihood that Williams will be able to set aside his disbarment on grounds that the services he provided were as an agent and not as an attorney?
c.   Assume that Williams is not an attorney. Do the services Williams provides for his athlete clients constitute the unauthorized practice of law?

See *In Matter of Horak*, 224 A.D.2d 47, 647 N.Y.S.2d 20 (1996); *In re Jackson*, 650 A.2d 675 (D.C. App. 1994); and the foregoing materials.

CHAPTER
9

Racial Equity Issues in Athletics

A. INTRODUCTION

Race remains a prevalent issue in sport, and one that is increasingly ambiguous and complex. Yet the role of race in sport often is overlooked until a particular event brings it into focus. The event may be a derisive comment made by a radio personality in reference to an athlete of color or an event that marks progress toward racial equity, such as the hiring of an African American NFL head coach. Events seemingly unrelated to sports may inspire discussion of race in sport. Following the election of President Barack Obama on November 4, 2008, for instance, commentators wondered if his achievement might increase access to administrative positions in sports for people of color. They also offered their views on whether the presence of African Americans in leadership positions in sports might have influenced Americans to vote for President Obama.

The goal of this chapter is to introduce you to some of the issues that arise when examining race in the sports context. It attempts to achieve this goal through commentary and leading cases that address race-related issues. The chapter begins with historical perspectives on the role of race in American sport.

B. HISTORICAL PERSPECTIVE

During the early years of professional and collegiate sports, a period extending from after the Civil War to the late 1800s and early 1900s, African Americans participated in organized sports at the amateur and professional levels, including boxing, horse racing, baseball, and cycling. The opportunity to participate during this period was not accompanied by equality of treatment. African Americans were both exploited for their athletic ability and subjected to the indignities that flowed from racial discrimination. To illustrate, African American athletes suffered the racial epithets of fans and opposing players and the discriminatory acts (e.g., physical attacks) of their own teammates.

The early years of inclusion in amateur and professional sports, albeit limited, were followed by a period during which formal and informal rules excluded blacks from organized professional and collegiate sports. One scholar cites two reasons for the segregation of sports:

> The most obvious [reason] was simply the desire of whites not to associate with African-Americans. . . . Associated with this desire for separation was . . . the other broad explanation: a view that African-Americans were inferior. This view, of course, finds its roots in slavery and provided a common excuse for separation of the races.

Kenneth L. Shropshire, In Black and White: Race and Sports in America 31 (1996). See generally Arthur Ashe, A Hard Road to Glory (1988) (discussing the history of African Americans in amateur and professional sports in America). This period of segregation was followed by what some have coined the reintegration of sports, which is discussed *infra*.

The following excerpt illustrates the web of formal and informal rules that historically prevented African American athletes from playing for white Southern colleges and universities and severely limited their ability to play for Northern colleges and universities. In reading these materials, be mindful that similar rules were used to enforce segregation in professional sports in America.

1. *Racial Segregation: Intercollegiate Athletics*[1]

a. **Formal Rules of Exclusion**

During the late nineteenth and early twentieth centuries, legally countenanced segregation impacted virtually every aspect of social behavior and interaction, including sport. In college sport, a series of rules and customs limited black participation to historically black colleges and a few predominantly white colleges located in the northern United States.

In the South, prohibitions against blacks attending white colleges and universities effectively excluded the black athlete from playing for predominantly white southern institutions. Moreover, Jim Crow laws enacted to prohibit whites and blacks from social interaction extended to bar direct sporting competition between them. For example, a Texas Penal Code provision, enacted in 1933, prohibited any "boxing, sparring or wrestling contest or exhibition between any person of the Caucasian or 'White' race and one of the African or 'Negro' race." Tex. Art. 614-11(f), Texas Penal Code (1933). Likewise, a 1932 Atlanta city ordinance prohibited amateur baseball clubs of different races from playing within two blocks of each other.

More broadly written statutes prohibited any form of athletic competition between whites and African Americans. Legislative Act 579 is illustrative. Enacted by the Louisiana legislature in 1956, the statute prohibited interracial sports participation. Although similar legislation was defeated in Mississippi, Mississippi state institutions adopted an "unwritten but ironclad segregation policy." Thomas E. Foreman, Discrimination Against the Negro in American Athletics 37 (1957). That such a policy was adopted with respect to sport may be explained by the fact that Mississippi led former states of the Confederacy

---

1. This section is adapted from Timothy Davis, *Myth of the Superspade: The Persistence of Racism in College Athletics*, 22 Fordham Urban L.J. 615 (1995).

in enacting laws and policies to "ensure effective apartheid." Wendy R. Brown, *The Convergence of Neutrality and Choice: The Limits of the State's Affirmative Duty to Provide Equal Educational Opportunity*, 60 Tenn. L. Rev. 63, 74 (1992).

One commentator observed, "What was left for blacks generally was participation of black against black and the formation of Negro leagues. At a less organized level, it meant acceptance of the Jim Crow laws which called for separate (but almost never equal) playgrounds, public parks, swimming pools, and other recreational facilities." John A. Lucas and Ronald A. Smith, Saga of American Sport 275 (1978). Under such a regime, the idea of competition in the South between white and black collegians was out of the question.

b. Informal Rules of Discrimination

During the late nineteenth and early twentieth centuries, blacks played sports for a limited number of northern colleges such as Harvard, Amherst, and Oberlin. Informal rules reinforced by social strictures, however, were as effective as legislation in limiting the opportunities available to black athletes to compete at predominantly white institutions outside the South.

These informal limitations appeared in various guises. In some instances, they were manifested as a virtual prohibition of African Americans from becoming student-athletes. For instance, few black students competed in sports for Catholic universities, because most such institutions excluded African American students during this period. Often informal Jim Crow laws prohibited blacks from playing sports for the schools that did admit black students.

African American students' experience at the University of Kansas is illustrative. No formal Jim Crow laws were passed in the state of Kansas. Nevertheless, the official policy of the university attempted to minimize the presence of black students in order to remove them from the mainstream of the school's social and extracurricular activities. One historian notes, "Blacks were denied practically every right except that of attending classes." Raymond Wolters, The New Negro on Campus: Black College Rebellions of the 1920s 316 (1975). The university's denial of African American students' rights to participate in most extracurricular activities included the right to participate on the university's athletic teams. The head of athletics at the University of Kansas in the 1930s insisted, "[N]o colored man will ever have a chance as long as [he is there]." Loren Miller, *The Unrest Among College Students*, 34 CRISIS 187 (1927). The situation at University of Kansas illustrates the lack of opportunity for black students to compete for northern universities, which often paralleled those institutions' attitudes and policies toward black students in general.

The environment encountered by black students and student-athletes at the University of Kansas was not unique. Certain athletic conferences, such as the Missouri Athletic Conference (with the exception of Nebraska) systematically excluded black athletes pursuant to so-called "gentlemen's agreements" that prohibited blacks from participating in league contests. These "gentlemen's agreements" constituted a series of written rules or tacit understandings precluding black participation in organized sport.

The reach and impact of "gentlemen's agreements" extended beyond the walls of the institutions that relied on them to exclude black athletes. These agreements severely impacted the few black athletes who were participating for northern universities. Prior to World War II, most northern teams with blacks on their rosters either did not schedule games against southern teams or would leave their African American players at home when the team traveled south. It has also been suggested that a promise to withdraw voluntarily from games against southern schools was an element of the consideration that some northern institutions extracted from their black athletes.

Illustrations abound of northern schools forcing black players to sit out games against southern teams. For instance, in 1916, Paul Robeson, a member of Rutgers University's football team, was barred from the field of play when Washington and Lee College threatened not to play if he was allowed to participate. Such racially exclusionary practices resulted in black colleges providing the only significant opportunities for the black athlete to compete in college athletics prior to the 1930s.

Northern institutions adopted other informal rules. These rules carried the weight of law and, thus, restricted the ability of black athletes to compete for white colleges and universities. Informal quotas typically restricted the slots open to black athletes to no more than one or two players on a team. In addition to numerical quotas, northern colleges imposed another requirement that limited the number of black student-athletes allowed to compete on their teams. Many of these institutions imposed a "superspade" requirement. In other words, the typical African American student-athlete playing for a predominantly white college prior to the 1930s tended to be an exceptionally talented starter.

Black student-athletes competing for the few predominantly white colleges willing to admit them were not spared the indignities of racism at their home institutions. Black athletes were excluded from the mainstream of campus social, academic, and athletic life. Black student-athletes were typically not permitted to reside in campus housing or otherwise engage in campus social life. They encountered demeaning comments from coaches, teammates, and other members of the university community, as well as the populace of the local communities in which those colleges were located. This sense of isolation was heightened by an absence of other black students, as well as black faculty, coaches, or administrators.

By the end of World War II, virtually every major collegiate program outside the South had opened its doors to permit at least one African American player to compete for it. Southern colleges and universities resisted this fundamental change in college sport and continued after World War II to exclude African American student-athletes. The integration of college sport at predominantly white colleges in the South did not begin until the latter part of the 1960s, but once it did the numbers of African American players competing for these institutions mushroomed. For discussions of the integration of intercollegiate sport, see Timothy Davis, *Myth of the Superspade: The Persistence of Racism in College Athletics*, 22 Fordham Urban L.J. 615, 633-637 (1995); see also Timothy Davis, *Race and Sports in America: An Historical Overview*, 7 Va. Sports & Ent. L.J. 291 (2008); Forest J. Berghorn, *Racial Participation and Integration in Men's and Women's Intercollegiate Basketball: Continuity and Change, 1958-1985*, 5 Soc. Sport J. 107, 111 (1988).

2. *Racial Segregation: Professional Sports*

Prior to World War II, the experiences of racial and ethnic minorities in professional sports largely paralleled those of their amateur counterparts. Baseball provides an excellent illustration of the experiences of African Americans in professional sports prior to World War II. It is estimated that approximately 24 blacks played in organized professional baseball during the 1880s. By the 1890s, however, segregation of professional baseball emerged pursuant to a gentleman's agreement that resulted in the total exclusion of black and dark-skinned Latino players from Major League Baseball (MLB). Fair-skinned Latinos were permitted to play, but they were subjected to images that depicted them as "lazy, passive, and inferior," and to other forms of discrimination that continued into the post–World War II era. In addition, fair-skinned Latinos who initially entered American professional baseball systematically received lower-paying contracts than their white counterparts.

Blacks and dark-skinned Latinos developed alternative venues in which to play. Principally, they played in the Negro Leagues and in Latin America, and they barnstormed against white players. (Opportunities for interracial play in a barnstorming capacity were reduced beginning in the 1920s, however, when MLB's first commissioner, Judge Kenesaw Landis, prohibited major league all-star teams from competing against Negro League teams.)

According to Professor Alfred Mathewson, the term "Negro Leagues" generally has been used somewhat casually to refer to teams that played in the United States between 1880 and 1995. Alfred D. Mathewson, *Major League Baseball's Monopoly Power and the Negro Leagues*, 35 Am. Bus. L.J. 291, 292 (1998). These leagues consisted primarily of black professional baseball players and black owners. *Id.* He goes on to note that although formal leagues existed, "particularly the Negro American and National Leagues," most Negro League teams were unaffiliated with a formal league and operated independently. *Id.* Professor Mathewson adds that most of these teams traveled throughout the United States engaging in "barnstorming sport" that resulted in them playing both black and white local teams. "Frequently, the games were significant social events in Black communities. Even those teams that were members of formal leagues barnstormed before, during and after joining leagues. The Kansas City Monarchs, who introduced night baseball in 1930, and the Indianapolis Clowns were two of the most successful barnstorming teams." *Id.* at 293.

Segregated baseball also provides insight into the inequity of separate but equal. Black ballplayers' salaries averaged less than half that of white major league ballplayers. While traveling, black players were confronted with inadequate transportation and substandard segregated accommodations. Negro League teams also encountered difficulty finding suitable playing facilities. Some facilities were off limits because of stereotypical fears of blacks. Although some Negro League teams constructed their own facilities, many teams rented major league stadiums at which they often encountered segregated seating restrictions. *Id.* at 294-295.

3. The Reintegration of Professional and Amateur Sports

Baseball would remain segregated until Jackie Robinson joined the Brooklyn Dodgers in 1947. The formal desegregation of baseball would not occur, however, until 1959, when the Boston Red Sox, the last major league baseball team to field an all white team, promoted Pumpsie Green to the major leagues. The National Football League (NFL) had been integrated from the year of its founding in 1920 until 1934, when a gentlemen's agreement between NFL owners, seeking to remake the league, banned the signing of black players. Daniel Coyle, *Invisible Men*, Sports Illustrated, Dec. 15, 2003, 124. The NFL was reintegrated in 1946 when Kenny Washington, who coincidentally had once roomed with Jackie Robinson at UCLA, joined the Los Angeles Rams. Similar to football, basketball had less of a history of exclusion than baseball. African Americans competed against whites in professional basketball up until World War I. In 1950, a year after the NBA was formed, Chuck Cooper, an African American, was selected in the draft by the Boston Celtics. In 1966, basketball also provided the first African American coach in a major professional sports league when Bill Russell became coach of the NBA's Boston Celtics. See Kenneth L. Shropshire, In Black and White: Race and Sports in America 29-31 (1996).

A confluence of social, political, and economic variables resulted in the integration of professional sports and broader American society. Significant among these variables are (1) expectations for desegregation created by the "democratic idealism spawned by World War II," (2) opportunities created by a shortage of players because of World War II's decimation of the talent pool of white athletes, (3) political activism by blacks and their white allies demanding the desegregation of professionals sports, (4) Supreme Court desegregation decisions, and (5) enactment of federal civil rights legislation. For informative discussions of the integration of major American sports leagues and the factors contributing to the end of segregation, see William C. Rhoden, Forty Million Dollar Slaves: The Rise, Fall, and Redemption of the Black Athlete (2006); Jules Tygiel, Baseball's Great Experiment: Jackie Robinson and His Legacy (1983); Paul Finkleman, *Baseball and the Rule of Law*, 46 Cleve. St. L. Rev. 239 (1998); J. Gordon Hylton, *Essay: American Civil Rights Law and the Legacy of Jackie Robinson*, 8 Marq. Sports L.J. 387 (1998); Shropshire, *supra*.

Additional factors converged to provide incentives for colleges and universities to recruit African American student-athletes, including political decisions, such as congressional passage of the G.I. Bill (which increased the presence of African Americans on college campuses) and the increased professionalism of college sports following World War II. Historian Adolph Grundman posits that colleges' recruitment of African Americans served a dual purpose: It helped these schools strengthen their athletic programs, while at the same time it promoted the advancement of race relations.

C. RACE AND RACIAL EQUITY IN MODERN SPORTS: AN EVOLVING DEBATE

The majority of players in professional basketball and football are African American. During the 2010-2011 season, African Americans accounted for 78 percent of NBA players and 67 percent of NFL players. Similarly, in 2009-2010, African American males made up a disproportionate number of student-athletes who played Division I football and men's basketball, at 45.8 percent and 60.9 percent, respectively. In 2009-2010, American Americans accounted for 24.9 percent of male athletes participating in Division I intercollegiate sports.[2]

---

2. See The Institute for Diversity and Ethics in Sport, The 2010 Racial and Gender Report Card: College Sport (Richard Lapchick, ed.) (March 3, 2011).

The disproportionate presence of African Americans in basketball and football is misleading to the extent that it suggests race has become a nonissue in American sports.[3] To the contrary, the debate regarding race has merely shifted from the question of distributive justice (e.g., participation opportunities for African Americans in the major sports) to other matters. These issues include (1) opportunities for minorities in administrative and coaching positions; (2) the underrepresentation of African American athletes in sports other than football, basketball, and to a lesser extent, baseball; (3) stereotype threat; (4) the underrepresentation of Latinos and Asians in intercollegiate athletics; (5) the persistence of racial stereotypes in sports media; and (6) the implications for sport when issues relating to race converge with those relating to gender, globalization, and economic exploitation. Timothy Davis, Foreward, *Losing to Win: Discussions of Race and Intercollegiate Sports*, 2 Wake Forest J L. & Pol'y 1 (2012); see also Andrew C. Billings, *Talking Around Race: Stereotypes, Media and the Twenty-First Century Collegiate Athlete*, 2 Wake Forest J.L. & Pol'y 199 (2012); Timothy Davis, *Race and Sports in America: An Historical Overview*, 7 Va. Sports & Ent. L.J. 291, 307-311 (2008). The following discussion illustrates the complex and evolving role of race in American sport.

1. Coaching and Administrative Opportunities

a. College Sports

i. Coaching Opportunities

In December 2003, Sylvester Croom became the first African American head football coach in the history of the Southeastern Conference (SEC) when he was hired to take the reins of Mississippi State University's football team. At the time of his hiring, Croom became the fifth active African American head football coach among the then 117 schools that made up the NCAA's Division I-A (now Football Bowl Subdivision (FBS)). Shortly after Croom was hired, the University of Georgia hired Damon Evans as its athletic director, making him the first African American to hold such a position in the SEC. The hiring of Croom and Evans were particularly significant given the SEC's history of being one of the last conferences to integrate its universities' athletics programs.

While these hirings represented progress, the celebration around them highlighted the broader problem. Croom and Evans were relative rarities; part of an extremely small group of African Americans in athletics leadership positions at Division I-A institutions. Lack of head coaching diversity in football (in which so many African Americans competed) was particularly troubling, and notwithstanding Croom's hiring, this lack of diversity prompted numerous initiatives. For instance, the Black Coaches' Association (which has since changed its name to Black Coaches and Administrators) in 2003 announced a framework for a report card that annually evaluates Division I institutions' search and hiring

---

3. See N. Jeremi Duru, *Friday Night Lite: How De-Racialization in the Motion Picture* Friday Night Lights *Disserves the Movement to Eradicate Racial Discrimination from American Sport*, 25 Cardozo Arts & Ent. L.J. 485, 487 (2007) (arguing "rather than signaling an end to discrimination in sports, [b]lack visibility in collegiate and professional sports has merely served to mask the racism that pervade[s] the entire sport establishment").

processes for head football coaches. Institutions are evaluated based on several factors, including an institution's contact with the BCA during the hiring process, the extent to which institutions make efforts to interview candidates of color, and the diversity of the hiring process. The late Myles Brand, then president of the NCAA, supported the BCA's efforts and also made an institutional commitment to address these concerns, creating an NCAA Diversity and Inclusion Department, which "is responsible for leading the Association in the development and implementation of strategies, policies and programs that promote diversity and inclusion throughout intercollegiate athletics." Through this department the NCAA has developed various programs aimed at addressing the shortage of ethnic minorities in collegiate coaching, including coaching symposia consisting of workshops emphasizing skill development in areas such as communications, booster/alumni relations, fiscal responsibility, moral and ethical considerations, and interview preparation.

Even in light of these efforts, there remained a dearth of coaches of color at American colleges and universities, and accompanying the release of its 2008 report card, the BCA called on the NCAA to initiate a college version of the NFL's Rooney Rule, which requires that each NFL team looking for a head coach interview at least one candidate of color before filling the position (the Rooney Rule is discussed in greater detail in section 1.b, below). In addition, the BCA threatened legal action to redress what it characterized as the continued segregation of college football at the head coach position. While the NCAA has taken no such action and the BCA has not brought suit, the Division I-A Athletic Directors Association stepped forward in 2008 and created a Rooney Rule-like "best practice" for all head football coaching searches in the FBS.[4] These efforts have proved successful. Between 2008 and 2011, the percentage of FBS collegiate head football coaches of color increased from 6.7 percent to 12.6 percent—by far the most substantial increase among college football's four divisions.[5]

Legislatures have gotten involved in efforts to ensure equal opportunity in collegiate football coaching as well. In July 2009, Oregon became the first state to enact Rooney Rule–like legislation that requires its seven public universities to interview minority candidates before hiring a head coach or athletic director. Rachel Bachman, *Kulongoski Signs Minority Coaching Bill*, Oregonian, July 23, 2009, 2009 WLNR 14214680. Since then, legislators in several other states, including Alabama, Florida, Tennessee, Arkansas, Mississippi, Georgia, New York, and Oklahoma, have indicated interest in following Oregon's lead.

These developments are promising, but head football coaching positions continue to be difficult for minorities to access, and football is not anomalous in this regard; overall, coaching opportunities for racial minorities in college sports present a bleak picture. For the 2008-2009 season, the racial demographics of combined head coaching positions in all Division I men's sports were as follows: whites, 89.3 percent; African Americans, 6.6 percent; Asian Americans, 0.7 percent; Latinos, 1.8 percent; and Native Americans, 0.3 percent.[6] Similar

4. N. Jeremi Duru, *Call in the Feds: Title VI as a Diversifying Force in the Collegiate Head Football Coaching Ranks*, 2 Wake Forest J.L. & Pol'y 143, 151 (2012).

5. *Id.* at 152. ("The percentage of Football Championship Subdivision (formerly Division I-AA) collegiate head football coaches of color increased by only one percentage point during that time, from 5.9% to 6.9%. And the percentage of head football coaches of color in divisions II and III actually dropped during that time: from 4.5% to 3% and from 3.7% to 2.9%, respectively").

6. NCAA, 2008-2009 NCAA Race and Gender Demographics Report, 96 (2010).

numbers are present in all Division I women's sports, where whites hold approximately 87.7 percent of head coaching positions.[7] Minority representation in the head coaching ranks is even lower for both men's and women's Division II and III sports.[8]

ii. Administrative Opportunities

Coaching is not the only realm of collegiate athletics in which minorities are underrepresented. Minorities are also underrepresented in various administrative aspects of collegiate sport, for example, athletic directors, conference commissioners, faculty athletics representatives (FAR), and game officials. A detailed discussion of the extent of this underrepresentation, given the breadth of administrative opportunities within intercollegiate athletics, is beyond the scope of this book. Comprehensive information in this regard, however, may be found at the Institute for Diversity and Ethics in Sport, The 2010 Racial and Gender Report Card: College Sport (Richard Lapchick, ed.) (March 3, 2011). This report notes, for example, that in 2009-2010, whites held 93.5 percent of the Division I-A FAR positions and 100 percent of the Division I-A conference commissioner positions.

Notably, while minorities remain underrepresented among administrators in collegiate sport, the NCAA's 2008-2009 Race and Gender Demographics Report, excerpted below, does show gains for minorities since 1995-1996, when the report was first compiled.[9]

Minorities in Leadership Roles, All Institutions
(Historically Black Institutions Excluded)

Position	1995-1996	2008-2009
Overall Percentages		
Director of Athletics	4.0	7.0
Associate Director of Athletics	7.4	11.0
Assistant Director of Athletics	7.9	10.3
Senior Woman Administrator	4.1	9.8
Academic Advisor	20.7	22.7
All Administrative Staff Positions[10]	7.8	12.2
Division I Percentages		
Director of Athletics	5.3	11.1
Associate Director of Athletics	7.9	11.5
Assistant Director of Athletics	9.3	11.6
Senior Woman Administrator	3.9	15.0
Academic Advisor	22.3	26.9
All Administrative Staff Positions	9.1	14.2

7. *Id.*

8. *Id.* at 108-119.

9. The complete document, Race and Gender Demographics: 2008-09 NCAA Member Institutions' Personnel Report (2010), is available online at http://www.ncaapublications.com/c-59-other.aspx.

10. "All Administrative Staff Positions" consists of those positions listed herein and additional positions cited in the report (e.g., Compliance Coordinator, Business Manager, Facility Manager).

b. Professional Sports

Minorities are beginning to make inroads in coaching and senior-level administrative positions in U.S. professional sports, but progress in the coaching ranks has generally outstripped progress at the senior administrative level. For instance, at the end of the 2010-2011 NBA regular season, people of color held 33 percent of the league's head coaching positions but just 11 percent of its CEO/president positions.[11] Similarly, at the end of the 2011 MLB season, people of color represented 16.7 percent of MLB managers, but only 9.7 percent of its general managers.[12]

With respect to both coaching and senior-level administrative diversity, the National Football League has historically lagged behind even the modest gains of the other major American professional sports leagues. This trend continued into the new millennium, prompting the most substantial equal opportunity challenge to an American sports league in recent decades. On September 20, 2003, attorneys Johnnie Cochran and Cyrus Mehri released *Black Coaches in the National Football League: Superior Performance, Inferior Opportunities*, a report concluding that African American football coaches are victims of discrimination with respect to hiring and firing notwithstanding their superior coaching performance. Following the report's release, Cochran and Mehri threatened to sue the NFL if it failed to take concrete steps to increase the number of African Americans among the league's head coaches. Shortly thereafter, an NFL committee issued guidelines as a part of an effort to foster greater opportunities for African Americans to gain head coaching positions. The guidelines, collectively known as the Rooney Rule, include provisions requiring that at least one person of color be interviewed as a candidate for all head coaching vacancies as well as documentation of each interview.

By most estimates the Rooney Rule has been extremely successful. Over the ten years between 2001 and 2011, the number of minority NFL head coaches increased from two to eight, and while no team in any of the first 40 Super Bowls were led by a head coach of color, Super Bowls XLI, XLIII, XLIV, and XLV (played in 2007, 2009, 2010, and 2011, respectively) featured head coaches of color. In 2007, recognizing the Rooney Rule's benefits for diversity in coaching, the NFL began suggesting that teams interview at least one minority candidate when searching for a general manager; and in 2009, the NFL officially extended the Rooney Rule to "include openings for general manager jobs and equivalent front office positions in addition to head coaching vacancies." A notable exception to the rule is that it will not apply when a "team's top front-office job is held or filled by the franchise's owner or a member of his or her family, or in a case in which a team has an existing contractual obligation to promote a member of its front-office staff." Mark Maske, *NFL Expands Rooney Rule to Cover Front-Office Hires*, WashingtonPost.com, June 16, 2009. Still, the Rooney Rule has been successful in expanding equal opportunity in NFL front offices: as of 2012, six NFL teams had general managers of color. Among these six is Jerry Reese, who helped construct the 2008 and 2012 Super Bowl winning New York Giants teams. For a thorough exploration of the Rooney Rule, its origins, and

---

11. Richard Lapchick, The 2011 Racial and Gender Report Card: National Basketball Association 22, 25 (June 16, 2011).

12. Richard Lapchick, The 2012 Racial and Gender Report Card: Major League Baseball 23, 27 (April 25, 2012).

its impact on the NFL and broader society, see N. Jeremi Duru, Advancing the Ball: Race, Reformation, and the Quest for Equal Coaching Opportunity in the NFL (Oxford University Press, 2011).

Although the foregoing progress is to be applauded, people of color continue to be underrepresented in administrative positions (e.g., general managers, coaches, team vice presidents) and ownership in professional sports. For comprehensive information in this regard, see the racial report cards for each major professional sport league generated annually by the Institute for Diversity and Ethics in Sport at the University of Central Florida. For discussions of racial equity relating to coaching and administrative positions in sports see N. Jeremi Duru, *The Fritz Pollard Alliance, the Rooney Rule, and the Quest to "Level the Playing Field" in the National Football League*, 7 Va. Sports & Ent. L.J. 179 (2008); Jacquelyn Bridgeman, *The Thrill of Victory and the Agony of Defeat: What Sports Tell Us About Achieving Equality in America*, 7 Va. Sports & Ent. L.J. 248 (2008); Robert E. Thomas and Bruce L. Rich, *Under the Radar: The Resistance of Promotion Biases to Market Forces*, 55 Syracuse L. Rev. 301 (2005).

2. *Intersections*

a. **Race and Gender**

The racial demographics of women who participate in college sports exemplify the intersection of race and gender. In 2009-2010, African American women accounted for approximately 51 percent of Division I basketball players and 29 percent of women track athletes.[13] The profile of women of color participating in Division I athletics overall during the 2009-2010 season was as follows: African American women composed approximately 16 percent, Latinas 4.2 percent, Asians 2.4 percent, and Native Americans 0.04 percent.[14]

The data suggests that minority women are not participating in the increased athletic opportunities created by sports such as rowing, golf, lacrosse, and soccer, which many institutions added in order to comply with Title IX. Consequently, women of color appear not to be in a position to derive the same level of benefits from Title IX as white women. Addressing this issue in the context of African American women, one scholar commented:

> African American women have encountered stereotyping and stacking within the sports world which steers them into basketball and track. The steering into basketball and track and away from other sports reduces the participation opportunities for which they may compete. . . . Training and development at the higher levels of competition in other sports depend upon access to the lower levels of organized competition in those sports. Sports such as ice hockey, field hockey, tennis, and golf have socio-economic dimensions that limit their accessibility to many black girls at the lower levels of the amateur systems.

Alfred D. Mathewson, *Black Women, Gender Equity and the Function at the Junction*, 6 Marq. Sports L.J. 239 (1996). Professor Marilyn Yarbrough identified race and

---

13. Richard Lapchick, The 2010 Racial and Gender Report Card: College Sport 37 (March 3, 2011).
    14. *Id.* at 38.

gender as the dual prohibitions that confront women of color in sports. Marilyn V. Yarbrough, *If You Let Me Play Sports*, 6 Marq. Sports L.J. 229 (1996). In this regard, two scholars recently wrote:

> For the African-American females who decide to pursue athletics, racism and patriarchy in the culture of sport present additional barriers to their continued participation. Consider, for example, that black females frequently are steered into particular sports or positions within sports. Black females are more prevalent in basketball or track. . . .
>
> [F]or African-American girls, gender, race, and class converge in ways that make participation in sports a gamble. They risk experiencing the isolation that results from being one of the few girls of color on a team and losing their "black lady" bona fides. At the same time, the persistence of stereotypes about black women's proper place in sport constrains the athletic opportunities deemed appropriate for them.

Deborah L. Brake and Verna L. Williams, *The Heart of the Game: Putting Race and Educational Equity at the Center of Title IX*, 7 Va. Sports & Ent. L.J. 199, 210-211 (2008). See Alfred D. Mathewson, *Remediating Discrimination Against African American Female Athletes at the Intersection of Title IX and Title IV*, 2 Wake Forest J L. & Pol'y 295 (2012); Lauren Smith, *Black Female Participation Languishes Outside Basketball and Track*, Chron. of Higher Educ. (June 29, 2007).

b.   Race and Economic Exploitation

Commentators have drawn attention to one possible example of the intersection of race and economic exploitation in examining whether African American student-athletes, who are disproportionately overrepresented in collegiate revenue-producing sports, are exploited. Professor Rodney Smith has written that practices in major college football programs foster the unequal treatment of athletes of color. Rodney K. Smith and Neil Millhiser, *The BCS and Big-Time Intercollegiate Football Receive an "F": Reforming a Failed System*, 2 Wake Forest J.L. & Pol'y 45 (2012); see Rodney K. Smith, *When Ignorance Is Not Bliss: In Search of Racial and Gender Equity in Intercollegiate Athletics*, 61 Mo. L. Rev. 329 (1996). Similarly, Professors Amy and Robert McCormick argue that the hyper-commercialization of college sports disadvantages African American athletes economically and academically. Amy C. McCormick and Robert A. McCormick, *Race and Interest Convergence in NCAA Sports*, 2 Wake Forest J.L. & Pol'y 17, 20 (2012). See also Ahmed E. Taha, *Are College Athletes Economically Exploited?*, 2 Wake Forest J.L. & Pol'y 69, 94 (2012) (applying an economic analysis and concluding that the "athletes that generate the most revenue for their colleges are disproportionately black"); Elisia J.P. Gatmen, *Academic Exploitation: The Adverse Impact of College Athletics on the Educational Success of Minority Student-Athletes*, 10 Seattle J. for Soc. Just. 509 (2011) (discussing the exploitation of student-athletes of color).

c.   Race and Globalization

As is true for many industries, American sport has been impacted by globalization. Illustrations include the worldwide televising of American professional sports, playing American professional sports in overseas venues, international sales of licensed merchandise, programs created to increase the popularity of American professional sports leagues, and the increasing numbers of foreign players who play in American professional sports leagues. The dramatic increase in the recruitment of Latino players by MLB raises the issue of the unsavory side of globalization. Commentators allege that MLB systematically affords Latino baseball prospects less favorable treatment than American baseball prospects. See Timothy Poydenis, *The Unfair Treatment of Dominican-Born Baseball Players: How Major League Baseball Abuses the Current System and Why It Should Implement a Worldwide Draft in 2012,* 18 Sports Law. J. 305 (2011); Adam Wasch, *Children Left Behind: The Effect of Major League Baseball on Education in the Dominican Republic,* 11 Tex. Rev. Ent. & Sports L. 99 (2009); Arturo J. Marcano and David P. Fidler, *The Globalization of Baseball: Major League Baseball and Mistreatment of Latin American Baseball Talent,* 6 Ind. J. Global Legal Stud. 511 (1999).

As described by some commentators, the inequitable treatment of Latino baseball prospects allegedly manifests in "MLB scouts getting Latino children to sign blank pieces of paper as 'contracts' to play professional baseball; MLB teams paying no or only paltry signing bonuses for Latino baseball prospects; and, MLB teams systematically discouraging Latino baseball prospects from retaining agents." Marcano and Fidler, *supra,* at 532. These and other commentators allege that such treatment would not be tolerated in the United States. They also contend that it represents a form of discrimination against Latino children.

Another race-related issue on the international stage is the racist behavior of players, coaches, officials, and fans with which players of color must contend, and efforts being made by teams and entities such as the European Union to combat racism in soccer. See Michael W. Ryan, *The European Union and Fan Racism in European Soccer Stadiums: The Time Has Come for Action,* 20 Fla. J. Int'l L. 245 (2009). Yet another issue that demonstrates the confluence of race and internationality are restrictions on the numbers of international players allowed on teams in certain leagues domestic and international. See, e.g., N. Jeremi Duru, *This Field Is Our Field: Foreign Players, Domestic Leagues, and the Unlawful Racial Manipulation of American Sport,* 84 Tul. L. Rev. 613 (2010).

NOTES AND QUESTIONS

1. Explanations that have been offered for the dearth of African American head football college coaches include interference by influential white alumni and fans that hinders the hiring of African American head football coaches; the refusal of athletic administrators to admit that a problem exists in hiring procedures; and black coaches' lack of experience because many did not play in central positions during college. Do you agree or disagree with any of the foregoing reasons? Are there other reasons for the underrepresentation of racial minorities in coaching and management positions in college and professional sports? Professor Kenneth Shropshire argues that the inability of African Americans to break into leadership is attributable in large part to negative stereotypes. These stereotypes, in conjunction with the "good old boy" system of hiring, result in lower numbers of blacks in authority positions in sports. Shropshire, *supra,* In Black and White 83-85.

2. *Stacking.* Stacking involves the assignment of certain individuals to specific athletic positions based on race or ethnicity rather than ability. The

following account, offered in 2002, describes the history of stacking in the NFL:

> During the 1960s, black NFL players were "stacked" in positions thought by white coaches to require mere raw talent, not talent and brains. Black players were channeled and confined to running back, wide receiver, cornerback, offensive tackle and defensive tackle. The "lily white triangle," the two guards, center and quarterback where the plays and line calls are made, was virtually all white. Of course there were no black quarterbacks. On the defensive side of the ball, virtually no black players played linebacker or safety.
>
> With the coming of the American Football League in 1960, the stereotypes of black football players began to break down. Competing head to head with the NFL, AFL teams were looking for legitimacy and superior football talent. The only issue regarding what position a black football player played in the new league, with the exception of quarterback, was whether or not he could perform.
>
> Ten years ago, there were eight black quarterbacks out of the NFL's 106 quarterbacks and three were starters. In 2002, out of the 104 NFL quarterbacks, 22 are black and nine are starters. Given the chance, black athletes certainly excel as NFL quarterbacks equally as well as their white counterparts.

David Meggyesy, *Let Players Decide Who Coaches Will Be*, Sports Bus. J., Oct. 21-27, 2002.

But are black quarterbacks truly given a chance? At the end of the 2011 season, the proportion of black quarterbacks in the NFL was almost exactly what it was when Meggyesy wrote the foregoing article in 2002 (roughly 20 percent) even though more than 70 percent of the league's overall players were of color. See Hub Arkush, *Why Does NFL Still Have Few Black QBs?*, Pro Football Weekly, Mar. 1, 2012 at 26. Why does such stacking continue? In what other sports and at what other positions is it evident? See Andrew C. Billings, *Talking Around Race: Stereotypes, Media and the Twenty-First Century Collegiate Athlete*, 2 Wake Forest J.L. & Pol'y 199, 210 (2012) (providing examples of stacking in college athletics).

3. The disproportionate number of African American men in basketball and football gives a false impression that they dominate the world of professional sports. With a couple of exceptions (e.g., baseball and soccer for Latino men), African American and other racial minorities are underrepresented in most other sports. What reasons exist for the absence of racial minorities in most sports other than basketball, football, baseball, and to some extent soccer? Recognizing the need for diversity, sports such as NASCAR have developed programs aimed at increasing minority representation within their sports. For example, NASCAR has developed Drive for Diversity, which seeks to find drivers and mechanics of color. In an effort to reverse the decline of black players, Major League Baseball has instituted programs including "Reviving Baseball in Inner Cities," and "Major League Baseball's Urban Youth Academies," both of which are aimed at developing a pipeline for players of color to eventually compete in the major leagues.

4. Another question that has been the subject of intense debate is whether sports are overemphasized in the African American community. (Interestingly, the same issue has been raised with respect to young prospective baseball players who live in Latin American countries.) Some commentators argue that far too many young African American males consider sports their "ticket to

upward mobility." The statistics paint a clear picture that very few athletes who compete in high school sports will play at the professional level. The NCAA estimates that the percentage of high school athletes who will play professional basketball is 0.03 percent. The figure for professional football is 0.08 percent.

One author notes, however, that the emphasis young African American males place on athletics is understandable given the historically high profile of blacks in sports.

> The list of black athletes who are revered as heroes is long—and impressive. Athletics is the ultimate meritocracy, and when black athletes won competitions against white athletes, African-Americans did more than cheer. They looked upon the victories as proof that they could compete in a white world that stretched beyond the playing fields. . . . As more black athletes succeeded, the expectations rose. . . .
>
> Given such a situation, researchers say, it's no surprise that even now there are more prominent and successful blacks in those areas than the business world or academia. And given how media—for better or worse—pay more attention to singers and football players, people who excel in such pursuits get more attention than teachers or accountants.

Lori Shontz, *Focus on Sports Hurts Blacks, Some Say*, St. Louis Post-Dispatch, Feb. 22, 2004, at A1. Reasons offered to explain the focus by young African Americans on sports include the devaluation of African American males' academic achievement and negative perceptions concerning the likelihood that African American males will succeed in enterprises outside sports. *Id.* Whatever reasons may underlie this untoward emphasis on sports, many commentators argue the situation must be turned around.

> As far as [Professor Henry Louis] Gates[, Jr.] is concerned, the reasons behind the athletic emphasis don't matter. Action must be taken to correct it. "The blind pursuit of attainment in sports is having a devastating effect on our people. . . . Imbued with a belief that our principal avenue to fame and profit is through sport, and seduced by a win-at-any-cost system that corrupts even elementary school students, far too many black kids treat basketball courts and football fields as if they were classrooms in an alternative school system. "OK, I flunked English," a young athlete will say. "But I got an A plus in slam-dunking."

Id.

D. CASE LAW

The cases that follow address four (among many) contexts in which race has emerged as an issue in sports: (1) the development and promulgation of NCAA initial eligibility rules; (2) employment discrimination claims asserted by minority coaches; (3) the use by American sports teams of Native American mascots, names, and symbols; and (4) racially hostile sports environments. Collectively, these cases provide a glimpse of the complexity of the race-related legal issues that arise in sports.

1. Academic Racism and Marginalization: NCAA Initial Eligibility Rules

PROBLEM 9-1

The NCAA is considering a number of proposals designed ostensibly to increase graduation rates of basketball players at the Division I level. The Black Coaches and Administrators (BCA) has asked for your advice regarding a couple of the proposals. One proposal is designed to improve graduation rates by creating disincentives for programs with lower graduation rates. The proposal in question would provide for a reduction of two scholarships for programs with graduation rates that fall below 50 percent and four scholarships for programs with graduation rates below 25 percent. A number of coaches fear that the proposals will harm their programs because they take players from weaker high schools, many of which are poorly funded inner-city schools in which a large percentage of the students are racial minorities. The coaches believe that it is more difficult to maintain the higher graduation standards with student-athletes from these poorer schools. As such, they believe that the proposal is questionable on racial equity grounds. A second proposal calls for incentives in the form of additional scholarships for schools with graduation rates above 60 percent (one new scholarship at 60 percent, two at 70 percent, and three at 80 percent or higher). Once again, many of the coaches believe that this requirement may benefit universities that recruit heavily from wealthier school districts, which include fewer minority students. A few coaches in the association disagree and argue that the graduation incentives and disincentives programs will ultimately increase the number of minority athletes graduating from universities. Are there legal or ethical problems with the proposals as outlined? What response should the BCA offer to such proposals at the legislative level within the NCAA? Consider the following materials.

PRYOR v. NCAA
288 F. 3d 548 (3d Cir. 2002)

MICHEL, Circuit Judge.

In this close and complex appeal, we must decide whether Plaintiffs have stated a claim for purposeful, racial discrimination under Title VI of the Civil Rights Act of 1964, 42 U.S.C. §2000d *et seq.* (1994) and 42 U.S.C. §1981 (1994), by alleging (among other things) that the National Collegiate Athletic Association adopted certain educational standards because of their adverse impact on black student athletes seeking college scholarships. We hold that they have sufficiently alleged a claim for relief.

As the complaint indicates, the NCAA purportedly tried to improve graduation rates among black student athletes by adopting Proposition 16, a facially neutral rule that establishes scholarship and athletic eligibility criteria for incoming student athletes. As a result of these criteria, Plaintiffs allege, Proposition 16 has caused increased numbers of black student athletes to lose eligibility for receiving athletic scholarships and for participating in intercollegiate athletics during their freshmen year. Plaintiffs further allege that defendant knew of these effects and intended them. And thus, Plaintiffs suggest that the NCAA actually adopted Proposition 16 to "screen out" more black student athletes from ever receiving athletic scholarships in the first place, with the asserted goal of increased graduation rates serving as a mere "pretext."

Because the complaint sufficiently avers that Proposition 16 has adversely impacted the number of black student athletes who qualify for athletic scholarships, and because it alleges the NCAA adopted this otherwise facially neutral policy "because of" this adverse, racial impact, we cannot agree that the Plaintiffs—African-American student athletes who failed to meet the eligibility criteria established by Proposition 16—have failed to state a claim for relief under the liberal notice-pleading requirements of Fed. R. Civ. P. 8(a). . . .

. . . [I]n 1986, the [NCAA's] Division I members adopted Proposition 48, which required incoming high school athletes to have a minimum grade point average of 2.0 and a minimum 700 score on the Scholastic Aptitude Test in order to practice, play and receive an athletic scholarship. As this court has previously stated, the Division I members implemented Proposition 48 to address the perception that its member schools were exploiting athletes "for their talents without concern for whether they graduated." *Cureton v. Nat'l Collegiate Athletic Assoc.*, 198 F.3d 107, 110 (3d Cir.1999). Following the implementation of Proposition 48, graduation rates among athletes, especially among black athletes, increased.

B

In 1992, the Division I schools voluntarily adopted the NCAA's Proposition 16, the provision at issue in this case. Proposition 16 modifies Proposition 48 by increasing the number of core high school courses in which a student athlete must have a minimum GPA, and it determines athletic eligibility based on a formula that combines a student-athlete's GPA and standardized test score. Proposition 16 essentially increases the minimum scores that a high school student athlete must attain to qualify for athletic scholarship aid and eligibility for practicing and competing as a college freshman. For example, if a student athlete had a 2.0 GPA in the core high school courses, he or she must score a 1010 on the SAT. The district court found in a similar case that Proposition 16 puts a greater emphasis on standardized test scores than did its predecessor (Proposition 48).

Cureton I

In 1997, counsel for Plaintiffs in this case sued the NCAA on behalf of different minority student athletes who claimed that Proposition 16 violated the regulations to Title VI of the 1964 Civil Rights Act. *Cureton v. Nat'l Collegiate Athletic Assoc.*, 198 F.3d at 111 (*"Cureton I"*). Specifically, the *Cureton* plaintiffs alleged a Title VI violation based on the theory that Proposition 16 creates a disparate impact on racial minorities. *Id.* . . . [T]he district court concluded that Proposition 16's disparate impact on African-American athletes violated the regulations to Title VI; and so, the court permanently enjoined the continued enforcement of Proposition 16. . . .

This court reversed and remanded with instructions for the entry of judgment for the NCAA. In the court's analysis, the regulations applied only to the specific programs or activities for which an entity uses federal funds, not to the entity at large. *See Cureton I*, 198 F.3d at 114. As a result, the court reasoned, even assuming the NCAA received federal funds, the Title VI regulations did not apply to the NCAA because the NCAA did not exercise "controlling authority" over its member institutions' "ultimate decision" about a student-athlete's eligibility to participate in collegiate athletics. *See id.* at 116-17 (citing and discussing *NCAA v. Tarkanian,* 488 U.S. 179, 197-99, 109 S.Ct. 454, 102 L.Ed.2d 469 (1988)). Roughly one year after this decision, the Supreme Court held that Title VI creates no claim for disparate impact, contrary to the theory alleged by the plaintiffs in *Cureton I:* "Title VI itself directly reach[es] only instances of intentional discrimination." *Alexander v. Sandoval,* 532 U.S. 275, 281, 121 S. Ct. 1511, 149 L.Ed.2d 517 (2001). . . .

C

This dispute very much resembles the *Cureton* case, with the variant that Plaintiffs here allege that the NCAA purposefully discriminated against them by adopting Proposition 16. . . .

According to the complaint, Plaintiff Kelly Pryor is an African-American student athlete recruited by San Jose State to play varsity soccer. Pryor has a learning disability. In 1999, as a high school athlete, she signed an agreement, called a National Letter of Intent ("NLI"), to play soccer on a scholarship at San Jose State beginning in the fall of 1999. Plaintiff Warren Spivey is an African-American student athlete who signed an NLI to play football at the University of Connecticut ("UConn"). As with the NLIs signed by all student athletes who receive athletic scholarships, the NLIs signed by Pryor and Spivey contain a condition that would render the agreement void if they failed to meet the eligibility requirements established in Proposition 16.

Neither Pryor nor Spivey met these requirements. Pryor, however, did petition for a waiver based on her learning disability. As a result, she received "partial qualifier" status, meaning she retained her athletic scholarship and could still practice with the San Jose State soccer team; she just could not compete in the team's games. . . .

Spivey himself, meanwhile, did not petition for a waiver; but UConn did so on his behalf, arguing that Spivey's record showed that he was prepared for the academic requirements of college. The NCAA denied this petition, as well as the appeal thereto, meaning Spivey could not receive athletically related financial aid or participate in varsity athletics during his freshman year. According to the complaint, Spivey still attends UConn, but he incurred substantial debt, *i.e.,* student loans, in order to pay his college tuition.

Under Proposition 16, student athletes who fail to meet the eligibility criteria as freshmen may still compete in varsity athletics beginning their sophomore year, provided they meet other minimum academic criteria. Also, Proposition 16 relates only to the award of athletic scholarships; no NCAA policy stops a university from giving a Proposition 16 "casualty" the financial aid that is available to all students. None of the post-freshmen year criteria are at issue in this case.

In February 2000, Pryor and Spivey sued the NCAA and sought to certify a class against it. Pryor alleged that Proposition 16 discriminated against her on account of her learning disability, in violation of the Americans with Disabilities Act and the Rehabilitation Act. . . . In addition, both Pryor and Spivey alleged that, by adopting Proposition 16, the NCAA intentionally discriminated against them on account of their race, in violation of Title VI of the Civil Rights Act and 42 U.S.C. §1981.

As support for their race-discrimination claims, Plaintiffs' complaint cites often to NCAA memoranda and other evidence obtained during the *Cureton* litigation. In particular, the complaint notes that the NCAA responded to an interrogatory about its reasons for adopting Proposition 16 by identifying (as one of its "top ten reasons") the goal that Proposition 16 would promote a higher graduation rate for black athletes and would thereby narrow the "Black/ White Gap" between black student-athlete graduation rates and white student-athlete graduation rates. (Pls.' Compl. ¶¶62-63.) Citing statements from the district court's now-vacated decision in *Cureton I*, the complaint asserts that Proposition 16's "explicit race-based goal stands in stark contrast to the characterization of Proposition 16 as a facially neutral rule." (*Id.* ¶64) quoting *Cureton v. NCAA*, 37 F.Supp.2d 687, 705 (E.D.Pa.1999)). Further, it professes a reliance, in part, on the "serious questions" the *Cureton* court itself had about whether Proposition 16 "function[ed] simply as a proxy for a racial quota." (*Id.* ¶64) (quoting *Cureton, supra.*)

In addition, the complaint identifies a memorandum from the NCAA dated July 1998 asserting that Proposition 48 and Proposition 16 have led to steady increases in the graduation rates for minorities and that no other proposed models would achieve that goal as well as Proposition 16 has. (*Id.* ¶65.) An affidavit from Graham Spanier, a former member of various NCAA committees, similarly avers that Proposition 48—the precursor to Proposition 16—had significantly improved graduation rates of student athletes, with the greatest increase coming among black student athletes. (*Id.* ¶66.) And another memorandum from an NCAA statistician . . . indicates that Proposition 16 projected the highest graduation rate for black and white athletes.

Liberally construed, the complaint maintains that Proposition 16 achieves the NCAA's stated goal of improving graduation rates for black athletes relative to white athletes by simply "screen[ing] out" greater numbers of black athletes from ever becoming eligible in the first place, *i.e.*, from ever receiving athletic eligibility and scholarship aid. (*E.g.*, Pls.' Compl. ¶¶20, 29, 66, 159, 162, 177.) Further, it maintains that although the NCAA knew that Proposition 16 would have a more adverse impact on black student athletes than on white student athletes, the NCAA went ahead and adopted Proposition 16 anyway, based on its "misguided view toward affecting African-American student-athletes' graduation rates by denying [scholarship] eligibility to greater numbers of" black student athletes. (*Id.* ¶¶69, 76.) As support for this assertion, the complaint points to various studies, research and reports by the NCAA showing that Proposition 16 and its precursor (Proposition 48) would disproportionately and negatively impact black student athletes. (*E.g.*, Pls.' Compl. ¶¶71-75.)

Citing these allegations, the complaint also lays out two theories of relief under Title VI and §1981. First, it asserts that because the NCAA adopted Proposition 16 knowing that it would adversely affect black student athletes, the NCAA thereby acted with "deliberate indifference" to Proposition 16's impact on African-American student athletes. (*Id.* ¶¶164-66, 178.) And that indifference, the theory goes, amounts to the purposeful discrimination proscribed by Title VI and §1981. (*See id.*) Alternatively, the complaint indicates that the evidence of the NCAA's knowledge about Proposition 16's impact as well as other "circumstantial evidence" establishes that the NCAA adopted this policy to intentionally deny athletic eligibility and scholarship aid to a greater number of black athletes. (*See, e.g.*, Pls.' Compl. ¶¶20, 81, 169.) "Any suggestion" that considerations of race did not at least partially motivate the NCAA's adoption of Proposition 16 is "pretextual." (*Id.* ¶¶83, 180.)

In response, the NCAA moved to dismiss Plaintiffs' complaint under Fed. R. Civ. P. 12(b)(6) or, alternatively, for summary judgment.

The District Court Grants the NCAA's Motion to Dismiss

In July 2001, the district judge—the same judge that handled the *Cureton* litigation—granted the NCAA's motion to dismiss. As to Pryor's ADA and Rehabilitation Act claims, the court determined that Pryor lacked standing to effectively remedy her asserted loss of freshman eligibility. . . .

In addition, the court dismissed the two theories that Pryor and Spivey advanced to show purposeful discrimination. . . . [The court's discussion of the district court's rationale for dismissing the Title VI claim is omitted.]

Finally, the district court dismissed Pryor and Spivey's §1981 claim. . . . [The court's discussion of the district court's rationale for dismissing Plaintiffs' §1981 claim is omitted.]

This appeal followed. We have jurisdiction under 28 U.S.C. §1291 (1994) and now affirm in part, reverse in part and remand. . . .

IV

B

As stated, Plaintiffs' complaint and attached exhibits sufficiently allege a claim for purposeful discrimination in the adoption of an otherwise facially neutral policy. In effect, the complaint states that the NCAA purposefully discriminated against black student athletes by adopting a policy with the intent to reduce the number of black athletes who could qualify for athletic scholarship aid. We address this theory first and Plaintiffs' "deliberate indifference" theory thereafter.

1

To recover under Title VI or §1981, Plaintiffs cannot simply assert that Proposition 16 has a disproportionate effect on certain minorities. . . . As the parties agree, Title VI and §1981 provide a private cause of action for intentional discrimination only.

To prove intentional discrimination by a facially neutral policy, a plaintiff must show that the relevant decisionmaker (*e.g.,* a state legislature) adopted the policy at issue "'because of,' not merely 'in spite of,' its adverse effects upon an identifiable group." *Personnel Administrator of Massachusetts v. Feeney*, 442 U.S. 256, 279, 99 S.Ct. 2282, 60 L.Ed.2d 870 (1979); *accord Gen. Bldg. Contractors Assoc.*, 458 U.S. at 391, 102 S.Ct. 3141. A mere awareness of the consequences of an otherwise neutral policy will not suffice. . . .

Once a plaintiff establishes a discriminatory purpose based on race, the decision-maker must come forward and try to show that the policy or rule at issue survives strict scrutiny, *i.e.,* that it had a compelling interest in using a race-based classification and this classification is narrowly tailored to achieve that compelling interest. . . . Racial classifications, well intentioned or not, must survive the burdensome strict scrutiny analysis because "'absent searching judicial inquiry . . . there is simply no way of determining what classifications are "benign" or "remedial" and what classifications are in fact motivated by illegitimate notions of racial inferiority or simple racial politics.'" This appeal involves only whether the NCAA intended to discriminate against black athletes by adopting Proposition 16, not whether that policy survives strict scrutiny.

"Determining whether invidious discriminatory purpose was a motivating factor [in the adoption of a facially neutral policy] demands a sensitive inquiry into such circumstantial and direct evidence of intent as may be available." *Arlington Heights*, 429 U.S. at 266, 97 S.Ct. 555. Although considering evidence of impact would seem to contradict the principle that no claim for disparate impact lies under Title VI or §1981 . . . , the Supreme Court has more directly stated that the "important starting point" for assessing discriminatory purpose is the "impact of the official action" and "whether it bears more heavily on one race than another." *Arlington Heights*, 429 U.S. at 266, 97 S.Ct. 555. As the Court has explained, the "impact of an official action is often probative of why the action was taken in the first place since people usually intend the natural consequences of their actions." *Bossier Parish School Bd.*, 520 U.S. at 487, 117S.Ct. 1491.

Other considerations relevant to the purpose inquiry include the "historical background of the . . . decision; [t]he specific sequence of events leading up to the challenged decision; [d]epartures from the normal procedural sequence; and[t]he legislative or administrative history, especially . . . [any] contemporary statements by members of the decisionmaking body." *Id.* . . . Owing perhaps to the principle that questions of intent and state of mind are ordinarily not amenable to summary adjudication . . . , courts have only reluctantly upheld the Rule 12(b)(6) dismissal of a claim alleging unlawful discrimination in the adoption of an otherwise facially neutral policy. . . .

2

In this case, Plaintiffs have stated a claim for purposeful discrimination. As we are reviewing this case at the Rule 12(b)(6) stage, we may affirm the judgment only if "it appears beyond doubt that no set of facts would entitle" Plaintiffs to relief. . . .

Here, it does not appear beyond doubt that Plaintiffs have failed to sufficiently allege facts showing purposeful discrimination by the NCAA. The complaint and attached exhibits make clear that the NCAA considered race as one of its reasons for adopting Proposition 16, with the NCAA stating explicitly that it believed the adoption of this policy would increase the graduation rates of black athletes relative to white athletes. Further, the complaint alleges that the NCAA purposefully discriminated against black student athletes (like Plaintiffs) when it adopted Proposition 16 because the NCAA knew—via various studies and report—that the heightened academic requirements of Proposition 16 would effectively "screen out" or reduce the percentage of black athletes who could qualify for athletic scholarships. In short, the complaint alleges that the NCAA adopted Proposition 16 because it knew that policy would prevent more black athletes from ever receiving athletic scholarship aid in the first place.

. . . [T]his is a case where, based on the face of the complaint and all reasonable inferences thereto, the NCAA at least partially intended to reduce the number of black athletes who could attend college on an athletic scholarship by adopting the heightened academic requirements of Proposition 16. And as the exhibits and complaint allege, the NCAA knew of this impact because of the pre-Proposition 16 studies informing them about this outcome. . . .

. . . [L]iberally construing the allegations, the complaint here conveys that the NCAA adopted Proposition 16 because it allegedly wanted to reduce the number of black athletes who could ever become eligible for athletic scholarships. The complaint further suggests that the NCAA's "stated goal" of wanting to improve graduation rates via Proposition 16 served as a mere "pretext" for its actual goal. . . .

Here . . . the complaint alleges that the NCAA purposefully adopted a policy because that policy would reduce the number of black athletes who could receive athletic scholarships and compete in intercollegiate athletics as freshmen. Further, the complaint indicates that the NCAA knew this policy, Proposition 16, would and has adversely affected black student athletes, not white student athletes, because of the pre-Proposition 16 studies that informed them of this outcome. In other words . . . , the complaint in this case does sufficiently state facts showing intentional, disparate treatment on account of race.

3

The NCAA asserts that both the complaint and the exhibits thereto show only that the NCAA intended to help black athletes by adopting Proposition 16, not harm them. In like vein, it claims that precedent from the Supreme Court, as well as from rulings by other circuit courts, consistently absolve decisionmakers from purposeful-discrimination liability so long as their intent was "benign" or (in the words of Plaintiffs' counsel in *Cureton*) "laudable." For two reasons, however, this argument is unconvincing.

First, as explained above, the complaint adequately alleges that the NCAA sought to achieve its stated goal of improving graduation rates by using a system that would exclude more African-American freshmen who, in the past, might have qualified for scholarships. Further, as the complaint and other exhibits suggest, the NCAA knew that using this approach would also screen out more black student athletes than white student athletes. So again, one could infer that, because the NCAA knew this, it was actually pursuing its stated goal and adopted means as a way to accomplish this sinister purpose while still seeming "laudable" and well intentioned. True, at first glance, some might well consider this theory far fetched. But we are reviewing this case at the pleading stage, not the summary judgment stage. Further, two allegations and the exhibits supporting them support the theory of the complaint: the NCAA openly considered race in formulating Proposition 16; and it had reason to know that the adoption of Proposition 16 would lead to the greater exclusion of black athletes from receiving college athletic scholarships.

Again, one may doubt that the NCAA harbored such ill motives. After all, many NCAA schools have long engaged in fierce recruiting contests to obtain the best high school athletes in the country, many of whom are black. And in today's world of collegiate athletics, better athletes can translate into more revenues and exposure for the schools that sign them. On the other hand, racial discrimination is nearly always irrational and thus, in the words of the Supreme Court, "odious" to our nation's principles of equality. . . . Further, neither our court nor the district court can render "findings" in this case—at least not yet. And findings of fact, of course, turn on evidence, not on one's speculations about the issue. Nothing in our decision today precludes either summary judgment or trial findings that conclude the NCAA did not intend to discriminate on the basis of race.

Second, even assuming the NCAA's assertion that it had only "laudable" goals in adopting Proposition 16 and that it actually wanted only to improve graduation rates among black student athletes, the NCAA has cited no authority holding that a claim for purposeful discrimination may lie only if the accused decision-maker had "bad intentions" or "animus." Quite the contrary. The Court has squarely held that, well-intentioned or not, express or neutral on its face, a law or policy that purposefully discriminates on account of race is presumptively invalid and can survive only if it withstands strict scrutiny review. . . .

Admittedly, this case is not subject to easy categorization. It differs from many Supreme Court precedents in that one could read the complaint and attached exhibits as showing that the NCAA adopted Proposition 16 to benefit the parties now suing for intentional discrimination. . . . And it differs from . . . reverse-discrimination cases in that Plaintiffs here are not, say, white student athletes claiming the NCAA adopted a race-based policy at their expense. Again, putting aside the more sinister theory about the NCAA purposefully using Proposition 16 as a means to discriminate against black athletes, Plaintiffs' complaint can also be read as alleging that (1) the NCAA considered race when it adopted Proposition 16; (2) it did so for the "benign" or "laudable" goal of improving graduation rates among black student athletes; but (3) the policy for achieving that goal—Proposition 16—backfired and has instead worked to the detriment of black athletes.

We need not address whether this theory fits within the analytical framework established by the Supreme Court. As stated earlier, liberally reading the complaint (as we must), Plaintiffs also sufficiently allege that the NCAA adopted Proposition 16 for the malevolent purpose of excluding black student athletes from receiving scholarship aid and athletic eligibility. In this regard, we merely reiterate the Supreme Court's established view that a claim for purposeful discrimination may lie even if the decisionmaker adopted the allegedly discriminatory policy or rule at issue for a "beneficial" or "laudable" purpose.

4

As Plaintiffs have sufficiently alleged a claim of purposeful discrimination under the analysis set forth above, they need not establish their alternative theory about the NCAA acting with "deliberate indifference" to the impact of Proposition 16 in order to secure reversal of the total dismissal of the complaint. But as they continue to press this alternative theory, we must address and reject it. The Supreme Court has recently re-affirmed the principle that Title VI of the Civil Rights Act "directly reaches only instances of intentional discrimination." *Alexander v. Sandoval*, 532 U.S. at 281, 121 S.Ct. 1511. Plaintiffs try to sidestep this holding by claiming that the NCAA was not just indifferent to Proposition 16's alleged disparate impact on black athletes; it was extremely indifferent to that impact even if it did not intend to discriminate. Frankly, we see no meaningful difference between the proffered "deliberate indifference" standard and the rule, well settled by the Supreme Court, that a decision maker will not commit purposeful discrimination if it adopts a facially neutral policy "in spite of" its impact, not "because of " that impact. . . . Accordingly, we reject Plaintiffs' "deliberate indifference" standard as a cognizable theory of relief under Title VI. . . .

c

Having determined that Plaintiffs have sufficiently alleged a claim for purposeful discrimination, we must also conclude that Plaintiffs have thereby satisfied two of the three elements of the §1981 analysis. To establish a right to relief under §1981, a plaintiff must show (1) that he belongs to a racial minority; (2) "an intent to discriminate on the basis of race by the defendant; and (3) discrimination concerning one or more of the activities enumerated in" §1981, including the right to make and enforce contracts. *Brown v. Philip Morris Inc.*, 250 F.3d at 797. The standard for establishing an "intent to discriminate on the basis of race" is identical in the Title VI and §1981 contexts.

Here, the district court granted the motion to dismiss Plaintiffs' §1981 claim because not only (in the court's view) did Plaintiffs fail to allege facts showing an intent to discriminate; but also because they failed to show that the NCAA had deprived them of their contract rights under the NLI. According to the district court, Plaintiffs agreed to the NLI condition that they satisfy the academic requirements of Proposition 16; and that Plaintiffs therefore received all their rights under their respective NLIs because they had simply failed to meet this condition, meaning the NLIs had by their own force become void.

This analysis is certainly logical. But it fails to account for the argument about the NLI condition resulting from the NCAA's alleged discrimination. . . . In our view, this argument is persuasive. A contract term or condition that violates public policy is void and is thus unenforceable.

In the realm of contract law, the doctrine of public policy reflects principles of law already enumerated by the Constitution and state and federal law. . . . It follows that this doctrine may also void a contract term if that term offends the laws prohibiting racial discrimination. . . .

In this case, we have already determined that Plaintiffs have stated a claim for purposeful discrimination, meaning Plaintiffs have alleged facts sufficient to meet the second prong of §1981 as well. Moreover, as the precedents above show, the NCAA could not avoid §1981 liability here simply because the Proposition 16 condition—an alleged product of purposeful discrimination—was not satisfied. . . . Rather, as Plaintiffs suggest, this condition is void on its face provided Plaintiffs can establish that the NCAA adopted Proposition 16 (and, thus, the condition contained in the Plaintiffs' NLIs) for the purpose of intentionally discriminating on the basis of race. For purposes of the NCAA's Rule 12(b)(6) motion, we hold that Plaintiffs have so established that point. Accordingly, the fact that the condition here was not performed does not serve as a basis for vitiating Plaintiffs' §1981 claim. We therefore reverse and remand Plaintiffs' §1981 claim too.

V

While we appreciate the NCAA's burden of having to tend to numerous lawsuits alleging purposeful discrimination in the adoption of Proposition 16, neither the courts nor the NCAA nor any other civil litigant is free to ignore the rules of procedure, including the notice pleading provisions of Fed. R. Civ. P. 8 and 9. By the same token, parties suing the NCAA for such claims must be prepared to present evidence at the summary judgment stage that would substantiate their allegations. We express no opinion about whether Plaintiffs in this case can carry that burden.

For the reasons stated above, we affirm the dismissal of Plaintiff Pryor's ADA and Rehabilitation Act claims for want of constitutional standing. But we reverse the Rule 12(b)(6) dismissal of Plaintiffs' Title VI and §1981 claims insofar as they rest on allegations of purposeful discrimination, not deliberate indifference. We remand for additional proceedings consistent with this opinion.

NOTES AND QUESTIONS

1. Identify the NCAA's goals in promulgating Proposition 16. Why did the court reject these goals as a basis for upholding the standardized test component of the NCAA's initial eligibility rules?

2. In 1997, minority student-athletes sued the NCAA claiming that Proposition 16 violated regulations promulgated under Title VI of the 1964 Civil Rights Act because of its disparate impact on African American athletes. The district court concluded that Proposition 16 had a disparate impact on African American athletes in violation of the regulations and permanently enjoined enforcement of Proposition 16. It did so even though it accepted the NCAA's stated justification that Proposition 16 was a way to raise all student-athletes' graduation rates. *Cureton v. NCAA*, 37 F. Supp. 2d 687 (E.D. Pa. 1999).

   On appeal, however, the Third Circuit reversed that decision. *Cureton v. NCAA*, 198 F.3d 107 (3d Cir. 1999). The appellate court concluded that the regulations in question applied only to specific programs or activities using federal funds and not to the whole entity. Because the NCAA program allegedly receiving direct funding was not at issue, the regulations could only become applicable if the NCAA had controlling authority over some relevant program receiving federal funding, such as a member school's athletic scholarship program. The court concluded that the NCAA did not exercise controlling authority over member institutions' ultimate decisions about student-athletes' eligibility to participate in athletics, and thus was not subject to the regulations.

   For discussions of *Cureton v. NCAA* and the controversy surrounding the standardized test component of the NCAA's initial eligibility rules, see Diane Heckman, *Tracking Challenges to NCAA's Academic Eligibility Requirements Based on Race and Disability*, 222 Ed. L. Rep. 1 (2007); Anneliese Munczinski, Note, *Interception! The Courts Get Another Pass at the NCAA and the Intentional Discrimination of Proposition 16 in* Pryor v. NCAA, 10 Vill. Sports & Ent. L.J. 389 (2003); Eli D. Oates, *Cureton v. NCAA: The Recognition of Proposition 16's Misplaced Use of Standardized Tests in the Context of Collegiate Athletics as a Barrier to Educational Opportunity for Minorities*, 35 Wake Forest L. Rev. 445 (2000); Kenneth L. Shropshire, *Colorblind Propositions: Race, the SAT and the NCAA*, 8 Stan. L. & Pol'y Rev. 141 (1997).

3. *Revised Initial Eligibility Standards.* In 2003, the NCAA reported that graduation rates of student-athletes who matriculated in 1996 rose to 61 percent, an all-time high. This was the first group of student-athletes who entered college subject to Proposition 16. Graduation rates for black male basketball players and football players increased. The rate increased for black male basketball players to 41 percent compared to 35 percent for black male basketball players who entered in 1995. For black football players the increase was from 46 percent to 49 percent. The graduation rate for all Division I football players was 54 percent. The rate for all Division I basketball players was 44 percent. The rate for women basketball players was 66 percent, a 1 percent increase over the 65 percent graduation rate for women basketball players who matriculated in 1995. The NCAA also reported that 3 percent fewer African American athletes entered colleges in 1996 as compared to 1995. NCAA graduation data released in 2008 showed that graduation rates for black football and basketball players remained much higher than pre-Proposition 16 rates. According to federal graduation data, 50 percent

of FBS black football players who entered college in 2001-2002 graduated (the Graduation Success Rate (GSR) compiled by the NCAA, which includes transfer students was 54 percent). The federal rate for black male basketball players was 44 percent (the GSR was 54 percent). The continued improvement in athlete graduation rates has been attributed to an increased emphasis on academics, the Academic Progress Rate (APR), and heightened initial eligibility requirements. See Chapter 3 for a discussion of the APR.

Proposition 16 was not the first major NCAA reform related to its initial eligibility requirements. In 1983, NCAA initial eligibility rules known as Proposition 48 were enacted to take effect in 1986. Proposition 48's minimum standards required that a student-athlete achieve a minimum of 2.00 GPA in at least 11 designated high school courses (core courses). In addition, it required a minimum combined score of 700 on the SAT or 15 on the ACT. As was true of Proposition 16, critics assailed Proposition 48's requirement as racially biased. They argued that heightened standards would reduce many black student-athletes' access to college; standardized tests are culturally biased against African Americans; and standardized tests fail to take into account the often unique circumstances of African American student-athletes. Proponents of stricter initial eligibility rules argued that such requirements would help to restore academic integrity to colleges and universities that had been undermined by scandals arising within intercollegiate athletics and represented a means of ensuring that student-athletes have a reasonable chance of obtaining a meaningful degree. Informative discussions of the debate surrounding the enactment of NCAA initial eligibility rules be found in Davis, *supra*, at 664-667; Kenneth L. Shropshire, *Colorblind Propositions: Race, the SAT and the NCAA*, 8 Stan L. & Pol'y Rev. 141 (1997).

4. What were the ramifications of the *Pryor* court's ruling? Will the ruling have harmful or beneficial effects on student-athletes? How will it affect intercollegiate athletics programs? In November 2002, the NCAA passed legislation that radically changed its initial eligibility rules. This legislation became effective with the class of student-athletes who matriculated in 2005 (students who entered prior thereto could gain eligibility under either the current or revised initial eligibility standards). In the same year, 2005, the SAT format changed. The implementation of a writing section increased the maximum achievable score from 1600 to 2400, but the new NCAA initial eligibility standards regard only the math and verbal sections and therefore remain on a 1600-point scale. In addition, the new initial eligibility standards eliminate the cutoff score for the standardized test component. For example, a student with a 3.0, or solid B, average needs to score 620 on the SAT to be eligible for competition and financial aid during his or her first year. (See Initial Eligibility Index, *infra*.) The minimum SAT score ranges from 400 (students with a 3.550 or above GPA) to 1010 (students with a 2.0 GPA). The number of core courses increased from 13 to 14 for student-athletes who matriculated in 2005. This number increased to 16 for students who entered college in 2008. Late NCAA president Myles Brand articulated the following rationale for the revised standard:

> The goal in developing the most recent eligibility models was to maximize graduation rates while minimizing disparate impact. . . . We believe that eliminating the test-score cut will increase access and that the new progress-toward-degree

benchmarks—particularly in the student-athlete's first two years—will put athletes on track to graduate at even higher rates than they already do.

Athlete Graduation Rates Continue to Climb, NCAA News, Sept. 1, 2003, at 1,
11. As discussed in Chapter 3, in 2011, the NCAA imposed more stringent
initial eligibility rules with respect to grade point averages in core courses.

2.   *Employment Discrimination: Title VII and Section 1981*

As discussed *supra*, race has been identified as a factor that limits access to
coaching and administrative positions and promotion opportunities for African
Americans in college and professional sports. In the few instances in which
minority coaches have alleged racial discrimination in hiring and promotion in
sports, they have resorted to Title VII and Section 1981 of the Civil Rights Act.
Title VII prohibits discrimination in employment. Under Title VII, a plaintiff
is likely to assert claims premised on disparate treatment (which focuses on
intentional racial discrimination) or disparate impact (which focuses on the
use of facially neutral employment practices) that unjustifiably discriminate
against members of a protected group. Section 1981 is broader in scope in that
it applies to the making, performance, and enforcement of all contracts, not
just employment contracts. Section 1981 proscribes intentional discrimination.
   The *Jackson* case, *infra*, provides a detailed discussion of the proof that plaintiffs must establish in order to prevail in Title VII and Section 1981 actions.
Jackson also reveals, however, that the proof required in order to establish a
cognizable Title VII or Section 1981 claim limits the effectiveness of these traditional antidiscrimination norms for those seeking redress for alleged racial
discrimination. See Neil Forester, Comment, *The Elephant in the Locker Room:
Does the National Football League Discriminate in the Hiring of Head Coaches?*, 34
McGeorge L. Rev. 877 (2003) (outlining the elements of Title VII and Section
1981 claims). Before reading *Jackson*, review the following comment that sheds
light on the reality of hiring in professional sports.

THE FRONT OFFICE AND ANTIDISCRIMINATION LAW[15]

The statistical composition of sports management's upper echelon would seem
to implicate at least one of [the antidiscrimination norms]. A key problem, however, lies in the informal nature of hiring practices in the sports industry. . . .
   Employers in sports tend to use a series of subjective criteria that vary among
employment decisions, with no elements necessarily being weighed more heavily than others. With no unique employment practice to target as discriminatory, it is difficult to bring an action under Title VII, no matter what the statistics
show regarding the under-representation of any group at any job level.
   The nature of the law indicates that the most viable suit for individuals is one
brought by a party denied a job opportunity on the basis of race or a discriminatory selection device or hiring practice. Thus if there is no party wronged, no person denied employment based on discriminatory criteria, then no viable cause

---

15. This excerpt was originally published in Kenneth L. Shropshire, In Black and White: Race
and Sports in America 65-68 (1996). Internal citations to authority have been omitted.

of action exists. . . . When those in power tap a friend or family member for a job opening, it is difficult to prove that a particular African-American candidate has been denied an opportunity for employment; in an industry run through contacts and word of mouth, it is likely that there were no other applicants. So, very often, no individual is harmed when a management position goes to yet another white male, because there were no other applicants who could prove that they were denied the job on the basis of race. And in many instances, race was not a factor. The *McDonnell Douglas* formula is wholly inapplicable because the African-American candidate rarely even gets into the pipeline. . . .

Complicating the difficulty in forming a successful discrimination lawsuit against the hiring practices in professional sports is the fact that at the management level, particularly in sports, many employment decisions rest significantly on factors not objectively quantifiable. Judges typically are reluctant to override an employer's decision and impose their own judgments of a candidate's qualifications, especially when the criteria are highly subjective. The instances of judges professing a lack of expertise or refusing to step in and overrule hiring decisions for high-level employment positions are legion in case law.

The sports industry has the added patina of unique talent-identification criteria, particularly for coaching and general manager positions. Courts have been particularly reluctant to interfere with purely sports-related decisions of private sporting enterprises. . . . Whether a specific African-American would be a better coach than the white applicant hired is not an issue in which a court is likely to become involved.

JACKSON v. UNIVERSITY OF NEW HAVEN
228 F. Supp. 2d 156 (D. Conn. 2002)

DRONEY, District Judge.

I. INTRODUCTION

James C. Jackson ("Jackson") brought this action against the University of New Haven ("UNH") and Deborah Chin, the Athletic Director of UNH, alleging racial discrimination in hiring in violation of 42 U.S.C. §981, 42 U.S.C. §000d (Title VI), and 42 U.S.C. §000e-5 (Title VII). . . . Jackson seeks damages as well as equitable relief, costs, and attorney's fees. Pending before the Court is Defendants' Motion for Summary Judgment. . . . For the following reasons, the motion is GRANTED.

II. FACTS

In February 1999 the head football coach at the University of New Haven ("UNH") left to take a position with the Cleveland Browns of the National Football League. This dispute arises out of the ensuing search for a new head coach at UNH.

Beginning in early February of 1999, UNH posted the head coach position both internally and with the "NCAA market," an online professional publication for university and college athletics. The postings for the head coaching position listed the following requirements:

> A bachelors degree is required, master's degree preferred. *Successful collegiate coaching experience required.* Experience in recruiting, game coaching and knowledge of NCAA rules and regulations is essential.

. . . Further, the duties were listed as follows:

> Implement and manage all aspects of a national caliber Division II football program in accordance with NCAA and university regulations. Areas of responsibility include, but are not limited to coaching, recruiting qualified student athletes, budget management, scheduling, hiring and supervising coaching staff, academically monitoring student-athletes, and promotions and fund-raising.

. . . After receiving 36 applications, UNH's Search Committee, which had been established to select a new head coach, decided to interview six applicants—all of whom had college coaching experience and are Caucasian. Jackson, an African-American, was not among the six applicants interviewed. Jackson had no college experience, but had been a professional minor league football coach, earned several "coach of the year" honors as such a coach, and was inducted into the minor league football hall of fame. The defendants assert that they decided not to interview Jackson because he lacked the requisite collegiate coaching experience. From the six applicants interviewed, the Search Committee ultimately selected Darren Rizzi, who had been an assistant coach at UNH for four years, to fill the position of head coach.

At the heart of this dispute lies the "collegiate coaching experience" requirement. The parties are in agreement that the posted job qualifications included that requirement and that all of the applicants selected for interviews possessed such experience. However, the parties differ markedly in their characterizations of that prior experience requirement. The defendants maintain that prior NCAA coaching experience was essential to ensure the selection of a candidate sufficiently well-versed in NCAA rules and regulations to both pass the NCAA's annual tests on such regulations and manage the UNH football team successfully. Jackson, however, asserts that the requirement of previous collegiate coaching experience was not necessary to ensure familiarity with NCAA rules and regulations and that it served to exclude otherwise qualified minority applicants, such as himself.

Jackson asserts that the requirement that applicants have prior college coaching experience amounts to discrimination in violation of 42 U.S.C. §1981, 42 U.S.C. §2000d (Title VI), and 42 U.S.C. §2000e-5 (Title VII).[3] Jackson asserts all three of these statutory causes of action against defendant UNH. However, only the §1981 claim is asserted against defendant Chin.

---

3. Title 42 U.S.C. §1981 provides that "[a]ll persons within the jurisdiction of the United States shall have the same right in every State and Territory . . . to the full and equal benefit of all laws." Title 42 U.S.C. §2000d (Title VI) provides that "No person in the United States shall, on the ground of race . . . be excluded from participation in, be denied any benefits of, or be subject to discrimination under any program or activity receiving Federal financial assistance." . . . Finally, Title VII prohibits certain "Unlawful employment practices," which include "fail[ing] or refus[ing] to hire or discharge any individual, or otherwise to discriminate against any individual . . . because of such individual's race. . . ." 42 U.S.C. §2000e-2.

Jackson appears to base his complaint on both the "disparate treatment" and "disparate impact" theories of recovery in that he alleges both that the challenged qualification had a discriminatory effect upon African Americans (disparate impact) and that the defendants intentionally discriminated against him based on his race (disparate treatment). . . .

IV. ANALYSIS

A. DISPARATE TREATMENT CLAIM

As mentioned, Jackson alleges that he has been discriminated against in violation of 42 U.S.C. §§1981, 2000d (Title VI), and 2000e-5 (Title VII). To the extent that he claims that he has been discriminated against intentionally, the U.S. Supreme Court has developed a "burden shifting framework" for claims brought under Title VII alleging "disparate treatment." *McDonnell Douglas Corp. v. Green*, 411 U.S. 792, 802, 93 S.Ct. 1817, 36L.Ed.2d 668 (1973). Courts have subsequently applied the same burden-shifting framework articulated in *McDonnell Douglas* to disparate treatment claims arising under 42 U.S.C. §§1981 and 2000d (Title VI). . . . Thus, because the test is the same under each of the three statutes, this Court will apply the same *McDonnell Douglas* burden-shifting framework to the plaintiff's disparate treatment claim.

Under the burden-shifting framework of *McDonnell Douglas*, a plaintiff alleging disparate treatment based on race and national origin must first establish a prima facie case of discrimination. 411 U.S. at 802, 93 S.Ct. 1817.[5] The burden then shifts to the defendant to offer a legitimate, nondiscriminatory rationale for its actions. *See James v. New York Racing Ass'n*, 233 F.3d 149, 154 (2d Cir. 2000). Finally, if the defendant does offer a non-discriminatory reason for its decision, the burden again shifts to the plaintiff to show that the defendant's stated reason is a mere pretext for discrimination. *See Id.* (citing *St. Mary's Honor Ctr. v. Hicks*, 509 U.S. 502, 506-10, 113 S.Ct. 2742, 125 L.Ed.2d 407 (1993)). In some circumstances, under *Reeves v. Sanderson Plumbing Products, Inc.*, 530 U.S. 133, 120 S.Ct. 2097, 147 L.Ed.2d 105, (2000), after the plaintiff offers evidence to show that the defendant's asserted non-discriminatory reason for the hiring is pretextual, the evidence that established the prima facie case will be sufficient to survive a summary judgment motion. . . . Here, the burden-shifting framework does not reach this stage because Jackson has failed to establish a prima facie case.

To establish a prima facie case of discrimination, a plaintiff must show (1) membership in a protected class, (2) qualification for the employment, (3) an adverse employment decision, and (4) circumstances that give rise to an inference of discrimination. *McDonnell Douglas*, 411 U.S. at 802, 93 S.Ct. 1817. . . . Courts have acknowledged this framework is "not inflexible," but that "in establishing a prima facie case the plaintiff must show that [he] applied for an available position for which [he] was qualified, but was rejected under circumstances that give rise to an inference of discrimination." *Brown v. Coach Stores, Inc.*, 163 F.3d 706, 710 (2d Cir.1998) (citing *Texas Dep't of Cmty. Affairs v. Burdine*, 450 U.S. 248, 253, 101 S.Ct. 1089, 67 L.Ed.2d 207 (1981)) (internal quotation marks omitted).

---

5. The *McDonnell Douglas* burden-shifting framework is only necessary when the plaintiff has failed to offer direct evidence of discriminatory intent. . . . Here, the plaintiff has not offered any evidence of discriminatory intent; thus, the *McDonnell Douglas* inquiry is appropriate.

The parties do not dispute that Jackson is a member of a protected class. Nor do they dispute that the defendants' decision to hire Rizzi instead of Jackson was adverse to him. However, the parties disagree as to whether Jackson meets the second prong of *McDonnell Douglas:* qualification for the position. In their Motion for Summary Judgment, the defendants assert that Jackson was not qualified because he failed to meet an express condition of the employment, that he did not have prior NCAA coaching experience. Although he maintains that he is qualified, Jackson does not dispute that prior collegiate coaching was an expressly listed qualification for the UNH head coach position, nor does he contend that he had any prior experience coaching in college. However, Jackson's subjective determination that he is qualified for the position is not enough to carry his burden of making out a prima facie case. The Second Circuit, in the context of an age discrimination suit, elaborated on the definition of the "qualification" requirement of the *McDonnell Douglas* prima facie case in *Thornley v. Penton Publ'g*, 104 F.3d 26 (2d Cir.1997): "As we understand this element, being 'qualified' refers to the criteria the employer has specified for the position." 104 F.3d at 29. The Court further explained that broad deference should be afforded to employers in selecting hiring criteria: "Absent a showing by the plaintiff that the employer's demands were made in bad faith . . . an employer . . . is not compelled to submit the reasonableness of its employment criteria to the assessment of either judge or jury." *Id.* . . .

Consistent with this understanding, courts have afforded employers considerable latitude in selecting employment qualifications. For example, in *Schaffner v. Glencoe Park Dist.*, 256 F.3d 616 (7th Cir.2001) the Seventh Circuit considered the "qualification prong" of the *McDonnell Douglas* burden-shifting framework in the context of an ADEA claim. 256 F.3d at 620. There the plaintiff was denied a promotion to the position of "program manager" for park recreational programs — a position that listed as one of its requirements one of several types of bachelor's degrees. The court held that the plaintiff failed to meet the qualification prong of the *McDonnell Douglas* test because she did not possess any of the specified degrees, and was therefore not qualified for the position.

. . . [D]eference must be given the defendants in selecting college coaching experience as a qualification for the position of head coach. Nor is it appropriate for this Court to mandate that the defendants equate Jackson's experience in coaching minor league football with college coaching experience. . . .

There are, however, limits to an employer's latitude in selecting hiring criteria. For example, in *Howley v. Town of Stratford*, 217 F.3d 141 (2d Cir.2000) the Second Circuit rejected the defendant's argument that the plaintiff, a female firefighter, was "ineligible" for a promotion to assistant-chief because she did not have the required four years of line-officer experience. 217 F.3d at 151. The Court acknowledged that the town was "entitled to set its own criteria" for the position, but held that because the Town had "relaxed" that standard for two male firefighters, the plaintiff's lack of experience should not have resulted in summary judgment for the defendant. *Id.* at 151-52.

Here there is no claim, and Jackson has put forth no evidence, that the defendants failed to apply the prior college coaching experience requirement uniformly to African-Americans and others. Absent any such showing, the defendants are entitled to the deference in selecting hiring criteria recognized in *Thornley*. Moreover, the prior college coaching experience requirement at issue here appears reasonable on its face. There is an obvious and significant nexus between the defendants' need to select a head coach well-versed in NCAA regulations and the requirement that candidates have actual experience in college coaching. Thus, Jackson has failed to make out a prima facie case of disparate treatment in that he has failed to demonstrate that he was qualified for the position of head coach. As Jackson has failed to meet his burden, this Court grants summary judgment as to his disparate treatment claim brought pursuant to 42 U.S.C. §§1981, 2000d (Title VI), and 2000e-5 (Title VII).

B. DISPARATE IMPACT

Unlike disparate treatment, in asserting a claim of disparate impact under Title VII a plaintiff need not allege that the discrimination was intentional. *Griggs v. Duke Power Co.*, 401 U.S. 424, 430-32, 91 S.Ct. 849, 28 L.Ed.2d 158 (1971) ("[G]ood intent or absence of discriminatory intent does not redeem employment procedures or testing mechanisms that operate as 'built in head winds'"). It is enough that a facially-neutral policy, such as the prior college coaching experience requirement at issue here, be shown to have an adverse impact on a protected group. . . .

However, unlike disparate treatment, the disparate impact theory of recovery is available only for claims brought pursuant to Title VII, and not for claims under 42 U.S.C. §1981 or §2000(d) (Title VI). The U.S. Supreme Court has held that these latter provisions can only be violated by intentional discrimination and that they therefore cannot support a "disparate impact" claim. *See Alexander v. Sandoval*, 532 U.S. 275, 280-85, 121 S.Ct. 1511, 149 L.Ed.2d 517 (2001) (holding that §2000d (Title VI) proscribes only intentional discrimination and therefore does not support a disparate impact theory of recovery) (citing *Regents of Univ. of Cal. v. Bakke*, 438 U.S. 265, 98 S.Ct. 2733, 57 L.Ed.2d 750 (1978)). . . . *General Bldg. Contractors Ass'n v. Pennsylvania*, 458 U.S. 375, 391, 102 S.Ct. 3141, 73 L.Ed.2d 835 (1982) (holding that §1981 is only violated by a showing of intentional discrimination). Thus, to the extent that Jackson alleges a disparate impact theory of recovery, his claim is cognizable only under Title VII.

Disparate impact cases, like disparate treatment cases, are governed by a "burden-shifting" framework. The Second Circuit reviewed the disparate impact burden-shifting framework in *NAACP, Inc. v. Town of East Haven*, 70 F.3d 219, 225 (2d Cir.1995):

> "[A] plaintiff may establish a prima facie case of disparate impact by showing that use of the test causes the selection of applicants . . . in a racial pattern that significantly differs from that of the pool of applicants." Such a showing can be established through the use of statistical evidence which discloses a disparity so great that it cannot reasonably be attributed to chance. To establish a prima facie case, the statistical disparity must be sufficiently substantial to raise an inference of causation. After a prima facie case is established, the employer has the burden of coming forward with evidence to show that the test has "'a manifest relationship to the employment in question.'" If the employer can make such a showing, the plaintiff may nonetheless prevail if he can suggest alternative tests or selection methods that would meet the employer's legitimate needs while reducing the racially disparate impact of the employer's practices. [Citations omitted.]

Id. at 225. . . . As the Court noted in *East Haven*, this framework was statutorily enacted by the Civil Rights Act of 1991. *Id.* at 225 fn. 6. *See also* 42 U.S.C. §2000e-2(k).

Here, as in the disparate treatment context, Jackson has failed to meet his burden of setting forth a prima facie case of disparate treatment. In making out a prima facie case for disparate impact under Title VII, the plaintiff bears the burden of demonstrating that a specific policy or practice of the defendant has had a disproportionately negative impact on the plaintiff's protected class. 42 U.S.C. Section 2000e-2(k)(1)(A) . . . ;[7] *Griggs*, 401 U.S. at 432, 91 S.Ct. 849. "To make this showing, a plaintiff must (1) identify a policy or practice, (2) demonstrate that a disparity exists, and (3) establish a causal relationship between the two." *Robinson*, 267 F.3d at 160 (citing 42 U.S.C. §2000e-2(k)(1)(A)(I)). *See also Brown v. Coach Stores, Inc.*, 163 F.3d 706, 712 (2d Cir.1998) ("plaintiff must show that a facially neutral employment policy or practice has a significant disparate impact"). Here, Jackson alleges that the defendants' facially neutral hiring criteria (requiring prior college coaching experience), had a discriminatory impact on African-Americans. Specifically, Jackson asserts that because African-Americans have historically been under-represented in the ranks of NCAA coaches this requirement disproportionately excludes African-Americans from consideration.

Statistics are often an important component of a disparate impact claim. *See Robinson*, 267 F.3d at 160 ("[S]tatistical proof almost always occupies center stage in a prima facie showing of a disparate impact claim"). . . .

The defendants here attack the sufficiency of the plaintiff's statistics. They argue that the plaintiff has not offered any statistical evidence to indicate a causal link between UNH's prior college coaching experience requirement and its negative impact on African-Americans. However, in its memorandum

7. The 1991 Civil Rights Act sets forth the burden of proof required in disparate impact cases at 42 U.S.C. §2000e2(k), which provides in relevant part:

(k) Burden of proof in disparate impact cases

(1)(A) An unlawful employment practice based on disparate impact is established under this chapter only if—

(i) a complaining party demonstrates that a respondent uses a particular employment practice that causes a disparate impact on the basis of race, color, religion, sex, or national origin and the respondent fails to demonstrate that the challenged practice is job related for the position in question and consistent with business necessity; or

(ii) the complaining party makes the demonstration described in subparagraph (C) with respect to an alternative employment practice and the respondent refuses to adopt such alternative employment practice. . . .

(C) The demonstration referred to by subparagraph (A)(ii) shall be in accordance with the law as it existed on June 4, 1989, with respect to the concept of "alternative employment practice."

. . . Even when the disparate impact case is argued on the basis of 42 U.S.C.2000e-2(k)(1)(A)(ii), the burden is still on the plaintiff to demonstrate that the challenged employment practice has an adverse impact on a protected group. In *Price v. City of Chicago*, 251 F.3d 656 (7th Cir.2001), the Title VII plaintiff argued that the 1991 Amendments "eliminated the requirement that the challenged practice has a disparate impact" and that it was enough that "an alternative employment practice with a lesser adverse impact exists and that the employer has failed to adopt it." 251 F.3d at 659. The Seventh Circuit rejected this argument, reasoning that the 1991 Amendments merely provided that "a plaintiff's demonstration shall be in accordance with the law as it existed prior to the Supreme Court's decision in *Wards Cove Packing Co. v. Atonio*, 490 U.S. 642, 109 S.Ct. 2115, 104 L.Ed.2d 733 (1989)." *Id.* at 660, 109 S.Ct. 2115. Case law prior to *Wards Cove*, the Court continued, "made it clear that an employer has no duty to justify its use of a particular employment practice *unless* the plaintiff establishes that the practice has a disparate impact." *Id.* (emphasis in original).

in opposition to the defendants' motion for summary judgment, Jackson does offer statistics suggesting a causal link between the prior experience requirement and its impact on African-Americans, by comparing the pool of applicants to those who were ultimately selected for interviews. Jackson notes that, of the 14 applicants whose race was identified, only 10% of the Caucasians (1 out of 10) did not have college coaching experience, but 50% of the African-American candidates (2 out of 4) did not have college coaching experience. Further, Jackson noted that all six of the applicants selected for interviews were Caucasian. However, this statistical evidence fails to establish a sufficient causal link between the defendants' employment criterion and its impact on African-Americans. The Second Circuit has recognized that exceedingly small sample sizes often result in statistically unreliable evidence. *Lowe v. Commack Union Free Sch. Dist.*, 886 F.2d 1364, 1371-72 (2d Cir.1989) (holding that the fact that two out of three candidates under age 40 received favorable ratings while only 16 out of 34 candidates over age 40 received such ratings did not support a disparate impact claim in part because of "the unreliability of such a small statistical sample") (superceded by statute on other grounds). The Second Circuit has also indicated that a plaintiff's statistics must meet a certain threshold level of substantiality. . . . Here, the relevant sample size is only 14 (of the 36 applicants, the race of only 14 has been identified), which is too small to yield a statistically significant result.

In *Smith* [*v. Xerox Corp.*, 196 F.3d 358 (2d Cir. 1999)], the Second Circuit cautioned that in assessing whether a statistical disparity is "sufficiently substantial to establish a prima facie case of disparate impact, there is no one test that always answers that question." *Smith*, 196 F.3d at 366. "Instead," the Court reasoned, "the substantiality of a disparity is judged on a case-be-case basis." *Id.* (citing *Watson v. Fort Worth Bank & Trust*, 487 U.S. 977, 996 n. 3, 108 S.Ct. 2777, 101 L.Ed.2d 827 (1988)). In this case, the plaintiff has failed to provide a sufficiently substantial disparity to survive summary judgment, because the sample is too small.

In addition to the statistics discussed above, the plaintiff has presented an article from the *Sports Business Journal*, which purportedly demonstrates the disparity of college football coaches that are African-American. However, this article—without more—does not present the type of substantial statistical evidence contemplated by the Second Circuit in *Smith*. It is only two pages long, and most of it is an opinion piece rather than a scientific statistical analysis. Even when the author does cite statistics, he does not disclose the basis for them or reveal their methodology. Also, the article fails to set forth the type of statistics that are appropriate in a disparate impact analysis. The only statistics in the article concern the percentages of coaches in the various NCAA divisions that are African-American. However, the essence of a disparate impact analysis is a *comparison*. In *Carter v. Ball*, 33 F.3d 450 (4th Cir.1994) the plaintiff brought a Title VII discrimination suit against the Secretary of the Navy. The plaintiff in that case attempted to offer statistical evidence "which purportedly demonstrate[d] a statistical imbalance in the Navy's promotional practices." 33 F.3d at 456. The Fourth Circuit upheld the district court's exclusion of the statistical evidence. In so holding, the Court emphasized that "[i]n a case of discrimination in hiring or promoting, the relevant comparison is between the percentage of minority employees and the percentage of potential minority applicants in the qualified labor pool. . . . The mere absence of minority employees in upper-level positions does not suffice to prove a *prima facie* case of discrimination without a comparison to the relevant labor pool." *Id.* . . .[8]

Finally, also in support of his disparate impact claim, the plaintiff asserts that the use of the prior college coaching experience requirement has yielded discriminatory results when applied to other athletic programs at UNH. The plaintiff contends that only one out of 23 coaches hired since 1993, when the plaintiff asserts the prior college coaching experience requirement was adopted for most head coaching positions at UNH, has been African-American. However, even if true, the Supreme Court held in *Wards Cove* that "[t]he percentage of nonwhite workers found in other positions in the employer's labor force is irrelevant to the question of a prima facie statistical case of disparate impact." 490 U.S. at 653, 109 S.Ct. 2115. Thus, the plaintiff has failed to meet his burden of establishing a prima facie case of disparate impact, and this Court also grants summary judgment as to that claim.

For the forgoing reasons, the defendant's Motion for Summary Judgment . . . is GRANTED and the case is DISMISSED.

NOTES AND QUESTIONS

1. *Analyzing* Jackson. The plaintiff based his complaint on "disparate treatment" and "disparate impact" grounds. What is the difference between these arguments as a factual and a legal matter? Which argument do you believe is stronger? What was the court's response to each argument? How much latitude should a university be given in setting coaching experience and related requirements? If you were representing a university involved in such a search, what would you recommend as a legal and practical matter?

2. *Case Law.* As in *Jackson*, other plaintiffs have encountered difficulty in convincing courts that their employment claims were meritorious. For example, in *Wallace v. Texas Tech. Univ.*, 80 F.3d 1042 (5th Cir. 1996), the head coach of Texas Tech's men's basketball team refused to renew the one-year contract of the plaintiff, an African American assistant coach of the team. The plaintiff had been admonished while serving as an assistant coach for becoming "too close" to basketball players. Asserting Title VII and Section 1981 and 1983 claims, the plaintiff alleged racial discrimination in retaliation for the exercise of his First Amendment right to advise African American players regarding their eligibility for financial assistance and for having a close, personal relationship with players.

---

8. The statistics offered by the plaintiff in *Carter* were in support of a disparate treatment claim, but the Court held that they would have been inadmissible in a disparate impact case for precisely the same reasons. The Court observed:

> the test for a disparate impact claim requires (1) that there is an underrepresentation of the qualified members in a protected class promoted to the positions at issue and (2) that specific elements of the employer's promotion criteria had a significant disparate impact on a protected class. Without any evidence of how many African-Americans were qualified for positions at the level to which [the plaintiff] sought to be promoted, there can be no reliable proof of underrepresentation.

Carter, 33 F.3d at 457 fn. 9. [Citations and internal quotation marks omitted.]

The Fifth Circuit upheld the district court summary judgment dismissing the plaintiff's claims. The Fifth Circuit adopted the standard that to succeed on claims of intentional discrimination under Title VII, Section 1981, and Section 1983, a plaintiff must prove a prima facie case of discrimination. It found that the plaintiff's bare assertions, unsupported by evidence on the record, that the head coach had used racial slurs were insufficient to meet the burden of proof. The court also concluded that the plaintiff failed to present sufficient evidence with respect to claims alleging disparate pay, disparate discipline, and hostile environment. See also *Wilson v. Lock Haven Univ.*, 2012 WL 1130593 (3d Cir. April 5, 2012) (affirming lower court's summary judgment rejection of African American coach's racial discrimination claim); *Moran v. Selig*, 447 F.3d 748 (9th Cir. 2006) (rejecting retired Caucasian and Latino professional baseball players' claims that Major League Baseball violated Title VII by excluding them from medical and supplemental income plans for former Negro League players, because "providing a remedy for past discrimination only to those who have been discriminated against does not constitute discriminatory conduct"); *Small v. Feather River College*, 2011 WL 1670236 (E.D. Cal. May 3, 2011) (discussing elements required to establish racially motivated retaliation claims under Title VII and Section 1981); *Moberly v. Univ. of Cincinnati Clermont College*, 2010 U.S. Dist. LEXIS 89974 (S.D. Ohio 2010) (rejecting racial discrimination and First Amendment claims of African American coach who alleged he was not reappointed because of his complaints regarding discriminatory treatment of African American players); *Zachery v. Crawford County Bd. of Educ.*, 2008 WL 4394736 (M.D. Ga. Sept. 24, 2008) (rejecting racial discrimination claim of African American with 36 years of teaching experience and success as basketball coach, the court accepted an explanation that school district's hiring of a white applicant as athletic director was a consequence of non-race-based reasons relating to the successful candidate's record including his possession of outstanding qualifications for the job, history as a successful football coach, desire of district to entice the person to return to the school district, and pressure from the community for the school district to do so); *Cowan v. Unified Sch. Dist. 501*, 316 F. Supp. 2d 1061 (D. Kan. 2004) (even though plaintiff established prima facie Title VII claim, defendant presented nondiscriminatory reason for hiring white applicant—the successful applicant's qualifications—that was not pretext for racial discrimination against African American candidate given the similarities in the candidates qualifications; however, inconsistencies in the reasons given by district for selecting candidates for interviews for another coaching position precluded summary judgment on whether reasons were pretext for race discrimination against plaintiff); but see *Banks v. Pocatella Sch. Dist. No. 25*, 429 F. Supp. 2d 1197 (D. Idaho 2006) (African American coach applicant could proceed on Title VII claim since he presented evidence that school district's asserted reasons for hiring other applicants, plaintiff's alleged poor organizational and communication skills, were pretextual); *McBryde v. Ritenour Sch. Dist.*, 207 S.W.3d 162 (Mo. App. Ct. 2006) (evidence sufficient to allow a jury to conclude that plaintiff, whose coaching contract was not renewed, suffered racial discrimination in violation of the Missouri Human Rights Act); *Hamilton v. Montgomery County Bd. of Educ.*, 122 F. Supp. 2d 1273 (M.D. Ala. 2000) (African American applicant for head basketball coach position at a high school presented sufficient evidence of racial discrimination to survive summary judgment). For a "reverse discrimination" case in which a court found that a white coach's claim that the hiring of a black woman coach instead of him had alleged sufficient facts to establish a violation of Title VII, see *Jacobeit v. Rich Twp. High Sch. Dist. 227*, 673 F. Supp. 2d 653 (N.D. Ill. 2009).

Do the subjective considerations that are relevant in hiring a coach present a virtually insurmountable obstacle to an unsuccessful coaching applicant prevailing in a race discrimination action? See Neil Forester, Comment, *The Elephant in the Locker Room: Does the National Football League Discriminate in the Hiring of Head Coaches?*, 34 McGeorge L. Rev. 877 (2003).

3. *Racial Composition of Teams and Leagues.* As these materials reflect, most scholars and sports law practitioners focus on the coaching and administrative contexts when examining race-based employment discrimination in sports, because of an assumption that racial discrimination with respect to players is a thing of the past. But is it? Although it is well documented that the quarterback position in football was for decades reserved largely for whites, most commentators believe NFL quarterbacking aspirants are now assessed strictly on the basis of skill. At the end of the 2011 season, however, only 20.6 percent of the NFL's quarterbacks were of color while more than 70 percent of the league's overall players were of color. See Hub Arkush, *Why Does NFL Still Have Few Black QBs?*, Pro Football Weekly, March 1, 2012 at 26. Is this disproportionality a coincidence? Might it signal the continued resonance of old stereotypes that African Americans are not well-suited to playing a cerebral position like quarterback?

What about league-wide eligibility rules and their racial implications? Both the NBA and WNBA are overwhelmingly composed of African American players. Both leagues also have eligibility rules permitting non-U.S. citizens to enter the leagues at a younger age than U.S. citizens. Given that the NBA's and WNBA's domestic player pools are largely African American and that their international player pools are largely non–African American, might these age eligibility rules be viewed as racially discriminatory? If so, could either league be vulnerable under a Title VII or Section 1981 lawsuit?

4. *Race-Related Health Complications.* After a 2007 game against the Denver Broncos, Pittsburgh Steelers safety Ryan Clark became life-threateningly ill, resulting in emergency surgery to remove both his gallbladder and spleen. Clark carries the trait for sickle cell anemia, a serious blood disorder that affects people of African descent, and while sickle cell trait carriers are generally asymptomatic, in rare cases factors such as extreme athletic exertion and altitude can cause them to become ill. Doctors concluded that these factors (Denver is well above sea level) combined to precipitate Clark's crisis. In 2012, when the Steelers traveled to Denver to face the Broncos in a play-off game, Steelers head coach Mike Tomlin expressed concern about Clark's health and refused to let him play. Clark accepted the decision and has not had sickle cell trait–related health problems since. He acknowledges, however, that his contract negotiations have been complicated by his condition.

If an NFL club developed a policy of disadvantaging sickle cell trait carriers in contract negotiations or completely refusing to hire players with sickle cell trait, might the club be vulnerable to a Title VII disparate impact racial discrimination lawsuit? It bears noting that a crisis like Clark's is extremely rare for a sickle cell trait carrier and of the estimated 90 sickle cell trait carriers playing in the NFL, none have ever suffered such an episode. Do these facts change your view? For a thorough exploration of these and other questions involving sickle cell trait–related employment complications in sports, see Chika Duru, *Out For Blood: Employment Discrimination, Sickle Cell Trait, and the NFL*, 9 Hastings Race and Poverty L. J. 265 (2012).

5. *Intersection of Race and Freedom of Expression.* Are African American athletes and coaches expected to behave in a way that dilutes their racial identity? For example, African Americans have complained that white coaches and players are afforded much greater latitude to express themselves than their African American counterparts. According to this view, African American athletes and coaches run the risk of incurring costly sanctions if they speak out on racially or politically sensitive issues. See Alfred D. Mathewson, *Grooming Crossovers*, 4 J. Gender Race & Just. 225 (2001) (discussing the role of black athletes in struggling for political, racial, and economic equity in sport). Such allegations lie at the core of two notable lawsuits that have been filed by an African American coach and player.

Nolan Richardson, an African American, was head coach of the University of Arkansas at Fayetteville's (UAF) men's basketball team from 1985 until he was fired in March 2002. *Richardson, Jr. v. Sugg*, 325 F. Supp. 2d 919 (E.D. Ark. 2004). Richardson alleged that "he was fired because of his race and because he spoke out on matters of public concern (race)." *Id.* at 922. With respect to his employment discrimination claims, Richardson alleged he was treated differently than white head coaches at UAF with respect to duties, authority, and pay. The court rejected this claim based on Richardson's failure to produce evidence to support his contention. It also rejected Richardson's claim that pay differences between basketball assistant coaches and football assistant coaches amounted to racial discrimination. The court found that notwithstanding an alleged promise by UAF's athletic director Frank Broyles that the football and basketball assistants would be paid the same, the disparity in pay did not by itself amount to sufficient evidence of discrimination because the positions were not comparable. The court noted that the salaries of assistant football coaches had increased dramatically because of market pressures, principally the recruitment of assistant football coaches by professional teams. *Id.* at 933-934. Richardson also alleged that attempts to insert a clause in his contract requiring goals for graduating basketball players demonstrated racial discrimination. He argued that basketball had been singled out because it was a sport dominated by African Americans. This claim also was dismissed for lack of evidence.

The district court also rejected Richardson's claim that his termination was racially motivated. UAF alleged that Richardson was fired because of statements he made, including the following, unprompted statement at a press conference: "If they go ahead and pay me my money, they can take the job tomorrow." *Id.* at 937. The court concluded that even though Richardson had established a *prima facie* case, UAF had articulated legitimate, nondiscriminatory reasons for firing Richardson. UAF asserted the preceding comment and others made by Richardson had led UAF officials to conclude that Richardson had lost interest in and was no longer committed to the program. UAF also asserted his comments undermined public confidence in the program and adversely affected recruiting in all sports at UAF.

As it relates to the intersection of race and the First Amendment, Richardson alleged, *inter alia*, that his termination was in retaliation for his making comments regarding (1) the difficulties of recruiting African Americans to UAF given Fayetteville's small black population and the social adjustment issues confronting African American athletes in the Fayetteville community, and (2) comments made by Richardson regarding the low graduation rates of UAF's men's basketball team.

In assessing Richardson's First Amendment claim, the court articulated the following standard:

> Courts generally use a three-step analysis when evaluating First Amendment retaliation claims. First, to prove a violation of her or his First Amendment rights, a public employee must demonstrate that the speech in which he is engaged is protected speech. To establish this, he must show that the speech can be "fairly characterized as constituting a matter of public concern," and not a matter of private interest. Speech is a "matter of public interest or concern" when it touches upon "any matter of political, social or other concern to the community." Opposition to racial discrimination *is* a "matter of inherently public concern." (internal footnotes omitted).

Id. at 941-942.

Applying the foregoing standard, the court found that Richardson's comments regarding the social environment at Fayetteville could not be regarded as attempts to raise the social consciousness of the public, or to challenge UAF for anything that it had either done or not done regarding the issue of race as it related to student athletes.

The district court opinion was affirmed in *Richardson v. Sugg*, 448 F.3d 1046 (8th Cir. 2006). With respect to Richardson's racial discrimination claim, the court held Richardson failed to produce evidence of racial animus sufficient to rebut defendant's legitimate nondiscriminatory reasons for firing him or establish that these reasons were pretext. The court ruled that Richardson's First Amendment claim was subject to dismissal for two reasons. First, his comments were not a matter of public concern since neither the context nor content of his statements addressed race or other matters of public concern. *Id.* at 1062-1063. In addition, the detrimental impact that Richardson's comments had on the university outweighed any free speech privilege he might have possessed. *Id.* at 1063.

Free speech considerations lie at the core of the issues raised in *Hodges v. National Basketball Association*, 1998 WL 26183 (N.D. Ill. 1998) as well. There, Craig Hodges alleged that the NBA conspired to keep him out of basketball because he was "an outspoken African-American activist" who commented on political issues, particularly those involving the African American community. *Id.* at *1. As framed by the court, Hodges asserted that "racial discrimination is at the root of the conspiracy, a conclusion supported by the fact that white players with backgrounds similar to his are free to express themselves politically without suffering any retaliation." *Id.* The court did not have an opportunity to address the merits of Hodges's claims. His suit was dismissed because it was not filed within the applicable two-year statute of limitations period.

Do African American participants in sport become the subject of criticism or retaliation if their behavior fails to conform to standards deemed acceptable by the majority? If so, what are the parameters of those standards?

PROBLEM 9-2

Midwestern State University, a Division I-A football power that had fallen on hard times, advertised for a new head football coach. The ad indicated that previous football coaching experience was required. Several applicants applied, including Coach Ross, the head football coach at another college, who was also a friend and former colleague of Midwestern's athletic director, Shoemaker. Ross, who had over 15 years of collegiate coaching experience, including 8 years as a head coach, applied after being persuaded by Shoemaker to do so. Ross and Shoemaker are both white.

A search committee, chaired by Shoemaker, reviewed numerous applications and invited two applicants for on-campus interviews. One applicant was Ross. The other was an African American, Coach Pegues, who had played college and professional football. Pegues coached at a Division I institution for four years, where he served first as running backs coach and then as wide receivers coach. From there Pegues moved to the NFL, where he coached for seven years for two teams. He served as the quarterbacks coach for the first team for two years. For the past five years, Pegues served as offensive coordinator of a highly regarded NFL team.

During the on-campus interviews, Ross and Pegues met with various constituencies, including football players, the search committee, a faculty committee, and athletic department personnel. Both received favorable responses from the groups with whom they met. However, the faculty, athletes, and athletic personnel stated that they preferred Pegues. During the deliberations of the search committee, Shoemaker stated, "Perhaps I shouldn't say this, but I have to be honest. I feel uneasy with Pegues. How do we know if he'll be outspoken like that Nolan Richardson? I'm also concerned with how the major donors to our football program will react to him. We wouldn't want to lose a major source of financial support by hiring this guy. It wouldn't be worth it." After vigorous debate, the search committee concluded that both candidates were qualified to serve as head football coach. The committee understood, however, that it served in an advisory capacity and the final decision rested with the athletic director, Shoemaker.

Shoemaker extended an offer to Ross, who declined. Shoemaker decided not to extend an offer to Pegues. In explaining why he did not, Shoemaker stated, "Pegues is highly qualified, and I wish him well. I simply don't think he is a good fit for our program."

Pegues has come to your office seeking advice on whether he should pursue an action for employment discrimination on account of race. How would you advise him?

3. Stereotypes: Racially Stereotyped Mascots — Racism or Pride?

PRO-FOOTBALL, INC. v. HARJO
284 F. Supp. 2d 96 (D.D.C. 2003)

KOLLAR-KOTELLY, District Judge.

[EDS. Pro-Football, Inc. (Pro-Football), which owns the NFL's Washington Redskins football team, holds six trademarks containing the word, or a derivative of the word, "redskin(s)" that are registered with the Patent and Trademark Office (PTO). The oldest of the six trademarks involved in the litigation was issued in 1967, and the newest was issued in 1990. In 1992, plaintiff and six other Native Americans petitioned the U.S. PTO's Trademark Trial and Appeal Board (the Board) to cancel the six federal trademark registrations held by Pro-Football. Plaintiffs argued that use of the word "redskin(s)" is "scandalous," "may . . . disparage" Native Americans, and may cast Native Americans into "contempt, or disrepute" in violation of section 2(a) of the Lanham Trademark Act of 1946 (Lanham Act or Act). In 1999, the Board canceled the registrations, finding that the marks "may disparage" Native Americans or "bring them into contempt or disrepute." *Harjo v. Pro-Football, Inc.*, 50 U.S.P.Q.2d 1705, 1749 (Trademark Tr. & App. Bd. 1999). Among the issues before the court was whether the Board's finding of disparagement was supported by substantial evidence. The court's conclusions regarding this issue are set forth below.]

2. THE DEROGATORY NATURE OF THE WORD "REDSKIN(S)"

The TTAB . . . concluded that "the word 'redskin(s)' has been considered by a substantial composite of the general population, *including by inference Native Americans,* a derogatory term of reference for Native Americans during the time period of relevance herein." *Id.* at 1746, 1999 WL 375907 (emphasis added). As the Court has already explained, the TTAB's decision to conflate the views of the general population with those of Native Americans cannot be supported by substantial evidence. Nevertheless, even a review of the evidence that supports this conclusion leads the Court to conclude that the TTAB's finding on this point was not supported by substantial evidence. The Court examines this evidence in turn.

a. *Dictionary Evidence*

In support of the proposition that the term "redskin(s)" was a derogatory term for Native Americans, the TTAB first turned its attention to the dictionary definitions that were in evidence. As discussed *supra,* the TTAB had refused to make findings about the expert testimony surrounding the definitions and therefore only had the dictionary definitions, themselves, to consider. The TTAB observed that half of the dictionaries in the record contained a usage label indicating, for example, that the word "redskin(s)" is "often offensive," "informal," or "offensive slang." Half of the dictionaries did not have any usage labels. Based solely on this evidence, the TTAB wrote that "from the fact that usage labels appear in approximately half of the dictionaries of record at any point in the time period covered, we can conclude that a not insignificant number of Americans have understood 'redskin(s)' to be an offensive reference to Native Americans since at least 1966." *Id.* at 1744, 1999 WL 375907.

There are a number of concerns that the Court has with this conclusion. First, the TTAB expressly found that it would not make findings on the conflicting linguistic expert testimony that related to the "significance to be attached to the usage labels, or the lack thereof." *Id.* at 1732, 1999 WL 375907. Even though it made this statement, the TTAB still made a finding about the significance to be attached to the usage labels in the dictionary. The TTAB's conclusion is without any basis because there is no evidence in the record that was credited as to the purpose and methodology for including or not including usage labels in dictionaries or an explanation as to the basis for their conclusion. There are no findings of fact to support the TTAB's conclusion; rather, it is mere speculation on the part of the TTAB that this is the case.

Second, the fact that a "not insignificant number of Americans have understood 'redskin(s)' to be an offensive reference to Native Americans," has nothing to do with whether Native Americans, themselves, consider the term "offensive," which would obviously be more probative or relevant. Third, the dictionary evidence only states that the term "redskin(s)" is "often offensive," which, as Pro-Football observes, means that in certain contexts the term "redskin(s)" was not considered offensive. Pl.'s Mot. at 27. In fact, the TTAB concluded that the term "redskin(s)" means both a Native American and the Washington-area professional football team. The fact that it is usually offensive may mean the term is only offensive in one of these contexts. There is not a discussion of this possibility in the TTAB's opinion. Moreover, as Defendants' own expert observed, "[d]isparaging and offensive are two different words and mean two different things." Pl.'s Stmt. ¶124.

Finally, the dictionary evidence was, at best, equivocal. The TTAB observed in a footnote that:

> In view of the contradictory testimony of the parties' linguistics experts regarding the significance of a lack of usage label for a dictionary entry, we cannot conclude that the lack of such labels in the other excerpts of record establishes that the word "redskin(s)" was *not* considered offensive during the relevant time period.

Harjo II, 50 U.S.P.Q.2d at 1744 n. 114, 1999 WL 375907 (emphasis in original). By the same token, however, the conflicting linguist expert testimony should not necessarily lead to a finding that usage labels establish that the term "redskin(s)" was necessarily considered offensive by the American public. Accordingly, the Court finds that the TTAB's findings related to the significance of the dictionary evidence are not supported by substantial evidence.

b.   *Historical Evidence*

The TTAB next deviated into a lengthy discussion of the history of the term "redskin(s)." The TTAB observed that it had found that during the late 1800's and early 1900's that the vast majority of evidence which included the word "redskin(s)" as a reference for Native Americans, portrayed Native Americans in a "derogatory manner." *Id.* at 1744, 1999 WL 375907. The TTAB then observed that the evidence demonstrates that by the 1930's through the late 1940's the word "redskin(s)" as a reference for Native Americans "reflect[ed] a slightly less disdainful, but still condescending, view of Native Americans." *Id.* at 1745, 1999 WL 375907. However, the TTAB then states that "[f]rom the 1950's forward, the evidence shows, and neither party disputes, that there are minimal examples of uses of the word 'redskin(s)' as a reference to Native Americans." *Id.* During this same time period the TTAB noted that the record reflects "significant occurrences of the word 'redskin(s)' as a reference to [Pro-Football's] football team." *Id.* From this latter evidence, the TTAB stated:

> [W]e conclude from the evidence of record that the word "redskin(s)" does not appear during the second half of this century in written or spoken language, formal or informal, as a synonym for "Indian" or "Native American" because it is, and has been since at least the 1960's, perceived by the general population, which includes Native Americans, as a pejorative term for Native Americans.

Id. The Court determines that this finding is also not supported by substantial evidence because no concrete evidence supports this conclusion.

First, the TTAB agreed with Pro-Football, that "the pejorative nature of 'red-skin(s)' in the early historical writings of record comes from the overall negative viewpoints of the writings." *Id.* Despite this finding, the TTAB merely assumed that because the term "redskin(s)" dropped out of use as a term for Native Americans it must have been because the term was derogatory. There is no evidence in the record to support this finding one way or the other. Concerned with adopting witness testimony that reached the ultimate legal question, the TTAB did not make findings regarding the significance of the use of the word from the 1960's onward. *Id.* at 1731, 1999 WL 375907. However, the ultimate legal inquiry is whether the six trademarks at issue may disparage Native Americans when used in connection with Pro-Football's services and during the relevant time frame. The ultimate legal inquiry is not whether the term "red-skin(s)" is a pejorative term for Native Americans. Accordingly, the TTAB's reluctance to make findings in this area deprives the Court of meaningful review. There is no evidence to support the conclusion that the drop-off of the use of the term "redskin(s)" as a reference for Native Americans is correlative with a finding that the term is pejorative. Accordingly, the Court finds that this finding is unsupported by substantial evidence. . . .

c. *Survey Evidence*

As discussed earlier, the Court found the TTAB's conclusion that the survey could be extrapolated to the Native American population as a whole to be unsupported by substantial evidence. Nevertheless, to the extent that the survey would be even included in the calculus, the Court determines that it does not support the TTAB's decision that the word "redskin(s)" was viewed by a substantial composite of Native Americans to be a derogatory term of reference for Native Americans from the mid-1960's to 1990. The survey measures attitudes of Native Americans about their perceptions of the term "redskin" as used as a reference to Native Americans in *1996.* The survey, therefore, is entirely irrelevant to the question before the Board.

. . . The TTAB has no evidence, therefore, to draw a conclusion that during the relevant time periods, *i.e.* 1967, 1974, 1978, and 1990, the term Native Americans was a pejorative term for Native Americans. . . . Putting aside the fact that the survey results have no bearing on Native Americans perceptions of the term "redskin(s)" as used in connection with the Pro-Football's professional sports team, the survey tells us nothing about the relevant time frame. Accordingly, it fails to support with substantial evidence the TTAB's finding that the term "redskin(s)" is viewed by a substantial composite of Native Americans as a derogatory term for Native Americans.[32]

---

32. The survey evidence, that Native Americans find the term "redskin(s)" offensive as a term for Native Americans, does not even represent a majority of Native Americans polled. Indeed only 36.6% of Native Americans agreed with that statement. While the TTAB found that 36.6% was a substantial composite, *Harjo II,* 50 U.S.P.Q.2d at 1746 n. 120, 1999 WL 375907 (quoting McCarthy, *supra,* §32.185) (noting that in cases dealing with likelihood of confusion, "an appreciable number of customers" may be less than a majority), the Court finds that conclusion difficult to support in the context of this case. The survey only found that 131 out of the 358 participants agreed that this term was offensive when used as a reference to Native Americans. This Court, accordingly, finds that the survey results do not demonstrate that a "substantial composite" of Native Americans found the term offensive as a reference for Native Americans.

3. THE WORD "REDSKIN(S)" AS A TERM OF DISPARAGEMENT

The TTAB next turned to the ultimate inquiry before the Board and found that "within the relevant time periods, the derogatory connotation of the word 'redskin(s)' in connection with Native Americans extends to the term 'Redskin(s)' as used in [Pro-Football's] marks in connection with the identified services, such that [Pro-Football's] marks may be disparaging of Native Americans to a substantial composite of this group of people." *Id.* at 1748, 1999 WL 375907. The crux of the TTAB's conclusion, therefore, is that the "derogatory connotation of the word 'redskin(s)'" extends to the term "Redskin(s)" as used in connection with Pro-Football's entertainment services. This finding is not supported by substantial evidence.

To reach its conclusion that the trademarks may disparage Native Americans, the TTAB essentially determined that because the *word* "redskin(s)" may be viewed by Native Americans as derogatory when used as a reference for Native Americans, the trademarks are disparaging because they use that word. The result of this analysis is that there is very little discussion of the use of the mark in connection with Pro-Football's product or services. Unlike in the *Doughboy* case, where the Examiner-in-Chief of the Patent Office stated that use of the term "Doughboy"—a reference for a World War I soldier—was disparaging when used to sell an anti-venereal prophylactic, *Doughboy*, 88 U.S.P.Q. at 228, 1951 WL 4167, in this case the TTAB did very little analysis of *how* the use of the trademarks in connection with Pro-Football's services disparages Native Americans. The Board was content with stating that because it found the name to be pejorative, the marks must be disparaging.

First, the TTAB observed that "[a]s we move through the 1960's to the present, the evidence shows increasingly respectful portrayal of Native Americans." *Id.* at 1746, 1999 WL 375907. The TTAB then noted that "*[t]he evidence herein shows a parallel development of [Pro-Football's] portrayal of Native Americans.*" *Id.* (emphasis added). What the TTAB found therefore, was that during the relevant time periods, the use of the term "redskin(s)" in connection with Pro-Football's marks was used in a respectful manner. Nevertheless, despite this stunning observation—that during the relevant time frame Pro-Football used Native American imagery in a respectful manner as connected to its entertainment services—the Board still concluded that the use of the term "redskin(s)" was disparaging when used in the context of Pro-Football's professional football club.

The TTAB apparently premised this conclusion on a number of factors. First, the TTAB discussed the fact that the media has used Native American imagery in connection with Pro-Football's football team, throughout the entire period, "in a manner that often portrays Native Americans as aggressive savages or buffoons." *Id.* at 1747, 1999 WL 375907 (noting newspaper headlines referring to Washington Redskins team, players or managers scalping opponents, seeking revenge on the warpath, holding pow wows, or using pidgin English). In addition, newspaper and video excerpts of games were presented showing Washington Redskins fans dressed "in costumes and engaging in antics that clearly poke fun at Native American culture and portrays [*sic*] Native Americans as savages and buffoons." *Id.* . . . From this evidence, the TTAB concluded that the term "redskin(s)" "retains its derogatory character as part of the subject marks and as used in connection with respondent's football team." *Id.*

The problem with this reasoning is twofold. First, the perceptions of the general public are irrelevant to determining if the marks are disparaging to Native Americans. In other words, this evidence is simply not relevant to the

legal question in the case. Second, and most importantly, this finding is logically flawed. At best, this evidence demonstrates that Pro-Football's fans and the
media continue to equate the Washington Redskins with Native Americans and
not always in a respectful manner. However, the evidence does not automatically
lead the Court to conclude that the word "redskin(s)" as used in Pro-Football's
marks is derogatory in character. Under the broad sweep of the TTAB's logic,
no professional sports team that uses Native American imagery would be permitted to keep their trademarks if the team's fans or the media took any action
or made any remark that could be construed as insulting to Native Americans.
The Court cannot accept such an expansive doctrine; particularly when premised on a finding that is not supported by any substantial evidence.

Clearly, the evidence relating to the media and fans has no bearing on whether
a substantial composite of Native Americans finds the term "redskin(s)" to be
disparaging when used in connection with Pro-Football's marks. In this regard,
the evidence the TTAB put forward comes nowhere close to meeting the substantial evidence test. First, the TTAB noted that the record contained the
testimony of the Defendants who stated that they were "seriously offended by
Pro-Football's use of the term in connection with its services." *Id.* This testimony,
however, is a reflection of their individual viewpoints and there is no evidence
that Defendants' views are a reasonable proxy for a substantial composite of the
entire Native American population. As Pro-Football's counsel stated at the July
23, 2003, motions hearing, "Do these seven petitioners strongly believe that our
famous football team mark Washington Redskins is disparaging? Apparently.
That's fine. They have an opinion, but they are representing themselves and no
one else. There are 2.41 million Native Americans in this country, Your Honor.
There are over 500 Native American tribes. So I ask, can petitioner's opinions,
no matter how stridently held, be extrapolated to even one additional Native
American by some method acceptable in a courtroom? The answer is, of course,
not at all." Tr. 7/23/2003 at 16.

To corroborate its ultimate conclusion, the TTAB cites to other evidence
which this Court views as irrelevant because it has no correlation to the relevant
time frame at issue and it does not add exponentially to the requirement that
the marks, when used in connection with Pro-Football's services, are considered
disparaging by a substantial composite of Native Americans. The TTAB noted
that the record includes Resolutions indicating a present objection to the use
of the word "redskin(s)" in connection with Pro-Football's services, from the
National Congress of American Indians ("NCAI"), "a broad-based organization
of Native American tribes and individuals" from the Oneida tribe, and from
Unity 94, "an organization including Native Americans." All of these resolutions
were made after the relevant time frame, with no explanation by the TTAB as to
how they "shed light" on the relevant time period, and thus, are irrelevant to the
calculus. *See* Pl.'s Mot. at 23. Indeed, all of these resolutions were adopted after
Defendants filed their Petition to Cancel. *Id.* at 24. Moreover, the TTAB made
no findings of fact about the strength of this evidence. For example, only two
Native Americans voted for the Unity 94 resolution. Pl.'s Stmt. ¶212.

In addition, the TTAB relies on "news articles," which appeared at various
times from 1969 to 1992, describing Native American objections to the team
name. *Harjo II*, 50 U.S.P.Q.2d at 1747, 1999 WL 375907. The TTAB does not
describe the contents of these news articles and it is impossible to determine if
they would represent a substantial composite of Native Americans. Moreover,
these articles were only introduced to demonstrate "the existence of a controversy

spanning over a long period of time." *Id.* Again, the existence of a controversy does not inform the Court as to whether the trademarks at issue are perceived of as disparaging by a substantial composite of Native Americans.

Finally, the TTAB relied on a letter written by Harold Gross in 1972 to Edward Bennett Williams, the then-team owner urging the team name be changed. *Id.* at 1747, 1999 WL 375907. The record also indicates that Mr. Gross and seven other colleagues from Native American organizations met with Mr. Williams to discuss the disparaging nature of the team's name. *Id.; see also* Pl.'s Stmt. ¶202. Again, this evidence does not represent a "substantial composite" of Native Americans.

The TTAB concluded that "the evidence of record establishes that, within the relevant time periods, the derogatory connotation of the words 'redskin(s)' in connection with Native Americans extends to the term 'Redskins,' as used in [Pro-Football's] marks in connection with the identified services, such that [Pro-Football's] marks may be disparaging of Native Americans to a substantial composite of this group of people." *Harjo II,* 50 U.S.P.Q.2d at 1748, 1999 WL 375907. The Court determines that this decision is not supported by substantial evidence. As such, the decision of the TTAB must be reversed. . . .

V.   Summary of Analysis

. . . The legal question before the TTAB was whether the six trademarks, when used in connection with Pro-Football's entertainment services, "may disparage" a substantial composite of Native Americans at the time the marks were registered starting in 1967. The findings do not come close to shedding any light on the legal inquiry. There is no evidence in the record that addresses whether the use of the term "redskin(s)" in the context of a football team and related entertainment services would be viewed by a substantial composite of Native Americans, in the relevant time frame, as disparaging. In addition, none of the TTAB's findings related to the linguists' expert testimony help explain whether the term "redskins," when used in connection with the "Washington Redskins" football team, disparaged Native Americans during the relevant time frame. . . .

This is undoubtedly a test case that seeks to use federal trademark litigation to obtain social goals. The problem, however, with this case is evidentiary. The Lanham Act has been on the books for many years and was in effect in 1967 when the trademarks were registered. By waiting so long to exercise their rights, Defendants make it difficult for any fact-finder to affirmatively state that in 1967 the trademarks were disparaging.

VI.   Conclusion

The TTAB's finding of disparagement is not supported by substantial evidence and must be reversed. . . .

NOTES AND QUESTIONS

1. The D.C. Circuit reversed the district court's ruling that the Native Americans' petition to cancel the Redskins trademarks was barred by

laches. The appellate court ruled that the district court applied the wrong standard when considering the laches defense and remanded the case for further proceedings. However, the D.C. Circuit did not disturb the district court's alternative ground for dismissing the plaintiffs' petition, which was that there is no substantial evidence that the Redskins trademarks disparage Native Americans. *Pro-Football, Inc. v Harjo*, 415 F.3d 44 (D.C. Cir. 2005).

Following remand, the district court reaffirmed in *Pro-Football, Inc. v. Harjo* (*Harjo III*), 567 F. Supp. 2d 46 (D.D.C. 2008) that the burden was on the plaintiff, Pro-Football, to prove the elements of laches: "(1) lack of diligence by the party against whom the defense is asserted; and (2) prejudice to the party asserting the defense." The court ultimately held that the defendant's eight-year delay in filing a petition with TTAB to cancel the Redskins trademarks represented an undue delay that subjected Pro-Football to a degree of trial and economic prejudice sufficient to support a laches argument and to reverse TTAB's cancellation of the trademarks. In particular, the court found that the defendant's delay frustrated Pro-Football's ability to build a defense based on survey data that might have been compiled to reflect the prevailing attitude of the public toward the Redskins name and trademarks and exposed the plaintiff to prejudice resulting from the intervening death of the franchise president during the eight-year delay. The court also concluded that the franchise was not provided timely notice of the need to retain certain documents and records that it might have used to defend the contested marks during the original TTAB proceeding. In addition, the court emphasized that Pro-Football significantly expanded its use of and investment in the disputed trademarks while the defendant slept on its rights.

In *Pro-Football, Inc. v. Harjo*, 565 F.3d 880 (2009 D.C. Cir), on appeal from the district court's decision in *Harjo III*, Harjo's codefendant Romero challenged the court's finding that Pro-Football suffered trial and economic prejudice sufficient to support a laches argument to reverse TTAB's cancellation of Pro-Football's Washington Redskins trademarks. The court of appeals held that the district court in *Harjo III* did not abuse its discretion when it found that Romero's delay was sufficient to support the plaintiff's laches argument. The court stressed that Romero's delay was lengthy, and therefore Pro-Football's showing that it continued to develop and invest in the disputed marks during the delay demonstrated adequate economic prejudice. For a discussion of the *Harjo* case, see John R. Wallace, *Discriminatory and Disparaging Team Names, Logos, and Mascots: Workable Challenges and the Misapplication of the Doctrine of Laches*, 12 Rutgers Race & L. Rev. 203 (2011).

2. Opponents of the use of Native American names and mascots argue that the symbols are disparaging to American Indians. Proponents argue that such symbols honor Native Americans. Should it matter that an entity that uses a Native America name or symbol does so with dignity? For instance, in *Harjo* the district court ruled that the plaintiffs were required to show that the use of the term "redskins" is offensive when used in the context of the services offered by Pro-Football. Do you agree or disagree? See Justin P. Grose, *Time to Bury the Tomahawk Chop: An Attempt to Reconcile the Differing Viewpoints of Native Americans and Sports Fans*, 35 Am. Indian L. Rev. 695, 696 (2011); J. Gordon Hylton, *Before the Redskins Were the Redskins: The Use of Native American Team Names in the Formative Era of American Sports, 1857-1933*, 86 N.D. L. Rev. 879 (2010) (providing an historical overview of the use of Native American team names).

3. Does Notre Dame's use of the "Fighting Irish" and Leprechaun mascots raise the same issues as a school's use of Native Americans as mascots? Why? Why not?

4. Should it matter if members of the general population or Native Americans find the use of such names and symbols offensive? In *Harjo*, the district court found that whether "redskins" is disparaging should be based not on whether the general population considers the term disparaging but whether Native Americans consider "redskins" disparaging. The court also found that the survey results failed to demonstrate that a "substantial composite" of Native Americans found "redskins" offensive as a reference for Native Americans. These results were consistent with a poll taken by *Sports Illustrated* in 2002, which revealed the following:

> Asked if high school and college teams should stop using Indian nicknames, 81% of Native American respondents said no. As for pro sports, 83% of Native American respondents said teams should not stop using Indian nicknames, mascots, characters and symbols. Opinion is far more divided on reservations, yet a majority (67%) there said the usage by pro teams should not cease, while 32% said it should.

S.L. Price, *The Indian Wars*, Sports Illustrated, March 4, 2002, at 67, 69.

The survey and poll results reveal the complexity of the issue. The *Sports Illustrated* article included statements by Native Americans that reflected the contrasting views. One commentator summarized the contrasting views as follows:

> Opposers . . . argue that such uses are stereotypical in that they promote misconceptions of Native Americans and their ways. This is harmful, Opposers claim, because it erodes tribal efforts to accurately preserve their culture. Opposers also insist that such uses are dehumanizing because they remove humane characteristics from Native Americans, depicting them instead as objects, cartoon characters, and savages. This has the detrimental affect of creating a perception of Native Americans as mythical ornaments, relegating them to an archaic, nonhuman, beastly status. . . .
>
> Opposers also believe that these teams are wrongly appropriating a people's identity and image for their own purposes. . . .
>
> One common response is that Indian mascots actually honor Native Americans by celebrating their culture and traditions. Supporters add that the use of Indian mascots actually helps to preserve Indian culture. Another response is that the users of Indian mascots do not intend any harm or ill will toward Native Americans. A related argument is that teams choose Indian mascots for the positive attributes associated with Native Americans. Supporters also argue that the Indian mascot is not a significant issue, in light of more urgent problems such as hunger and homelessness, and that their schools' mascots are protected by the First Amendment. [Citations omitted.]

Jeff Dolley, *The Four R's: Use of Indian Mascots in Educational Facilities*, 32 J.L. & Educ. 21, 26-27 (2003). Contrasting scholarly views on the use of Native American mascots may be found in Symposium, *Braves or Cowards? Use of Native American Images and Symbols as Sports Nicknames*, 1 Va. Sports & Ent. L.J. 257 (2002); see also Jeremy Daniel Heacox, *Wisconsin Legislature Employs Halftime Adjustment: How Wisconsin's "New" Indian Mascot Law Changes the Outlook for Future Challenges to the Use of Discriminatory Nicknames, Mascots, and*

Logos in Wisconsin Schools, 22 Marq. Sports L. Rev. 651 (2012) (addressing the societal issues implicating the debate).

5. Despite these contrasting views, efforts to end the use of Native American names and mascots have been successful. One report revealed that between 1969 and 2001, more than 1,200 schools had discontinued use of Indian mascots. Dolley, *supra*, at 24, n.12.

In late 2003, the Executive Committee of the NCAA declined to pass a recommendation of its Subcommittee on Gender and Diversity that would have required the elimination of all Native American nicknames, mascot names, and logos in NCAA publications and announcements. The committee approved, however, recommendations requesting that member institutions using Native American mascots, nicknames, or logos undertake a self-analysis to determine if the use might be deemed offensive.

In August 2005, however, the NCAA Executive Committee approved a policy that "prohibits NCAA colleges and universities from displaying hostile and abusive racial/ethnic/national origin mascots, nicknames or imagery at any of the 88 NCAA championships" unless the schools identified made changes prior to February 1, 2006. Gary T. Brown, *Policy Applies Core Principles to Mascot Issue*, 42 NCAA News, 1, 19 (Aug. 15, 2005). This restriction has three components. First, any institution that hosts a NCAA championship competition must cover up any and all offensive references at the site of the competition. Second, institutions can no longer have offensive references on "team mascots, cheerleaders, dance teams, [or] band uniforms" that travel to NCAA championships beginning August 1, 2008. Effective February 1, institutions with offensive references on their competitive uniforms were prohibited from wearing or displaying them at NCAA-sponsored championships.

The policy allowed institutions to appeal the categorization of their school as one "whose mascots are considered hostile or abusive." *Id.* The NCAA stated that it would find any evidence that a namesake tribe had "formally approved of the use of the mascot, name, and imagery by the institution" to be compelling evidence. *NCAA Executive Committee Approves Native American Mascot Review Process*, NCAA, Aug. 19, 2005, http://fs.ncaa.org/Docs/PressArchive/2005/Announcements/NCAA%2BExecutive%2BCommittee%2BApproves%2BNative%2BAmerican%2BMascot%2BAppeals%2BProcess.html. Several institutions, including Florida State University, Central Michigan University, and the University of Utah, established to the satisfaction of the NCAA's Executive Committee that their use of a Native American name, mascot, or symbol was inoffensive. Others such as the University of North Dakota had their appeals rejected. Rebecca Aronauer, *Tribes' Views on Mascot Names Hold Sway with NCAA*, Chron. Higher Educ., Oct. 15, 2005. In each instance in which the NCAA accepted an appeal, the institution had support from Native American tribe(s), such as the Seminole Tribe of Florida and the Seminole Nation of Oklahoma, which both supported Florida State's appeal. In contrast, two Sioux tribes expressed opposition to the University of North Dakota's use of the "Fighting Sioux." *Id.*

In contrast to Florida State, the NCAA denied an appeal by the University of North Dakota (UND). After the NCAA denied its appeal, UND sued the NCAA. In late 2007, the parties agreed to a settlement under which UND would have three years within which to obtain namesake tribe approval of its nickname and related imagery. If such approval was not granted after three years, UND agreed to transition to a new nickname and logo.

In April 2010, the North Dakota Supreme Court ruled that the North Dakota Board of Higher Education had valid authority to choose to discontinue using UND's "Fighting Sioux" nickname prior to the expiration of this three-year deadline, which the board had voted to do. The university's action to discontinue use of the mascot appeared to resolve the issue. In 2011, however, the North Dakota legislature passed a law, which was signed by the governor, that banned higher education and university officials from taking action to discontinue use of the name. Emma G. Fitsimmons, *North Dakota and N.C.A.A. Are at Odds Again over University's Sioux Mascot*, N.Y. Times, July 12, 2011. However, the Board of Higher Education announced that it would not comply with this law and would require UND to discontinue usage of the "Fighting Sioux" nickname and imagery by August 2011, and UND's president, Robert Kelley, stated that the university would comply with the board's instructions. In February 2012, President Kelley publicly stated that the university would continue to use the "Fighting Sioux" while the issue was put to a state vote. The NCAA responded by indicating that they intended to continue to punish UND for using the nickname. In June 2012, the citizens of North Dakota voted overwhelmingly to abolish the "Fighting Sioux" mascot. See Levi Rickert, *North Dakotans Vote to Get Rid of "Fighting Sioux" Mascot by a 2 to 1 Margin*, Native News Network, June 13, 2012, http://www.nativenewsnet work.com/north-dakotans-vote-to-get-rid-of-fighting-sioux-mascot-by-2-to-1-margin.html.

6. *Free Speech*. In *Crue v. Akin*, 204 F. Supp. 2d 1130 (C.D. Ill. 2002), certain faculty and students at the University of Illinois expressed interest in contacting prospective student-athletes in order to inform them about the controversy surrounding the university's use of a Native American mascot, Chief Illiniwek. Shortly thereafter, the university's chancellor sent an e-mail to faculty, staff, and students requiring them to obtain the clearance of the university's athletic director before contacting prospective student-athletes. The stated purpose of the preclearance directive was to avoid violation of NCAA rules that impose limits on the extent to which universities can contact prospective student-athletes. Students and faculty members sued alleging that their First Amendment rights to free speech were chilled by the preclearance directive. The district court found that the chancellor's ban imposed a substantial burden on a particular kind of expressive speech. *Id.* at 1138.

Before the Seventh Circuit, the university again argued, *inter alia*, that the directive enabled it to adhere to NCAA recruiting rules and thus avoid subjecting the university's athletic program to possibly severe sanctions. *Crue v. Akin*, 370 F.3d 668 (7th Cir. 2004). In rejecting this argument, the Seventh Circuit first articulated the governing standard — "because we are dealing with a significant prior restraint on speech, we must determine whether the impact of the speech on the actual operation of the university and its athletic program outweighs the plaintiffs' right to free expression on the matter which is, as we have noted, a clear issue of public concern." *Id.* at 679. Applying this balancing test, the court held that the "free-speech interest of the plaintiffs — members of a major public university community — in questioning what they see as blatant racial stereotyping is substantial. That interest is not outweighed by fear that an athletic association might not approve of what they say. . . . For these reasons, we conclude that the district court correctly found that the plaintiffs' free-speech rights were infringed by the

March 2 pre-clearance directive." *Id.* at 680. The court buttressed its holding by pointing to the NCAA's assurance, given in response to an inquiry from plaintiffs, that plaintiffs could send letters to prospective student-athletes regarding the controversy without causing sanctions to be imposed on the university. The court noted that even if the university faced possible sanctions based on plaintiffs' activities, it might reach the same result.

For analysis of *Harjo, Crue,* and the NCAA's mascot policy, see Glenn George, *Playing Cowboy and Indians,* 6 Va. Sports & Ent. L.J. 90 (2006); Kelly P. O'Neill, *Sioux Unhappy: Challenging the NCAA's Ban of Native American Imagery,* 42 Tulsa L. Rev. 171 (2006); Timothy M. Keegan, *Harsh Reality: The Prior Restraint Doctrine and the Free Speech Rights of Employees of Public Colleges and Universities,* 33 J.C. & U.L. 625, 627 (2007).

7. *Action by Private Citizen.* In a unique case, *DuPuis v. Board of Trustees,* 128 P.3d 1010 (Mont. 2006), the board of trustees for a school district, following a public hearing, decided to allow a middle school to continue to use Native American symbols on its gymnasium floor. Thereafter, a citizen filed suit attempting to overturn the board's decision. Plaintiff alleged that the use of the mascots within the school district created a hostile environment and violated human dignity provisions of the Montana Constitution. The court dismissed plaintiff's claims finding that she failed to exhaust administrative remedies by not bringing her claims before the Montana Human Rights Commission. *Id.* at 1013-1014.

PROBLEM 9-3

In 2008, Donor gave $10 million to University. In 2012, Donor pledged another $50 million to University to be used for the construction of a new state-of-the-art hockey facility for the school and possibly fund another program. Well into the construction of the facility, controversy erupted concerning whether University should change its nickname, the "Battling Cherokee," and its logo, a majestic Indian head that was designed three years ago by a highly regarded Native American artist. University is one of the country's leading schools in Native American studies and graduates an estimated 25 percent of the Native American doctors in the United States. The controversy arose when a group of white and Native American students and nonstudents protested the nickname and logo. The controversy was only heightened after Donor entered the fray. Donor threatened to halt construction if the school did not retain the name and logo. As legal counsel for University, how would you advise University to proceed? Are there ethical issues to consider?

4. Racially Hostile Environments and Conduct

PROBLEM 9-4

A highly paid and very talented African American NFL running back, Jerome Crawford, had a reputation for being outspoken on what he believed were racial inequities within American society. This resulted in conflicts between Crawford and his teammates and management. During an away game, Crawford was subjected to verbal abuse from fans. Although most of the fans' statements were not racially based, a few were. The latter included threats, such as "we will kill you," and a dummy in blackface with Crawford's number on it. The player reacted by directing an obscene gesture toward the fans. Because of his response, the player was fined $10,000 by the NFL for a lack of professionalism. The player refused to play until the league and individual teams implemented measures to protect African American and other minority football players from racially motivated abuse by fans. You are general counsel for the team on which Crawford plays. What advice should you give to team management as to how it should respond to Crawford's refusal to perform?

Problem 9-4 illustrates what Professor Phoebe Williams characterizes as the overlooked issue of racially hostile environments created by fans. Phoebe Williams, *Racially Hostile Environments*, 6 Marq. Sports L.J. 287, 289 (1996). Several issues emerge when examining fan-based racial animus against athletes, including the following:

a. In the professional sports setting, to what extent do leagues and teams owe a responsibility to athletes to address racial harassment?

b. How pervasive is racially motivated fan conduct against athletes of color? With respect to Problem 9-4, assume that the fans' conduct toward Crawford was not overtly racist. Also assume that Crawford was not outspoken but was having a season in which he had severely underperformed. To what extent is fan criticism of athletes race-based even though it is not accompanied by obviously racist conduct? Are black athletes, particularly those who are highly paid, subjected to a double standard as it relates to their on-the-field performance? On the other hand, are athletes of color overly sensitive to harsh criticism of fans? Are athletes of color too quick to assume that criticism of them is motivated in part by racial attitudes?

   Professor Williams notes the difficulty in determining when harassment of players is racially motivated. "Where the taunts are not obviously racial but disparately based on race, the motivation of the parties will be difficult to establish." *Id.* at 312. Is racial harassment one of the tools fans use in an effort to assist their team in winning? Is racial harassment simply a part of the game?

c. What reasonable reaction should leagues and teams expect of athletes who are on the receiving end of overtly racial statements and conduct? When confronted with racial hostility, should minority athletes be expected to behave as "model citizens"? Professor Williams argues that when confronted with racial hostility "African-American athletes are expected to endure and defer to racially hostile environments without protest." *Id.* at 308. Professor Williams adds that "standards of professionalism become a metaphor for condoning unlawful racist activity." *Id.* According to Williams, the prevailing attitude is that it becomes the obligation of the athlete as a professional not to lose control. Consequently, professionalism shifts responsibility "for providing an environment free of racial harassment from the employer to the athlete player." *Id.* at 311.

d. What steps might team owners take to eliminate racial harassment in sports venues? Eject fans? Revoke season tickets? Limit the consumption of alcohol? See Williams, *supra.*

e. Should team owners and league administrators hold fans accountable for racial abuse stemming from activity during a game but expressed through social media outlets such as Twitter or Facebook? During the 2012 NHL play-offs, the Washington Capitals Joel Ward, one of the NHL's few black players, scored a Game 7 overtime goal to propel the Capitals past the Boston Bruins and into the Eastern Conference Semifinals. A "racist tweet storm" followed in which Ward was menacingly threatened and derided by Bruins fans. See Cindy Boren, *Racist Tweet Storm About Joel Ward Prompted by Bruins' Loss to Capitals*, Wash. Post, April 26, 2012, http://www.washingtonpost .com/blogs/early-lead/post/racist-tweets-about-joel-ward-after-bruins-loss-to-capitals-is-another-ugly-mark-for-nhl/2012/04/26/gIQAjfZQjT_blog .html. The next day Ted Leonsis, the Capitals' owner, issued the following statement:

> Shame on these folks who decided to take to their keyboards and show their ignorance and their racism and hate. What these people have said and done is unforgivable. I hope they are now publicly identified and pay a huge price for their beliefs. There should be zero tolerance for this kind of hate mongering.

If those who tweeted the racial abuse are publicly identified, should part of the "huge price" Ted Leonsis calls for include league-enforced discipline such as a prohibition on attending future NHL games?

The problem is just as profound when the racially hostile sports environment emanates not from fans but from teammates, management, opposing players, or some combination thereof. In *Priester*, a teammate is the source of the racial hostility. Nevertheless, similar issues emerge, including the legal duty of institutions to stymie racially motivated conduct against athletes of color and the adequacy of the law to address racial hostility in sport.

PRIESTER v. LOWNDES COUNTY

354 F.3d 414 (5th Cir. 2004)

STEWART, Circuit Judge.

FACTUAL AND PROCEDURAL BACKGROUND

. . . On September 14, 1999, Terry, an African-American tenth-grade student at New Hope High School, sustained a serious eye injury during football practice allegedly caused by a white teammate Eli Ward ("Ward"). Leading up to the injury, Ward slapped Terry on the back of the head and derided him in the locker room and during warm-up drills on matters such as his weight and race. On previous occasions, the head football coach Rick Cahalane ("Cahalane") subjected Terry to numerous racial epithets and derogatory comments concerning his weight.[2] After hearing such comments from Cahalane, Ward used the same derogatory terms toward Terry. The day of the injury, Ward also approached Terry and, without provocation, hit him on the helmet with a rock. Terry was also hit in a similar manner by another fellow player. Cahalane allegedly heard

---

2. The record shows that Terry Priester was subjected to such derogatory terms as "nigger" and "fat black ass."

the statements and witnessed the assaults, but he did nothing to protect Terry or take the necessary actions that could stop or prevent the recurrence of the incident. Terry's mother witnessed these events and immediately informed the high school principal, who said he would handle the problem in the morning.

In the midst of a full-contact drill during football practice, the injury occurred subsequent to Terry's successful block of Ward. In response, Cahalane walked over to Ward to "get on to him" about the previous play. While Cahalane and Ward talked, Ward apparently looked at Terry throughout the conversation. Immediately following the conversation, Ward told Terry that he "had something for him." On the next play from scrimmage, Terry alleges that Ward lunged toward him, thrust his hands through his helmet, and gouged his eye. Terry's injury resulted in permanent damage including a torn right lower eyelid, a laceration to his lower punctum and caniliculus (tear duct), chronic tearing, and blurry vision. The school's response was two-fold. First, upon interviewing the coaches and players, New Hope High School principal Mike Halford compiled a report of the incident. In the report, however, no one admitted seeing anyone hit Terry. Second, the school declined to pay Terry's medical bills.

On January 8th, 2001, Eve Priester, individually and as the next friend of her son Terry Priester, pursuant to section 1983, filed suit in federal district court. . . . Priester alleged an agreement between Ward and the coaches to deprive her son of his rights under the Due Process and Equal Protection Clauses of the U.S. Constitution's Fourteenth Amendment.[4] Additionally, she alleged state-law claims of negligence and intentional torts resulting in emotional distress and physical injury.

On February 2, 2001, Priester amended her complaint to include Ward as a defendant, alleging that Ward, motivated by racial animus, subjected Priester to physical and verbal assaults. Ward moved for a Rule 56 summary judgment to dismiss the claim. On August 15, 2001, Ward was dismissed as a defendant by order of the district court because he was not a state actor under Section 1983 and the one-year statute of limitations tolled on September 14, 2000, for the applicable Mississippi tort.

The remaining defendants moved for summary judgment arguing, *inter alia*, that Priester failed to allege any state action to support her section 1983 claim. The district court granted the defendants' motion finding no requisite fair attribution or special relationship between the school and Priester, and thus, an absence of state action to support a section 1983 claim. The district court dismissed the remaining state law claims without prejudice. Priester timely filed a notice of appeal. . . .

DISCUSSION

I. DISMISSAL OF WARD PURSUANT TO STATE STATUTE OF LIMITATIONS

On appeal, Priester contends that the district court erred in dismissing the former defendant Ward under the one-year statute of limitations for an intentional tort, rather than a theory of negligence. Specifically, Priester argues that the

4. Although the district court did not construe Eve Priester's complaint as asserting an equal protection claim, she raises this issue on appeal, arguing that New Hope High School did not pay for her son's medical expenses nor did the school respond to their complaints of racial harassment.

three-year statute of limitations should apply, instead of a one-year statute of limitations, because of both the civil rights nature of this case and the policy of not allowing states to circumvent section 1983 by adopting shorter statute of limitations standards. A close scrutiny of the record, however, reveals that Priester has misconstrued the district court's opinion dismissing the claims stemming from Ward's actions. The district court dismissed Ward as a defendant on two theories; the intentional tort claims were dismissed pursuant to the one-year statute of limitations, while the section 1983 claims were dismissed for lack of state action.

A.   Intentional Tort Claims

We find that the district court correctly construed Priester's amended complaint as stating a claim under an intentional tort theory rather than a negligence theory. Priester's complaint states that Ward's alleged actions, "Ward put both of his hands through Priester's helmet and planted his finger in Terry Priester's eye and pulled it as hard as he could," are in the form of an intentional tort rather than negligence. Under the applicable state statute, intentional torts have a one-year statute of limitations period. Thus, the district court correctly found that Priester's claim stated an intentional tort, and that the applicable statute of limitations had run because the amended complaint was filed on February 2, 2001, well over a year from September 14, 1999, the date upon which the alleged injuries occurred during football practice.

B.   Section 1983 Claims

To state a cause of action under section 1983 the appellant must allege that the person who deprived him of a federal right was acting under color of law. *Cinel v. Connick*, 15 F.3d 1338, 1342 (5th Cir.1994). For a private citizen, such as Ward, to be held liable under section 1983, the plaintiff must allege that the citizen conspired with or acted in concert with state actors. *Mylett v. Jeane*, 879 F.2d 1272, 1275 (5th Cir.1989).

This court has held that a non-state actor may be liable under 1983 if the private citizen was a "willful participant in joint activity with the State or its agents." *Cinel*, 15 F.3d at 1343. The plaintiff must allege: (1) an agreement between the private and public defendants to commit an illegal act and (2) a deprivation of constitutional rights. *Id.* Allegations that are merely conclusory, without reference to specific facts, will not suffice. *Brinkmann v. Johnston*, 793 F.2d 111, 113 (5th Cir.1986). The district court correctly determined Priester's complaint failed to allege a conspiracy. The complaint alleges that the coaches either ignored or "encouraged and/or allowed" Ward's behavior; however, the complaint does not allege an agreement between Ward and the coaches to commit an illegal act, nor does it allege specific facts to show an agreement. Therefore, we uphold the district court's dismissal of Ward for failure to state a claim under Rule 12(b)(6).

II.   DISMISSAL OF SCHOOL DISTRICT OFFICIALS UNDER SECTION 1983

Priester also argues that under section 1983, the district court erred in granting summary judgment to the defendants on two accounts. First, Priester alleges that the school officials' failure to protect Priester from violence during a school activity violates the Due Process clause. Second, Priester contends that the school officials' use of racial epithets and their refusal to both pay for her son's medical expenses and respond to her complaints of racial harassment deprives Priester of his clearly established rights, and thus, violates the Equal Protection clause.

A.   Substantive Due Process

Pursuant to the Due Process Clause, Priester argues that the district court erred in summarily dismissing her claim as failing to have the requisite state action. To state a claim under section 1983, a plaintiff must: (1) allege a violation of rights secured by the Constitution of the United States or laws of the United States; and (2) demonstrate that the alleged deprivation was committed by a person acting under color of state law. *McKinney v. Irving Ind. Sch. Dist.*, 309 F.3d 308 (5th Cir.2002). As for the first prong of *McKinney*, Priester's allegations indicate that her complaint falls under the substantive component of the Due Process Clause. *See Leffall v. Dallas Indep. Sch. Dist.*, 28 F.3d 521, 526 (5th Cir.1994) (finding a substantive due process claim when the plaintiff alleged that the state had a duty to provide students protection from injury at a school dance). Thus, the district court correctly construed Priester's allegations that the coaches and school officials failed to protect Priester from the attack, as essentially a claim under the substantive component of the Due Process Clause.

As for the second prong of *McKinney*, because the Fourteenth Amendment protects liberty and property interests only against invasion by a state, a section 1983 plaintiff, alleging the deprivation of Due Process under the Fourteenth Amendment, must also show that state action caused his injury. *Bass v. Parkwood Hosp.*, 180 F.3d 234, 241 (5th Cir.1999). In such cases, the "under color of law" and state action inquiries merge into one. *Id.* This court has consistently held that "the right to be free of state-occasioned damage to a person's bodily integrity is protected by the [F]ourteenth [A]mendment's guarantee of due process." *Doe v. Taylor Ind. Sch. Dist.*, 15 F.3d 443, 450-51 (5th Cir.1994); *Petta v. Rivera*, 143 F.3d 895 (5th Cir.1998) (finding that a constitutional right under the Due Process Clause requires more than merely a non-physical harm to give rise to a constitutional tort). Considering that the bodily integrity of Terry was indisputably damaged by Ward's act, he suffered an unquestionable harm to his property. The issue in this case, therefore, is whether the harm to Terry's property was caused by state action.

As a general rule, the state's failure to protect an individual from private violence does not violate the Due Process Clause. . . . This court has clearly held, that absent "certain limited circumstances," substantive due process "does not confer an entitlement to governmental aid as may be necessary to realize the advantages of liberty guaranteed by the Clause." *Walton v. Alexander*, 44 F.3d 1297, 1302 (5th Cir.1995). Therefore, for Priester to overcome the district court's grant of summary judgment in favor of the defendants, she must show that the alleged harm to her son fits one of those "certain limited circumstances."

i.   Special Relationship Exception

Priester contends that the coaches were effectively state actors because a "special relationship" exists between students and teachers, and thus, the coaches were cloaked with a certain public trust and responsibility to protect her son from harm. We have recognized that when the "special relationship" between the person and the state imposes upon the state a constitutional duty to protect that individual from known threats of harm by private actors, this circumstance constitutes an exception to the general rule that a state has no affirmative duty to protect an individual from private violence. *Walton*, 44 F.3d at 1299. . . .

The special relationship exception, however, has been narrowly construed when applied to school sponsored activities. This court has held that no such special relationship exists between a school district and its students during a school sponsored activity "held outside the time during which students are required to attend school for non-voluntary activities." *Leffall*, 28 F.3d at 529. In *Leffall*, an eighteen-year-old student, named Dameon Steadham, was fatally shot by random gunfire in the parking lot of a public high school after a school dance. *Id.* at 523. The court reasoned that no special relationship existed between the student and the school, because although the student may have been "compelled to attend school during the day, any special relationship that may have existed lapsed when compulsory attendance ended." *Id.* at 530. In other words, "the State does not become the permanent guarantor of an individual's safety by having once offered him shelter." *DeShaney*, 489 U.S. at 201, 109 S.Ct. 998.

In the present case, Priester's claim that lack of supervision during football practice is gross negligence wrongfully rests upon a characterization of the State as a permanent guarantor of a student's safety. It is undisputed that Terry's injuries did not occur during regular school hours, when students are arguably compelled to attend public schools. Rather, Terry's injury occurred after regular school hours during football practice, and thus, at the time his injuries occurred, no special relationship existed between him and the school. Moreover, Priester fails to show that her son was compelled or restrained against his will. High school football practice is a voluntary extra-curricular activity, and thus, Priester cannot claim that her son was in any ways compelled by the school to participate. Priester has cited no relevant case law which supports her special relationship claims. Therefore, because no special relationship exists between a school district and its students during a school-sponsored football practice held outside of the time during which students are required to attend school for non-voluntary activities, the district court did not err in finding no requisite state action under section 1983. . . .

iii.   Fair Attribution Standard

Despite the absence of any exception to the general rule, Priester contends that Ward's actions should be attributed to the school officials because of both: the alleged conspiracy between Cahalane and Ward to gouge her son's eye, and the history of unpunished racial bullying, which she argues was an official endorsement that facilitated Terry's injury. For the purpose of section 1983, private action may be deemed state action when the defendant's conduct is "fairly attributable to the State." *Bass*, 180 F.3d at 241 (5th Cir.1999). Under the "fair attribution" test, the plaintiff must show: (1) that the deprivation was caused by the exercise of some right or privilege created by the state or by a rule of conduct imposed by the state, or by a person for whom the state is responsible, and (2) that the party charged with the deprivation may fairly be said to be a state actor. *Daniel v. Ferguson*, 839 F.2d 1124, 1130 (5th Cir.1988). State action will not accrue merely because of government acquiescence or approval of the private entity's actions. *Yeager v. City of McGregor*, 980 F.2d 337, 342 (5th Cir.1993). A party may fairly be said to be a state actor only when "he has acted with or has obtained significant aid from state officials, or because his conduct is otherwise chargeable to the State." *Daniel*, 839 F.2d at 1130; *Bass*, 180 F.3d at 242 (stating that a "State normally can be held responsible for a private decision only when it has exercised coercive power or has provided such significant encouragement

[or] where the government has so far insinuated itself into a position of interdependence . . . that it was a joint participant in the enterprise").

On the facts *sub judice*, Ward's conduct cannot be fairly attributable to the state. Although Priester asserts an alleged conspiracy between Cahalane and Ward, the record shows no evidence of the content of the conversation nor does it highlight any actual agreement. Without knowledge of the content of the conversation or any objective evidence of an agreement, Priester's assertion is nothing more than conclusory. Due to the pleading and proof requirements to present a prima facia case of conspiracy, . . . this evidence is legally insufficient to overcome summary judgment.

Moreover, although the district court did not address Priester's contention that the school officials' failure to adequately respond to either her son's history of racial abuse at the school or Ward's assault on Priester is tantamount to state endorsement, her argument fails to overcome the burden of summary judgment. The record is devoid of any active participation or significant encouragement of the alleged racial abuse by the school officials. Rather than any affirmative act, Priester alleges omissions; the school's inaction and indifference, although morally reprehensible, do not rise to the level of legal action under the fair attribution standard. Nor does the record show any evidence that Ward and the school officials shared the common objective of gouging Terry's eye, as is required to qualify as joint participation. Therefore, Ward's seemingly private conduct may not be charged to the state because the school officials' mere indifference does not arise to the level of fair attribution.

B.   Equal Protection

Priester asserts that the school officials use of racial epithets, their inability or unwillingness to respond to complaints of racial mistreatment, and their failure to pay her son's medical expenses violated Priester's equal protection rights. To state a claim of racial discrimination under the Equal Protection Clause and section 1983, the plaintiff "must allege and prove that he received treatment different from that received by similarly situated individuals and that the unequal treatment stemmed from a discriminatory intent." *Taylor v. Johnson*, 257 F.3d 470, 473 (5th Cir. 2001). A discriminatory purpose "implies that the decision maker singled out a particular group for disparate treatment and selected his course of action at least in part for the purpose of causing its adverse effect on an identifiable group." *Id.*

Priester contends that the use of racial epithets, combined with other conduct, deprived her son of his clearly established rights. This court has held that the use of a racial epithet without harassment or other conduct depriving the victim of his established rights does not constitute an equal protection violation. *Williams v. Bramer*, 180 F.3d 699, 706, *clarified*, 186 F.3d 633 (5th Cir. 1999) ("Where the conduct at issue consists solely of speech, there is no equal protection violation"). Assuming arguendo that Cahalane used racial epithets, Priester must also demonstrate additional genuine issues of material fact, where school officials participated in actions that deprived Terry of his constitutional rights.

Priester argues that the additional evidence of racial animus stemmed from the high school principal's failure to conduct an investigation in regards to Priester's racial harassment complaints. While the record does not show whether school officials investigated Priester's twice-weekly complaints of harassment, the record does indicate that Halford investigated and completed a report on Terry's injury, resolved a complaint regarding his grades, and investigated

Priester's complaint regarding harassment of her son during a field trip. Thus, while the school officials may not have adequately responded to all of Priester's numerous complaints, the record does not show that the officials' inaction on some of the complaints rises to the level of an equal protection violation. Moreover, Priester presents no evidence establishing that the alleged racial harassment went unpunished while other types of misconduct was punished or that the school did not document the racial harassment in its records. . . .

CONCLUSION

For the foregoing reasons, the judgment of the district court is AFFIRMED. . . .

NOTES AND QUESTIONS

1. *Analysis of* Priester. On what basis did the court affirm the dismissal of Defendant Ward on statute of limitations grounds? When an intentional tort has its basis in racial animus, should the statute of limitations be tolled on public policy grounds (i.e., a racially motivated intentional tort sufficiently different than other intentional torts to warrant special treatment in terms of applying the statute of limitations)? After the decision in the *Priester* case, even if you believed that the statute of limitations could not be tolled under existing law, would you support legislative action to toll the statute of limitations in cases of intentional torts based on racial animus or to extend the length of time in which such claims could be brought?

   Neither the coach (Cahalane) nor the player (Ward) was held to be a state actor or to have acted under color of state law under Section 1983. Why wasn't the coach held to be a state actor or to have acted under the color of state law? Isn't he clearly a state actor? Does the fact that practices were "voluntary" and held after school render the special relationship between a teacher and student different from the relationship that exists during school hours? Is this a case in which sport is simply being insulated from liability (i.e., the court is being deferential to sport in refusing to find that the coach is a state actor)? If the coach were held to be a state actor, what would the plaintiff have to plead to link the player's actions to the coach and the school? Did the plaintiff in this case simply fail to plead an agreement between the coach and the player? What would have to be pled in this regard? Would it be sufficient to plead the existence of an implied or tacit agreement? In effect, didn't the coach's failure to intervene constitute just such an agreement?

   The court recognized that a party may assert a violation of substantive due process when the state has a duty to protect students from injury at school. Doesn't a coach have a duty to protect his players in a case like *Priester*? Why did the court refuse to find such a duty to protect the plaintiff from invasion of his bodily integrity? The court notes, "The record is devoid of any active participation or significant encouragement of alleged racial abuse by the school officials." Do you agree with this statement? What about the concerns raised by the student-athlete's mother and the failure of the school to investigate those concerns?

The court also refused to find an equal protection violation in this case. What would the plaintiff have to allege and ultimately prove to be able to prevail on equal protection grounds? The court acknowledges that school officials "may not have adequately responded to all of Priester's numerous complaints," but concludes that "the record does not show that the officials' inaction on some of the complaints rises to the level of an equal protection violation." What would the plaintiff have to prove? Was it enough that the school documented the racial harassment in its records? The court seems to imply that the plaintiff would have to prove that racial harassment was treated differently from other forms of misconduct. Is the court saying that other forms of misconduct also went unpunished or that the plaintiff failed to assert that other forms of misconduct had in fact been treated differently? Given the court's decision, would a school district be advised to take care not to take a hands-off approach to misconduct (i.e., to treat all misconduct equally by failing to punish misconduct generally)?

In *Priester* the court analyzed each issue in seriatim fashion in dispensing with the plaintiff's case. At many points, the court appears to be quite deferential to the school in operating its athletic program. Have they given coaches too much deference in such matters? What are they protecting — the right of participants or the interests of the school to run an unfettered athletic program?

2. *Title VI as a Remedial Option.* In a case involving alleged opponent-to-opponent racial discrimination, the plaintiffs sought recovery pursuant to Title VI, which prohibits discrimination in programs receiving federal financial assistance. In *Malcolm v. Novato Unified School District*, 2002 WL 31770392 (Cal. App. 1 Dist.) (not selected for official publication), the plaintiffs, two African American high school basketball players, were subjected to racial harassment by fans of San Marin High School, the opponent home team. About 20 fans attended the game dressed in costumes, which included racial depictions of blacks. Fans also directed racial slurs toward plaintiffs and other African American players on the visiting team. In asserting their Title VI claim, the plaintiffs alleged that the defendant school district had actual knowledge of the racially hostile environment at San Marin and had failed to take adequate steps to address it. While acknowledging that efforts undertaken by the school district to address racial hostility were not ideal, the court concluded that the district's remedial action was not unreasonable. The court framed the appropriate standard as follows:

> The issue is not whether district officials could have done more or acted more effectively. They could have. Under the current state of the law, however, school districts are not liable for damages because their response to inappropriate behavior is ill advised, ineffective or inept.
> . . . The United States Supreme Court has made clear that an action for damages under the federal civil rights legislation invoked here is not [cognizable] unless the school district's role or response is so clearly unreasonable as to reflect deliberate indifference.

Id. at *10. *See Garvey v. Unified School Dist.*, 2005 WL 2548332 (D. Kan. Oct. 12, 2005) (a high school basketball player denied position on boys' basketball team alleged school engaged in racial discrimination in selecting members of team. The court found that the plaintiff could sue for intentional discrimination under Title VI, but the statute allows for neither a disparate impact claim nor the recovery of punitive damages). See *Scott v. State of Hawaii Dept. of Educ.*, 2009 WL 564709 (D. Haw.) (African American athlete kicked off high school football team failed to present evidence establishing disciplinary rules were applied to him in a discriminatory manner—other students received less harsh punishment for similar violations—and therefore could not sustain a Title VI racial discrimination claim); *Williams v. U.S. Tennis Assn.*, 2009 WL 5088727 (N.D. Cal. Dec. 17, 2009) (tennis player and her mother failed to allege facts sufficient to support their claim that the daughter was a victim of racial discrimination based on the defendant association's failure to respond to hostile comments made by another player and her mother).

3. *Fans as Victims.* In an interesting twist on the issue of fan harassment, a university was sued on the basis of discrimination in public accommodations when the student manager of its basketball team shouted racial slurs and threats to spectators. *Hawai'i v. Hoshijo*, 102 Haw. 307, 76 P.3d 550 (2003). In holding the university liable, the Hawaii Supreme Court deemed the University of Hawaii to be the owner and operator of a place of public accommodation by virtue of its ownership of a sports facility. It concluded that the student manager was an agent of the university and, at the time, was acting within the scope of his authority. The court held that liability for violation of Hawaii's statute barring discrimination in public accommodations should attach to the university pursuant to *respondeat superior. Id.* at 564. The court also held that the manager's racial slurs did not constitute protected speech under the First Amendment. *Id.* at 564-565.

CHAPTER
10

Gender Equity Issues in Athletics

A. INTRODUCTION

In this chapter, we explore issues related to gender equity in athletics. We also explore intersections between racial and gender equity. While the focus is largely on developments in the United States, global issues are raised on occasion as well. A brief history is followed by sections focusing on the development of the law in this area over the past four decades. Gender discrimination issues were first raised through federal equal protection claims, with additional regulation for school-based sports programs coming from Title IX of the Educational Amendments of 1972, 20 U.S.C. §1681, and the various regulations, policy interpretations, and other documents issued by the Office of Civil Rights (OCR) of the U.S. Department of Education. Increasing athletics participation opportunities for girls and women has introduced other gender-based legal issues such as sexual harassment and pregnancy discrimination to the world of sports. Although much of the focus on gender equity in athletics has centered on female participants, gender discrimination issues also exist for women who wish to work in sports, including as administrators, coaches, officials, and journalists.

B. HISTORICAL PERSPECTIVE

Globally, gender inequity has been present in athletics for centuries. Much of the following chronology is based on an informative website titled *History of Women in Sports Timeline* at http://www.northnet.org/stlawrenceaauw/timeline.htm. In the first Olympics, held in ancient Greece in 776 B.C., women were excluded, so they were relegated to competing in their own games every four years to honor the Greek goddess who ruled over women and earth. In 392 B.C., even after women were permitted to participate in the ancient Olympics, Kyniska, a Spartan princess, won an Olympic chariot race but was not permitted to receive her prize in person. Even though women made periodic strides toward equity in their participation in athletics in the ensuing centuries, it was not until 1900 that 16 women were permitted to participate in three sports—tennis, golf, and croquet—in the modern Olympic Games. In 1914, however, the U.S. Olympic Committee formally opposed participation by women athletes in the Olympics, with the only exception being the floor exercise, in which women were expected to wear long skirts.

The battle for gender equity in the Olympics persists. In *Martin v. IOC*, 740 F.2d 670 (9th Cir. 1984), the Ninth Circuit affirmed the denial of a preliminary injunction to require the organizers of the 1984 Los Angeles Summer Olympic Games to include the same 5,000- and 10,000-meter track events for women as existed for men. The court rejected plaintiffs' claims that the failure to include these events constituted illegal gender discrimination, even though "the women runners made a strong showing that the early history of the modern Olympic Games was marred by blatant discrimination against women." *Id.* at 673. The majority explained, "[W]e find persuasive the argument that a court should be wary of applying a state statute to alter the content of the Olympic Games. The Olympic Games are organized and conducted under the terms of an international agreement—the Olympic Charter. We are extremely hesitant to undertake the application of one state's statute to alter an event that is staged with competitors from the entire world under the terms of that agreement." *Id.* at 677.

The *Martin* dissenting judge argued:

> The IOC made concessions to the widespread popularity of women's track and field by adding two distance races this year. The IOC refused, however, to grant women athletes equal status by including all events in which women compete internationally. In so doing, the IOC postpones indefinitely the equality of athletic opportunity that it could easily achieve this year in Los Angeles. When the Olympics move to other countries, some without America's commitment to human rights, the opportunity to tip the scales of justice in favor of equality may slip away. Meanwhile, the Olympic flame—which should be a symbol of harmony, equality, and justice—will burn less brightly over the Los Angeles Olympic Games.

Id. at 683.

In *Sagen v. Vancouver Organizing Committee for the 2010 Olympic & Paralympic Games*, 98 B.C.L.R. 4th 141 (Can. B.C.), the British Columbia Court of Appeal rejected a similar gender discrimination claim and ruled that the International Olympic Committee's (IOC's) decision not to include women's ski jumping as an event in the Vancouver Olympic Games, while including men's ski jumping events, did not violate Canadian Charter of Rights and Freedoms. In opposing the inclusion of women's ski jumping as an Olympic sport in 2005, Gian Franco Kasper—an IOC member and President of the International Ski Federation—opined that ski jumping is physically taxing and seems "not to be appropriate for ladies from a medical point of view." Reflecting its paternalistic views, the IOC allowed Vancouver to add women's ski cross, a less physically taxing sport, even though ski cross was not as popular among women participants worldwide. *Why Can't Women Ski Jump?*, Time, 2012, http://www.time.com/time/specials/packages/article/0,28804,1963484_1963490_1963447,00.html.

Kasper's statement and the IOC's decision to add ski cross rather than ski jumping as a women's Olympic sport underscores the persistence of medically unsupportable views that often hinder the creation and development of women's athletic participation opportunities and progress. Ultimately, the IOC approved women's ski jumping for the 2014 Olympics in Sochi, Russia, indicating that while the *Martin* dissent's inclusive view did not prevail as a legal matter, it did ultimately win the day. Nevertheless, myths about women's athletic capabilities and interests will no doubt continue to arise, globally and within the United States.

Despite historically limited participation opportunities, women's Olympic athletic achievements have been quite notable, particularly in recent years. Reacting to significant successes on the part of women athletes, *USA Today* columnist Christine Brennan noted, "The 2012 Olympic Games are over, and while nations will debate and discuss their performances in the weeks and months to come, there can be no doubt about one overriding topic: women were the big winners." Christine Brennan, *American Women Rule the London Olympics—Now What?*, USA Today, Aug. 12, 2012, http://www.usatoday.com/sports/olympics/london/story/2012-08-12/London-Olympics-womens-sports-Christine-Brennan-Title-IX/57016306/1. It is clear that women were major winners in the London Games, with women from over 200 nations participating, including Brunei, Quatar, and Saudi Arabia, which had steadfastly resisted sending female participants on largely religious grounds. Nearly 45 percent of the participants in the 2012 Olympics from all nations were women. Over half of the members of the United States Olympic team were women. Indeed, the American women won more gold medals (29) than all other nations, with the exception of China and Great Britain (they tied with Great Britain). Brennan and others have referred to the American women Olympians as "team Title IX." *Id.* They won a total of 58 medals (56 percent of the United States' total of 104), which is a significant increase from the 1972 Munich Olympics (the year in which Title IX was enacted) when they won 22 (23 percent) of all medals won by the United States team.

Participation by American women in the 2012 London Games is evidence of increasing gender equity in the United States and a tribute to Title IX, which has been the primary engine of increased participation opportunities for women in the United States. Within the United States gender equity in athletics has come slowly and has not yet been fully achieved as evidenced by the following chronology.

In the United States, the first interscholastic athletic activity—gymnastics—occurred at the Latin School for girls in Salem, Massachusetts, in 1821. Progress, in terms of participation for women, was slow during the nineteenth century. In 1866, Vassar College formed the first two women's amateur baseball teams; in 1867, the first women's professional baseball team was formed, the Dolly Vardens, which was made up of African American women from Philadelphia. In 1874, Mary Ewing Outerbridge introduced tennis to the United States. The first athletic games for women in the United States were held in 1882 at the YWCA in Boston. *Physical Education*, a journal published in 1896 by the YMCA, devoted a full issue to women. In 1896, the University of California–Berkeley and Stanford University played the first women's intercollegiate basketball game, with Stanford winning 2-1 before 700 fans.

Progress came slowly in the twentieth century, as well. It was not until the 1920s that some of the cultural opposition to the involvement of women in athletics began to dissipate. In 1920, female swimmers became the first American women to be accorded full Olympic status. There were only three swimming events for women in the 1920 Olympiad, and Ethelda Bleibtrey entered all of them, winning three gold medals. By 1924, Sybil Bauer became the first woman to break an existing men's swimming record with her record-breaking win in the 100-meter backstroke. However, because women had only limited opportunities to participate in the Olympics, the first *Olympiades Feminines,* an alternative competition for women, was held in 1921. In the same year, the National Women's Athletic Association was organized. The National Amateur Athletic Federation also was founded in 1921, with women being afforded "equal footing [with men] with the same standards, the same program and the same regulations." The Amateur Athletic Union (AAU) added track and field for women in 1922, and it held the first national basketball tournament for women, with six teams participating in 1924. By 1922, 22 percent of U.S. colleges were offering some varsity team sports for women. In 1928, Olympic track and field events were open to women, and American Betty Robinson became the first woman to win a gold medal with her victory in the 100-meter race. Finally, in 1929, Tuskegee Institute in Alabama awarded scholarships to women participating on its track team and hosted a women's track meet.

In 1931, Virne Beatrice "Jackie" Mitchell, a 17-year-old woman pitching for the Chattanooga Lookouts, struck out Babe Ruth and Lou Gehrig in an exhibition game. Baseball commissioner Judge Kenesaw Mountain Landis responded by banning women from professional baseball on the grounds that it was "too strenuous" for them to participate. In 1936, Sally Sterns became the first woman coxswain of a male rowing team at Rollins College. The All American Red Heads Basketball Team was also formed in 1936 and won more than 85 percent of its games against male teams over a 50-year period. Women's gymnastics was added to the Olympic Games in 1936.

Some advances in athletics participation opportunities for women occurred after World War II, although progress remained slow. For example, in 1954, the Iowa Girls' High School Athletic Association established a statewide program that placed girls on equal footing with boys in high school athletics. By 1959, women were permitted to participate in the international cycling championships.

In the 1960s, women made some significant strides in terms of their participation opportunities in competitive athletic events. In 1966, for example, the first intercollegiate women's basketball tournament was played in Pennsylvania, and the Commission on Intercollegiate Athletics for Women (CIAW) was established by the Division for Girl's and Women's Sports in 1967. The CIAW was formed for the purpose of increasing participation by women in competitive sports, which led to the first women's national intercollegiate championship competition in 1969 in the sport of gymnastics.

The 1970s proved to be an historic decade in the evolution of gender equity in athletics for women in the United States. In 1971, the Association for Intercollegiate Athletics for Women (AIAW) was formed, replacing the CIAW and offering seven national championships for women. However, in 1972, only a small number of colleges offered varsity sports for women, with the National Collegiate Athletic Association (NCAA) reporting that only 30,000 women were participating in collegiate varsity and recreational sports. Welch Suggs, *Title IX at 30,* Chron. Higher Educ., June 21, 2002, at 38. In the 1970s the AIAW was the only major national intercollegiate athletic governing association for women's sports. In 1980, however, the NCAA began offering national championships for women in all three of its divisions. The AIAW brought an unsuccessful antitrust action against the NCAA in an effort to prevent the NCAA from absorbing women's athletics at the intercollegiate level. See *Association of Intercollegiate Athletics for Women v. National Collegiate Athletic Assn.,* 735 F.3d 577 (D.C. Cir. 1984). Thereafter, the AIAW was soon disbanded.

The historic congressional enactment of Title IX of the Education Amendments of 1972, which in 2002 was renamed the Patsy T. Mink Equal Opportunity in Education Act in honor of the Hawaiian congresswoman who was instrumental in its passage, provided significant momentum for increased participation for women in organized athletics at the interscholastic and intercollegiate levels. Ironically, Title IX was "slipped into a civil-rights law because conservative Southerners thought the idea of granting equal opportunities for women would derail the bill." *Id.* Senators Edith Green of Oregon and Birch Bayh of Indiana, however, took the initiative and guided the bill into law. On June 23, 1972, Title IX, 20 U.S.C. §1681, was signed into law by President Richard M. Nixon. The legislation does not specifically mention athletics, but it did require the promulgation of regulations to achieve gender equity in educational opportunities. Title IX gender equity regulations relating to athletics became effective on July 21, 1975, and are codified in 34 C.F.R. Pt. 106.

In an effort to limit the scope of Title IX as applied to intercollegiate athletics, two bills were proposed in Congress in 1975 and 1977. In H.R. 8394, Representative O'Hara sought to require that revenues generated by men's sports be used for their funding before being used to support other sports. Senators Tower, Bartlett, and Hruska proposed Senate Bill 2106, which would have excluded revenue-producing sports from Title IX coverage. These legislative efforts, however, were unsuccessful and did not result in any changes to Title IX or its regulations.

In 1978, the Department of Health, Education, and Welfare (HEW), the government agency originally responsible for governmental enforcement of Title IX, issued a set of proposed policy interpretations regarding the application of Title IX to athletics. More than 700 comments were received, and HEW's final policy interpretations were adopted on December 11, 1979. In 1980, HEW was reorganized, and the Department of Education (DOE) was formed. The DOE's Office of Civil Rights (OCR) was charged with responsibility for enforcing Title IX. On July 28, 1980, the OCR, in one of its first official acts, issued an interim manual dealing with Title IX and athletics.

However, Title IX was not vigorously enforced during the 1980s. The administrations of Presidents Carter, Reagan, and Bush were subjected to strong pressure from various groups opposed to Title IX. Walter F. Byers, former executive director of the NCAA, has noted that the NCAA and many of its member universities argued from the inception of Title IX that, "to decree that football and women's field hockey immediately deserved the same per capita Title IX expenditures was financial lunacy. We contended that income-producing sports should be exempted." Walter Byers, Unsportsmanlike Conduct 243 (1995).

In *Grove City College v. Bell*, 465 U.S. 555 (1984), the Supreme Court held that Title IX applied only to programs that benefited directly from federal funds. The *Grove City* decision seriously limited OCR's jurisdiction over university athletic programs, virtually none of which receive any federal funding. Subsequently, however, the Civil Rights Restoration Act of 1987 was passed as Congress overrode a presidential veto. This act mandates that all departments and programs of educational institutions that receive federal funds, including their athletics departments, are bound by the requirements of Title IX. Because the vast majority of educational institutions receive some federal funding, virtually all high school and college athletics programs are covered by Title IX. Thereafter, the OCR began to enforce Title IX more aggressively.

In *Franklin v. Gwinnett County Public Schools,* 503 U.S. 60 (1992), the Supreme Court unanimously held that prevailing plaintiffs may recover monetary damages and attorney fees for intentional violations of Title IX. The *Gwinnett* decision, coupled with increased enforcement activity on the part of OCR, contributed to a significant rise in the number of Title IX cases in the athletics context. See generally Paul M. Anderson and Barbara Osborne, *A Historical Review of Title IX Litigation,* 18 J. Legal Aspects of Sport 127 (Winter 2008).

In 1994 Congress passed the Equity in Athletics Disclosure Act (EADA), 20 U.S.C. §1092, which requires all federally funded institutions of higher education to disclose information regarding their athletics programs, including athletic participation opportunities for men and women. Initial EADA reports were due on October 1, 1996, and these reports have provided a source of information that has increased public awareness and provided a better evidentiary basis for quantifying gender inequities.

On January 16, 1996, OCR issued *Clarification of Intercollegiate Athletics Policy Guidance: The Three-Part Test,* the application of which in determining the existence of equal athletic participation opportunities has been the source of much Title IX litigation beginning in the mid- to late 1990s and continuing until the present. Private litigation and government enforcement activity under Title IX has resulted in increased athletic participation opportunities for women and increased gender equity. Nevertheless, women continue to be underrepresented in intercollegiate and interscholastic athletics, and they still do not have access to equivalent athletic facilities, equipment, and other resources.

This federal legal mandate to achieve gender equity in athletics has been affected by reduced funding for education, which has been exacerbated by the worldwide recession that began in 2008. With declining state revenues, many higher educational institutions have faced significant cuts in their overall budgets with corresponding cuts in their athletics programs, placing increasing pressure on those programs to produce revenues to cover existing expenses and the costs of expanding opportunities for women athletes.

On March 25, 2005, the Department of Education issued modified guidelines for determining compliance with the third prong of the OCR's three-part test. Under these guidelines, educational institutions may use an Internet or e-mail survey to determine whether the athletic interests and abilities of the underrepresented gender have been effectively accommodated. On June 22, 2005, NCAA president Myles Brand reissued an April 2005 resolution passed by the NCAA Executive Committee on behalf of the NCAA membership "reiterating the NCAA's commitment to strong enforcement of Title IX and the Association's opposition to the new [DOE modified guideline]" and urging the DOE to honor its prior commitments to strongly enforce the standards of long-standing Title IX athletics policies. The NCAA also urged its own members to decline to rely on an e-mail survey as the sole measure of women's interest in athletics. NCAA News Release, June 22, 2005. In April 2010, the Department of Education withdrew its 2005 policy that allowed colleges to comply with Title IX by simply using electronic surveys to gauge the interest of female students in playing sports.

Since the 1972 enactment of Title IX, the number of girls participating in interscholastic athletics has increased from 294,015 (7 percent of total participants) to 3,207,533 (42 percent of total participants). However, this is still significantly less than the 3,666,917 boys participating in interscholastic athletics in 1972 and the 4,484,987 male participants in 2012. Similarly, although Title IX has increased female intercollegiate athletics participation opportunities, men have substantially more opportunities; of the 453,347 NCAA student-athletes who competed in NCAA intercollegiate athletics during the 2011-2012 year, 195,657 (43.2 percent) of them were women and 257,690 (56.8 percent) were men. Thus, it is generally undisputed that the goal of gender equity in athletics has not been fully achieved. Women continue to be underrepresented in both high school and college athletics, and they do not have universal access to equivalent athletic facilities, equipment, and other resources.

In 2010, the National Women's Law Center (NWLC) filed administrative complaints with the U.S. Department of Education's OCR against 12 secondary school districts, including some of the nation's largest ones, alleging that they were not providing equal opportunities, on a proportional basis, for girls to play interscholastic sports. In July 2012, the OCR reached agreements with four school districts that ensure girls will receive equal athletic participation opportunities as male students. Each school agreed to assess whether there are unmet interests and abilities among its female student body and to develop a procedure whereby students may request the addition of new sports. If there are unmet interests and abilities, appropriate remedial steps will be taken (e.g., the addition of new sports for girls). At the time this book went to press, OCR complaints against the New York City Department of Education, Chicago Public School District 299, and a number of other districts remain open.

The issue of how gender is determined for purposes of athletic eligibility is becoming increasingly significant issue in the twenty-first century and requires exploration of the corresponding medical, legal, and policy issues. The issue of verification of "gender"—what methods we use to define a woman for the purpose of participation in women's sports—is increasingly controversial. The controversy surrounding Caster Semenya, South African women's middle-distance runner and 2009 world champion in the 800 meters, calls into question definitions of gender and sex verification methods and raises significant ethical issues. Erin Buzuvis, *Caster Semenya and the Myth of a Level Playing Field,* 6 Mod. Am. 36 (2010). See also Pablo S. Torre and David Epstein, *The Transgender Athlete,* Sports Illustrated, May 28, 2012, http://sportsillustrated.cnn.com/vault/article/magazine/MAG1198744/index.htm; Juliet Macur, *I.O.C. Adopts Policy for Deciding Whether an Athlete Can Compete as a Woman,* N.Y. Times, June 23, 2012, http://www.nytimes.com/2012/06/24/sports/olympics/ioc-adopts-policy-for-deciding-whether-athletes-can-compete-as-women.html?_r=0; Elliott Almond, *Stanford Bioethicist Challenges Controversial Olympics Gender-Testing Policy,* MercuryNews.com, June 24, 2012, http://www.mercurynews.com/other-sports/ci_20929583/stanford-bioethicist-challenges-controversial-olympics-gender-testing-policy. On November 30, 2010, the Ladies Professional Golfers Association changed its "female at birth" requirement to allow transgender membership in response to a federal lawsuit filed by a transgendered woman in a California case, *Lawless v. LPGA et al.,* Case No. 4:10CV04599 (N.D. Cal. 2010). These developments are significant and may have a far-reaching impact on the development of women's athletic participation opportunities.

The following materials and problems consider the legal, practical, and policy aspects of gender equity issues in connection with intercollegiate and interscholastic athletics. Title IX litigation regarding intercollegiate athletics has often focused on gender equity in terms of athletic participation opportunities, whereas the emphasis in interscholastic athletics litigation has focused on providing women with access to equal sports facilities and other benefits of athletic participation. Nevertheless, all aspects of Title IX are fully applicable to all levels of interscholastic and intercollegiate sports as well as high school and university intramural and recreational athletic programs.

NOTES AND QUESTIONS:

1. *Adding New Sports.* An increasing number of high school athletic associations now recognize cheer and dance as a competitive sport. Florida and Alaska now offer state championships at the high school level in women's flag football (which is becoming very popular and is a significant part of many educational institutions' intramural and club sports programs for women), bowling, rugby, and weightlifting. Texas recognizes women's wrestling. Despite their professed support for gender equity in athletics and Title IX, the NCAA and other intercollegiate athletic associations have not been as willing as their high school association counterparts to recognize new women's sports. Why does the NCAA continue to oppose the addition of new sports such as women's football, wrestling, rugby, and dance and cheer, despite the growing interest in those sports on the part of women, while encouraging competition in synchronized swimming, tennis, and other sports that seem to appeal to women of a higher socioeconomic status? The efforts of some universities to characterize dance and cheer as an intercollegiate sport were unsuccessful in *Biediger v. Quinnipiac University, infra,* in which the Second Circuit found that women's cheer at Quinnipiac University was not a sport for the purposes of Title IX. The NCAA Committee on Women's Athletics (CWA) is charged with identifying and managing progress of emerging sports for women. There are three emerging sports recognized by the Committee: rugby, sand volleyball, and equestrian. *Emerging Sports for Women,* NCAA, July 16, 2012, http://www.ncaa.org/wps/wcm/connect/ public/NCAA/Resources/Emerging+Sports+for+Women. Do you agree that these are the appropriate sports for the NCAA to focus on? Do sports like sand volleyball and equestrian favor the wealthy?

2. *Gender Discrimination Based on Pregnancy.* On June 25, 2007, a letter was sent by the OCR to university leaders emphasizing the Department of Education's responsibility to enforce 34 C.F.R. §106.40(a) of the Title IX regulation, which prohibits recipients of federal funds from applying "any rule concerning a student's actual or potential parental, family or marital status which treats students differently on the basis of sex." The regulation specifically states, "A recipient shall not discriminate against any student, or exclude any student from its education program or activity, including any class or extracurricular activity, on the basis of such student's pregnancy, childbirth, false pregnancy, termination of pregnancy or recovery therefrom, unless the student requests voluntarily to participate in a separate portion of the program or activity of the recipient." 34 C.F.R. §106.40(b)(1). In the letter, Assistant Secretary Stephanie Monroe noted her "concern over recent media reports regarding the current or past practice of some postsecondary education institutions to terminate scholarships of female athletes on the basis of pregnancy and the impact that this has had on female athletic participation. Some reports also indicate that some female athletes are choosing to terminate their pregnancy for fear of losing their athletic scholarships." It is clear from that letter that the OCR will enforce these provisions in such

instances. See also *Debate over Student-Athlete Pregnancy Issue to Intensify*, 44 NCAA News 1 (June 18, 2007). Questions have also arisen as to whether fathers are covered by Title IX's pregnancy regulations. In *Butler v. NCAA*, 2006 WL 2398683 (D. Kan. 2006), the court observed that the NCAA permits exceptions to its five-year eligibility rule to be made for female student-athletes "for reasons of pregnancy." Noting that a waiver "for reasons of pregnancy" is different from "reasons of maternity or paternity," the court held that a male student-athlete (i.e., a father) seeking to be treated the same as a pregnant female student-athlete for purposes of the five-year eligibility rule did not establish a substantial likelihood of success on the merits for his claim that the NCAA's refusal to grant him a waiver violated his right to equal protection under the law.

C. GENDER-BASED EXCLUSION FROM A PARTICULAR SPORT

The first sports-related gender equity cases were brought by female students in the 1970s and 1980s seeking the opportunity to play an interscholastic sport traditionally offered only for males. Historically, boys have had a wider variety of high school sports to participate in than girls, particularly contact sports. Even if there was not a girls' team, athletic governing body or school district rules often prohibited girls from playing on boys' teams regardless of their ability level. The following case illustrates that courts generally held that such exclusion is illegal sex discrimination.

FORCE v. PIERCE CITY R-VI SCHOOL DISTRICT

570 F. Supp. 1020 (W.D. Mo. 1983)

ROBERTS, District Judge.

[EDS. Nichole Force, a 13-year-old female student enrolled in the eighth grade at Pierce City Junior High School in Missouri, sought an injunction that would have allowed her to compete for a place on the school's eighth-grade football team. She had already been involved to a considerable extent in athletics (swimming, diving, organized softball, organized basketball, and elementary school football), and she had grown up with two brothers who excelled at football and who encouraged and helped her in her own athletic endeavors.

Pierce City Junior High School is a public school facility made up of the seventh, eighth, and ninth grades that sponsors an interscholastic athletics program. Boys could participate in football during the fall, basketball during the winter, and track during the spring. The corresponding sports for girls were volleyball, basketball, and track.

The boys' athletics coach for the school said he would let Nichole participate if school administration officials approved. However, school board members expressed concern over the potential precedent involved in granting her request (e.g., the possibility that boys would wish to participate on the girls' volleyball team and that high school girls might wish to play on the high school football team), the potential safety risk to a female competing in a contact sport with males, the administrative difficulties that might ensue (arrangements for locker room facilities, etc.), and that, at least as some board members understood it, the applicable provisions of Title IX and its regulations or Section 1.6 of the Missouri State High School Activities Association (MSHSAA) rules might be violated by permitting coeducational participation in a contact sport. The board voted unanimously to deny the request. While "they all agreed" Nichole would be a good football player and would have no problems playing, if she were permitted to play, the same allowance would have to be made for all other girls as well.

Nichole contended that this refusal to allow her an opportunity to play football was based solely upon the fact that she was a female rather than a male, and that this sex-based determination violated her right to the equal protection of the laws under the Fourteenth Amendment and 42 U.S.C. §1983.]

II. Discussion

The record makes clear, and I find, that defendants' refusal to grant plaintiff's request is the product of a gender-based classification. Stated simply, only males are permitted to compete for a place on the Pierce City Junior High School eighth grade football team. Since Nichole is a female, that opportunity is denied to her.

The principles which must govern in this situation are summarized in the opening passages of Section II of the Supreme Court's recent decision in *Mississippi University For Women v. Hogan,* 458 U.S., 102 S.Ct. 3331, 73 L.Ed.2d 1090 (1982). I can do no better than to quote those passages here:

> Because the challenged policy expressly discriminates among applicants on the basis of gender, it is subject to scrutiny under the Equal Protection Clause of the Fourteenth Amendment. Our decisions also establish that the party seeking to uphold a statute that classifies individuals on the basis of their gender must carry the burden of showing an "exceedingly persuasive justification" for the classification. The burden is met only by showing at least that the classification serves "important governmental objectives and that the discriminatory means employed" are "substantially related to the achievement of those objectives."
>
> Although the test for determining the validity of a gender based classification is straightforward, it must be applied free of fixed notions concerning the roles and abilities of males and females. Care must be taken in ascertaining whether . . . the objective itself reflects archaic and steretypic notions. Thus if the . . . objective is to exclude or "protect" members of one gender because they are presumed to suffer from an inherent handicap or to be innately inferior, the objective itself is illegitimate.
>
> If the State's objective is legitimate and important, we next determine whether the requisite direct, substantial relationship between objective and means is present. The purpose of requiring that close relationship is to assure that the validity of the classification is determined through reasoned analysis rather than through the mechanical application of traditional, often inaccurate, assumptions about the proper roles of men and women. . . .

Defendants do not quarrel with the fact that the present case must be governed by these principles; indeed they candidly acknowledge that fact. They argue, rather, that in the circumstances shown here a gender-based classification fully satisfies those principles. To that end, they identify four "important governmental objectives" which are said to be at stake: (a) maximization of equal athletic educational opportunities for all students, regardless of gender; (b) maintenance of athletic educational programs which are as safe for participants as possible; (c) compliance with Title IX of the Educational Amendments of 1972 and the regulations thereunder; and (d), compliance with the constitution and by-laws of MSHSAA. According to defendants, there is a "substantial relationship" between each of these objectives and a gender based classification which would prevent any female from competing with males for a place on the Pierce City Junior High School eighth grade football team.

Defendants' suggestion with respect to the necessity of compliance with Title IX can, I think, be dealt with in relatively short order. There is in fact nothing whatsoever in Title IX, or in its implementing regulations (34 C.F.R. §106.41(b)), which would mandate the action defendants have taken here.[3] To the contrary, Title IX's regulations leave each school free to choose whether co-educational participation in a contact sport will be permitted. Allowing Nichole Force to compete with males for a place on the Pierce City Junior High School eighth grade football team would no more violate those regulations than would refusing her that opportunity. Title IX simply takes a neutral stand on the subject.

Nor in my judgment can defendants' point regarding compliance with MSHSAA rules withstand scrutiny.[5] A school can hardly validate an otherwise unconstitutional act (assuming for the moment that there is one here) by noting that it has agreed with other schools to commit that act. There can be no doubt, of course, that MSHSAA performs a valuable and needed service for the schools and citizens of this state. But its rules cannot transcend constitutional requirements, and a member school's adherence to those rules cannot make constitutional that which is not.

I accordingly reject defendants' "objectives" (c) and (d) as providing any sort of appropriate predicate for the action taken here. Defendants' first two points, however, have more meat to their bones, and are deserving of more detailed treatment. Each will be examined separately below.

---

3. 34 C.F.R. §106.41(b) reads as follows: "(b) Separate teams. Notwithstanding the requirements of paragraph (a) of this section, a recipient may operate or sponsor separate teams for members of each sex where selection for such teams is based upon competitive skill or the activity involved is a contact sport. However, where a recipient operates or sponsors a team in a particular sport for members of one sex but operates or sponsors no such team for members of the other sex, and athletic opportunities for members of that sex have previously been limited, members of the excluded sex must be allowed to try-out for the team offered unless the sport involved is a contact sport. For the purposes of this part, contact sports include boxing, wrestling, rugby, ice hockey, football, basketball and other sports the purpose or major activity of which involves bodily contact."

5. Section 1.6 of the MSHSAA by-laws, in pertinent part, reads as follows:

A school, at its own discretion, may allow a student to compete on a team with the opposite sex in baseball, cross country, golf, gymnastics, soccer, softball, swimming, tennis, track or volleyball, provided the school does not offer interscholastic competition for both sexes in that sport.

This language obviously does not directly prohibit co-educational participation in contact sports. The parties have stipulated, however, that "as applied to the facts of this case, [the rule] does not permit members of the opposite sex to compete on the same team in interscholastic football."

A. MAXIMIZING PARTICIPATION IN ATHLETICS

One might wonder, at first blush, how denying all females the right to participate in a sport—which is the case here, since Pierce City eighth grade girls are not allowed to compete for a place on the only football team which might be available to them—will result in maximizing the participation of both sexes in athletics. And the short answer is that it probably does not. Defendants' argument in this regard, however, is sufficiently sophisticated to merit more than first blush treatment.

That argument proceeds on three interrelated theories. Defendants suggest, first, that males (as a class) will outperform females (as a class) in most athletic endeavors, given male size, speed and greater ratio of lean body mass. That being so, the argument proceeds, the best way in which to encourage and maximize female participation in athletics is by providing separate male and female teams, where males compete only against males and females only against females, since otherwise males will dominate the competition and ultimately discourage female participation. Pursuant to this idea, defendants have established separate inter-scholastic athletic programs for the two sexes in the Pierce City secondary schools, with the fall season sport being football for males and volleyball for females. But if (second) Nichole Force is permitted to compete for a place on the football team, then other girls must be accorded the same privilege, and boys must be allowed to compete for positions on the volleyball team. When (third) that happens, the girls will lose their best athletes, the boys will come to dominate volleyball, and overall female participation will ultimately wither.

Based upon the expert testimony presented in this case I am willing to accept the proposition that the average male, even at age 13, will to some extent outperform the average female of that age in most athletic events, although the matter may be open to some dispute. And I note, without being called upon to decide the issue, that a number of courts have held that the establishment of separate male/female teams in a sport is a constitutionally permissible way of dealing with the problem of potential male athletic dominance. . . . Beyond these two points, however, I am unable to accept defendants' argument.

The principal difficulty with the remaining portions of that argument, it seems to me, is that the various hypotheses used to bind it together are just that—hypotheses, and nothing more. There is, for example, no factual indication that the girls' eighth grade volleyball team will be blighted by the defection of its best players to the football field, if Nichole Force is allowed to play football. To the contrary, defendants' own testimony is that Nichole Force is the first and only girl, at any grade level, who has ever made a request to play football. And for that matter, if defendants are correct in their position that females are unable to compete successfully with males in athletics, particularly in contact sports, it is to be expected that such defections would be short-lived in any event, and that the situation would prove to be self-regulating. [Citation omitted.]

Nor is there any factual indication that eighth grade boys at Pierce City Junior High School are waiting eagerly for volleyball to be desegregated. Again to the contrary, there is no indication that any boy has ever expressed a desire to play on the volleyball team. . . . And in any event, it is by no means clear that the District would be constitutionally required to permit boys to participate in girls' volleyball, even if girls were allowed to participate in football. See *Clark v. Arizona Interscholastic Association*, 695 F.2d 1126, 1131-32 (9th Cir.1982); *Petrie v. Illinois High School Association*, 75 Ill.App.3d 980, 31 Ill.Dec. 653, 394 N.E.2d 855 (1979) (both holding, on a theory similar to that utilized in *Regents of the University of California v. Bakke*, 438 U.S. 265, 98 S.Ct. 2733, 57 L.Ed.2d 750 (1978), that the governmental interest in redressing past discrimination against women in athletics is sufficient to justify a regulation which excludes boys from participating on girls' teams, even though girls are allowed to compete on boys' teams).

Finally, even if by some chance defendants' worst case scenario should be realized, there might still be no need for the general breakdown which defendants postulate. For example, if a sufficient number of girls wish to play football, one obvious solution would be to organize a girls' football team; or if so many boys wish to play volleyball that they would dominate the girls' competition in that sport, to form a boys' volleyball team. . . .

There is, however, a further point implicit in defendants' argument on this subject which should be addressed before passing on: the apparent assumption that if, in the interest of maximizing equal athletic opportunities, it is constitutionally permissible to establish separate male and female teams in a given sport and to exclude each sex from the other's team, cases *supra*, then it is equally permissible, in that same interest, to designate separate male and female sports and to exclude each sex from participation in the other's sport. That is a proposition I am unwilling to accept, at least as a general matter. [Citations omitted.]

Each sport has its own relatively unique blend of requirements in terms of skills and necessary physical attributes, and each person, male or female, will for a variety of reasons probably find one or another sport more enjoyable and rewarding than others. In point of fact, volleyball is *not* football; and baseball is *not* hockey; and swimming is *not* tennis. Accordingly, if the idea is to "maximize educational athletic opportunities for all students, regardless of gender," it makes no sense, absent some substantial reason, to deny all persons of one sex the opportunity to test their skills at a particular sport. Of course there may be certain exceptional instances in which there is a "substantial reason" for such an exclusion, as for example where peculiar safety and equipment requirements demand it, see *Lafler v. Athletic Board of Control*, 536 F.Supp. 104 (W.D.Mich.1982) (boxing), or perhaps where excluding males is necessary to redress past inequality and to foster female participation, see *Clark v. Arizona Interscholastic Association, supra; Petrie v. Illinois High School Association, supra*. But those instances would, I think, be relatively rare, and would need to be factually established. And that is precisely where defendants' present argument fails, as far as the instant case is concerned.

I do not question the idea that maximizing the participation of both sexes in interscholastic athletic events is a worthy, and important, governmental objective. Nor do I question the sincerity of defendants' efforts in that regard. In the circumstances of this case, however, I must and do hold that the gender based classification used by defendants does not bear a sufficiently "substantial" relationship to that objective to withstand a constitutional challenge.

not a sufficient objective

B.   SAFETY

Neither do I question the fact that the "maintenance of athletic educational programs which are as safe for participants as possible" is an "important governmental objective." Indeed, that would seem obvious. Again, however, the facts of this case do not demonstrate a sufficiently "substantial" relationship between that objective and a blanket rule which prohibits all eighth grade females from competing for a place on the Pierce City Junior High School eighth grade football team.

There is no evidence, or even any suggestion, that Nichole Force herself could not safely participate in that football program. And while I do find, from the expert testimony presented, that a "typical" (i.e., average) 13 year old female would in fact, to some degree, have a higher potential for injury in mixed-sex football than would a "typical" (i.e., average) 13 year old male, this does not in my judgment greatly assist the defendants' argument. The problem, of course, is that not all 13 year old females are "typical," any more than all 13 year old males are "typical." Indeed, as defendants' own expert candidly admitted, some 13 year old females could safely play eighth grade football in mixed sex competition, and some 13 year old males could not. And yet I note that the Pierce City R-VI School District permits *any* male to compete in football, regardless of his size, speed, body type, lean body mass, fat body mass, bone structure, "Q" angle measurement or any other factor which might have a bearing on his potential for injury.

In short, the "safety" factor which defendants would utilize to prevent any female from playing eighth grade football—including those who could play safely—is not applied to males at all, even to those who could not play safely. All this tends to suggest the very sort of well-meaning but overly "paternalistic" attitude about females which the Supreme Court has viewed with such concern.[13] See, e.g., *Frontiero v. Richardson*, 411 U.S. 677, 684-87, 93 S.Ct. 1764, 1769-71, 36 L.Ed.2d 583 (1973). . . .

. . . I reject it here for the simple reason that it is sophistry to suggest a concern with the "administrative burden" of weeding out physically unfit 13 year old females in connection with a football program when there is no concern at all with weeding out physically unfit 13 year old males involved in the same program. In fact, I think, it might be rather difficult to sustain a requirement that females competing for a place on a particular athletic team be subjected to a fitness screening program, when males competing for a place on the same team are subjected to none at all.

I conclude, accordingly, that there is an insufficient relationship between defendants' announced goal of "safety" and a rule which automatically excludes all eighth grade females from competing with eighth grade males for a place on a football team. That holding, I note, is consistent with the result reached by virtually every other court which has considered this same sort of "safety" argument in connection with male/female competition in contact sports. . . .

Conclusion

Nichole Force obviously has no legal entitlement to a starting position on the Pierce City Junior High School eighth grade football team, since the extent to which she plays must be governed solely by her abilities, as judged by those who coach her. But she seeks no such entitlement here.

Instead she seeks simply a chance, like her male counterparts, to display those abilities. She asks, in short, only the right to try.

---

13. The reference here is to governmental attitudes, not parental attitudes. Any parent who feels that his or her child should not play football, or any other interscholastic sport for that matter, remains quite free to withhold consent to that child's participation. The school requires such parental consent before any child is permitted to compete on one of the interscholastic teams.

I do not suggest there is any such thing as a constitutional "right to try." But the idea that one should be allowed to try—to succeed or to fail as one's abilities and fortunes may dictate, but in the process at least to profit by those things which are learned in the trying—is a concept deeply engrained in our way of thinking; and it should indeed require a "substantial" justification to deny that privilege to someone simply because she is a female rather than a male. I find no such justification here.

[The court enjoined defendants from refusing to allow Nichole Force to compete for membership on the Pierce City Junior High School eighth-grade interscholastic football team on the same basis that males are allowed to compete.]

_____

Similarly, male athletes have challenged rules prohibiting their ability to compete on all-girls teams when a school does not offer a boys' team in a particular sport.

WILLIAMS v. SCHOOL DISTRICT OF BETHLEHEM, PA
998 F.2d 168 (3d Cir. 1993)

SLOVITER, Chief Judge.
Can high school field hockey be considered a contact sport? . . .

I. FACTS AND PROCEDURAL HISTORY

When John Williams was fourteen years old and in ninth grade, he presented himself for the girls' field hockey team tryouts at Liberty High School, a public school in the School District of Bethlehem, Pennsylvania. He had played intramural coed field hockey when he was in eighth grade at a middle school in the School District, but the high school has only a girls' field hockey team. After the tryouts, the coach made tentative position and team assignments based on each player's abilities. John, whose skills were average, would probably have played goalie on the junior varsity team. However, after school officials learned that John and another boy had been issued uniforms, the boys were instructed that they could not play on the girls' field hockey team.

John's parents, plaintiffs Sarah and Wayne Williams, filed this action in October 1990 against the School District of Bethlehem, challenging John's exclusion from the girls' field hockey team. They made claims alleging violations of title IX . . . ; the Equal Protection and Due Process clauses of the federal Constitution, under 42 U.S.C. §1983; and the Equal Rights Amendment to the Pennsylvania Constitution (E.R.A.), Pa. Const. art. I, §28. . . .

Based on the undisputed facts that the School District limits player participation on the field hockey team to females and that John was not permitted to be a part of the Liberty High School team only because of that policy, the district court granted summary judgment . . . in favor of the plaintiffs, permanently enjoining the School District from excluding John from the Liberty High School girls' field hockey team. . . .

II.   Discussion

A.   Title IX

1.   *Contact Sport*

Because field hockey is not one of the sports expressly specified in the regulation as a contact sport, whether it can be so deemed depends on whether it is a sport "the purpose or major activity of which involves bodily contact." 34 C.F.R. §106.41(b). . . . [P]laintiffs introduced the affidavits of four experts, each of whom concluded that field hockey is not a contact sport. . . .[5] All of these experts relied on the rules of play for field hockey promulgated by the National Federation of State High School Associations, which provide that almost all bodily contact or threatened bodily contact between players is a violation or foul. . . .

[The School District's two experts testified that because of the nature of field hockey, there inevitably will be contact among the players.]

It is not insignificant that the National Federation rules, introduced by the School District, require mouth protectors and shin guards, prohibit spiked shoes, require that artificial limbs be padded, and prohibit wearing jewelry. These rules suggest that bodily contact does in fact occur frequently and is expected to occur during the game. . . .

. . . We hold only that there is sufficient evidence on this record to preclude summary judgment for plaintiffs on that issue.

2.   *Previously Limited Athletic Opportunities*

If it is determined that field hockey is a contact sport, no other inquiry is necessary because that will be dispositive of the title IX claim. Even if a sport is not a contact sport, and there is no team for the other sex in that sport, the implementing regulation requires that members of the excluded sex be permitted to try out for a single-sex team only if their athletic opportunities have "previously been limited." 34 C.F.R. §106.41(b). In interpreting that language, the district court considered the composition of the athletic program at Liberty High School, which mirrors the team offerings in the School District of Bethlehem overall. The court compared the number of teams for boys and those for girls, noting that as of 1989, each of the two high schools in the School District has had ten boys' teams, ten girls' teams, and two coed teams. The court found that athletic opportunities for girls have surpassed those of boys because girls are permitted to try out for all twenty-two teams whereas boys may try out for only twelve, and it thus concluded that athletic opportunities for boys have "previously been limited."

Plaintiffs argue that even if we find that athletic opportunities for boys at Liberty High School have not been limited, the School District would still be in violation of title IX because it is clear that opportunities for boys in the sport of field hockey have previously been limited. Plaintiffs thus would interpret the

---

5. Plaintiffs also argue on appeal that field hockey should not be considered a contact sport because it is played coed at the adult level and because there will be no bodily contact with John Williams, who plays goalie. Assuming *arguendo* that John was slated as goalie on the junior varsity team, a matter which is not free from doubt, neither argument is relevant to the threshold question whether field hockey is a contact sport for purposes of the implementing regulation.

regulation's inquiry with respect to prior opportunities as sports-specific, in this case focusing on boys' opportunities in a traditionally female sport. This reading of the regulation language was adopted by the court in *Gomes v. Rhode Island Interscholastic League*, 469 F.Supp. 659, 664 (D.R.I.). . . .

We believe that the contrary interpretation adopted by the New York and New Hampshire courts is more persuasive. In *Mularadelis v. Haldane Central School Board*, 74 A.D.2d 248, 427 N.Y.S.2d 458, 461-64 (1980), the court looked at the phrase at issue in the context of the entire regulation. The court noted that the first clause expressly refers to a "particular sport" ("where a recipient operates or sponsors a team in a particular sport"), and the second clause uses broad and general language, defining the inquiry as whether "athletic opportunities" for members of the excluded sex have previously been limited. *Id.* If Congress had intended the inquiry into "athletic opportunities" to be limited to a "particular sport," it would have so stated, particularly since the phrase "particular sport" was used earlier in the same sentence. *Id.*

This analysis convinced the Superior Court of New Hampshire, which adopted it in *Gil v. New Hampshire Interscholastic Athletic Association*, No. 85-E-646, slip op. at 31-32. We agree. As the School District argues, if the plaintiffs' construction were adopted, there could never be a situation in a non-contact sport in which a team was limited to a single sex without a corresponding team for the other sex because, by definition, the opportunities in that particular sport will be limited for the excluded sex. It would mean that boys will always be able to argue that they had previous limited athletic opportunities just because certain sports have traditionally been considered women's sports, such as field hockey. This would render nugatory the purpose of the phrase in question, which was intended to authorize single-sex teams in certain circumstances.

We believe the district court was correct in implicitly rejecting the plaintiffs' sports-specific interpretation, and in looking instead to the overall athletic opportunities.

We conclude, however, that the district court applied a flawed analysis in holding as a matter of law that athletic opportunities for boys were previously limited at Liberty High School because girls have been able to try out for more teams than boys for almost two decades. The mere opportunity to try out for a team, which the district court found tipped the balance in favor of girls in the School District, is not determinative of the question of "previously limited" athletic opportunities under title IX. "Athletic opportunities" means real opportunities, not illusory ones. If, to satisfy title IX, all that the School District were required to do was to allow girls to try out for the boys' teams, then it need not have made efforts, only achieved in 1989, to equalize the numbers of sports teams offered for boys and girls.

The School District produced evidence that its decision in or about 1975 to allow girls the right to try out for all twenty-two teams did not equalize athletic opportunities between the sexes. . . .

Whether the opportunity for girls to try out for a boys' team is a realistic athletic opportunity with respect to that particular sport may turn on whether there are real and significant physical differences between boys and girls in high school. There was conflicting evidence introduced by the parties on this issue.

Plaintiffs offered evidence to show that the physical differences between boys and girls of high school age are negligible. . . .

It follows that in determining whether boys' athletic opportunities at Liberty have previously been limited, the factfinder must decide whether meaningful physiological differences between boys and girls of high school age negate the significance of allowing girls to try out for boys' teams but not allowing the reverse.

Because the district court erred in finding dispositive the mere opportunity for girls to try out without acknowledging that the School District had created a material issue of fact as to the effect of that opportunity, we will reverse the grant of summary judgment on the plaintiffs' title IX claim and remand for further factual development on the issue whether athletic opportunities for boys have previously been limited. . . .

B.   FEDERAL CONSTITUTIONAL CLAIMS

. . . The School District argues that the plaintiffs' constitutional claims under 42 U.S.C. §1983 are precluded because they are based on a matter fully addressed by the comprehensive scheme in title IX.

The Supreme Court has made clear that where a federal statute provides its own comprehensive enforcement scheme, Congress intended to foreclose a right of action under section 1983. *Middlesex County Sewerage Auth. v. National Sea Clammers Ass'n*, 453 U.S. 1, 20-21, 101 S.Ct. 2615, 2626-27, 69 L.Ed.2d 435 (1981). This court recently addressed the applicability of the *Sea Clammers* doctrine to cases in which plaintiff asserts a claim under title IX and the federal Constitution. In *Pfeiffer v. Marion Center Area School District*, 917 F.2d 779, 789 (3d Cir.1990), we held that the constitutional claims are "subsumed" in title IX, and that the district court, having addressed the title IX claim, properly refused to hear plaintiff's section 1983 claim. Plaintiffs argue that the *Sea Clammers* doctrine is inapplicable where an injunction is sought, but in *Pfeiffer* plaintiff also sought an injunction, and we are bound by that holding.

The district court in the instant case acknowledged that *Sea Clammers* rendered its discussion of the constitutional claims unnecessary, but chose to proceed, *inter alia*, "for the sake of completeness." . . . The court should have been guided instead by the Supreme Court's admonition that courts should exercise restraint before reaching federal constitutional claims. We will therefore not reach the constitutional issues, and will vacate the district court's judgment on the section 1983 claim.

C.   PENNSYLVANIA EQUAL RIGHTS AMENDMENT

The Pennsylvania E.R.A. provides that "[e]quality of rights under the law shall not be denied or abridged in the Commonwealth of Pennsylvania because of the sex of the individual." Pa. Const. art. I, §28. . . .

Although the Supreme Court of Pennsylvania has not addressed the E.R.A. in the context of interscholastic athletics, in a thoughtful opinion the Commonwealth Court made clear that if the classification between boys and girls in connection with team sports is based on impermissible assumptions and stereotypes about the comparative characteristics or abilities of boys and girls, the E.R.A. will be violated. *Commonwealth ex rel. Packel v. Pennsylvania Interscholastic Athletic Ass'n*, 18 Pa.Cmwlth. 45, 334 A.2d 839, 843 (1975) (athletic league provision barring girls from participating in sports with boys violates E.R.A. because it embodies the stereotype that girls are generally weaker and boys generally more skilled at athletics). However, after the Commonwealth Court's decision in *Packel*, the Pennsylvania Supreme Court decided *Fischer v. Department of Public Welfare*, 509 Pa. 293, 502 A.2d 114 (1985), where it accepted the view prevailing among jurisdictions with a state E.R.A. that the E.R.A. does not prohibit differential treatment among the sexes when, as here[,] that treatment is reasonably and genuinely based on physical characteristics unique to one sex.

Id. 502 A.2d at 125. [Quotation omitted.]

In defending the E.R.A. claim, the School District argued that because of the undeniable physical differences between girls and boys of high school age, sex was the only classification feasible for accomplishing, *inter alia,* the legitimate and substantial interest of promoting athletic opportunities for girls. As we noted in our discussion of title IX, the parties introduced conflicting evidence on the extent of physical differences between boys and girls at the high school level. . . .

The validity of the School District's policy excluding boys from the field hockey team depends on whether there are "physical characteristics unique to [boys]" which warrant differential treatment. If there are real physical differences between high school boys and high school girls, then the sexes are "not similarly situated as they enter into most athletic endeavors," *Petrie v. Illinois High School Ass'n*, 75 Ill.App.3d 980, 31 Ill.Dec. 653, 661, 394 N.E.2d 855, 863 (1979), and exclusion based on sex may be justified. . . .

Ultimately, the validity of the classification will depend on the relationship between the classification and the government interest. . . .

We will therefore remand the E.R.A. claim to the district court for factfinding as to whether there are any real physical differences between boys and girls that warrant different treatment, and whether boys are likely to dominate the school's athletic program if admitted to the girls' teams. Only then will it be possible to determine whether the School District's policy of excluding boys from girls' teams is necessary to the School District's recognized interest in preserving meaningful athletic opportunities for girls, . . . and/or whether there is a current need to rectify the admittedly pervasive past discrimination against female high school students with respect to athletic opportunities. . . .

NOTES AND QUESTIONS

1. *Equal Protection.* Why did the *Force* court find that categorically excluding girls from playing high school football violated the Equal Protection Clause? Would it be appropriate for the court to reach this conclusion if boys and girls had proportionately equal athletic participation opportunities on a program-wide basis?

Because Title IX provides a comprehensive enforcement scheme for gender discrimination in athletics, the *Williams* court refused to consider a male athlete's claim that his exclusion from the girls' field hockey team violated the equal protection clause of the federal constitution. However, other courts have reached a contrary conclusion. See *Communities for Equity v. Michigan High Sch. Athletic Assn.*, 459 F.3d 676, 690 (6th Cir. 2006), *cert. denied*, 127 S. Ct. 1912 (2007) ("The fact that the Supreme Court implied a private remedy in *Cannon* gives strength to the argument that Congress did not intend for the termination of federal funds — the only remedy explicitly authorized by Title IX — to serve as a comprehensive or exclusive remedy"); *Alston v. Virginia High Sch. League, Inc.*, 176 F.R.D. 220, 223 (W.D. Va. 1997) ("Title IX claim does not preclude or 'subsume' a §1983 claim for redress of the same underlying conduct"); *Leffel v. Wisconsin Interscholastic Athletic Assn.*, 444 F. Supp. 1117, 1120 (E.D. Wis. 1978) ("The enactment of Title IX did not remove the problem of sex discrimination from constitutional concern; congressional enactments cannot preempt provisions of the Constitution"). In *Fitzgerald v. Barnstable School Committee*, 555 U.S. 246 (2009), the Supreme Court resolved this split among lower courts by holding that Title IX does not preclude a plaintiff from bringing a denial of equal protection claim against a public school to gender discrimination under the broader civil rights statute, 42 U.S.C. §1983. The Court explained:

> A comparison of the substantive rights and protections guaranteed under Title IX and under the Equal Protection Clause lends further support to the conclusion that Congress did not intend Title IX to preclude §1983 constitutional suits. Title IX's protections are narrower in some respects and broader in others. Because the protections guaranteed by the two sources of law diverge in this way, we cannot agree with the Court of Appeals that "Congress saw Title IX as the sole means of vindicating the constitutional right to be free from gender discrimination perpetrated by educational institutions."

Id. at 256.

2. *Title IX.* Title IX's regulations do not require that members of the opposite sex be permitted to try out for unisex contact sports. See *Barnett v. Texas Wrestling Assn.*, 16 F. Supp. 2d 690 (N.D. Tex. 1998) (holding that Title IX was not violated when girls were denied permission to participate against boys at a wrestling tournament). However, in *Yellow Springs Exempted Village School District Board of Education v. Ohio High School Athletic Assn.*, 647 F.2d 651 (6th Cir. 1981), the Sixth Circuit held that a state athletics governing body's rule prohibiting coed teams in contact sports violates Title IX by inhibiting its member schools' ability to provide equal athletic opportunity for girls.

In construing Title IX, what limitation does the *Williams* court impose on the opportunities that boys will have to play on all-girls teams? According to the court, what is required by Title IX regarding the athletic participation opportunities offered for boys and girls? For interesting discussions of what constitutes a contact sport, see Suzanne Sangree, *Title IX and the Contact Sports Exemption: Gender Stereotypes in a Civil Rights Statute*, 32 Conn. L. Rev. 381 (2000); Renee Forseth and Walter Toliver, *The Unequal Playing Field-Exclusion of Male Athletes from Single-Sex Teams*, 2 Vill. Sports & Ent. L.F. 99 (1995).

During 2010, 1,561 women participated on their "men's" high school football team, which constitutes a 17.5 percent increase over a four-year period. *Trivia: Girls and High School Football*, Sportsmanship Blog, Oct. 31, 2011, http://josephsoninstitute.org/sports/pvwh-sportsmanship/2011/10/trivia-girls-and-high-school-football/. In 2006 and 2007, Holly Mangold, the 5'9", 315-pound sister of New York Jets center Nick Mangold, won two varsity letters in football as an offensive line player for prep football powerhouse Kettering Alter in Ohio. In its 2010-2011 release, the NFHS High School Athletics Participation Survey statistics revealed that the number of female high school wrestlers grew to 7,351 athletes, an increase of 1,217 wrestlers from the previous year (a 19.8 percent increase). Joseph Santoliquito, *Girls High School Wrestling Grows Rapidly at National Level*, MaxPreps, March 27, 2012, http://www.maxpreps.com/news/EYvdhNqZb069CZgu3ryckA/

girls-high-school-wrestling-grows-rapidly-at-national-level.htm.   In   2006, Michaela Hutchinson became the first girl to win a state wrestling championship by defeating a boy in the 103-pound finals of Alaska's large-school wrestling championships; subsequently, at least two other girls have won state championships while competing against boys.

3. *Separate but Equal.* Both the Equal Protection Clause and Title IX's regulations permit "separate but equal" athletic teams in the same sport for both sexes. As one court explained:

> Given the lack of athletic opportunity for females in past years, the encouragement of female involvement in sports is a legitimate objective and separation of teams may promote that purpose. . . .
>
> Separate soccer teams for males and females would meet the constitutional requirement of equal opportunity if the teams were given substantially equal support and if they had substantially comparable programs. There may be differences depending upon the effects of such neutral factors as the level of student interest and geographic locations. Accordingly, the standard should be one of comparability, not absolute equality.

Hoover v. Meiklejohn, 430 F. Supp. 164, 170 (D. Colo. 1977).

In *O'Connor v. Board of Education,* 645 F.2d 578 (7th Cir. 1981), the court, despite undisputed testimony rating her ability as equal to a male eighth-grade player, held that a girl did not have the right to try out for boys' sixth-grade basketball team. Is there a valid reason for prohibiting an exceptionally talented girl from having an opportunity to play on the boys' basketball team?

4. *State Constitutional Law.* The *Williams* case illustrates that state constitutional law may provide a basis for remedying gender inequities in interscholastic or intercollegiate athletics. See also *Haffer v. Temple Univ. of the Commonwealth System of Higher Educ.,* 678 F. Supp. 517, 536 (E.D. Pa. 1987) ("it is clear that judicial scrutiny of programs challenged under [state] ERA is at least as searching as that employed in an equal protection analysis"); *Blair v. Washington State Univ.,* 108 Wash. 2d 558, 740 P.2d 1379 (1987).

MERCER v. DUKE UNIVERSITY
190 F.3d 643 (4th Cir. 1999)

Girl who wants to be the kicker, makes the team, and then gets dismissed

LUTTIG, Circuit Judge.

Appellee Duke University operates a Division I college football team. . . . Before attending Duke, [Heather Sue] Mercer was an all-state kicker at Yorktown Heights High School in Yorktown Heights, New York. Upon enrolling at Duke in the fall of 1994, Mercer tried out for the Duke football team as a walk-on kicker. Mercer was the first—and to date, only—woman to try out for the team. Mercer did not initially make the team, and instead served as a manager during the 1994 season; however, she regularly attended practices in the fall of 1994 and participated in conditioning drills the following spring.

In April 1995, the seniors on the team selected Mercer to participate in the Blue-White Game, an intrasquad scrimmage played each spring. In that game, Mercer kicked the winning 28-yard field goal, giving the Blue team a 24-22 victory. . . . The kick was subsequently shown on ESPN, the cable television sports network. Soon after the game, [Duke head football coach] Goldsmith told the news media that Mercer was on the Duke football team, and Fred Chatham, the Duke kicking coach, told Mercer herself that she had made the team. . . .

Although Mercer did not play in any games during the 1995 season, she again regularly attended practices in the fall and participated in conditioning drills the following spring. Mercer was also officially listed by Duke as a member of the Duke football team on the team roster filed with the NCAA and was pictured in the Duke football yearbook.

During this latter period, Mercer alleges that she was the subject of discriminatory treatment by Duke. Specifically, she claims that Goldsmith did not permit her to attend summer camp, refused to allow her to dress for games or sit on the sidelines during games, and gave her fewer opportunities to participate in practices than other walk-on kickers. In addition, Mercer claims that Goldsmith made a number of offensive comments to her, including asking her why she was interested in football, wondering why she did not prefer to participate in beauty pageants rather than football, and suggesting that she sit in the stands with her boyfriend rather than on the sidelines.

At the beginning of the 1996 season, Goldsmith informed Mercer that he was dropping her from the team. Mercer alleges that Goldsmith's decision to exclude her from the team was on the basis of her sex because Goldsmith allowed other, less qualified walk-on kickers to remain on the team. Mercer attempted to participate in conditioning drills the following spring, but Goldsmith asked her to leave because the drills were only for members of the team. Goldsmith told Mercer, however, that she could try out for the team again in the fall.

. . . [R]ather than try out for the team again, Mercer filed suit against Duke and Goldsmith, alleging sex discrimination in violation of Title IX. . . .

. . . 34 C.F.R. §106.41 . . . reads in relevant part as follows:

ATHLETICS.

   (a) General. No person shall, on the basis of sex, be excluded from participation in, be denied the benefits of, be treated differently from another person or otherwise be discriminated against in any interscholastic, intercollegiate, club or intramural athletics offered by a recipient, and no recipient shall provide any such athletics separately on such basis.

   (b) Separate teams. Notwithstanding the requirements of paragraph (a) of this section, a recipient may operate or sponsor separate teams for members of each sex where selection for such teams is based upon competitive skill or the activity involved is a contact sport. However, where a recipient operates or sponsors a team in a particular sport for members of one sex but operates or sponsors no such team for members of the other sex, and athletic opportunities for members of that sex have previously been limited, members of the excluded sex must be allowed to try out for the team offered unless the sport involved is a contact sport. For the purposes of this part, contact sports include boxing, wrestling, rugby, ice hockey, football, basketball and other sports the purpose or major activity of which involves bodily contact.

34 C.F.R. §106.41(a)-(b). . . . The district court held, and appellees contend on appeal, that, under this regulation, "contact sports, such as football, are specifically excluded from Title IX coverage." We disagree.

Subsections (a) and (b) of section 106.41 stand in a symbiotic relationship to one another. Subsection (a) establishes a baseline prohibition against sex discrimination in intercollegiate athletics, tracking almost identically the language in the parallel statutory provision prohibiting discrimination by federally funded educational institutions. In addition to generally barring discrimination on the basis of sex in intercollegiate athletics, subsection (a) specifically prohibits any covered institution from "provid[ing] any such athletics separately on such basis."

Standing alone, then, subsection (a) would require covered institutions to integrate all of their sports teams. In order to avoid such a result—which would have radically altered the face of intercollegiate athletics—HEW provided an explicit exception to the rule of subsection (a) in the first sentence of subsection (b), allowing covered institutions to "operate or sponsor separate teams for members of each sex where selection for such teams is based upon competitive skill or the activity involved is a contact sport." By its terms, this sentence permits covered institutions to operate separate teams for men and women in many sports, including contact sports such as football, rather than integrating those teams.

The first sentence of subsection (b), however, leaves unanswered the question of what, if any, restrictions apply to sports in which a covered institution operates a team for one sex, but operates no corresponding team for the other sex. HEW addressed this question in the second sentence of subsection (b).

This second sentence is applicable only when two predicate criteria are met: first, that the institution in question "operates or sponsors a team in a particular sport for members of one sex but operates or sponsors no such team for members of the other sex," and second, that "athletic opportunities for members of that sex have previously been limited." In this case, appellees do not dispute that athletic opportunities for women at Duke have previously been limited, and thus we assume that the second condition has been met. Further, we assume, without deciding, that Duke operated its football team "for members of one sex"—that is, for only men—but did not operate a separate team "for members of the other sex," and therefore that the first condition has also been satisfied. Thus, insofar as the present appeal is concerned, we consider the predicate conditions to application of the sentence to have been met.

Provided that both of the conditions in the protasis of the second sentence of subsection (b) have been met, the apodosis of the sentence requires that "members of the excluded sex must be allowed to try out for the team offered unless the sport involved is a contact sport." The text of this clause, on its face, is incomplete: it affirmatively specifies that members of the excluded sex must be allowed to try out for single-sex teams where no team is provided for their sex except in the case of contact sports, but is silent regarding what requirements, if any, apply to single-sex teams in contact sports. As to contact sports, this clause is susceptible of two interpretations. First, it could be read to mean that "members of the excluded sex must be allowed to try out for the team offered unless the sport involved is a contact sport, *in which case the anti-discrimination provision of subsection (a) does not apply at all.*" Second, it could be interpreted to mean that "members of the excluded sex must be allowed to try out for the team offered unless the sport involved is a contact sport, *in which case members of the excluded sex need not be allowed to try out.*"

Appellees advocate the former reading, arguing that HEW intended through this clause to exempt contact sports entirely from the coverage of Title IX. We believe, however, that the latter reading is the more natural and intended meaning. The second sentence of subsection (b) does not purport in any way to state an exemption, whether for contact sports or for any other subcategory, from the general antidiscrimination rule stated in subsection (a). And HEW certainly knew how to provide for a complete exemption had it wished, Congress itself having provided a number of such exemptions in the very statute implemented by the regulation. Rather, the sentence says, and says only, that covered institutions must allow members of an excluded sex to try out for single-sex teams in non-contact sports. Therefore, the "unless" phrase at the end of the second clause of the sentence cannot (logically or grammatically) do anything more than except contact sports from the tryout requirement that the beginning of the second clause of the sentence imposes on all other sports.

Contrary to appellees' assertion, this reading of the regulation is perfectly consistent with the evident congressional intent not to require the sexual integration of intercollegiate contact sports. If a university chooses not to permit members of the opposite sex to try out for a single-sex contact-sports team, this interpretation respects that choice. At the same time, however, the reading of the regulation we adopt today, unlike the one advanced by appellees, ensures that the likewise indisputable congressional intent to prohibit discrimination in all circumstances where such discrimination is unreasonable—for example, where the university itself has voluntarily opened the team in question to members of both sexes—is not frustrated.

We therefore construe the second sentence of subsection (b) as providing that in non-contact sports, but not in contact sports, covered institutions must allow members of an excluded sex to try out for single-sex teams. Once an institution has allowed a member of one sex to try out for a team operated by the institution for the other sex in a contact sport, subsection (b) is simply no longer applicable, and the institution is subject to the general anti-discrimination provision of subsection (a). To the extent that the Third Circuit intended to hold otherwise in *Williams v. School Dist. of Bethlehem, Pa.*, 998 F.2d 168, 174 (3d Cir. 1993), with its lone unexplained statement that, "[if] it is determined that [a particular sport] is a contact sport, no other inquiry is necessary because that will be dispositive of the title IX claim," we reject such a conclusion as inconsistent with the language of the regulation.

Accordingly, because appellant has alleged that Duke allowed her to try out for its football team (and actually made her a member of the team), then discriminated against her and ultimately excluded her from participation in the sport on the basis of her sex, we conclude that she has stated a claim under the applicable regulation, and therefore under Title IX. We take to heart appellees' cautionary observation that, in so holding, we thereby become "the first Court in United States history to recognize such a cause of action." Br. of Appellees at 20. Where, as here, however, the university invites women into what appellees characterize as the "traditionally all-male bastion of collegiate football," *id.* at 20 n.10, we are convinced that this reading of the regulation is the only one permissible under law.

The district court's order granting appellees' motion to dismiss for failure to state a claim is hereby reversed, and the case remanded for further proceedings.

NOTES AND QUESTIONS

1. *Contact Sport Exception.* What is the scope of the contact sport exception as construed by *Mercer*? From a practical perspective, does the result in *Mercer* represent a victory for women athletes attempting to try out for a single-sex contact sports team? After the decision in *Mercer*, if you were an athletic director or coach at a public high school or state university, what would you do if a woman asked to try out for football, wrestling, or some other contact sport?

On remand to the district court, a judgment was rendered in favor of Mercer in the amount of $1 in compensatory damages and $2 million in punitive damages. The Fourth Circuit vacated the punitive damages award and found that punitive damages are unavailable in private actions brought to enforce Title IX. *Mercer v. Duke Univ.*, 50 Fed. Appx. 643 (4th Cir. 2002). The court's holding was premised on the similarity between Title IX and Title VI and the Supreme Court's ruling in *Barnes v. Gorman*, 536 U.S. 181 (2002), that punitive damages are not recoverable in private actions brought under Title VI. In January 2004, a federal judge awarded Mercer $349,243 in attorney fees. *Mercer v. Duke Univ.*, 301 F. Supp. 2d 454, 470 (M.D.N.C. 2004), *aff'd*, 401 F.3d 199 (4th Cir. 2005), which illustrates the costs and risks of Title IX litigation. A few women have participated in NCAA college football games as place kickers. In September 2003, Tonya Butler kicked a field goal for West Alabama University in a Division II Gulf South Conference game against Stillman University. Other women have kicked extra points during games.

2. *State Action and Private Universities.* Private universities such as Duke are not state actors subject to federal constitutional rights claims, although state gender discrimination laws may apply to their conduct. For commentary regarding *Mercer*, see Kimberly Capadona, Comment, *The Scope of Title IX Protection Gains Yardage as Courts Continue to Tackle the Contact Sports Exception*, 10 Seton Hall J. Sports L. 415 (2000); Abigail Crouse, Comment, *Equal Athletic Opportunity: An Analysis of* Mercer v. Duke University *and a Proposal to Amend the Contact Sport Exception to Title IX*, 84 Minn. L. Rev. 1655 (2000); Suzanne Sangree, *Title IX and the Contact Sports Exemption: Gender Stereotypes in a Civil Rights Statute*, 32 Conn. L. Rev. 381 (2000).

PROBLEM 10-1

Your 14-year-old daughter wants to try out for the boys' wrestling team and is not interested in participating in any other sports. She is an exceptionally talented athlete who has regularly lifted weights for the past two years and is in excellent physical condition. Although she has no prior experience in wrestling, her dream is to one day earn a gold medal as a member of the U.S. Olympic women's wrestling team. No other girls at her high school are interested in wrestling. For the past three years the boys' wrestling team has won the state championship, and several wrestlers have earned college athletic scholarships. The team's coach, whose decision is supported by the school's principal and athletic director, has refused to allow your daughter to try out for the team. Would you allow your daughter to participate in wrestling? Are you willing to file a lawsuit on her behalf to challenge her exclusion? Evaluate the merits of her potential legal claims.

STOP

D.   EQUAL ATHLETIC PARTICIPATION OPPORTUNITIES, BENEFITS, AND TREATMENT

In the 1980s, women began successfully challenging gender discrimination in intercollegiate athletics on a program-wide basis on federal and state equal protection grounds. See, e.g., *Haffer v. Temple Univ.*, 678 F. Supp. 517 (E.D. Pa. 1987); *Blair v. Wash. State Univ.*, 108 Wash. 2d 558, 740 P.2d 1379 (1987). Although Title IX was enacted in 1972, its application to intercollegiate and interscholastic athletics was not clearly established until 1987. *Bennett v. West Texas State Univ.*, 799 F.2d 155 (5th Cir. 1986) (relying on *Grove City College v. Bell* to hold that Title IX coverage does not extend to college athletic programs that do not receive federal funds). The Civil Rights Restoration Act of 1987 reversed the Supreme Court's 1984 *Grove City College* ruling that Title IX applies only if a specific educational program receives federal funds. As a result, college and university athletic programs now are covered if any part of the educational institution directly or indirectly receives federal funds. For cases considering whether an athletics governing body is subject to Title IX, see *NCAA v. Smith*, 525 U.S. 459 (1999); *Horner v. Kentucky High Sch. Athletic Assn.*, 43 F.3d 265 (6th Cir. 1994); *Alston v. Va. High Sch. League, Inc.*, 144 F. Supp. 2d 526 (W.D. Va. 1999).

Title IX currently is the law most frequently utilized to remedy sex discrimination in interscholastic or intercollegiate athletics. Title IX litigation in the interscholastic area has occurred with less regularity than litigation in the intercollegiate athletics context, but it is anticipated that this federal law will be invoked by private parties at all levels of athletic participation with greater regularity in the future. Thus far, most college cases have involved claims that women are not being provided with equal athletic participation opportunities in comparison to men. At the high school level, most litigation to date has come in the form of claims that female athletes are not provided equivalent treatment and benefits vis-à-vis male athletes. An illustrative sampling of cases addressing alleged unequal athletic participation opportunities, benefits, and treatment follows.

1.   *Equal Athletic Participation Opportunities*

In this subsection, we examine in detail four of the leading cases in the intercollegiate context: *Cohen v. Brown University*, *Biediger v. Quinnipiac University*, *Boucher v. Syracuse University*, and *Pederson v. Louisiana State University*. As you read these cases, carefully consider how the legal doctrines have developed in this area. Because lawyers often become involved in Title IX disputes long before the filing of a lawsuit, reflect on what guidance developing legal doctrine provides to prevent or remedy a Title IX violation.

COHEN v. BROWN UNIVERSITY
101 F.3d 155 (1st Cir. 1996), *cert. denied*, 520 U.S. 1186 (1997)

BOWNES, Senior Circuit Judge.

This is a class action lawsuit charging Brown University, its president, and its athletics director (collectively "Brown") with discrimination against women in the operation of its intercollegiate athletics program, in violation of Title IX. . . .

This suit was initiated in response to the demotion in May 1991 of Brown's women's gymnastics and volleyball teams from university-funded varsity status to donor-funded varsity status. Contemporaneously, Brown demoted two men's teams, water polo and golf, from university-funded to donor-funded varsity status. As a consequence of these demotions, all four teams lost, not only their university funding, but most of the support and privileges that accompany university-funded varsity status at Brown. . . .

I

. . . Brown operates a two-tiered intercollegiate athletics program with respect to funding: although Brown provides the financial resources required to maintain its university-funded varsity teams, donor-funded varsity athletes must themselves raise the funds necessary to support their teams through private donations. The district court noted that the four demoted teams were eligible for NCAA competition, provided that they were able to raise the funds necessary to maintain a sufficient level of competitiveness, and provided that they continued to comply with NCAA requirements. The court found, however, that it is difficult for donor-funded varsity athletes to maintain a level of competitiveness commensurate with their abilities and that these athletes operate at a competitive disadvantage in comparison to university-funded varsity athletes. . . .

Brown's decision to demote the women's volleyball and gymnastics teams and the men's water polo and golf teams from university-funded varsity status was apparently made in response to a university-wide cost-cutting directive. . . .

Plaintiffs alleged that, at the time of the demotions, the men students at Brown already enjoyed the benefits of a disproportionately large share of both the university resources allocated to athletics and the intercollegiate participation opportunities afforded to student athletes. Thus, plaintiffs contended, what appeared to be the even-handed demotions of two men's and two women's teams, in fact, perpetuated Brown's discriminatory treatment of women in the administration of its intercollegiate athletics program.

. . . The district court . . . summarized the history of athletics at Brown, finding, . . . that, while nearly all of the men's varsity teams were established before 1927, virtually all of the women's varsity teams were created between 1971 and 1977, after Brown's merger with Pembroke College. The only women's varsity team created after this period was winter track, in 1982.

In the course of the trial on the merits, the district court found that, in 1993-94, there were 897 students participating in intercollegiate varsity athletics, of which 61.87% (555) were men and 38.13% (342) were women. During the same period, Brown's undergraduate enrollment comprised 5,722 students, of which 48.86% (2,796) were men and 51.14% (2,926) were women. The district court found that, in 1993-94, Brown's intercollegiate athletics program consisted of 32 teams, 16 men's teams and 16 women's teams. Of the university-funded teams, 12 were men's teams and 13 were women's teams; of the donor-funded teams, three were women's teams and four were men's teams. At the time of trial, Brown offered 479 university-funded varsity positions for men, as compared to 312 for women; and 76 donor-funded varsity positions for men, as compared to 30 for women. In 1993-94, then, Brown's varsity program—including both university- and donor-funded sports—afforded over 200 more positions for men than for women. Accordingly, the district court found that Brown maintained a 13.01% disparity between female participation in intercollegiate athletics and female student enrollment. . . .

In computing these figures, the district court counted as participants in intercollegiate athletics for purposes of Title IX analysis those athletes who were members of varsity teams for the majority of the last complete season. . . .

The district court found from extensive testimony that the donor-funded women's gymnastics, women's fencing and women's ski teams, as well as at least one women's club team, the water polo team, had demonstrated the interest and ability to compete at the top varsity level and would benefit from university funding.

The district court did *not* find that full and effective accommodation of the athletics interests and abilities of Brown's female students would disadvantage Brown's male students. *would not disadvantage males*

II

Title IX . . . specifies that its prohibition against gender discrimination shall not "be interpreted to require any educational institution to grant preferential or disparate treatment to the members of one sex on account of an imbalance which may exist" between the total number or percentage of persons of that sex participating in any federally supported program or activity, and "the total number or percentage of persons of that sex in any community, State, section, or other area." 20 U.S.C.A. §1681(b) (West 1990). Subsection (b) also provides, however, that it "shall not be construed to prevent the consideration in any . . . proceeding under this chapter of statistical evidence tending to show that such an imbalance exists with respect to the participation in, or receipt of the benefits of, any such program or activity by the members of one sex." *law*

Applying §1681(b), the prior panel held that Title IX "does not mandate strict numerical equality between the gender balance of a college's athletic program and the gender balance of its student body." The panel explained that, while evidence of a gender-based disparity in an institution's athletics program is relevant to a determination of noncompliance, "a court assessing Title IX compliance may not find a violation solely because there is a disparity between the gender composition of an educational institution's student constituency, on the one hand, and its athletic programs, on the other hand." . . .

[A 1978 OCR] Policy Interpretation establishes a three-part test, a two-part test, and factors to be considered in determining compliance under 34 C.F.R. §106.41(c)(1) [which provides a non-exhaustive list of ten factors to be considered in determining whether equal athletics are available to both genders.] At issue in this appeal is the proper interpretation of the first of these, the so-called three-part test, which inquires as follows:

3 part test!

(1) Whether intercollegiate level participation opportunities for male and female students are provided in numbers substantially proportionate to their respective enrollments; or

(2) Where the members of one sex have been and are underrepresented among intercollegiate athletes, whether the institution can show a history and continuing practice of program expansion which is demonstrably

responsive to the developing interests and abilities of the members of that sex; or

(3) Where the members of one sex are underrepresented among intercollegiate athletes, and the institution cannot show a continuing practice of program expansion such as that cited above, whether it can be demonstrated that the interests and abilities of the members of that sex have been fully and effectively accommodated by the present program.

44 Fed. Reg. at 71, 418.

The district court held that, "because Brown maintains a 13.01% disparity between female participation in intercollegiate athletics and female student enrollment, it cannot gain the protection of prong one." Nor did Brown satisfy prong two. While acknowledging that Brown "has an impressive history of program expansion," the district court found that Brown failed to demonstrate that it has "maintained a continuing practice of intercollegiate program expansion for women, the under-represented sex." . . . [T]he fact that Brown has eliminated or demoted several men's teams does not amount to a continuing practice of program expansion for women. As to prong three, the district court found that Brown had not "fully and effectively accommodated the interest and ability of the under-represented sex" to the extent necessary to provide equal opportunity in the selection of sports and levels of competition available to members of both sexes. . . .

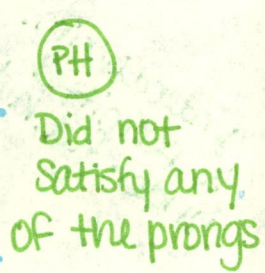

IV

Brown contends that the district court misconstrued and misapplied the three-part test. Specifically, Brown argues that the district court's interpretation and application of the test is irreconcilable with the statute, the regulation, and the agency's interpretation of the law, and effectively renders Title IX an "affirmative action statute" that mandates preferential treatment for women by imposing quotas in excess of women's relative interests and abilities in athletics. Brown asserts, in the alternative, that if the district court properly construed the test, then the test itself violates Title IX and the United States Constitution. . . .

A

Brown's talismanic incantation of "affirmative action" has no legal application to this case and is not helpful to Brown's cause. . . . True affirmative action cases have historically involved a voluntary undertaking to remedy discrimination (as in a program implemented by a governmental body, or by a private employer or institution), by means of specific group-based preferences or numerical goals, and a specific timetable for achieving those goals. . . .

Title IX is not an affirmative action statute; it is an anti-discrimination statute, modeled explicitly after another anti-discrimination statute, Title VI. No aspect of the Title IX regime at issue in this case—inclusive of the statute, the relevant regulation, and the pertinent agency documents—mandates gender-based preferences or quotas, or specific timetables for implementing numerical goals.

Like other anti-discrimination statutory schemes, the Title IX regime permits affirmative action. In addition, Title IX, like other anti-discrimination schemes, permits an inference that a significant gender-based statistical disparity may indicate the existence of discrimination. Consistent with the school desegregation cases, the question of substantial proportionality under the Policy Interpretation's three-part test is merely the starting point for analysis, rather than the conclusion; a rebuttable presumption, rather than an inflexible requirement. In short, the substantial proportionality test is but one aspect of the inquiry into whether an institution's athletics program complies with Title IX. . . .

From the mere fact that a remedy flowing from a judicial determination of discrimination is gender-conscious, it does not follow that the remedy constitutes "affirmative action." Nor does a "reverse discrimination" claim arise every time an anti-discrimination statute is enforced. While some gender-conscious relief may adversely impact one gender—a fact that has not been demonstrated in this case—that alone would not make the relief "affirmative action" or the consequence of that relief "reverse discrimination." To the contrary, race- and gender-conscious remedies are both appropriate and constitutionally permissible under a federal anti-discrimination regime, although such remedial measures are still subject to equal protection review.

B

[In this section the court notes, "*Cohen II* held that the Policy Interpretation is entitled to substantial deference because it is the enforcing agency's 'considered interpretation of the regulation.'"] . . .

F

Brown has contended throughout this litigation that the significant disparity in athletics opportunities for men and women at Brown is the result of a gender-based differential in the level of interest in sports and that the district court's application of the three-part test requires universities to provide athletics opportunities for women to an extent that exceeds their relative interests and abilities in sports. . . .

We view Brown's argument that women are less interested than men in participating in intercollegiate athletics, as well as its conclusion that institutions should be required to accommodate the interests and abilities of its female students only to the extent that it accommodates the interests and abilities of its male students, with great suspicion. To assert that Title IX permits institutions to provide fewer athletics participation opportunities for women than for men, based upon the premise that women are less interested in sports than are men, is (among other things) to ignore the fact that Title IX was enacted in order to remedy discrimination that results from stereotyped notions of women's interests and abilities.

Interest and ability rarely develop in a vacuum; they evolve as a function of opportunity and experience. The Policy Interpretation recognizes that women's lower rate of participation in athletics reflects women's historical lack of opportunities to participate in sports. . . . [T]here exists the danger that, rather than providing a true measure of women's interest in sports, statistical evidence purporting to reflect women's interest instead provides only a measure of the very discrimination that is and has been the basis for women's lack of opportunity to participate in sports. Prong three requires some kind of evidence of interest in athletics, and the Title IX framework permits the use of statistical evidence in assessing the level of interest in sports. Nevertheless, to allow a numbers-based lack-of-interest defense to become the instrument of further discrimination against the under-represented gender would pervert the remedial purpose of Title IX. We conclude that, even if it can be empirically demonstrated that, at a particular time, women have less interest in sports than do men, such evidence, standing alone, cannot justify providing fewer athletics opportunities for women than for men. Furthermore, such evidence is completely irrelevant where, as here, viable and successful women's varsity teams have been demoted or eliminated.

Finally, the tremendous growth in women's participation in sports since Title IX was enacted disproves Brown's argument that women are less interested in sports for reasons unrelated to lack of opportunity. . . .

Brown's relative interests approach is not a reasonable interpretation of the three-part test. This approach contravenes the purpose of the statute and the regulation because it does not permit an institution or a district court to remedy a gender-based disparity in athletics participation opportunities. Instead, this approach freezes that disparity by law, thereby disadvantaging further the under-represented gender. Had Congress intended to entrench, rather than change, the status quo—with its historical emphasis on men's participation opportunities to the detriment of women's opportunities—it need not have gone to all the trouble of enacting Title IX.

VII

. . . Brown may achieve compliance with Title IX in a number of ways: It may eliminate its athletic program altogether, it may elevate or create the requisite number of women's positions, it may demote or eliminate the requisite number of men's positions, or it may implement a combination of these remedies. I leave it entirely to Brown's discretion to decide how it will balance its program to provide equal opportunities for its men and women athletes. I recognize the financial constraints Brown faces; however, its own priorities will necessarily determine the path to compliance it elects to take. . . .

. . . Brown's proposed compliance plan stated its goal as follows: The plan has one goal: to make the gender ratio among University-funded teams at Brown substantially proportionate to the gender ratio of the undergraduate student body. To do so, the University must disregard the expressed athletic interests of one gender while providing advantages for others. The plan focuses only on University-funded sports, ignoring the long history of successful donor-funded student teams. . . .

Brown states that it "seeks to address the issue of proportionality while minimizing additional undue stress on already strained physical and fiscal resources."

The general provisions of the plan may be summarized as follows: (i) Maximum squad sizes for men's teams will be set and enforced. (ii) Head coaches of all teams must field squads that meet minimum size requirements. (iii) No additional discretionary funds will be used for athletics. (iv) Four new women's junior varsity teams—basketball, lacrosse, soccer, and tennis—will be university-funded. (v) Brown will make explicit a de facto junior varsity team for women's field hockey.

The plan sets forth nine steps for its implementation, and concludes that "if the Court determines that this plan is not sufficient to reach proportionality, phase two will be the elimination of one or more men's teams."

The district court found Brown's plan to be "fatally flawed" for two reasons. First, despite the fact that 76 men and 30 women participated on donor-funded varsity teams, Brown's proposed plan disregarded donor-funded varsity teams. Second, Brown's plan "artificially boosts women's varsity numbers by adding junior varsity positions on four women's teams." As to the propriety of Brown's proposal to come into compliance by the addition of junior varsity positions, the district court held:

> Positions on distinct junior varsity squads do not qualify as "intercollegiate competition" opportunities under the Policy Interpretation and should not be included in defendants' plan. . . . "[I]ntercollegiate" teams are those that "regularly participate in varsity competition." See 44 Fed. Reg. at 71,413 n.l. Junior varsity squads, by definition, do not meet this criterion. Counting new women's junior varsity positions as equivalent to men's full varsity positions flagrantly violates the spirit and letter of Title IX; in no sense is an institution providing equal opportunity if it affords varsity positions to men but junior varsity positions to women.

The district court found that these two flaws in the proposed plan were sufficient to show that Brown had "not made a good faith effort to comply with this Court's mandate." . . .

The district court ordered Brown to "elevate and maintain women's gymnastics, women's water polo, women's skiing, and women's fencing to university-funded varsity status." . . .

We agree with the district court that Brown's proposed plan fell short of a good faith effort to meet the requirements of Title IX as explicated by this court in *Cohen II* and as applied by the district court on remand. . . .

It is clear, nevertheless, that Brown's proposal to cut men's teams is a permissible means of effectuating compliance with the statute. . . . [A]lthough the district court's remedy is within the statutory margins and constitutional, we think that the district court was wrong to reject out-of-hand Brown's alternative plan to reduce the number of men's varsity teams. After all, the district court itself stated that one of the compliance options available to Brown under Title IX is to "demote or eliminate the requisite number of men's positions." Our respect for academic freedom and reluctance to interject ourselves into the conduct of university affairs counsels that we give universities as much freedom as possible in conducting their operations consonant with constitutional and statutory limits.

Brown therefore should be afforded the opportunity to submit another plan for compliance with Title IX. . . . Accordingly, we remand the case to the district court so that Brown can submit a further plan for its consideration. In all other respects the judgment of the district court is affirmed. . . .

VIII

There can be no doubt that Title IX has changed the face of women's sports as well as our society's interest in and attitude toward women athletes and women's sports. . . . In addition, there is ample evidence that increased athletics participation opportunities for women and young girls, available as a result of Title IX enforcement, have had salutary effects in other areas of societal concern.

One need look no further than the impressive performances of our country's women athletes in the 1996 Olympic Summer Games to see that Title IX has had a dramatic and positive impact on the capabilities of our women athletes, particularly in team sports. These Olympians represent the first full generation of women to grow up under the aegis of Title IX. The unprecedented success of these athletes is due, in no small measure, to Title IX's beneficent effects on women's sports, as the athletes themselves have acknowledged time and again. What stimulated this remarkable change in the quality of women's athletic competition was not a sudden, anomalous upsurge in women's interest in sports, but the enforcement of Title IX's mandate of gender equity in sports.

Affirmed in part, reversed in part, and remanded for further proceedings. . . .

———————————

After *Cohen*, budgetary constraints made it difficult for universities to comply with the proportionality provision, creating pressure to provide more opportunities for women by adding sports for women or cutting men's sports. Additionally, concerns as to what is required in terms of proportionality have persisted. The following case examines proportionality issues. It also raises issues regarding what women's sports should be added and under what circumstances. The NCAA has recommended three emerging sports for women: equestrian, sand volleyball, and rugby. These sports present both financial and access issues for institutions. For example, there are serious questions about the socioeconomic ramifications of adding sand volleyball and equestrian, two sports that are generally played by women in wealthier areas but not by women from poorer high school districts.

Recognizing the athleticism involved in women's cheer (tumbling and dance), a competitive activity offered at many high schools and universities, Quinnipiac University sought recognition for its women's cheer team as a sport for Title IX purposes.

BIEDIGER v. QUINNIPIAC UNIVERSITY

691 F.3d 85 (2d Cir. 2012)

RAGGI, Circuit Judge.

. . . Quinnipiac argues that the injunction [issued by the trial court], which prohibits any such future discrimination, should be vacated because it is based on a Title IX ruling infected by errors in counting the varsity athletic participation opportunities afforded Quinnipiac's female students in the 2009-10 school year. Specifically, Quinnipiac faults the district court for excluding from its count of the total athletic participation opportunities afforded female students: (1) 11 roster positions on the women's indoor and outdoor track and field teams, held by members of Quinnipiac's women's cross-country team who were required to join the track teams even though they were unable to compete in 2009-10 because they were injured or "red-shirted"; and (2) all 30 roster positions on Quinnipiac's nascent women's competitive cheerleading team, based on a finding that the team did not afford the athletic participation opportunities of a varsity sport. Quinnipiac further contends that, even if these 41 roster positions should not count as varsity athletic participation opportunities for women, the district court erred in concluding that (3) the resulting 3.62% disparity between the percentage of all participation opportunities in varsity sports afforded female students (58.25%) and the percentage of enrolled

△ female undergraduates (61.87%) established a Title IX violation warranting the challenged injunctive relief. . . . *error*

I. BACKGROUND

A. QUINNIPIAC'S DECISION TO ELIMINATE WOMEN'S VOLLEYBALL PROMPTS THIS TITLE IX ACTION

This lawsuit has its origins in Quinnipiac's March 2009 announcement that in the 2009-10 academic year, it would eliminate its varsity sports teams for women's volleyball, men's golf, and men's outdoor track and field, while simultaneously creating a new varsity sports team for women's competitive cheerleading. Plaintiffs, five Quinnipiac women's volleyball players and their coach, Robin Sparks, filed this action in April 2009, charging the university with violating Title IX by denying women equal varsity athletic participation opportunities, and seeking an injunction that, among other things, prevented Quinnipiac from eliminating its women's volleyball team. After a hearing, the district court preliminarily enjoined Quinnipiac from withdrawing support from its volleyball team, finding that Quinnipiac systematically and artificially increased women's teams' rosters and decreased men's teams' rosters to achieve the appearance of Title IX compliance. . . .

B. STATUTORY AND REGULATORY BACKGROUND

[The appellate court provides an excellent general summary of the statutory and regulatory background to Title IX, which is followed by a summary of specific materials related to the issue of whether cheer is a sport for Title IX purposes.]

In a 2008 letter, OCR explained that a genuine athletic participation opportunity must take place in the context of a "sport." Letter from Stephanie Monroe, Assistant Sec'y for Civil Rights, OCR, U.S. DOE, to Colleagues, at 1-2 (Sept. 17, 2008) ("2008 OCR Letter"). If a school is a member of a recognized intercollegiate athletic organization, such as the National Collegiate Athletic Association ("NCAA"), that subjects the activity at issue to its organizational requirements, OCR will "presume" that the activity is a sport and that participation can be counted under Title IX. But if that presumption does not apply or has been rebutted, OCR will determine whether the activity qualifies as a sport by reference to several factors relating to "program structure and administration" and "team preparation and competition." . . .

[I]n 2000, OCR had issued two letters stating that cheerleading, whether of the sideline or competitive variety, was presumptively not a sport, and that team members could not be counted as athletes under Title IX. While the letters indicated OCR's willingness to review particular cheerleading programs on a case-by-case basis, the parties stipulated in the district court that, since 2000, OCR has never recognized an intercollegiate varsity cheerleading program to be a sport for Title IX purposes. . . . Nor has Quinnipiac ever sought OCR recognition of its competitive cheerleading program as a sports activity. . . .

Once the numbers of real athletic participation opportunities afforded men and women have been determined in light of these principles, the next step of Title IX effective-accommodation analysis considers whether the numbers are substantially proportionate to each sex's enrollment. . . .

OCR affords schools considerable "flexibility and choice" in deciding how to provide substantially proportionate athletic opportunities to students of both sexes. . . .

C.   THE DISTRICT COURT RULING

At trial, Quinnipiac maintained that it offered athletic participation opportunities to male and female undergraduates substantially proportionate to their respective enrollments. In support, it pointed to evidence showing that, of the 5,686 students enrolled in Quinnipiac's undergraduate programs in the 2009-10 academic year, 3,518 were female and 2,168 were male. Varsity rosters for the first day of team competitions in 2009-10 listed 440 varsity athletes, of whom 274 were female and 166 were male. Thus, Quinnipiac maintained that women represented 61.87% of the total student body and 62.27% of all varsity athletes, while men represented 38.13% of the student body and 37.73% of all varsity athletes. . . .

Plaintiffs challenged Quinnipiac's count of its varsity athletes, arguing that (1) the university manipulated its team rosters to produce artificially undersized men's teams and artificially oversize women's teams; (2) counting the same women's membership on cross-country, indoor track, and outdoor track teams as three distinct athletic participation opportunities was unwarranted because Quinnipiac's indoor and outdoor track teams did not afford cross-country athletes genuine and distinct benefits; and (3) women who participated on the competitive cheerleading team should not be counted at all because the activity had not yet achieved the status of an intercollegiate varsity sport.

After trial, the district court issued a detailed memorandum of decision in favor of plaintiffs . . . reject[ing] plaintiffs' contention that, in setting roster targets for each of its teams, Quinnipiac had manipulated the rosters so as to undercount male participants and overcount female participants, or to set artificially high targets for women's teams that denied women participants genuine athletic opportunities. . . . The district court also decided that none of the 30 roster positions assigned to women's competitive cheerleading should be counted because the activity did not yet afford genuine athletic participation opportunities in a varsity sport. . . .

The district court observed that "in strictly numerical terms," a 3.62% disparity between Quinnipiac's women's 58.25% varsity athletic participation and their 61.87% representation in the undergraduate population reflected only "a borderline case of disproportionate athletic opportunities for women." Id. Nevertheless, the district court concluded that the disparity was significant enough to support judgment in favor of plaintiffs because (1) the disparity was caused by Quinnipiac's own actions and not by natural fluctuations in enrollment; and (2) it was reasonable to expect Quinnipiac to close the gap because the 38 roster positions needed for that purpose would be enough to field a viable women's athletic team, and such a team already existed in the form of the women's volleyball team. . . .

Accordingly, the district court entered a declaratory judgment finding Quinnipiac to have violated Title IX and its implementing regulations by discriminating against women in failing to provide equal athletic participation opportunities to female students, and it permanently enjoined Quinnipiac from continuing to discriminate in this manner. The district court ordered Quinnipiac to submit a plan for complying with the injunction, which plan was to provide for continuation of the women's volleyball team during the 2010-11 athletic season. . . .

II.   DISCUSSION

A.   QUINNIPIAC'S ARGUMENT AND THE STANDARD OF REVIEW

[The court reviews the award of permanent injunctive relief for abuse of discretion only for clear error and its conclusions of law de novo.]

[handwritten: mixed standard]

B.   DEFERENCE TO AGENCY INTERPRETATION OF TITLE IX'S IMPLEMENTING REGULATIONS

In addressing Quinnipiac's arguments, we note at the outset that no party challenges the district court's reliance on agency policy statements and letters . . .

Here, Quinnipiac elected to defend against plaintiffs' discrimination claim only by reference to the first safe harbor created by the three-part test, arguing that its athletics program provided "substantially proportionate" athletic participation opportunities [for women]. In sum, as a matter of Quinnipiac's litigation strategy, resolution of this case effectively turned on whether Quinnipiac's sex based treatment of varsity athletes provided its female students with genuine athletic participation opportunities substantially proportionate to their enrollment. . . .

[handwritten: Ⓘ]

C.   ATHLETIC PARTICIPATION OPPORTUNITIES FOR WOMEN RUNNERS: DISCOUNTING THE REPORTED NUMBERS FOR INDOOR AND OUTDOOR TRACK

Before the district court, plaintiffs argued that Quinnipiac should not be allowed to count as 54 athletic participation opportunities the cross-country, indoor track, and outdoor track roster positions held by the same 18 women. As the district court recognized, the issue admitted no easy resolution. The 1996 Clarification plainly states that "an athlete who participates in more than one sport will be counted as a participant in each sport in which she participates." 1996 Clarification at 3. But the trial evidence reflected circumstances not addressed in the 1996 Clarification: Quinnipiac's women cross-country runners were not afforded a choice as to whether to participate in more than one sport; they were required to do so. . . . As the district court recognized, these circumstances raise questions as to whether simultaneous participation on the women's cross-country, indoor track, and outdoor track teams at Quinnipiac represented three genuine athletic opportunities, or whether cross-country runners' mandated participation on the indoor and outdoor track teams was simply a form of alternative off-season training for the cross-country runners, one that allowed Quinnipiac to inflate the rosters of its women's indoor and outdoor track teams. . . .

[handwritten: π]

[handwritten: interesting! No choice but to participate]

D.   ATHLETIC PARTICIPATION OPPORTUNITIES FOR WOMEN IN COMPETITIVE CHEERLEADING: THE DETERMINATION THAT THE ACTIVITY DOES NOT YET QUALIFY AS A "SPORT"

Competitive cheerleading, which Quinnipiac decided to create as a new women's varsity sport team for 2009-10, is a late twentieth-century outgrowth of traditional sideline cheerleading. Whereas sideline cheerleaders generally strive to entertain audiences or solicit crowd reaction at sport or school functions, a competitive cheerleading team seeks to pit its skills against other teams for the purpose of winning. Thus, to distinguish the two activities, competitive cheerleaders do not attempt to elicit crowd response; generally do not use pom-poms, megaphones, signs, or other props associated with [sideline] cheerleading teams; wear uniforms consisting of shorts and jerseys, much like what women's volleyball players don; and emphasize the more gymnastic elements of sideline cheerleading, such as aerial maneuvers, floor tumbling, and balancing exercises, to the exclusion of those activities intended to rally the watching audience.

The district court nevertheless concluded that the 30 roster positions that Quinnipiac assigned competitive cheerleading for 2009-10 could not be counted under Title IX because the activity did not yet afford the participation opportunities of a varsity "sport."

Preliminary to reaching this conclusion, the district court observed that competitive cheerleading is not yet recognized as a "sport," or even an "emerging sport," by the NCAA, action that would have triggered a presumption in favor of counting its participants under Title IX.

Mindful of these circumstances, the district court proceeded carefully to review the structure, administration, team preparation, and competition of Quinnipiac's competitive cheerleading program to determine whether it nevertheless qualified as a sport whose athletic participation opportunities should be counted for purposes of Title IX. Again, we only briefly summarize the district court's detailed findings, which find ample support in the record evidence. The district court found that in terms of the team's operating budget, benefits, services, and coaching staff, competitive cheerleading was generally structured and administered by Quinnipiac's athletics department in a manner consistent with the school's other varsity teams. The district court noted two "minor" exceptions to this conclusion: Quinnipiac did not afford its competitive cheerleading team locker space; and because the NCAA did not recognize competitive cheerleading as a sport, the team did not receive NCAA catastrophic injury insurance and had to obtain it from a separate provider. With respect to factors relating to the team's preparation and competition, the district court found that the competitive cheerleading team's practice time, regimen, and venue were consistent with other varsity sports. Further, as with other varsity sports, the length of the competitive cheerleading season and the minimum number of competitions in which a team would participate were pre-determined by a governing athletic organization, the recently formed National Competitive Stunt and Tumbling Association, of which Quinnipiac was a founding member. Finally, the purpose of the team—to compete athletically at the intercollegiate varsity level—was akin to that of other varsity sports.

At the same time, however, the district court identified a number of circumstances that sufficiently distinguished Quinnipiac's competitive cheerleading program from traditional varsity sports as to "compel[ ] the decision that, for the 2009-10 season," the program could not "be counted as a varsity sport for purposes of Title IX." First, Quinnipiac did not—and, in 2009-10, could not—conduct any off-campus recruitment for its competitive cheerleading team, in marked contrast not only to the school's other varsity sports teams but also to a typical NCAA Division I sports program. The district court explained the significance of this circumstance: "Although the women on the Quinnipiac competitive cheer team were athletically able, they would have been all the more talented had [Coach] Powers been able to seek out the best competitive cheerleaders around the country, as any other varsity coach would have been able to do."

More important, no uniform set of rules applied to competitive cheerleading competition throughout the 2009-10 season. Indeed, in the ten competitions in which the Quinnipiac team participated during the regular season, it was judged according to five different scoring systems. Further, in these competitions, Quinnipiac did not face only varsity intercollegiate competitive cheerleading teams. Rather, it was challenged by "a motley assortment of competitors," including collegiate club opponents who did not receive varsity benefits, collegiate sideline cheerleading teams, and all-star opponents unaffiliated with a particular academic institution, some of whom may still have been high-school age. As the district court observed, "application of a uniform set of rules for competition and the restriction of competition to contests against other varsity opponents" are the "touchstones" of a varsity sports program. "Those features ensure that play is fair in each game, that teams' performances can be compared across a season, and that teams can be distinguished in terms of quality."

The concerns raised by these irregularities in season competition were only aggravated by aspects of post-season play. Notably, competitive cheerleading offered no progressive playoff system leading to a championship game. Rather, it provided an open invitational, which neither excluded any team on the basis of its regular season performance nor ranked or seeded participating teams on that basis. Instead, all entrants competed in a single championship round in which the team with the highest score won. That round, moreover, was subject to a new rule of competition that had not applied to Quinnipiac in any of its regular season competitions: a mandatory 45-60 second "spirit" segment in which a team was judged by the intensity of the response it elicited from the crowd and the number of the sponsoring brand's props that it employed, features that Quinnipiac's coach confirmed were more characteristic of sideline rather than competitive cheerleading. Viewing the totality of these circumstances, the district court concluded that the competitive cheerleading team's post-season competition did not conform to expectations for a varsity sport.

Most other varsity sports would have used some system to separate teams and competitors in terms of quality, and would have ranked, seeded, or excluded teams on the basis of their performances during the regular season. Moreover, any other varsity sport would not have imposed new rules of competition in the post-season that teams did not follow during the regular season.

Based on these findings, as well as those pertaining to regular season play, the district court concluded that Quinnipiac's competitive cheerleading team did not compete in circumstances indicative of varsity sports. Thus, it ruled that Quinnipiac's 30 roster positions for competitive cheerleading could not be counted for Title IX purposes because the activity did not yet afford women genuine participation opportunities in a varsity sport.

In challenging this conclusion, Quinnipiac questions the weight the district court assigned the various factors it identified as supporting or undermining recognition of competitive cheerleading as a genuine varsity sport. Quinnipiac argues that this court should decide the question de novo. . . . [E]ven assuming that de novo review were warranted, we conclude for the same reasons stated in detail by the district court and summarized in this opinion that, although there are facts on both sides of the argument, in the end, the balance tips decidedly against finding competitive cheerleading presently to be a "sport" whose participation opportunities should be counted for purposes of Title IX. Like the district court, we acknowledge record evidence showing that competitive cheerleading can be physically challenging, requiring competitors to possess "strength, agility, and grace." Similarly, we do not foreclose the possibility that the activity, with better organization and defined rules, might some day warrant recognition as a varsity sport. But, like the district court, we conclude that the record evidence shows that "that time has not yet arrived."

Accordingly, we conclude that the district court was correct not to count the 30 roster positions assigned to competitive cheerleading in determining the number of genuine varsity athletic participation opportunities that Quinnipiac afforded female students.

E.   FINDING A TITLE IX VIOLATION BASED ON A 3.62% DISPARITY

Having reduced Quinnipiac's claimed athletic participation opportunities for women by 41—representing 30 competitive cheerleaders and 11 cross-country runners required to join the indoor and outdoor track teams but unable to compete on those teams because of their injuries or red-shirt status—the district court correctly found that the school had a total of 400 varsity athletic participation opportunities, of which 233, or 58.25%, were assigned to women. Because enrollment data established that 61.87% of Quinnipiac's undergraduate population were women, this indicated a 3.62% disparity in the athletic opportunities that Quinnipiac afforded women. See id. The district court concluded that this disparity was sufficient to support a finding that Quinnipiac had failed to afford female students varsity athletic participation opportunities substantially proportionate to their enrollment. See id. at 113.

Quinnipiac argues that a 3.62% disparity is too small to support such a finding. In any event, it submits that the district court erred in holding Quinnipiac responsible for the disparity in light of fluctuations in enrollment and Quinnipiac's good faith reliance on the district court's statement at the time of the preliminary injunction decision that it would likely count all women members of the cross-country, indoor track, outdoor track, and competitive cheerleading teams as athletic participants for purposes of Title IX. Further, Quinnipiac contends that the district court erroneously accorded dispositive weight to the fact that the number of additional female roster spots needed to achieve exact proportionality—38—would have been sufficient for Quinnipiac to field an additional varsity team.

Quinnipiac's arguments fail to persuade. First, its emphasis on the relatively small percentage of disparity is unwarranted. The district court itself recognized that "in strictly numerical terms," a 3.62% disparity presents "a borderline case of disproportionate athletic opportunities." . . . While a district court outside this circuit reports finding no case in which a disparity of two percentage points or less has been held to manifest a lack of substantial proportionality, see Equity in Athletics, Inc. v. DOE, 675 F.Supp.2d 660, 682-83 (W.D.Va.2009), aff'd, 639 F.3d 91 (4th Cir.2011), we do not pursue the issue because the disparity in this case is greater than 2%, and we do not, in any event, understand the 1996 Clarification to create a statistical safe harbor at this or any other percentage. Instead, the Clarification instructs that substantial proportionality is properly determined on a "case-by-case basis" after a careful assessment of the school's "specific circumstances," including the causes of the disparity and the reasonableness of requiring the school to add additional athletic opportunities to eliminate the disparity.

Specifically, the district court pointed to record evidence showing that the 3.62% identified disparity was almost entirely attributable to Quinnipiac's own careful control of its athletic rosters. . . .

Accordingly, we reject Quinnipiac's challenge to the district court's finding that the school engaged in sex discrimination in violation of Title IX, and we affirm the order enjoining Quinnipiac from continuing such discrimination.

[handwritten: There was sex discrim.]

The following case, *Boucher v. Syracuse*, lacks weight as precedent, but it is included in the text because it offers an example of the kind of analysis that courts are likely to engage in when considering the history and continuing practice of program expansion prong of the OCR's three-part test.

BOUCHER v. SYRACUSE UNIVERSITY

1998 WL 167296 (N.D.N.Y. 1998), *vacated in part and appeal dismissed in part,*
164 F.3d 113 (2d Cir. 1999)

SCULLIN, J.

[handwritten: why was this softball player suing?]

[handwritten: women's club lacrosse team + 1 softball sue school for ineffective accomodation of student int. + ability]

FACTUAL BACKGROUND

The eight named [Plaintiffs] are undergraduate students at Syracuse University, seven of which are, or were, members of the women's club lacrosse team. The other plaintiff is a member of the women's club softball team. . . .

[handwritten: 7 - lacrosse, 1 - softball]

In 1971, Syracuse University ("Syracuse") established a women's intercollegiate athletics program, creating women's varsity basketball, fencing, swimming, tennis and volleyball teams. Field hockey replaced fencing in 1972. Syracuse added women's varsity crew in 1977 and indoor and outdoor track in 1981. In 1982, Syracuse merged its male and female varsity athletic programs into a single all-sport intercollegiate Athletic Department. From 1980 through 1982, the Office of Civil Rights ("OCR") performed a Title IX compliance review and found that Syracuse's intercollegiate program was in compliance with Title IX. In 1996 Syracuse added a women's varsity soccer team, and in 1997 Syracuse added a women's varsity lacrosse team; both of which are receiving the benefits of varsity status, including facilities and scholarships.

With the establishment of these two additional women's sports, Syracuse now offers 21 varsity sports — ten men's varsity sports and eleven women's varsity sports. As stated, Syracuse has also announced its plan to implement women's softball as a varsity sport beginning the 1999-2000 academic year.

All other sport teams are "club" sport teams which are student run and primarily student funded. Any financial assistance Syracuse provides to club sports comes from Recreation Services, an office within the Division of Student affairs. The Athletic Department does not provide any funding for club sports. . . .

I.   TITLE IX

. . . The Department of Education, through its Office of Civil Rights ("OCR") promulgated regulations and a "Policy Interpretation" to clarify the responsibilities of institutions subject to the mandates of Title IX. See 44 Fed.Reg.

71,413-23. This Court has previously found that these regulations are a "reasonable interpretation of the statute, and consequently, affords them controlling weight." The Court further found that it would afford substantial deference to the Policy Interpretation where it "reasonably interprets the regulations." The regulations which are applicable to claims of gender bias in athletics fall within three categories: (1) equality in Athletic Financial Assistance (Scholarships), 34 C.F.R. §106.37(c); (2) Equivalence in Other Athletic Benefits and Opportunities, 34 C.F.R. §106.41(c)(2)-(10); and (3) Effective Accommodation of Student Interests and Abilities, 34 C.F.R. §106.41(c)(1). Presently, Plaintiffs assert that Defendants are in violation of the third category; ineffective accommodation of student interests and abilities.

[margin note: categories of claims of gender bias]

[margin note: π]

A. Effective Accommodation

An institution is in violation of Title IX where it does not provide effective accommodation, regardless of whether that institution satisfies the other two categories of compliance. See *Cohen v. Brown University*, 897 F.2d 888, 897 (1st Cir.1993). An institution cannot satisfy the statute by merely bolstering those programs already in existence or by reducing the opportunities of the overrepresented gender.

To survive a motion for summary judgment against an effective accommodation claim, a plaintiff must establish that a question of material fact exists with regard to whether:

(1) intercollegiate level participation opportunities for male and female students are not provided in numbers substantially proportionate to their respective enrollment; and
(2) the interests and abilities of the sex under represented among intercollegiate athletes have not been effectively accommodated by the present program.

[margin note: π must show]

Even if Plaintiffs can raise an issue of fact with regard to either of these two elements, Defendants may still succeed on their motion if they can establish, without dispute, that they qualify under any part of Title IX's three-part test, more commonly known as Title IX's "safe harbor" provisions. . . . According to the Policy Interpretation promulgated by the OCR, an institution will be found to be in compliance with Title IX if it falls within any one of the following "safe harbors":

[margin note: Δ must show]

(1) where the institution can show that intercollegiate level participation opportunities for male and female students are provided in numbers substantially proportionate to their respective enrollments; or
(2) where the members of one sex have been and are under represented among intercollegiate athletes, but the institution can show a history and continuing practice of program expansion which is demonstrably responsive to the developing interest and abilities of the members of that sex; or
(3) where the members of one sex are under represented among intercollegiate athletes, and the institution cannot show a continuing practice of program expansion such as that cited above, but the institution can demonstrate that the interests and abilities of the members of that sex have been fully and effectively accommodated by the present program.

[margin note: Δ wins under these Safe Harbors]

In the present case, Defendants argue as an affirmative defense that they fall within the second "safe harbor" provision; that Syracuse has a history and continuing practice of program expansion. Defendants have the burden of demonstrating to this Court that there is no material factual dispute as to whether they qualify for this "safe harbor" immunity.

B.   Safe Harbor as an Affirmative Defense

To succeed on their affirmative defense, Defendants must show (1) a history of Program expansion, i.e. that their past actions expanded participation opportunities for the under represented sex in a manner that was demonstrably responsive to their developing interests and abilities; and (2) a continuing practice, i.e. that they continue their practice of program expansion in response to its student bodies abilities and interests.

1.   History of Program Expansion

In January of 1996, the OCR issued a letter entitled, "Clarification of Intercollegiate Athletics Policy Guidance: The Three Part Test" (the "Clarification") which further explained the safe harbor provisions. In doing so it identified three factors that the Court may consider in determining whether an institution has established a history of program expansion:

(1)   the institution's record of adding intercollegiate teams, or upgrading teams to intercollegiate status, for the under represented sex;

(2)   an institution's record of increasing the number of participants in intercollegiate athletics who are members of the under represented sex; and

(3)   an institution's affirmative response to requests by students or others for addition or elevation of sports. OCR Clarification, p. 6.

As set forth in the facts, from 1971 to 1982, Syracuse had a strong history of adding women's sports programs. While it is true that between 1982 and 1995 no new women's teams were added, during this period Syracuse continuously increased the number of women's scholarships and otherwise enhanced its women's programs by providing improved facilities, enhanced coaching staffs, and providing more elaborate support services. Between 1982 and 1995, the number of female participants in varsity sports increased from 148 to 217; an increase of forty-seven percent (47%). During this period, male participation in varsity sports only increased three percent (3%). Since 1995, Syracuse has added two additional women's athletic teams, lacrosse and soccer, and is planning the induction of a third team, softball, by the year 1999. The Court finds as a matter of law that Syracuse has a sufficient history of expanding opportunities for its women student-athletes so to satisfy the first prong of its affirmative defense.

2.   Continuing Practice of Program Expansion

In evaluating whether an institution has complied with the second requirement, that of demonstrating a continuing practice of program expansion, the Court may consider whether there are any formal policies in place which might indicate that the institution is monitoring the pulse of its students' interests in anticipation of expansion. This is particularly relevant where there is no actual expansion currently taking place. However, the best evidence of continued expansion is expansion itself. While Defendants have not established, to the

Court' satisfaction, that any formal policy was in place whereby students could voice their interests to the institution, the undisputed testimony of Athletic Director Crouthamel shows that Syracuse did expand its women's athletic program by adding two women's varsity teams with plans of creating a third team by the year 1999. Furthermore, according to Crouthamel's affidavit, these additions were in response to his monitoring of and gathering information regarding club participation at Syracuse; prospective competition with other schools; and the developing interests and abilities at national, regional, and local levels of competition, including information regarding the interest and abilities of the University's feeder schools. Additionally, it is evident from the multiple affidavits submitted by both parties that there are informal means by which self-motivated students bring their interests to Defendants' attention.

[handwritten: considered club participation]

The Court does believe that the spirit of Title IX would be better served were the institution to implement a more formal policy by which students could bring their interests and abilities to the attention of the administration. However, notwithstanding this lack of formal policy, the Court is convinced that taken as a whole, Defendants have continued a practice of program expansion which is responsive to the abilities and interests of its student body. Accordingly, the Court finds that Defendants fall within the second safe harbor provision of Title IX.

[handwritten: Δ fall w/in SH #2]

C. Elevation of Club Sports

Plaintiffs' only remaining claim relates to treatment of female athletes vis-a-vis male athletes in club sports. To date, Plaintiffs have not provided the Court with any evidence that Defendant Syracuse treats men's club teams any different from women's club teams or that Defendant Crouthamel has anything to do with club sports. Nor do Plaintiff's dispute that the club teams are organized, operated and substantially funded by the student body.

[The court granted Defendants' motion for summary judgment and dismissed Plaintiffs' complaint.] *[handwritten: Dismissed complaint.]*

NOTES AND QUESTIONS

1. *Substantial Proportionality. Cohen, Biediger,* and *Boucher* make it clear that courts have accepted the three-prong test for evaluating equal athletics participation opportunities in the OCR's 1979 Policy Interpretation. How did the *Cohen* and *Biediger* courts apply the "substantial proportionality" prong of the test? This prong is often very difficult to satisfy, particularly in an era of rising female undergraduate enrollment and if an institution has a football program with a significant number of male participants. See also *Roberts v. Colorado State Bd. of Agric.*, 998 F.2d 824, 830 (10th Cir. 1993), *cert. denied*, 510 U.S. 1004 (1993) ("substantial proportionality entails a fairly close relationship between athletic participation and undergraduate enrollment"; not satisfied by 10.5 percent disparity between enrollment and athletic participation for women); *Brust v. University of Calif.*, 2007 WL 4365521 (E.D. Cal.) (whether 6 percent disparity between female undergraduate enrollment and intercollegiate athletic participation opportunities satisfies substantial proportionality test is a question of fact); *Miller v. University of Cincinnati*, 2008 WL 203025 (S.D. Ohio 2008) (1 percent disparity between male undergraduate enrollment and intercollegiate athletic participation

opportunities complies with substantial proportionality requirement; observing that Department of Education permits multisport athlete to be counted as a participant for each sport).

2. *U.S. Women's Olympic Success Continues.* The *Cohen* court lauds the successful performance of U.S. women's athletes in the 1996 Atlanta Olympics, which it attributes to Title IX. That success continues. More women than men represented the United States in the 2012 London games, and they won many more total and gold medals (58, 29) than the men (45, 17). Indeed, in the London Olympics, if the American women had competed as their own country, they would have finished fifth in total medals and third in gold medal production.

3. *Equal Protection Analysis.* In *Cohen,* why did the court reject Brown University's assertion that the lower court was imposing an unconstitutional quota or affirmative action requirement regarding athletic participation opportunities for women? Do you agree with the court's analysis?

In terms of equal protection analysis, strict scrutiny applies in the race discrimination area. A less restrictive test applies in the gender context, however, and permits greater latitude in fashioning affirmative action programs to achieve gender equity. In *United States v. Virginia*, 518 U.S. 515 (1996), the Supreme Court held that equal protection clause of the Fourteenth Amendment precluded the State of Virginia from reserving exclusively to men the unique educational experience offered by the Virginia Military Institute. Writing for the Court, Justice Ginsburg applied intermediate scrutiny, which requires that the gender classification serve important governmental objectives and that the discriminatory means are substantially related to achievement of those objectives. However, she appears to have added extra bite to this intermediate test by stating that the state actor must offer an "exceptionally persuasive justification" in support of its discriminatory policy, stating that "[t]he burden of justification is demanding and it rests entirely on the State." *Id.* at 532. She asserted, "The justification must be genuine, not hypothesized or invented post hoc in response to litigation . . . [and the state] must not rely on overbroad generalizations about the different talents, capacities, or preferences of males and females." *Id.* Acknowledging that application of a strict scrutiny test like that used in the racial context does not apply, she noted that the test used by the Court does not make gender "a proscribed classification." *Id.* at 533.

The strict scrutiny test applied to racial discrimination claims makes it very difficult for the state actor to take affirmative steps to aid a disadvantaged ethnic or racial group (i.e., to engage in affirmative action). Indeed, if the strict scrutiny test was applied to Title IX gender discrimination claims, the substantial proportionality prong of the OCR's three-part test (which essentially establishes a gender-based quota) would be found to be unconstitutional on equal protection grounds. Put simply, strict scrutiny in the racial discrimination context largely prohibits affirmative action by state actors, whereas intermediate scrutiny permits affirmative action in the context of gender discrimination.

Affirmative action and efforts to ensure gender equity under the auspices of Title IX have clearly contributed to increased opportunities for women to participate in interscholastic and intercollegiate athletics. One might argue, however, that strict scrutiny has harmed minorities (including student-athletes) by limiting the capacity of state actors to affirmatively aid groups historically discriminated against based on race. Are there sound reasons for analyzing the constitutionality of gender and racial discrimination differently in the athletics context?

4. *Effective Accommodation.* To prove compliance with Title IX's effective accommodation requirement, a school may establish that it has a history and continuing practice of adding sports for the underrepresented gender, which is usually female student-athletes. Why did Brown University fail to prove compliance on this ground? The *Cohen* court's requirement that a school "march uninterruptedly in the direction of equal athletic opportunity" is difficult to prove. 101 F.3d at 176. However, *Boucher* illustrates how an educational institution can satisfy part two of the three-part test, which requires an examination of the entire history of the school's women's athletics program. But see *Mansourian v. Regents of Univ. of Calif.*, 816 F. Supp. 2d 869 (E.D. Cal. 2011) (prong two not satisfied if significant number of women given opportunity to participate in university's intercollegiate athletics program declines).

[handwritten: haven't added in a while]

In the decade after Title IX was adopted, female athletics participation opportunities were regularly added by many institutions. Beginning in the mid-1980s, however, institutions entered what has been called the "cost-containment era"—a time when many schools, particularly public institutions, faced serious budget cuts. As university budgets were cut, it became increasingly difficult for schools to add women's sports, which generally do not generate sufficient revenues to pay their operating expenses. Thus, there was a hiatus in terms of the addition of women's sports, which began in the mid-1980s, and which has been exacerbated to some extent with the national economic downturn following September 11, 2001. As one court explained:

> We recognize that in times of economic hardship, few schools will be able to satisfy Title IX's effective accommodation requirement by continuing to expand their women's athletics programs. Nonetheless, the ordinary meaning of the word "expansion" may not be twisted to find compliance under this prong when schools have increased the relative percentages of women participating in athletics by making cuts in both men's and women's sports programs. Financially strapped institutions may still comply with Title IX by cutting athletic programs such that men's and women's athletic participation rates become substantially proportionate to their representation in the undergraduate population.

Roberts v. Colorado State Bd. of Agric., 998 F.2d 824, 830 (10th Cir. 1993), *cert. denied*, 510 U.S. 1004 (1993).

5. *Interest Accommodation.* Given the difficulties of proving prongs one or two of the three-part test, universities are increasingly attempting to prove compliance by establishing that the athletic participation interests of women athletes are being fully and effectively accommodated. Why did *Cohen* hold that Brown University failed to establish compliance under the third part of the test? See also *Barrett v. West Chester Univ. of Pa.*, 2003 WL 22803477 (E.D. Pa. 2003) (finding that elimination of viable women's intercollegiate athletic teams violates prong three).

6. *Fashioning a Plan.* Why does the First Circuit provide Brown University with another opportunity to prepare a plan to comply with Title IX? If you were representing Brown University, how would you fashion a new compliance

plan? In doing so, consider the potential economic and political implications of your recommended compliance plan within the university community.

7. *Emerging Sports.* In *Biediger*, the court held that women's cheer was not a "sport" for Title IX purposes. What reasons did the court offer to support its decision? What might an institution do in the future to ensure that women's cheer will be recognized as a sport for Title IX purposes? In *Biediger*, the court notes that there is a presumption that a sport qualifies for Title IX purposes if it is recognized by the NCAA; which women's cheer has not been. The NCAA currently recognizes three emerging sports: equestrian, rugby, and sand volleyball. *Emerging Sports for Women*, NCAA, July 16, 2012, http://www.ncaa.org/wps/wcm/connect/public/NCAA/Resources/ Emerging+Sports+for+Women.

In a news release on August 16, 2011, the NCAA Committee on Women's Athletics indicated that it "will watch for continued growth and development in a new sport that combines elements of gymnastics and competitive cheerleading after two different groups requested emerging-sport status for slightly different versions." Michelle Brutlag Hosick, *NCAA Committee Looks into New Sport*, NCAA.com, Aug. 16, 2011, http://www.ncaa.com/news/ ncaa/2011-08-16/ncaa-committee-looks-new-sport. That release refers to a letter sent to groups representing Stunt and Tumbling, each of which had requested recognition as an emerging sport, asking the two groups to jointly submit a single proposal for consideration by the NCAA membership. Should the NCAA recognize cheer in some form as an emerging sport, given that, according to the National Federation of State High School Associations, approximately 123,000 students participated in competitive cheer in 2009 and 29 state high school athletic associations recognize it as a sport? What other sports should be recognized by the NCAA?

In June 2012, a group of concerned African American women gathered at the Schomburg Center for Research in Black Culture in Harlem for a forum in which they argued that Title IX discriminates against black women, raising the issue of most scholarships going to white women. *Black Women Say Title IX Discriminates Against Them*, Atlanta Black Star, June 11, 2012, http:// atlantablackstar.com/2012/06/11/black-women-say-title-ix-discriminate- against-them/. Should the NCAA consider racial equity issues in placing its imprimatur on certain emerging sports?

PEDERSON v. LOUISIANA STATE UNIVERSITY

213 F.3d 858 (5th Cir. 2000)

STEWART, Circuit Judge:

We must today determine whether the largest public university in Louisiana has discriminated against women under Title IX in the provision of facilities and teams for intercollegiate athletic competition. . . .

B.   TITLE IX VIOLATION

Appellees argue brazenly that the evidence did not demonstrate sufficient interest and ability in fast-pitch softball at LSU and that, therefore, they cannot be liable under Title IX. The heart of this contention is that an institution with no coach, no facilities, no varsity team, no scholarships, and no recruiting in a given sport must have on campus enough national-caliber athletes to field a competitive varsity team in that sport before a court can find sufficient interest and abilities to exist. It should go without saying that adopting this criteria would eliminate an effective accommodation claim by any plaintiff, at any time. . . . Having reviewed the record, we determine that the district court did not clearly err because there was ample indication of an interest by women in fast-pitch softball. . . .

[T]he student population of LSU is 51% male and 49% female, the population participating in athletics is 71% male and 29% female. Given this breakdown, [appellees] argue that it is improper to consider proportionality, because to do so would be to impose quotas, and that the evidence shows that female students are less interested in participating in sports than male students. The law suggests otherwise. Title IX provides that the district court may consider disproportionality when finding a Title IX violation:

> This subsection shall not be construed to prevent the consideration in any hearing or proceeding under this chapter of statistical evidence tending to show that such an imbalance exists with respect to the participation in or receipt of the benefits of any such program or activity by the members of one sex.

20 U.S.C. §1681(b). LSU's hubris in advancing this argument is remarkable, since of course fewer women participate in sports, given the voluminous evidence that LSU has discriminated against women in refusing to offer them comparable athletic opportunities to those it offers its male students.

Nevertheless, Appellees persist in their argument by suggesting that the district court's reliance on the fact that LSU fields a men's baseball team as evidence of discrimination was improper because there is no requirement that the same sports be offered for both men and women and because LSU offers nine sports for women and only seven for men. We find that it was indeed proper for the district court to consider the fact that LSU fields a men's baseball team while declining to field a comparable team for women despite evidence of interest and ability in fast-pitch softball at LSU.

Appellees finally contest the district court's determination that LSU's decision to add fast-pitch softball and soccer was not for the purpose of encouraging women's athletics. They challenge the district court's finding that LSU did not attempt to determine the interest and ability level of its female student population, contending that there is evidence in the record that shows that LSU does analyze the interest level of its female student athletes. Our review of the record demonstrates no such analysis on the part of LSU. . . . [T]he district court correctly found that LSU did not have a history of expanding women's athletic programs and had not presented credible evidence regarding the interests and abilities of its student body. These findings were not clearly erroneous. . . .

C.   INTENTIONAL DISCRIMINATION

The district court found that LSU had violated and continued to violate the prescriptions of Title IX. The trial judge further concluded that, notwithstanding this threshold finding, a Title IX claimant must additionally prove intentional discrimination on the part of a recipient before she may recover monetary damages. With respect to the claims at issue in this case, the district court considered the question to be a "very close one" but eventually held that LSU did not intentionally violate Title IX. . . . We find that LSU did intentionally violate Title IX, thus we reverse that ruling.

The district court stated that Appellees' actions were not a result of intentional discrimination but rather of "arrogant ignorance, confusion regarding the practical requirements of the law, and a remarkably outdated view of women and athletics which created the byproduct of resistance to change." *Id.* The district court reasoned, inter alia, that, because Athletic Director Dean testified that he believes that his "women's athletics" program is "wonderful" and because he was ignorant of the program's state of compliance with Title IX, Appellees did not intentionally discriminate against women. . . .

If an institution makes a decision not to provide equal athletic opportunities for its female students because of paternalism and stereotypical assumptions about their interests and abilities, that institution intended to treat women differently because of their sex. Moreover, Appellees' ignorance about whether they are violating Title IX does not excuse their intentional decision not to accommodate effectively the interests of their female students by not providing sufficient athletic opportunities.

Apparently, Dean "believed his program to be so wonderful that he invited an investigator from the Department of Education's Office of Civil Rights to visit LSU to evaluate the athletics program's compliance with Title IX." That representative's findings confirmed Dean's ignorance of the actual state of compliance with Title IX by his athletic program but the district court nonetheless reasoned that Dean's testimony was "credible" because "otherwise he would not have invited OCR to LSU to assess the program." This conclusion ignores the fact that, already on notice of potential violations, Dean and others continued to adhere to deprecatory nomenclature when referring to female athletes, refused to authorize additional sports for women, and instead seemed content that the "women's teams fielded [by LSU] during the relevant time frame performed well in competition." This assessment of the athletics program is not merely "arrogance," as the district court concluded, it belies an intent to treat women differently in violation of the law.

It bears noting that the provisions of Title IX and its attendant regulations are not merely hortatory; they exist, as does any law, to sculpt the relevant playing field. Consequently, Appellees' alleged ignorance of the law does not preclude our finding that LSU acted intentionally. Appellees need not have intended to violate Title IX, but need only have intended to treat women differently. . . . Appellees' outdated attitudes about women amply demonstrate this intention to discriminate, and the district court squarely found that LSU's treatment of women athletes was "remarkably outdated," "archaic," and "outmoded." Well-established Supreme Court precedent demonstrates that archaic assumptions such as those firmly held by LSU constitute intentional gender discrimination. [Citations omitted.] We conclude that, because classifications based on "archaic" assumptions are facially discriminatory, actions resulting from an application of these attitudes constitutes intentional discrimination.

In addition to the district court's evaluation of LSU's attitudes as "archaic," our independent evaluation of the record and the evidence adduced at trial supports the conclusion that Appellees persisted in a systematic, intentional, differential treatment of women. For instance, in meetings to discuss the possibility of a varsity women's soccer team, Dean referred to [one female athlete] repeatedly as "honey," "sweetie," and "cutie" and negotiated with her by stating that "I'd love to help a cute little girl like you." Dean also opined that soccer, a "more feminine sport," deserved consideration for varsity status because female soccer players "would look cute running around in their soccer shorts." Dean, charismatically defending LSU's chivalry, later told the coach of the women's club soccer team that he would not voluntarily add more women's sports at LSU but would "if forced to." Among many other examples, [one student] testified that, when she met with representatives of the Sports and Leisure Department to request the implementation of an intramural fast-pitch softball team, she was told that LSU would not sponsor fast-pitch softball because "the women might get hurt."

LSU perpetuated antiquated stereotypes and fashioned a grossly discriminatory athletics system in many other ways. For example, LSU appointed a low-level male athletics department staff member to the position of "Senior Women's Athletic Administrator," which the NCAA defines as the most senior women in an athletic department. LSU consistently approved larger budgets for travel, personnel, and training facilities for men's teams versus women's teams. The university consistently compensated coaches of women's team's at a rate far below that of its male team coaches.

Appellees have not even attempted to offer a legitimate, nondiscriminatory explanation for this blatantly differential treatment of male and female athletes, and men's and women's athletics in general; they merely urge that "archaic" values do not equate to intentional discrimination. . . . Appellees must have been aware that they were discriminating on the basis of sex by not effectively accommodating the interests and abilities of its female student-athletes.

. . . The proper test is not whether [the institution] knew of or is responsible for the actions of others, but is whether Appellees intended to treat women differently on the basis of their sex by providing them unequal athletic opportunity, and, as we noted above, we are convinced that they did. Our review of the record convinces us that an intent to discriminate, albeit one motivated by chauvinist notions as opposed to one fueled by enmity, drove LSU's decisions regarding athletic opportunities for its female students. . . .

NOTES AND QUESTIONS

1. *Offering Practical Counsel.* What arguments did LSU raise in support of its efforts to achieve gender equity in its intercollegiate athletics program, and why did the *Pederson* court reject them? What practical advice would you give to LSU to help bring the school into compliance with Title IX requirements?

Regarding how to determine women's athletic participation interests, the *Pederson* district court explained:

LSU could have obtained this information in a variety of ways, including, *but not limited* to: (1) Requests by students that a sport be added; (2) Requests that an existing club sport be elevated; (3) Participation levels in club or intramural sports; (4) Interviews with students, admitted students, coaches, administrators or others regarding interest in a particular sport; (5) Results of questionnaires of students and admitted students regarding interest in particular sports; and (6) Participation levels in interscholastic sports by admitted students. Information also could be obtained through discussions with amateur athletic associations or community sports leagues or, perhaps the simplest solution, the inclusion of a "participation and interest" question on the admissions form to the university. However, there was no testimony to support that any credible attempt was made to gather such information.

[handwritten: LSU made no attempt]

912 F. Supp. at 915, n.61.

2. *Successful Aftermath.* LSU initially argued that there was a lack of interest on the part of women at LSU in developing a nationally prominent softball program. However, it added women's softball as a varsity sport prior to the final resolution of the *Pederson* case. Ironically, the women's softball team quickly rose to national prominence, winning the Southeastern Conference Championship in May 1999. In 2001, the team tied for third place in the Women's College World Series.

[handwritten: added softball]

3. *Discretion in the Offering of Sports.* If both sexes' athletic participation interests are not effectively accommodated, *Cohen v. Brown University, supra,* illustrates that courts generally give a school some measure of discretion regarding the specific sports to offer. Note that the 1979 OCR Title IX policy interpretation provides:

> In the selection of sports, the regulation does not require institutions to integrate their teams nor to provide exactly the same choice of sports to men and women. However, where an institution sponsors a team in a particular sport for members of one sex, it may be required either to permit the excluded sex to try out for the team or to sponsor a separate team for the previously excluded sex.
>
> a. Contact Sports—Effective accommodation means that if an institution sponsors a team for members of one sex in a contact sport, it must do so for members of the other sex under the following circumstances: (1) The opportunities for members of the excluded sex have historically been limited; and (2) There is sufficient interest and ability among the members of the excluded sex to sustain a viable team and a reasonable expectation of intercollegiate competition for that team.
>
> b. Non-Contact Sports—Effective accommodation means that if an institution sponsors a team for members of one sex in a non-contact sport, it must do so for members of the other sex under the following circumstances:(1) The opportunities for members of the excluded sex have historically been limited; (2) There is sufficient interest and ability among the members of the excluded sex to sustain a viable team and a reasonable expectation of intercollegiate competition for that team; and (3) Members of the excluded sex do not possess sufficient skill to be selected for a single integrated team, or to compete actively on such a team if selected.

See http://www.ed.gov/about/offices/list/ocr/docs/t9interp.html.

4. *Intentional Discrimination.* In *Pederson,* the Fifth Circuit held that LSU had intentionally engaged in gender discrimination in the operation of its intercollegiate athletics program. Sufficient proof of intentional discrimination enables a plaintiff to recover compensatory damages. According to the court, what is the legal standard for proving that an institution intentionally violated Title IX?

[handwritten: If the inst. makes a decision to not provide equal opportunities]

The *Pederson* court seemed to be particularly concerned by comments made by LSU athletics personnel to female student-athletes. As legal counsel for an institution, how would you counsel coaches and other athletics personnel to prevent any intentional violations of Title IX?

In *Barrett v. West Chester University of Pennsylvania*, 2003 WL 22803477 at *12 (E.D. Pa. 2003), the court observed that "[i]n the athletic realm of Title IX, intent is found on the face of most decisions." However, in *Horner v. Kentucky High School Athletic Assn.*, 206 F.3d 685 (6th Cir. 2000), the Sixth Circuit held that a facially neutral policy for determining the sports for which state championships would be sanctioned is not intentional discrimination. The court concluded: "Plaintiffs have simply not established that Defendants had actual knowledge of the discriminatory effect of their facially neutral rule, yet failed to remedy the violation." *Id.* at 697.

5. *Eleventh Amendment.* Courts have held that the Eleventh Amendment is no bar to private suits brought against states under Title IX of the Education Amendments of 1972. See *Litman v. George Mason Univ.*, 186 F.3d 544 (4th Cir. 1999), *cert. denied*, 528 U.S. 1181 (2000); *Franks v. Kentucky Sch. for the Deaf*, 142 F.3d 360, 363 (6th Cir. 1998); *Doe v. University of Ill.*, 138 F.3d 653, 660 (7th Cir. 1998), vacated and remanded, 119 S. Ct. 2016 (1999), *reinstated in pertinent part*, 200 F.3d 499 (7th Cir. 1999); *Crawford v. Davis*, 109 F.3d 1281, 1283 (8th Cir. 1997).

6. *Title IX Denial of Athletic Participation Opportunities at the High School Level.* In *Oliver v. Sweetwater Union High School District*, 604 F. Supp. 2d 1264 (S.D. Cal. 2009), the court dealt with a claim by a high school student that her participation in sports was limited in violation of Title IX. The court rejected the defendant school district's argument that participation opportunities for girls were "substantially proportionate" because they were below a 10.5 percent alleged benchmark and found that the defendants had failed to provide female students with substantially proportionate athletic opportunities. The court also rejected the defendant school district's attempt to show that its history and continuing practice of program expansion satisfied Title IX. The district argued that by providing opportunities in new female sports, it had satisfied the continuing practice of program expansion prong, but the court rejected this argument because the focus should not be on the number of sports played, but on the number of females being afforded participation opportunities. Finally, the court rejected the district's argument that the plaintiffs had failed to provide evidence that specific girls or groups of girls had the necessary interest and ability to field competitive, approved interscholastic sports teams. The court found that the plaintiffs had provided evidence that demonstrated sufficient female interest in playing certain sports and their viability, and rejected the district's defense that it could not find a coach for those sports as insufficient.

7. *Legal Challenge to the Three-Prong Test.* In *Equity in Athletics, Inc. v. U.S. Department of Education*, 639 F.3d 91 (4th Cir. 2011), James Madison University announced plans to eliminate seven men's and three women's athletic teams in order to come into compliance with the substantial proportionality prong of OCR's three prong test for Title IX compliance. At the time, women represented 61 percent of the university's undergraduate student population but constituted only 50.7 percent of student-athletes. Opponents challenged the cuts and sought injunctive relief precluding the university from implementing them. In rejecting the plaintiffs' claims, the court held that (1) the use of the substantial proportionality standard does not violate Title IX inasmuch as it neither imposes a mandatory disparate

impact requirement nor unlawfully authorizes intentional discrimination; (2) like other courts to consider the issue, requiring substantial proportionality does not violate the Equal Protection Clause because taking gender into account when decreasing athletic opportunities does not violate the U.S. Constitution; and (3) elimination of the men's teams does not violate due process because generally student-athletes possess no property interest in intercollegiate athletic participation.

8. *Notice and Opportunity to Cure as Title IX Requirements?* In *Mansourian v. Regents of University of California*, 602 F.3d 957 (9th Cir. 2010), a group of female students, who had wrestled in high school, alleged their exclusion from the University of California at Davis wrestling team violated Title IX and the Equal Protection Clause. After their matriculation at the university, the women participated on the varsity wrestling team and enjoyed the benefits that accompanied their participation (e.g., training, coaching, and academic tutoring). The university had one wrestling team on which men and a few women participated. During the 2000-2001 academic term, the university eliminated women from the team. Following protests, the university again permitted women to participate on the team conditioned on their "ability to beat male wrestlers in their weight class, using men's collegiate wrestling rules. (Prior to their elimination from the team, women wrestlers at UCD had competed only against other women and used international freestyle rules). As a result of the new requirement that they compete against men and under men's rules, the female students were unable to participate on the wrestling team." *Id.* at 962.

The women filed a class action suit seeking relief under Title IX and the Equal Protection Clause. The district court dismissed the plaintiff's Title IX claim holding that "notice and an opportunity to cure a violation is an essential precursor to a sexual harassment suit for damages under Title IX." *Id.* at 966. The Ninth Circuit disagreed. In so doing it initially distinguished the case before it from cases in which plaintiffs had sought monetary damages pursuant to Title IX for sexual harassment. The court found that "[p]roof of actual notice is required only when the alleged Title IX violation consists of an institution's indifference to acts that 'do not involve official policy of the recipient entity.' In sexual harassment cases, it is the deliberate failure to curtail known harassment, rather than the harassment itself, that constitutes the intentional Title IX violation." *Id.* at 967. The court explained that the "Supreme Court has made it clear that no notice requirement is applicable to Title IX claims that rest on an affirmative institutional policy." *Id.* The court concluded that "[a]thletic programs that fail effectively to accommodate students of both sexes thus represent 'official policy of the recipient entity' and so are not covered by [the] notice requirement." *Id.* at 968. The Ninth Circuit also reasoned that a notice requirement would be superfluous given universities' continuing obligations to certify their programs for Title IX compliance and to track gender equity data. For these reasons, the court concluded that "pre-litigation notice and opportunity to cure are not necessary in cases alleging unequal provision of athletic opportunities in violation of Title IX." *Id.*

On February 16, 2012, the University of California and the three former UC Davis female student wrestlers announced that they had settled the case, with payment by the university of $1.35 million to the plaintiffs' counsel for attorney fees and costs incurred in the lengthy course of the case.

Law. Rev. comment

9.   *Sexual Harassment and Denial of Educational Opportunity.* Relying on Title IX, students (primarily female) have asserted denial of access to educational benefits because their colleges and universities failed to respond appropriately to student-on-student sexual harassment. For a discussion of the circumstances under which an institution might be subject to Title IX liability, see *Williams v. Board of Regents Univ. of Georgia Sys.*, 477 F.3d 1282 (11th Cir 2007); *Roe ex rel Callahan v. Gustine Unified Sch. Dist.*, 678 F. Supp. 2d 1008 (E.D. Cal. 2009); *J.K. v. Arizona Bd. of Regents*, 2008 U.S. Dist. Lexis 83855 (D. Ariz); Timothy Davis and Keith E. Smith, *Eradicating Student-Athlete Sexual Assault of Women: Section 1983 and Personal Liability Following* Fitzgerald v. Barnstable, 2009 Mich. State U. L. Rev. 629. In *Summa v. Hofstra University*, 2011 WL 1343058 (E.D. N.Y.), a former student-athlete who was employed by the university asserted that she experienced sexual harassment in violation of Title IX. Noting a split of authority on the question of whether employees can assert sexual harassment claims under Title IX, the court ruled it would limit the plaintiff's legal means of redress to Title VII of the Civil Rights Act, which prohibits employment discrimination. Providing an alternative basis for rejecting the plaintiff's Title IX claim, the court ruled that the plaintiff failed to meet the standard required to establish a cognizable Title IX sexual harassment claim. It found that the events of which the plaintiff complained were not so severe or pervasive as to violate Title IX.

look @ these

PROBLEM 10-2

You have been retained as legal counsel by a mid-level Division I university with a very successful men's basketball team that generates net revenues of approximately $2.5 million. The basketball coach is paid $2 million per year—a substantial portion of which comes from privately raised funds. The men's basketball coach has also insisted that to remain competitive in a recruiting sense, he needs the use of a private jet and improved practice and training facilities for his team. With the hiring of a new coach, at a nationally competitive salary ($1.5 million annually, plus some incentives), the men's football program has been improving, and that has had a positive economic impact. Three years ago, the men's football team was operating at a loss of over $1 million per year, but it is now losing only $300,000 per year. The women's basketball team produces revenue, but it operates at a net loss of over $250,000 per year. Other men's and women's athletics programs generate very little revenue. The net result is that the athletic program is being run at a deficit of approximately $1 million per year. The president of the university has been pressured by state legislators and is required by mandate from the university's board of trustees to operate the university's athletic program with a balanced budget. The president has communicated this mandate to the athletics director and has made it clear that the athletics budget needs to be balanced within two years.

Currently, 61 percent of the students at the university are women and 39 percent are men. Participation figures in intercollegiate athletics are almost reversed, with 63 percent male and 37 percent female participation in intercollegiate athletics. The football team has 110 participants, including a number of walk-ons. The school is considering adding women's swimming or women's softball, and its athletics conference recognizes both sports. The university has pool facilities that can easily be converted to use for a women's swimming team, but there is only limited interscholastic competition in swimming in the general geographical area of the university. There is interscholastic competition in the softball in the area, but there are no facilities at the university. Building new facilities would involve substantial costs and the cost of operating the softball team would be slightly higher per student-athlete than operating a swimming program. An interest survey indicates somewhat more interest in participating in softball than swimming on the part of women attending the university.

There has been some talk of dropping the men's track team, which would help some in terms of proportionality, but concerns have been raised in the community that such an act would eliminate a disproportionate number of athletes of color. Men's baseball might also be cut, but it is quite popular with the chairperson of the university's board of trustees, whose son plays on the team.

From time to time, some of the coaches of the women's teams have complained that they are paid less than their male counterparts, their teams receive less academic support (e.g., the men's basketball team takes two tutors with them on trips that exceed two days, but no other teams are permitted to bring tutors on trips), their practice and training facilities are not as good as those used by the men, and they are not given the same amount of support in terms of fund-raising and media coverage.

Based on these, facts, what advice would you give? What additional facts would you want to know? What practical problems may arise as you deal with the legal issues raised in this problem?

2. *Equal Benefits and Treatment*

The following cases illustrate how courts have responded to female athletes' claims that, because of their gender, they have been denied treatment and benefits equivalent to those provided to male athletes.

MCCORMICK v. SCHOOL DISTRICT OF MAMARONECK

370 F.3d 275 (2d Cir. 2004)

STRAUB, Circuit Judge.

[EDS. Plaintiffs Katherine McCormick and Emily Geldwert assert that the Mamaroneck and Pelham school districts' scheduling of girls' high school soccer in the spring and boys' high school soccer in the fall deprives girls, but not boys, of the opportunity to compete in the New York regional and state championships in soccer, in violation of Title IX. Both are current students and soccer players at these schools.

The New York State Public High School Athletic Association (NYSPHSAA) has approximately 750 members across the state, including the Pelham and Mamaroneck high schools. The NYSPHSAA divides its members into 11 sections and leaves the decision regarding which sports are played in which season to the individual sections. Section I, to which Pelham and Mamaroneck belong, leaves those season scheduling decisions to individual school districts. In New York 714 public schools offer girls' soccer, 649 of which offer it in the fall. The regional and state championships are scheduled at the end of the fall season.

Some girls' soccer teams at Section I schools began playing in the spring 15 years ago because of the popularity of girls' field hockey in the region. The girls' soccer teams in Pelham and Mamaroneck have an opportunity to compete in the Section I spring league championships, in which 19 other schools participate. However, even if they win the sectional championship, they cannot compete at the regional or state championships, as those games are in the fall. Because the school districts schedule boys' soccer in the fall, the boys have a chance to compete in the regional and state championships for boys' soccer which are held at the end of the fall season. Girls' soccer is the only sport at the Pelham and Mamaroneck high schools that is scheduled out of the state championship game season.

Both McCormick and Geldwert qualified in 2003 for the Olympic Development Program (ODP), a program for girls with exceptional ability in soccer. ODP schedules practices and tournaments in the spring based on the assumption that there will be no conflicts with high school soccer, which is typically scheduled in the fall. ODP tryouts are in the fall, but practices do not begin until the winter. Boys in Pelham and Mamaroneck who qualify for ODP do not face the same conflicts between ODP and high school soccer, because they play high school soccer in the fall.

Both McCormick and Geldwert also play soccer for the Eastchester Patriots club team, a private soccer team that competes in various high-level soccer tournaments. Club soccer has practices and tournaments throughout the year. Neither McCormick nor Geldwert planned to play on their high school teams in the spring of 2003 because neither wanted to play high school, club, and ODP soccer at the same time. In the spring of 2002, Geldwert's participation on the club team caused her to miss some Mamaroneck high school games. McCormick and Geldwert would play for their high school soccer teams if girls' soccer were moved to the fall season and have expressed that they want a chance to compete in the regional and state championships.]

B.   THE REGULATIONS AND THE POLICY INTERPRETATION

[Title IX] regulations state that "[a] recipient which operates or sponsors interscholastic, intercollegiate, club or intramural athletics shall provide equal athletic opportunity for members of both sexes." *Id.* §106.41(c). In determining whether equal opportunities exist, the Department of Education's Office for Civil Rights ("OCR") considers, among other factors:

(1) Whether the selection of sports and levels of competition effectively accommodate the interests and abilities of members of both sexes;
(2) The provision of equipment and supplies;
(3) *Scheduling of games and practice time;*
(4) Travel and per diem allowance;
(5) Opportunity to receive coaching and academic tutoring;
(6) Assignment and compensation of coaches and tutors;
(7) Provision of locker rooms, practice and competitive facilities;
(8) Provision of medical and training facilities and services;
(9) Provision of housing and dining facilities and services;
(10) Publicity.

Id. §106.41(c) (emphasis added). Plaintiffs in this case assert that the School Districts do not provide equal opportunities to girls and boys under factor three, "[s]cheduling of games and practice time." . . .

C.   THE DISPARITY IN ATHLETIC OPPORTUNITY

[Under the OCR's 1979] Policy Interpretation, a disparity in one program component (i.e., scheduling of games and practice time) can alone constitute a Title IX violation if it is substantial enough in and of itself to deny equality of athletic opportunity to students of one sex at a school. Under the Policy Interpretation, a disparity is a difference, on the basis of sex, in benefits, treatment, services, or opportunities that has a negative impact on athletes of one sex when compared with benefits, treatment, services, or opportunities available to athletes of the other sex. A disparity does not mean that benefits, treatment, services, or opportunities are merely different. . . .

. . . [T]he Policy Interpretation makes clear that identical scheduling for boys and girls is not required. Rather, compliance is assessed by first determining whether a difference in scheduling has a negative impact on one sex, and then determining whether that disparity is substantial enough to deny members of that sex equality of athletic opportunity.

Moreover, the Policy Interpretation contemplates that a disparity disadvantaging one sex in one part of a school's athletics program can be offset by a comparable advantage to that sex in another area. *See* Policy Interpretation, 44 Fed.Reg. at 71,415 ("Institutions will be in compliance if the compared program components are equivalent, that is, equal or equal in effect. Under this standard, identical benefits, opportunities, or treatment are not required, provided the *overall effect* of any differences is negligible.") (emphasis added). The Policy Interpretation explains also that compliance should not be measured by a "sport-specific comparison" but rather by examining "program-wide benefits and opportunities." *Id.* at 71,422.

Schools thus have considerable flexibility in complying with Title IX. For example, a school that provides better equipment to the men's basketball team than to the women's basketball team would be in compliance with Title IX if it provided comparably better equipment to the women's soccer team than to the men's soccer team. . . .

In the present case, scheduling girls' soccer in the spring clearly creates a disparity—boys can strive to compete in the Regional and State Championships in soccer and girls cannot. Without a doubt, this difference has a negative impact on girls. The School Districts have not pointed to—in their submissions to the District Court or to us—any areas in which female athletes receive comparably better treatment than male athletes at their schools. Thus, the disadvantage that girls face in the scheduling of soccer has not been offset by any advantages given to girls as compared to boys in the Mamaroneck and Pelham athletics programs. Moreover, girls' soccer is the only sport at these schools scheduled in a season that precludes championship game play. Male athletes do not suffer from any comparable disadvantage.

D.   THE SIGNIFICANCE OF THE DISPARITY

Because the School Districts have not come forth with evidence that the disparity in this case has been offset by some comparable advantage to girls or disadvantage to boys, we must determine whether the disparity is "substantial enough" by itself to deny girls at the Mamaroneck and Pelham schools equality of athletic opportunity. We conclude that the disparity meets that threshold.

The School Districts attempt to downplay their denial of opportunity to the girls by arguing that it is unlikely that the girls' teams would even qualify for the

[handwritten margin note: downplay]

championship games. They point out that the Pelham and Mamaroneck teams did not even win their sectional championship in 2002. We are not persuaded by this argument.

[handwritten margin note: not about possible game outcomes]

First, a team that is bad one year can be a championship contender the next year. Second, even if any of the individual teams in this litigation are less likely than some others to make the State Championships, as counsel for McCormick and Geldwert stated at oral argument, "a girl's reach should exceed her grasp." The greater the potential victory, the greater the motivation to the athletes. Any championship motivates, but a great championship motivates more. . . . Winning the State Championship in New York means being the best team out of 649 teams in the state. Winning the Section I spring soccer championships, which is the best the girls in Pelham and Mamaroneck can hope for, means being the best team out of 19 (or possibly 13) teams. . . . The scheduling of soccer in the spring, therefore, places a ceiling on the possible achievement of the female soccer players that they cannot break through no matter how hard they strive. The boys are subject to no such ceiling. Treating girls differently regarding a matter so fundamental to the experience of sports—the chance to be champions—is inconsistent with Title IX's mandate of equal opportunity for both sexes. Scheduling the girls' soccer season out of the championship game season sends a message to the girls on the teams that they are not expected to succeed and that the school does not value their athletic abilities as much as it values the abilities of the boys.

[handwritten margin note: good argument!]

Nor do we place great weight on the School Districts' argument that these girls are simply not interested in winning. . . .

Moreover, we note that girls and women were historically denied opportunities for athletic competition based on stereotypical views that participating in highly competitive sports was not "feminine" or "ladylike." . . . Despite substantial progress in attitudes about women and sports, the competitive accomplishments of male athletes may continue to be valued more than the achievements of female athletes. The different value that society may place on the competitive success of female athletes as compared to male athletes, however, must not play a role in our assessment of the significance of the denial of opportunity to the female athletes in this case. . . .

E. JUSTIFICATION FOR DISPARITY

The Policy Interpretation states that "[i]f comparisons of program components reveal that treatment, benefits, or opportunities are not equivalent in kind, quality or availability, a finding of compliance may still be justified if the differences are the result of nondiscriminatory factors." Policy Interpretation, 44 Fed. Reg. at 71,415. The Policy Interpretation lists "[s]ome of the factors that may justify these differences." Although none of the particular factors listed in the Policy Interpretation are relevant in this case, the list does not purport to be exhaustive. However, we conclude that the School Districts have not adequately justified the scheduling of girls' soccer in the spring.

The School Districts offer several reasons for why girls' soccer is scheduled in the spring and why moving it to the fall would be a problem. First, the schools assert that if girls' soccer is moved, there will not be enough field space, they will have to hire another coach, and there might be a shortage of officials. These reasons are not the kind of nondiscriminatory factors that can justify inferior treatment of female athletes. Hiring a new coach and finding more officials may cost money, but the fact that money needs to be spent to comply with Title IX is obviously not a defense to the statute. The schools will have to make some adjustments in order to provide field space to the girls' soccer teams for practices and games. However, the schools have not demonstrated that finding field space for practices will be impossible or will result in significantly shorter or more infrequent practices. In any event, all of these administrative problems could be avoided by moving boys' soccer to the spring. There is no reason that the boys' soccer teams should be entitled to the fields, coaches, and officials in the fall simply because they were in the fall first. The School Districts could comply with Title IX by offering soccer to boys and girls in the fall in alternating years (or every two years) — as long as the girls, who have been thus far denied the fall season, are scheduled in the upcoming 2004 fall season. Because the School Districts could avoid the administrative problems they complain about by alternating boys' and girls' soccer in the fall season, this case does not require us to decide the availability of an "administrative hardship defense," if any, or the threshold that would suffice to justify a significant disparity in equal athletic opportunity on the basis of such a defense.

Second, the School Districts assert that moving soccer to the fall will hurt girls because it will force them to choose between soccer and other fall sports. However, all students athletes must make choices about which sports to play. Currently, the girls at these schools have to choose between soccer and the other sports offered in the spring. If soccer is moved, they will have to pick among fall sports. . . .

everyone always has to choose which sport

Third, the School Districts assert that girls have been playing soccer in the spring for fifteen years because of the "popularity in our region of the girls' field hockey program." The School Districts complain that a "ramification of the ruling below would be the gradual elimination of the girls soccer program because of the lack of participants due to field hockey's allure." . . . The School Districts claim that if soccer is moved, there might not be a sufficient number of athletes to fill out the girls' teams in the fall. However, the School Districts do not offer persuasive data to support this point.

Fourth, the School Districts assert that moving soccer to the fall will result in fewer opportunities for girls to participate in sports in the spring. According to the School Districts, if soccer is moved "a lot of girls may do nothing in the spring." . . . The School Districts have not offered persuasive evidence that the other sports the schools offer in the spring will not be able to accommodate the girls; nor have they claimed an inability to add another spring sport.

Thus, we conclude that none of the reasons offered by the School Districts justify their decisions to schedule girls' soccer in the spring thereby denying the girls' soccer teams the opportunity to compete in the Regional and State Championships. We do not intend to foreclose the possibility that scheduling a sport outside the season of championship game play, may, under certain circumstances, be permissible under Title IX. As mentioned, a school that denied comparable championship opportunities to boys and girls in equal numbers would not be in violation of Title IX. In addition, off-season scheduling that disadvantaged members of only one sex might be permissible if supported by greater justification than that advanced here. We conclude in this case, however, that the School Districts have not adequately justified the unequal provision of competitive opportunities to girls and boys. The denial of equality of athletic opportunity therefore violates Title IX. . . .

terrible justifications

violation of Title IX!

G. COMPLIANCE PLAN

. . . Moving girls' soccer permanently to the fall, the same season as boys' soccer, would seem to be the easiest way for the School Districts to comply with Title IX. However, as discussed, the School Districts would be in compliance with Title IX if they offered soccer to girls and boys on a rational alternating basis—as long as girls are scheduled in the upcoming fall 2004 season. The relevant inquiry is whether girls and boys are given equal opportunities for post-season competition—not whether the sports are scheduled in the same season. We are aware of, and have noted, the problems with the option of alternating the fall season between boys' and girls' soccer. . . .

CONCLUSION

To summarize, we affirm the District Court's holding that the decisions by the School Districts of Mamaroneck and Pelham to schedule girls' high school soccer in the spring and boys' high school soccer in the fall, which deprives girls but not boys of the opportunity to compete in the New York Regional and State Championships in soccer, violates Title IX. . . . However, we modify the District Court's injunction to allow the School Districts to submit a plan that either alternates the fall soccer season between the girls and the boys or moves girls' soccer permanently to the fall. . . . *can submit a new plan!*

DANIELS v. SCHOOL BOARD OF BREVARD COUNTY, FLORIDA (DANIELS I)

985 F. Supp. 1458 (M.D. Fla. 1997)

This case is about the facilities of a baseball program v. softball program that est. gender inequality

CONWAY, District Judge.

The Plaintiffs in this action are Jessica and Jennifer Daniels, and their father, Daniel Daniels. Jessica and Jennifer are seniors at Merritt Island High School ("MIHS"). They both are members of the girls' varsity softball team.

Plaintiffs have sued the Defendant, School Board of Brevard County, based *Claim* on disparities between the MIHS girls' softball and boys' baseball programs. They assert claims pursuant to 20 U.S.C. §1681 ("Title IX") and the Florida Educational Equity Act, Fla.Stat. §228.2001 ("the Florida Act"). . . . *2 claims*

IV. ANALYSIS

A. SUBSTANTIAL LIKELIHOOD OF SUCCESS ON THE MERITS

Plaintiffs assert that the following inequalities exist at the MIHS softball and baseball facilities, and that these disparities violate Title IX and the Florida Act.

Electronic Scoreboard

It is undisputed that the boys' baseball field has an electronic scoreboard, and that the girls' field has no scoreboard at all. At the preliminary injunction hearing, Defendant's counsel argued that a scoreboard is inessential to varsity softball play. The Court disagrees. A scoreboard is of obvious benefit to players who must keep track of the score, the innings, and the numbers of outs, balls and strikes at any given moment. The prestige factor of a scoreboard is also obvious. As with all the differences the Court addresses in this Order, the fact that the boys have a scoreboard and the girls do not sends a clear message to players, fellow students, teachers and the community at large, that girls' varsity softball is not as worthy as boys' varsity baseball.

Batting Cage

It is also undisputed that the boys' baseball team has a batting cage and the girls' softball team does not. The use of a batting cage sharpens hitting skills. The girls' softball team is technically disadvantaged by the absence of such equipment. At the hearing, Plaintiffs' counsel represented that it would be difficult for the two teams to share one batting cage as a result of differences in the pitching machines each team uses. Accordingly, it appears that sharing the existing batting cage is not feasible. *OMG — no it's not — can share cages!*

Bleachers

Photographs submitted by Plaintiffs starkly illustrate that the bleachers on the girls' softball field are in worse condition, and seat significantly fewer spectators, than the bleachers on the boys' field. In fact, at the preliminary injunction hearing, Defendant's counsel admitted that the girls' bleachers are actually "hand-me-downs" that the boys' team passed on to the girls' team after the boys' team received new bleachers. Again, the message this sends the players, spectators and community about the relative worth of the two teams is loud and clear.

Signs

A sign reading "Merritt Island Baseball" is emblazoned in very large letters on the side of a portable structure adjacent to the boys' baseball field. The sign faces MIHS' student parking lot. This sign clearly publicizes only the boys' baseball team. Another sign is located just outside the left field fence of the boys' field. This billboard-type sign reads "Home of the Mustangs;" it faces toward the boys' field. Due to its location, the effect of this second sign is to advertise the boys' baseball team. There are no signs publicizing the girls' softball team.

Bathroom Facilities

There are no restrooms located on the girls' softball field. Restrooms are located on the boys' baseball field. A fence separates the girls' field from the restrooms. There is a dispute concerning whether the coach of the girls' team has been provided with a key to a gate in the fence. Equal access to restroom facilities is such a clearly established right as to merit no further discussion.

Concession Stand/Press Box/Announcer's Booth

A combination concession stand/press box/announcer's booth is located on the boys' baseball field. There is no such structure on the girls' softball field. These facilities affect player and spectator enjoyment of a sport, as well as attendance.

Field Maintenance

The photographs submitted by Plaintiffs facially suggest that the girls' softball field is not as well-maintained as the boys' baseball field. However, at the preliminary injunction hearing, Defendant's counsel stated that the photographs were misleading because MIHS was in the process of reconditioning the girls' field at the time the photographs were taken. Defense counsel maintains that the reconditioning process continues. Accordingly, at this juncture, it is difficult for the Court to evaluate the comparative level of field maintenance.

Lighting

The boys' baseball field is lighted for nighttime play; the girls' softball field is not. Apparently, this single factor was the impetus for this lawsuit. *[main reason for lawsuit]*

Nighttime play affects spectator attendance, parental involvement, and player and spectator enjoyment. Nighttime games have a "big league" quality not associated with daytime play. Additionally, lighting affords more flexibility regarding practice scheduling. The absence of lighting on the girls' softball field detrimentally affects the girls' team in all these respects.

After Plaintiffs filed suit, the Brevard County School Board voted to install lighting at MIHS' girls softball field. Plaintiffs contend that they have not received assurance that the lighting will be in place by January 26, 1998, the beginning of the girls' season. . . . Unless the lighting is in place by January 26, 1998, MIHS will be enjoined from using the lights on the boys' baseball field.

The Court determines that the cumulative effect of the inequalities in the two athletic programs is so significant as to give Plaintiffs a substantial likelihood of success on the merits of the Title IX and Florida Act claims. The Defendant has chosen to favor the boys' baseball team with a lighted playing field, a scoreboard, a batting cage, superior bleachers, signs publicizing the team, bathroom facilities, and a concession stand/press box/announcer's booth, but has not seen fit to provide the girls softball team with any of these things. This disparity implicates several of the considerations listed in 34 C.F.R. §106.41. *See* §106.41(2) ("provision of equipment and supplies"), (3) ("[s]cheduling of games and practice times"), (7) ("[p]rovision of . . . practice and competitive facilities"), (8) ("[p]rovision of . . . training facilities"), and (10) ("[p]ublicity"). A balance of the relevant factors favors the Plaintiffs.

The Defendant seeks to avoid liability on the basis that it provides equal funding for the boys' and girls' programs. According to the Defendant, each team has a separate booster club which engages in separate fund-raising activities. The Defendant suggests that it cannot be held responsible if the fund-raising activities of one booster club are more successful than those of another. The Court rejects this argument. It is the Defendant's responsibility to ensure equal athletic opportunities, in accordance with Title IX. This funding system is one to which Defendant has acquiesced; Defendant is responsible for the consequences of that approach.

B. SUBSTANTIAL THREAT OF IRREPARABLE INJURY

Plaintiffs have also demonstrated a substantial threat of irreparable injury. Each day these inequalities go unredressed, the members of the girls' softball team, prospective members, students, faculty and the community at large, are sent a clear message that girls' high school varsity softball is not as worthy as boys' high school varsity baseball, i.e., that girls are not as important as boys. . . . Further, Jessica and Jennifer are seeking athletic scholarships, many of which, Plaintiffs maintain, are not decided until after the softball season is over. Accordingly, it is critical that the two girls do their best during their final season. *[not a fundamental right!]*

C.   RELATIVE HARM/PUBLIC INTEREST

Since these inequalities should have long ago been rectified, the Court is unsympathetic to Defendant's claims that it will be unduly harmed by the expenditure of funds necessary to level the playing field for girls' softball athletes. For too long, the girls' softball team has been denied athletic opportunity equal to the boys' baseball team. The harm associated with that treatment as second-class athletes is significant. In short, the balance of harms favors Plaintiffs. The players and all others associated with these programs, the school system as a whole, and the public at large, will benefit from a shift to equal treatment.

[The court determined that plaintiffs are entitled to a preliminary injunction to remedy these gender inequities. Because public funds are at stake, the court afforded Defendant an opportunity to submit a plan addressing how it proposes to remedy them.]

DANIELS v. SCHOOL BOARD OF BREVARD COUNTY, FLORIDA (DANIELS II)

995 F. Supp. 1394 (M.D. Fla. 1997)

CONWAY, District Judge.

II.   THE SCHOOL BOARD'S PLAN

[EDS. The school board proposes not to spend any funds to remedy the inequities identified in the prior order because of "financial limitations and tight budgetary constraints under which the School Board is forced to operate. Any monies spent on athletics must obviously be taken from another area of operations which is already lacking in funds."]

The School Board proposes the following remedial measures regarding the specific inequities identified in the prior Order:

Electronic Scoreboard

The School Board says it is not feasible to move the electronic scoreboard on the boys' baseball field back and forth between the baseball field and the girls' softball field. Accordingly, the Board proposes to disallow use of the scoreboard on the boys' field "until such time as the girls' field has a comparable scoreboard."

Batting Cage

The School Board contends that the design and structure of the batting cage on the boys' field precludes moving it back and forth between the two fields. The Board proposes to co-locate the girls' and boys' separate pitching machines so that both teams can use the batting cage on alternate weeks.

Bleachers

The School Board maintains it is not feasible to relocate bleachers from the boys' field to the girls' field. Accordingly, "[u]ntil such time as funds may be raised for the purchase of additional bleachers or bleachers are donated so that the girls' field has bleachers essentially equal in number and quality to the boys' bleachers," the School Board proposes to rope off the boys' bleachers so that "the only area used during games shall be equivalent in size and seating number to those bleachers which presently exist on the girls' softball field."

Signs

The School Board proposes altering the "Merritt Island Baseball" sign facing the student parking lot, to read "Merritt Island Baseball and Softball." Alternatively, the Board proposes to either eliminate all lettering or change the sign to "Merritt Island Athletics." The School Board also proposes to remove the donated "Home of the Mustangs" sign which faces the boys' baseball diamond, and to leave in place a second, gender neutral sign located outside the boys' field.

Bathroom Facilities

The School Board proposes to remove a portion of the fence separating the boys' and girls' fields, so as to permit equal access to the restrooms.

Concession Stand/Press Box/Announcer's Booth

The Board proposes to close down this building until such time as a comparable facility is constructed on the girls' field.

Lighting

The School Board has already approved the installation of lights on the MIHS girls' softball field. The Board anticipates the installation process will be complete by the beginning of the girls' season. If it is not, the Board proposes to disallow use of the lights on the boys' field until the lights on the girls' field are in place.

These suggestions are terrible for the boys!

III. PLAINTIFFS' RESPONSE TO THE PLAN

Plaintiffs' basic position is that the School Board should be required to remedy the inequities by spending the funds necessary to improve the MIHS girls' softball program, rather than denying the boys' baseball team facilities it already enjoys. . . . Plaintiffs also assert that the School Board's "take it away from the boys" approach is actually designed to generate "backlash" against the girls' softball team. Further, Plaintiffs contend that the Board's plan is inadequate to remedy the perception of inequality because even if the boys are not allowed to use certain facilities—such as the electronic scoreboard, bleachers, lighting and concession stand/press box/announcer's booth—those facilities will remain in place as symbols of inequality. Accordingly, Plaintiffs urge the Court to require the School Board to either completely remove those facilities from the boys' field or provide the girls with equal facilities on their field. Finally, Plaintiffs decry the School Board's claim of "tight budgetary constraints;" they maintain that the Board is slated to receive at least $43 million from the Florida Department of Education for capital improvements.

will create backlash against girls!

IV. ANALYSIS

In giving the School Board the opportunity to submit a plan, the Court had hoped for constructive input, such as a long-range fiscal plan to remedy the inequities identified in the Court's prior Order. Unfortunately, the Board's plan leaves much to be desired; it creates the impression that the Board is not as sensitive as it should be regarding the necessity of compliance with Title IX. The Court is inclined to agree with Plaintiffs that many of the Board's proposals seem more retaliatory than constructive. The Board's approach essentially imposes "separate disadvantage," punishing both the girls and the boys, rather than improving the girls' team to the level the boys' team has enjoyed for years. The Court is sensitive to the financial constraints imposed upon public educational institutions in this day and age; that is yet another reason the Court gave the Board an opportunity to submit a remedial plan, rather than simply entering an injunction decreeing the expenditure of funds by a date certain. However, the fact remains that Plaintiffs have presented substantial evidence that the School Board has violated, and continues to violate, an Act of Congress mandating gender equality in public education.

However, the inquiry does not end here. Before the School Board's response to the Court's November 25 Order was due, Plaintiffs altered the playing field dramatically by filing a separate suit seeking class action status and challenging the Board's treatment of girls' softball on a county-wide basis. . . . On the heels of this filing, a different group of parents and children commenced yet another action claiming gender equity violations with respect to girls' softball programs throughout the county. . . .

As a result of these latest two cases, the Title IX focus has expanded from the softball facilities at one high school to girls' softball programs throughout Brevard County. In the instant suit, two high school girls and a parent sought to force expenditures to improve one softball field. The two subsequent cases presumably seek to force, *inter alia*, the construction of softball fields at three other high schools. These developments dramatically alter the potential financial impact on the School Board.

At this juncture, the Court cannot make a reasoned determination concerning the amount of additional funds the School Board should be required to expend to remedy the inequities present at Plaintiffs' particular high school. The extent to which the Board must further appropriate funds to correct the situation at MIHS must be considered in the context of the two related cases which seek class action treatment and the expenditure of funds on a county-wide basis. Accordingly, with the exception of lighting on the MIHS girls' softball field, which the School Board has already committed to install, for the moment, the Court will impose injunctive measures which do not require additional funding.

V.   PRELIMINARY INJUNCTION

Based on the foregoing, it is ORDERED as follows:
1. Before January 26, 1998, the School Board shall make the following changes at Merritt Island High School:
    a. Remove a portion of the fence separating the boys' baseball field and girls' softball field, so that the restroom facilities are readily accessible to players and spectators at both fields.
    b. Co-locate the girls' and boys' pitching machines so that both teams can use the batting cage, and establish a schedule allowing both teams equal use of the cage.

c. Change the "Merritt Island Baseball" sign facing the student parking lot, so that it reads "Merritt Island Baseball and Softball," and remove the donated "Home of the Mustangs" sign which faces the boys' baseball diamond.

d. Install lighting on the girls' softball field.

2. During the pendency of this action and the two related cases, the School Board is not required to deny the boys' baseball team and its spectators use of the electronic scoreboard, existing bleachers and the concession stand/press box/announcer's booth. The Board is also not required to deny the boys' baseball team use of the lights on the baseball field, since the Board is required to install lighting on the girls' softball field by January 26, 1998. Finally, the Board is not required to remove the gender-neutral sign located outside the boys' baseball field.

NOTES AND QUESTIONS

1. *Standing and Mootness.* As a threshold matter, the *McCormick* court held that plaintiffs had standing to bring their Title IX claims although they did not play soccer for their respective schools in 2003. Their claims were not moot because they would have an opportunity to play soccer during their senior year if the sport were played in the fall. 370 F.3d at 284-285. A plaintiff only has standing to assert claims to remedy specific harm that arises out of his or her current or future participation in the school's athletic program. *Boucher v. Syracuse Univ.*, 164 F.3d 113 (2d Cir. 1999); *Cook v. Colgate Univ.*, 992 F.2d 17 (2d Cir. 1993). Without any individualized harm, he or she does not have standing to generally challenge inequitable treatment or the provision of benefits on the basis of gender in connection with a school's entire athletics program. *Pederson v. Louisiana State Univ.*, 213 F.3d 858, 871-872 (5th Cir. 2000).

What is the specific harm that plaintiffs suffered in *McCormick* as a result of being treated unequally? In *Daniels P.*

In *Horner v. Kentucky High School Athletic Assn.*, 206 F.3d 685 (6th Cir. 2000), plaintiffs alleged that a high school athletic association's failure to sanction fast-pitch softball for girls violated Title IX. Instead, the association sanctioned slow-pitch softball because only 17 percent of its member schools expressed an interest in offering fast-pitch softball. Association rules required that at least 25 percent of its members indicate a desire to participate in a sport before it will be sanctioned. This allegedly diminished female players' ability to compete for college fast-pitch softball scholarships in comparison to male baseball players, who had an opportunity to develop their skills and earn college baseball scholarships.

Before this case was finally resolved, the Kentucky legislature enacted a statute directing the Kentucky board of education and high school athletic association to promulgate regulations requiring schools to offer, as between one of two similar sports, the sport for which NCAA universities offer athletic scholarships. In response, the association amended its bylaws accordingly and expressly identified girls' fast-pitch softball as the sport for which NCAA universities offer athletic scholarships. However, the Sixth Circuit found that plaintiffs' lawsuit was not "an important and necessary factor in changing the law"; therefore, they were not entitled to recover their attorney fees as a prevailing party in Title IX litigation. *Id.* at 698. Consider the policy implications of the court's ruling: will it discourage female student-athletes from bringing Title IX claims?

2. *Disparate Treatment of the Same Sport.* Although compliance with Title IX requires a comparison of boys' and girls' sports on program-wide basis, *McCormick* and *Daniels I* demonstrate that disparate treatment of male and female teams for the same sport may violate this law. What constitutes an illegal disparity for purposes of Title IX?

Female athletes have prevailed in unequal treatment claims. For a recent case, see *Ollier v. Sweetwater High School District,* No. 07-714 (S.D. Cal. Feb. 9, 2012), in which a federal district court in California ruled that a school district violated the Title IX rights of female student-athletes because of the unequal treatment and benefits afforded the girls' softball program in comparison to those afforded the boys' baseball program. The plaintiffs were awarded declaratory and injunctive relief, and the court ordered the parties jointly to prepare a proposed compliance plan. The court also found that the school district was liable for retaliation under Title IX for firing the girls' softball coach, who complained about the unequal facilities.

In *Parker v. Franklin County Community School,* 667 F.3d 910 (7th Cir. 2012), the Court of Appeals for the Seventh Circuit reversed the district court's granting of the school district's summary judgment motion and colorfully framed the issue: "A packed gymnasium, cheerleaders rallying the fans, the crowd on their feet supporting their team, and the pep band playing the school song: these are all things you might expect to see at an Indiana high school basketball game on a Friday night. The crowd becomes part of the game; they provide motivation, support, and encouragement to the players. After all, what would a spectator sport be without the spectators? Unfortunately, this is a question the Franklin County High School girls' basketball teams must answer every season because half their games have been relegated to non-primetime nights (generally Monday through Thursday) to give preference to the boys' Friday and Saturday night games. Non-primetime games result in a loss of audience, conflict with homework, and foster feelings of inferiority. The question we're asked to decide in this appeal is whether such discriminatory scheduling practices are actionable under Title IX. . . . We think the plaintiffs have presented a genuine question of fact that such practices violate the statute, and therefore we vacate the district court's entry of summary judgment in favor of the defendants." *Id.* at 913. In October 2012, the parties reached a court-approved agreement that provides for a plan that will improve the scheduling of girls' varsity basketball games through 2017, requiring that more women's games will need to be scheduled at "prime times," which is defined in the Consent Decree as days "when school is not scheduled the next day." See *Parker v. Indiana High School Athletic Association Consent Decree,* http://www.scribd .com/doc/116857761/Parker-v-Franklin-Consent-Decree.

As was the case in *Parker* and *Daniels II,* courts are reluctant to order a school to take specific action to remedy gender-based unequal treatment that violates Title IX. Note that some courts have encouraged the parties to mutually resolve Title IX litigation by using a professional facilitator with expertise in improving equality of athletic opportunities for males and females. See *Ridgeway v. Montana High Sch. Assn.,* 858 F.2d 579 (9th Cir. 1988).

3. *Override of a Scholarship Proposal.* In an interesting development, in July 2005, a total of 116 NCAA Division I institutions voted to override a legislative proposal adopted in April that would have increased the maximum number of grants-in-aid in women's gymnastics from 12 to 14, in women's basketball from 12 to 13, in women's cross country/track and field from 18 to 20, and in women's soccer from 12 to 14. This is the first time since Division I went to a representative governance structure in 1997 that the membership has exercised its override option. Institutions favoring the override were concerned with cost-containment and competitive equity issues related to the increase in women's scholarships in the named sports. This override evidences an increasing concern with cost containment, at the expense of gender equity, at the university level. Is this a wise choice? Does this evidence a diminishing concern with gender equity, or is it more indicative of general concern over financial issues in intercollegiate athletics at the NCAA Division I level?

E. ADVERSE EFFECTS OF TITLE IX AND POLICY IMPLICATIONS

Faced with budgetary constraints, many educational institutions have cut men's sports or athletics programs in an effort to comply with Title IX. The following case is a gender reverse-discrimination lawsuit in which male college athletes allege that the discontinuance of their sport violates Title IX and their federal equal protection rights.

NEAL v. BOARD OF TRUSTEES OF THE CALIFORNIA STATE UNIVERSITIES

198 F.3d 763 (9th Cir. 1999)

HALL, Circuit Judge:

[This] suit alleged that the decision of California State University, Bakersfield ("CSUB") to reduce the number of spots on its men's wrestling team, undertaken as part of a university-wide program to achieve "substantial proportionality" between each gender's participation in varsity sports and its composition in the campus's student body, violated Title IX and the Equal Protection Clause of the United States Constitution. . . .

Defendant/Appellant CSUB is a large public university where female students outnumbered male students by roughly 64% to 36% in 1996. The composition of CSUB's varsity athletic rosters, however, was quite different. In the 1992-93 academic year, male students took 61% of the university's spots on athletic rosters and received 68% of CSUB's available athletic scholarship money.

This imbalance helped prompt a lawsuit by the California chapter of the National Organization for Women, alleging that the California State University system was violating a state law that is similar to the federal government's Title IX. That lawsuit eventually settled, resulting in a consent decree mandating, *inter alia*, that each Cal State campus have a proportion of female athletes that was within five percentage points of the proportion of female undergraduate students at that school. This portion of the consent decree was patterned after the first part of the three-part Title IX compliance test promulgated by the Department of Education's Office for Civil Rights ("OCR").

When the university agreed to the consent decree, California was slowly emerging from a recession, and state funding for higher education was declining. As a result, CSUB administrators were seriously constrained in what they could spend on athletic programs. The university chose to adopt squad size targets, which would encourage the expansion of the women's teams while limiting the size of the men's teams. In order to comply with the consent decree, CSUB opted for smaller men's teams across the board, rejecting the alternative of eliminating some men's teams entirely. CSUB's plan was designed to bring it into compliance with the consent decree by the 1997-98 academic year, meaning that female students would fill at least 55% of the spaces on the school's athletic teams.[1]

As part of this across-the-board reduction in the number of slots available to men's athletic teams, the size of the men's wrestling team was capped at 27. Although the reduction was protested vigorously by wrestling coach Terry Kerr, and team captain Stephen Neal expressed concerns that a smaller squad would prove less competitive, the smaller CSUB team performed exceptionally well, winning the Pac-10 Conference title and finishing third in the nation in 1996. In 1996-97, the men's wrestling roster was capped at 25, and four of these spots went unused. Nevertheless, in response to the rumored elimination of the men's wrestling team, on January 10, 1997, the team filed the instant lawsuit . . .

. . . . The district court initially granted a temporary restraining order preventing the reductions, then granted a preliminary injunction to prevent CSUB from reducing the size of the wrestling team. . . .

Appellees recognize that . . . it would be imprudent to argue that Title IX prohibits the use of all gender-conscious remedies. Appellees therefore suggest that gender-conscious remedies are appropriate only when necessary to ensure that schools provide opportunities to males and females in proportion to their relative levels of interest in sports participation. By contrast, Appellants contend that schools may make gender-conscious decisions about sports-funding levels to correct for an imbalance between the composition of the undergraduate student body and the composition of the undergraduate student athletic participants pool. This disagreement has real significance: Men's expressed interest in participating in varsity sports is apparently higher than women's at the present time—although the "interest gap" continues to narrow—so permitting gender-conscious remedies until the proportions of students and athletes are roughly proportional gives universities more remedial freedom than permitting remedies only until expressed interest and varsity roster spots correspond. . . .

In other words, Appellees' interpretation of Title IX would have allowed universities to do little or nothing to equalize men's and women's opportunities if they could point to data showing that women were less interested in sports. But a central aspect of Title IX's purpose was to *encourage* women to participate in sports: The increased number of roster spots and scholarships reserved for

---

1. This figure assumed 60 percent female enrollment for that year.

women would gradually increase demand among women for those roster spots and scholarships.[4] . . . *changing!*

Title IX is a dynamic statute, not a static one. It envisions continuing progress toward the goal of equal opportunity for all athletes and recognizes that, where society has conditioned women to expect less than their fair share of the athletic opportunities, women's interest in participating in sports will not rise to a par with men's overnight. The percentage of college athletes who are women rose from 15% in 1972 to 37% in 1998, and Title IX is at least partially responsible for this trend of increased participation by women. . . . Title IX has altered women's preferences, making them more interested in sports, and more likely to become student athletes. *women more interested b/c of title IX*

Adopting Appellees' interest-based test for Title IX compliance would hinder, and quite possibly reverse, the steady increases in women's participation and interest in sports that have followed Title IX's enactment. *I get this*

A number of courts of appeals have addressed another potentially dispositive issue in this appeal—namely, whether Title IX permits a university to diminish athletic opportunities available to men so as to bring them into line with the lower athletic opportunities available to women. Every court, in construing the Policy Interpretation and the text of Title IX, has held that a university may bring itself into Title IX compliance by increasing athletic opportunities for the underrepresented gender (women in this case) *or* by decreasing athletic opportunities for the overrepresented gender (men in this case). [Citations omitted.] An extensive survey of Title IX's legislative history and the regulations promulgated to apply its provisions to college athletics concluded that boosters of male sports argued vociferously before Congress that the proposed regulations would require schools to shift resources from men's programs to women's programs, but that Congress nevertheless sided "with women's advocates" by deciding not to repeal the HEW's athletics-related Title IX regulations. Mary Jo Festle, Playing Nice: Politics and Apologies in Women's Sports 171-76 (1996). Congress thus appears to have believed that Title IX would result in funding reductions to male athletic programs. If a university wishes to comply with Title IX by leveling down programs instead of ratcheting them up, as Appellant has done here, Title IX is not offended. *not fair!*

There is a second reason why a reversal of the district court's order granting injunctive relief on the Title IX claim is warranted. The district court failed to defer properly to the interpretation of Title IX put forward by the administrative agency that is explicitly authorized to enforce its provisions. It is well-established that the federal courts are to defer substantially to an agency's interpretation of its own regulations. . . .

We also note that Appellees' interpretation of Title IX's text has been rejected explicitly by the Seventh Circuit . . . as well as the OCR, and implicitly rejected by the other circuits that have held that a school may cut the number of male athletic slots in order to bring itself into compliance with Title IX. . . .

4. That is, the creation of additional athletic spots for women would prompt universities to recruit more female athletes, in the long run shifting women's demand curve for sports participation. As more women participated, social norms discouraging women's participation in sports presumably would be further eroded, prompting additional increases in women's participation levels. . . .

would encourage female participation

Finally, the district court below rejected the interpretation of Title IX advocated by the OCR and Appellants on the ground that such a reading of the statute might violate the Constitution. In the court's words, OCR's interpretation would effectively transform Title IX from an anti-discrimination statute to a statute enacted to remedy past discrimination, thus subjecting it to heightened scrutiny. Without speculating whether Title IX would survive such searching constitutional scrutiny, the court notes that it remains unsatisfied with the [*Cohen v. Brown Univ.*, 991 F.2d 888 (1st Cir. 1993)] majority's treatment of these important questions. The court is satisfied that avoiding serious constitutional questions such as an equal protection challenge to a very important Congressional statute is itself ample reason for rejecting the safe harbor idea as part of Title IX.

The district court thus strained to interpret Title IX in a way that ostensibly would avoid these concerns. . . .

The First and Seventh Circuits both have considered at length the constitutionality of the first prong of the OCR's test. In [*Cohen v. Brown Univ.* (*Cohen I*), 991 F.2d 888 (1st Cir. 1993), *Cohen v. Brown Univ.* (*Cohen II*), 101 F.3d 155 (1st Cir. 1996), and *Kelley v. Board of Trustees*, 35 F.3d 265 (7th Cir. 1994)] the courts emphatically rejected the claim that the Policy Interpretation was unconstitutional under the Fourteenth Amendment. The separate reasoning in the two *Cohen* opinions is particularly well-developed. It applied intermediate scrutiny, which we would also do were we addressing the constitutional merits. *See Coalition for Econ. Equity v. Wilson*, 122 F.3d 692, 702 (9th Cir.1997) ("When the government classifies by gender, it must demonstrate that the classification is substantially related to an important governmental interest, requiring an 'exceedingly persuasive' justification."). *Cohen II* noted that the Policy Interpretation furthered the "clearly important" objectives of "avoid[ing] the use of federal resources to support discriminatory practices, and provid[ing] individual citizens effective protection against those practices." Moreover, it found that "judicial enforcement of federal anti-discrimination statutes is at least an important governmental objective." And *Cohen II* held that the district court's relief, which was essentially identical to what the OCR Policy Interpretation calls for, was "clearly substantially related" to these objectives. . . . Along the same lines, the Seventh Circuit has held that "the remedial scheme established by Title IX and the applicable regulation and policy interpretation are clearly substantially related to" the objective of prohibiting "educational institutions from discriminating on the basis of sex." We adopt the reasoning of *Cohen I*, *Cohen II*, and *Kelley*, and hold that the constitutional analysis contained therein persuasively disposes of any serious constitutional concerns that might be raised in relation to the OCR Policy Interpretation. The district court's final basis for rejecting the OCR's interpretation of Title IX was therefore erroneous. . . .

This past summer, 90,185 enthusiastic fans crowded into Pasadena's historic Rose Bowl for the finals of the Women's World Cup soccer match. An estimated 40 million television viewers also tuned in to watch a thrilling battle between the American and Chinese teams. The match ended when American defender Brandi Chastain fired the ball past Chinese goalkeeper Gao Hong, breaking a 4-4 shootout tie. . . . The victory sparked a national celebration and a realization by many that women's sports could be just as exciting, competitive, and lucrative as men's sports. And the victorious athletes understood as well as anyone the connection between a 27-year-old statute and tangible progress in women's athletics. . . . Title IX has enhanced, and will continue to enhance, women's opportunities to enjoy the thrill of victory, the agony of defeat, and the many tangible benefits that flow from just being given a chance to participate in intercollegiate athletics. Today we join our sister circuits in holding that Title IX does not bar universities from taking steps to ensure that women are approximately as well represented in sports programs as they are in student bodies.

We REVERSE, and VACATE the preliminary injunction.

can cut men's programs if women are underrepresented

NOTES AND QUESTIONS

1. *Capping and Title IX.* In *Neal*, why does the Ninth Circuit reject plaintiffs' claim that capping rosters for men's sports or eliminating men's teams violates Title IX? For purposes of federal equal protection, do you agree with *Neal's* holding that cutting men's sports (gender-based conduct) is substantially related to an important government interest? The court states that "women's sports could be just as exciting, competitive, and lucrative as men's sports." What is the role of Title IX in achieving this objective?

By saying it is fine as long as women are underrepresented. No!

Title IX played a role by getting women interested and now more play, which creates opport. like the world cup

More than 10 years ago, Donna Lopiano, a well-known advocate for gender equity and former chief executive officer of the Women's Sports Foundation, cited statistics evidencing that "(1) Most schools are adding women's sports without cutting men's sports. (2) The richest schools are the ones that are cutting men's sports. (3) Men's sports participation has continued to increase (not decrease) as women's sports participation grows. At the college level, there are still 30 percent more male than female participants. (4) Some men's and women's sports have been cut from college programs, many simply because of lack of interest." *It's Time for Straight Talk About Title IX*, SportsBus. J., April 30-May 6, 2001, at 33. She asserts that some NCAA Division I universities are making a "status decision" to have "a gender equitable program at the highest competitive level with fewer teams, spending more money on each team." She points out the alternatives of moving down to a lower level of competition and continuing to afford all teams, or conducting an athletic program with multiple funding tiers.

2. *Cutting Sports.* Consistent with *Neal*, courts have uniformly held that cutting men's sports in an effort to achieve substantial proportionality in athletic participation opportunities does not violate Title IX or male athletes' equal protection rights. See, e.g., *Miami Univ. Wrestling Club v. Miami Univ.*, 302 F.3d 608 (6th Cir. 2002); *Chalenor v. University of N.D.*, 291 F.3d 1042 (8th Cir. 2002); *Boulahanis v. Board of Regents*, 198 F.3d 633 (7th Cir. 1999); *Kelly v. Board of Trustees*, 35 F.3d 265 (7th Cir. 1994); *Equity in Athletics v. Department of Educ.*, 505 F. Supp. 2d 88 (W.D. Va. 2007); *Gonyo v. Drake Univ.*, 879 F. Supp. 1000 (S.D. Iowa 1995). Legal scholars have observed:

> [C]ourts have recognized that budget reductions and constraints are a reality at many schools and that Title IX must be interpreted to reflect that reality. While everyone would prefer that schools remedy their past discrimination and reach equity by increasing female opportunities to the level males have long enjoyed (and most schools do so), schools with dwindling budgets cannot always do this. The law allows schools to decide their own level of commitment to athletics and to set their own budgets. As courts have reiterated, Title IX does not dictate these choices and is not the cause of these schools' decision-making; it merely requires that they equitably allocate the opportunities and resources that they have.

I think it does dictate!

Jocelyn Samuels and Kristen Galles, *In Defense of Title IX: Why Current Policies Are Required to Ensure Equality of Opportunity*, 14 Marq. Sports L. Rev. 11, 31 (2003).

A lawsuit by several associations representing men's collegiate wrestling coaches, athletes, and alumni claimed that the three-part test in the OCR's 1979 Policy Interpretation and its 1996 Clarification of Title IX and its regulations is illegal. Plaintiffs sought to enjoin the Department of Education from enforcing Title IX in a manner that allegedly discriminated against male athletes. This lawsuit was dismissed on the grounds that the plaintiffs lacked standing and the federal Administrative Procedure Act barred their claims. *National Wrestling Coaches Assn. v. United States Dept. of Educ.*, 366 F.3d 930 (D.C. Cir. 2004), *cert. denied.*, 545 U.S. 1104 (2005). See also *Cobb v. U.S. Dept. of Educ. Office for Civil Rights*, 487 F. Supp. 2d 1049 (D. Minn. 2007) (no private right to force OCR to withhold federal funds to violator school but recognizing a private-party claim against OCR if it "assists" violation of Title IX contrary to its legal duty to eliminate discrimination).

The best way to avoid elimination of men's nonrevenue sports may be to raise private funds to support them. In April 2002 University of Minnesota administrators announced plans to cut men's golf and the men's and women's gymnastics teams in an effort to more closely comply with gender equity guidelines and to help erase a projected $21 million deficit in the athletic department. A grassroots drive by university alumni, fans, and parents raised $900,000 by the end of June to keep these sports alive for another year. Ironically, the men's golf team won its first NCAA national championship that same month — the first Northern university to do so in more than 20 years.

3. *Title IX at 30 Report.* On February 28, 2003, the Secretary of Education's Commission on Opportunity in Athletics issued its report "Open to All: Title IX at Thirty." The Commission held several public meetings, heard testimony from more than 50 expert witnesses, and reviewed thousands of documents submitted by experts and citizens nationwide. It found that "[a]fter 30 years of Title IX, great progress has been made, but more needs to be done to create opportunities for women and girls and retain opportunities for boys and men." It adopted 23 specific recommendations, including that the Office of Civil Rights should aggressively enforce Title IX standards and policies (but make clear that cutting teams is disfavored) while seeking sanctions for noncompliance. The Commission made a series of recommendations concerning new ways of measuring Title IX compliance, while also recommending that the Department of Education encourage universities and national governing bodies to consider ways of reducing excessive expenditures in college athletics.

Two commission members, Donna de Varona and Julie Foudy, disagreed with the commission's report and issued a separate report expressing their minority viewpoint. They expressed concern that the commission had focused on addressing the loss of men's teams rather than whether discrimination against women persists and how it can be remedied. They opposed several specific Commission recommendations to make it easier for educational institutions to comply with the three-part test, on the ground that implementing them might prevent the objective of ultimately achieving equal athletic participation opportunities for girls and women.

Both reports are reproduced in the appendix to *Symposium: Title IX at Thirty,* 14 Marq. Sports L. Rev. 1 (2003), which provides extensive scholarly commentary regarding the application and effects of Title IX.

4. *Title IX and Economic Policy.* Professor Richard A. Epstein has argued, on legal and economic grounds, that we should "scrap Title IX altogether and rely on schools to allocate their athletic funds as they see fit, spurred by the current powerful social consensus behind the equal-opportunity norm." Richard A. Epstein, *Law and Economics: Just Scrap Title IX,* Nat'l L.J., Oct. 14, 2002. In making this argument, Epstein asserts:

I like him!

> Co-ed institutions bidding for students have every incentive to set the right internal sports balance.
>
> That sensible equilibrium cannot be maintained under the proportionality tests read into Title IX. Instead of maximizing total participation regardless of sex, Title IX, as now construed, is committed to minimizing the differences in participation by sex. Ironically, this is most easily met by shutting down all varsity sports. Few colleges wish to go to that extreme. Yet given the strong differences in demand, this federal mandate instantly creates male queues and female shortages.

Id.

Colleges have two ways to respond to this imbalance: pay to increase the number of women athletes or cut the number of men without charge. With constrained budgets, it's no surprise that colleges slash slots from nonrevenue men's sports, such as wrestling and gymnastics, and use the savings to add far fewer female slots in, say, ice hockey or golf. The marginal male athlete begs for a chance to clean up the locker room to wrestle without a scholarship; the marginal female athlete receives a large scholarship to induce her to participate.

= true!

It is not surprising, therefore, that Professor Epstein concludes:

> Defenders of Title IX will howl in protest that all the recent gains in female athletics are attributable to the statute. Poppycock. With or without Title IX, we would have seen a steep rise in women's sports through the 1970s because the law passed just when social attitudes toward women were radically changing. Private and state institutions are not impervious to student demands; nor should women be painted as society's perpetual victims, unable to speak and act for themselves. Women no longer need Title IX to be heard loud and clear.

I agree!

Id.

For a contrary view, see Daniel R. Marburger and Nancy Hogshead-Makar, *Is Title IX Really to Blame for the Decline in Intercollegiate Men's Nonrevenue Sports?,* 14 Marq. Sports L. Rev. 65 (2003). Professors Marburger and Hogshead-Makar begin their analysis by distinguishing between the perspectives relied on at the Division I, II, and III levels:

> Inferring the relative emphasis on the consequentialist/utilitarian perspectives, Division I overtly favors promoting intercollegiate athletics as spectator sports, with the income potential of football and basketball specifically identified in its statement of philosophy. In emphasizing the spectator-orientation of sports, the philosophy specifically notes the goal of a self-financing athletic department. Division II and III members, in contrast, explicitly assert that the primary goal of their athletic programs is to benefit the student-athletes.

Id. at 77.

After examining how the Division I arm's race—the need to provide better facilities and other amenities for revenue-producing football and men's basketball programs to remain competitive in those sports—the authors examine extensive data regarding participation of men and women in intercollegiate athletics at the Division I, II, and III levels. They conclude that placing the blame on Title IX for the decrease in participation opportunities for male athletes may be misplaced:

> As long as football and men's basketball budgets [at the Division I level, in particular] are essentially exempted from budgetary restraints, Title IX proportionality burdens are shifted to nonrevenue sports. This begs the question: is Title IX responsible for a sport's discontinuation, or is it the incentive to favor the growth in the football/men's basketball budget? In answering this question, we should note that the net decrease in men's nonrevenue sports occurred only at the Division I level despite the fact that football and men's basketball are frequently in a position to cross-subsidize the nonrevenue sports. At the Division III level, whether expenditures per participant are substantially more equal between "revenue" and nonrevenue sports, and also between men's and women's sports in general, the net change in the number of men's sports is positive.
>
> If the analysis provided in this study is correct, weakening the proportionality component of Title IX will not spare men's nonrevenue sports at the Division I level. Rather, it will only serve to further accelerate the arms race, with men's and women's nonrevenue sports experiencing equivalent budgetary casualties.

Id. at 93.

Has Title IX been responsible for reducing men's opportunities to participate in intercollegiate athletics, or has the Division I emphasis on marketing and promoting football and men's basketball as spectator and revenue-producing sports in a highly competitive market been the primary cause of such reductions? Is it fair to use revenues produced by Division I football and men's basketball teams to provide athletic participation opportunities for men and women in non-revenue-producing sports? In contrast, at the Division II and III levels of athletic competition, participation is emphasized in competitive sports by many students rather than only elite student-athletes. It is not uncommon for a small university or college to have as many as 30 percent to 40 percent of its students participating in intercollegiate athletics, which provides a significant tool to recruit students to Division II and III educational institutions. What, if anything, can or should be done at the Division I level to address the problems that arise in the gender and racial equity contexts because of the emphasis on a more commercial, revenue-producing and self-funding model of intercollegiate athletics?

5. *The* Simpson *Case.* In *Simpson v. University of Colorado Boulder*, 500 F.3d 1170 (10th Cir. 2007), two women claimed that they were sexually assaulted by University of Colorado football players and recruits and brought an action against the university under Title IX.. The district court granted the university's motion for summary judgment. On appeal, the Tenth Circuit articulated the test for institutional liability:

[Whether] a funding recipient can be said to have "intentionally acted in clear violation of Title IX," *Davis*, 526 U.S. at 642, 119 S.Ct. 1161, when the violation is caused by official policy, which may be a policy of deliberate indifference to providing adequate training or guidance that is obviously necessary for implementation of a specific program or policy of the recipient. Implementation of an official policy can certainly be a circumstance in which the recipient exercises significant "control over the harasser and the environment in which the harassment occurs."

Id. at 1178.

After examining the facts, the Tenth Circuit concluded:

[T]he evidence before the district court would support findings that by the time of the assaults on Plaintiffs, (1) Coach Barnett [the head coach], whose rank in the CU hierarchy was comparable to that of a police chief in a municipal government, had general knowledge of the serious risk of sexual harassment and assault during college-football recruiting efforts; (2) Barnett knew that such assaults had indeed occurred during CU recruiting efforts; (3) Barnett nevertheless maintained an unsupervised player-host program to show high-school recruits "a good time"; and (4) Barnett knew, both because of incidents reported to him and because of his own unsupportive attitude, that there had been no change in the atmosphere since 1997 (when the prior assault occurred) that would make such misconduct less likely in 2001. A jury could infer that "the need for more or different training [of player-hosts] so obvious, and the inadequacy so likely to result in [Title IX violations], that [Coach Barnett could] reasonably be said to have been deliberately indifferent to the need.

Id. at 1184.

Prior to the assaults in this case, and based on a previous case of assault, Assistant District Attorney Mary Keenan had met with CU officials and recommended that "CU adopt a policy of zero tolerance for alcohol and sex in the recruiting program, develop written policies and procedures for supervising recruits, and offer football players annual training by the DA on sexual assault." *Id.* at 1182. The court reports that Coach Barnett resisted recruiting reform efforts and claimed that "at schools all over the country recruits were shown 'a good time,' met young women, and went to parties, and if such activities weren't allowed at CU, it would be a 'competitive disadvantage' for the football team." *Id.* at 1184. In its opinion, the Tenth Circuit noted:

A recent three-year study conducted by the National Institute of Mental Health found that athletes participated in one-third of the 862 sexual assaults on college campuses. Another study conducted at Towson State University's Center for the Study and Prevention of Campus Violence found that athletes are 5.5 times more likely to commit date rape.

Id. at 1181.

Would policies like the one suggested by Ms. Keenan have been a strong deterrent to the assaults that provided the basis for this case? Considering that CU paid $2.85 million to settle the *Simpson* case, if you were counsel to a major university, would you advise that it adopt such policies? If not, *[handwritten margin note, top left:]* Fire coach to show that approval of this type of behavior will not be tolerated

[handwritten, top:] Zero tolerance — coach should have done something when he knew

what would you recommend that the university do to prevent the type of conduct that gave rise to *Simpson*? Is this another area in which the revenue-producing and spectator-driven nature of Division I athletics places significant pressure on legal counsel, athletic directors, and coaches to be reluctant to lead and take steps to prevent misconduct by student-athletes who participate in sports such as football and basketball? Is this an area in which the NCAA Division I leadership should establish a rule limiting or prohibiting practices such as showing recruits "a good time" during their campus visits?

[handwritten:] It's not like the NCAA condones this activity, it just happens.

[handwritten margin, left:] ① ② ans. for class

PROBLEM 10-3

If you were a member of a newly formed Commission on Opportunity in Athletics appointed by President Obama, what reforms, if any, of current Title IX law, including its regulations and policy interpretations, would you suggest? For example, a number of individuals have recommended that men's football be exempt from Title IX considerations. Would you support such a proposal? Others have argued that the requirements of Title IX are, in some senses, "an unfunded mandate." If so, do you believe funding to achieve equal athletic participation opportunities for both sexes should be provided at the school, state, or federal levels, or by private donors?

[handwritten:] A proposal to exempt only the # of FB slots, not facilities, $, etc.
Should be provided at school level, BUT can be supplemented w/ the other 2.

PROBLEM 10-4

One of the authors of this textbook has suggested that affirmative efforts to achieve gender equity sometimes have racial implications that need to be considered. Rodney K. Smith, *When Ignorance Is Not Bliss: In Search of Racial and Gender Equity in Intercollegiate Athletics*, 61 Mo. L. Rev. 329 (1996). He argues that a high percentage of athletes participating in the major revenue-producing intercollegiate sports are athletes of color from disadvantaged socioeconomic backgrounds, and the funds produced by those sports are being used to fund women's sports (archery, badminton, bowling, equestrian, rugby, squash, synchronized swimming, and team handball) that are played primarily, if at all, by upper-middle-class white women. Do gender equity efforts raise racial equity issues? If so, how should those issues be resolved as a matter of policy? He suggests that women's football be added as an interscholastic and intercollegiate sport. Rodney K. Smith, *Solving the Title IX Conundrum with Women's Football*, 38 S. Tex L. Rev. 1057 (1997). Do you agree that women's football should be sanctioned as a sport by the NCAA? Alternatively, what other women's sports should be added and why? *[handwritten:]* No! Not enough interest, Beach volleyball

[handwritten margin, left:] I don't think so! If so, then over time survey to establish if it is happening and if it is, then modify Title IX to eliminate discrepencies.

What strategies would you employ to persuade the NCAA to adopt football, cheer, or another sport as an emerging sport? Sports recognized by the NCAA are frequently also the major sports added at high schools because high school administrators and coaches want to offer sports that provide girls with college athletics scholarship opportunities.

Colleges and universities have also been named as defendants in lawsuits when student-athletes have raped other students, both on and off campus. In *Williams v. Board of Regents of the University System of Georgia*, 477 F.3d 1282 (11th Cir. 2007), a female student was allegedly gang raped by three male student-athletes in an

[handwritten, bottom:] History shows that females' interest ↑ which will happen w/ football

on-campus dormitory. The plaintiff argued that the university was liable under Title IX because the coach, athletics director, and university president were all aware that the student–athlete who attacked the plaintiff had a history of sexual assaults before he was recruited and admitted to the university. The Eleventh Circuit held that given the past history of the recruited student-athlete, the institution had "before the fact notice" and should have made efforts to prevent future harassment from occurring.

It is important to note that individual school officials (such as coaches or athletics administrators) can also be held personally liable for acts of harassment under §1983 for violating a student's civil rights in addition to Title IX claims made against the school. Timothy Davis and Keith E. Smith, *Eradicating Student-Athlete Sexual Assault of Women: Section 1983 and Personal Liability Following* Fitzgerald v. Barnstable, 2009 Mich. St. L. Rev. 629.

F.   GENDER-BASED EMPLOYMENT DISCRIMINATION IN ATHLETICS[1]

Gender discrimination affects not only student-athletes; it can also adversely affect coaches and violate Title IX and employment discrimination laws.

Since 1977, Vivien Acosta and Linda Jean Carpenter have conducted a longitudinal study, *Women in Intercollegiate Sport* (see http://acostacarpenter.org/AcostaCarpenter2012.pdf). According to the study, there are more women currently employed in administrative and coaching positions in intercollegiate athletics than ever before. However only 19.1 percent of athletics directors are women, which is dramatically lower than the 90 percent representation in the 1970s, when most colleges and universities had separate men's and women's athletics departments. There are no female administrators at all in 13.2 percent of college athletics programs. Less than half (42.6 percent) of women's athletics teams have a female head coach even though the majority (57.1 percent) of paid assistant coaches of women's teams are women. The gender barrier for female coaches is apparent, as less than 3 percent of men's teams are coached by a female head coach. Sports medicine and sports information lag woefully behind, with only 28 percent of women employed as head athletics trainers. Athletics communications appears to mirror the professional sports media, as only 11.9 percent of sports information directors are women.

Fuhr v. School District of Hazel Park, 364 F.3d 753 (6th Cir. 2004), illustrates the sports cultural bias against hiring female coaches. Geraldine Fuhr had significant experience as the girls' varsity basketball coach at Hazel Park High School for ten years, and concurrently as the assistant boys' varsity basketball coach for eight years. Fuhr applied for the boys' varsity coach position, and only one other candidate, a teacher who had been coaching the boys' freshman basketball team for the past two years, also applied. Both candidates were interviewed,

1. Some of the material in this section is from Matthew Mitten, Timothy Davis, Kenneth L. Shropshire, Barbara Osborne, and Rodney K. Smith, Sports Law: Governance and Regulation (Wolters Kluwer 2013) and was drafted by Barbara Osborne. The authors of this text express their appreciation to Professor Osborne.

and the Superintendent of Schools informed the search committee that several members of the school board did not want Fuhr as the boys' coach and that they had to honor their wishes. The president of the school board announced that he "was very concerned about a female being the head boys' basketball coach in Hazel Park." *Id.* at 757. Barnett was hired, and Fuhr sued the school district for sex discrimination under Title VII and the Elliot-Larsen Act, a Michigan civil rights act that prohibits discrimination. A jury held in Fuhr's favor, awarding her $455,000 in damages. Subsequently, the district court ordered Hazel Park to hire Fuhr as the boys' varsity basketball coach. Hazel Park appealed, but the Sixth Circuit affirmed, finding that Hazel Park had intentionally discriminated against Fuhr on the basis of sex by not hiring her as the head boys' basketball coach.

In addition to barriers in employing women in college athletics programs, a gender gap also exists in salaries, with female coaches earning on average only 62 percent of what male coaches make. Barbara Osborne and Marilyn V. Yarbrough. *Pay Equity for Coaches and Athletic Administrators: An Element of Title IX?*, 34 U. Mich. J. Law Reform 231 (2001). In the mid-1990s, two cases were decided that marked important victories for plaintiffs alleging gender-based employment discrimination in intercollegiate athletics. In *Tyler v. Howard University*, No. 91-CA11239 (D.C. June 28, 1993), a women's basketball coach claimed that the disparity between her salary and that of the men's basketball coach and the difference in their office facilities violated Title IX, the Equal Pay Act, and state law. The Howard men's basketball coach was paid $34,500 more annually than Tyler and had a spacious office, while Tyler's office was in a storage room. The jury awarded Tyler $2.34 million in damages, although the judge eventually reduced the award to $250,000. This case marked the first time a plaintiff had received a jury award based on such allegations. Similarly, in *Pitts v. Oklahoma State University*, No. CIV-93-1341-A (W.D. Okla. 1994), another jury awarded damages of $36,000 to a women's college golf coach because her salary was $28,000 a year less than the men's golf coach. She alleged that this disparity violated Title IX and other laws.

The following cases consider potential remedies for gender-based wage discrimination or retaliation by educational institutions against those seeking to ensure compliance with Title IX in the context of athletics.

1.   Wage Discrimination

DELI v. UNIVERSITY OF MINNESOTA

863 F. Supp. 958 (D. Minn. 1994)

Magnuson, District Judge.

Background

Plaintiff Katalin Deli is the former head coach of the University of Minnesota (University) women's gymnastics team. In June 1992, the University terminated her employment. Ms. Deli challenged this dismissal through the University grievance procedure. After review, the University upheld the termination, finding there existed just cause for her termination.

. . . Deli filed the present action against the University, alleging the University improperly paid her less than head coaches of several men's athletic teams. Deli contends that this pay differential, allegedly based on the gender of the athletes she coached, constituted prohibited discrimination on the basis of sex, in violation of Title VII of the Civil Rights Act, 42 U.S.C. §2000e; the Equal Pay Act, 29 U.S.C. §206(d); and Title IX . . .

. . . Plaintiff contends the Defendant discriminated in the compensation it paid her on the basis of the gender of the athletes she coached. Significantly, Plaintiff does not claim that the University discriminated against her on the basis of Plaintiff's gender, i.e. she does not claim that the University's motivation for paying her less money than the coaches of men's sports was the fact that Plaintiff was a woman and the coaches of men's sports were men. Plaintiff also does not challenge in this action the circumstances, justification or legality of her discharge from employment by the University. . . .

DISCUSSION

I.   TITLE VII CLAIM

Title VII prohibits employers from "discriminating against any individual with respect to his compensation . . . *because of such individual's* race, color, religion, sex or national origin. . . ." 42 U.S.C. §2000e-2(a)(1) (1981). [Emphasis added.] The clear terms of the statute prohibit discrimination in compensation based on the sex of the recipient. The statute does not proscribe salary discrimination based on the sex of other persons over whom the employee has supervision or oversight responsibilities. Even assuming, arguendo, that the University did discriminate in payment of salaries on the basis of the gender of the athletes the Plaintiff coached, such discrimination is not within the scope of Title VII, which prohibits discrimination based on the claimant employee's gender. See *Jackson v. Armstrong School Dist.*, 430 F. Supp. 1050, 1052 (W.D. Pa. 1977) (to be actionable under Title VII, claim must be that claimant was victim of discrimination on basis of claimant's gender, not that of athletes coached by claimant). Plaintiff has failed to state a Title VII claim on which relief can be granted and Defendant is entitled to judgment as a matter of law on Count II of the Complaint.

II.   EQUAL PAY ACT CLAIMS

A.   *"Factor Other Than Sex" Exception*

Plaintiff Deli also claims the Defendant violated the Equal Pay Act because it paid Plaintiff less than the coaches of men's athletics teams, thus discriminating against her on the basis of the gender of the athletes she supervised. Again assuming arguendo that the Defendant did discriminate in the payment of salary based on the gender of athletes supervised, such action would not support this Plaintiff's claim for violation of the Equal Pay Act.

The Equal Pay Act (EPA) prohibits an employer from discriminating between employees on the basis of sex by paying wages to employees . . . at a rate less than the rate at which [the employer] pays wages to employees of the opposite sex . . . for equal work on jobs the performance of which requires equal skill, effort, and responsibility, and which are performed under similar working conditions, except where such payment is made pursuant to . . . (iv) a differential based on any other factor other than sex. 26 U.S.C. §206(d)(1) . . . After review of the admittedly less-than-clear language of the statute and its history, this Court concurs with the reasoning of the Seventh Circuit—the EPA prohibits discrimination based on the gender of the claimant only and does not reach compensation differentials based on the gender of student athletes coached by a claimant. Such compensation differentials are based on a "factor other than sex" and thus are not proscribed by the EPA. Because Plaintiff's Complaint alleges discrimination based on the gender of the athletes she coached, she has failed to state an actionable claim under the Equal Pay Act and Defendant's motion for summary judgment on Plaintiff's EPA claims will be granted.

B.   *Position Not Substantially Equal*

Even if Plaintiff had alleged discrimination in salary based on her own gender, her claim could not withstand summary judgment. . . . [T]he Ninth Circuit recently held that a women's basketball coach who was paid less than a men's basketball coach at the same university failed to show that she would likely prevail on her claims for violation of the Equal Pay Act or Title IX. *Stanley v. University of Southern California*, 13 F.3d 1313 (9th Cir. 1994). The Ninth Circuit affirmed that, consistent with the Equal Pay Act, an employer may pay different salaries to coaches of different genders if the coaching positions are not substantially equal in terms of skill, effort, responsibility, and working conditions. . . . In order to state an Equal Pay Act claim, a Plaintiff must show her position was substantially equal to that of the comparator positions with respect to each of the foregoing attributes.

The comparators Deli has chosen in this suit are the coaches of the men's football, hockey and basketball teams. Defendant has presented evidence to show that all three of those teams are larger than the women's gymnastics team. The University also proffers evidence that the head coaches in those sports supervise more employees than Deli supervised. Further, Defendant has provided evidence to show that the three teams enjoy significantly greater spectator attendance and generate substantially more revenue for the University than the women's gymnastics team. Finally, the University has alleged and provided evidence to support its contention that the coaches of the three men's athletic teams have greater responsibility for public and media relations than Deli had as the coach of the women's gymnastics team. The foregoing evidence alone, if undisputed, is enough to show the Plaintiff's job and that of the head coaches of men's basketball, football and hockey are not "substantially equal" in terms of responsibility and working conditions. See *Stanley*, 13 F.3d 1313, 1322 (finding substantial difference in responsibility based on essentially same factors as those listed above).

Deli offers no evidence to refute the foregoing. . . .

III.   TITLE IX CLAIMS

. . . Plaintiff's Title IX claims fail on the merits. Courts are to accord the authoritative Department of Education Office of Civil Rights (OCR)'s Policy Interpretation and Title IX Investigator's Manual substantial deference in determining the appropriate application of Title IX. Plaintiff alleges Defendant violated Title IX by compensating her at a lower level than coaches of certain men's sports. According to the OCR Policy Interpretation, differential compensation of coaches violates Title IX "only where compensation or assignment policies or practices deny male and female athletes coaching of equivalent quality, nature or availability" 44 Fed. Reg. at 71416. More generally, according to Title IX implementing regulations, "unequal aggregate expenditures for members of each sex or unequal expenditures for male and female teams [alone] . . . will not constitute noncompliance with [Title IX]" 34 C.F.R. §106.41(c). The Investigator's Manual confirms that the crux of the inquiry is whether differentials in coaches' compensation result in denial of equal athletic opportunity for athletes:

> If availability and assignment of coaches to both programs are equivalent, it is difficult . . . to assert that the lower compensation for coaches in, for example, the women's program, negatively affects female athletes. The intent of [the regulation implementing Title VII] is for equal athletic opportunity to be provided to participants, not coaches.

OCR Title IX Investigator's Manual (1990) at 58.

Plaintiff does not assert in her Complaint or elsewhere that the athletes she supervised received lesser quality coaching as a result of the difference between Plaintiff's salary and salaries paid to coaches of the men's football, hockey and basketball teams. To the contrary, the record shows Plaintiff contends she provided superior coaching and opportunities for the athletes she coached, as evidenced by her coaching honors and the accomplishments of her athletes. . . . Because Plaintiff does not claim or provide any evidence to suggest that due to her receipt of a lower salary than that received by coaches of some men's athletic teams, Plaintiff's coaching services were inferior in "quality, nature or availability" to those provided to the men's teams, she has failed to make out a prima facie claim for violation of Title IX. The Defendant is entitled to summary judgment on Plaintiff's Title IX claims. . . .

NOTES AND QUESTIONS

1. *Unequal Pay Claims.* Why did *Deli* reject the plaintiff's EPA and Title IX claims? What would a plaintiff have to plead and prove to establish successful claims under each of these federal statutes?

When asserting a Title IX violation because of unequal pay, the plaintiff must assert that the disparity is a result of the gender of the *team* coached, rather than the coach's gender. Under such a theory, the plaintiff coach could be male or female. Cathryn L. Claussen, *Title IX and Employment Discrimination in Coaching Intercollegiate Athletics*, 12 U. Miami Ent. & Sports L. Rev. 149, 150 (1994).

After the *Stanley* decision relied on by the *Deli* court, the EEOC revised its guidelines to clarify how the EPA should be applied in such cases. The guidelines require that an educational institution provide a non-gender-based reason for paying a male coach more than a female coach. Men and women involved in coaching are to be evaluated based on their duties, not their sports. Should the EEOC adopt further guidelines to address what many female coaches refer to as the "chicken and egg" problem—that is, if they were paid more and given more resources to market their programs, would they be able to overcome social inequities developed over a long period of time and develop programs that would be as successful as men's programs? A pertinent Title IX regulation states:

A recipient shall not make or enforce any policy or practice which, on the basis of sex: (a) Makes distinctions in rates of pay or other compensation; (b) Results in the payment of wages to employees of one sex at a rate less than that paid to employees of the opposite sex for equal work on jobs the performance of which requires equal skill, effort, and responsibility, and which are performed under similar working conditions.

34 C.F.R. §106.54 (2003).

2. *Women Coaching Men's Sports?* Female athletes often state that they prefer male coaches, and most male athletes state that they prefer male coaches. Is this a justification for hiring a male coach over a female coach? Why or why not? Men regularly coach women's teams, but women seldom coach men's teams. Why are there not more objections to this disparity (inequity)? What can or should be done to increase the number of women working in sports?

[handwritten: Yes!]

[handwritten left margin: I think so. The athletes' opinions should be taken into consideration!]

[handwritten: STOP]

[handwritten: Probably b/c women know men don't want to be coached by women and women do not have as much of an interest in coaching men.]

PROBLEM 10-5

You represent a Division I-A institution that has a history of being competitive in men's and women's basketball. In fact, your men's basketball team has made the NCAA play-offs six out of the past nine years, and your women's team has made the play-offs eight out of the past nine years. Both programs have been in the revenue-producing category. The women's program currently operates at a slight loss ranging from under $25,000 last year, when the team went to the Sweet Sixteen with a record of 24-6, to just over $100,000 three years ago, when the team was rebuilding and had a record of 14-12. In the past three years, attendance has increased significantly at home games, and the university has just entered into a local television contract for the women's team, including a coach's show, like the one available to the men's coach. The television revenues should make the program profitable if the team remains successful. Indeed, revenues as a percentage have increased more rapidly over the past decade for the women's program than for the men's program.

The women's coach has also been trying to build strong external funding for the program, with increasing but still fairly minimal success in terms of dollars raised for the program. The men's program has operated at a net profit, averaging over $1.5 million each of the past three years. The women's coach received a $10,000 increase in base salary after her successful season and is currently paid $175,000 per year in base salary, with an additional $75,000 per year from other sources of income, including television appearances, camps, apparel contracts, and other activities.

The men's basketball coach left to take a head coaching position in the NBA, and the university is in negotiations with a candidate to replace him. The coach who left for the NBA was paid $1.5 million per year ($300,000 in base salary and $1.2 million from other sources). The new men's coach candidate is demanding a base salary of $500,000 per year with a guarantee of $1.5 million from other sources, for a total of $2 million, and average salaries for his assistants of $105,000 per year.

The women's coach has been increasingly vocal about the importance of equal treatment for her program, including equity in salary for herself and her assistant coaches (the average salary for women's assistant coaches was $35,000 last year, and the average for assistant coaches for the men's team was $78,000). The men's football coach is the second-highest-paid coach at the university. He makes $250,000 in base salary and $750,000 from other sources, for a total of $550,000. His assistants average $90,000 per year. The football team has operated at a loss, losing an average of $500,000 per year for the past three years and has made it to a bowl game in only one of those years. The team was 6-5 this year in a rebuilding year, and a strong incoming class has been recruited. The football coach was given a $25,000 raise in base pay.

As general counsel for the university, you have been asked for your advice as to how the university should proceed. If the university meets the new coaching candidate's demands, as the university would like to do (it is getting strong pressure from boosters to hire the coach), do you have a legal or moral obligation to increase salaries for the coaches of the women's team? How would you advise that the university deal with practical problems, for example, with the media and morale in the athletics department?

2.   *Retaliatory Discharge or Punitive Action*

Both male and female coaches have asserted that they have been discharged in retaliation for complaining about gender disparities in institutions' athletic programs. The following case addresses the elements of Title VII and IX retaliatory discharge claims.

LOWREY v. TEXAS A&M UNIVERSITY SYSTEM
11 F. Supp. 2d 895 (S.D. Tex. 1998)

LAKE, Judge.

I.   BACKGROUND

Tarleton State University (Tarleton) is a four-year coeducational institution of higher education located in Stephenville, Texas. . . . Tarleton is managed and controlled by the Board of Regents of the Texas A&M University System. . . . Dr. Dennis McCabe is the President of Tarleton. Lonn Reisman is Men's Basketball Coach and Athletics Director. Dr. Lamar Johanson is Dean of the College of Arts and Sciences and Tarleton's Faculty Representative to the NCAA. Jim Johnson is the Men's Athletics Coordinator and the NCAA Compliance Coordinator for Tarleton and a physical education teacher.

A.   TWENTY YEARS OF COACHING

Jan Lowrey became Women's Basketball Coach at Tarleton in the fall of 1976. Over the next twenty years Lowrey's teams were very successful. Her teams won twenty or more games in each of her first nine years as coach. They won several conference championships, and in 1992 the team placed second in the Division II national women's basketball tournament.

Lowery's success did not lead to improved conditions for the women's basketball team. For example, the locker room used by the women's team from the early 1980s was the former men's visiting-team dressing room. The room had "a 'gang' shower, four urinals and one toilet, one sink, no dressing tables, no outlets for hair dryers, no storage, and inadequate lockers." Tarleton repeatedly ignored requests from Lowrey for renovations. Lowrey and the team manager ultimately installed shower rods and curtains to divide the showers. Tarleton finally removed the urinals in 1996, but it did not install toilets to replace them.

In 1988 Tarleton hired Lonn Reisman as Men's Basketball Coach. During his first year Reisman's salary was less than Lowrey's. The year before Reisman was hired the men's team won three games and lost twenty-five. In Reisman's first year (1988-89) the men's team improved its record to eighteen wins and eleven losses. The women's team had twenty wins and ten losses that year. Both Lowrey and Reisman received a $1,400 raise in salary as a reward for their winning seasons. In the Spring of 1989 then-Tarleton President Barry Thompson created the position of Assistant Athletics Director and appointed Reisman to the post. Tarleton did not give Lowrey an opportunity to apply for this position. Reisman then held the positions of Assistant Athletics Director, Men's Basketball Coach, and a physical education instructor. By the 1989-90 fiscal year, Reisman's second year at Tarleton and his first year as Assistant Athletics Director, Tarleton was paying Reisman a higher salary than it paid Lowrey, who by then had coached and taught at the university for thirteen years. Tarleton paid Reisman $36,899 and Lowrey $31,137 that year.

On August 27, 1993, Dr. Ron Newsome, Tarleton's Athletics Director, resigned. Although Lowrey was a head coach in the Athletics Department, she learned of Newsome's resignation through the press, not from the university. Over the next few days a Tarleton search committee interviewed three candidates to fill the vacancy: Reisman, Lowrey, and the new football coach, Ronnie Roemisch. On September 1, 1993, McCabe offered the position of Athletics Director to Reisman. Dr. McCabe explained to Lowrey that although she was equally qualified for the position, "he 'was going with Lonn.'"

Lowrey asked Reisman and McCabe to create the position of Associate Athletics Director for her, with a raise in pay commensurate with the duties and responsibilities of such an office. Instead, Reisman offered her the position of Women's Athletics Coordinator. Although this position required Lowrey to assume several new duties, the evidence is unclear whether she received an increase in pay for taking this position.

Earlier that year, on January 28, 1993, McCabe had appointed Lowrey to a special task force to study gender equity at Tarleton. On November 17, 1993, Dr. Janet Schmelzer, an Associate Professor of History at Tarleton, filed a complaint with the Department of Justice's Office of Civil Rights (OCR) alleging sex discrimination at Tarleton in violation of Title IX of the Education Amendments of 1972, 20 U.S.C. §§1681-1688 (1994). Schmelzer's complaint included several allegations of Title IX violations in Tarleton's Athletics Department. In May of 1994, Schmelzer agreed to withdraw her complaint while the parties attempted to mediate the dispute.

Beginning in April of 1994 Reisman began filing several "incident reports" in Lowrey's personnel file, noting among other problems, days when Lowrey was absent from work, arrived late, or left early without notifying Reisman. On September 29, 1994, Reisman conducted a performance review of Lowrey and gave her an average rating of 2.0 on a scale of 1 to 5 (lowest to highest) in nine categories. Reisman sent a copy of the review to Lowrey on

October 3, 1994. On October 5, 1994, Reisman recommended that McCabe terminate Lowrey as Women's Athletics Coordinator. Reisman did not notify Lowrey of his recommendation. Reisman reiterated his views in an October 26, 1994, memorandum to McCabe, stating that he "strongly recommended the reassignment of Ms. Jan Lowrey from Women's Athletics Coordinator/ Head Women's Basketball Coach, effective immediately, to Head Women's Basketball Coach."

In an October 28, 1994, letter Schmelzer reminded McCabe of his promise not to allow retaliation against persons who spoke to her regarding matters raised by her OCR complaint and warned him that Title VI would forbid such retaliation regardless of McCabe's promises. On November 4, 1994, President McCabe reassigned Lowrey. She remained Women's Basketball Coach and an instructor in the Physical Education Department, and her salary did not change. Eventually, Lowrey sought employment elsewhere. She resigned from Tarleton on July 15, 1996, and took the head coach's position for the San Jose Lasers, a professional women's basketball team. The Lasers released her from her two-year contract after her first year with the club. . . .

IV. Retaliation

Lowrey alleges that defendants are liable are under Title VII, Title IX, and 42 U.S.C. §1983 and the First and Fourteenth Amendments to the Constitution for retaliating against her in response to comments she made criticizing the university and its officials on gender equity issues.

A. Title VII

Title VII prohibits employers from retaliating against employees for filing a discrimination charge or otherwise exercising their rights under Title VII. See 42 U.S.C. §2000e-3 (1994). To establish a prima facie case of retaliation under Title VII a plaintiff must show that:

(1) she engaged in activity protected by Title VII;
(2) her employer took an adverse employment action against her; and
(3) a causal connection exists between the protected activity and the adverse employment action.

See *Mattern v. Eastman Kodak Co.*, 104 F.3d. 702, 705 (5th Cir), cert. denied, 139 L. Ed. 2d 260, 118 S. Ct. 336 (1997). The "adverse employment action" must be an "ultimate employment decision," such as hiring, granting leave, discharging, promoting, or compensating. 104 F.3d at 707; *Dollis v. Rubin*, 77 F.3d 777, 782 (5th Cir. 1995). The only adverse action Lowrey identifies . . . is her removal as Women's Athletics Coordinator.

Tarleton argues that Lowrey cannot make a prima facie case of Title VII retaliation because her removal as Women's Athletics Coordinator was not an adverse employment action. Title VII's antiretaliation provisions address ultimate employment decisions, not "interlocutory or mediate" decisions that might lead to ultimate decisions. *Mattern*, 104 F.3d at 708. Employment actions having only a tangential effect on an ultimate decision are not sufficient to raise a claim of retaliation under Title VII. *Dollis*, 77 F.3d at 781-82. Tarleton argues that because Lowrey's demotion was not one of the five employment actions classified as adverse in *Mattern* (i.e., hiring, granting leave, discharging, promoting, and compensating), it does not constitute an ultimate employment decision.

Demotion is the opposite of promotion. If promotion is an ultimate employment decision, so is demotion. . . . Tarleton does not challenge the remaining elements of Lowrey's prima facie case and has not offered any legitimate, nondiscriminatory reasons for Lowrey's demotion. The court will therefore deny summary judgment on her Title VII retaliation claim.

B. TITLE IX

1. *Legal Standards*

In *Lakoski v. James*, 66 F.3d 751, 758 (5th Cir. 1995), *cert. denied*, 117 S. Ct. 357 (1996), the court held that Title IX does not imply a cause of action for employment discrimination because Title VII already prohibits such conduct. However, in an appeal from Lowrey's first suit, the Fifth Circuit held that "Title IX affords a right of action for retaliation against employees of federally funded educational institutions." *Lowrey I*, 117 F.3d 242, 249 (5th Cir. 1997) (emphasis added). The *Lowrey I* court examined Department of Education regulations promulgated under Title IX and concluded that they implied a cause of action for retaliation. . . .[62]

While the *Lowrey I* court held that Title IX implies a retaliation claim, the court did not address what substantive legal standards apply to such a claim. Tarleton contends that this court should apply the same rules that courts use for Title VII retaliation claims. After carefully reviewing *Lowrey I* and the treatment of Title IX retaliation claims by other courts, the court generally agrees with Tarleton.

The *Lowrey I* court stated that courts should interpret the antiretaliation provisions of Title IX and 34 C.F.R. §100.7(e) in accordance with the antiretaliation provisions of Title VII and the Age Discrimination in Employment Act (ADEA), 29 U.S.C. §623(e) (1994). . . . Several other circuit and district courts have applied Title VII's burden-shifting scheme and prima facie case requirements to the Title IX retaliation claims before them. [Citations omitted.] The court concludes that Lowrey's Title IX retaliation claim is best analyzed under the standard *Burdine-McDonnell Douglas* burden-shifting scheme for employment discrimination claims. Absent direct evidence of retaliaton, Lowrey has the initial burden of establishing a prima facie case of retaliation in violation of Title IX. If she meets this burden Tarleton may rebut her prima facie case by articulating legitimate, nondiscriminatory reasons for its conduct. If Tarleton meets its burden, the inference of unlawful retaliation dissolves and Lowrey must establish that Tarleton's proffered reasons are pretexts for unlawful behavior. [Citations omitted.]

Tarleton argues that in a Title IX retaliation case the court should require the same three elements of a prima facie case that are required for Title VII retaliation claims. While that test provides a helpful guide for establishing a prima

---

62. 34 C.F.R. §100.7(e) (1997), states:

Intimidatory or retaliatory acts prohibited. No recipient or other person shall intimidate, threaten, coerce, or discriminate against any individual for the purpose of interfering with any right or privilege secured by section 601 of the Act or this part, or because he has made a complaint, testified, assisted, or participated in any manner in any investigation, proceeding or hearing under this part. . . .

facie case under Title IX, the court must modify it to comply with *Lowrey I* and to conform to the specific activities governed by Title IX.

Because a Title IX retaliation claim only covers conduct protected by Title IX, a plaintiff may only recover under Title IX when the defendant retaliated against her "solely as a consequence of complaints alleging noncompliance with the substantive provisions of Title IX." [Citation omitted.] Therefore Lowrey must first establish as part of her prima facie case that she engaged in activity protected by Title IX, not Title VII.

A Title IX retaliation claim is not limited to actions by an employer against an employee. If Title IX retaliation claims were so limited, students who are not employed by an educational institution would have no protection under Title IX against retaliation by their school. Title IX protects "any individual" who complains about or helps investigate alleged violations of Title IX. [Citations omitted.] In addition, while Title VII protects against employment discrimination, Title IX prohibits gender discrimination in educational programs. [Citation omitted.] *Lakoski v. James*, 66 F.3d 751, 753 (5th Cir. 1995). Retaliation claims brought under Title IX protect against a broad array of retaliatory conduct unrelated to employment.

With these distinctions in mind, the court concludes that in order to establish a prima facie case of retaliation under Title IX Lowrey must show that:

(1) she engaged in activities protected by Title IX;
(2) Tarleton took adverse action against her; and
(3) a causal connection exists between her protected activities and Tarleton's adverse action.

2.   Analysis

(a)   Prima Facie Case

Tarleton argues that Lowrey cannot establish a prima facie case of retaliation because

(1) its actions do not constitute an ultimate employment decision; . . .
(2) Lowrey could not articulate any discriminatory actions against her at her deposition; . . . and
(3) there was no causal connection between Tarleton's failure to promote her and her activities protected by Title IX. . . .

Because Tarleton does not deny that Lowrey engaged in activities protected by Title IX, the court's evaluation of Tarleton's arguments must focus on the second and third elements of Lowrey's prima facie case.

(1)   Adverse Action

Tarleton proceeds under the mistaken assumption that Title IX only protects against adverse employment actions that constitute ultimate employment decisions. As explained above, Title IX is not limited to employment decisions; it protects against a broader range of retaliatory conduct.

Lowrey alleges that after she spoke out on Title IX issues Tarleton:

(1) did not promote her to Athletics Director;
(2) limited her authority as Women's Athletics Coordinator;

(3) increased her duties as Women's Athletics Coordinator without a commensurate increase in compensation;
(4) unjustifiably reprimanded her;
(5) isolated and harassed her in the workplace;
(6) withdrew staff support for her;
(7) withdrew support for the women's basketball team; and
(8) demoted her from the position of Women's Athletics Coordinator.

Lowrey fails to explain or support with . . . evidence many of these allegations. She does not explain how Tarleton limited her authority, increased her duties, or isolated and harassed her. Her complaints regarding withdrawn support for her and her team focus on personality conflicts and personal behavior, which are not the type of adverse actions protected by Title IX.

Tarleton admits that it did not promote Lowrey to Athletics Director, and the court has already concluded that Lowrey's alleged demotion was an adverse action. The record also reflects that Lowrey received a reprimand in the fall of 1994 as a result of a secondary violation of NCAA recruiting regulations. Lowrey argues and has submitted evidence that this disciplinary action was more severe than appropriate under the circumstances and was an act of retaliation against her. The court therefore concludes that Lowrey has satisfied the adverse action element of her prima facie case as to three allegedly retaliatory acts:

(1) Tarleton's failure to promote her to Athletics Director;
(2) her demotion from the position of Women's Athletics Coordinator; and
(3) Tarleton's reprimand of Lowery.

(2) Causal Connection

Lowrey never explains or offers evidence showing how her Title IX activities led to the reprimand she received after the recruiting violation. Although Lowrey attempts to show a causal connection between Tarleton's failure to promote her to Athletics Director, she fails to submit sufficient evidence to raise an issue of fact.

In January of 1993 President McCabe appointed Lowrey to the newly formed Special Task Force to Study Gender Equity. In February of 1993 Lowrey sent a letter to McCabe complaining of continuing gender-equity problems in the Athletics Department. McCabe responded by a February 16, 1993 memorandum, copying Dr. Koy Floyd. Because McCabe sent a copy of his memorandum to Dr. Floyd, a jury could infer that McCabe had also communicated Lowrey's gender-equity complaints to Dr. Floyd. Dr. Floyd was a member of the committee charged with recommending the new Athletics Director. Lowrey thus raises the question whether Dr. Floyd was biased against her because of her advocacy of gender equity issues when the committee met to recommend the new Athletics Director.

This is the only admissible evidence offered by Lowrey that any of the committee members failed to recommend her for Athletics Director because of her gender-equity complaints. . . .

Aside from her allegations regarding Dr. Floyd, who was only one of the four members of the selection committee, Lowrey offers no other admissible evidence that the committee was biased against her, let alone that such bias resulted from her Title IX activities. Lowrey presents no evidence that Dr. Floyd carried his alleged bias into the selection process or that he persuaded the other members of the committee not to recommend her for Athletics Director. The court concludes that Lowrey has failed to establish a causal link between her protected Title IX conduct and Tarleton's failure to promote her to Athletics Director.

Lowrey does offer evidence raising an issue of fact as to the causal link between her Title IX conduct and her demotion. On October 26, 1994, Reisman sent a memorandum to President McCabe recommending Lowrey's reassignment. In this memorandum Reisman complained that "Ms. Lowrey has taken her concerns, complaints, and issues directly to others on campus outside the Athletics Department since the beginning, effectively undermining any viable working relationship we might have had." McCabe acted on Reisman's recommendation and demoted Lowrey. There is thus some evidence that Reisman based his demotion recommendation in part on his displeasure with Lowrey's Title IX conduct.

In summary, Tarleton does not deny that Lowrey engaged in conduct protected by Title IV, and Lowrey has established issues of fact as to whether Tarleton took adverse action against her in the form of her demotion, her reprimand, and Tarleton's failure to promote her to Athletics Director. However, Lowrey has only offered evidence of a causal link between her protected Title IX conduct and her demotion. Lowrey has therefore established a prima facie case only as to her demotion.

(b)   Tarleton's Reasons for Its Action

Under *Burdine* and *McDonnell Douglas*, the burden shifts to Tarleton to articulate legitimate, nondiscriminatory reasons for Lowrey's demotion. Because Tarleton has not attempted to do so the court will deny summary judgment on Lowrey's Title IX retaliatory demotion claim. The court will grant summary judgment as to the remainder of Lowrey's Title IX retaliation claim.[80] . . .

NOTES AND QUESTIONS

1. *Private Right of Action for Retaliation Under Title IX.* A threshold issue is whether there is an implied private right of action under Title IX for retaliation on behalf of employees of educational institutions who raise concerns regarding compliance with the substantive provisions of Title IX. In *Jackson v. Birmingham Board of Education*, 544 U.S. 167 (2005), in a 5-4 decision, the Supreme Court resolved a split in the circuits when it held that Title

---

80. Tarleton has articulated legitimate, nondiscriminatory reasons for its decision not to promote Lowrey to Athletics Director. Tarleton lists the following reasons why McCabe decided to promote Reisman to Athletics Director instead of Lowrey:

(1)   the selection committee recommended Reisman;
(2)   Reisman had prior administrative experience as Assistant Athletics Director at Tarleton;
(3)   Reisman was familiar with different levels of intercollegiate athletics;
(4)   Reisman had coached at six different universities, including Tarleton, as well as at the high school level;
(5)   Reisman showed fundraising potential; and
(6)   Reisman had "cogently and compellingly" articulated an attractive vision for Tarleton athletics.

IX's private right of action encompasses retaliation against an employee who complains about gender-based discrimination. With the retirement of Justice O'Connor, who cast the deciding vote for the majority, it is not clear whether this issue will be decided the same way if it is raised before the Supreme Court in the future.

2. *Retaliation Under Title VII.* Denying the defendant's motion for summary judgment on the plaintiff's retaliation claim under Title VII, the *Lowrey* court states that a demotion should be treated the same as a promotion for Title VII purposes. What else must the plaintiff prove to establish a retaliation claim under Title VII? What proof will be sufficient to prove causality in a retaliation claim?

3. *Retaliation Under Title IX.* How does a Title IX retaliation claim differ, as a matter of legal doctrine, from a Title VII retaliation claim? Why does the *Lowrey* court refuse to require that retaliation claims be limited to employee claims against an employer? If a student prevails in a claim under Title IX, what relief may the student be awarded?

In *Bryant v. Gardner*, 587 F. Supp. 2d 951 (E.D. Ill. 2008), a coach brought a civil action under Title IX against his high school's principal and the Chicago Board of Education alleging his termination as head coach of the men's basketball team was a result of retaliation against him for complaining about unequal treatment of male and female athletes at his high school. He asserted that female players were allowed to participate in open gym, while male players were prohibited from doing so. The defendants moved for summary judgment, which the court denied, holding that a reasonable jury might find that the board's reasons for terminating the coach were merely a pretext designed to cover a retaliatory motive.

Fresno State University has been involved in litigation related to gender discrimination for much of the past decade. First, Diane Milutinovich, an athletics administrator, was dismissed from her position after she complained about inequities in the men's and women's athletics programs. Then the women's volleyball coach, Lindy Vivas, and women's basketball coach, Stacy Johnson-Klein, were fired after questioning administrators and complaining about inequities in facilities, staffing, and employment between the men's and women's athletics programs. Fresno State settled with Milutinovich for $3.5 million. Juries in separate trials found that the university intentionally discriminated against the coaches and awarded $5.85 million to Vivas and $19.1 million to Johnson-Klein.

PROBLEM 10-6

Mark Smith is a basketball player at a small Division II highly regarded private school that offers limited athletic scholarships that substantially cover both tuition and room and board. Upon observing what he believes to be a Title IX violation, Mark mentioned, in passing, the situation to his ethics professor, who reports the violation without Mark's knowledge. The professor's report, however, makes it clear that Mark was the source of the information on which the professor based his complaint.

The athletic director was clearly angered by the disclosure and initially offered vehement denials, although he eventually acknowledged the problem and allocated revenues to deal with the inequities disclosed by the professor. Shortly after the professor's disclosure, Mark was called into the head coach's office and informed that he will no longer be on scholarship because of recent cutbacks in funding.

Mark was one of five scholarship players (three will be graduating, and one is a returning all-conference player who will retain his scholarship). Mark was heavily recruited the prior year as a freshman, and he started in 17 of the 25 games played. Mark has also learned that the coach is planning on using two of the three scholarships lost through graduation to fund recruiting for the entering class. Without the scholarship, Mark is compelled to leave school and return to a less expensive public junior college. He will lose a full semester of 16 credits in the transfer, and will have to work full-time to pay his tuition and room and board at the junior college, which means that it will take him at least two more years to graduate than would have been necessary had he been able to keep his scholarship.

Mark has asked whether he has legal recourse against the university and whether you are willing to represent him in such a matter. What advice do you give Mark?

CHAPTER
11

Health, Safety, and Risk Management
Issues in Sports

A.   INTRODUCTION

This chapter illustrates the wide range of health and safety issues, and the corresponding need for careful risk management, that arise in a variety of sports-related contexts. Initially we will explore how common law tort principles are used to allocate the risks of injury and establish liability rules for injuries occurring while observing or participating in sporting events. The materials demonstrate judicial recognition that the unique characteristics and features of athletic competition may require modification of general tort principles to further various policy objectives. Also, courts have uniquely applied criminal law principles to determine what injury-causing conduct constitutes criminally culpable behavior between participants in sporting events. In addition to tort and criminal law principles, state and federal statutes (e.g., workers' compensation and disability antidiscrimination statutes) are increasingly being used to regulate relationships among sports organizations, clubs, and teams and their respective athletes that present health and safety issues. Examples include the means of compensating professional athletes for injuries and the participation rights of athletes who potentially pose a health risk to themselves and others.

B.   TORT AND CRIMINAL LIABILITY FOR
ATHLETICS-RELATED INJURIES

1.   *Injury to Spectators*

EDWARD C. v. CITY OF ALBUQUERQUE ET AL.

241 P.3d 1086 (N.M. 2010)

CHÁVEZ, Justice.

 . . . The question we must answer is what duty do owner/occupants of commercial baseball stadiums have to protect spectators from projectiles leaving the field of play. The district court applied the most limited duty, which is followed in a minority of jurisdictions, commonly referred to as the "baseball rule." The district court held that the duty was limited to providing screening for the area of the field behind home plate for as many spectators as may reasonably be expected to desire such protection. Because Isotopes stadium has such screening, the district court granted summary judgment to Defendants.

On appeal, the Court of Appeals reversed summary judgment regarding the City and the Isotopes "on the ground that, under the particular circumstances alleged, there are issues of material fact precluding summary judgment" and rejected application of a limited-duty baseball rule, holding instead that these Defendants owed a duty to exercise ordinary care. *Crespin v. Albuquerque Baseball Club*, LLC, 2009-NMCA-105, ¶¶ 1, 13, 147 N.M. 62, 216 P.3d 827. We granted certiorari to decide whether New Mexico should recognize a limited duty for owner/occupants of commercial baseball stadiums.

Considering the nature of the sport of baseball, which involves spectator participation and a desire to catch balls that leave the field of play, contrary to the Court of Appeals majority opinion, we believe that a limited-duty rule, albeit not the one argued for by Defendants, is warranted by sound policy considerations. Accordingly, we hold that an owner/occupant of a commercial baseball stadium owes a duty that is symmetrical to the duty of the spectator. The spectator must exercise ordinary care to protect himself or herself from the inherent risk of being hit by a projectile that leaves the field of play and the owner/occupant must exercise ordinary care not to increase that inherent risk.

In this case, it is alleged that the injured child was not in an area dedicated solely to viewing the game, but was in the picnic area with tables positioned perpendicular to the field of play. This type of area can be described as a multipurpose area. It is alleged that, without warning, batting practice commenced when the child was hit by a baseball that left the field of play. Given the scope of duty that we define today and Plaintiffs' allegations, we conclude that, on the record before us, Defendants did not make a prima facie showing entitling them to summary judgment.

I. BACKGROUND

Plaintiffs and their four-year-old son, Emilio, two-year-old daughter, Rachel, and ten-year-old daughter, Cassandra, were attending a Little League party at Isotopes stadium. The City owns the stadium, which is leased by the Isotopes. Plaintiffs were in the stadium's picnic area, located beyond the left field wall in fair ball territory. They "had just sat down with [their] hot dogs and drinks" and had "just begun to eat [their] meals, when without a warning from anyone at the ball park a baseball struck Emilio in the head." During pregame batting practice, New Orleans Zephyrs player Dave Matranga batted a ball out of the park into the picnic area, striking Emilio "in the upper right portion of his head fracturing his skull." The picnic tables in the left field stands are arranged in alignment with the left field foul line, so that seated individuals are not directly facing the field of play, but face perpendicular to the action. Isotopes stadium has a screen or protective netting between home plate and the seats behind home plate, but has no screen or protective netting between home plate and the seats beyond the left field wall. . . .

II. A LIMITED DUTY FOR OWNER/OCCUPANTS OF BASEBALL STADIUMS IS APPROPRIATE

What duty should owner/occupants of a baseball stadium in New Mexico have to protect spectators from projectiles that leave the field of play? The question of the existence and scope of a defendant's duty of care is a legal question that depends on the nature of the sport or activity in question, the parties' general relationship to the activity, and public policy considerations. . . .

"As a general rule, an individual has no duty to protect another from harm." Grover v. Stechel, 2002–NMCA–049, ¶ 11, 132 N.M. 140, 45 P.3d 80. Certain relationships, such as a possessor of land and a visitor, however, give rise to such a duty. *Id.* The special relationship between Defendants, as owners and occupants of Isotopes stadium, and Plaintiffs, as visitors, places Defendants' duty within the first category. Indeed, Defendants do not dispute that a duty is owed; they simply argue that the scope of that duty should be limited.

New Mexico generally applies a "single standard of reasonable care under the circumstances" to landowners or occupants. *Ford v. Bd. of Cnty. Comm'rs*, 118 N.M. 134, 138, 879 P.2d 766, 770 (1994) (abolishing the distinction between invitees and licensees but not trespassers, because trespassers have "no basis for claiming extended protection" and such "would place an unfair burden on a landowner who has no reason to expect a trespasser's presence" (internal quotation marks and citation omitted)). In *Ford*, we articulated the standard of reasonable care as follows:

> A landowner or occupier of premises must act as a reasonable man in maintaining his property in a reasonably safe condition in view of all the circumstances, including the likelihood of injury to another, the seriousness of the injury, and the burden of avoiding the risk. This duty of care shall extend to all persons, other than trespassers, who enter property with the defendant's consent, express or implied.

Id. at 139, 879 P.2d at 771. Accordingly, our jury instructions provide that "[a]n [owner] [occupant] owes a visitor the duty to use ordinary care to keep the premises safe for use by the visitor[, whether or not a dangerous condition is obvious]." UJI 13-1309 NMRA. UJI 13-1603 NMRA provides guidance on what constitutes "ordinary care."

> "Ordinary care" is that care which a reasonably prudent person would use in the conduct of the person's own affairs. What constitutes "ordinary care" varies with the nature of what is being done.
>
> As the risk of danger that should reasonably be foreseen increases, the amount of care required also increases. In deciding whether ordinary care has been used, the conduct in question must be considered in the light of all the surrounding circumstances.

Id.

The Court of Appeals determined that ordinary care was the applicable standard because "Emilio and his injury were [ ]foreseeable," and "[c]onsequently, all Defendants owed Emilio a duty to exercise ordinary care for his safety." *Crespin*, 2009-NMCA-105, ¶ 13, 147 N.M. 62, 216 P.3d 827. Foreseeability, however, is but one factor to consider when determining duty and not the principal question. See Restatement (Third) of Torts: Liability for Physical and Emotional

Harm § 7 cmt. j (2010) (disapproving the use of foreseeability to limit liability in preference for "articulat[ing] polic[ies] or principle[s] . . . to facilitate more transparent explanations of the reasons for a no-duty [or limited-duty] ruling and to protect the traditional function of the jury as factfinder"). Instead, "duty is a policy question that is answered by reference to legal precedent, statutes, and other principles of law." *Herrera*, 2003-NMSC-018, ¶ 7, 134 N.M. 43, 73 P.3d 181 (internal quotation marks and citation omitted).

In considering the policy implications of adopting the baseball rule, the Court of Appeals determined "that there is no compelling reason to immunize the owners/occupiers of baseball stadiums" because "[c]omparative negligence principles allow the fact finder to take into account the risks that spectators voluntarily accept when they attend baseball games as well as the ability of stadium owners to guard against unreasonable risks that are not essential to the game itself." *Crespin*, 2009-NMCA-105, ¶ 23, 147 N.M. 62, 216 P.3d 827. . . .

To determine whether New Mexico's duty of ordinary care for owners/occupants is appropriate in the context of commercial baseball, we will review baseball spectator injury cases from other jurisdictions for comparison to our owner/occupant duty framework. In doing so, we look for instances where courts have imposed a duty other than the duty to exercise ordinary care that are supported by sound policy consistent with New Mexico's pure comparative fault system and a general interest in promoting safety, welfare, and fairness.

III. The History and Development of a Baseball Rule

[Eds. After reviewing baseball spectator cases, the court concluded that initially jurisdictions adopted the baseball rule premised on the doctrines of assumption of the risk and contributory negligence. The court found that "in its most limited form, the baseball rule held:

> that where a proprietor of a ball park furnishes screening for the area of the field behind home plate where the danger of being struck by a ball is the greatest and that screening is of sufficient extent to provide adequate protection for as many spectators as may reasonably be expected to desire such seating in the course of an ordinary game, the proprietor fulfills the duty of care imposed by law and, therefore, cannot be liable in negligence.

Akins v. Glens Falls City Sch. Dist., 53 N.Y.2d 325, 441 N.Y.S.2d 644, 424 N.E.2d 531, 534 (1981)."

Based on its survey of baseball spectator cases the court concluded that while the *Akins* baseball rule arguably once represented a majority approach across jurisdictions to baseball spectator injury claims, a wide variation in the formulation of the baseball rule now exists, making the *Akins* rule the minority approach. It noted that some jurisdictions impose duties on stadium owners greater than those pronounced in *Akins*, yet less onerous than a general duty of ordinary care.

The court attributed the shift to a move away from the absolute defenses of contributory negligence and assumption of risk, which functioned as complete bars to plaintiff recovery, to comparative fault tort systems. Aside from shifts in tort law, advances in the game and the business of baseball have also been significant factors contributing to court modification of the traditional baseball rule. It concluded that the common theme among contemporary cases modifying the traditional baseball rule is that spectators injured by baseballs are generally allowed to advance their claim when the injury is the result of some circumstance, design, or conduct neither necessary nor inherent in the game. Quoting the New Jersey Supreme Court in *Masionave v. Newark Bears Prof'l Baseball Club, Inc.*, 881 A.2d 700 (N.J. 2005), the court stated, "It would be unfair to hold owners and operators [of baseball stadiums] liable for injuries to spectators in the stands when the potential danger of fly balls is an inherent, expected, and even desired part of the baseball fan's experience." Accordingly, the court applied the Akins baseball rule only within the stands—areas "dedicated solely to viewing the game" (*Id.* at 707), where fly balls are inherent, expected, and even desired. "In contrast, multi-purpose areas, such as concourses and playground areas, are outside the scope of the rule" (*Id.* at 707) and are subject to "a duty of reasonable care" (*Id.* at 709). In these multipurpose areas, "[t]he validity of the baseball rule diminishes" because "[f]ans foreseeably and understandably let down their guard when they are in other areas of the stadium" where the fan "is no longer trying to catch foul balls or even necessarily watching the game" (*Id.* at 708), and so fly balls are neither expected nor desired.]

. . . From these seminal and contemporary baseball spectator injury cases, it is clear that the baseball rule, rigid as it may be for injuries arising from necessary and inherent aspects of the game, historically has not been applied to preclude recovery for spectators injured in extraordinary circumstances, where conduct or situations—even stadium design flaws—leading to injury were beyond the norm. Therefore, when a stadium owner or occupant has done something to increase the risks beyond those necessary or inherent to the game, or to impede a fan's ability to protect himself or herself, the courts have generally, and we believe correctly, allowed claims to proceed for a jury to determine whether the duty was breached.

After reviewing the history of baseball spectator injury cases and the rationale and policy choices motivating those decisions, we believe that commercial baseball stadium owners/occupants owe a duty to their fans that is justifiably limited given the unique nature of their relationship, as well as the policy concerns implicated by this relationship. Accordingly, New Mexico's traditional common-law framework for land owners and occupants that would otherwise prescribe a standard duty of ordinary care is inapposite in the limited circumstance of spectator injuries resulting from the play of commercial baseball. At the same time, we reject the baseball rule pronounced in Akins because of its extreme and unyielding results. Instead, we modify the duty owed by commercial baseball stadium owners/occupants.

We hold, therefore, that an owner/occupant of a commercial baseball stadium owes a duty that is symmetrical to the duty of the spectator. Spectators must exercise ordinary care to protect themselves from the inherent risk of being hit by a projectile that leaves the field of play and the owner/occupant must exercise ordinary care not to increase that inherent risk. This approach recognizes the impossibility of playing the sport of baseball without projectiles leaving the field of play. This approach also balances the competing interests of spectators who want full protection by requiring screening behind home plate consistent with the *Akins* approach and allowing other spectators to participate in the game by catching souvenirs that leave the field of play. In addition, it balances the practical interest of watching a sport that encourages players to strike a ball beyond the field of play in fair ball territory to score runs with the safety and entertainment interests of the spectators in catching such balls. As long as the owner/occupant exercises ordinary care not to increase the inherent risk of being hit by a projectile leaving the field, he or she need not be concerned about adverse social and economic impacts on the citizens of New Mexico. While not of paramount concern, this approach will bring New Mexico in line with the vast majority of jurisdictions that have considered the issue. . . .

IV.   Defendants Did Not Make a Prima Facie Case Entitling Them to Summary Judgment

. . . Here, it was insufficient for Defendants' prima facie case to simply rely on an affidavit that established their compliance with the baseball rule we have rejected. To make their prima facie case, Defendants must establish that there is not a genuine issue of material fact and that they are entitled to a judgment as a matter of law, based on the limited duty we announce today. We therefore remand this matter to the district court for proceedings consistent with this Opinion.

V.   Conclusion

The Court of Appeals rejection of a limited-duty rule is reversed. We adopt a limited-duty rule that applies to owner/occupants of a commercial baseball facility. Under the duty we adopt, an owner/occupant of a commercial baseball stadium owes a duty that is symmetrical to the duty of the spectator. Spectators must exercise ordinary care to protect themselves from the inherent risk of being hit by a projectile that leaves the field of play and the owner/occupant must exercise ordinary care not to increase that inherent risk. Defendants did not make a prima facie case for their entitlement to a summary judgment under the limited duty we announce today, and therefore this matter is remanded to the district court for further proceedings consistent with this Opinion.

IT IS SO ORDERED.

NOTES AND QUESTIONS

1. *General Duty of Reasonable Care to Spectators.* Liability is imposed on a sports facility operator for spectator injury only if there is breach of a legal duty of care.

   Courts have rejected attempts to hold facility operators strictly liable for spectator injuries by refusing to characterize a sporting event such as a baseball game as an ultrahazardous activity, or considering the sale of a ticket to be the sale of a product subject to strict products liability. *Romeo v. Pittsburgh Assocs.*, 787 A.2d 1027 (Pa. Super. Ct. 2001). Sports event spectators generally are characterized as invitees, meaning they are invited to enter a venue to view a game or event (usually as a paying customer), and "the owner of a [sports] facility has a duty of reasonable care under the circumstances to invitees." *Allred v. Capital Area Soccer League, Inc.*, 669 S.E.2d 777, 779 (N.C.

App. 2008). This duty requires a facility owner or operator to maintain the premises and equipment therein in a reasonably safe condition to prevent spectator injury from normal use of the facility. If this duty is breached and causes harm to a spectator, there is potential liability for negligence. See, e.g., *Pryor v. Iberia Parish Sch. Bd.*, 42 So. 3d 1015, 1021 (La. App. 2010) (rejecting argument that the defendant should be absolved of liability where the danger to the plaintiff was "open and noxious" [defective bleachers], but the defect was found to present an unreasonable harm); *Gray v. Louisiana Downs*, 585 So. 2d 1238 (La. Ct. App. 1991) (racetrack owner/operator liable for patron's fall caused by failure to reasonably inspect for and remove discarded concessions, packing, and other debris); *Rockwell v. Hillcrest Country Club, Inc.*, 181 N.W.2d 290 (Mich. App. 1970) (negligent failure to warn golf tournament spectators of bridge's maximum capacity or restrict number of persons on it).

A facility operator or club also may be liable for failing to use reasonable care in regulating crowd control and fan conduct during sporting events, although it should be noted that the doctrine of sovereign immunity may preclude a negligence suit against a public entity for inadequate crowd control or policing of spectator conduct. See, e.g., *Eneman v. Richter*, 577 N.W.2d 386, 1998 WL 50414 (Wis. App. 1998).

Some courts have held that injury caused by fellow spectators while pursuing a ball that goes into the stands as a souvenir is not an inherent risk of attending and observing a game. *Hayden v. University of Notre Dame*, 716 N.E.2d 603 (Ind. App. 1999); *Telega v. Security Bureau, Inc.*, 719 A.2d 372 (Pa. Sup. Ct. 1998). Ruling that a university has a legal duty to protect spectators against a foreseeable risk of such harm, the *Hayden* court explained:

> We find that the totality of the circumstances establishes that Notre Dame should have foreseen that injury would likely result from the actions of a third party in lunging for the football after it landed in the seating area. As a result, it owed a duty to Letitia Hayden to protect her from such injury. The Haydens were seated in Notre Dame's stadium to watch a football game. Notre Dame well understands and benefits from the enthusiasm of the fans of its football team. It is just such enthusiasm that drives some spectators to attempt to retrieve a football to keep as a souvenir. There was evidence that there were many prior incidents of people being jostled or injured by efforts of fans to retrieve the ball. Letitia Hayden testified that she and her husband had attended Notre Dame football games for many years, and that she witnessed footballs land in the seating area around her many times. On numerous occasions, she saw people jump to get the ball. She testified that she witnessed another woman injured a number of years earlier when people in the crowd attempted to retrieve a football, and that she was knocked off her seat earlier in the game by crowd members attempting to retrieve the ball prior to the incident in which she was injured.

716 N.E.2d at 606. However, in *Telega*, which involved similar facts, the dissenting judge observed: "[t]he risk faced in the case at bar was quite common and customary to the football game and reasonably foreseeable based on past experience. Appellants assumed the risk of being injured by displaced fans pursuing a souvenir football." 719 A.2d at 378. With which judicial view do you agree?

2. *Limited Duty Rule.* The duty of a facility owner or operator to exercise reasonable care to protect invitees does not extend to protect spectators attending sporting events against risks inherent to a particular sport. As it relates to the liability of a stadium owner, player, or team to an injured spectator, the majority of courts have adopted what is frequently referred to as the "limited duty" rule. Pursuant to this rule, "there is no legal duty to protect or warn spectators about the 'common, frequent, and expected' inherent risks of observing a sporting event such as being struck by flying objects that go into the stands." *Jones v. Three Rivers Mgmt. Corp.*, 394 A.2d 546, 551 (Pa. 1978).

A rationale frequently articulated in support of the limited duty rule is that spectators assume injury-causing risks that are an inherent part of the activity in question. Another rationale rests on the protection of consumer preference. Proponents of this view argue that not imposing a duty on facility owners for risks inherent in the game promotes allowing owners to construct facilities that enhance consumer choice. Consumers may elect to sit in protected seats or find seats in unprotected areas where their view may be unobstructed and they can become more intimately involved in the particular game.

What policy considerations led the New Mexico Supreme Court in *Edward C.* to reject the limited liability rule known as the "baseball rule" and to adopt a different limited duty rule? For a discussion of the *Edward C.* case, see Christopher McNair, Edward C. v. City of Albuquerque*: The New Mexico Supreme Court Balks on the Baseball Rule*, 41 N.M. L. Rev. 539 (2011).

Although facility operators and teams generally are not liable for spectator injuries resulting from on-field play, they have a legal duty not to increase the inherent risks of injury from watching a game or athletic event. In *Lowe v. California League of Professional Baseball*, 65 Cal. Rptr. 2d 105 (Cal. App. 1997), the court recognized the existence of a legal duty not to increase the inherent risks to which spectators are regularly exposed and which they knowingly and voluntarily assume. While sitting in his assigned seat, the plaintiff was facing forward and watching a baseball game when the team mascot, a seven-foot-tall caricature of a dinosaur, suddenly and without warning began touching him from behind with a tail protruding from his costume. As plaintiff turned to see what was touching him, he was struck in the face by a foul ball and suffered serious injury. The court found that the presence of a team mascot is not an integral part of the game of baseball. It held that the mascot's antics in hitting plaintiff with his tail, while the game was being played, created a triable issue of fact whether the club increased the inherent risks of watching a baseball game by distracting plaintiff and preventing him from seeing and protecting himself from injury by a batted ball. See also *Gil de Rebollo v. Miami Heat Assns., Inc.*, 137 F.3d 56 (1st Cir. 1998) (club liable for mascot's negligent antics during timeout entertainment routine that caused injury to spectator); but see *Harting v. Dayton Dragons Prof. Baseball Club*, 870 N.E.2d 766 (Ohio App. 2007) (spectator assumed risk of injury from foul ball by watching mascot perform rather than game).

Is *Lowe* consistent with cases holding there is no legal duty to ensure that vendors or other patrons do not obscure the view of the spectators? *Clapman v. City of New York*, 468 N.E.2d 697 (N.Y. 1984); *Nemarnik v. L.A. Kings Hockey Club, L.P.*, 127 Cal. Rptr. 2d 10, 15 (Cal. App. 2002). How would you advise club management to protect against liability for the conduct of its mascot? What should a code of conduct for the team mascot require and prohibit?

Courts have also addressed whether the limited duty rule applies to pregame activities and injuries to spectators that occur off the field of play. In *Allred v. Capital Area Soccer League, Inc.*, 669 S.E.2d 777, 781 (N.C. App. 2008), the court stated "principles of assumption of the risk apply not only to being struck during the course of a game, but also to preliminary and warm-up activities."

In *Pickel v. Springfield Stallions, Inc.*, 926 N.E.2d 877, 1075 (Ill. App. 2010), an Illinois appellate court ruled:

> We concede that football players, like basketball players, commonly run out of bounds and that anyone standing on or near the sidelines, with nothing between them and the football players but thin air, should reasonably perceive the danger of getting hit. We cannot legitimately take judicial notice, however, that in arena football games, football players tumble over walls and into spectators with great frequency, the way basketball players run out of bounds and collide with spectators sitting out in the open, at court level, with no barrier between them and the players. In other words, defendants' equation of standing on the sidelines with standing behind a wall is problematic. It is unclear that, in indoor football, spectators watching from behind a wall get hit by football players with such frequency as to warrant the conclusion that these player-spectator collisions are inherent in the sport, or in the very nature of football, and that defendants therefore owe the spectators no duty to take reasonable precautions to protect them against such collisions.

3. *Evolving Common Law Duty of Care.* In contrast to baseball, courts initially refused to hold that spectators assumed the risk of being hit by hockey pucks that flew into the stands. *Morris v. Cleveland Hockey Club, Inc.*, 98 N.E.2d 49 (Ohio Ct. App. 1951); *Thurman v. Ice Palace*, 97 P.2d 999, 1001 (Cal. App. 1939) ("It is not common knowledge that pucks used in ice hockey game are liable to be batted into the section occupied by the spectators"). However, now "it is undisputed that ice hockey spectators face a known risk of being hit by a flying puck," and a facility operator has no legal duty to eliminate this inherent risk. *Nemarnik v. L.A. Kings Hockey Club, L.P.*, 127 Cal. Rptr. 2d 10, 15 (Cal. App. 2002). See also *Hurst v. East Coast Hockey League*, 637 S.E.2d 560, 562 (S.C. 2006) ("risk of being injured by a foul ball at a baseball game and the risk of being injured by a flying puck at a hockey game are similar risks"). See also Brett Celedonia, *Flying Objects: Arena Liability for Fan Injuries in Hockey and Other Sports*, 15 Sports Law. J. 115, 119 (2008) (discussing the evolution of the standard of care involving injuries to spectators observing hockey matches).

On March 16, 2002, a 13-year-old girl was struck in the head by a deflected hockey puck while watching a National Hockey League (NHL) game between the Columbus Blue Jackets and the Calgary Flames in Columbus, Ohio. Two days later, she died from a blood clot caused when her head violently snapped back when hit by the puck, the first spectator to be fatally injured in the NHL's 85-year history. Phil Taylor, *Death of a Fan*, Sports Illustrated, April 1, 2002 at 58. Her parents received a $1.2 million settlement from the NHL and the arena in which the game was played. Following a common practice in European hockey rinks, the NHL subsequently required its member clubs to install protective netting approximately 30 feet in height and 120 feet in width behind the goals in their playing facilities.

Was the NHL legally required to take this action? In *Nemarnik, supra,* the court observed "if we were to impose a duty upon defendants to eliminate all risk of injury from flying pucks, we would force defendants to do either of two things: provide a floor to ceiling protective screen around the rink, thereby reducing the quality of everyone's view; or increase the price of tickets to cover the increased liability costs . . . we find neither alternative to be acceptable." 127 Cal. Rptr. 2d at 17. What other factors may have motivated the NHL's decision? In responding, consider *Allred v. Capital Area Soccer League, Inc.,* 669 S.E.2d 777 (N.C. App. Ct. 2008) (plaintiff's lack of actual or constructive knowledge of risks associated with attending a soccer match may remove assumption of risk as bar to cognizable negligence claim).

Even if the facility operator or club is not liable for a spectator's initial injury from being struck by a flying ball or puck, *Fish v. Los Angeles Dodgers Baseball Club,* 128 Cal. Rptr. 807 (Cal. App. 1976), illustrates potential liability for negligent medical care rendered to an injured spectator. In *Fish,* the court held that a club may be liable for negligently failing to ascertain the nature and extent of a spectator's symptoms after being struck by a foul ball and consequent need for immediate hospitalization. Expert medical testimony established that the spectator might have survived if his injuries had been properly diagnosed and treated.

4. *Establishing Legal Duty of Care by Statute.* Some jurisdictions limit sports facility owner and operator liability by statute. For example, the Illinois Baseball Facility Liability Act requires a spectator injured by a baseball or bat to prove that the screen or backstop behind which he or she was sitting is defective (in a manner other than width or height) because of the facility owner or operator's negligence or that his or her injury was caused by willful or wanton conduct. 745 Ill. Comp. Stat. §38/10 (West 2008). The Illinois Hockey Facility Liability Act creates a similar immunity for spectator injuries caused by being hit by a hockey stick or puck. 745 Ill. Comp. Stat. §52/10 (West 2008). Rejecting a challenge to the constitutionality of the Baseball Facility Liability Act, the Illinois court of appeals stated:

> We believe the sport of baseball does have unique characteristics that would reasonably prompt a legislature to enact limited liability legislation. . . . Foul balls traveling at high speeds are common at baseball games. The speed and frequency of foul balls distinguish baseball from most other spectator sports. In this respect, basketball and football spectators, for example, are not similarly situated.

Jasper v. Chicago Nat'l League Ball Club, Inc., 722 N.E.2d 731, 735 (Ill. App. 1999).

In *Sciarrotta v. Global Spectrum,* 944 A.2d 630 (N.J. 2008), a plaintiff, who was seated in an unscreened area of a stadium, suffered injuries after being struck by a hockey puck that caromed into the stands during the warm-up period. Relying in part on the New Jersey Baseball Spectator Safety Act of 2006, the court held that the limited duty rule applies to all on-the-field activities including practice and warm-up periods before a game has begun and "does not encompass a separate duty to warn of the peril of objects leaving the field of play." *Id.* at 632. According to the court, "[I]f a sports venue owner or operator complies with the limited duty rule, it has satisfied its duty of care to patrons in the stands and, in those circumstances, no action in negligence will lie for the peril of objects leaving the field of play." *Id.* See C. Peter Goplerud III and Nicolas P. Terry, *Allocation of Risk Between Hockey Fans and Facilities: Tort Liability After the Puck Drops*, 38 Tulsa L. Rev. 445, 471-480 (2003) (discussing sport projectile legislation). Other states adopting sport-specific legislation include Arizona, Ariz. Rev. Stat. §12-554 (West 2003), Colorado, Colo. Rev. Stat. §13-21-120 (2002), and Utah, Utah Code Ann. §78B-4-508 (LexisNexis 2008).

5. *Liability Waivers.* Should a printed warning on an admission ticket impact the viability of the limited duty rule? In *Edward C.*, assume the back of the plaintiffs' ticket contained a printed warning stating, "The holder of this ticket assumes all risk and danger incidental to the game of baseball . . . including specifically (but not exclusively) the danger of being injured by thrown bats, thrown or batted balls . . . and agrees that the participating clubs or their officials, agents and players are not liable for injury related from such causes." Should the court legally recognize and enforce a contractual modification of the defendants' tort duty? See C. Peter Goplerud III and Nicolas P. Terry, *Allocation of Risk Between Hockey Fans and Facilities: Tort Liability After the Puck Drops*, 38 Tulsa L. Rev. 445, 458-459 (2003) (noting that in invalidating disclaimers in cases involving spectators, courts have resorted to theories, such as unconscionability and public policy, and have interpreted disclaimers not to apply to willful and wanton conduct).

PROBLEM 11-1

Bobby Baron has been baseball's reigning home run king over the last five years. At a game played two nights ago, Baron hit a home run that matched the most home runs ever hit by a major league ballplayer. Over the past week, attendance at baseball games in which Baron's team, the Quest, played has been tremendous given the anticipation that Baron might match and surpass the record.

The Quest home game on July 15 was a sellout. In the fourth inning, Baron hit his record-shattering home run into the right outfield stands. Jimmy Hands attempted to catch the ball, but it hit him in the face and fell under his seat. As a result of being struck by the ball, Hands required extensive surgery to reconstruct his nose and repair an injury to his eye. To make matters worse for Hands, after the ball fell under his seat, another fan, Harry, violently pushed Hands out of his seat in order to retrieve the ball. As a result of being pushed, Hands suffered a broken arm and lacerations. In the ensuing melee caused by attempts to retrieve the ball, several other fans were injured.

Harry and several other fans who were involved in efforts to retrieve the ball consumed an inordinate amount of alcohol that they had purchased during the game from vendors at Quest Ballpark. The owners of Quest Ballpark had become increasingly concerned with improper fan behavior that stemmed, in part, from the consumption of alcohol. Last year, Quest Ballpark instituted a policy that forbids the sale of alcohol after the seventh inning, but placed no strict limits on the amount of alcohol consumed prior to the seventh inning.

Discuss who, if anyone, may be potentially liable for the injuries suffered by Hands and the other fans. What additional facts might aid you in completing your analysis?

2. *Injury to Athletes*

a.   **Co-participant Liability**

i.   *Tort Liability*

HACKBART v. CINCINNATI BENGALS, INC. (HACKBART I)
435 F. Supp. 352 (D. Colo. 1977)

MATSCH, Judge

The case arises as a result of an incident which occurred in the course of a professional football game played between the Denver Broncos and the Cincinnati Bengals, in Denver, Colorado, on September 16, 1973. . . .

The incident which gave rise to this lawsuit occurred near the end of the first half of the game at a time when the Denver team was leading by a score of 21 to 3. Dale Hackbart was playing a free safety position on the Broncos' defensive team and Charles Clark was playing fullback on the Bengals' offensive team. The Cincinnati team attempted a forward pass play during which Charles Clark ran into a corner of the north end zone as a prospective receiver. That took him into an area which was the defensive responsibility of Mr. Hackbart. The thrown pass was intercepted near the goal line by a Denver linebacker who then began to run the ball upfield. The interception reversed the offensive and defensive roles of the two teams. As a result of an attempt to block Charles Clark in the end zone, Dale Hackbart fell to the ground. He then turned and, with one knee on the ground and the other leg extended, watched the play continue upfield. Acting out of anger and frustration, but without a specific intent to injure, Charles Clark stepped forward and struck a blow with his right forearm to the back of the kneeling plaintiff's head with sufficient force to cause both players to fall forward to the ground. Both players arose and, without comment, went to their respective teams along the sidelines. They both returned to play during the second half of the game.

Because no official observed it, no foul was called on the disputed play and Dale Hackbart made no report of this incident to his coaches or to anyone else during the game. Mr. Hackbart experienced pain and soreness to the extent that he was unable to play golf as he had planned on the day after the game, he did not seek any medical attention and, although he continued to feel pain, he played on specialty team assignments for the Denver Broncos in games against the Chicago Bears and the San Francisco Forty-Niners on successive Sundays. The Denver Broncos then released Mr. Hackbart on waivers and he was not claimed by any other team. After losing his employment, Mr. Hackbart sought medical assistance, at which time it was discovered that he had a neck injury. When that information was given to the Denver Broncos Football Club, Mr. Hackbart received his full payment for the 1973 season pursuant to an injury clause in his contract.

The claim of the plaintiff in this case must be considered in the context of football as a commercial enterprise. The National Football League (NFL) is an organization formed for the purpose of promoting and fostering the business of its members, the owners of professional football "clubs" with franchises to operate in designated cities. . . .

A collective bargaining contract between that association and the National Football League Player Relations Association, as bargaining agent for the member clubs, was in effect during 1973. . . . There is no provision for disputes between players of different teams. . . .

Football is a contest for territory. The objective of the offensive team is to move the ball through the defending team's area and across the vertical plane of the goal line. The defensive players seek to prevent that movement with their bodies. Each attempted movement involves collisions between the bodies of offensive and defensive players with considerable force and with differing areas of contact. The most obvious characteristic of the game is that all of the players engage in violent physical behavior.

The rules of play which govern the method and style by which the NFL teams compete include limitations on the manner in which players may strike or otherwise physically contact opposing players. During 1973, the rules were enforced by six officials on the playing field. The primary sanction for a violation was territorial with the amounts of yardage lost being dependent upon the particular infraction. Players were also subject to expulsion from the game and to monetary penalties imposed by the league commissioner.

The written rules are difficult to understand and, because of the speed and violence of the game, their application is often a matter of subjective evaluation of the circumstances. Officials differ with each other in their rulings. The players are not specifically instructed in the interpretation of the rules, and they acquire their working knowledge of them only from the actual experience of enforcement by the game officials during contests.

Many violations of the rules do occur during each game. Ordinarily each team receives several yardage penalties, but many fouls go undetected or undeclared by the officials.

Disabling injuries are also common occurrences in each contest. Hospitalization and surgery are frequently required for repairs. Protective clothing is worn by all players, but it is often inadequate to prevent bodily damage. Professional football players are conditioned to "play with pain" and they are expected to perform even though they are hurt. The standard player contract imposes an obligation to play when the club physician determines that an injured player has the requisite physical ability.

The violence of professional football is carefully orchestrated. Both offensive and defensive players must be extremely aggressive in their actions and they must play with a reckless abandonment of self-protective instincts. The coaches make studied and deliberate efforts to build the emotional levels of their players to what some call a "controlled rage."

The large and noisy crowds in attendance at the games contribute to the emotional levels of the players. Quick changes in the fortunes of the teams, the shock of violent collisions and the intensity of the competition make behavioral control extremely difficult, and it is not uncommon for players to "flare up" and begin fighting. The record made at this trial indicates that such incidents as that which gave rise to this action are not so unusual as to be unexpected in any NFL game.

The end product of all of the organization and effort involved in the professional football industry is an exhibition of highly developed individual skills in coordinated team competition for the benefit of large numbers of paying spectators, together with radio and television audiences. It is appropriate to infer that while some of those persons are attracted by the individual skills and precision performances of the teams, the appeal to others is the spectacle of savagery.

While a theory of intentional misconduct is barred by the applicable statute of limitations, the plaintiff contends that Charles Clark's foul was so far outside of the rules of play and accepted practices of professional football that it should be characterized as reckless misconduct. . . .

Alternatively, the plaintiff claims that his injury was at least the result of a negligent act by the defendant. The difference in these contentions is but a difference in degree. Both theories are dependent upon a definition of a duty to the plaintiff and an objective standard of conduct based upon the hypothetical reasonably prudent person. Thus, the question is what would a reasonably prudent professional football player be expected to do under the circumstances confronting Charles Clark in this incident?

Two coaches testified at the trial of this case. Paul Brown has had 40 years of experience at all levels of organized football, with 20 years of coaching professional football. Both Mr. Brown and Mr. Ralston emphasized that the coaching and instructing of professional football players did not include any training with respect to a responsibility or even any regard for the safety of opposing players. They both said that aggressiveness was the primary attribute which they sought in the selection of players. Both emphasized the importance of emotional preparation of the teams. Mr. Brown said that flare-up fighting often occurred, even in practice sessions of his teams.

It is wholly incongruous to talk about a professional football player's duty of care for the safety of opposing players when he has been trained and motivated to be heedless of injury to himself. The character of NFL competition negates any notion that the playing conduct can be circumscribed by any standard of reasonableness.

Both theories of liability are also subject to the recognized defenses of consent and assumption of the risk. Here the question is what would a professional football player in the plaintiff's circumstances reasonably expect to encounter in a professional contest?

All of the witnesses with playing or coaching experience in the NFL agreed that players are urged to avoid penalties. The emphasis, however, is on the unfavorable effects of the loss of yardage, not the safety of the players. It is undisputed that no game is without penalties and that players frequently lose control in surges of emotion.

The conflict in the testimony is the difference in the witnesses' opinions as to whether Mr. Clark's act of striking the plaintiff on the back of the head in reaction to anger and frustration can be considered as "a part of the game." Several former players denounced this incident and said that Mr. Clark's conduct could not be considered customary or acceptable.

It is noteworthy that while this incident was clearly shown on the Denver Broncos' defensive game films, which were routinely reviewed by the defensive players and coaching staff, none of them made it a matter of special attention or concern.

Upon all of the evidence, my finding is that the level of violence and the frequency of emotional outbursts in NFL football games are such that Dale

Hackbart must have recognized and accepted the risk that he would be injured by such an act as that committed by the defendant Clark on September 16, 1973. Accordingly, the plaintiff must be held to have assumed the risk of such an occurrence. Therefore, even if the defendant breached a duty which he owed to the plaintiff, there can be no recovery because of assumption of the risk. . . . *assumption of risk*

While the foregoing findings of fact and conclusions of law are determinative of the claim made by Dale Hackbart against Charles Clark and his employer, this case raises the larger question of whether playing field action in the business of professional football should become a subject for the business of the courts. . . . *Next ①*

To this time professional football has been a self-regulated industry. The only protection which NFL contract players have beyond self-defense and real or threatened retaliation is that which is provided by the league rules and sanctions. It may well be true that what has been provided is inadequate and that these young athletes have been exploited and subjected to risks which should be unacceptable in our social order. . . .

Football has been presumed to be lawful and, indeed, professional football has received the implicit approval of government because these contests take place in arenas owned by local governments and the revenues are subject to taxation. Like coal mining and railroading, professional football is hazardous to the health and welfare of those who are employed as players.

What is the interest of the larger community in limiting the violence of professional football? That question concerns not only the protection of the participants, but also the effects of such violence on those who observe it. Can the courts answer this question? I think not. An ordinary citizen is entitled to protection according to the usages of the society in which he lives, and in the context of common community standards there can be no question but that Mr. Clark's blow here would generate civil liability. It would involve a criminal sanction if the requisite intent were present. The difference here is that this blow was delivered on the field of play during the course of action in a regularly scheduled professional football game. . . . *cannot compare football to other civil claims*

There is no discernible code of conduct for NFL players. The dictionary definition of a sportsman is one who abides by the rules of a contest and accepts victory or defeat graciously. Webster's Third New International Dictionary, p. 2206 (1971). That is not the prevalent attitude in professional football. There are no Athenian virtues in this form of athletics. The NFL has substituted the morality of the battlefield for that of the playing field, and the "restraints of civilization" have been left on the sidelines.

Mr. Justice Holmes' simple statement of the function of tort law ["The business of the law of torts is to fix the dividing line between those cases in which a man is liable for harm which he has done, and those in which he has not." Justice O.W. Holmes, The Common Law (1881)] and the evidentiary record now before me clearly reveal the density of the thicket in which the courts would become entangled if they undertook the task of allocation of fault in professional football games. The NFL rules of play are so legalistic in their statement and so difficult of application because of the speed and violence of the play that the differences between violations which could fairly be called deliberate, reckless or outrageous and those which are "fair play" would be so small and subjective as to be incapable of articulation. The question of causation would be extremely difficult in view of the frequency of forceful collisions. The volume of such litigation would be enormous and it is reasonable to expect that the court systems of the many states in which NFL games are played would develop differing and conflicting principles of law. It is highly unlikely that the NFL could continue to produce anything like the present games under such multiple systems of overview by judges and juries. If there is to be any governmental involvement in this industry, it is a matter which can be best considered by the legislative branch.

My conclusion that the civil courts cannot be expected to control the violence in professional football is limited by the facts of the case before me. I have considered only a claim for an injury resulting from a blow, without weaponry, delivered emotionally without a specific intent to injure, in the course of regular play in a league-approved game involving adult, contract players. Football as a commercial enterprise is something quite different from athletics as an extension of the academic experience and what I have said here may have no applicability in other areas of physical competition. . . .

HACKBART v. CINCINNATI BENGALS, INC. (HACKBART II)

601 F.2d 516 (10th Cir. 1979)

DOYLE, Circuit Judge.

The question in this case is whether in a regular season professional football game an injury which is inflicted by one professional football player on an opposing player can give rise to liability in tort where the injury was inflicted by the intentional striking of a blow during the game. . . .

The evidence at the trial uniformly supported the proposition that the intentional striking of a player in the head from the rear is not an accepted part of either the playing rules or the general customs of the game of professional football. . . .

[T]he district court's assumption was that Clark had inflicted an intentional blow which would ordinarily generate civil liability and which might bring about a criminal sanction as well, but that since it had occurred in the course of a football game, it should not be subject to the restraints of the law; that if it were it would place unreasonable impediments and restraints on the activity. The judge also pointed out that courts are ill-suited to decide the different social questions and to administer conflicts on what is much like a battlefield where the restraints of civilization have been left on the sidelines. . . .

Plaintiff, of course, maintains that tort law applicable to the injury in this case applies on the football field as well as in other places. On the other hand, plaintiff does not rely on the theory of negligence being applicable. This is in recognition of the fact that subjecting another to unreasonable risk of harm, the essence of negligence, is inherent in the game of football, for admittedly it is violent. . . .

[T]here are no principles of law which allow a court to rule out certain tortious conduct by reason of general roughness of the game or difficulty of administering it.

Indeed, the evidence shows that there are rules of the game which prohibit the intentional striking of blows. Thus, Article 1, Item 1, Subsection C, provides that: All players are prohibited from striking on the head, face or neck with the heel, back or side of the hand, wrist, forearm, elbow or clasped hands.

Thus the very conduct which was present here is expressly prohibited by the rule which is quoted above.

The general customs of football do not approve the intentional punching or striking of others. That this is prohibited was supported by the testimony of all of the witnesses. They testified that the intentional striking of a player in the face or from the rear is prohibited by the playing rules as well as the general customs of the game. Punching or hitting with the arms is prohibited. Undoubtedly these restraints are intended to establish reasonable boundaries so that one football player cannot intentionally inflict a serious injury on another. Therefore, the notion is not correct that all reason has been abandoned, whereby the only possible remedy for the person who has been the victim of an unlawful blow is retaliation. . . .

The Restatement of Torts Second, § 500, distinguishes between reckless and negligent misconduct. Reckless misconduct differs from negligence, according to the authors, in that negligence consists of mere inadvertence, lack of skillfulness or failure to take precautions; reckless misconduct, on the other hand, involves a choice or adoption of a course of action either with knowledge of the danger or with knowledge of facts which would disclose this danger to a reasonable man. Recklessness also differs in that it consists of intentionally doing an act with knowledge not only that it contains a risk of harm to others as does negligence, but that it actually involves a risk substantially greater in magnitude than is necessary in the case of negligence. The authors explain the difference, therefore, in the degree of risk by saying that the difference is so significant as to amount to a difference in kind.

Subsection (f) also distinguishes between reckless misconduct and intentional wrongdoing. To be reckless the *act* must have been intended by the actor. At the same time, the actor does not intend to cause the harm which results from it. It is enough that he realized, or from the facts should have realized, that there was a strong probability that harm would result even though he may hope or expect that this conduct will prove harmless. Nevertheless, existence of probability is different from substantial certainty which is an ingredient of intent to cause the harm which results from the act.

Therefore, recklessness exists where a person knows that the act is harmful but fails to realize that it will produce the extreme harm which it did produce. It is in this respect that recklessness and intentional conduct differ in degree.

In the case at bar the defendant Clark admittedly acted impulsively and in the heat of anger, and even though it could be said from the admitted facts that he intended the act, it could also be said that he did not intend to inflict serious injury which resulted from the blow which he struck.

In ruling that recklessness is the appropriate standard and that assault and battery is not the exclusive one, we are saying that these two liability concepts are not necessarily opposed one to the other. Rather, recklessness under § 500 of the Restatement might be regarded, for the purpose of analysis at least, a lesser included act.

Assault and battery, having originated in a common law writ, is narrower than recklessness in its scope. In essence, two definitions enter into it. The assault is an attempt coupled with the present ability to commit a violent harm against another. Battery is the unprivileged or unlawful touching of another. Assault and battery then call for an intent, as does recklessness. But in recklessness the intent is to do the act, but without an intent to cause the particular harm. It is enough if the actor knows that there is a strong probability that harm will result. Thus, the definition fits perfectly the fact situation here. Surely, then, no reason exists to compel appellant to employ the assault and battery standard which does not comfortably apply fully in preference to the standard which meets this fact situation. . . .

The cause is reversed and remanded for a new trial. . . .

[handwritten margin note: This should be decided by a court. (Torts)]

SHIN v. AHN
165 P.3d 581 (Cal. 2007)

CORRIGAN, J.

In *Knight v. Jewett* (1992) 3 Cal.4th 296, 11 Cal.Rptr.2d 2, 834 P.2d 696 (*Knight*), we considered the duty of care that should govern the liability of sports participants. We recognized that careless conduct by co-participants is an inherent risk in many sports, and that holding participants liable for resulting injuries would discourage vigorous competition. Accordingly, those involved in a sporting activity do not have a duty to reduce the risk of harm that is inherent in the sport itself. They do, however, have a duty not to increase that inherent risk. Thus, sports participants have a limited duty of care to their co-participants, breached only if they intentionally injure them or "engage[ ] in conduct that is so reckless as to be totally outside the range of the ordinary activity involved in the sport." (*Knight*, at p. 320, 11 Cal.Rptr.2d 2, 834 P.2d 696, fn. omitted.) This application of the *primary assumption of risk doctrine* recognizes that by choosing to participate, individuals assume that level of risk inherent in the sport.

[handwritten margin note: (R)]

This case represents the next generation of our *Knight* jurisprudence. *Knight* involved touch football. We expressly left open the question whether the primary assumption of risk doctrine should apply to noncontact sports, such as golf. We address that question here. We hold that the primary assumption of risk doctrine does apply to golf and that being struck by a carelessly hit ball is an inherent risk of the sport. As we explain, whether defendant breached the limited duty of care he owed other golfers by engaging in conduct that was "so reckless as to be totally outside the range of the ordinary activity involved in [golf]" depends on resolution of disputed material facts. Thus, defendant's summary judgment motion was properly denied. . . .

[handwritten margin notes: (I) (H) language]

I.   FACTUAL AND PROCEDURAL BACKGROUND

Plaintiff and defendant were playing golf with Jeffrey Frost at the Rancho Park Golf Course in Los Angeles. Defendant, the first of the threesome to complete the 12th hole, went to the 13th tee box. Plaintiff and Frost then finished putting and followed him. Frost took the cart path to the 13th tee box, which placed him perpendicular to, or slightly behind, defendant and to his right. Plaintiff took a shortcut, which placed him in front of defendant and to his left. Plaintiff stopped there to get a bottle of water out of his golf bag and to check his cell phone for messages. He did so even though he knew (1) that he was in front of the tee box, (2) that defendant was preparing to tee off, and (3) that he should stand behind a player who was teeing off. Defendant inadvertently "pulled" his tee shot to the left, hitting plaintiff in the temple. When struck, plaintiff was 25 to 35 feet from defendant, at a 40- to 45-degree angle from the intended path of the ball. Plaintiff claims his injuries were "disabling, serious, and permanent. . . ."

In his declaration, plaintiff's expert stated that golf etiquette requires that a player ensure that no one is in a position to be struck when he or she hits the ball. (See USGA, The Rules of Golf, *supra*, § 1, Etiquette, p. 1.) If defendant knew plaintiff was in jeopardy, he should have shouted a warning before teeing off. (*Ibid.*)

When plaintiff sued for negligence, defendant sought summary judgment, relying on the primary assumption of risk doctrine. The trial court initially agreed that the doctrine applied, found no triable issue of material fact, and granted summary judgment. However, the trial court later reversed itself, concluding that triable issues remained.

The Court of Appeal affirmed, holding that the primary assumption of risk doctrine did not apply. . . . The Court of Appeal applied general negligence principles and concluded that defendant breached a general duty of care owed to a member of his own playing group by failing to ascertain where he was before teeing off.

We reject the duty analysis of the Court of Appeal and conclude that the primary assumption of risk doctrine regulates the duty a golfer owes both to playing partners and to other golfers on the course. Defendant's summary judgment motion was, however, properly denied. Material questions of fact remain bearing on whether defendant breached his limited duty of care to plaintiff by engaging in conduct that was so reckless as to be totally outside the range of the ordinary activity involved in golf.

II.   DISCUSSION

Generally, one owes a duty of ordinary care not to cause an unreasonable risk of harm to others. The existence of a duty is not an immutable fact of nature, but rather an expression of policy considerations providing legal protection. Thus, the existence and scope of a defendant's duty is a question for the court's resolution. When a sports participant is injured, the considerations of policy and duty necessarily become intertwined with the question of whether the injured person can be said to have assumed the risk.

California's abandonment of the doctrine of contributory negligence in favor of comparative negligence led this court to revisit the assumption of risk doctrine in *Knight, supra*, 3 Cal.4th 296, 11 Cal.Rptr.2d 2, 834 P.2d 696.

A.   *KNIGHT* AND ITS PROGENY IN THIS COURT

In *Knight, supra*, the plurality noted that there are two types of assumption of risk: primary and secondary. Under the primary assumption of risk doctrine, the defendant owes *no duty* to protect a plaintiff from particular harms arising from ordinary, or simple negligence. In a sports context, the doctrine bars liability because the plaintiff is said to have assumed the particular risks inherent in a sport by choosing to participate. Thus, "a court need not ask what risks a particular plaintiff subjectively knew of and chose to encounter, but instead must evaluate the fundamental nature of the sport and the defendant's role in or relationship to that sport in orto determine whether the defendant owes a duty to protect a plaintiff from the particular risk of harm." ([*Knight, supra*, 3 Cal.4th] at 313, 315–317.) . . .

The *Knight* court used baseball as an example. In baseball, a batter is not supposed to carelessly throw the bat after getting a hit and starting to run to first base. However, the primary assumption of risk doctrine recognizes that vigorous bat deployment is an integral part of the sport and a risk players assume when they choose to participate. Especially in the heat of competition, and in an effort to get to first base quickly, a batter may be careless in freeing himself or herself from the bat's encumbrance. Thus, under the doctrine, a batter does not have a duty to another player to avoid carelessly throwing the bat after getting a hit.

In *Knight, supra,* 3 Cal.4th 296, 11 Cal.Rptr.2d 2, 834 P.2d 696, we stressed the chilling effect that would flow from imposing liability on touch football players for ordinary careless conduct. "[E]ven when a participant's conduct violates a rule of the game and may subject the violator to internal sanctions prescribed by the sport itself, imposition of legal liability for such conduct might well alter fundamentally the nature of the sport by deterring participants from vigorously engaging in activity. . . ." (*Id.* at pp. 318-319, 11 Cal.Rptr.2d 2, 834 P.2d 696, italics omitted.) Accordingly, we concluded that coparticipants' limited duty of care is to refrain from intentionally injuring one another or engaging in conduct that is "so reckless as to be totally outside the range of the ordinary activity involved in the sport." (*Id.* at p. 320, 11 Cal.Rptr.2d 2, 834 P.2d 696, fn. omitted.)

A majority of this court has since extended *Knight's* application of the primary assumption of risk doctrine to other sports. (citations omitted). . . .

Cheong v. Antablin, 946 P.2d 817 (1997) involved skiing. One skier sued another for injuries he suffered when the other skier turned and unintentionally ran into him. We concluded that, "under the applicable common law principles, a skier owes a duty to fellow skiers not to injure them intentionally or to act recklessly, but a skier may not sue another for simple negligence. . . ." Because there was no evidence that the defendant acted recklessly or intentionally injured the plaintiff, we concluded that the defendant's motion for summary judgment was properly granted. . . .

Avila v. Citrus Community College Dist., 38 Cal. 4th 148, 41 Cal.Rptr.3d 299, 131 P.3d 383, involved intercollegiate baseball. A pitcher on the Rio Hondo Community College team (Rio Hondo) hit a batter on the Citrus Community College team (Citrus). The next inning the Citrus pitcher allegedly retaliated by hitting a Rio Hondo batter with a "beanball." The Rio Hondo player sued the Citrus Community College District for negligence. We held the suit was barred by the primary assumption of risk doctrine. It is against the rules of baseball to intentionally throw at a batter. Nevertheless, "being intentionally thrown at is a fundamental part and inherent risk of the sport of baseball. It is not the function of tort law to police such conduct."

B.   COURT OF APPEAL CASES APPLYING *KNIGHT* TO GOLF

In *Knight, supra,* 3 Cal.4th 296, 11 Cal.Rptr.2d 2, 834 P.2d 696, we expressly left open the question whether the primary assumption of risk doctrine should be applied to sports like golf. (*Id.* at p. 320, fn. 7, 11 Cal.Rptr.2d 2, 834 P.2d 696.) . . .

D.   SISTER-STATE DECISIONS

The first court to apply the reckless disregard or intentional conduct standard to golf appears to have been the Supreme Court of Ohio in *Thompson v. McNeill* (1990) 53 Ohio St.3d 102, 559 N.E.2d 705 (*Thompson*). (*Schick v. Ferolito* (2001) 167 N.J. 7, 767 A.2d 962, 966 (*Schick*).) In *Thompson,* at page 706, the defendant "shanked" a shot. The plaintiff, a member of the defendant's foursome, was standing at a 90-degree angle to the intended path of a ball that struck her. The Ohio Supreme Court held that "only injuries caused by intentional conduct, or in some instances reckless misconduct, may give rise to a cause of action [by one golfer against another]." (*Thompson*, at p. 706.)

Applying that standard, the *Thompson* court affirmed a grant of summary judgment in the defendant's favor. "Shanking the ball is a foreseeable and not uncommon occurrence in the game of golf. The same is true of hooking, slicing, pushing, or pulling a golf shot. We would stress that '[i]t is well known that not every shot played by a golfer goes to the point where he intends it to go. If such were the case, every player would be perfect and the whole pleasure of the sport would be lost. It is common knowledge, at least among players, that many bad shots must result although every stroke is delivered with the best possible intention and without any negligence whatsoever.'" *Benjamin v. Nernberg* (1931), 102 Pa.Super. 471, 475-476, 157 A. 10, 11. (*Thompson, supra*, 559 N.E.2d at p. 709.)

In *Schick, supra*, 167 N.J. 7, 767 A.2d 962, the New Jersey Supreme Court followed *Thompson, supra*, 53 Ohio St.3d 102, 559 N.E.2d 705. In *Schick*, at page 963 the defendant hit a second tee shot, or "mulligan," striking a member of his foursome. The New Jersey Supreme Court applied the reckless or intentional misconduct standard. "We perceive no persuasive reason to apply an artificial distinction between 'contact' and 'noncontact' sports. In fact, only a minority of courts do so. [Citations.]" (*Id.* at p. 968.) The New Jersey Supreme Court went on to hold that the trial court erred in granting the defendant's motion for summary judgment because the facts would have supported a verdict of recklessness. The court pointed to "defendant's own testimony that he perceived plaintiff to be in the 'line of fire' and that he waved plaintiff off in an effort to induce plaintiff to move from his location." (*Id.* at p. 970.) Plaintiff did not move. The defendant did not wait for him to do so and hit his shot anyway. The court held, "[t]hat scenario presents a set of facts that a jury could find constitutes reckless conduct because it may reflect a conscious choice of a course of action with knowledge or reason to know that the action will create serious danger to others." (*Ibid.*) . . .

In *Yoneda v. Tom* (2006) 110 Hawai'i 367, 133 P.3d 796, the plaintiff was struck by a ball hit by a golfer in another group. The plaintiff sued the other golfer as well as the owner and operator of the golf course. The Hawaii Supreme Court concluded that the primary assumption of risk doctrine applied to define the defendant golfer's duty, relying in part on *Knight, supra*, 3 Cal.4th 296, 11 Cal. Rptr.2d 2, 834 P.2d 696. . . . Upholding a grant of summary judgment for the defendant golfer, the Hawaii Supreme Court ruled that no one could have reasonably anticipated that a person in the plaintiff's location was in danger of being struck by the defendant's shot. (*Id.* at p. 809.) . . .

E.   APPLICATION OF THE PRIMARY ASSUMPTION OF RISK DOCTRINE

The lesson to be drawn from *Knight* and its progeny, as well as the weight of authority in sister states, is that the primary assumption of risk doctrine should be applied to golf. Thus, we hold that golfers have a limited duty of care to other players, breached only if they intentionally injure them or engage in conduct that is "so reckless as to be totally outside the range of the ordinary activity involved in the sport."

The Court of Appeal relied too heavily on one of golf's rules of etiquette involving safety. Golf's first rule of etiquette provides that "[p]layers should ensure that no one is standing close by or in a position to be hit by the club, the ball or any stones, pebbles, twigs or the like when they make a *stroke* or practice swing." (USGA, The Rules of Golf, *supra*, § 1, Etiquette, p. 1.) The Court of concluded that "[t]his duty included the duty to ascertain Shin's whereabouts before hitting the ball."

Rules of etiquette govern socially acceptable behavior. The sanction for a violation of a rule of etiquette is social disapproval, not legal liability. This is true, generally, of the violation of the rules of a game. "The cases have recognized that, [in sports like football or baseball], even when a participant's conduct violates a rule of the game and may subject the violator to internal sanctions prescribed by the sport itself, imposition of legal liability for such conduct might well alter fundamentally the nature of the sport by deterring participants from vigorously engaging in activity that falls close to, but on the permissible side of, a prescribed rule." . . .

G.   DEFENDANT'S SUMMARY JUDGMENT MOTION

Here, summary judgment was properly denied because there are material questions of fact to be adjudicated.

In determining whether defendant acted recklessly, the trier of fact will have to consider both the nature of the game and the totality of circumstances surrounding the shot. In making a golf shot the player focuses on the ball, unlike other sports in which a player's focus is divided between the ball and other players. That is not to say that a golfer may ignore other players before making a shot. Ordinarily, a golfer should not make a shot without checking to see whether others are reasonably likely to be struck. Once having addressed the ball, a golfer is not required to break his or her concentration by checking the field again. Nor must a golfer conduct a headcount of the other players in the group before making a shot.

Many factors will bear on whether a golfer's conduct was reasonable, negligent, or reckless. Relevant circumstances may include the golfer's skill level; whether topographical undulations, trees, or other impediments obscure his view; what steps he took to determine whether anyone was within range; and the distance and angle between a plaintiff and defendant.

Here plaintiff testified at his deposition that he and defendant made eye contact "as I was cutting up the hill." He did not make clear, however, how far he had proceeded up the hill, how far away he was from the defendant, or whether he was stationary when the eye contact occurred. At his deposition, defendant said he looked to see if the area "directly ahead" of him was clear. It is not apparent just how broad or limited that area was. This record is simply too sparse to support a finding, as a matter of law, that defendant did, or did not, act recklessly. This will be a question the jury will ultimately resolve based on a more complete examination of the facts. We do not suggest that cases like this can never be resolved on summary judgment, only that this record is insufficient to do so. . . .

The judgment of the Court of Appeal is affirmed. The case is remanded with directions that litigation should continue under the primary assumption of risk doctrine.

NOTES AND QUESTIONS

1. *Professional Sports.* Is there a sufficient public interest in using the tort system to regulate violence in a "commercial enterprise" such as professional

football? Or do you agree with Judge Matsch's view in *Hackbart I* that "[t]he NFL has substituted the morality of the battlefield for that of the playing field, and the 'restraints of civilization' have been left on the sidelines?"

Does an internal disciplinary system administered by the sport's commissioner or governing body combined with the availability of contractual benefits and workers' compensation for injuries eliminate the need to provide tort recovery for player injuries? For professional team sports, would an arbitration process established by the collective bargaining process be a better alternative than judicial resolution? See Jeffrey M. Schalley, *Eliminate Violence from Sports Through Arbitration, Not the Civil Courts*, 8 Sports Law. J. 181, 199 (2001) (observing that CBA providing for "arbitration of injuries resulting from intentional or reckless violence . . . may result in reduced violence as players view torts as a contract violation"); Benjamin C. Thompson, *Personal Foul . . . 15 Years in Jail: Sports' Problem with Excessive Violence and the Severe Punishment Solution*, 76 UMKC L. Rev. 769, 775 (2008) (providing illustrations of excessive violence in sports).

Consistent with *Hackbart II*, courts generally require professional athletes to prove intentional or reckless conduct by a co-participant in order to recover for playing field injuries. *Turcotte v. Fell*, 502 N.E.2d 964 (N.Y. 1986); *McKichan v. St. Louis Hockey Club, L.P.*, 967 S.W.2d 209 (Mo. App. 1998); *Averill v. Luttrell*, 311 S.W.2d 812 (Tenn. App. 1957). See also Thompson, *supra*, at 774 (analyzing *MiKichan* and addressing the recklessness standard). Although courts such as *Babych v. McRae*, 567 A.2d 1269 (Conn. Super. Ct. 1989) have recognized a cause of action for negligence, there is judicial reluctance to do so.

> Manifestly a professional athlete is more aware of the dangers of the activity, and presumably more willing to accept them in exchange for a salary, than is an amateur. . . .
>
> Plaintiff does not claim that Fell intentionally or recklessly bumped him, he claims only that as a result of carelessness, Fell failed to control his mount as the horses raced for the lead and a preferred position on the track. While a participant's "consent" to join in a sporting activity is not a waiver of all rules infractions, nonetheless a professional clearly understands the usual incidents of competition resulting from carelessness, particularly those which result from the customarily accepted method of playing the sport, and accepts them. They are within the known, apparent and foreseeable dangers of the sport and not actionable and thus plaintiffs' complaint against Fell was properly dismissed.

Turcotte, 502 N.E.2d at 969-970. See Timothy Davis, *Tort Liability of Coaches for Injuries to Professional Athletes: Overcoming Policy and Doctrinal Barriers*, 76 UMKC L. Rev. 571, 579-580 (2008) (discussing liability of co-participants engaged in professional sports).

2. *Co-participant Civil Liability.* Do you agree with the *Shin* court's extension of the limited duty rule to golf? For scholarly commentary regarding this issue, see Joseph M. Hnylka, *California Drops the Ball: The Lack of a Clear Approach to Recklessness in Sport Injury Litigation*, 11 Va. Sports & Ent. L.J. 77, 87 (2011); Brian P. Harlan, *The California Supreme Court Should Take a Mulligan: How the Court Shanked by Applying the Primary Assumption of Risk Doctrine to Golf*, 29 Loy. L.A. Ent. L. Rev. 91 (2009).

Most jurisdictions permit recovery in sports injury cases between co-participants only for intentional or reckless conduct regardless of the level of competition, age or experience of the participants, or organizational structure of the sport. See, e.g., *Cole v. Boy Scouts of Am.,* 725 S.E.2d 476, 478 (S.C. 2011) (holding that a co-participant in a pick-up softball game assumed the risk of injury resulting from a collision at home plate). A minority of courts apply a negligence standard that is premised on the duty of reasonable care that one person owes to guard against foreseeable injuries to others. One of the significant differences between the application of the intentional/recklessness and negligence standards is that mere careless or rough play does not establish liability under the intentional/recklessness standard. After the Wisconsin Supreme Court in *Lestina v. West Bend Mutual Insurance Co.,* 501 N.W.2d 28, 33 (Wis. 1993), held that "the negligence standard, properly understood and applied is suitable for cases involving recreational team contact sports," the state legislature enacted a statute establishing liability "only if the participant who caused the injury acted recklessly or with intent to cause injury" in a "recreational activity that includes physical contact between persons in a sport involving amateur teams" or "professional teams in a professional league." Wisc. Stat. Ann. §895.525(4m)(a) and (b). See *Noffke v. Bakke,* 760 N.W.2d 156 (Wis. 2009) (characterizing high school cheerleading as a contact sport under Wisc. Stat. Ann. §895.525, which immunizes cheerleader from negligence liability for injury to fellow cheerleader while performing a practice stunt before a basketball game).

On May 18, 2011, in *Pfenning v. Lineman,* 947 N.E.2d 392 (Ind. 2011), the Indiana Supreme Court adopted a variation on the limited duty rule. In *Pfenning,* a minor was struck in the mouth by a golf ball while operating a beverage cart at a golf outing. The court rejected, as inconsistent with comparative fault, the rule that a co-participant in a "sporting event owes no duty of care to protect others from inherent risks" of a sport. Rather than focusing on the existence or nonexistence of a duty, the court reasoned that emphasis should be placed on whether a duty was breached. It held that:

> In negligence claims against a participant in a sports activity, if the conduct of such participant is within the range of ordinary behavior of participants in the sport, the conduct is reasonable as a matter of law and does not constitute a breach of duty.
>
> In any sports activity, however, a participant's particular conduct may exceed the ambit of such reasonableness as a matter of law if the "participant either intentionally caused injury or engaged in [reckless] conduct." (citation omitted). Such intentional or reckless infliction of injury may be found to be a breach of duty. A defendant is entitled to summary judgment when a "sports participant is within the range of ordinary behavior of participants in the sport and therefore is reasonable as a matter of law."
>
> As to the golfer's hitting an errant drive which resulted in the plaintiff's injury, such conduct is clearly within the range of ordinary behavior of golfers and thus is reasonable as a matter of law and does not establish the element of breach required for a negligence action.

Id. at 404. See also *Welch v. Young,* 950 N.E.2d 1283, 1289 (Ind. Ct. App. 2011) (discussing *Pfenning* and providing illustrations of risks that are within the realm of ordinary risks assumed by co-participants).

3. *Different Standards for Amateur and Professional Sports?* As a matter of policy, should the liability standard for co-participant injuries occurring in amateur sports be the same as for professional sports? In determining the appropriate standard, should any distinction be drawn among adult recreational or intramural sports, intercollegiate athletics, high school sports, and youth sandlot games? Why or why not? Consider whether the possibility of tort liability actually deters socially undesirable conduct or changes how a particular sport is played.

4. *Different Standards for Contact and Noncontact Sports?* Should the co-participant liability standard be the same for all sports? Or can a principled distinction be drawn between different sports based on the inherent risks of physical contact among participants or with the sport's playing equipment or other instrumentalities?

    As reflected in *Shin*, the trend is toward the abandonment of the contact versus noncontact sport distinction and toward a focus on whether the injury-causing risk is inherent to the sporting activity. In *Shin*, the court relied on an Ohio Supreme Court decision wherein the court explained:

> [T]here are different duties and risks appropriate to different sports, but the contact-non-contact distinction does not sufficiently take into account that we are dealing with a spectrum of duties and risks rather than an either-or distinction. Is golf a contact sport? Obviously, a golfer accepts the risk of coming in contact with wayward golf shots on the links, so golf is more dangerous than table tennis, for instance, but certainly not as dangerous as kickboxing. Analyzing liability for injuries inflicted in sports in terms of a continuum along which the standard of care rises as the inherent danger of the sport falls is more useful than distinguishing sports by applying a black-and-white distinction between contact and non-contact sports.

Thompson v. McNeill, 559 N.E.2d 705, 709 (Ohio 1990). See generally John J. Kircher, *Golf and Torts: An Interesting Twosome*, 12 Marq. Sports L. Rev. 347 (2001) (discussing the applicable standard of care for co-participant liability in golf).

Illinois courts historically applied an intentional or reckless conduct standard for contact sports and a negligence standard for noncontact sports. See *Zurla v. Hydel*, 681 N.E.2d 148, 152 (Ill. App. 1997). Whether the contact versus noncontact distinction will survive is doubtful after *Karas v. Strevell*, 884 N.E. 2d 122 (Ill. 2008), in which the Illinois Supreme Court ruled, "We agree and . . . conclude that, in a full contact sport such as ice hockey or tackle football, a participant breaches a duty of care to a coparticipant only if the participant intentionally injures the coparticipant or engaged in conduct 'totally outside the range of the ordinary activity involved in the sport.'" *Id.* at 134. Notwithstanding the *Karas* court's apparent affirmation of the contact/noncontact distinction in a case involving a contact sport, hockey, it is unclear whether the court will apply a negligence standard if presented, in the future, with a case involving co-participant liability in the context of a noncontact sport. The uncertainty arises from the court's endorsement of the standard of care as articulated in jurisdictions such as California, which have adopted the primary assumption of the risk standard. Indeed, the *Karas* court noted that whether couched in terms of a contact rule exception or primary assumption of the risk, courts rely on similar policies to justify adherence to an intentional/reckless standard. "Regardless of the precise wording, these standards all draw a line in a way that permits recovery for extreme misconduct during a sporting event that causes injury while at the same time foreclosing liability for conduct which, although it may amount to an infraction of the rules, is nevertheless an inherent and inevitable part of the sport." *Id.* See *Feld v. Borkowski*, 790 N.W.2d 72 (Iowa 2010) (recognizing the distinction between contact and noncontact sports but finding that a question of fact existed as to whether a batter, whose errant bat struck a player on an opposing team, acted recklessly).

5. *Relationship Between Plaintiff's Assumption of Risk and Defendant's Legal Duty of Care.* Prior to the widespread adoption of comparative fault principles, the focus was on the plaintiff's subjective awareness of the inherent risks of injury from voluntarily participating in a sporting event, which was an affirmative defense barring a negligence action. In most jurisdictions, as summarized by the *Shin* court, the focus now is on the nature of the defendant's legal duty to protect a co-participant from injury during competition, which is part of the plaintiff's *prima facie* case. The question of duty is often articulated in the guise of primary assumption of the risk.

> Primary assumption of the risk focuses not on whether the plaintiff voluntarily assumed a known risk, but on the question of duty. Did the defendant possess a duty to protect the plaintiff from the risk of harm resulting in injury. . . . If the risk causing the injury is an inherent part of the activity, the defendant owed no duty to the plaintiff, and there is no liability.

Timothy Davis, Avila v. Citrus Community College District: *Shaping the Contours of Immunity and Primary Assumption of the Risk*, 17 Marq. Sports L. Rev. 259, 270 (2006). See also *Anand v. Kapoor*, 942 N.E.2d 295 (N.Y. 2010) (in granting defendant's motion for summary judgment, the court holds that golfer's failure to warn plaintiff, a fellow golfer who was struck by an errant ball, did not unreasonably increase the inherent risk of being struck that plaintiff had assumed).

6. *Rules of the Game Violations.* Under a recklessness standard, a violation of a game rule intended to protect the health and safety of participating athletes (e.g., no touching the face mask in football) will not necessarily result in liability. As stated by the Illinois Supreme Court:

> [A] majority of courts have concluded that "rules violations are inherent and anticipated aspects of sports contests" and, thus, insufficient to establish sports liability by themselves. T. Davis, *Avila v. Citrus Community College District: Shaping the Contours of Immunity and Primary Assumption of the Risk*, 17 Marq. Sports L. Rev. 259, 274 (2006). . . . In games . . . , it is reasonable to assume that the competitive spirit of the participants will result in some rules violations and injuries. That is why there are penalty boxes, foul shots, free kicks, and yellow cards. (citations omitted).
>
> Policy reasons also justify the holding that rules violations, by themselves, are insufficient to impose liability in a contact sport: "Even when a participant's conduct violates a rule of the game and may subject the violator to internal sanctions prescribed by the sport itself, imposition of *legal liability* for such conduct might well alter fundamentally the nature of the sport by deterring participants from vigorously engaging in activity that falls close to but on the permissible side of, a prescribed rule." (Emphasis in original).

Karas, 884 N.E.2d at 133-134.

intent ?

     Consider whether any of the following conduct should give rise to tort liability:

   a. A professional boxer throws a third below-the-belt punch in a match, is disqualified by the referee, and seriously injures his opponent.
   b. An NHL player strikes an opposing player in the head with his fist during a fight and renders him unconscious. *Inherent risk.*
   c. A college hockey player breaks an opponent's nose during a fight and is given a three-game suspension for violating league rules prohibiting any fighting. *Inherent risk*

        STOP

ii.   Criminal Liability

In *People v. Fitzsimmons,* 34 N.Y.S. 1102, 1109 (1895), the court instructed the jury as follows in a case involving the prosecution of a professional boxer for a blow that killed his opponent during a sparring exhibition:

> The public has an interest in the personal safety of its citizens, and is injured where the safety of any individual is threatened, whether by himself or another. A game which involves a physical struggle may be a commendable and manly sport, or it may be an illegal contest. This depends upon whether it is a game which endangers life. Thus, in the prosecution for a death which was caused accidentally in playing the game of football, it was left to the jury to say whether the game was dangerous; for, if so, consent on the part of the players to submit to what the game had in store for them would not protect a player from prosecution.
>
> In other words, gentlemen, nine men, or whatever constitutes a team of football, cannot lawfully engage in a contention upon the green with the idea that the result may terminate in the death or serious injury of one-half of them; but, if the rules of the game and the practices of the game are reasonable, are consented to by all engaged, are not likely to induce serious injury, or to end life, if then, as a result of the game, an accident happens, it is excusable homicide.
>
> No rules or practice of any game whatever can make that lawful which is unlawful by the law of the land, and the law of the land says you shall not do that which is likely to cause the death of another.

The jury acquitted the defendant of manslaughter.

The following cases provide a modern view of criminal liability for injuries that occur on the athletic playing field. Consider whether the law has changed or remained the same since *Fitzsimmons*.

PEOPLE v. SCHACKER

670 N.Y.S.2d 308 (N.Y. Dist. Ct. 1998)

DONOHUE, Judge.

The defendant moved to dismiss the misdemeanor information in the interest of justice pursuant to CPL 170.40. . . .

The defendant is charged with Assault in the Third Degree in violation of Penal Law 120.00.1. The factual portion of the information reads as follows:

> [A]t the Superior Ice Rink . . . the defendant Robert Schacker during an ice hockey game and after a play was over and the whistle had blown, did come up

behind Andrew Morenberg who was standing near the goal net and did strike him on the back of the neck and caused him to strike his head on the crossbar of the net, causing him to sustain a concussion, headaches, blurred vision, and memory loss. Injuries had been treated at St. John's Hospital, Smithtown.

Both an X-ray and a CAT scan showed no damage. The final diagnosis was "Contusion Forehead." Thus the medical records show only minor injuries.

Since the defendant had pled "not guilty," the people are required to prove that the defendant possessed the conscious intent to cause physical injury to the complainant. The fact that the act occurred in the course of a sporting event is a defense that tends to deny that the requisite intent was present.

As Chief Judge Benjamin Cardozo said in *Murphy v. Steeplechase Amusement Co.*, 250 N.Y. 479, 482-483, 166 N.E. 173: "One who takes part in such a sport accepts the dangers that inhere in it so far as they are obvious and necessary, just as a fencer accepts the risk of a thrust by his antagonist or a spectator at a ball game the chance of contact with the ball. A different case would be here if the dangers inherent in the sport were obscure or unobserved or so serious as to justify the belief that precautions of some kind must have been taken to avert them." See DeSantis, *Assumption of Risk Doctrine Is Alive and Well*, NYLJ, Dec. 2, 1997, at 1, col. 1. Persons engaged in athletic competition are generally held to have legally assumed the risk of injuries which are known, apparent and reasonably foreseeable consequences of participation. Hockey players assume the risk of injury by voluntarily participating in a hockey game at an ice rink.

This tort rule states a policy "intended to facilitate free and vigorous participation in athletic activities." *Benitez v. New York City Board of Education*, 73 N.Y.S. 2d 650, 657, 543 N.Y.S.2d 29, 541 N.E.2d 29. This policy would be severely undermined if the usual criminal standards were applied to athletic competition, especially ice hockey. If cross checking, tripping and punching were criminal acts, the game of hockey could not continue in its present form.

The complainant does not assume the risk of reckless or intentional conduct. However, it must be recognized that athletic competition includes intentional conduct that has the appearance of criminal acts. In fact, in many sporting events, physical injuries are caused by contact with other players. However, the players are "legally deemed to have accepted personal responsibility for" the risks inherent in the nature of sport. This includes intentional acts which result in personal injury. Thus, in order to allege a criminal act which occurred in a hockey game, the factual portion of the information must allege acts that show that the intent was to inflict physical injury which was unrelated to the athletic competition. Although play may have terminated, the information herein does not show that the physical contact had no connection with the competition. Furthermore, the injuries must be so severe as to be unacceptable in normal competition, requiring a change in the nature of the game. That type of injury is not present in this case. Firstly, the physical injury resulted from hitting the net, not from direct contact with the defendant. Secondly, the hospital records do not indicate severe trauma to the complainant.

The idea that a hockey player should be prosecuted runs afoul of the policy to encourage free and fierce competition in athletic events. The People argued at the hearing that this was a non-checking hockey league. While the rules of the league may prohibit certain conduct, thereby reducing the potential injuries, nevertheless, the participant continues to assume the risk of a strenuous and competitive athletic endeavor. The normal conduct in a hockey game cannot be the standard for criminal activity under the Penal Law, nor can the Penal Law be imposed on a hockey game without running afoul of the policy of encouraging athletic competition.

For the foregoing reasons, the interest of justice requires a dismissal of this charge pursuant to CPL 170.40.

REGINA v. MCSORLEY

2000 British Columbia Provincial Ct. 0116 (Criminal Div. 2000)

KITCHEN, Judge.

This is my decision on the charge against Marty McSorley that he assaulted Donald Brashear with his hockey stick during a hockey game on February 21, 2000. . . .

Some may view the matter as a trial of the game of hockey itself. If that is the expectation, my decision will be a disappointment. My only concern is whether Marty McSorley is guilty of the specific charge alleged against him. . . .

In the context of this case, it is especially important for the public to understand how these proceedings were initiated. The question has been asked, "Why are the courts bringing these proceedings?" The answer of course is that the courts had no part in laying the charge. Judges have little or no control over intake into the justice system. Crown Counsel, in their discretion to prosecute, decide which complaints will result in criminal charges.

Mr. Hicks, in his submission, explained why the act of McSorley in striking Brashear resulted in this charge being laid. It was as follows:

> In our submission, that act is precisely why the law, the criminal law, has a place in the hockey rink. It is why the law refuses to sanction those acts as a matter of public policy. It is particularly significant when that act is carried out in the National Hockey League at the highest level of the game in circumstances that are watched by millions of people for whom the game is important, many of whom play that game at a whole variety of levels. That's why the public policy issue justifies the criminal law's involvement, and that's why these rules as to the application of the criminal law are present. Our submission is that this is precisely the kind of case, precisely the fact situation that the criminal law is intended and has a place to deal with. It is way beyond the scope of this game. It is irrelevant. It is an act that is completely irrelevant to the game that is taking place on the ice. Mr. McSorley may have felt that there was a need to deliver a message to his team that we don't quit, but you don't deliver that message by putting another player's health and safety at risk, and that is what happened in this case, we submit, and that is why it is a criminal act.

The power exercised by the Crown in proceeding with matters such as this has been endorsed many times by the courts. As an example, our present Associate Chief Justice Dohm made these comments in 1976 in *R. v. Henderson*, [1976] 4 W.W.R. 119 at 127:

> I fully realize that if too many legal restrictions are placed upon those who participate in sports where the very nature of the game precipitates bodily contact, the game will soon lose not only players but also spectators. It certainly is not my plan in any way to inhibit the interaction between players, but what is society to do when those interactions between participants lead to conduct which, if it were anywhere

but in the arena or on a playing field, would attract criminal sanctions without any delay on the part of the authorities? Surely the authorities are not to turn a blind eye while the law of the jungle prevails. Quite the contrary, where there are obvious infractions of the criminal law, the authorities are duty-bound to take whatever action is necessary to prevent a repetition of such conduct.

A related issue includes the question of whether the criminal law process should be pre-empted where discipline procedures have been taken by the hockey authorities. Again, I must emphasize that this is not an issue related to a determination of whether Mr. McSorley has committed a crime.

There are many groups that claim authority to discipline their members. Some are statutory, such as law societies and judicial councils, and some exist by virtue of private contractual arrangements such as in the case of the National Hockey League. Even where the disciplinary body is statutory, its status is often very controversial. There have been many cases before police discipline tribunals and medical licensing authorities where the public has been suspicious of the process, fearing that those involved are getting special treatment or that the truth is being concealed. In my view, there should be a heavy onus on those purporting to pre-empt the normal criminal process, particularly where it is a private organization such as a group of hockey owners. Statutory bodies must act in the public interest; businessmen have no such obligation.

Comments by judges in two previous cases reflect this. In one of the first cases involving NHL players, *R. v. Maki*, (1970) 1 C.C.C. (2d) 333 at 336, the following comments were made by the trial judge:

> Although no criminal charges have been laid in the past pertaining to athletic events in this country, I can see no reason why they could not be in the future where the circumstances warrant and the relevant authorities deem it advisable to do so. No sports league, no matter how well organized or self-policed it may be, should thereby render the players in the league immune from criminal prosecution.

And in *R. v. Watson*, (1975) 26 C.C.C. (2d) 150 at 156, the judge said:

> Hockey is a fast, vigorous, competitive game involving much body contact. Were the kind of body contact that routinely occurs in a hockey game to occur outside the playing area or on the street, it would, in most cases, constitute an assault to which the sanctions of the criminal law would apply. Patently, when one engages in a hockey game, one accepts that some assaults, which would otherwise be criminal, will occur and consents to such assaults. It is equally patent, however, that to engage in a game of hockey is not to enter a forum to which the criminal law does not extend. To hold otherwise would be to create the hockey arena a sanctuary for unbridled violence to which the law of Parliament and the Queen's justice could not apply. . . .

Obviously, the object of the game is to put the puck in the net—the opposing net. Many of the written rules of the game deal with the legitimate means by which that may be done. Many other written rules deal with the consequences that will follow if the rules are not obeyed. All of these rules are codified in the NHL Official Rules, a copy of which is an exhibit in these proceedings.

But those written rules are only part of the picture. There is also an unwritten code of conduct, agreed to by the players and officials, that is superimposed on the written rules. This code of conduct deals mainly with situations where the written rules are breached, and the code then comes into play. For example, the written rules prohibit slashing with the stick, but the unwritten code says that slashing is permissible as long as it is during play, and not to the head. Of course, when a slash is employed, and it is observed by the referee, there are consequences; a penalty is called. . . .

So I conclude there is an unwritten code of conduct agreed to by the players and the officials. This amalgam of written rules and the unwritten code leads to composite rules, such as the following. It is a legitimate game strategy to slash another player, but if done with sufficient force, and if the referee sees it, then the offender's team plays one player short for two minutes. It is a legitimate game strategy to fight another consenting player, but the offenders are kept off the ice for a period of time determined by the referee.

There is a further complication. The referees and linesmen exercise considerable discretion in assessing penalties. This exercise of discretion is seen by them as setting guidelines for the players so that the players will know what tolerance there will be for breaches of the written rules. Presumably the players are then expected to govern themselves accordingly. This requires the players to have a thorough knowledge of the written rules, a familiarity with the unwritten code, and an understanding of the guidelines the referee is signaling to the players during the game through his assessment and non-assessment of penalties. . . .

So the rules of the NHL game of hockey consist of the written rules in the rulebook, a co-existing unwritten code of conduct impliedly agreed to by the players and officials, and guidelines laid down by the officials from game to game. It is within this somewhat indefinite framework that players must play the game. . . .

[EDS. The Vancouver Canucks and the Boston Bruins were both struggling to make the play-offs. Early during the game's first period, McSorley and Brashear engaged in a fight, consisting mainly of clutching and grappling while blows were exchanged. Brashear was much more successful at this than McSorley, delivering several heavy lefts to the side and top of McSorley's head but with surprisingly little effect. The fight ended with Brashear apparently delivering a heavy body blow and wrenching McSorley to the ice surface. McSorley did react to this; it is clear he was in considerable pain at this time. He promptly came to his feet after the linesmen intervened and skated off to the penalty box, showing no adverse effects from the encounter. Brashear, for his part, skated past the Boston bench "dusting off" his hands, suggesting he had made short work of McSorley. This was obviously intended to upset the Boston players.

At the midpoint of the first period, McSorley again attempted to fight with Brashear. McSorley approached Brashear from behind and cross-checked him to the ice. As Brashear was coming to his feet, helmet off, McSorley used his glove to swat Brashear about the head several times. Brashear failed to respond to this and attempted to skate away. The referee gave McSorley three penalties for this—back-to-back two-minute minors for cross-checking and roughing and a ten-minute major for inciting. Shortly afterward, Brashear himself was penalized for interfering with the Boston goalie during play.

From the Brashear penalty in the middle of the first period until the middle of the third period, the game had settled down and play between the two teams had evened out. During the third period, Brashear was making a play to come from the corner to the front of the Boston net. A Bruin slashed Brashear to prevent this and was given a penalty. During the stoppage in play, Brashear returned to the Vancouver bench, performing what witnesses described as a

Hulk Hogan pose for the benefit of the Boston bench. Once again this was an obvious attempt to antagonize the opposing players, and it was effective. Boston complained to the referee, but no action was taken; it was determined that the Boston players had been mocking him at the same time.

With 20 seconds left in the game, which the Canucks were certain to win, McSorley was sent on to the ice by the Bruins coach to regain Boston pride by challenging Brashear to fight again. McSorley unsuccessfully tried to do so. With only three seconds left to play, McSorley, while skating up from behind him, struck Brashear in the head with his stick, bringing it around with his hands together on a horizontal plane like a baseball bat swing. As he was struck on the side of the head, Brashear's helmet was lifted out of position and his shoulder shrugged upward, an apparent reflex reaction to the blow of the stick. The blow was of significant force and caused Brashear to fall to the ice and strike his head. As he collapsed to the ice, he had a grand mal seizure before recovering consciousness. Brashear suffered a grade three concussion and could not continue with physical activity for another month.]

It is the position of the Crown that this body of evidence permits only two possibilities—that McSorley deliberately struck Brashear to the head without Brashear's consent, or that he recklessly struck him to the head, not necessarily aiming for the head directly. Recklessness in this case may be likened to willful blindness—ignoring a known risk. . . .

If the blow to the head was intentional, it is common ground that it was an assault. Brashear himself said in evidence that he did not consent to being struck in that manner. The other witnesses agreed that stick blows to the head were not permitted in either the written rules, or the unwritten code . . . players in the NHL would not accept a blow such as that as part of the game.

McSorley's evidence . . . was to the effect that he intended to slash Brashear on the shoulder to get his attention so that they would fight. Brashear, when cross-examined by Mr. Smart, agreed with the proposition that it was a deliberate blow to the head that he found objectionable. Implicit in this response was the likelihood that he would accept an accidental blow to the head, aimed elsewhere, as a risk of the game.

In addition there was a considerable body of evidence . . . in which witnesses agreed that slashes and cross-checks to various parts of the body, including the shoulders, were recognized as legitimate means of initiating fights. When they saw Brashear and McSorley on the ice together in the dying moments of the game, [referees] were both even expecting that McSorley might deliver a slash or cross-check to Brashear to start something.

If the slash was intended for the shoulder, delivered with the intention of starting a fight, my conclusion would be that it was within the common practices and norms of the game. . . .

The question is, was the slash to the shoulder worth the risk, given all of the circumstances, including what had happened previously, and the time of the game?

The Boston team had come out flat. McSorley had fought Brashear, trying to fire up his team, but it failed to inspire them. Brashear had riled the Boston bench with his hand dusting, Hulk Hogan pose, and goalie interference, but he had clearly declined subsequent opportunities to fight. At the end of the game, with about twenty seconds left, McSorley was put on the ice by his coach, Jacques Laperriere, to regain Boston pride by challenging Brashear once more. McSorley tried to lure Brashear by taking the puck himself, but Brashear turned away, clearly showing once again that he was not interested in a confrontation. There was too little time left — only seconds. McSorley had to act quickly to avoid being suspended by the league for fighting at the end of the game. Whatever he chose to do would be rushed. The most dangerous of permissible options would be to slash to the shoulder area, endangering the head. In fact, McSorley's stated target was even more indefinite — "High in the body, upper arm, shoulder area." This danger was compounded by the fact Brashear would be struck from behind, allowing no opportunity to defend himself. At that time of the game, it was likely that all of the players were letting their guards down.

Because Brashear was not interested in confrontation, only a very major slash might force him to respond, but this increased the danger of injury. The only benefit to be gained from all of this was that perhaps Boston might walk out of the building with a little more pride. The risk was not worth it. . . .

This certainly does not conclude the matter. I have only concluded that a slash aimed at the shoulder was too dangerous for the players to consent to it. . . .

I therefore come to the final issue — what did Marty McSorley intend to do? I have said that if he intended to strike Brashear in the head, he is guilty of assault.

Of course, if I have a doubt as to what his intent was, he will be acquitted on either Crown theory; the Crown must prove a culpable state of mind beyond a reasonable doubt. . . .

McSorley said that Brashear was now skating away from him and the end of the game was fast approaching. If he was to start a fight, it would have to be before the end of the game or he would be heavily penalized. He was concerned that Brashear would get away from him and, in an attempt to force Brashear to turn and face him, he slashed at his shoulder. He said it was not an unusual slash — he maintained his hands in the normal position on the stick. He knew he struck Brashear, but he did not see that it was to the head and he had no idea it had injured him. He circled around and went to Brashear, still thinking they would fight, but when he bent over Brashear, he saw that something was wrong. . . .

Based on the evidence I am left to consider, I conclude that the following occurred.

McSorley had fought Brashear and he had been briefly hurt. He was nevertheless prepared to fight him again, but Brashear frustrated his attempts to do so. Brashear taunted the Boston players and was seen to be responsible for taking the Boston goalie out of the game. This was all fairly routine for McSorley. He was credible when he said he was prepared to let things wind down at the end of the game.

Then Laperriere effectively directed him to get Brashear with about twenty seconds left. This was really too little time to fight but he felt himself pressured to do something. He found himself gliding in from centre ice toward Brashear, sizing him up for possible ways to confront him. Brashear crossed directly in front of him, presenting an easy target. Brashear was the focus of all of McSorley's and Boston's frustrations. McSorley had to do something; he might still be able to start a fight. In the words of McSorley, "It has to be an instantaneous reaction." He had an impulse to strike him in the head. His mindset, always tuned to aggression, permitted that. He slashed for the head. A child, swinging as at a Tee ball, would not miss. A housekeeper swinging a carpetbeater would not miss. An NHL player would never, ever miss. Brashear was struck as intended.

Mr. McSorley, I must find you guilty as charged.

PEOPLE v. HALL
999 P.2d 207 (Col. 2000)

BENDER, Justice.

We hold that Nathan Hall must stand trial for the crime of reckless manslaughter. While skiing on Vail mountain, Hall flew off of a knoll and collided with Allen Cobb, who was traversing the slope below Hall. Cobb sustained traumatic brain injuries and died as a result of the collision. The People charged Hall with felony reckless manslaughter. . . .

The charge of reckless manslaughter requires that a person "recklessly cause the death of another person." For his conduct to be reckless, the actor must have consciously disregarded a substantial and unjustifiable risk that death could result from his actions. We hold that, for the purpose of determining whether a person acted recklessly, a particular result does not have to be more likely than not to occur for the risk to be substantial and unjustifiable. A risk must be assessed by reviewing the particular facts of the individual case and weighing the likelihood of harm and the degree of harm that would result if it occurs. Whether an actor consciously disregarded such a risk may be inferred from circumstances such as the actor's knowledge and experience, or from what a similarly situated reasonable person would have understood about the risk under the particular circumstances.

We hold that under the particular circumstances of this case, whether Hall committed the crime of reckless manslaughter must be determined by the trier of fact. Viewed in the light most favorable to the prosecution, Hall's conduct—skiing straight down a steep and bumpy slope, back on his skis, arms out to his sides, off-balance, being thrown from mogul to mogul, out of control for a considerable distance and period of time, and at such a high speed that the force of the impact between his ski and the victim's head fractured the thickest part of the victim's skull—created a substantial and unjustifiable risk of death to another person. A reasonable person could infer that the defendant, a former ski racer trained in skier safety, consciously disregarded that risk. For the limited purposes of a preliminary hearing, the prosecution provided sufficient evidence to show probable cause that the defendant recklessly caused the victim's death. . . .

Like other activities that generally do not involve a substantial risk of death, such as driving a car or installing a heater, "skiing too fast for the conditions" is not widely considered behavior that constitutes a high degree of risk. However, we hold that the specific facts in this case support a reasonable inference that Hall created a substantial and unjustifiable risk that he would cause another's death.

Several witnesses stated that Hall was skiing very fast. Allen and the other eyewitnesses all said that Hall was travelling too fast for the conditions, at an excessive rate of speed, and that he was out of control. Allen said that Hall passed him on the slope travelling three times faster than Allen, himself an expert skier. Sandberg presented testimony that Hall was a ski racer, indicating that Hall was trained to attain and ski at much faster speeds than even skilled and experienced recreational skiers. The witnesses said that Hall was travelling straight down the slope at such high speeds that, because of his lack of control, he would not have been able to stop or avoid another person.

In addition to statements of witnesses, the nature of Cobb's injuries and other facts of the collision support the inference that Hall was skiing at an inordinately high speed when he struck Cobb. As Dr. Galloway testified, the severe injuries Cobb sustained were consistent with a person being thrown from a moving automobile during a crash. The coroner said that although he could not estimate Hall's speed from Cobb's injuries, Hall must have been travelling with "a significant amount of speed" to generate sufficient force to cause a basal skull fracture and brain injuries like Cobb's. Additionally, Hall crashed through Lemaner's skis and poles after he struck Cobb—breaking one of the poles in half—indicating a very high speed and great deal of force. Hall came to rest over eighty feet past Cobb's body, further suggesting that Hall was skiing at exceptionally high speeds. Thus, based on the testimony of the witnesses and the coroner's examination of Cobb's body, a reasonable person could conclude that Hall was skiing at very high speeds, thereby creating a risk of serious injury or death in the event of a skier-to-skier collision.

In addition to Hall's excessive speed, Hall was out of control and unable to avoid a collision with another person. All the witnesses said Hall was not traversing the slope and that he was skiing straight down the fall line. Hall was back on his skis, with his ski tips in the air and his arms out to his sides to maintain balance. Allen said that Hall was bounced around by the moguls on the slope rather than skiing in control and managing the bumps. Hall admitted to Deputy Mossness that he first saw Cobb when he was airborne and that he was unable to stop when he saw people below him just before the collision. Hence, in addition to finding that Hall was skiing at a very high rate of speed, a reasonably prudent person could have concluded that Hall was unable to anticipate or avoid a potential collision with a skier on the trail below him.

While skiing ordinarily carries a very low risk of death to other skiers, a reasonable person could have concluded that Hall's excessive speed, lack of control, and improper technique for skiing bumps significantly increased both the likelihood that a collision would occur and the extent of the injuries that might result from such a collision, including the possibility of death, in the event that a person like Cobb unwittingly crossed Hall's downhill path. McWilliam testified that he was aware of only two other deaths from skier collisions on Vail mountain in the past eleven years, but a reasonable person could have determined that Hall's conduct was precisely the type of skiing that risked this rare result.

We next ask whether a reasonable person could have concluded that Hall's creation of a substantial risk of death was unjustified. To the extent that Hall's extremely fast and unsafe skiing created a risk of death, Hall was serving no direct interest other than his own enjoyment. Although the sport often involves high speeds and even moments where a skier is temporarily out of control, a reasonable person could determine that the enjoyment of skiing does not justify skiing at the speeds and with the lack of control Hall exhibited. Thus, a reasonable person could have found that Hall's creation of a substantial risk was unjustifiable.

In addition to our conclusion that a reasonable person could have entertained the belief that Hall's conduct created a substantial and unjustifiable risk, we must ask whether Hall's conduct constituted a "gross deviation" from the standard of care that a reasonable law-abiding person (in this case, a reasonable, law-abiding, trained ski racer and resort employee) would have observed in the circumstances.

As we noted, the nature of the sport involves moments of high speeds and temporary losses of control. However, the General Assembly imposed upon a skier the duty to avoid collisions with any person or object below him. Although this statute may not form the basis of criminal liability, it establishes the minimum standard of care for uphill skiers and, for the purposes of civil negligence suits, creates a rebuttable presumption that the skier is at fault whenever he collides with skiers on the slope below him. A violation of a skier's duty in an extreme fashion, such as here, may be evidence of conduct that constitutes a "gross deviation" from the standard of care imposed by statute for civil negligence. . . .

Having determined that Hall's conduct created a substantial and unjustified risk of death that is a gross deviation from the reasonable standard of care under the circumstances, we next ask whether a reasonably prudent person could have entertained the belief that Hall consciously disregarded that risk. Hall is a trained ski racer who had been coached about skiing in control and skiing safely. Further, he was an employee of a ski area and had a great deal of skiing experience. Hall's knowledge and training could give rise to the reasonable inference that he was aware of the possibility that by skiing so fast and out of control he might collide with and kill another skier unless he regained control and slowed down.

Thus, both Hall's subjective knowledge and the awareness that a reasonable person with Hall's background would have had support the inference that Hall consciously disregarded the risk he created by acting despite his awareness of the risk.

Thus, interpreting the facts presented in the light most favorable to the prosecution, we hold that a reasonably prudent and cautious person could have entertained the belief that Hall consciously disregarded a substantial and unjustifiable risk that by skiing exceptionally fast and out of control he might collide with and kill another person on the slope.

Obviously, this opinion does not address whether Hall is ultimately guilty of any crime. Rather, we hold only that the People presented sufficient evidence to establish probable cause that Hall committed reckless manslaughter, and the court should have bound Hall's case over for trial. . . .

NOTES AND QUESTIONS

1. *Policy Considerations.* When, if ever, is it appropriate to criminally prosecute for player conduct that occurs during competitive sporting events? Can a principled factual or legal distinction be drawn between *Schacker* and *McSorley*? Should the level of competition and age or maturity level of the participants make a difference? What other factors should be considered? Will the possibility of criminal liability have the detrimental effect of chilling vigorous participation and competition in athletic activities? On the other hand, what socially desirable effects may result? See generally *State v. Guidugli*, 811 N.E.2d 567, 574-575 (2004) (stating that "given the unique social dynamics involved in sports, criminal prosecution of sports participants for conduct that occurs with the playing of the game is rare"); Jeffrey Standen, *The Manly Sports: The Problematic Use of Criminal Law to Regulate Sports Violence*, 99 J. Crim. L. & Criminology 619, 634 (2009) (discussing *Schacker* and the principles on which courts rely determining whether to apply criminal sanctions in the athletics context); Jeff Yates and William Gillespie, *The Problem of Sports Violence and the Criminal Prosecution Solution*, 12 Cornell J.L. & Pub. Pol'y 145, 168 (2002) ("Criminal prosecutions can be an effective means by which to

send the message that society will not tolerate acts of unnecessary violence by sports participants"); Charles Harary, *Aggressive Play or Criminal Assault? An In-Depth Look at Sports Violence and Criminal Liability*, 25 Colum. J.L. & Arts 197, 214 (2002) ("any sport league, whether professional, collegiate, or recreational, should defer all cases of violent conduct to the state criminal system. . . . As long as the league is the sole penal enforcer, the violence will never stop").

2. *Tort Versus Criminal Liability*. The same playing field conduct may give rise to both tort and criminal liability, although that is not necessarily the case. How do the elements and burdens of proof differ for tort and criminal liability?

Similar to tort law, physical contact resulting in even severe injury is not criminal if it is "part of the game." Consent is a defense to alleged criminal assault, and it is necessary to determine "whether the conduct of defendant constituted foreseeable behavior in the play of the game" and whether a plaintiff's injury "occurred as a by-product of the game itself." *State v. Shelley*, 929 P.2d 489, 493 (Wash. Ct. App. 1997). Courts have affirmed criminal convictions for injuries caused by intentionally thrown punches during basketball and football games. See, e.g., *Shelley*, 929 P.2d at 493 ("There is nothing in the game of basketball, or even rugby or hockey, that would permit consent as a defense to such conduct"); *State v. Floyd*, 466 N.W.2d 919 (Iowa Ct. App. 1990); *People v. Freer*, 381 N.Y.S.2d 976 (N.Y. Dist. Ct. 1976). In 2009, a Canadian high school rugby player was found guilty of manslaughter for an opponent's death, which was caused by fatal injuries resulting from the player's lifting his opponent into the air with his feet facing upward and driving him head first into the ground. The trial judge found that the "defendant intentionally applied force that was outside the rules of the game or any standard by which the game is played." See *Canadian Player Guilty of Manslaughter over Spear Tackle*, New Zealand Herald, May 29, 2009, http://www.nzherald.co.nz/world/news/article.cfm?c_id=2&objectid=10575238.

Another important case was the reckless homicide prosecution of David Stinson, the former head football coach at Pleasure Park High School in Kentucky, for the death of a player from heat stroke during an August 2008 practice. The prosecution of Stinson marked the first time a coach was criminally charged for his on-field conduct. See Zac DesAutels, *Changing the Play: Football and the Criminal Law After the Trial of Jason Stinson*, 8 Willamette Sports L.J. 29, 30 (2010). Stinson was indicted following an incident in which a player collapsed, and later died, after running a series of sprints on a hot Kentucky afternoon. *Id.* at 29. Although Stinson was acquitted on charges of reckless homicide and wanton endangerment, the case marked the first instance in which a court was forced to address the societal issues surrounding assigning criminal liability to athletic coaches.

Should the Stinson trial be viewed as establishing a credible threat of criminal liability for athletic coaches? For perspectives on this question and the societal issues at play in the Stinson trial, see DesAutels, *supra*.

Would criminal liability be appropriate under *Hackbart*'s facts?

3. People v. Hall. This case illustrates the possibility of criminal liability for engaging in dangerous conduct during recreational sports. Would you convict the defendant of reckless manslaughter under the facts in *Hall*? Why or why not?

4. *Appropriate Sentences for Criminal Convictions.* After finding Marty McSorley guilty of assaulting Donald Brashear with a weapon (a hockey stick), Judge Kitchen provided the following explanation for the sentence he imposed:

> The finding of guilt is the real consequence here; the further step of entering a conviction is not necessary. I have concluded that specific deterrence and rehabilitation are served by this. I have concluded that protection of the public is a lesser consideration here. The real concern is that such a sentence may not send the correct message to the community. It must be kept in mind that the consequences to Mr. McSorley are already considerable. He has been without income since the incident, and he has had significant expense in preparing his defence. He has had to endure embarrassing publicity, much more than would be the situation in other assault matters. He will carry the stigma of this with him for the rest of his career; even the rest of his life. If that is not enough to convince anyone that such an offence is to be avoided, there is nothing more a court can do to persuade such a person otherwise.
>
> Before I impose sentence, I have these comments. In 1979, Judge Shaw of this court dealt with the matter of several New Westminster Bruins having engaged in an attack on players of the opposing team. The beatings to the other players were cowardly and brutal. Incidentally, he also found discharges appropriate. After imposing sentence, he said this:
>
>> As a judge I am but a spectator at hockey games. Yet we are all continuing spectators and participants in the serious game of life. I say to the owners, managers and coaches, to those who guide our youngsters from the midget level, through the intermediate levels and on into the teens: "You're playing a dangerous game in advocating intimidation and violence above the basic sporting skills. You do these men, the game of hockey, and Canada itself a terrible disservice."
>
> His comments appear not to have been heeded. I have learned from that. If the game is to become less violent, it will likely only be in response to pressure brought by the fans.
>
> Mr. McSorley, you are a man of influence in the game. You were a players' representative. You have had men of high regard in the game stand behind you. You could use your influence to effect changes to the game. The written rules are not realistic. The penalties do not deter. But please — one way or the other, we need fewer penalties, not more. There is work to be done. The game deserves it.
>
> I grant you a conditional discharge for 18 months. You must keep the peace and be of good behaviour. You are bound by a condition that you will not engage in any sporting event where Donald Brashear is on the opposition.
>
> That is my sentence.

Regina v. McSorley, 2000 B.C.P.C. 0117 (Oct. 6, 2000). By comparison, consider the following sentences for criminal convictions resulting from on-field conduct:

a. In 1988 Minnesota North Star player Dino Ciccarelli was sentenced to one day in jail and fined $1,000 for striking an opposing player several times in the head with his stick during a National Hockey League game.

b. In February 2001, after being convicted of criminally negligent homicide for striking and killing a fellow skier while speeding recklessly down a ski slope with alcohol in his system, Nathan Hall was sentenced to 90 days in jail, ordered to perform 240 hours of community service, and was barred from drinking alcohol and recreational skiing during a probationary term.

c. In February 2000, Tony Limon, a Texas high school basketball player, was sentenced to five years in the state penitentiary for deliberately elbowing an opponent (who suffered a concussion and fractured nose as a result) during a game. This conduct was unrelated to any ongoing play, but no foul was called. Limon had previously pled guilty to burglary and was given four years' probation, but had no prior history of violent behavior.

d. In September 2000, a 16-year-old Illinois high school hockey player was sentenced to two years' probation, ordered not to participate in any contact sports during that time, and required to perform 120 hours of community service after entering an Alford plea (no admission of guilt but acknowledgment that sufficient evidence to convict exists) to a misdemeanor battery charge. The prosecution and sentence resulted from the player's actions as a hockey game was ending: he cross-checked an opposing player from behind, causing the opposing player to crash headfirst into the boards, which permanently paralyzed him from the chest down.

Does the punishment fit the crime in each of these cases? In these examples, what may account for the significant disparities in the sentences imposed? Is there seemingly a different standard for professional athletes as compared to amateur and recreational athletes?

PROBLEM 11-2

During his warm-up between innings, a college pitcher deliberately throws at an opposing team player standing in the on-deck circle 24 feet away from the batter's box. The player was attempting to gauge the speed and time of the pitches, but did not see the thrown ball in time to avoid it. A high-speed fastball hit him in the face, causing a broken cheekbone and orbital fracture. He now has two permanent blind spots in his left eye. The pitcher's coach told his pitchers to "brush back" any opponents attempting to time their pitches. Although admitting an effort to intimidate his opponent, the pitcher denied he was trying to hit him with the thrown ball.

Would you recommend that the pitcher be criminally prosecuted? As a juror, would you convict him? What would be an appropriate sentence?

C. LIABILITY OF EDUCATIONAL INSTITUTIONS

1. High School

a. Legal Duty of Care

A high school is not an insurer of a student-athlete's safety and is not strictly liable for his or her injuries. To recover for an injury, a high school athlete is required to prove tortious conduct on the part of a school district or its employees. Negligence is the theory traditionally relied on by student-athletes who sue their high schools for sports-related injuries. For example, in *Beckett v. Clinton Prairie School Corp.*, 504 N.E.2d 552, 553 (Ind. 1987), the court held that high school personnel have a duty to exercise ordinary and reasonable care for the safety of student-athletes under their authority. See also *Benitez v. New York City Bd. of Educ.*, 541 N.E.2d 29, 32, 543 N.Y.S.2d 29 (1989) (high school owed student-athlete voluntarily competing in interscholastic football game a duty to protect against injuries arising from unassumed, concealed, or unreasonably increased risks). Absent state law immunity from tort liability, a school may be liable for the negligent conduct of employees such as coaches, trainers, and administrative personnel under vicarious liability principles.

Notwithstanding the foregoing authority, courts increasingly have limited the range of risks for which high schools will incur tort liability to their student-athletes. This is, in part, because of judicial extension of the reckless and intentional conduct standard adopted in co-participant injury cases (see *supra*) to limit the liability of coaches and trainers for certain forms of conduct that result in injury to high school student-athletes. Similarly, courts' increased willingness to enforce liability waivers against high school student-athletes has limited institutions' tort liability. See, e.g., *Sharon v. City of Newton*, 769 N.E.2d 738 (2002).

For discussions of the liability of high schools to student-athletes, see generally Timothy Davis, Avila v. Citrus Community College District: *Shaping the Contours of Immunity and Primary Assumption of the Risk*, 17 Marq. Sports L. Rev. 259 (2006); Timothy B. Fitzgerald, *The "Inherent Risk" Doctrine, Amateur Coaching Negligence, and the Goal of Loss Avoidance*, 99 Nw. U. L. Rev. 889 (2005); Thomas R. Hurst and James N. Knight, *Coaches' Liability for Athletes' Injuries and Deaths*, 13 Seton Hall J. Sport L. 27 (2003); Matthew J. Mitten, *Emerging Legal Issues in Sports Medicine: A Synthesis, Summary, and Analysis*, 76 St. John's L. Rev. 5 (2002).

In determining the appropriate liability standard for injuries suffered while participating in interscholastic athletics, the following case illustrates that courts must strike a balance between the responsibility that arises out of the custodial relationship between schools and their student-athletes (most of whom are minors) and the participants' assumption of the risk of injury inherent in athletic participation. Other relevant policy considerations include the age, skill, and experience levels of those involved in the activity and the extent to which imposing liability may fundamentally alter the nature of the sport.

KAHN v. EAST SIDE UNION HIGH SCHOOL DISTRICT

75 P.3d 30 (Cal. 2003)

GEORGE, C.J.

This case presents a question concerning the proper application of the doctrine of primary assumption of risk. At the time of her injury, plaintiff was a 14-year-old novice member of defendant school district's junior varsity swim team. She was participating in a competitive swim meet when she executed a practice dive into a shallow racing pool that was located on defendant school district's property and broke her neck. She alleged that the injury was caused in part by the failure of her coach, a district employee, to provide her with any instruction in how to safely dive into a shallow racing pool. She also alleged lack of adequate supervision and further that the coach breached the duty of care owed to her by insisting that she dive at the swim meet despite her objections, her lack of expertise, her fear of diving, and the coach's previous promise to exempt her from diving.

In *Knight v. Jewett* (1992) 3 Cal.4th 296, 11 Cal.Rptr.2d 2, 834 P.2d 696 (*Knight*), we considered the proper duty of care that should govern the liability of a sports participant for an injury to a coparticipant. We concluded that, in recognition of the circumstance that some risk of injury is inherent in most sports, and in order to avoid the detriment to a sport that would arise from discouraging participants from vigorously engaging in the activity, it is appropriate to hold that a participant breaches a duty of care to a coparticipant only if he or she "intentionally injures another player or engages in conduct that is so reckless as to be totally outside the range of the ordinary activity involved in the sport." In the present case, we recognize that the relationship of a sports instructor or coach to a student or athlete is different from the relationship between coparticipants in a sport. But because a significant part of an instructor's or coach's role is to challenge or "push" a student or athlete to advance in his or her skill level and to undertake more difficult tasks, and because the fulfillment of such a role could be improperly chilled by too stringent a standard of potential legal liability, we conclude that the same general standard should apply in cases in which an instructor's alleged liability rests primarily on a claim that he or she challenged the player to perform beyond his or her capacity or failed to provide adequate instruction or supervision before directing or permitting a student to perform a particular maneuver that has resulted in injury to the student. A sports instructor may be found to have breached a duty of care to a student or athlete only if the instructor intentionally injures the student or engages in conduct that is reckless in the sense that it is "totally outside the range of the ordinary activity" involved in teaching or coaching the sport.

Applying this standard to the present case, we conclude that, on the basis of the declarations and deposition testimony filed in support of and in opposition to defendants' motion for summary judgment, the Court of Appeal majority erred in determining that the doctrine of primary assumption of risk warranted entry of summary judgment in defendants' favor. We conclude that the totality of the circumstances precludes the grant of defendants' motion for summary judgment. Specifically, we refer to evidence of defendant coach's failure to provide plaintiff with training in shallow-water diving, his awareness of plaintiff's intense fear of diving into shallow water, his conduct in lulling plaintiff into a false sense of security by promising that she would not be required to dive at competitions, his last-minute breach of this promise in the heat of a competition, and his threat to remove her from competition or at least from the meet if she refused to dive. Plaintiff's evidence supports the conclusion that the maneuver of diving into a shallow racing pool, if not done correctly, poses a significant risk of extremely serious injury, and that there is a well-established mode of instruction for teaching a student to perform this maneuver safely. The declarations before the trial court raise a disputed issue of fact as to whether defendant coach provided any instruction at all to plaintiff with regard to the safe performance of such a maneuver, as well as to the existence and nature of the coach's promises and threats. Under these circumstances, the question whether the coach's conduct was reckless in that it fell totally outside the range of ordinary activity involved in teaching or coaching this sport cannot properly be resolved on summary judgment. Accordingly, the judgment of the Court of Appeal is reversed. . . .

[T]here are circumstances in which the relationship between defendant and plaintiff gives rise to a duty on the part of the defendant to use due care not to increase the risks inherent in the plaintiff's activity. For example, a purveyor of recreational activities owes a duty to a patron not to increase the risks inherent in the activity in which the patron has paid to engage. [Citations.] Likewise, *a coach or sport instructor owes a duty to a student not to increase the risks inherent in the learning process undertaken by the student.* . . .

The general proposition that a sports instructor or coach owes a duty of due care not to increase the risk of harm inherent in learning an active sport is consistent with a growing line of Court of Appeal opinions that have applied the *Knight* analysis to claims against such defendants. In these cases, the reviewing courts examined the particular circumstances of the sport, its inherent risks, and the relationship of the parties to the sport and to each other. Most also examined the question whether imposing broader liability on coaches and instructors would harm the sport or cause it to be changed or abandoned. In each instance, the Courts of Appeal have agreed that although the coach or athletic instructor did not have a duty to eliminate the risks presented by a sport, he or she did have a duty to the student not to increase the risk inherent in learning, practicing, or performing in the sport.

Subsequent decisions have clarified that the risks associated with *learning* a sport may themselves be inherent risks of the sport, and that an instructor or coach generally does not increase the risk of harm inherent in learning the sport simply by urging the student to strive to excel or to reach a new level of competence. This line of cases analyzes and articulates an important and appropriate limitation on the duty of a sports instructor. The cases point out that instruction in a sport frequently entails challenging or "pushing" a student to attempt new or more difficult feats, and that "liability should not be imposed simply because an instructor asked the student to take action beyond what, with hindsight, is found to have been the student's abilities." (*Bushnell v. Japanese-American Religious & Cultural Center, supra*, 43 Cal.App.4th at p. 532, 50 Cal.Rptr.2d 671.) As a general matter, although the nature of the sport and the relationship of the parties to it and to each other remain relevant, a student's inability to meet an instructor's legitimate challenge is a risk that is inherent in learning a sport. To impose a duty to mitigate the inherent risks of learning a sport by refraining from challenging a student, as these cases explain, could have a chilling effect on the enterprise of teaching and learning skills that are necessary to the sport. At a competitive level, especially, this chilling effect is undesirable. . . .

[E]ven keeping in mind the role of the coach or sports instructor, the imposition of a duty to avoid challenging a student to perform beyond his or her current capacity would have a chilling effect on the enterprise of teaching and learning skills that are necessary to the sport . . . a coach or athletic instructor must challenge his or her students, and . . . learning itself can be a risky process, sometimes unavoidably so. . . . [W]hile a student is engaged in the process of learning, he or she frequently is at greater risk than a proficient athlete would be, and a coach does not have a duty to eliminate all the risks presented by inexperience.

We agree that the object to be served by the doctrine of primary assumption of risk in the sports setting is to avoid recognizing a duty of care when to do so would tend to alter the nature of an active sport or chill vigorous participation in the activity. This concern applies to the process of learning to become competent or competitive in such a sport. Novices and children need instruction if they are to participate and compete, and we agree with the many Court of Appeal decisions that have refused to define a duty of care in terms that would inhibit adequate instruction and learning or eventually alter the nature of the sport. Accordingly, we believe that the standard set forth in *Knight* as it applies to coparticipants, generally should apply to sports instructors, keeping in mind, of course, that different facts are of significance in each setting. In order to support a cause of action in cases in which it is alleged that a sports instructor has required a student to perform beyond the student's capacity or without providing adequate instruction, it must be alleged and proved that the instructor acted with intent to cause a student's injury or that the instructor acted recklessly in the sense that the instructor's conduct was "totally outside the range of the ordinary activity" involved in teaching or coaching the sport.

Plaintiff's allegations and supporting evidence . . . went far beyond a claim that the coach made an ordinary error of judgment in determining that she was ready to perform the shallow-water dive.

The Red Cross teaching manual submitted by plaintiff acknowledged that the principal danger faced by persons learning to compete in swimming is the shallow-water dive. The risk presented is not simply that the swimmer might suffer bruises or even break an arm; the risk is that the student may sustain serious head and spinal cord injuries by striking the bottom of the pool. Plaintiff presented evidence, both documentary and expert, that a settled progression of instruction in the dive is considered essential to a student's safety. Her own declaration and deposition testimony was that she had not received any instruction at all from her coaches or teammates on the performance of the shallow-water dive. She also claimed that she had expressed a mortal fear of performing the shallow-water dive and that she had been assured by the coach that she would not be required to perform it. Her evidence was that the coach made a last-minute demand that she take a position in the relay race that would require her to dive, threatening that if she did not comply, either she would be dropped from the team or she would not be permitted to compete that day.

With respect to the issue of causation . . . there was a conflict in the evidence on the question whether plaintiff had been instructed not to practice dives on her own. Under the allegations and evidence provided by plaintiff, it was reasonably foreseeable that when the coach told plaintiff she would have to dive (for the first time) at the meet, she would see a need for practice. Under these circumstances and those referred to above, sufficient facts were produced that would support a determination that the absence of prior instruction was the proximate cause of plaintiff's injury.

Applicable California authority establishes that defendants had a duty of supervision that included an obligation to offer plaintiff some protection against her own lack of mature judgment. . . . We do not believe it can be determined as a matter of law that plaintiff's decision to practice shallow-water dives with the help of other students, after the coach unexpectedly told her she was to dive that day, was conduct beyond what the coach should have foreseen and forestalled. . . .

We believe that triable issues of material fact exist regarding the question whether coach McKay breached a duty of care owed to plaintiff, thereby causing her injury, by engaging in conduct that was reckless in that it was totally outside the range of ordinary activity involved in teaching or coaching the sport of competitive swimming. . . .

Concurring Opinion by WERDEGAR, J.

I therefore agree with the majority that an instructor should be liable for a student's injury in the course of learning a sport only if the instructor's conduct is found to have been "'totally outside the range of the ordinary activity' involved in teaching or coaching the sport." Although the majority also adopts *Knight*'s label of such conduct as "reckless," I do not understand our standard, at least in the instructional context, to be equivalent to recklessness as it is sometimes understood, i.e., as the "wilful or wanton misconduct" shown when an actor has "'intentionally done an act of an unreasonable character in disregard of a risk known to him or so obvious that he must be taken to have been aware of it, and so great as to make it highly probable that harm would follow.'" Rather, I believe a coach or instructor departs from the range of ordinary instructional activities, increasing the risks of injury beyond those inherent in teaching a sport, and is therefore subject to liability, when his or her conduct constitutes a gross or extreme departure from the instructional norms. . . .

I believe we must recognize a somewhat greater duty on the part of instructors, especially teachers and coaches of minor students, than the duty participants in a sport owe one another. A school football *coach*, while far from being the insurer of students' safety, is also very differently situated in knowledge, training, experience, and responsibilities from the casual football *player* whose duty we considered in *Knight.* . . . [A] coach or instructor stands somewhat apart from the fray; the coach's role includes observing and directing the competition, and he or she is expected to keep a cooler head than the competitors themselves. When the instructor or coach is a school teacher, moreover, the safety of the minor students will usually be a primary consideration. Society expects—legitimately, in my view—more from instructors and coaches than merely that they will refrain from harming a student intentionally or with wanton disregard for safety. An instructor's gross or extreme lack of care for student safety is not an inherent risk of school athletics programs.

Finally, I believe a standard akin to gross negligence will provide sufficient protection against unfair second-guessing of the instructor's judgment and, therefore, will not unduly chill participation in sports instruction. . . .

Concurring and Dissenting Opinion by KENNARD, J.

I would hold high school coaches to the general standard of ordinary care. . . . I would require the injured plaintiff to establish only negligence, not recklessness. . . .

Thus, defendant coach in this case should be held liable if, in teaching plaintiff the requisite skills of competitive swimming and in supervising her progress, the coach's conduct fell short of that of a *reasonable* coach of student athletes in similar circumstances.

Persons participating in active sports have to expect that a coparticipant may play too roughly and thus cause injury. By contrast, coaches of student athletes teach them the skills necessary to perform their sport of choice safely and effectively. Because student athletes, particularly minors, often consider their coach a mentor or role model, they trust the coach not to carelessly and needlessly expose them to injury. The majority's decision puts an end to that trust: Coaches are under no legal obligation to use reasonable care in training their students how best to perform a sport without incurring personal injury.

The concurring opinion agrees with the majority that a coach incurs liability to a student athlete only for conduct "'totally outside the range'" of ordinary coaching activity. But it objects to the majority's labeling such conduct "'reckless,'" preferring to call it "gross negligence." Whatever one chooses to call it, the standard the majority imposes is dangerously lax; it puts concern for the physical safety of children far down on a secondary school coach's list of priorities. . . .

Because participation in active sports always entails some risk of harm, the traditional negligence standard imposes liability on an athletic coach only for conduct that exposes players to an *"unreasonable* risk" of such harm. . . . Thus, contrary to the majority's view, applying the negligence standard here would leave coaches free to challenge or push their students to advance their skills level as long as they do so without exposing the student athletes to an unreasonable risk of harm. . . .

NOTES AND QUESTIONS

1. *Determining Inherent Risks.* A school is not liable for a player's injury resulting from the inherent risks of a sport if it has used reasonable care in conducting the activity. Determining the inherent risks of a sport requires a fact-specific analysis of what activities are "part of the game," and which risks of injury are assumed by all participants. An inherent risk is one that is indivisible from the sport. In other words, the inherent risk inquiry focuses on whether the activity at issue constitutes a risk that is among the consequences attendant to normal competition in a sport. For instance, the risk of being hit by a ball is a consequence of playing baseball. However, there are some risks that are divisible from competition within a sport; because such risks are not inherent to the sport, they fall outside the scope of primary implied assumption of the risk. For example, a faulty helmet is a "divisible risk" because the defect arose from the manufacturing process and not from participation in an athletic event. Risks deemed not to be inherent to sports activities include defective equipment, substandard medical treatment, and intentional torts. Marc J. Dobberstein, *"Give Me the Ball, Coach": A Scouting Report on the Liability of High Schools and Coaches for Injuries to High School Pitchers' Arms*, 14 Sports Law. J. 49, 53 (2007).

   However, an athlete does not assume all risks of injury from playing a sport, regardless of how they occur. In this regard, coaches must act neither recklessly nor in a manner that increases risks inherent in an athletic activity. See, e.g., *Koffman v. Garnett*, 265 Va. 12, 574 S.E.2d 258, 261 (2003) (coach who unexpectedly lifted a 13-year-old football player and slammed him to the ground as part of demonstration on tackling techniques acted imprudently and in "utter disregard" of the student's safety); see also *Patrick v. Great Valley Sch. Dist.*, 296 Fed. App. 258 (3d Cir. 2008) (although coach's conduct in pairing student wrestler with a teammate who was 90 pounds heavier might constitute deliberate indifference to his health and safety, school could not be held liable for violating student's §1983 liberty interest without due process unless facts established that the coach's conduct represented unofficial custom so pervasive as to carry the force of law).

2. *Inadequate Instruction and Training.* Which of the three liability standards considered in *Kahn* strikes the appropriate balance between enabling coaches to promote athletic performance and protecting young athletes from increased risks of injury? Considering the objectives of competitive

interscholastic athletics, what policy considerations should be given paramount weight? Should injury resulting from negligent coaching be an inherent risk of playing a sport that is assumed by a young athlete? See Joseph M. Hnylka, *California Drops the Ball: The Lack of a Clear Approach to Recklessness in Sport Injury Litigation*, 11 Va. Sports & Ent. L.J. 77 (2011) (discussing *Kahn, Knight,* and *Shin* and providing comprehensive discussion of California's application of assumption of risk in sport cases).

Relying on the reasoning of the *Kahn* majority, a Maryland appellate court held that a 13-year-old softball player assumed the risk of her injury, a fractured ankle, while attempting to tag an opposing player who slid into her at second base. Plaintiffs claimed that the coach failed to adequately instruct her not to block the base path. The court stated: "Inadequate instruction and training claims have progressed to trial only when a coach provided little or no training before asking the injured athlete to engage in a significantly dangerous play, and compounded that omission by failing to adequately supervise that play." *Kelly v. McCarrick,* 841 A.2d 869, 886-887 (Md. Ct. Spec. App. 2004). Other courts recently have adopted a similar standard. See, e.g., *Karas v. Strevell,* 884 N.E.2d 122 (Ill. 2008). But see *Wilson v. O'Gorman High School,* 2008 WL 2571833 at *4 (D. S.D. 2008) (concluding that "the South Dakota Supreme Court would not adopt the *Kahn* standard, but rather would apply the general negligence standard"); *Morales v. Beacon City Sch. Dist.,* 44 A.D.3d 724, 726 (N.Y. Sup. Ct. 2007) ("plaintiff raised a triable issue of fact as to whether the coach failed to properly train and supervise the plaintiff, and whether this failure unreasonably increased the plaintiff's risk of injury"); see also *Sherry v. East Suburban Football League,* 807 N.W.2d 859, 862 (Mich. App. 2011) (applying negligence standard in case alleging coach failed to properly train and supervise cheerleaders engaged in "privately sponsored recreational activities").

Pushing a high school athlete beyond his or her endurance level may be actionable if doing so exposes the athlete to an unreasonably enhanced risk of injury during competition. In *Vargo v. Svitchan,* 301 N.W.2d 1 (Mich. Ct. App. 1980), a Michigan appellate court held that urging a high school football player to push "himself to and beyond his limits" with resulting injury may establish negligence liability. *Id.* at 3.

There also is potential liability for improperly warning students regarding the need for and appropriate use of protective equipment during athletics. Indeed, these cases appear to represent an exception to the intentional/recklessness standard. *Henney v. Shelby City Sch. Dist.* 2006 WL 747475, at *3 (Ohio Ct. App. March 23, 2006) (coach can be held negligent for failing to supply proper athletic equipment); *Moose v. Massachusetts Inst. Tech.,* 683 N.E.2d 706 (Mass. App. 1997) (adopting negligence as standard to determine liability of coach for supplying defective equipment to player); *Zides v. Quinnipiac Univ.,* 2006 WL 463182 (Conn. Super. Ct. Feb. 7, 2006) (question of fact whether assistant coach could be held liable in negligence for alleged failing to supply adequate equipment); *Baker v. Briarcliff Sch. Dist.,* 613 N.Y.S.2d 660, 663 (N.Y. App. Div. 1994) (assumption of risk unavailable as a defense if proved that coach inadequately warned players about the "risks involved in not wearing a mouthpiece . . . thereby exposing [plaintiff] to unreasonably increased risks of injury").

Notwithstanding the potential liability that may ensue from institutions supplying athletes with defective sporting equipment, courts have drawn a distinction between accidents resulting from defective equipment and those resulting from suboptimal playing conditions. *Bukowski v. Clarkson University*, 19 N.Y.3d 353, 357 (N.Y. June 5, 2012), is illustrative. Plaintiff, an experienced college baseball player, was struck by a batted ball during a pitching exercise. *Id.* at 355. The court held that the player assumed the inherent risk of being hit by a line drive, despite the absence of a protective L-screen and low lighting in the facility. *Id.* at 356. The court stated that although the lack of adequate lighting and protective screen may be considered "less than optimal for baseball, they still did not constitute risks beyond those assumed by the [player]." *Id.* at 357. The court further distinguished *Baker* because the player in *Bukowski* did not "assert that the Clarkson coaching staff violated any established safety protocol or the NCAA Rulebook by holding their indoor pitching practices without an L-Screen or a dark backdrop." *Id.*

3. *Aggravation of Existing Injury.* Requiring a high school athlete to continue playing with a known injury may create tort liability for aggravation of the injury. In *Morris v. Union High School District A*, 294 P. 998 (Wash. 1931), the Washington Supreme Court held that a school district was liable for a coach's negligence in inducing a student to continue playing football with a back injury. The court ruled, "[If] the coach knew that a student in the school was physically unable to play football, or in the exercise of reasonable care should have known it, but nevertheless permitted, persuaded, and coerced such student to play, with the result that he sustained injuries, the district would be liable." *Id.* at 999. See also *Summers v. Milwaukie Union High Sch. Dist. No. 5*, 481 P.2d 369 (Or. Ct. App. 1971). But see *Christian v. Eagles Landing Christian Acad., Inc.*, 303 Ga. App. 113, 117, 692 S.E.2d 745, 749 (2010) (granting summary judgment on behalf of defendant because the coach did not encourage or grant permission to cheerleading squad to perform the stunt that resulted in an injury to a cheerleader); *Hale v. Davies*, 70 S.E. 2d 923 (Ga. Ct. App. 1952) (dismissing complaint alleging that a coach negligently ordered a student to practice with an injury).

    Permitting an injured athlete to return to play without using reasonable care to determine his or her medical condition also may result in institutional liability. *Jarreau v. Orleans Parish Sch. Bd.*, 600 So. 2d 1389 (La. Ct. App. 1992). However, in *Cerny v. Cedar Bluffs Junior/Senior Public School*, 679 N.W.2d 198 (Neb. 2004), the Nebraska Supreme Court affirmed the lower court's finding that a coach exercised reasonable care by properly evaluating a high school football player for symptoms of a concussion and allowing him to reenter a game. See also *Zemke v. Arreola*, 2006 WL 1587101 (Cal. Ct. App. June 12, 2006) (coaches not liable for brain injury caused by second impact syndrome, which was not foreseeable, because student did not appear to have or report symptoms of initial head injury).

4. *Duty to Provide Emergency Medical Care.* High school personnel have a duty to promptly obtain emergency medical care for an injured athlete. *Mogabgab v. Orleans Parish Sch. Bd.*, 239 So. 2d 456, 460-461 (La. Ct. App. 1970) (noting that because coaches did not seek medical attention for an injured athlete until two hours after his symptoms appeared, they were negligent in causing his death). Although lay athletic personnel are not charged with the knowledge of medical experts, they must recognize a medical emergency and act reasonably under the circumstances. *Pirkle v. Oakdale Union Grammar Sch. Dist.*, 253 P.2d 1, 4 (Cal. 1953); *Kersey v. Harbin*, 531 S.W.2d 76, 80-81 (Mo.

Ct. App. 1975). Courts have found coaches liable for improperly providing first aid that worsens an injured athlete's condition. See *Halper v. Vayo*, 568 N.E.2d 914 (Ill. App. Ct. 1991); *Gahan v. Mineola Union Free Sch. Dist.*, 660 N.Y.S.2d 144 (N.Y. App. Div. 1997).

5. *Duty of State High School Athletic Association to Protect Athlete's Health and Safety.* State high school athletic associations often promulgate competition and equipment rules for interscholastic sports played within their respective jurisdictions. Courts have held that these governing bodies have a legal duty to exercise reasonable care when formulating safety rules governing high school athletic competition. See, e.g., *Mohr v. St. Paul Fire & Marine Ins. Co.*, 674 N.W.2d 576 (Wis. App. 2003); *Wissel v. Ohio High Sch. Athletic Assn.*, 605 N.E.2d 458 (Ohio App. 1992). As a policy matter, what should a state high school athletic association do to protect the health and safety of those students participating in interscholastic athletics? See *Mohr, supra* (Wisconsin Interscholastic Athletic Association may be liable for adopting national organization of high school athletic associations' rule without independent inquiry into whether starting a competitive swimming race in 3.5 feet of water is safe).

b.   Sovereign Immunity

PRINCE v. LOUISVILLE MUNICIPAL SCHOOL DISTRICT
741 So. 2d 207 (Miss. 1999)

Waller, Justice:

This case arose out of a suit filed by Richard Prince on April 11, 1994, against the Louisville Municipal School District (the District), David Chambiss and Bobby Bowman for injures suffered while Prince was a member of the Nanih Waiya High School football team. . . .

Prince alleged he suffered a heat stroke during football practice at Nanih Waiya High School on August 29, 1991, due to the negligence of football coaches Bowman and Chambliss. Prince further alleged Bowman and Chambliss negligently failed to keep a proper monitor on his health and condition, failed to provide necessary liquids and failed to provide necessary medical care in a timely manner. Prince required hospitalization for his injury and claims to have suffered permanent injuries. . . .

Bowman, Chambliss and the District moved to dismiss Prince's claim [and] . . . claimed (1) Prince's complaint failed to state a claim on which relief could be granted; (2) the defendants were protected by sovereign immunity or qualified sovereign immunity; and (3) based on the pleadings, there was no material issue in dispute and the defendants were entitled to summary judgment. . . .

For the District, the doctrine of sovereign immunity mandates a finding of non-liability.

For Bowman and Chambliss individually, "[p]re-*Pruett* common law mandates a finding of whether the act involved is a discretionary function or a ministerial function. . . . An official will be immune when the act being performed is discretionary."

In *Quinn v. Mississippi State University*, 720 So.2d 843 (Miss.1998), we were faced with a factual situation comparable to the present case. Bobby Quinn was injured June 22, 1992, while participating in a summer baseball camp at Mississippi State University. An instructor at the camp hit Quinn with a baseball bat during a hitting demonstration. Quinn lost one tooth and suffered permanent damages to four other teeth. Quinn sued the university President, the head baseball coach and an assistant baseball coach, who was also director of the camp.

We affirmed the trial court's granting of summary judgment for the three defendants stating "limited immunity applies to actions by a state agency, an arm of the state or local government and the members thereof, who either for remuneration or as a public service, engage in discretionary functions for which the agency or governmental arm was formed." *Id.* at 849. (citations omitted). The three defendants in *Quinn* were not present at the time of the injury, but they were "engaged in hiring employees, and coordinating, and supervising the baseball program either directly or indirectly. The motion for summary judgment was correctly granted as [the defendants] were engaged in a discretionary activity that served a public interest." *Id.*

In a case even more factually akin to the case at bar, *Lennon v. Petersen*, 624 So.2d 171 (Ala.1993), the Alabama Supreme Court addressed the effect of qualified immunity on a negligence action brought against a soccer coach and university trainer by an injured soccer player. Patrick Lennon alleged his coach was negligent in not recognizing his injuries and providing the proper treatment. Lennon experienced sharp pain in his hip and groin during soccer practice and received treatment from the University of Alabama at Huntsville athletic trainer, Debbie Lee. Lee diagnosed his injury as "groin strain" and treated him with ice and electricity. Lennon's injury persisted and he sought treatment from a physician after the season ended. Lennon's physician diagnosed his condition as avascular necrosis which had worsened because of the treatment he received during the course of the soccer season from Lee and under the direction of Peterson, his soccer coach. Lennon required surgery to help his problem, but was forced to avoid any activities that could cause a jarring of his hip bones. He also faced the prospect of premature arthritis and a hip joint replacement in the future.

In addressing the negligence claim against Lennon's coach, the Alabama Supreme Court stated:

> Petersen's actions clearly fall into the category of discretionary acts. Petersen had to rely on his own judgment and discretion in making difficult decisions while performing his job. He had to determine what drills his players needed and how long the drills should last. He also had to evaluate his players to determine if they were playing to the best of their ability. He had to make difficult decisions in determining whether a player was injured and should report to the trainer or whether the player was merely faking an injury to avoid practice. He also had to be aware that some players would hide their injuries so that they would be allowed to practice or to play in a game. He was responsible for motivating the players and evaluating their performance. Petersen was acting within his authority in using his discretion in such matters, and he is entitled to discretionary function immunity.

Id. at 174.

Like the defendants in *Quinn*, high school football coaches Bowman and Chambliss were responsible for coordinating and supervising the football program at Nanih Waiya High School. Bowman and Chambliss also faced the same daily coaching decisions as did Coach Peterson in *Lennon*. The Alabama Supreme

Court's description of the nature of a coach's job is important to consider. In a typical practice there are strains, sprains and complaints from a coach's players. A coach must consider the good order and discipline of the team when confronted with situational complaints by the players. A coach must use his discretion in judging whether or not an individual player is injured and then, whether the player should report to a trainer or seek other medical aid. There was no evidence presented in the lower court to show that either Bowman or Chambliss did anything beyond exercising ordinary discretion in supervising the Nanih Waiya football practice on August 29, 1991. Prince produced no facts that evidenced any disregard for his health or any other outrageous action on the part of Bowman or Chambliss that might have warranted a departure from our previous holdings. The trial court correctly found the coaches were protected by qualified immunity. . . .

We affirm the trial court's granting of summary judgment in favor of the District because the District was protected by sovereign immunity. Following our prior decision in *Quinn v. Mississippi State University* and the approach of the Alabama Supreme Court in *Lennon v. Petersen*, we affirm the trial court's granting of summary judgment to Bowman and Chambliss based on the protection of qualified immunity. . . .

BANKS, Justice, concurring in part and dissenting in part:

In *Womble v. Singing River Hosp.*, 618 So.2d 1252 (Miss.1993), this Court removed a then relatively recently discovered blanket immunity for "discretionary" medical decisions. We concluded that medical treatment decisions, however discretionary, were not governmental policy decisions and, therefore, no immunity attached. *Womble* put medical personnel, back on an even footing with all other governmental personnel, where they had always been and where they belonged. Today's decision elevates athletic coaches to the same perch from which we removed medical personnel.

Administrators, commissioners, etc., are immune for policy-making decisions, such as how much money to allocate to particular objectives. Neither they nor other government employees should be immune for breaches of the duty of reasonable care when dealing directly with individuals to whom such a duty is owed. The Alabama Supreme Court construing Alabama law reaches a different result, *Lennon v. Petersen*, 624 So.2d 171 (Ala.1993), but that simply is not our law.

The majority's reliance upon *Quinn v. Mississippi State University*, 720 So.2d 843 (Miss.1998), is also misplaced. There we held that the president of the university, the university head baseball coach and the assistant head baseball coach who also directed the baseball camp enjoyed qualified immunity from liability with respect to an injury to a participant in the baseball camp. Neither of these defendants, however, was shown to have had or exercised direct supervisory responsibility for the particular activities out of which the injury arose. These individuals would be counterparts to the hospital administrators and perhaps, chiefs of various medical disciplines as opposed to treating physicians as in the case of *Womble*. No one contends that administrative decisions fall outside the ambit of qualified immunity. The decisions here involved were not administrative.

In my view the football coach and trainer in the instant case owed a duty of reasonable care to the player, the breach of which should incur liability from which there is no immunity. That is not to say that they were, in fact, negligent in breach of their duty. Perhaps what they did was fully in keeping with reasonable care under the circumstances. All I say is that there should be no immunity. . . .

McRae, Justice, concurring in part and dissenting in part:
   [T]he coaches were acting in their ministerial capacities, not with discretion. Qualified immunity is not warranted. . . . Coaches Chambliss and Bowman maintained duties to manage their players. Randall Prince suffered harm because his coaches failed to perform their duties such that he suffered heatstroke, and because those same coaches failed to take proper actions afterwards. As coaches directly responsible for serving the general needs of Prince while he is under their power as a football player, the coaches should have more closely monitored Prince's condition. When it became possible that Prince was a candidate for heatstroke, the coaches should have given him rest out of the sun, provided him additional liquids, or simply excused him from practice. There are no means by which to grant qualified immunity. The instant case deals with an extracurricular activity internal to the school, not a promotion of government policy and public good. Accordingly, I dissent to affirming summary judgment for the coaches and the school district.

what does he concur with ?

NOTES AND QUESTIONS

1. *Sovereign Immunity for Public Schools.* As illustrated in *Prince*, under the doctrine of *sovereign immunity*, a public school district, as a subsidiary agency of the state, may be immune from tort liability for negligent acts of its employees causing injury to a high school athlete. See also *Evans v. Oaks Mission Pub. Sch.*, 945 P.2d 492 (Okla. 1997); *Grandalski v. Lyons Township High Sch. Dist. 204*, 711 N.E.2d 372 (Ill. App. Ct. 1999). The scope of this immunity varies on a state-by-state basis.
      Courts generally hold that the operation of an interscholastic athletics program is a governmental function that is covered by sovereign immunity rather than a proprietary function, which is not immune. *Fowler v. Tyler Indep. Sch. Dist.*, 232 S.W.3d 335 (Tex. Ct. App. 2007); *Limerick v. Euclid Bd. of Educ.*, 591 N.E.2d 1299 (Ohio Ct. App. 1990). In *Lovitt v. Concord School District*, 228 N.W.2d 479 (Mich. Ct. App. 1975), a Michigan court of appeals held that a public high school football program was a physical education activity encompassed within the governmental function of providing education. Finding that the district's athletics program had been operating at a deficit for five years, the court rejected plaintiff's claim that the football program was a proprietary function because an admission fee was charged to games. For discussions of sovereign immunity in the athletic context, see Davis, *Avila v. Citrus College, supra*, at 260-263; Thomas R. Hurst and James N. Knight, *Coaches' Liability for Athletes' Injuries and Deaths*, 13 Seton Hall J. Sport L. 27, 44-47 (2003); Anthony S. McCaskey and Kenneth W. Biedzynski, *A Guide to the Legal Liability of Coaches for a Sports Participant's Injuries*, 6 Seton Hall J. Sport L. 7, 73, 66-77 (1996); William H. Baker, *Injuries to College Athletes: Rights & Responsibilities*, 97 Dick. L. Rev. 655, 656-660 (1993); see also *Ward v. Michigan State Univ.*, 782 N.W.2d 514 (Mich. App. 2010) (university's operation of hockey rink constituted a governmental function because it did not operate the rink primarily to generate a profit).

2. *Qualified Immunity for Public School Employees.* The doctrine of *qualified immunity* may protect public school employees such as coaches and athletic trainers from negligence liability when they are exercising a discretionary act, but not a ministerial act. The disagreement between the majority and dissenting judges in *Prince* relates to whether coaches act in a ministerial or discretionary capacity when supervising a sport and making decisions about medical matters involving athletes. How does one distinguish the performance of a ministerial function from a discretionary function? In *Lennon v. Petersen*, 624 So. 2d 171 (Ala. 1993), the Alabama Supreme Court stated, "A discretionary function does not include ministerial tasks like the mere filling out of a form, nor does it include acts made 'fraudulently, in bad faith, beyond [the actor's] authority, or . . . under a mistaken interpretation of the law.' . . . Although discretionary functions do not include unauthorized acts, they do include acts that require 'personal deliberation, decision and judgment.'" *Id.* at 173-174. Accord *Feagins v. Waddy*, 978 So. 2d 712 (Ala. 2007). Considering the underlying policy reasons for qualified immunity, is this the appropriate distinction to be made in the context of high school athletics?

In reaffirming *Prince*, the Mississippi Supreme Court expressed the following concern if the state's tort claims act is not construed to provide immunity to a public school and coaches:

> High school football coaches around the state would lose their ability to control their football teams. Discipline of a football team would become nonexistent. If a coach refused a player's request for a water break—to see a trainer—to not have to run any more wind sprints—to not have to do any more one-on-one blocking drills, because of that player's complaint of "feeling weak" or "not feeling good" or simply "not feeling like it," that coach would be very much aware of the fact that he/she would be running the risk of being successfully sued . . . should that player later suffer physical/medical problems related to the coach's failure to cow to the player's every whim and wish. On the other hand, if the coach, in fear of a successful lawsuit, should cow to the player's every whim, wish and demand, then the coach would lose the respect of the players, and discipline and morale would be lost.

Harris v. McCray, 867 So. 2d 188, 193 (Miss. 2003); accord *Covington County Sch. Dist. v. Magee*, 29 So. 3d 1, 6 (Miss. 2010), *reh'g denied* (Mar. 18, 2010).

In *Yanero v. Davis*, 65 S.W.3d 510 (Ky. 2001), a high school baseball player who was not wearing a batting helmet was injured after being struck in the head by a ball thrown by a classmate. Although the Kentucky Supreme Court adopted the doctrine of qualified immunity, it refused to allow it to shield a coach from negligence related to his failure to supervise the plaintiff so as to require that he wear a batting helmet. "The performance of that duty in this instance was a ministerial, rather than a discretionary, function in that it involved only the enforcement of a known rule requiring that student athletes wear batting helmets during baseball batting practice. The promulgation of such a rule is a discretionary function; the enforcement of it is a ministerial function." *Id.* at 529. See also *Covington County Sch. Dist. v. Magee*, 29 So. 3d 1 (Miss. 2010) (school district was immunized from tort liability relating to the heat-stroke death of a high school football player during practice; a coach's decision to hold practice was considered a discretionary act); *Harris v. McCray*, 867 So. 2d 188, 193 (Miss. 2003) (coach and school district immune from liability for injuries student-athlete suffered from heat stroke where acts performed by coach in his position as coach were discretionary). But see *Elston v. Howland Local Schools*, 865 N.E.2d 845 (Ohio 2007) (where there was no showing that a coach's position involves policy-making, planning, or enforcement powers, his position did not involve "the exercise of a high degree of official judgment or discretion"; therefore immunity was not an available defense); accord *Karalyos v. Board of Educ. of Lake Forest Community High Sch. Dist.*, 788 F. Supp. 2d 727, 731 (2011) (a discretionary act involves an act of discretion and a policy decision). For commentary regarding institutional liability for heat-related deaths, see David Feingold, *Who Takes the Heat? Criminal Liability for Heat-Related Deaths in High School Athletics*, 17 Cardozo J.L. & Gender 359, 373 (2011) (discussing the immunity of high school coaches in cases involving heat-related deaths).

Should courts be more concerned with team discipline rather than players' health and safety?

3. *Alleging Federal Constitutional Violation to Avoid Sovereign Immunity Defense.* Courts generally have rejected athletes' efforts to avoid the application of state law tort immunity by seeking recovery for negligent injury treatment rendered by public school personnel under the guise of federal constitutional rights violations. In *Burden v. Wilkes-Barre Area School District*, 16 F. Supp. 2d 569 (M.D. Pa. 1998), a federal district court rejected plaintiff's contention that an educational institution's decision not to hire a certified athletic trainer to protect the health and safety of students participating in competitive sports violated an athlete's constitutional right to life and liberty. See also *Livingston v. Desoto Indep. School Dist.*, 391 F. Supp. 2d 463 (N.D. Tex. 2005) (despite egregious facts of case, public high school, coach, and athletic trainer are immune from §1983 liability because court concluded their alleged improper first aid did not establish deliberate indifference to student's constitutionally protected liberty interest in health and bodily integrity). But see *Roventini v. Pasadena Indep. Sch. Dist.*, 981 F. Supp. 1013 (S.D. Tex. 1997) (holding that allegations of a high school football player's death caused by heat stroke, suffered during a practice in which no certified athletic trainer was present and in which the only persons providing medical assistance were untrained teenage team managers, stated a claim for violation of the decedent's federal constitutional rights), *vacated*, 183 F.R.D. 500 (S.D. Tex. 1998); *Davis v. Carter*, 555 F.3d 979 (5th Cir. 2009) (rejecting parents' constitutional claims as means of circumventing immunity defense in case in which minor football player died during intense voluntary workout; evidence failed to establish coaches acted willfully or maliciously).

4. *Imminent Harm Exception.* Some statutes carve out a limited exception to state tort immunity defenses for plaintiffs "when the circumstances make it apparent to the public officer that his or her failure to act would be likely to subject an identifiable person [or member of an identifiable class of foreseeable persons] to imminent harm." See *Prescott v. City of Meriden*, 873 A.2d 175 (Conn. 2005) (holding that a parent who sustained injuries when he fell on the bleachers at his son's football game does not come within the imminent harm exception since he is not within the class of foreseeable victims—schoolchildren—attending public schools during school hours).

c.   The Validity of Liability Waivers

The following materials explore the enforceability of pre-injury contracts pursuant to which a person agrees to release a school district or its employees from liability for negligent failure to use reasonable care to protect the health and safety of students during athletic activities. Differing terminology, including exculpatory clauses, releases, covenants not to sue, and hold harmless agreements, is used to refer to such contracts. Although technical differences exist in specific types of such contracts, what lies at their core is an agreement by one party to accept the risk of harm resulting from another's conduct. If enforceable, these waivers of liability bar a plaintiff's ability to seek recovery from the defendant for harm caused by certain tortious conduct. Determining the validity of liability waivers requires judicial reconciliation of a fundamental tension between contract and tort law.

A basic premise of tort law holds a party responsible for his or her own negligent or intentional misconduct that causes harm to another. An equally fundamental tenet of contract law provides that a competent party has the freedom to construct his or her own bargains and agreements. The Colorado Supreme Court has described a release as standing "at the crossroads of two competing principles: freedom of contract and responsibility for damages caused by one's own negligent acts." Mary A. Connell and Frederick G. Savage, *Releases: Is There Still a Place for Their Use by Colleges and Universities?*, 29 J.C. & U.L. 579, 580 (2003). Helpful discussions of the validity of waivers appear in Elisa Lintemuth, *Parental Rights v. Parens Patriae: Determining the Correct Limitations on the Validity of Pre-Injury Waivers Effectuated by Parents on Behalf of Minor Children*, 2010 Mich. St. L. Rev. 169 (2010); Robert S. Nelson, Comment, *The Theory of the Waiver Scale: An Argument Why Parents Should Be Able to Waive Their Children's Tort Liability Claims*, 36 U.S.F.L.R. 535 (2002); Mario R. Arango and William R. Trueba, Jr., *The Sports Chamber: Exculpatory Agreements Under Pressure*, 14 U. Miami Ent. & Sports L. Rev. 1 (1997).

Some courts have refused to enforce pre-injury waivers on the grounds that they violate public policy. In one group of cases, which probably represents the majority view, courts rely on public policy grounds to refuse to permit a high school to enforce waivers against a student-athlete or his or her parents or guardian who signed it. In what can be characterized as an intermediate approach, other jurisdictions allow high schools to enforce such waivers against a parent or guardian who signs it, but not against a minor. A minority of jurisdictions has adopted a position that permits parents to sign a release that binds both the parent and minor. The cases that follow, *Wagenblast* and *Sharon*, represent contrasting perspectives on the validity of liability waivers.

WAGENBLAST v. ODESSA SCHOOL DISTRICT NO. 105-157-166J

110 Wash. 2d 845, 758 P.2d 968 (Wash. 1988)

ANDERSEN, Justice.

Can school districts require public school students and their parents to sign written releases which release the districts from the consequences of all future school district negligence, before the students will be allowed to engage in certain recognized school related activities, here interscholastic athletics?

We hold that the exculpatory releases from any future school district negligence are invalid because they violate public policy. (H)

The courts have generally recognized that, subject to certain exceptions, parties may contract that one shall not be liable for his or her own negligence to another. . . .

In accordance with the foregoing general rule, appellate decisions in this state have upheld exculpatory agreements where the subject was a toboggan slide, a scuba diving class, mountain climbing instruction, an automobile demolition derby, and ski jumping.

As Prosser and Keeton . . . observe, however, there are instances where public policy reasons for preserving an obligation of care owed by one person to another outweigh our traditional regard for the freedom to contract. . . .

Probably the best exposition of the test to be applied in determining whether exculpatory agreements violate public policy is that stated by the California Supreme Court. In writing for a unanimous court, the late Justice Tobriner outlined the factors in *Tunkl v. Regents of Univ. of Cal.*, 60 Cal.2d 92, 383 P.2d 441, 32 Cal.Rptr. 33, 6 A.L.R.3d 693 (1963):

> Thus the attempted but invalid exemption involves a transaction which exhibits some or all of the following characteristics. It concerns a business of a type generally thought suitable for public regulation. The party seeking exculpation is engaged in performing a service of great importance to the public, which is often a matter of practical necessity for some members of the public. The party holds himself out as willing to perform this service for any member of the public who seeks it, or at least for any member coming within certain established standards. As a result of the essential nature of the service, in the economic setting of the transaction, the party invoking exculpation possesses a decisive advantage of bargaining strength against any member of the public who seeks his services. In exercising a superior bargaining power the party confronts the public with a standardized adhesion contract of exculpation, and makes no provision whereby a purchaser may pay additional reasonable fees and obtain protection against negligence. Finally, as a result of the transaction, the person or property of the purchaser is placed under the control of the seller, subject to the risk of carelessness by the seller or his agents.

[Footnotes omitted.] *Tunkl*, 60 Cal.2d at 98-101, 383 P.2d 441, 32 Cal.Rptr. 33. We agree. . . .

Obviously, the more of the foregoing six characteristics that appear in a given exculpatory agreement case, the more likely the agreement is to be declared invalid on public policy grounds. . . .

1. *The agreement concerns an endeavor of a type generally thought suitable for public regulation.*

Regulation of governmental entities usually means self-regulation. Thus, the Legislature has by statute granted to each school board the authority to control, supervise, and regulate the conduct of interscholastic athletics. In some situations, a school board is permitted, in turn, to delegate this authority to the Washington Interscholastic Activities Association (WIAA) or to another voluntary nonprofit entity. In the cases before us, both school boards look to the WIAA for regulation of interscholastic sports. The WIAA handbook contains an extensive constitution with rules for such athletic endeavors. . . .

Clearly then, interscholastic sports in Washington are extensively regulated, and are a fit subject for such regulation.

2.   *The party seeking exculpation is engaged in performing a service of great importance to the public, which is often a matter of practical necessity for some members of the public.*

This court has held that public school students have no fundamental right to participate in interscholastic athletics. Nonetheless, the court also has observed that the justification advanced for interscholastic athletics is their educational and cultural value. As the testimony of then Seattle School Superintendent Robert Nelson and others amply demonstrate, interscholastic athletics is part and parcel of the overall educational scheme in Washington. The total expenditure of time, effort and money on these endeavors makes this clear. The importance of these programs to the public is substantive; they represent a significant tie of the public at large to our system of public education. Nor can the importance of these programs to certain students be denied; as Superintendent Nelson agreed, some students undoubtedly remain in school and maintain their academic standing only because they can participate in these programs. Given this emphasis on sports by the public and the school system, it would be unrealistic to expect students to view athletics as an activity entirely separate and apart from the remainder of their schooling. . . .

In sum, under any rational view of the subject, interscholastic sports in public schools are a matter of public importance in this jurisdiction.

3.   *Such party holds itself out as willing to perform this service for any member of the public who seeks it, or at least for any member coming within certain established standards.*

Implicit in the nature of interscholastic sports is the notion that such programs are open to all students who meet certain skill and eligibility standards. This conclusion finds direct support in the testimony of former Superintendent Nelson and the WIAA eligibility and nondiscrimination policies set forth in the WIAA handbook.

4.   *Because of the essential nature of the service, in the economic setting of the transaction, the party invoking exculpation possesses a decisive advantage of bargaining strength against any member of the public who seeks the services.*

Not only have interscholastic sports become of considerable importance to students and the general public alike, but in most instances there exists no alternative program of organized competition. For instance, former Superintendent Nelson knew of no alternative to the Seattle School District's wrestling program. While outside alternatives exist for some activities, they possess little of the inherent allure of interscholastic competition. Many students cannot afford private programs or the private schools where such releases might not be employed. In this regard, school districts have near-monopoly power. And, because such programs have become important to student participants, school districts possess a clear and disparate bargaining strength when they insist that students and their parents sign these releases.

5.   *In exercising a superior bargaining power, the party confronts the public with a standardized adhesion contract of exculpation, and makes no provision whereby a purchaser may pay additional reasonable fees and obtain protection against negligence.*

Both school districts admit to an unwavering policy regarding these releases; no student athlete will be allowed to participate in any program without first signing the release form as written by the school district. In both of these cases, students and their parents unsuccessfully attempted to modify the forms by deleting the release language. In both cases, the school district rejected the attempted modifications. Student athletes and their parents or guardians have no alternative but to sign the standard release forms provided to them or have the student barred from the program.

6.   *The person or property of members of the public seeking such services must be placed under the control of the furnisher of the services, subject to the risk of carelessness on the part of the furnisher, its employees or agents.*

A school district owes a duty to its students to employ ordinary care and to anticipate reasonably foreseeable dangers so as to take precautions for protecting the children in its custody from such dangers. This duty extends to students engaged in interscholastic sports. As a natural incident to the relationship of a student athlete and his or her coach, the student athlete is usually placed under the coach's considerable degree of control. The student is thus subject to the risk that the school district or its agent will breach this duty of care.

   In sum, the attempted releases in the cases before us exhibit all six of the characteristics denominated in [*Tunkl*]. Because of this, and for the aforesaid reasons, we hold that the releases in these consolidated cases are invalid as against public policy.

   Having decided the case on this basis, only two remaining aspects of the cases require discussion.

   The first of these aspects is the relationship of this decision to the doctrine of ① assumption of risk. Another name for a release of the sort presented here is an express assumption of risk. If a plaintiff has released a defendant from liability for a future occurrence, the plaintiff may also be said to have assumed the risk of the occurrence. If the release is against public policy, however, it is also against public policy to say that the plaintiff has assumed that particular risk. This court has implicitly recognized that an express assumption of risk which relieves the defendant's duty to the plaintiff may violate public policy. Accordingly, to the extent that the release portions of these forms represent a consent to relieve the school districts of their duty of care, they are invalid whether they are termed *invalid (AoR)* releases or express assumptions of risk. . . .

   The remaining aspect of these appeals which merits discussion is the Legislature's role in deciding such matters of public policy. . . . [S]ince ter- ritorial days, the State Legislature has generally followed a policy of holding school districts accountable for their negligence. Our decision today is in general accordance with that policy.

   Legislative policies may, of course, change with changing conditions. This opinion is not to be construed as precluding school districts from attempting to convince the Legislature that their problems in this area require a legislative response of one kind or another. The Legislature through its hearing processes is well suited to making such inquiries and has tools and resources adequate to the task. . . .

SHARON v. CITY OF NEWTON
437 Mass. 99, 769 N.E.2d 738 (2002)

CORDY, Judge.

(I) In this case, we consider the question of the validity of a release signed by the parent of a minor child for the purpose of permitting her to engage in public school extra-curricular sports activities. The question is one of first impression in the Commonwealth. *Hasn't been decided on in this jurisdiction before.*

A. BACKGROUND

On November 8, 1995, sixteen year old Merav Sharon was injured while participating in a cheerleading practice at Newton North High School. Merav fell from a teammate's shoulders while rehearsing a pyramid formation cheer and sustained a serious compound fracture to her left arm that required surgery. At the time of her injury, Merav had had four seasons of cheerleading experience at the high school level.

[D]uring the course of discovery, the city came across a document entitled "Parental Consent, Release from Liability and Indemnity Agreement" signed by Merav and her father in August, 1995, approximately three months prior to the injury. The relevant part of the release reads as follows:

> [I] the undersigned [father] . . . of Merav Sharon, a minor, do hereby consent to [her] participation in voluntary athletic programs and do forever RELEASE, acquit, discharge, and covenant to hold harmless the City of Newton . . . from any and all actions, causes of action, [and] claims . . . on account of, or in any way growing out of, directly or indirectly, all known and unknown personal injuries or property damage which [I] may now or hereafter have as the parent . . . of said minor, and also all claims or right of action for damages which said minor has or hereafter may acquire, either before or after [she] has reached [her] majority resulting . . . from [her] participation in the Newton Public Schools Physical Education Department's athletic programs. . . .

(language)

The city filed a motion for summary judgment raising the signed release as a defense. . . .

2. SUMMARY JUDGMENT

We conclude that the facts Merav contends are in dispute are not material, enforcement of the release is consistent with our law and public policy, and Newton is entitled to judgment as a matter of law.

a. Merav's Factual Contentions

Merav first argues that there are disputed issues of material fact regarding her understanding of the release and its voluntariness. She contends that neither she nor her father realized that by signing the release they were waiving their future claims against the school, and that their understanding of what they signed is a matter of fact to be decided by a jury. As the motion judge properly noted, "it is a rule in this Commonwealth that the failure to read or to understand the contents of a release, in the absence of fraud or duress, does not avoid its effects." *Lee v. Allied Sports Assocs., Inc.*, 349 Mass. 544, 550, 209 N.E.2d 329-551 (1965). The undisputed evidence supports the conclusion that both Merav and her father had ample opportunity to read and understand the release before signing it, and they are therefore deemed to have understood it. . . .

The release is a clearly labeled, two-sided document, which Merav brought home from school for her parents to review. Merav and her father both signed the front of the release, which they indicated was for the sport of "cheerleading." In addition, they filled out the back of the release that called for information regarding Merav's address, date of birth, health insurance provider, and emergency contacts, and which provided for the purchase of optional student accident insurance through the school (an option which they explicitly declined on the form). Her father also signed the back of the release giving parental consent to a physical examination of Merav prior to her participation in the cheerleading program. In these respects, the circumstances differ substantially from the so-called "baggage check" or "ticket" cases relied on by Merav in which a customer merely purchases a ticket or receives a receipt that contains release language. . . .

The release at issue here was clearly labeled as such and was filled out and signed by Merav and her father for the purpose of ensuring that she would be permitted to participate in an ongoing extracurricular activity. These are not circumstances likely to mislead a person of ordinary intelligence as to whether a limitation of liability might be included in the type of document being executed. There is no dispute that Merav and her father had ample opportunity to review and understand the release. Their failure to do so does not avoid its effects as a matter of law. . . .

b. *Public Policy*

Merav next contends that enforcement of the release against her claims would constitute a gross violation of public policy. This argument encompasses at least three separate public policy contentions: first, that it is contrary to public policy to permit schools to require students to sign exculpatory agreements as a prerequisite to participation in extracurricular school sports; second, that public policy prohibits a parent from contracting away a minor child's right to sue for a future harm; and third, that the enforcement of this release would undermine the duty of care that public schools owe their students. . . .

(1) Releases. Massachusetts law favors the enforcement of releases. . . . "There can be no doubt . . . that under the law of Massachusetts . . . in the absence of fraud a person may make a valid contract exempting himself from any liability to another which he may in the future incur as a result of his negligence or that of his agents or employees acting on his behalf." *Schell v. Ford*, 270 F.2d 384, 386 (1st Cir. 1959). Whether such contracts be called releases, covenants not to sue, or indemnification agreements, they represent "a practice our courts have long found acceptable." (citations omitted). . . .

Although Merav has suggested that, if the release at issue here is valid, there is nothing to prevent cities or towns from requiring releases for "simply allowing a child to attend school," such a conclusion does not necessarily follow. We have not had occasion to rule on the validity of releases required in the context of a compelled activity or as a condition for the receipt of essential services (e.g., public education, medical attention, housing, public utilities), and the enforceability of mandatory releases in such circumstances might well offend public policy. . . . In this case, Merav's participation in the city's extracurricular activity of cheerleading was neither compelled nor essential, and we conclude that the public policy of the Commonwealth is not offended by requiring a release as a prerequisite to that participation.

(2) *Parent's waiver of a minor's claim.* Merav contends that a parent cannot waive, compromise, or release a minor child's cause of action, and that enforcement of such a release against the child would violate public policy.

While the common-law rule has been narrowed somewhat by statute, . . . it remains our law that the contract of a minor is generally voidable when she reaches the age of majority. Merav unequivocally repudiated the release (to the extent it might be deemed a contract executed by her) by filing suit against the city. The city concedes that Merav effectively disaffirmed the release, but contends that insofar as the release is signed by the parent and purports to release the school from any claim that might accrue to the minor, it remains valid because the parent can do what the minor cannot.

The purpose of the policy permitting minors to void their contracts is "to afford protection to minors from their own improvidence and want of sound judgment." *Frye v. Yasi,* 327 Mass. 724, 728, 101 N.E.2d 128 (1951). . . . Moreover, our law presumes that fit parents act in furtherance of the welfare and best interests of their children, . . . and with respect to matters relating to their care, custody, and upbringing have a fundamental right to make those decisions for them.

In the instant case, Merav's father signed the release in his capacity as parent because he wanted his child to benefit from participating in cheerleading, as she had done for four previous seasons. He made an important family decision cognizant of the risk of physical injury to his child and the financial risk to the family as a whole. In the circumstance of a voluntary, nonessential activity, we will not disturb this parental judgment. This comports with the fundamental liberty interest of parents in the rearing of their children, and is not inconsistent with the purpose behind our public policy permitting minors to void their contracts.

c.   The Encouragement of Athletic Activities for Minors

Our views with respect to the permissibility of requiring releases as a condition of voluntary participation in extracurricular sports activities, and the enforceability of releases signed by parents on behalf of their children for those purposes, are also consistent with and further the public policy of encouraging athletic programs for the Commonwealth's youth. This policy is most clearly embodied in statutes that exempt from liability for negligence: nonprofit organizations and volunteer managers and coaches who offer and run sports programs for children under eighteen years of age (*G. L. c. 231, § 85V*), and owners of land (including municipalities) who permit the public to use their land for recreational purposes without imposing a fee (*G. L. c. 21, § 17C*). . . .

To hold that releases of the type in question here are unenforceable would expose public schools, who offer many of the extracurricular sports opportunities available to children, to financial costs and risks that will inevitably lead to the reduction of those programs.[11] It would also create the anomaly of a minor who participates in a program sponsored and managed by a nonprofit organization not having a cause of action for negligence that she would have had had she participated in the same program sponsored as an extracurricular activity by the local public school. This distinction seems unwarranted, inevitably destructive to school-sponsored programs, and contrary to public interest.

Merav contends that to enforce the release would convey the message that public school programs can be run negligently, in contravention of the well-established responsibility of schools to protect their students. We disagree. There are many reasons aside from potential tort liability why public schools will continue to take steps to ensure well-run and safe extracurricular programs—not the least of which is their ownership by, and accountability to, the citizens of the cities and towns they serve. Moreover, the Legislature has already made the judgment that the elimination of liability for negligence in nonprofit sports programs is necessary to the encouragement and survival of such programs. . . . The enforcement of the release is consistent with the Commonwealth's policy of encouraging athletic programs for youth and does not contravene the responsibility that schools have to protect their students.

d.   Massachusetts Tort Claims Act

Merav's reliance on *G. L. c. 258, § 2*, to support her claim that cities and towns should not be permitted to require or enforce releases regarding their negligent conduct, is misplaced. While the purpose of the Act may be to provide a remedy for persons injured as a result of the negligence of government entities, . . . it does so by abrogating sovereign immunity only within a narrow statutory framework. . . . Because releases of liability for ordinary negligence involving private parties are valid as a general proposition in the Commonwealth, it is not contrary to the purposes of the Act to allow municipalities to use releases as a precondition for the participation in voluntary, nonessential activities they may sponsor.

e.   Consideration

Merav last argues that the release she signed is void because it was not supported by proper consideration. The motion judge properly concluded that the benefit bargained for, in this case Merav's participation in the cheerleading program, was adequate consideration for the release. . . .

C.   CONCLUSION

For the reasons set forth above, we conclude that Merav's father had the authority to bind his minor child to an exculpatory release that was a proper condition of her voluntary participation in extracurricular sports activities offered by the city. Summary judgment for the city that was entered on the basis of the validity of that release is therefore affirmed. . . .

11. The fact that *G. L. c. 258, § 2*, limits the financial exposure of municipalities to $100,000 an occurrence (plus defense costs) does not insulate them from the deleterious impact of inherently unquantifiable financial risk. Consequently, in times of fiscal constraint, those programs are often the targets of budget reductions. A decision exposing school systems to further financial costs and risk for undertaking such programs cannot help but accelerate their curtailment.

NOTES AND QUESTIONS

1. *Comparison of* Wagenblast *and* Sharon. In *Wagenblast,* the Washington Supreme Court held that requiring a student and his parent or guardian to sign a standard form releasing the school district from liability for negligence in connection with the student's participation in interscholastic athletics violated public policy. Which of the factors articulated in *Tunkl v. University of California* appear most critical as a basis for invalidating waivers in the realm of high school athletics? According to the *Wagenblast* court, is participation in high school sports an important public and practical necessity?

   The *Sharon* court recognized the ability of a minor to void a contract. It upheld a waiver, however, because it had been signed by the minor's parent. Which factors most influenced the court's decision? Which court, *Wagenblast* or *Sharon*, most effectively reconciles the competing public policies regarding whether pre-injury liability waivers should be enforced?

   How critical is the inability of minors or their parents to negotiate the terms of a waiver to determining the enforceability of such a provision? Do minors and their parents possess a realistic opportunity to negotiate the terms of waivers of liability for athletic injury?

2. *Developing Law in Other Jurisdictions.* Other courts have exhibited a willingness to enforce liability waivers for negligent injury to minors participating in competitive or recreational sports. *Mohney v. USA Hockey, Inc.*, 5 Fed. Appx. 450 (6th Cir. 2001) (release, signed by minor hockey player and his father, was valid and applied to injuries sustained by the player); *Zivich v. Mentor Soccer Club, Inc.*, 696 N.E.2d 201 (Ohio 1998) (release, signed by mother of injured child, barred child's claim for negligence against volunteers and sponsors of nonprofit sport activities). In *Platzer v. Mammoth Mountain Ski Area*, 128 Cal. Rptr. 2d 885 (Cal App. 2002), a mother who enrolled her eight-year-old son in a ski resort's sports school signed a form assuming the risk of injury associated, among other things, with use of the chairlifts. Her son fell from a lift during a lesson. In upholding the validity of the exculpatory clause, the court rejected plaintiff's argument that public policy precluded enforcement of the release. It noted that California courts have consistently refused to invalidate exculpatory agreements in the recreational sports context. See also *Pollock v. Highlands Ranch Community Assn., Inc.*, 140 P.3d 351 (Colo. App. 2006) (discussing statute superseding case that had invalidated a release waiving minor child's negligence claim).

   It would be premature to conclude at this point in time that *Sharon* and these cases represent an emerging trend of greater enforcement of exculpatory clauses signed by parents on behalf of their minor children. Although these judicial decisions represent an erosion of the majority rule, other cases demonstrate that many jurisdictions remain reluctant to enforce waiver clauses. See, e.g., *Galloway v. State*, 790 N.W.2d 252, 258 (Iowa 2010) (holding public policy precludes the enforceability of pre-injury waiver a parent signs on behalf of child and characterizing *Sharon* as reflective of the minority rule); *J.T. ex rel. Thode v. Monster Mountain, LLC*, 754 F. Supp. 2d 1323, 1327 (M.D. Ala. 2010) (refusing to enforce liability waiver where court approval had not been obtained); *Hawkins v. Blair Peart*, 37 P.3d 1062, 1066 (Utah 2001) (invalidating on public policy grounds a waiver of liability and indemnity agreement signed by parent on behalf of minor child); *Rice v. American Skiing Co.*, 2000 Me. Super. LEXIS 90 (holding that an unambiguous release of negligence claims given by a mother on behalf of her child is invalid as to the child but is binding against his mother); *Childress v. Madison County*, 777 S.W.2d 1, 7-8 (Tenn. Ct. App. 1989) (holding the same); *Hojnowski v. Vans Skate Park*, 868 A.2d 1087, 1096 (N.J. Super. App. Div. 2005) ("without statutory authority or judicial authorization, a parent has no ability to release a claim properly belonging to a child; therefore liability waiver signed by parent of minor is unenforceable"). See also *Atkins v. Swimwest Family Fitness Center*, 691 N.W.2d 334 (Wis. 2005) (refusing to enforce exculpatory language in liability release because it does not adequately inform parents of rights being waived on minor's behalf).

3. *Other Grounds for Invalidating Waivers.* In jurisdictions in which a release of liability for negligence is enforceable, one that attempts to relieve a defendant of liability for its willful misconduct, gross negligence, and intentional torts is invalid. Connell and Savage, *supra*, at 603. Courts will also resort to contract interpretation as a mechanism for invalidating waivers that are ambiguous and inconspicuous. Strict interpretation of contracts eases the burden on courts to reconcile the tensions between contract and tort. *Id.* at 605-606. See *Eriksson v. Nunnink*, 120 Cal. Rptr. 3d 90 (Cal. App. 2011) (a finding that an equestrian coach was grossly negligent in selecting an unfit horse for the plaintiff would invalidate a liability waiver).

2. College or University

Like the body of law defining a high school's legal duty to protect its students' health and safety, the nature and scope of a university's corresponding legal duty also is rapidly developing. As you read the following cases, consider how the differences between intercollegiate and interscholastic athletics as well as the nature of the relationship between a university and its student-athletes influence judicial definition of the parameters of this duty. In the context of health and safety, should a distinction be drawn between the duty of care owed by colleges to student-athletes and high schools to their student-athletes?

KLEINKNECHT v. GETTYSBURG COLLEGE

989 F.2d 1360 (3d Cir. 1993)

HUTCHINSON, Circuit Judge.

II.   FACTUAL HISTORY

In September 1988, Drew Kleinknecht was a twenty-year-old sophomore student at [Gettysburg] College, which had recruited him for its Division III intercollegiate lacrosse team. . . .

Lacrosse is a contact sport. In terms of sports-related injuries at the College, it ranked at least fourth behind football, basketball, and wrestling, respectively. Lacrosse players can typically suffer a variety of injuries, including unconsciousness, wooziness, concussions, being knocked to the ground, and having the wind knocked out of them. Before Drew died, however, no athlete at the College had experienced cardiac arrest while playing lacrosse or any other sport. . . .

Because lacrosse is a spring sport, daily practices were held during the spring semester in order to prepare for competition. Student trainers were assigned to cover both spring practices and games. Fall practice was held only for the players to learn "skills and drills," and to become acquainted with the other team members. No student trainers were assigned to the fall practices.

Drew participated in a fall lacrosse practice on the afternoon of September 16, 1988. Coaches Janczyk and Anderson attended and supervised this practice. It was held on the softball fields outside Musselman Stadium. No trainers or student trainers were present. Neither coach had certification in CPR. Neither coach had a radio on the practice field. The nearest telephone was inside the training room at Musselman Stadium, roughly 200-250 yards away. The shortest route to this telephone required scaling an eight-foot high cyclone fence surrounding the stadium. According to Coach Janczyk, he and Coach Anderson had never discussed how they would handle an emergency during fall lacrosse practice.

no cell phones

The September 16, 1988 practice began at about 3:15 p.m. with jogging and stretching, some drills, and finally a "six on six" drill in which the team split into two groups at opposite ends of the field. Drew was a defenseman and was participating in one of the drills when he suffered a cardiac arrest. According to a teammate observing from the sidelines, Drew simply stepped away from the play and dropped to the ground. Another teammate on the sidelines stated that no person or object struck Drew prior to his collapse.

After Drew fell, his teammates and Coach Janczyk ran to his side. Coach Janczyk and some of the players noticed that Drew was lying so that his head appeared to be in an awkward position. No one knew precisely what had happened at that time, and at least some of those present suspected a spinal injury. . . .

According to the College, Coach Janczyk acted in accordance with the school's emergency plan by first assessing Drew's condition, then dispatching players to get a trainer and call for an ambulance. Coach Janczyk himself then began to run toward Musselman Stadium to summon help. . . .

[T]he team captain, ran toward the stadium, where he knew a training room was located and a student trainer could be found. . . . [He] scaled a chain link fence that surrounded the stadium and ran across the field, encountering student trainer Traci Moore outside the door to the training room. He told her that a lacrosse player was down and needed help. . . . [He] continued into the training room where he told the student trainers there what had happened. One of them phoned Plank Gymnasium and told Head Trainer Donolli about the emergency.

[A]nother team member ran toward . . . the College Union Building. He told the student at the front desk of the emergency on the practice field . . . and she immediately telephoned for an ambulance.

Student trainer Moore was first to reach Drew. . . . Because Drew was breathing, she did not attempt CPR or any other first aid technique, but only monitored his condition, observing no visible bruises or lacerations.

By this time, Coach Janczyk had entered the stadium training room and learned that Donolli had been notified and an ambulance called. Coach Janczyk returned to the practice field at the same time Donolli arrived in a golf cart.

Donolli saw that Drew was not breathing, and turned him on his back to begin CPR with the help of a student band member who was certified as an emergency medical technician and had by chance arrived on the scene. The two of them performed CPR until two ambulances arrived at approximately 4:15 p.m. Drew was defibrillated and drugs were administered to strengthen his heart. He was placed in an ambulance and taken to the hospital, but despite repeated resuscitation efforts, Drew could not be revived. He was pronounced dead at 4:58 p.m.

As the district court observed, the parties vigorously dispute the amount of time that elapsed in connection with the events following Drew's collapse. . . .

The Kleinknechts further maintain, and the College does not dispute, that at least five minutes elapsed from the time that Drew was first observed on the ground until Head Trainer Donolli began administering CPR. Thus, the Kleinknechts contend that evidence exists from which a jury could infer that as long as twelve minutes elapsed before CPR was administered. They also estimate that roughly ten more minutes passed before the first ambulance arrived on the scene.

Prior to his collapse on September 16, 1988, Drew had no medical history of heart problems. The Kleinknechts themselves describe him as "a healthy, physically active and vigorous young man" with no unusual medical history until his death. Brief for Appellants at 3-4. In January 1988, a College physician had examined Drew to determine his fitness to participate in sports and found him to be in excellent health. The Kleinknecht's family physician had also examined Drew in August 1987 and found him healthy and able to participate in physical activity.

Medical evidence indicated Drew died of cardiac arrest after a fatal attack of cardiac arrhythmia. Post-mortem examination could not detect the cause of Drew's fatal cardiac arrhythmia. An autopsy conducted the day after his death revealed no bruises or contusions on his body. This corroborated the statements by Drew's teammates that he was not in play when he suffered his cardiac arrest and dispelled the idea that contact with a ball or stick during the practice might have caused the arrhythmia. . . .

IV. ANALYSIS

1. THE DUTY OF CARE ISSUE

Whether a defendant owes a duty of care to a plaintiff is a question of law. . . .

a. Special Relationship

The Kleinknechts argue that . . . a college or university owes a duty to its intercollegiate athletes to provide preventive measures in the event of a medical emergency.

In support of their argument, the Kleinknechts cite the case of *Hanson v. Kynast*, No. CA-828 (Ohio Ct.App. June 3, 1985), *rev'd on other grounds*, 24 Ohio St.3d 171, 494 N.E.2d. 1091 (1986). In *Hanson* an intercollegiate, recruited lacrosse player was seriously injured while playing in a lacrosse game against another college. The plaintiff alleged that his university breached its legal duty to have an ambulance present during the lacrosse game. The trial court granted the defendant's motion for summary judgment based on its holding, *inter alia*, that

There is no duty as a matter of law for the Defendant College or other sponsor of athletic events to have ambulances, emergency vehicles, trained help or doctors present during the playing of a lacrosse game or other athletic events, and the failure to do so does not constitute negligence as a matter of law.

Id. at 10. The court of appeals reversed, concluding, "[I]t is a question of fact for the jury to determine whether or not appellee University acted reasonably in failing to have an ambulance present at the field or to provide quick access to the field in the event of an emergency." *Id.* at 6. By directing the trial court to submit the case to a jury, the court of appeals implicitly held that the university owed a duty of care to the plaintiff.

Although the *Hanson* court did not specify the theory on which it predicated this duty, we think it reached the correct result, and we predict that the Supreme Court of Pennsylvania would conclude that a similar a duty exists on the facts of this case. Like the lacrosse student in *Hanson*, Drew chose to attend Gettysburg College because he was persuaded it had a good lacrosse program, a sport in which he wanted to participate at the intercollegiate level. Head Trainer Donolli actively recruited Drew to play lacrosse at the College. At the time he was stricken, Drew was not engaged in his own private affairs as a student at Gettysburg College. Instead, he was participating in a scheduled athletic practice for an intercollegiate team sponsored by the College under the supervision of College employees. On these facts we believe that the Supreme Court of Pennsylvania would hold that a special relationship existed between the College and Drew that was sufficient to impose a duty of reasonable care on the College. Other states have similarly concluded that a duty exists based on such a relationship. . . .

Drew was not acting in his capacity as a private student when he collapsed. Indeed, the Kleinknechts concede that if he had been, they would have no recourse against the College. There is a distinction between a student injured while participating as an intercollegiate athlete in a sport for which he was recruited and a student injured at a college while pursuing his private interests, scholastic or otherwise. This distinction serves to limit the class of students to whom a college owes the duty of care that arises here. Had Drew been participating in a fraternity football game, for example, the College might not have owed him the same duty or perhaps any duty at all. There is, however, no need for us to reach or decide the duty question either in that context or in the context of whether a college would owe a duty towards students participating in intramural sports. On the other hand, the fact that Drew's cardiac arrest occurred during an athletic event involving an intercollegiate team of which he was a member does impose a duty of due care on a college that actively sought his participation in that sport. We cannot help but think that the College recruited Drew for its own benefit, probably thinking that his skill at lacrosse would bring favorable attention and so aid the College in attracting other students. . . .

b.   Foreseeability

This does not end our inquiry, however. The determination that the College owes a duty of care to its intercollegiate athletes could merely define the class of persons to whom the duty extends, without determining the nature of the duty or demands it makes on the College. . . .

Although the district court correctly determined that the Kleinknechts had presented evidence establishing that the occurrence of severe and life-threatening injuries is not out of the ordinary during contact sports, it held that the College had no duty because the cardiac arrest suffered by Drew, a twenty-year old athlete with no history of any severe medical problems, was not reasonably foreseeable. Its definition of foreseeability is too narrow. Although it is true that a defendant is not required to guard against every possible risk, he must take reasonable steps to guard against hazards which are generally foreseeable. Though the specific risk that a person like Drew would suffer a cardiac arrest may be unforeseeable, the Kleinknechts produced ample evidence that a life-threatening injury occurring during participation in an athletic event like lacrosse was reasonably foreseeable. In addition to the testimony of numerous medical and athletic experts, Coach Janczyk, Head Trainer Donolli, and student trainer Moore all testified that they were aware of instances in which athletes had died during athletic competitions. The foreseeability of a life-threatening injury to Drew was not hidden from the College's view. Therefore, the College did owe Drew a duty to take reasonable precautions against the risk of death while Drew was taking part in the College's intercollegiate lacrosse program.

Having determined that it is foreseeable that a member of the College's inter-scholastic lacrosse team could suffer a serious injury during an athletic event, it becomes evident that the College's failure to protect against such a risk is not reasonable. The magnitude of the foreseeable harm—irreparable injury or death to one of its student athletes as a result of inadequate preventive emergency measures—is indisputable. With regard to the offsetting cost of protecting against such risk, the College prophesied that if this Court accepts that the College owed the asserted duty, then it will be required "to have a CPR certified trainer on site at each and every athletic practice whether in-season or off-season, formal or informal, strenuous or light," and to provide similar cardiac protection to "intramural, club sports and gym class." This "slippery slope" prediction reflects an unwarranted extension of the holding in this case. First, the recognition of a duty here is limited to intercollegiate athletes. No other scenario is presented, so the question whether any of the other broad classes of events and students posited by the College merit similar protection is not subject to resolution. Second, the determination whether the College has breached this duty at all is a question of fact for the jury. This Court recognizes only that under the facts of this case, the College owed a duty to Drew to have measures in place at the lacrosse team's practice on the afternoon of September 16, 1988 in order to provide prompt treatment in the event that he or any other member of the lacrosse team suffered a life-threatening injury. . . .

It may be that the emergency medical measures the College had in place were sufficient to fulfill this duty. It is also possible that the College could not foresee that its failure to provide emergency medical services other than those which it already had in place would substantially contribute to the death of an apparently healthy student. . . .

Our holding is narrow. It predicts only that a court applying Pennsylvania law would conclude that the College had a duty to provide prompt and adequate emergency medical services to Drew, one of its intercollegiate athletes, while he was engaged in a school-sponsored athletic activity for which he had been recruited. Whether the College breached that duty is a question of fact. . . .

NOTE AND QUESTIONS

What is the holding in *Kleinknecht*? What policy reasons justify holding the university liable for the student-athlete's death, particularly since his cardiac arrest was unforeseeable? Does a university sponsoring intercollegiate athletics have a legal duty to have a certified athletic trainer present at all games, practices, and training sessions? See *Kennedy v. Syracuse Univ.*, 1995 WL 548710, at 1-3 (N.D. N.Y. Sept. 12, 1995) (the court dismissed an athlete's claim that the university was negligent for failing to have an athletic trainer present at gymnastics team practices, without considering a university's duty to do so, because there was no proof that inadequate emergency care given by coaches or teammates caused plaintiff's injury).

Consistent with *Kleinknecht*, in *Stineman v. Fontbonne College*, 664 F.2d 1082 (8th Cir. 1981), the Eighth Circuit held that a university has a duty to refer an injured intercollegiate athlete to a physician for medical treatment. The plaintiff was struck in the eye by a ball thrown during softball practice. The team's coaches did not recommend that plaintiff see a physician for treatment of her injury. Because of a delay in obtaining medical treatment, the plaintiff lost the vision in her eye. Without considering the plaintiff's potential contributory negligence, the court awarded her damages of $600,000.

In the summer of 2005, Northwestern University paid $16 million to settle a lawsuit alleging that its employees provided negligent emergency medical treatment to Rashidi Wheeler, a football player with a known asthmatic condition, after he collapsed during a preseason workout, which caused his death.

Kleinknecht has potentially broad implications regarding the nature and scope of a university's duty to protect the health and safety of its intercollegiate athletes. However, outside the context of emergency medical care, *Orr* and *Searles* illustrate that courts currently are divided regarding the scope of a university's duty to protect its student-athletes from harm.

ORR v. BRIGHAM YOUNG UNIVERSITY

960 F. Supp. 1522 (D. Utah 1994), *aff'd*, 108 F.3d 1388 (10th Cir. 1997)

SAM, District Judge.

This case raises issues regarding the duty of care owed by a university to one of its football players.

[EDS. Plaintiff Vernon Peter Orr attended Brigham Young University (BYU) from the fall of 1988 until April 1990, and played on the varsity football team for two football seasons. Prior to attending BYU, Orr attended Dixie College in St. George, Utah, and played for two years on the football team. Orr denied having any lower back pain or injury prior to attending BYU. In August 1988, Orr felt pain in his back during a practice drill with a blocking sled during a BYU football practice. He received treatment for his injuries by BYU's athletic trainer while he continued to practice and play in football games during the 1988 season. During the 1989 season, Orr experienced back pain and stiffness but, despite the football coach's directive, did not see the team's athletic trainers for treatment because the pain was not bad and he still felt "pretty much 100%." For the remainder of the 1989 season, Orr had mild episodes of back pain but could not remember if they were reported to the coaching staff or the medical staff.

In the last regular season game of the 1989 season, Orr complained of back pain at halftime and was examined and treated by two orthopedic specialists. Orr returned to play with the instruction that he was to leave the game if the pain increased or changed. Orr played the remainder of the game. After the game, all players who had been injured were instructed to report to the medical clinic in the athletic training room the next day. Orr did not report.

During postseason bowl practice two weeks later, Orr suffered a back injury. He was referred to the medical staff. Examination revealed reticular pain, and he was sent for radiological imaging, which showed three herniated discs. Orr was immediately referred to a neurological surgeon, who performed surgical repair of the herniated discs. At the close of BYU's 1991 winter semester, Orr left BYU to play professional football in Finland. Orr did not return to BYU to complete his education.]

Orr asserts that BYU negligently breached its duty of care owed to him in one or more of the following respects:

a.   engendering a win-at-all-cost mentality;
b.   excessively pressuring players to perform;
c.   using psychological pressure to increase performance at the sacrifice of his health;
d.   creating disincentives to report injuries or seek medical attention;
e.   conditioning payment for medical services on an athletic trainer's determination of medical need;
f.   employing unqualified persons to diagnose and treat football related injuries;
g.   allowing unqualified personnel to evaluate his medical fitness to play football;
h.   misdiagnosing his injuries;
i.   failure of the trainers to refer him to a team physician for diagnosis and treatment;
j.   failing to hire a full-time team physician responsible for diagnoses and treatment in lieu of unqualified trainers;
k.   approving and encouraging him to play after being injured;
l.   using pain killing injections to enable him to continue to play without completely diagnosing his injury;
m.   placing greater emphasis on winning football games than on his physical and mental health;
n.   losing interest in him and failing to assist him further in his education;
o.   failing to act to preserve his health, and to treat his injuries in his long term personal best interest, to see that his educational needs were met; and,
p.   engaging in the unauthorized practice of medicine.

BYU argues that "[e]xcept for those duties relating to claims of medical negligence or violations of medical standards of care, the long list of alleged duties owed to Orr and breached by BYU are ones that have never been identified or recognized as duties owed as a matter of law."

Much of Orr's claim of negligence is based upon the breach of purported duties of care created by the special relationship between a university and its student athletes. . . .

Orr, in essence, urges that BYU, having recruited him to play football, assumed the responsibility for his safety and deprived him of the normal opportunity for self protection. . . .

The Utah Supreme Court has not been called upon to rule on the precise issue presented here. However, direction is provided by analogous authority found in several Utah Supreme Court cases, although factually distinguishable. For example, the plaintiff in *Beach v. University of Utah*, 726 P.2d 413 (Utah 1986), alleged breach of a duty of care based upon a special relationship between the university and the student, injured while intoxicated on a field trip sponsored by the university and supervised by a university professor. After examining the relationship of a university and its students, the Utah Supreme Court concluded that the relationship was not custodial in nature and that law and society increasingly recognized the modern college student as an adult and not a child in need of custodial care. The analysis of *Beach* concerning the nature of the parties' relationship is helpful in evaluating Orr's relationship with BYU. . . .

Arguably, Orr, as a collegiate football player, had both demands and advantages distinct from those of the average college student. However, in the court's view, any distinctions are more of a contractual nature than a custodial nature mandating special duties of care and protection beyond those traditionally recognized under a simple negligence theory of liability. BYU, in exchange for a student's promise to play football, agrees to provide the student with such benefits as special consideration in meeting entrance requirements, financial assistance, training table meals, training equipment, medical services, and academic support. Certainly when training and medical services are provided and then negligently performed, liability could result under existing theories of negligence. However, nothing in the facts supports Orr's contentions that, by playing football for BYU, he became in essence a ward of the university without any vestige of free will or independence. At the time Orr began attending BYU he was twenty-two years old, married with one child. The court finds no facts which suggest that Orr's relationship with BYU was custodial in nature.

An athlete's choice to participate in a sport is not coerced. Voluntary association with a collegiate athletic team does not make the student less of "an autonomous adult or the institution more a caretaker." *Beach*, 726 P.2d at 419. n. 5. As noted earlier, the court views any distinctions between a regular student and a student athlete as more contractual in nature than custodial. In short, the court finds no compelling reasons to impose upon colleges and universities additional duties beyond those owed to other students or those presently recognized and available to collegiate athletes under acknowledged legal theories.

Based upon the analysis of the Utah Supreme Court in the analogous case of *Beach v. University of Utah*, the absence of facts supporting a custodial relationship, as well as for sound policy reasons, the court concludes that the supreme court of Utah would reject Orr's claim that duties are owed to him on the basis of a special relationship with the university by virtue of his football player status. . . .

[EDS. The court granted BYU's motion for summary judgment on all of Orr's claims except any arising out of the alleged negligent provision of medical care. BYU conceded it has a duty to conform to the standard of reasonable care when voluntarily providing sports medical care to its student-athletes. The court found that disputed issues of material fact existed as to Orr's claims based on BYU's alleged breach of its duty of care to Orr in diagnosing and treating his medical injuries.]

SEARLES v. TRUSTEES OF ST. JOSEPH'S COLLEGE

695 A.2d 1206 (Me. 1997)

LIPEZ, Justice.

Paul Searles . . . alleged that while playing basketball for St. Joseph's College the negligence of the defendants caused him permanent injuries and that they breached a contract to pay the medical expenses related to his injuries. Because we conclude that genuine issues of material fact exist on Searles's negligence claims, we vacate the judgment in part.

Searles entered St. Joseph's College as a freshman in 1988, having been awarded an athletic scholarship. Searles alleges that while playing basketball he began experiencing pain in his knees during the fall semester of 1988. In January 1989 Searles was diagnosed with patellar tendinitis. He continued to play basketball for the remainder of the school year, and he returned to play for the 1989-1990 season. He stopped playing in 1990 and had surgery on his knees in 1990 and again in 1991.

Searles filed the present action against St. Joseph's College, Rick Simonds, the school's basketball coach, and Peter Wheeler, the athletic trainer, alleging that "[d]espite medical advice and information suggesting that the Plaintiff should not be playing basketball, Defendant Simonds insisted that Paul Searles play. [As a] result, Paul Searles's knees became permanently impaired." . . .

We previously stated that a college has a legal duty to exercise reasonable care towards its students. *Isaacson v. Husson College*, 297 A.2d 98, 103 (Me.1972). . . . That duty encompasses the duty of college coaches and athletic trainers to exercise reasonable care for the health and safety of student athletes. . . .

Searles alleged that Simonds "knew or should have known Paul Searles should not have been playing basketball in his condition, and should not have played plaintiff." Searles's response to the summary judgment motion included citations to the deposition testimony of Peter Wheeler, St. Joseph's trainer, who stated that he recognized the nature of Searles's problem, was concerned that Searles's continued play would result in greater injury to his knee, and that he discussed Searles's medical problem with Coach Simonds. Searles also alleged that on more than one occasion he advised Simonds that his knees were bothering him, but Simonds "continued to play Plaintiff in games despite knowledge of Plaintiff's condition and general knee soreness as early as January, 1989." The record before the court contains sufficient evidence to raise an issue of material fact as to Simonds's breach of his duty to exercise reasonable care for the health and safety of Searles. . . .

Searles presented medical testimony from Dr. John Herzog that his condition was likely due to "history overuse" and that "the more you play, the longer it's going to hurt and you may have a chronic problem develop." Searles presented evidence that Simonds was aware of his knee injury and continued to play him in games. Searles further alleges that Simonds was so intent on keeping Searles in games that he allowed him to skip basketball practices to preserve his knees for games. Searles himself testified as to the painful injuries he suffered playing basketball. The medical testimony and Searles's own account of his condition create a genuine issue of material fact as to whether he suffered permanent injury as a result of playing basketball at St. Joseph's. . . .

The gravamen of Searles's allegations against Wheeler, set forth in Counts VI and VII of his complaint, involves more than a claim that Wheeler negligently conducted a course of treatment of Searles's injuries that contributed to a worsening of his condition, or that he failed to appreciate the seriousness of Searles's condition. Searles claims that Wheeler "failed to advise Coach Simonds that Paul Searles should not be playing basketball and the condition of Paul Searles's knees was such that continued play before complete healing will likely cause permanent injury." The deposition of Wheeler demonstrates an awareness of the acuteness of Searles's knee problems. Simonds states in his deposition that he was never advised by Wheeler that Searles could be permanently impaired by continued play, and he does not recall the trainer suggesting that Searles should not play. He also asserts that the trainer decided whether an injured player could play basketball, not the coach. To the extent that Searles's claim of negligence against Wheeler involves a failure by Wheeler to communicate to Simonds the nature and extent of Searles's knee problems, or a failure by Wheeler to advise Searles that he should not play basketball in light of Wheeler's knowledge of Searles's medical condition, Searles did not have to provide expert testimony about the standard of care applicable to an athletic trainer. Jurors could apply their common knowledge in determining whether such failures, if they occurred, constituted a breach by Wheeler of his duty to exercise reasonable care for the health and safety of Searles. . . .

[EDS. Searles "[also] alleged that he entered into a contract with St. Joseph's [C]ollege, through its agents, under which the college promised to pay Paul's medical bills if he continued to play for the basketball team." Searles asserted, "Coach Simonds told my parents and me that the school's insurance would pay for all of the medical bills relating to my knee problems." Assuming that Simonds did state to Searles's parents that the school would pay Searles's medical bills, such a statement was deemed insufficient to constitute an offer to enter into a contract. There was no evidence as to the terms of the "offer" purportedly made by Simonds and no evidence that Searles and Simonds had an agreement that Searles had to continue to play basketball in exchange for the payment of his medical expenses. The court found the record did not contain evidence of the existence of a contract and that a judgment had been properly entered in favor of St. Joseph's on the contract claim.]

NOTES AND QUESTIONS

1. *Comparison of* Searles *and* Orr. The *Searles* court ruled that a university has a general legal duty to exercise reasonable care to protect the health and safety of injured student-athletes, whereas *Orr* declines to impose such a broad duty on a university. What reasoning underlies these courts' differing conclusions? According to the *Orr* court, under what limited circumstances might a university be held liable in tort to an injured student-athlete? Consistent with *Searles*, other courts have held that a university has a legal duty not to pressure or permit an injured athlete to return to a game. In *Lamorie v. Warner Pacific College*, 850 P.2d 401 (Or. Ct. App. 1993), a scholarship basketball player asserted that his coach negligently required him to play with a nose and eye injury in violation of a physician's orders. Because the plaintiff feared losing his scholarship if he did not play, he participated in a team scrimmage and reinjured his eye. Reversing the grant of summary judgment for defendants, an Oregon appellate court ruled that a jury could reasonably find that the player's reinjury of his eye was a foreseeable risk of

being directed to resume playing basketball, for which the university could be held liable.

2. *University "Special Relationship" with Student-Athletes.* Should there be a legally recognized special relationship between a university and its student-athletes that imposes a duty to protect their health and safety? If so, what should be the parameters of such a relationship? For commentary regarding whether a special relationship provides the basis for imposing tort liability on universities vis-à-vis their student-athletes, see Brian C. Root, *How the Promises of Riches in Collegiate Athletics Lead to the Compromised Long-Term Health of Student-Athletes: Why and How the NCAA Should Protect Its Student-Athletes' Health*, 19 Health Matrix 279, 295 (2009) (discussing *Kleinknecht* and other cases raising the issue addressed therein); James J. Hefferan, Jr., Note, *Taking One for the Team:* Davidson v. University of North Carolina *and the Duty of Care Owed by Universities to Their Student-Athletes*, 37 Wake Forest L. Rev. 589 (2002); Michelle D. McGirt, Comment, *Do Universities Have a Special Duty of Care to Protect Student-Athletes from Injury?*, 6 Vill. Sports & Ent. L.J. 219 (1999); Timothy Davis, *Examining Educational Malpractice Jurisprudence: Should a Cause of Action Be Created for Student-Athletes?*, 69 Denv. U. L. Rev. 57 (1992).

In *Davidson v. University of North Carolina at Chapel Hill*, 543 S.E.2d 920 (N.C. App. 2001), *cert. denied*, 550 S.E.2d 771 (N.C. 2001), a North Carolina appellate court followed *Kleinknecht* and found the existence of a special relationship between the university and a member of a school-sponsored intercollegiate team. Plaintiff, a member of the University of North Carolina's junior varsity cheerleading squad, suffered permanent brain damage and serious bodily injury resulting from a fall that occurred while she was performing a cheerleading stunt called a "two-one-chair" pyramid. The appellate court concluded that a "special relationship" existed between UNC and the plaintiff because of the parties' mutual dependence and the considerable degree of control the university exercised over the plaintiff. In addition, the court found that the "voluntary undertaking" by UNC to "advise and educate its cheerleaders regarding safety," created a duty of care that arose independently of the special relationship between the plaintiff and UNC. *Id.* at 28. But see *McFadyen v. Duke Univ.*, 2011 WL 1260207 (M.D. N.C. March 31, 2011) (court rules university was not in a special relationship with members of lacrosse team on the basis of their status as students; the extent of any special relationship that might have arisen between players and university would be limited to the lacrosse team context. Consequently, the university was not insurer of the safety of team members in other facets of their university experience); *Sandford v. Long*, 2012 WL 874678 (Cal. App. 4 Dist. March 15, 2012) (rejecting student-athlete's argument that special relationship between university and student-athlete imposed duty of coach to protect athlete against the intentional conduct of a teammate).

Other courts have focused on the inherent risks of a sport, rather than the existence of a special relationship, when defining the scope of a university's duty to protect its student-athletes' safety. *Bukowski v. Clarkson Univ.*, 2012 WL 1986521, *3 (N.Y. June 5, 2012) (coach and university not liable for injuries sustained by pitcher who was hit by a line drive during indoor practice; the player, who was a knowledgeable and experienced baseball player, assumed the inherent risk of being hit by a line drive); *Geiersbach v. Friej*, 807 N.E.2d 114, 120 (Ind. Ct. App. 2004) (finding university had a duty "to avoid reckless or malicious behavior or intentional injury" when conducting sporting events and practices).

3. *National Collegiate Athletic Association Efforts to Protect Student-Athletes' Health and Safety.* The NCAA publishes a sports medicine handbook available on its website that provides guidelines for protecting the health and safety of student-athletes and for minimizing the risk of significant injury for participants in intercollegiate athletics. These guidelines may be relevant in determining the nature and scope of a university's duty to use reasonable care in connection with sports medicine issues affecting its athletics program. See *Wallace v. Broyles*, 961 S.W.2d 712, 713-716 (Ark. 1998) (asserting that a university may be liable for negligently permitting student-athletes, in violation of NCAA guidelines, to have access to controlled substances in athletic department facilities without prescriptions, labels, instructions, or warnings regarding the dangers or side effects of usage).

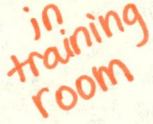 *in training room*

Like state high school athletics governing bodies, the NCAA has a legal duty to use reasonable care when promulgating rules to protect athletes' safety. *Sanchez v. Hillerich & Bradsby Co.*, 128 Cal. Rptr. 2d 529 (Cal. App. 2002) (NCAA may be liable for approving baseball bat if its performance capabilities are proved to increase unreasonably a pitcher's inherent risk of being hit by a batted ball). *like composite*

4. *University Duty to Protect Opponents' Health and Safety.* The law continues to develop regarding the scope of a university's legal duty to prevent one of its athletes from injuring an opposing player. Courts have refused to recognize that a special relationship exists between a university and student-athletes at another school or that a university is vicariously liable for its student-athletes' torts; see *Trujillo v. Yeager*, 642 F. Supp. 2d 86, 91 (D. Conn. 2009) ("holding coaches liable in negligence, particularly to players on a different college's team, would unreasonably threaten to chill competitive play"); *Avila v. Citrus Community College Dist.*, 38 Cal. 4th 148, 131 P.3d 383, 41 Cal. Rptr. 3d 299 (Cal. 2006) (although university has a legal duty not to increase the risks inherent in an intercollegiate sport, it has no legal duty to prevent its pitcher from intentionally throwing at an opposing team's batter because "being intentionally thrown at is a fundamental part and inherent risk" of baseball); *Kavanagh v. Trustees of Boston Univ.*, 795 N.E.2d 1170, 1178 (Mass. 2003) (university "would have to have specific information about a player suggesting a propensity to engage in violent conduct" to be held directly liable); and the *Fox v. Board of Supervisors of La. State Univ.* 576 So. 2d 978 (La. 1991) (university possessed no duty to supervise activities of LSU club rugby team to protect player on opposing team from injury because no special relationship existed between LSU and plaintiff).

5. *Validity of Liability Waivers.* In the preceding discussion of interscholastic sports, we note the majority rule that invalidates liability waivers executed by minors and their parents. Should a different rule apply for waivers executed by adult college student-athletes? See *Roe v. St. Louis University*, 2012 WL 6757558 at *1 (E.D. Mo.) (upholding waiver that releases university of liability for negligence that "may rise by or in connection with [student-athlete's] participation in any activities related to Saint Louis University intercollegiate athletic teams").

6. *Tort Immunity Issues.* Like a public high school system and its employees, a public university and its employees may be immune from liability for

negligence in connection with the operation of its athletic program under the doctrines of sovereign and qualified immunity, respectively. *Lennon v. Petersen*, 624 So. 2d 171, 173-175 (Ala. 1993). Immunity from tort liability may be waived to the extent that negligent conduct arising out of a public university's sports program is covered by insurance. *Shriver v. Athletic Council of Kan. State Univ.*, 564 P.2d 451, 455 (Kan. 1977). See also *Wallace v. Broyles*, 961 S.W.2d 712, 714 (Ark. 1998) (holding that an athletic trainer may be liable for negligence to the extent of his insurance coverage). Tortious conduct more culpable than mere negligence, such as malicious acts or omissions, may not be immunized. See *Wallace*, 961 S.W.2d, at 717.

Some courts have held that sponsoring revenue-generating sports such as intercollegiate football is a proprietary function of a public university that is not protected by sovereign immunity. *Brown v. Wichita State Univ.*, 540 P.2d 66, 86-89 (Kan. 1975). Thus, sovereign immunity would not bar tort suits by athletes injured while participating in these sports. But see *Harris v. University of Mich. Bd. of Regents*, 558 N.W.2d 225, 228 (Mich. Ct. App.1996) (holding that university sponsorship of intercollegiate athletics is a governmental, not a proprietary, function of a public university, even if some sports generate revenue); *Ward v. Michigan State Univ.* (*on remand*), 782 N.W.2d 514, 520 (Mich. App. 2010) *appeal denied*, 798 N.W.2d 766 (Mich. 2011) (holding the same); *University of Texas at El Paso v. Moreno*, 172 S.W.3d 281 (Tex. Ct. App. 2005) (university entitled to immunity from liability for claims filed by fan who asserted he was injured by conduct of other fans after he streamed onto football field and hung from goal post following postgame celebration).

Private universities may be protected from negligence suits by intercollegiate athletes by the doctrine of charitable immunity. Application of this doctrine varies by jurisdiction. See *Gilbert v. Seton Hall Univ.*, 332 F.3d 105 (2d Cir. 2003) (applying conflicts of law principles to determine applicability of charitable immunity doctrine in suit by injured club team player against private university).

PROBLEM 11-3

Amos is a scholarship athlete who is the star wide receiver at Big U, a private NCAA FBS powerhouse whose football program generates approximately $50 million in annual revenues. The week before the game with Large U, Big U's hated rival, Amos suffered a very painful neck injury that prevented him from practicing. Although Big U's team physician recommended that Amos not play, Big U's coach pressured Amos to play because the Large U game would decide the conference championship.

During the game Amos suffered a broken neck causing permanent paralysis when he was injured in a vicious helmet-to-helmet tackle by Brutus, a Large U defensive back. Large U was penalized 15 yards for Brutus's personal foul, which was characterized by the referees as illegal "spearing."

It is anticipated that Amos will require lifetime care and incur significant medical expenses. During the recruiting process, Big U's head coach told Amos that the university would "take care" of him if he was injured while playing football. Discuss Amos's potential claims for recovery for his injuries.

D.   SPORTS MEDICINE MALPRACTICE LIABILITY

Professional teams and collegiate educational institutions generally hire a physician or group of physicians to provide medical care to their athletes. Many high schools also select a physician to provide pre-participation physical examinations and emergency medical care to athletes participating in interscholastic athletics.

A "team physician" provides medical services to athletes that are arranged for, or paid for, at least in part, by an institution or entity other than the patient or his parent or guardian. Joseph H. King, Jr., *The Duty and Standard of Care for Team Physicians*, 18 Hous. L. Rev. 657, 658 (1981).

The team physician's primary responsibility is to provide for the physical well-being of athletes. The team physician must provide medical treatment and advice consistent with an individual athlete's best health interests because there is a physician-patient relationship between them. Although one of the team physician's objectives is to avoid the unnecessary restriction of athletic activity, his paramount responsibility should be to protect the competitive athlete's health. Matthew J. Mitten, *Team Physicians and Competitive Athletes: Allocating Legal Responsibility for Athletic Injuries*, 55 U. Pitt L. Rev. 129, 140-141 (1993). Team physicians may face extreme pressure from coaches, team management, fans, or the athlete to provide medical clearance to participate or treatment enabling immediate return to play. For scholarly commentary discussing the potential conflicts inherent in the team physician's dual obligations to an athletic team and its athletes, see Twila Keim, Comment, *Physicians for Professional Sports Teams: Health Care Under the Pressure of Economic and Commercial Interests*, 9 Seton Hall J. Sport L. 196 (1999); Scott Polsky, Comment, *Winning Medicine: Professional Sports Team Doctors' Conflicts of Interest*, 14 J. Contemp. Health L. & Pol'y 503 (1998); Hayden Opie, *The Team/ Doctor/Athlete Legal Relationship*, 2 Sports Training, Med. & Rehab. 287 (1991).

As the following case illustrates, the team physician's judgment should be governed only by medical considerations, not the team's need for the services of the player or the athlete's strong desire to play.

KRUEGER v. SAN FRANCISCO FORTY NINERS
234 Cal. Rptr. 579 (Cal. App. 1987)

(In denying review, the California Supreme court ordered that this opinion not be officially published.)

NEWSOM, Associate Justice.

Appellant Charles Krueger began playing professional football with the San Francisco 49'ers (hereafter respondent or the 49'ers) in 1958. He was a defensive lineman for the 49'ers until retiring in 1973, missing only parts of two seasons due to injuries. During his career, however, appellant played despite suffering numerous injuries. He broke his arm and the ring finger on each hand, cracked or broke his nose "innumerable times," suffered multiple dislocations of the fingers and thumbs on both hands, incurred a "blow-out" fracture of the right ocular orbit, developed an eye infection or "pterygium" caused by a foreign substance becoming lodged in the eye, sprained his right knee, and developed hypertension, among other maladies.

[EDS. Injuries and damages to appellant's left knee were the focus of the suit. In October 1963, he ruptured the medial collateral ligament in his left knee. Dr. Taylor, the Forty Niners' team physician, performed an operation on the knee, which, Krueger was told, effectuated a "good repair." Dr. Taylor noted in his report of the operation that the anterior cruciate ligament—the function of which is to prevent the tibia from shifting forward on the femur—"appeared to be absent" from appellant's left knee. Such an injury can produce instability in the knee, particularly if combined with other injuries. According to Krueger, he was not told that his left knee evidently lacked the anterior cruciate ligament.

During subsequent seasons Krueger experienced pain and considerable swelling in his left knee. He received treatment from physicians retained by the 49'ers, which consisted of aspiration of bloody fluid from the knee by means of a syringe and contemporaneous injection of Novocain and cortisone, a steroid compound. Appellant testified that he received approximately 50 such "Kepplemann" treatments during 1964, and an average of 14 to 20 per year from 1964 to 1973. He testified that he was never advised by the 49'ers medical staff of the dangers associated with steroid injections in the knee, such as possible rupturing of tendons, weakening of joints and cartilage, and destruction of capillaries and blood vessels. At trial, Krueger offered expert medical testimony that the number of steroid injections appellant claimed to have undergone would have been inappropriate and quite "unusual." X-rays taken between 1964 and 1971 revealed "degenerative post-traumatic changes" in appellant's left knee joint. Appellant's uncontradicted testimony was that he was not told of either of these afflictions by the 49'ers medical staff.

Krueger also testified that he suffered a "hit" on the outside of his knee during a game in 1970 and felt a piece of the knee break off. Notwithstanding the obvious severity of the injury, he was given Empirin codeine and directed to return to the game. For the remainder of the season, he could feel a "considerable piece of substance" dislodged on the outside of his left knee joint; nevertheless, he played the remaining five games of the season. At no time did the team doctors ever advise him that he risked permanent injury by continuing to play without surgery. Krueger testified unequivocally that, had he been advised not to play, he would have followed that advice.

Appellant retired from football following the 1973 season. At the time of his lawsuit, he suffered from traumatic arthritis and a crippling degenerative process in his left knee. He could not stand up for prolonged periods and could not run. He was also unable to walk on stairs without severe pain. His condition was degenerative and irreversible.]

Appellant's action was for fraud or deceit. . . .

The elements of a cause of action for fraud or deceit are as follows: a misrepresentation or suppression of a material fact; knowledge of any falsity; intent to induce reliance; actual and justifiable reliance; and resulting damages. Deceit may be negative as well as affirmative; it may consist in suppression of that which it is one's duty to disclose, as well as in the declaration of that which is false. . . . [T]he intentional concealment of a material fact is actionable fraud only if there is a fiduciary relationship giving rise to a duty to disclose it. The relationship between physician and patient is fiduciary in nature and creates a duty to disclose.

Respondent submits that the record fails to substantiate appellant's claim that material medical information was concealed from him. We disagree. Appellant testified unequivocally that the team's physicians never disclosed to him the adverse effects of steroid injections, or the true nature and extent of the damage to his left knee, particularly the dangers associated with the prolonged violent traumatic impact inherent in professional football. Nor, he testified, was he informed that x-rays taken of his legs revealed the severely degenerated condition of his left knee. . . .

If the case were simply one of conflicting evidence, we would of course affirm the judgment. As to the crucial issue of full disclosure, however, we find the evidence uncontradicted; as will appear, the requisite disclosure was never made. That the team physicians *withheld* no material information from Krueger is not, in our view, the proper focus of inquiry. The critical question is whether full *disclosure* of his medical condition was ever made to Krueger. . . .

In our opinion, the duty of full disclosure within the context of a doctor-patient relationship defines the test for concealment or suppression of facts under Civil Code section 1710, subdivision (3). The failure to make such disclosure constitutes not only negligence, but—where the requisite intent is shown—fraud or concealment as well. A physician cannot avoid responsibility for failure to make full disclosure by simply claiming that information was not withheld.

The testimony that, following his knee surgery in 1963, Krueger was not advised of the adverse effects of steroid injections, or of the risks associated with the continued pursuit of his profession, was uncontradicted. That is, while respondent produced testimony that the physicians treating appellant told him of the general nature of his injury, and did not *conceal* certain information from him, there is no evidence that appellant was ever informed of the continuing risks associated with his injuries. Hence, the requisite disclosure was never made. . . .

[W]e think the record unequivocally demonstrates that, in its desire to keep appellant on the playing field, respondent consciously failed to make full, meaningful disclosure to him respecting the magnitude of the risk he took in continuing to play a violent contact sport with a profoundly damaged left knee. The uncontradicted record shows that Krueger was in acute pain from 1963 on, that he was regularly anesthetized between and during games, and endured repeated, questionable steroid treatments administered by the team physician. X-rays had been taken which fully depicted the extent of his degenerative condition, but he was never so informed. In 1970, part of his knee broke away and yet he was still not given an honest assessment of the seriousness of his condition. Respondent's claim of no concealment cannot be substituted for the professional warnings to which Krueger was at this point so clearly entitled. And it is in this palpable failure to disclose, viewed in the light of the 49'ers compelling obvious interest in prolonging appellant's career, that we find the intent requisite for a finding of fraudulent concealment.

Respecting the element of reliance, appellant's testimony was that he accepted and acted upon the medical advice of the physicians as provided by respondent. No contradictory evidence appears. "'[P]atients are generally persons unlearned in the medical sciences, . . .'" and consequently are entitled to rely upon physicians for full disclosure of material medical information. (*Truman v. Thomas*, supra, 27 Cal.3d 285, 291, 165 Cal.Rptr. 308, 611 P.2d 902.) Reliance is thus established.

Respondent contends that appellant was or should have been cognizant of the seriousness and permanent nature of the injury to his left knee, but we find no credible evidence supportive of this claim. Certainly, appellant knew that his injury was serious. He was entitled, however, to rely upon respondent's physicians for medical treatment and advice without consulting outside sources or undertaking independent investigation.

Turning to the issues of proximate cause and damages, we note the trial court's finding that appellant's desire to continue playing was so intense that he would have continued even had he been informed of the magnitude of the risk involved. This finding seems to us mere conjecture. Appellant demonstrated throughout his football career a courageous—some might say foolhardy—willingness to endure pain and injuries for the sake of his team and employer, but no credible evidence suggests that he ever assessed and accepted the prospect of permanent disability. On the contrary, he testified that he would have retired had respondent's physicians recommended that course of action, and no contrary evidence was offered by respondent.

Accordingly, we conclude there is no substantial evidence to support the judgment entered by the trial court; and conversely, that appellant established all the elements of a fraudulent concealment case based upon nondisclosure of material medical information. . . .

NOTES AND QUESTIONS

1. *Informed Consent Doctrine.* Why was the team physician found liable in *Krueger*? General informed consent principles apply in the sports medicine context and govern the required disclosure of information by the team physician to a competitive athlete. One commentator has suggested:

> A team physician or consulting specialist should fully disclose to an athlete the material medical risks of playing with an injury, illness or physical abnormality, and the potential health consequences of a given medication or treatment. To enable the athlete to make an informed decision, a physician should clearly warn of all material short and long-term medical risks of continued athletic participation and medical treatment under the circumstances, including any potentially life-threatening or permanently disabling health consequences. . . . To minimize potential legal liability, information concerning the athlete's medical condition, proposed treatment and alternatives, probability of injury or re-injury, severity of harm and potential long-term health effects should be tape recorded when provided verbally and also should be given in writing.

Matthew J. Mitten, *Emerging Legal Issues in Sports Medicine: A Synthesis, Summary, and Analysis,* 76 St. John's L. Rev. 5, 26-27 (2002).

In other cases, athletes have been unable to prove that a physician violated the informed consent doctrine. In *Martin v. Casagrande,* 559 N.Y.S.2d 68 (N.Y. App. Div. 1990), a New York appellate court rejected a professional hockey player's claim that a physician intentionally concealed the condition of his knee to induce him to continue playing hockey. Because x-rays and tests performed by the physician did not indicate ligament or meniscal damage to the player's knee, the court held there was no basis for finding that the physician fraudulently withheld this information. The court observed that, at most, the player might have a negligence claim against the physician for failing to properly diagnose the condition of his knee.

To prevail against a team physician for negligent or fraudulent failure to disclose medical information, *Krueger* holds that an athlete must prove he would not have played or undergone the medical treatment that caused his harm if he had been properly informed of the material risks. Should this be an objective or subjective standard?

Krueger ultimately was awarded $2.36 million in damages by a trial court, but settled his claim for between $1 million and $1.5 million. See Jennifer L. Woodlief, *The Trouble with Charlie—Fraudulent Concealment of Medical Information in Professional Football*, 9 Ent. & Sports Law 3 (1991).

2. *Physician Standard of Care.* There are few reported cases discussing the appropriate standard of care for malpractice in the sports medicine setting. In malpractice suits involving a medical specialist, the trend is to apply a national standard of care because national specialty certification boards exist to ensure standardized training and certification procedures. Team physicians generally are internists, family practitioners, or orthopedic surgeons. Other specialists such as cardiologists and pediatricians also provide sports medicine care to athletes. See *Pratt v. Weiss* 53 So. 3d 395 (Fla. App. 2011) (holding that pediatric emergency medicine specialist who frequently treats injured football players in hospital emergency room is expert qualified to testify regarding orthopedic surgeon's negligent treatment of injured football player on field).

Historically, courts ruled that sports medicine is not a separate medical specialty, because no national medical specialty board certification or standardized training previously existed. See, e.g., *Fleischmann v. Hanover Ins. Co.*, 470 So. 2d 216, 217 (La. Ct. App. 1985) (refusing to recognize subspecialty in sports medicine). This judicial view, however, is changing as sports medicine becomes a recognized and accepted area of specialization within the medical profession. The American Osteopathic Association has a certification board for sports medicine, and the specialty boards for family practice, internal medicine, emergency medicine, and pediatrics within the American Board of Medical Specialties now recognize sports medicine as a subspecialty. See *Gibson v. Digiglia*, 980 So. 2d 739 (La. App. 2008) (dismissing athlete's malpractice claim because plaintiff presented "no evidence to establish the standard of care required of a 'team medical director/coordinator' nor have they presented any evidence to support a claim that Dr. Digiglia's actions fell below the standard of care for that alleged sub-specialty of physicians"). If a team physician holds himself out as having special competence in sports medicine, he should be treated as a specialist and held to an awareness of "fundamentals which all practicing specialists in sports medicine should know, based on the types of athletes with whom the physician is involved." Charles V. Russell, *Legal and Ethical Conflicts Arising from the Team Physician's Dual Obligations to the Athlete and Management*, 10 Seton Hall Legis. J. 299, 306-307 (1987).

Sports medicine malpractice cases adopt an "accepted practice" standard of care in determining physician liability. *Mikkelsen v. Haslam*, 764 P.2d 1384, 1386 (Utah Ct. App. 1988) (upholding jury verdict imposing liability on orthopedist on grounds that advice to a patient with a total hip replacement that snow skiing was permissible was "a departure from orthopedic medical profession standards"); *Classen v. Izquierdo*, 520 N.Y.S.2d 999, 1002 (N.Y. Sup. Ct. 1987) (physician who treats an athlete must "practice in accordance with good and accepted standards of medical care"). Under this standard, acceptable or reasonable medical practices (rather than what has been customary) define the boundaries of a physician's legal duty of care in treating athletes.

See generally Mitten, *supra*, at 8-30 (providing overview of team physician malpractice liability issues).

Some groups of sports medicine physicians and hospitals are paying professional teams and universities a significant sponsorship fee to treat their players and for the right to advertise themselves as the team's official sports medicine care provider. Do these arrangements create an unethical conflict of interest for physicians? Is evidence of a sponsorship agreement relevant evidence of malpractice in a suit by an athlete against the team physician?

3. *Athletic Trainers.* Athletic trainers typically provide a variety of sports medicine services to athletes, such as physical conditioning, injury prevention, emergency medical care, and injury rehabilitation—which may give rise to legal liability if rendered improperly. See, e.g., *Howard v. Missouri Bone and Joint Center, Inc.*, 615 F.3d 991 (8th Cir. 2011) (expert testimony establishes athletic trainer's negligence in conducting workout program that caused injury to college athlete); *Ramsey v. Gamber*, 2011 WL 486139 (M.D. Ala.) (former athletic trainer could not be held liable in tort for weight-lifting injury on basis of respondeat superior where plaintiff presented no proof that trainer had the ability to select or terminate employment of weight room assistants); *Searles v. Trustees of St. Joseph's College*, 695 A.2d 1206, 1210 (Me. 1997) (an athletic trainer "has the duty to conform to the standard of care required of an ordinary careful trainer" when providing care and treatment to athletes); *Jarreau v. Orleans Parish Sch. Bd.*, 600 So. 2d 1389 (La. Ct. App. 1992) (court upheld a jury finding that a high school football team's trainer negligently failed to refer a player with a wrist injury to an orthopedist until after the season ended. The athletic trainer's delay in referring the player for treatment of his fracture necessitated an extended period of treatment and caused a permanent disability).

4. *Athlete's Contributory Negligence.* An athlete has a legal duty to use reasonable care to protect his own health and safety. For example, he must truthfully disclose his medical history and physical symptoms to the team physician. In *Jarreau, supra*, the court, applying contributory negligence principles, found an injured high school football player to be one-third at fault for failing to consult his own physician or requesting that he be referred to a school physician. See *McGee v. Covington County Sch. Dist.*, 2012 WL 48026 (Miss. App.) (absolving nurse practitioner, who conducted pre-participation physical examination of high school student-athlete who later died during practice, from liability where athlete and his mother failed to truthfully disclose the athlete's medical history).

An athlete generally may rely on the recommendations of the team physician or his designated consulting specialists regarding when it is appropriate to return to play after an injury without seeking a second medical opinion. His reliance on the team physician's recommendations ordinarily is considered reasonable because of the doctor's sports medicine expertise, and the athlete is not required to obtain a confirming medical opinion. *Mikkelsen v. Haslam*, 764 P.2d 1384, 1388 (Utah Ct. App. 1988); *Krueger v. S.F. Forty Niners*, 234 Cal. Rptr. 579, 584 (Cal. Ct. App. 1987).

On the other hand, an athlete's failure to follow his physician's instructions constitutes contributory negligence that may reduce or bar his recovery. In *Gillespie v. Southern Utah State College*, 669 P.2d 861 (Utah 1983), a college basketball player was found to be solely responsible for aggravating an ankle injury by not following physician instructions concerning proper treatment and rehabilitation. See also *Holtman v. Reese*, 460 S.E.2d 338 (N.C. Ct. App. 1995) (engaging in high-impact aerobics, snow skiing, and water-skiing contrary to chiropractor's advice). *Starnes v. Caddo Parish Sch. Bd.*, 598 So. 2d 472 (La. Ct. App. 1992) (playing volleyball without wearing knee brace against doctor's advice).

An athlete does not assume the risk of injury from negligent emergency medical care rendered by a physician during a sporting event. In *Classen v. Izquierdo*, 520 N.Y.S.2d 999 (N.Y. Sup. Ct. 1987), the court denied a summary judgment motion by a ringside physician who allegedly was negligent in allowing a boxer to continue fighting and thereby receive injuries that caused his death.

PROBLEM 11-4

Midway during the college basketball season, Star Player was diagnosed with a potentially life-threatening heart rhythm disorder. The university's team physician referred him to a prominent cardiologist who medically cleared him to participate with prescribed medication and careful monitoring. The medication made Star Player feel sluggish, and he was unable to play at his previously high level of competition while taking it. This concerned both Star Player, who had aspirations of a future career as a player in the National Basketball Association (NBA), and his college basketball coach, who needed him to perform well during the upcoming NCAA basketball tournament for the team to make the Final Four. After conferring with the university's team physician and head basketball coach, the cardiologist reduced the level of Star Player's medication. Thereafter, he played much better but occasionally was winded and felt light-headed during the first two games of the NCAA tournament. Star Player, who was concentrating on helping his team make the Final Four and impressing NBA scouts, did not tell anyone how he was feeling. While playing a game in the Sweet Sixteen round, Star Player collapsed and died from cardiac arrest.

In a lawsuit by his heirs, consider who may be legally liable for Star Player's death and any defenses that may be raised by defendants.

E.   INJURY COMPENSATION FOR PROFESSIONAL ATHLETES

Like other athletes, professional athletes generally assume the inherent risks of injury while participating in their respective sports. However, the league collective bargaining agreement and standard player contract generally establish a contractual right of professional athletes to receive team-provided or paid medical care and rehabilitation for injuries suffered during training and games. Major league professional athletes also have contractual injury protection guarantees and benefits for career-ending injuries and sport-related disabilities. See, e.g., *Courson v. Bert Bell NFL Player Ret. Plan*, 214 F.3d 136 (3d Cir. 2000) (discussing the disability benefits plan for NFL players). Disputes between a player and team concerning the parties' respective rights and responsibilities under these agreements generally must be submitted to binding arbitration.

Smith v. Houston Oilers, Inc., 87 F.3d 717 (5th Cir. 1996); *Sherwin v. Indianapolis Colts, Inc.*, 752 F. Supp. 1172 (N.D.N.Y. 1990). But see *Hendy v. Losse*, 925 F.2d 1470 (9th Cir. 1991) (state tort law claims against club alleging negligent hiring and retention of team physician actionable because they arose independent of CBA and do not require construction of its terms for resolution); *Jurevicius v. Cleveland Browns Football Co. LLC*, 2010 WL 8461220 (N.D. Ohio Mar. 31, 2010) (refusing to dismiss a player's negligence against the Cleveland Browns because CBA provisions regarding player health and safety related only to a player's physical condition, and not to management of the training facility); *Brown v. NFL*, 219 F. Supp. 2d 372 (S.D.N.Y. 2002) (former player's claim against NFL for injury caused by referee arises out of common law tort duty, not terms of CBA); *Bentley v. Cleveland Browns Football Co.*, 2011 WL 2652343 (Ohio App. July 7, 2011) (club's alleged fraudulent and negligent misrepresentations regarding its postoperative rehabilitation facility for players do not require interpretation of NFL CBA and are not required to be submitted to arbitration).

As employees, athletes on professional teams also may be eligible to recover state workers' compensation benefits for injuries or diseases arising from playing a sport. Workers' compensation laws provide a simple and inexpensive method for employees to obtain compensation and medical expenses for work-related injuries and illnesses. The theory underlying these laws is that businesses should bear the burden of industrial accidents as a component of the cost of production. Thus, workers' compensation is premised on the idea that workplace accidents are a cost of doing business and therefore should be borne by the enterprise that engendered them. In this sense, workers' compensation is a transfer of economic losses from injured workers to industry and, ultimately, to the public.

Under workers' compensation legislation, benefits are available to injured workers without having to prove an employer's common law tort or other statutory liability. Defenses available in common law tort actions, such as contributory negligence, assumption of risk, and the fellow servant rule, are unavailable to employers in workers' compensation actions. The removal of such requirements enables injured employees to avoid the impediments that left many workers uncompensated under the common law.

Employees obtain the security of workers' compensation benefits on a no-fault basis in exchange for relinquishing rights to pursue tort actions against their employers. A worker who accepts workers' compensation benefits or has successfully prosecuted a workers' compensation claim is barred from bringing a common law tort action. Limitations are also imposed on the amount of damages that workers can recover. For example, workers' compensation statutes generally preclude employees from recovering for pain and suffering or punitive damages. Available remedies are typically limited to compensation for disability, medical, death, and burial expenses. Thus, employees waive tort claims against their employers in exchange for a simplified but limited recovery under workers' compensation laws.

State statutes are generally the source of employee rights to workers' compensation benefits. Typically, the right of an employee to receive benefits under workers' compensation laws is dependent on two important criteria: (1) Is the person seeking benefits an "employee" as defined by the relevant state statute? (2) Is the injury for which compensation is sought work-related, or as is commonly stated, did the injury "arise out of" and "in the course of" the claimant's employment? A helpful review and analysis of general workers' compensation principles is provided in Arthur Larson, Larson's Workers' Compensation Law (LEXIS 2008).

Although professional athletes most often can readily establish the existence of an employee/employer relationship, this characterization sets the stage for the introduction of a myriad of other legal issues that potentially affect injured athletes' entitlement to workers' compensation benefits against their teams. The legal issues related to workers' compensation prevalent in professional sports are too numerous to provide an exhaustive examination in this text. For a general discussion of the law of workers' compensation as it applies to professional athletes, see Gerald Herz, *Professional Athletes and the Law of Workers' Compensation: Rights and Remedies*, in Law of Professional and Amateur Sports 17-1 (Gary A. Uberstine ed., West Group 2002); Matthew J. Mitten, *Team Physicians As Co-Employees: A Prescription That Deprives Professional Athletes of an Adequate Remedy for Sports Medicine Malpractice*, 50 St. Louis U. L.J. 211 (2005); Matthew J. Mitten, *Emerging Legal Issues in Sports Medicine: A Synthesis, Summary, and Analysis*, 76 St. John L. Rev. 5, 44-49, 57-59 (2002); Nick DiCello, *No Pain, No Gain, No Compensation: Exploiting Professional Athletes Through Substandard Medical Care Administered by Team Physicians*, 49 Clev. St. L. Rev. 507, 526-533 (2001).

Bodily injury caused by negligent medical treatment is compensable under workers' compensation statutes. See *DePiano v. Montreal Baseball Club, Ltd.*, 663 F. Supp. 116, 117 (W.D. Pa. 1987). But see *Brinkman v. Buffalo Bills Football Club*, 433 F. Supp. 699, 702 (W.D.N.Y. 1977) (holding that a tort claim for bodily injury from negligent medical treatment was barred by workers' compensation laws). A professional athlete may receive workers' compensation benefits for aggravation of an injury caused by improper treatment by the team's medical personnel. See *Bayless v. Philadelphia Nat'l League Club*, 472 F. Supp. 625, 629 (E.D. Pa. 1979) ("Once an employer undertakes, through its physicians, to provide proper medical care for any on-the-job illnesses, any harm resulting from the failure to do so is compensable under [state workers' compensation law]"). Aggravation of a player's existing injury caused by a professional team's requirement that the player continue or resume playing is compensable damage under workers' compensation law. See *DePiano*, 663 F. Supp. at 117-118.

The following material provides an introduction to illustrate contemporary issues involving workers' compensation and professional athletics. The principal cases and notes primarily address four issues: (1) the injuries that are compensable under workers' compensation statutes, (2) the constitutionality of workers' compensation statutes that impose limitations on the benefits recoverable by professional athletes, (3) exceptions to the exclusivity of workers' compensation benefits system as the sole state law remedy for player injuries, and (4) the validity of forum selection clauses designating the state in which a player can assert a workers' compensation claim.

PRO-FOOTBALL, INC. v. UHLENHAKE

558 S.E. 2d 571 (Va. App. 2002)

BENTON, Judge.

The Workers' Compensation Commission entered an award of permanent partial disability benefits in favor of Jeffrey A. Uhlenhake, a professional football player, for injury to his left foot and denied him an award of benefits for injury to his left knee. Pro-Football, Inc., trading as the Washington Redskins, contends that injuries to a professional football player are not covered by the Act and, alternatively, that the evidence does not support the award of benefits for injury to Uhlenhake's left foot. Uhlenhake contends the evidence proved a compensable injury to his left knee. For the reasons that follow, we affirm the commission's award. . . .

Uhlenhake testified that he sustained an injury on September 28, 1997, during a regularly scheduled game when another player fell on his left ankle and foot. Uhlenhake reported the injury to the team's trainer and continued in the game. The team's physician, Dr. Gordon Lee Avery, an orthopaedic surgeon, examined Uhlenhake and noted a left ankle sprain with swelling, bruising, and pain but no instability. Uhlenhake applied ice to the injury and did not return to Dr. Avery for further treatment for the sprain.

Uhlenhake testified that during a regularly scheduled game on November 9, 1997, he felt a "pop and pain" in his left knee when he "twisted or hyper-extended or did something" while blocking an opposing player. He testified that he continued in the game and reported the incident to the training staff the following day. Uhlenhake saw Dr. Avery a few days later because of an extreme amount of swelling. He testified that Dr. Avery gave him a brace and treatments of icing and electrical stimulation. Although Uhlenhake testified that he had no popping or pain in his knee before this incident, he recalled having some bursa sac problems two weeks prior to the November 9 incident.

The assistant trainer's report indicates that Uhlenhake had "moderate effusion of his left knee" and "did not remember when he injured the knee." Dr. Avery examined Uhlenhake on November 12 and reported the following: [Uhlenhake] has been having some vague discomfort about the left knee for the past two weeks with some associated swelling. He does not recall a particular injury, however. On careful questioning he has had the feeling that the knee is not stable. [Uhlenhake] gives a past history of an ACL reconstruction back in 1992, and states that he had his knee arthroscoped at least three times, but he is not certain how much chondral damage or meniscal damage had occurred.

Dr. Avery "suggested that [Uhlenhake] try again wearing his ACL brace to . . . stabilize the knee" and warned that if "the knee is subluxing . . . he needs to stop playing."

Uhlenhake testified that he wore his brace in a regularly scheduled game on November 23. During the game, he "had a pop and some pain." Dr. Avery examined him three days later and noted Uhlenhake had pain "in the postero-lateral corner" and renewed "ACL deficiency." He "explained to [Uhlenhake] that if he continues to sublux he is damaging the knee and should stop playing." Uhlenhake participated in two more games that season. Dr. Avery reported "an episode of subluxation of the left knee" on December 3. At the end of the 1997 football season, Uhlenhake had surgery to repair the ACL on his left knee. Dr. Joseph D. Linehan, an orthopaedic surgeon, examined Uhlenhake in 1999 and opined that he had a permanent impairment of his left ankle due to arthritis and of his left knee due to the ACL injury.

Uhlenhake filed a claim for permanent partial disability benefits based upon injuries to his left ankle and foot and to his left knee. . . .

Upon its review, the commission rejected Pro-Football's "argument that none of the alleged injuries are compensable because they were not 'accidental' within the meaning of the . . . Act." In pertinent part, the commission ruled as follows: An injury sustained while playing football may be a frequent occurrence, but we disagree that it is a probable, intended, and designed consequence of the employment. . . . The nature of the employment and the foreseeability of a potential injury does not determine whether an injury sustained in the ordinary course of an employee's duties is an accident.

As to Uhlenhake's foot and ankle injury, the commission made the following ruling: [Uhlenhake] credibly testified to an event on September 28, 1997, that caused injury. Dr. Avery examined him on September 28, 1997, because he had inverted his left foot during the game. [Uhlenhake] was diagnosed with a sprain. On September 29, 1997, [the assistant trainer] noted an injury to the left foot and ankle area at the previous game. Dr. Linehan assessed a five percent loss of use to the left lower extremity due to post-traumatic arthritis. [Pro-Football] presented no testimony or other medical evidence to the contrary. Accordingly, [Uhlenhake] is entitled to medical benefits and permanent partial disability benefits.

In addition, the commission denied an award of benefits for Uhlenhake's knee injury. The commission found that "at most, the evidence established that [Uhlenhake] suffered a gradual stretching injury of the ACL graft which progressively worsened during the season." The commission made special note of Uhlenhake's extensive history of knee problems, Dr. Avery's testimony that the ACL injury was the result of "multiple episodes of trauma," and Dr. Jackson's testimony that the MRI showed that the ACL was stretched. Both parties appeal from these rulings.

Pro-Football contends that "injuries resulting from voluntary participation in activities where injuries are customary, forseeable, and expected are not accidental within the meaning of the Virginia Workers' Compensation Act." It argues that "in determining whether an injury is accidental, the relevant focus is upon the predictability of the injury based upon the activity performed."

As a guiding principle, the Workers' Compensation Act provides that "'injury' means only injury by accident arising out of and in the course of employment." Code § 65.2-101.

The Act does not . . . specifically define the term "injury by accident." Consequently, the phrase has been the subject of judicial interpretation. . . .

To establish an "injury by accident," a claimant must prove (1) that the injury appeared suddenly at a particular time and place and upon a particular occasion, (2) that it was caused by an identifiable incident or sudden precipitating event, and (3) that it resulted in an obvious mechanical or structural change in the human body. . . .

Pro-Football initially posits that Uhlenhake seeks to recover for "injuries resulting from *voluntary* participation in activities." (Emphasis added.) The evidence proved, however, that Uhlenhake was engaged in an activity required by his employment. He was employed by Pro-Football to train, practice, and play in football games, which is the business of Pro-Football. No evidence proved Uhlenhake undertook a voluntary task when he engaged in the activity, which he alleges caused his injury. This is not a case of an injury "resulting from an employee's voluntary participation in employer-sponsored off-duty recreational activities which are not part of the employee's duties." Code § 65.2-101 (specifying an exclusion from injury by accident). Likewise, this is not a case in which the "injury was the direct result of [an employee] taking a risk of his own choosing, independent of any employment requirements, and one that was not an accepted and normal activity at the place of employment." *Mullins v. Westmoreland Coal Co.*, 10 Va. App. 304, 308, 391 S.E.2d 609, 611 (1990). Uhlenhake was at all relevant times engaged in an activity within the scope of his employment contract.

Pro-Football argues that by engaging in conduct which is physically dangerous and which has a high likelihood of injury, Uhlenhake must "automatically expect to be injured." In support of its contentions, Pro-Football cites two appellate court decisions in other jurisdictions, *Rowe v. Baltimore Colts*, 53 Md. App. 526, 454 A.2d 872 (Md. App. 1983), and *Palmer v. Kansas City Chiefs Football Club*, 621 S.W.2d 350 (Mo. App. 1981), and argues that a football player's traumatic injury is not an injury by accident as contemplated by the Act. We decline to so hold.

In *Rowe*, the court specifically noted "that the parties, as well as the Commission and the trial court, seemed to accept the fact that professional football players are within the purview of [Maryland's] Workmen's Compensation Law." 454 A.2d at 878. Thus, the court held that whether "professional football players are entitled to full coverage under the Workmen's Compensation Law" was not an issue raised by the appeal. 454 A.2d at 878-79. Applying Maryland compensation law, the court "held that an injury sustained by a professional football player as the result of legitimate and usual physical contact with other players, whether under actual or simulated game conditions, cannot be said to be an 'accidental injury' within the meaning of the Maryland Workmen's Compensation Law." 454 A.2d at 878. Significantly, the court noted, however, that Maryland law was changed after the filing of the claim to provide that "'Compensation may not be denied to an employee because of the degree of risk associated with the employment.'" *Id.* 454 A.2d at 878 n.7. Presumably, the court did not apply the revised statute because it was not in effect at the time of the injury.

In *Palmer*, the issue posed on appeal was the sufficiency of the evidence to prove a professional football player sustained "an accident within the terms of the [Missouri] compensation law." 621 S.W.2d at 353. The Missouri statute at issue specifically provided that "the word 'accident' as used in this chapter shall . . . be construed to mean an unexpected or unforeseen event happening suddenly and violently, with or without human fault, and producing at the time objective symptoms of an injury." *Id.* at 353 n.2. The court held that under Missouri's "abnormal strain doctrine the [employee] must show that the usual occupation was done in an unusual manner or that the work was not the usual occupational task—or that some other unexpected source of strain produced the injury." *Id.* at 354. Applying its statute, the court held that the "strain [Palmer experienced] was an expected incident of the usual work task done in the usual way," *id.* at 356, and was not "trauma from an unexpected or unforeseen event in the usual course of occupation." *Id.*

The *Rowe* and *Palmer* decisions are contrary to the decisions in the great majority of jurisdictions. "Injuries in [professional] sports are so routinely treated as compensable in the great majority of jurisdictions that they seldom appear in reported appellate decisions." 2 Arthur Larson, Workers' Compensation Law § 22.04[1][b] (2001). Referencing the Maryland statutory changes, which was cited in *Rowe* but not in effect when the claim arose, Larson's notes that *Palmer* "is the only surviving appellate decision denying compensation for injury in a professional team sport." *Id.*

Moreover, no evidence in this record established that Uhlenhake performed his employment tasks with the intent or design to bring on an injury. [citation omitted.] Indeed, the record establishes that Uhlenhake was performing the tasks he was employed to perform when he was injured. Pro-Football offered no proof that he was doing anything other than his required employment tasks in the manner required.

Pro-Football nevertheless asserts that "professional football players must accept the risk of injury if they wish to play the game" and argues that "the commission's broadened definition will extend compensability to . . . others who voluntarily participate in employment where injury is either highly probable or certain." It has long been understood, however, that the legislature abolished various common law doctrines, including assumption of the risk, when it adopted the Workers' Compensation Act. . . . In effect, Pro-Football's argument, if accepted, would introduce into the workers' compensation law the concept of assumption of the risk for a hazard that is undisputedly an incident of a worker's occupation.

"To say that football injuries are not accidental because of the probability of injury is, if one looks at it more closely, no more than to say that any activity with a high risk factor should be ruled noncompensable." 2 Larson at § 22.04[1][b]. The commission properly rejected this misguided notion and ruled that "the nature of the employment and the foreseeability of a potential injury does not determine whether an injury sustained in the ordinary course of an employee's duties is an accident." The business of Pro-Football is to engage in the activity of professional football. It employs individuals to constantly perform in a strenuous activity that has risks and hazards. As with coal miners, steel workers, firefighters, and police officers, who are covered by the Act, other classes of employees are regularly exposed to known, actual risks of hazards because "the employment subjects the employee to the particular danger." *Olsten v. Leftwich*, 230 Va. 317, 319, 336 S.E.2d 893, 894 (1985). The commission correctly ruled that professional football players are not exempt from the coverage of the Act when they suffer injuries in the game they are employed to perform.

Pro-Football does not dispute that Uhlenhake sprained his ankle on September 28, 1997, and reported the injury immediately. It contends that the injury was minor and that no credible evidence supports the award of permanent partial disability. . . .

[EDS. Based on the foregoing standard of review, the court found that credible evidence supported the commission's finding awarding Uhlenhake permanent partial disability benefits for loss of use of his left foot. The court next considered Uhlenhake's challenge of the sufficiency of the evidence to support the commission's finding that his left knee injury resulted from cumulative trauma and, therefore, is not compensable. Noting that the employee bears the burden of proving by a preponderance of the evidence that an injury by accident occurred, the court concluded that credible evidence supported the commission's finding that the "that the [knee] injury was the result of cumulative events" and consequently was not compensable.]

For these reasons, we affirm all aspects of the commission's decision.

NOTES AND QUESTIONS

1. *Covered Injuries.* Describe the team's arguments in support of its contention that Uhlenhake was not entitled to workers' compensation benefits. Is the court's rejection of the team's arguments consistent with the

principles and policies that underlie workers' compensation systems? Is a professional hockey player entitled to receive workers' compensation benefits for injuries suffered in a fight with an opposing player during a game, which was ordered by his coach? *Norfolk Admirals v. Jones*, 2005 WL 2847392 (Va. App. Nov. 1, 2005) (yes). Do you agree? See *Pro-Football, Inc. v. Tupa*, 14 A.3d 678 (Md. App. 2011) (adopting the approach articulated in *Uhlenhake* on what constitutes an accidental injury for workers' compensation purposes; also invalidating a forum selection clause articulating the jurisdiction in which injured athlete would be required to file a workers' compensation claim).

2. *Statutory Exclusion.* As noted by the court in *Uhlenhake*, absent a specific exclusion under a particular state's law, injured professional athletes normally are eligible to receive workers' compensation benefits. See *Pro-Football Inc. v. McCants*, No. 116 (Md. Aug. 23, 2012) (finding professional athlete a "covered employee" for purposes of workers' compensation statute, where athlete "was regularly employed in Maryland while playing football games . . . presence in other jurisdictions for practice or playing purposes necessarily was merely incidental or occasional"). A few states exclude professional athletes from the definition of employee for workers' compensation purposes or otherwise severely limit the extent to which workers' compensation benefits are available to professional athletes. See, e.g., Fla. Stat. Ann. §440.02(17)(c)(3) (West 2009); Mass. Gen. Laws Ann. Ch. 152, §1(4)(b) (West 2000 & Supp. 2012); Wyo. Stat. Ann. §27-14-102(vii)(F) (LexisNexis 2011). The Florida and Wyoming statutes provide coverage for professional athletes when their team purchases insurance for the specific purpose of providing workers' compensation benefits for its athletes. What justifies excluding professional athletes from the scope of workers' compensation systems? Do exclusions reflect bias against athletes? If so, what might underlie such bias?

3. *Notice Requirements.* Finding that Uhlenhake failed to establish a connection between the knee injury and a compensable event, the court upheld the denial of workers' compensation for injury to his left knee. Uhlenhake's ability to recover would have been enhanced if he had provided timely notice of the injury. Generally, an injured employee must provide timely notice to his or her employer and file a claim within the time frame established by the relevant workers' compensation statute. What is the purpose of the notice requirement? According to a prominent commentator, "The purpose is dual: First, to enable the employer to provide immediate medical diagnosis and treatment with a view to minimizing the seriousness of the injury; and second, to facilitate the earliest possible investigation of the facts surrounding the injury." Arthur Larson, Larson's Workers' Compensation Law (2002) at §126.01.

To whom should notice be given? Will notice given to a team physician or trainer comply with this procedural requirement? See *Pittsburgh Steelers Sports, Inc. v. Workers' Comp. Appeal Bd.*, 814 A.2d 788 (Pa. Commw. Ct. 2002) (notification of injury given to team trainer is sufficient to meet statutory notice requirements for workers' compensation). A workers' compensation claim must be filed within the relevant statutory time period or it will be barred. *Adams v. N.Y. Giants*, 362 N.J. Super. 101, 827 A.2d 299 (2003).

4. *Forum Selection Clauses.* Notwithstanding choice of law and forum clauses stipulating the jurisdiction within which professional athletes should file workers' compensation claims, athletes have asserted the right to have their workers' compensation claims decided by the law of jurisdictions other than those specified in the parties' contract. Consequently, courts have adjudicated the enforceability of these provisions in player/team contracts. The workers' compensation claim of Bruce Matthews is illustrative.

Matthews, who was a member of the NFL's Tennessee Titans (which, before 1997, went by the name Houston Oilers) from 1983 to 2002, filed a workers' compensation claim in California. In 2011, a California federal district court upheld a choice of law provision in Matthews's contract that provided that any matter relating to workers' compensation benefits would be determined exclusively by the laws of Tennessee. Confirming an arbitration award that Mathews's workers' compensation was governed by Tennessee law, the court found that the provision was not contrary to California law or public policy. *National Football League Players Assn. v. National Football League Mgmt. Council,* 2011 WL 31068, at 5 (S.D. Cal. Jan. 5, 2011). The Ninth Circuit upheld the lower court ruling finding Matthews had failed to demonstrate that the choice of law provision "violate[d] an explicit, well-defined and dominant public policy of the state of California." *Matthews v. National Football League Mgmt. Council,* 688 F.3d 1107(9th Cir. 2012). Accord *Chicago Bears Football Club, Inc. v. Haynes,* 816 F. Supp. 2d 534, 538 (N.D. Ill. 2011) (upholding choice of law and forum selection provisions in the contracts between the Chicago Bears and three of its players; the court concluded that the provisions were "consistent with Illinois law and, presumably, its public policy").

The dearth of cases and the existence of contrary authority make it premature to conclude that the decisions of the California and Illinois courts represent the majority approach. Maryland courts have less favorably viewed the enforceability of choice of law and forum clauses as pertaining to workers' compensation claims. See *Pro-Football, Inc. v. Tupa,* 197 Md. App. 463 (Md. Ct. Spec. App. 2011). Punter Thomas Tupa suffered a back injury while employed by the Washington Redskins of the National Football League. *Id.* at 466. The Maryland Court of Special Appeals invalidated a forum selection clause in the Redskins/Tupa contract because the enforcement of the clause would have contravened Maryland's public policy. *Id.* at 477-478. See also Md. Code Ann., Lab. & Empl. §9-104(a)(1)-(2) (West 2012). It found that Maryland public policy precludes a forum selection clause exempting the Redskins from paying workers' compensation benefits.

5. *Off-Season Injuries.* The time of the occurrence of an injury may impact a player's right to workers' compensation benefits. See, e.g., *Dandenault v. Workers' Compensation Appeals Bd.,* 728 A.2d 1001 (Pa. Commw. Ct. 1999) (professional ice hockey player's participation in a summer hockey league to get into shape for the upcoming season was not within the scope of employment when there was no evidence that the player's team either required or encouraged him to engage in that activity). But see *Farren v. Baltimore Ravens,* 720 N.E. 2d 590 (Ohio Ct. App. 1998) (summary judgment inappropriate where player, who was injured during the off-season while between contracts, received ambiguous communications and instructions from the team concerning his employment status, thereby creating a question of fact as to his employment status).

LYONS v. WORKERS' COMPENSATION APPEAL BOARD
(PITTSBURGH STEELERS SPORTS, INC.)

803 A.2d 857 (Pa. Commw. Ct. 2002)

SMITH-RIBNER, Judge.

Mitchell W. Lyons appeals from an order of the Workers' Compensation Appeal Board (Board) that affirmed the decision of a Workers' Compensation Judge (WCJ) which granted Lyons' claim petition but limited his benefits in accordance with Section 308.1 of the Workers' Compensation Act (Act), Act of June 2, 1915, P.L. 736, *as amended*, added by Section 10 of the Act of July 2, 1993, P.L. 190, 77 P.S. § 565. Lyons is a former professional football player for Pittsburgh Steelers' Sports, Inc. (Steelers), which is a franchise of the National Football League (NFL). Lyons contends that Section 308.1 violates equal protection of the law by imposing an artificially low average weekly wage on certain professional athletes.

[EDS. Before his injury, Lyons played professional football for the Steelers as a tight end and as a special teams player. As a result of a blow to his knee that occurred during a game, Lyons was diagnosed as having sustained a dislocated left knee, with tears of the posterior cruciate ligament, the anterior cruciate ligament, and medial collateral ligament, and possible damage to the meniscus and possible other damage to the interior. As a professional football player, Lyons needed to be able to run; make sudden stops, sharp turns, twists, and quick starts; and be prepared to be tackled when handling the football. Because he could no longer do those things, Lyons was unable to return to his career as a professional football player.]

At the time of his injury, Lyons' actual weekly wage was $8,075.90, and he was paid that wage through February 9, 2000. Since October 31, 2000, Lyons has been gainfully employed by AXA Advisors, a financial planner in Grand Rapids Michigan, with a weekly income of $1,000. Due to the operation of Section 308.1 of the Act, Lyons' partial disability benefit rate is calculated based upon an average weekly wage of $1,176.00 (two times the statewide average weekly wage of $588) rather than Lyons' actual average weekly wage of $8,075.90. The parties stipulated to the facts of Lyons' injury and that, under the Act, Lyons is entitled to partial disability benefits at the rate of $117.33 per week from November 1, 2000 to date and continuing. The $117.33 figure is calculated as two thirds of the difference between Lyons' weekly income of $1,000 and the average weekly wage of $1,176.00 imposed by Section 308.1.

Under the stipulation, Lyons reserved the right to challenge the constitutionality of Section 308.1. . . .

Section 308.1 of the Act limits the amount of partial disability benefits received by professional athletes who are employed by franchises of certain enumerated professional athletic organizations and whose average weekly wage is more than eight times the Statewide average weekly wage. When calculating such benefits, Section 308.1 imposes an artificial average weekly wage equal to two times the Statewide average weekly wage. . . .

Lyons contends that Section 308.1 violates his right to equal protection under the law as guaranteed by the Fourteenth Amendment of the United States Constitution and by Article 1, Section 26 of the Pennsylvania Constitution. The same standards apply when analyzing claims brought under the equal protection provisions of the Pennsylvania Constitution and claims brought under the equal protection provisions of the United States Constitution. *Commonwealth v. Albert*, 563 Pa. 133, 758 A.2d 1149 (2000). The essence of those standards is that the law should treat similarly situated people in similar ways, but the standard allows the legislature to treat people with different needs differently and to classify people for purposes of receiving treatment. *Id.*

The first step in an equal protection analysis is to determine which of three types of scrutiny the reviewing court should apply to the challenged classification: strict scrutiny, intermediate scrutiny or rational basis scrutiny. . . .

Professional athletes are neither a suspect class nor a sensitive classification, and Section 308.1 implicates no fundamental or important right. The right at issue is purely economic, and therefore the rational basis scrutiny applies. . . .

A classification satisfies rational basis scrutiny so long as the legislative distinction has some rational ground that relates to a legitimate state purpose. . . . A law will not be found to violate equal protection under rational basis scrutiny simply because the classifications drawn by the legislature are imperfect or result in some inequality. . . .

Lyons argues that he is being treated disparately because he receives less benefits than a worker earning the same wage in any other line of work. He contends that even among professional athletes the treatment is disparate because Section 308.1 targets only certain athletic organizations; for example, it does not apply to professional athletes who play soccer or to professional athletes who play football but are employed by a start-up league. Lyons further contends that there is no logical reason to distinguish between professional athletes who receive eight times the statewide average weekly wage and those who receive less than that amount, and he suggests that the only purpose served by Section 308.1 is to confer an economic benefit upon the owners of the athletic organizations that the law targets.[2]

The District Court of Appeals of Florida considered a similar constitutional challenge to the Florida workers' compensation statute in *Rudolph v. Miami Dolphins, Ltd.*, 447 So. 2d 284 (Fla. Dist. Ct. App. 1983). The statute in question provided that the term employment did not include service performed by a professional athlete, such as a professional football player. Among other things, the claimants in that case argued that the exclusion was unconstitutional in violation of the equal protection clause of the Fourteenth Amendment and the corresponding equal protection guarantee in the state constitution. In upholding the constitutionality of the exclusion, the Florida court provided the following explanation for the basis of the classification:

> The professional athlete exclusion is not a wholly arbitrary one. Professional football players incur serious injuries on a regular, frequent, and repetitive basis. They are generally well paid, and as the NFL contracts in these cases exemplify, they willfully hold themselves out as well-skilled in the sport of their choice. They make a conscious decision to use their skills in an occupation involving a high risk of frequent, repetitive, and serious injury. We cannot say that the legislature's exclusion of this voluntary, though highly dangerous, activity from the worker[s'] compensation act fails to bear some reasonable relationship to a legitimate state purpose

2. The Steelers correctly note that Section 308.1 affects only professional athletes who have demonstrated an ability to secure post-injury wages with gainful employment. The Section has no effect on an athlete's right to receive total disability benefits or to receive medical treatment.

and is so completely arbitrary and lacking in equality of application to all persons similarly situated as to violate the cited constitutional provisions.

Id. at 291-292.

The explanation supplied by the Florida court offers a rational basis for treating professional athletes differently that equally supports Section 308.1. The Court agrees that professional athletes willfully hold themselves out to risk of frequent, repetitive and serious injury in exchange for lucrative compensation. While other occupations are also rewarded for facing risk, professional athletes employed in the major professional sports represent a distinctive blend of risk combined with lucrative compensation. It is also worth observing that professional athletes undergo this risk in order to provide entertainment. While the Court has great respect for professional athletes, the legislature could have rationally placed a different value on those who risk bodily harm to provide entertainment from those, such as police officers and fire fighters, who risk bodily harm to protect society.

Although these characteristics may apply equally to some other occupations, the fact that a classification is imperfect does not render it arbitrary. *McCusker.* Likewise, the legislature could rationally have concluded that professional athletes paid less than eight times the statewide average weekly wage have a greater need for partial disability benefits than athletes who receive greater compensation. The cut-off chosen by the legislature need not be mathematically perfect in order to withstand rational basis scrutiny. *Id.* For the foregoing reasons, the Court affirms the order of the Board.

NOTES AND QUESTIONS

1. *Statutory Limitations on Benefits.* Like the statute upheld in *Lyons,* other statutes impose limitations specifically directed toward professional athletes. To prevent professional athletes from receiving benefits for the same injury from two different sources, some states limit the amount of recoverable workers' compensation benefits. In *Gulf Ins. Co. v. Hennings,* 2008 WL 256828 (Tex. App.-Waco Jan. 30, 2008), a Texas court interpreted several provisions of the Texas workers' compensation act. The court concluded that because the income and medical benefits Hennings received under his contract and collective bargaining agreement were not equal to or in excess of the corresponding workers' compensation benefits, he was not required to elect between the two. Thus, Hennings was entitled to receive both his workers' compensation benefits and his employment-related benefits. Noting the insurer's failure to cite to any authority to support its contention, the court also rejected Gulf's claim that it was entitled to a set-off against the amounts it had paid in benefits and the medical and income benefits Hennings received under the terms of both his contract and the NFL CBA. See, e.g., Tex. Lab. Code Ann. §406.095 (West 2008) (athletes are required to elect to receive workers' compensation benefits or benefits available pursuant to contract or collective bargaining agreement where applicable).

    Other states statutorily require that benefits payments from an athlete's team be set off against any workers' compensation benefits awarded to the athlete. See, e.g., Ohio Rev. Code Ann. §§4123.56-4123.58 (West 2011). In states with such provisions, litigation often arises over what parts of a team's benefits payments should be set off and whether the team is entitled to a dollar-for-dollar or a week-for-week set-off. *Lincoln Hockey, LLC v. D.C. Dept. of Employment Servs.*, 810 A.2d 862 (D.C. App. 2002) (limiting the types of payments to be set off under D.C. Code 32-1515(j)); *Smith v. Richardson Sports Ltd.*, 616 S.E.2d 245 (N.C. App. 2005) (noting complex interaction between North Carolina workers' compensation statute and injury compensation benefits paid by club pursuant to NFL collective bargaining agreement and his individual player contract in determining club's credits against injured player's workers' compensation benefits). Although a team's benefits payments may be deemed advance payments of workers' compensation benefits, those payments may not have the same tax-exempt status as workers' compensation benefits. See *Wallace v. United States*, 139 F.3d 1165 (7th Cir. 1998) (interpreting 26 U.S.C. §104(a)(1) not to exempt a team's benefits payments that had been deemed advanced payments of workers' compensation). The amount to which an athlete is entitled under the workers' compensation statute is often litigated. *Farquhar v. New Orleans Saints*, 16 So. 3d 404 (La. App. Ct. 2009), illustrates the types of computation issues that arise. There the court held that the workers' compensation amount due to the athlete should be based on the amount that he actually earned from playing prior to his injury and not the contract amount. Accord *Hoffman v. New Orleans Saints*, 56 So. 3d 446 (La. App. 5 Cir. 2011).

2. *Intentional Injury Exception.* Rather than seeking the no-fault fixed benefits provided by workers' compensation, an injured player instead may prefer trying to obtain an uncertain, but potentially much larger, judgment in tort litigation. The exclusive remedy provisions of workers' compensation laws will not bar a tort action against an employer for harm caused by conduct that is intended to injure an employee. If the requisite intent is established, an employee may elect to either receive workers' compensation benefits or bring a tort claim.

   Even in jurisdictions that recognize the intentional injury exception to the exclusivity effect of workers' compensation laws, however, courts generally are not receptive to a professional athlete's claim that his team "intended" his injury and are rather exacting with regard to the burden imposed on the employee. See, e.g., *DePiano v. Montreal Baseball Club, Ltd.*, 663 F. Supp. 116, 117 (W.D. Pa. 1987) ("In order to constitute an intentional tort, the conduct must be engaged in with the desire to bring about the consequences of the act. A mere knowledge and appreciation of a risk is not the same as the intent to cause injury"); *Brocail v. Detroit Tigers, Inc.* 268 S.W.3d 90, 108 (Tex. App. 2008) ("An employer is deemed to have intended to injure if he had actual knowledge that an injury was certain to occur and willfully disregarded that knowledge. . . . A plaintiff may establish a corporate employer's actual knowledge by showing that a supervisory or managerial employee had actual knowledge that an injury would follow from what the employer deliberately did or did not do"). See also Timothy Davis, *Tort Liability of Coaches for Injuries to Professional Athletes: Overcoming Policy and Doctrinal Barriers*, 76 UMKC L. Rev. 571, 587-590 (2008) (discussing the intentional conduct exception to the exclusivity of workers' compensation remedies).

3. *Fraudulent Misrepresentation Exception.* Even if a club does not intend to injure a player, in some jurisdictions it may be subject to tort liability for fraudulent concealment of material medical information concerning a player's fitness to play. In *Krueger v. San Francisco Forty Niners*, 234 Cal. Rptr. 579 (Cal.

Ct. App. 1987), discussed *supra*, the court held that a professional football team fraudulently failed to disclose that a player risked permanent disability by continuing to play with a chronic knee condition. Evidence established that the team "consciously failed" to disclose that the player's knee lacked the anterior cruciate ligament, that steroid injection treatments might have adverse effects, and that he risked permanent injury by continuing to play without surgery. The exclusivity provisions of the California workers' compensation statute were inapplicable because they expressly permitted the recovery of tort damages if the employee's injury was aggravated by the employer's fraudulent concealment of the existence of the injury. Absent a statutory exception to the workers' compensation bar to employee tort claims, however, courts have refused to allow a player to bring a fraud action against a team for misrepresenting or failing to disclose material information about a physical condition that increased the risk of harm from continued play.

In *Gambrell v. Kansas City Chiefs Football Club, Inc.*, 562 S.W.2d 163 (Mo. Ct. App. 1978), a football player alleged that his team and two of its physicians conspired to falsely represent that he was medically fit to play football based on the results of his physical examination. He allegedly was unfit to play because of preexisting back, neck, and spine injuries. After receiving medical clearance to play, the plaintiff severely aggravated an existing injury during a game and was permanently disabled. The court observed that the alleged fraud preceded, and helped to produce, the aggravation of the plaintiff's injury; therefore, the subsequent aggravation merged into the preexisting injury, for which the plaintiff had previously received workers' compensation benefits. Concluding that the player was entitled to only one recovery for his injury, the court found his tort claim barred by the exclusivity provision of the Missouri workers' compensation law.

4. *Workers' Compensation Co-Employee Bar.* In an effort to assert claims for sports medicine malpractice, players have attempted to characterize the team physician as an independent contractor rather than a team employee to avoid the workers' compensation bar to tort against co-employees. Despite earlier authority adopting such a characterization, see *Bryant v. Fox*, 515 N.E.2d 775 (Ill. App. Ct. 1987), recent case law has rejected it. In *Hendy v. Losse*, 819 P.2d 1 (Cal. 1991), a professional football player sued team physicians for negligently diagnosing and treating a knee injury suffered during a game and for advising him to continue playing football. In dismissing these claims, the California Supreme Court held that California's workers' compensation law bars tort suits between co-employees for injuries caused within the scope of employment. The court found that the plaintiff and defendant were both employed by the San Diego Chargers and that the defendant acted within the scope of his employment in treating the plaintiff. Thus, the plaintiff's exclusive remedy for his harm was workers' compensation. See also *Lotysz v. Montgomery*, 766 N.Y.S.2d 28 (N.Y. App. Div. 2003) (athlete's tort claim against physician barred by workers' compensation statute); *Daniels v. Seattle Seahawks*, 968 P.2d 883 (Wash. App. Ct. 1998) (same). Accord *Stringer v. Minnesota Vikings Football Club, LLC*, 705 N.W.2d 746 (Minn. 2005) (workers' compensation co-employee doctrine bars tort claim against NFL club's athletic trainers for alleged improper treatment of player who died from heat stroke during preseason practice). See generally Matthew J. Mitten, *Team Physicians as Co-Employees: A Prescription That Deprives Professional Athletes of an*

Adequate Remedy for Sports Medicine Malpractice, 50 St. Louis U. L.J. 211 (2006) (critiquing these cases); Dennis Durao, *An Endangered Species: Professional Sports Team Physicians*, 15 Quinnipiac Health L.J. 33, 45 (2012) (examining the liability of team physicians).

Some state workers' compensation laws do not bar tort claims against team physicians for work-related injuries that are aggravated by fraudulent concealment of the existence of the injury. For example, claims against professional team physicians for fraudulent concealment of medical information, similar to those raised in *Krueger v. S.F. Forty Niners, supra*, are actionable.

F. PARTICIPATION RIGHTS OF ATHLETES WITH PHYSICAL OR MENTAL IMPAIRMENTS

1. Enhanced Risk of Harm to Oneself

Athletes are risk takers by nature and accept some risk of injury merely by playing competitive sports. The possibility of bumps, bruises, and even broken bones during the course of play is a known inherent risk willingly assumed by all athletes. In addition to assuming normal inherent risks of injury, athletes with a physical impairment or abnormality may expose themselves to increased risk or severity of injury by participating in competitive sports. Such athletes—if nevertheless physically capable of playing a sport—sometimes are willing to accept an enhanced risk of injury or potential significant harm to themselves. Although most athletes accept the team physician's medical recommendation not to play competitive sports to avoid exposure to significant health risks, some have resorted to litigation in an effort to continue playing a desired sport.

Beginning in the mid-1970s, athletes with a missing or nonfunctioning paired organ (e.g., an eye or kidney) began asserting a legal right not to be medically excluded from participating in contact sports. In *Neeld v. American Hockey League*, 439 F. Supp. 459 (W.D.N.Y. 1977), the court enjoined enforcement of a professional league bylaw prohibiting one-eyed athletes from playing hockey. The court ruled that this bylaw violated New York's Human Rights Law prohibiting employees from discrimination based on disability unless the characteristic is a bona fide occupational qualification. There was no evidence that blindness in one eye substantially detracted from the plaintiff's ability to play hockey. However, in *Neeld v. NHL*, 594 F.2d 1297 (9th Cir. 1979), the Ninth Circuit rejected the same plaintiff's claim that this bylaw violates the federal antitrust laws. The court concluded that the bylaw's primary purpose of promoting safety outweighed any *de minimis* anticompetitive effect on excluded athletes.

Courts generally have rejected claims by physically impaired athletes that exclusion from athletics violates the federal constitution. *Grube v. Bethlehem Area Sch. Dist.*, 550 F. Supp. 418, 423 (E.D. Pa. 1982) (expressing doubt that excluding handicapped students from high school athletics denies equal protection of the laws); *Neeld v. American Hockey League*, 439 F. Supp. 459 (W.D.N.Y. 1977) (professional league's bylaw a product of private conduct, not state action subject to constitutional scrutiny). The Supreme Court has ruled that handicapped persons are not a suspect or quasi-suspect class justifying a heightened scrutiny of alleged discrimination. *City of Cleburne v. Cleburne Living Ctr., Inc.*, 473 U.S. 432

(1985). Even if state action exists, exclusion of physically impaired athletes is legally justifiable if the decision of the governing body, educational institution, or team is rationally related to a legitimate objective. Reliance on the team physician's medical recommendation that an athlete not play rationally furthers the permissible purpose of ensuring the health and safety of its athletes. See generally Matthew J. Mitten, *Amateur Athletes with Handicaps or Physical Abnormalities: Who Makes the Participation Decision?*, 71 Neb. L. Rev. 987, 1004-1007 (1992).

Physically impaired athletes have asserted that their exclusion from athletics, even if based on the team physician's medical recommendation, violates §504(a) of the Rehabilitation Act of 1973, 29 U.S.C.A. §§701 et seq., a federal statute that prohibits discrimination against persons with a disability. The following case considers whether the Rehabilitation Act provides an athlete with a legal right to participate in intercollegiate athletics if medical opinions are divided regarding whether doing so will expose him to an enhanced risk of serious injury or death.

KNAPP v. NORTHWESTERN UNIVERSITY

101 F.3d 473 (7th Cir. 1996), *cert. denied*, 520 U.S. 1274 (1997)

EVANS, Circuit Judge.

Nicholas Knapp wants to play NCAA basketball for Northwestern University—so badly that he is willing to face an increased risk of death to do so. Knapp is a competent, intelligent adult capable of assessing whether playing intercollegiate basketball is worth the risk to his heart and possible death, and to him the risk is acceptable. Usually, competent, intelligent adults are allowed to make such decisions. This is especially true when, as here, the individual's family approves of the decision and the individual and his parents are willing to sign liability waivers regarding the worst-case scenario should it occur.

Northwestern, however, refuses to allow Knapp to play on or even practice with its men's basketball team. Knapp, currently a sophomore at Northwestern, has the basketball skills to play at the intercollegiate level, but he has never taken the court for his team. Although Northwestern does not restrict him from playing pick-up basketball games, using recreational facilities on campus, or exerting himself physically on his own, the university disqualified Knapp from playing on its intercollegiate basketball team. The issue in this case boils down to whether the school—because of § 504 of the Rehabilitation Act of 1973, as amended, 29 U.S.C. § 794—will be forced to let Knapp don a purple uniform and take the floor as a member of Northwestern's basketball team.

[EDS. As a high school senior, Knapp suffered sudden cardiac arrest while playing recreational basketball, which required cardiopulmonary resuscitation and defibrillation to restart his heart. Thereafter, he had an internal defibrillator implanted in his abdomen, which detects heart arrhythmia and delivers a shock to convert heart rhythm back to normal. He subsequently played competitive recreational basketball without any incidents of cardiac arrest and received medical clearance to play college basketball from three cardiologists who examined him.

Northwestern agreed to honor its preexisting commitment to provide Knapp with an athletic scholarship, although he was medically disqualified from playing intercollegiate basketball. Its team physician's recommendation was based on Knapp's medical records and history, the 26th Bethesda Conference guidelines for athletic participation with cardiovascular abnormalities, and opinions of two consulting cardiologists who concluded that Knapp would expose himself to a significant risk of ventricular fibrillation or cardiac arrest during competitive athletics.

All medical experts agreed on the following facts: Knapp had suffered sudden cardiac death because of ventricular fibrillation; even with the internal defibrillator, playing college basketball placed Knapp at a higher risk of sudden cardiac death as compared with other male college basketball players; the internal defibrillator had never been tested under the conditions of intercollegiate basketball; and no person currently played or had ever played college or professional basketball after suffering sudden cardiac death or after having a defibrillator implanted. However, they disagreed regarding whether Knapp should be medically cleared to play intercollegiate basketball. Northwestern's Presidential Directive on Self-Regulation of Intercollegiate Athletics, the Big Ten Conference's Handbook Agreements for Men's Programs, and the NCAA's Constitution and Sports Medicine Handbook all give the team physician sole responsibility to decide whether a student is medically eligible to compete on the basketball team.]

The district court held a hearing solely to determine whether Knapp presently is medically eligible to play intercollegiate basketball. Presented with conflicting evidence, the district court found Knapp medically eligible and Northwestern in violation of the Rehabilitation Act. [It] . . . entered a permanent injunction prohibiting Northwestern from excluding Knapp from playing on its basketball team for any reason related to his cardiac condition. . . .

To prevail on his claim for discrimination under the Act, Knapp must prove that: (1) he is disabled as defined by the Act; (2) he is otherwise qualified for the position sought; (3) he has been excluded from the position solely because of his disability; and (4) the position exists as part of a program or activity receiving federal financial assistance. Northwestern does not dispute that it receives federal financial assistance and that it has excluded Knapp from its intercollegiate basketball program solely because of his cardiac condition, so our focus is on whether Knapp is an "otherwise qualified individual with a disability."

To show that he is disabled under the terms of the Act, Knapp must prove that he (i) has a physical . . . impairment which substantially limits one or more of [his] major life activities, (ii) has a record of such an impairment, or (iii) is regarded as having such an impairment. 29 U.S.C. § 706(8)(B). Knapp satisfies the first element of part (i) of this definition. A cardiovascular problem constitutes a physical impairment under § 706(8)(B). 34 C.F.R. § 104.3(j)(2)(i)(A); 45 C.F.R. § 84.3(j)(2)(i)(A). Northwestern does not dispute this fact, but it instead zeros in on the second element of the disability definition: whether playing intercollegiate basketball is part of a major life activity and, if so, whether its diagnosis of Knapp's cardiac condition substantially limits Knapp in that activity.

In determining whether a particular individual has a disability as defined in the Rehabilitation Act, the regulations promulgated by the Department of Health and Human Services with the oversight and approval of Congress are of significant assistance. Those regulations define "major life activities" as basic functions of life "such as caring for one's self, performing manual tasks, walking, seeing, hearing, speaking, breathing, learning, and working." 34 C.F.R. § 104.3(j)(2)(ii); 45 C.F.R. § 84.3(j)(2)(ii). Regulations regarding equal employment opportunities under the Americans with Disabilities Act, 42 U.S.C. §§ 12101 *et seq.*, adopt the same term and definition and an interpretive note provides a bit more guidance: "'Major life activities' are those basic activities that the average person in the general population can perform with little or no difficulty." 29 C.F.R. pt. 1630, app. § 1630.2. . . .

Knapp contends that playing an intercollegiate sport is an integral part of his major life activity of learning and that his education will be substantially limited if he cannot play on the team. He states that he does not believe he can obtain confidence, dedication, leadership, perseverance, discipline, and teamwork in any better way. The district court agreed with him, determining that *for Knapp*, playing on the Northwestern basketball team was part of the major life activity of learning and that he was substantially limited from such learning by the university. . . .

We do not think that the definition of "major life activity" can be as particularized as Knapp wants it to be. Playing intercollegiate basketball obviously is not in and of itself a major life activity, as it is not a basic function of life on the same level as walking, breathing, and speaking. Not everyone gets to go to college, let alone play intercollegiate sports. We acknowledge that intercollegiate sports can be an important part of the college learning experience for both athletes and many cheering students—especially at a Big Ten school. Knapp has indicated that such is the case for him. But not every student thinks so. Numerous college students graduate each year having neither participated in nor attended an inter-collegiate sporting event. Their sheepskins are no less valuable because of the lack of intercollegiate sports in their lives. Not playing intercollegiate sports does not mean they have not learned. Playing or enjoying intercollegiate sports therefore cannot be held out as a *necessary* part of learning for *all* students.

A few cases, none of them binding on us, have considered school team sports a major life activity in and of themselves. *See Pahulu v. University of Kansas*, 897 F.Supp. 1387 (D.Kan.1995) (intercollegiate football may be a major life activity); *see also Sandison v. Michigan High School Athletic Assn., Inc.*, 863 F.Supp. 483, 489 (E.D.Mich.1994) (participation on the cross-country and track teams an important and integral part of education and a major life activity), *rev'd on other grounds*, 64 F.3d 1026 (6th Cir.1995). . . . Because intercollegiate athletics may be *one part* of the major life activity of learning for *certain* students, the parties here have framed the analysis of what constitutes a major life activity into a choice between a subjective test or an objective test—whether we look at what constitutes learning for Nick Knapp or what constitutes learning in general for the average person. The Rehabilitation Act and the regulations promulgated under it give little guidance regarding whether the determination of what constitutes a major life activity turns on an objective or subjective standard. And while we have previously said that whether a person is disabled is "an individualized inquiry, best suited to a case-by-case determination," we have also indicated that "the definition of 'major life activity' in the regulations 'cannot be interpreted to include working at the specific job of one's choice,'" *Byrne*, 979 F.2d at 565. Other courts have been across the board on whether the test is objective or subjective. *Compare Pahulu*, 897 F.Supp. at 1393 ("for Pahulu, intercollegiate football may be a major life activity, i.e., learning"), and *Sandison*, 863 F.Supp. at 489 (participation on high school teams is "as to them a major life activity") with *Welsh v. City of Tulsa, Okla.*, 977 F.2d 1415, 1417 (10th Cir.1992) (major life activity of working does not necessarily mean working at the job of one's choice).

We decline to define the major life activity of learning in such a way that the Act applies whenever someone wants to play intercollegiate athletics. A "major life activity," as defined in the regulations, is a basic function of life "such as caring for one's self, performing manual tasks, walking, seeing, hearing, speaking, breathing, learning, and working." 34 C.F.R. § 104.3(j)(2)(ii); 45 C.F.R. § 84.3(j)(2)(ii). These are basic functions, not more specific ones such as being an astronaut, working as a firefighter, driving a race car, or learning by playing Big Ten basketball. . . .

Because learning through playing intercollegiate basketball is only one part of the education available to Knapp at Northwestern, even under a subjective standard, Knapp's ability to learn is not substantially limited. Knapp's scholarship continues, allowing him access to all academic and—except for intercollegiate basketball—all nonacademic services and activities available to other Northwestern students, in addition to all other services available to scholarship athletes. Although perhaps not as great a learning experience as actually playing, it is even possible that Knapp may "learn" through the basketball team in a role other than as a player. Knapp is an intelligent student and athlete, and the inability to play intercollegiate basketball at Northwestern forecloses only a small portion of his collegiate opportunities. . . .

Even if we were inclined to find Knapp disabled under the Rehabilitation Act, he would still come up short because we also hold as a matter of law that he is not, under the statute, "otherwise qualified" to play intercollegiate basketball at Northwestern. . . .

Section 794 does not compel educational institutions to disregard the disabilities of disabled persons. *Southeastern Community College v. Davis*, 442 U.S. 397, 405, 99 S.Ct. 2361, 2366, 60 L.Ed.2d 980 (1979). It requires only that an "otherwise qualified" disabled person not be excluded from participation in a federally funded program solely because of the disability. *Id.* In other words, although a disability is not a permissible ground for assuming an inability to function in a particular context, the disability is not thrown out when considering if the person is qualified for the position sought. *Id.* at 405-06, 99 S.Ct. at 2366-67. "An otherwise qualified person is one who is able to meet all of a program's requirements in spite of his handicap," *id.* at 406, 99 S.Ct. at 2367, with reasonable accommodation, *see Arline*, 480 U.S. at 287-88 n. 17, 107 S.Ct. at 1131 n. 17 ("when a handicapped person is not able to perform the essential functions of the job, the court must also consider whether any reasonable accommodation by the employer would enable the handicapped person to perform those functions").

Legitimate physical qualifications may in fact be essential to participation in particular programs. . . .

A significant risk of personal physical injury can disqualify a person from a position if the risk cannot be eliminated. But more than merely an elevated risk of injury is required before disqualification is appropriate. Any physical qualification based on risk of future injury must be examined with special care if the Rehabilitation Act is not to be circumvented, since almost all disabled individuals are at a greater risk of injury. . . .

[Eds. In this case, the severity of the potential injury was as high as it could have been—death. In regard to the probability of injury, Knapp's experts testified that playing intercollegiate basketball would expose him to a risk of death between 1 in 34 and 1 in 100. These estimates took into account Knapp's internal defibrillator, apparently the only "accommodation" possible for Knapp's condition. Although these numbers were merely estimates, all of them agreed that the risk to Knapp is higher than to the average male collegiate basketball player. Knapp's experts believed it was an acceptable level of risk. Northwestern's experts agreed with the school's team doctor that although the precise risk cannot be quantified, Knapp's participation in competitive Big Ten basketball significantly increases his risk of death to an unacceptable degree.]

The district court judge in this case believed that in the face of conflicting opinion evidence regarding risk, and the fact that no scientific data existed to quantify that risk, the decision on whether Knapp should play falls in the lap of the court. . . .

We disagree with the district court's legal determination that such decisions are to be made by the courts and believe instead that medical determinations of this sort are best left to team doctors and universities as long as they are made with reason and rationality and with full regard to possible and reasonable accommodations. In cases such as ours, where Northwestern has examined both Knapp and his medical records, has considered his medical history and the relation between his prior sudden cardiac death and the possibility of future occurrences, has considered the severity of the potential injury, and has rationally and reasonably reviewed consensus medical opinions or recommendations in the pertinent field—regardless whether conflicting medical opinions exist—the university has the right to determine that an individual is not otherwise medically qualified to play without violating the Rehabilitation Act. The place of the court in such cases is to make sure that the decision-maker has reasonably considered and relied upon sufficient evidence specific to the individual and the potential injury, not to determine on its own which evidence it believes is more persuasive.

Other courts have held the same. In *Pahulu*, for instance, an intercollegiate football player presented testimony of three specialists in an attempt to show that his risk of permanent neurological injury was no greater than any other player's and that the University of Kansas declared him physically ineligible based on misconceptions. The Kansas district court nevertheless found that "the conclusion of the KU physicians, although conservative, is reasonable and rational . . . and is supported by substantial competent evidence for which the court is unwilling to substitute its judgment." *Pahulu*, 897 F.Supp. at 1394. We reject those cases intimating that a school's rational decision has no weight. *See Poole v. South Plainfield Bd. of Educ.*, 490 F.Supp. 948, 954 (D.N.J.1980) (school board incorrectly "insisted nonetheless in imposing its own rational decision over the rational decision of the Pooles"). . . .

We do not believe that, in cases where medical experts disagree in their assessment of the extent of a real risk of serious harm or death, Congress intended that the courts—neutral arbiters but generally less skilled in medicine than the experts involved—should make the final medical decision. Instead, in the midst of conflicting expert testimony regarding the degree of serious risk of harm or death, the court's place is to ensure that the exclusion or disqualification of an individual was individualized, reasonably made, and based upon competent medical evidence. So long as these factors exist, it will be the rare case regarding participation in athletics where a court may substitute its judgment for that of the school's team physicians. . . .

In closing, we wish to make clear that we are *not* saying Northwestern's decision necessarily is the right decision. We say only that it is not an illegal one under the Rehabilitation Act. On the same facts, another team physician at another university, reviewing the same medical history, physical evaluation, and medical recommendations, might reasonably decide that Knapp met the physical qualifications for playing on an intercollegiate basketball team. Simply put, all universities need not evaluate risk the same way. What we say in this case is that if substantial evidence supports the decision-maker—here Northwestern—that decision must be respected.

Section 794 prohibits authorities from deciding without significant medical support that certain activities are too risky for a disabled person. Decisions of this sort cannot rest on paternalistic concerns. Knapp, who is an adult, is not in need of paternalistic decisions regarding his health, and his parents—more entitled to be paternalistic toward him than Northwestern—approve of his decision. . . . But here, where Northwestern acted rationally and reasonably rather than paternalistically, no Rehabilitation Act violation has occurred. The Rehabilitation Act "is carefully structured to replace . . . reflexive actions to actual or perceived handicaps with actions based on reasoned and medically sound judgments. . . ." *Arline*, 480 U.S. at 284-85, 107 S.Ct. at 1129. . . .

Reversed.

NOTES AND QUESTIONS

1. *Purpose of the Rehabilitation Act.* The Supreme Court has observed that the Rehabilitation Act's objective is to prevent discrimination based on an assumed "inability to function in a particular context." *Southeastern Community College v. Davis*, 442 U.S. 397, 405 (1979). The act is primarily intended to provide handicapped or impaired persons with an opportunity to participate fully in activities in which they have the physical capability and skill to perform. Section 504 of the act is patterned after similar federal statutes prohibiting racial and sexual discrimination. Regulations promulgated under the act by the Department of Education specifically prohibit colleges and high schools from discriminating against qualified handicapped athletes. Qualified handicapped athletes must be given an "equal opportunity for participation" in interscholastic and intercollegiate athletics. 34 C.F.R. §§104.37(c) and 104.47(a); 45 C.F.R. §§84.37(c) and 84.47(a).
2. *Entities Covered by the Rehabilitation Act.* If any part of an educational institution receives federal financial assistance, all of its operations and programs are covered by the Rehabilitation Act. 29 U.S.C.A. §794(b). Thus, virtually all university and high school athletics programs are covered by the act.
3. *Persons Protected by the Rehabilitation Act.* Why did *Knapp* hold that the plaintiff was not entitled to the act's protection? Would the court's holding be different if Northwestern University refused to honor his athletic scholarship?
    One scholar asserts:

    In determining whether an individual athlete's exclusion from athletics substantially limits a major life activity, courts should accord greater weight to the importance of athletic competition in high school and college education. . . . Whether exclusion from intercollegiate or interscholastic athletics substantially limits one's opportunity to learn must necessarily be considered on an individualized basis. Even if there are other educational benefits available to excluded physically impaired athletes, they are being denied an equal opportunity to participate fully in all of an educational institution's programs and activities which are generally available to all persons with the requisite skills and abilities. If physically impaired high school and college athletes are not covered by the Act, such an athlete is deprived of his or her federal right to have one's medical condition individually evaluated as well as the full potential educational benefits of competitive athletics if he or she is found to be "otherwise qualified" under the Act. Accordingly, it would further the Act's objectives of prohibiting medically unjustified discrimination against physically impaired persons by ensuring that these athletes are protected by the Act.

Matthew J. Mitten, *Enhanced Risk of Harm to One's Self as a Justification for Exclusion from Athletics*, 8 Marq. Sports L.J. 189 (1998). Do you agree?

4. *"Excluded . . . Solely Because of His Disability."* An educational institution might fear tort liability if it permits an athlete to play a sport contrary to the recommendations of its team physician and the athlete suffers a serious injury or dies while doing so. Is this a valid justification for exclusion given that Nicholas Knapp and his parents were willing to release Northwestern University from any potential liability if a "worst-case scenario" occurred? *Grube v. Bethlehem Area Sch. Dist.*, 550 F. Supp. 418, 424 (E.D. Pa. 1982) (suggesting that fear of contractual liability does not justify excluding impaired athlete willing to waive future tort claims against school for permitting participation). What advice would you give to the university?

5. *"Otherwise Qualified" to Participate.* An individual is "otherwise qualified" if "able to meet all of a program's requirements in spite of his handicap." *Southeastern Community College v. Davis*, 442 U.S. 397, 406 (1979). An athlete is not "otherwise qualified" if physically unable to perform or function effectively in a particular sport.

How does *Knapp* construe this statutory language as it applies to athletics? According to the Seventh Circuit, what standard must be satisfied to justify an educational institution's exclusion of a physically impaired athlete from competitive sports?

Other courts have accorded significant weight to an impaired athlete's interest in individual autonomy by concluding:

> Life has risks. The purpose of [the Act], however, is to permit handicapped individuals to live life as fully as they are able, without paternalistic authorities deciding that certain activities are too risky for them . . . The [school's] responsibility is to see that he does not pursue this course in a foolish manner. They therefore have a duty to alert Richard and his parents to the dangers involved and to require them to deal with the matter rationally.

Poole v. S. Plainfield Bd. of Educ., 490 F. Supp. 948, 953-954 (D. N.J. 1980). In *Poole*, the court declined to dismiss an athlete's complaint that his high school's refusal to permit him to wrestle with only one kidney violated the act. The court rejected the school's argument that the athlete was not "otherwise qualified" because he was unable to pass the team physician's examination with one kidney. The court found that the plaintiff was qualified to wrestle because he was capable of meeting the sport's training requirements and another "respectable medical authority" cleared him for participation. *Id.* at 953. See generally Adam A. Milani, *Can I Play? The Dilemma of the Disabled Athlete in Interscholastic Sports*, 49 Ala. L. Rev. 817, 904-905 (1998) ("If the student-athlete can compete at the same level as his peers, a school has 'neither the duty nor the right' to bar a student from playing once it is satisfied that he and his family know of the dangers involved and rationally reach a decision to continue playing").

Judicial opinion is divided regarding whether the exclusion of athletes with missing or nonfunctioning paired organs from contact sports violates the Rehabilitation Act. Some courts hold that doing so violates this federal law. *Kampmeier v. Nyquist*, 553 F.2d 296 (2d Cir. 1977); *Grube v. Bethlehem Area School Dist.*, 550 F. Supp. 418 (E.D. Pa. 1982); *Wright v. Columbia Univ.*, 520 F. Supp. 789 (E.D. Pa. 1981); *Poole v. S. Plainfield Bd. of Educ.*, 490 F. Supp. 948 (D. N.J. 1980).

6. *Reasonable Accommodation Requirement.* The Rehabilitation Act requires a covered entity to make reasonable accommodations or modifications to its program's participation requirements to enable an athlete to play sports. *Alexander v. Choate*, 469 U.S. 287, 300 (1985) ("while a [school] need not be required to make 'fundamental' or 'substantial' modifications to accommodate the handicapped, it may be required to make 'reasonable' ones"); *Grube v. Bethlehem Area Sch. Dist.*, 550 F. Supp. 418, 424 (E.D. Pa.1982) (permitting a high school student with one kidney to play football if he wore a protective flak jacket was a required reasonable accommodation).

Do you agree with the Seventh Circuit's holding that the Rehabilitation Act did not require the university to allow Knapp to play intercollegiate basketball with an internal defibrillator?

7. *Aftermath of* Knapp. After his unsuccessful litigation against Northwestern, Nicholas Knapp transferred to Northeastern Illinois University, which permitted him to play on its basketball team. However, his internal defibrillator malfunctioned before a practice three games into the 1997-1998 basketball season, and he sat out the rest of the year. Because Northeastern Illinois discontinued its intercollegiate basketball program after that season, Knapp transferred to Ashland University, where he played for two seasons. Knapp quit playing during his third year after his defibrillator again malfunctioned; at a later time it was removed, but he has not experienced any additional heart problems. Kathryn Kranhold and Kevin Helliker, *Cardiologist Helps Athletes Get Back in the Game*, Pittsburgh Post-Gazette, July 25, 2006, http://www.post-gazette.com/stories/news/health/cardiologist-helps-athletes-get-back-in-the-game-443447/.

2.   Enhanced Risk of Harm to Others

A physically impaired athlete's medical condition may expose other participants to an enhanced risk of harm beyond what is inherent in a particular sport. For example, there have been concerns expressed by some athletes about perceived health risks from playing contact sports with an athlete who has tested positive for human immunodeficiency virus (HIV), which causes the fatal disease acquired immunodeficiency syndrome (AIDS). Despite a consensus among medical experts that the risk of HIV transmission during an athletic event is extremely low, some fear that HIV infection may occur from exposure to an HIV-positive athlete's blood during a game. See Karen Ahearn, *HIV-Positive Athletes*, 7 Sports L.J. 279 (2000); Anthony DiMaggio, *Suffering in Silence: Should They Be Cheered or Feared? (Mandatory HIV Testing of Athletes as a Health and Safety Issue)*, 8 Seton Hall J. Sport L. 663 (1998); John T. Wolohan, *An Ethical and Legal*

Dilemma: Participation in Sports by HIV Infected Athletes, 7 Marq. Sports L.J. 373 (1997); Matthew J. Mitten, *AIDS and Athletics*, 3 Seton Hall J. Sport L. 5 (1993).

This issue came to the forefront of public attention with former Los Angeles Lakers superstar player Earvin "Magic" Johnson's November 1991 announcement that he was retiring from the NBA because he tested positive for HIV. Thereafter, Johnson returned to basketball and won the Most Valuable Player award at the 1992 NBA All-Star Game and led the United States men's basketball team to the gold medal in the 1992 Summer Olympics. In September 1992, Johnson announced his decision to rejoin the Lakers, making him the first player to play a professional sport while known to be HIV positive. Prior to the 1992-1993 NBA season, Johnson again retired because of opposing players' concerns that competing against him would expose them to the risk of HIV infection. These fears were exacerbated by a cut on Johnson's arm suffered during a preseason NBA basketball game. Even prior to this incident, one Australian Olympic basketball team member said if his team were scheduled to play the United States for the gold medal, he would prefer to skip the game and accept the silver medal rather than play against Magic Johnson. In 1996 this issue resurfaced when the Nevada State Athletic Commission suspended professional boxer Tommy Morrison from fighting after he tested positive for HIV.

The following case considers whether it is legal to exclude an athlete known to be HIV positive from participation in competitive sports.

MONTALVO v. RADCLIFFE

167 F.3d 873 (4th Cir.), *cert. denied*, 528 U.S. 813 (1999)

NIEMEYER, Circuit Judge.

Michael Montalvo, a 12-year old boy with AIDS, was denied admission to a traditional Japanese style martial arts school because of his HIV-positive status. In this action, brought under Title III of the Americans with Disabilities Act (prohibiting discrimination on the basis of disability by places of public accommodation), the district court denied Montalvo relief because his condition posed a significant risk to the health or safety of other students and no reasonable modification could sufficiently reduce this risk without fundamentally altering the nature of the program. We affirm.

Southside Virginia Police Karate Association, Inc. operates a karate school in Colonial Heights, Virginia, known as U.S.A. Bushidokan, which is owned by James P. Radcliffe, II. The school teaches exclusively traditional Japanese, combat-oriented martial arts rather than the more prevalent, family-oriented fitness programs offered by most martial arts schools. Within the first three weeks of lessons at U.S.A. Bushidokan, students learn techniques that involve substantial body contact, and within the first few months they apply these techniques to spar in actual combat situations. Radcliffe testified at trial that the sparring often results in injuries which, while minor, are bloody. . . .

He explained that to progress "through the belt," a level of achievement, a student must "engage in combat activity fighting. You have to do the self-defense. It involves contact, that's what we do." Radcliffe noted that inherent in this form of karate are "consistently scratched skin, scratches, gouges, bloody lips, bloody noses, things of that nature."

In May 1997, Luciano and Judith Montalvo applied to enter their 12-year old son, Michael, into group karate classes at U.S.A. Bushidokan because Michael wanted to learn karate with some friends who had already begun lessons there. Luciano Montalvo signed a "Membership Application and Agreement" form in which he warranted that Michael was "in good health and that [he] suffer[ed] from no illness or condition . . . which would possibly be infectious to others" and that the Montalvos understood that "no member [would] use the facilities with any open cuts, abrasions, open sores, infections, [or] maladies with the potential of harm to others." In fact, however, Michael had AIDS. The Montalvos did not disclose that fact to U.S.A. Bushidokan because they were afraid that U.S.A. Bushidokan would not enroll Michael if it knew of his HIV-positive status, [but U.S.A. Bushidokan] received information [of Michael's HIV status] from an anonymous source . . . .

Title III of the Americans with Disabilities Act ("ADA") was enacted to facilitate disabled individuals' access to places of public accommodation. Consistent with this goal, the Act states broadly:

> No individual shall be discriminated against on the basis of disability in the full and equal enjoyment of the goods, services, facilities, privileges, advantages, or accommodations of any place of public accommodation by any person who owns, leases (or leases to), or operates a place of public accommodation.

42 U.S.C. § 12182(a). The ADA defines "denial of participation" in a program offered by a place of public accommodation to be an act of discrimination. 42 U.S.C. § 12182(b)(1)(A)(i).

Recognizing that the need to protect public health may at times outweigh the rights of disabled individuals, Congress created a narrow exception to this broad prohibition against discrimination based on disability in places of public accommodation. Thus, a place of public accommodation is entitled to exclude a disabled individual from participating in its program "where such individual poses a *direct threat* to the health or safety of others." 42 U.S.C. § 12182(b)(3) (emphasis added). The Act defines "direct threat" as "a significant risk to the health or safety of others that cannot be eliminated by a modification of policies, practices, or procedures or by the provision of auxiliary aids or services." *Id.* When determining whether an individual poses a "direct threat," a place of public accommodation must not base its calculus on stereotypes or generalizations about the effects of a disability but rather must make "an individualized assessment, based on reasonable judgment that relies on current medical knowledge or on the best available objective evidence." 28 C.F.R. § 36.208(c). The relevant factors which the place of public accommodation must weigh and balance are "the nature, duration, and severity of the risk [and] the probability that the potential injury will actually occur." *Id.; see also* 28 C.F.R. Pt. 36, App. B, p. 598 (1998) (noting that the direct threat provision in Title III of the ADA codifies *School Bd. of Nassau County v. Arline,* 480 U.S. 273, 287-88, 107 S.Ct. 1123, 94 L.Ed.2d 307 (1987) (delineating criteria for determining whether, under § 504 of the Rehabilitation Act, a tubercular teacher posed a significant risk to the school community).

If the place of public accommodation determines that the individual would pose a significant risk to the health and safety of others, it must then ascertain "whether reasonable modifications of policies, practices, or procedures will mitigate the risk," 28 C.F.R. § 36.208(c), to the point of "eliminat[ing]" it as a "significant risk," 42 U.S.C. § 12182(b)(3). . . . Under the ADA, a failure to make a reasonable modification is itself an act of discrimination unless the place of public accommodation can demonstrate that implementing the modification would fundamentally alter the nature of the program. *See* 42 U.S.C. § 12182(b)(2)(A)(ii).

In this case, U.S.A. Bushidokan concedes that its karate school is a place of public accommodation subject to the requirements of Title III and that Michael Montalvo is disabled for purposes of the ADA by virtue of being HIV-positive or having AIDS. U.S.A. Bushidokan also concedes that it denied Michael participation in group karate classes on the basis of his HIV-positive status, the condition that concededly constitutes his disability. But U.S.A. Bushidokan contends that its exclusion of Michael was legally justified because Michael posed a "direct threat" to other members of the karate class. This contention presents two issues: (1) whether Michael's condition posed a significant risk to the health or safety of others and (2) whether reasonable modifications of policies, practices, or procedures were available to eliminate the risk as a significant one.

While the question of whether Michael's HIV-positive status posed a significant risk to the health or safety of others is a "fact intensive determination," the evidence in the record before us is ample to support the district court's conclusion that Michael posed such a risk.

First, both the Montalvos' and U.S.A. Bushidokan's medical experts testified that blood-to-blood contact is a means of HIV transmission, and both experts agreed that AIDS is inevitably fatal. In addition, U.S.A. Bushidokan's expert testified without challenge that it was possible to become infected with the virus from blood splashing into the eyes or onto seemingly intact skin.

Second, the type of activity offered at U.S.A. Bushidokan emphasized sparring, attack drills, and continuous body interaction with the result that the participants frequently sustained bloody injuries, such as nose bleeds, cuts inside the mouth, and external abrasions. Radcliffe testified that blood from those injuries is "extremely likely" to come in contact with other students' skin. Even though U.S.A. Bushidokan had a policy of constantly monitoring for bloody injuries and removing for treatment participants with those injuries, the fast-paced, continuous combat exercises hampered U.S.A. Bushidokan's efforts to eliminate contact when such injury occurred. . . .

The nature, duration, and severity of the risk and probability of transmission—factors outlined by *Arline* and the ADA regulations—indicate that a significant risk to the health and safety of others would exist if Michael were allowed to participate in the group karate classes. The nature of the risk, which *Arline* defines as the mode of transmission of the disease, is blood-to-blood or blood-to-eye contact, according to the testimony of both sides' experts. The duration of the risk, which *Arline* defines as how long the carrier is infectious, is for the length of Michael's life. The severity of the risk is extreme because there is no known cure for AIDS, and, as the Montalvos concede, AIDS is inevitably fatal. And although the exact mathematical probability of transmission is unknown, the mode of transmission is one which is likely to occur in U.S.A. Bushidokan's combat-oriented group karate classes because of the frequency of bloody injuries and body contact. Thus, the nature of the risk, combined with its severity, creates a significant risk to the health and safety of hard-style karate class members.

When balancing the *Arline* factors to determine whether a risk is significant, one need not conclude that each factor is significant on its own. Rather, the gravity of one factor might well compensate for the relative slightness of another. Thus, when the disease at risk of transmission is, like AIDS, severe and inevitably fatal, even a low probability of transmission could still create a significant risk. In this case, therefore, we agree with the district court that Michael's condition posed a significant risk to the health and safety of others. . . .

The experts in this case agreed that HIV can be transmitted through blood-to-blood contact, and the evidence showed that this type of contact occurred frequently in the karate classes at U.S.A. Bushidokan. Thus, the district court's finding that Michael Montalvo posed a significant risk to the health or safety of others is amply supported by the evidence.

Even though Michael Montalvo's condition posed a significant risk to the health or safety of others, U.S.A. Bushidokan would still be required to admit him to group karate classes if a reasonable modification could have eliminated the risk as a significant one. The only modification which was both effective in reducing risk to an insignificant level and in maintaining the fundamental essence of U.S.A. Bushidokan's program was its offer of private karate classes to Michael.

In considering other modifications, U.S.A. Bushidokan was entitled to reject the modification that would soften the teaching style of its program. U.S.A. Bushidokan's unique niche in the martial arts market was its adherence to traditional, "hard-style" Japanese karate, and the contact between participants, which causes the bloody injuries and creates the risk of HIV transmission, was an integral aspect of such a program. To require U.S.A. Bushidokan to make its program a less combat-oriented, interactive, contact intensive version of karate would constitute a fundamental alteration of the nature of its program. The ADA does not require U.S.A. Bushidokan to abandon its essential mission and to offer a fundamentally different program of instruction.

Similarly, U.S.A. Bushidokan was not required to implement further "universal precautions" such as using eye coverings and wearing gloves. The district court found as a fact that these modifications would not accomplish their goal of eliminating or reducing the otherwise significant risk Michael would pose to his classmates. As Radcliffe testified on behalf of U.S.A. Bushidokan, the suddenness of injuries, the tendency of some wounds to splatter blood, the continuing movement and contact, and the inability to detect injuries immediately all would undermine the effectiveness of these precautions, particularly for places not protected by eye coverings, gloves, or other similar coverings. . . .

Accordingly, we conclude that U.S.A. Bushidokan, in excluding Michael Montalvo from participating in its combat-oriented group karate classes, did not violate Title III of the ADA because Michael posed a significant risk to the health and safety of others that could not be eliminated by a reasonable modification.

The judgment of the district court is *AFFIRMED.*

NOTES AND QUESTIONS

1. *Scope of ADA's Coverage.* Unlike *Knapp*, which was a Rehabilitation Act case, *Montalvo* was brought pursuant to the Americans with Disabilities Act of 1990 (ADA), 42 U.S.C. §§12101 et seq. The ADA is patterned after the Rehabilitation Act, has similar policy objectives, and extends the coverage of federal legal protection of the rights of handicapped and disabled persons. However, the ADA's scope of coverage is broader than that of the

Rehabilitation Act because it covers private entities that do not receive federal funding, such as professional sports leagues and their member teams. Courts generally construe the ADA's substantive provisions in a manner consistent with judicial interpretations of the Rehabilitation Act. *Bragdon v. Abbott*, 524 U.S. 624, 631-632 (1998).

Three sections of the ADA are particularly relevant in the context of athletics. The ADA applies to public entities, 42 U.S.C. §§12131 and 12132, and employers with 15 or more employees engaged in industries affecting interstate commerce. 42 U.S.C. §12111(5)(A). Persons that own, lease, or operate a place of public accommodation also are subject to the ADA. 42 U.S.C. §12182(a). A place of public accommodation includes "a gymnasium, health spa, bowling alley, golf course, or other place of exercise or recreation." 42 U.S.C. §12181(7)(L). Virtually all public and private grade schools, high schools, colleges, universities, professional teams, and operators of sporting events held in facilities open to the public are subject to the ADA. Under which provision was the *Montalvo* defendant covered by the ADA?

2. *Individuals Protected by ADA.* Although they were both excluded from desired athletic participation, why was Michael Montalvo protected by federal disability discrimination laws, whereas Nicholas Knapp was not? Note that strict judicial application of the "substantially limits a major life activity" requirement can lead to the ironic result that certain physically impaired athletes are covered by the ADA and Rehabilitation Act, but others are not. For example, a blind or deaf athlete is "disabled" because being blind or deaf substantially limits, respectively, the major life activities of seeing or hearing. On the other hand, an athlete with a cardiovascular abnormality or certain other physical impairments may not be able to prove that this medical condition substantially limits a major life activity. Yet blind or deaf athletes are legally entitled to an individualized evaluation of their respective medical conditions, whereas other athletes are not. Is there is a principled justification for protecting some physically impaired athletes but not others? Consider that effective January 1, 2009, Congress amended the ADA to provide that "[t]he definition of disability in this Act shall be construed in favor of broad coverage of individuals under this Act, to the maximum extent permitted by the terms of this Act." 42 U.S.C. §12102(4)(A).

3. *Medical Justification for Exclusion.* What is the legal standard for excluding an athlete with an infectious disease from participation in a sport? In *Montalvo*, was the medical evidence of record sufficient to satisfy this standard? See *Bragdon v. Abbott*, 524 U.S. 624, 626-627 (1998) (assessment of risk of HIV transmission "is based on the medical or other objective, scientific evidence available . . . not simply on . . . good-faith belief that a significant risk existed").

Prior to *Montalvo*, two federal district courts held that the exclusion of HIV-positive elementary school students from participation in school-sponsored contact sports does not violate the Rehabilitation Act. *Doe v. Dolton Elementary Sch. Dist. No. 148*, 694 F. Supp. 440, 449 (N.D. Ill. 1988); *Ray v. School Dist.*, 666 F. Supp. 1524, 1537 (M.D. Fla. 1987). These courts, however, failed to cite or rely on any medical evidence finding that there is a significant risk of HIV transmission during contact sports. See *Anderson v. Little League Baseball, Inc.*, 794 F. Supp. 342 (D. Ariz. 1992) (baseball league's blanket policy prohibiting coaches in wheelchairs from being on the field violates the ADA because there was no individualized assessment of safety risks).

In *Doe v. Woodford County Board of Education*, 213 F.3d 921 (6th Cir. 2000), the Sixth Circuit ruled that placing a member of a high school's junior varsity basketball team who suffered from hepatitis B on "hold" status pending receipt of medical clearance from his physician did not violate the act. The court explained:

> It is entirely reasonable for defendants to be concerned and arguably were obligated to be concerned with limiting risk of exposure of any contagion to others as well as limiting any injury that John may suffer. In an effort to ensure that John's participation in practice would not pose a threat to the safety and well being of John as well as other players, the school requested plaintiff to present some objective medical evidence to that effect. After receiving a very general letter from John Doe's doctor, defendants asked for a more definitive statement as to the safety of John's participation on the team. For purposes of liability, it does not matter that defendants eventually determined, according to its inter-office memorandum, that John should be allowed to fully participate on the basketball team. Rather, defendants, during this "hold" status period, were simply trying to balance the need of protecting the public health with John's rights not to be treated differently due to his disability.

Id. at 926.

The *Woodford County* court observed that "defendants faced potential liability from other students and parents if they allowed John to play on the team and another student accidentally became exposed to John's contagious condition." *Id.* This is a valid concern because courts have held that an athletic event sponsor has a legal duty to use reasonable care to prevent the transmission of contagious diseases during competition. See, e.g., *Joseph E.G. v. E. Irondequoit Cent. Sch. Dist.*, 708 N.Y.S.2d 537 (N.Y. App. Div. 2000) (reversing summary judgment for defendant school district because its affidavits did not address its alleged negligent failure to clean wrestling mats properly after a wrestler sustained a bloody nose); *Silver v. Levittown Union Free Sch. Dist.*, 692 N.Y.S.2d 886 (N.Y. Sup. Ct. 1999) (finding that an athlete may be liable for the negligent transmission of a contagious disease during a wrestling match).

4. *Comparative Law Perspective.* An Australian federal law, the Equal Opportunity Act of 1995, prohibits discrimination against physically impaired persons unless reasonably necessary to protect the health and safety of others. In *Hall v. Victorian Amateur Football Association* EOC ¶92-997 (1999), the Victorian Civil and Administrative Tribunal held that a sports league illegally discriminated against an HIV-positive athlete by excluding him from participating in amateur football, although it had a genuine belief that it was reasonably necessary based on available medical evidence. The tribunal found the risk of HIV transmission "so low" that it is not reasonably necessary to ban him from playing football. It observed that there is no documented case of HIV transmission during sports competition and that neither the Australian Sports Medicine Federation nor the league's infectious disease policy required the player's exclusion. Although medical experts calculated the risk of HIV transmission to be between 1/6,000 and 1/1,250,000 per player per game, the tribunal concluded the "calculated risk is much greater than the real risk." Compliance with the league's blood-borne infectious disease policy would reduce the risk of HIV transmission posed by the plaintiff's participation in the sport. The tribunal noted that even if he were prohibited from

playing football, the risk of HIV transmission from other unknown HIV-positive football players would still exist. For an in-depth discussion of the legality of excluding HIV-positive athletes from sports under Australian law, see Roger S. Magnusson and Hayden Opie, *HIV and Hepatitis in Sport: An Australian Legal Framework for Resolving Hard Cases*, 5 Seton Hall J. Sport L. 69 (1995).

PROBLEM 11-5

A local public school board voted to bar a parent from continuing to coach his son's high school football team. The parent is a former paramedic who apparently contracted HIV several years ago while treating an auto accident victim subsequently discovered to be HIV positive. School board members are concerned that the parent could transmit HIV to players while coaching or rendering first aid to injured players. One board member who is a physician does not think it is a good idea for the parent to continue coaching. Does the school board's action violate the ADA or Rehabilitation Act?

3. Modification of Rules of the Game

The essence of sports is competition by all participants in accordance with uniform playing rules and eligibility requirements. In the following case, the Supreme Court considers whether the federal disability discrimination laws require the rules of the game to be modified to enable an athlete with a mental or physical impairment to participate in a sport. Its decision also provides guidance regarding whether eligibility rules must be modified to permit athletes covered by the ADA or Rehabilitation Act to participate in competitive sports, as illustrated by *Cruz v. Pennsylvania Interscholastic Athletic Assn.*, Inc., 157 F. Supp. 2d 485 (E.D. Pa. 2001), *infra*.

PGA TOUR, INC. v. MARTIN
532 U.S. 661 (2001)

Justice STEVENS delivered the opinion of the Court.

Petitioner PGA TOUR, Inc., a nonprofit entity formed in 1968, sponsors and cosponsors professional golf tournaments conducted on three annual tours. About 200 golfers participate in the PGA TOUR; about 170 in the NIKE TOUR; and about 100 in the SENIOR PGA TOUR. PGA TOUR and NIKE TOUR tournaments typically are 4-day events, played on courses leased and operated by petitioner. . . .

Three sets of rules govern competition in tour events. First, the "Rules of Golf," jointly written by the United States Golf Association (USGA) and the Royal and Ancient Golf Club of Scotland, apply to the game as it is played, not only by millions of amateurs on public courses and in private country clubs throughout the United States and worldwide, but also by the professionals in the tournaments conducted by petitioner, the USGA, the Ladies' Professional Golf Association, and the Senior Women's Golf Association. Those rules do not prohibit the use of golf carts at any time.

Second, the "Conditions of Competition and Local Rules," often described as the "hard card," apply specifically to petitioner's professional tours. The hard cards for the PGA TOUR and NIKE TOUR require players to walk the golf course during tournaments, but not during open qualifying rounds. On the SENIOR PGA TOUR, which is limited to golfers age 50 and older, the contestants may use golf carts. Most seniors, however, prefer to walk.

Third, "Notices to Competitors" are issued for particular tournaments and cover conditions for that specific event. Such a notice may, for example, explain how the Rules of Golf should be applied to a particular water hazard or man-made obstruction. It might also authorize the use of carts to speed up play when there is an unusual distance between one green and the next tee.

The basic Rules of Golf, the hard cards, and the weekly notices apply equally to all players in tour competitions. . . .

Casey Martin is a talented golfer. As an amateur, he won 17 Oregon Golf Association junior events before he was 15, and won the state championship as a high school senior. He played on the Stanford University golf team that won the 1994 National Collegiate Athletic Association (NCAA) championship. As a professional, Martin qualified for the NIKE TOUR in 1998 and 1999, and based on his 1999 performance, qualified for the PGA TOUR in 2000. . . .

Martin is also an individual with a disability as defined in the Americans with Disabilities Act of 1990 (ADA or Act). Since birth he has been afflicted with Klippel-Trenaunay-Weber Syndrome, a degenerative circulatory disorder that obstructs the flow of blood from his right leg back to his heart. The disease is progressive; it causes severe pain and has atrophied his right leg. During the latter part of his college career, because of the progress of the disease, Martin could no longer walk an 18-hole golf course. Walking not only caused him pain, fatigue, and anxiety, but also created a significant risk of hemorrhaging, developing blood clots, and fracturing his tibia so badly that an amputation might be required. For these reasons, Stanford made written requests to the Pacific 10 Conference and the NCAA to waive for Martin their rules requiring players to walk and carry their own clubs. The requests were granted.

When Martin turned pro and entered petitioner's Q-School, the hard card permitted him to use a cart during his successful progress through the first two stages. He made a request, supported by detailed medical records, for permission to use a golf cart during the third stage. Petitioner refused to review those records or to waive its walking rule for the third stage. . . .

At trial, petitioner did not contest the conclusion that Martin has a disability covered by the ADA, or the fact "that his disability prevents him from walking the course during a round of golf." 994 F.Supp. 1242, 1244 (D.Or.1998). Rather, petitioner asserted that the condition of walking is a substantive rule of competition, and that waiving it as to any individual for any reason would fundamentally alter the nature of the competition. Petitioner's evidence included the testimony of a number of experts, among them some of the greatest golfers in history. Arnold Palmer, Jack Nicklaus, and Ken Venturi explained that fatigue can be a critical factor in a tournament, particularly on the last day when psychological pressure is at a maximum. Their testimony makes it clear that, in their view, permission to use a cart might well give some players a competitive advantage over other players who must walk. They did not, however, express any opinion on whether a cart would give Martin such an advantage.

[T]he District Court . . . judge found that the purpose of the rule was to inject fatigue into the skill of shotmaking, but that the fatigue injected "by walking the course cannot be deemed significant under normal circumstances." *Id.*, at 1250. Furthermore, Martin presented evidence, and the judge found, that even with the use of a cart, Martin must walk over a mile during an 18-hole round,[17] and that the fatigue he suffers from coping with his disability is "undeniably greater" than the fatigue his able-bodied competitors endure from walking the course. *Id.*, at 1251. . . .

As we have noted, 42 U.S.C. § 12182(a) sets forth Title III's general rule prohibiting public accommodations from discriminating against individuals because of their disabilities. The question whether petitioner has violated that rule depends on a proper construction of the term "discrimination," which is defined by Title III to include: "a failure to make reasonable modifications in policies, practices, or procedures, when such modifications are necessary to afford such goods, services, facilities, privileges, advantages, or accommodations to individuals with disabilities, unless the entity can demonstrate that making such modifications would fundamentally alter the nature of such goods, services, facilities, privileges, advantages, or accommodations." § 12182(b)(2)(A)(ii) [Emphasis added.]

Petitioner does not contest that a golf cart is a reasonable modification that is necessary if Martin is to play in its tournaments. Martin's claim thus differs from one that might be asserted by players with less serious afflictions that make walking the course uncomfortable or difficult, but not beyond their capacity. In such cases, an accommodation might be reasonable but not necessary. In this case, however, the narrow dispute is whether allowing Martin to use a golf cart, despite the walking requirement that applies to the PGA TOUR, the NIKE TOUR, and the third stage of the Q-School, is a modification that would "fundamentally alter the nature" of those events.

In theory, a modification of petitioner's golf tournaments might constitute a fundamental alteration in two different ways. It might alter such an essential aspect of the game of golf that it would be unacceptable even if it affected all competitors equally; changing the diameter of the hole from three to six inches might be such a modification. Alternatively, a less significant change that has only a peripheral impact on the game itself might nevertheless give a disabled player, in addition to access to the competition as required by Title III, an advantage over others and, for that reason, fundamentally alter the character of the competition. We are not persuaded that a waiver of the walking rule for Martin would work a fundamental alteration in either sense.

As an initial matter, we observe that the use of carts is not itself inconsistent with the fundamental character of the game of golf. From early on, the essence of the game has been shotmaking — using clubs to cause a ball to progress from the teeing ground to a hole some distance away with as few strokes as possible. . . . There is nothing in the Rules of Golf that either forbids the use of carts or penalizes a player for using a cart. That set of rules, as we have observed, is widely accepted in both the amateur and professional golf world as the rules of the game. . . .

Indeed, the walking rule is not an indispensable feature of tournament golf either. As already mentioned, petitioner permits golf carts to be used in

---

17. "In the first place, he does walk while on the course — even with a cart, he must move from cart to shot and back to the cart. In essence, he still must walk approximately 25% of the course. On a course roughly five miles in length, Martin will walk 1 1/4 miles." 994 F. Supp., at 1251.

the SENIOR PGA TOUR, the open qualifying events for petitioner's tournaments, the first two stages of the Q-School, and, until 1997, the third stage of the Q-School as well. Moreover, petitioner allows the use of carts during certain tournament rounds in both the PGA TOUR and the NIKE TOUR. In addition, although the USGA enforces a walking rule in most of the tournaments that it sponsors, it permits carts in the Senior Amateur and the Senior Women's Amateur championships.

Petitioner, however, distinguishes the game of golf as it is generally played from the game that it sponsors in the PGA TOUR, NIKE TOUR, and (at least recently) the last stage of the Q-School—golf at the "highest level." According to petitioner, "[t]he goal of the highest-level competitive athletics is to assess and compare the performance of different competitors, a task that is meaningful only if the competitors are subject to identical substantive rules." The waiver of any possibly "outcome-affecting" rule for a contestant would violate this principle and therefore, in petitioner's view, fundamentally alter the nature of the highest level athletic event. The walking rule is one such rule, petitioner submits, because its purpose is "to inject the element of fatigue into the skill of shot-making," and thus its effect may be the critical loss of a stroke. As a consequence, the reasonable modification Martin seeks would fundamentally alter the nature of petitioner's highest level tournaments even if he were the only person in the world who has both the talent to compete in those elite events and a disability sufficiently serious that he cannot do so without using a cart.

The force of petitioner's argument is, first of all, mitigated by the fact that golf is a game in which it is impossible to guarantee that all competitors will play under exactly the same conditions or that an individual's ability will be the sole determinant of the outcome. For example, changes in the weather may produce harder greens and more head winds for the tournament leader than for his closest pursuers. A lucky bounce may save a shot or two. Whether such happen-stance events are more or less probable than the likelihood that a golfer afflicted with Klippel-Trenaunay-Weber Syndrome would one day qualify for the NIKE TOUR and PGA TOUR, they at least demonstrate that pure chance may have a greater impact on the outcome of elite golf tournaments than the fatigue resulting from the enforcement of the walking rule.

Further, the factual basis of petitioner's argument is undermined by the District Court's finding that the fatigue from walking during one of petitioner's 4-day tournaments cannot be deemed significant. . . . And even under conditions of severe heat and humidity, the critical factor in fatigue is fluid loss rather than exercise from walking. . . .

Even if we accept the factual predicate for petitioner's argument—that the walking rule is "outcome affecting" because fatigue may adversely affect performance—its legal position is fatally flawed. Petitioner's refusal to consider Martin's personal circumstances in deciding whether to accommodate his disability runs counter to the clear language and purpose of the ADA. . . . An individualized inquiry must be made to determine whether a specific modification for a particular person's disability would be reasonable under the circumstances as well as necessary for that person, and yet at the same time not work a fundamental alteration.

To be sure, the waiver of an essential rule of competition for anyone would fundamentally alter the nature of petitioner's tournaments. As we have demonstrated, however, the walking rule is at best peripheral to the nature of petitioner's athletic events, and thus it might be waived in individual cases without working a fundamental alteration. Therefore, petitioner's claim that all the substantive rules for its "highest-level" competitions are sacrosanct and cannot be modified under any circumstances is effectively a contention that it is exempt from Title III's reasonable modification requirement. But that provision carves out no exemption for elite athletics, and given Title III's coverage not only of places of "exhibition or entertainment" but also of "golf course[s]," 42 U.S.C. §§ 12181(7)(C), (L), its application to petitioner' tournaments cannot be said to be unintended or unexpected, see §§ 12101(a)(1), (5). . . .[51]

Under the ADA's basic requirement that the need of a disabled person be evaluated on an individual basis, we have no doubt that allowing Martin to use a golf cart would not fundamentally alter the nature of petitioner's tournaments. As we have discussed, the purpose of the walking rule is to subject players to fatigue, which in turn may influence the outcome of tournaments. Even if the rule does serve that purpose, it is an uncontested finding of the District Court that Martin "easily endures greater fatigue even with a cart than his able-bodied competitors do by walking." 994 F.Supp., at 1252. The purpose of the walking rule is therefore not compromised in the slightest by allowing Martin to use a cart. A modification that provides an exception to a peripheral tournament rule without impairing its purpose cannot be said to "fundamentally alter" the tournament. What it can be said to do, on the other hand, is to allow Martin the chance to qualify for, and compete in, the athletic events petitioner offers to those members of the public who have the skill and desire to enter. That is exactly what the ADA requires. As a result, Martin's request for a waiver of the walking rule should have been granted.

The ADA admittedly imposes some administrative burdens on the operators of places of public accommodation that could be avoided by strictly adhering to general rules and policies that are entirely fair with respect to the able-bodied but that may indiscriminately preclude access by qualified persons with disabilities. But surely, in a case of this kind, Congress intended that an entity like the PGA not only give individualized attention to the handful of requests that it might receive from talented but disabled athletes for a modification or waiver of a rule to allow them access to the competition, but also carefully weigh the purpose, as well as the letter, of the rule before determining that no accommodation would be tolerable.

The judgment of the Court of Appeals is affirmed.

Justice SCALIA, with whom Justice THOMAS joins, dissenting.

In my view today's opinion exercises a benevolent compassion that the law does not place it within our power to impose. The judgment distorts the text of Title III, the structure of the ADA, and common sense. I respectfully dissent.

Nowhere is it writ that PGA TOUR golf must be classic "essential" golf. Why cannot the PGA TOUR, if it wishes, promote a new game, with distinctive rules (much as the American League promotes a game of baseball in which the

---

51. Hence, petitioner's questioning of the ability of courts to apply the reasonable modification requirement to athletic competition is a complaint more properly directed to Congress, which drafted the ADA's coverage broadly, than to us. . . . While Congress expressly exempted "private clubs or establishments" and "religious organizations or entities" from Title III's coverage, 42 U.S.C. § 12187, Congress made no such exception for athletic competitions, much less did it give sports organizations *carte blanche* authority to exempt themselves from the fundamental alteration inquiry by deeming any rule, no matter how peripheral to the competition, to be essential. . . .

pitcher's turn at the plate can be taken by a "designated hitter")? If members of the public do not like the new rules—if they feel that these rules do not truly test the individual's skill at "real golf" (or the team's skill at "real baseball") they can withdraw their patronage. But the rules are the rules. They are (as in all games) entirely arbitrary, and there is no basis on which anyone—not even the Supreme Court of the United States—can pronounce one or another of them to be "nonessential" if the rulemaker (here the PGA TOUR) deems it to be essential. . . .

Is someone riding around a golf course from shot to shot *really* a golfer? The answer, we learn, is yes. The Court ultimately concludes, and it will henceforth be the Law of the Land, that walking is not a "fundamental" aspect of golf.

Either out of humility or out of self-respect (one or the other) the Court should decline to answer this incredibly difficult and incredibly silly question. To say that something is "essential" is ordinarily to say that it is necessary to the achievement of a certain object. But since it is the very nature of a game to have no object except amusement (that is what distinguishes games from productive activity), it is quite impossible to say that any of a game's arbitrary rules is "essential." Eighteen-hole golf courses, 10-foot-high basketball hoops, 90-foot baselines, 100-yard football fields—all are arbitrary and none is essential. The only support for any of them is tradition and (in more modern times) insistence by what has come to be regarded as the ruling body of the sport—both of which factors support the PGA TOUR's position in the present case. (Many, indeed, consider walking to be *the central feature* of the game of golf—hence Mark Twain's classic criticism of the sport: "a good walk spoiled.") . . .

Because step one of the Court's two-part inquiry into whether a requested change in a sport will "fundamentally alter [its] nature," § 12182(b)(2)(A)(ii), consists of an utterly unprincipled ontology of sports (pursuant to which the Court is not even sure whether golf's "essence" requires a 3-inch hole), there is every reason to think that in future cases involving requests for special treatment by would-be athletes the second step of the analysis will be determinative. In resolving that second step—determining whether waiver of the "nonessential" rule will have an impermissible "competitive effect"—by measuring the athletic capacity of the requesting individual, and asking whether the special dispensation would do no more than place him on a par (so to speak) with other competitors, the Court guarantees that future cases of this sort will have to be decided on the basis of individualized factual findings. Which means that future cases of this sort will be numerous, and a rich source of lucrative litigation. One can envision the parents of a Little League player with attention deficit disorder trying to convince a judge that their son's disability makes it at least 25% more difficult to hit a pitched ball. (If they are successful, the only thing that could prevent a court order giving the kid four strikes would be a judicial determination that, in baseball, three strikes are metaphysically necessary, which is quite absurd.)

The statute, of course, provides no basis for this individualized analysis that is the Court's last step on a long and misguided journey. The statute seeks to assure that a disabled person's disability will not deny him *equal access* to (among other things) competitive sporting events—not that his disability will not deny him an *equal chance to win* competitive sporting events. The latter is quite impossible, since the very *nature* of competitive sport is the measurement, by uniform rules, of unevenly distributed excellence. This unequal distribution is precisely what determines the winners and losers—and artificially to "even out" that distribution, by giving one or another player exemption from a rule that emphasizes his particular weakness, is to destroy the game. . . . In the Court's world, there is one set of rules that is "fair with respect to the able-bodied" but "individualized" rules, mandated by the ADA, for "talented but disabled athletes." The ADA mandates no such ridiculous thing. . . .

My belief that today's judgment is clearly in error should not be mistaken for a belief that the PGA TOUR clearly *ought not* allow respondent to use a golf cart. *That* is a close question, on which even those who compete in the PGA TOUR are apparently divided; but it is a *different* question from the one before the Court. Just as it is a different question whether the Little League *ought* to give disabled youngsters a fourth strike, or some other waiver from the rules that makes up for their disabilities. In both cases, whether they *ought* to do so depends upon (1) how central to the game that they have organized (and over whose rules they are the master) they deem the waived provision to be, and (2) how competitive—how strict a test of raw athletic ability in all aspects of the competition—they want their game to be. . . .

And it should not be assumed that today's decent, tolerant, and progressive judgment will, in the long run, accrue to the benefit of sports competitors with disabilities. Now that it is clear courts will review the rules of sports for "fundamentalness," organizations that value their autonomy have every incentive to defend vigorously the necessity of every regulation. They may still be second-guessed in the end as to the Platonic requirements of the sport, but they will *assuredly* lose if they have at all wavered in their enforcement. The lesson the PGA TOUR and other sports organizations should take from this case is to make sure that the same written rules are set forth for all levels of play, and never voluntarily to grant any modifications. The second lesson is to end open tryouts. I doubt that, in the long run, even disabled athletes will be well served by these incentives that the Court has created. . . .

NOTES AND QUESTIONS

1. *Applicability of the ADA.* Because Casey Martin is an independent contractor who qualified for the Professional Golfers' Association (PGA) Tour because of his playing skills rather than an employee of the PGA, Title I's prohibition against employment discrimination was inapplicable. Because the PGA Tour is not a public entity, Title II did not apply. Therefore, Martin had to fit his disability discrimination claim under Title III, which covers places of public accommodation.

   The PGA initially argued it is a "private club" exempt from coverage under Title III pursuant to 42 U.S.C. §12187, or alternatively, that the playing area "behind the ropes" that is open only to the competitors is not a "place of public accommodation." Rejecting the first argument, the district court held that the PGA is appropriately characterized as a commercial enterprise operating in the entertainment industry for the economic benefit of its members rather than as a private club. 121 S. Ct. at 1886. The Ninth Circuit declined to accept the second argument because all members of the public who satisfy certain requirements are eligible to qualify for the PGA Tour and play in its tournaments.

   In a vigorous dissent, Justice Scalia argued that in the context of athletics, Title III's coverage is limited to clients and customers of places of public accommodation, not professional athletes seeking to provide entertainment services therein. In response, the majority found that Congress's intent was that the ADA be liberally construed to provide broad protection for all disabled persons and concluded that the PGA, as an operator of a place of public accommodation during its golf tournaments, "may not discriminate against either spectators or competitors on the basis of disability." 121 S. Ct. at 1892, n.34. With which view do you agree?

2. *Reasonable Accommodation or Fundamental Alteration of the Sport?* According to the *Martin* majority, when is a sport's governing body required to modify its playing rules to enable an impaired athlete to participate in the sport? Is there a principled judicial basis for distinguishing between "an essential rule of competition" and one that is merely nonessential or has a peripheral impact on the game? Does the majority provide a convincing response to the dissent's assertion that the essence of sport is that everyone plays by the same rules?

Should the federal disability discrimination laws be construed to permit judicial modification of uniform and neutral playing rules on a case-by-case basis? If not, what is an effective alternative means of ensuring that impaired persons have an equal opportunity to participate in athletics commensurate with their interests, skills, and abilities?

The following two cases decided prior to *Martin* illustrate the nature of the individualized inquiry that must be undertaken to determine whether requested rules modifications by impaired athletes would "fundamentally alter" the nature of a particular sport. Are these cases consistent with *Martin*?

In *Shultz v. Hemet Youth Pony League, Inc.*, 943 F. Supp. 1222 (C.D. Cal. 1996), an 11-year-old boy with a medical condition that severely affected the functioning of his leg muscles sought to play baseball in an age division reserved for children younger than him. The sport's governing body refused to modify its rules to permit him to do so. Although the boy was physically able to play baseball with the use of crutches, the governing body was concerned that permitting him to "play down" would create a possible risk of harm to himself and other players, and have adverse ramifications on its liability insurance coverage. The court found that the requested modification had been denied without any consideration of the boy's ability to run or engage in reflexive action or of what significant risks existed because he used crutches to play baseball. It held that the governing body violated the ADA by failing to even attempt to determine whether the game could be modified to accommodate his ability.

In *Elitt v. U.S.A. Hockey*, 922 F. Supp. 217 (E.D. Mo. 1996), the national governing body for amateur hockey denied the request of a youth hockey player with attention deficit disorder that his father or one of his brothers be permitted on the ice with him during practices and scrimmages to help keep him focused on the game. It also denied his request to "play down" to a lower age group. The court held that the denial of the requested modifications did not violate the ADA. Allowing the plaintiff's father or brother to be on the ice during scrimmages would fundamentally alter the nature of the game by disrupting the flow of play and preventing other players from experiencing actual game conditions. Permitting plaintiff to "play down" to the Squirt level was not required because:

> U.S.A. Hockey's age levels are important because they group players who are roughly the same skill and size. . . . Mark has focusing problems and would generally be larger than the average Squirt level player. These two factors would increase the chances of accidental collision as well as the risk of injury to younger and smaller-sized children. In short, Mark's participation in the lower age group would be too disruptive, thus fundamentally altering the house program.

Id. at 225. See generally Paul M. Anderson, *A Cart That Accommodates: Using Case Law to Understand the ADA, Sports, and Casey Martin,* 1 Va. Sports & Ent. L. J. 211 (2002) (observing that "[t]he cases that have followed Martin have simply refined the analysis that was already there").

In May 2007, the Ladies Professional Golfers Association allowed MacKinzie Kline, a 15-year-old golfer with a congenital heart condition that prevented her from walking long distances without becoming fatigued, to ride in a cart and use an oxygen delivery system when necessary during an LPGA Tour event. LPGA commissioner Carolyn Bivens determined that these accommodations would not provide her with an unfair competitive advantage.

In *Barron v. PGA Tour, Inc.,* 670 F. Supp. 2d 674 (W.D. Tenn. 2009), the court held that the PGA Tour did not violate a professional golfer's rights under the ADA by suspending him for one year for testing positive for exogenous testosterone, a banned substance under its anti-doping program, and refusing to grant him a therapeutic use exemption. Plaintiff alleged he suffers from abnormally low testosterone, which causes him to have a reduced sex drive, experience fatigue, and have a compromised immune system, and that by refusing to allow him to take medically prescribed exogenous testosterone and suspending him for using it, the PGA Tour discriminated against him in violation of the ADA. The court concluded that he had not shown a likelihood of success on his claim:

> Barron has not shown that the "reasonable accommodation" he has requested (allowing him to continue taking exogenous Testosterone) is necessary in order for him to continue playing golf in PGA Tour events. His complaint and post-hearing brief, at most, claim that he needs these Testosterone shots to address specific medical concerns relating to a reduced sex drive, fatigue, and a compromised immune system-not to play golf. While Barron's abnormally low Testosterone may in some way cause him to be a less competitive golfer than he would be if he were permitted to take the Testosterone injections, [the ADA] simply does not provide a remedy under those circumstances.

Id. at 685-686. After his suspension ended, the PGA Tour granted Barron a therapeutic use exemption to use testosterone while attempting to qualify for the 2011 PGA Tour, which was based on new medical information he submitted. See generally Travis Tygart and Anthony R. Ten Haagen, *The Americans With Disabilities Act, The United States Anti-Doping Agency, and the Effort Toward Equal Opportunity: A Case Study of the* United States Anti-Doping Agency v. George Hartman *Matter,* 2 Harv. J. Sports & Ent. L. 199 (2011) (discussing ADA's reasonable accommodation requirement as applied to athlete's therapeutic use of synthetic testosterone).

3. *Competition Between Able-Bodied and Disabled Athletes.* South African Oscar Pistorius had both legs amputated below the knee when he was 11 months

old, because he was born without the fibula in his lower legs and had other defects in his feet. Running with "Cheetah" prosthetic legs—a pair of J-shaped carbon fiber blades that touch only a few inches of ground and that attach to his knees—he easily won the 100- and 200-meter sprints at the 2007 Paralympic World Cup. He has set world record performances for disabled athletes in the 100, 200, and 400 meters, all of which would have won him gold medals in equivalent women's events at the 2004 Olympics. Currently, there are limited biomechanical studies of amputee runners, and his speed on prosthetic legs cannot be precisely compared with what his speed would be on natural legs.

In 2008, the Court of Arbitration for Sport ruled that Pistorius was eligible to run in International Association of Athletics Federations sanctioned track events with his prosthetic legs. *Pistorius v. IAAF*, CAS 2008/A/1480, award of 16 May 2008. An IAAF rule prohibited the use of "any technical device that incorporates springs, wheels or any other element that provides the user with an advantage over another athlete not using such a device." However, the CAS panel rejected the IAAF's argument that the use of a technical device providing an athlete "with any *advantage*, however small, in any part of a competition . . . must render that athlete ineligible to compete regardless of any compensating disadvantages." It concluded that the use of a passive device such as the "Cheetah" prosthetic legs does not violate this rule "without convincing scientific proof that it provides him with *an overall net advantage* over other athletes." The panel concluded that because scientific evidence did not prove that Pistorius obtained a metabolic or biomechanical advantage from using the "Cheetah" prosthetic legs, his exclusion would not further the rule's purpose of ensuring fair competition among athletes. Pistorius was unable to qualify for the 2008 Beijing Olympics, but four years later he qualified for the 2012 London Olympics, representing South Africa in both the 400-meter individual race and the 4×400-meter relay.

Are the federal disability laws violated if a U.S. athletic governing body refuses to allow Pistorius to compete in track events against able-bodied male runners? See *McFadden v. Grasmick*, 485 F. Supp. 2d 642 (D. Md. 2007) (court previously granted injunctive relief allowing "world class" Olympic wheelchair racer to compete alongside footed athletes in races within school district, but denies preliminary injunction seeking to require state high school athletic association to allow her to earn points in separate wheelchair racing events that count in determining team track and field state champion); *Badgett v. Alabama High School Athletic Assn.*, 2007 WL 2461928 (N.D. Ala.) (refusing to grant preliminary injunction to enable wheelchair athlete to compete against able-bodied runners in state track and field championship, because doing so would raise legitimate competitive fairness and safety concerns).

In response to a June 2010 United States Government Accountability Office report finding that public elementary and secondary school students with disabilities do not have an equal opportunity to participate in extracurricular sports, the Department of Education's Office for Civil Rights (OCR), which is responsible for enforcing Section 504 of the Rehabilitation Act and Title II of the ADA, issued on January 25, 2013, written guidance regarding the obligations of covered elementary, secondary, and postsecondary educational institutions to provide students with disabilities the opportunity to participate in interscholastic, intercollegiate, club, and intramural athletics. Department of Education, Office for Civil Rights, January 25, 2013, Directive. The directive states that educational institutions must provide "qualified students with disabilities an equal opportunity for participation in extracurricular athletics in an integrated manner to the maximum extent appropriate to the needs of the student." *Id.* at 7. An educational institution is required to create additional athletic participation opportunities (e.g., wheelchair basketball or tennis) for students with disabilities who are unable to participate in its existing extracurricular athletics program even with reasonable modifications thereto.

4. *Disabled Spectator Protections.* Disabled spectators have experienced mixed success in bringing ADA or Rehabilitation Act discrimination claims against professional leagues or operators of sports venues. See, e.g., *Paralyzed Veterans of America v. D.C. Arena L.P.*, 117 F.3d 579 (D.C. Cir. 1997) (violation not to provide line of sight over standing spectators for those in wheelchairs); *Stoutenborough v. NFL*, 59 F.3d 580 (6th Cir. 1995) (NFL television "blackout" rule does not discriminate against hearing-impaired persons); *Feldman v. Pro Football, Inc.*, 2008 U.S. Dist. Lexis 85149 (D. Md.) at *31 (ADA requires NFL club and stadium operator to provide equal access to aural information broadcast over FedExField public address system, including "music with lyrics, play information, advertisements, referee calls, safety/emergency information, and other announcements"); *Access Now Inc. v. S. Fla. Stadium Corp.*, 161 F. Supp. 2d 1357 (S.D. Fla. 2001) (stadium has reasonable number of wheelchair seating spaces; no evidence that plaintiff's proposed facility modifications would actually make stadium more accessible to disabled); *Cortez v. NBA*, 960 F. Supp. 113 (W.D. Tex. 1997) (rejecting hearing-impaired patron's demand for captioning and interpretative services while attending NBA games). See also *Celano v. Marriott Int'l, Inc.*, 2008 WL 239306 (N.D. Cal.) (failure to provide "accessible" or "single-rider" carts to enable disabled persons to play golf at defendant's courses violates ADA).

PROBLEM 11-6

Able is a paraplegic and a nationally ranked player in wheelchair racquetball competitions. He wants to play in an A-level open tournament with footed players, but asks that he be permitted two bounces to hit the ball. The Official Rules of Racquetball require the ball to be returned on one bounce in a game between footed players, but allow for two bounces if both participants are playing in wheelchairs.

The general manager of the Metropolis Athletic Club, which is organizing the tournament, has refused to grant Able's request. However, she will allow him to play in a novice league with footed players and be given only one bounce, or set up a wheelchair league if there are a sufficient number of other wheelchair players. Some footed players have expressed concern about whether it would be safe to play against Able in tournament competition. Able rejected these proposed alternatives and insists on being placed in the A League and given two bounces.

Does Able have a valid disability discrimination claim against the Metropolis Athletic Club for refusing to allow him to participate in its A League tournament with his requested rules modification?

4.   *Modification of Eligibility Requirements*

Students with mental impairments sometimes take longer to complete their schooling than students without such impairments and therefore find themselves too old to participate in interscholastic athletics as juniors or seniors in high school. Consider Eric Dompierre, a Michigan high school athlete with Down syndrome. Dompierre played sports throughout his childhood in Ishpeming, Michigan. When he entered Ishpeming High School as a freshman, Dompierre joined the football and basketball teams. Because of his Down syndrome, however, Dompierre progressed through his academic career more slowly than his non–mentally impaired age mates and by January 2012—the second semester of his junior year—he was already 19 years old. This made him ineligible under a Michigan High School Athletic Association rule prohibiting any student who turns 19 before September 1 of his or her senior year from participating in interscholastic athletics. See Tim Rohan, *Age Is Obstacle for Athlete with Down Syndrome,* N.Y. Times, April 12, 2012, at B13. In response to a national outcry spurred by an Internet and social media campaign to "Let Eric Play!" the MHSAA member schools voted in May 2012 to enact a waiver provision to permit age-ineligible athletes to participate if:

> 1) [The applicant's educational progress] was delayed prior to initial enrollment in the ninth grade solely because of a medically documented disability under the federal Americans with Disabilities Act or Michigan's Persons With Disabilities Civil Rights Act; and
> 2) At the time of the waiver request, [the] student [has] a defined disability documented to diminish both physical and either intellectual or emotional capabilities, does not create a health or safety risk to participants, and does not create a competitive advantage for the team.

See MHSAA Regulation 1 §2(B) (2011-2012). Although Dompierre's athletic eligibility status was resolved without litigation, consider how a court may have decided a federal disability discrimination claim by Dompierre against the MHSAA.

CRUZ v. PENNSYLVANIA INTERSCHOLASTIC ATHLETIC ASSN., INC.

157 F. Supp. 2d 485 (E.D. Pa. 2001)

Buckwalter, District Judge.

[Eds. Luis Cruz was a 19-year-old public school special education student who was educable mentally retarded in his fourth year at Ridley High School, a recipient of federal funding. He had played several sports in his first three years at Ridley High School, including football, wrestling, and track. Because he was a student with a disability, Luis Cruz was educated in accordance with an individualized education program (IEP), pursuant to the federal Individuals with Disabilities Education Act (IDEA). As a "non-graded" student, Luis Cruz was not enrolled in a particular numerical grade. His window of opportunity to participate in high school instruction and sports at an earlier age was limited and he did not have comparable opportunities as non-special education children, since due to his intellectual limitations he entered elementary school between ages eleven and twelve, rather than at the customary younger age, and then stayed an additional two years over the regular education students.

The defendant was the Pennsylvania Interscholastic Athletic Association, Inc. (P.I.A.A.), a Pennsylvania nonprofit membership corporation composed of most public and many private high schools in Pennsylvania, for a total of approximately 1,350 schools. A purpose of P.I.A.A. is to develop and apply rules regulating interscholastic athletic competition among its members. The P.I.A.A.'s "Age Rule" provided that "[a] pupil shall be ineligible for interscholastic athletic competition upon attaining the age of nineteen years, with the following exception: If the age of 19 is attained on or after July 1, the pupil shall be eligible, age-wise, to compete through that school year."

A school was required to forfeit a contest for using an ineligible coach or contestant. P.I.A.A. rules permitted students to participate in eight semesters of interscholastic sports; however, Cruz was only been permitted to participate in six semesters. The Director of Special Education Services observed that he still needed the remaining two semesters of interscholastic sports activities to interact with peers and adults, familiarize himself with demands and responsibilities, and develop interpersonal skills that would help him maintain employment after high school. Participation in these activities was vitally important to the development of his self-esteem and self-confidence. Although there was a provision for waiving either the eight-semester or transfer rules, with the key issue usually being "athletic intent," there was no waiver provision for the age rule. This was only the second time the P.I.A.A. had received a request for a waiver of this rule by a student with an IEP.]

The purposes of [the age rule] are: (1) to protect high school athletes of customary age from the dangers and unfairness of participation with those who are older and thus perhaps physically larger, stronger, and more mature and experienced; (2) to limit the possibility that the team with the over-age student will gain an unfair competitive advantage over opponents; (3) to have available the maximum number of team positions for high school athletes who are of customary age for students in high school; and (4) to maintain uniformity of standards with regard to the age of participants. . . .

[According to Bradley Cashman, the P.I.A.A.'s executive director, the age rule did not provide for any waivers because it would be an overly burdensome task to evaluate competitive advantage in individual cases.] An assessment of whether the student would "skew the overall competitiveness of the particular activity" or whether the student would constitute a competitive advantage would have to be looked at not only sport by sport, but individual by individual. Such an assessment would involve examining the individual in comparison with members of his or her own team, and in comparison with members of opposing teams. Such an assessment would involve projecting future athletic performance, at a time in the student's life when athletic ability is changing. This would be a very difficult, complex, and burdensome assessment involving many variables, including both objective and subjective elements, according to Mr. Cashman. . . .

P.I.A.A. estimates that it would have to significantly increase the size of its staff, doubling or tripling it, in order to perform assessments of whether a student would "skew the overall competitiveness of the particular activity" or whether the student would constitute a competitive advantage.

Luis Cruz is not a "star" player in any of his interscholastic sports. Luis Cruz has been included in the football program for an inclusive experience. He is a marginal player and appeared in football games on a very limited basis such as a few kickoffs where the performance apparently was not critical. At the same time, the non-special education students of Ridley High School are attempting to be inclusive. They have rallied around him, as he is a "great team player."

Luis Cruz is not more experienced than other players. In fact, he is less experienced and therefore has played football only on a very limited basis. Further, he is five foot three inches tall and weighs 130 pounds, which is by no means greater than the average height and weight of other, even younger, participants. It is thus readily apparent that there is no safety threat to others or competitive advantage in the situation presented here. Also, again, there is no "cut" policy on the football squad, so Luis Cruz is not replacing any other student who would otherwise have an opportunity to play.

Luis Cruz has "good basic skills" in wrestling, but there are "a lot of better wrestlers than him." He is not a safety risk factor, but he may have a competitive advantage based on his outstanding dual meet record.

In track, where there is also a no-cut policy, Luis Cruz is not a fast runner, does not displace other students, has no competitive advantage and represents no safety risk. He runs a minute behind qualifying time in the mile. He has been unable to earn points in dual meets and would only place by default.

The plaintiffs claim that defendant has violated . . . Section 504 of the Rehabilitation Act of 1973, 29 U.S.C. § 794, *et. seq.* [and] the Americans with Disabilities Act (ADA), 42 U.S.C. § 12101, *et. seq.* . . . .

With respect to the Rehabilitation Act, 29 U.S.C. § 794(a) provides in part that no individual with a disability shall be subjected to discrimination under any program or activity receiving federal financial assistance. There is no evidence that the defendant receives federal financial assistance. . . .

The only remaining claim of plaintiff is under the ADA. The P.I.A.A. is, in my opinion, a public entity under Title II of that Act and plaintiff's claim should be viewed according to its provisions. . . .

[T]his court was waiting for the decision in *PGA Tour, Inc. v. Casey Martin*, 531 U.S. 1049, 121 S.Ct. 1879, 149 L.Ed.2d 904 (2001), decided by the Supreme Court on May 29, 2001. The opinion is not directly on point with this case. First, it concerns Title III of the ADA, and second, the causal connection between the disability and the exclusion from an activity is more direct in the *Martin* case. But in *Martin*, the Supreme Court made clear that a basic requirement of the ADA is the evaluation of a disabled person on an individual basis. According to *Martin*, three inquiries are contemplated by ADA: (1) whether the requested modification is reasonable; (2) whether it is necessary for the disabled individual; and (3) whether it would fundamentally alter the nature of the competition. The case presently before this court, it seems to me, requires the same analysis.

It is clear from the findings of fact that Luis Cruz would not fundamentally alter the nature of the competition in football and track and that the modification of the age rule is necessary for him to be able to play in interscholastic competition in those two sports. What is more difficult to assess is whether the modification is reasonable. Initially, that involves a determination as to whether the age rule is essential to the P.I.A.A. sports program. . . .

It now seems clear that a rule is essential to a program unless it can be shown that the waiver of it would not fundamentally alter the nature of the program.

This determination must be made on an individual basis. The court has looked at the specific facts applicable to Luis Cruz in reaching its conclusion stated earlier in this opinion. In doing so in this case, it is clear that Luis Cruz playing on the football team and track team would not fundamentally alter the nature of P.I.A.A. interscholastic competition.

There is another consideration regarding reasonable modification and that is the burden that would be placed upon the P.I.A.A. to administer a waiver rule in connection with age. P.I.A.A. claims that a procedure by which Cruz would be granted a waiver of the age rule would be an undue burden on it. Specifically, the P.I.A.A. argues that requiring it to develop a waiver system which would assess whether an over-age student would have a competitive advantage over opponents in a given sport would be unreasonable as it would require complex fact-finding as well as extremely difficult judgments about leadership skills, motivational abilities, physical maturity, benefits of experience, quickness, agility, strength, and sport-specific abilities which are extremely difficult to measure. . . .

In light of the other waivers which the P.I.A.A., through district committees, routinely considers, namely transfer and 8 term waivers (some of which require the determination of athletic intent), and in view of the apparent ability of the P.I.A.A. to make what must be very difficult decisions in those waiver cases, I do not believe that an age waiver rule would put an undue burden on the P.I.A.A. The statistics to date suggest that there may not be many occasions for the age waiver to be requested. On the present record, it does not appear that a waiver process would place an unreasonable burden on the P.I.A.A. Indeed, the waiver process proposed by plaintiffs would require initially that the student seeking the waiver have an IEP which requires participation in interscholastic sports. Again, on this record, the P.I.A.A. should not be unreasonably burdened by such a process. . . .

[EDS. The court issued the following order: "(1) Defendant is restrained and prohibited from application and enforcement of its by-law as to age ineligibility with respect to Luis Cruz, unless done so pursuant to a waiver rule which provides for an individual evaluation of him. (2) Thus, as to any interscholastic sports in which Luis Cruz wishes to participate, the defendant must entertain an application for waiver of its by-laws as to age ineligibility rules pursuant to procedures that it establishes. (3) Failure to adopt such waiver procedures in a timely manner as to Luis Cruz will result under this opinion in his being eligible to participate in interscholastic football and track for the 2001-2002 school year."]

NOTES AND QUESTIONS

1. *Application of ADA and Rehabilitation Act to Amateur Athletics Governing Bodies.* Cruz held that the Pennsylvania Interscholastic Athletic Association is not covered by the Rehabilitation Act because it does not receive federal funding, but it is covered as a public entity under Title II of the ADA. Other courts have found that a state high school athletic association is covered by Title II, *Washington v. Indiana High Sch. Athletic Assn., Inc.,* 181 F.3d 840 (7th Cir. 1999), or assume such coverage. *Sandison v. Michigan High Sch. Athletic Assn., Inc.,* 64 F.3d 1026 (6th Cir. 1995). This conclusion was strengthened by the Supreme Court's holding that a state high school athletic association may be a state actor exercising public governance over interscholastic sports. *Brentwood Acad. v. Tennessee Secondary Sch. Athletic Assn.,* 531 U.S. 288 (2001). Moreover, state disability discrimination laws may apply and provide

[handwritten margin note: May not be bound by Rehab Act, but could be under the ADA.]

a similar measure of protection to disabled athletes. *Baisden v. West Virginia Secondary Schs. Activities Comm'n*, 568 S.E.2d 32 (W. Va. 2002).

Although the NCAA is not subject to the Rehabilitation Act unless it receives federal financial assistance, *NCAA v. Smith*, 525 U.S. 459 (1999), courts have found coverage under Title III of the ADA based on its control of its members' athletic programs through its student-athlete eligibility requirements. *Matthews v. NCAA*, 179 F. Supp. 2d 1209 (E.D. Wash. 2001); *Bowers v. NCAA*, 118 F. Supp. 2d 494 (D. N.J. 2000); *Tatum v. NCAA*, 992 F. Supp. 1114 (E.D. Mo. 1998). The United States Olympic Committee is subject to the Rehabilitation Act if it receives funding from Congress or other federal agencies. *Shepherd v. USOC*, 94 F. Supp. 2d 1136 (D. Colo. 2000), *aff'd on other grounds*, 513 F.3d 1191 (10th Cir. 2008).

2. *When Are Modifications to Athlete Eligibility Rules Required?* Prior to *Martin*, courts were divided on whether a student-athlete's compliance with a maximum age limit is an essential eligibility requirement. See, e.g., *Washington v. Indiana High Sch. Athletic Assn., Inc.*, 181 F.3d 840 (7th Cir. 1999) (no); *Sandison v. Michigan High Sch. Athletic Assn., Inc.*, 64 F.3d 1026 (6th Cir. 1995) (yes); *Pottgen v. Missouri State High Sch. Activities Assn.*, 40 F.3d 926 (8th Cir. 1994) (yes). How does the *Cruz* court apply *Martin* to athlete eligibility standards?

After *Martin*, are uniform athletic eligibility rules applied without any exceptions effectively per se illegal under the federal disability discrimination laws? What are valid legal justifications for refusing to grant a waiver in an individual case? What practical advice would you give to an athletic governing body's management regarding how to ensure compliance with the ADA and Rehabilitation Act?

[handwritten margin note: Cruz was a fact-specific inquiry.]

It is important to note that student-athletes with the same disability may not be entitled to the same scope of protection under the federal disability discrimination laws. For example, in determining whether granting a waiver would fundamentally alter the nature of a sport by providing a competitive advantage or would adversely affect other participants' safety, an athlete's individual size, skills, and athletic prowess will be the dispositive factors. *Cruz* illustrates that this is a fact-specific inquiry and that the outcome will vary based on the individual athlete and subject sport.

In *Baisden v. West Virginia Secondary Schs. Activities Comm'n*, 568 S.E.2d 32, 44 (W. Va. 2002), the West Virginia Supreme Court explained:

> While we decide, through this opinion, that individualized assessments are required in cases of this nature and that reasonable accommodations may be made through waiver of the age nineteen rule under certain circumstances, we do not believe that the facts of this case justify waiver as an accommodation. Mr. Baisden turned nineteen on July 27, 2001. He is six feet four inches tall and weighs 280 pounds. He runs the forty-yard-dash in 5.3 seconds. His participation in high school football would permit him to compete in this contact sport against students approximately five years younger. The safety of younger, smaller, more inexperienced students would be unreasonably compromised. In our view, this would fundamentally alter the structure of the interscholastic athletic program, a result which is not required by reasonable accommodation standards in anti-discrimination law.

3. *Legal Challenges to NCAA Academic Eligibility Standards.* Over the years there have been several ADA challenges to the NCAA's initial academic eligibility

requirements based on a sliding scale consisting of a student-athlete's grade point average in designated high school core courses and standardized test scores. See, e.g., *Cole v. NCAA*, 120 F. Supp. 2d 1060 (N.D. Ga. 2000); *Tatum v. NCAA*, 992 F. Supp. 1114 (E.D. Mo. 1998); *Bowers v. NCAA*, 974 F. Supp. 459 (D. N.J. 1997); *Ganden v. NCAA*, 1996 WL 680000 (N.D. Ill. 1996). See also *Matthews v. NCAA*, 179 F. Supp. 2d 1209 (E.D. Wash. 2001) (challenging NCAA's 75/25 rule, designed to ensure student-athletes maintain a course load equivalent to the general student body during the normal school year). See generally Maureen A. Weston, *Academic Standards or Discriminatory Hoops? Learning-Disabled Student-Athletes and the NCAA Initial Academic Eligibility Requirements*, 66 Tenn. L. Rev. 1049 (1999).

As the *Cole* court explained:

> Defendant NCAA's minimum academic scores, which are set by representatives of member institutions, are an essential eligibility requirement. See e.g., Ganden, 1996 WL 680000 at 15 (finding "little doubt" that the eligibility requirements "serve important interests of the NCAA athletics"). The criteria are designed to ensure that an entering student-athlete is academically prepared, in light of the rigors of intercollegiate athletic competition, to succeed in his or her educational endeavors. The initial-eligibility requirement is also integral to the NCAA's mission of maintaining amateurism in intercollegiate sports. The purpose of the NCAA's academic eligibility requirements is to ensure that students are not merely admitted to universities to participate in intercollegiate sports, but also are admitted to promote and develop educational leadership and scholarship.

120 F. Supp. 2d at 1071. The court held that "[a]bandoning the eligibility requirements altogether for this or any athlete is unreasonable as a matter of law and is not required by the ADA." *Id.* However, the ADA requires the NCAA to make reasonable modifications for student-athletes with learning disabilities on an individualized basis.

On May 27, 1998, the NCAA and Department of Justice entered into a consent decree regarding the application of NCAA initial eligibility bylaws to learning-disabled student-athletes. It provides that mere designation as a remedial or special education course does not preclude it from satisfying a NCAA core course requirement (depending on its content, certain remedial courses may be substituted for core courses); the waiver committee will include experts in learning disabilities and consider certain factors in individual circumstances; and student-athletes who did not satisfy initial academic eligibility requirements are permitted to regain a fourth season of athletic eligibility by satisfactory college academic performance. See http://www.usdoj.gov/crt/ada/ncaa.htm#anchor36919.

CHAPTER
12

Intellectual Property Issues in Sports

A. INTRODUCTION

The licensing and sale of sports-related intellectual property rights such as trademarks, service marks, and copyrights generate billions of dollars in annual revenues for professional leagues and clubs, the United States Olympic Committee, the National Collegiate Athletic Association (NCAA), university and high school athletics programs, and other sports organizations such as the National Association of Stock Car Auto Racing (NASCAR) and the Professional Golfers Association (PGA). These revenues are derived from various sources, such as the sale of television, radio, and Internet broadcasting rights for sports events; trademark and team logo licensing agreements; and league, team, or event sponsorship deals with advertisers. In addition, popular athletes and coaches license various aspects of their identity, such as their name or photo, to others for commercial purposes, thereby earning a substantial amount of money for endorsing various products and services.

Sports event broadcasting rights are a multibillion-dollar source of revenue. For example, the NFL's television contracts with Fox, CBS, and NBC that will take effect after the 2013 football season will pay the NFL an average of $3.1 billion a year in rights fees over the life of these nine-year deals through 2022. Major League Baseball's television contracts with media entities will generate approximately $5.3 billion through 2013. In April 2010 the NCAA entered into an agreement with CBS and Turner Sports pursuant to which they will pay almost $11 billion for the television rights to the "Final Four" men's basketball tournament for 14 years.

The licensing and merchandising of sports brands (i.e., trademarks and logos) also generate billions of dollars in aggregate revenues for professional and amateur sports leagues and other entities. The estimated value of collegiate sports licensing revenues alone is more than $3 billion. Plunkett Research estimates that companies and businesses spend approximately $32 billion annually for sports-related advertising in the United States, which includes naming rights and sponsorship of professional, Olympic, and intercollegiate sports events and organizations, professional leagues and their member clubs, colleges and universities, and others.

Well-known athletes and coaches have entered into lucrative deals to promote and endorse a wide variety of products and services. In some instances, income earned from the licensing of a player's identity to sell products and services may be greater than that derived from his or her athletic ability or success. For example, Michael Jordan signed his first Nike endorsement contract in 1985 for $2.5 million, and he has earned more money from endorsement deals than from playing NBA basketball. Before ever playing in a NBA game, LeBron James signed a five-year, $5 million endorsement deal with Upper Deck trading cards and a seven-year shoe endorsement deal with Nike worth more than $90 million. In 2011, Tiger Woods earned approximately $55 million in endorsement income, Roger Federer earned $45 million, and David Beckham earned $37 million; Maria Sharapova earned $23.5 million from endorsements, and Danica Patrick earned $12.5 million. In February 2012 Derrick Rose signed a 14-year, $260 million endorsement contract with Adidas; two months earlier he signed a 5-year, $95 million contract extension with the Chicago Bulls.

One commentator notes that "[e]very traditional area of intellectual property has a basis for application in the sporting arena," and advises "those wishing to seriously consider venturing into the nebulous world of 'sports law' to acquaint themselves with these nexus of intellectual property and sport." Darryl C. Wilson, *The Legal Ramifications of Saving Face: An Integrated Analysis of Intellectual Property and Sport*, 4 Vill. Sports & Ent. L.J. 227, 275-276 (1997). At a 2001 National Sports Law Institute conference held at Marquette University Law School, NFL executive vice president and league counsel Jeff Pash remarked: "Professional sports league general counsel used to focus on antitrust and labor issues, now their focus is on intellectual property issues."

This chapter initially considers how trademark and unfair competition law protects the owners of sports-related trademarks, logos, and other identifying insignia from infringement and economic harm to their rights. Next, the nature and scope of legal protection for game accounts and broadcasting of sporting events under federal copyright law as well as state misappropriation and unfair competition laws is addressed. Finally, an athlete's protected interests in his or her privacy, reputation, and identity is considered.

B.   TRADEMARKS, LOGOS, AND OTHER IDENTIFYING INSIGNIA

1.   Trademark Infringement

Common law trademark and service mark rights are acquired by first usage of a name, logo, or other symbol to identify one's products or services, to distinguish them from those of others, and to denote a consistent level of quality of the product or service identified by the mark. In *White v. Board of Regents of University of Nebraska*, 614 N.W.2d 330 (Neb. 2000), the court determined that a university acquired rights in "Husker Authentics" by virtue of its first use of this mark in connection with the advertising and sale of products to season ticket holders, alumni, and boosters. Professor Thomas McCarthy observes that "the exclusive 'property' right of a trademark is defined by consumer perception."

1 J.T. McCarthy, McCarthy on Trademarks and Unfair Competition (4th ed.), §2:14 (West 2012). In other words, the nature and scope of one's property interest in a trademark generally is only the right to prevent consumer confusion. As the Seventh Circuit explained: "the trademark laws exist not to 'protect' trademarks, but . . . to protect the consuming public from confusion, concomitantly protecting the trademark owner's right to a non-confused public." *James Burrough, Ltd. v. Sign of the Beefeater, Inc.*, 540 F.2d 266, 276 (7th Cir. 1976).

A sports team's name functions as a trademark or a service mark by virtue of public association of that name with a particular team. Sports team names generally are either inherently distinctive or have acquired "secondary meaning," therefore entitling them to trademark protection. An inherently distinctive mark is one that is coined or arbitrary in relation to the goods or services it identifies such as "Miami Dolphins" for an NFL club, or suggestive of the club's desired characteristics such as "Tennessee Titans." See *In re WNBA Enterprises LLC*, 70 U.S.P.Q.2d 1153 (TTAB 2003) (finding "Orlando Miracle" to be an inherently distinctive mark for Women's National Basketball Association club in Orlando). As one court explained: "Secondary meaning is the consuming public's understanding that the mark, when used in context, refers, not to what the descriptive word ordinarily describes, but to the particular business that the mark is meant to identify." *Maryland Stadium Authority v. Becker*, 806 F. Supp. 1236, 1241 (D. Md. 1992) (finding that public identifies "Camden Yards" with a Baltimore baseball stadium).

Courts have recognized that the popularity of NFL football combined with its extensive media coverage and advertising creates a public association of its team names with its member clubs, *NFL Properties, Inc. v. N.J. Giants, Inc.*, 637 F. Supp. 507 (D. N.J. 1986), which also is true of any of the other U.S. major professional leagues. Sports team logos such as the Oakland Raiders' pirate and The Ohio State University's "Brutus Buckeye" function as trademarks that identify particular teams. Distinctive helmet and uniform designs and colors also can function as trademarks. See, e.g., *Board of Supervisors of the La. State Univ. v. Smack Apparel Co.*, 550 F.3d 465 (5th Cir. 2008) (finding that well-known and long-used color schemes, logos, and designs identify university's sports teams); *Dallas Cowboys Cheerleaders, Inc. v. Pussycat Cinema, Ltd.*, 604 F.2d 200, 204 n.5 (2d Cir. 1979) (finding trademark rights in uniform "universally recognized as the symbol of the Dallas Cowboys Cheerleaders").

Trademark rights exist indefinitely as long as the mark continues to be used and serves as an indication of the source of the seller's goods or services. *Boston Prof'l Hockey Assn. v. Dallas Cap & Emblem Mfg., Inc.*, 510 F.2d 1004, 1011 (5th Cir. 1975) ("[T]here is no reason why trademarks should ever pass into the public domain by the mere passage of time."). However, such rights are lost if usage of the mark to identify, advertise, or promote the seller's goods or services is discontinued.

The Lanham Act, 15 U.S.C. §1051, et seq., provides nationwide legal protection for federally registered trademarks. Federal registration provides *prima facie* evidence of the registrant's ownership and exclusive right to use of the mark for the subject goods or services as well as the validity of the registration. Legal proceedings to prevent and remedy infringement of federally registered marks may be brought in federal courts.

Infringement of the prior user's rights occurs if another's use of the same or similar mark creates a likelihood of consumer confusion regarding the source, affiliation, endorsement, or sponsorship of sports-related products or services.

For example, in *Champions Golf Club, Inc. v. Champions Golf Club, Inc.*, 78 F.3d 1111 (6th Cir. 1996), the court found a likelihood of consumer confusion regarding the (nonexistent) affiliation between two independently owned and operated golf courses located in Nicholasville, Kentucky, and Houston, Texas, that were concurrently using the "Champions" mark.

a.   As Name of Sports Team or Event

While reading the following case, consider whether you agree with the court's view regarding the scope of the plaintiffs' exclusive rights in the "Colts" mark and whether the evidence establishes infringement of their trademark rights by the defendant.

INDIANAPOLIS COLTS, INC. v. METROPOLITAN BALTIMORE FOOTBALL CLUB LIMITED PARTNERSHIP

34 F.3d 410 (7th Cir. 1994)

POSNER, Chief Judge.

The Indianapolis Colts and the National Football League, to which the Colts belong, brought suit for trademark infringement (15 U.S.C. §§ 1051 *et seq.*) against the Canadian Football League's new team in Baltimore, which wants to call itself the "Baltimore CFL Colts." . . .

A bit of history is necessary to frame the dispute. In 1952, the National Football League permitted one of its teams, the Dallas Texans, which was bankrupt, to move to Baltimore, where it was renamed the "Baltimore Colts." Under that name it became one of the most illustrious teams in the history of professional football. In 1984, the team's owner, with the permission of the NFL, moved the team to Indianapolis, and it was renamed the "Indianapolis Colts." The move, sudden and secretive, outraged the citizens of Baltimore. The city instituted litigation in a futile effort to get the team back—even tried, unsuccessfully, to get the team back by condemnation under the city's power of eminent domain—and the Colts brought a countersuit that also failed.

Nine years later, the Canadian Football League granted a franchise for a Baltimore team. Baltimoreans clamored for naming the new team the "Baltimore Colts." And so it was named—until the NFL got wind of the name and threatened legal action. The name was then changed to "Baltimore CFL Colts" and publicity launched, merchandise licensed, and other steps taken in preparation for the commencement of play this summer. . . . [S]ince the Canadian Football League is not well known in the United States—and "CFL" has none of the instant recognition value of "NFL"—the inclusion of the acronym in the team's name might have little impact on potential buyers even if prominently displayed. Those who know football well know that the new "Baltimore Colts" are a new CFL team wholly unrelated to the old Baltimore Colts; know also that the rules of Canadian football are different from those of American football and that teams don't move from the NFL to the CFL as they might from one conference within the NFL to the other. But those who do *not* know these things—and we shall come shortly to the question whether there are many of these football illiterates—will not be warned off by the letters "CFL." The acronym is a red herring, and the real issue is whether the new Baltimore team can appropriate the name "Baltimore Colts." . . .

No one questions the validity of "Indianapolis Colts" as the trademark of the NFL team that plays out of Indianapolis and was formerly known as the Baltimore Colts. If "Baltimore CFL Colts" is confusingly similar to "Indianapolis Colts" by virtue of the history of the Indianapolis team and the overlapping product and geographical markets served by it and by the new Baltimore team, the latter's use of the abandoned mark would infringe the Indianapolis Colts' new mark. The Colts' abandonment of a mark confusingly similar to their new mark neither broke the continuity of the team in its different locations—it was the same team, merely having a different home base and therefore a different geographical component in its name—nor entitled a third party to pick it up and use it to confuse Colts fans, and other actual or potential consumers of products and services marketed by the Colts or by other National Football League teams, with regard to the identity, sponsorship, or league affiliation of the third party, that is, the new Baltimore team. . . .

A professional sports team is like Heraclitus's river: always changing, yet always the same. When Mr. Irsay transported his team, the Baltimore Colts, from Baltimore to Indianapolis in one night in 1984, the team remained, for a time anyway, completely intact: same players, same coaches, same front-office personnel. With the passage of time, of course, the team changed. Players retired or were traded, and were replaced. Coaches and other nonplaying personnel came and went. But as far as the record discloses there is as much institutional continuity between the Baltimore Colts of 1984 and the Indianapolis Colts of 1994 as there was between the Baltimore Colts of 1974 and the Baltimore Colts of 1984. . . . The Colts were Irsay's team; it was moved intact; there is no evidence it has changed more since the move than it had in the years before. There is, in contrast, no continuity, no links contractual or otherwise, nothing but a geographical site in common, between the Baltimore Colts and the Canadian Football League team that would like to use its name. Any suggestion that there is such continuity is false and potentially misleading.

Potentially, for if everyone *knows* there is no contractual or institutional continuity, no pedigree or line of descent, linking the Baltimore-Indianapolis Colts and the new CFL team that wants to call itself the "Baltimore Colts" (or, grudgingly, the "Baltimore CFL Colts"), then there is no harm, at least no harm for which the Lanham Act provides a remedy, in the new Baltimore team's appropriating the name "Baltimore Colts" to play under and sell merchandise under. If not everyone knows, there is harm. . . .

The legal standard under the Act has been formulated variously, but the various formulations come down to whether it is likely that the challenged mark if permitted to be used by the defendant would cause the plaintiff to lose a substantial number of consumers. Pertinent to this determination is the similarity of the marks and of the parties' products, the knowledge of the average consumer of the product, the overlap in the parties' geographical markets, and the other factors that the cases consider. The aim is to strike a balance between, on the one hand, the interest of the seller of the new product, and of the consuming public, in an arresting, attractive, and informative name that will enable the new product to compete effectively against existing ones, and, on the other hand, the interest of existing sellers, and again of the consuming public, in consumers being able to know exactly what they are buying without having to incur substantial costs of investigation or inquiry.

To help judges strike the balance, the parties to trademark disputes frequently as here hire professionals in marketing or applied statistics to conduct surveys of consumers. . . .

The plaintiffs' study, conducted by Jacob Jacoby, was far more substantial and the district judge found it on the whole credible. The 28-page report with its numerous appendices has all the trappings of social scientific rigor. Interviewers showed several hundred consumers in 24 malls scattered around the country, shirts and hats licensed by the defendants for sale to consumers. The shirts and hats have "Baltimore CFL Colts" stamped on them. The consumers were asked whether they were football fans, whether they watched football games on television, and whether they ever bought merchandise with a team name on it. Then they were asked, with reference to the "Baltimore CFL Colts" merchandise that they were shown, such questions as whether they knew what sport the team played, what teams it played against, what league the team was in, and whether the team or league needed someone's permission to use this name, and if so whose. . . . [A]nother group of mallgoers was asked the identical questions about a hypothetical team unappetizingly named the "Baltimore Horses." The idea was by comparing the answers of the two groups to see whether the source of confusion was the name "Baltimore Colts" or just the name "Baltimore," in which event the injunction would do no good since no one suggests that the new Baltimore team should be forbidden to use "Baltimore" in its name, provided the name does not also include "Colts." . . .

Jacoby's survey of consumers' reactions to the "Baltimore CFL Colts" merchandise found rather astonishing levels of confusion not plausibly attributable to the presence of the name "Baltimore" alone, since "Baltimore Horses" engendered much less. . . . Among self-identified football fans, 64 percent thought that the "Baltimore CFL Colts" was either the old (NFL) Baltimore Colts or the Indianapolis Colts. But perhaps this result is not so astonishing. Although most American football fans have heard of Canadian football, many probably are unfamiliar with the acronym "CFL," and as we remarked earlier it is not a very conspicuous part of the team logo stamped on the merchandise. Among fans who watch football on television, 59 percent displayed the same confusion; and even among those who watch football on cable television, which attracts a more educated audience on average and actually carries CFL games, 58 percent were confused when shown the merchandise. Among the minority not confused about who the "Baltimore CFL Colts" are, a substantial minority, ranging from 21 to 34 percent depending on the precise subsample, thought the team somehow sponsored or authorized by the Indianapolis Colts or the National Football League. . . .

[W]e cannot say that the district judge committed a clear error in crediting the major findings of the Jacoby study and inferring from it and the other evidence in the record that the defendants' use of the name "Baltimore CFL Colts" whether for the team or on merchandise was likely to confuse a substantial number of consumers. . . .

AFFIRMED.

NOTES AND QUESTIONS

Why did the NFL and its Indianapolis club have the right to prevent unauthorized use of "Baltimore Colts" by a Canadian Football League club even after the NFL club left Baltimore? How did they prove that the Baltimore CFL Colts team violated its trademark rights?

Consistent with *Indianapolis Colts*, the Seventh Circuit held that the NFL's Los Angeles Rams club retained its rights to continue using "Rams" to identify the team name even though it was relocating to St. Louis. *Johnny Blastoff, Inc. v. L.A. Rams Football, Co.*, 188 F.3d 427 (7th Cir. 1999). Observing that the franchise was founded in 1937 as the Cleveland Rams, moved to become the Los Angeles Rams in 1946, and was again moving to become the St. Louis Rams in 1995, the court concluded, "[T]he Rams organization and the NFL had a long-established priority over the use of the 'Rams' name in connection with the same professional football team, regardless of urban affiliation." *Id.* at 435.

However, other courts have expressed a narrow view regarding the scope of a club's protectable rights in its name after it relocates. In *Major League Baseball Properties, Inc. v. Sed Non Olet Denarius, Ltd.*, 817 F. Supp. 1103 (S.D.N.Y. 1993), *vacated pursuant to settlement*, 859 F. Supp. 80 (S.D.N.Y. 1994), the court held that discontinued use of the "Brooklyn Dodgers" trademark after the club relocated to Los Angeles in 1958 constituted an abandonment of rights in this composite mark and that a Brooklyn restaurant may use the name "The Brooklyn Dodger." The court found that "[i]n Brooklyn, the 'Los Angeles Dodgers' and the 'Brooklyn Dodgers' are seen as two separate entities which have been wholly unrelated for more than 30 years." *Id.* at 1125. The court concluded that "Brooklyn is more than a geographic designation or appendage to the word 'Dodgers.' The 'Brooklyn Dodgers' was a non-transportable cultural institution separate from the 'Los Angeles Dodgers' or the 'Dodgers' who play in Los Angeles." *Id.* at 1128.

Legal considerations aside, business reasons may justify treating the favorable goodwill developed by a popular local sports franchise over the years as "a non-transportable cultural institution." For example, the NFL decided to leave the "Browns" identity in Cleveland when the franchise relocated to Baltimore in 1996. The franchise formerly named the "Cleveland Browns" established a new identity as the "Baltimore Ravens." The NFL expansion club that began playing in Cleveland in 1999 is named the "Cleveland Browns." See *Hawaii-Pacific Apparel Group, Inc. v. Cleveland Browns Football Co. LLC*, 418 F. Supp. 2d 501 (S.D.N.Y. 2006) (holding that, by enforcing its claimed trademark rights during four-year period in which Browns franchise did not play in Cleveland, the NFL retained rights in DAWG POUND mark).

However, the use of the same trademark or service mark by different teams, even if playing the same sport, does not inevitably create a likelihood of consumer confusion. Rather, a fact-specific inquiry must be made on a case-by-case basis. In *Harlem Wizards Ent. Basketball, Inc. v. NBA Props., Inc.*, 952 F. Supp. 1084 (D. N.J. 1997), the court held that a NBA club's proposed name change to the "Washington Wizards" would not infringe a "show basketball" team's prior use of "Harlem Wizards." Unlike the Washington NBA club, the Harlem club is not a competitive sports team that plays in a professional league. The Harlem Wizards combine trick basketball and comedic basketball in a form of entertainment similar to that of the world famous Harlem Globetrotters. Although the Harlem club has the right to use "Wizards" for its entertainment services, the court concluded that the NBA club's concurrent use of the same mark will not create a likelihood of confusion among basketball fans. The teams do not compete with each other for fan patronage. The Harlem club markets its games to event organizers at high schools, colleges, and charitable organizations through direct mail, trade shows, and trade magazines, whereas the NBA club advertises its games directly to fans. Survey results evidenced that consumer familiarity with the Harlem Wizards team "is almost nonexistent." *Id.* at 1098. There is a significant disparity between the parties' respective ticket prices, and the court found "it unlikely that consumers will attend a Harlem Wizards' game expecting to see NBA basketball or purchase NBA tickets expecting to see the Harlem Wizards perform show basketball." *Id.*

b.   Affixation of Sports-Related Mark to Merchandise

The following materials consider the nature and scope of legal protection provided to owners of sports team names, logos, and other identifying insignia and whether unauthorized usage by third parties in connection with the advertising and sale of collateral or promotional merchandise (e.g., wearing apparel) constitutes trademark infringement or otherwise violates their rights.

North American consumers annually purchase billions of dollars' worth of merchandise bearing the names and logos of their favorite teams. For 2010, it was estimated that the retail value of merchandise licensed by the National Football League (NFL), National Basketball Association (NBA), National Hockey League (NHL), and Major Leagur Baseball (MLB) was approximately $7.83 billion, which constitutes a substantial part of the estimated $12.5 billion retail value of all merchandise licensed by sports leagues, teams, and individual personalities in the United States and Canada. Consider why consumers buy merchandise bearing the names and logos of their favorite teams: because of their desire to identify with the team, to purchase goods produced or licensed by the team, or for other reasons?

In *National Football League Properties, Inc. v. Consumer Enterprises, Inc.,* 327 N.E.2d 242, 246 (Ill. App. 1975), the court observed that the NFL's "trademarks are associated with highly successful football teams that enjoy tremendous notoriety. Through the extensive licensing arrangements developed and perpetuated by [the NFL] and its licensees, the buying public has come to associate the trademark with the sponsorship of the NFL or the particular member team involved." It concluded "that the trademarks of the teams copied by defendant indicate sponsorship or origin in addition to their ornamental value." See also *University Bookstore v. Board of Regents of the Univ. of Wis. Sys.,* 33 U.S.P.Q.2d 1385, 1405 (T.T.A.B. 1994) ("[T]he mark of a university on clothing can signify that the university endorses and licenses the sale of such wearing apparel by the manufacturer. . . . It is a question of fact as to whether consumers view such indicia as 'merely ornamental' or as symbols that identify a secondary source of sponsorship").

On the other hand, "[m]any trademark law scholars oppose expanding the traditional scope of trademark law protection, which is limited to preventing a likelihood of consumer confusion regarding the source or origin of a product or service, simply to prevent 'free riding' (that is, misappropriation of the goodwill associated with a trademark and perceived unjust enrichment from its unauthorized use on collateral or promotional products unrelated to the mark owner's primary business activities). Doing so creates inappropriately broad property rights in trademarks, with resulting trademark monopolies and reduced market competition that increases consumer prices for collateral products." Matthew J. Mitten, *From* Dallas Cap *to* American Needle *and Beyond: Antitrust Law's Limited Capacity to Stitch Consumer Harm from Professional Sports Club Trademark Monopolies*, 86 Tul. L. Rev. 901, 914-915 (2012). See also Mark A. Kahn, *May the Best Merchandise Win: The Law of Non-Trademark Uses of Sports Logos*, 14 Marq. Sports L. Rev. 283, 317 (2004) ("Sports logos on merchandise do not indicate a certain quality level to consumers. Therefore, the logos are not operating as trademarks. To prohibit such behavior under existing federal trademark law is to misapply the law."). Some have argued:

> This type of protection is unnecessary for the production of sporting events and only results in a transfer of additional revenue to the teams and their licensees. Permitting fans to purchase unlicensed clothing bearing the name or logo of their favorite team would make it easier for less economically well-off fans to express their support for their teams. It would allow a larger number of individuals to participate in the communal act of supporting a particular team or club. Teams would still be able to market their own merchandise . . . but they would not be able to exercise monopoly control over their names and symbols.

J. Gordon Hylton, *The Over-Protection of Intellectual Property Rights in Sport in the United States and Elsewhere*, 21 J. Legal Aspects Sport 43, 49-50 (2011). Nevertheless, "[r]egardless of scholarly concerns over whether merchandising rights are in accordance with the purpose of trademark law, trademark merchandising has long represented a 'fait accompli' in trademark practice." Irene Calboli, *The Case for a Limited Protection of Trademark Merchandising*, 2011 U. Ill. L. Rev. 865, 890.

Regarding the requisite "likelihood of confusion" that must be shown to prove trademark infringement under the Lanham Act or similar state trademark infringement laws, in *Board of Governors of the University of North Carolina v. Helpingstine*, 714 F. Supp. 167, 172 (M.D. N.C. 1989), the court observed:

> While cases have indicated at one extreme that an alleged infringer's use of a mark with the knowledge that the public will be aware of the mark's origin is enough to establish likelihood of confusion, . . . and at the other that likelihood of confusion occurs only where there would be confusion as to the origin of the goods themselves, . . . the majority of courts have taken the middle ground on this issue. This middle position, which both parties recognize in this case, is that the requisite likelihood of confusion will exist where there is likelihood of confusion as to source, sponsorship or endorsement of the goods.

The following case illustrates how courts apply a multifactor test to determine whether the unauthorized usage of a sports team mark on collateral or promotional merchandise creates a likelihood of consumer confusion.

NATIONAL FOOTBALL LEAGUE PROPERTIES, INC. v. NEW JERSEY GIANTS, INC.

637 F. Supp. 507 (D. N.J. 1986)

BARRY, District Judge.

[EDS. Plaintiff, the New York Football Giants, Inc., owned and operated the New York Giants, an NFL team that had played all of its home games at Giants' Stadium in East Rutherford, New Jersey, since 1976. In what was then the New

York Football Giants' 60-year history, home games had been played at several locations in the New York metropolitan area, including in Connecticut and New Jersey. To maintain continuity of tradition, the club always had used the name "New York Giants," which along with "Giants" is a federally registered trademark under the Lanham Act and under New Jersey and New York state law.

Plaintiff National Football League Properties, Inc. (NFLP), is the marketing arm of the NFL's member clubs, and is licensed by the clubs to use their trademarks and is authorized to protect them from infringement. NFLP licensed selected companies to use the "Giants" and "New York Giants" marks on a wide variety of merchandise, including T-shirts, sweatshirts, caps, jackets, and other wearing apparel. NFLP had a quality control program in which it supervised and approved the conception, design, color combinations, production, and distribution of all merchandise licensed to bear the marks of the Giants and other NFL clubs.

Defendant, the New Jersey Giants, Inc., in an effort to exploit the anomaly of a team bearing the name of one state while playing in another, began to sell various items of inferior quality sports-related apparel bearing the words "New Jersey GIANTS" without authorization from NFLP or the New York Giants club.]

Defendant's "New Jersey GIANTS" merchandise competes directly with licensed NFL merchandise bearing the New York Football Giants' marks, because NFLP has licensed the same types of merchandise sold by defendant. Moreover, defendant's "New Jersey GIANTS" merchandise is likely to confuse consumers into believing that it is part of the wide array of licensed merchandise sponsored and approved by the New York Football Giants and available to the public through NFLP's licensing program.

But the Giants and NFLP have no control over defendant's business activities or over the nature and clearly inferior quality of the merchandise sold by defendant and, indeed, the quality of that merchandise does not satisfy the quality control standards imposed by NFLP on its licensees. The sale of inferior quality merchandise bearing the NFL marks, or colorable imitations thereof, will adversely affect NFLP's business including the poor impression of the NFL and its Member Clubs that will be held by the consumer.

Because the demand for merchandise bearing the NFL marks is finite, any sales of unlicensed merchandise bearing those marks will cause direct economic harm to NFLP's licensees thus reducing the royalties payable by licensees to NFLP and reducing the size of the fund available for NFL Charities. Defendant's activities in the sale of its "New Jersey GIANTS" merchandise will interfere, as well, with NFLP's business and cause harm to its reputation and goodwill with licensees and retailers actively promoting the products of NFLP's licensees. If NFLP is unable to abide by its agreement to protect licensees from companies that use the NFL marks without authorization, licensees will lose confidence in the NFLP's licensing program and the value of a license will be impaired thus harming the business of NFLP.

Defendant's use of its trade name and the solicitation and sale of "New Jersey GIANTS" merchandise is also likely to confuse the public into believing that the New York Football Giants has changed the team's name to the New Jersey Giants or does not object to being referred to by that name. Neither is true, of course, and while one may wonder why the New York Giants resist a new name and may wish, perhaps, that it were otherwise, the fact remains that the Giants have the right to retain the long-standing goodwill and reputation they have developed in the name "New York Giants" and efforts in that regard will be undermined were defendant's conduct permitted to continue. . . .

In a case for service mark or trademark infringement and unfair competition, a plaintiff is entitled to a permanent injunction against a defendant by showing that that defendant's activities are likely to confuse consumers as to the source or sponsorship of the goods. In order to be confused, a consumer need not believe that a plaintiff actually produced a defendant's merchandise and placed it on the market. Rather, a consumer's belief that a plaintiff sponsored or otherwise approved the use of the mark satisfies the confusion requirement.

In a suit, as here, involving competing goods, the relevant factors to be considered in a determination as to whether a likelihood of confusion exists are:

(1)   The degree of similarity between the owner's mark and the alleged infringing mark;
(2)   The strength of the owner's mark;
(3)   The price of the goods and other factors indicative of the care and attention expected of consumers when making a purchase;
(4)   The length of time the defendant has used the mark without evidence of actual confusion;
(5)   The intent of the defendant in adopting the mark;
(6)   The evidence of actual confusion.

Defendant's mark "New Jersey GIANTS" is similar to the Giants' registered marks "New York Giants" and "Giants" and the dominant element of the mark — "Giants" — is identical, rendering those marks particularly confusing. . . .

The second . . . factor is similarly satisfied. Through extensive media coverage and commercial use, the NFL marks, including those of the Giants, are extremely strong, and, accordingly, are entitled to a wide range of protection.

With reference to the third . . . factor, the likelihood of confusion in this case is enhanced because both NFLP's licensed apparel bearing the Giants' marks and defendant's apparel, which is the same type of apparel, are low to moderately priced and purchasers will not exercise a high degree of care in determining whether the merchandise has been sponsored or approved by the NFL and the Giants.

Defendant, which only began selling its merchandise in 1982 and had total sales of less than $5000.00 at the time its activities were halted by the restraining order, used the mark without evidence of actual confusion. In establishing the existence of a likelihood of confusion in actions such as this, however, there is no requirement that incidents of actual confusion be shown and such evidence is unnecessary where other factors so strongly suggest the likelihood of confusion.

However, the consumer survey conducted by Dr. Jacoby and Guideline Research demonstrated substantial actual confusion and a substantial potential for further actual confusion. The results of the survey, which found that over 57% of respondents were actually and likely confused and that football fans were confused in even higher percentages (67%), is extremely strong evidence of likely confusion, and far in excess of the evidence relied upon by courts for this purpose. . . .

Defendant's intentional, willful, and admitted adoption of a mark closely similar to the existing marks "Giants" and "New York Giants" manifested . . . an intent to confuse . . .

Defendant's use of the Giants' marks is likely to cause confusion or mistake or deceive purchasers of such merchandise as to the source, sponsorship or approval by the NFL and the Giants. . . .

[The court concluded defendant's conduct constituted unfair competition in violation of federal and New Jersey law as well as tortious misappropriation of plaintiffs' goodwill and interference with their business relationships.]

NOTES AND QUESTIONS

1. *The Application of Likelihood of Confusion Standard.* The *New Jersey Giants* case identifies several factors relevant to whether defendant's unauthorized usage of a sports team mark creates a likelihood of confusion. Why was defendant's use of "New Jersey Giants" on apparel found to infringe the New York Giants marks for "entertainment services in the form of professional football games and exhibitions"?

   Whether the requisite likelihood of confusion exists is a question of fact decided on a case-by-case basis. Examples of infringement include *Johnny Blastoff, Inc. v. L.A. Rams Football Co.*, 188 F.3d 427 (7th Cir. 1999) (use of "St. Louis Rams" for a fictional, cartoon sport team); *NFL v. Coors Brewing Co.*, 205 F.3d 1324 (2d Cir. 1999) (advertising Coors beer as "Official Beer of the NFL Players" without NFL's permission); *Boston Athletic Assn. v. Sullivan*, 867 F.2d 22 (1st Cir. 1989) (unauthorized use of "Boston Marathon" to sell T-shirts); *University of Ga. Athletic Assn. v. Laite*, 756 F.2d 1535 (11th Cir. 1985) (use of University of Georgia bulldog mark and logo portraying an English bulldog for "Battlin' Bulldog Beer"); *Acushnet Co. v. 100GolfClubs.com*, 2012 WL 692187 (S.D. Fla.) (unauthorized use of golf club manufacturers' marks on counterfeit golf equipment); *Ohio State Univ. v. Thomas*, 738 F. Supp. 2d 743 (S.D. Ohio 2010) (unauthorized use of Ohio State trademarks, including university colors, in connection with website and electronic magazines covering university sports teams); *Auburn Univ. v. Moody*, 2008 WL 4877542 (M.D. Ala.) (unauthorized use of Auburn's trademarks on six-finger foam hands).

   To avoid weakening valuable trademark rights that may be licensed and generate substantial revenues, professional teams and educational institutions must carefully monitor unauthorized third-party usage of their trademarks and take timely, necessary steps to prevent infringement of its marks. The affirmative defense of laches may bar or limit monetary recovery for infringement if a mark owner's delay in asserting its trademark rights prejudices an infringer that detrimentally relied on such inaction. *University of Pittsburgh v. Champion Prods. Inc.*, 686 F.2d 1040 (3d Cir. 1982), *cert. denied*, 495 U.S. 1087 (1982) (university's 36-year delay in objecting to unauthorized sale of clothing and novelty items bearing its name and panther mascot bars an accounting for past infringement but not an injunction against future unauthorized use).

2. *Collective Licensing of League Clubs' Trademarks.* Major professional sports leagues such as the NFL, NBA, NHL, and MLB currently market, license, and enforce their clubs' trademark rights collectively through a central

league-operated entity. To maximize the revenues from its national sponsorship agreements, which generally are distributed pro rata to its member clubs, a sports league may have exclusive agreements with its official sponsors and corresponding limits on its member clubs' individual sponsorships with other companies. A club that violates league restrictions on its local sponsorship agreements may be liable for breach of contract and fiduciary duty, tortious interference with contractual relationships, and trademark infringement. See *NFL Properties, Inc. v. Dallas Cowboys Football Club, Ltd.*, 922 F. Supp. 849 (S.D.N.Y. 1996). See Chapter 6, section D.3.b.iii for a discussion of antitrust law challenges to a professional league's exclusive control and licensing of its member clubs' trademarks.

3. *Primacy of the First Amendment.* In *University of Alabama Board of Trustees v. New Life, Inc.*, 683 F.3d 1266 (11th Cir. 2012), the University of Alabama alleged that an artist's paintings, prints, and calendars infringed its trademarks because his unauthorized inclusion of the university's crimson and white uniforms and helmets therein created a likelihood of consumer confusion that it sponsored or endorsed these products. Characterizing the paintings, prints, and calendars as expressive speech protected by the First Amendment, the Eleventh Circuit held it "should construe the Lanham Act narrowly when deciding whether an artistically expressive work infringes a trademark." *Id.* at 1278. Such usage does not violate the Lanham Act "unless the use of the mark has no artistic relevance to the underlying work whatsoever, or, if it has some artistic relevance, unless it explicitly misleads as to the source or the content of the work." *Id.* at 1278. Applying this standard, the court concluded: "The depiction of the University's uniforms in the content of these items is artistically relevant to the expressive underlying works because the uniforms' colors and designs are needed for a realistic portrayal of famous scenes from Alabama football history. Also there is no evidence that Moore ever marketed an unlicensed item as 'endorsed' or 'sponsored' by the University, or otherwise explicitly stated that such items were affiliated with the University. . . . Even if 'some members of the public would draw the incorrect inference that [the University] had some involvement with [Moore's paintings, prints, and calendars,] . . . that risk of misunderstanding, not engendered by any overt [or in this case even implicit] claim . . . is so outweighed by the interest in artistic expression as to preclude' any violation of the Lanham Act." *Id.* at 1278-1279.

4. *Fair Use or Parody of a Trademark.* In *WCVB-TV v. Boston Athletic Association*, 926 F.2d 42, 46 (1st Cir. 1991), the First Circuit explained: "In technical trademark jargon, the use of words for descriptive purposes is called a 'fair use,' and the law usually permits it even if the words themselves also constitute a trademark." The court held that a television station's use of "Boston Marathon" to describe its unlicensed broadcast of the event is not trademark infringement, although another local television station was exclusively authorized to broadcast this event. This was judicially characterized as fair use of the Boston Marathon mark merely to describe the event defendant was broadcasting that did not create any viewer confusion. See also *Dream Team Collectibles, Inc. v. NBA Props., Inc.*, 958 F. Supp. 1401, 1421 (E.D. Mo. 1997) (use of NBA team name on framed collage of trading cards depicting players in team uniforms "not likely to cause confusion, but is a simply a way to identify a particular NBA team").

Would a state lottery based on the unauthorized use of regular season NFL game scores constitute trademark infringement or fair use? See *NFL v. Governor of Del.*, 435 F. Supp. 1372, 1380 (D. Del. 1977) (permissible to truthfully describe services offered, but creating false public impression that mark owner authorizes or approves such services is prohibited). The Professional and Amateur Sports Act, 28 U.S.C. §3701 et seq., enacted in 1992, now prohibits lotteries, sweepstakes, and gambling based on the results of professional and amateur sports games, although Delaware, Montana, Nevada, and Oregon have grandfathered rights.

For the same reason that underlies the fair use defense, the parody of a trademark is not infringing. In *Cardtoons, L.C. v. Major League Baseball Players Assn.*, 95 F.3d 959 (10th Cir. 1996), the Tenth Court held that parody trading cards with caricatures of baseball players and critical commentary does not create public confusion regarding the source of the cards. The court explained that "as with all successful parodies, the effect of the cards is to amuse rather than confuse." *Id.* at 967.

2.   *Trademark Dilution*

The Trademark Dilution Revision Act of 2006 (TDRA), which is part of the Lanham Act, protects the owner of a "famous mark" from unauthorized use of its mark or a similar mark that is likely to cause dilution of the mark's distinctiveness. 15 U.S.C. §1125(c). Proof that the defendant's unauthorized usage creates an actual or likelihood of confusion or actual economic injury is not required. The statute provides a remedy for tarnishing the goodwill associated with a famous mark by using it in a disparaging manner outside the context of permissible parody, or a blurring of the mark's distinctiveness because it is used to identify a wide range of unrelated goods and services.

To be "famous," the mark must be "widely recognized by the general consuming public of the United States as a designation of source of the goods or services of the mark's owner." 15 U.S.C. §1125(c)(2)(A). The trademarks and logos of major U.S. sports events such as the Indianapolis 500 auto race, Kentucky Derby horse race, and Masters golf tournament as well as those of major league professional teams, sports governing bodies such as the United States Olympic Committee, National Collegiate Athletic Association, NASCAR, and many universities with successful football and basketball teams are well known among sports fans and probably are "famous" marks. In *New York City Triathlon LLC v. NYC Triathlon Club Inc.*, 95 U.S.P.Q.2d 1451 (S.D.N.Y. 2010), the court ruled that the "New York City Triathlon," "NYC Triathlon," and "NYC Tri" marks are famous because of their extensive national and international promotion and recognition. See also *Dallas Cowboys Football Club, Ltd. v. America's Team Properties*, 616 F. Supp. 2d 622 (N.D. Tex. 2009) (Dallas Cowboys' "long duration and geographic reach" of "America's Team" mark in connection with various products advertised and sold to public combined with survey evidence showing recognition of mark among a relevant consumer base establishes that the mark is "famous" under federal dilution statute).

In *Dallas Cowboys Football Club, Ltd. v. America's Team Properties*, the court ruled that the unauthorized use of "America's Team" on apparel "blurs the uniqueness" of the mark and tarnishes it because it is used in connection with the defendant's inferior goods. Similarly, in *New York City Triathlon LLC v. NYC Triathlon*

Club Inc., another court held that defendant's unauthorized usage of the "New York City Triathlon" marks as the name of its athletic club blurred and tarnished their distinctiveness in violation of the dilution statute by creating a negative association because of defendant's reputation for poor customer service.

The following cases, which were decided prior to enactment of the TDRA, provide graphic examples of usages that tarnish sports marks. In *NBA Properties v. Untertainment Records LLC*, 1999 WL 335147 (S.D.N.Y. 1999), a federal district court held that the unauthorized use of an altered NBA logo showing a silhouetted basketball player dribbling a basketball with a handgun in his other hand to advertise a rap album violates the federal dilution statute. Because "linking the NBA Logo with violence and drugs will adversely color the public's impressions of the NBA," the court concluded that "[a]ny suggestion that the NBAP or the NBA endorses violence, gunplay or drug use, or that they have chosen to associate themselves with those who do, will likely tarnish their reputation with their corporate customers and partners, as well as the public at large." Similarly, in *Dallas Cowboys Cheerleaders, Inc. v. Pussycat Cinema, Ltd.*, 604 F.2d 200, 205 (2d Cir. 1979), the Second Circuit ruled that the unauthorized use of female actors wearing well-known Dallas Cowboys Cheerleaders uniforms in a "sexually depraved film . . . has 'tendency to impugn (plaintiff's services) and injure plaintiff's business reputation.'" See also *Boston Red Sox Baseball Club LP v. Sherman*, 88 U.S.P.Q.2d 1581 (T.T.A.B. 2008) (affirming refusal to register "Sex Rod" for clothing because it would disparage MLB club's well-known "Red Sox" mark).

3. Anticybersquatting Consumer Protection Act of 1999

The significant expansion and use of the Internet in recent years has given rise to "cybersquatting," which is the registration of well-known trademarks (including those of sports teams and events) as domain names (i.e., website addresses) by those who are not the trademark owners. Their objectives usually are to try to sell rights to the domain names back to the trademark owners at a profit or to attract Internet users to their websites, such as online sports gambling. Cybersquatting that creates a likelihood of consumer confusion constitutes trademark infringement and unfair competition. See, e.g., *March Madness Athletic Assn. v. Netfire, Inc.*, 2003 WL 22047375 (N.D. Tex. 2003) (www.marchmadness.com infringes NCAA's federally registered March Madness mark for basketball tournament); *Quokka Sports, Inc. v. Cup Int'l Internet Ventures*, 99 F. Supp. 2d 1105 (N.D. Cal. 1999) (defendants' www.americascup.com website, "masquerading as an official site associated with the America's Cup event," located at www.americascup.org, infringes registered mark "America's Cup"). It also may constitute trademark dilution and violate the Anticybersquatting Consumer Protection Act (ACPA) of 1999, 15 U.S.C. §1129.

The ACPA provides a trademark owner with a cause of action against a defendant for bad-faith registration or use of a domain name that is (1) identical to or confusingly similar to a distinctive mark or (2) identical to or confusingly similar to, or dilutes, a famous mark. 15 U.S.C. §1125 (d)(1). See *March Madness Athletic Assn. v. Netfire, Inc.*, 2003 WL 22047375 (N.D. Tex.) (finding that defendants' registration and use of www.march-madness.com violates ACPA, entitling NCAA to injunctive relief). In addition to available remedies under the Lanham Act, the ACPA provides for statutory damages for bad-faith registration of domain names after the November 29, 1999, effective date of the statute. 15 U.S.C. §1117(d). The ACPA also authorizes an action against the domain name itself for forfeiture or transfer to the trademark owner if the domain name registrant cannot be located or is not subject to personal jurisdiction by an American court. 15 U.S.C. §1125(d)(2)(A).

As a faster and less expensive alternative to litigation against a cybersquatter under the Lanham Act or ASCP, a mark owner may choose to instead utilize arbitration procedures under the Uniform Domain Name Dispute Resolution Policy (UDRP). The domain name registration agreement incorporates the terms of the UDRP, which governs disputes between the domain name registrant and others concerning the registration and use of a domain name. Several sports-related domain name disputes have been resolved by UDRP proceedings, including the first decided case under this procedure. See *World Wresting Fed'n Ent., Inc. v. Bosman*, WIPO, Case No. D99-0001, Jan. 14, 2000, available at http://pub.bna.com/ptcj/d990001.htm (finding bad-faith registration and use of worldwrestlingfederation.com domain name, which is identical or confusingly similar to federally registered World Wrestling Federation trademark and service mark, and ordering transfer of domain name registration to owner of marks). See also *June Bug Enterprises v. Kyamko*, 73 U.S.P.Q.2d 1310 (2004) (ordering operator of a pornography site to transfer its "magicjohnson.com" domain name to plaintiff June Bug Enterprises, the owner of former NBA player Earvin Johnson's federally registered "MAGIC JOHNSON" mark). The UDRP provides for judicial review of arbitration decisions in national courts. Under U.S. law, a UDRP arbitration proceeding does not preclude an ACPA lawsuit over the domain name. *Sallen v. Corinthians Licenciamentos LTDA*, 273 F.3d 14 (1st Cir. 2001).

4. Ted Stevens Olympic and Amateur Sports Act: Olympic Marks

The United States Olympic Committee (USOC) owns the exclusive right to use and license the Olympic marks within the United States. *United States Olympic Comm. v. Intelicense Corp., S.A.*, 737 F.2d 263 (2d Cir. 1984), *cert. denied*, 469 U.S. 982 (1984). The Ted Stevens Olympic and Amateur Sports Act (ASA) prohibits the unauthorized usage of the Olympic name and marks, including the five-ring Olympic symbol, "for the purpose of trade, to induce the sale of any goods or services, or to promote any theatrical exhibition, athletic performance, or competition." 36 U.S.C. §220506(c). The ASA extended the USOC's exclusive property rights to include the "Pan-American" and "Paralympiad" marks, which are now protected to the same extent as the Olympic marks. *United States Olympic Comm. v. Toy Truck Lines, Inc.*, 237 F.3d 1331 (Fed. Cir. 2001).

The Olympic marks have a broader scope of protection under federal law beyond that generally provided to other trademarks and service marks. In *San Francisco Arts & Athletics, Inc. v. United States Olympic Committee*, 483 U.S. 522 (1987), the Supreme Court held that the ASA's language and legislative intent evidenced Congress's intent to grant the USOC exclusive rights to control use of the Olympic marks regardless of whether their unauthorized usage creates a likelihood of confusion. The Court explained:

> One reason for Congress to grant the USOC exclusive control of the word "Olympic," as with other trademarks, is to ensure that the USOC receives the

benefit of its own efforts so that the USOC will have an incentive to continue to produce a "quality product," that, in turn, benefits the public. See 1 J. McCarthy, Trademarks and Unfair Competition § 2:1, pp. 44-47 (1984). But in the special circumstance of the USOC, Congress has a broader public interest in promoting, through the activities of the USOC, the participation of amateur athletes from the United States in "the great four-yearly sport festival, the Olympic Games." . . . The USOC's goal under the Olympic Charter, Rule 24(B), is to further the Olympic movement, that has as its aims: "to promote the development of those physical and moral qualities which are the basis of sport"; "to educate young people through sport in a spirit of better understanding between each other and of friendship, thereby helping to build a better and more peaceful world"; and "to spread the Olympic principles throughout the world, thereby creating international good-will." Congress' interests in promoting the USOC's activities include these pur-poses as well as those specifically enumerated in the USOC's charter. Section 110 directly advances these governmental interests by supplying the USOC with the means to raise money to support the Olympics and encourages the USOC's activi-ties by ensuring that it will receive the benefits of its efforts.

Id. at 537-538. Defendant's unauthorized use of "Gay Olympic Games" for an athletics competition in San Francisco was found to be infringing regardless of whether it tends to cause any confusion. See also *USOC v. Tobyhanna Camp Corp.*, 2010 WL 4617429 (M.D. Pa.) (use of "Camp Olympik" and non-interlocked five-ring Olympic symbol for children's summer camp infringing); *USOC v. Xclusive Leisure & Hospitality Ltd.*, 2008 WL 3971120 (N.D. Cal.) (enjoining unauthor-ized usage of Olympic marks in United States to advertise and sell tickets and hospitality packages to the Beijing Olympics).

The ASA "grandfathers" the rights of those who lawfully used the Olympic marks prior to 1950 (the date the ASA's predecessor statute was enacted) to advertise and sell their goods or services. However, such users may not expand the scope of their goods or services sold under the Olympic mark, or adopt new marks with the word "Olympic" therein. In *O-M Bread, Inc. v. United States Olympic Committee*, 65 F.3d 933 (Fed. Cir. 1995), the Federal Circuit held that the pro-posed use of "Olympic Kids" for bakery products is not a permitted extension of a prior user's grandfathered right to use the Olympic mark for bakery products. The court found these "different marks present a different commercial impres-sion and are not legal equivalents." *Id.* at 938. It concluded that "commercial growth into new 'Olympic'-based marks is outside the letter of the statute, as well as outside its spirit.

The ASA does not prohibit all unauthorized uses of the Olympic marks. As one court observed, "because the [ASA] grants the USOC rights over and above both the common law and [the Lanham Act], the language and scope of the Act must be strictly construed." *United States Olympic Committee v. American Media, Inc.*, 156 F. Supp. 2d 1200, 1209 (D. Colo. 2001). For example, the media may report about Olympic sports competitions, which would include use of the word "Olympic" and competition photographs containing Olympic marks in news reporting. In *American Media*, the court ruled that the mere publication of an Olympic preview magazine titled "Olympics USA" is noncommercial speech that does not infringe the USOC's rights under the ASA. However, the publisher's usage of the Olympic marks in a manner falsely suggesting that the USOC offi-cially endorses or authorizes its magazine would violate the Lanham Act.

Unless a likelihood of public confusion as to origin, sponsorship, or affilia-tion is created, the Olympic mark may be used for purely expressive purposes.

In *Stop the Olympic Prison v. United States Olympic Committee*, 489 F. Supp. 1112 (S.D.N.Y. 1980), the court found that publication and distribution of a poster with the words "Stop the Olympic Prison" to marshal public opposition to the planned conversion of the Lake Placid Olympic Village into a prison after the 1980 Olympics does not violate the Stevens Act. The publisher was not using the Olympic mark to make a profit; its only purpose was to disseminate its political views in an effort to change future plans for the Olympic Village. The poster is not likely to be viewed as a commercial advertisement for the sale of any goods or services, and it was not used to promote any theatrical exhibition or athletic competition.

PROBLEM 12-1

a. Ohio State University (OSU) and University of Michigan (UM) authorize each other to use their registered marks for nonprofit purposes. OSU sells "Go Bucks, Beat Michigan" buttons and "Beat Michigan Week" T-shirts, with all proceeds going to the university's cancer hospital. If a Columbus, Ohio, business sells "Beat Michigan" T-shirts, golf balls, license plate holders, and beer mugs without UM's authorization, does this infringe UM's trademark rights?

b. Does the University of Michigan have a legal right to prevent the NCAA Division I-AA Delaware University Blue Hens from using its well-known blue and gold "winged tips" helmet design as part of its football team uniform? Would it be able to prevent a Wisconsin high school football team from doing so?

c. Can the NFL prevent a women's professional football league from identifying itself as the "National Women's Football League" and calling its championship game the SupHer Bowl?

d. In 1994 Marquette University, whose school colors are blue and gold, changed the name of its athletic teams from the "Warriors" to the "Golden Eagles" to discontinue using a potentially disparaging characterization of Native Americans. (See Chapter 9 for an in-depth discussion of this issue.) Does Marquette have the right to prohibit an off-campus bookstore from selling blue and gold Marquette Warriors T-shirts?

e. A nutrition supplement manufacturer includes the statement "This product does not contain any substances banned by the National Collegiate Athletic Association" on the label of its product. Does this violate the Lanham Act?

f. Consider whether any of the following unauthorized usages violates the USOC's rights in the Olympic marks:

   i.   An Iowa farmer prunes his cornfield into the shape of the interlocking Olympic rings during the summer before the 2002 Salt Lake City Winter Olympics. Does your determination depend on whether he charges a fee to enter his cornfield and view the Olympic rings?

   ii. To stimulate local interest in a student science project, a high school district dubs a series of races by mice through an obstacle course the "Rat Olympics."

   iii. The "Redneck Olympics" features the cigarette flip, bobbing for pigs' feet, mud pit belly flop, toilet seat throwing, big hair contest, and seed spitting.

5. Ambush Marketing

Ambush marketing is a creative advertising practice by a business other than an official sponsor that seeks to create an association with a sports event without using the event's name, trademarks, or logos. It encompasses "intentional efforts to weaken [a] competitor's official association with a sport organization, which has been acquired through the payment of sponsorship fees" as well as seeking "to capitalize on the goodwill, reputation and popularity of a particular sport or event by creating an association without the authorization or consent of the necessary parties." Steve McKelvey and John Grady, *Ambush Marketing: The Legal Battleground for Sports Marketers*, 21 Ent. & Sports Law 8, 9 (2004).

Official event sponsors claim that ambush marketing dilutes the value of their sponsorships. Ambush marketing may harm event organizers, which need sponsorship money to fund production of a sporting event. When ambush marketers receive commercial benefits by free-riding on an event's popularity or goodwill, the value of an official sponsorship may be significantly reduced. This creates an economic disincentive to be an official event sponsor, with a corresponding incentive to engage in ambush marketing instead. This in turn reduces the value of official sponsorships and causes sports event organizers to lose sponsorship revenues. See *United States Olympic Comm. v. American Media, Inc.*, 156 F. Supp. 2d 1200, 1204 (D. Colo. 2001) (alleging that defendant's ambush marketing will encourage other companies to do so, which will adversely affect USOC's ability to fund United States' participation in the Olympic Games). Successful ambush marketing campaigns also may harm consumers of sporting events. A decrease in sponsorship revenues could force event organizers to find new revenue sources (e.g., cable or pay-per-view television broadcasts rather than free-to-air telecasts), or possibly result in the discontinuance of sports events that lack adequate commercial sponsorship support.

Despite ambush marketing's potential adverse economic effects on the official sponsorship of sporting events, one commentator has observed:

> Sports organizations, however, remain reluctant to challenge ambush marketing campaigns legally for several reasons: limited case law exists regarding ambush marketing; corporations have successfully defended ambush marketing claims with claims of commercial free speech or fair use; most ambush campaigns are short-lived; an adverse court decision could create an onslaught of ambush campaigns; and courts support of the use of disclaimers, thus allowing ambush companies to make limited use of a registered trademark so long as they avoid creating consumer confusion.

Lori Bean, Note, *Ambush Marketing: Sports Sponsorship Confusion and the Lanham Act*, 75 B.U. L. Rev. 1099, 1101-1102 (1995). Another observes, "While many people complain that [ambush marketing] involves a question of business ethics, others say it is aggressive advertising. Thus, smart lawyers can devise strategies for corporate clients that stay on the legal side." Robert N. Davis, *Ambushing the Olympic Games*, 3 Vill. Sports & Ent. L.J. 423, 430 (1996).

Under current U.S. law, ambush marketing is illegal only if it creates a likelihood of consumer confusion. In *Federation Internationale De Football v. Nike, Inc.*, 285 F. Supp. 2d 64 (D.D.C. 2003), the court refused to preliminarily enjoin Nike's use of "USA 03" to advertise and sell various products in connection with its sponsorship of the U.S. Women's National Soccer Team. Plaintiff Federation

Internationale De Football (FIFA) used "USA 2003" in connection with its 2003 women's soccer World Cup held in the United States. Nike was not a World Cup sponsor and was not authorized to use FIFA's marks. Although Nike did not use FIFA's name or refer to the World Cup, FIFA alleged that Nike's usage of "USA 03" is infringing and illegally interfered with its official sponsorship contracts.

Holding that FIFA has not shown a substantial likelihood of success on the merits of its claims, the court observed:

> Nike argues that its use of "USA 03" (or "United States 2003") is innocent, given the company's sponsorship of the Women's National Team. After all, the team that Nike is backing is the United States team for the year 2003, and therefore, "USA 03" is an appropriate and understandable way for Nike to associate itself with that group of players. The Court agrees that Nike's preexisting and entirely legitimate relationship with the Women's World Cup provides an important context for its use of the disputed marks. For there can be little doubt, in light of the success that the U.S. women enjoyed in the 1999 World Cup, that the team and the event are already linked in the public mind. As such, Nike's careful use of a mark that might be affiliated with both is not necessarily an indication of bad faith, but instead of savvy marketing. Whenever that team plays in this country, it is to be expected that the sponsors of both the team and the event would want to use trademarks that reflect the United States and that emphasize this year's date. Nike's doing so here thus may not indicate a deliberate attempt to deceive the buying public.

Id. at 73-74.

Even if there currently are only limited legal remedies for combating ambush marketing, a sports event organizer can minimize its successful use and resulting detrimental effects by developing a comprehensive anti-ambush marketing plan. For example, it can contractually prohibit broadcasters from selling commercial time to the competitors of official sponsors. Nonsponsor advertisements and signage in connection with a sporting event should be carefully monitored to ensure that the event's name, marks, and logos are not included therein. See generally Anne M. Wall, *The Game Behind the Games,* 12 Marq. Sports L. Rev. 557 (2002) (detailing Olympic governing bodies' defensive strategies to deter ambush marketing and protect exclusive contractual rights of official sponsors).

Courts will enforce contract rights to prevent unfair competition that causes a likelihood of consumer confusion. In *Mastercard International, Inc. v. Sprint Communications Co.,* 1994 WL 97097 (S.D.N.Y.), *aff'd,* 23 F.2d 397 (2d Cir. 1994), an international soccer federation granted exclusive rights to Mastercard to use the 1994 World Cup Soccer Tournament trademarks on "all card-based payment and account access devices." The court held that Mastercard's contract rights precluded the United States Local Organizing Committee from authorizing Sprint Communications to use and imprint those marks on phone cards. Finding that Sprint's conduct violated the Lanham Act, the court concluded, "Sprint wishes to use the World Cup marks to convey to the world the false impression that its use of the marks on calling cards is officially sanctioned by the World Cup organization. Clearly, that is not the case, and Mastercard, which has the exclusive right to use the mark for such purposes, is entitled to enjoin this deceptive use."

PROBLEM 12-2

a. Zeebok paid a $25 million sponsorship fee to the International Olympic
    Committee to be designated as the official sneaker of the Olympic Games
    which will be held in the United States. One week before the Games begin,
    Badidas, a rival athletic footwear company, begins airing a series of commer-
    cials with scenes from past Olympic Games showing medal-winning track
    athletes wearing its sneakers. Consider whether Badidas's ambush market-
    ing campaign is illegal and what additional information might be needed to
    make this determination.
b. Koors Brewing Company provides free NCAA men's basketball "Final
    Four" tickets as grand prizes to winners of its "Koors Light Tourney Time
    Sweepstakes" beer promotion held during the month of March. The back of
    each ticket states, "Unless specifically authorized in advance by the NCAA,
    this ticket may not be offered in a commercial promotion or as a prize in
    a sweepstakes or contest." The NCAA permits only official sponsors of its
    "Final Four" men's basketball tournament to do so, and it refuses to allow
    any manufacturers of alcoholic beverages to become official sponsors. Is
    Koors's conduct legal?

C.   REAL-TIME GAME ACCOUNTS AND
BROADCASTING RIGHTS

1.   *Historical Background*

Historically, producers of sporting events sought to protect live game accounts
and play-by-play descriptions from unauthorized viewer usage under state misappropriation, unfair competition, and contract laws. The then-current federal copyright laws did not provide any legal protection for sporting events or
simultaneously recorded broadcasts. Relying primarily on the misappropriation doctrine established by the Supreme Court in *International News Service v.
Associated Press*, 248 U.S. 215 (1918), courts broadly held that the creator of a
game or athletic event has an exclusive property right in its commercial value.
Recognizing that the production of athletic events requires the expenditure of
substantial time, effort, and money, these courts prohibited observers and listeners—whether inside or outside the facility in which the event occurred—from
unauthorized transmission of live game accounts to the public for commercial
benefit. See, e.g., *National Exhibition Co. v. Fass*, 143 N.Y.S.2d 767 (N.Y. Sup. Ct.
1955); *Pittsburgh Athletic Co. v. KQV Broad. Co.*, 24 F. Supp. 490 (W.D. Pa. 1938);
Twentieth Century Sporting Club v. Transradio Press Service, Inc., 300 N.Y.S. 159 (N.Y.
Sup. Ct. 1937). See generally Bruce P. Keller, *Condemned to Repeat the Past: The
Reemergence of Misappropriation and Other Common Law Theories of Protection for
Intellectual Property*, 11 Harv. J.L. & Tech. 401 (1998) (tracing historical reliance
on state misappropriation law to protect sports-related intellectual property
rights).

In *Pittsburgh Athletic Co. v. KQV Broadcasting Co.*, the court held: "the Pittsburgh
Athletic Company [owner of the Pittsburgh Pirates professional baseball club],

by reason of its creation of the game, its control of the park, and its restriction of the dissemination of news therefrom, has a property right in such news, and the right to control the use thereof for a reasonable time following the games." 24 F. Supp. at 492. The Pittsburgh Athletic Company sold the exclusive rights to broadcast Pirates games played at Forbes Field to General Mills, Inc. The defendant broadcast play-by-play accounts of Pirates games as described by observers stationed outside Forbes Field who were able to see them being played. Finding that the defendant's conduct violated the baseball club's property rights, the court ruled that its unauthorized broadcast of Pirates games constitutes misappropriation, unfair competition, and unlawful interference with the parties' contract rights.

2. *Nature and Scope of Copyright Law Protection*

To encourage creative expression such as books, movies, music, and other works, the federal Copyright Act of 1976 protects only "original works of authorship fixed in any tangible medium of expression." 17 U.S.C. §102(a).

Copyright law does not protect ideas, procedures, systems, or methods of operation "regardless of the form in which it is described, explained, illustrated, or embodied." 17 U.S.C. §102(b). Thus, neither the underlying idea for a type of athletic event nor a system or method of playing a sport is copyrightable. 1 M. Nimmer and D. Nimmer, *Nimmer on Copyright* §2.18[H][3][a] (2004). In *Hoopla Sports and Entertainment, Inc. v. Nike, Inc.*, 947 F. Supp. 347 (N.D. Ill. 1996), the court held that the concept of an international high school all-star basketball game is not copyrightable and plaintiff cannot prevent defendant from using its idea to conduct a similar event. The court observed that "the methods or rules of playing basketball games are not generally copyrightable." *Id.* at 354. See also *Seltzer v. Sunbrock*, 22 F. Supp. 621 (S.D. Cal. 1938) (rejecting plaintiff's claim that his idea of a system for staging a transcontinental roller-skating race is protected by copyright law; "[a] system, as such, can never be copyrighted. If it finds any protection, it must come from the patent laws"). *Id.* at 630.[1]

The following case considers the nature and scope of protection that federal copyright law provides to the producer of a sports event.

NBA v. MOTOROLA, INC.

105 F.3d 841 (2d Cir. 1997)

WINTER, Circuit Judge.

The facts are largely undisputed. Motorola manufactures and markets the SportsTrax paging device while STATS supplies the game information that is transmitted to the pagers. The product became available to the public in January 1996, at a retail price of about $200. SportsTrax's pager has an inch-and-a-half by

---

1. To be a patentable invention under the federal Patent Act, a sport or game must be useful, non-obvious, and novel, which are difficult statutory requirements to satisfy. 35 U.S.C. §100, et seq. For example, the Patent Office issued U.S. Patent No. 4,911,433 to the Arena Football League for its unique system for playing indoor professional football. See generally Carl A. Kukkonen, III, *Be a Good Sport and Refrain from Using My Patented Putt: Intellectual Property Protection for Sports Related Movements*, 80 J. Pat. & Trademark Off. Soc'y 808 (Nov. 1998).

inch-and-a-half screen and operates in four basic modes: "current," "statistics," "final scores" and "demonstration." It is the "current" mode that gives rise to the present dispute. In that mode, SportsTrax displays the following information on NBA games in progress: (i) the teams playing; (ii) score changes; (iii) the team in possession of the ball; (iv) whether the team is in the free-throw bonus; (v) the quarter of the game; and (vi) time remaining in the quarter. The information is updated every two to three minutes, with more frequent updates near the end of the first half and the end of the game. There is a lag of approximately two or three minutes between events in the game itself and when the information appears on the pager screen.

SportsTrax's operation relies on a "data feed" supplied by STATS reporters who watch the games on television or listen to them on the radio. The reporters key into a personal computer changes in the score and other information such as successful and missed shots, fouls, and clock updates. The information is relayed by modem to STATS's host computer, which compiles, analyzes, and formats the data for retransmission. The information is then sent to a common carrier, which then sends it via satellite to various local FM radio networks that in turn emit the signal received by the individual SportsTrax pagers. . . .

COPYRIGHTS IN EVENTS OR BROADCASTS OF EVENTS

The NBA asserted copyright infringement claims with regard both to the underlying games and to their broadcasts. . . .

INFRINGEMENT OF A COPYRIGHT IN THE UNDERLYING GAMES

In our view, the underlying basketball games do not fall within the subject matter of federal copyright protection because they do not constitute "original works of authorship" under 17 U.S.C. § 102(a). Section 102(a) lists eight categories of "works of authorship" covered by the act, including such categories as "literary works," "musical works," and "dramatic works." The list does not include athletic events, and, although the list is concededly non-exclusive, such events are neither similar nor analogous to any of the listed categories.

Sports events are not "authored" in any common sense of the word. There is, of course, at least at the professional level, considerable preparation for a game. However, the preparation is as much an expression of hope or faith as a determination of what will actually happen. Unlike movies, plays, television programs, or operas, athletic events are competitive and have no underlying script. Preparation may even cause mistakes to succeed, like the broken play in football that gains yard-age because the opposition could not expect it. Athletic events may also result in wholly unanticipated occurrences, the most notable recent event being in a championship baseball game in which interference with a fly ball caused an umpire to signal erroneously a home run.

What "authorship" there is in a sports event, moreover, must be open to copying by competitors if fans are to be attracted. If the inventor of the T-formation in football had been able to copyright it, the sport might have come to an end instead of prospering. Even where athletic preparation most resembles authorship—figure skating, gymnastics, and, some would uncharitably say, professional wrestling—a performer who conceives and executes a particularly graceful and difficult—or, in the case of wrestling, seemingly painful—acrobatic feat cannot copyright it without impairing the underlying competition in the future. A claim of being the only athlete to perform a feat doesn't mean much if no one else is allowed to try.

For many of these reasons, *Nimmer on Copyright* concludes that the "[f]ar more reasonable" position is that athletic events are not copyrightable. 1 M. Nimmer & D. Nimmer, *Nimmer on Copyright* § 2.09[F] at 2-170.1 (1996). *Nimmer* notes that, among other problems, the number of joint copyright owners would arguably include the league, the teams, the athletes, umpires, stadium workers and even fans, who all contribute to the "work."

Concededly, caselaw is scarce on the issue of whether organized events themselves are copyrightable, but what there is indicates that they are not. In claiming a copyright in the underlying games, the NBA relied in part on a footnote in *Baltimore Orioles, Inc. v. Major League Baseball Players Assn.*, 805 F.2d 663, 669 n. 7 (7th Cir.1986), *cert. denied*, 480 U.S. 941, 107 S.Ct. 1593, 94 L.Ed.2d 782 (1987), which stated that the "[p]layers' performances" contain the "modest creativity required for copyright ability." However, the court went on to state, "Moreover, even if the [p]layers' performances were not sufficiently creative, the [p]layers agree that the cameramen and director contribute creative labor to the telecasts." *Id.* This last sentence indicates that the court was considering the copyright ability of telecasts—not the underlying games, which obviously can be played without cameras.

We believe that the lack of caselaw is attributable to a general understanding that athletic events were, and are, uncopyrightable. . . .

INFRINGEMENT OF A COPYRIGHT IN THE BROADCASTS OF NBA GAMES

As noted, recorded broadcasts of NBA games—as opposed to the games themselves—are now entitled to copyright protection. The Copyright Act was amended in 1976 specifically to insure that simultaneously-recorded transmissions of live performances and sporting events would meet the Act's requirement that the original work of authorship be "fixed in any tangible medium of expression." 17 U.S.C. § 102(a). . . . Congress specifically had sporting events in mind: [T]he bill seeks to resolve, through the definition of "fixation" in section 101, the status of live broadcasts—sports, news coverage, live performances of music, etc.—that are reaching the public in unfixed form but that are simultaneously being recorded. H.R. No. 94-1476 at 52, *reprinted in* 1976 U.S.C.C.A.N. at 5665. The House Report also makes clear that it is the broadcast, not the underlying game, that is the subject of copyright protection. . . .

Although the broadcasts are protected under copyright law, the district court correctly held that Motorola and STATS did not infringe NBA's copyright because they reproduced only facts from the broadcasts, not the expression or description of the game that constitutes the broadcast. The "fact/expression dichotomy" is a bedrock principle of copyright law that "limits severely the scope of protection in fact-based works." *Feist Publications, Inc. v. Rural Tel. Service Co.*, 499 U.S. 340, 350, 111 S.Ct. 1282, 1290, 113 L.Ed.2d 358 (1991). "'No author may copyright facts or ideas. The copyright is limited to those aspects of the work—termed "expression"—that display the stamp of the author's originality.'" *Id.* (quoting *Harper & Row, Publishers, Inc. v. Nation Enter.*, 471 U.S. 539, 547, 105 S.Ct. 2218, 2224, 85 L.Ed.2d 588 (1985)).

We agree with the district court that the "[d]efendants provide purely factual information which any patron of an NBA game could acquire from the arena without any involvement from the director, cameramen, or others who contribute to the originality of a broadcast." Because the SportsTrax device and AOL site reproduce only factual information culled from the broadcasts and none of the copyrightable expression of the games, appellants did not infringe the copyright of the broadcasts . . .

NOTES AND QUESTIONS

1. *Sports Events and Performances.* Why did the *Motorola* court hold that a sports event or performance is not subject to protection under federal copyright law? Considering that elite athletic performance on either an individual or team basis normally involves significant creative activity and generally has substantial commercial value, was the *Motorola* court's conclusion correct? See *National Assn. of Broadcasters v. Copyright Royalty Tribunal,* 675 F.2d 367, 377 and n.16 (D.C. Cir. 1982) (noting apparent understanding of Congress during hearings on Copyright Act of 1976 that "the mere performance of a sport or game could not be copyrighted at common law"). As one noted commentator observes:

> Although the commercial value of professional sports cannot be doubted, and although judges should not determine copyrightability according to their subjective evaluation of an artistic work, nonetheless copyright extends only to "works of authorship," not to every commercially valuable activity. Failure to appreciate that distinction would result in according copyright protection not only to athletic events, but also to a heart surgeon's operation on diseased tissue or the twisting of knobs in the control center of a nuclear power plant—both important and commercially valuable activities, to be sure, but neither remotely capable of copyright protection.

1 M. Nimmer and D. Nimmer, *Nimmer on Copyright* §2.09[F] at 2-168 (2004). But see Richard A. Posner, *Misappropriation: A Dirge,* 40 Hous. L. Rev. 621, 632-633 (2003) (based on economic analysis, "it is arguable that games should be copyrightable").

2. *Sports Broadcasts.* The *Motorola* court ruled that the Copyright Act of 1976 protects the broadcast of a sporting event, even though it does not protect the underlying event itself. Is there a principled basis for drawing this distinction?

The Copyright Act of 1976 grants a copyright owner the exclusive right to use and authorize others to use the work in five statutorily defined ways, including the right to copy or duplicate a copyrighted broadcast of a sports event and to "publicly perform" it 17 U.S.C. §106. The act provides that anyone who violates any of these exclusive rights engages in copyright infringement. 17 U.S.C. §501(a). The owner of a copyright has a variety of available remedies for infringement including injunctive relief and the recovery of actual or statutory damages, the infringer's profits, and attorney fees. 17 U.S.C. §§502-505.

Why didn't the *Motorola* defendants' conduct constitute infringement of the copyright in the broadcast of NBA games?

3. *Ownership of Sports Broadcast Copyright.* A threshold issue is who owns the copyright to the broadcast of a sporting event—the clubs playing the particular game, the league, the broadcaster of the game, or the players participating in the game? In general, ownership of a copyright initially vests in the author(s) of the work. 17 U.S.C. §201(a). The Copyright Act recognizes that a work may be jointly authored and its copyright co-owned. 17 U.S.C. §201(a). Within a sports league, broadcasting rights and copyright ownership of broadcast games generally are determined by contract. *Chi. Prof'l Sports Ltd. Partnership v. NBA*, 874 F. Supp. 844, 850-851 (N.D. Ill. 1995), *reversed on other grounds*, 95 F.3d 593 (7th Cir. 1996). A broadcaster's camera angles, types of shots, use of instant replays, split screens, special effects, and commentary supplies the creativity necessary for "authorship" of a broadcast sports event. *Baltimore Orioles, Inc. v. Major League Baseball Players Assn.*, 805 F.2d 663, 668-669 (7th Cir. 1986); *National Assn. of Broadcasters v. Copyright Royalty Tribunal*, 675 F.2d 367, 377-379 (D.C. Cir. 1982). Ownership of the copyright for a sports broadcast vis-à-vis the league/clubs and the broadcaster generally is contractually determined. See, e.g., *NFL v. Insight Telecomm. Corp.*, 158 F. Supp. 2d 124, 128 (D. Mass. 2001) ("The NFL owns the copyright in all regular season and post-season NFL game telecasts, as confirmed by the League's contracts with the networks").

   In *Baltimore Orioles, Inc. v. Major League Baseball Players Assn.*, 805 F. 2d 663, 670 (7th Cir. 1986), the Seventh Circuit held: "Because the Players are employees and their performances before broadcast audiences are within the scope of their employment, the telecasts of major league baseball games, which consist of the Players' performances, are works made for hire within the meaning of § 201(b). . . . Thus, in the absence of an agreement to the contrary, the Clubs are presumed to own all of the rights encompassed in the telecasts of the games. The district court found that there was no written agreement that the Clubs would not own the copyright to the telecasts, and, therefore, that the copyright was owned by the Clubs." See also *Big Fights Inc. v. Ficara*, 40 U.S.P.Q.2d 1377, 1378 (S.D.N.Y. 1996) (promoter of a professional boxing match, not boxers, owns copyright in film of the match). Cf. *Ettore v. Philco Television Broad. Corp.*, 229 F.2d 481 (3d Cir. 1956) (boxer contracts to receive 20 percent of all proceeds derived from sale of motion picture rights to boxing match in which he participated).

4. *Sports Scores and Statistics.* Federal copyright law provides limited protection for compilations of game scores and statistics. Although mere facts such as game scores and statistics are not copyrightable, their original and creative compilation is a form of expression that is copyrightable. In *Feist Publications, Inc. v. Rural Telephone Service Co., Inc.*, 499 U.S. 340, 344-345 (1991), the Supreme Court explained:

   "No one may claim originality as to facts." [Citation omitted.] This is because facts do not owe their origin to an act of authorship. The distinction is one between creation and discovery: The first person to find and report a particular fact has not created the fact; he or she has merely discovered its existence. . . . Factual compilations, on the other hand, may possess the requisite originality. The compilation author typically chooses which facts to include, in what order to place them, and how to arrange the collected data so that they may be used effectively by readers. These choices as to selection and arrangement, so long as they are made independently by the compiler and entail a minimal degree of creativity, are sufficiently original that Congress may protect such compilations through the copyright laws.

Id. at 347-348. See *Kregos v. Associated Press*, 3 F.3d 656, 663 (2d Cir. 1993) (although pitching form with compiled selection of statistics for MLB pitchers is copyrightable, no infringement found because defendant's form differed by "more than a trivial degree").

In *NFL v. McBee & Bruno's, Inc.*, 792 F.2d 726 (8th Cir. 1986), the court ruled that a sports bar's unauthorized interception of the broadcast of a sports event through the use of satellite dish antennae and its showing to patrons, which occurred in the mid-1980s, constitutes copyright infringement. It explained, "The Copyright Act protects 'original works of authorship fixed in any tangible medium,' 17 U.S.C. § 102(a), including 'motion pictures and other audiovisual works,' 17 U.S.C. § 102(a)(6). As for live broadcasts, such as the football games at issue here, the Act states that '[a] work consisting of sounds, images, or both, that are being transmitted, is "fixed" . . . if a fixation of the work is being made simultaneously with its transmission,' 17 U.S.C. § 101; '[t]o "transmit" is defined as "to communicate . . . by any device or process whereby images or sounds are received beyond the place from which they are sent."'" *Id.* at 731-732. This was an unauthorized "public performance" of a copyrighted sports broadcast, which the Copyright Act defines as a display "at a place open to the public or at any place where a substantial number of persons outside of a normal circle of a family and its social acquaintances is gathered." 17 U.S.C. §101. See also *NFL v. PrimeTime 24 Joint Venture*, 211 F.3d 10, 13 (2d Cir. 2000), *cert. denied*, 532 U.S. 941 (2001) ("PrimeTime's uplink transmission of signals captured in the United States is a step in the process by which NFL's protected work wends its way to a public audience [in Canada] . . . and [b]ecause PrimeTime did not have authorization to make such a public performance, PrimeTime infringed the NFL's copyright").

The following case illustrates that the Internet provides a modern means for infringing copyrighted sports event broadcasts and enables unauthorized webcasts to occur throughout the world—conduct that violates U.S. law but possibly not foreign laws.

NFL v. TVRADIONOW CORP.
53 U.S.P.Q.2d 1831 (W.D. Pa. 2000)

ZIEGLER, J.

This is a civil action for money damages and equitable relief, filed by the National Football League ("NFL"), National Basketball Association ("NBA"), and NBA Properties, Inc. ("NBA Properties") (collectively "the Sports Leagues") . . . contending that defendants violated the Copyright Act, 17 U.S.C. Section 106. . . .

The gravamen of this dispute concerns the public performance of plaintiffs' copyrighted programming from Toronto, Canada, to computer users in the United States since November 30, 1999, over the Internet. Specifically, defendants have streamed copyrighted professional football and basketball games as well as copyrighted programs such as "60 Minutes," "Ally McBeal," and "Star Trek Voyager," framed with advertisements obtained by defendants. Plaintiffs allege that defendants have captured United States programming from television stations in Buffalo, New York and elsewhere, converted these television signals into computerized data and streamed them over the Internet from a website called iCraveTV.com. According to plaintiffs, any Internet user may access iCraveTV.com by simply entering three digits of any Canadian area code, one of which is provided to the user on the site itself, and by clicking two other buttons. Further, Internet users from the United States and elsewhere easily may revisit the site because iCraveTV causes a small file, or cookie, to be deposited in a user's computer during his or her initial visit so that the user can automatically bypass defendants' screening process. . . . [T]he Court is mindful of the long-standing precept that the United States copyright laws do not have extraterritorial operation. *See Allarcom Pay Television, Ltd. v. General Instrument Corp.*, 69 F.3d 381 [36 USPQ2d 1654] (9th Cir.1995).

Defendants argue that their website is for Canadian viewers only and it is not intended for citizens of the United States and elsewhere. Thus, the argument continues, the alleged improper acts are limited to Canada.

Plaintiffs have presented testimony, sworn affidavits and declarations establishing that Pennsylvania residents have accessed defendants' website and viewed the programs which were streamed thereon. Further, defendants posted an article on the Website by a United States citizen noting that access to defendants' website could be obtained by any United States citizen with little or no difficulty.

Accordingly, when an allegedly infringing act occurring without the United States is publicly performed within the United States, the Copyright Act is implicated and a district court possesses jurisdiction. [Citations omitted.] Subject matter jurisdiction exists because, although the streaming of the plaintiffs' programming originated in Canada, acts of infringement were committed within the United States when United States citizens received and viewed defendants' streaming of the copyrighted materials. These constitute, at a minimum, public performances in the United States. . . .

The plaintiffs have established without rejoinder from the defendants that they have copyright . . . ownership of several items, including, among others, the Super Bowl, the NBA Finals, and the NFL playoff games and regular League games. . . .

Defendants do not deny that they have copied these items, represented themselves as the authors and that they have publicly performed them over the Internet. Rather, defendants argue that there is no desire on the part of defendants for any United States residents to access iCraveTV. Notwithstanding defendants' intentions, the Court finds that plaintiffs have presented sufficient facts to establish their claims of copyright . . . infringement. . . .

A January 25, 2000 breakdown of "impressions" and "clicks" onto the iCraveTV website, generated by a private ad serving system (DART) utilized by Cox, reported 1.6 million impressions (page views) from United States visitors on the iCraveTV website. This figure was second only to the figure for Canada, which was 2.0 million.

Defendants also use a "Real Video" server to stream video programming through their website. This server maintains "logs" of the Internet Protocol addresses of computers that contact defendants' server to obtain access to video programming. An analysis of the Real Video server logs shows that substantial numbers of persons in the United States received the streaming of programming, including programming in which plaintiffs own copyrights. [E]vidence in the record shows that plaintiffs are likely to succeed in showing that defendants are unlawfully publicly performing plaintiffs' copyrighted works in the United States. Defendants do so by transmitting (through use of "streaming" technology) performances of the works to the public by means of the telephone lines and computers that make up the Internet. 17 U.S.C. Section 101. This activity violates plaintiffs' rights to perform their works publicly and to authorize others to do so. 17 U.S.C. Sections 106, 501(a). . . .

Defendants have submitted a declaration of a Canadian law professor, Michael Geist, which argues that defendants' activities are permissible under Canadian law. However, because plaintiffs seek relief under U.S. law for infringements of the U.S. Copyright Act, there is no need for this Court to address any issue of Canadian law. . . .

[The court preliminarily and permanently enjoined defendants from infringing plaintiffs' copyrighted works through streaming or otherwise into the United States via the iCraveTV.com site or any other Internet site or online facility without plaintiffs' prior consent.]

NOTES AND QUESTIONS

1. Why does the defendants' conduct constitute copyright infringement? See also *Live Nation Motor Sports, Inc. v. Davis*, 2006 WL 3616983 (N.D. Tex. 2006) (providing unauthorized access to motorcycle racing producer's live webcasts through defendant's website is copyright infringement). See generally Michael J. Mellis, *Internet Piracy of Live Sports Telecasts*, 18 Marq. Sports L. Rev. 259 (2008).

   The Internet enables unauthorized webcasts to occur throughout the world, but currently there is not a uniform global scope of copyright law protection for sports broadcasts. For example, an Israeli court refused to grant the English Football Association Premier League's request for an ex parte injunction against unauthorized Internet broadcasting of its games because of judicial uncertainty whether such conduct violates Israel's recently amended copyright law. In *Football Association Premier League Ltd v. Netvision 013 Barack Ltd.*, MCA 011646/08 (Dist. Ct. Tel Aviv, July 16, 2008) (unofficial English translation), the court concluded:

   > From a preliminary review of the new law I believe that, in light of the new balance created by the legislat[ure], it cannot be determined that copyright applies to filming a sports game for live broadcast. In fact, what interests the TV viewers is the game itself, and there is almost no importance in the "original work", i.e. photography angles and replays. It is a fact that the audience views the game during any broadcast and at any photographic angle whatsoever. What is important is the progress of the game and mainly the results in real time (and in this matter, see the threatened claim against the broadcasters of the 2008 Euro Cup games during which, due to a malfunction, one of the goals in the semi-finals between Turkey and Germany was not shown). It appears that replays, and mainly the integrated videos of the players and the teams, are added almost in order to create copyright from nothing. The Applicant itself did not argue that copyright was applicable to the "clean"

live broadcast, but only to the international live broadcast which included all those additions. It seems artificial to grant copyright to TV photography. In actual fact, there is nothing original in the photography, it is just a documentation of the game itself to which, as all agree, copyright does not apply.

2. Tape recording of televised sports broadcasts for solely in-home, personal use is not copyright infringement. *Sony Corp. of Am. v. Universal City Studios, Inc.*, 464 U.S. 417, 449 (1984) (characterizing this activity as "time-shifting for private home use" that is noninfringing fair use of copyrighted broadcast pursuant to §107 of Copyright Act).

    However, the unauthorized public performance of taped broadcasts of sports events (which would include posting on YouTube) constitutes copyright infringement. In *New Boston Television, Inc. v. Entertainment Sports Programming Network, Inc.*, 215 U.S.P.Q. 755 (D. Mass. 1981), ESPN contended that its rebroadcast of taped sports event highlights is permissible fair use. Rejecting this alleged defense and finding copyright infringement, the court stated:

    > While protection of the public right of access to [newsworthy] information is a primary justification for the fair use defense, this right is sufficiently protected merely by enabling defendants to report the underlying facts which the plaintiff's videotapes record. It does not however permit defendants to appropriate the plaintiff's expression of that information by copying the plaintiff's films themselves.

    Id. at 756.

    In *Viacom Int'l v. YouTube, Inc.*, 718 F. Supp. 2d 514 (S.D.N.Y. 2010), *aff'd and reversed and remanded on other grounds*, 676 F.3d 19 (2d Cir. 2012), a federal district court held that the Digital Millenium Copyright Act does not require YouTube to self-police its website for infringing content posted by third parties such as copyrighted broadcast and webcast sports events. YouTube is required to remove copyrighted material in accordance with this federal law only when it has actual knowledge that a specific posting contains copyrighted material that has been posted without the copyright owner's authorization.

3. In *WPIX, Inc. v. IVI, Inc.*, 691 F.3d 275 (2d Cir. 2012), a significant case protecting the ability of producers of broadcast sports events to maximize their economic value, the Second Circuit ruled that the unauthorized streaming of copyrighted television programming over the Internet is not noninfringing retransmission of copyrighted programming protected by §111 of the Copyright Act's compulsory licensing provisions for cable television systems. Section 111 permits "cable systems to publicly perform and retransmit signals of copyrighted television programming to its subscribers, provided they pay royalties at government-regulated rates and abide by the statute's procedures." *Id.* at *2. The court concluded that Congress "has not codified a statutory provision for Internet retransmissions, nor has it included the 'Internet' as an acceptable communication channel under § 111" and "did not . . . intend for § 111's compulsory license to extend to Internet transmissions." *Id.* at *5-6.

    The Second Circuit expressed concern that the plaintiffs' "desire to create original television programming surely would be dampened if their creative works could be copied and streamed over the Internet in derogation of their exclusive property rights." *Id.* at *11. It affirmed the district court's preliminary injunction against defendant's unauthorized streaming because this infringing conduct irreparably harms plaintiffs:

> The value of plaintiffs' programming would also be harmed by the impact on advertising revenue. Broadcast television stations and networks earn most of their revenues from advertising. Plaintiffs argue—persuasively—that advertisers pay substantial fees to target specific audiences; such fees are often determined by the number of viewers and their demographic profiles. [Defendant's] retransmissions of plaintiffs' copyrighted programming over the Internet increases the number of Internet viewers and reduces, "fragments," and diverts the number of "local viewers." As a result, [defendant'] retransmissions weaken plaintiffs' negotiating position with advertisers and reduce the value of its local advertisements.

Id.

3. Misappropriation of Real-Time Game Accounts and Scores

In *NBA v. Motorola, Inc., supra,* the Second Circuit ruled that federal copyright law preempted (i.e., barred or precluded) the NBA's state law commercial misappropriation claim because the defendants' collection and dissemination of "strictly factual information about the games" was obtained from NBA games broadcast on television and radio, which was information already in the public domain. The court explained:

> When Congress amended the Copyright Act in 1976, it provided for the preemption of state law claims that are interrelated with copyright claims in certain ways. Under 17 U.S.C. § 301, a state law claim is preempted when: (i) the state law claim seeks to vindicate "legal or equitable rights that are equivalent" to one of the bundle of exclusive rights already protected by copyright law under 17 U.S.C. § 106—styled the "general scope requirement"; and (ii) the particular work to which the state law claim is being applied falls within the type of works protected by the Copyright Act under Sections 102 and 103—styled the "subject matter requirement."
>
> The district court concluded that the NBA's misappropriation claim was not preempted because, with respect to the underlying games, as opposed to the broadcasts, the subject matter requirement was not met. . . . We hold that where the challenged copying or misappropriation relates in part to the copyrighted broadcasts of the games, the subject matter requirement is met as to both the broadcasts and the games. . . .
>
> Although game broadcasts are copyrightable while the underlying games are not, the Copyright Act should not be read to distinguish between the two when analyzing the preemption of a misappropriation claim based on copying or taking from the copyrightable work. . . .
>
> Copyrightable material often contains uncopyrightable elements within it, but Section 301 preemption bars state law misappropriation claims with respect to uncopyrightable as well as copyrightable elements. . . .
>
> It is often difficult or impossible to separate the fixed copyrightable work from the underlying uncopyrightable events or facts. Moreover, Congress, in extending copyright protection only to the broadcasts and not to the underlying events, intended that the latter be in the public domain. . . .

105 F.3d at 848-849.

Although the *Motorola* court held that a state law "hot-news" misappropriation claim was not preempted, it determined all its elements were not satisfied because the defendants' collection and dissemination of only real-time factual information did not have an adverse economic effect on the production or broadcasting of NBA games:

> We therefore find the extra elements—those in addition to the elements of copyright infringement—that allow a "hot-news" claim to survive preemption are: (i) the time-sensitive value of factual information, (ii) the free-riding by a defendant, and (iii) the threat to the very existence of the product or service provided by the plaintiff.
>
> We conclude that Motorola and STATS have not engaged in unlawful misappropriation under the "hot-news" test set out above. To be sure, some of the elements of a "hot-news" *INS* claim are met. The information transmitted to SportsTrax is not precisely contemporaneous, but it is nevertheless time-sensitive. Also, the NBA does provide, or will shortly do so, information like that available through SportsTrax. . . .
>
> However, there are critical elements missing in the NBA's attempt to assert a "hot-news" *INS*-type claim. As framed by the NBA, their claim compresses and confuses three different informational products. The first product is generating the information by playing the games; the second product is transmitting live, full descriptions of those games; and the third product is collecting and retransmitting strictly factual information about the games. The first and second products are the NBA's primary business: producing basketball games for live attendance and licensing copyrighted broadcasts of those games. The collection and retransmission of strictly factual material about the games is a different product: e.g., box-scores in newspapers, summaries of statistics on television sports news, and real-time facts to be transmitted to pagers. In our view, the NBA has failed to show any competitive effect whatsoever from SportsTrax on the first and second products and a lack of any free-riding by SportsTrax on the third.
>
> With regard to the NBA's primary products—producing basketball games with live attendance and licensing copyrighted broadcasts of those games—there is no evidence that anyone regards SportsTrax or the AOL site as a substitute for attending NBA games or watching them on television. In fact, Motorola markets SportsTrax as being designed "for those times when you cannot be at the arena, watch the game on TV, or listen to the radio. . . ."
>
> The NBA argues that the pager market is also relevant to a "hot-news" *INS*-type claim and that SportsTrax's future competition with Gamestats satisfies any missing element. We agree that there is a separate market for the real-time transmission of factual information to pagers or similar devices, such as STATS's AOL site. However, we disagree that SportsTrax is in any sense free-riding off Gamestats.
>
> An indispensable element of an *INS* "hot-news" claim is free riding by a defendant on a plaintiff's product, enabling the defendant to produce a directly competitive product for less money because it has lower costs. SportsTrax is not such a product. The use of pagers to transmit real-time information about NBA games requires: (i) the collecting of facts about the games; (ii) the transmission of these facts on a network; (iii) the assembling of them by the particular service; and (iv) the transmission of them to pagers or an on-line computer site. Appellants are in no way free-riding on Gamestats. Motorola and STATS expend their own resources to collect purely factual information generated in NBA games to transmit to SportsTrax pagers. They have their own network and assemble and transmit data themselves.

105 F.3d at 853-854.

If athletic events and factual accounts of games are not copyrightable, why are some state law remedies for their unauthorized commercial appropriation preempted by §301 of the Copyright Act? Although it found a separate commercial market for the real-time transmission of game accounts, why did the court hold that defendants' conduct was not infringing the NBA's rights?

Consistent with *Motorola*, courts have held that unauthorized commercial usage of sports statistics that are in the public domain does not violate state misappropriation law, although it is impermissible to do so in a manner that creates a likelihood of consumer confusion regarding authorization or sponsorship, which would constitute trademark infringement and/or unfair competition. In *National Football League v. Governor of the State of Delaware*, 435 F. Supp. 1372 (D. Del. 1977), the NFL sought to enjoin the unauthorized use of its game schedules and scores as the basis for a Delaware state football lottery. Although defendants profited from public popularity generated by NFL games, the court found no misappropriation of the league's property:

> The only tangible product of plaintiffs' labor which defendants utilize in the Delaware Lottery are the schedule of NFL games and the scores. These are obtained from public sources and are utilized only after plaintiffs have disseminated them at large and no longer have any expectation of generating revenue from further dissemination.

Id. at 1377.

The following case illustrates that the producer of a sports event may limit access to real-time scores and game information by contract (for example, by allowing admission only if ticket holders or members of the media agree to comply with certain conditions).

MORRIS COMMUNICATIONS CORP. v. PGA TOUR, INC.

235 F. Supp. 2d 1269 (M.D. Fla. 2002), *aff'd*, 364 F.3d 1288
(11th Cir.), *cert. denied*, 543 U.S. 919 (2004)

SCHLESINGER, District Judge.

At issue in this case is the extent to which the PGA Tour may be allowed to limit the access of Morris [Communications Corporation ("Morris")] and other media entities to its own private golf tournaments. Specifically, the Court must resolve whether the PGA Tour may legally condition access to its tournaments on Morris's agreement not to syndicate "real-time" golf scores obtained from an on-site media center. . . .

The parties' dispute in this case concerns the on-line publication of "real-time" golf scores [which] are scores that are transmitted electronically nearly contemporaneously to their actual occurrence on the golf course. In this way, Internet users are able to track during a golf tournament each participating player's progress on a hole-by-hole basis. In order to improve its scoring capabilities for its tournaments, including transmission of real-time golf scores over the Internet, the PGA Tour has designed and implemented an elaborate electronic relay known as the Real-Time Scoring System ("RTSS").

RTSS works as follows: During a given golf tournament, volunteer workers called "hole reporters" follow each group of golfers on the golf course and tabulate the scores of each player at the end of each hole. The scores are then collected by other volunteers located at each of the eighteen greens on the golf course, who, with the aid of hand-held wireless radios, relay the scoring information to a remote production truck staffed by personnel employed by the PGA Tour.[6] The scores of all participating golfers are then processed at the remote production truck and transmitted by the PGA Tour to its Internet web-site, pga tour.com. The PGA Tour claims that it takes "about five minutes" for the information to be routed from the production truck to pgatour.com. At the same time, real-time scores are also transmitted to an on-site media center where accredited members of the media are able to access the scores. The same information is also transmitted to various electronic "leaderboards" located throughout the golf course for public viewing by spectators. The leaderboards do not simultaneously show the real time scores of all participating golfers. Rather, they typically show only the top ten or fifteen scores.

Due to the nature and size of golf courses, which may span as much as 150 acres, comprehensive real-time scores—that is, up-to-the-minute scores of every competitor—can only be compiled using a relay system such as RTSS. During a golf tournament, different groups of players compete contemporaneously at different holes such that any one spectator can only view a limited number of players at any one of the eighteen holes. Thus, in order to generate real-time scores, it is necessary to have individuals stationed at each hole as the tournament progresses so that the entire golf course can be monitored simultaneously. Acknowledging that some kind of relay system is needed to generate the type of real-time scoring information it wishes to syndicate, Morris submits that it is unable to implement such a system itself due to the PGA Tour rules prohibiting unauthorized use of wireless communication devices on the golf course at its tournaments. . . .

[Morris' federal and state antitrust claims] alleged that the PGA Tour possesses monopoly power over access to its golf tournaments and has unfairly used that power by attempting to stifle competition in the separate market for syndicated real-time golf scores. In response, the PGA Tour argued that it enjoys a property right in RTSS and that its regulations restricting the syndication of real-time golf scoring information gathered and generated by RTSS constitute a reasonable safeguard against would-be free riders seeking to unfairly capitalize on its product. . . .

Morris asks the Court to force the PGA Tour to provide Morris with the compilation of scores, for which the PGA Tour spends considerable money and time creating, at no cost to Morris. . . .

Morris contends that it is not free-riding . . . [In *NBA. v. Motorola, Inc.*, 105 F.3d 841(2d Cir.1997)] the court found that Motorola did not free-ride when it created a network that disseminated scores from NBA basketball games. Three distinctions between Motorola and the instant case make Morris's claim untenable. First, the *Motorola* court used a very high standard for free-riding that is applicable only in cases with the hot-news exception . . . More importantly, the information that Motorola used to create its product was in the public domain, having been broadcast on television or radio. Specifically, Motorola-paid

---

6. Under newly developed technology known as "Shotlink," the walking scorers themselves will be able to relay scores directly to the production truck. In addition, the new technology allows the scorers to transmit additional data such as club selection, the lie of the ball, and the distance to the pin. Morris has not sought to syndicate any information obtainable from Shotlink other than the raw score.

reporters, who had heard the radio or television broadcast scores, reported the information to a central location and merely relayed what had been known to the world. Golf, unlike basketball, precludes a single person gathering all the information occurring on all 18 holes. So when television and radio cover a basketball game, the score is presented to the public through those media outlets, allowing Motorola to obtain the information and republish it. If Morris were able to gather scores from all 18 holes through a television or radio broadcast, Morris could then republish that information, absent a hot-news exception. However, golf's atypical format prevents any single television or radio broadcast from providing results from all 18 holes live. The PGA Tour does publish the scores in the media center,[18] but the media cannot disseminate that information except as the PGA Tour's press credentials allow them to do.[19] As a result, the scores, which are not protected by copyright, remain outside the public domain and within the PGA Tour's control, because the PGA Tour provides access with certain restrictions.[20] Finally, Motorola benefited from the NBA's costs in producing and marketing the games and from the radio and television stations who paid for broadcast rights: that is Motorola capitalized on the NBA's positive externalities. However, the NBA and the broadcast stations had already reaped the profits of their investment, and the information was in the public domain at the moment of broadcasting. Additionally, once in the public domain, Motorola "expend[ed] their own resources to collect purely factual information generated in NBA games." *Id.* at 854. While here, Morris does not expend its own resources in gathering information, which is not in the public domain, but instead free-rides on the PGA Tour's compilation of scores. . . .

The PGA Tour claims that the restrictions have a valid business justification, because they are necessary to protect a property right in the scores that it compiled by use of RTSS. Morris argues that the PGA Tour lacks a property right in the score, thus negating the claimed business justification. For the following reasons, the Court finds that the PGA Tour does have a property right in the scores compiled by the use of RTSS, but that property right vanishes when the scores are in the public domain.

The PGA Tour's property right does not come from copyright law, as copyright law does not protect factual information, like golf scores. *See Feist Publications v. Rural Tel. Serv. Co.*, 499 U.S. 340, 348, 111 S.Ct. 1282, 113 L.Ed.2d 358 (1991). However, the PGA Tour controls the right of access to that information and can place restrictions on those attending the private event, giving the PGA Tour a property right that the Court will protect. . . . [T]he instant case deals with facts that are not subject to copyright protection. The compiler of the information . . . collects information, which it created, at a cost. Also the events occur on private property to which the general public does not have unfettered access, and the creator of the event can place restrictions upon those who enter the

---

18. The PGA Tour also publishes the scores of the top players to the spectators, who are present under a license from the PGA Tour which prevents their dissemination of the scores off the course.

19. Currently, the PGA Tour allows Morris to publish the scores as quickly as it can re-key them from the media center, but the PGA Tour does not allow Morris to sell or syndicate that information. Also, a compiler of information can limit the dissemination of that information through contracts, including contracts found on tickets. *See ProCD v. Zeidenberg*, 86 F.3d 1447, 1451 (7th Cir. 1996).

20. Even if the information were in the public domain, the PGA Tour would have the ability to limit the use of the information it provides to Morris under contract law. [Citation omitted.]

private property. The vastly increased speed that the Internet makes available does not change the calculus or the underlying property right. Accordingly, the PGA Tour . . . has a property right in the compilation of scores, but that property right disappears when the underlying information is in the public domain.

Whether the PGA Tour has a separate right to license or sell broadcast rights on the Internet, like sports and entertainment producers currently enjoy in dealing with television and radio, is a novel question. . . .

Both parties would certainly agree that the Internet provides an opportunity to profit from a product by selling advertisement. Television, radio, and print media operate on a similar, if not identical, principle: the selling of advertisement to viewers, listeners, or readers of entertainment, be it sports, entertainment, or news. Therefore, the Court finds that the PGA Tour has a right to sell or license its product, championship golf, and its derivative product, golf scores, on the Internet in the same way the PGA Tour currently sells its rights to television broadcasting stations. . . .

Accordingly, the Court finds that the PGA Tour is justified in its restrictions because (1) Morris free-rides on the PGA Tour's efforts, (2) the PGA Tour has a property right in the scores before they are in the public domain, and (3) the PGA Tour has the right to license or sell broadcasting rights of its products over the Internet. . . .

[I]n this case, Morris is seeking access to the media center and the scoring system at no cost, putting it at a competitive advantage to the PGA Tour. The PGA Tour offers access to the scores through a license as evidenced by its contract with USA Today, and Morris is free to negotiate for the purchase of a license which would put it on a competitive plane with the PGA Tour. . . .

[The court granted the PGA Tour's summary judgment motion and dismissed Morris's antitrust claims.]

NOTE AND QUESTIONS

Why does the PGA Tour have a property right in its real-time golf scores, and how long does this right last? Is *Morris Communications* consistent with *Motorola's* holding that the NBA did not have a protectable property interest in its real-time game scores?

In *Morris Communications Corp. v. PGA Tour, Inc*, 364 F.3d 1288, 1298 (11th Cir. 2004), the Eleventh Circuit affirmed that the PGA Tour's property right in compiled real-time golf scores enables it to prevent their unauthorized commercial usage:

> The district court correctly found that a company—even a monopolist company—that expends time and money to create a valuable product does not violate the antitrust laws when it declines to provide that product to its competitors for free. PGA has accommodated Morris at every step along the way, has agreed to sell its product to Morris, and has acted appropriately to protect its economic interests and investments. Yet Morris demands that it be given access to the product of PGA's proprietary RTSS, without compensating PGA, so that Morris can then sell that product to others for a fee. That is the classic example of "free-riding."

In *Wisconsin Interscholastic Athletic Assn. v. Gannett Co., Inc.*, 658 F.3d 614 (7th Cir. 2011), the Seventh Circuit held that a high school athletic association, which the parties stipulated is a state actor, has a property right in its tournament games and that its exclusive contract to stream games over the Internet does not violate the First Amendment. Relying on *Zacchini v. Scripps-Howard Broadcasting Co.*, the court ruled that the "WIAA has the right to package and distribute its performance; nothing in the First Amendment confers on the media an affirmative right to broadcast entire performances." *Id.* at 622. It explained:

> The idea that reporting and streaming are synonymous is also at odds with experience in the private sector. There, everyone understands that there is a difference between a description of an event like the Super Bowl, Women's World Cup, or the College World Series and the right both to videotape that entertainment and then to publish it as one sees fit. In each of these situations the producer of the entertainment—the NFL, FIFA, or the NCAA—normally signs a lucrative contract for exclusive, or semi-exclusive, broadcast rights for the performance. Meanwhile, all media report on the events. *Cf. Home Box Office*, 587 F.2d at 1253 ("Contracts conferring the exclusive right to broadcast sporting events and artistic or theatrical performances are commonplace."). Gannett's argument boils down to an assertion that a government actor cannot, under any circumstances, act like the NFL, FIFA or NCAA. But the First Amendment does not require such a draconian rule. . . . WIAA is not prohibiting the media from reporting on its events, nor is it imposing outrageous fee for media members to have access to games. It does not require the media to submit stories or blog post to its editors before they are published. Any of these actions would make this a significantly different case.

Id. at 628-629.

The *Morris Communications* district court observes that contract law may be used to limit event spectators' use of scores and accounts of live sporting events. On behalf of a sports team, draft appropriate language for spectator admission tickets and event signage to prohibit unauthorized use of such information, including a description of any action that may be taken for noncompliance with these terms.

PROBLEM 12-3

a. Since 1914, several private rooftop clubs that overlook Wrigley Field have sold tickets for fans to watch Chicago Cubs home baseball games live or on television. Cubs home games generally are sold out, and all games are televised. These rooftop clubs have business licenses issued by the City of Chicago. All of them have spectator capacities of at least 30 persons, and some charge patrons as much as $150 per game. Consider the likely success of the Cubs' lawsuit alleging that the rooftop clubs' conduct constitutes copyright infringement and misappropriation. Also consider the Cubs' potential nonlegal remedies and how this dispute might be amicably resolved from the perspective of all parties. See *Detroit Baseball Club v. Deppert*, 27 N.W. 856 (Mich. 1886); Ronnie Bitman, Note, *Rocking Wrigley: The Chicago Cubs' Off-Field Struggle to Compete for Ticket Sales with Its Rooftop Neighbors*, 56 Fed. Comm. L.J. 377 (2004).

b. MLB Advanced Media, Major League Baseball's Internet subsidiary, claims ownership of all real-time data used by sports websites to provide live graphical simulations of baseball games over the Internet. However, some webcasters operate sites providing very detailed game accounts, including the location of each pitch, that are updated every 30 to 90 seconds. Some web-casters obtain this information from employees who are present at MLB games; whereas others get their data from employees who are watching tele-vised games or listening to radio broadcasts. One webcaster is licensed to use the real-time data from MLB games, but no others are willing to pay the fee for obtaining licensing rights. Evaluate whether the unauthorized description of a baseball game infringes MLB's intellectual property rights.

D.   ATHLETE'S LANHAM ACT AND STATE LAW PRIVACY, REPUTATION, AND PUBLICITY RIGHTS

Today's professional athlete is a celebrity and probably attains that status, at least locally, much earlier than the onset of his or her professional career. The best-known athletes have entered into lucrative deals to promote and endorse a wide variety of products and services. Income earned from the licensing of a player's identity to sell products and services may be greater than that derived from his or her athletic earnings. For example, the most elite and widely rec-ognized male and female athletes, such as LeBron James, Tiger Woods, David Beckham, Maria Sharapova, and Danica Patrick earn millions annually, far sur-passing their income from purely athletic accomplishments. All of them have multiple endorsement deals carefully crafted by their representatives. The evo-lution of the various laws protecting an athlete's personality rights requires con-sideration of trademark and unfair competition under the federal Lanham Act, which was previously considered in this chapter, as well as state defamation, privacy, and publicity laws as well.

1.   Lanham Act

The unauthorized misappropriation of an athlete's name, likeness, or other aspects of his or her identity violates §43(a) of the Lanham Act, 15 U.S.C. §1125(a), if it causes consumer confusion regarding whether he or she has endorsed or sponsored particular products and services. This federal statutory claim provides a consumer protection-based cause of action, and state trade-mark and unfair competition laws establish a similar standard. As the Ninth Circuit has observed: "Many people may assume that when a celebrity's name is used in a television commercial, the celebrity endorses the product advertised. Likelihood of confusion as to endorsement is therefore a question for the jury." *Abdul Jabbar v. General Motors Corp.*, 85 F.3d 407, 413 (9th Cir. 1996).

In *Hillerich & Bradsby v. Christian Brothers*, 943 F. Supp. 1136 (D. Minn. 1996), defendant was selling its Pro-Rite hockey blades with the name "Messier" clearly affixed on the blade and product label without the permission of Mark Messier, one of professional hockey's most recognized players who led the Edmonton Oilers and the New York Rangers to a total of six Stanley Cup championships and was twice voted the most valuable player in the National Hockey League. The court ruled that this unauthorized commercial use of Messier's name created the false impression that he endorsed defendant's hockey blades in violation of

§43(a) and enjoined defendant from using Messier's name on its products or in connection with their advertising and sale without his express permission.

An athlete may use his or her name as a trademark or service mark, and it may be federally registered under the Lanham Act after acquiring secondary meaning as the source or origin of goods or services (i.e., it functions as a brand name that the public associates with an identifiable athlete). For example, the name "Tiger Woods" has been federally registered as a trademark for art prints, calendars, mounted photographs, notebooks, pencils, pens, posters, trading cards, and unmounted photographs. Unauthorized usage of an athlete's federally registered name that creates a likelihood of consumer confusion regarding the source or sponsorship of goods or services constitutes trademark infringement and unfair competition in violation of the Lanham Act and virtually all state laws.

Courts require that a person's photo, image, likeness, or distinguishing characteristic actually function as a trademark to be protected by the Lanham Act's provisions prohibiting trademark infringement. In *ETW Corp. v. Jireh Publishing, Inc.*, 332 F.3d 915, 922 (6th Cir. 2003), the Sixth Circuit observed:

> Here, ETW claims protection under the Lanham Act for any and all images of Tiger Woods. This is an untenable claim. ETW asks us, in effect, to constitute Woods himself as a walking, talking trademark. Images and likenesses of Woods are not protectable as a trademark because they do not perform the trademark function of designation. They do not distinguish and identify the source of goods. They cannot function as a trademark because there are undoubtedly thousands of images and likenesses of Woods taken by countless photographers, and drawn, sketched, or painted by numerous artists, which have been published in many forms of media, and sold and distributed throughout the world. No reasonable person could believe image, they all originated with Woods.

See also *Pirone v. Macmillan, Inc.*, 894 F.2d 579, 583 (2d Cir. 1990) ("[u]nder some circumstances, a photograph of a person may be a valid trademark—if, for example, a particular photograph was consistently used on specific goods").

In recent years, well-known athletes have sought to federally register their nicknames or other unique identifying characteristics. Heisman trophy winner and NFL quarterback Tim Tebow is seeking to register "Tebowing," which depicts him in the Christian athlete practice of dropping to one knee in prayer. Anthony Davis, who led the University of Kentucky to the 2012 NCAA men's basketball championship and was the first pick in the 2012 NBA draft, is claiming trademark rights in the phrases "Fear the Brow" and "Raise the Brow," hoping to commercially exploit his unibrow (i.e., attached-in-the-center eyebrows). Texas A&M quarterback Johnny Manziel, the 2012 Heisman trophy recipient, filed an intent to use application under the Lanham Act for "Johnny Football," which provides constructive notice of his claimed trademark rights, although the NCAA's amateurism rules prohibit him from commercially benefiting from the usage or licensing of this mark until after his college career ends.

2. State Laws

In the United States, state laws protecting the reputation, privacy, and publicity rights of celebrities, including athletes, are still developing and vary by jurisdiction. The First Amendment of the U.S. Constitution, which protects freedom of speech and expression, as well as state constitutional provisions, provides a significant limit on the ability of state laws to recognize and protect reputation, privacy, and publicity rights and must always be considered.

a. Defamation

The tort of defamation includes both oral (slander) and written (libel) statements. The scope of its legal protection is not limited to celebrities, but defamation assumes special significance in this context. Professional athletes are written about all the time in various forms of media, including blogs, Twitter, and many others. Their lives, both professionally and personally, are scrutinized, at times to excruciating degrees. Thus, one must be mindful of the basics of defamation.

Although there are variations in state law definitions and approaches to defamation, a general definition of defamation is set forth in the Restatement (Second) of Torts, §558 (1977), which provides, "To create liability for defamation, there must be: (a) a false and defamatory statement concerning another; (b) an unprivileged communication to a third party; (c) fault amounting at least to negligence on the part of the publisher; and (d) either actionability of the statement irrespective of special harm or the existence of special harm caused by the publication."

Several observations can be made about this definition regarding the world of sports. Statements must be both false and defamatory, meaning they tend to damage the reputation of the person identified by the statement in the minds of others. Not included in the definition but generally accepted as a part thereof is that the false statement must be one of fact, not merely opinion. Most of what is written about the professional performance of athletes is opinion, which is not legally actionable even if it harms his or her reputation. See, e.g., *Time, Inc. v. Johnston*, 448 F.2d 378, 380 (4th Cir. 1971) ("as a paid performer," professional athlete "assumed the risk of publicity, good or bad, . . . so far as it concerned his public performance"); *Washington v. Smith*, 893 F. Supp. 60 (D.D.C. 1995), *aff'd*, 80 F.3d 555 (D.C. Cir. 1996) (statement in newspaper article that coach "usually finds a way to screw things up" and "[t]his season will be no different" is nonactionable opinion regarding team's potential for upcoming season and coach's ability); *Parks v. Steinbrenner*, 520 N.Y.S.2d 374 (N.Y. App. Div. 1987) ("'rhetorical hyperbole' that generally accompany the communication of displeasure at an umpire's 'calls'" is statement of opinion, not fact).

On the other hand, asserting that an athlete "fixed" a boxing match and used cocaine with his opponent thereafter, or knowingly used "loaded" gloves are statements of fact that harm one's professional reputation and may cause resulting economic loss. *Cobb v. Time, Inc.*, 278 F.3d 629 (6th Cir. 2002); *Dempsey v. Time Inc.*, 252 N.Y.S.2d 186 (N.Y. Sup. Ct. 1964). See also *Faigin v. Kelly*, 978 F. Supp. 420 (D. N.H. 1997), *aff'd*, 184 F.3d 67 (1st Cir. 1999) (pro football player's charge that former agent engaged in untrustworthy conduct in handling his business affairs). False factual statements about an athlete's personal life such as alleged criminal conduct also are defamatory.

During the past 50 years, the traditional state law elements of defamation have been modified by federal constitutional law; therefore, First Amendment issues must also be considered. A prominent athlete is considered to be a "public figure" who must prove by clear and convincing evidence that a defamatory statement was made with "actual malice," meaning the defendant had knowledge of its falsity or a reckless disregard regarding whether or not it was true. See, e.g, *Cobb v. Time, Inc.*, 278 F.3d 629 (6th Cir. 2002); *Cepeda v. Cowles Magazines and Broadcasting*, 392 F.2d 417 (9th Cir. 1968). Thus, although athletes receive some protection through the laws of defamation, it is not the chief legal theory used to protect most invasions of an athlete's rights.

b.   Right of Privacy

The right of privacy, as a distinct concept of legal protection, was first enunciated in a famous law review article by Samuel Warren and Louis Brandeis that was published in the *Harvard Law Review* in 1890. Warren and Brandeis argued that a distinct tort protecting a person's right to privacy existed at common law and should be recognized:

> Later, there came a recognition of man's spiritual nature, of his feelings and his intellect. Gradually, the scope of these legal rights broadened; and now the right to life has come to mean the right to enjoy life, the right to be let alone; the right to liberty secures the exercise of extensive civil privileges; and the term "property" has grown to comprise every form of possession—intangible, as well as tangible.

Samuel D. Warren and Louis D. Brandeis, *The Right to Privacy*, 4 Harv. L. Rev. 193 (1890).

A further impetus to the development of the right of privacy occurred many years later through the various writings of Professor William Prosser. He identified four separate categories that he advocated should be subsumed under a general concept of privacy: (1) protection against intrusion into one's private affairs; (2) avoidance of disclosure of one's embarrassing private facts; (3) protection against publicity placing one in a false light in the public eye; and (4) remedies for appropriation, usually for commercial advantage, of one's name or likeness. William Prosser, *Privacy*, 48 Cal. L. Rev. 383 (1960). These four categories of torts have largely been adopted in most states, though there is hardly unanimity as to the nature and scope of their common law development by courts. In some states, statutes have codified these torts.

The first three torts concern intrusions into one's private life and affairs, and athletes have relied on one or more of these legal theories in asserting various invasion of privacy claims. In some early cases, athletes asserted that the unauthorized use of their name or likeness in connection with the advertising or sale of products violated their common law privacy rights. *O'Brien v. Pabst Sales Co.*, 124 F.2d 167 (5th Cir. 1941), illustrates that courts generally were not receptive to these claims. In *O'Brien*, a famous professional football player alleged that the unauthorized use of his photograph in a calendar advertising defendant's beer invaded his right of privacy. Because he was not a private person and "the publicity he got was only that which he had been constantly seeking and receiving," the Fifth Circuit ruled, "Considered from the standpoint merely of an invasion of plaintiff's right of privacy, no case was made out, because plaintiff was an outstanding national football figure and had completely publicized his name and his pictures." *Id.* at 169-170.

However, courts have recognized claims for publicity placing an athlete in a false light in the public eye. See, e.g., *Spahn v. Julian Messner, Inc.*, 286 N.Y.S.2d 832 (N.Y. 1967) (publication of unauthorized fictionalized biography of well-known baseball player violates statutory privacy law). In addition, an NFL club was found liable for its team physician's known false published statement that a player had a fatal blood disease. *Chuy v. Phila. Eagles Football Club*, 595 F.2d 1265 (3d Cir. 1979) (intentional infliction of emotional distress).

The fourth privacy tort is readily distinguishable from the others because of its recognition of the commercial value in one's name or likeness. Today, it is the basis for a separate tort know as the "right of publicity," which is recognized in a majority of states by common law or statute.

c.   Right of Publicity

Courts initially refused to characterize celebrity names and likenesses as protectable property rights. In *Hanna Mfg. Co. v. Hillerich & Bradsby Co.*, 78 F.2d 763, 766 (5th Cir. 1935), the Fifth Circuit held that "fame is not merchandise." It concluded that an athlete has a valid claim for unauthorized commercial use of his name only if such usage falsely suggests that he uses or endorses the product, thereby constituting unfair competition.

In 1953, a U.S. court recognized the right of publicity for the first time. *Haelan Laboratories, Inc. v. Topps Chewing Gum, Inc.*, 202 F.2d 866 (2d Cir. 1953), *cert. denied*, 346 U.S. 816 (1953). The case involved a dispute over the rights to use baseball players' images on bubblegum trading cards. One company had been assigned these rights by the players; however, the defendant produced its own cards without the players' permission. One of the central issues was whether the players' rights, if any, were assignable—or were they strictly personal to the player. The Second Circuit held that New York law recognized a common law right of publicity, which is a freely transferable property right, not just a personal right. The court explained "in addition to and independent of the right of privacy . . . a man has a right in the publicity value of his photograph, i.e., the right to grant the exclusive privilege of publishing his picture." *Id.* at 868. See generally J. Gordon Hylton, *Baseball Cards and the Birth of the Right of Publicity: The Curious Case of* Haelan Laboratories v. Topps Chewing Gum, 12 Marq. Sports L. Rev. 273 (2001).

Since the *Haelan* decision 50 years ago, there has been a lot of litigation to determine if a common law right of publicity exists in a particular jurisdiction. The common law development of the right of publicity certainly has not been uniform nationwide. In many states the right of publicity has been created and defined by statute. See generally 1 J. Thomas McCarthy, *Rights of Publicity and Privacy* (2d ed.), §§6:1-6.9 (West Group 2012).

By common law or statute, a majority of states (but not all) now recognize a right of publicity property-based claim for unauthorized commercial use of an athlete's identity. As one court observed, "a celebrity has a legitimate proprietary interest in his public personality. A celebrity must be considered to have invested his years of practice and competition in a public personality which eventually may reach marketable status. . . . A name is commercially valuable as an endorsement of a product or for use for financial gain only because the public recognizes it and attributes good will and feats of skill or accomplishments of one sort or another to that personality." *Uhlaender v. Henricksen*, 316 F. Supp. 1277, 1282-1283 (D. Minn. 1970).

The right of publicity is a property right that may be transferred and is descendible (if the jurisdiction recognized such right at the time of the person's death). By contrast, defamation and privacy rights generally are personal in nature, cannot be assigned, and expire when the person dies.

i.　Elements of a Right of Publicity Claim

NEWCOMBE v. ADOLF COORS CO.

157 F.3d 686 (9th Cir. 1998)

HUG, Chief Judge.

[Don] Newcombe is a former major league baseball all-star who pitched for the Brooklyn Dodgers and other teams from 1949 until 1960. He had previously starred in the so-called Negro leagues and was one of the first African-American players to play in the major leagues after Jackie Robinson broke the color barrier in 1947. Newcombe is the only player in major league history to have won the Most Valuable Player Award, the Cy Young Award, and the Rookie of the Year Award. . . .

Newcombe's baseball career was cut short due to his service in the Army and a personal battle with alcohol. He is a recovering alcoholic and he has devoted a substantial amount of time using his fame to advocate the dangers of alcohol. . . .

Killian's Irish Red Beer, owned by Coors Brewing Co., published an advertisement in the February 1994 *Sports Illustrated* "swimsuit edition" that featured a drawing of an old-time baseball game. The drawing was on the left half of the full-page advertisement while the right half was filled with text and a picture of a glass of beer. The baseball scene focused on a pitcher in the windup position and the background included a single infielder and an old-fashioned outfield fence. The players' uniforms did not depict an actual team, and the background did not depict an actual stadium. However, Newcombe, along with family, friends and former teammates, immediately recognized the pitcher featured in the advertisement as Newcombe in his playing days.

Newcombe filed suit . . . alleging that his identity had been misappropriated in violation of California statutory and common law, that the advertisement was defamatory because it portrayed him—a recovering alcoholic—as endorsing beer, that the advertisement was negligently created, and that the defendants intentionally inflicted emotional distress upon him. He sought to enjoin the advertisement from future publication, and he asked for $100,000,000 in damages. . . .

While denying that the pitcher in the advertisement was a "likeness" of Newcombe, Coors admitted that the drawing in the color advertisement was based on a newspaper photograph of Newcombe pitching in the 1949 World Series. The drawing and the newspaper photograph are virtually identical, as though the black and white newspaper photo had been traced and colored in. The only major differences between the newspaper photograph of Newcombe and the drawing of him are that the pitcher's uniform number has been changed from "36" to "39," and the bill of the hat in the drawing is a different color from the rest of the hat. Otherwise, the drawing in the advertisement appears to be an exact replica of the newspaper photograph of Newcombe. . . .

CAL. CIV. CODE § 3344 AND COMMON LAW MISAPPROPRIATION

Newcombe contends that the defendants violated his right of privacy and used his likeness and identity to their commercial advantage in violation of his statutory rights under Cal. Civ.Code § 3344 and common law right of privacy. California has long recognized a common law right of privacy for the protection of a person's name and likeness against appropriation by others for their advantage. *Eastwood v. Superior Court of Los Angeles County,* 149 Cal.App.3d 409, 416, 198 Cal.Rptr. 342 (1983). This California common law cause of action has been complemented by the enactment of Cal. Civ.Code § 3344. That section neither replaces nor codifies the common law cause of action. Section 3344(g) specifically provides that the statutory remedies of the section are cumulative and in addition to any others provided by law.

To sustain a common law cause of action for commercial misappropriation, a plaintiff must prove: "(1) the defendant's use of the plaintiff's identity; (2) the appropriation of plaintiff's name or likeness to defendant's advantage, commercially or otherwise; (3) lack of consent; and (4) resulting injury." *Eastwood,* 149 Cal.App.3d at 417, 198 Cal.Rptr. 342.

Cal. Civ.Code § 3344 provides in relevant part, "Any person who knowingly uses another's name, voice, signature, photograph, or likeness, in any manner . . . for purposes of advertising . . . without such person's prior consent . . . shall be liable for any damages sustained by the person." Cal. Civ.Code § 3344(a). Section 3344, unlike a common law claim, thus requires a plaintiff to establish: (1) a "knowing" use; (2) for purposes of advertising, and (3) a direct connection between the use and the commercial purpose.

[W]e must first decide whether Newcombe's likeness was actually used. Necessarily, we must address how identifiable an image must be to constitute a likeness under the common law and section 3344. Neither the common law nor section 3344 indicate to whom or to what degree the plaintiff must be identifiable from the alleged likeness.

We find a useful definition in section 3344 itself. Section 3344(b) states that a photograph must be "readily identifiable" as the plaintiff in order for the plaintiff to prevail. A person is deemed to be readily identifiable from a photograph "when one who views the photograph with the naked eye can reasonably determine that the person depicted in the photograph is the same person who is complaining of its unauthorized use." Cal. Civ.Code § 3344(b)(1). Because a likeness and a photograph are so similar—a photograph is a visual image that is obtained by using a camera while a likeness is a visual image of a person other than a photograph—we find application of this standard appropriate to likenesses as well as photographs. Therefore, we hold that in order to constitute Newcombe's likeness, the pitcher depicted in the advertisement must be readily identifiable as Newcombe.

Having viewed the advertisement, we hold that a triable issue of fact has been raised as to whether Newcombe is readily identifiable as the pitcher in the advertisement. Initially, we note that the drawing in the advertisement and the newspaper photograph of Newcombe upon which the drawing was based are virtually identical. The pitcher's stance, proportions and shape are identical to the newspaper photograph of Newcombe; even the styling of the uniform is identical, right down to the wrinkles in the pants. The defendants maintain that stance alone cannot suffice to render a person readily identifiable, and that even if it could, the drawing of the pitcher in the advertisement was essentially generic and could have been any one of thousands of people who have taken to the pitcher's mound to throw a baseball. We disagree.

It may be the case that Newcombe's stance is essentially generic, but based on the record before us, Newcombe is the only one who has such a stance. The record contains pictures of other pitchers in the windup position but none of these pitchers has a stance similar to Newcombe's, thus giving us no basis to reach the conclusion proposed by the defendants that the pitcher in the advertisement is "generic." . . . [T]here is a genuine issue of material fact as to whether Newcombe's stance was so distinctive that the defendants used his likeness by using a picture of Newcombe's stance.

In addition to the identifiability of the pitcher in the advertisement as Newcombe based on the pitcher's stance, the pitcher's skin is moderately dark, which is quite similar to Newcombe's skin color. A jury could rationally find from this that Newcombe was readily identifiable, even though his facial features were not entirely visible.

Furthermore, while the drawing in the advertisement was slightly altered from the newspaper photograph, that does not alter our conclusion that there is a genuine issue of material fact as to whether the advertisement made use of Newcombe's likeness. For example, the uniform number in the advertisement ("39") is only slightly different than Newcombe's number ("36") — the first number is the same and the second number is simply inverted and the advertisement utilized the same block style numbers that were used on Newcombe's jersey — and it is arguable that the similarity in numbers could either consciously or subconsciously conjure up images of Newcombe. *See Motschenbacher v. R.J. Reynolds Tobacco Co.*, 498 F.2d 821, 822 & 827 (9th Cir.1974) (plaintiff's identity had been used despite fact that number on the plaintiff's car had also been changed from "11" to "71"). Also, we do not find persuasive the fact that the coloring of the bill of the hat in the advertisement is different, in light of the fact that the rest of the uniform is identical to the uniform in the newspaper photograph of Newcombe. *See id.* (plaintiff's identity had been used even though exterior of the car had been altered). . . .

As to the remaining factors for a common law misappropriation claim, the second prong of the *Eastwood* test has been met in that Newcombe's likeness was certainly used to Coors' and Belding's commercial advantage as the drawing which resembled Newcombe was a central figure in the advertisement and the purpose of the advertisement was to attract attention. *See Eastwood*, 149 Cal. App.3d at 420, 198 Cal.Rptr. 342 ("one of the primary purposes of advertising is to motivate a decision to purchase a particular product or service. The first step toward selling a product or service is to attract the consumers' attention."). . . .

The third and fourth prongs of the *Eastwood* test were satisfied with respect to Coors . . . because Newcombe did not consent to the use of his likeness, and he was injured because he was not compensated for the use of his likeness. As a result, we hold that summary judgment was improper as to Coors and Belding on Newcombe's common law misappropriation claim.

With regard to Newcombe's statutory claim, the district court alternatively held that summary judgment was appropriate because Newcombe had failed to establish a direct connection between the use of his likeness and defendants' commercial purpose. Section 3344(e) states that not all uses of likeness are a "use" that requires consent; only those uses where the "likeness was so directly connected with the commercial sponsorship" constitute a "use" under § 3344(a). However, whether such a connection is present "shall be a question of fact." Cal.

Civ.Code § 3344(e). Despite the express command that the connection between defendants' use of Newcombe's likeness and the commercial sponsorship of Killian's Red Beer is a matter of fact, the district court concluded that summary judgment in favor of defendants was appropriate as "it is beyond dispute that defendants were not trying to use plaintiff's identity to sell beer." We disagree. It would not be unreasonable for a jury to conclude that there was a direct connection between Newcombe, as the central feature of the advertisement, and the commercial sponsorship of Killian's Red. . . .

[EDS. The Ninth Circuit reversed the trial court's grant of summary judgment in favor of defendant Coors and the advertisement's creator on Newcombe's common law and statutory right of publicity claims. However, it affirmed the granting of summary judgment on his defamation, false light, negligence, and international infliction of emotional distress claims.]

NOTES AND QUESTIONS

1. *Which State's Law Applies?* In our modern technological age, a right of publicity claim may potentially exist in many jurisdictions. An advertisement that inappropriately uses the likeness of an athlete may be published nationwide, not just in one state. Conflicts of laws principles generally provide that the state law of the plaintiff's domicile governs. As illustrated by *Newcombe*, California recognizes both a common law and statutory right of publicity, but each has differing elements. How do they differ? Some states do not recognize a common law or statutory right of publicity. In several other states, a right of publicity may have been recognized by a federal court, which merely predicts the nature and scope of state law. These cases may be subject to effective reversal by state courts as happened in New York when the state's highest court rejected *Haelan*'s creation of a common law right of publicity under state law. Today, New York recognizes only a statutory right of publicity.

2. *Scope of Protectable Publicity Rights.* What aspects of Don Newcombe's identity were used in the subject advertisement? Courts have broadly defined the protected aspects of an athlete's identity to encompass more than merely his or her name or photo. See, e.g., *Abdul-Jabbar v. Gen. Motors Corp.*, 85 F.3d 407 (9th Cir. 1996) (birth name of Lew Alcindor not abandoned as indicia of identity despite name change to Kareem Abdul-Jabbar after conversion to Islam); *Ventura v. Titan Sports, Inc.*, 65 F.3d 725 (8th Cir. 1995) (voice); *White v. Samsung Elecs. Am., Inc.*, 971 F.2d 1395 (9th Cir. 1992) (robotic caricature); *Motschenbacher v. R.J. Reynolds Tobacco Co.*, 498 F.2d 821 (9th Cir. 1974) (distinctive car driven by professional racer); *Ali v. Playgirl, Inc.*, 447 F. Supp. 723 (S.D.N.Y. 1978) (facial features and moniker "The Greatest"); *Hirsch v. S.C. Johnson & Son, Inc.*, 280 N.W.2d 129 (Wis. 1979) ("Crazy Legs" nickname).

   A state statutory or common law right of publicity may even protect an athletic performance. *Zacchini v. Scripps-Howard Broadcasting Co.*, 433 U.S. 562 (1977). However, federal copyright law preempts a right of publicity claim that is equivalent to any of the exclusive rights within the general scope of copyright protection. In *Baltimore Orioles, Inc. v. Major League Baseball Players Assn.*, 805 F.2d 663 (7th Cir. 1986), the MLB players union claimed that the clubs' unauthorized telecasts of games in which they played violated their publicity rights. Finding that the clubs owned the copyright to televised baseball games, the Seventh Circuit held that the players' publicity rights in their game performances are preempted by the Copyright Act. The court explained:

> [O]nce a performance is reduced to tangible form, there is no distinction between the performance and the recording of the performance for the purpose of preemption under § 301(a). Thus, if a baseball game were not broadcast or were telecast without being recorded, the Players' performances similarly would not be fixed in tangible form and their rights of publicity would not be subject to preemption. [Citation omitted.] By virtue of being videotaped, however, the Players' performances are fixed in tangible form, and any rights of publicity in their performances that are equivalent to the rights contained in the copyright of the telecast are preempted.

Id. at 675. See also *Ventura v. Titan Sports, Inc.*, 65 F.3d 725, 730 n. 6 (8th Cir. 1995) (observing that publicity rights in videotaped commentary of sports event may be preempted). But see *Facenda v. NFL Films, Inc.*, 542 F.3d 1007, 1029 (3d Cir. 2008) ("when defendants use [copyrighted] work 'for the purposes of trade,' such as an advertisement, plaintiffs' right-of-publicity claims have not been held to be preempted").

3. *Unauthorized Commercial Use of an Athlete's Identity, or Use for Purposes of Advertising or Trade. Newcombe* demonstrates that infringement of an athlete's right of publicity occurs if an aspect of one's identity is used to advertise and sell a product or service without permission. Examples of infringing commercial usage include incorporating an athlete's photo into a product such as sports trading cards, drinking glasses, or clothing. *Haelan Labs., Inc. v. Topps Chewing Gum*, 202 F.2d 866 (2d Cir. 1953); *Vinci v. American Can Co.*, 459 N.E.2d 507 (Ohio 1984); *Shamsky v. Garan, Inc.*, 632 N.Y.S.2d 930 (N.Y. Sup. Ct. 1995).

   Courts have applied the "first-sale doctrine" to the right of publicity, which enables the purchaser of authorized sports trading cards or other products bearing an athlete's likeness to resell them or incorporate them into other sports memorabilia such as framed displays. *Allison v. Vintage Sports Plaques*, 136 F.3d 1443 (11th Cir. 1998); *Upper Deck Authenticated, Ltd. v. CPG Direct*, 971 F. Supp. 1337 (S.D. Cal. 1997); *Major League Baseball Players Assn. v. Dad's Kid Corp.*, 806 F. Supp. 458 (S.D.N.Y. 1992). As the Eleventh Circuit explained:

> [A] decision by this court not to apply the first-sale doctrine to right of publicity actions would render tortious the resale of sports trading cards and memorabilia. . . . Such a holding presumably also would prevent, for example, framing a magazine advertisement that bears the image of a celebrity and reselling it as a collector's item, reselling an empty cereal box that bears a celebrity's endorsement, or even reselling a used poster promoting a professional sports team. . . . A holding that the first-sale doctrine does limit the right of publicity, on the other hand, would not eliminate completely a celebrity's control over the use of her name or image; the right of publicity protects against unauthorized use of an image, and a celebrity would continue to enjoy the right to license the use of her image *in the first instance*—and thus enjoy the power to determine when, or if, her image will be distributed. Appellants in this case, for example, have received sizable royalties from the use of their images on the trading cards at issue, images that could not have been used in the first place without permission.

Allison, 136 F.3d at 1449.

Courts generally refuse to characterize the use of a famous athlete's name or identity in connection with the sale of a product as legally permissible incidental or informational use. Rather, such usage is unauthorized commercial appropriation of the athlete's persona. In *Abdul-Jabbar v. Gen. Motors Corp.*, 85 F.3d 407 (9th Cir. 1996), the Ninth Circuit held that, although such information is newsworthy, an auto manufacturer's use of Lew Alcindor's name and college basketball records in a television advertisement is commercial usage. The auto manufacturer gained a commercial advantage from the advertisement, which attracted the attention of television viewers of the 1993 NCAA men's basketball tournament. See also *Town & Country Properties, Inc. v. Riggins*, 457 S.E.2d 356 (Va. 1995) (use of former NFL player's name in flyer to sell his former home violates his publicity rights).

Unauthorized usage of one's identity is a necessary element of a claim for infringement of publicity rights. An athlete's consent to the use of his or her identity for commercial purposes may be either express or implied under the circumstances. The scope of such consent is necessarily determined on a case-by-case basis and requires careful contract drafting to delineate which rights are conferred. See, e.g., *Cepeda v. Swift & Co.*, 415 F.2d 1205 (8th Cir. 1969); *O'Brien v. Pabst Sales Co.*, 124 F.2d 167 (5th Cir. 1941); *Sharman v. C. Schmidt & Sons, Inc.*, 216 F. Supp. 401 (E.D. Pa. 1963); *Andretti v. Rolex Watch U.S.A., Inc.*, 437 N.E.2d 264 (N.Y. 1982).

For a discussion of available remedies for violation of one's publicity rights, see Laura L. Stapleton and Matt McMurphy, *The Professional Athlete's Right of Publicity*, 10 Marq. Sports L. Rev. 23, 53-62 (1999).

4. *Limitations Imposed to Maintain High School and College Athletes' "Amateur" Status.* Although college and high school athletes may have legally protectable publicity rights, the NCAA and state high school athletics governing bodies generally prohibit their exercise in order to be eligible to participate in intercollegiate or interscholastic sports competition. See generally Sean Hanlon and Ray Yasser, *"J.J. Morrison" and His Right of Publicity Lawsuit Against the NCAA*, 15 Vill. Sports & Ent. L.J. 241 (2008). For example, to retain his eligibility to play football for the University of Colorado, the NCAA prohibited U.S. Olympic moguls skier Jeremy Bloom from earning future endorsement and modeling contract income needed to finance his training. See *Bloom v. NCAA*, 93 P.3d 621 (Colo. App. 2004) (upholding NCAA bylaws prohibiting student-athletes from being paid for advertisements and product endorsements). In December 2011, to prevent the amateur eligibility of cornerback Tyrann Mathieu (nicknamed "Honey Badger" for his defensive plays comparing him to the fearless small animal of the same name) from being potentially compromised, Louisiana State University's compliance office sent cease and desist notices and published an advisory warning local retailers not to sell items with "Honey Badger" combined with Mathieu's name or image or LSU's marks or colors. NCAA rules require student-athletes to take steps to prevent their names or images from being used for commercial purposes other than by their respective universities. Several former student-athletes recently have filed pending lawsuits alleging that the NCAA and others are unlawfully profiting from the unauthorized commercial use of their identities even after their intercollegiate playing careers have ended, which are discussed *infra*.

In 2003, the Ohio High School Athletic Association (OHSAA) declared LeBron James ineligible to continue playing high school basketball for violating its rule prohibiting "capitalizing on athletic fame by receiving money or gifts of monetary value." James had accepted two "throwback" jerseys worth a combined $845 from an Akron sporting goods store for posing for photos to be displayed on its walls. Although an Ohio trial court ultimately enjoined the OHSAA from enforcing its rule, James was required to serve a two-game suspension for his conduct.

ii.   First Amendment Limitations

The First Amendment of the United States Constitution limits the protection of publicity rights under state law. In *Titan Sports, Inc. v. Comics World Corp.*, 870 F.2d 85, 88 (2d Cir. 1989), the Second Circuit noted the "inherent tension between the protection of an individual's right to control the use of his likeness and the constitutional guarantee of free dissemination of ideas, images, and newsworthy matter in whatever form it takes." Courts have struggled to draw the line between unauthorized commercial use of one's identity that may be prohibited by state law and communicative or expressive use protected by the First Amendment.

In *Zacchini v. Scripps-Howard Broadcasting, Inc.*, 433 U.S. 562 (1977), the Supreme Court held that the media's right to report newsworthy events does not permit the unauthorized broadcast of a performer's entire act, which threatens harm to its economic value. A local Ohio television station sent a news crew to film the act of Hugo Zacchini, the "human cannonball," who was performing at a county fair. This was done despite Zacchini's request that his performance not be filmed. His entire 15-second performance was shown on the evening news. In a 5-4 decision, the Court ruled that showing his entire act is not permitted by the First Amendment's protection of news reporting. Under the majority's view, the television station's broadcast is not protected by the United States Constitution, because it reduces the commercial value of Zacchini's entertainment product and corresponding economic incentive to produce his performance. However, the dissenting justices concluded that the First Amendment broadly protects the media from a right of publicity or commercial appropriation claim "absent a strong showing . . . that the news broadcast was a subterfuge or cover for private or commercial exploitation." *Id.* at 581.

The *Zacchini* case is notable, not for the clarity of its line-drawing, but for its clear demonstration that such line-drawing regarding the scope of First Amendment protections is one that is often difficult and likely to be criticized, whatever the result reached. When the usage of an athlete's identity moves from the purely commercial, as is most likely the case in the advertising or sale of a product or service, to more of a mixed medium—such as films, television, radio, newspapers and other literary works—the more likely that First Amendment issues will arise.

The First Amendment broadly immunizes the media from state law liability for infringement of publicity rights, even though media publications and broadcasts usually are for-profit commercial activity. The media may use a celebrity's name, photograph, and other aspects of his or her identity in connection with truthful news reporting. Courts have extended constitutional protection to media republications of news coverage of sporting events and athletic accomplishments even if used for advertising purposes. For example, in *Montana v. San Jose Mercury News, Inc.*, 34 Cal. App. 4th 790 (Cal. Ct. App. 1995), the court held that a newspaper may contemporaneously reproduce a full-page account of the San Francisco Forty-Niners four Super Bowl victories in the 1990s in poster form for public sale without violating the publicity rights of Joe Montana, the team's quarterback. Even though his name and likeness appeared on the posters, they were depictions of newsworthy events in which Montana had played a prominent role. See also *Namath v. Sports Illustrated*, 371 N.Y.S.2d 10 (App. Div. 1975), *aff'd*, 352 N.E.2d 584 (N.Y. 1976) (dismissing athlete's right of publicity claim against magazine for using his photograph in advertisements to promote subscriptions).

On the other hand, the use of news coverage of an athletic event incorporating an athlete's name or likeness to advertise or sell unrelated products is not constitutionally protected. In *Pooley v. National Hole-in-One Association*, 89 F. Supp. 1108 (D. Ariz. 2000), the defendant made a videotape of a professional golfer's hole-in-one and used his name to promote its hole-in-one fundraising competitions. Denying defendant's motion to dismiss plaintiff's right of publicity claim, the court ruled:

> [W]hile Plaintiff's hole-in-one at the Bay Hill Classic was open to national observation and public videotaping, its *subsequent* unauthorized reproduction was not automatically privileged simply because the hole-in-one continued to be a "newsworthy" event. Defendant did not create the videotape in connection with a news account. Defendant did not include Plaintiff's name and videotape footage simply to communicate an idea. It capitalized on Plaintiff's name, reputation, and prestige in the context of an advertisement. The promotional videotape went one step further and implied a false connection between the Plaintiff and its business. The Court finds that the use of Plaintiff's identity was strictly commercial and not protected by the First Amendment.

Id. at 1114.

In *ETW v. Jireh Publishing, Inc.*, 332 F.3d 915 (6th Cir. 2003), the Sixth Circuit held that the First Amendment protects a sports artist's freedom of expression to include the likenesses of famous professional athletes (e.g., Tiger Woods and other legendary professional golfers) in a painting commemorating Woods's historic victory in the 1997 Masters Tournament, reprints of which were sold to the public. The court explained that the First Amendment protects expressive materials "including music, pictures, films, photographs, paintings, drawings, engravings, prints, and sculptures," which is not limited even if it is sold. Observing that famous athletes, "through their pervasive presence in the media . . . have come to symbolize certain ideas and values in our society and have become a valuable means of expression in our culture," the court concluded: "While the right of publicity allows celebrities like Woods to enjoy the fruits of their labors, here Rush has added a significant creative component of his own to Woods's identity. Permitting Woods's right of publicity to trump Rush's right of freedom of expression would extinguish Rush's right to profit from his creative enterprise." *Id.* at 938. But see *Doe a/k/a Tony Twist v. TCI Cablevision*, 110 S.W.3d 363, 374 (Mo. 2003), *cert. denied*, 540 U.S. 1106 (2004) (unauthorized metaphorical reference to Tony Twist, an ex-NHL player known as an on-ice "enforcer," in a comic book with a fictional Mafia don with a long list of evil deeds "has very little literary value compared to its commercial value" and "free speech must give way to the right of publicity").

In *Cardtoons, L.C. v. Major League Baseball Players Assn.*, 95 F.3d 959 (10th Cir. 1996), the Tenth Circuit recognized a parody defense based on the First Amendment to a right of publicity claim. Cardtoons produced a series of baseball cards that lampooned MLB players and allowed identification of the individual players. The court explained:

> Cardtoons' parody trading cards receive full protection under the First Amendment. The cards provide social commentary on public figures, major league baseball players, who are involved in a significant commercial enterprise, major league baseball. While not core political speech (the cards do not, for example, adopt a position on the Ken Griffey, Jr., for President campaign), this type of commentary on an important social institution constitutes protected expression.

Id. at 969.

As you read the following case, consider whether courts are applying a consistent legal principle that appropriately balances an athlete's economic interest in preventing unauthorized use of his identity for commercial purposes with the First Amendment's protection of freedom of expression.

C.B.C. DISTRIBUTION AND MARKETING, INC. v. MLBAM

505 F.3d 818 (8th Cir. 2007), *cert. denied*, 128 S. Ct. 2872 (2008)

ARNOLD, Circuit Judge.

C.B.C. Distribution and Marketing, Inc., brought this action for a declaratory judgment against Major League Baseball Advanced Media, L.P., to establish its right to use, without license, the names of and information about major league baseball players in connection with its fantasy baseball products. Advanced Media counterclaimed, maintaining that CBC's fantasy baseball products violated rights of publicity belonging to major league baseball players and that the players, through their association, had licensed those rights to Advanced Media, the interactive media and Internet company of major league baseball. . . .

I.

CBC sells fantasy sports products via its Internet website, e-mail, mail, and the telephone. Its fantasy baseball products incorporate the names along with performance and biographical data of actual major league baseball players. Before the commencement of the major league baseball season each spring, participants form their fantasy baseball teams by "drafting" players from various major league baseball teams. Participants compete against other fantasy baseball "owners" who have also drafted their own teams. A participant's success, and his or her team's success, depends on the actual performance of the fantasy team's players on their respective actual teams during the course of the major league baseball season. Participants in CBC's fantasy baseball games pay fees to play and additional fees to trade players during the course of the season.

From 1995 through the end of 2004, CBC licensed its use of the names of and information about major league players from the Players Association pursuant to license agreements that it entered into with the association in 1995 and 2002. The 2002 agreement, which superseded in its entirety the 1995 agreement, licensed to CBC "the names, nicknames, likenesses, signatures, pictures, playing records, and/or biographical data of each player" (the "Rights") to be used in association with CBC's fantasy baseball products.

In 2005, after the 2002 agreement expired, the Players Association licensed to Advanced Media, with some exceptions, the exclusive right to use baseball players' names and performance information "for exploitation via all interactive media." Advanced Media began providing fantasy baseball games on its website, MLB.com, the official website of major league baseball. It offered CBC, in exchange for a commission, a license to promote the MLB.com fantasy baseball games on CBC's website but did not offer CBC a license to continue to offer its own fantasy baseball products. This conduct by Advanced Media prompted CBC to file the present suit, alleging that it had "a reasonable apprehension that it will be sued by Advanced Media if it continues to operate its fantasy baseball games."

The district court granted summary judgment to CBC. It held that CBC was not infringing any state-law rights of publicity that belonged to major league baseball players. The court reasoned that CBCs fantasy baseball products did not use the names of major league baseball players as symbols of their identities and with an intent to obtain a commercial advantage, as required to establish an infringement of a publicity right under Missouri law (which all parties concede applies here). The district court further held that even if CBC were infringing the players' rights of publicity, the first amendment preempted those rights. . . .

II.

A.

An action based on the right of publicity is a state-law claim. *See Zacchini v. Scripps-Howard Broad. Co.,* 433 U.S. 562, 566, 97 S.Ct. 2849, 53 L.Ed.2d 965 (1977). In Missouri, "the elements of a right of publicity action include: (1) That defendant used plaintiff's name as a symbol of his identity (2) without consent (3) and with the intent to obtain a commercial advantage." *Doe v. TCI Cablevision,* 110 S.W.3d 363, 369 (Mo.2003), *cert. denied,* 540 U.S. 1106, 124 S.Ct. 1058, 157 L.Ed.2d 892 (2004). The parties all agree that CBC's continued use of the players' names and playing information after the expiration of the 2002 agreement was without consent. The district court concluded, however, that the evidence was insufficient to make out the other two elements of the claim, and we address each of these in turn.

With respect to the symbol-of-identity element, the Missouri Supreme Court has observed that "'the name used by the defendant must be understood by the audience as referring to the plaintiff.'" The state court had further held that "[i]n resolving this issue, the fact-finder may consider evidence including 'the nature and extent of the identifying characteristics used by the defendant, the defendant's intent, the fame of the plaintiff, evidence of actual identification made by third persons, and surveys or other evidence indicating the perceptions of the audience.'" *Doe,* 110 S.W.3d at 370 (quoting Restatement (Third) of Unfair Competition § 46 cmt. d).

Here, we entertain no doubt that the players' names that CBC used are understood by it and its fantasy baseball subscribers as referring to actual major league baseball players. CBC itself admits that: In responding to the appellants' argument that "this element is met by the mere confirmation that the name used, in fact, refers to the famous person asserting the violation," CBC stated in its brief that "if this is all the element requires, CBC agrees that it is met." We think that by reasoning that "identity," rather than "mere use of a name," "is a critical element of the right of publicity," the district court did not understand that when a name alone is sufficient to establish identity, the defendant's use of that name satisfies the plaintiff's burden to show that a name was used as a symbol of identity.

It is true that with respect to the "commercial advantage" element of a cause of action for violating publicity rights, CBC's use does not fit neatly into the more traditional categories of commercial advantage, namely, using individuals' names for advertising and merchandising purposes in a way that states or intimates that the individuals are endorsing a product. But the Restatement, which the Missouri Supreme Court has recognized as authority in this kind of case, *see Doe*, 110 S.W.3d at 368, also says that a name is used for commercial advantage when it is used "in connection with services rendered by the user" and that the plaintiff need not show that "prospective purchasers are likely to believe" that he or she endorsed the product or service. Restatement (Third) of Unfair Competition § 47 & cmt. a. We note, moreover, that in Missouri, "the commercial advantage element of the right of publicity focuses on the defendant's intent or purpose to obtain a commercial benefit from use of the plaintiff's identity." *Doe*, 110 S.W.3d at 370-71. Because we think that it is clear that CBC uses baseball players' identities in its fantasy baseball products for purposes of profit, we believe that their identities are being used for commercial advantage and that the players therefore offered sufficient evidence to make out a cause of action for violation of their rights of publicity under Missouri law.

B.

CBC argues that the first amendment nonetheless trumps the right-of-publicity action that Missouri law provides. Though this dispute is between private parties, the state action necessary for first amendment protections exists because the right-of-publicity claim exists only insofar as the courts enforce state-created obligations that were "never explicitly assumed" by CBC.

The Supreme Court has directed that state law rights of publicity must be balanced against first amendment considerations, *see Zacchini v. Scripps-Howard Broad.*, 433 U.S. 562, 97 S.Ct. 2849, 53 L.Ed.2d 965 (1977), and here we conclude that the former must give way to the latter. First, the information used in CBC's fantasy baseball games is all readily available in the public domain, and it would be strange law that a person would not have a first amendment right to use information that is available to everyone. It is true that CBC's use of the information is meant to provide entertainment, but "[s]peech that entertains, like speech that informs, is protected by the First Amendment because '[t]he line between the informing and the entertaining is too elusive for the protection of that basic right.'" *Cardtoons, L.C. v. Major League Baseball Players Ass'n*, 95 F.3d 959, 969 (10th Cir.1996) (quoting *Winters v. New York*, 333 U.S. 507, 510, 68 S.Ct. 665, 92 L.Ed. 840 (1948)); *see also Zacchini*, 433 U.S. at 578. We also find no merit in the argument that CBC's use of players' names and information in its fantasy baseball games is not speech at all. We have held that "the pictures, graphic design, concept art, sounds, music, stories, and narrative present in video games" is speech entitled to first amendment protection. *See Interactive Digital Software Ass'n v. St. Louis County, Mo.*, 329 F.3d 954, 957 (8th Cir.2003).

Similarly, here CBC uses the "names, nicknames, likenesses, signatures, pictures, playing records, and/or biographical data of each player" in an interactive form in connection with its fantasy baseball products. This use is no less expressive than the use that was at issue in *Interactive Digital*.

Courts have also recognized the public value of information about the game of baseball and its players, referring to baseball as "the national pastime." A California court, in a case where Major League Baseball was itself defending its use of players' names, likenesses, and information against the players' asserted rights of publicity, observed, "Major league baseball is followed by millions of people across this country on a daily basis. . . . The public has an enduring fascination in the records set by former players and in memorable moments from previous games. . . . The records and statistics remain of interest to the public because they provide context that allows fans to better appreciate (or deprecate) today's performances." *Gionfriddo v. Major League Baseball*, 94 Cal.App.4th 400, 411, 114 Cal.Rptr.2d 307 (2001). The Court in *Gionfriddo* concluded that the "recitation and discussion of factual data concerning the athletic performance of [players on Major League Baseball's website] command a substantial public interest, and, therefore, is a form of expression due substantial constitutional protection." We find these views persuasive.

In addition, the facts in this case barely, if at all, implicate the interests that states typically intend to vindicate by providing rights of publicity to individuals. Economic interests that states seek to promote include the right of an individual to reap the rewards of his or her endeavors and an individual's right to earn a living. Other motives for creating a publicity right are the desire to provide incentives to encourage a person's productive activities and to protect consumers from misleading advertising. But major league baseball players are rewarded, and handsomely, too, for their participation in games and can earn additional large sums from endorsements and sponsorship arrangements. Nor is there any danger here that consumers will be misled, because the fantasy baseball games depend on the inclusion of all players and thus cannot create a false impression that some particular player with "star power" is endorsing CBC's products.

Then there are so-called non-monetary interests that publicity rights are sometimes thought to advance. These include protecting natural rights, rewarding celebrity labors, and avoiding emotional harm. We do not see that any of these interests are especially relevant here, where baseball players are rewarded separately for their labors, and where any emotional harm would most likely be caused by a player's actual performance, in which case media coverage would cause the same harm. We also note that some courts have indicated that the right of publicity is intended to promote only economic interests and that non-economic interests are more directly served by so-called rights of privacy. . . .

Because we hold that CBC's first amendment rights in offering its fantasy baseball products supersede the players' rights of publicity, we need not reach CBC's alternative argument that federal copyright law preempts the players' state law rights of publicity.

[The court's analysis of the breach of contract issues is omitted.]

NOTES AND QUESTIONS

1. *Scholarly Commentary Regarding* CBC. Legal scholars are sharply divided regarding whether *CBC* was decided correctly. See, e.g., Matthew J. Mitten,

A Triple Play for the Public Domain: From Delaware Lottery to Motorola to C.B.C., 11 Chapman L. Rev. 569, 579 (2008) ("Extending the right of publicity to require CBC to pay a licensing fee would create an exclusive property right that precludes or severely limits the commercial use of public domain information, reduces the availability of collateral products, and/or increases their costs to consumers. Such a broad, state-created 'right of publicity on steroids' is legally and economically unjustified"); Richard T. Karcher, *The Use of Players' Identities in Fantasy Sports Leagues: Developing Workable Standards for Right of Publicity Claims,* 111 Penn. St. L. Rev. 557, 572 (2007) ("[T]he players are providing the content for the fantasy sports league industry which is a huge profit-making service industry, and the players should be compensated for the use of that content by fantasy operators"). Which view is correct?

Applying *C.B.C. Distribution,* in *CBS Interactive Inc. v. National Football League Players Assn., Inc.,* 259 F.R.D. 398 (D. Minn. 2009), a Minnesota district court ruled that the unauthorized use of NFL players' names and statistics in connection with fantasy football game does not violate players' publicity rights because "package of player information" consisting of "names, player profiles, up-to-date statistics, injury reports, participant blogs, pictures, images, and biographical information" is no different.

2. *Unauthorized Use of Athletes' Persona in Video Games.* Courts are split regarding whether the unauthorized use of identifiable traits and characteristics of athletes in video games are protected by the First Amendment. In *Keller v. Electronic Arts, Inc.,* 2010 WL 530108 (N.D. Cal.), a New Jersey district court refused to dismiss the claims of former Arizona State quarterback Sam Keller alleging that an NCAA college football video game produced by Electronic Arts violated his right of publicity. It ruled that "EA's depiction of Plaintiff in 'NCAA Football' is not sufficiently transformative to bar his California right of publicity claims as a matter of law. In the game, the quarterback for Arizona State University shares many of Plaintiff's characteristics. For example, the virtual player wears the same jersey number, is the same height and weight and hails from the same state. . . . EA does not depict Plaintiff in a different form; he is represented as he what he was: the starting quarterback for Arizona State University. Further . . . the game's setting is identical to where the public found Plaintiff during his collegiate career: on the football field." *Id.* at *5. This case subsequently was consolidated with a class action suit by former UCLA basketball player Ed O'Bannon on behalf of himself and former NCAA Division I basketball players and Football Bowl Subdivision football players in a California federal court asserting that the NCAA and its licensing arm, Collegiate Sports Licensing, have violated the antitrust laws by "foreclos[ing] class members from receiving compensation in connection with the commercial exploitation of their images following their cessation of intercollegiate athletic competition." See *In re NCAA Student-Athlete Name & Likeness Licensing Litigation,* 2012 WL 1745593 (N.D. Cal.).

In *Hart v. Electronic Arts, Inc.,* 808 F. Supp. 2d 757 (D. N.J. 2011), a New Jersey district court ruled that Electronic Arts' First Amendment right to free expression outweighs the right of publicity claims of Ryan Hart, a former Rutgers University quarterback, as a matter of law. The court applied the transformative use test, which permits the use of one's likeness as "raw material" in a creative work such as a video game:

[T]hat Hart's image is placed in a college football game is problematic for EA's assertion of a transformative defense. Placing present and former college athletes, including Hart, into the fittingly-titled *NCAA Football* game setting strongly suggests that the goal of the game is to capitalize upon the fame of those players. Indeed, "[i]t seems ludicrous to question whether video game consumers enjoy and, as a result, purchase more EA-produced video games as a result of the heightened realism associated with actual players." This, alone, however, does not mean that EA's use of Hart's image was not transformative. *See Winter, supra* at 889, 134 Cal.Rptr.2d 634, 69 P.3d 473 ("[i]f it is determined that a work is worthy of First Amendment protection because added creative elements significantly transform the celebrity depiction, then independent inquiry into whether or not that work is cutting into the market for the celebrity's images . . . appears to be irrelevant.") (citation omitted). Nevertheless, a game developer that bases its work on real players, in the context of the games that bring them notoriety, may walk a fine line between using reality as a building block for the developer's own creative work and exploiting the hard-earned reputations of college players for its own profit.

For this reason, the Court appreciates the plight of college players who are prohibited by NCAA bylaws from entering into licensing agreements and other "commercial opportunities" during their playing years. Hart Decl., ¶ 5. In this connection, Hart argues that EA has a practice of paying professional football players for the use of their images in EA's professional football video games, suggesting that it is disingenuous for EA to refuse to pay college athletes for the use of their images. . . .

That EA may license professional player images, as well as team intellectual property from the N.C.A.A., yet refuse to license former college athlete images may suggest an element of unfairness. Nevertheless, it bears not on the question before this Court here—whether or not EA's use of Hart's image is protected by the First Amendment.

Viewed as a whole, there are sufficient elements of EA's own expression found in the game that justify the conclusion that its use of Hart's image is transformative and, therefore, entitled to First Amendment protection. For one, the game includes several creative elements apart from Hart's image. Similar to the *Madden NFL* video game, as described in a case dismissing a former professional football player's Lanham Act claim, *Brown v. Electronic Arts, supra*, the *NCAA Football* game contains "virtual stadiums, athletes, coaches, fans, sound effects, music, and commentary, all of which are created or compiled by the games' designers." Furthermore, as explained by Jeremy Strauser, an Executive Producer at EA responsible for the development of *NCAA Football*, "[t]he virtual world of *NCAA Football* is constructed from a vast array of graphics, sound and other material. Once a user chooses two college teams to compete against another, the video game assigns a stadium for the match-up and populates it with players, coaches, referees, mascots, cheerleaders and fans—all designed and rendered by EA's artists. Each game has over 100 virtual teams and thousands of virtual players." Strauser Decl., ¶ 4. The Court's own review of the video games confirms Mr. Strauser's description.

Even focusing on Hart's virtual image alone, it is clear that the game is transformative. It is true that the virtual player bears resemblance to Hart and was designed with Hart's physical attributes, sports statistics, and biographical information in mind. However, as noted, the game permits users to alter Hart's virtual player, control the player's throw distance and accuracy, change the team of which the player is a part by downloading varying team names and rosters, or engage in "Dynasty" mode, in which the user incorporates players from historical teams into the gameplay. *See id.* at ¶¶ 6-8. That the user is able to change the image's features, statistics, and teammates distinguishes *NCAA*

Football from the game at issue in *No Doubt,* where the characters were immutable. These aspects also distinguish the video game from the greeting card in *Hilton,* where Paris Hilton's photograph was used in a single, static setting.

To be clear, it is not the user's alteration of Hart's image that is critical. What matters for my analysis of EA's First Amendment right is that EA created the mechanism by which the virtual player may be altered, as well as the multiple permutations available for each virtual player image. Since the game permits the user to alter the virtual player's physical characteristics, including the player's height, weight, hairstyle, face shape, body size, muscle size, and complexion, *see e.g.,* Strauser Decl., Exh. F at 4 (Part I) (displaying "Edit Player-Appearance" screenshot), it follows that EA's artists created a host of physical characteristic options from which the user may choose. For example, EA artists created the several different hairstyles that can be morphed onto the image. *See id.* The Court's review of the game revealed eight such hairstyle options: fade 1, fade 2, close crop, buzzout 1, buzzout 2, afro, balding 1, and balding 2. In my view, the creation of these varied potential formulations of each virtual player alone makes the game a transformative use of Hart's image.

Id. at 783-785.

PROBLEM 12-4

Consider whether the following use of player names and identities without authorization from the player, players association, or league violate any legally protected rights:

a.   A minor league baseball league affixes the names and photos of members of its all-star team to merchandise such as T-shirts, mugs, and other souvenirs that are sold in the venue hosting its all-star game.
b.   A company makes and sells bobblehead dolls depicting famous professional athletes and identifies them by name in the product's packaging.
c.   A car dealer's giveaway of a football autographed by the starting quarterback of the local NFL team, who is paid to endorse another local dealer's vehicles, is advertised on the radio. The dealer was the successful bidder for the football at a local charity's fund raiser. All prospective customers who visit its showroom are eligible to win this prize.
d.   A nationally circulated sports magazine does a feature story on the rigorous off-season workout program of an All-Pro NFL linebacker, which includes a sentence stating that he takes daily protein supplements. Next to the story, there is a paid advertisement for Brand X protein supplements. This player does use Brand Y protein supplements but is not an endorser of any brand of protein supplements.

TABLE OF CASES

Principal cases are italicized.

INDEX